Women's Lives
Multicultural Perspectives

Gwyn Kirk

Margo Okazawa-Rey

Mayfield Publishing Company
Mountain View, California
London • Toronto

Library of Congress Cataloging-in-Publication Data
Kirk, Gwyn.
    Women's lives : multicultural perspectives / Gwyn Kirk, Margo
  Okazawa-Rey
      p. cm.
    Includes bibliographical references.
    ISBN 1-55934-748-1
    1. Women — United States — Social conditions.   2. Women — United
States — Economic conditions.   3. Feminism — United States.
I. Okazawa-Rey, Margo.   II. Title.
HQ1421.K573   1997
305.42′0973 — DC21   97-27096
                                                CIP

Manufactured in the United States of America
10   9   8   7   6   5   4   3   2   1

Mayfield Publishing Company
1280 Villa Street
Mountain View, CA 94041

Sponsoring editor, Franklin C. Graham; production editor, Julianna Scott Fein; manuscript editor, Jamie Fuller; design manager, Jean Mailander; text designer, Carolyn Deacy; cover designer, Laurie Anderson; cover art, Mary Grigoriadis (American, b. 1942), *Persian Steep*, 1977, oil on canvas, 66 × 66 in. The National Museum of Women in the Arts. Gift of Minnie B. Odoroff; art manager, Robin Mouat; manufacturing manager, Randy Hurst. The text was set in 9/11 Palatino by ColorType and printed on acid-free 45# Chromatone Matte by Banta Book Group.

To those who connect us to the past,
our mothers,
who birthed us, raised us, taught us, inspired us, and took no nonsense from us
Edwina Davies, Kazuko Okazawa, Willa Mae Wells
and to those who connect us to the future
Charlotte Elizabeth Andrews-Briscoe
Gabrielle Raya Clancy-Humphrey
Camille Celestina Stovall-Ceja

Contents

CHAPTER 1

♦♦♦

Theory and Theorizing: Integrative Frameworks for Understanding 7

CHAPTER 2

♦♦♦

Identities and Social Locations: Who Am I? Who Are My People? 51

CHAPTER 3

◆◆◆

Body Politics 103

CHAPTER 4

◆◆◆

Relationships, Families, and Households 132

CHAPTER 5

◆◆◆

Living in a Global Economy 182

The Global Factory 182

The Profit Motive 183

Consumerism, Expansionism, and Waste 184

The Myth of Progress 184

Emphasis on Immediate Costs 184

The Global Economy 184

Complex Inequalities 184

Legacies of Colonialism 185

External Debt 187

Implications of Global Economic Inequalities 189

Connections to U.S. Policy Issues 189

International Alliances Among Women 190

The Seeds of a New Global Economy 191

CHAPTER 6

◆◆◆

Work, Wages, and Welfare 217

Defining Women's Work 217

Women in the U.S. Workforce 218

Women's Wages: The Effects of Gender, Race, Class, and Disability 219

Discrimination Against Working Women:
Sexual Harassment, Age, and Disability 220

Balancing Home and Work 221

Organized Labor 222

Pensions, Disability Payments, and Welfare 223

Pensions and Retirement 224

Disability Payments 225

Welfare 225

Feminist Approaches to Women's Work and Income 225

Comparable Worth 225

Feminization of Poverty 226

Impact of Class 226

Policy Implications and Activist Projects 227

Promoting Greater Economic Security for Women 227

CHAPTER 7

◆◆◆

Women's Health 265

CHAPTER 8

◆◆◆

Women, Crime, and Criminalization 331

CHAPTER 9

◆◆◆

Women and the Military 376

CHAPTER 10

◆◆◆

Women and the Environment 406

Theoretical and Activist Perspectives 407

Deep Ecology 407

Ecofeminism 408

Environmental Justice 409

Connectedness and Sustainability 410

CHAPTER 11

◆◆◆

Creating Change: Theory, Vision, and Action   450

Preface

An introductory course is perhaps the most challenging women's studies course to conceptualize and teach. Depending on their overall goals for the course, instructors must make difficult choices about what to include and what to leave out. Students come into the course for a variety of reasons and with a range of expectations and prior knowledge, and most will not major in women's studies. The course may fulfill a distribution requirement for them, or it may be a way of taking one women's studies course during their undergraduate education out of a personal interest to broaden their knowledge of women's lives. For women's studies majors, the course plays a very different role, offering a foundation for their area of study.

Several factors related to the wider university setting and societal context also shape women's studies in the late 1990s. There is increasing awareness of the difficulties of what it means for mainly White instructors to teach about the broad diversity of women's experiences in the United States. Women's studies programs continue to build their reputations in terms of academic rigor and scholarly standards. Outside the academy, a range of economic changes and government policies have made many women's lives more difficult in the United States—a loss of factory and office work as jobs continue to be moved overseas or become automated; government failure to introduce a health care system that will benefit everyone or to introduce an adequate system of childcare; cuts in Aid to Families with Dependent Children and other welfare programs; greater restriction of government support to immigrants and their families; and a dramatic increase in the number of women now incarcerated compared with a decade ago.

This text started out as two separate readers that we used in our classes at Antioch College (Gwyn Kirk) and San Francisco State University (Margo Okazawa-Rey). Serendipitously, as it seemed at the time, we were introduced to each other by a mutual friend. We began to talk about our teaching and discovered many similarities in approach despite our very different institutional settings. We decided to take what we thought were the best parts of our readers and combine them into a book that would work for an introductory course.

What We Want in an Introductory Women's Studies Book

Several key issues concern us as teachers. We want to present a broad range of women's experiences to our students in terms of class, race, culture, disability, age, and sexual orientation. We assume that hierarchies based on these factors create systems of disadvantage as well as systems of privilege and that women's multiple positions along these dimensions shape our life experiences in important and unique ways. Although the national discourse on race, for example, is presented in Black/White terms, we want teaching materials that do justice to the diversity and complexity of race and ethnicity in this country. We also want materials that address the location of the United States in the global economy. Students need to understand the economic forces that affect the availability of jobs in this country and elsewhere.

They also need to understand the significance of U.S. dominance abroad in terms of language and popular culture, the power of the dollar and U.S.-based corporations, and the prevalence of the U.S. military.

In our introductory courses, we both included some discussion of theory because a basic understanding of various theoretical frameworks is a powerful tool not only for women's studies courses but for other courses students take. Another shared concern we have is women's activism. As women's studies has become more established and professionalized, it has tended to grow away from its roots in the women's liberation movement, a trend that greatly troubles us. As we talked about our own lives, it was clear that we both value our involvements in political movements. This activism has taught us a great deal and provided us with vital communities of like-minded people. Currently, there are myriad women's activist and advocacy projects across the country, but many students do not know about them. In our teaching, we make it a point to include examples of women's activism and urge students to think of themselves as people who can make a difference in their own lives and in the world around them. Much of the information that students learn in women's studies concerning the difficulties and oppression of women's lives can be discouraging. Knowing about women's activism can be empowering, even in the face of daunting realities. This knowledge reinforces the idea that current inequalities and problems are not fixed but have the potential to be changed.

Linking Individual Experiences to National and International Trends and Issues

We are both trained in sociology. We have noticed that students coming into our classes are much more familiar with psychological explanations for behavior and experience rather than structural explanations. They invariably enjoy first-person accounts of women's experiences, but a series of stories, even wonderfully insightful stories, leaves us unsatisfied. In class, we provide a context for the various issues students study. Taking a story about a woman with cancer, for example, we add details about how many

women in the United States have cancer, possible explanations for this, the effects of age, race, and class on treatment and likelihood of recovery. The overview essay for each chapter provides some broader context for the personal accounts. We have tried to integrate the many aspects of women's lives. We abandoned our earlier sections on aging and disability in favor of threading these aspects of women's experience through each chapter. We've included readings that reflect the complexity of women's identities, where the authors wrote, for example, about being Chinese American, working-class, and lesbian in an integrated way. We added a section on crime and criminalization in response to the great increase in women caught up in the criminal justice system in the past decade, and added a chapter on women and the environment.

Challenges for the Twenty-First Century: Security and Sustainability

We find ourselves thinking about the challenges facing women and men in the twenty-first century: challenges concerning work and livelihood, personal and family relationships, violence on many levels, and the fragile physical environment. These issues pose major questions concerning the distribution of resources, personal and social values, and the definition of security. How is our society going to provide for its people in the years to come? What are the effects of the increasing polarization between rich and poor in the United States and between rich and poor countries of the world? Genuine security—at personal, community-wide, national, and planetary levels—is a key issue for the future, and, similarly, sustainability. These themes of security and sustainability provide a wider framework for the book.

As teachers, we are concerned with students' knowledge and understanding, and beyond that, with their aspirations, hopes, and values. One of our goals for this book is to provide a series of lenses that will help students understand their own lives and the lives of others, especially women. The second goal is that, through this understanding, they will be able to participate in some way in the creation of a secure and sustainable future.

Acknowledgments

Many people made it possible for us to complete this book, some four years in the making, especially our students at Antioch College and San Francisco State University who first inspired us to do it.

In terms of practical support, several people helped us get through the day-to-day tasks of writing, preparing the manuscript, and staying healthy: Alice Feldman, Trina Histon, Erwin Morgenthaler, Alan Ng and Mark Gin at Copy Edge, Diane Sabin, and the School of Social Work at San Francisco State University. Research assistants Marieka Brown, Anna Lisa Couturier, and Carolyn Reyes were part of this team.

The following people pushed us intellectually, read parts of the manuscript, or provided new ideas and information: Molly Andrews, Grace Lee Boggs, Alice Cook, Annette Dula, Vitka Eisen, Ann Filemyr, Jewelle Gomez, Mark Gross, Anna Gruver, Ynestra King, Martha Matsuoka, Chandra Talpade Mohanty, Cassandra O'Neill, Freddy Paine, Megan Reynolds, Eric Rofes, Anne Simon, and Sondra Stein. Other friends supported and encouraged us: D. Kamili Anderson, Ondwéwe Chymes, Adrienne Cool, Crispin Hollings, Catherine Joseph, Nancy Knipe, Nobu Tomita, Julie Torgeson, and Lisa Vuong.

We acknowledge those who wrote pieces especially for this volume: Lynore B. Gause, Barbara Bloom, Cynthia Cohen, Monique Corbin, Eric De-Meulenaere, Jean Grossholtz, Teresa Luftus, Shannon Murray, Carolyn Reyes, Melinda Smith-Wells, Rita Takahashi, Elizabeth Wilson-Compton, and Wendy A. Young. We also appreciate all the feminist scholars and activists whose work we have reprinted here and those whose research and writings have informed not only our work but also shaped the field of women's studies.

We are grateful to everyone at Mayfield who so thoughtfully worked to put our manuscript be-tween covers: Franklin Graham, our editor, whose confidence in our ideas never wavered and whose light hand on the steering wheel and clear sense of direction helped get us to this point; especially Julianna Scott Fein, production editor, who kept track of the details as well as the big picture; the production team; Jamie Fuller, copyeditor extraordinaire; Sara Early, editorial assistant, who waded through early drafts; and Serina Beauparlant, Mayfield's new women's studies editor. We are also grateful to outside reviewers Teri Ann Bengiveno, San Jose State University; Shamita Das Dasgupta, Rutgers University; Torry Dickinson, Kansas State University; Dana Dunn, University of Texas at Arlington; and Patricia Huckle, San Diego State University, who asked good questions and made useful suggestions.

We also thank our teachers, from whom we've learned information and new ways of thinking, and those key people who provided support and opportunities at various turning points in our lives: Il Soon Ahn, the late James Boggs, Lillian Gonzalez Brown, Steve Brown, Charlotte Bunch, Bryan Burdick, Kathleen Casey, Susan Cavin, Max Culver, Eleanor Duckworth, Kat Duff, Margaret Duncombe, Carolyn Francis, G. William Freeman, Virginia Glennon, Rachel Hare-Mustin, Joseph Jordan, Josephine Lambert, Yoko Lee, Sara Lawrence Lightfoot, Donald Oliver, Grace Paley, Shirley Royster, Josephine Shaddock, David O. Shipp, Judith Sturnick, Suzuyo Takazato, Wendy Grayson Thunderchief, and the late James C. Wells.

We continue to be inspired by the cultural work of Sweet Honey in the Rock, whose blend of music and politics touches the head, heart, and hands, and also by the "sociological imagination"—C. Wright Mills' concept—that draws on the need for complex social analysis in order to make change.

Our very sincere thanks to all of you and to each other.

We have chosen each other
and the edge of each other's battles
the war is the same
if we lose
someday women's blood will congeal
upon a dead planet
if we win
there is no telling
we seek beyond history
for a new and more possible meeting.

— AUDRE LORDE

◆◆◆

The Framework of This Book

The Focus of Women's Studies

To study alongside men, to have access to the same curriculum, and to be admitted to male professions were goals that dominated women's education in the United States for several generations, from the early nineteenth century onward. In the late 1960s and early 1970s, however, the gendered nature of knowledge itself—with its focus on white, male, and middle-class perspectives that are assumed to be universal—was called into question by feminists. The early 1970s saw the start of many women's studies programs across the country, building on the insights and energies of the women's liberation movement. Early courses had titles like "Women's Liberation," "The Power of Patriarchy," or "Sexist Oppression and Women's Empowerment." Texts often included mimeographed articles from feminist newsletters and pamphlets, as there was so little appropriate material in books. By contrast, women's studies is now an established field of study with over six hundred programs nationwide in universities and colleges and a rapidly growing and extensive body of literature (National Women's Studies Association 1994). Women's studies graduates are employed in many fields, including law, business, publishing, health, social and human services, and education and library work (Luebke and Reilly 1995). Students report that women's studies courses are in-

formative and empowering; they provide a perspective on one's own life and on other college courses in ways that are often life-changing (Luebke and Reilly 1995; Musil 1992).

Women's studies seeks new ways of understanding—more comprehensive than those offered by traditional academic disciplines that so often view women in stereotypical ways, if at all. In addition, women's studies goes beyond description and analysis to focus on the consequences and applications of knowledge. In a women's studies class you are encouraged to share your own experiences and to relate the readings and discussions to your own life. Women's studies courses provide data that are often absent in the rest of the curriculum. You may be challenged by this and pushed to rethink some of your assumptions about gender, your own experiences of schooling, family, and relationships, and your positions on a number of complex issues. This kind of study often evokes strong emotional reactions, as your own life may be deeply affected by issues under discussion. These aspects of women's studies have given rise to criticisms that it is too "touchy-feely," more like therapy than serious study, or that it is an extended gripe session against men. We discuss these criticisms later in this introduction. Women's studies also often generates anger in students at the many forms of women's oppression, at other students' ignorance or lack of concern

1

for this, at being female in a male-dominated world, and at the daunting nature of the issues and problems faced by women that become problems for all of society.

The Framework for This Book: Collective Action for a Sustainable Future

This book is concerned with women in the United States and the rich diversity of their life experiences. We have selected readings that reflect this diversity, women speaking for themselves, telling what their lives are like. Each chapter also includes an overview essay to give some historical and contemporary context for the specific readings. As writers and editors, a big challenge for us has been to choose effective writings and salient facts from the vast wealth of materials available. There has been a groundswell of women's writing and publishing in the past twenty-five years, as well as a proliferation of popular and scholarly books and journals on issues of interest to women's studies students. When opinion polls, academic studies, government data, public debates, and grassroots research, available in print and through electronic media, are added to this, it is easy to be swamped with information and opposing viewpoints.

In making our selections we have filtered this wealth of material according to a number of principles—our particular road map.

An Activist Approach

We argue that women and men in the United States face a range of serious problems in the years ahead if we are to sustain our lives and the lives of our children. Although some women have benefited from greater opportunities for education and wage earning in recent years, many are now working harder, or working longer hours than their mothers did, under pressure to keep a job and to juggle their work lives with family responsibilities. In the 1980s and 1990s a range of economic changes and government policies have made many women's lives more difficult. Examples include a loss of factory and office work as jobs are moved overseas or become automated; government failure to introduce an adequate system of child care or a health-care system that

will benefit everyone; cuts in welfare and Aid to Families with Dependent Children; greater restriction of government support to immigrants and their families; and a dramatic increase in the number of women now incarcerated compared with the number from a decade ago. While the U.S. military budget consumes a massive 49 percent of federal income tax, according to the War Resisters League (1997), and some states spend more public money on new jails and prisons than on higher education, countless thousands of people are homeless, inner-city schools lack basic resources, and Head Start and other preschool programs are cut back. Individual women and men are personally affected by these changes and policies as they negotiate intimate relationships and family life.

We see collective action for progressive social change as a major goal of scholarly work, and thus, in the face of these economic and political trends, we take a deliberately activist approach in this book. We mention many practical projects and organizations to give students a sense of how much activist work is going on that is often not visible in the mainstream media. Throughout our discussion we emphasize the diversity of women's experiences. These differences have often divided women. We assume no easy "sisterhood" across lines of race, class, age, or sexual orientation, for example, but we do believe that alliances built firmly on the recognition and understanding of such differences make collective action possible.

A Sustainable and Secure Future

We see sustainability and security as central issues for the twenty-first century. These involve questions about the distribution of wealth, both within the United States and between the rich and poor countries of the world, and about the direction of future economic development. Another concern is the rapid deterioration of the physical environment on our overburdened planet. In many chapters security is an underlying theme. This includes the individual security of knowing who we are; having secure family relationships; living in freedom from threats, violence, or coercion; having adequate income or livelihood; and enjoying health and well-being. It also involves security for the community, the nation, and the planet, and includes issues like crime, the role of the military, and the crucial importance of the physical environment. Throughout the book we emphasize severe structural inequalities between people: women and men, white people and people of color, older people and young people, for example. We see these inequalities as a major threat to long-term security because they create literal and metaphorical walls, gates, and fences that separate people and maintain hierarchies among us. We also argue that a more sustainable future means re-thinking materialism and consumerism and finding new ways to distribute wealth so that everyone has the basics of life. These issues affect not only women, of course, and are not solely the responsibility of women, but women are actively involved in community organizing and movements for economic and environmental justice in the United States and many other countries, often in greater numbers than men.

The United States in a Global Context

This is not a book about global feminism. Its focus is on the United States, but we also comment on the wider global context within which the United States operates. We recognize the racial and ethnic diversity of this country; many people in the United States were not born here and come with hopes for a better future, but they also have no illusions about inequalities in the United States. We argue that people in the United States need to understand the significance of this country's preeminence in the world, manifested culturally—through the dominance of the English language and in widespread distribution of U.S. movies, pop music, books, and magazines—as well as economically, through the power of the dollar as an international currency and the impact of U.S.-based corporations abroad. We need to understand the significance of the globalization of the economy for people in the United States as well as throughout the world. We must understand the connections between domestic policy issues like health care, child care, and welfare, and foreign policy issues, such as military expenditures and foreign aid.

Linking the Personal and the Global

Throughout the book we use the terms **micro level** (personal or individual), **meso level** (community, neighborhood, or school, for example), **macro level** (national), and **global level.** To understand people's

experiences or the complexity of a particular issue, it is necessary to look at all these levels and how they interconnect. For instance, a personal relationship between two people might be thought to operate on a micro level. However, both partners bring all of themselves to the relationship. Thus, in addition to micro-level factors such as appearance, generosity, or their determination not to repeat the mistakes of their parents' relationships, there are also meso-level factors—such as their connections to people of other faiths or races—and macro-level factors—such as the obvious or hidden ways in which men or White people are privileged in this society. As editors we have made these connections in our overview essays and looked for writings that make these links between levels of analysis.

A Matrix of Oppressions

Underlying our analysis throughout the book is the concept of oppression, which we see as a group phenomenon, regardless of whether individuals in a group think they are oppressed or want to be in dominant positions. Men, as a group, are advantaged by sexism, for example, while women, as a group, are disadvantaged. Every form of oppression—for instance, **sexism, racism, classism, heterosexism, anti-Semitism, able-bodyism**—is rooted in our **social institutions**—such as the family, education, religion, and the media. Oppression, then, is systemic, and it is systematic. It is used consistently by one group of people—those who are dominant in this society—to rule, control, and exploit (to varying degrees) another group—those who are subordinate—for the benefit of the dominant group. Oppression works through systems of inequality, as well as the dominance of certain values, beliefs, and assumptions about people and how society should be organized. These are institutional and ideological controls. Members of dominant groups generally have built-in economic, political, and cultural benefits and power, regardless of whether they are aware of, or even want, these benefits. This process of accruing benefits and power from institutional inequalities is often referred to as **privilege.** Those most privileged are often those least likely to be aware of it or to recognize it (McIntosh 1988). Oppression works on personal (micro), community (meso), national (macro), and global levels.

Oppression involves **prejudice,** which we define as unreasonable, unfair, and hostile attitudes toward people, and **discrimination,** differential treatment favoring those who are in positions of dominance. But oppression reaches beyond individual bigotry or good intentions: it is promoted by the **ideologies** and practices of every institution we encounter and are part of and cannot be fully changed without fundamental changes in these institutions (Anderson and Collins 1995). Our definition of oppression assumes that everyone is socialized to participate in oppressive practices, thereby helping to maintain them. People may be involved as direct perpetrators or passive beneficiaries, or they may direct **internalized oppression** at members of their own group. Oppression results in appropriation—the loss—both voluntary and involuntary—of voice, identity, and agency of oppressed peoples.

It is important to think about oppression as an intricate system, at times blatantly obvious and at others subtly nuanced, rather than an either/or dichotomy of privileged/disadvantaged or oppressor/oppressed. We use the term **matrix of oppression** to describe the interconnection and interrelatedness of various forms of oppression. People can be privileged in some respects (race or gender, for example) and disadvantaged in others (class or sexual orientation, for example).

Feminisms: Tangling with the "F" Word

Whether or not you consider yourself a feminist as a matter of personal identity, in women's studies you will study feminist perspectives and theories because these seek to understand and explain gender. Feminism is a term with a great deal of baggage. For some it is positive and empowering. For others it conjures up negative images of "ugly" women in overalls and flannel shirts, women who do not wear makeup or shave their legs or underarms and who are said to be lesbians, man-haters, or "ball-busters." Many women do not want to be associated with the label feminist. They may agree that women deserve higher pay, sexual freedom, or greater opportunity, "but they are careful to start their comments with a disclaimer: 'I'm not a feminist, but. . . .'"

In the past few years virtually every major U.S. publication has published a "feminism has gone too far" piece. Some lament the difficulties of being White and male in the 1990s; others blame women's dissatisfactions on "too much equality"; and still others equate feminism with a "victim" mentality. A number of women are highly visible in this discourse, courted by talk-show hosts and interviewed in the Sunday newspapers. Naomi Wolf (1993), for example, promotes "power feminism"—the idea that real feminists are go-getting, smart, and equal contenders for power with men. Karen Lehrman (1993) attempts to discredit women's studies as unacademic, inappropriately personal, providing easy credits, and selling women short in terms of education. Elizabeth Fox-Genovese (1994) criticizes "the new Puritanism" of feminism. Katie Roiphe (1993) attacks "rape crisis feminism." Camille Paglia (1990) says that women who go to frat houses on campus deserve to be raped. An *Esquire* magazine article talked approvingly of "do me feminism" and quotes a woman academic who claims that there are a lot of "homely girls" in women's studies (Quindlen 1994). When women talk of violence—battering, incest, rape, sexual abuse, and harassment—or racism, or living in poverty, or aging without health insurance, they are said to be "victim" feminists, or perhaps worse, "feminazis"—anti-sex, no fun, whining critics who are out to destroy men and the male establishment. This is part of what Faludi (1991) means when she talks of a backlash against feminism and women's rights and an erosion of the gains made for and by women in the past twenty-five years or so. In our society, women are socialized to care for men and to spare their feelings, but recognizing and discussing institutional inequalities between women as a group and men as a group are very different from "man-bashing." This garbled, trivializing media framework contributes to the many myths and misunderstandings about women's studies on the part of students and scholars in other fields. We consider three of these myths here.

Myth 1: Women's Studies Is Ideological

Some people assume that women's studies is not "real" scholarship but feminist propaganda. Yet feminist inquiry, analysis, and activism have arisen from real problems experienced by real women, from well-documented inequalities and discrimination. For instance, data on women's wages recorded for more than one hundred years in the United States show that women's wages, on average, have never risen above 70 percent of what men earn on average — that is, on average, women earn seventy cents for every dollar earned by men. And women of color fare much worse in this respect than White women. As we mentioned above, women's studies arose out of feminist organizing, and it values scholarly work that is relevant to activist concerns. Women's studies courses and projects seek to link intellectual, experiential, and emotional forms of connected knowing with the goal of improving women's lives. Women's studies is a rigorous endeavor, but its conception of rigor differs from that of much traditional scholarship, which values abstract, in-depth knowledge, narrowly defined. Knowledge is never neutral, and in women's studies this is made explicit.

To some students and scholars, feminism is something to believe in because it provides a perspective that makes sense of the world and is personally empowering. But students who blithely blame everything on "rich White men," or "the patriarchy" without taking the trouble to read and think critically are anti-intellectual and inadvertently reinforce the notion that women's studies is anti-intellectual.

Myth 2: Women's Studies Is a White, Middle-Class Thing

Some White middle-class feminists have made, and still make, untenable claims about all women based on their own, necessarily partial, experience. Since the writings of Aphra Behn in the early 1600s, however, there have been White women who have thought about race and class as well as gender. Some White feminists worked against slavery in the nineteenth century, organized against the Ku Klux Klan, and participated in the civil rights movement of the 1950s and 1960s. Indeed, the 1970s revitalization of feminism in the United States came out of civil rights organizing. In the past twenty-five years or so, White feminists like Charlotte Bunch, Ruth Frankenberg, Peggy McIntosh, Minnie Bruce Pratt, Adrienne Rich, and Mab Segrest have worked to integrate race and gender in their work. Much more can be done in this regard, but there is a foundation to build on. Many notable scholars, writers, and activists of color are also feminists. Among African-Americans these include Toni Cade Bambara, Linda Burnham, Patricia Hill Collins, Angela Davis, bell hooks, June Jordan, Audre Lorde, Barbara Omolade, Sonia Sanchez, and Barbara Smith; among Asian-Americans, Maxine Hong Kingston, Janice Mirikitani, Miriam Ching Louie, Chandra Talpade Mohanty, Sonia Shah, Nellie Wong, and Merle Woo; among Latinas, Gloria Anzaldua, Aida Hurtado, Elizabeth Martinez, Cherrie Moraga, and Aurora Levins Morales; among Native Americans, Paula Gunn Allen, Beth Brant, Chrystos, and Joy Harjo. Many of these writers are included in this anthology.

Myth 3: Women's Studies Is Narrowly Concerned with Women's Issues

Although women's studies aims to focus on women's experiences — in all their diversity — we do not see this as catering to narrow "special interests." On the contrary, feminist analyses provide a series of lenses to examine many topics and academic disciplines, including psychology, sociology, anthropology, political science, law, international relations, economic development, national income accounting, human biology, philosophies of science, and physics. Feminist scholarship is on the cutting edge of many academic fields, especially literature, history, philosophy, and film and media studies. It also raises crucial questions about teaching and learning, research design and methodologies, and theories of knowledge. At root, women's studies is concerned with thinking critically about the world in all its complexity.

Scope of the Book

The book is concerned with the project of theorizing about the oppressive conditions facing women today and the long-term work of transforming those conditions. Therefore, we begin with a discussion about the process of theory making and the importance of theory for social change. In the next three chapters we analyze women's experiences of self and home in terms of identity, body politics, and relationships and families. We then examine, in Chapter 5, the significance of living in a global economy and what it means, at all the levels of analysis mentioned earlier, to be a part of the United States. This discussion of the global economy is part of the theoretical framework for understanding women's experiences of work, wages, and welfare, health, crime and criminalization, the military, and the environment; these are treated in Chapters 6–10. We end, in Chapter 11, with a discussion of social change and focus on the importance of theories, visions, and action for creating change. Our overall argument is that to improve the lives of women in the United States also means redefining security and directing ourselves, our communities, this society, and the wider world toward a more sustainable future.

◆◆◆

CHAPTER ONE

Theory and Theorizing:
Integrative Frameworks for Understanding

W hy are girls in the United States generally better at creative writing than at math? Has this always been so? Is this difference inevitable? Is rape about sexuality? Power? Both? Or neither? What is pornography? Is it the same as erotica? Do lesbians really want to be men? Why do so many marriages end in divorce? Why are so many children in the United States brought up in poverty? Why are more women going to jail than ever before?

People often say that facts speak for themselves. On the contrary, we argue that facts are always open to interpretation. They are "made to speak" according to your particular point of view. This is why we open this book about U.S. women's lives with a chapter on theory and theory making. How you think about women's situations and experiences affects what you see and what you understand by what you see. This chapter may seem abstract in the beginning, and you may want to return to it as you work with the material in the book. It would also be a good idea to review it at the end of your course. In this chapter we look at theory and theory making in general terms and give a brief account of feminist theoretical perspectives in preparation for understanding and interpreting women's experiences and issues presented in the rest of the book. During the course of the discussion we will consider these questions: What is a theory? Who creates theory, and how is it created? What is the purpose of theory?

Definition of a Theory

Consider the following assertion about poverty that many people in our society make: Poor people are poor because they are lazy. Think about the following questions:

1. What is the purpose of this statement?

2. What are the underlying assumptions on which it is based?

3. If the statement were true, what would it imply about action that should be taken?

4. Who came up with this idea, under what circumstances, and when?

5. How did this idea become popular?

6. What would you need to know to decide whether this statement is really true?

The statement above is a theory. It is one explanation of poverty, of why people are poor. It is built on a set of assumptions, or certain factors taken for granted. For example, this theory assumes there are well-paying jobs for all who want to work and that everyone meets the necessary requirements for those jobs, such as education, skills, or a means of providing for child care. These factors are proposed as facts or truths. This explanation of poverty takes a moral perspective. A psychological explanation of poverty may argue that people are poor because they have low self-esteem, lack self-confidence, and take on self-defeating behaviors. A sociological explanation might conclude that structures in our society, such as the educational and economic systems, are organized to exclude certain groups from being able to live above the poverty line. Each theory explicitly or implicitly suggests how to address the problem, which could then lead to a particular set of actions. If the problem is defined in terms of laziness, a step to ending poverty might be to punish people who are poor; if it is defined in psychological terms, assertiveness training or counseling might be suggested; and if it is defined in terms of structural inequality, ending discrimination would be the answer.

Every human being participates in theorizing, the activity of creating theory. For instance, we analyze the causes of poverty in our communities, the impact of immigration on the state we live in, or the experience of date rape. Theories generated by ordinary people, however, are not regarded as worthy of consideration beyond their own spheres of influence, among friends or coworkers, for example. Historically, Western, university-educated men from the upper classes—most often academics—and their theories, which are supported by societal institutions such as education and government, have had the greatest impact on how human beings and social phenomena are explained and understood. Their considerable influence, indeed, has even compelled many people simply to accept what is presented to them as conventional wisdom. For instance, a proposition that most people apparently agree with is "there will always be poverty," though this is not necessarily true. In the following sections, we discuss how only certain kinds of theories have been legitimized in this society and suggest another way of theorizing and developing knowledge that engages ordinary people.

Theory, Theorizing, and Ways of Knowing

The Dominant Perspective

From the perspective of the **dominant culture**—the values, symbols, means of expression, language, and interests of the people in power in this society—

only certain types of theories have authority. Generally, the authoritativeness of a theory about human beings and society is evaluated primarily along two dimensions. One is its degree of formality, which is determined according to how closely its development followed a particular way of theorizing, the so-called scientific method, the basics of which most of us learned in high school science classes. The second is the scope and generality of the theory (Smelser 1994).

Although in practice there are several variations of the scientific method, key elements must be present for a theory to fit in this category. The scientific method, originally devised by natural scientists, rests on the presumption of **objectivity,** "an attitude, philosophy, or claim . . . independent of the individual mind [through emotional detachment and social distance] . . . verified by a socially agreed-upon procedure such as those developed in science, mathematics, or history" (Kohl 1992, p. 84). Objectivity is seen as both a place to begin the process of theorizing and the outcome of that process. It has been long argued that "if done properly, [science] is the epitome of objectivity" (Tuana 1989, p. xi). Therefore, theories developed correctly using the scientific method are held out as value-free and neutral. The method is also empirical. That is, for something to be a fact, it must be physically observable and countable or measurable. This proposition is extended to include the notion that something is either true or not true, fact or not fact. Last, the experimental method, commonly used in science, "attempts to understand a whole by examining its parts, asking how something works rather than why it works, and derives abstract formulas to predict future results" (Duff 1993, p. 51). In summary, these elements add up to research methods that

> generally require a distancing of the researcher from her or his subjects of study; . . . absence of emotions from the research process; ethics and values are deemed inappropriate in the research process, either as the reason for scientific inquiry or as part of the research process itself; . . . adversarial debates, whether written or oral, become the preferred method of ascertaining truth: the arguments that can withstand the greatest assault and survive intact become the strongest truth.
>
> *(Collins 1990, p. 205)*

The scientific method was adopted by theorists in the social sciences as a way to validate and legitimate social scientific knowledge beginning in the late nineteenth century, as disciplines such as psychology and sociology were being developed. Since that time, many other academic disciplines, like education, nursing, and social work, have also adopted it as the primary method with which to develop new knowledge in their fields.

The second dimension for evaluating and judging theory is concerned with its scope and generality. The range is from the most concrete explanation with the narrowest scope and most limited generality to the other end of the continuum, the general theory, which is the most abstract and is assumed to have the most general application (Smelser, 1994). Many general theories have been promoted and accepted as being universally applicable. One of them, **biological determinism,** holds that a group's biological or genetic makeup shapes its social, political, and economic destiny; this theory is critiqued by Ruth Hubbard in Reading 3.

Alternative Perspectives

Evaluating and judging theories according to the scientific method have come under heavy criticism from theorists who typically have been viewed as outsiders to traditional academic circles, such as scholars in women's studies, ethnic studies, gay/lesbian studies, and some mainstream academics. These theorists have seen the fallacies, biases, and harmful outcomes of that way of creating knowledge. The primary criticisms are that knowledge created by the scientific method is not value-free, neutral, or generalizable to the extent it is claimed to be. Science, as with other academic disciplines, is "a cultural institution and as such is structured by the political, social, and economic values of the culture within which it is practiced" (Tuana 1989, p. xi). As Hubbard (1989) argues:

> to be believed, scientific facts must fit the worldview of the times. Therefore, at times of tension and upheaval, such as during the last two decades, some researchers always try to prove that differences in the social, political, and economic status of women and men, blacks and whites, poor people and rich people, are inevitable because they are the results of people's

inborn qualities and traits. Such scientists have tried to "prove" that blacks are innately less intelligent than whites, or that women are innately weaker, more nurturing, less good at math than men.

(p. 121)

Rather than being neutral, all knowledge is socially constructed, value-laden, and biased and reflects and serves the interests of the culture that produced it, in this case the dominant culture. Anne Fausto-Sterling makes this point in Reading 7.

The problem is not that theories are value-laden or biased, but that the values and biases of many theories are hidden under the cloak of "scientific objectivity." Moreover, there is the assumption that "if the science is 'good,' in a professional sense [following closely the rules of scientific method], it will also be good for society" (Hubbard 1989, p. 121). Many theories are applied not only to the United States but also to the rest of the world, often without acknowledgment that they primarily serve the interests of the dominant group in the United States. These theories are used to justify the inequalities in our society as well as differences and inequalities between the United States and other societies. Despite claims to the contrary, general theories created by mainstream scholars serve a political purpose in addition to whatever other purpose they are intended to serve. And, as Collins (1990) asserts, "Because elite white men and their representatives control structures of knowledge validation, white male interests pervade thematic content of traditional scholarship" (p. 201).

We further argue that theorizing is a political project, regardless of whether the politics is acknowledged. Social theories—explaining the behavior of human beings and society—serve to support the existing social order or can be used to challenge it. For women and men of color, White women, poor people, members of oppressed groups, and people with privilege who are interested in progressive social change, the political work of theorizing is to generate knowledge that challenges conventional wisdom and those formal theories that do not explain their real lived experiences, provide satisfactory solutions to their difficulties, or lead to their liberation. Charlotte Bunch and Aida Hurtado make this point in Readings 1 and 4, respectively.

"Socially Lived" Theorizing As discussed earlier, traditional scholarship primarily validates knowledge that is produced, using some form of the scientific method, by White men and others who form an elite group of scholars or subscribe to their views and approaches. We argue that theorizing is not the sole domain of elites. Catharine MacKinnon (1991) talks about "articulating the theory of women's practice — resistance, visions, consciousness, injuries, notions of community, experiences of inequality. By practic[e], I mean socially lived" (p. 20). In the following pages, we present our framework for theory making, drawing from the work of MacKinnon and other scholars in women's studies, ethnic studies, and other disciplines who have challenged traditional academic ways of knowing and understanding the social world. We begin with the following assumptions:

- All knowledge is socially constructed; there is no value-free or neutral knowledge.

- Everyone has the capacity to be a creator of knowledge.

- What one knows comes out of a specific historical and cultural context, whether one is an insider or outsider to that context.

- It is the responsibility of everyone to reflect on, evaluate, and judge the world around us, and our places in that world, as an essential element of theorizing.

- Knowledge should be used for the purposes of helping to liberate oppressed people and to transform the current social and economic structures of inequality into a sustainable world for all people.

As Catharine MacKinnon remarks, "It is common to say that something is good in theory but not in practice. I always want to say, then it is not such a good theory, is it?" (1991, p. 1).

Knowing and Understanding In writing about the Holocaust — the mass murder primarily of Jewish people but also of gypsies, people with disabilities, and gay people in Europe during World War II — Alan Rosenberg (1988) makes a profound distinction between knowing and understanding something. According to Rosenberg, knowing is having the facts about a particular event or condition. One knows the Holocaust happened: Eight million people were murdered, and countless others were tortured, raped, and otherwise devastated; the Nazis, under the leadership of Adolph Hitler, were the perpetrators; others, both inside and outside Germany, including the United States initially, were unable or refused to help; the result was the genocide of the Jewish people. Traditional educational practices, epitomized by the scientific method, teach us primarily to know. For Rosenberg, knowing is the first step to understanding, a much deeper process that, in the case of the Holocaust, involves not only comprehending its significance and longer-term effects but also trying to discover how to prevent similar injustices in the future.

> Knowing . . . refers to factual information or the process by which it is gathered. Understanding refers to systematically grasping the significance of an event in such a way that it becomes integrated into one's moral and intellectual life. Facts can be absorbed without their having any impact on the way we understand ourselves or the world we live in; facts in themselves do not make a difference. It is the understanding of them that makes a difference.
>
> *(Rosenberg 1988, p. 382)*

Recognizing theory making as a political project helps us understand, in the way Rosenberg describes it, the conditions facing not only women in particular but all oppressed peoples. So how do we begin to understand?

Early in the U.S. women's liberation movement of the sixties and seventies, the slogan "the personal is political" was popularized to validate individual women's personal experiences as a starting point for recognizing and understanding discrimination against women as a group. This promoted the practice of "starting from one's own experiences" as a legitimate way to theorize and create new knowledge. This practice was also useful in counteracting the dominant view of theorizing that personal experience, along with emotions and values, contaminates the "purity" of the scientific method. As a first step, starting from what we know the most about — our experiences, our **subjectivity** — is helpful, but it also contains obvious problems. On the one hand, there is self-centeredness, as reflected in comments such as "I can only know my experience," "I can only speak for myself," and "What does all this have to do with me?" On the other hand, a naive generalization like "As a woman, I assume that all women have experienced the same things I have" also limits the extent to which we can understand women's experiences in all their complexity. More recently, theorists critical of dominant perspectives have talked about **situated knowledge,** knowledge and ways of knowing that are specific to a particular context. What we know is the direct result of our experience, is understood in a specific historical and cultural context, and cannot be generalized. For instance, the experience of being a single mother as a poor teenager in a rural community in the mid-1990s would be quite different from being a single mother as an established professional in a big city. One could not apply her experience to the other, and neither could speak authoritatively about being a single mother in the 1960s.

Our task of socially lived theorizing involves several important challenges. We are faced with the self-centeredness of pure subjectivity, "in which knowledge and meaning [are] lodged in oneself and one's own experiences" (Maher and Tetreault 1994, p. 94). We must also negotiate the problem of the cultural relativism of situated knowledge, where the authenticity of subjective knowledge is not challenged because it is seen as someone's, or some group's, "real experience," and consequently, others do not have the authority to question it. Thus, the white supremacist views of Ku Klux Klan members might be considered equally as valid as those held by antiracist activists, or a New York judge could sentence a Chinese immigrant man to five years' probation for killing his wife on the argument that the murder was the result of "cultural differences" (Yen 1989). Given these major challenges arising out of pure subjectivity and cultural relativism, how can we generate knowledge that reflects the perspectives and interests of a broad range of people, communities, and life circumstances, that is visionary, not just reactive, and that could lead to social change? Socially lived theorizing requires a methodology that includes collective dialogue and **praxis**—reflection and action upon the world in order to transform it. Paulo Freire (1989) calls this methodology **conscientization,** or gaining a "critical consciousness," and describes it as "learning to perceive social, political, and economic contradictions, [the effects of the push and pull of opposing forces], and to take action against the oppressive elements of this reality" (p. 19).

"Learning to perceive social, political, and economic contradictions" is a tall order for many of us who have been formally educated by what Freire calls the "banking method," whereby teachers deposit knowledge—dates, historical facts, formulas for problem solving, for example—into the minds of students and expect them to be able to withdraw this information at a given time, such as during exams, quizzes, and class presentations. During our schooling most of us have never been asked such questions as, What are the assumptions in the statement you are making? How do you know what you know? Why do you think so? What are the implications of your position? Many of us have sat in class listening to a teacher or other students and have kept quiet when we knew what was being said did not match our experience. When we put forward our ideas and observations, they might have been shot down as silly, naive, or too idealistic. We were expected to back up our experience with facts. We were encouraged to accept facts and ideas as they were given to us and to accept social conditions as they are. Indeed, we may often have accepted things as they are without thinking about them, or simply not noticed injustices happening around us. Most likely, too, we have had little opportunity to engage in honest dialogue with others—both people like ourselves and those from different backgrounds—about important issues.

Having honest dialogues and asking critical questions move us beyond excessive subjectivity because we are compelled to see and understand many different sides of the same subject. Creating theory for social change—something that will advance human development and create a better world for all—gives us a basis for making critical judgments of facts and experiences. This in turn provides a framework for deciding where to draw the line on cultural relativism. Through ongoing, detailed discussion and conscientious listening to others we can generate a carefully thought-out set of principles that lead to greater understanding of issues and of acceptable actions in a given situation.

Many assume that the scientific method involves authoritativeness and rigor. We believe this alternative way of theorizing redefines rigor by demanding the engagement of our intellectual, emotional, and spiritual selves. It compels us to think systematically and critically, requires us to face the challenges of talking about our differences, and obligates us to consider the real implications and consequences of our theories. Knowledge created in this way helps us "to systematically grasp . . . the significance of an event in such a way that it becomes integrated into [our] moral and intellectual life, " also a form of rigor (Rosenberg 1988, p. 382).

In her essay "The Body Politic" (Reading 2), Abra Chernik discusses her personal struggle with an eating disorder. The subject matter of this essay is also relevant in Chapter 3, Body Politics, but we include it here because her process of coming to understand this issue provides an excellent example of socially lived theorizing at a personal and macro level.

Feminist Theories

Feminist theories seek to understand and explain women's experiences and differences between women and men. The following very brief discussion of various strands of feminist thought serves as a reference for the readings included in this book. Individual writers and activists with an interest in women's issues may draw on more than one of these strands, but we separate them here for ease of explanation. Although some writers and activists do not use these labels to describe their views, much women's studies literature does use these categories, and we expect that readers will want to return to this section from time to time. Throughout this book we refer to theoretical perspectives in the context of specific issues, but here we set out some baseline understandings by way of preparation.

An abstract discussion of theoretical strands may appear rather fixed and static. Bear in mind that these ideas are more dynamic and varied, and often less "pure" in practice, as activists may be prepared to compromise longer-term goals for short-term gains. The complexities of contentious issues like pornography or prostitution, for example, may defy easy analysis. As ideas inform activism, and vice versa, people may shift and modify their earlier views. Many of these perspectives overlap in places, making for the possibility of broad alliances and coalitions, which we discuss further in Chapter 11.

Liberal Feminism

A **liberal feminist** draws on ideas of political liberalism (Bird and Briller 1969; Friedan 1963; Steinem 1983) and sees the oppression of women in terms of inequality between women and men. Liberal feminists are concerned that women have equal rights, equal representation, and equal access to opportunities, for example, in education, politics, law, the military, the professions, and blue-collar trades. They focus on women's being treated as equals with men within existing economic and social structures. They often subscribe to the idea that private matters (relationships and family life, for example) are separate from public issues (law, politics, religion). Although these two spheres affect each other, they are governed by different rules, attitudes, and behavior. The family, for example, is the place where love, caring, and sensitivity come first. The National Organization for Women is an example of liberal feminist practice.

Radical Feminism

A **radical feminist** sees the oppression of women in terms of patriarchy, a system of male authority over women, especially manifested in sexuality, personal relationships, and the family (Daly 1976; Echols 1989; Harne and Miller 1996). This patriarchal power also carries over into the male-dominated world of work, government, religion, and law. Some radical feminists are involved in creating "women's culture" — music, art, performance, writing, and dance — and in celebrating women's lives, women's friendships, women's ways of thinking and knowing, and women's history. They have founded women's newsletters, presses, recording studios, bookstores, and music festivals. Radical feminists who argue that women should live entirely apart from men are called separatists. Because radical feminists are often lesbians, there is the saying that "feminism is the theory; lesbianism is the practice." Not all feminists are lesbians, and not all lesbians are feminists.

Socialist Feminism

A **socialist feminist** sees the oppression of women in terms of our subordinate position in a system defined as both patriarchal and capitalist (Eisenstein 1979; Mitchell 1990; Roberts and Mizuta 1993). In this view, capitalism is an economic system involving the class oppression of workers by the owners of capital. "Socialist . . . feminists argue that the capitalist mode of production is structured by a patriarchal sexual division of labor" (Humm 1992, p. 159). Theorists vary in their understanding of the precise relationship between capitalism and patriarchy. Socialist feminists seek to change social structures by redefining how women's work (paid and unpaid) is rewarded and valued. These feminists seek to create a more egalitarian society, with transformed relationships between women and men, and among workers, managers, and investors. Manual and mental work would be valued, and everyday culture would not be commercialized and commodified in the way it is under the current economic system.

Ecofeminism

Ecofeminism links the domination of women and the domination of nature (Diamond and Orenstein 1990; Merchant 1980; Mies and Shiva 1993). A core point in ecofeminist analysis involves the concept of dualism, where various attributes are thought of in terms of oppositions: culture/nature, mind/body, male/female, civilized/primitive, sacred/profane, subject/object, self/other, and so on. Val Plumwood (1993) argues that these dualisms are mutually reinforcing and should be thought of as an interlocking set. In each pair, one side is valued over the other. Culture, mind, male, civilized, for example, are valued over nature, body, female, primitive, which are thought of as "other" and inferior. Plumwood argues that dualism is the logic of hierarchical systems of thought—colonialism, racism, sexism, or militarism, for example—which rely on the idea of "otherness," enemies, and inferiority to justify superiority and domination. So ecofeminism is concerned with racism and economic exploitation as well as the domination of women and nature. This perspective is explored in more detail in Chapter 10.

Post-Modern Feminisms

Post-modern feminisms repudiate the broad-brush "universal" theorizing of liberalism, radical feminism, or socialism. Post-modern feminists emphasize the particularity of women's experiences in specific cultural and historical contexts (Ferguson and Wicke 1992; Nicholson 1990). This has led to detailed scholarship into the specifics of women's lives and subjective experiences. Some post-modern thinkers advocate abandoning the category "woman"

altogether because it implies some shared experience and leads to the false notion of collectivity—"women."

Integrative Feminism

In the 1970s and 1980s, women of color in the United States, White working-class women, and feminists from Third World countries criticized much U.S. feminism for emphasizing gender at the expense of race and class, and for putting forward the experiences of White, middle-class women as the experience of all women (Collins 1990; Davis 1983b; hooks 1984; Mohanty, Russo, and Torres 1991; Moraga and Anzaldua 1983; Smith 1983). They argue that women's experiences are structured by their class, race, ethnicity, and culture, as much as, sometimes perhaps more than, by gender. There can be no talk of gender as an autonomous category and no easy sisterhood among women unless these differences between us are recognized and acknowledged. In addition, since many U.S. feminists of color were also connected to liberation movements in Africa, Asia, and Central America, they integrated an explicitly anti-imperialist strand into their analysis. The Combahee River Collective Statement, written in the late 1970s by a group of Black feminists in the Boston area (Reading 5) is an example of an integrative perspective that draws on gender, race, and class at the same time. Writing in the early 1990s, Sonia Shah (Reading 6) points out that from the perspectives of Asian-American women, African-American women's theorizing has much to offer but is too narrowly focused on the experiences of Black women.

Such an integrative perspective is not only the prerogative of women of color, of course. It is a fundamental assumption throughout this anthology and one of the principles that guided our selection of writings. We argue for the specificity of individual experiences and for collective action, based on an understanding of differences. Kalima Rose exemplifies this approach in her account of the 1995 Beijing women's conference (Reading 8).

In attempting to understand any particular theoretical perspective, one should consider the following questions:

1. What does the theory aim to explain?

2. How does it do this?

3. Why is this of interest?

4. What are the basic arguments and assumptions?

5. What is the cultural and historical context giving rise to the theory?

6. What are the starting points and why?

7. What does the theory focus on? What does it ignore?

8. What key writers and activists are associated with it? Who are they in terms of gender, race, class, nation, sexual orientation?

9. Who are their critics? What is the criticism based on?

10. Do you find this perspective useful? Why?

11. Are you convinced by the arguments? Why? Why not?

12. What kinds of research questions does this perspective generate?

13. What kind of actions and projects follow from a particular theoretical perspective?

14. What situations or issues can you think of that are not addressed by this theoretical approach?

15. What is your theoretical framework?

16. How do you explain inequality between women and men, for example? Between White people and people of color? How do you explain poverty?

17. What is your theory of social change? How does social change happen? How is knowledge related to social change?

ONE

◆◆◆

Not by Degrees
Feminist Theory and Education
Charlotte Bunch

The development of feminist theory and a rigorous analysis of society are more important for us today than ever before. Feminists need to understand the forces working against us, as well as to analyze our experiences as a movement, if we are to survive the antiwoman backlash and keep our visions alive. When feminists despair, burn out, or give up, it is often because the forces against us are strong and because our theoretical framework does not give us a sense of how individual activities contribute to significant victories in the future. A solid feminist theory would help us understand present events in a way that would enable us to develop the visions and plans for change that sustain people engaged in day-to-day political activity.

When I left the university to do full-time work in "the movement" in the 1960s, it didn't occur to me that I would return one day to teach or write feminist theory. Like many others who chose to become movement activists then, I felt that I was leaving behind not only the academic world, but also what I saw as irrelevant theorizing. However, as I experienced the problems of movement organizing when an overall analysis was lacking, felt the frustration of conflicts where issues were not clear, and observed people dropping out of political activity, I became aware of the critical role of theory in the movement. I began to see feminist theory not as academic, but as a process based on understanding and advancing the activist movement.

While my growing sense of the importance of theory applied to all my feminist work, the urgency that I felt about it became clearest during my involvement with lesbian-feminism. When the lesbian issue became a major controversy in the women's movement in the early 1970s, I realized that in order for lesbians to function openly, we would have to understand *why* there was so much resistance to this issue. It was not enough to document discrimination against homosexuals or to appeal to fairness. We had to figure out why lesbianism was taboo, why it was a threat to feminists, and then devise strategies accordingly. I saw that my life as a lesbian in the movement depended on, among other things, the development of a theory that would explain our immediate conflicts in the context of a long-term view of feminism. This theoretical perspective developed along with our activism, but it required us to consciously ask certain questions, to look at our experiences in and out of the movement, and to consider existing feminist theory in new ways. Through this process, new interpretations of the relationship between lesbianism and feminism, and new strategies for ending lesbian oppression emerged.

For example, as we examined feminists' fear of being called lesbians, we were able to confront directly the role that such name-calling played in the oppression of all women. Having a theory about lesbian oppression did not tell us what to do tactically, but it did provide a framework for understanding situations, for placing them in a broader context, and for evaluating possible courses of action. This experience showed me that theory was not simply intellectually interesting, but was crucial to the survival of feminism.

The Functions of Feminist Theory

Theory enables us to see immediate needs in terms of long-range goals and an overall perspective on the world. It thus gives us a framework for evaluating various strategies in both the long and the short run, and for seeing the types of changes that they are likely to produce. Theory is not just a body of facts or a set of personal opinions. It involves explanations and hypotheses that are based on available knowledge and experience. It is also dependent on conjecture and insight about how to interpret those facts and experiences and their significance.

No theory is totally "objective," since it reflects the interests, values, and assumptions of those who created it. Feminist theory relies on the underlying assumption that it will aid the liberation of women. Feminist theory, therefore, is not an unengaged study of women. It is an effort to bring insights from the movement and from various female experiences together with research and data-gathering to produce new approaches to understanding and ending female oppression.

While feminist theory begins with the immediate need to end women's oppression, it is also a way of viewing the world. Feminism is an entire world view or *gestalt*, not just a list of "women's issues." Feminist theory provides a basis for understanding every area of our lives, and a feminist perspective can affect the world politically, culturally, economically, and spiritually. The initial tenets of feminism have already been established — the idea that power is based on gender differences and that men's illegitimate power over women taints all aspects of society, for instance. But now we face the arduous task of systematically working through these ideas, fleshing them out and discovering new ones.

When the development of feminist theory seems too slow for the changes that we seek, feminists are tempted to submerge our insights into one of the century's two dominant progressive theories of reality and change: democratic liberalism or Marxist socialism. However, the limitations of these systems are increasingly obvious. While feminism can learn from both of them, it must not be tied to either because its greatest strength lies in providing an alternative view of the world.

The full implications of feminism will evolve over time, as we organize, experiment, think, analyze, and revise our ideas and strategies in light of our experiences. No theory emerges in full detail overnight; the dominant theories of our day have expanded and changed over many decades. That it will take time should not discourage us. That we might fail to pursue our ideas — given the enormous need for them in society today — is unconscionable.

Because feminist theory is still emerging and does not have agreed-upon answers (or even approaches to many questions), it is difficult to work out strategies based on that theory. This difficulty can lead feminists to rely on the other theories of change or to fall into the "any action/no action" bind. When caught in this bind, one may go ahead with action — any action — for its own sake, or be paralyzed, taking no action for lack of a sense of what is "right." To escape this bind, we must remember that we do not need, and indeed never will have, all the answers before we act, and that it is often only through taking action that we can discover some of them. The purpose of theory, then, is not to provide a pat set of answers about what to do, but to guide us in sorting out options, and to keep us out of the "any action/no action" bind. Theory also keeps us aware of the questions that need to be asked, so that what we learn in each activity will lead to more effective strategies in the future. Theory thus both grows out of and guides activism in a continuous, spiraling process.

In pursuing feminist theory as an activist, I have become increasingly aware of the need to demystify it. Theory is not something set apart from our lives. Our assumptions about reality and change influence our actions constantly. The question is not whether we have a theory, but how aware we are of the assumptions behind our actions, and how conscious we are of the choices we make daily among different theories. For example, when we decide whether to put our energies into a rape-crisis center or into efforts to change rape laws, we are acting according to certain theories about how service projects and legislation affect change. These theories may be implicit or explicit, but they are always there.

A Model for Theory

Theory doesn't necessarily progress in a linear fashion, but examining its components is useful in understanding existing political theory as well as in developing new insights. In the model I have developed, I divide theory into four interrelated parts: description, analysis, vision, and strategy.

1. Description: *Describing what exists* may sound simple, but the choices that we make about interpreting and naming reality provide the basis for the rest of our theory. Changing people's perceptions of the world through new descriptions of reality is usually a prerequisite for altering that reality. For example, fifteen years ago, few people would say that women in the United States were oppressed. Today, the oppression of women is acknowledged by a large number of people, primarily because of feminist work which described that oppression in a number of ways. This work has involved consciousness-raising, as well as gathering and interpreting facts about women in order to substantiate our assertions. Description is necessary for all theory; unfortunately for feminism, much of our work has not yet gone beyond this point.

2. Analysis: *Analyzing why that reality exists* involves determining its origins and the reasons for its perpetuation. This is perhaps the most complex task of theory and is often seen as its entire function. In seeking to understand the sources of women's oppression and why it is perpetuated, we have to examine biology, economics, psychology, sexuality, and so on. We must also look at what groups and institutions benefit from oppression, and why they will, therefore, strive to maintain it. Analyzing why women are oppressed involves such things as sorting out how the forms of oppression change over time while the basic fact of oppression remains, or probing how the forms of oppression vary in different cultures while there are cross-cultural similarities.

Analysis of why something happens sometimes gets short-circuited by the temptation to ascribe everything to one single factor, such as capitalism or motherhood. In developing an analysis, I find that it is useful to focus initially on a phenomenon in a limited context and consider a wide range of factors that may affect it. Then, as that context is understood, the analysis can be expanded. Above all, we need not feel that we must answer the "why" of everything all at once with a single explanation.

3. Vision: *Determining what should exist* requires establishing principles (or values) and setting goals. In taking action to bring about change, we operate consciously or unconsciously out of certain assumptions about what is right or what we value (principles), and out of our sense of what society ought to be (goals). This aspect of theory involves making a conscious choice about those principles in order to make our visions and goals concrete. We must look at our basic assumptions about such things as "human nature" and how it can be changed, about the relationships of individuals to groups, about whether men and women are essentially different, for example. We may choose not to address some of these issues yet, but since every action carries implicit assumptions, we must be conscious of them so that we do not operate out of old theoretical frameworks by default. The clearer we are about our principles—for example, whether we think that women should gain as much power as possible in every area, or believe, instead, that power itself should be eliminated— the more easily we can set our long-term goals. Im-

mediate goals can then be based on an assessment of what can be accomplished that may be short of our long-term vision, but moves toward, not away, from it. Visions, principles, and goals will change with experience, but the more explicit we make them, the more our actions can be directed toward creating the society we want, as well as reacting to what we don't like.

4. Strategy: *Hypothesizing how to change what is to what should be* moves directly into questions of changing reality. Some people see strategy not as part of theory, but rather as a planning process based on theory. But I include strategy here in its broadest sense — the overall approach one takes to how to accomplish one's goals. The descriptive and analytic process of theory help develop a more systematic understanding of the way things work, but they usually do not make obvious what one should do. Developing a strategy requires that we draw out the consequences of our theory and suggest general directions for change.

Like the other aspects of theory, this involves a combination of information-gathering and creative speculation. It entails making judgments about what will lead to change — judgments that are based both on description and analysis of reality, and on visions, principles, and goals. Developing a strategy also involves examining various tools for change — legislative, military, spiritual — and determining which are most effective in what situations. There are many questions to consider, such as what sectors of society can best be mobilized to carry out which types of action. In working out which strategies will be most effective, the interaction between developing theory and actively experimenting with it becomes most clear. For in all aspects of theory development, theory and activism continually inform and alter each other.

Using the Model

This four-part model for theory can be used in many ways. In my feminist-theory classes, we have tried to understand different theories by outlining how various authors address each of its developmental parts. For example, we take Shulamith Firestone's *Dialectic of Sex* and discuss her approach to descrip-

tion, analysis, vision, and strategy. Then we compare her ideas in each area with those of other radical feminists, in an effort to see the common tenets of radical feminism, the important areas of disagreement, and the strategy implications of those differences. We then take the same approach to socialist-feminist authors, compare them to each other and to radical feminist works, and so on.

Another way to use this approach to theory is to examine possible ways of addressing a specific issue in terms of these processes. For example, on the issue of reproductive freedom, we can use theoretical work to understand the implications behind various strategies. Considerable work has been done detailing the variety of ways in which women lack control over reproduction, from forced sterilization to negligence in the development of contraceptives. Several analyses of why women do not have control over our bodies have been suggested. These range from the idea that men fear women's powers to create life and therefore compensate by controlling reproduction, to the proposition that capitalism is the primary cause because it must control the number of workers produced, to the view that the Catholic Church is the dominant perpetuator of this situation because its control over reproduction and matters of family life is central to its power. Most analyses also look at which institutions are most influential and which are most vulnerable to change, and the relations between them — e.g., how the Catholic Church affects hospital and government policies.

There are considerable differences of opinion about how reproduction should be treated. Some feminists argue that women should have absolute control over our bodies and reproduction at all times and in all circumstances. Others contend that there can be some legitimate limits on an individual woman's control; in the case of abortion, for example, limiting a woman's right to abortion on demand to the first trimester. Some argue that the state should prescribe standards of control that "protect" women such as the requirement of a thirty-day waiting period for any sterilization; and still others hold that a woman's control must be subordinate to the obligation of government to supervise overall population growth.

The practical consequences of these differences in theory become clear when strategies for gaining women's reproductive rights are discussed. Even among those who agree that women's lack of control over reproduction is central to our oppression, there are differences in strategy based on differences in analysis and vision. Those who think that the Catholic Church is the primary enemy of women's reproductive rights may focus on efforts to remove Church influence on the state, the fight against religious tax exemptions, and so on, while those who see multinational corporations as the primary controller of population issues would focus on them. The controversy among feminists over whether having the government require a thirty-day waiting period for all sterilizations would protect women or further abridge our rights to control our bodies illustrates how disagreement over vision and goals leads to different strategies and often to conflict over what we will demand.

This example, though simplified here, illustrates how the four-part model in particular, and theory in general, can be used to clarify practical political problems. When we understand the basis of our disagreements and the nature of the forces against us, we are better equipped to come to some agreement or to realize when compromise may not be possible. Theory helps clarify how things work and what our choices are, and thus aids in determining where to put our energies and how to challenge the sources of our oppression most effectively.

Theory is also a tool for passing on the knowledge we have gained from our life experiences and movement projects. Feminists need to analyze personal experiences as well as political developments—to sort out our initial assumptions about goals and analysis, to look at the strategies we used and why, and to evaluate the results in terms of what could be learned for the future.

T W O

◆◆◆

The Body Politic

Abra Fortune Chernik

My body possesses solidness and curve, like the ocean. My weight mingles with Earth's pull, drawing me onto the sand. I have not always sent waves into the world. I flew off once, for five years, and swirled madly like a cracking brown leaf in the salty autumn wind. I wafted, dried out, apathetic.

I had no weight in the world during my years of anorexia. Curled up inside my thinness, a refugee in a cocoon of hunger, I lost the capacity to care about myself or others. I starved my body and twitched in place as those around me danced in the energy of shared existence and progressed in their lives. When I graduated from college crowned with academic honors, professors praised my potential. I wanted only to vanish.

It took three months of hospitalization and two years of outpatient psychotherapy for me to learn to nourish myself and to live in a body that expresses strength and honesty in its shape. I accepted my right and my obligation to take up room with my figure, voice and spirit. I remembered how to tumble forward and touch the world that holds me. I chose the ocean as my guide.

Who disputes the ocean's fullness?

Growing up in New York City, I did not care about the feminist movement. Although I attended an all-girls high school, we read mostly male authors and studied the history of men. Embracing mainstream culture without question, I learned about womanhood from fashion magazines, Madison Avenue and Hollywood. I dismissed feminist alternatives as foreign and offensive, swathed as they were in stereotypes that threatened my adolescent need for conformity.

Puberty hit late; I did not complain. I enjoyed living in the lanky body of a tall child and insisted on the title of "girl." If anyone referred to me as a "young woman," I would cry out, horrified, "Do not call me the *W* word!" But at sixteen years old, I could no longer deny my fate. My stomach and breasts rounded. Curly black hair sprouted in the most embarrassing places. Hips swelled from a once-flat plane. Interpreting maturation as an unacceptable lapse into fleshiness, I resolved to eradicate the physical symptoms of my impending womanhood.

Magazine articles, television commercials, lunchroom conversation, gymnastics coaches and write-ups on models had saturated me with diet savvy. Once I decided to lose weight, I quickly turned expert. I dropped hot chocolate from my regular breakfast order at the Skyline Diner. I replaced lunches of peanut butter and Marshmallow Fluff sandwiches with small platters of cottage cheese and cantaloupe. I eliminated dinner altogether and blunted my appetite with Tab, Camel Lights, and Carefree bubble gum. When furious craving overwhelmed my resolve and I swallowed an extra something, I would flee to the nearest bathroom to purge my mistake.

Within three months, I had returned my body to its preadolescent proportions and had manipulated my monthly period into drying up. Over the next five years, I devoted my life to losing my weight. I came to resent the body in which I lived, the body that threatened to develop, the body whose hunger I despised but could not extinguish. If I neglected a workout or added a pound or ate a bite too many, I would stare in the mirror and drown myself in a tidal wave of criticism. Hatred of my body generalized to hatred of myself as a person, and self-referential labels such as "pig," "failure" and "glutton" allowed me to believe that I deserved punishment. My self-hatred became fuel for the self-mutilating behaviors of the eating disorder.

As my body shrank, so did my world. I starved away my power and vision, my energy and inclinations. Obsessed with dieting, I allowed relationships, passions and identity to wither. I pulled back from the world, off of the beach, out of the sand. The waves of my existence ceased to roll beyond the inside of my skin.

And society applauded my shrinking. Pound after pound the applause continued, like the pounding ocean outside the door of my beach house.

The word "anorexia" literally means "loss of appetite." But as an anorexic, I felt hunger thrashing inside my body. I denied my appetite, ignored it, but never lost it. Sometimes the pangs twisted so sharply, I feared they would consume the meat of my heart. On desperate nights I rose in a flannel nightgown and allowed myself to eat an unplanned something.

No matter how much I ate, I could not soothe the pangs. Standing in the kitchen at midnight, spotlighted by the blue-white light of the open refrigerator, I would frantically feed my neglected appetite: the Chinese food I had not touched at dinner; ice cream and whipped cream; microwaved bread; cereal and chocolate milk; doughnuts and bananas. Then, solid sadness inside my gut, swelling agitation, a too-big meal I would not digest. In the bathroom I would rip off my shirt, tie up my hair, and prepare to execute the desperate ritual, again. I would ram the back of my throat with a toothbrush handle, crying, impatient, until the food rushed up. I would vomit until the toilet filled and I emptied, until I forgave myself, until I felt ready to try my life again. Standing up from my position over the toilet, wiping my mouth, I would believe that I was safe. Looking in the mirror through puffy eyes in a tumescent face, I would promise to take care of myself. Kept awake by the fast, confused beating of my heart and the ache in my chest, I would swear I did not miss the world outside. Lost within myself, I almost died.

By the time I entered the hospital, a mess of protruding bones defined my body, and the bones of my emaciated life rattled me crazy. I carried a pillow around because it hurt to sit down, and I shivered with cold in sultry July. Clumps of brittle hair clogged the drain when I showered, and blackened eyes appeared to sink into my head. My vision of reality wrinkled and my disposition turned mercurial as I slipped into starvation psychosis, a condition associated with severe malnutrition. People told me that I resembled a concentration camp prisoner, a chemotherapy patient, a famine victim or a fashion model.

In the hospital, I examined my eating disorder under the lenses of various therapies. I dissected my childhood, my family structure, my intimate relationships, my belief systems. I participated in experiential therapies of movement, art and psychodrama. I learned to use words instead of eating patterns to communicate my feelings. And still I refused to gain more than a minimal amount of weight.

I felt powerful as an anorexic. Controlling my body yielded an illusion of control over my life; I received incessant praise for my figure despite my sickly mien, and my frailty manipulated family and friends into protecting me from conflict. I had reduced my world to a plate of steamed carrots, and over this tiny kingdom I proudly crowned myself queen.

I sat cross-legged on my hospital bed for nearly two months before I earned an afternoon pass to go to the mall with my mother. The privilege came just in time; I felt unbearably large and desperately wanted a new outfit under which to hide gained weight. At the mall, I searched for two hours before finally discovering, in the maternity section at Macy's, a shirt large enough to cover what I perceived as my enormous body.

With an hour left on my pass, I spotted a sign on a shop window: "Body Fat Testing, $3.00." I suggested to my mother that we split up for ten minutes; she headed to Barnes & Noble, and I snuck into the fitness store.

I sat down in front of a machine hooked up to a computer, and a burly young body builder fired questions at me:

"Age?"

"Twenty-one."

"Height?"

"Five nine."

"Weight?"

"Ninety-nine."

The young man punched my statistics into his keyboard and pinched my arm with clippers wired to the testing machine. In a moment, the computer spit out my results. "Only ten percent body fat! Unbelievably healthy. The average for a woman your age is twenty-five percent. Fantastic! You're this week's blue ribbon winner."

I stared at him in disbelief. *Winner? Healthy? Fantastic?* I glanced around at the other customers in the store, some of whom had congregated to watch my testing, and I felt embarrassed by his praise. And then I felt furious. Furious at this man and at the society that programmed him for their ignorant approbation of my illness and my suffering.

"I am dying of anorexia," I whispered. "Don't congratulate me."

I spent my remaining month in the hospital supplementing psychotherapy with an independent examination of eating disorders from a social and political point of view. I needed to understand why society would reward my starvation and encourage my vanishing. In the bathroom, a mirror on the open door

behind me reflected my backside in a mirror over the sink. Vertebrae poked at my skin, ribs hung like wings over chiseled hip bones, the two sides of my buttocks did not touch. I had not seen this view of myself before.

In writing, I recorded instances in which my eating disorder had tangled the progress of my life and thwarted my relationships. I filled three and a half Mead marble notebooks. Five years' worth of: *I wouldn't sit with Daddy when he was alone in the hospital because I needed to go jogging; I told Derek not to visit me because I couldn't throw up when he was there; I almost failed my comprehensive exams because I was so hungry; I spent my year at Oxford with my head in the toilet bowl; I wouldn't eat the dinner my friends cooked me for my nineteenth birthday because I knew they had used oil in the recipe; I told my family not to come to my college graduation because I didn't want to miss a day at the gym or have to eat a restaurant meal.* And on and on for hundreds of pages.

This honest account of my life dissolved the illusion of anorexic power. I saw myself naked in the truth of my pain, my loneliness, my obsessions, my craziness, my selfishness, my defeat. I also recognized the social and political implications of consuming myself with the trivialities of calories and weight. At college, I had watched as classmates involved themselves in extracurricular clubs, volunteer work, politics and applications for jobs and graduate schools. Obsessed with exercising and exhausted by starvation, I did not even consider joining in such pursuits. Despite my love of writing and painting and literature, despite ranking at the top of my class, I wanted only to teach aerobics. Despite my adolescent days as a loud-mouthed, rambunctious class leader, I had grown into a silent, hungry young woman.

And society preferred me this way: hungry, fragile, crazy. *Winner! Healthy! Fantastic!* I began reading feminist literature to further understand the disempowerment of women in our culture. I digested the connection between a nation of starving, self-obsessed women and the continued success of the patriarchy. I also cultivated an awareness of alternative models of womanhood. In the stillness of the hospital library, new voices in my life rose from printed pages to echo my rage and provide the conception of my feminist consciousness.

I had been willing to accept self-sabotage, but now I refused to sacrifice myself to a society that profited from my pain. I finally understood that my eating disorder symbolized more than "personal psychodynamic trauma." Gazing in the mirror at my emaciated body, I observed a woman held up by her culture as the physical ideal because she was starving, self-obsessed and powerless, a woman called beautiful because she threatened no one except herself. Despite my intelligence, my education, and my supposed Manhattan sophistication, I had believed all of the lies; I had almost given my life in order to achieve the sickly impotence that this culture aggressively links with female happiness, love and success. And everything I had to offer to the world, every tumbling wave, every thought and every passion, nearly died inside me.

As long as society resists female power, fashion will call healthy women physically flawed. As long as society accepts the physical, sexual and economic abuse of women, popular culture will prefer women who resemble little girls. Sitting in the hospital the summer after my college graduation, I grasped the absurdity of a nation of adult women dying to grow small.

Armed with this insight, I loosened the grip of the starvation disease on my body. I determined to recreate myself based on an image of a woman warrior. I remembered my ocean, and I took my first bite.

Gaining weight and getting my head out of the toilet bowl was the most political act I have ever committed.

I left the hospital and returned home to Fire Island. Living at the shore in those wintry days of my new life, I wrapped myself in feminism as I hunted sea shells and role models. I wanted to feel proud of my womanhood. I longed to accept and honor my body's fullness.

During the process of my healing, I had hoped that I would be able to skip the memory of anorexia like a cold pebble into the dark winter sea. I had dreamed that in relinquishing my obsessive chase after a smaller body, I would be able to come home to rejoin those whom I had left in order to starve, rejoin them to live together as healthy, powerful women. But as my body has grown full, I have sensed a hollowness in the lives of women all around me that I had not noticed when I myself stood hollow. I have made it home only to find myself alone.

Out in the world again, I hear the furious thumping dance of body hatred echoing every place I go. Friends who once appeared wonderfully carefree in ordering late-night french fries turn out not to eat breakfast or lunch. Smart, talented, creative women talk about dieting and overeating and hating the beach because they look terrible in bathing suits. Famous women give interviews insulting their bodies and bragging about bicycling twenty-four miles the day they gave birth.

I had looked forward to rejoining society after my years of anorexic exile. Ironically, in order to preserve my health, my recovery has included the development of a consciousness that actively challenges the images and ideas that define this culture. Walking down Madison Avenue and passing emaciated women, I say to myself, *those women are sick.* When smacked with a diet commercial, I remind myself, *I don't do that anymore.* I decline invitations to movies that feature anorexic actors, I will not participate in discussions about dieting, and I refuse to shop in stores that cater to women with eating-disordered figures.

Though I am critical of diet culture, I find it nearly impossible to escape. Eating disorders have woven their way into the fabric of my society. On television, in print, on food packaging, in casual conversation and in windows of clothing stores populated by ridiculously gaunt mannequins, messages to lose my weight and control my appetite challenge my recovered fullness. Finally at home in my body, I recognize myself as an island in a sea of eating disorder, a sea populated predominantly by young women.

A perversion of nature by society has resulted in a phenomenon whereby women feel safer when starving than when eating. Losing our weight boosts self-esteem, while nourishing our bodies evokes feelings of self-doubt and self-loathing.

When our bodies take up more space than a size eight (as most of our bodies do), we say, *too big.* When our appetites demand more than a Lean Cuisine, we say, *too much.* When we want a piece of a friend's birthday cake, we say, *too bad.* Don't eat too much, don't talk too loudly, don't take up too much space, don't take from the world. Be pleasant or crazy, but don't seem hungry. Remember, a new study shows that men prefer women who eat salad for dinner over women who eat burgers and fries.

So we keep on shrinking, starving away our wildness, our power, our truth.

Hiding our curves under long T-shirts at the beach, sitting silently and fidgeting while others eat dessert, sneaking back into the kitchen late at night to binge and hating ourselves the next day, skipping breakfast, existing on diet soda and cigarettes, adding up calories and subtracting everything else. We accept what is horribly wrong in our lives and fight what is beautiful and right.

Over the past three years, feminism has taught me to honor the fullness of my womanhood and the solidness of the body that hosts my life. In feminist circles I have found mentors, strong women who live with power, passion and purpose. And yet, even in groups of feminists, my love and acceptance of my body remains unusual.

Eating disorders affect us all on both a personal and a political level. The majority of my peers—including my feminist peers—still measure their beauty against anorexic ideals. Even among feminists, body hatred and chronic dieting continue to consume lives. Friends of anorexics beg them to please start eating; then these friends go home and continue their own diets. Who can deny that the millions of young women caught in the net of disordered eating will frustrate the potential of the next wave of feminism?

Sometimes my empathy dissolves into frustration and rage at our situation. For the first time in history, young women have the opportunity to create a world in our image. But many of us concentrate instead on recreating the shape of our thighs.

As young feminists, we must place unconditional acceptance of our bodies at the top of our political agenda. We must claim our bodies as our own to love and honor in their infinite shapes and sizes. Fat, thin, soft, hard, puckered, smooth, our bodies are our homes. By nourishing our bodies, we care for and love ourselves on the most basic level. When we deny ourselves physical food, we go hungry emotionally, psychologically, spiritually and politically. We must challenge ourselves to eat and digest, and allow society to call us too big. We will understand their message to mean too powerful.

Time goes by quickly. One day we will blink and open our eyes as old women. If we spend all our energy keeping our bodies small, what will we have to show for our lives when we reach the end? I hope we have more than a group of fashionably skinny figures.

THREE

◆◆◆

Science, Facts, and Feminism

Ruth Hubbard

The Facts of Science. The Brazilian educator, Paulo Freire, has pointed out that people who want to understand the role of politics in shaping education must "see the reasons behind facts" (Freire 1985, 2). I want to begin by exploring some of the reasons behind a particular kind of facts, the facts of natural science. After all, facts aren't just out there. Every fact has a factor, a maker. The interesting question is: as people move through the world, how do we sort those aspects of it that we permit to become facts from those that we relegate to being fiction—untrue, imagined, imaginary, or figments of the imagination—and from those that, worse yet, we do not even notice and that therefore do not become fact, fiction, or figment? In other words, what crite-

ria and mechanisms of selection do scientists use in the making of facts?

One thing is clear: making facts is a social enterprise. Individuals cannot just go off by themselves and dream up facts. When people do that, and the rest of us do not agree to accept or share the facts they offer us, we consider them schizophrenic, crazy. If we do agree, either because their facts sufficiently resemble ours or because they have the power to force us to accept their facts as real and true—to make us see the emperor's new clothes—then the new facts become part of our shared reality and their making, part of the fact-making enterprise.

Making science is such an enterprise. As scientists, our job is to generate facts that help people understand nature. But in doing this, we must follow rules of membership in the scientific community and go about our task of fact-making in professionally sanctioned ways. We must submit new facts to review by our colleagues and be willing to share them with qualified strangers by writing and speaking about them (unless we work for private companies with proprietary interests, in which case we still must share our facts, but only with particular people). If we follow proper procedure, we become accredited fact-makers. In that case our facts come to be accepted on faith and large numbers of people believe them even though they are in no position to say why what we put out are facts rather than fiction. After all, a lot of scientific facts are counterintuitive, such as that the earth moves around the sun or that if you drop a pound of feathers and a pound of rocks, they will fall at the same rate.

What are the social or group characteristics of those of us who are allowed to make scientific facts? Above all, we must have a particular kind of education that includes graduate, and post-graduate training. That means that in addition to whatever subject matter we learn, we have been socialized to think in particular ways and have familiarized ourselves with that narrow slice of human history and culture that deals primarily with the experiences of western European and North American upper class men during the past century or two. It also means that we must not deviate too far from accepted rules of individual and social behavior and must talk and think in ways that let us earn the academic degrees required of a scientist.

Until the last decade or two, mainly upper-middle and upper class youngsters, most of them male and white, have had access to that kind of education. Lately, more white women and people of color (women and men) have been able to get it, but the class origins of scientists have not changed appreciably. The scientific professions still draw their members overwhelmingly from the upper-middle and upper classes.

How about other kinds of people? Have they no role in the making of science? Quite the contrary. In the ivory (that is, white) towers in which science gets made, lots of people are from working class and lower-middle class backgrounds, but they are the technicians, secretaries, and clean-up personnel. Decisions about who gets to be a faculty-level fact-

maker are made by professors, deans, and university presidents who call on scientists from other, similar institutions to recommend candidates who they think will conform to the standards prescribed by universities and the scientific professions. At the larger, systemic level, decisions are made by government and private funding agencies which operate by what is called peer review. What that means is that small groups of people with similar personal and academic backgrounds decide whether a particular fact-making proposal has enough merit to be financed. Scientists who work in the same, or related, fields mutually sit on each other's decision making panels and whereas criteria for access are supposedly objective and meritocratic, orthodoxy and conformity count for a lot. Someone whose ideas and/or personality are out of line is less likely to succeed than "one of the boys"—and these days some of us girls are allowed to join the boys, particularly if we play by their rules.

Thus, science is made, by and large, by a self-perpetuating, self-reflexive group: by the chosen for the chosen. The assumption is that if the science is "good," in a professional sense, it will also be good for society. But no one and no group are responsible for looking at whether it is. Public accountability is not built into the system.

What are the alternatives? How could we have a science that is more open and accessible, a science *for* the people? And to what extent could—or should—it also be a science *by* the people? After all, divisions of labor are not necessarily bad. There is no reason and, indeed, no possibility, that in a complicated society like ours, everyone is able to do everything. Inequalities which are bad, come not from the fact that different people do different things, but from the fact that different tasks are valued differently and carry with them different amounts of prestige and power.

For historical reasons, this society values mental labor more highly than manual labor. We often pay more for it and think that it requires more specifically human qualities and therefore is superior. This is a mistake especially in the context of a scientific laboratory, because it means that the laboratory chief—the person "with ideas"—often gets the credit, whereas the laboratory workers—the people who work with their hands (as well as, often, their imaginations)—are the ones who perform the operations and make the observations that generate new hypotheses and that permit hunches, ideas, and hypotheses to become facts.

But it is not only because of the way natural science is done that head and hand, mental and manual work, are often closely linked. Natural science requires a conjunction of head and hand because it is an understanding of nature *for use*. To understand nature is not enough. Natural science and technology are inextricable, because we can judge that our understanding of nature is true only to the extent that it works. Significant facts and laws are relevant only to the extent that they can be applied and used as technology. The science/technology distinction, which was introduced one to two centuries ago, does not hold up in the real world of economic, political and social practices.

Woman's Nature: Realities versus Scientific Myths. As I said before, to be believed, scientific facts must fit the world-view of the times. Therefore, at times of tension and upheaval, such as the last two decades, some researchers always try to "prove" that differences in the political, social, and economic status of women and men, blacks and whites, or poor people and rich people, are inevitable because they are the results of people's inborn qualities and traits. Such scientists have tried to "prove" that blacks are innately less intelligent than whites, or that women are innately weaker, more nurturing, less good at math than men. If, for the purposes of this discussion, we focus on sex differences, it is clear that the ideology of woman's nature can differ drastically from the realities of women's lives and indeed be antithetical to them. In fact, the ideology functions, at least in part, to obscure the ways women live and to make people look away from the realities or ask misleading questions about them. So, for example, the ideology that labels women as the natural reproducers of the species, and men as producers of goods, has not been used to exempt women from also producing goods and services, but to shunt us out of higher paying jobs, the professions, and other kinds of work that require continuity and provide a measure of power over one's own and, at times, other people's lives. Most women who work for pay do so in job categories, such as secretary or nurse, which often involve a great deal of concealed responsibility, but are underpaid. This is one reason why insisting on equal pay *within* job categories cannot remedy women's economic disadvantage. Women will continue to be underpaid as long as women's jobs are less well paid than men's jobs and as long as access to traditional men's jobs is limited by social pressures, career counseling, training and hiring practices, trade union policies, and various other subtle and not so subtle societal mechanisms, such as research that "proves" that girls are not as good as boys at spatial perception, mathematics and science. An entire range of discriminatory practices is justified by the claim that they follow from the limits that biology places on women's capacity to work. Though exceptions are made during wars and other emergencies, they are forgotten as soon as life resumes its normal course. Then women are expected to return to their subordinate roles, not because the quality of their work during the emergencies has been inferior, but because these roles are seen as natural.

A few years ago, a number of women employees in the American chemical and automotive industries were actually forced to choose between working at relatively well-paying jobs that had previously been done by men or remaining fertile. In one instance, five women were required to submit to sterilization *by hysterectomy* in order to avoid being transferred from work in the lead pigment department at the American Cyanamid plant in Willow Island, West Virginia to janitorial work at considerably lower wages and benefits (Stellman and Henifin 1982). Even though none of these women was pregnant or planning a pregnancy in the near future (indeed, the husband of one had had a vasectomy), they were considered "potentially pregnant" unless they could prove that they were sterile. This goes on despite the fact that exposure to lead can damage sperm as well as eggs and can affect the health of workers (male and female) as well as a "potential fetus." It is as though fertile women are at all times potential parents; men, never. But it is important to notice that this vicious choice is being forced only on women who have recently entered relatively well-paid, traditionally male jobs. Women whose work routinely involves reproductive hazards because it exposes them to chemical or radiation hazards, but who have traditionally female jobs such as nurses, X-ray technologists, laboratory technicians, cleaning women in surgical operating rooms, scientific laboratories or the chemical and biotechnology industries, beauticians, secretaries, workers in the ceramics industry, and domestic workers are not warned about the chemical or physical hazards of their work to their health or to that of a fetus, should they be pregnant. In other words, scientific knowledge about fetal susceptibility to noxious chemicals and radiation is used to keep women out of better paid job categories from which they had previously been excluded by discriminatory employment practices, but, in general, women (or, indeed, men) are not protected against health endangering work.

The ideology of woman's nature that is invoked at these times would have us believe that a woman's capacity to become pregnant leaves her always physically disabled by comparison with men. The scientific underpinnings for these ideas were elaborated in the nineteenth century by the white, university-educated, mainly upper class men who made up the bulk of the new professions of obstetrics and gynecology, biology, psychology, sociology and anthropology. These professionals used their theories of women's innate frailty to disqualify the girls and women of their own race and class who would have been competing with them for education and professional status. They also realized that they might lose the kinds of personal attention they were accustomed to get from mothers, wives, and sisters if women of their own class gained access to the professions. They did not invoke women's weakness when it came to poor women spending long hours working in the homes and factories belonging to members of the upper classes, nor against the ways black slave women were made to work on the plantations and in the homes of their masters and mistresses.

Nineteenth century biologists and physicians claimed that women's brains were smaller than men's and that women's ovaries and uteruses required much energy and rest in order to function properly. They "proved" that therefore young girls must be kept away from schools and colleges once they begin to menstruate and warned that without this kind of care women's uteruses and ovaries will shrivel and the human race die out. Yet again, this analysis was not carried over to poor women, who were not only required to work hard, but often were said to reproduce *too* much. Indeed, scientists interpreted the fact that poor women could work hard and yet bear many children as a sign that they were more animal-like and less highly evolved than upper class women.

During the past decade, feminists have uncovered this history. We have analyzed the self-serving theories and documented the absurdity of the claims as well as their class and race biases and their glaringly political intent (Hubbard and Lowe 1979; Lowe and Hubbard 1983; Bleier 1984; Fausto-Sterling 1985). But this kind of scientific mythmaking is not past history. Just as in the nineteenth century medical men and biologists fought women's political organizing for equality by claiming that our reproductive organs made us unfit for anything but childbearing and childrearing, just as Freud declared women to be intrinsically less stable, intellectually inventive and productive than men, so beginning in the 1970's, there has been a renaissance in sex differences research that has claimed to prove scientifically that women are innately better than men at home care and mothering while men are innately better fitted than women for the competitive life of the market place.

Questionable experimental results obtained with animals (primarily that prototypic human, the white laboratory rat) are treated as though they can be applied equally well to people. On this basis, some scientists are now claiming that the secretion of different amounts of so-called male hormones (androgens) by male and female fetuses produces lifelong differences in women's and men's brains. They claim not only that these (unproved) differences in fetal hormone levels exist, but imply (without evidence) that they predispose women and men *as groups* to exhibit innate differences in our abilities to localize objects in space, in our verbal and mathematical aptitudes, in aggressiveness and competitiveness, nurturing ability, and so on (Money and Ehrhardt 1972; Goy and McEwen 1980; *Science* 1981, 1263–1324). Sociobiologists claim that some of the sex differences in social behavior that exist in Western, capitalist societies (such as, aggressiveness, competitiveness, and dominance among men; coyness, nurturance, and submissiveness among women) are human universals that have existed in all times and cultures. Because these traits are said to be ever-present, sociobiologists deduce that they must have evolved through Darwinian natural selection and are now part of our genetic inheritance (Wilson 1975).

Sociobiologists have tried to prove that women's disproportionate contributions to child- and home-care are biologically programmed because women have a greater biological "investment" in our children than men have. They offer the following rationale: an organism's biological fitness, in the Darwinian sense, depends on producing the greatest possible number of offspring, who themselves survive long enough to reproduce, because this is what determines the frequency with which an individual's genes will be represented in successive generations. Following this logic a step further, sociobiologists argue that women and men must adopt basically different strategies to maximize opportunities to spread our genes into future generations. The calculus goes as follows: Eggs are larger than sperm and women can produce many fewer of them than men can sperm. Therefore each egg that develops into a child represents a much larger fraction of the total number of children a woman can produce, hence of her "reproductive fitness," than a sperm that becomes a child does of a man's "fitness." In addition, women "invest" the nine months of pregnancy in each child. Women must therefore be more careful than men to acquire well-endowed sex partners who will be good providers to make sure that their few investments (read, children) mature. Thus, from seemingly innocent biological asymmetries between sperm and eggs flow such major social consequences as female fidelity, male promiscuity, women's disproportional contribution to caring for home and children, and the unequal distribution of labor by sex. As sociobiologist, David Barash, says, "mother nature is sexist," so don't blame her human sons (Dawkins 1976; Barash 1979, esp. 46–90).

In devising these explanations, sociobiologists ignore the fact that human societies do not operate with a few superstuds; nor do stronger or more powerful men as a rule have more children than weaker ones. Men, in theory, could have many more children than women can, but in most societies equal numbers of men and women engage in producing children, though not in caring for them. These kinds of absurdities are useful to people who have a stake in maintaining present inequalities. They mystify procreation, yet have a superficial ring of plausibility and thus offer naturalistic justifications for discriminatory practices.

As the new scholarship on women has grown, a few anthropologists and biologists have tried to mitigate the male bias that underlies these kinds of theories by describing how females contribute to social life and species survival in important ways that are overlooked by scientists who think of females only in relation to reproduction and look to males for everything else (Lancaster 1975; Hrdy 1981, 1986; Kevles 1986). But, unless scientists challenge the basic premises that underlie the standard, male-centered descriptions and analyses, such revisions do not offer radically different formulations and insights. (For examples of more fundamental criticisms of evolutionary thinking and sociobiology, see Lowe and Hubbard 1979; Hubbard 1982; Lewontin, Rose and Kamin 1984).

Subjectivity and Objectivity. I want to come back to Paulo Freire, who says: "Reality is never just simply the objective datum, the concrete fact, but is also people's [and I would say, certain people's] perception of it." And he speaks of "the indispensable unity between subjectivity and objectivity in the act of knowing" (Freire 1985, 51).

The recognition of this "indispensable unity" is what feminist methodology is about. It is especially necessary for a feminist methodology in science because the scientific method rests on a particular definition of objectivity, that we feminists must call into question. Feminists and others who draw attention to the devices that the dominant group has used to deny other people access to power — be it political power or the power to make facts — have come to understand how that definition of objectivity functions in the processes of exclusion I discussed at the beginning.

Natural scientists attain their objectivity by looking upon nature (including other people) in small chunks and as isolated objects. They usually deny, or at least do not acknowledge, their relationship to the "objects" they study. In other words, natural scientists describe their activities as though they existed in a vacuum. The way language is used in scientific writing reinforces this illusion because it implicitly denies the relevance of time, place, social context, authorship, and personal responsibility. When I report a discovery, I do not write, "One sunny Monday after a restful weekend, I came into the laboratory, set up my experiment and shortly noticed that . . ." No; proper style dictates, "It has been observed that . . ." This removes relevance of time and place, and implies that the observation did not originate in the head of a human observer, specifically my head, but out there in the world. By deleting the scientist-agent as well as her or his participation as observer, people are left with the concept of science as a thing in itself, that truly reflects nature and that can be treated as though it were as real as, and indeed equivalent to, nature.

A blatant example of the kind of context-stripping that is commonly called objectivity is the way E. O. Wilson opens the final chapter of his *Sociobiology: The New Synthesis* (Wilson 1975, 547). He writes: "Let us now consider man in the free spirit of natural history, as though we were zoologists from another planet completing a catalog of social species on earth." That statement epitomizes the fallacy we need to get rid of. There is no "free spirit of natural history," only a set of descriptions put forward by the mostly white, educated, Euro-American men who have been practicing a particular kind of science during the past two hundred years. Nor do we have any idea what "zoologists from another planet" would have to say about "man" (which, I guess is supposed to mean "people") or about other "social species on earth," since that would depend on how these "zoologists" were used to living on their own planet and by what experiences they would therefore judge us. Feminists must insist that subjectivity and context cannot be stripped away, that they must be acknowledged if we want to use science as a way to understand nature and society and to use the knowledge we gain constructively.

For a different kind of example, take the economic concept of unemployment which in the United States has become "chronic unemployment" or even "the normal rate of unemployment." Such pseudo-objective phrases obscure a wealth of political and economic relationships which are subject to social action and change. By turning the activities of certain people who have the power to hire or not hire other people into depersonalized descriptions of economic fact, by turning activities of scientists into "factual" statements about nature or society, scientific language helps to mystify and intimidate the "lay public," those anonymous others, as well as scientists, and makes them feel powerless.

Another example of the absurdity of pretended objectivity, is a study that was described in the *New York Times* in which scientists suggested that they had identified eight characteristics in young children that were predictive of the likelihood that the children would later develop schizophrenia. The scientists were proposing a longitudinal study of such children

as they grow up to assess the accuracy of these predictions. This is absurd because such experiments cannot be done. How do you find a "control" group for parents who have been told that their child exhibits five out of the eight characteristics, or worse yet, all eight characteristics thought to be predictive of schizophrenia? Do you tell some parents that this is so although it isn't? Do you not tell some parents whose children have been so identified? Even if psychiatrists agreed on the diagnosis of schizophrenia — which they do not — this kind of research cannot be done objectively. And certainly cannot be done ethically, that is, without harming people.

The problem is that the context-stripping that worked reasonably well for the classical physics of falling bodies has become the model for how to do every kind of science. And this even though physicists since the beginning of this century have recognized that the experimenter is part of the experiment and influences its outcome. That insight produced Heisenberg's uncertainty principle in physics: the recognition that the operations the experimenter performs disturb the system so that it is impossible to specify simultaneously the position and momentum of atoms and elementary particles. So, how about standing the situation on its head and using the social sciences, where context stripping is clearly impossible, as a model and do all science in a way that acknowledges the experimenter as a self-conscious subject who lives, and does science, within the context in which the phenomena she or he observes occur? Anthropologists often try to take extensive field notes about a new culture as quickly as possible after they enter it, before they incorporate the perspective and expectations of that culture, because they realize that once they know the foreign culture well and feel at home in it, they will begin to take some of its most significant aspects for granted and stop seeing them. Yet they realize at the same time that they must also acknowledge the limitations their own personal and social backgrounds impose on the way they perceive the foreign society. Awareness of our subjectivity and context must be part of doing science because there is no way we can eliminate them. We come to the objects we study with our particular personal and social backgrounds and with inevitable interests. Once we acknowledge those, we can try to understand the world, so to speak, from inside instead of pretending to be objective outsiders looking in.

The social structure of the laboratory in which scientists work and the community and inter-personal relationships in which they live are also part of the subjective reality and context of doing science. Yet, we usually ignore them when we speak of a scientist's scientific work despite the fact that natural scientists work in highly organized social systems. Obviously, the sociology of laboratory life is structured by class, sex, and race, as is the rest of society. We saw before that to understand what goes on in the laboratory we must ask questions about who does what kinds of work. What does the lab chief — the person whose name appears on the stationery or on the door — contribute? How are decisions made about what work gets done and in what order? What role do women, whatever our class and race, or men of color and men from working class backgrounds play in this performance?

Note that women have played a very large role in the production of science — as wives, sisters, secretaries, technicians, and students of "great men" — though usually not as accredited scientists. One of our jobs as feminists must be to acknowledge that role. If feminists are to make a difference in the ways science is done and understood, we must not just try to become scientists who occupy the traditional structures, follow established patterns of behavior, and accept prevailing systems of explanation; we must understand and describe accurately the roles women have played all along in the process of making science. But we must also ask why certain ways of systematically interacting with nature and of using the knowledge so gained are acknowledged as science whereas others are not.

I am talking of the distinction between the laboratory and that other, quite differently structured, place of discovery and fact-making, the household, where women use a different brand of botany, chemistry, and hygiene to work in our gardens, kitchens, nurseries, and sick rooms. Much of the knowledge women have acquired in those places is systematic and effective and has been handed on by word of mouth and in writing. But just as our society downgrades manual labor, it also downgrades knowledge that is produced in other than professional settings, however systematic it may be. It downgrades the orally transmitted knowledge and the unpaid observations, experimentation and teaching that happen in the household. Yet here is a wide range of systematic, empirical knowledge that has gone unnoticed and unvalidated (in fact, devalued and invalidated) by the institutions that catalog and describe, and thus define, what is to be called knowledge. Men's explorations of nature also began at home, but later were institutionalized and professionalized. Women's explorations have stayed close to home and their value has not been acknowledged.

What I am proposing is the opposite of the project the domestic science movement put forward at the turn of the century. That movement tried to make women's domestic work more "scientific" in the traditional sense of the word (Newman 1985, 156–191). I am suggesting that we acknowledge the scientific value of many of the facts and knowledge that women have accumulated and passed on in our homes and in volunteer organizations.

I doubt that women as gendered beings have something new or different to contribute to science, but women as political beings do. One of the most important things we must do is to insist on the political content of science and on its political role. The pretense that science is objective, apolitical and value-neutral is profoundly political because it obscures the political role that science and technology play in underwriting the existing distribution of power in society. Science and technology always operate in somebody's interest and serve someone or some group of people. To the extent that scientists are "neutral" that merely means that they support the existing distribution of interests and power.

If we want to integrate feminist politics into our science, we must insist on the political nature and content of scientific work and of the way science is taught and otherwise communicated to the public. We must broaden the base of experience and knowledge on which scientists draw by making it possible for a wider range of people to do science, and to do it in different ways. We must also provide kinds of understanding that are useful and useable by a broad range of people. For this, science would have to be different from the way it is now. The important questions would have to be generated by a different social process. A wider range of people would have to have access to making scientific facts and to understanding and using them. Also, the process of validation would have to be under more public scrutiny, so that research topics and facts that benefit only a small elite while oppressing large segments of the population would not be acceptable.

Our present science, which supposedly exists to explain nature and let us live more comfortably in it, has in fact mystified nature. As Virginia Woolf's Orlando says as she enters a department store elevator:

> The very fabric of life now . . . is magic. In the eighteenth century, we knew how everything was done; but here I rise through the air; I listen to voices in America; I see men flying— but how it's done, I can't even begin to wonder. (Woolf 1928, 300)

Other ways to do Science? The most concrete examples of a different kind of science that I can think of come from the women's health movement and the process by which the Boston Women's Health Book Collective's (1984) *The New Our Bodies, Ourselves* or the Federation of Feminist Women's Health Centers' (1981) *A New View of a Woman's Body* have been generated. These groups have consciously tried to involve a range of women in setting the agenda, as well as in asking and answering the relevant questions. But there is probably no single way in which to change present-day science, and there shouldn't be. After all, one of the problems with science, as it exists now, is that scientists narrowly circumscribe the allowed ways to learn about nature and reject deviations as deviance.

Of course it is difficult for feminists who, as women, are just gaining a toehold in science, to try to make fundamental changes in the ways scientists perceive science and do it. This is why many scientists who are feminists live double-lives and conform to the pretenses of an apolitical, value-free, meritocratic science in our working lives while living our politics elsewhere. Meanwhile, many of us who want to integrate our politics with our work, analyze and critique the standard science, but no longer do it. Here again, feminist health centers and counselling groups come to mind as efforts to integrate feminist inquiry and political praxis. It would be important for feminists, who are trying to reconceptualize reality and reorganize knowledge and its uses in areas other than health, to create environments ("outstitutes") in which we can work together and communicate with other individuals and groups, so that people with different backgrounds and agendas can exchange questions, answers, and expertise.

References

Barash, D. 1979. *The whispering within*. New York: Harper & Row.

Bleier, R. 1984. *Science and gender*. New York: Pergamon.

Boston Women's Health Book Collective. 1984. *The new our bodies, ourselves*. New York: Simon and Schuster.

Dawkins, R. 1976. *The selfish gene*. New York: Oxford University Press.

Fausto-Sterling, A. 1985. *Myths of gender*. New York: Basic Books.

Federation of Feminist Women's Health Centers. 1981. *A new view of a woman's body*. New York: Simon and Schuster.

Freire, P. 1985. *The politics of education*. South Hadley, MA: Bergin and Garvey.

Goy, R. W. and B. S. McEwen. 1980. *Sexual differentiation of the brain*. Cambridge, MA: M.I.T. Press.

Hrdy, S. B. 1981. *The woman that never evolved*. Cambridge, MA: Harvard University Press.

———. 1986. Empathy, polyandry, and the myth of the coy female. In *Feminist approaches to science*, ed. R. Bleier, 119–146. New York: Pergamon.

Hubbard, R. 1982. Have only men evolved? In *Biological woman—The convenient myth*, ed. R. Hubbard, M. S. Henifin and B. Fried, 17–46. Cambridge, MA: Schenkman.

Hubbard, R. and M. Lowe, eds. 1979. *Genes and gender II: Pitfalls in research on sex and gender*. Staten Island, NY: Gordian Press.

Kevles, B. 1986. *Females of the species*. Cambridge, MA: Harvard University Press.

Lancaster, J. B. 1975. *Primate behavior and the emergence of human culture*. New York: Holt, Rinehart and Winston.

Lewontin, R. C., S. Rose and L. J. Kamin. 1984. *Not in our genes*. New York: Pantheon.

Lowe, M. and R. Hubbard, 1979. Sociobiology and biosociology: Can science prove the biological basis of sex differences in behavior? In *Genes and gender II: Pitfalls in research on sex and gender*, ed. R. Hubbard and M. Lowe, 91–112. Staten Island, NY: Gordian Press.

Lowe, M. and R. Hubbard, eds. 1983. *Woman's nature: Rationalizations of inequality*. New York: Pergamon.

Money, J. and A. A. Ehrhardt. 1972. *Man & woman, boy & girl*. Baltimore: Johns Hopkins University Press.

Newman, L. M., ed. 1985. *Men's ideas/Women's realities: Popular science, 1870–1915*. New York: Pergamon.

Science. 1981. *211*, pp. 1263–1324.

Stellman, J. M. and M. S. Henifin. 1982. No fertile women need apply: Employment discrimination and reproductive hazards in the workplace. In *Biological woman—The convenient myth*, ed. R. Hubbard, M. S. Henifin and B. Fried, 117–145. Cambridge, MA: Schenkman.

Wilson, E. O. 1975. *Sociobiology: The new synthesis*. Cambridge, MA: Harvard University Press.

Woolf, V. 1928. *Orlando*. New York: Harcourt Brace Jovanovich; Harvest Paperback Edition.

FOUR

◆◆◆

Theorizing by Feminists of Color

Aída Hurtado

Regardless of the exclusion of feminists of Color by practices within women's studies (Zinn, Cannon, Higginbotham, and Dill 1986) and academic publishing outlets, women of Color have always theorized about their gender subordination, although not always in traditionally academic forms (Collins 1991). The history of women of Color's feminism has gone largely undocumented because, in order to garner the true complexity of women of Color's experiences, it becomes necessary to tap into sources of knowledge not used by scholars steeped in mainstream positivist ideology. Yet . . . this lack of documentation does not mean a lack of action by feminists of Color on behalf of women's issues.

Feminists of Color's theorizing, as mentioned earlier, has been constrained by their access to academic resources, but within these constraints they have produced impressive frameworks that contribute to our understanding of gender subordination (Cotera 1977; Zavella 1988; Fernández 1994). They have theorized not only about structures of oppression but have simultaneously tried to devise methods of deconstructing the very structures they are discovering and all within the framework of intergroup ethnic/racial solidarity—no easy task indeed.

Women of Color in the United States have been forced to resist gender subordination within their own communities as well as gender, class, and race/ethnic discrimination in society at large (Zavella 1987, 1988). Women of Color's "triple" oppression has resulted in earning less, receiving less education, and having more children to support than whites or than men within their own groups. The core issues of women of Color feminists are material conditions such as employment, poverty, education, health, child care, and reproductive rights (Zavella 1988, 125). Their political mobilization historically has not only revolved around these material conditions, issues that affect them disproportionately, but also has involved matters of political empowerment for themselves and their communities. A model of this type of leadership is exhibited by Antonia Pantoja, founder of the Puerto Rican Association for Community Affairs who echoes the Black feminist organizers of the antislavery movement in emphasizing collective decisionmaking, the development of new leaders, especially among the youth, and the good of the group over the personal gain of the individual. The concerns of feminists of Color have always been intimately tied to those of their communities (Zavella 1988; Fernández 1994).

Because U.S. women of Color are composed of native-born individuals as well as immigrants, their feminism has been influenced by the history of other lands as well as experiences in the United States. A case in point are Latinas. Some Latinas are recent immigrants, and others are descendants of the original Mexicans who resided in the Southwest since 1848, when the Treaty of Guadalupe Hidalgo ended the Mexican American War and Mexico lost over 50 percent of its territory to the United States. Most Latinas reside in the five southwestern states (California, Texas, Arizona, New Mexico, and Colorado). There are, however, a sizable number of Latinas of Puerto Rican descent in New York, of Cuban descent in Miami, and of Mexican and Puerto Rican descent in Chicago. The complexity of Latinas' feminism in the United States is represented in their history of struggle (Zavella 1988). For example, many Latinas have fought side by side in revolutionary struggles in Cuba, Nicaragua, or El Salvador and have worked to unionize miners and farmworkers in the Southwest as well as garment workers in the Northeast. From Dolores Huerta in California, one of the foremost leaders of the United Farmworkers Union, to Esperanza Martell, cofounder of the Latin Women's Collective in New York City, their political efforts on behalf of women's issues have been embedded in their political activities on behalf of their entire communities.

Historically, all communities of Color in the United States have had strong women leaders. For example, in the Latino community there are such leaders as Emma Tenayuca, a famous labor leader in Texas, and María Mercedes Barbudo, who was jailed in 1824 in Puerto Rico for conspiring against the Spanish colonizers, to *las soldaderas,* who fought in the Mexican Revolution of 1910. *Soldadera* literally means "female soldier." *Soldaderas* helped democratize Mexico from a feudal country to one in which land was distributed among peasants.

Currently, there is a flurry of academic and artistic production from feminists of Color who are making connections with activists in the United States and in the rest of the Americas. Some of the most exciting work is being created by feminists of Color who are questioning the sexism (Zavella 1988, 126–27) and heterosexism in their communities and documenting the lives of lesbians of Color (Trujillo 1991). These scholars are also working to form domestic and international alliances around women's issues. In the domestic arena organizations such as the Women of Color Resource Center in Oakland, California, are committed to creating inclusive political agendas that span ethnic and cultural differences. International alliances have been built between women of Color in the United States and those in other countries such as in Latin America through scholarly conferences and political mobilization along the U.S.-Mexico border.

Feminists of Color residing on the mainland, for example, have been cultivating cultural and political alliances with feminists residing in Puerto Rico.

In summary the impetus for much of the theorizing by women of Color has been political mobilization, largely around labor issues (Zavella 1987). Their theorizing and political praxis are not separate, however, and feminists of Color have made impressive inroads in the number of organizations they have built (Fernández 1994, 29), their artistic production, as well as their scholarly output. Regardless of their diversity, there are some overarching principles that characterize their theorizing about gender subordination. First, almost all feminists of Color resist arranging their derogated group memberships into a hierarchy of oppressions; instead, they insist on deciphering the complexity of their gender, class, and ethnic/racial status simultaneously (Zavella 1988, 126). Second, almost all feminists of Color claim their individual group's history as part of their activist legacy. They see the connections between their current political activism as being part of their group's historical trajectory of resistance. For groups that have a history of forced and semiforced migration, it includes struggles in their native lands. Third, almost all feminists of Color do not make a distinction between theorizing that emerges in the academy and theorizing that emerges from political organizing, everyday interaction, and artistic production. Feminist theorizing by women of Color is trying to build a paradigm that is inclusive in nature, nonelitist, and does not reside exclusively within the academy. Fourth, currently there is an emphasis on attacking head-on the previously taboo subject of heterosexism in their communities. These emphases, which are not exhaustive, provide a valuable road map for the work of a multicultural feminism. Among the principles that can be gleaned from the extensive and diverse writings of feminists of Color are: strength and pragmatism, predisposition to political coalitions, and an inclusive paradigm.

References

Collins, P. H. (1991). *Black feminist thought.* New York: Routledge.

Cotera, M. (1977). *Chicana feminism.* Austin, Tex.: Information System Development.

Fernández, R. (1994). Abiendo-caminos in the brotherland: Chicana writers respond to the ideology of literary nationalism. *Frontiers—A Journal of Women's Studies* 14(2), 23–50.

Trujillo, C. (1991). *Chicana lesbians: The girls our mothers warned us about.* Berkeley, Calif.: Third Woman Press.

Zavella, P. (1987). *Women's work and Chicano families: Cannery workers of the Santa Clara Valley.* Ithaca, N.Y.: Cornell University Press.

Zavella, P. (1988). The problematic relationship of feminism and Chicana studies. *Women's Studies* 17, 123–34.

Zinn, M. B., L. W. Cannon, E. Higginbotham, and B. T. Dill. (1986). The costs of exclusionary practices in women's studies. *Signs: Journal of Women in Culture and Society* 11(21), 290–303.

F I V E

◆◆◆

A Black Feminist Statement

*Combahee River Collective**

We are a collective of Black feminists who have been meeting together since 1974.[1] During that time we have been involved in the process of defining and clarifying our politics, while at the same time doing political work within our own group and in coalition with other progressive organizations and movements. The most general statement of our politics at the present time would be that we are actively committed to struggling against racial, sexual, heterosexual, and class oppression and see as our particular task the development of integrated analysis and practice based upon the fact that the major systems of oppression are interlocking. The synthesis of these oppressions creates the conditions of our lives. As Black women we see Black feminism as the logical political movement to combat the manifold and simultaneous oppressions that all women of color face.

We will discuss four major topics in the paper that follows: (1) the genesis of contemporary Black feminism; (2) what we believe, i.e., the specific province of our politics; (3) the problems in organizing Black fem-

inists, including a brief herstory of our collective; and (4) Black feminist issues and practice.

1. The Genesis of Contemporary Black Feminism

Before looking at the recent development of Black feminism we would like to affirm that we find our origins in the historical reality of Afro-American women's continuous life-and-death struggle for survival and liberation. Black women's extremely negative relationship to the American political system (a system of white male rule) has always been determined by our membership in two oppressed racial and sexual castes. As Angela Davis points out in "Reflections on the Black Woman's Role in the Community of Slaves," Black women have always embodied, if only in their physical manifestation, an adversary stance to white male rule and have actively resisted its inroads upon them and their communities in both dramatic and subtle ways. There have always been Black women activists— some known, like Sojourner Truth, Harriet Tubman, Frances E. W. Harper, Ida B. Wells Barnett, and Mary Church Terrell, and thousands upon thousands unknown—who had a shared awareness of how their sexual identity combined with their racial identity to make their whole life situation and the focus of their political struggles unique. Contemporary Black fem-

---

*The Combahee River Collective is a Black feminist group in Boston whose name comes from the guerrilla action conceptualized and led by Harriet Tubman on June 2, 1863, in the Port Royal region of South Carolina. This action freed more than 750 slaves and is the only military campaign in American history planned and led by a woman.

inism is the outgrowth of countless generations of personal sacrifice, militancy, and work by our mothers and sisters.

A Black feminist presence has evolved most obviously in connection with the second wave of the American women's movement beginning in the late 1960s. Black, other Third World, and working women have been involved in the feminist movement from its start, but both outside reactionary forces and racism and elitism within the movement itself have served to obscure our participation. In 1973 Black feminists, primarily located in New York, felt the necessity of forming a separate Black feminist group. This became the National Black Feminist Organization (NBFO).

Black feminist politics also have an obvious connection to movements for Black liberation, particularly those of the 1960s and 1970s. Many of us were active in those movements (civil rights, Black nationalism, the Black Panthers), and all of our lives were greatly affected and changed by their ideology, their goals, and the tactics used to achieve their goals. It was our experience and disillusionment within these liberation movements, as well as experience on the periphery of the white male left, that led to the need to develop a politics that was antiracist, unlike those of white women, and antisexist, unlike those of Black and white men.

There is also undeniably a personal genesis for Black feminism, that is, the political realization that comes from the seemingly personal experiences of individual Black women's lives. Black feminists and many more Black women who do not define themselves as feminists have all experienced sexual oppression as a constant factor in our day-to-day existence. As children we realized that we were different from boys and that we were treated differently. For example, we were told in the same breath to be quiet both for the sake of being "ladylike" and to make us less objectionable in the eyes of white people. As we grew older we became aware of the threat of physical and sexual abuse by men. However, we had no way of conceptualizing what was so apparent to us, what we *knew* was really happening.

Black feminists often talk about their feelings of craziness before becoming conscious of the concepts of sexual politics, patriarchal rule, and most importantly, feminism, the political analysis and practice that we women use to struggle against our oppression. The fact that racial politics and indeed racism are pervasive factors in our lives did not allow us, and still does not allow most Black women, to look more deeply into our own experiences and, from that sharing and growing consciousness, to build a politics that will change our lives and inevitably end our oppression. Our development must also be tied to the contemporary economic and political position of Black people. The post World War II generation of Black youth was the first to be able to minimally partake of certain educational and employment options, previously closed completely to Black people. Although our economic position is still at the very bottom of the American capitalistic economy, a handful of us have been able to gain certain tools as a result of tokenism in education and employment which potentially enable us to more effectively fight our oppression.

A combined antiracist and antisexist position drew us together initially, and as we developed politically we addressed ourselves to heterosexism and economic oppression under capitalism.

2. What We Believe

Above all else, our politics initially sprang from the shared belief that Black women are inherently valuable, that our liberation is a necessity not as an adjunct to somebody else's but because of our need as human persons for autonomy. This may seem so obvious as to sound simplistic, but it is apparent that no other ostensibly progressive movement has ever considered our specific oppression as a priority or worked seriously for the ending of that oppression. Merely naming the pejorative stereotypes attributed to Black women (e.g. mammy, matriarch, Sapphire, whore, bulldagger), let alone cataloguing the cruel, often murderous, treatment we receive, indicates how little value has been placed upon our lives during four centuries of bondage in the Western hemisphere. We realize that the only people who care enough about us to work consistently for our liberation is us. Our politics evolve from a healthy love for ourselves, our sisters and our community which allows us to continue our struggle and work.

This focusing upon our own oppression is embodied in the concept of identity politics. We believe that the most profound and potentially the most radical politics come directly out of our own identity, as opposed to working to end somebody else's oppression. In the case of Black women this is a particularly repugnant, dangerous, threatening, and therefore revolutionary concept because it is obvious from looking at all the political movements that have preceded us that anyone is more worthy of liberation than ourselves. We reject pedestals, queenhood, and walking ten paces behind. To be recognized as human, levelly human, is enough.

We believe that sexual politics under patriarchy is as pervasive in Black women's lives as are the politics of class and race. We also often find it difficult to separate race from class from sex oppression because in our lives they are most often experienced simultaneously. We know that there is such a thing as racial-sexual oppression which is neither solely racial nor solely sexual, e.g., the history of rape of Black women by white men as a weapon of political repression.

Although we are feminists and lesbians, we feel solidarity with progressive Black men and do not advocate the fractionalization that white women who are separatists demand. Our situation as Black people necessitates that we have solidarity around the fact of race, which white women of course do not need to have with white men, unless it is their negative solidarity as racial oppressors. We struggle together with Black men against racism, while we also struggle with Black men about sexism.

We realize that the liberation of all oppressed peoples necessitates the destruction of the political-economic systems of capitalism and imperialism as well as patriarchy. We are socialists because we believe the work must be organized for the collective benefit of those who do the work and create the products, and not for the profit of the bosses. Material resources must be equally distributed among those who create these resources. We are not convinced, however, that a socialist revolution that is not also a feminist and antiracist revolution will guarantee our liberation. We have arrived at the necessity for developing an understanding of class relationships that takes into account the specific class position of Black women who are generally marginal in the labor force, while at this particular time some of us are temporarily viewed as doubly desirable tokens at white-collar and professional levels. We need to articulate the real class situation of persons who are not merely raceless, sexless workers, but for whom racial and sexual oppression are significant determinants in their working/economic

lives. Although we are in essential agreement with Marx's theory as it applied to the very specific economic relationships he analyzed, we know that his analysis must be extended further in order for us to understand our specific economic situation as Black women.

A political contribution which we feel we have already made is the expansion of the feminist principle that the personal is political. In our consciousness-raising sessions, for example, we have in many ways gone beyond white women's revelations because we are dealing with the implications of race and class as well as sex. Even our Black women's style of talking/testifying in Black language about what we have experienced has a resonance that is both cultural and political. We have spent a great deal of energy delving into the cultural and experiential nature of our oppression out of necessity because none of these matters has ever been looked at before. No one before has ever examined the multilayered texture of Black women's lives. An example of this kind of revelation/conceptualization occurred at a meeting as we discussed the ways in which our early intellectual interests had been attacked by our peers, particularly Black males. We discovered that all of us, because we were "smart" had also been considered "ugly," i.e., "smart-ugly." "Smart-ugly" crystallized the way in which most of us had been forced to develop our intellects at great cost to our "social" lives. The sanctions in the Black and white communities against Black women thinkers is comparatively much higher than for white women, particularly ones from the educated middle and upper classes.

As we have already stated, we reject the stance of lesbian separatism because it is not a viable political analysis or strategy for us. It leaves out far too much and far too many people, particularly Black men, women, and children. We have a great deal of criticism and loathing for what men have been socialized to be in this society: what they support, how they act, and how they oppress. But we do not have the misguided notion that it is their maleness, per se—i.e., their biological maleness—that makes them what they are. As Black women we find any type of biological determinism a particularly dangerous and reactionary basis upon which to build a politic. We must also question whether lesbian separatism is an adequate and progressive political analysis and strategy, even for those who practice it, since it so completely denies any but the sexual sources of women's oppression, negating the facts of class and race.

3. Problems in Organizing Black Feminists

During our years together as a Black feminist collective we have experienced success and defeat, joy and pain, victory and failure. We have found that it is very difficult to organize around Black feminist issues, difficult even to announce in certain contexts that we *are* Black feminists. We have tried to think about the reasons for our difficulties, particularly since the white women's movement continues to be strong and to grow in many directions. In this section we will discuss some of the general reasons for the organizing problems we face and also talk specifically about the stages in organizing our own collective.

The major source of difficulty in our political work is that we are not just trying to fight oppression on one front or even two, but instead to address a whole range of oppressions. We do not have racial, sexual, heterosexual, or class privilege to rely upon, nor do we have even the minimal access to resources and power that groups who possess any one of these types of privilege have.

The psychological toll of being a Black woman and the difficulties this presents in reaching political consciousness and doing political work can never be underestimated. There is a very low value placed upon Black women's psyches in this society, which is both racist and sexist. As an early group member once said, "We are all damaged people merely by virtue of being Black women." We are dispossessed psychologically and on every other level, and yet we feel the necessity to struggle to change the condition of all Black women. In "A Black Feminist's Search for Sisterhood," Michele Wallace arrives at this conclusion:

> "We exist as women who are Black who are feminists, each stranded for the moment, working independently because there is not yet an environment in this society remotely congenial to our struggle — because, being on the bottom, we would have to do what no one else has done: we would have to fight the world."[2]

Wallace is pessimistic but realistic in her assessment of Black feminists' position, particularly in her

allusion to the nearly classic isolation most of us face. We might use our position at the bottom, however, to make a clear leap into revolutionary action. If Black women were free, it would mean that everyone else would have to be free since our freedom would necessitate the destruction of all the systems of oppression.

Feminism is, nevertheless, very threatening to the majority of Black people because it calls into question some of the most basic assumptions about our existence, i.e., that sex should be a determinant of power relationships. Here is the way male and female voices were defined in a Black nationalist pamphlet from the early 1970s.

> "We understand that it is and has been traditional that the man is the head of the house. He is the leader of the house/nation because his knowledge of the world is broader, his awareness is greater, his understanding is fuller and his application of this information is wiser . . . After all, it is only reasonable that the man be the head of the house because he is able to defend and protect the development of his home . . . Women cannot do the same things as men — they are made by nature to function differently. Equality of men and women is something that cannot happen even in the abstract world. Men are not equal to other men, i.e. ability, experience or even understanding. The value of men and women can be seen as in the value of gold and silver — they are not equal but both have great value. We must realize that men and women are a complement to each other because there is no house/family without a man and his wife. Both are essential to the development of any life."[3]

The material conditions of most Black women would hardly lead them to upset both economic and sexual arrangements that seem to represent some stability in their lives. Many Black women have a good understanding of both sexism and racism, but because of the everyday constrictions of their lives cannot risk struggling against them both.

The reaction of Black men to feminism has been notoriously negative. They are, of course, even more threatened than Black women by the possibility that Black feminists might organize around our own needs. They realize that they might not only lose valuable and hard-working allies in their struggles but that they might also be forced to change their habitually sexist ways of interacting with and oppressing Black women. Accusations that Black feminism divides the Black struggle are powerful deterrents to the growth of an autonomous Black women's movement.

Still, hundreds of women have been active at different times during the three-year existence of our group. And every Black woman who came, came out of a strongly-felt need for some level of possibility that did not previously exist in her life.

When we first started meeting early in 1974 after the NBFO first eastern regional conference, we did not have a strategy for organizing, or even a focus. We just wanted to see what we had. After a period of months of not meeting, we began to meet again late in the year and started doing an intense variety of consciousness-raising. The overwhelming feeling that we had is that after years and years we had finally found each other. Although we were not doing political work as a group, individuals continued their involvement in Lesbian politics, sterilization abuse and abortion rights work, Third World Women's International Women's Day activities, and support activity for the trials of Dr. Kenneth Edelin, Joan Little, and Inéz García. During our first summer, when membership had dropped off considerably, those of us remaining devoted serious discussion to the possibility of opening a refuge for battered women in a Black community. (There was no refuge in Boston at that time.) We also decided around that time to become an independent collective since we had serious disagreements with NBFO's bourgeois-feminist stance and their lack of a clear political focus.

We also were contacted at that time by socialist feminists, with whom we had worked on abortion rights activities, who wanted to encourage us to attend the National Socialist Feminist Conference in Yellow Springs. One of our members did attend and despite the narrowness of the ideology that was promoted at that particular conference, we became more aware of the need for us to understand our own economic situation and to make our own economic analysis.

In the fall, when some members returned, we experienced several months of comparative inactivity and internal disagreements which were first conceptualized as a Lesbian-straight split but which

were also the result of class and political differences. During the summer those of us who were still meeting had determined the need to do political work and to move beyond consciousness-raising and serving exclusively as an emotional support group. At the beginning of 1976, when some of the women who had not wanted to do political work and who also had voiced disagreements stopped attending of their own accord, we again looked for a focus. We decided at that time, with the addition of new members, to become a study group. We had always shared our reading with each other, and some of us had written papers on Black feminism for group discussion a few months before this decision was made. We began functioning as a study group and also began discussing the possibility of starting a Black feminist publication. We had a retreat in the late spring which provided a time for both political discussion and working out interpersonal issues. Currently we are planning to gather together a collection of Black feminist writing. We feel that it is absolutely essential to demonstrate the reality of our politics to other Black women and believe that we can do this through writing and distributing our work. The fact that individual Black feminists are living in isolation all over the country, that our own numbers are small, and that we have some skills in writing, printing, and publishing makes us want to carry out these kinds of projects as a means of organizing Black feminists as we continue to do political work in coalition with other groups.

4. Black Feminist Issues and Projects

During our time together we have identified and worked on many issues of particular relevance to Black women. The inclusiveness of our politics makes us concerned with any situation that impinges upon the lives of women, Third World and working people. We are of course particularly committed to working on those struggles in which race, sex and class are simultaneous factors in oppression. We might, for example, become involved in workplace organizing at a factory that employs Third World women or picket a hospital that is cutting back on already inadequate health care to a Third World community, or set up a rape crisis center in a Black neighborhood. Organizing around welfare and daycare concerns might also be a focus. The work to be done and the countless issues that this work represents merely reflect the pervasiveness of our oppression.

Issues and projects that collective members have already worked on are sterilization abuse, abortion rights, battered women, rape and health care. We have also done many workshops and educationals on Black feminism on college campuses, at women's conferences, and most recently for high school women.

One issue that is of major concern to us and that we have begun to publicly address is racism in the white women's movement. As Black feminists we are made constantly and painfully aware of how little effort white women have made to understand and combat their racism, which requires among other things that they have a more than superficial comprehension of race, color, and Black history and culture. Eliminating racism in the white women's movement is by definition work for white women to do, but we will continue to speak to and demand accountability on this issue.

In the practice of our politics we do not believe that the end always justifies the means. Many reactionary and destructive acts have been done in the name of achieving "correct" political goals. As feminists we do not want to mess over people in the name of politics. We believe in collective process and a nonhierarchical distribution of power within our own group and in our vision of a revolutionary society. We are committed to a continual examination of our politics as they develop through criticism and self-criticism as an essential aspect of our practice. In her introduction to *Sisterhood Is Powerful* Robin Morgan writes:

> "I haven't the faintest notion what possible revolutionary role white heterosexual men could fulfill, since they are the very embodiment of reactionary-vested-interest-power."

As Black feminists and Lesbians we know that we have a very definite revolutionary task to perform and we are ready for the lifetime of work and struggle before us.

Endnotes

1. This statement is dated April 1977.
2. Michele Wallace, "A Black Feminist's Search for Sisterhood," The Village Voice, 28 July 1975, pp. 6–7.
3. Mumininas of Committee for Unified Newark, Mwanamke Mwananchi (The Nationalist Woman), Newark, N.J., © 1971, pp. 4–5.

S I X

◆◆◆

Presenting the Blue Goddess
Toward a National Pan-Asian Feminist Agenda
Sonia Shah

We all laughed sheepishly about how we used to dismiss the South Asian women in our lives as doormats irrelevant to our feminist lives. For most of us in that fledgling South Asian American women's group in Boston, either white feminists or black feminists had inspired us to find our Asian feminist heritage. Yet neither movement had really prepared us for actually finding any. The way either group defined feminism did not, could not, define our South Asian feminist heritages. That, for most of us, consisted of feisty immigrant mothers, ball-breaking grandmothers, Kali-worship (Kali is the blue goddess who sprung whole from another woman and who symbolizes "shakti" — Hindi for womanpower), social activist aunts, freedom-fighting/Gandhian great-aunts. In many ways, white feminism, with its "personal is political" maxim and its emphasis on building sisterhood and consciousness raising, had brought us together. Black feminism, on the other hand, had taught us that we could expect more — that feminism can incorporate a race analysis. Yet, while both movements spurred us to organize, neither included our South Asian American agendas — toward battery of immigrant women, the ghettoization of the Indian community, cultural discrimination, bicultural history and identity.

I felt we were starting anew, starting to define a South Asian American feminism that no one had articulated yet. As I began to reach out to other Asian American women's groups over the years and for this chapter, however, that sense faded a bit. Asian American women have been organizing themselves for decades, with much to show for it.

Our shakti hasn't yet expressed itself on a national stage accessible to all of our sisters. But we are entering a moment in our organizing when we will soon be able to create a distinctly Asian American feminism — one that will be able to cross the class and culture lines that currently divide us.

The first wave of Asian women's organizing, born of the women's liberation and civil rights movements of the 1960s, created established groups like Asian Women United in San Francisco, Asian Sisters in Action in Boston, and other more informal networks of primarily professional, East Asian American women. They focused on empowering Asian women economically and socially and accessing political power. Asian Women United, for example, has produced videos like "Silk Wings," which describes Asian women in non-traditional jobs, and books like *Making Waves,* an anthology of Asian American women's writing.

In contrast, the second wave of organizing, politicized by the 1980s multicultural movements, includes the many ethnically specific women's groups that tend to start out as support networks, some later becoming active in the battered women's movement (like Manavi in New Jersey, Sneha in Hartford, and the New York Asian Women's Center, which offer battery hotlines and shelter for Asian women) and others working in the woman-of-color and lesbian/gay liberation movements. Culturally, these groups are Korean, Indian, Cambodian, Filipina, and from other more recently arrived immigrant groups who may not have felt part of the more established, primarily East Asian women's networks. These different groups are divided by generation, by culture, and by geographic location. Anna Rhee, a cofounder of the Washington Alliance of Korean American Women

(WAKAW), a group of mostly 1.5 generation (those who emigrated to the United States in early adulthood) and second generation Korean American women, with an average age of 27 to 28, says she felt "we were starting anew, because of the focus on English speaking Korean women, which was different from any other group we had seen." WAKAW, like many similar groups, started as a support group, but has since evolved into activism, with voter registration and other projects.

Talking to different Asian American women activists, I was inspired by the many projects these activists have undertaken, and impressed with the overwhelming sense women had that the Asian American women's community today stands at a crossroads ripe with possibility. The New York Asian Women's Center, which runs several programs fighting violence against Asian women, just celebrated its 10th birthday. The Pacific Asian American Women's Bay Area Coalition honors Asian American women with Woman Warrior (à la Maxine Hong Kingston's novel) leadership awards, catapulting their honorees on to other accolades. Indian Subcontinent Women's Alliance for Action (ISWAA) in Boston just assembled a grassroots arts exhibit of works by and for South Asian women. Asian Women United, in addition to several other videos, is working on a video of Asian American visual artists. The Washington Alliance for Korean American Women is taking oral histories of Korean mothers and daughters. Everyone has a story of another group starting up, another exciting Asian American woman activist.

So far, Asian American women activists have used two general organizing models. The first is based on the fact that Asian women need each other to overcome the violence, isolation, and powerlessness of their lives; no one else can or will be able to help us but each other. The groups that come together on this basis focus on the immediate needs of the community: housing battered women, finding homes for abandoned women and children, legal advocacy for refugee women, etc.

The second model uses the basis of shared identity and the realization that both Asian and U.S. mainstream cultures make Asian American women invisible as organizing principles. The groups that come together on this basis work on articulating anger about racism and sexism, like other women of color groups, but also on fighting the omniscient and seductive pressure to assimilate, within ourselves and for our sisters.

Today, our numbers are exploding, in our immigrant communities and their children, and subsequently, in our activist communities. Our writers, poets, artists, and filmmakers are coming of age. Our activist voices, against anti-Asian violence, battery, and racism, are gaining legal, political, and social notice. We still have much ground to cover in influencing mainstream culture: we must throw those exoticizing books about Asian women off the shelf and replace them with a slew of works on pan-Asian feminism; women of color putting together collections of radical essays must be able to "find" Asian American feminists; *Ms.* magazine must offer more than a colorful photo of an Indian mother and daughter with less than three lines about them in a related cover article; critics must stop touting Asian American women's fiction as "exotic treasures"; Fifth Avenue advertising executives must stop producing ads that exploit tired stereotypes of Asian female "exotic beauty" and "humble modesty" with images of silky black hair and Asian women demurely tucking tampons into their pockets.

Our movement faces crucial internal challenges as well. Longtime Asian American feminist activists, such as Helen Zia, a contributing editor to *Ms.*, wonder, "What makes us different from white feminists or black feminists? What can we bring to the table?" and complain that "these questions haven't really been developed yet." Others, such as Jackie Church, a Japanese American activist, state that "there just aren't enough Asian American feminists who aren't doing five different things at once."

On the one hand, our national Asian women's groups, while inclusive across Asian ethnicities, haven't yet developed an Asian feminism *different* from black or white feminism. On the other, our ethnically specific groups, while emotionally resonant and culturally specific, are still remote and inaccessible to many of our sisters.

The movements of the 1960s colluded with the mainstream in defining racism in black and white terms; racism is still defined as discrimination based on skin color, i.e. race. They also, to some extent, elevated racism, defined in this way, to the top of layers of oppression. This narrow definition has distorted mainstream perception of anti-Asian racism

and even our perception of ourselves — as either non-victims of racism or victims of racism based on skin color. By these assumptions, an Indian assaulted because she "dresses weird" is not a victim of racism; a Chinese shopkeeper harassed because she has a "funny accent" is not a victim of racism. Mainstream culture finds neither of these incidents as disturbing, unacceptable, or even downright "evil" as racism. By this definition, one must either be in the black or white camp to even speak about racism, and we are expected to forget ourselves. Whites try to convince us we are really *more like them;* depending upon our degree of sensitivity toward racist injustice, we try to persuade blacks that we are more like them.

For example, many Asian American women have described Asian women's experience of racism as a result of stereotypes about "exotica" and "china dolls," two stereotypes based on our looking different from white people. But our experiences of racism go far beyond that. Rather than subvert the definition of racism itself, or uncover new layers of oppression just as unacceptable and pernicious as racism but based on what I call cultural discrimination, we have attempted to fit our experience of discrimination into the given definition. We too assume that racism is the worst kind of oppression, by emphasizing that racism against us is based on skin color and racial differences. Indeed, when we forged our first wave of women's movement, solidarity with other people of color whose activism revolved around black/white paradigms of oppression was a matter of survival. And organizing around racially based oppressions served as common ground for all ethnic Asians.

Yet our experiences of oppression are, in many qualitative ways, different from black and white people. For me, the experience of "otherness," the formative discrimination in my life, has resulted from culturally different (not necessarily racially different) people thinking they were culturally central: thinking that *my* house smelled funny, that *my* mother talked weird, that *my* habits were strange. They were normal; I wasn't.

Today, a more sophisticated understanding of oppression is emanating from all people of color groups. The L.A. riots, among other ethnic conflicts, unmasked to belated national attention the reality of an ethnic conflict (between blacks and browns, as well as between the white power structure and oppressed people of color) impossible to explain away simply as white-against-black racism. Multicultural movements and growing internationalism have raised questions about our hierarchy of oppressions. Asian American men and women activists are beginning to create legal and social definitions of cultural discrimination. Our movement can march beyond black/white paradigms that were once useful, and start to highlight cultural discrimination — our peculiar blend of cultural and sexist oppression based on our accents, our clothes, our foods, our values, and our commitments. When we do this successfully, we will have not just laid a common ground for all ethnic Asian women for the practical goal of gaining power, we will have taken an important political step toward understanding and, from there, struggling against the many layers of oppression.

The search for identity that has compelled Asian American women to separate into cultural-, age-, generation-, class-, and geographic-specific groups will ensure that the emerging pan-Asian-American feminism retains emotional resonance. Although the very specificity that makes them so useful limits these groups, as their numbers grow, coalition building and networking become not only viable options, but necessary for advancing difficult agendas requiring extensive resources and support. These coalitions and networks must struggle to find common ground that retains emotional resonance while being inclusive.

Our common ground must be more than our simply being "Asian," which encompasses so much diversity as to be practically useless as an ethnic category, particularly since our specific cultural heritages are so much more meaningful. The general "feminist" agenda, commonly understood as that of the mainstream white middle-class women's movement, is also problematic. The racism and classism of the traditional white women's movement, as well as the threat of violence from our community's patriarchy, has sometimes held us back from calling ourselves "feminists." "The whole attitude" of white feminism, says Sunita Mani of Indian Subcontinent Women's Alliance for Action, "is that my strong-mindedness is my American-ness, not my Asian-ness." The heightened demand for specificity that grows out of groups like ISWAA makes the simple grafting of the feminist label onto our organizing untenable: We need something that recognizes our

Asian activist heritage and our cultural specificity. As Carol Ito, a board member of the Pacific Asian American Women's Bay Area Coalition in San Francisco says, "We didn't want to called feminist." "Feminism was seen as a white, middle-class concern," says Korean American Elaine Kim, literary critic and a member of Asian Women United. "Race discrimination was much more vivid than sexism."

Our movement owes much to black feminism. But, while white feminism seemed to ignore race and culture analyses, black feminism, on the other hand, worked under the black/white paradigms and according to a hierarchy of oppressions, which Asian American women can neither accurately nor powerfully organize under. The black/white paradigms of both feminist and civil rights struggles create false divisions and false choices for Asian American women. Recently, a group of 1.5 generation South Asian women who organize against battery held a conference on South Asian women. This group, demographically, having emigrated later than the parents of second-generation South Asian Americans, tends to hail from greater class privilege. Second-generation South Asian American activists boycotted the conference, charging that the organizers, because of their class privilege and their relative newness to the Asian American community, sidelined issues of U.S.-based racism and discrimination.

This is a false division, especially dangerous in such a relatively small activist community. When first faced with American racism and its black/white constructs, immigrants with class privilege, even activist ones, are apt to dismiss racism as "not their problem." (As the mainstream defines it, strictly speaking, it isn't.) Efforts by second-generation activists and beyond, confined as we have been to black/white paradigms, to convince our sisters at other locations on the culture/class continuum that what we suffer is similar to what the black community suffers will necessarily be difficult if not impossible. Yet we are natural allies, given a broader critique of oppression that includes cultural discrimination and an accurate portrayal of our own experiences of racism on a continuum of oppressions linked to imperialism, immigration policy, and sexism: across real divisions of immigration status and class and certainly across the false divisions of black/white race analysis and black/white feminism.

As Asian Americans, Asians in America, Americans of Asian descent, or however we choose to think of ourselves, we all grapple with conflicting signals and oppressions in our lives because we are all situated, to differing degrees, in both Asian and American cultural milieus. As any of these, we not only suffer cultural discrimination as men also do, but our own form of cultural schizophrenia, from the mixed and often contradictory signals about priorities, values, duty, and meaning our families and greater communities convey. We encounter sexist Asian tradition, racist and sexist white culture, anti-racist non-feminist women heroes, racist feminist heroes, strong proud Asian women who told us not to make waves, strong proud non-Asian women who told us *to* make waves, and on and on.

Black/white paradigms have informed the conception of cultural or racial difference as well: White people are all white, black people are all black. No room exists for cultural duality in a world where one is automatically relegated to one camp or another based on biology. Yet the problems of cultural duality as well as the concomitant experience of cultural discrimination are exactly what unite the Asian American women's community across our differences. We all reconcile these tensions and oppressions in different ways, by acting out a model minority myth, for some; by suffering silently, for others; by being activist, for still others. As we grapple with conflicting signals and oppressions in our lives with the support of our sisters, as well as struggle against cultural discrimination, we can reimagine and reinvent ourselves and our priorities. We can politicize the process of cultural reconciliation, and tag it for feminism and liberation.

This broader critique that the Asian American women's community is groping toward does and must continue to include this empowering and activist commonality among Asian American women: Not just the fact and nature of our oppressions, but the nature of our responses to oppression, what I call bicultural feminism.

The plea for bicultural feminism is not simply that Asian American women activists call themselves bicultural feminists. It is a call for an agenda that subverts the black/white paradigms, articulates cultural discrimination and how it illuminates and connects to other processes of oppression, and politicizes the process of cultural reconciliation for feminism and liberation.

A poor immigrant Asian woman follows an abusive husband to the United States; she doesn't speak English and is cut off from the women who supported her in her home country; she is beaten nearly to death by her one contact to the outside world. This woman needs a bicultural feminism. Within black/white constructs of racism, she cannot name the threats to her with the authority that racism carries. Within narrow white feminist paradigms and essentialist notions of cultural difference, she is presented with false choices for liberation: Either become a prototypical "American" woman, with all the alien cultural cues that implies, or go back to Asia. She needs an activism that struggles against the danger she encounters as a non-English speaking Asian woman in America; she needs an activism that empowers her to liberate herself in this country (with money, legal services, shelter, and support) while recognizing and politicizing the cultural reconciliation she must undergo to liberate herself (by reimagining her duty as an Asian wife as a duty to herself, for example).

When my little sister, who is just beginning to see herself as a sexual person, thinks she is a "slut" for wearing tight jeans, she needs this bicultural feminism. Not a mainstream white feminism, which might suggest she throw away her tight jeans because she is objectifying herself, nor one that simply suggests she revert to the dress of her "homeland" and wear a revealing sari—but one that would affirm that she doesn't have to abandon Indian values or filial respect of whatever it is that makes her fear appearing "slutty."

It is possible that first-generation Indians reject the trappings of American sexuality, such as tight jeans, as culturally alien. The subsequent interpretation by their children and their greater American communities, however, that they are anti-sexuality stems from the dominant paradigm of a monoculture: white culture and black culture, which is simply the poor, darker version of the white culture. An Asian American feminism that emphasized cultural duality and reconciliation would subvert this notion. There are many cultures, many sexualities, and many trappings of such. My sister needs to name the cultural conflicts she is involved in for what they are, and reconcile her visions of sexuality and empowerment within the cultural confines of white patriarchy and Indian patriarchy. A bicultural feminism would ensure that she does this in a feminist, liberated way.

As bicultural feminists, we are empowered to enter the broader discussion and struggles around us with something more substantial than identity politics and our slightly different take on racism within the black/white dichotomy. As we approach the concept and practice of the extended family, for example, we can apply our critical reinventions to the struggle for accessible child care, by shifting the turgid debate away from paid care and toward building cooperative care centers and work-sharing. As we approach social and linguistic difference within Asian American families, we can apply our insights to the current debates about gay parents raising potentially straight children, or to white families raising children of color, for example, by advocating for the fitness of the child's cultural community rather than for the "fitness" of the parent. As we remember our histories as Asian women, we can apply our sense of outrage, over the internment, the brain drain, and the treatment of refugees, to the struggle for just immigration policy. We can reinterpret Asian paradigms of filial and familial duty as social responsibility. We can use anti-materialism as a basis for building an ecological society.

I remember, in that South Asian American women's group, we were all looking forward to Mira Nair's film, "Mississippi Masala." We took Nair as a kind of model — a seemingly progressive Indian woman filmmaker who had gained the kind of financial backing necessary for reaching wide sectors of the South Asian community. "Masala" was the first film we knew of that would portray an Indian American woman in her cultural milieu as the protagonist.

I don't know what Nair's intentions were, but her Indian American protagonist was little more than a standard Western-defined beauty, her biculturalism little more than occasional bare feet and a chureedar thrown over her shoulder. Although a refugee from Uganda living in Mississippi with Indian parents, she was phenomenally unconcerned with issues of race, history, culture, and gender. Given the dearth of accessible activist commentary on biculturalism and feminism beyond the black/white divide, even a sympathetic "opinion-maker" like Nair can hurt our movement by portraying us as little more than exotic, browner versions of white women, who by virtue of a little color can bridge the gap between black and white (not through activism, of course, just romantic love). If Asian American women's movements can effectively unite within bicultural feminist agendas, we can snatch that power away from those willing to trivialize us, and "Masala" and our less sympathetic foes beware.

SEVEN

◆◆◆

The Five Sexes
Why Male and Female Are Not Enough
Anne Fausto-Sterling

In 1843 Levi Suydam, a twenty-three-year-old resident of Salisbury, Connecticut, asked the town board of selectmen to validate his right to vote as a Whig in a hotly contested local election. The request raised a flurry of objections from the opposing party, for reasons that must be rare in the annals of American democracy: it was said that Suydam was more female than male and thus (some eighty years before suffrage was extended to women) could not be allowed to cast a ballot. To settle the dispute a physician, one William James Barry, was brought in to examine Suydam. And, presumably upon encountering a phallus, the good doctor declared the prospective voter male. With Suydam safely in their column the Whigs won the election by a majority of one.

Barry's diagnosis, however, turned out to be somewhat premature. Within a few days he discovered that, phallus notwithstanding, Suydam menstruated regularly and had a vaginal opening. Both his/her physique and his/her mental predispositions were more complex than was first suspected. S/he had narrow shoulders and broad hips and felt occasional sexual yearnings for women. Suydam's "feminine propensities, such as a fondness for gay colors, for pieces of calico, comparing and placing them together, and an aversion for bodily labor, and an inability to perform the same, were remarked by many," Barry later wrote. It is not clear whether Suydam lost or retained the vote, or whether the election results were reversed.

Western culture is deeply committed to the idea that there are only two sexes. Even language refuses other possibilities; thus to write about Levi Suydam I have had to invent conventions — *s/he* and *his/her* — to denote someone who is clearly neither male nor female or who is perhaps both sexes at once. Legally, too, every adult is either man or woman, and the difference, of course, is not trivial. For Suydam it meant the franchise; today it means being available for, or exempt from, draft registration, as well as being subject, in various ways, to a number of laws governing marriage, the family and human intimacy. In many parts of the United States, for instance, two people legally registered as men cannot have sexual relations without violating anti-sodomy statutes.

But if the state and the legal system have an interest in maintaining a two-party sexual system, they are in defiance of nature. For biologically speaking, there are many gradations running from female to male; and depending on how one calls the shots, one can argue that along that spectrum lie at least five sexes — and perhaps even more.

For some time medical investigators have recognized the concept of the intersexual body. But the standard medical literature uses the term *intersex* as a catch-all for three major subgroups with some mixture of male and female characteristics: the so-called true hermaphrodites, whom I call herms, who possess one testis and one ovary (the sperm- and egg-producing vessels, or gonads); the male pseudohermaphrodites (the "merms"), who have testes and some aspects of the female genitalia but no ovaries; and the female pseudohermaphrodites (the "ferms"), who have ovaries and some aspects of the male genitalia but lack testes. Each of those categories is in itself complex; the percentage of male and female characteristics, for instance, can vary enormously among members of the same subgroup. Moreover, the inner lives of the people in each subgroup — their special needs and their problems, attractions and repulsions — have gone unexplored by science. But on the basis of what is known about them I suggest that the three intersexes, herm, merm and ferm, deserve to be considered additional sexes

each in its own right. Indeed, I would argue further that sex is a vast, infinitely malleable continuum that defies the constraints of even five categories.

Not surprisingly, it is extremely difficult to estimate the frequency of intersexuality, much less the frequency of each of the three additional sexes; it is not the sort of information one volunteers on a job application. The psychologist John Money of Johns Hopkins University, a specialist in the study of congenital sexual-organ defects, suggests intersexuals may constitute as many as 4 percent of births. As I point out to my students at Brown University, in a student body of about 6,000 that fraction, if correct, implies there may be as many as 240 intersexuals on campus — surely enough to form a minority caucus of some kind.

In reality though, few such students would make it as far as Brown in sexually diverse form. Recent advances in physiology and surgical technology now enable physicians to catch most intersexuals at the moment of birth. Almost at once such infants are entered into a program of hormonal and surgical management so that they can slip quietly into society as "normal" heterosexual males or females. I emphasize that the motive is in no way conspiratorial. The aims of the policy are genuinely humanitarian, reflecting the wish that people be able to "fit in" both physically and psychologically. In the medical community, however, the assumptions behind that wish — that there be only two sexes, that heterosexuality alone is normal, that there is one true model of psychological health — have gone virtually unexamined.

The word *hermaphrodite* comes from the Greek names Hermes, variously known as the messenger of the gods, the patron of music, the controller of dreams or the protector of livestock, and Aphrodite, the goddess of sexual love and beauty. According to Greek mythology, those two gods parented Hermaphroditus, who at age fifteen became half male and half female when his body fused with the body of a nymph he fell in love with. In some true hermaphrodites the testis and the ovary grow separately but bilaterally; in others they grow together within the same organ, forming an ovo-testis. Not infrequently, at least one of the gonads functions quite well, producing either sperm cells or eggs, as well as functional levels of the sex hormones — androgens or estrogens. Although in theory it might be possible for a true hermaphrodite to become both father and mother to a child, in practice the appropriate ducts and tubes are not configured so that egg and sperm can meet.

In contrast with the true hermaphrodites, the pseudohermaphrodites possess two gonads of the same kind along with the usual male (XY) or female (XX) chromosomal makeup. But their external genitalia and secondary sex characteristics do not match their chromosomes. Thus merms have testes and XY chromosomes, yet they also have a vagina and a clitoris, and at puberty they often develop breasts. They do not menstruate, however. Ferms have ovaries, two X chromosomes and sometimes a uterus, but they also have at least partly masculine external genitalia. Without medical intervention they can develop beards, deep voices and adult-size penises.

No classification scheme could more than suggest the variety of sexual anatomy encountered in clinical practice. In 1969, for example, two French investigators, Paul Guinet of the Endocrine Clinic in Lyons and Jacques Decourt of the Endocrine Clinic in Paris, described ninety-eight cases of true hermaphroditism — again, signifying people with both ovarian and testicular tissue — solely according to the appearance of the external genitalia and the accompanying ducts. In some cases the people exhibited strongly feminine development. They had separate openings for the vagina and the urethra, a cleft vulva defined by both the large and the small labia, or vaginal lips, and at puberty they developed breasts and usually began to menstruate. It was the oversize and sexually alert clitoris, which threatened sometimes at puberty to grow into a penis, that usually impelled them to seek medical attention. Members of another group also had breasts and a feminine body type, and they menstruated. But their labia were at least partly fused, forming an incomplete scrotum. The phallus (here an embryological term for a structure that during usual development goes on to form either a clitoris or a penis) was between 1.5 and 2.8 inches long; nevertheless, they urinated through a urethra that opened into or near the vagina.

By far the most frequent form of true hermaphrodite encountered by Guinet and Decourt — 55 percent — appeared to have a more masculine physique. In such people the urethra runs either through or

near the phallus, which looks more like a penis than a clitoris. Any menstrual blood exits periodically during urination. But in spite of the relatively male appearance of the genitalia, breasts appear at puberty. It is possible that a sample larger than ninety-eight so-called true hermaphrodites would yield even more contrasts and subtleties. Suffice it to say that the varieties are so diverse that it is possible to know which parts are present and what is attached to what only after exploratory surgery.

The embryological origins of human hermaphrodites clearly fit what is known about male and female sexual development. The embryonic gonad generally chooses early in development to follow either a male or a female sexual pathway; for the ovotestis, however, that choice is fudged. Similarly, the embryonic phallus most often ends up as a clitoris or a penis, but the existence of intermediate states comes as no surprise to the embryologist. There are also uro-genital swellings in the embryo that usually either stay open and become the vaginal labia or fuse and become a scrotum. In some hermaphrodites, though, the choice of opening or closing is ambivalent. Finally, all mammalian embryos have structures that can become the female uterus and the fallopian tubes, as well as structures that can become part of the male sperm-transport system. Typically either the male or the female set of those primordial genital organs degenerates, and the remaining structures achieve their sex-appropriate feature. In hermaphrodites both sets of organs develop to varying degrees.

Intersexuality itself is old news. Hermaphrodites, for instance, are often featured in stories about human origins. Early biblical scholars believed Adam began life as a hermaphrodite and later divided into two people — a male and a female — after falling from grace. According to Plato there once were three sexes — male, female and hermaphrodite — but the third sex was lost with time.

Both the Talmud and the Tosefta, the Jewish books of law, list extensive regulations for people of mixed sex. The Tosefta expressly forbids hermaphrodites to inherit their fathers' estates (like daughters), to seclude themselves with women (like sons) or to shave (like men). When hermaphrodites menstruate they must be isolated from men (like women); they are disqualified from serving as witnesses or as priests (like women), but the laws of pederasty apply to them.

In Europe a pattern emerged by the end of the Middle Ages that, in a sense, has lasted to the present day: hermaphrodites were compelled to choose an established gender role and stick with it. The penalty for transgression was often death. Thus in the 1600s a Scottish hermaphrodite living as a woman was buried alive after impregnating his/her master's daughter.

For questions of inheritance, legitimacy, paternity, succession to title and eligibility for certain professions to be determined, modern Anglo-Saxon legal systems require that newborns be registered as either male or female. In the U.S. today sex determination is governed by state laws. Illinois permits adults to change the sex recorded on their birth certificates should a physician attest to having performed the appropriate surgery. The New York Academy of Medicine, on the other hand, has taken an opposite view. In spite of surgical alterations of the external genitalia, the academy argued in 1966, the chromosomal sex remains the same. By that measure, a person's wish to conceal his or her original sex cannot outweigh the public interest in protection against fraud.

During this century the medical community has completed what the legal world began—the complete erasure of any form of embodied sex that does not conform to a male–female, heterosexual pattern. Ironically, a more sophisticated knowledge of the complexity of sexual systems has led to the repression of such intricacy.

In 1937 the urologist Hugh H. Young of Johns Hopkins University published a volume titled *Genital Abnormalities, Hermaphroditism and Related Adrenal Diseases*. The book is remarkable for its erudition, scientific insight and open-mindedness. In it Young drew together a wealth of carefully documented case histories to demonstrate and study the medical treatment of such "accidents of birth." Young did not pass judgment on the people he studied, nor did he attempt to coerce into treatment those intersexuals who rejected that option. And he showed unusual even-handedness in referring to those people who had had sexual experiences as both men and women as "practicing hermaphrodites."

One of Young's more interesting cases was a hermaphrodite named Emma who had grown up as a female. Emma had both a penis-size clitoris and a vagina, which made it possible for him/her to have "normal" heterosexual sex with both men and women. As a teenager Emma had had sex with a number of girls to whom s/he was deeply attracted; but at the age of nineteen s/he had married a man. Unfortunately, he had given Emma little sexual pleasure (though *he* had no complaints), and so throughout that marriage and subsequent ones Emma had kept girlfriends on the side. With some frequency s/he had pleasurable sex with them. Young describes his subject as appearing "to be quite content and even happy." In conversation Emma occasionally told him of his/her wish to be a man, a circumstance Young said would be relatively easy to bring about. But Emma's reply strikes a heroic blow for self-interest:

> Would you have to remove that vagina? I don't know about that because that's my meal ticket. If you did that, I would have to quit my husband and go to work, so I think I'll keep it and stay as I am. My husband supports me well, and even though I don't have any sexual pleasure with him, I do have lots with my girlfriends.

Yet even as Young was illuminating intersexuality with the light of scientific reason, he was beginning its suppression. For his book is also an extended treatise on the most modern surgical and hormonal methods of changing intersexuals into either males or females. Young may have differed from his successors in being less judgmental and controlling of the patients and their families, but he nonetheless supplied the foundation on which current intervention practices were built.

By 1969, when the English physicians Christopher J. Dewhurst and Ronald R. Gordon wrote *The Intersexual Disorders*, medical and surgical approaches to intersexuality had neared a state of rigid uniformity. It is hardly surprising that such a hardening of opinion took place in the era of the feminine mystique—of the post–Second World War flight to the suburbs and the strict division of family roles according to sex. That the medical consensus was not quite universal (or perhaps that it seemed poised to break apart again) can be gleaned from the near-hysterical tone of Dewhurst and Gordon's book, which contrasts markedly with the calm reason of Young's founding work. Consider their opening description of an intersexual newborn:

> One can only attempt to imagine the anguish of the parents. That a newborn should have a deformity . . . [affecting] so fundamental an issue as the very sex of the child . . . is a tragic event which immediately conjures up visions of a hopeless psychological misfit doomed to live always as a sexual freak in loneliness and frustration.

Dewhurst and Gordon warned that such a miserable fate would, indeed, be a baby's lot should the case be improperly managed; "but fortunately," they wrote, "with correct management the outlook is infinitely better than the poor parents — emotionally stunned by the event — or indeed anyone without special knowledge could ever imagine."

Scientific dogma has held fast to the assumption that without medical care hermaphrodites are doomed to a life of misery. Yet there are few empirical studies to back up that assumption, and some of the same research gathered to build a case for medical treatment contradicts it. Francies Benton, another of Young's practicing hermaphrodites, "had not worried over his condition, did not wish to be changed, and was enjoying life." The same could be said of Emma, the opportunistic hausfrau. Even Dewhurst and Gordon, adamant about the psychological importance of treating intersexuals at the infant stage, acknowledged great success in "changing the sex" of older patients. They reported on twenty cases of children reclassified into a different sex after the supposedly critical age of eighteen months. They asserted that all the reclassifications were "successful," and they wondered then whether reregistration could be "recommended more readily than [had] been suggested so far."

The treatment of intersexuality in this century provides a clear example of what the French historian Michel Foucault has called biopower. The knowledge developed in biochemistry, embryology, endocrinology, psychology and surgery has enabled physicians to control the very sex of the human body. The multiple contradictions in that kind of power call for some scrutiny. On the one hand, the medical "management" of intersexuality certainly developed as part of an attempt to free people from perceived

psychological pain (though whether the pain was the patient's, the parents' or the physician's is unclear). And if one accepts the assumption that in a sex-divided culture people can realize their greatest potential for happiness and productivity only if they are sure they belong to one of only two acknowledged sexes, modern medicine has been extremely successful.

On the other hand, the same medical accomplishments can be read not as progress but as a mode of discipline. Hermaphrodites have unruly bodies. They do not fall naturally into a binary classification; only a surgical shoehorn can put them there. But why should we care if a "woman," defined as one who has breasts, a vagina, a uterus and ovaries and who menstruates, also has a clitoris large enough to penetrate the vagina of another woman? Why should we care if there are people whose biological equipment enables them to have sex "naturally" with both men and women? The answers seem to lie in a cultural need to maintain clear distinctions between the sexes. Society mandates the control of intersexual bodies because they blur and bridge the great divide. Inasmuch as hermaphrodites literally embody both sexes, they challenge traditional beliefs about sexual difference: they possess the irritating ability to live sometimes as one sex and sometimes the other, and they raise the specter of homosexuality.

But what if things were altogether different? Imagine a world in which the same knowledge that has enabled medicine to intervene in the management of intersexual patients has been placed at the service of multiple sexualities. Imagine that the sexes have multiplied beyond currently imaginable limits. It would have to be a world of shared powers. Patient and physician, parent and child, male and female, heterosexual and homosexual — all those oppositions and others would have to be dissolved as sources of division. A new ethic of medical treatment would arise, one that would permit ambiguity in a culture that had overcome sexual division. The central mission of medical treatment would be to preserve life. Thus hermaphrodites would be concerned primarily not about whether they can conform to society but about whether they might develop potentially life-threatening conditions — hernias, gonadal tumors, salt imbalance caused by adrenal malfunction — that sometimes accompany hermaphroditic development. In my ideal world medical intervention for intersexuals would take place only rarely before the age of reason; subsequent treatment would be a cooperative venture between physician, patient and other advisers trained in issues of gender multiplicity.

I do not pretend that the transition to my utopia would be smooth. Sex, even the supposedly "normal," heterosexual kind, continues to cause untold anxieties in Western society. And certainly a culture that has yet to come to grips—religiously and, in some states, legally—with the ancient and relatively uncomplicated reality of homosexual love will not readily embrace intersexuality. No doubt the most troublesome arena by far would be the rearing of children. Parents, at least since the Victorian era, have fretted, sometimes to the point of outright denial, over the fact that their children are sexual beings.

All that and more amply explains why intersexual children are generally squeezed into one of the two prevailing sexual categories. But what would be the psychological consequences of taking the alternative road—raising children as unabashed intersexuals? On the surface that tack seems fraught with peril. What, for example, would happen to the intersexual child amid the unrelenting cruelty of the school yard? When the time came to shower in gym class, what horrors and humiliations would await the intersexual as his/her anatomy was displayed in all its nontraditional glory? In whose gym class

would s/he register to begin with? What bathroom would s/he use? And how on earth would Mom and Dad help shepherd him/her through the mine field of puberty?

In the past thirty years those questions have been ignored, as the scientific community has, with remarkable unanimity, avoided contemplating the alternative route of unimpeded intersexuality. But modern investigators tend to overlook a substantial body of case histories, most of them compiled between 1930 and 1960, before surgical intervention became rampant. Almost without exception, those reports describe children who grew up knowing they were intersexual (though they did not advertise it) and adjusted to their unusual status. Some of the studies are richly detailed—described at the level of gym-class showering (which most intersexuals avoided without incident); in any event, there is not a psychotic or a suicide in the lot.

Still, the nuances of socialization among intersexuals cry out for more sophisticated analysis. Clearly, before my vision of sexual multiplicity can be realized, the first openly intersexual children and their parents will have to be brave pioneers who will bear the brunt of society's growing pains. But in the long view—though it could take generations to achieve—the prize might be a society in which sexuality is something to be celebrated for its subtleties and not something to be feared or ridiculed.

E I G H T

◆◆◆

Taking on the Global Economy

Kalima Rose

The rain was with us everyday, washing us, a metaphor for the tears of women from across the planet who came to share the pains and victories of

Kalima Rose attended the NGO Forum of the United Nations Fourth World Conference on Women in Beijing, in 1995. She reports on theoretical perspectives discussed by participants, focusing on the globalization of the economy and its implications for women in the U.S.

their peoples. The earth turned to bog, wheelchairs became stranded and events were canceled. For some, the inconvenience of incessant rain symbolized the expected relegation of women to substandard facilities. For others, we felt the monsoon working on us, softening the definitions of land and boundaries of peoples, preparing the ground for the new seed that women carried here to share.

The distributed seeds held the kernels of analysis that women first brought to trial at the 1985 world women's conference in Nairobi. There, women from countries of the south were raising their analysis of the social disinvestment that was making women poorer in their countries. The disinvestment they experienced in '85 was a result of their countries' overdue foreign debts. The financial institutions that could help them out were dictating structural adjustment policies which compelled them to restructure their economies along free market principles to help exact the debt payments. Things like food, health, and other social infrastructure subsidies were jettisoned to meet these alignments. In 1985, this was news to women from the U.S., where, by the way, the financial institutions enforcing these policies are located.

A Tighter Analysis

At the Beijing conference in 1995, women from around the world, and particularly women of color, carried a further-developed version of this analysis. Structural adjustment policies were only one component of what women could now more specifically name as the detrimental aspects of the globalization of the economy. They brought criticism of the destructive nature of a world economic system that is driven by consumption and western industrial values. By 1995, women were much more unified in their understanding of the global deregulation that allows market capitalism to run more freely in its pursuit of "maximizing profits." From country after country, women reported disinvestment in social support programs, privatization, increasing domination by western media, and the "westernizing-down" of cultural integrity because of these influences. It was this discussion, about the effects of globalization on communities around the world, that marked a defining change in the world women's movement. World economic issues were now women's issues.

Winona LaDuke, an Anishinabe of the White Earth reservation in northern Minnesota, rejected any notion of gender equity within western, consumer, industrial development, which continually exploits the lands and natural resources of others. She noted the inherent difficulties of seeking gender equity within a system based on exploitation, that denies self-determination of peoples.

Vandana Shiva, a scientist from India associated with the international Women's Environment and

Development Organization (WEDO), brought an understanding of how transnational corporations are using intellectual property rights, a particularly western notion of "owning" information, to privatize collective knowledge. For example, if a corporation names the genetics of a seed, or the chemical structure of a medicine, it can then copyright it and claim royalty rights. Farmers saving seed from crops they have grown can now be charged royalty payments, and medicines developed by women in communities as collective knowledge must be purchased.

Margaret Prescod, an African American member of the International Wages for Housework campaign, carried the analysis that economies are supposed to facilitate the exchange of goods and services necessary in caring for societies. But our contemporary economic system commodifies everything except caretaking work, which largely falls to and is carried out by women. Because it has no value, anyone performing that work is impoverished and anyone out working to earn a living can minister little caretaking. This campaign succeeded in persuading the official conference to adopt their position that governments should start quantifying and keeping account in national accounting systems of all the caretaking work that women do.

Regulating the Corporate Rampage

A common analysis that emerged from these women, is that we need ways of internationally and personally monitoring and regulating an out-of-control, profit-driven system. This has special meaning for women in the U.S., because while we are victims of this growing capitalism, we are also residents of its home territory. So while we can learn from women in other countries who deal with more extreme versions of increasing poverty, social dissolution, forced migration and homelessness, and share strategies to fight these trends, one of the key things we will learn from them is that we also need to rein in our own.

Consider, for example, that while the negative effects of the globalization of the economy was one of the largest issue areas raised at the conference, it got zero press coverage in the U.S. press. Human rights and violence against women got a lot more ink here, but the analysis of human rights is intimately linked to economic rights: women's experiences of violence are interwoven with economic insecurity and militarism. The western media drops its human rights coverage when women leaders challenge how the sacred tenets of capitalism feed human rights abuses.

While women at the NGO forum dealt significantly with this issue, and while the Platform for Action (the official document emerging from the UN forum) was supposed to address problems of poverty, the Clinton administration opposed including language advocating international regulation of transnational corporations, or investigation of the links between the structural adjustment policies of international financial institutions and the increasing poverty of people living under those policies. Our administration also opposed language that affirmed the importance of including environmental and labor protections in trade agreements. So you can see that the solutions that women presented from around the world to deal with the social disenfranchisement codified by a global economy are in direct opposition to the direction that our congress and our administration propose.

Though the Platform was supposed to address women's increasing poverty, solutions focus on improving women's access to credit and markets. This assumes that the problem is discrimination against women and not in how markets inherently work. Women from the Economic Justice Caucus (an international coalition of women's nongovernmental organizations that work on economic justice issues) tried to raise the issue that there are also inherent problems in the nature of the markets. This is a very important issue for women in the U.S. to continue to raise. Because, while the document specifically mentions providing adequate safety nets; doing macroeconomic analysis that includes a gender analysis; exploring how excess military spending, arms production, and trade contribute to women's poverty; and ensuring the full human rights of all migrants (not just the documented), the current federal government is actually undoing those things.

Strategies on the Homefront

What does this suggest that we should do here in the U.S.? First, we must develop an astute political and economic analysis of the global economy. We must not simply swallow the conservative rhetoric that

decries the role of governments and characterizes regulations that protect the interests of citizens as bad. Every economy of every country on earth is undergoing dramatic changes that have to do with commodifying goods and services, specializing the products of each country, and using women as much of the labor force in this specialization, in low-paid and unpaid ways.

Second, we must analyze the kinds of democratic structures that can uphold community visions of what values we want our economy to serve. This means looking at policies that deal with both access and protection. While the U.S. signs international documents that endorse "access," it at the same time is actively undoing "access" regulations that we have in place (affirmative action). And current public rhetoric opposes regulating toxics, protecting workers or ecosystems, or targeting human rights abuses within our own borders.

Third, we should deeply question the idealized industrial model of development whose central tenet is profits dependent on increasing consumption throughout the world. Women from India sang a powerful song, "Coca cola, Pepsi cola, whatever cola, Why can I get any brand of cola, but when I turn on the tap, nothing comes out?" They boycotted the opening of Kentucky Fried Chicken in south India, and they clearly do not think that it is an improvement that western commercials can now be beamed into any hut in India, promoting Nikes, Reeboks, and Levis, along with the panoply of violent U.S. television shows.

Finally, we can strengthen our commitments to democracy, diversity, and human rights by building on the strengths of women. I believe these strengths include tremendous intelligence and the ability to carry cultural relevance and celebration from one generation to the next. Women from South Africa were a tremendous inspiration. They had just participated in drafting the most progressive constitution on earth, where gender rights were codified. The highest ranking member of the ANC gave a rousing analysis of involving women in democratic participation, then she proceeded to embrace all the other women leaders who were on her panel, and later that night led the dance of women from South Africa in the cultural celebration. While that was an inspiring display of the rich gifts women leaders bring, our job is more challenging here at home. In the regional tents where cultural celebrations were rampant, the North American/Europe tent was anemic, to be generous. Factory clothes, no food, little art, no music. Our insipid cultural expression is closely linked with our consumerism.

So I close with an offering of the seeds passed to me in the rain of China. Like my sisters from other parts, I urge you to buck these trends. Educate yourself on these issues, educate other women, make friends and do organizing with people of other races, ages, abilities. It will expand your humanity. Bring celebrations to this work across difference, encourage art and music within it. Take a new track by looking deeply inside the negative values American "democracy" is pursuing. Do your best to change them. Forward yourself and encourage other women forward to take on these challenges. Because despite the power and inspiration of gatherings like this Fourth World Conference on Women, despite the important advances made in naming and overcoming the inequities faced by women around the world, we return home to an increasing military budget, decreasing investment in education and jobs, greater poverty and more obscene wealth, more goods and less natural beauty—and these decisions still made mostly by men.

CHAPTER TWO

Identities and Social Locations:
Who Am I? Who Are My People?

Our identity is a specific marker of how we define ourselves at any particular moment in life. Discovering and claiming our unique identity is a process of growth, change, renewal, and regeneration throughout our lifetime. As a specific marker, identity may seem tangible and fixed at any given point. Over the life span, however, identity is more fluid. For example, an able-bodied woman who suddenly finds herself confined to a wheelchair after an automobile accident, an assimilated Jewish woman who begins the journey of recovering her Jewish heritage, an immigrant woman from a traditional Guatemalan family "coming out" as a lesbian in the United States, or a young, middle-class college student, away from her sheltered home environment for the first time and becoming politicized by an environmental justice organization on campus, will probably find herself redefining who she is, what she values, and what "home" and "community" are.

Identity formation is the result of a complex interplay among individual decisions and choices, particular life events, community recognition and expectations, and societal categorization, classification, and socialization. It is an ongoing process that involves several key questions:

Who am I? Who do I want to be?

Who do others think I am and want me to be?

Who and what do societal and community institutions, such as schools, religious institutions, the media, and the law, say I am?

Where/what/who are my "home" and "community"?

Which social group(s) do I want to affiliate with?

Who decides the answers to these questions, and on what basis?

Answers to these questions form the core of our existence. In this chapter, we examine the complex issue of identity and its importance in women's lives.

The American Heritage Dictionary (1993) defines *identity* as

the collective aspect of the set of characteristics by which a thing is definitely known or recognizable;

a set of behavioral or personal characteristics by which an individual is recognizable as a member of a group;

the distinct personality of an individual regarded as a persisting entity;

individuality.

The same dictionary defines *to identify* as "to associate or affiliate (oneself) closely with a person or group; to establish an identification with another or others."

These definitions point to the connections between us as individuals and how we are perceived by other people and classified by societal institutions. They also involve a sense of individual agency and choice regarding affiliations with others. Gender, race, ethnicity, class, nationality, sexual orientation, age, religion, disability, and language are all significant social categories by which people are recognized by others. Indeed, on the basis of these categories alone, others often think they know who we are and how we should behave. Personal decisions about our affiliations and loyalties to specific groups are also shaped by these categories. For example, in many communities of color women struggle over the question of race versus gender. Is race a more important factor than gender in shaping their lives? If a Latina speaks out publicly about sexism within the Latino community, is she betraying her people? This separation of categories, mirrored by our segregated social lives, tends to set up false dichotomies in which people often feel that they have to choose one aspect of their identity over another. It also presents difficulties for mixed-race or bisexual people, who do not fit neatly into such narrow categories.

In order to understand the complexity and richness of women's experiences, we must examine them from the micro, meso, macro, and global levels of social relations. Each level involves the standards — beliefs, behaviors, customs, and worldview — that people value. But it is important to emphasize that in a society marked by serious social and economic inequality, such as the United States, oppressed peoples rarely see their values reflected in the dominant culture. Indeed, this absence is an important aspect of their oppression.

Critically analyzing the issue of identity at all these levels will allow us to see that identity is much more than an individual decision or choice about who we are in the world. Rather, it is a set of complex and often contradictory and conflicting psychological, physical, geographical, political, cultural, historical, and spiritual factors, as shown in the readings that follow.

Being Myself: The Micro Level

At the micro level, individuals usually feel the most comfortable as themselves. Here one can say, for example, "I am a woman, heterosexual, middle-class, with a movement disability; but I am also much more than those categories." At this level we define ourselves and structure our daily activities according to our own preferences. At the micro level we can best feel and experience the process of identity formation, which includes naming specific forces and events that shape our identities. At this level we also seem to have more control of the process, although there are always interconnections between events and experiences at this level and the other levels.

Critical life events, such as entering kindergarten, losing a parent through death, separation, or divorce, or the onset of puberty, may all serve as catalysts for a shift in how we think about ourselves. A five-year-old Vietnamese-American child from a traditional home and community may experience the first challenge to her sense of identity when her kindergarten teacher admonishes her to speak only in English. A White, middle-class professional woman who thinks of herself as "a person" and a "competent attorney" may begin to see the significance of gender and "the glass ceiling" for women when she witnesses younger, less experienced male colleagues in her law office passing her by for promotions. A woman who has been raped who attends her first meeting of a campus group organizing against date rape feels the power of connection with other rape survivors and their allies. An eighty-year-old woman, whose partner of fifty years has just died, must face the reality of having lost her lifetime companion, friend, and lover. Such experiences shape each person's ongoing formulation of self, whether or not the process is conscious, deliberate, reflective, or even voluntary.

Identity formation is a lifelong endeavor that includes discovery of the new, recovery of the old, forgotten, or appropriated, and synthesis of the new and old. At especially important junctures during the process, individuals mark an identity change in concrete ways. An African-American woman may change her name from the anglicized Susan to Aisha, with roots in African culture. A Chinese-Vietnamese immigrant woman, on the other hand, may adopt an anglicized name, exchanging Nu Lu for Yvonne Lu as part of becoming a U.S. citizen. Another way of marking and effecting a shift in identity is by altering your physical appearance: changing your wardrobe or makeup; cutting your hair very short, wearing it natural rather than permed or pressed, dyeing it purple, or letting the gray show after years of using hair coloring. More permanent changes might include having a tattoo, having your body pierced, having a face lift or tummy tuck, or, for Asian-American women, having eye surgery to "Europeanize" their eyes. Transsexuals — female to male and male to female — have surgery to make their physical appearance congruent with their internal sense of self. Other markers of a change in identity include redecorating your home, setting up home for the first time, or physically relocating to another neighborhood, another city, or another part of the country in search of a new home.

For many people home is where we grow up until we become independent, by going to college, for example, or getting married; where our parents, siblings, and maybe grandparents are; where our needs for safety, security, and material comfort are met. In reality, what we think of as home is often a complicated and contradictory place where some things we need are present and others are not. Some people's homes are comfortable and secure in a material sense but are also places of emotional or physical violence and cruelty. Some children grow up in homes that provide emotional comfort and a sense of belonging, but as they grow older and their values diverge from those of their parents, home becomes a source of discomfort and alienation.

Regardless of such experiences — perhaps because of them — most people continue to seek places of comfort and solace and others with whom they feel they belong and with whom they share common values and interests. Home may be a geographic, social, emotional, and spiritual space where we hope to find safety, security, familiarity, continuity, acceptance, and understanding, and where we can feel and be our best, whole selves. Home may be in several places at once or in different places at different times of our lives. Some women may have a difficult time finding a home, a place that feels comfortable and familiar, even if they know what it is. Finally, this search may involve not only searching outside ourselves but also piecing together in some coherent way the scattered parts of our identities — an inward as well as an outward journey.

Community Recognition, Expectations, and Interactions: The Meso Level

It is at the meso level — at school, in the workplace, or on the street — that people most frequently ask "Who are you?" or "Where are you from?" in an attempt to categorize us and determine their relationship to us. Moreover, it is here that people experience the complexities, conflicts, and contradictions of multiple identities, which we consider later.

The single most visible signifier of identity is physical appearance. How we look to others affects their perceptions, judgments, and treatment of us. Questions such as "Where do you come from?" and questioning behaviors, such as feeling the texture of your hair or asking if you speak a particular language, are commonly used to interrogate people whose physical appearances especially, but also behaviors, do not match the characteristics designated as belonging to established categories. At root, we are being asked, "Are you one of us or not?" These questioners usually expect singular and simplistic answers, assuming that everyone will fit existing social categories, which are conceived of as undifferentiated and unambiguous. Among people with disabilities, for example, people wanting to identify each other may expect to hear details of another's disability rather than the fact that the person being questioned also identifies equally strongly as, say, a woman who is White, working-class, and bisexual.

Community, like home, may be geographical and emotional, or both, and provides a way for people to express group affiliations. "Where are you from?" is a commonplace question in the United States among strangers, a way to break the ice and start a conversation, expecting answers like "I'm from Tallahassee, Florida," or "I'm from the Bronx." Community might also be an organized group like Alcoholics Anonymous, a religious group, or a political organization like the African-American civil rights organization, the National Association for the Advancement of Colored People (NAACP). Community may be something much more abstract, as in "the women's community" or "the queer community," where there is presumed to be an identifiable group. In all these examples there is an assumption of some kind of shared values, goals, interests, culture, or language.

At the community level, individual identities and needs meet group standards, expectations, obligations, responsibilities, and demands. You compare yourself with others and are subtly compared. Others size up your clothing, accent, personal style, and knowledge of the group's history and culture. You may be challenged directly, "You say you're Latina. How come you don't speak Spanish?" "You say you're working-class. What are you doing in a professional job?" These experiences may both affirm our identities and create or highlight inconsistencies, incongruities, and contradictions in who we believe we are, how we are viewed by others, our role and status in the community, and our sense of belonging. Some individuals experience **marginality** if they can move in two or more worlds and, in part, be accepted as insiders (Stonequist 1937). Examples include bisexuals, mixed-race people, and immigrants, who all live in at least two cultures. Margaret, a White, working-class woman, for instance, leaves her friends behind after high school graduation as she goes off to an elite university. Though excited and eager to be in a new setting, she often feels alienated at college because her culture, upbringing, and level of economic security differ from those of the many upper-middle-class and upper-class students. During the winter break she returns to her hometown, where she discovers a gulf between herself and her old friends who remained at home and took full-time jobs. She notices that she is now speaking a slightly different language from them and that her interests and preoccupations are different from theirs. Margaret has a foot in both worlds. She has become sufficiently acculturated at college to begin to know that community as an insider, and she has retained her old community of friends, but she is not entirely at ease or wholly accepted by either community. Her identity is complex, composed of several parts.

One aspect of marginality, then, is how an individual experiences herself. Lisa Kahaleole Chang Hall (1996) describes herself as "a woman on the edge." A Hawai'ian with Black, Chinese, and White ancestry, she is a person who has a foot in several worlds. The complexity of her identity is rarely understood by other people who look for single categories and often treat her in simplistic or insensitive ways. She comments: "In Hawai'i the centuries of racial mixture are like the Caribbean, there is both language and a finely honed recognition of racial features. In the United States I am a constant question" (p. 243).

First-generation immigrants invariably experience marginality. Sangeeta Tyagi, an Indian woman who immigrated to the United States at an early age, comments:

My parents did what they could to provide roots within an Indian cultural heritage and yet there were certain deep contradictions with my other socializing influence, my schooling. Is it possible to support the weight of one civilization without, to some extent, letting go of another? How could I truly love English literature without participating in the sense of racial superiority embedded within its view of the rest of the world? And having sensed the devaluation of my culture at that level, did the privileges of class blunt the anger?

(Tyagi 1996, pp. 49–50)

Social Categories, Classifications, and Structural Inequality: Global and Macro Levels

Classifying and labeling human beings, often according to real or assumed physical, biological, or genetic differences, is a way to distinguish who is included and who is excluded from a group, to ascribe particular characteristics, to prescribe social roles, and to assign status, power, and privilege. People are to know their places. Thus social categories such as gender, race, and class are used to establish and maintain a particular kind of social order. The classifications and their specific features, meanings, and significance are socially constructed through history, politics, and culture. The specific meanings and significance were often imputed to justify the conquest, colonization, domination, and exploitation of entire groups of people, and although the specifics may have changed over time, this system of categorizing and classifying remains intact. For example, Native American people were described as brutal, uncivilized, and ungovernable savages in the writings of early colonizers on this continent. This justified the genocide of Native Americans by White settlers and the U.S. military and public officials, as well as the breaking of treaties between the U.S. government and Native American tribes (Zinn 1995). Today, Native Americans are no longer called savages but are often thought of as a vanishing species, or a nonexistent people, already wiped out, thereby rationalizing their neglect by the dominant culture and erasing their long-standing and continuing resistance.

These social categories are at the foundation of the structural inequalities present in our society. In each category there is one group of people deemed superior, legitimate, dominant, and privileged while others are relegated — whether explicitly or implicitly—to the position of inferior, illegitimate, subordinate, and disadvantaged.

Category	Dominant	Subordinate
Gender	Men	Women, Transgender
Race	White	Peoples of Color
Class	Middle and Upper Class	Poor, Working-Class
Nation	U.S./First World	Second, Third Worlds
Ethnicity	European	All other ethnicities
Sexual orientation	Heterosexual	Lesbian, Gay, Bisexual
Religion	Christian	All other religions
Physical ability	Able-bodied	Persons with disabilities
Age	Youth	Elderly persons
Language	English	All other languages

Maintaining Systems of Structural Inequality

Maintaining this system of inequality requires the objectification and dehumanization of subordinated peoples. Appropriating their identities is a particularly effective method of doing this, for it defines who the subordinated group/person is or ought to be. This happens in several ways:

Using the values, characteristics, features of the dominant group as the supposedly neutral standard against which all others should be evaluated. For example, men are generally physically larger and stronger than women. Many of the clinical trials for new pharmaceutical drugs are conducted using men's bodies and activities as the standard. The results, however, are applied equally to both men and women. Women are often prescribed the same dosage of a medication as men are even though their physical makeup is not the same. Thus women, as a distinct group, do not exist in this research.

Using terms that distinguish the subordinate from the dominant group. Terms such as "non-White" and "minority" connote a relationship to another group,

White in the former case and majority in the latter. A non-White person is the negative of the White person; a minority person is less than a majority person. Neither has an identity on her or his own terms.

Stereotyping. Stereotyping involves making a simple generalization about a group and claiming that all members of the group conform to this generalization. Stereotypes are behavioral and psychological attributes; they are commonly held beliefs about groups rather than individual beliefs about individuals; and they persist in spite of contradictory evidence. Lesbians hate men. Latinas are dominated by macho Latinos. Women with physical disabilities are asexual. Fat women are good-humored but not healthy. As Andre (1988) asserts, "[a] 'stereotype' is pejorative; there is always something objectionable in the beliefs and images to which the word refers" (p. 260).

Exoticizing and romanticizing. These two forms of appropriation are particularly insidious because on the surface there is an appearance of appreciation. For example, Asian-American women are described as personifying the "mysterious orient," Native American women as "earth mothers" and the epitome of spirituality, and Black women as perpetual towers of strength. In all three cases, seemingly positive traits and cultural practices are identified and exalted. This "positive" stereotyping prevents people from seeing the truth and complexity of who these women are.

Another way to think about the appropriation of identity concerns representation—the images that are circulated and popularized about a group of people. How are various groups of women typically depicted in this society? The fundamental problem with the representation of women, as with all oppressed peoples, is that "they do not have central control over the production of images about themselves" (McCarthy & Crichlow 1993, p. xvii). The four processes of identity appropriation described above are used to project images of women that generally demean, dehumanize, denigrate, and otherwise violate their basic humanity, a point elaborated in Chapter 3.

In the face of structural inequalities, the issue of identity and representation can literally and metaphorically be a matter of life and death for members of subordinated groups for several reasons. They are reduced to the position of the "other"—that is, fundamentally unlike "us"—made invisible, misunderstood, misrepresented, and often feared.

Equally significant, designating a group as "other" justifies its exploitation, its exclusion from whatever benefits the society may offer, and the violence and, in extreme cases, genocide committed against it. Therefore, at the global and macro levels, identity is a matter of collective well-being and survival. Individual members of subordinate groups tend to be judged by those in dominant positions according to negative stereotypes. If any young African-American women, for example, are poor single mothers, they merely reinforce the stereotype the dominant group holds about them. When young African-American women hold advanced degrees and are economically well off, they are regarded as exceptional by those in the dominant group, who rarely let disconfirming evidence push them to rethink their stereotypes.

Given the significance of identity appropriation as an aspect of oppression, it is not surprising that many liberation struggles have included projects and efforts aimed at changing identities and taking control of the process of positive identity formation and representation. Before liberation struggles, oppressed people often use the same terminology to name themselves as the dominant group uses to label them. One crucial aspect of liberation struggles is to get rid of pejorative labels and use names that express, in their own terms, who people are in all their humanity. Thus the name a group uses for itself gradually takes on more of an insider perspective that fits the evolving consciousness growing out of the political movement. As with individual identity, naming ourselves collectively is an important act of empowerment. One example of this is in the evolution of the names African Americans have used to identify themselves, moving from Colored, to Negro, to Black, to Afro-American, and African American. Similarly, Chinese Americans gradually rejected the derogatory label "Chink," preferring to be called Orientals and now Chinese Americans or Asians. These terms are used unevenly, sometimes according to the age and political orientation of the person or the geographic region, where one usage may be more popular than another. Among the very diverse group of people connected historically, culturally, and linguistically to Spain, Portugal, and their former colonies (parts of the United States, Mexico, the Caribbean, and Central and South America), some use more inclusive terms such as Latino or Hispanic; others prefer more specific names such as Chicano, Puerto Rican, Nicaraguan, Cuban, and so on.

Colonization, Immigration, and the U.S. Landscape of Race and Class

Other macro-level factors affecting people's identities include colonization and immigration. Popular folklore would have us believe that the United States has welcomed "the tired, huddled masses yearning to breathe free" (Young 1997). This ideology that the United States is "a land of immigrants" obscures several important issues excluded from much mainstream debate about immigration: not all Americans came to this country voluntarily. Native American peoples and Mexicans were already here on this continent, but the former experienced near-genocide and the latter were made foreigners in their own land. African peoples were captured, enslaved, and forcibly imported to this country to be laborers. All were brutally exploited and violated — physically, psychologically, culturally, and spiritually — to serve the interests of those in power. The relationships between these groups and this nation and their experiences in the United States are fundamentally different from the experiences of those who chose to immigrate here, though this is not to negate the hardships the latter may have faced. These differences profoundly shaped the social, cultural, political, and economic realities faced by these groups throughout history and continue to do so today.

Robert Blauner (1972) makes a useful analytical distinction between colonized minorities, whose original presence in this nation was involuntary, and all of whom are people of color, and immigrant minorities, whose presence was voluntary. According to Blauner, colonized minorities faced insurmountable structural inequalities, based primarily on race, that have prevented their full participation in social, economic, political, and cultural arenas of U.S. life. Early in the history of this country, for example, the Naturalization Law of 1790 (which was repealed as recently as 1952) prohibited peoples of color from becoming U.S. citizens, and the Slave Codes restricted every aspect of life for enslaved African peoples. These laws made race into an indelible line that separated "insiders" from "outsiders." White people were designated insiders and granted many privileges while all others were confined to systematic disadvantage.

Studies of U.S. immigration "reveal discrimination and unequal positioning of different ethnic groups" (Yans-McLaughlin 1990, p. 6), challenging

An Outline of U.S. Immigration Law and Policy*

Throughout U.S. history tens of millions of newcomers have made their way to the United States, sometimes at the express invitation of the government and sometimes not. The United States has resettled on a permanent basis more refugees fleeing persecution than any other industrialized nation. By contrast with other countries, it is relatively easy to qualify for and obtain U.S. citizenship. These newcomers have transformed and invigorated their adopted country; the United States would not be what it is today without them. At the same time U.S. immigration law and policy have not always been fairly or evenly applied. Particularly in times of economic stress or when there is a perceived threat to national security, the United States has quickly turned inward and raised legal barriers to the admission of individuals from other countries. Blaming immigrants for the country's economic and social problems is nothing new.

1790   The first immigration law, the Naturalization Law of 1790, which was not repealed until 1952, limited naturalization to "free white persons" who had resided in the United States for at least two years. Slave Codes restricted every aspect of life for enslaved African peoples.

1875   The Immigration Act of 1875 denied admission to individuals considered "undesirable," including revolutionaries, prostitutes, and those carrying "loathsome or dangerous contagious diseases."

1882   The Chinese Exclusion Act, one of the most blatant racially biased immigration laws in U.S. history, was adopted and subsequently upheld by the U.S. Supreme Court; variations were enforced until 1943. The act was a response to fear of the large numbers of Chinese laborers brought to the United States to lay railroads and work in the mines.

1917   Congress designated Asia (with the exception of Japan and the Philippines) as a barred zone from which no immigrants were to be admitted.

1921   The Immigration Act of 1921 set an overall cap on the number of immigrants admitted each year and established a nationalities quota system that strongly favored northern Europeans at the expense of immigrants from southern and eastern Europe and Asia.

1924   The Immigration Act of 1924 (the Johnson-Reed Act) based immigration quotas on the ethnic composition of the U.S. population in 1920; it also prohibited Japanese immigration.

1945   President Harry Truman issued a directive after World War II allowing for the admission of 40,000 refugees.

1946   The War Brides Act permitted 120,000 foreign wives and children to join their husbands in the United States.

1948   The Displaced Persons Act of 1948 permitted entry to an additional 400,000 refugees and displaced persons as a result of World War II.

1952   The Immigration and Nationality Act of 1952 (the McCarren-Walter Act) was a response to U.S. fear of communism and barred the admission of anyone who might engage in acts "prejudicial to the public interest, or that endanger the welfare or safety of the United States." It allowed immigration for all nationalities, however, thus opening the doors to immigrants previously excluded on racial grounds; it also established family connections as a criterion for immigrant eligibility.

1953   The Refugee Relief Act of 1953 admitted another 200,000 individuals, including

*Thanks to Wendy A. Young for this material.

(continued)

An Outline of U.S. Immigration Law and Policy (continued)

Hungarians fleeing Communism and Chinese emigrating after the Chinese revolution.

1965   The Immigration Act of 1965, which established an annual quota of 120,000 immigrants from the Eastern Hemisphere, increased the number of Asian immigrants, especially middle-class and upper-middle-class people.

1980   The Refugee Act of 1980 codified into U.S. law the 1951 United Nations Convention Relating to the Status of Refugees and its 1967 Protocol; it includes a definition of a refugee as a person who is outside her or his country of nationality and has a well-founded fear of persecution on account of race, religion, nationality, political opinion, or membership in a particular social group.

1986   The Immigration Reform and Control Act of 1986 was introduced to control the growth of illegal immigrants by introducing an "amnesty" program to legalize undocumented people resident in the United States before January 1, 1982, and imposing sanctions against employers who knowingly employ undocumented workers.

1990   The Immigration Act of 1990 affirmed family reunification as the basis for most immigration cases; redefined employment-based immigration; created a new system to diversify the nationalities immigrating to the United States,

ostensibly to compensate for the domination of Asian and Latin American immigration that had occurred since 1965; and created new mechanisms to provide refuge to those fleeing civil strife, environmental disasters, or other forms of upheaval in their homelands.

1996   The Illegal Immigration Reform and Immigrant Responsibility Act was adopted, the first legislation in recent years to target both legal and illegal immigration. It provides for increased border controls and penalties for document fraud; changes in employer sanctions; restrictions on immigrant eligibility for public benefits, including benefits for those lawfully in the United States; and drastic streamlining of the asylum system.

The "pull" factors drawing immigrants to the United States include the possibility of better-paying jobs, better education — especially for children — and greater personal freedom. "Push" factors include poverty, the dire effects of wars, political upheaval, authoritarian regimes, and fewer personal freedoms in the countries they have left. Immigration will continue to be a thorny issue in the United States as the goals of global economic restructuring, filling the country's need for workers, and providing opportunities for family members to live together are set off against the fears of those who see continued immigration as a threat to the country's prosperity and to the dominance of European Americans.

the myth of equal opportunity for all. According to Fuchs (1990), "freedom and opportunity for poor immigrant Whites in the seventeenth and eighteenth centuries were connected fundamentally with the spread of slavery" (p. 294). It was then that European immigrants, such as the Irish, Poles, and Italians, began to learn to be White (Roediger 1991). Thus, the common belief among descendants of European im-

migrants that the successful assimilation of their foremothers and forefathers against great odds is evidence that everyone can pull themselves up by the bootstraps if they work hard enough does not take into account the racialization of immigration that favored White people.

On coming to the United States, immigrants are drawn into the racial landscape of this country. In media debates and official statistics this is still dominated by a Black/White polarization in which everyone is assumed to fit into one of these two groups. Demographically, the situation is much more complex and diverse, but people of color, who comprise the more inclusive group, are still set off against White people, the dominant group. Immigrants identify themselves according to nationality—for example, as Cambodian or Guatemalan. Once in the United States they learn the significance of racial divisions in this country and may adopt the term *people of color* as an aspect of their identity here.

This emphasis on race tends to mask differences based on class, another important distinction among immigrant groups. For example, the Chinese and Japanese people who came in the nineteenth century and early twentieth century to work on plantations in Hawai'i, as loggers in Oregon, or building roads and railroads in several western states were poor and from rural areas of China and Japan. The 1965 immigration law made way for "the second wave" of Asian immigration (Takaki 1987). It set preferences for professionals, highly skilled workers, and members of the middle and upper-middle classes, making this group "the most highly skilled of any immigrant group our country has ever had" (quoted in Takaki 1987, p. 420). The first wave of Vietnamese refugees who immigrated between the mid-1970s and 1980 were from the middle and upper classes, and many were professionals; by contrast, the second wave of immigrants from Vietnam was composed of poor and rural people. The class backgrounds of immigrants affect not only their sense of themselves and their expectations but also how they can succeed as strangers in a foreign land. For example, a poor woman who arrives with no literacy skills in her own language will have a more difficult time learning to become literate in English than one who has several years of formal schooling in her country of origin that may have included basic English.

Multiple Identities, Social Location, and Contradictions

The social features of one's identity incorporate individual, community, societal, and global factors, as discussed throughout this chapter. The point where all the features embodied in a person overlap is called **social location.** Imagine a diagram made up of overlapping circles, with a circle representing one specific feature of identity such as gender, class, ability, age, and so on. A person's social location is the point at which a part of each circle touches all others—where all elements are present simultaneously. Social location is a way of expressing the core of a person's existence in the social and political world. It places us in particular relationships to others, to the dominant culture of the United States, and to the rest of the world. It determines the kinds of power and privilege we have access to and can exercise, as well as situations in which we have less power and privilege.

Because social location is where all the aspects of one's identity meet, our experience of our own complex identities is sometimes contradictory, conflictual, and paradoxical. We live with multiple identities that can be both enriching and contradictory and that push us to confront questions of loyalty to individuals and groups. It is also in this place that we are forced to differentiate our inclinations, behaviors, self-definition, and politics from how we are classified by larger societal institutions. An inclination toward bisexuality, for example, does not mean that one will necessarily act on that inclination. Defining oneself as working-class does not necessarily lead to activity in progressive politics based on a class consciousness.

Social location is also where we meet others socially and politically. Who are we in relation to people who are both like us and different from us? How do we negotiate the inequalities in power and privilege? How do we both accept and appreciate who we and others are, and grow and change to meet the challenges of a multicultural world? In the readings that follow the writers note significant changes in the way they think about themselves over time. Some mention difficulties in coming to terms with who they are, describing things that have happened to them and the complexities of their contradictory positions. They also write about the empowerment that comes from a deepening understanding of identity, enabling them to claim their place in the world.

As you read and discuss the readings in this chapter, think about the following questions:

1. Where do you come from? Who are you? How has your identity changed? How do you figure out your identity?

2. Which parts of your identity do you emphasize? Which do you underplay?

3. Who are your "people"? Where or what are your "home" and "community"? How do you know? How have you learned who you are and where home and community are? How can you find out if you do not know?

4. How many generations have your family members been in the United States? What was their first relationship to it? Under what conditions did they become a part of the United States?

5. What do you know of your family's culture and history before it became a part of the United States?

6. How does your own social location place you in relation to people of colonized minorities and immigrant minorities? What repercussions does this have for you today?

7. Which of the social dimensions of your identity provide power and privilege? Which provide less power and disadvantage?

NINE

◆◆◆

White Trash
An Autobiography

Carol Tarlen

Part I: 1948: Dysentery in the First World

My daddy was a truck driver. In Salinas he hauled
    lettuce.
When I was five, we lived in a three-room trailer:
my mother who played little squirrels with us
when it rained—my brother, sister and I who
    pretended
we lived in trees, gathered nuts and it was never
    winter,
we always ate—and my father who never went to
    high school,
who wasn't a vet because he had been kicked out
of the army on a Section 8, who once was a fireman
on the railroad, who was a Teamster,
who never crossed a picket line, never scabbed.
Our friends were Mexicans, Indians, Okies,
farmworkers, gas station attendants, taxi drivers,
carpenters, communists, ex-cons, out of work,
Red, Brown and White Trash.

We didn't have lawns, instead we shared the gravel,
the wash tubs, the showers, the toilets.
My little brother and I played in the fields
behind the trailer court.

We found an irrigation ditch to wade in.
I pushed my brother, he fell down,
stuck his hands into the slimy water,
lifted his fingers to his mouth, licked.
That night he awoke with a belly ache and diarrhea.
It lasted a week. I watched from my bunk bed
as he sat on a pot in the middle of the room,
his shit turning to blood,
blood turning to a thin clear liquid.
His ribs protruded from his white skin.
His red hair shone luminous in the dark.
Sores grew on his lips. He was all the time thirsty.
He went to the hospital.
After two weeks the doctors told my mother
to take him home to die.
Instead she took him to a university medical center.
He was given antibiotics and lived.

He got lots of toys.
One was a stringed horse that wobbled and danced
when you pushed the wooden knob it stood on.
His favorite was a book called The Little Pond.
It had pictures of animals with their faces
dipped in bright blue water:
deer, raccoon, sparrows, rabbits.
Mommy tried to read it to us when he was well,

but she always cried. She said that when he
    was sick
she sat by his bed day and night and
listened to him beg for water.

Summer came. The lettuce shriveled in the fields.
Daddy got laid off and we moved to Redding.
The trailer park we lived in had grass and oak trees.
In the evening, when the air cooled,
we sat with the neighbors under the oaks.
The women talked. The men played dominoes.
The children ran, pushed, shouted.
Lizards climbed our legs. Giggling, we shook
    them off.
Daddy lost his job. We moved to Folsom.
Hospital bills followed us up and down California.
We never paid.

Part II: Irvington Square
(1958–1959)

When I was fifteen, my best friend was named
    Diane.
She was French Canadian and Indian,
but everyone thought she was Mexican.
Daddy drove a big diesel rig.
We lived in a house in Irvington Square. It was
    small,
square and painted turquoise. It had one bath-
    room,
a cement block tile floor and no foundation.
Our neighbors worked in the GM plant.
They were Okies and Chicanos.
All the houses were identical.
The streets were named for movie stars:
Elizabeth, Gina, Rita, Marilyn, Hudson, Hunter,
Wayne, Dean, Lancaster. I lived on Gina.
Diane's father drove up and down Irvington Square
in a blue pickup like it was a hot rod.
The girls thought he was cute. He had a duck tail.
Diane's mother was dark, thin, beautiful,
with a straight nose, small hands.
One night her father didn't come home,
but the neighbors saw him driving around with
    a girl
snuggled close. They said she was 16 and pregnant,
like his oldest daughter,
the one who was married to Ernie Jimenez,

the one who lived in Decoto, the one who was
    pregnant.
Ernie was in the joint for Mary Jane possession.

Diane and I went to the baby shower.
While her sister opened presents,
we walked around Decoto's dirt streets,
watched the children and dogs run in the road,
pretended to ignore the cute guys when they
    whistled.
Diane said she liked it when they called to her,
Heeey Chicana. The rest she didn't understand
because she didn't speak Spanish.
I wrote Ernie to cheer him up.
He said jail wasn't so bad because there were lots
    of books.
His letters were full of big words:
effervescent simultaneous coherence rapport
    amiability.

One day Diane's father came home, said
he wanted to see his baby son. His teenaged
    girlfriend
sat outside in the passenger seat of the pickup.
Diane's beautiful mother threw a milk bottle at
    his head.
She chased him outside with a butcher knife,
tried to open the pickup door,
slashed at the windows with the big, steel blade.
The girl locked the doors and cried.
Diane's father grabbed the knife,
threw his wife down on the asphalt,
then drove his 16 year-old pregnant lover some-
    place safe,
while Diane's mother chased them, screaming,
How many babies will you give her, you bastard,
    how many?
Diane ran after her, shouting,
Get out of the street, Mama, Mama, get inside.
The neighbors stood on their lawns. No one said
    anything.
Diane's little brother and sister huddled in the
    doorway,
crying. Diane got suspended for smoking in the
    bathroom.
She flunked English, General Math, Health
    Education.
She quit going to school. She was fifteen.
The bank foreclosed on the house. The social
    workers came.

Diane, her mother, little sister and brother
moved to the projects in Oakland.
Ernie got out of jail. The older sister stayed in
    Decoto.
Louie, the older brother,
parked his car by the Safeway and lived in it,
painted a picture of a Mohawk Indian on the pas-
    senger door.
He was 6 feet tall, with shimmering brown skin
    and black hair
that flowed into a waterfall over his forehead
and almost touched the arch of his long, curving
    nose.
Everyone called him Chief.

Part III: Two Virgins (1958)

Diane had strong, long legs that swung from
    wide hips.
Her brown hair was cut short and curly on top of
    her head
and straight in back. It fell to a point
between her shoulder blades.
She helped me cut my blonde hair the same.
Her eyes were slanted brown above her high
    cheekbones.
She was French Canadian and Indian.
She wanted to be Chicano.
When I first saw her I was afraid. I thought she was
Queen of the Pachucas. I thought she was bad and
    beautiful.
I thought she would choose me out.
I thought she would beat me up.

One evening I met her at the grocery store.
She was trying to buy cigarettes. I helped her steal
    a pack.
We ran to her house and locked the door. No one
    followed.
I stayed for dinner: Hot dogs and Hormel chili.
When it was dark we went for a walk and talked.
We walked to Mission San Jose, talking all the way.
Men and boys followed us in their cars,
asked if we needed a ride. We laughed at them,
called them ignorant fools, kept walking,
flaunted our unattainability. We were proud
    virgins.

The houses in Mission San Jose had family rooms,
    dens,
double garages, two and one-half bathrooms,
newly mowed lawns.
We pretended we were married, had three children.
We discussed what our husbands did for a living:
Fireman, auto worker, teacher (that was me),
never businessman or cop.
We chose the homes we would live in,
when we were mothers, when we were married,
when our husbands brought home paychecks.
In the daytime we walked to newly constructed
    houses
and pretended we were buying the model with an
enclosed dining area and sunken living room.
The salesmen ignored us as we sat for hours
on the Montgomery Ward Sofa.

We hiked to Niles Canyon and had a picnic.
We talked about the ghost who appeared every
    Halloween,
a teenaged girl killed on her way to a dance
    10 years before,
who sat on a rock in the middle of Niles Creek
    and wept
for the children and husband she would never
    have,
a house with a separate dining room.

Two kids got killed driving 100 miles per hour
around the Canyon's curves. The grieving father
towed the wreck to the high school parking lot
as a lesson. Everyone stood around
looking for blood and bits of flesh, but nobody
    spoke.
A few hours later, when he left, he was crying.

Diane and I didn't have boyfriends with cars.
Day and night we walked. One night, as we
    walked on
Mission San Jose Boulevard's gravel shoulder,
a car followed us. We ignored its headlights.
It stopped. We weren't afraid. We never were
    afraid.
A man stepped out, said he was a cop, showed
    us a badge.
He asked for our names, took down our
    descriptions.

(Two female juveniles:
one dark, medium frame; one fair, slight frame.)
He called on his unmarked car's radio.
We checked out, we weren't runaways.
But you have a reputation for walking around, he
  said.
He let us go. We kept walking.

Part IV: The Projects (1960)

I took the bus to Oakland to spend the weekend
  with Diane.
The projects were rows of wood framed barracks,
once painted white.
Children played in the trash sprouted lawns.
Teenaged girls gathered in bunches along the
  sidewalks,
whispered and taunted us
as we walked past on our way to the corner store
  for cokes.
Diane and I sat on her front step and filed our nails.
We stared back with cold and menacing eyes
as we slowly ran the metal points over our
  thumbs.
Sharp dudes with slicked back black hair, thin
  moustaches,
their eyes covered with shades,
drove past in raked '56 Chevies.
Sunlight gleamed on the white walled tires,
silver spikes twirled from the hubcaps.
Hey Sheena, one yelled to me, you Queen of the
  Jungle?
I hate that blond puta,
a girl hissed from across the street.
Diane and I looked at one another and filed our
  nails.
We didn't giggle in the presence of the enemy.
Her sister used to go steady with Johnny Moreno,
Diane whispered, but now he goes with me.

Diane walked me to the bus stop so I wouldn't get
  hassled.
She was wearing pedal pushers, a black sweater,
black flat-heeled shoes, no lipstick.
Her hair was in rollers.
I have a date with Johnny tonight, she explained.
She said she liked Oakland, liked the guys,
felt she belonged.

I promised to visit again, but I didn't know when.
You know, I said, school.
I thought the projects were scary, but I didn't say so.
See you around, she said, turned and walked away.
I waited for the bus by myself.

I became friends with Becky Martinez
who lived on Rita Street, but we didn't walk
  around.
We played records in her bedroom with the door
  closed.
We called boys on the phone and hung up when
  they answered.
The football team yelled yahoo baby at me
in the school hallways. I didn't know what they
  meant.
I hid in the bathroom.

I was put in college preparatory classes.
The girls asked what housing tract I lived in.
When I said Irvington Square, they stopped talk-
  ing to me.
When they got bad grades, they said,
Watch it, you'll end up waiting tables, or
You don't want to marry a truck driver, do you?
No one asked me to school dances.
But why? Becky asked. You're pretty. Sometimes
a boy from another school would take me to a
  movie.
Becky started going steady with Bobby Gomez.
I stayed home and read:
The Amboy Dukes. Knock On Any Door.
I discovered Theodore Dreiser, Richard Wright,
  George Orwell.
I read about drama during the Thirties.
I read Waiting for Lefty.
I wanted to join the Group Theatre in New York.
I wanted to join Hemingway in Spain.
I wanted to read Brecht,
but he wasn't in the school library.

Louie visited. He asked to stay for supper.
He hadn't bathed in weeks.
He said Diane was pregnant.
Her boyfriend stole a car and was in jail.
Write her, he said.
I didn't. I didn't know what to say.
Becky married Bobby Gomez.
I went to junior college.

T E N

◆◆◆

Letter to Ma

Merle Woo

January, 1980

Dear Ma,

I was depressed over Christmas, and when New Year's rolled around, do you know what one of my resolves was? Not to come by and see you as much anymore. I had to ask myself why I get so down when I'm with you, my mother, who has focused so much of her life on me, who has endured so much; one who I am proud of and respect so deeply for simply surviving.

I suppose that one of the main reasons is that when I leave your house, your pretty little round white table in the dinette where we sit while you drink tea (with only three specks of Jasmine) and I smoke and drink coffee, I am down because I believe there are chasms between us. When you say, "I support you, honey, in everything you do except . . . except . . ." I know you mean except my speaking out and writing of my anger at all those things that have caused those chasms. When you say I shouldn't be so ashamed of Daddy, former gambler, retired clerk of a "gook suey" store, because of the time when I was six and saw him humiliated on Grant Avenue by two white cops, I know you haven't even been listening to me when I have repeatedly said that I am not ashamed of him, not you, not who we are. When you ask, "Are you so angry because you are unhappy?" I know that we are not talking to each other. Not with understanding, although many words have passed between us, many hours, many afternoons at that round table with Daddy out in the front room watching television, and drifting out every once in a while to say "Still talking?" and getting more peanuts that are so bad for his health.

We talk and we talk and I feel frustrated by your censorship. I know it is unintentional and unconscious. But whatever I have told you about the classes I was teaching, or the stories I was working on, you've always forgotten within a month. Maybe you can't listen — because maybe when you look in my eyes, you will, as you've always done, sense more than what we're actually saying, and that makes you fearful. Do you see your repressed anger manifested in me? What doors would groan wide open if you heard my words with complete understanding? Are you afraid that your daughter is breaking out of our shackles, and into total anarchy? That your daughter has turned into a crazy woman who advocates not only equality for Third World people, for women, but for gays as well? Please don't shudder, Ma, when I speak of homosexuality. Until we can all present ourselves to the world in our completeness, as fully and beautifully as we see ourselves naked in our bedrooms, we are not free.

After what seems like hours of talking, I realize it is not talking at all, but the filling up of time with sounds that say, "I am your daughter, you are my mother, and we are keeping each other company, and that is enough." But it is not enough because my life has been formed by your life. Together we have lived one hundred and eleven years in this country as yellow women, and it is not enough to enunciate words and words and words and then to have them only mean that we have been keeping each other company. I desperately want you to understand me and my work, Ma, to know what I am doing! When you distort what I say, like thinking I am against all "caucasians" or that I am ashamed of Dad, then I feel anger and more frustration and want to slash out, not at you, but at those external forces which keep us apart. What deepens the chasms between us are our different reactions to those forces. Yours has been one of silence, self-denial, self-effacement; you believing it is your fault that you never fully experienced self-pride and freedom of choice. But listen, Ma, only with a deliberate consciousness is my reaction different from yours.

When I look at you, there are images: images of you as a little ten-year-old Korean girl, being sent alone from Shanghai to the United States, in steerage with only one skimpy little dress, being sick and lonely on Angel Island for three months; then growing up in a "Home" run by white missionary women. Scrubbing floors on your hands and knees, hauling coal in heavy metal buckets up three flights of stairs, tending to the younger children, putting hot bricks on your cheeks to deaden the pain from the terrible toothaches you always had. Working all your life as a maid, waitress, salesclerk, office worker, mother. But throughout there is an image of you as strong and courageous, and persevering: climbing out of windows to escape from the Home, then later, from an abusive first husband. There is so much more to these images than I can say, but I think you know what I mean. Escaping out of windows offered only temporary respites; surviving is an everyday chore. You gave me, physically, what you never had, but there was a spiritual, emotional legacy you passed down which was reinforced by society: self-contempt because of our race, our sex, our sexuality. For deeply ingrained in me, Ma, there has been that strong, compulsive force to sink into self-contempt, passivity, and despair. I am sure that my fifteen years of alcohol abuse have not been forgotten by either of us, nor my suicidal depressions.

Now, I know you are going to think I hate and despise you for your self-hatred, for your isolation. But I don't. Because in spite of your withdrawal, in spite of your loneliness, you have not only survived, but been beside me in the worst of times when your company meant everything in the world to me. I just need more than that now, Ma. I have taken and taken from you in terms of needing you to mother me, to be by my side, and I need, now, to take from you two more things: understanding and support for who I am now and my work.

We are Asian American women and the reaction to our identity is what causes the chasms instead of connections. But do you realize, Ma, that I could never have reacted the way I have if you had not provided for me the opportunity to be free of the binds that have held you down, and to be in the process of self-affirmation? Because of your life, because of the physical security you have given me: my education, my full stomach, my clothed and starched back, my piano and dancing lessons—all those gifts you never received—I saw myself as having worth; now I begin to love myself more, see our potential, and fight for just that kind of social change that will affirm me, my race, my sex, my heritage. And while I affirm myself, Ma, I affirm you.

Today, I am satisfied to call myself either an Asian American Feminist or Yellow Feminist. The two terms are inseparable because race and sex are an integral part of me. This means that I am working with others to realize pride in culture and women and heritage (the heritage that is the exploited yellow immigrant: Daddy and you). Being a Yellow Feminist means being a community activist and a humanist. It does not mean "separatism," either by cutting myself off from non-Asians or men. It does not mean retaining the same power structure and substituting women in positions of control held by men. It does mean fighting the whites and the men who abuse us, straightjacket us and tape our mouths; it means changing the economic class system and psychological forces (sexism, racism, and homophobia) that really hurt all of us. And I do this, not in isolation, but in the community.

We no longer can afford to stand back and watch while an insatiable elite ravages and devours resources which are enough for all of us. The obstacles are so huge and overwhelming that often I do become cynical and want to give up. And if I were struggling alone, I know I would never even attempt to put into action what I believe in my heart, that (and this is primarily because of you, Ma) Yellow Women are strong and have the potential to be powerful and effective leaders.

I can hear you asking now, "Well, what do you mean by 'social change and leadership'? And how are you going to go about it?" To begin with we must wipe out the circumstances that keep us down in silence and self-effacement. Right now, my techniques are education and writing. Yellow Feminist means being a core for change, and that core means having the belief in our potential as human beings. I will work with anyone, support anyone, who shares my sensibility, my objectives. But there are barriers to unity: white women who are racist, and Asian American men who are sexist. My very being declares that those two groups do not share my complete sensibility. I would be fragmented, mutilated, if I did not fight against racism and sexism together.

And this is when the pain of the struggle hits home. How many white women have taken on the responsibility to educate themselves about Third World people, their history, their culture? How many white women really think about the stereotypes they retain as truth about women of color? But the perpetuation of dehumanizing stereotypes is really very helpful for whites; they use them to justify their giving us the lowest wages and all the work they don't want to perform. Ma, how can we believe things are changing when as a nurse's aide during

World War II, you were given only the tasks of changing the bed linen, removing bed pans, taking urine samples, and then only three years ago as a retired volunteer worker in a local hospital, white women gave themselves desk jobs and gave you, at sixty-nine, the same work you did in 1943? Today you speak more fondly of being a nurse's aide during World War II and how proud you are of the fact that the Red Cross showed its appreciation for your service by giving you a diploma. Still in 1980, the injustices continue. I can give you so many examples of groups which are "feminist" in which women of color were given the usual least important tasks, the shitwork, and given no say in how that group is to be run. Needless to say, those Third World women, like you, dropped out, quit.

Working in writing and teaching, I have seen how white women condescend to Third World women because they reason that because of our oppression, which they know nothing about, we are behind them and their "progressive ideas" in the struggle for freedom. They don't even look at history! At the facts! How we as Asian American women have always been fighting for more than mere survival, but were never acknowledged because we were in our communities, invisible, but not inaccessible.

And I get so tired of being the instant resource for information on Asian American women. Being the token representative, going from class to class, group to group, bleeding for white women so they can have an easy answer—and then, and this is what really gets to me—they usually leave to never continue their education about us on their own.

To the racist white female professor who says, "If I have to watch everything I say I wouldn't say anything," I want to say, "Then get out of teaching."

To the white female poet who says, "Well, frankly, I believe that politics and poetry don't necessarily have to go together," I say, "Your little taste of white privilege has deluded you into thinking that you don't have to fight against sexism in this society. You are talking to me from your own isolation and your own racism. If you feel that you don't have to fight for me, that you don't have to speak out against capitalism, the exploitation of human and natural resources, then you in your silence, your inability to make connections, are siding with a system that will eventually get you, after it has gotten me. And if you think that's not a political stance, you're more than simply deluded, you're crazy!"

This is the same white voice that says, "I am writing about and looking for themes that are 'universal.'" Well, most of the time when "universal" is used, it is just a euphemism for "white": white themes, white significance, white culture. And denying minority groups their rightful place and time in U.S. history is simply racist.

Yes, Ma, I am mad. I carry the anger from my own experience and the anger you couldn't afford to express, and even that is often misinterpreted no matter how hard I try to be clear about my position. A white woman in my class said to me a couple of months ago, "I feel that Third World women hate me and that *they* are being racist; I'm being stereotyped, and I've never been part of the ruling class." I replied, "Please try to understand. Know our history. Know the racism of whites, how deep it goes. Know that we are becoming ever more intolerant of those people who let their ignorance be their excuse for their complacency, their liberalism, when this country (this world!) is going to hell in a handbasket. Try to understand that our distrust is from experience, and that our distrust is power*less*. Racism is an essential part of the status quo, power*ful*, and continues to keep us down. It is a rule taught to all of us from birth. Is it no wonder that we fear there are no exceptions?"

And as if the grief we go through working with white women weren't enough; so close to home, in our community, and so very painful, is the lack of support we get from some of our Asian American brothers. Here is a quote from a rather prominent male writer ranting on about a Yellow "sister":

> . . . I can only believe that such blatant sucking off of the identity is the work of a Chinese American woman, another Jade Snow Wong Pochahontas yellow. Pussywhipped again. Oh, damn, pussywhipped again.

Chinese American woman: "another Jade Snow Wong Pochahontas yellow." According to him, Chinese American women sold out—are contemptuous of their culture, pathetically strain all their lives to be white, hate Asian American men, and so marry white men (the John Smiths)—or just like Pochahontas: we rescue white men while betraying our fathers; then marry white men, get baptized, and go to dear old England to become curiosities of the civilized world. Whew! Now, that's an indictment! (Of all women of color.) Some of the male writers in the Asian American community seem never to support us. They always expect us to support them, and you know what? We almost always do. Anti-Yellow men? Are they kidding? We go to their readings, buy and read and comment on their books, and try to keep up a dialogue. And they accuse us of betrayal, are resentful because we do readings together as Women, and so often do not come to our performances. And all the while we hurt because we are rejected by our brothers. The Pochahontas image used by a Chinese American man points out a tragic truth: the white man and his ideology are still over us and between us. These men of color, with clear vision, fight the racism in white society, but have bought the white male definition of "masculinity": men only should take on the leadership in the community because the qualities of "originality, daring, physical courage, and creativity" are "traditionally masculine."[1]

Some Asian men don't seem to understand that by supporting Third World women and fighting sexism, they are helping themselves as well. I understand all too clearly how dehumanized Dad was in this country. To be a Chinese man in America is to be a victim of both racism and sexism. He was made to feel he was without strength, identity, and purpose. He was made to feel soft and weak, whose only job was to serve whites. Yes, Ma, at one time I was ashamed of him because I thought he was "womanly." When those two white cops said, "Hey, fat boy, where's our meat?" he left me standing there on Grant Avenue while he hurried over to his store to get it; they kept complaining, never satisfied, "That piece isn't good enough. What's the matter with you, fat boy? Don't you have respect? Don't wrap that meat in newspapers either; use the good stuff over there." I didn't know that he spent a year and a half on Angel Island; that we could never have our right names; that he lived in constant fear of being deported; that, like you, he worked two full-time jobs most of his life; that he was mocked and ridiculed because he speaks "broken English." And Ma, I was so ashamed after that experience when I was only six years old that I never held his hand again.

Today, as I write to you of all these memories, I feel even more deeply hurt when I realize how many people, how so many people, because of racism and sexism, fail to see what powe sacrifice by not joining hands.

But not all white women are racist, and not all Asian American men are sexist. And we choose to trust them, love and work with them. And there are visible changes. Real tangible, positive changes. The changes I love to see are those changes within ourselves.

Your grandchildren, my children, Emily and Paul. That makes three generations. Emily loves herself. Always has. There are shades of self-doubt but much less than in you or me. She says exactly what she thinks, most of the time, either in praise or in criticism of herself or others. And at sixteen she goes after whatever she wants, usually center stage. She trusts and loves people, regardless of race or sex (but, of course, she's cautious), loves her community and works in it, speaks up against racism and sexism at school. Did you know that she got Zora Neale Hurston and Alice Walker on her reading list for a Southern Writers class when there were only white authors? That she insisted on changing a script done by an Asian American man when she saw that the depiction of the character she was playing was sexist? That she went to a California State House Conference to speak out for Third World students' needs?

And what about her little brother, Paul? Twelve years old. And remember, Ma? At one of our Saturday Night Family Dinners, how he lectured Ronnie (his uncle, yet!) about how he was a male chauvinist? Paul told me once how he knew he had to fight to be Asian American, and later he added that if it weren't for Emily and me, he wouldn't have to think about feminist stuff too. He says he can hardly enjoy a movie or TV program anymore because of the sexism. Or comic books. And he is very much aware of the different treatment he gets from adults: "You have to do everything right," he said to Emily, "and I can get away with almost anything."

Emily and Paul give us hope, Ma. Because they are proud of who they are, and they care so much about our culture and history. Emily was the first to write your biography because she knows how crucial it is to get our stories in writing.

Ma, I wish I knew the histories of the women in our family before you. I bet that would be quite a story. But that may be just as well, because I can say that *you* started something. Maybe you feel ambivalent or doubtful about it, but you did. Actually, you should be proud of what you've begun. I am. If my reaction to being a Yellow Woman is different than yours was, please know that that is not a judgment on you, a criticism or a denial of you, your worth. I have always supported you, and as the years pass, I think I begin to understand you more and more.

In the last few years, I have realized the value of Homework: I have studied the history of our people in this country. I cannot tell you how proud I am to be a Chinese/Korean American Woman. We have such a proud heritage, such a courageous tradition. I want to tell everyone about that, all the particulars that are left out in the schools. And the full awareness of being a woman makes me want to sing. And I do sing with other Asian Americans and women, Ma, anyone who will sing with me.

I feel now that I can begin to put our lives in a larger framework. Ma, a larger framework! The outlines for us are time and blood, but today there is a breadth possible through making connections with others involved in community struggle. In loving ourselves for who we are — American women of color —

we can make a vision for the future where we are free to fulfill our human potential. This new framework will not support repression, hatred, exploitation and isolation, but will be a human and beautiful framework, created in a community, bonded not by color, sex or class, but by love and the common goal for the liberation of mind, heart, and spirit.

Ma, today, you are as beautiful and pure to me as the picture I have of you, as a little girl, under my dresser-glass.

I love you,
Merle

Reference

1. *Aiieeeee! An Anthology of Asian American Writers*, editors Frank Chin, Jeffrey Paul Chan, Lawson Fusao Inada, Shawn Wong (Howard University Press, 1974).

◆◆◆

ELEVEN

Mary Peterson
A Life of Healing and Renewal
Joanne B. Mulcahy with Mary Peterson

Introduction

Kodiak Island lies in the heart of the Gulf of Alaska almost two hundred and fifty miles southwest of Anchorage. The rich waters surrounding the island and its central location have made Kodiak a crossroads for trade and cultural exchange since the early days of exploration. Beginning with Russian contact in the late eighteenth century, the indigenous Alutiiq people have adopted aspects of Russian, European, and American cultures into their hunting and fishing culture, often through force by the colonizing group. Today, the island's Native population lives poised between the modernity of Kodiak's lucrative fishing industry and the maintenance of traditional ways. From new bilingual programs to recreating traditional dances, Native people are now reclaiming aspects of their cultural identity lost or suppressed during the past two centuries.[1]

When I moved to Kodiak in 1979, I knew little about the cultural or natural landscape I would encounter. I was soon spending hours in the Alaska collection at the local library, gleaning what I could from the diaries of the Russian fur traders and missionaries who had colonized much of southwestern Alaska. They recorded a romantic and exciting history of clashes between the human and natural worlds and between cultural groups vying for economic resources. I was struck by the absence of women from both archival sources and more recent popular literature. Later, when I began working as the Program Coordinator for the Kodiak Women's Resource Center (KWRC), I traveled to the six Native villages which ring the island and had the opportunity to meet many Native women whose ancestors had lived on Kodiak for centuries. I visited with them in their homes, picked berries and grass for basketmaking, and sometimes helped them escape a cycle of violence wrought by the cultural changes of the last century. Their stories of life on the island stood in marked contrast to what I had been reading. Their focus was the everyday world of giving birth, raising families, and subsistence living. They also chronicled the importance of women's practice as healers in roles which had continued until well into the 1960s, a version of medical history which differed substantially from the written literature. I collected oral histories from women all over Kodiak between 1979 and 1981 and when I returned on field trips every two years throughout the 1980s. I began to piece together other versions of history which traced the continuity in women's roles as healers and their strength in facing social problems. Of all of the remarkable women that I came to know, the memory of Mary Peterson Simeonoff stayed with me.

I met Mary in the summer of 1980. In my position at the KWRC, I was responsible for the arrangement of safe homes for women in danger from domestic violence. One night, through efforts coordinated with the Kodiak Area Native Association (KANA), a woman in her fifties from the village of Akhiok was flown in, silent and afraid. I still recall my amazement that such a young-looking woman had endured the hardships she described with so few visible scars. I could envision the life she was escaping: nights spent cowering, sometimes beneath the bed, other times under the floorboards of the house, to escape the wrath and beatings — and even once the knife — of a man transformed by alcohol, an otherwise good husband. She would try to hide in a treeless terrain where there were no hiding places, a small village where everyone knew the circumstances of her life. She would wait — for daybreak, for him to sober up — so that she could go and make breakfast, ready the kids for school, and prepare for her own long morning as a kindergarten teacher. Afternoons she worked at the clinic as the community health aide, a position that links villages throughout Alaska with the centralized health care system. As dusk approached, so did the familiar feelings of dread and anticipation of another night of violence and fear.

Mary left Kodiak for the shelter in Anchorage, and I often pondered her fate. Several years later, in 1985, I was looking for a Mary Peterson whom I had been advised to seek out for her knowledge of traditional healing. I was amazed to discover the Mary

Simeonoff that I knew from Akhiok, now using her maiden name. Living in Anchorage, she had begun a new life. . . .

Early Memories and Traditional Life

Mary Peterson was born in 1927 near Akhiok, a village on the southern tip of Kodiak Island. As she describes her home, it was at Red River or "Ayakulik" between a settlement called Carmel and the present-day village of Karluk. Originally she had eighteen brothers and sisters, but the toll of disease and hardship gradually reduced their number to eight. They lived in the early years with her grandparents, who had a fox and mink farm, and then moved with the fishing and hunting seasons. Her father fished in Karluk in the summers, and she moved back and forth between Akhiok and Ayakulik until she began school in Karluk when she was six. Some of her strongest and happiest memories recreate life in the villages, particularly events surrounding the Russian Orthodox holidays. The religious rituals and sense of community fostered by the Church connected the diverse places of Mary's childhood. The calendar divides into summers at fishcamps and the central celebration of light in the winter darkness, Christmas "starring." This Slavonic folk tradition is named for the large, brightly decorated and tinsel laden stars villagers carry as they travel from house to house celebrating in prayer and song. "Starring," referred to in Western Alaska as "Selaviq" (from the Russian, "Slavit," "praise or glory"), illustrates the common integration of Russian and indigenous traditions on Kodiak and in other areas of Alaska. . . .

Mary also recalls the finale to the season's festivities, the "devil dance," which inaugurated the new year on the night of January 14th as the ghost of the old year was banished by the "devils." Her memories of these ritual events create a rich tapestry of Native life in the villages well after the U.S. purchase of Alaska in 1867. Despite attempts by the government to eradicate the Native language and culture, Mary's stories — part of an ongoing oral tradition — attest to the tenacity of many cultural practices well into the twentieth century. Moving from the public arena of ritual, her stories of everyday, private life open another whole arena of memory, one shaped by and expressive of women's reality.

"Helping" and Traditional Healing

A central and enduring metaphor for women's lives on Kodiak emerges from Mary's stories of healing and of "helping" other women through her practice as a midwife. Women throughout the island articulate enormous respect for the village midwife and her role as an everyday healer. These reflections carry the threads of historical memory back to the earliest women healers, who provided a general knowledge of herbs and medicinal plants. Midwives continued to practice in the Kodiak villages well into the 1960s, long after it was assumed the practice had died out. As with childbirth in many other traditional cultures, midwives provided prenatal care in the steambath ("banya" from the Russian for "bath"), repositioned the fetus through massage, eased women through the process of birth, and stayed with a woman for a week or more beyond the birth to provide care and support. Women's stories of the midwives take shape around several recurring images, especially that of the "knowing" midwife "helping" women through the birth ritual.

Becoming a midwife was a natural transition for Mary from her early days of simply being with the old people, "helping" in whatever ways she could. From her first recall, she knew that she wanted to be a nurse and just "be among the old people because they used to tell stories." "Helping" was later formalized into working as a midwife and community health aide. Her understanding of many herbal treatments and cures was bound to a belief in the good health and superior knowledge of the elders.

> Ever since I could remember,
> I was taking care of old people,
> helping them spill their spit cans.
> Even if they're not sick,
> I like to be around them
> and HELP them.
> Just be among them.
> Everybody learned from each other,
> from the elder people.
> They would tell them what to do,
> and try to keep each other fed good, you know.
> If anybody got sick,
> the older people would tell them what to do.
> They used vinegar and water,
> soak a piece of rag
> and wrap it around their feet for fever.

> Or they would use potatoes,
> put it in a rag,
> put it on the bottom of the feet.
> When they use those potatoes,
> they turn real black.
> That means it's pulling the fever down real fast.
> If they don't get black,
> then it's not working.
> If they stay white,
> they know they're gonna lose that person.

Mary learned to use chamomile and a variety of other herbs that are common throughout the island. But the strongest "medicine from the land" that she remembers is the fern-like plant that grows amidst the blackberry bushes up in the hills, the one they call "mogulnik" on the north end of the island. The plant is a strong symbol in Mary's mind, opening a floodgate of memories about the older healers she learned from. When she returns to the village now, she goes up on the mountain to find this medicine, which cured her when doctors told her she had tuberculosis. Affirming the many stories about the superiority of Native healing, Mary insisted that the medical doctors did not know how she had been cured. "The next time they checked on it," she said, "it was gone. I guess because I BELIEVE in it." As a symbol, it recreates all that is good about life in the village, connecting past and future. . . .

These memories are congruent with those of other villagers — the use of "medicine from the land," stories of using potatoes and vinegar to draw out fever, the triumph of traditional healing over Western medicine. However, Mary's understanding of healing bridges two worlds. She relates stories about Katya, a "blind old lady" from Karluk who cured her of an eye ailment when she was a child. Following her advice, Mary's father cleaned her eyes first with a newborn boy's urine and then with salt water from the ocean. "That ocean water must have been good," she said, "that and the urine. I was thinking it's sterile, you know, and clean." She displays an awareness of Western scientific thinking in noting the presumed sterility of the urine. Similarly, she explains that people were seldom sick in the old days because they ate the moldy dried fish they saved for winter. "When I found out that penicillin was made out of mold, I was thinking no wonder they never got sick!"

. . . In describing her own ways of "helping" people, Mary stressed the intuitive part of knowledge and a respect for learning from lived experience. She described the early days when the chief would call the whole community to decide on a midwife if there weren't enough women practicing. The degree of formal initiation varied in the villages; for Mary, it was a relatively informal process. She became a midwife in 1947 when she was twenty years old. She stressed that "nobody really showed me anything, but I just KNEW what to do because I had so many brothers and sisters." She had watched other midwives deliver children, and, even where apprenticeship patterns are more formalized, Mary believes that certain aspects of healing cannot be learned. This belief in "knowing" as an intuitive, often religiously inspired knowledge, is central to the oral tradition about women healers on Kodiak. It is evident in Mary's memory of her first birth, where she reveals belief to be pivotal:

> First time by myself, I happened to be home alone
> > when one of the girls was ready to have her baby.
> > I guess it was one of my sisters.
> So, I delivered her baby,
> > and it was like I had been doing it for a longtime.
> I just KNEW, you know,
> > knew what to do,
> Like there was somebody with me
> > but using my hands and my mind.
> No fear,
> > or worry
> > or excitement.
> Only after the baby was born,
> > when I got everything done,
> > got the mother settled and drinking tea,
> then I started shaking and sweating ALL OVER!
> When I think about it,
> > it was like coming out of a trance,
> > like it wasn't me.
> I always think that God was using my hands to
> > help this lady.

Mary's stories of births were, like narratives from all over the island, accounts of creating a warm atmosphere for a woman, a place of privacy and comfort. She reinforced the view held throughout the island that banyas were essential. The only problem she had in bearing eighteen children was during one pregnancy, when they could not get wood for the banya. Women she helped started coming to the banyas on a weekly basis at about five months.

"If it's too small, then the heat might make you start bleeding." She used heat to detect both pregnancy and the position of the fetus, saying that "without hot packing, you can't press down and feel it too easy." Oleanna had also taught her how to feel for the heartbeat, checking consistently throughout the pregnancy. When a woman was ready to deliver, a sheet was hung on the window to alert the midwife to come. If too many people knew a woman was in labor, she related, "you'll labor long because they're sitting, worrying, wondering." During delivery, if a woman did "labor long," she usually squatted to speed the process. Generally the midwife would hold her hand, support her legs, and help her through what Mary insists were generally short and uncomplicated labors. "Back then, you start laboring and have it in a couple of hours . . . maybe three, because the midwives took care of them." After the delivery, she would stay for the first night, then return each morning to change and bathe the baby "until the navel dries out." She also wrapped infants in pieces of sheets cut to the width of ace bandages to keep them from moving around while sleeping.

The continuum of Mary's life was marked by her role as "helper" in many aspects of village life. It is so central to her self-image that she laughed when I asked when she "became" the health aide. "I don't know. I always was! My whole life, really, since I was young, I just wanted to help." She tried to foster the same sense of warmth that she created in the birthsetting in the clinic, in her other job as a kindergarten teacher, and in her home life. The last arena proved to be the most difficult. Her first marriage at fifteen, she reported, was arranged by her father in the hopes that he would have fewer mouths to feed. The pattern of choosing a man considerably older was common, Mary said, so that "he could take care of her." "Back then," she recalled, "as soon as a girl starts her menstruation, they marry her off."

Mary, in recalling how young women were treated during menarche, describes puberty seclusion as part of the "way things were." Documentation by early explorers describes the isolation of a young woman in a small, low hut for at least six months as the norm. After that time, she was welcomed back to her parent's home, fully initiated as a woman. During subsequent periods, a woman was sequestered for only the duration of the bleeding, after which she would wash herself and return to the village. . . .

They made a tent for us in the corner of the house.
· We couldn't see anyone.
And they don't let you see the light for five days.
    If you do,
      you might get blind.
They don't want you around people.
They didn't let you on a skiff
    or around fish
      especially summertime.
Even older women,
    after they have babies,
    they won't let them on the skiff
    or go to fishcamp
   · when they're having their period.
They said that the odor of the blood is strong!
In the spring,
    why do you get a cold?
    Why do you get sick?
Cause the ground is thawing,
    and you see heat coming up.
All that bacteria is coming up from the ground,
    and we get sick.
That's how they felt about a woman when she's
    having her period.
And because of the odor,
    and what we call bacteria.
If I had TB now,
    I couldn't even talk to you.
    I'd have to wear a mask.

That's how they felt about a woman with her period.
Especially the new ones,
    when they first start.
For a whole year,
    they wouldn't go traveling in a boat.
After a year,
    when they're not having their period,
    they could go.
Now, the real old people, they say,
    no wonder everything is disappearing . . .
People get SICK all the time
    because the young girls are here and there . . .
And the fish is disappearing.
    We don't have fish like we used to.
They blame it on the girls traveling around
    when they're having their period.
The old people get SO mad.

Mary's recollections about menarche reflect Kodiak women's ambivalence about cultural change.

On one hand, "the way things were" is viewed with longing. However, traditional marriage patterns and Mary's father's plan to "marry her off" began a cycle of pain from which she only recently escaped. Initially, the plan backfired. Mary's first husband was not much of a provider, and she was soon back in her parents' house with her two young children. When her husband drowned a few years after their marriage, she remarried another man from the village.

Change: The Roots of Violence

Mary's other memories of village life are equally complex, full of bittersweet longing and painful recollection. On one hand, there are memories of the bountiful days of plenty from the land and the sea. These were times infused with ritual, when everyone helped one another and people were much healthier. . . .

Memories of violence in her own home emerge when Mary talks about changes in village life. She cannot fix a point in her own past when things began to be different, but she related the stories of things she has "always heard."

The old people,
    the way they talked about it,
      the Russians started it.
    They came and traded stuff.
One old man used to say
    that they had foxes all over the village.
They'd dry the furs, you know,
    and pile them as tall as a rifle or a shotgun.
For those, they'd get the gun.
They got gypped so much!
They brought diseases, all kinds.
    The White people brought them in,
    drinking and diseases.
We'd be better off without the White people.
They came and changed our way of life.
    "You'll be better off with this and that."
They try and make money out of us.
They didn't do so much drinking before,
    but I remember it already with my dad.
    I remember I was always scared.
My dad gets jealous
    even when he's not drunk
    and beats up on my mom.
But she never left him,
    and as he grew older,
      he got better.

The mark of violence on Mary's life, both as a child and as an adult, has become increasingly typical in Alaska for both Native and non-Native women, in villages and towns. Statewide patterns are reflected on Kodiak, where social problems wrought by the extreme weather conditions, an erratic economy, and a transient fishing population have made violence endemic to life in town. Over half the reported cases are alcohol-related. Those problems were finally being addressed when I began working for the Kodiak Women's Resource Center in 1979. The center had been founded by a group of volunteers in 1976 as a grass-roots community project to address women's needs. They began with a crisis line and were eventually brought under the umbrella of a statewide network of women's organizations. Emergency aid to rape and domestic-violence victims was the funding priority, and most of the center's efforts were initially concentrated in town. Outreach to the villages, which began later, was an equally important but problematic arena. There was an understandable degree of mistrust of outside social service agencies, which had suppressed Native culture in the name of reform over a number of years. But through cooperation with KANA, the KWRC was eventually able to offer services to women in the villages.

At about the time that KWRC was beginning to reach the villages, Mary was working in the school until noon, then in the clinic until six in the evening. She would often be up all night with a patient, work all day, and return to a night of violence and fear. Of Mary's original eighteen children, the eleven who lived to adulthood were raised in the alcoholic household of her second marriage. She has nightmarish memories of never knowing what would happen, when and to where she would have to flee. Recounting nights of sleeping outside, hiding, running out in her nightgown without shoes, she says, "Oh, when I think about it, sometimes I wonder if it were true!"

When she married for the second time, Mary was unaware of the problems she would encounter. She had developed an "immunity," she said, "because I grew up in that kind of violent life." But her husband was also a radically different individual when he was sober. Mary tried to stay with him for the sake of the children and grandchildren and because, like so many abused women, she hoped he would change. . . .

When Mary finally left that August night in 1980, she called the number on one of the small, yellow, crisis-line cards distributed by the Kodiak Women's Resource Center. A KANA employee who also served on the board of KWRC went down to the village to help, and she sought shelter first in Kodiak. "I didn't know anyone could help," she now says, "I lived in a village my whole life and I didn't know that people outside could be so nice." It was then that I initially heard pieces of her story, one that is both typical and unique. She came to Kodiak as one of an increasing number of village women who were beginning to discover that they could leave. Mary Peterson, however, was different in an essential way. Frequently, women from the villages seek temporary shelter and return home within a few days, often to the same violent situation. But Mary got on a plane to Anchorage, leaving her children and the village existence whose structure and rhythms had given her life meaning for so many years. I wondered then if she knew how much she would miss that life. The other feeling which assailed me that night when she first spoke of her past was one of tragic irony. I was amazed that women so powerful and central to village life had come to find themselves in such an extremely vulnerable position. As she took up the story when we met in 1985, unaware that I was the person she had met that summer night, an eerie sense of déjà-vu took hold.

> They always ask me how did I do it.
>> How did I get the mind and strength to leave?
> I was getting to where I was scared all the time.
>> I couldn't stand the drinking all the time.
> I tried it,
>> but I don't know how people could go
>> for days and days and days . . .
> I was getting sick and scared,
>> and he kicked me out.
> I knew I had to make a move sometime, I guess.
>> I thought, "It's now or never."
> I decided.

Living in Exile

Mary Peterson is no longer afraid. "It feels so good not to be in fear now!" she says. "I do what I want to, and I'm not afraid and thinking, 'Oh, I shouldn't do that. He'll be mad.'" She has settled into her life in Anchorage now and recreated pieces of village life there. But it has taken time and painful years of readjustment. After the shock of leaving, the women from the shelter extended support, and her children in Anchorage helped as much as they could. But when the chaos settled, longing set in: longing for the fishing camp and the sweetness of salmon berries in summer, the Christmas traditions that she had lived for, and the satisfaction of her work as a mid-wife and health aide. She hated leaving behind her work and the familiar surroundings of village life, but those things, she says, she can recreate. "But me, I can't bring myself back."

Mary's escape from an abusive setting is also ex-pressed in terms of "helping" others—in this case, protecting her children from trouble. She feared that in trying to protect her, they might instead have harmed themselves. Thus she views her departure not as cutting bonds, but rather of strengthening them.

> *My kids will feel hurt*
> *and blame their dad forever for it,*
> *and they might even hurt HIM.*
> *They always told him not to touch mom on the face,*
> *you know.*
> *So to save him*
> *and to save my sons from getting thrown in jail*
> *and save myself,*
> *I HAVE to get out.*
> *I HAVE to keep my sons from getting into trouble.*

Fear of repercussions kept Mary from returning to Akhiok that first year. She met some new people among the city's large Native population and often saw her children who lived in Anchorage. The oth-ers flew the several hundred miles from Kodiak whenever they could, bringing fish and berries. She could not get the "tea" she missed so badly, the "medicine from the land," but she was managing. She got to church at St. Nicholas whenever she could find a ride. It was not the same—a big church, a big city—but she was getting by, until the holidays came. Then, she says, "Oh, when the holidays came, I just hurt! And I could just see it, just right there, picture it . . . right at twelve o'clock, the bell is ring-ing. . . ." Mary grows very distant when she de-scribes the yearning she experiences for the village. It is in the years of embedded memory, of knowing the landscape intimately—where the fish are, where

to find the "medicine from the land," the steps fol-lowed from house to house behind the Russian "star." The pain is visceral, as raw as the violence that drove her away.

She now returns to the village at least twice a year, for Russian Orthodox holidays and in the sum-mer to fish. She was afraid of seeing her ex-husband the first two years that she went back for the holi-days, but now the fear has subsided. There is a sense of mission in Mary's return each year. Initially, she says, she went back because "they kept calling me to lead the 'starring' and I had to go because I want them to learn." She is firmly devoted to helping transmit the Native traditions which the village is so fearful of losing. She hopes that the Alutiiq language she once taught in a bilingual pilot program will start up again, but that is contingent upon govern-ment funds. She can teach the Alutiiq and Slavonic "starring" songs which have given her so much joy. In summer, she can climb the hills to look for herbs and medicines, maybe teaching her grandchildren how to spot the small, white flowers which promise good health. Fishing is again a central part of her year, as well as an economic necessity. . . .

Mary has changed, grown stronger in the time away. Living in Anchorage, she has also come to value her privacy after so many years of caring for others. Having raised eleven children and worked for years as a health aide and a village midwife, she had forgotten what it felt like to be alone. When I asked if she would consider going back for good or moving to Kodiak, she responded negatively. "If I do, you know what will happen to me. My house will be full all the time, and I will have no peace." She also cited the proximity to her ex-husband as a reason. He still bothers her when she is in the village if he has been drinking. "Here," she said, "at least I'm a little protected."

But Mary also realizes that village life has changed. Some of the changes, she hopes, will be positive, especially for women who are suffering from the effects of the kind of violence and alco-holism that ruled her life for so long. She also hopes that her example will help others to leave or take ac-tion in the face of violence. She does not want her daughters to live in the same cycle that she saw per-petuated from her earliest days in Karluk through her adult years in Akhiok. . . . The Women's Re-source Center has grown and built a permanent shel-ter since the days when Mary sought help in Kodiak.

They have changed their name to the Kodiak Women's Resource and Crisis Center. They work in close contact with KANA on outreach to the villages, where violence is now on the decline. Perhaps the new health programs geared to cultural awareness have served to benefit women's safety by raising the level of self-esteem among men and women. Or perhaps, as Mary suggests, women are just "getting smarter." On another level, Mary knows that changes in the village have made it a place that she's not sure she could go back to. Life is not easy there for older people. "Helping" has been supplanted by cash exchange. "I can't roll a drum of oil," Mary says, "I'd have to hire someone. I have sons, but my mom, she has to holler and scream to get anything done. She has to cut her own wood. If I went back, I'd have the same problems. It's so HARD because they don't help each other like they used to." Other changes, in the realm of values, are less concrete. Mary believes that people think differently today, despite recent efforts to reinstitute Native traditions. Like other elders throughout Kodiak, she cites the unwillingness of the next generation to "listen" the biggest problem. "They're getting so sassy now, you can't talk to them. If you try to tell them something, they say, 'Oh don't be so old-fashioned!' It's not old-fashioned. 'Old-fashioned people lived better than you do now,' I tell them."

Mary's account becomes part of the collective perspective of elders all over Kodiak: balancing the superiority of "old-fashioned" village life with the benefits of change. Like so many other women, she adamantly defends the "old ways," especially those surrounding midwifery, childbirth, and healing. But deeper in memory is lodged the recall of violence and unhappiness in her own home, even in the "old days." Change has intensified those problems, but also brought help in the form of outside agencies like KWRC. Life is better now, she tells herself, since she can live out her Native traditions at least part of the year in Akhiok and bring back the bits of village life that she selects. Her freezer in Anchorage is stocked with salmon and halibut, and there is a full supply of smoked and canned fish for winter. Perhaps she also knows that her exile is not simply from a place, but from a time—a mental landscape of the past where village life revolved around the dictum to "help" and to share, where healing worked because people believed, and the Church's role was, like its placement in the village, central.

> The old people,
>> telling me stories,
>> telling me what not to do . . .
> Sometimes, now, when I'm by myself, you know,
>> and I go back,
> I wish,
>> Ooh, I wish them days were here now!
>> I WISH it was those days now!
> And summertime.
> Then I get to go by myself and pick berries
>> and I go fishing by myself,
>> no husband around.
> And then putting fish away.
> And Christmas.
>> They're the happiest.
>> They're the happiest.

. . . Mary's belief constitutes an entire world of cultural values which have sustained her through a life of hardships, informing her ability to heal as a midwife and a health aide. Her greatest struggle now is to provide a critical link to the next generation by transmitting those values, a role she once filled as midwife and one from which she is now physically as well as emotionally displaced. Like many of the elders on Kodiak, she insists that the next generation just doesn't "listen." But as Native people throughout Alaska draw from the wellspring of tradition to find sources of strength to combat the social ills of alcoholism, violence, and cultural disruption, there is every reason to believe that this generation will turn once again to the ways of "helping" and "knowing" which informed the world of their grandmothers.

Epilogue: April 25, 1992

At 11:30 P.M. on a cool, clear spring night, I am preparing to attend the midnight service in celebration of Russian Orthodox Easter in the village of Akhiok. The small church on a bluff overlooking the water is already filling with people; preparations have begun for tomorrow's feast. In a small house in the center of the village where she now lives, Mary Peterson is making *kulich*, an elaborately decorated Russian Easter bread. For the first time in over a decade, she is spending Easter in her Native village, a place she never thought could be safe enough for her return. "It feels so good to be back," she says.

Earlier in the spring, Mary came back to a village transformed by sobriety. The Akhiok that she returned to is not the village of her youth, but far closer to a genuine community, one built on Native values and reciprocity rather than the alienated group of individuals that she left in 1980. The sobriety movement, which had taken hold in the 1980s, was temporarily disrupted by the Exxon Valdez oil spill and clean-up efforts, but now has gained momentum. Few villagers are drinking; most contribute to the collective story of how Akhiok is healing from the wounds of cultural destruction, fragmented family life, alcohol abuse, and violence.

Mary returned to a village equally transformed by a revitalization of Native life. Part of the recovery story is a renewed pride in what it means to be Alutiiq. As proclaimed on a t-shirt produced for a recent elders conference, Native people are "healing through our culture." In the past decade, villagers in Akhiok have stopped drinking, recreated a sense of their Native identity, and relearned a number of traditional skills. Beyond the Orthodox church sits a "barabara," a traditional sod house constructed with grant funds from the Department of Health and Human Services. Masks and kayaks, replicas of artifacts used by their ancestors, are being built by students in the village school. The Kodiak Area Native Association has instituted an Alutiiq Studies Program that includes bilingual curriculum taught by village elders as well as via computer. All of these changes have strengthened Native identity and self-esteem and helped transform Akhiok into a village where Mary Peterson can again reside and participate in community life. This is the realization of many years of longing—to contribute once again to traditional life, to help ensure the maintenance of her Native language, to lead the Christmas "starring," to search for "medicine from the land."

In addition, Mary went back to Akthiok to work as the community health aide, a newer position in villages throughout Alaska that strongly resembles the role of the traditional midwife. Mary has come full cycle in her self perception as "helper" in realizing this continuity in women's roles as healers. As the health aide, she is once again a healer in a literal way. In a broader, metaphoric sense, she is contributing to the "healing through culture" that characterizes the contemporary movement among Alaska's Native people to reclaim their collective heritage. A central part of that process is the telling of stories, narratives of healing and renewal from which examples of how to live can be drawn. In searching for models, younger Natives are turning to the stories of elders like Mary Peterson, individuals who can provide an avenue for change as well as the knowledge of traditions. The Akhiok of 1992 to which Mary returned is, above all, a setting where her story can be heard, a place where she no longer needs to be silent and afraid.

Note

1. Kodiak Natives employ "Aleut," "Alutiiq," and "Koniag" as terms of self-reference for their unique cultural identity. The elders in particular use "Aleut" to refer to their culture and language.

TWELVE

◆◆◆

Transubstantiation:
This Is My Body, This Is My Blood

Jewelle Gomez

I was raised a Black Catholic in a white Catholic town. This was not the most emotionally well-integrated space for a young girl in the 1950s and '60s to occupy. The conflicts were innumerable. I saw the participation by members of the Catholic church in the Civil Rights Movement and at the same time watched the nuns in my St. Francis de Sales' catechism class systematically ignore the few Black students in their charge. I listened to sermons on charity and watched the parish offer fewer and fewer social services as more people of color moved in, and overheard the nuns complain about the "them" who were seeking entrance to the parochial school. Unlike most young Catholic girls I was never inspired to have a crush on my nun.

My great-grandmother insisted on my faithful attendance at mass, but she seemed to adhere to an internal spiritualism grounded elsewhere, maybe in her Ioway roots. She kept a bible and rosary beads nearby, as if living in Boston for more than fifty years caused her to evolve into a Catholic, but she rarely attended mass. My grandmother believed in the Catholic church because of the missionary work on the Indian reservations and because Father Francis and Monsignor Kelly were handsome and debonaire. She found the passion of the church fit well with her own passions.

I, too, was drawn to the passion. Catholicism is grounded in a melodramatic round of torture and desire that must have kept the Marquis de Sade perpetually erect. As a kid I pondered deeply the martyrdom of St. Teresa of Avila, founder of numerous convents, subject to wild moments of mystical ecstasy and profound depression.

And the Christians, thrown to the lions in the Roman circus, captured my imagination. I repeatedly put the question to myself: Would I profess my faith in Jesus or bow to the hegemony of the Emperor? The sensation of facing such a fate vacillated between pride, humility, and an agitation that can only be called arousal. The mythology of the saints and the unknown faithful who chose the lions was seared into my spirit. It was a mythology of ordinary people doing extraordinary things, transcending their natural sense of preservation, clinging to faith.

At the moment in the mass when the priest raised the small round wafer and chalice of wine to the parishioners, the bell rang, and he pronounced the words of Christ—"This is my body, this is my blood"—my heart would pound with the magnificence of such a sea change, such an offering. An edible disk the consistency of styrofoam and a dusty jug wine were miraculously turned into the sacred body and blood of the Son of God, and we were going to eat and drink it! It all appealed to the child's sense of the grotesque, as well as a need for the safety of an authority figure and belief in magic and myth.

As time passed, the miracles recounted by the priest during each mass felt to me much more an indication of the power that lay in the human spirit

rather than in the hands of God. I became less certain that one was the creation of the other. In fact, the church looked less like an agent of change or comfort than the bedrock supporting the suppression of independent thought.

There came a moment one Saturday afternoon when I was leaving confession. I'd already figured out that I didn't have to confess the lesbian relationship I'd been having for several years since no one ever mentioned that specifically. But sleeping with a married man was expressly forbidden. I'd just confessed to that sin for about the twentieth time and done the requisite ten Hail Marys and ten Our Fathers before being picked up by my boyfriend (my sinner consort) outside the church when a larger reality dawned on me: I didn't think God really cared. At least not in the way the nuns would have us believe. My teenage confusions seemed transitory and mild in comparison with the transgressions of white Southern sheriffs, the Boston School committee, and the U.S. soldiers who participated in the My Lai massacre, or people like Jesse Helms, who was a narrow-minded demagogue even then. My heart told me that I did believe in the concept of sin, that it was wrong to do damaging things to others, but my intellect told me the definitions given me by the church were highly subjective.

The interpretation of sin was even more unreliable in light of those doing the interpreting. Although my parish tried, no one could ever make me believe it would be a sin for me to be a maid of honor for my best friend's wedding in her Baptist church. The primitive jealousy with which the church guarded its property—me—even when it wasn't certain it wanted me, made the exultation of the Baptist choir and the expansive socializing of the Episcopal Youth Club irresistible.

I do not now call myself a lapsed or fallen-away Catholic, as the church would have me do, because that sounds too passive. My faith in Catholicism or any western religion did not slip out of my grasp. My faith was stripped away by the years of revelation about the horrors that had been done in the name of those religions. The missionary work, examined more closely, looked like colonialism; the catechism lessons sounded like patriarchy. My faith was rejected vehemently. And even now, with the development of institutions like the gay-identified Metropolitan Community Church, and groups like Dignity that interpret Catholic precepts with lesbians and gays at the center, I find that my spirit does not rest peacefully in any of that religious ground.

The passion of faith stayed with me over time even if Catholicism did not. The church mythology, deeply embedded in my imagination, depicted a passionate commitment to a higher power. That passion was transformed into a belief in human rights and the interconnection of all living things. There's no reason to believe that the weekly stories I saw on TV had less influence on me than the weekly stories (the Gospel) I heard in church. St. Teresa keeping her faith and Robert Culp sticking by Bill Cosby dying in an episode of "I Spy." I'm certain I developed my idea of sin and redemption as much from some of the television shows my great-grandmother and I used to watch—"Route 66," "Perry Mason," "Star Trek"—as I did from the weekly sermons. The passions were the same. It was just the focus that was different.

The first story I published was about a young deaf woman who inherits a Cape Cod cottage from her grandmother and retreats there in isolation, missing her grandmother and the imaginary friends she had as a child. It ends with her happily crossing over into the "Twilight Zone," so to speak. Her belief in the imaginary friends in a painting brings them to life. Speaking to her in sign language, accepting her as she is, they draw her into the painting with them and create a new family for them all. I was writing a story of faith and the redemptive power of love.

My writing and my activism have become a continuing pursuit of that same faith: looking for the redemptive family, whether it is political or social, that will accept and support me. When I wrote my coming-out story in 1988, I was again responding to the need I felt to celebrate the enduring bond I experienced with my grandmother and mother. I was insistent that the commitment was there, just as it had been between the TV characters, just as it had been with St. Teresa, just as it had been with my great-grandmother, who always stood by me. My coming out confirmed that faith.

Over the past twenty-five years that faith has been sorely tested. Not primarily within my immediate family, but more in the political arena. My sense of myself grows explicitly out of what it is to have a special "American" persona. There is a combination of elements that make me individual: African-American, Ioway, Wampanoag, Bostonian, lesbian, welfare-raised, artist, activist. But the combination is at odds with the monolithic picture many

people would like to have of themselves and of others. Blacks don't want lesbians to exist publicly. Gays don't want lesbians to exist publicly. Many white lesbians don't know what to do with Black lesbians either publicly or privately. I'm left to wrestle with who I'm writing for and speaking to. I keep faith with the idea that my life can have meaning for others just as the lives of those who went before have meaning in my life. I must insist that the combination of factors that make me who I am are as natural as the two *H*s and the *O* constituting water. My family taught me that, and it is a belief I hold passionately. I am a product of so many influences: Grace, Lydia, Dolores, Henrietta, Duke, Aunt Irene, Billie Holiday, Lorraine Hansberry, Judy Holliday, Fyodor Dostoevsky, Dorothy Dandridge, James Dean, Audre Lorde, Mr. Spock, James Caine, Metro-Goldwyn-Mayer, and Barbara Streisand. I can only show you where they pop out. I cannot excise them from my cultural inner life, nor do I feel the need to do so.

In fact, my joy is figuring out how they are all interconnected. I feel like I'm trying to take all those pieces, all those stories, ones I've lived and ones I've heard about, and transform them into food for others in my writing.

In the early 1980s I started writing some vampire fiction, which would turn into my novel, *The Gilda Stories*. The book began as simple adventure—a heroic Black woman using her powers to save people, even though she was eternally damned because of her gift of long life. But as the book progressed I began to see that I was reaching for more than an adventure. I was creating a character who, like me, was perpetually seeking that sense of family, something she could commit to. As a writer I liked the challenge of taking a Victorian, predatory myth and recreating it so that it embodied the principles of lesbian feminism that were at the center of my life and politics. Since vampire mythology exists in most cultures, not just Bram Stoker's England, it felt as much mine as anyone else's to tinker with, to reconstruct. And its grand passions mirrored those I'd been raised on in the Catholic church.

Somewhere in the process I understood that my fascination with the vampire myth was connected to several pivotal elements in my life. The death of my great-grandmother in 1971 left me devastated, although it took me years to let that devastation in close enough to recognize it. My loss felt, like that of most people who lose a parent, cataclysmic, as if the world should stand at rest for a moment. In that pain I was seeking a myth that would allow everyone I loved to live forever. Once obtained, the ability to live an earthly life forever was, of course, a curse — I was raised Catholic. The splendid timbre of the priest's voice announcing, *This is my blood,* rang in my ears as I considered the vampiric possibilities. That women have a natural monthly blood cycle made a female vampire irresistible once I started to really consider the idea. The sense of mythology, grand passion, and faith all came together for me in the creation of that character, Gilda, and those she chose as her family.

And under it all was the reality that historically the creation of the vampire mythology was a response to a fear of death. Within that dread was often embedded a fear of life. The preoccupation with the past, yearning for "the way things were," living eternally, were each ways of avoiding the change and loss of the future. In my writing and life I retreated to the pleasures of family life of the past. My family became mythic, transforming for me. This retreat was, I think, at the same time, a rejection of my present and the possibilities it presented.

Gilda eventually had to come to terms with not just her power over life and death, but the places where her power was superfluous, the interaction born of human nature. She needed to learn, as did I, that the connection between people is independent of time and space. Her love of humankind was a highly abstract concept, but in my writing its manifestations had to be specific, grounded in worldly circumstance. Gilda could not kill every time she took blood nor create vampires each time she had an interest in someone. The moral dilemmas she faced were those I'd heard discussed around my kitchen table as a child — family connections, responsibility, our role in society. In the creation of that character, and others, I am able to explore the passion and faith I've come to believe are necessary for living a full life.

As I go into my middle years I find I'm unprepared for the hormonally induced introspection and reevaluations. I was just starting to get comfortable with where I was. After I finished *The Gilda Stories* I was faced with the question confronting many first novelists: what to do with the remaining typewriter ribbons. I was terrified I'd spend the rest of my career writing pieces with titles like "Feminist Performance in the Year 2000 — Art or Fad," or the already used "Lesbian Chic." My dilemma is intensified by

the fact that I still feel young, or new to all of this — writing, living, loving. I have only one novel, no academic appointments, no *New York Times* reviews, no movie contract. I don't feel blasé about anything I've ever accomplished. I still feel passionate about the commitments to social change I made thirty years ago. This is my blood.

Making a bridge for myself between that youthful fire and the smoldering embers of the present is frightening, as if embracing the more low-key yet persistent faith of the present could deny the validity of the past. The passion I'd learned to live by was being subsumed under the tiny physical ailments that plague us all eventually. And the realization that there were only so many years left to accomplish everything.

I read a lot of detective fiction and among my favorite characters is world-weary, middle-aged Travis McGee, created by John D. MacDonald. In one book Travis observes that we get about eighty Septembers in a lifetime, if we're lucky. And, put that way, it seemed a crime to waste any one of them. It struck me that by his reckoning, at that time, I had only thirty-seven Septembers left. Crude and sentimental, but I was jolted. My fear of dying leapt out at me, and with it a fear of living I would have never suspected was mine. I think it is my continually renewed commitment to change that keeps that fear of death and of life at bay.

In the early '80s, when the Women Against Pornography activists began campaigning against what they believed to be material harmful to women, some of them used rationales and tactics that were, to my mind, distinctly unfeminist. The efforts reminded me of *The Pilot,* the national Catholic newspaper that regularly published a list of movies too sexy for good Catholics to see. To do so was to commit mortal sin. While I did appreciate the attention to the issue of violence against women engendered by WAP's campaign, their stance was too much like the autocratic denouncements featured in the pages of that newspaper. They had made a decision about what was good for me and what was not. Their activism, and the response of the Feminist Anti-Censorship Taskforce (FACT), inspired me (and quite a few others) to write erotica for the first time. I made myself work at interpreting the experience of physical desire and presenting it without romance or a happy ending. The experience of pure desire, if only on paper, reawakened my world of passion.

I began to look at the struggle for liberation from yet another perspective. Because where are those things — passion and faith — located really? In both the heart and the body. I felt driven to keep safe the literature of desire so any of us might have the experience of passion simply by reading a book. And I knew that space for passion must always be kept open in my own life.

The love of humankind was never an abstract concept in the catechism. They said that Jesus actually hung on a cross for days, not berating his torturers, probably thinking good thoughts (if you don't count the *Father, why hast thou forsaken me* lapse toward the end). This is a very specific physical manifestation of faith and passion. My concern that I be able to face the lions was really a need to hold on to faith and passion. Always it comes back to my work — writing about physical desire or political movements. The two will continue to be interlocked for me. The dominant culture — the U.S. government, the church, mass media, capitalism — has had too much to say about my body and my desire as a Black woman and as a lesbian for me to ever be wholly comfortable with it. Agitation for examination of the status quo is air to me. This is my blood.

By the time *The Pilot* list arrived at St. Francis de Sales I had usually seen the forbidden movies already, and the nuns did not look kindly on my questioning exactly what about Elizabeth Taylor or Tennessee Williams might send me to hell. My own family's acceptance of independent thought helped me to locate the sin not in the content of Hollywood classics about desire but rather in the Catholic church's underestimation of my intelligence.

I was fortunate that the family in which I landed was able to give of themselves in a way that showed the value of passionate beliefs and the importance of connections. My Aunt Irene was not too timid to shout at the police, my great-grandmother wouldn't let all the racist remarks about Indians on television pass without comment, and my father cared enough about my cousin, Allan, to ask about him with almost his last breath. When I'm writing I want to know how I can keep those connections going, how I can ask the questions that will inspire the next generation to keep asking questions.

In the writing, when I'm tackling big issues or recreating a larger-than-life mythology, the most effective arena of discussion for me remains highly personal, small, familiar. My fictional characters, even

when they're vampires, are always placed within a recognizable context. It is there that the ordinary events of living are made into mythology as I draw upon my own experience to make the ideas come alive. The key is in the sea change: the place where the small incident is transformed into the belief, the daily wine into the blood. In that change I am learning to treasure the things of my past without being limited by them. To use the things of my past without needing to relive them. To make the past a dimension of my life, but not the only perspective from which I view it. In that way my youth is not more important than my middle years; my father was not a god but simply a man able to be special to me; my knowledge is not better or truer than anyone else's, its value comes when it is made useful to others.

For my great-grandmother all things were connected, the past with the present, the present with the future. What she did in her childhood on the reservation in Iowa would relate to my childhood in Boston. My faith may have been momentarily placed in the statue of the Virgin Mary, standing strategically outside the confessional at St. Francis de Sales church, but eventually the faith found its way to my ancestors. It is the same faith, finding its way home. My passion for social change and for the fulfillment of physical desire are the same passion, made manifest in many different ways. On the wall over my desk I keep a changing selection of knickknacks, but always there is a large wooden stake (greatly resembling what Dr. Van Helsing carried into the crypt in pursuit of Dracula), a gift from two friends when I began writing my vampire fiction. Hanging from it is the string of rosary beads given to me by my stepfather, Peachy, for my Confirmation, the ceremony in which young Catholics reconfirm their faith. The rosary had been his for many years, and he was so proud to have me as his stepdaughter, the worn beads might as well have been platinum. I keep these two entwined in my work space to remind me of the power of faith and mythology. And to remind myself of the need to reconfirm my faith and passion with every word I write.

After I left home the church sold the land and buildings of St. Francis de Sales to the city for a new school complex. I was stunned because I thought it was almost impossible to "decommission" a church. I suppose the complexion of the parishioners made its value less certain. I only recently learned that St. Francis de Sales is the patron saint of writers.

◆◆◆

THIRTEEN

Immigrants

Aurora Levins Morales

For years after we left Puerto Rico for the last time, I would wake from a dream of something unbearably precious melting away from my memory as I struggled desperately to hold on, or at least to remember that I had forgotten. I am an immigrant, and I forget to feel what it means to have left. What it means to have arrived.

There was hail the day we got to Chicago and we joked that the city was hailing our arrival. The brown brick buildings simmered in the smelly summer, clenched tight all winter against the cold and the sooty sky. It was a place without silence or darkness, huddled against a lake full of dying fish whose corpses floated against the slime-covered rocks of the south shore.

Chicago is the place where the slack ended. Suddenly there was no give. In Indiera there was the farm: the flamboyan tree, the pine woods, the rainforest hillsides covered with alegría, the wild joyweed that in English is called impatiens. On the farm there were hideouts, groves of bamboo with the tiny brown hairs that stuck in your skin if you weren't careful. Beds of sweet-smelling fern, drowsymaking under the sun's heat, where the new leaves uncurled from fiddleheads and tendrils climbed and tangled in a spongy mass six feet deep. There were still hillsides, out of range of the house, where I could watch lizards hunt and reinitas court, and stalk the wild cuckoos, trying to get up close. There were mysteries and consolations. There was space.

Chicago was a wasteland. Nowhere to walk that was safe. Killers and rapists everywhere. Police sirens. Ugly, angry looks. Bristling hostility. Worst of all, nowhere to walk. Nowhere to go if it was early morning and I had to get out. Nowhere to go in the late afternoon or in the gathering dusk that meant fireflies and moths at home. Nowhere to watch animal life waking into a new day. The animal life was rats and dogs, and they were always awake because it never got dark here; always that sickly purple and orange glow they call sky in this place. No forest to run wild in. Only the lot across 55th Street with huge piles of barren earth, outlines of old cellars, and a few besieged trees in a scraggly row. I named one of them Ceres, after the goddess of earth and plenty who appeared in my high school production of *The Tempest:* bounteous Ceres, queen of the wasteland. There were no hills to race down, tumbling into heaps of fern, to slide down, on a slippery banana leaf; no place to get muddy. Chicago had grime, but no mud. Slush, but no slippery places of the heart, no genuine moistness. Only damp alleyways, dank brick, and two little humps in the middle of 55th Street over which grass had been made to grow. But no real sliding. No slack.

There are generations of this desolation behind me, desolation, excitement, grief, and longing all mixed in with the dirty air, the noise, seasickness, and the strangeness of wearing a winter coat.

My grandmother Lola was nineteen the day she married my grandfather and sailed away to Nueva York in 1929. She had loved someone else, but his family disapproved and he obeyed their orders to leave for the States. So her family married her to a son of a neighboring family because the family store was doing poorly and they could no longer support so many children. Two months after her first love left, she found herself married and on the boat. She says: "I was a good Catholic girl. I thought it was my duty to marry him, that it was for the good of my family." I have pictures of her, her vibrant beauty wrapped up but not smothered in the winter coats and scarves, in my grandfather's violent possessiveness and jealousy. She is standing in Central Park with her daughters, or with her arms around a friend or cousin. Loving the excitement. Loving the neighbors and the hubbub. In spite of racist landlords. In spite of the girdle factory. In spite of Manolin's temper and the poverty and hunger. Now, retired to Manolin's dream of a little house in Puerto Rico with a yard and many plants to tend, she longs for New York or some other U.S. city where a woman can go out and about on her own, live among many voices speaking different languages, out of the stifling air of that house, that community, that family.

My mother, the child in that Central Park photo, grew up an immigrant child among immigrants. She went to school speaking not a word of English, a small Puerto Rican girl scared out of her wits, and learned fast: learned accentless English in record time, the sweet cadence of her mother's open-voweled words ironed out of her vocabulary, the edges flattened down, made crisp, the curls and flourishes removed. First generation.

The strangeness. The way time worked differently. The way being on time mattered. Four second bells. Four minutes of passing time between classes. A note from home if you were ten minutes late, which you took to the office and traded for a late pass. In Indiera the classroom emptied during coffee season, and they didn't bother to send the inspector up unless we were out for longer than four or five weeks. No one had a clock with a second hand. We had half days of school because there were only four rooms for six grades. Our room was next to the bakery, and the smell of the warm pan de agua filled our lungs and stomachs and mouths. Things happened when they were ready, or "cuando Dios quiere." The público to town, don Paco's bread, the coffee ripening, the rain coming, growing up.

The stiffness. The way clothing mattered with an entirely different kind of intensity. In Indiera, I wore the same wine-colored jumper to school each day with the same white blouse, and only details of the buttons or the quality of the cloth or the presence or absence of earrings, only the shoes gave information about the homes we left at dawn each day, and I was grateful to be able to hide my relative wealth. In Chicago, there were rituals I had never heard of. Knee socks and plaid skirts and sweaters matching each other according to a secret code I didn't understand. Going steady and wearing name tags. First date, second date, third date, score. The right songs to be listening to. The right dances. The coolness.

In the middle of coolness, of stiffness, of strangeness, my joyful rushing up to say, "I come from Puerto Rico, a nest of beauty on the top of a mountain range." Singing "beauty, beauty, beauty." Trying to get them to see in their minds' eyes the perfect edge of a banana leaf against a tropical blue sky, just wanting to speak of what I longed for. Seeing embarrassed faces turning away, getting the jeering voices, singing "Puerto Riiiico, my heart's devotion . . . let it sink into the ocean!" Learning fast not to talk about it, learning excruciatingly slowly how to

dress, how to act, what to say, where to hide. The exuberance, the country-born freshness going quietly stale. Made flat. Made palatable. Made unthreatening. Not different, really. Merely "exotic."

I can remember the feelings, but I forget to give them names. In high school we read novels about immigrant families. In college we discussed the problems of other first generations, talked about displacement, talked about families confused and divided, pride and shame. I never once remembered that I was an immigrant, or that both my parents are the first U.S.-born generations of their families.

My father is the First American Boy. His mother, Ruth, was born in Russia. Took the boat with her mother, aunt, and uncle when she was two. My grandfather Reuben was the second son of Lev Levinsky, the first one born in the new country, but born into the ghetto. Lev and the first son, Samuel, were orthodox, old-country Jews, but Reuben and his younger brother Ben went for the new. They worked three or four jobs at once. They ran a deli in shifts and went to law school in their free hours. So Rube grew up and out of the immigrant poverty, still weak and bent from childhood hungers, still small and vulnerable. The sicker he got, the harder he worked to safeguard his wife and sons, adding on yet another job, yet another project until he worked himself to death at the age of forty-six.

My father was the First American Boy: the young genius, the honors student, the PhD scientist. Each milestone recorded in home movies. His letters and report cards hoarded through the decades, still exhibited to strangers. The one who knew what was what. The expert. The one who carried the family spark, the one to boast about. The one with the weight of the family's hope on his shoulders. First generation.

And what am I?

The immigrant child of returned immigrants who repeated the journey in the second generation. Born on the island with first-hand love and the stories of my parents' Old Country — New York: and behind those, the secondhand stories of my mother's father, of the hill town of his long-ago childhood, told through my mother's barrio childhood. Layer upon layer of travel and leaving behind, an overlay of landscapes, so that I dream of all the beloved and hated places, and endlessly of trains and paths and roads and ships docking and leaving port and a multitude of borders and officials waiting for my little piece of paper.

I have the passport with which my great-grandmother Leah, traveling as Elisavieta, and her sister Betty (Rivieka) and her brother Samuel and her mother Henke and my grandmother Riva, a round two-year-old to be known all her life as Ruth, and a neighbor who traveled with them as a relative, all came together into New York. I touch the seal of Russia, the brown ink in which their gentile names were recorded, the furriness of the old paper, the place where the date is stamped: June 1906. My great-grandfather Abe had come alone, fleeing the draft, by way of England and Canada, two years earlier.

I don't know what it looked like, the Old Country they left, the little farm in the Ukraine. I will never know. The town of Yaza was utterly destroyed in two gory days in 1942, eight thousand shot and buried in long trenches. My aunt Betty was unable to speak by the time I wanted to ask her: What was it like, a girl of fifteen, to come from that countryside to New York, to suddenly be working ten hours a day in a factory? I have the tiniest fragments, only the dust clinging to their shoes. The dreamy look on my great-grandmother's face one morning when I was ten, watching me play jacks. "There was a game we used to play on the farm, just like that, but with round little stones from the river, tossed from the fronts to the backs of our hands: how many times before they fall?" Pop's, my great-grandfather's painting of the farm he grew up on, and a dozen pages he left in phonetic yiddishy English about the place he grew up in, the horses, the pumpkins, the pota-toes, the family decision for him to marry, to flee to New York, where you had to use *tsikolodzi* (psychology) to stay on top.

My grandmother Ruth unexpectedly answering my questions about her earliest memories with a real story, one whole, shining piece of her life: "*Dancing. We were on the boat from Russia. The sun was shining. The place we slept was smelly, stuffy, dark, so all the people were out on the deck as much as possible, sharing food, talking, laughing, playing music. Some of the other passengers were playing accordions and fiddles and I began to dance in the middle of the deck. I danced and danced and all the people around me were laughing and clapping and watching me as I spun round and round in my short skirts. It was the happiest moment of my life!*"

My children will be born in California. It's not strange anymore, in this part of the world, in this time, to be born a thousand miles from the birthplace of your mother. My children will hear stories about the coquís and coffee flowers, about hurricanes and roosters crowing in the night, and will dig among old photographs to understand the homesick sadness that sometimes swallows me. Living among these dry golden hills, they will hear about rain falling for months, every afternoon at two o'clock, and someday I'll take them there, to the farm on the top of Indiera, redolent of my childhood, where they can play, irreverent, in the ruins of my house. Perhaps they will lie in bed among the sounds of the rainforest, and it will be the smell of eucalyptus that calls to them in their dreams.

FOURTEEN

◆◆◆

Boundaries
Arab/American

Lisa Suhair Majaj

. . . I was born in 1960, in the small farming community of Hawarden, on Iowa's western border. My mother, Jean Caroline Stoltenberg, in whose hometown I was born, was American, of German descent. From her I take my facial structure and features, the color of my hair, and more: an awkward shyness, a certain naiveté, but also a capacity for survival and adaptation that exceeds my own expectations. I learned from her to value both pragmatism and a sense of humor. She liked to say that she was of farming stock, plain but sturdy. Twenty-three years in Jordan did not greatly alter her midwestern style; she met the unfamiliar with the same resolution and forthrightness with which she turned to her daily tasks. Despite her willing adjustment to Middle Eastern life, she never quite relinquished her longing for the seasonal landscapes of her Iowa childhood — summer's lush greenness, the white drifts of winter. Although I experienced her primarily against a Jordanian backdrop, my memories of her evoke midwestern images and echoes: fragrant platters of beef and potatoes, golden cornfields beneath wide, sultry skies, the strident music of crickets chanting at dusk.

My father, Isa Joudeh Majaj, a Palestinian of the generation that had reached young adulthood by the time of Israel's creation from the land of Palestine, was born in Bir Zeit, in what is now the occupied West Bank. From him I take the olive tinge to my skin, the shape of my hands and nose, the texture of my hair, and a tendency toward inarticulate and contradictory emotion. From him, too, I take a certain stubbornness, and what he used to call "Palestinian determination." Named Isa, Arabic for Jesus, by his widowed mother in fulfillment of a vow, my father grew from childhood to adolescence in Jerusalem, that city where so many histories intersect. Although distanced from each other by geographical origin, culture, and more, my parents held in common their respect for the earth and for the people who till it. My father, never quite reconciled to his urban life, spoke longingly of the groves of orange and olive trees, the tomato plants and squash vines, by which Palestinian farmers live. He could identify the crop of a distant field by its merest wisp of green, had learned the secrets of grafting, knew when to plant and when to harvest. His strong attachment to the earth — an emotion I have come to recognize among Palestinians — made me understand his dispossession as a particular form of violence. I associate his life with loss and bitterness, but also with a life-bearing rootedness reminiscent of those olive trees in Jerusalem that date back to the time of Christ, or of jasmine flowering from vines twisted thick as tree trunks.

After a youth punctuated by the devastating events leading up to Israel's creation in 1948, during which he fought against the British and saw relatives lose both homes and lives, my father worked his way to the United States for a college education. In Sioux City, Iowa he attended Morningside College, shovelling mounds of hamburger in the stockyards during school breaks. At a YMCA dance he met my mother, a quiet young woman working as a secretary in a legal firm. A year later the two were married.

I do not know what drew my parents together. My father may have seen and valued in my mother both the shy pliancy cultivated by girls of her generation and the resilience learned in a farming family. Though he seemed to take her strength for granted, he assumed she would mold herself to his delineation. My mother, who by her own account had grown up imbued with visions of true romance, may have seen in my father an exemplar of the tall dark stranger. At their wedding she vowed both to love and to obey. My parents' marriage, complex from its outset, promised the richness of cultural interaction, but bore as well the fruit of much cultural contradiction. It is the complexity and contradictions of their relationship that I have inherited, and that mediate my interactions in the societies, Arab and American, that I claim as birthright, but experience all too often as alienation.

When I was born my mother claimed me in a gesture that in later years I understood to have been quite remarkable. The birth of my older sister three years previously had disappointed my father in his desire for a son and the title *"Abu-Tarek,"* father of Tarek. Forced by his work to be absent before my own birth, he refused to choose a girl's name before he left — hoping, no doubt, that this second child would be a boy, as the first one had not been. I was born, and my mother called me Lisa Ann. But my father asserted his will over my identity from many thousands of miles away. Upon learning of my birth, he sent a telegram congratulating my mother on the arrival of Suhair Suzanne — *Suhair,* a name meaning "little star in the night"; *Suzanne,* an Americanization of the Arabic *Sausan* — in what he may have thought would be a cultural compromise. By the time she received the telegram my mother must have had me home, Lisa Ann firmly inscribed in the hospital records. But this did not deter my father, always a stubborn man. On his return I was baptized Suhair Suzanne. In the one picture I possess of the event, I am cradled plumply in the arms of my aunt, indifferent to the saga of fractured identity about to ensue.

My mother, however, must have been stronger-willed than anyone expected. She acquiesced to the baptism, but her dutiful letters to the relatives in Jordan relate news of baby Lisa Suhair, with "Lisa" crossed out by her own pen. This marvelously subversive gesture allowed her to appear to abide by my father's wishes while still wedging her own claims in. And somehow her persistence won out. My earliest memories are of myself as Lisa: birthday cards and baby books all confirm it. Even my father only called me Suhair to tease me. But if my mother claimed victory in the colloquial, his was the legal victory. Both passport and birth certificate identified me as Suhair Suzanne, presaging a schism of worlds which would widen steadily as I grew.

When my sister and I were still very young, my parents moved first to Lebanon, then to Jordan. My father had had much difficulty finding work in the midwestern United States: people were suspicious of foreigners, and frequently anti-Semitic, and he was often assumed to be a Jew. Moving to the west coast did not greatly improve his opportunities. Finally, however, he was hired by a moving and packing firm that sent him to Beirut. From there we moved to Amman, where his mother and brother lived. By my fourth birthday we were settled in the small stone house, in what is now thought of as "old" Amman, where we were to live for the next twenty years.

Despite the semblance of rootedness this move to Jordan offered, my childhood was permeated with the ambience of exile. If to my mother "home" was thousands of miles away, beyond the Atlantic, to my father it was tantalizingly close, yet maddeningly unattainable —just across the Jordan River. My early years were marked by a constant sense of displacement, the unsettling quality of which determined much of my personal ambivalence and sense of confusion, as well as a certain flexibility I have come to value. I learned at an early age that there is always more than one way of doing things, but that this increased my awareness of cultural relativity has often meant a more complicated, and painful, existence. I learned to live as if in a transitional state, waiting always for the time that we would go to Palestine, to the United States, to a place where I would belong. But trips to Iowa and to Jerusalem taught me that once I got there, "home" slipped away inexplicably, materializing again just beyond reach. If a sense of rootedness was what gave life meaning, as my parents' individual efforts to ward off alienation implied, this meaning seemed able to assume full import only in the imagination.

The world of my growing-up years consisted of intersecting cultural spheres that often harmonized, but more frequently, particularly as my sister and I grew older, clashed. Home provided, naturally enough, the site of both the greatest cultural intermingling and the most intense contradiction. My mother worked, despite my father's objections, at the American Community School in Amman from the time I entered kindergarten until several years before her death in 1986. Though in later years she began to articulate the independence she had muted for years, for most of her married life she acquiesced to a hierarchical structuring of family codes. Although the prime agent of my sister's and my own socialization, my mother transmitted to us largely those lessons of my father's choosing. But my father's failure to fully explain his assumptions often resulted in a gap in the cultural translation from Arab to American. Thus, only *after* I had been away at college for some time did I explicitly learn that I should never go out except in large groups — a rule at the heart of which was a ban upon interactions with men. But such expectations hardly needed to be spelled out. My restricted upbringing and my own desire to maintain familial harmony had resulted in such an effective internalization of my father's expectations, most of which had to do with the maintenance of honor, that I lived them out almost unconsciously.

Looking back on our family life from the perspective of a painfully won feminism, the gender dynamics pervading our household seem unambiguously problematic. In addressing them, however, I find myself becoming defensive, wanting to preserve my deep-rooted family loyalties, however conflicted. I had learned to understand my relationship to others through the medium of Arab cultural norms filtered through an uneven Americanization. My childhood was permeated by the lesson, incessantly reinforced, that family is not just vital to self, but is so inherent that family and self are in a sense one and the same. I am more familiar than I would choose to be with the constrictions implicit in such celebration of family ties. But the mesh of familial expectations stressed in Arab culture provided a sense of security not readily apparent in my experience of American relationships, with their emphasis on individualism. However restrictively articulated, the stable definitions of self available in my childhood context held a certain appeal for me, caught as I was in a confusion of cultures.

I have come to understand the pressures that governed my life not as an innate characteristic of Arab culture, but as a particular, and gendered, product of cross-cultural interactions. In my experience, male children of mixed marriages are often able to claim both the rights of Arab men and an indefinable freedom usually attributed to western identity. Although the cultural mix imposes its burdens, a boy's situatedness between Arab and American identities is not debilitating. But for girls, relegated to the mother's sphere, the implications of a western identity in an Arab context can be so problematic that claustrophobic familial restrictions are often the result. Although modesty is required of all girls, those with American blood are at particular risk and must be doubly protected, so that there is neither opportunity nor basis for gossip.

As a child, however, I was aware only that being Arab, even in part, mandated a profound rejection of any self-definition that contradicted the claims of familial bonds. When I wished, as an adult, to marry a non-Arab man against my father's wishes, and engaged in a bitter, painful attempt to do so without irrevocably severing family ties, some friends seemed unable to understand why I would not rebel simply and cleanly, claiming my life and my feminist principles on my own terms. But to do so would have meant the abrogation not just of emotional connections, but of my very identity. Such absolute definitions make it extremely difficult for those of us caught between cultures to challenge restrictive cultural codes: without the security of being able to first lay full claim to the identity one rejects, rebellion becomes precarious and difficult.

Although I lived in an Arabic-speaking country, in my private world English was the main language of communication. My Arab relatives (who had all, except for my grandmother, learned English at school) wished to make my mother welcome by speaking her language, and wished as well to practice their skills in English—the use of which, in a residue of colonialism, still constitutes a mark of status in Jordan. Though I learned "kitchen Arabic" quite early, and could speak with my grandmother on an elementary level, I never became proficient in the language that should have been mine from childhood. This lack resulted in my isolation from the culture in which I lived. I was unable to follow conversations in family gatherings when people did not speak English. I could not understand Arabic television shows or news broadcasts, was unable to speak to storekeepers or passersby, or to develop friendships with Arab children. As a result I remained

trapped in a cultural insularity—articulated through the American school, American church, and American friends constituting my world—which now mortifies me. My father's habit of speaking only English at home played a large part in this deficiency; it seems never to have occurred to him that my sister and I would *not* pick up Arabic. Perhaps he thought that language skills ran in the blood. Indeed, during my college years he once sent me an article in Arabic, and was surprised and dismayed at my inability to read it: he had expected me to be literate in his language.

These linguistic deficiencies, though partly self-willed, have come to haunt me. I mourned with particular potency when my grandmother died shortly after I started studying Arabic for the specific purpose of communicating with her more meaningfully. As a child I had received occasional Arabic lessons from a relative at home and during special lunch-hour classes at school. During my teens and early twenties, embarrassed by the limitations of mono-lingualism, I took various courses in spoken and written Arabic. Despite my efforts, however, I retained little of what I learned, and my father, perhaps taking my knowledge for granted, offered little reinforcement. During bursts of enthusiasm or guilt I would ask him to speak Arabic to me on a daily basis. But such resolutions rarely lasted. He was too busy and too impatient for my faltering efforts, and I must have harbored more internal resistance to learning Arabic than I then realized.

Similarly, my father seemed to believe that knowledge of Palestinian history was a blood inheritance. I therefore had only my personal experience of events such as the Six Day War, or Black September, and a basic awareness of key dates—1948, 1967, 1970, 1973—to guide me though this history that so defined my father's life, and my own.* Only when challenged by my college peers in Lebanon did I begin to educate myself about my

---

*The state of Israel was established in 1948, dispossessing 750,000 Palestinians, more than 80 percent of the Arab inhabitants of the land that became Israel. The Six Day War of 1967 resulted in Israel's seizure of land from Jordan, Egypt, and Syria. During Black September of 1970 the Jordanian army killed thousands of Palestinians; militants who were not killed or captured fled to Lebanon. In 1973 war again broke out, this time between Israel, Egypt, Syria, and Iraq.

Palestinian background, a task that assumed more urgency when I moved to the United States. Indeed, in a pattern that continues to repeat itself, I have come to understand myself primarily in oppositional contexts: in Jordan I learned the ways in which I am American, while in the United States I discovered the ways in which I am Arab.

Though my father's cultural codes regulated everything from the length of my hair to the friends I was permitted to visit, the surface texture of my life was indisputably American. I grew up reading Mother Goose, singing "Home on the Range," reciting "The Ride of Paul Revere," and drawing pictures of Pilgrims and Indians, Christmas trees and Santa Clauses, Valentines and Easter bunnies. At school I learned the standard colonialist narrative of white Pilgrims settling an empty new land, struggling bravely against savage Indians. Yet into this world came many Arab elements. My relatives would fill the house with their Palestinian dialect, the men arguing in loud voices, slamming the *tric trac* stones on the board, while the women chatted on the veranda or in the kitchen. Although my mother took advantage of my father's frequent business trips to serve meatloaf and potatoes, the plain American food she craved, much of the food we ate was Arabic: I grew up on *yakhni* and *mahshi, wara'dawali* and *ma'aloubi*. My father had taught my mother to cook these dishes when they lived in the United States: hungry for the food of his childhood, he was willing to enter the kitchen to teach her the art of rolling grapeleaves or hollowing squash. In Jordan my grandmother took over her culinary education, the two of them communicating through hand gestures and my mother's broken Arabic.

But even food was a marker of both integration and conflict. To my father's dismay, I learned from my mother to hate yoghurt, a staple of Middle Eastern diets. He took this as a form of betrayal. Holidays became arenas for suppressed cultural battles, as my father insisted that my mother prepare time-consuming pots of rolled grapeleaves and stuffed squash in addition to the turkey and mashed potatoes, sweet potatoes and cranberry sauce; or that she dispense with the bread stuffing and substitute an Arabic filling of rice, lamb meat, and pine nuts. For periods of my childhood, having two cultural backgrounds seemed merely to mean more variety from which to choose, like the holiday dinners with two complete menus on the table. I learned to like

both cuisines, and to this day crave the potent garlic, the distinctive cinnamon and allspice of the Arabic dishes I rarely, for lack of time, make. But early on I learned that cultures, like flavors, often clash. And my sister and I, occupying through our very existence the point of tension where my mother's and father's worlds met, often provided the ground for this conflict.

Moving through childhood between the insular worlds of school and home, I remained constantly aware of the ways in which I was different. My relatively light skin and hair, while failing to grant me entrance to the blond, blue-eyed company of "real" Americans, set me apart from my Arab neighbors. There must have been some difference about me more elusive than that, however, for despite the fact that I knew Arabs with skin or hair lighter than my own, when I walked down the street I would hear the murmurs: *ajnabi*, foreigner. Even my body language marked me. When I was in my teens an Arab man once told me he would recognize my walk from blocks away. "You don't walk like an Arab girl," he said. "You take long steps; there's a bounce to your stride."

Instead of taking offense at what was in fact a criticism of my lack of "femininity," I hopefully interpreted this description to mean that perhaps I was, after all, American. I still clung to some shred of that old longing to be as confidently unambiguous as the diplomat kids who rode the Embassy bus, their lunchboxes filled with commissary treats—Oreos, Hershey bars—that we "locals" could never obtain. I wanted an American life like the ones I read about in the books I helped my mother unpack for the school library each year, the odor of glue and paper filling me with longing. I wanted an American father who would come home for dinner at 6 P.M., allow me to sleep over at friends' houses, speak unaccented English and never misuse a colloquialism; who would be other than what he indisputably was—a Palestinian. As a child I convinced myself that we lived in Jordan by mistake, and that soon we would return to the United States, where I would become my true self: American, whole. I wanted to believe that my confusion and fragmentation were merely temporary.

Meanwhile, I searched for someone to explain me to myself. I knew that Arabs—my relatives as much as neighbors and shopkeepers and strangers—thought me foreign, while "real" Americans thought me foreign as well. I knew, too, the subtle hierarchies implicit in these assessments. At school the social order was clear: Embassy Americans, then non-Embassy Americans, and finally those of us with mixed blood, whose claim to the insular world of overseas Americans was at best partial. At the interdenominational church we attended, my mother and sister and I fielded the solicitude of missionaries who never quite believed that my father was not Muslim. When, after exhausting the resources of the American school, I transferred to a Jordanian high school offering courses in English, I learned that there too I was an outsider. My father's name didn't change the fact that I couldn't speak Arabic, lacked the cultural subtleties into which an Arab girl would have been socialized, and as an American female had automatically suspect morals.

I see now how orientalist representations of the Arab world find echoes in occidentalist perceptions of the west. When I walked down the streets of Amman I was categorized as foreign, female; a target of curiosity and harassment. My appearance alone in public and my foreignness seemed to suggest sexual availability; whispers of *charmoota*, prostitute, echoed in my burning ears. The insidious touch of young men's hands on my body pursued me, their eyes taunting me in mock innocence when I whirled to confront them. Once, when a young man crowded me against a wall, brushing my hips with his hand as he passed, I cried out wildly and swung my bag at him. But he advanced threateningly toward me, shouting angrily at my effrontery. If I had spoken Arabic to him he might have retreated in shame. Because I did not he must have seen me simply as a foreign woman, flaunting a sexuality unmediated by the protection of men, the uncles and brothers and cousins whom an Arab woman would be assumed to have.

Despite such experiences, early in my teens I claimed walking as a mark of my individuality. Determined to assert my difference since I could not eradicate it, I walked everywhere, consciously lengthening my stride and walking with a freedom of motion I longed to extend to the rest of my life. Walking offered a means both of setting myself off from and of confronting the Arab culture that I felt threatened to overwhelm me. I wanted to insist that I was "other" than these people whose language I barely spoke, even though they were my relatives; that I was American—as was, for that matter, my father. Lacking an understanding of his history, I remained

oblivious to his awareness of his American citizenship as a bitter acquiescence to the realities of international politics and the denial of Palestinian identity. Instead, I clung to markers of our mutual Americanness. Didn't we cross the bridge to the West Bank with the foreigners, in air-conditioned comfort, instead of on the suffocatingly hot "Arab" side, where Palestinians returning to the Occupied Territories had to strip naked and send their shoes and suitcases to be x-rayed? Didn't we go to the Fourth of July picnics and Christmas bazaars? Weren't we as good as other Americans?

While my father shared my anger at being marginalized in the American community, he did not appreciate my attempts to reject his heritage. Despite his esteem for certain aspects of American culture—his fondness of small midwestern towns, his fascination with technological gadgetry, his admiration of the American work ethic—as I grew older he grew ever more disapproving of my efforts to identify as an American. Although he had left much of my sister's and my own upbringing to my mother, he had assumed that we would arrive at adolescence as model Arab girls: when we did not he was puzzled and annoyed. As walking became a measure of my independence, it became as well a measure of our conflict of wills. He did not like my "wandering in the streets"; it was not "becoming," and it threatened his own honor. I stole away for walks, therefore, during the drowsy hours after the heavy midday meal when most people, my father included, were either at work or at siesta. Walking in the early afternoon, especially during the summer months, accentuated my difference from the Jordanian culture I had determined to resist. A young woman walking quickly and alone through still, hot streets, past drowsy guards and bored shopkeepers, presented an anomaly: Arab girls, I had been told both subtly and explicitly, did not do such things—a fact that pleased me.

As my sister and I entered the "dangerous age," when our reputations were increasingly at stake and a wrong move would brand us as "loose," my father grew more and more rigid in his efforts to regulate our self-definitions. Our options in life were spelled out in terms of whom we would be permitted to marry. A Palestinian Christian, I knew, was the preferred choice. But even a Palestinian Muslim, my father said—though I did not quite believe him, conscious of the crucial significance of religious distinctions in the Middle East—would be better than a Jordanian. (I think of Black September, the days spent below window level, the nights of guns and mortars, my grandmother's house burned after soldiers learned of my cousins' political affiliations, the horror of Palestinian families massacred in their homes by the Jordanian army, and I begin to understand.) To marry an American, or Britisher, or Canadian was out of the question. Westerners, I heard repeatedly, had no morals, no respect for family, no sense of honor—an opinion that seemed to derive in part from observations of real cultural differences between Arabs and westerners, in part from the weekly episodes of Peyton Place and other English-language programs aired on Jordan television. (I have been asked by Arabs whether Americans really get divorced six or seven times, abandon their elderly parents, and are all wealthy. And I have been asked by Americans whether Arabs really ride camels to work, live in tents, and have never seen planes or hospitals.) Though I now appreciate the difficult balance my father sought to maintain in his identity as a Christian Palestinian in Muslim Jordan, between the American characteristics he had embraced after years in the United States and the cultural requirements of Jordanian society, at the time I experienced his expectations as unreasonable and contradictory. Most difficult to accept was the implicit portrayal of my mother's American identity as a misfortune for which we all, she included, had to compensate. On constant trial to prove my virtue and held to a far stricter standard of behavior than my Arab cousins, I both resented and felt compelled to undertake the ongoing task of proving that I wasn't, in fact, American.

In my experience cultural marginality has been among the most painful of alienations. My childhood desire, often desperate, was not so much to be a particular nationality, to be American or Arab, but to be wholly one thing or another: to be *something* that I and the rest of the world could understand, categorize, label, predict. Although I spent years struggling to define my personal politics of location, I remained situated somewhere between Arab and American cultures—never quite rooted in either, always constrained by both. My sense of liminality grew as I became more aware of the rigid nature of definitions: Arab culture simultaneously claimed and excluded me, while the American identity I longed for retreated inexorably from my grasp.

My experiences in the United States in many ways reinforced this sense of exclusion. Upon arriving in Michigan for graduate school, after four years at the American University of Beirut during which both my American and Palestinian identities had been inevitably politicized, I yearned, yet again, for the simplicity of belonging. Consciously drawing as little attention as possible to my name, my family, my background, I avoided Middle Eastern organizations, and made no Arab friends at all. A few days after my arrival in the United States, when a man asked me provocatively why I wore a "map of Israel" around my neck, I answered briefly that it was a map of historic Palestine and then retreated from his attempts to draw me into debate, shrinking deep into a cocoon of silence.

"Passing demands a desire to become invisible," writes Michelle Cliff. "A ghost-life. An ignorance of connections."* While the incidents that first made me afraid to reveal myself in the United States were minor—pointed questions, sidelong glances, awkward silences—they were enough to thrust me firmly back into a desire for invisibility. I sought anonymity, as if trying to erode the connections that had brought me, juncture by juncture, to where and who I was, the product of histories I could no more undo than I could undo my bone structure.

But passing, as I was to learn, wreaks implicit violence upon the lived reality of our experiences. "Passing demands quiet," Cliff warns. "And from that quiet—silence." I have learned to understand silence as something insidious. As a child, lost between the contradictory demands of the worlds I moved between, I claimed silence as a tool of survival; I honed it still further in my American context. What I did not then realize was that silence, with time, atrophies the voice—a loss with such grave consequences that it is a form of dispossession. Silence made it possible for me to blend into my surroundings, chameleon-like; it enabled me to absorb without self-revelation what I needed to know. But its implications were disastrous. Silence wrapped itself around my limbs like cotton wool, wound itself

---

*Michelle Cliff, *Claiming an Identity They Taught Me to Despise* (Watertown, MA: Persephone Press, 1980), 5.

into my ears and eyes, filled my mouth and muffled my throat. I do not know at what point I began to choke. Perhaps there was never a single incident, just a slow deposition of sediment over time. Until one day, retching, I spat out some unnameable substance. And I attempted to speak.

By this time I was beginning to claim the tools of feminism. In Beirut I had pored over a copy of *The Feminine Mystique,* startled by the wave of recognition it evoked. Later, graduate school exposed me to the analytical training and the affirmation of voice that I had been lacking. Although I eventually discovered its cultural insensibilities, American feminism enabled me to begin interrogating the entanglement of gender and culture in a search for my own definitions. While much in my experience had tempted me to reject Arab culture as misogynist, my growing awareness of the ways in which my experiences represented not Arab culture *per se,* but a conflicted interaction between Arab and American, led me to explore my Palestinian background for positive symbols, not just nationalistic but gendered, on which to draw for identification and strength.

This exploration reinforced my acute awareness of the representation and misrepresentation of Arab culture in the United States. There are ways in which Palestinian women escape the typical stereotypes of Arab women — exotic, sensualized, victimized — only to be laden with the more male-coded, or perhaps merely generic, images of irrational terrorists and pathetic refugees. But none of these images reflect the Arab women I know: my widowed Palestinian grandmother, who raised three boys and buried two girls, raising two grandchildren as well after their mother was killed by a Zionist group's bomb, whose strength and independence people still speak of with awe; or my Lebanese aunt, a skilled nurse who ran a Jerusalem hospital ward for years, raised four children, gracefully met the social requirements of her husband's busy political and medical careers, and now directs a center for disabled children. My increasing anger at the portrayal of the Middle East as a chaotic realm outside the boundaries of rational Western comprehension, and a slowly developing confidence in my own political and cultural knowledge, came together with my burgeoning feminism to make possible an articulation that, although tentative, was more empowering than anything I had experienced.

At some point I began to feel anger. At the jokes about *kalashnikovs* in my backpack, grenades in my purse. At the sheer amazement of a woman who asked my mother, "But why did you marry a terrorist?" At an acquaintance's incredulous look when I spoke of Arab feminism. At the comments that it must be dangerous to live in Jordan "because of all the terrorism." At the college professor who did not believe that Arabs could be Christians. At the knowledge that when I posted announcements of Arab cultural events on campus they would be torn down moments later. At the look of shock and dismay, quickly masked, on the face of a new acquaintance just learning of my Palestinian background. At the startled response of someone who, having assumed my Arab name to be my spouse's, learned that I chose to keep an *Arab* name. At the conversations in which I am forced to explain that Palestinians do indeed exist; that they claim a long history in Palestine.

And with the anger has come fear. Of the unknown person in my apartment building who intercepted packages I had ordered from an Arab-American organization, strewing their contents, defaced with obscenities, at my door. Of the hostility of airport security personnel once they know my destination or origin point: the overly thorough searches, the insistent questions. Of the anonymous person who dialed my home after I was interviewed by my local paper, shouting "Death to Palestinians!" Of the unsigned, racist mail. Of the mysterious hit-and-run driver who smashed my car as it was parked on a quiet residential street, a Palestine emblem clearly visible through the window of the car door.

Such actions inscribe their subjects within a singular, predetermined identity, and often elicit responses validating precisely this identity. However, such exclusionary identification remains, finally, untenable. During the Gulf War a radio commentator proclaimed, "In war there are no hyphenated Americans, just Americans and non-Americans." It is a familiar, and chilling, sentiment: Japanese-Americans in particular can speak to its implications. But what is to become of those of us in-between, those of us who are neither "just" Americans, nor "just" non-Americans? I could say that I opposed the Gulf War as a human being first, as an American second, and only third as a Palestinian. But in fact my identities cannot be so neatly divided. I am never *just* an American, any more than I am *just* a Palestinian. Yet

I am not therefore any *less* of an American, or *less* of a Palestinian. As I was rarely given the choice in the Middle East to claim or not to claim my American identity, so I am not often given the choice in my American context to be or not to be Palestinian. At best I can attempt to pass, suppressing my identity and resorting to silence. And when this strategy fails—*or when I reject it*—then I am forced to take responsibility for *both* American and Palestinian histories in their contradictory entireties—histories articulated through idealism, but resorting too often to violence. And in so doing I come to a fuller understanding of the contradictions, the excesses, which spill over the neat boundaries within which I am often expected to, and sometimes long to, reside.

It has taken personal loss to bring me to a fuller understanding of the connections and contradictions forming the warp and weft of my experience. The devastation I experienced at my parents' deaths, at the foreclosing of their attempts to negotiate difference in their lives together, compels me to claim and validate their legacy—the textured fabric of my own life. I look in the mirror and recognize their mingled features in my own; I lift my hair and note the curl, the color bequeathed by their mixed genes. My skin, lighter now since my years away from the strong sun of Jordan and Lebanon, retains the faint tinge of olive that set me apart from my white-skinned playmates even in babyhood. Tata Olga, my Palestinian grandmother, used to lament my propensity to stay in the sun. "You'll never find a husband, dark like this," she would scold, speaking the words of internalized racism and sexism. But I search now for color in my life. On the shelf above my desk I keep a card depicting a small Maldivian girl whose richly hued skin, deep brown eyes, and dark, unkempt hair compel me with their beauty. The Lebanese-American poet who gave me this card recently adopted a vibrant Guatemalan child; the girl in the picture reminds me of his daughter. She reminds me as well of a group of Maldivian students from American University of Beirut whose embracing presence and steady endurance during our exodus from Lebanon sustained and comforted me. And she brings to mind all the small girls growing up in a world where women are less valued than men, dark skin less valued than light skin, poor people less valued than wealthy people, non-western cultures less valued than western cultures.

She reminds me, too, that it is through a willing encounter with difference that we come to a fuller realization of ourselves. I possess no representative photograph of a Palestinian-American, no non-personal touchstone of my mixed heritage. And despite my longing for such tokens, perhaps they are unnecessary. Although I remain acutely aware of the importance of communal symbols in affirming individual and group consciousness, I find glimmers of myself in people I do not recognize, in faces that share with mine only questions. No closed circle of family or tribe or culture reflects from the Maldivian girl's eyes. She looks slightly away from the camera, her gaze directed wistfully at something just over my left shoulder, something I cannot see and that she may not be able to claim. The card identifies her as Laila, from a Maldive fishing family, noting that Maldivians are a mix of Arab, Singhalese, and Malaysian: there are, after all, some connections between us. But I cannot intercept her gaze. Laila looks steadily beyond me, light planing her pensive face. Whatever she sees remains unspoken. I look at her often, remembering how much I do not know.

Like my parents, I am grounded in both history and alienation. But if it is true that we are ideologically determined, it is also true that our choices allow us a measure of resistance against the larger patterns that map us, a measure of self-creation. Constructed and reconstructed, always historically situated, identities embody the demarcation of possibilities at particular junctures. I claim the identity "Arab-American" not as a heritage passed from generation to generation, but rather as an on-going negotiation of difference. My parents articulated their relationship oppositionally, assumptions colliding as they confronted each other's cultural boundaries. Child of their contradictions, I seek to transform that conflict into a constant motion testing the lines that encircle and embrace me, protect and imprison me. I am caught within a web: lines fade and reappear, forming intricate patterns, a maze. I live at borders that are always overdetermined, constantly shifting. Gripped by the logic of translation, I still long to find my reflection on either side of the cultural divide. But the infinitely more complex web of music beckons, speaking beyond translation. Who can say how this will end?

◆◆◆

FIFTEEN

Defining Genealogies
Feminist Reflections on Being South Asian in North America
Chandra Talpade Mohanty

My local newspaper tells me that worldwide migration is at an all-time high in the early 1990s. Folks are moving from rural to urban areas in all parts of the Third World, and from Asia, Africa, the Caribbean and Latin America to Europe, North America and selected countries in the Middle East. Apparently two percent of the world's population no longer lives in the country in which they were born. Of course, the newspaper story primarily identifies the "problems" (for Europe and the USA) associated with these transnational migration trends. One such "problem" is taking jobs away from "citizens." I am reminded of a placard carried by Black and Third World people at an anti-racism rally in London: We Are Here Because You Were There. My location in the USA then, is symptomatic of large numbers of migrants, nomads, immigrants, workers across the globe for whom notions of home, identity, geography and history are infinitely complicated in the late twentieth century. Questions of nation(ality), and of "belonging" (witness the situation of South Asians in Africa) are constitutive of the Indian diaspora. This essay is a personal, anecdotal meditation on the politics of gender and race in the construction of South Asian identity in North America.

On a TWA flight on my way back to the U.S. from a conference in the Netherlands, the professional white man sitting next to me asks: a) which school do I go to? and b) when do I plan to go home?—all in the same breath. I put on my most professional demeanor (somewhat hard in crumpled blue jeans and cotton T-shirt—this uniform only works for white male professors, who of course could command authority even in swimwear!) and inform him that I teach at a small liberal arts college in upstate New York, and that I have lived in the U.S. for fifteen years. At this point, my work is in the U.S., not in India. This is no longer entirely true—my work is also with feminists and grassroots activists in India, but he doesn't need to know this. Being "mistaken" for a graduate student seems endemic to my

existence in this country—few Third World women are granted professional (i.e. adult) and/or permanent (one is always a student!) status in the U.S., even if we exhibit clear characteristics of adulthood, like grey hair and facial lines. He ventures a further question: what do you teach? On hearing "women's studies," he becomes quiet and we spend the next eight hours in polite silence. He has decided that I do not fit into any of his categories, but what can you expect from a *Feminist* (an *Asian* one!) anyway? I feel vindicated and a little superior—even though I know he doesn't really feel "put in his place." Why should he? He has a number of advantages in this situation: white skin, maleness and citizenship privileges. From his enthusiasm about expensive "ethnic food" in Amsterdam, and his J. Crew clothes, I figured class difference (economic or cultural) wasn't exactly an issue in our interaction. We both appeared to have similar social access as "professionals."

I have been asked the "home" question (when are you going home) periodically for fifteen years now. Leaving aside the subtly racist implications of the question (go home—you don't belong), I am still not satisfied with my response. What is home? The place I was born? Where I grew up? Where my parents live? Where I live and work as an adult? Where I locate my community—my people? Who are "my people"? Is home a geographical space, an historical space, an emotional, sensory space? Home is always so crucial to immigrants and migrants—I even write about it in scholarly texts, perhaps to avoid addressing it as an issue that is also very personal. Does two percent of the world's population think about these questions pertaining to home? This is not to imply that the other ninety-eight percent does not think about home. What interests me is the meaning of home for immigrants and migrants. I am convinced that this question—how one understands and defines home—is a profoundly political one.

Since settled notions of territory, community, geography, and history don't work for us, what does it really mean to be "South Asian" in the USA? Obviously I was not South Asian in India—I was Indian. What else could one be but "Indian" at a time when a successful national independence struggle had given birth to a socialist democratic nation-state? This was the beginning of the decolonization of the Third World. Regional geographies (South Asia) appeared less relevant as a mark of identification than citizenship in a post-colonial independent nation on the cusp of economic and political autonomy. However, in North America, identification as South Asian (in addition to Indian, in my case) takes on its own logic. "South Asian" refers to folks of Indian, Pakistani, Sri Lankan, Bangladeshi, Kashmiri, and Burmese origin. Identifying as South Asian rather than Indian adds numbers and hence power within the U.S. State. Besides, regional differences among those from different South Asian countries are often less relevant than the commonalities based on our experiences and histories of immigration, treatment and location in the U.S.

Let me reflect a bit on the way I identify myself, and the way the U.S. State and its institutions categorize me. Perhaps thinking through the various labels will lead me back to the question of home and identity. In 1977, I arrived in the USA on an F1 visa—a student visa. At that time, my definition of myself—a graduate student in Education at the University of Illinois, and the "official" definition of me (a student allowed into the country on an F1 visa) obviously coincided. Then I was called a "foreign student," and expected to go "home" (to India— even though my parents were in Nigeria at the time) after getting my Ph.D. Let's face it, this is the assumed trajectory for a number of Indians, especially the post-independence (my) generation, who come to the U.S. for graduate study.

However, this was not to be my trajectory. I quickly discovered that being a foreign student, and a woman at that, meant being either dismissed as irrelevant (the quiet Asian woman stereotype), treated in racist ways (my teachers asked if I understood English and if they should speak slower and louder so that I could keep up—this in spite of my inheritance of the Queen's English and British colonialism!), or celebrated and exoticized (you are so smart! your accent is even better than that of Americans— a little Anglophilia at work here, even though all my Indian colleagues insist we speak English the Indian way!).

The most significant transition I made at that time was the one from "foreign student" to "student of color." Once I was able to "read" my experiences in terms of race, and to read race and racism as it is written into the social and political fabric of the U.S., practices of racism and sexism became the analytic and political lenses through which I was able to anchor myself here. Of course, none of this happened in isolation—friends, colleagues, comrades, classes, books, films, arguments, and dialogues were constitutive of my political education as a woman of color in the U.S.

In the late 1970s and early 1980s feminism was gaining momentum on American campuses—it was in the air, in the classrooms, on the streets. However, what attracted me wasn't feminism as the mainstream media and white Women's Studies departments defined it. Instead, it was a very specific kind of feminism, the feminism of U.S. women of color and Third World women, that spoke to me. In thinking through the links between gender, race and class in their U.S. manifestations, I was for the first time enabled to think through my own gendered, classed post-colonial history. In the early 1980s, reading Audre Lorde, Nawal el Sadaawi, Cherríe Moraga, bell hooks, Gloria Joseph, Paula Gunn Allen, Barbara Smith, Merle Woo and Mitsuye Yamada, among others, generated a sort of recognition that was intangible but very inspiring. A number of actions, decisions and organizing efforts at that time led me to a sense of home and community in relation to women of color in the U.S. Home not as a comfortable, stable, inherited and familiar space, but instead as an imaginative, politically charged space where the familiarity and sense of affection and commitment lay in shared collective analysis of social injustice, as well as a vision of radical transformation. Political solidarity and a sense of family could be melded together imaginatively to create a strategic space I could call "home." Politically, intellectually and emotionally I owe an enormous debt to feminists of color—and especially to the sisters who have sustained me over the years. Even though our attempt to start the Women of Color Institute for Radical Research and Action fell through, the spirit of this vision, and the friendships it generated, still continue to nurture me. A number of us, including Barbara Smith, Papusa Molina, Jacqui Alexander, Gloria Joseph, Mitsuye Yamada, Kesho Scott, and myself, among others met in 1984 to discuss the possibility of such an Institute. The Institute never really happened, but I still hope we will pull it off one day.

For me, engagement as a feminist of color in the U.S. made possible an intellectual and political genealogy of being Indian that was radically challenging as well as profoundly activist. Notions of home and community began to be located within a deeply political space where racialization and gender and class relations and histories became the prism through which I understood, however partially, what it could mean to be South Asian in North America. Interestingly, this recognition also forced me to re-examine the meanings attached to home and community in India.

What I chose to claim, and continue to claim, is a history of anti-colonialist, feminist struggle in India. The stories I recall, the ones that I retell and claim as my own, determine the choices and decisions I make in the present and the future. I did not want to accept a history of Hindu chauvinist (bourgeois) upward mobility (even though this characterizes a section of my extended family). We all choose partial, interested stories/histories — perhaps not as deliberately as I am making it sound here. But consciously, or unconsciously, these choices about our past(s) often determine the logic of our present.

Having always kept my distance from conservative, upwardly mobile Indian immigrants for whom the South Asian world was divided into green-card holders and non-green-card holders, the only South Asian links I allowed and cultivated were with Indians with whom I shared a political vision. This considerably limited my community. Racist and sexist experiences in graduate school and after made it imperative that I understand the U.S. in terms of its history of racism, imperialism and patriarchal relations, specifically in relation to Third World immigrants. After all, we were into the Reagan-Bush years, when the neo-conservative backlash made it impossible to ignore the rise of racist, anti-feminist, and homophobic attitudes, practices and institutions. Any purely culturalist or nostalgic/sentimental definition of being "Indian" or "South Asian" was inadequate. Such a definition fueled the "model minority" myth. And this subsequently constituted us as "outsiders/foreigners" or as interest groups who sought or had obtained the American dream.

In the mid-1980s, the labels changed: I went from being a "foreign student" to being a "resident alien." I have always thought that this designation was a stroke of inspiration on the part of the U.S. State, since it accurately names the experience and status of immigrants — especially immigrants of color. The flip side of "resident alien" is "illegal alien," another inspired designation. One can be either a resident or illegal immigrant, but one is always an alien. There is no confusion here — no melting pot ideology or narratives of assimilation — one's status as an "alien" is primary. Being legal requires identity papers. (It is useful to recall that the "passport" — and by extension the concept of nation-states and the sanctity of their borders — came into being after World War I.)

One must be stamped as legitimate (that is, not-gay-or-lesbian and not-communist!) by the Immigration and Naturalization Service (INS). The INS is one of the central disciplinary arms of the U.S. State. It polices the borders and controls all border crossings — especially those into the U.S. In fact, the INS is also one of the primary forces which institutionalizes race differences in the public arena, thus regulating notions of home, legitimacy and economic access to the "American dream" for many of us. For instance, carrying a green card documenting resident alien status in the U.S. is clearly very different from carrying an American passport, which is proof of U.S. citizenship. The former allows one to enter the U.S. with few hassles; the latter often allows one to breeze through the borders and ports of entry of other countries, especially countries which happen to be trading partners (much of Western Europe and Japan, among others) or in an unequal relationship with the U.S. (much of the noncommunist Third World). At a time when notions of a capitalist free-market economy seem (falsely) synonymous with the values attached to democracy, an American passport can open many doors. However, just carrying an American passport is no insurance against racism and unequal and unjust treatment within the U.S. It would be important to compare the racialization of first-generation immigrants from South Asia to the racialization of second-generation South Asian Americans. For example, one significant difference between these two generations would be between experiencing racism as a phenomenon specific to the U.S., versus growing up in the ever-present shadow of racism in the case of South Asians born in the U.S. This suggests that the psychic effects of racism would be different for these two constituencies. In addition, questions of home, identity and history take on very different meanings for South Asians born in North America. But to be fair, this comparison requires a whole other reflection that is beyond the scope of this essay.

Rather obstinately, I have refused to give up my Indian passport and have chosen to remain as a resident alien in the U.S. for the last decade or so. Which leads me to reflect on the complicated meanings attached to holding Indian citizenship while making a life for myself in the USA. In India, what does it mean to have a green card — to be an expatriate? What does it mean to visit Bombay every two to four years, and still call it home? Why does speaking in Marathi (my mothertongue) become a measure and confirmation of home? What are the politics of being a part of the majority and the "absent elite" in India, while being a minority and a racialized "other" in the U.S.? And does feminist politics, or advocating feminism, have the same meanings and urgencies in these different geographical and political contexts?

Some of these questions hit me smack in the face during my last visit to India, in December 1992 — post-Ayodhya (the infamous destruction of the Babri Masjid in Ayodhya by Hindu fundamentalists on 6 December 1992). In earlier, rather infrequent visits (once every four or five years was all I could afford), my green card designated me as an object of envy, privilege and status within my extended family. Of course the same green card has always been viewed with suspicion by left and feminist friends who (quite understandably) demand evidence of my ongoing commitment to a socialist and democratic India. During this visit, however, with emotions running high within my family, my green card marked me as an outsider who couldn't possibly understand the "Muslim problem" in India. I was made aware of being an "outsider" in two profoundly troubling shouting matches with my uncles, who voiced the most incredibly hostile sentiments against Muslims. Arguing that India was created as a secular state and that democracy had everything to do with equality for all groups (majority and minority) got me nowhere. The very fundamentals of democratic citizenship in India were/are being undermined and redefined as "Hindu."

Bombay was one of the cities hardest hit with waves of communal violence following the events in Ayodhya. The mobilization of Hindu fundamentalists, even paramilitary organizations, over the last half century and especially since the mid-1980s had brought Bombay to a juncture where the most violently racist discourse about Muslims seemed to be woven into the fabric of acceptable daily life. Racism was normalized in the popular imagination such that it became almost impossible to publicly raise questions about the ethics or injustice of racial/ethnic/religious discrimination. I could not assume a distanced posture towards religion any more. Too many injustices were being done in my name.

Although born a Hindu, I have always considered myself a non-practicing one — religion had always felt rather repressive when I was growing up. I enjoyed the rituals but resisted the authoritarian hierarchies of organized Hinduism. However, the Hinduism touted by fundamentalist organizations like the RSS (Rashtriya Swayamsevak Sangh, a paramilitary Hindu fundamentalist organization founded in the 1930s) and the Shiv Sena (a Maharashtrian chauvinist, fundamentalist, fascist political organization that has amassed a significant voice in Bombay politics and government) was one that even I, in my ignorance, recognized as reactionary and distorted. But this discourse was real — hate-filled rhetoric against Muslims appeared to be the mark of a "loyal Hindu." It was unbelievably heart-wrenching to see my hometown become a war zone with whole streets set on fire, and a daily death count to rival any major territorial border war. The smells and textures of Bombay, of home, which had always comforted and nurtured me, were violently disrupted. The scent of fish drying on the lines at the fishing village in Danda was submerged in the smell of burning straw and grass as whole bastis (chawls) were burned to the ground. The very topography, language and relationships that constituted "home" were quietly but surely exploding. What does community mean in this context? December 1992 both clarified as well as complicated for me the meanings attached to being an Indian citizen, a Hindu, an educated woman/feminist, and a permanent resident in the U.S. in ways that I have yet to resolve. After all, it is often moments of crisis that make us pay careful attention to questions of identity. Sharp polarizations force one to make choices (not in order to take sides, but in order to accept responsibility) and to clarify our own analytic, political and emotional topographies.

I learned that combating the rise of Hindu fundamentalism was a necessary ethical imperative for all socialists, feminists and Hindus of conscience. Secularism, if it meant absence of religion, was no longer a viable position. From a feminist perspective, it became clear that the battle for women's minds and hearts was very much center-stage in the Hindu fundamentalist strategy. Feminists in India have written extensively about the appeal of fundamentalist rhetoric and social position to women. (The journals *The Economic and Political Weekly of India* and *Manushi* are good sources for this work.)

Religious fundamentalist constructions of women embody the nexus of morality, sexuality and Nation — a nexus of great importance for feminists. Similar to Christian, Islamic and Jewish fundamentalist discourses, the construction of femininity and masculinity, especially in relation to the idea of the Nation, are central to Hindu fundamentalist rhetoric and mobilizations. Women are not only mobilized in the "service" of the Nation, but they also become the ground on which discourses of morality and nationalism are written. For instance, the RSS mobilizes primarily middle-class women in the name of a family-oriented, Hindu nation, much like the Christian Right does in the U.S. But discourses of morality and nation are also embodied in the normative policing of women's sexuality (witness the surveillance and policing of women's dress in the name of morality by the contemporary Iranian State). Thus, one of the central challenges Indian feminists face at this time is how to rethink the relationship of nationalism and feminism in the context of religious identities. In addition to the fundamentalist mobilizations tearing the country apart, the recent incursions of the International Monetary Fund and the World Bank with their structural adjustment programs which are supposed to "discipline" the Indian economy, are redefining the meaning of post-coloniality and of democracy in India. Categories like gender, race, caste/class are profoundly and visibly unstable at such times of crisis. These categories must thus be analyzed in relation to contemporary reconstructions of womanhood and manhood in a *global* arena increasingly dominated by religious fundamentalist movements, the IMF and the World Bank, and the relentless economic and ideological colonization of much of the world by multinationals based in the U.S., Japan and Europe. In all these global economic and cultural/ideological processes, women occupy a crucial position.

In India, unlike most countries, the sex ratio has declined since the early 1900s. According to the 1991 census, the ratio is now 929 women to 1000 men, one of the lowest (if not *the* lowest) sex ratios in the world. Women produce seventy to eighty percent of all the food in India, and have always been the hardest hit by environmental degradation and poverty. The contradictions between civil law and Hindu and Muslim personal laws affect women — rarely men. Horrific stories about the deliberate genocide of female infants as a result of sex determination procedures like amniocentesis, and recent incidents of sati (self-immolation by women on the funeral pyres of their husbands) have even hit the mainstream American media. Gender and religious (racial) discrimination are thus urgent, life-threatening issues for women in India. In 1993, politically-conscious Indian citizenship necessitates taking such fundamentally feminist issues seriously. In fact, these are the very same issues South Asian feminists in the U.S. need to address. My responsibility to combat and organize against the regressive and violent repercussions of Hindu fundamentalist mobilizations in India extends to my life in North America. After all, much of the money which sustains the fundamentalist movement is raised and funneled through organizations in the U.S.

Let me now circle back to the place I began: the meanings I have come to give to home, community and identity. By exploring the relationship between being a South Asian immigrant in America and an expatriate Indian citizen in India, I have tried, however partially and anecdotally, to clarify the complexities of home and community for this particular feminist of color/South Asian in North America. The genealogy I have created for myself here is partial, interested and deliberate. It is a genealogy that I find emotionally and politically enabling — it is part of the genealogy that underlies my self-identification as an educator involved in a pedagogy of liberation. Of course, my history and experiences are far messier and not at all as linear as this narrative makes them sound. But then the very process of constructing a narrative for oneself — of telling a story — imposes a certain linearity and coherence that is never entirely there. But that is the lesson, perhaps, especially for us immigrants and migrants: i.e., that home, community and identity all fall somewhere between the histories and experiences we inherit and the political choices we make through alliances, solidarities and friendships.

One very concrete effect of my creating this particular space for myself has been my recent involvement in two grassroots organizations, one in India and the other in the U.S. The former, an organization called *Awareness,* is based in Orissa and works to empower the rural poor. Their focus is political education (similar to Paolo Freire's notion of "conscientization"), and they have recently begun to very consciously organize rural women. *Grassroots Leadership of North Carolina* is the U.S. organization I work with. It is a multiracial group of organizers (largely African American and White) working to build a poor and working peoples movement in the American South. While the geographical, historical and political contexts are different in the case of these two organizations, my involvement in them is very similar, as is my sense that there are clear connections to be made between the work of the two organizations. In addition, I think that the issues, analyses and strategies for organizing for social justice are also quite similar. This particular commitment to work with grassroots organizers in the two places I call home is not accidental. It is very much the result of the genealogy I have traced here. After all, it has taken me over a decade to make these commitments to grassroots work in both spaces. In part, I have defined what it means to be South Asian by educating myself about, and reflecting on, the histories and experiences of African American, Latina, West Indian, African, European American, and other constituencies in North America. Such definitions and understandings do provide a genealogy, but a genealogy that is always relational and fluid as well as urgent and necessary.

This essay is dedicated to the memory of Lanubai and Gauribai Vijaykar, maternal grandaunts, who were single, educated, financially independent, and tall (over six feet) at a time when it was against the grain to be any one of these things; and to Audre Lorde, teacher, sister, friend, whose words and presence continue to challenge, inspire and nurture me.

◆◆◆

SIXTEEN

An Unforgettable Journey

Maijue Xiong

I was born in a small village called Muong Cha in Laos on April 30, 1972. At the time I was born, my father was a soldier actively fighting alongside the American Central Intelligence Agency against the Communists. Although a war was in progress, life seemed peaceful. We did not think of ever leaving Laos, but one day our lives were changed forever. We found ourselves without a home or a country and with a need to seek refuge in another country. This period of relocation involved a lot of changes, adjustments, and adaptations. We experienced changes in our language, customs, traditional values, and social status. Some made the transition quickly; others have never fully adjusted. The changes my family and I experienced are the foundation of my identity today.

After Laos became a Communist country in 1975, my family, along with many others, fled in fear of persecution. Because my father had served as a commanding officer for eleven years with the American Central Intelligence Agency in what is known to the American public as the "Secret War," my family had no choice but to leave immediately. My father's life was in danger, along with those of thousands of others. We were forced to leave loved ones behind, including my grandmother who was ill in bed the day we fled our village. For a month, my family walked through the dense tropical jungles and rice fields, along rugged trails through many mountains, and battled the powerful Mekong River. We traveled in silence at night and slept in the daytime. Children were very hard to keep quiet. Many parents feared the Communist soldiers would hear the cries of their young children; therefore, they drugged the children with opium to keep them quiet. Some parents even left those children who would not stop crying behind. Fortunately, whenever my parents told my sisters and me to keep quiet, we listened and obeyed.

I do not remember much about our flight, but I do have certain memories that have been imprinted in my mind. It is all so unclear — the experience was like a bad dream: when you wake up, you don't remember what it was you had dreamed about but recall only those bits and pieces of the dream that stand out the most. I remember sleeping under tall trees. I was like a little ant placed in a field of tall grass, surrounded by a dense jungle with trees and bushes all around me — right, left, in the back, and in front of me. I also remember that it rained a lot and that it was cold. We took only what we could carry and it was not much. My father carried a sack of rice, which had to last us the whole way. My mother carried one extra change of clothing for each of us, a few personal belongings, and my baby sister on her back. My older sister and I helped carry pots and pans. My stepuncle carried water, dried meat, and his personal belongings.

From the jungles to the open fields, we walked along a path. We came across a trail of red ants and, being a stubborn child, I refused to walk over them. I wanted someone to pick me up because I was scared, but my parents kept walking ahead. They kept telling me to hurry up and to step over the ants, but I just stood there and cried. Finally, my father came back and put me on his shoulders, along with the heavy sack of rice he was carrying. My dad said he carried me on his back practically all the way to Thailand.

I also recall a car accident we had. My father had paid a truck-driver to take my family and relatives to a nearby town. There were about fifteen of us in the truck. My father, along with the driver and my pregnant aunt, sat in front. The rest of us were in the bed of the truck. While going up a steep mountain, the truck got out of control and, instead of going uphill, started sliding downhill and off the road. Everyone was terrified, but with the help of God, the truck was stopped by a tree stump. Everyone panicked and scrambled out, except for my pregnant aunt who was trapped on the passenger's side because the door was jammed. The impact affected her so much that she could not crawl from her seat to the driver's side in order to get out. My father risked his life to save hers. The rest of us stood back and waited breath-

lessly as he tried to open the jammed door. He managed to free her just as the truck slid down the hill.

Our adventure did not end then — many nights filled with terror were yet to come. After experiencing many cold days and rainy nights, we finally saw Thailand on the other side of the Mekong River. My parents bribed several fishermen to row us across. The fishermen knew we were desperate, yet, instead of helping us, they took advantage of us. We had to give them all our valuables: silver bars, silver coins, paper money, and my mother's silver wedding necklace, which had cost a lot of money. When it got dark, the fishermen came back with a small fishing boat and took us across the river. The currents were high and powerful. I remember being very scared. I kept yelling, "We're going to fall out! We're going to fall into the river!" My mom tried to reassure me but I kept screaming in fear. Finally, we got across safely. My family, along with many other families, were picked up by the Thai police and taken to an empty bus station for the night.

After a whole month at this temporary refugee camp set up in the bus station, during which we ate rice, dried fish, roots we dug up, and bamboo shoots we cut down, and drank water from streams, we were in very poor shape due to the lack of nutrition. Our feet were also swollen from walking. We were then taken to a refugee camp in Nongkhai, where disease was rampant and many people got sick. My family suffered a loss: my baby sister, who was only a few months old, died. She had become very skinny from the lack of milk, and there was no medical care available. The memory of her death still burns in my mind like a flame. On the evening she died, my older sister and I were playing with our cousins outside the building where we stayed. My father came out to tell us the sad news and told us to go find my stepuncle. After we found him, we went inside and saw our mother mourning the baby's death. Fortunately, our family had relatives around to support and comfort us.

Life in the refugee camp was very difficult. Rice, fish, vegetables, and water were delivered to the camp, but the ration for each family was never enough. Many times, the food my family received did not last until the next delivery. My parents went out to work in the fields to earn a little extra money to buy food. As a child, I did not understand why we had to work so hard and live so poorly.

When I left Laos, I was only three years old. I do not remember much of our life there, but my parents have told me that our family had been quite well off. We had our own house, cattle, rice fields, and a garden where all our vegetables were grown. The money my father received for serving in the army was saved, for there was little need for money. We had enough to eat because we grew our own food. The poor life in the camp is the only life I can remember. I saw my parents' suffering, but I was too young to understand why life was so difficult. Only later did I realize that I and thousands of other young children were victims of a cruel war. Our family remained in Nongkhai for three agonizing years, with our fate uncertain and our future obscure.

Our family life in the camp was very unstable, characterized by deprivation and neglect. My older sister and I were left alone for days while my parents were outside the camp trying to earn money to buy extra food. My parents fought a lot during this period, because we were all under such stress. They knew that if we remained in Thailand, there would be no telling what would become of us. We *had* to find a better life. Some people in the camp were being sponsored to go to the United States. The news spread that anyone who had served in the military with the CIA could apply to go to America. Since my stepuncle had already gone there two years earlier, he sponsored my family. Because my father had been in the military and we had a sponsor, it took only six months to process our papers when usually it took a year or more.

I can still recall the process of leaving the camp. Our relatives, whom we were leaving behind, walked my family from our house to the bus that was to take us to Bangkok. We boarded the bus with our few belongings. People hung out of the windows to touch loved ones for the last time. They cried, knowing they might never meet again. As the buses slowly made their way through the crowd, people ran after them calling out the names of their relatives. "Have a safe trip to your new home!" they shouted. "Don't forget us who are left behind! Please write and tell us about your new life!" Quickly the camp vanished out of sight . . . forever. The moments filled with laughter and tears shared with close friends and relatives were now just faint memories.

It took a full day to travel to Bangkok, where we stayed for four nights. The building we stayed in was one huge room. It was depressing and nerve-wracking. I especially remember how, when we got off the bus to go into the building, a small child about my age came up to my family to beg for food. I recall the exact words she said to my father, "Uncle, can you give me some food? I am hungry. My parents are dead and I am here alone." My dad gave her a piece of bread that we had packed for our lunch. After she walked away, my family found an empty corner and rolled out our bedding for the night. That night, the same child came around again, but people chased her away, which made me sad.

In the morning, I ran to get in line for breakfast. Each person received a bowl of rice porridge with a few strips of chicken in it. For four days, we remained in that building, not knowing when we could leave for the United States. Many families had been there for weeks, months, perhaps even years. On the fourth day, my family was notified to be ready early the next morning to be taken to the airport. The plane ride took a long time and I got motion sickness. I threw up a lot. Only when I saw my stepuncle's face after we landed did I know we had come to the end of our journey. We had come in search of a better life in the "land of giants."

On October 2, 1978, my family arrived at Los Angeles International Airport, where my uncle was waiting anxiously. We stayed with my uncle in Los Angeles for two weeks and then settled in Isla Vista because there were already a few Hmong families there. We knew only one family in Isla Vista, but later we met other families whom my parents had known in their village and from villages nearby. It was in Isla Vista that my life really began. My home life was now more stable. My mother gave birth to a boy a month after we arrived in the United States. It was a joyous event because the first three children she had were all girls. [Boys are desired and valued far more than girls in Hmong culture.] My family also accepted Christ into our lives. My parents still fought once in a while, but these fights were never like those they had in Thailand. The birth of my brother marked the beginning of a new life for us all.

I entered kindergarten at Isla Vista Elementary School. The first day was scary because I could not speak any English. Fortunately, my cousin, who had been in the United States for three years and spoke English, was in the same class with me. She led me to the playground where the children were playing.

I was shocked to see so many faces of different colors. The Caucasian students shocked me the most. I had never seen people with blond hair before. The sight sent me to a bench, where I sat and watched everyone in amazement. In class, I was introduced to coloring. I did not know how to hold a crayon or what it was for. My teacher had to show me how to color. I also soon learned the alphabet. This was the beginning of my lifelong goal to get an education.

I loved it in Isla Vista. When my family first settled there, we shared a three-bedroom apartment with another family. Altogether, there were fifteen of us. My family of five shared one room. A few years later, our family shared another three-bedroom apartment with two other families. There were twenty of us in this household. By then, I had four sisters and a brother; we all lived in the same room. I never knew what it was like to have my own room or bed. From this experience of living with so many people, I learned many valuable lessons that helped me to grow. I learned how to share but at the same time to respect the privacy of others. I also realized the uniqueness of my people. No matter how tough a situation is, we all stick together and help each other get through it. So long as there are other Hmong around, no individual Hmong will starve in the streets.

The rising rents in Isla Vista soon made it impossible for my family to continue living there. We moved to Lompoc, which is where my family now lives. There is a sizable Hmong community in Lompoc today. I now have eight sisters and one brother. I am the second oldest. People are usually shocked to hear there are so many of us. I believe that being part of such a large family has helped shape the person that I am today. My willingness to share was reinforced because there were so many of us to care for. I also learned to value many aspects of life that many people take for granted. My family is not rich. We live on the meager salary that my father brings home each week, which is never enough. For as long as I can remember, we got new clothes on only two special occasions: on our traditional Hmong New Year and at the beginning of each school year. There was always food on the table, but just enough that we did not go hungry. We could never afford snacks like cookies, chips, sodas, or fruits. Toys were unknown to me as a child. I never had a Barbie doll or a playhouse — things one might assume every child [in America] has.

My family is very patriarchal. Very early in my life, I was taught the manners that any proper Hmong female should have. I was taught the duties of a daughter. In the Hmong community, there is a clear and stereotypical understanding of how a daughter should act and what duties she must perform. In other words, all Hmong daughters are expected to be alike. A Hmong daughter should know how to cook and clean. She must get up earlier than her parents in the morning. If she doesn't, she is considered lazy. No girl wants that reputation because every girl is taught that if she is known to be lazy, no man would want her. A daughter is expected to stay home to help with the chores. During her free time, she has to occupy herself with needlework, which is called *pangdao*. Sons, on the other hand, are free to do whatever they choose. They are never expected to cook or help around the house.

When I became a teenager, I was never allowed to go out with a boy alone. When I got older and proved to my parents that I was responsible enough to have a boyfriend, they did not object, but still, we could not go out on dates by ourselves. Some of my sisters or my brother always had to go along, or I had to be with a large group. But having adopted the American belief that an individual should be free to choose his or her friends, many times I have gone out behind my parents' back. I believe it is wrong of me to do so, but because I am not allowed to go out even with people I trust, I feel I have no choice. If my parents were not so strict about dating, I would not go against their wishes. In a sense, their attitude drove me to rebel. Although I disagree with the restrictions they impose on me, I understand their reasoning. My parents feel a need to restrict my sisters and me because they fear they would lose control over us otherwise. They want to protect us from embarrassment and shame.

Although my parents have always been very strict, I was really surprised that they did not object at all when I wanted to go to college. In my culture, girls get married at a very young age. So, even though my parents encouraged me to get a higher education, they do not feel certain that I shall complete my studies. Since they came to America, they have seen many Hmong girls start college, but then get married and leave school before completing their degrees. They cannot grasp the idea that one can still get a college education after one gets married. My parents believe that a college education, which they understand serves as a ticket to a secure and comfortable future, is possible only when one is still single. They think once a young woman starts a family, she would not have time for school and a career.

As the first child in my family to go to college, and as a daughter, I face a lot of pressure. I feel it is my duty to prove, not only to my parents but also to other Hmong parents, that a daughter can do anything that a son can do—perhaps even more. My parents are very old-fashioned and set in their ways. In many respects, they raised us as they themselves were raised, but at the same time, they have pushed us toward a life they have never known. They do not understand that there is a gap between their generation and ours. Growing up in American society, I am caught between two very different cultures.

The kind of physical affection and words of praise that many American parents express are unknown in my family. My parents seldom converse with my sisters, brother, and me. They are very indirect in their communication and actions. They never tell us they love us, nor do they congratulate us when we accomplish something. They believe strongly that people should not show their feelings and emotions. I don't remember ever touching my parents' hands or embracing them. It is sad, but it would be awkward to hug them or hold their hands. Americans touch and hug each other all the time. In my culture, if a married man or woman hugs someone of the opposite sex, it is assumed the two individuals are in love, and rumors would fly, and jealousy would grow. Even married couples do not walk side by side. One, usually the husband, must walk in front of the other. It is considered disrespectful to elders if we touch them or walk in front of them.

My father never says much when he is home, but when he does talk to us, we know it must be serious. Because my father has to drive an hour each way to Goleta to get to work, our family sees him only for a few hours a night. On the weekends, he is too tired to spend time with his children. He hardly ever smiles. Many times, I think to myself, "He must be a sad and lonely man because he is one of only two survivors in his family as the result of a cold and deadly war." I feel sorry for him.

In one year, he lost two older brothers, whom we had left behind in Laos. One of them died after months of suffering. He had been in a car accident, but there was no medical care available to help him recover. My other uncle, after five years in a refugee camp in Thailand, decided he wanted to come to the United States. After studying for six months to prepare himself for the dramatic changes he and his family would encounter, he died suddenly in his sleep. This Sudden Unexplained Nocturnal Death Syndrome has affected many Hmong. We do not know the cause of his death, only that he died in peace. He went to bed and never woke up again. When my father received the news, he cried so much. It made me really sad to see him cry, because even though he has always looked sad to me, he has never said anything about how he feels or shown the pain he carries in his overburdened heart. Having learned the American way of expressing myself, I wanted to say something to him or just to hold him to let him know that I love him, but I could not bring myself to do so.

I felt awkward expressing my love to him either verbally or physically because my parents have never told us in words that they love us, nor have they shown any appreciation for the good deeds or services we have performed or for our achievements at school. They express their love only by the food they provide us with at each meal and the roof over our heads. It was not until this past summer (1992) that I learned that my parents in fact long to hear us children tell them, *"Niam thiab txiv, kuv hlub neb"* (Mom and Dad, we love you). This past summer, when I was at Maranatha Bible Camp in Nebraska for an annual conference held by the Hmong Youth Rally Zone, one of the pastors' sermons made me realize that should anything happen to my parents, I would not be able to live with the guilt of never having told them that I love them. That night, I called home and talked to my parents. And yes, I told them that for the past twenty years of my life, I have loved them with all my heart. In reply, my mother said that they loved me also and that they thought they would never hear any of us children tell them that.

My mother is very different from my father. She talks a lot and she is always complaining about how hard life is in America. She cannot go anywhere by herself because she cannot speak English well enough. My older sister and I have always been her interpreters and translators. For as long as I can remember, we have taken turns taking my mother to the grocery store, to parent–teacher conferences, to the doctor, and to other events that require communication. Every month when the utility bills come or when rent is due, she fusses about how we have so many bills to pay in the United States. She is right, of course. My mother is always making a comparison between our old life back in Laos and our new life here in California. "We didn't have to pay rent because we had built our own house. Electricity and gas were not available, yet we managed to survive. We had to haul water from nearby springs, but there was plenty of it. There were always fresh vegetables from our garden and our cattle provided milk and meat. We had no worries about what we would eat the next day or whether we had enough money to pay the bills."

Although her complaints get to me sometimes, I see in her a very courageous and caring woman. She has, in a single lifetime, gone through the worst I can imagine. When she shares with me her life story, I wish I had been there to help her in times of hardship. My grandparents divorced when my mother was only a few months old. She never knew her father. Her mother remarried shortly afterward. My grandmother died when my mother was only eleven or twelve years old, leaving her with her stepsister, who was five or six, and her stepbrother, who was a few months old. My stepgrandfather had two other wives, so these women were asked to care for my mother and her siblings, but they made my mother into their slave. My mother practically raised her brother and sister until she married my father at the age of sixteen. Even after her marriage, she worked hard. Throughout her life, she has never had a break. And now, she has ten children. Imagine how hectic that must be, especially in the United States, when the average number of children in a family is only two or three.

My mother is my mentor, my guide, and my shelter. Although I know I can never make up for the hard life she has led, I thank her for bringing me into this world. She has taught me to see through all the hatred and suffering in this world and to look at the good side that I know how to appreciate: my family.

When I was younger, lectures from my parents were dreadful to listen to. As I recall, the themes running through all their lectures were: "Don't forget where you came from and who you are! Nothing comes easy without sweat from your brow! Study hard and pursue your education to the best of your ability!" When I was young, I thought I knew everything about life. Those words of wisdom meant nothing to me. I was too busy trying to become a typical American girl, going out on dates, wearing nice clothes and makeup, and voicing my opinion when I felt my parents were wrong to tell me what to do and what not to do. I was ashamed of my heritage, of where I had come from, of who I was, and even of my parents who could not speak good English. I found it embarrassing and even shameful to speak my native language. I wanted so much to be like my "Americanized" Hmong-American friends. I felt I had to change my identity or risk rejection from my peers.

Now that I am older, I treasure the long but valuable lessons my parents tried to teach us — lessons that gave me a sense of identity as a Hmong. "Nothing comes easy. . . . ," my parents always said. As I attempt to get a college education, I remember how my parents have been really supportive of me financially throughout my schooling, but because they never had a chance to get an education themselves, they were not able to help me whenever I could not solve a math problem or write an English paper. Although they cannot help me in my schoolwork, I know in my heart that they care about me and want me to be successful so that I can help them when they can no longer help themselves. Therefore, I am determined to do well at the university. I want to become a role model for my younger brother and sisters, for I am the very first member of my family to attend college. I feel a real sense of accomplishment to have set such an example.

♦♦♦

CHAPTER THREE

Body Politics

Our bodies grow and develop from the first moments of life; they provide us with a living, physical basis for our identity where all aspects of our selves are literally embodied. The life cycle — from birth to youth to aging to dying — plays itself out through our bodies, minds, and emotions as we experience these life stages. Through our bodies we feel pain, and we experience sexuality, healing, and the complex physical, hormonal, neurological, and emotional changes that come with menstruation and menopause, pregnancy, and aging. Many of us develop and experience physical strength, stamina, agility, concentration, and coordination through exercise, dance, sports, martial arts, and outdoor activities. We show our dexterity in such things as handling tools, from kitchen knives to hammers and saws, or in fixing cars. We experience our bodies' suppleness through yoga. Pregnancy and childbirth provide intense understanding of our elasticity, strength, and stamina and the wonder of being able to sustain another body developing inside us. We have an awareness of our bodily rhythms throughout the day or through the menstrual cycle — the ups and downs of mental and physical energy, tiredness, stiffness, and cramps — and of bodily changes that are part of growing older.

Although there are physiological, financial, and technological limits to how much we can shape them, up to a point our bodies are malleable and we can change how we look, who we are, or who we appear to be. We make choices about clothing, hair, makeup, tattoos or piercing, as well as gestures and mannerisms. We may diet or exercise, use skin-lightening creams or tanning salons, have a nose job or tummy tuck, and consciously adopt particular postures and body language. We may have corrective surgeries for disabilities; our bodies may be altered by mastectomy due to breast cancer; we may need to use reading glasses, wheelchairs, or hearing aids. Transsexual people may choose to have surgery to make their physical appearance congruent with their internal sense of self. Others may deliberately defy cultural boundaries of sex and gender by looking as androgynous as possible or by changing their appearance in "gender-bending" ways.

The dominant culture often reduces women to bodies, valuing us only as sex objects or as bearers of children. Postmenopausal women, for example, are sometimes thought of as no longer "real" women, their lifework over. This chapter is concerned with how we as women think and feel about our bodies, the impact of idealized images of beauty, and the ways gender and sexuality are both grounded in our bodies and socially constructed. Something as intimate and personal as how we feel about our bodies is thus also profoundly cultural and political.

In *The Second Sex*, Simone de Beauvoir (1973) argued that gender is neither biological nor natural but learned; she concluded that one is not born a woman but, rather, becomes one. The body is the place where biological sex and socially constructed gender come together. In Chapter 1 Anne Fausto-Sterling describes how intersexual people challenge the binary categories of male/female in a fundamental way. Their social and surgical treatment—being pressured to choose a specific gender and stick with it—shows how important this dichotomy is in our society. Judith Butler (1990) notes that gender is usually thought of as a noun—a quality or characteristic that people possess. Against this, she argues that gender is performative, a verb, "a doing" (p. 25), and that we all "do" gender all the time, styling our bodies and behavior, putting on costume and makeup, playing our roles, so that over time gender seems natural.

The Beauty Ideal

Starting in childhood with dolls like Barbie, women and girls in the United States are bombarded with images showing what they should look like and how to achieve this look. Movies, TV programs, posters, billboards, magazine articles, and ads all portray images of the "perfect" woman. She is young and tall, with long legs, small breasts and hips, smooth skin, and well-groomed hair. Her body is trim, toned, and very lean. In some years cleavage is the desired trait; in others, it may be fuller lips; but the basic formula holds. Thus, Wolf (1991) notes that "450 full time American fashion models who constitute the elite corps [are] deployed in a way that keeps 150 million women in line" (p. 41). In most of these images the women are White. Where women of color are used, they are often light-skinned and conform to this same body type.

By contrast, in real life women come in all shapes, sizes, and skin tones. Many of us have rounded—even sagging—breasts and stomachs. We may have varicose veins, scars, stretch marks, warts, wrinkles, or blemishes, and definitely body hair. Many are short and stocky and will never look tall and willowy no matter how many diets and exercise routines they follow. The ideal standard of beauty is one that even the models themselves cannot achieve. Magazine ads and feature photos are airbrushed and enhanced photographically using computer-based image processing to get rid of imperfections and promote the illusion

of flawlessness (Dziemianowicz 1992). Not only do these images show no blemishes; they rarely even show pores.

Because this ideal of beauty is all around us it is not surprising that many women and girls—including models and film stars—think there is something wrong with their bodies and work hard, even obsessively, to eliminate, or at least reduce their "flaws" (Naidus 1993; Lakoff and Scherr 1984). As girls and teenagers many of us learn to inspect our bodies critically and to loathe ourselves. Many young children pick up the idea that fat is bad; girls aged eight or nine are on self-imposed diets; many teenage girls think they are overweight, and by college age one in eight young women in the United States is bulimic, imagining herself to be much fatter than she actually is. Jen Hill (1993) describes her struggle to like her looks in her teens:

> I began this journey in the tenth grade when I stopped wearing makeup in a compulsory fashion. I used to be addicted to it; it was my self-made face and the cover I told the world was me. As long as I could control what I thought of myself, I could control what others thought of me, because, after all, weren't they the same thing? . . . Sometimes [these] top layers were precarious, especially if I caught myself in the mirror at the wrong time in the wrong, unplanned position or looked at the wrong photographs when my eyes were looking elsewhere, and then I could see what I thought I had successfully killed. I'd have to go mirror-dance and pose it off until the power came back.
>
> *(p. 1)*

In Reading 18 Meredith Lee describes the self-acceptance and empowerment she felt when, as a college student who had often felt bad about her body, she dared to pose nude for a friend's photography project and also shaved her head.

The Beauty Business

Ideal standards of beauty are reinforced by, and a necessary part of, the multibillion-dollar beauty industry that sees women's bodies only in terms of a series of problems in need of correction. These notions of ideal beauty are a very effective way for men—as well as women—to compare and judge women and to keep them on the treadmill of "body management."

The beauty business creates needs by playing on our insecurities about our bodies and selling us creams, lotions, sprays, and handy roll-ons to improve our complexions, deodorize body scents, curl, color, condition, and straighten hair, or get rid of unwanted body hair altogether. Americans spend more than $10 billion a year on diet drugs, exercise tapes, diet books, diet meals, weight-loss classes, diet doctors, diet surgery, and fat farms even though research reveals that most diets don't work (Fraser 1997). We buy exercise equipment and pay for fitness classes or to join a gym. We buy magazines that continually urge us to improve ourselves.

Bored with your looks? Create a new you

Work off those extra pounds! Be a successful eater

Do you have lazy skin? The over-40 look is over

Do you dress to hide your body? Shape up for Summer

Learn to dress thin

Women's magazines suggest that anyone who is comfortable with her body must be lazy or undisciplined, "letting herself go" rather than "making the best of herself." Laura Fraser (1997) describes women's attempts to be thin as a third job, in addition to being a desirable woman, wife, and mother and to working for a living.

Despite the fact that genes, metabolism, shape, and size set limits on the possibilities for drastic bodily changes, new technologies such as surgery and hormone therapies are pushing back the boundaries of what once was possible, defying natural processes. Liposuction, for example, described in ads as body "sculpting," is designed to remove unwanted body fat from people of normal weight and is one of the fastest-growing operations in the country, at a cost of some $5,000 per procedure. About 94 percent of liposuction patients are women (LaVigne 1989, p. 12). Ads emphasize the benefits of slimmer knees and thighs or smoother hips, but like any surgery, liposuction has risks: the chance of injuries to capillaries, nerves, and skin or the possibility of infection. Such risks, together with greater public discussion

Comparing Priorities

- An estimated 40,000–50,000 children worldwide, but mainly in Africa and Asia, die each day from malnutrition and a lack of clean water.

- Ten million women in the world need wheelchairs and do not have them. Ninety percent of women with disabilities worldwide are unemployed (Mobility International USA).

- Many rural women in Africa, Asia, Latin America, and the Caribbean get plenty of exercise, walking miles each day in search of firewood and water, which they carry home on their backs or their heads. They do laundry by hand, carrying it to rivers and ponds. They do heavy farm work, carry surplus produce to local markets, and pound flour for daily household use from rice, maize, or millet (Agarwal 1992; Dankelman and Davidson 1988).

- The dominance of Hollywood movies and U.S. magazines and TV shows means that the ideal images of beautiful White women appear around the world—despite the fact that White women are a small minority of the world's women. Skin-lightening creams and hair straighteners are produced in West Africa, for example, and eyelid operations are the most common form of cosmetic surgery in East Asian countries.

of the dangers of silicone breast implants, for example, have not stopped women from wanting surgical procedures to achieve their desired body profiles.

Commodification and Co-option

Striving to achieve and then maintain a perfect body is an ongoing project that takes time, energy, money, and determination. Our bodies become objects, commodities, somehow separate from ourselves, something to deplore and strive to change. We learn to see ourselves as disconnected parts: ankles, thighs, hips, bottoms, breasts, upper arms, noses, and chins, all in need of improvement; and this **objectification** of women by the advertising media paves the way for women's dismemberment (literal and figurative) in pornography. While women's bodies are used in ads to sell "beauty" products, they are also used to sell virtually everything else: soft drinks, beer, tires, cars, fax machines, chain saws, or gun holsters. The underlying message in a Diet Coke ad is: If someone as beautiful as this drinks Diet Coke, you should, too. You can look like this if you drink Diet Coke. The smiling women draped over cars or caressing fax machines in ads have nothing to do with the product; they are merely tools to draw men's attention and increase sales.

Ads are costly to produce and carefully thought out, with great attention to every detail: the style of the product, its name, color, the shape of the packaging, and the text and layout of the ads. Ad designers make it their business to know women's interests and worries, which they use, co-opt, and undermine. The Nike slogan "Just Do It!" appeals to women's sense of independence and self-directedness while co-opting it for the consumption of products. Another slogan, "Running like a Girl," takes the commonplace put-down and turns it into a compliment. Over twenty years ago Virginia Slims pioneered this kind of co-option with "You've Come a Long Way, Baby," to advertise a new brand of cigarettes designed specifically for women. The use of the word "Slims" is no accident, as many women smoke to control their weight. Wendy Chapkis (1986) notes that 1970s feminists' insistence that a woman is beautiful just as she naturally appears has also been co-opted by the cosmetics industry and "re-written in a commercial translation as the Natural Look. The horrible irony of this is, of course, that only a handful of women have the Natural Look naturally" (p. 8).

Whites Only? Forever Young? Always Able?

These ideal notions of beauty are racist, ageist, and ableist. Even though White women are held to unreasonable beauty standards, they see beauty all around them defined as White. Women of color, on the other hand, rarely see themselves reflected in mainstream images. Veronica Chambers (1995) criticizes White women who do not acknowledge or un-

derstand that this may make women of color hate their looks. "To say simply, 'I don't look like Cindy Crawford either,' or 'I think Whitney Houston is really beautiful,' doesn't address the real pain that many black women have experienced. We are still acculturated to hate our dark skin, our kinky hair, our full figures" (p. 26). For example, Naomi Wolf (1991) discusses how expectations of beauty affect women in the paid workforce but does not refer to African-American women. Chambers criticizes Wolf for failing to

> give voice to the many ways that black women are instructed to look as "white" as possible, especially with regard to their hair. She doesn't mention the African American flight attendant who brought a famous suit against her employers, who had fired her because she wore braids. She doesn't mention how often braids, dreads and even Afros are strictly prohibited in many workplaces, forcing black women to straighten their hair and wear styles that are more "mainstream".
>
> (p. 27)

Indeed, White standards of beauty together with internalized racism are responsible for a hierarchy of value based on color among some people of color in the United States. Reading 20, "The Coming of Maureen Peal," an excerpt from Toni Morrison's novel *The Bluest Eye*, shows the affirmation and validation given to a light-skinned African-American girl by her teachers, other adults, and her peers. In Reading 19 Nellie Wong describes the pain of having wanted to look White.

This ideal standard of beauty is also ageist. It emphasizes youth and associates youth with sexuality, especially for women. Gray-haired men are often thought distinguished or wise; women are urged to look young and are thought old at least a decade before men of the same age. The phrase "old woman" is used negatively in mainstream culture. Many middle-aged women do not like others to know their age or are flattered to be told that they look younger than they are. A combination of beauty products, diet, exercise, surgery, and wealth has made movie stars in their fifties, like Raquel Welch, Sophia Loren, and Jane Fonda, look much younger than their years. These women have redefined standards of beauty for middle-aged women in general and have sold thousands of copies of their exercise videos and other products. Oprah Winfrey's accounts of her struggles with diet, exercise, and weight losses and gains have also become best sellers. Books, tapes, and magazine articles advise women in their sixties and seventies about fitness, nutrition, and sexuality, with an emphasis on new interests, productive lives, and personal growth. Although these images are positive, they assume that older women have the money for dancing lessons, vacations, and retirement financial planning, for example, and give no suggestion that many older women live in poverty and poor health.

Aging is a lifelong process from birth onward. Most people have less physical energy, poorer eyesight and hearing, or weaker immune systems as they age. Eleanor Palo Stoller and Rose Campbell Gibson (1994) note that contemporary U.S. culture reflects mixed images of older people — as wise, understanding, generous, happy, knowledgeable, and patriotic, but also as forgetful, lonely, dependent, demanding, complaining, senile, selfish, and inflexible. Aging is a fact of life that cannot be prevented, despite face creams, hair dyes, or hormone treatments. Not all middle-aged or older women, however, mourn the passing of their youth. Many in their forties, fifties, or older feel that they have really come into themselves, into their own voice, with newfound confidence and purpose (Bird 1995). They find that these years may be a time of self-definition and autonomy in which they can resist earlier pressures to conform to dominant beauty standards or to set a good example. At the same time older women must come to terms with their changing looks, physical limitations, and loss of independence and loved ones. Elders are highly respected among many cultural groups, including Native Americans, African-Americans, Latinas, and Asian-Americans, by contrast with White U.S. society. In these cultures gray hair is a mark of honor associated with experience and wisdom, which, if they are lucky, young people may be able to share. In Reading 21 Barbara Macdonald discusses the process of aging. Annette Dula's description of "Miss Mildred," an elderly African-American woman, included in Chapter 7, is also relevant here.

In addition to being racist and ageist, this ideal standard of beauty is profoundly ableist. Even if one is not born with a disability, everyone ages and dies. Ynestra King (1991) notes:

The common ground for the person — the human body — is a shifting sand which can fail us at any time. It can change shape and properties without warning and this is an essential truth of embodied existence. Of all the ways of becoming "other" in our society, disability is the only one that can happen to anyone, in an instant, transforming their lives and their identity forever. Bodily life is provisional.

(p. 12)

In *Aché: A Journal for Lesbians of African Descent,* Aisha (1991) writes:

I personally feel that we all have challenges, some are visible and some are hidden, mine just happens to be physical but yours is still there! . . . Get in touch with the ways in which you are challenged by being able to share openly my challenge . . . and not become frightened by FEAR (False Evidence Appearing Real) superiority and bigotry. . . .

(p. 28)

Thanks to untiring campaigning on the part of people with disabilities and their nondisabled allies, the U.S. government passed the Americans with Disabilities Act in 1990, the only piece of legislation quite like it in the world, though its provisions are not universally observed or enforced. Roughly 20 percent of people in this country have some form of disability, including movement and orthopedic problems, poor physical or mental health that is disabling in some way, blindness, deafness, and learning disabilities (Mainstream 1997, p. 14). Despite their numbers, people with disabilities are largely absent from the mainstream media, or portrayed as pitiful victims — helpless and passive — or freaks. In the readings that follow, Ernestine Patterson (Reading 22) and Donna Walton (Reading 23) argue that they are handicapped by the mental limitations of nondisabled people.

Resisting Beauty Stereotypes

Many women struggle long and hard to reconcile who they are and what their bodies are like with the commercial ideal of beauty. Others do not buy into it but may need to make concessions occasionally, such as wearing appropriate clothes and makeup for work or family gatherings.

As discussed earlier, beauty standards are always cultural constructions. For instance, in African-American communities, very thin, boyish-looking women are not necessarily thought beautiful. Queen T'hisha notes,

> Racism and sexism as practiced in America [include] body hostilities. I didn't grow up with the belief that fat women were to be despised. The women in my family were fat, smart, sexy, employed, wanted, married, and the rulers of their households.
>
> *(Quoted in Edison and Notkin 1994, p. 106)*

Extreme thinness may be associated with poverty, malnutrition, and illnesses such as cancer or AIDS, which eat the body away from the inside. Women who are large, fleshy, and rounded embody strength, sexiness, comfort, and nurturance. United States Jewish culture has the word *zaftig*, a positive term for voluptuous women.

Large women challenge many stereotypes and taken-for-granted assumptions: that they are undisciplined, depressed, sexless, unwanted, or unhealthy; that they have only themselves to blame for letting themselves go. Elise Matthesen argues,

> We have a right to take up space. We have a right to stretch out, to be big, old, to be "too much to handle." To challenge the rest of the world to grow up, get on with it, and become big enough themselves to 'handle' us. . . .
>
> *(Quoted in Edison and Notkin 1994, p. 107)*

And Dora Dewey-McCracken confounds common assumptions about fatness with regard to health:

> I've been diabetic since I was nineteen. . . . All my life I gained and lost at least sixty pounds each year. . . . I tried all diets, eating disorders, and fasts, only to gain the fat back, and more each time. I'm the fattest I've ever been, and yet my diabetic blood work is the best it's ever been. My doctor once told me, "As long as your disease is controlled and your blood chemistry is good, your fat is just a social issue." I'm extremely lucky to have this doctor; with most doctors, fat-phobia is the rule, not

the exception. They see the fat and their brains turn off. . . .

(Quoted in Edison and Notkin 1994, p. 104)

Feminist Perspectives on Body Politics

Women tend to be viewed from the outside, in terms of how they look, while men are judged in terms of what they do. Constantly promoting an ideal body image is a very effective way of oppressing women and girls, taking up time, money, and attention that could be devoted to other aspects of their lives, like education or self-development, or to wider issues such as the need for affordable health care, child care, elder care, and jobs with decent pay and benefits. Striving for a better body keeps us in check. Although ideals of beauty—and fashions in clothes, makeup, hairstyles, and body shape—are not new, Hesse-Biber (1991) notes that they have become increasingly stringent and elusive, where the goal is a body that is not only slender but also sculpted and firm, with a smooth, sleek profile. Over the past twenty-five years or so women in the United States have made gains toward greater equality with men in education and admission to professions and manual trades with higher pay scales. But, as Faludi (1991) notes in her analysis of the backlash against women's progress, as women have gained more independence socially and economically, body standards have become harder to achieve.

Susan Bordo (1993) notes the contradictory ideals and directives girls and women receive about femininity from contemporary culture that may affect women's attitude to food and eating. She argues that the **gendered division of labor,** under which women have the main responsibility for home and nurturing and men are mainly active in the public sphere, has barely changed despite women's entry into jobs and professions once closed to them. Women in the United States are supposed to nurture and care for men—their fathers, brothers, boyfriends, husbands, lovers, bosses, colleagues, and sons. Thus women learn to feed others—emotionally and literally—rather than themselves. Young, White middle-class women and upper-middle-class women in the United States are severely affected by eating disorders like anorexia and bulimia (Thompson 1994; Russell 1995; Fraser 1997). Abra Chernik's article in

Chapter 1 about her experience with anorexia is relevant here.

At the same time, Bordo (1989) notes that women who aspire to be successful professionally "must also learn to embody the 'masculine' language and values of that arena — self control, determination, cool, emotional discipline, mastery, and so on" (pp. 18–19). The boyish body ideals of current fashion ads suggest a new freedom from the limitations of reproductive femininity, but when placed next to solid, muscular male models, these ultra-slim women also look fragile and powerless. Part of their allure, it seems, is in this relative powerlessness, in their image as little girls who will never grow up to be true equals. As sex objects, women are commonly portrayed as playthings, an image accentuated by doll-like or childlike images.

Many women flout dominant beauty standards: by not using makeup, for example, by wearing sensible shoes and practical clothes, or by showing hairy legs and underarms. Some breast cancer survivors who have had one or both breasts removed have chosen to go without artificial breasts or have had their mastectomy scars tattooed. Some women challenge conventional standards by gender-bending, pushing the boyish look beyond the dictates of current mainstream fashion into a more genuinely androgynous area. Sexual orientation is very significant here. Idealized beauty standards are one aspect of the oppression of women; another related aspect is what Rich (1986b) has called compulsory heterosexuality. Judith Butler (1990) considers "the binary framework for both sex and gender" to be "regulatory fictions" that consolidate and naturalize the power of masculine and heterosexist oppression (p. 33). Similarly, Wittig (1992) argues that "the straight mind" assumes that heterosexuality is at the core of society; gender conformity is a powerful means of social control over women — and men.

There are many ways to be a woman, a spectrum of looks and behaviors, ranging from the conventionally feminine at one end to being able to pass for a man at the other, with various ambiguous femme/butch combinations in between. Lesbians in the 1950s and 1960s, for example, who identified themselves as butch or femme, adopted dress and hairstyles accordingly. Joan Nestle (1992) argues that this was not a replication of heterosexual gender polarization but "a lesbian-specific way of deconstructing gender that radically reclaims women's erotic energy" (p. 14). Many 1970s lesbian feminists saw idealized notions of beauty as oppressive to women and also critiqued butch-femme roles as inherently patriarchal. They adopted flannel shirts, overalls, and short hair almost as a uniform, in rejection of conventional womanly looks. Current fashion includes practical boots and shoes and leather jackets for women, and fashion ads portray androgynous women, suggesting bisexuality or lesbianism. Lesbian and gay characters are turning up in films and TV shows, and *Vanity Fair* has done an issue on "lesbian chic." As women push the boundaries of gender and sexual categories, this is represented in the media and also co-opted.

Butler's (1990) conception of gender as performative both allows and requires us to think of gender more fluidly than rigid gender categories permit. It also opens up the possibility that, under less repressive circumstances, people would have a much wider repertoire of gender behaviors than they currently do. Those who refuse to tailor their looks and actions to conventional categories — butch lesbians, cross-dressers, drag queens, and queers, described by Feinberg (1996) as "transgender warriors" — are involved in something profoundly transgressive and challenging in this culture. Drag, for example, plays with the idea of appearance as an illusion, mimics and parodies conventions, and raises questions as to who the person really is — in terms of both outside appearance and inner identity (Garber 1992). Young people are reclaiming the word *queer,* which for many older lesbians and gay men was a hateful and oppressive term, and see transgenderism as experimental, playful, and fun (Bernstein and Silberman 1996). At the same time, Butler notes that people "who fail to do their gender right" (p. 140), by the standards held to be appropriate in specific contexts and at particular times, may be punished for it, through name calling, discrimination, hate, and outright violence.

Feinberg (1996) sees transgenderism as a cutting-edge development, but for Raymond (1994) it involves "more style than substance" (p. xxxv). She argues that transgenderism is not a transformative movement because it does not deal with structural inequalities of power between men and women. Whether it can do so raises the question of how personal freedoms, played out through sexuality and the body, are connected to other political issues and other progressive groups in society.

The Sexual Body

Exploring and Defining Sexuality

Sexual attitudes and behaviors vary considerably from society to society (Caplan 1987). According to Katz (1995) heterosexuality is a relatively recent concept. First used in the 1890s, it was an obscure medical term applied to nonprocreative sex — that is, sex for pleasure — which was considered a deviant idea, showing "abnormal or perverted appetite toward the opposite sex" (p. 86). Webster's dictionary first included the word in 1934, and it gradually came into common usage in the United States as a "stable sign of normal sex" (p. 40).

In the 1960s there was much talk of a sexual revolution, partly made possible by the availability of contraceptive pills for the first time. In practice this "revolution" was very much on men's terms, though women have also become more aware and vocal about their own sexual needs and preferences (Ehrenreich, Hess, and Jacobs 1986). Women's magazines are one forum for this discourse, as are women's erotica (Reynolds 1992; Bright and Blank 1991). These developments are liberating to women but may also be co-opted and undermined by masculinist interests, which applaud women wanting sex on their own terms as "do me feminism," for example.

There is much hype about sex in this society, and there are many taboos about it; though there is a great deal of pressure on young people to be sexually active, there is a dearth of detailed information about women's sexuality. Shere Hite, one of the few popular researchers to have conducted extensive surveys of men's and women's sexual experiences and preferences, included the following questions for women in one of her surveys:

Is sex important to you? What part does it play in your life?

Who sets the pace and style of sex—you or your partner or both? Who decides when it's over?

Do you think your genital area and vagina are ugly or beautiful?

If you are sexually active do you ever fake orgasms? Why?

What are your best sex experiences? What would you like to try that you never have?

What is it about sex that gives you the greatest pleasure? Displeasure?

Have you chosen to be celibate at any point? What was/is that like for you?

In the best of all possible worlds what would sexuality be like?

Do you know as much as you'd like to know about your own body? Orgasm? Conception and pregnancy? Safe sex?

Do your partners know about your sexual desires and your body? If not, do you ask for it or act yourself to get it?

(1994, pp. 17–22)

To explore your sexuality, ideally you need a comfortable, safe place and freedom from worries about being attractive, getting pregnant, or getting sexually transmitted diseases. You also need time, self-awareness, and a cooperative partner to work out what you want sex to be for you. Sexuality is not instinctive but is learned from popular culture, negotiations with partners, and listening to our own bodies. Over the course of our lives it may take very different forms and take on different degrees of significance. Lillian Gonzales Brown of the Institute on Disability Culture (Las Cruces, New Mexico) notes the change in attitude for people with disabilities as a result of the disability rights activism, from shame to assimilationism to pride and celebration of difference. In workshops on sexuality for women with disabilities she urges participants to explore their sexuality and to see themselves as sexual beings (L. G. Brown, personal communications, October, 1996).

Lesbians and gay men have challenged the legitimacy and "normalcy" of heterosexuality. More recently, bisexual people have argued for greater fluidity in sexual desire and behaviors (Weise 1992). Eridani (1992) suggests that sexual orientation, meaning a "deeply rooted sense . . . that serious relationships are possible only with persons of the opposite sex or the same sex" (p. 174), is in itself a male perspective. She argues that many women are probably bisexual and do not fit into a gay/straight categorization. Transsexuals who choose sexual reassignment surgery to bring their bodies into line with how they think about themselves both challenge binary gender categories and reinforce them (Burke 1996). Janice Raymond (1994) sees reliance on surgery as avoiding a more public, political resistance to the limitations of current gender categories. She comments: "Although popular literature on transsexualism implies that Nature has made a mistake with transsexuals, it is really society that has made the mistake by producing conditions that create the transsexual body/mind split" (p. 115). She argues that defining transsexualism in medical terms means that people who think they are in the "wrong" bodies are not encouraged to question polarized gender roles. She uses the term "male to constructed female" to emphasize all those aspects of gender that are learned and cannot be transmitted through surgery or hormone treatments.

Sexuality and Power

Compared with men, most women in the United States have little structural power in terms of money, professional status, inherited wealth, or political influence. Women who are considered beautiful, though, have this personal power, which may help them "catch" a man but is no guarantee that he will stay. Robin Lakoff and Raquel Sherr (1984) argue that this power is more illusory than real when compared with material wealth and political clout. Moreover, beauty, as conventionally defined, does not last; to the extent that beautiful women have personal power they will probably lose it as they age.

In ads and popular culture, sexuality is only for the young and slender and usually heterosexual. Ads that use women's bodies to sell products also sell an idea of women's sexuality as passivity. Typically, men are the initiators in heterosexual encounters. A woman's role is to lure men, to fend them off, and only to give in when the time is right. Like beauty, sexuality is an important power and one of the few most women have. Because this economic system tends to turn everything into a commodity for sale, it is no surprise that sexuality is also commodified through sex work, and that there is an eroticization of power, played out through sexual dominance and submission. It is also important to note that many girls and women experience coercion and abuse — whether in childhood or as adults — in some cases struggling for many years with the devastating effects of sexual abuse on their confidence, trust, sexuality, and sense of themselves in the world. We take up this issue further in the next chapter.

Writing about the erotic as power, Lorde (1984) uses a very broad definition of the erotic. She sees "the erotic [as] a measure between our sense of self and the chaos of our strongest feelings" and notes that women have been "taught to separate the erotic . . . from most vital areas of our lives other than sex" (p. 55). By contrast, she writes: "When I speak of the erotic . . . I speak of it as an assertion of the life-force of women; of that creative energy empowered, the knowledge and use of which we are now reclaiming in our language, our history, our dancing, our loving, our work, our lives . . ." (p. 55).

Body Politics and Activist Groups

Numerous women's organizations and projects across the country are working on the issues raised in this chapter. Organizations that challenge sexist media images, for example, include the Body Image Task Force (Santa Cruz, Calif.), Challenging Media Images of Women (Framingham, Mass.), and Media Watch and Media Action Alliance (Circle Pines, Minn.). Those challenging fat oppression include the Boston Area Fat Liberation (Cambridge, Mass.), the Council on Size and Weight Discrimination (Mount Marion, N.Y.), Largess — the Network for Size Esteem (New Haven, Conn.), and the National Association to Advance Fat Acceptance (Sacramento, Calif.). The Grey Panthers (Washington, D.C.) and the Older Women's League (Washington, D.C.) both have many local chapters that advocate for older women around a range of issues, including prejudice and discrimination based on age and looks. Senior Action in a Gay Environment (New York) and the National Pacific/Asian Resource Center on Aging (Seattle, Wash.) support particular groups. Centers for Independent Living in many cities work with women with disabilities, as do projects like the Disabled Women's Theater Project (New York), and dance groups for women with disabilities.

As you read and discuss the readings that follow, consider these questions:

1. How do you feel about your own body? Have you always felt this way? Do you expect to always feel about your body as you do today?

2. What is your idea of a beautiful woman? Have you always thought this?

3. Do you think that makeup, piercing, tattooing, dieting, and body building make women look beautiful? Sexy? Are they the same thing?

4. Think about the ways that glamour photos of stars and advertising images of women affect how you feel about your own body.

5. Where do the concepts of underweight and overweight come from?

6. How do you feel good about your own body? About yourself? Are they different?

7. What do/can you do to feel good about your body?

8. How do you react to images of women who do not fit the feminine stereotype — for example, women with facial hair, women who are old, fat, mannish, or in wheelchairs?

9. What images of women do you consider positive? Where do you find them?

10. How can you contribute to the public display of positive images of women and girls?

11. What is old to you? What does aging mean to you?

12. What can/can't you do now that you could/couldn't do earlier in life? (Think of physical, mental, emotional, and spiritual aspects.)

13. What are the meanings of old age reflected in birthday cards?

14. What are positive images of aging? How can aging be celebrated in women's lives?

15. What images of older women would you have liked to have seen when you were younger?

16. What questions would you like to ask older women?

17. How would you organize activities on campus or in your own home community to draw attention to the issue of body image and to challenge common stereotypes?

18. How can women with disabilities and nondisabled women work together on this issue?

19. How can young women and older women work together on this issue?

20. Why is there currently no significant political movement/activism against this ideal of bodily perfection?

21. How much did you eat while reading this section? How much exercise did you do?

S E V E N T E E N

◆◆◆

Phenomenal Woman

Maya Angelou

Pretty women wonder where my secret lies.
I'm not cute or built to suit a fashion model's size
But when I start to tell them,
They think I'm telling lies.
I say,
It's in the reach of my arms,
The span of my hips,
The stride of my step,
The curl of my lips.

I'm a woman
Phenomenally.
Phenomenal woman,
That's me.

I walk into a room
Just as cool as you please,
And to a man,
The fellows stand or

Fall down on their knees.
Then they swarm around me,
A hive of honey bees.
I say,
It's the fire in my eyes,
And the flash of my teeth,
The swing in my waist,
And the joy in my feet.
I'm a woman
Phenomenally.
Phenomenal woman,
That's me.

Men themselves have wondered
What they see in me.
They try so much
But they can't touch
My inner mystery.
When I try to show them
They say they still can't see.
I say,
It's in the arch of my back,
The sun of my smile,

The ride of my breasts,
The grace of my style.
I'm a woman
Phenomenally.
Phenomenal woman,
That's me.

Now you understand
Just why my head's not bowed.
I don't shout or jump about
Or have to talk real loud.
When you see me passing
It ought to make you proud.
I say,
It's in the click of my heels,
The bend of my hair,
The palm of my hand,
The need for my care.
'Cause I'm a woman
Phenomenally.
Phenomenal woman,
That's me.

EIGHTEEN

◆◆◆

Outrageous Acts[*]

Meredith Lee

Body image has been a lifelong issue for me. I have always felt fat and ugly. I am proud to say I am learning to love my body and I am unlearning what society has taught me is beautiful. I have always seen beauty in womyn of all colors, shapes, and sizes, but I thought "Well, that's only my idea of beauty." I did not realize that body image is an issue for all womyn. I grew up thinking I was alone feeling fat and ugly. Now I know I am not. I have learned from talking to other womyn that we can help ourselves overcome our negative images of ourselves, and begin accepting our bodies. I have become very empowered talking to other womyn. I have become empowered learning to love myself the way I am.

I have empowered myself through two outrageous acts at college this quarter that have helped me create a positive body image. One I shaved my head, and two I posed nude for my friend's photography project. I have wanted to shave my head for six years, and I never in my wildest dreams imagined posing nude for anything. Hell, I did not wear a bathing suit until two summers ago. I did not even wear tank tops because I thought my arms were too fat. I was scared to pose nude, but I knew it would be a great experience for me. I was right.

I always felt that I was not pretty enough, or skinny enough to shave my head. I always felt my hair was the best part of my physical appearance, it was some sort of security I guess. I wanted to

---

[*]Dedicated to my mother.

quit chopping myself into pieces, "I like this, I hate this. . . ." Taking off my hair took away the only thing I felt was beautiful about my appearance, it forced me to look at myself as a whole. I will never forget how I felt when I looked into the mirror for the first time with a shaved head, I felt *beautiful.*

Posing nude was scary, but not nearly as bad as I had anticipated. What was most terrifying was waiting to see the pictures, and knowing that they would be hanging in an art show on campus. I have since seen the photos, I only really did not like four, that is not too bad considering there are about seventy. I had expected to hate all of them, and expected to regret that I posed. I actually liked a lot of the pictures, and I am psyched that I posed. Seeing myself nude in photos, as opposed to the mirror, helped me realize that I am beautiful the way I am. Just like a womyn I know said, "It's your house, you live in it, be proud."

♦♦♦

NINETEEN

When I Was Growing Up

Nellie Wong

I know now that once I longed to be white.
How? you ask.
Let me tell you the ways.

> when I was growing up, people told me
> I was dark and I believed my own darkness
> in the mirror, in my soul, my own narrow vision

>> when I was growing up, my sisters
>> with fair skin got praised
>> for their beauty, and in the dark
>> I fell further, crushed between high walls

> when I was growing up, I read magazines
> and saw movies, blonde movie stars, white skin,
> sensuous lips and to be elevated, to become
> a woman, a desirable woman, I began to wear
> imaginary pale skin

>> when I was growing up, I was proud
>> of my English, my grammar, my spelling
>> fitting into the group of smart children
>> smart Chinese children, fitting in,
>> belonging, getting in line

> when I was growing up and went to high school,
> I discovered the rich white girls, a few yellow girls,
> their imported cotton dresses, their cashmere sweaters,

their curly hair and I thought that I too should have
what these lucky girls had

>> when I was growing up, I hungered
>> for American food, American styles,
>> coded: white and even to me, a child
>> born of Chinese parents, being Chinese
>> was feeling foreign, was limiting,
>> was unAmerican

> when I was growing up and a white man wanted
> to take me out, I thought I was special,
> an exotic gardenia, anxious to fit
> the stereotype of an oriental chick

>> when I was growing up, I felt ashamed
>> of some yellow men, their small bones,
>> their frail bodies, their spitting
>> on the streets, their coughing,
>> their lying in sunless rooms,
>> shooting themselves in the arms

when I was growing up, people would ask
if I were Filipino, Polynesian, Portuguese.
They named all colors except white, the shell
of my soul, but not my dark, rough skin

>> when I was growing up, I felt
>> dirty. I thought that god
>> made white people clean

and no matter how much I bathed,
I could not change, I could not shed
my skin in the gray water

when I was growing up, I swore
I would run away to purple mountains,
houses by the sea with nothing over
my head, with space to breathe,

uncongested with yellow people in an area
called Chinatown, in an area I later learned
was a ghetto, one of many hearts
of Asian America

I know now that once I longed to be white
How many more ways? you ask.
Haven't I told you enough?

T W E N T Y

◆◆◆

The Coming of Maureen Peal

Toni Morrison

My daddy's face is a study. Winter moves into it and presides there. His eyes become a cliff of snow threatening to avalanche; his eyebrows bend like black limbs of leafless trees. His skin takes on the pale, cheerless yellow of winter sun; for a jaw he has the edges of a snowbound field dotted with stubble; his high forehead is the frozen sweep of the Erie, hiding currents of gelid thoughts that eddy in darkness. Wolf killer turned hawk fighter, he worked night and day to keep one from the door and the other from under the windowsills. A Vulcan guarding the flames, he gives us instructions about which doors to keep closed or opened for proper distribution of heat, lays kindling by, discusses qualities of coal, and teaches us how to rake, feed, and bank the fire. And he will not unrazor his lips until spring.

Winter tightened our heads with a band of cold and melted our eyes. We put pepper in the feet of our stockings, Vaseline on our faces, and stared through dark icebox mornings at four stewed prunes, slippery lumps of oatmeal, and cocoa with a roof of skin.

But mostly we waited for spring, when there could be gardens.

By the time this winter had stiffened itself into a hateful knot that nothing could loosen, something did loosen it, or rather someone. A someone who splintered the knot into silver threads that tangled us, netted us, made us long for the dull chafe of the previous boredom.

This disrupter of seasons was a new girl in school named Maureen Peal. A high-yellow dream child with long brown hair braided into two lynch ropes that hung down her back. She was rich, at least by our standards, as rich as the richest of the white girls, swaddled in comfort and care. The quality of her clothes threatened to derange Frieda and me. Patent-leather shoes with buckles, a cheaper version of which we got only at Easter and which had disintegrated by the end of May. Fluffy sweaters the color of lemon drops tucked into skirts with pleats so orderly they astounded us. Brightly colored knee socks with white borders, a brown velvet coat trimmed in white rabbit fur, and a matching muff. There was a hint of spring in her sloe green eyes, something summery in her complexion, and a rich autumn ripeness in her walk.

She enchanted the entire school. When teachers called on her, they smiled encouragingly. Black boys didn't trip her in the halls; white boys didn't stone her, white girls didn't suck their teeth when she was assigned to be their work partners; black girls stepped aside when she wanted to use the sink in the girls' toilet, and their eyes genuflected under sliding lids. She never had to search for anybody to eat with in the cafeteria—they flocked to the table of her choice, where she opened fastidious lunches, shaming our jelly-stained bread with egg-salad sandwiches cut into four dainty squares, pink-frosted cupcakes, sticks of celery and carrots, proud, dark apples. She even bought and liked white milk.

Frieda and I were bemused, irritated, and fascinated by her. We looked hard for flaws to restore our equilibrium, but had to be content at first with uglying up her name, changing Maureen Peal to Meringue Pie. Later a minor epiphany was ours when we discovered that she had a dog tooth—a charming one to be sure—but a dog tooth nonetheless. And when we found out that she had been born with six fingers on each hand and that there was a little bump where each extra one had been removed, we smiled. They were small triumphs, but we took what we could get—snickering behind her back and calling her Six-finger-dog-tooth-meringue-pie. But we had to do it alone, for none of the other girls would cooperate with our hostility. They adored her.

When she was assigned a locker next to mine, I could indulge my jealousy four times a day. My sister and I both suspected that we were secretly prepared to be her friend, if she would let us, but I knew it would be a dangerous friendship, for when my eye traced the white border patterns of those Kelly-green knee socks, and felt the pull and slack of my brown stockings, I wanted to kick her. And when I thought of the unearned haughtiness in her eyes, I plotted accidental slammings of locker doors on her hand.

As locker friends, however, we got to know each other a little, and I was even able to hold a sensible conversation with her without visualizing her fall off a cliff, or giggling my way into what I thought was a clever insult.

One day, while I waited at the locker for Frieda, she joined me.

"Hi."

"Hi."

"Waiting for your sister?"

"Uh-huh."

"Which way do you go home?"

"Down Twenty-first Street to Broadway."

"Why don't you go down Twenty-second Street?"

" 'Cause I live on Twenty-first Street."

"Oh. I can walk that way, I guess. Partly, anyway."

"Free country."

Frieda came toward us, her brown stockings straining at the knees because she had tucked the toe under to hide a hole in the foot.

"Maureen's gonna walk part way with us."

Frieda and I exchanged glances, her eyes begging my restraint, mine promising nothing.

It was a false spring day, which, like Maureen, had pierced the shell of a deadening winter. There

were puddles, mud, and an inviting warmth that deluded us. The kind of day on which we draped our coats over our heads, left our galoshes in school, and came down with croup the following day. We always responded to the slightest change in weather, the most minute shifts in time of day. Long before seeds were stirring, Frieda and I were scruffing and poking at the earth, swallowing air, drinking rain. . . .

As we emerged from the school with Maureen, we began to molt immediately. We put our head scarves in our coat pockets, and our coats on our heads. I was wondering how to maneuver Maureen's fur muff into a gutter when a commotion in the playground distracted us. A group of boys was circling and holding at bay a victim, Pecola Breedlove.

Bay Boy, Woodrow Cain, Buddy Wilson, Junie Bug—like a necklace of semiprecious stones they surrounded her. Heady with the smell of their own musk, thrilled by the easy power of a majority, they gaily harassed her.

"Black e mo. Black e mo. Yadaddsleepsnekked. Black e mo black e mo ya dadd sleeps nekked. Black e mo . . ."

They had extemporized a verse made up of two insults about matters over which the victim had no control; the color of her skin and speculations on the sleeping habits of an adult, wildly fitting in its incoherence. That they themselves were black, or that their own father had similarly relaxed habits was irrelevant. It was their contempt for their own blackness that gave the first insult its teeth. They seemed to have taken all of their smoothly cultivated ignorance, their exquisitely learned self-hatred, their elaborately designed hopelessness and sucked it all up into a fiery cone of scorn that had burned for ages in the hollows of their minds—cooled—and spilled over lips of outrage, consuming whatever was in its path. They danced a macabre ballet around the victim, whom, for their own sake, they were prepared to sacrifice to the flaming pit.

Black e mo Black e mo Ya daddy sleeps nekked.
Stch ta ta stch ta ta
stach ta ta ta ta ta

Pecola edged around the circle crying. She had dropped her notebook, and covered her eyes with her hands.

We watched, afraid they might notice us and turn their energies our way. Then Frieda, with set lips and Mama's eyes, snatched her coat from her head and threw it on the ground. She ran toward them and brought her books down on Woodrow Cain's head. The circle broke. Woodrow Cain grabbed his head.

"Hey, girl!"

"You cut that out, you hear?" I had never heard Frieda's voice so loud and clear.

Maybe because Frieda was taller than he was, maybe because he saw her eyes, maybe because he had lost interest in the game, or maybe because he had a crush on Frieda, in any case Woodrow looked frightened just long enough to give her more courage.

"Leave her 'lone, or I'm gone tell everybody what you did!"

Woodrow did not answer; he just walled his eyes.

Bay Boy piped up, "Go on, gal. Ain't nobody bothering you."

"You shut up, Bullet Head." I had found my tongue.

"Who you calling Bullet Head?"

"I'm calling you Bullet Head, Bullet Head."

Frieda took Pecola's hand. "Come on."

"You want a fat lip?" Bay Boy drew back his fist at me.

"Yeah. Gimme one of yours."

"You gone get one."

Maureen appeared at my elbow, and the boys seemed reluctant to continue under her springtime eyes so wide with interest. They buckled in confusion, not willing to beat up three girls under her watchful gaze: So they listened to a budding male instinct that told them to pretend we were unworthy of their attention.

"Come on, man."

"Yeah. Come on. We ain't got time to fool with them."

Grumbling a few disinterested epithets, they moved away.

I picked up Pecola's notebook and Frieda's coat, and the four of us left the playground.

"Old Bullet Head, he's always picking on girls."

Frieda agreed with me. "Miss Forrester said he was incorrigival."

"Really?" I didn't know what that meant, but it had enough of a doom sound in it to be true of Bay Boy.

While Frieda and I clucked on about the near fight, Maureen, suddenly animated, put her velvet-sleeved arm through Pecola's and began to behave as though they were the closest of friends.

"I just moved here. My name is Maureen Peal. What's yours?"

"Pecola."

"Pecola? Wasn't that the name of the girl in *Imitation of Life*?"

"I don't know. What is that?"

"The picture show, you know. Where this mulatto girl hates her mother 'cause she is black and ugly but then cries at the funeral. It was real sad. Everybody cries in it. Claudette Colbert too."

"Oh." Pecola's voice was no more than a sigh.

"Anyway, her name was Pecola too. She was so pretty. When it comes back, I'm going to see it again. My mother has seen it four times."

Frieda and I walked behind them, surprised at Maureen's friendliness to Pecola, but pleased. Maybe she wasn't so bad, after all. Frieda had put her coat back on her head, and the two of us, so draped, trotted along enjoying the warm breeze and Frieda's heroics.

"You're in my gym class, aren't you?" Maureen asked Pecola.

"Yes."

"Miss Erkmeister's legs sure are bow. I bet she thinks they're cute. How come she gets to wear real shorts, and we have to wear those old bloomers? I want to die every time I put them on."

Pecola smiled but did not look at Maureen.

"Hey." Maureen stopped short. "There's an Isaley's. Want some ice cream? I have money."

She unzipped a hidden pocket in her muff and pulled out a multifolded dollar bill. I forgave her those knee socks.

"My uncle sued Isaley's," Maureen said to the three of us. "He sued the Isaley's in Akron. They said he was disorderly and that that was why they wouldn't serve him, but a friend of his, a policeman, came in and beared the witness, so the suit went through."

"What's a suit?"

"It's when you can beat them up if you want to and won't anybody do nothing. Our family does it all the time. We believe in suits."

At the entrance to Isaley's, Maureen turned to Frieda and me, asking, "You all going to buy some ice cream?"

We looked at each other. "No," Frieda said.

Maureen disappeared into the store with Pecola.

Frieda looked placidly down the street; I opened my mouth, but quickly closed it. It was extremely important that the world not know that I fully expected Maureen to buy us some ice cream, that for the past 120 seconds I had been selecting the flavor, that I had begun to like Maureen, and that neither of us had a penny.

We supposed Maureen was being nice to Pecola because of the boys, and were embarrassed to be caught—even by each other—thinking that she would treat us, or that we deserved it as much as Pecola did.

The girls came out. Pecola with two dips of orange-pineapple, Maureen with black raspberry.

"You should have got some," she said. "They had all kinds. Don't eat down to the tip of the cone," she advised Pecola.

"Why?"

"Because there's a fly in there."

"How you know?"

"Oh, not really. A girl told me she found one in the bottom of hers once, and ever since then she throws that part away."

"Oh."

We passed the Dreamland Theatre, and Betty Grable smiled down at us.

"Don't you just love her?" Maureen asked.

"Uh-huh," said Pecola.

I differed. "Hedy Lamarr is better."

Maureen agreed. "Ooooo yes. My mother told me that a girl named Audrey, she went to the beauty parlor where we lived before, and asked the lady to fix her hair like Hedy Lamarr's, and the lady said, 'Yeah, when you grow some hair like Hedy Lamarr's.'" She laughed long and sweet.

"Sounds crazy," said Frieda.

"She sure is. Do you know she doesn't even menstrate yet, and she's sixteen. Do you, yet?"

"Yes." Pecola glanced at us.

"So do I." Maureen made no attempt to disguise her pride. "Two months ago I started. My girl friend in Toledo, where we lived before, said when she started she was scared to death. Thought she had killed herself."

"Do you know what it's for?" Pecola asked the question as though hoping to provide the answer herself.

"For babies." Maureen raised two pencil-stroke eyebrows at the obviousness of the question. "Babies need blood when they are inside you, and if you are having a baby, then you don't menstrate. But when you're not having a baby, then you don't have to save the blood, so it comes out."

"How do babies get the blood?" asked Pecola.

"Through the like-line. You know. Where your belly button is. That is where the like-line grows from and pumps the blood to the baby."

"Well, if the belly buttons are to grow like-lines to give the baby blood, and only girls have babies, how come boys have belly buttons?"

Maureen hesitated. "I don't know," she admitted. "But boys have all sorts of things they don't need." Her tinkling laughter was somehow stronger than our nervous ones. She curled her tongue around the edge of the cone, scooping up a dollop of purple that made my eyes water. We were waiting for a stop light to change. Maureen kept scooping the ice cream from around the cone's edge with her tongue; she didn't bite the edge as I would have done. Her tongue circled the cone. Pecola had finished hers; Maureen evidently liked her things to last. While I was thinking about her ice cream, she must have been thinking about her last remark, for she said to Pecola, "Did you ever see a naked man?"

Pecola blinked, then looked away. "No. Where would I see a naked man?"

"I don't know. I just asked."

"I wouldn't even look at him, even if I did see him. That's dirty. Who wants to see a naked man?" Pecola was agitated. "Nobody's father would be naked in front of his own daughter. Not unless he was dirty too."

"I didn't say 'father.' I just said 'a naked man.'"

"Well . . ."

"How come you said 'father'?" Maureen wanted to know.

"Who else would she see, dog tooth?" I was glad to have a chance to show anger. Not only because of the ice cream, but because we had seen our own father naked and didn't care to be reminded of it and feel the shame brought on by the absence of shame. He had been walking down the hall from the bathroom into his bedroom and passed the open door of our room. We had lain there wide-eyed. He stopped and looked in, trying to see in the dark room whether we were really asleep—or was it his imagination that opened eyes were looking at him? Apparently he convinced himself that we were sleeping. He moved away, confident that his little girls would not lie open-eyed like that, staring, staring. When he had moved on, the dark took only him away, not his nakedness. That stayed in the room with us. Friendly-like.

"I'm not talking to you," said Maureen. "Besides, I don't care if she sees her father naked. She can look at him all day if she wants to. Who cares?"

"You do," said Frieda. "That's all you talk about."

"It is not."

"It is so. Boys, babies, and somebody's naked daddy. You must be boy-crazy."

"You better be quiet."

"Who's gonna make me?" Frieda put her hand on her hip and jutted her face toward Maureen.

"You all ready made. Mammy made."

"You stop talking about my mama."

"Well, you stop talking about my daddy."

"Who said anything about your old daddy?"

"You did."

"Well, you started it."

"I wasn't even talking to you. I was talking to Pecola."

"Yeah. About seeing her naked daddy."

"So what if she did see him?"

Pecola shouted, "I never saw my daddy naked. Never."

"You did too," Maureen snapped. "Bay Boy said so."

"I did not."

"You did."

"I did not."

"Did. Your own daddy, too!"

Pecola tucked her head in—a funny, sad, helpless movement. A kind of hunching of the shoulders, pulling in of the neck, as though she wanted to cover her ears.

"You stop talking about her daddy," I said.

"What do I care about her old black daddy?" asked Maureen.

"Black? Who you calling black?"

"You!"

"You think you so cute!" I swung at her and missed, hitting Pecola in the face. Furious at my clumsiness, I threw my notebook at her, but it caught her in the small of her velvet back, for she had turned and was flying across the street against traffic.

Safe on the other side, she screamed at us, "I *am* cute! And you ugly! Black and ugly black e mos. I *am* cute!"

She ran down the street, the green knee socks making her legs look like wild dandelion stems that had somehow lost their heads. The weight of he remark stunned us, and it was a second or two before Frieda and I collected ourselves enough to shout, "Six-finger-dog-tooth-meringue-pie!" We chanted this most powerful of our arsenal of insults as long as we could see the green stems and rabbit fur.

Grown people frowned at the three girls on the curbside, two with their coats draped over their heads, the collars framing the eyebrows like nuns' habits, black garters showing where they bit the tops of brown stockings that barely covered the knees, angry faces knotted like dark cauliflowers.

Pecola stood a little apart from us, her eyes hinged in the direction in which Maureen had fled. She seemed to fold into herself, like a pleated wing. Her pain antagonized me. I wanted to open her up, crisp her edges, ram a stick down that hunched and curving spine, force her to stand erect and spit the misery out on the streets. But she held it in where it could lap up into her eyes.

Frieda snatched her coat from her head. "Come on, Claudia. 'Bye, Pecola."

We walked quickly at first, and then slower, pausing every now and then to fasten garters, tie shoelaces, scratch, or examine old scars. We were sinking under the wisdom, accuracy, and relevance of Maureen's last words. If she was cute—and if anything could be believed, she *was*—then we were not. And what did that mean? We were lesser. Nicer, brighter, but still lesser. Dolls we could destroy, but we could not destroy the honey voices of parents and aunts, the obedience in the eyes of our peers, the slippery light in the eyes of our teachers when they encountered the Maureen Peals of the world. What was the secret? What did we lack? Why was it important? And so what? Guileless and without vanity, we were still in love with ourselves then. We felt comfortable in our skins, enjoyed the news that our senses released to us, admired our dirt, cultivated our scars, and could not comprehend this unworthiness. Jealousy we understood and thought natural—a desire to have what somebody else had; but envy was a strange, new feeling for us. And all the time we knew that Maureen Peal was not the Enemy and not worthy of such intense hatred. The *Thing* to fear was the *Thing* that made *her* beautiful, and not us.

T W E N T Y - O N E

◆◆◆

Do You Remember Me?

Barbara Macdonald

I am less than five feet high and, except that I may have shrunk a quarter of an inch or so in the past few years, I have viewed the world from this height for sixty-five years. I have taken up some space in the world; I weigh about a hundred and forty pounds and my body is what my mother used to call dumpy. My mother didn't like her body and so, of course, didn't like mine. "Dumpy" was her word and just as I have had to keep the body, somehow I have had to keep the word — thirty-eight inch bust, no neck, no waistline, fat hips — that's dumpy.

My hair is grey, white at the temples, with only a little of the red cast of earlier years showing through. My face is wrinkled and deeply lined. Straight lines have formed on the upper lip as though I had spent many years with my mouth pursed. This has always puzzled me and I wonder what years those were and why I can't remember them. My face has deep lines that extend from each side of the nose down the face past the corners of my mouth. My forehead is wide, and the lines across my forehead and between my eyes are there to testify that I was often puzzled and bewildered for long periods of time about what was taking place in my life. My cheekbones are high and become more noticeably so as my face is drawn further and further down. My chin is small for such a large head and below the chin the skin hangs in a loose vertical fold from my chin all the way down my neck, where it meets a horizontal scar. The surgeon who made the scar said that the joints of my neck were worn out from looking up so many years. For all kinds of reasons, I seldom look up to anyone or anything anymore.

My eyes are blue and my gaze is usually steady and direct. But I look away when I am struggling with some nameless shame, trying to disclaim parts of myself. My voice is low and my speech sometimes clipped and rapid if I am uncomfortable; otherwise, I have a pleasant voice. I like the sound of it from in here where I am. When I was younger, some people, lovers mostly, enjoyed my singing, but I no longer have the same control of my voice and sing only occasionally now when I am alone.

My hands are large and the backs of my hands begin to show the brown spots of aging. Sometimes lately, holding my arms up reading in bed or lying with my arms clasped around my lover's neck, I see my arm with the skin hanging loosely from my forearm and cannot believe that it is really my own. It seems disconnected from me; it is someone else's, it is the arm of an old woman. It is the arm of such old women as I myself have seen, sitting on benches in the sun with their hands folded in their laps; old women I have turned away from. I wonder now, how and when these arms I see came to be my own — arms I cannot turn away from. . . .

I have grown to like living in Cambridge. I like the sharp lines of the reality of my life here. The truth is I like growing old. Oh, it isn't that I don't feel at moments the sharp irrevocable knowledge that I have finally grown old. That is evident every time I stand in front of the bathroom mirror and brush my teeth. I may begin as I often do, wondering if those teeth that are so much a part of myself, teeth I've clenched in anger all my life, felt with my own tongue with a feeling of possession, as a cat licks her paw lovingly just because it is hers — wondering, will these teeth always be mine? Will they stay with me loyally and die with me, or will they desert me before the Time comes? But I grow dreamy brushing my teeth and find myself, unaware, planning — as I always have when I brush my teeth — that single-handed crossing I plan to make. From East to West, a last stop in the Canaries and then the trade winds. What will be the best time of year? What boat? How much sail? I go over again the list of supplies, uninterrupted until some morning twinge in my left shoulder reminds me with uncompromising regret that I will never make that single-handed crossing — probably. That I have waited too long. That there is no turning back.

But I always say probably. Probably I'll never make that single-handed crossing. Probably, I've waited too long. Probably, I can't turn back now. But I leave room now, at sixty-five, for the unexpected. That was not always true of me. I used to feel I was in a kind of linear race with life and time. There were no probably's, it was a now or never time of my life. There were landmarks placed by other generations, and I had to arrive on time or fail in the whole race. If I didn't pass—if the sixth grade went on to the seventh without me, I would be one year behind for the rest of my life. If I graduated from high school in 1928, I had to graduate from college in 1932. When I didn't graduate from college until 1951, it took me another twenty years to realize the preceding twenty years weren't lost. But now I begin to see that I may get to have the whole thing, and that no experience longed for is really going to be missed.

"I like growing old." I say it to myself with surprise. I had not thought that it could be like this. There are days of excitement when I feel almost a kind of high with the changes taking place in my body, even though I know the inevitable course my body is taking will lead to debilitation and death. I say to myself frequently in wonder, "This is my body doing this thing." I cannot stop it, I don't even know what it is doing, I wouldn't know how to direct it. My own body is going through a process that only my body knows about. I never grew old before; never died before. I don't really know how it's done. . . .

So often we think we know how an experience is going to end so we don't risk the pain of seeing it through to the end. We think we know the outcome so we think there is no need to experience it, as though to anticipate an ending were the same as living the ending out. . . .

Of course, this time, for me, I am not going to live beyond this ending. The strangeness of that idea comes to me at the most unexpected moments and always with surprise and shock; sometimes, I am immobilized by it. Standing before the mirror in the morning, I feel that my scalp is tight. I see that the skin hangs beneath my jaw, beneath my arm; my breasts are pulled low against my body; loose skin hangs from my hips, and below my stomach a new horizontal crease is forming over which the skin will hang like the hem of a skirt turned under. A hem not to be "let down," as once my skirts were, because I was "shooting up," but a widening hem to "take up" on an old garment that has been stretched. Then I see that my body is being drawn into the earth—muscle, tendon, tissue and skin is being drawn down by the earth's pull back to the loam. She is pulling me back to herself; she is taking back what is hers. . . .

I think a lot about being drawn into the earth. I have the knowledge that one day I will fall and the earth will take back what is hers. I have no choice, yet I choose it. Maybe I won't buy that boat and that list of supplies; maybe I will. Maybe I will be able to write about my life; maybe I won't. But uncertainty will not always be there, for this is like no other experience I have ever had—I can count on it. I've never had anything before that I could really count on. My life has been filled with uncertainties, some were not of my making and many were: promises I made myself I did not keep; promises I made others I did not keep; hopes I could not fulfill; shame carried like a weight heavier each year, at my failure, at my lack of clear purpose. But this time I can rely on myself, for life will keep her promise to me. I can trust her. She isn't going to confuse me with a multitude of other choices and beckon me down other roads with vague promises. She will give me finally only one choice, one road, one sense of possibility. And in exchange for the multitude of choices she no longer offers, she gives me, at last, certainty. Nor do I have to worry this time that I will fail myself, fail to pull it off. This time, for sure I am going to make that single-handed crossing.

TWENTY-TWO

◆◆◆

Glimpse into a Transformation

Ernestine Amani Patterson

Even today, a little over four years after I began having my hair braided in cornrows, a few nervy women still come up to me and say: "Your hair is very pretty. But it's too bad you can't see how nice the style is and how colorful the beads are." And while I'm used to having insults veiled in compliments passing my way, I kinda thought I would never hear *that* one in connection with my blindness and the re-discovery of the African hairstyle which continues to be a source of great personal happiness to me. But having answered so many, many questions like it, I always say nowadays: "But each style has its own shape. And though the beads are a different color, many of them also have their own touch." This is quite true, because they are glass, wood, and plastic beads. These are further divided into varying tactile textures. And although I haven't gotten into them yet, you can purchase semi-precious gem beads, and they have their flavor, too.

And if I am wearing bells in my hair when these remarks are made, I shake my head a little so they can hear the jingle; hopefully they'll get the message. In fact, it was because I had encountered a young woman at school whose braids fairly sang with bells that I vowed I would quit pressing my hair for at least one time and try the cornrows. And as a kind of good omen, my classmate, one day when the lecture was over, gave me a small plastic bag containing about fifty sweet, high-noted pieces of bell-shaped metal. *That* did it. There was no way I was going to let such wonderful objects go unused. In my spare time, I would rattle them, listening to the beautiful notes they made, and was reminded of what I was seeking.

My quest was not easy, though. Beauticians and everyday people gave me a boatload of information, some of it deliberately discouraging, the rest offered out of ignorance. They'd say: "I've never seen anybody I liked that style on. It makes you look — I don't know — just doesn't look right." Others would say: "I heard you lose a lot of your hair, and people say it itches, too, whenever you get them — so badly that you have to take them down." But the worst was: "Your hair is too short."

This short hair business always caused me grief. The people unmistakably referred to the short stubborn crop of peculiar hair in the very back, close to my neck. It was said more than once to me that my being mischievous with the scissors as a youngster stunted its growth, and I had always felt guilty about having done it. My classmate said, however, that cornrowing was just what the back of my hair needed. Nobody paid the least bit of attention to this assertion, least of all me.

By the time I had resigned myself to being trapped in failure, I ran across someone I'd met several years previously. She was Mrs. Eunice Younger, a Liberian woman, who owned a most exotic African artifacts shop near my neighborhood. She had married a Black American and seemed to be doing quite well for herself. I had thought her shop sold only imports. But as a friend and I talked with her, and I discovered she did this kind of braiding, I immediately made an appointment with her for the end of that week.

"You know," I said, somewhat disappointed about having to remove my head from the dryer, "I really wish I could have braids. But you can press it as we planned until it grows out." I was admiring the warm and friendly fragrances of oil, shampoo, and conditioners that beauty parlors seem to love to stock.

I suspect she was just as eager for me to have braids as I was to get them, because she said: "Let's try it." It was a happy shock for me. I certainly didn't think I'd actually leave there wearing braids. It would come to my mind as she worked: *What if we come to the point where we must break off?* The back *was* a problem, because it really was too short to braid. But since she had already braided the rest, and was such a clever styler — an artist, really — she pinned the back portion into curls with small bobby-pins.

"When you take these out," she said, referring to the bobby-pins, "the curls will last for awhile. Then they'll come out, but that will be because your hair is growing. Next time, I think I'll be able to braid the back."

The compliments on my new look were so overwhelming that, when the curls did come out and I got a few uncharitable remarks about what remained of them, I put it down to pettiness. And though I experienced some itching, I told my hair: "You're only adjusting to this new way; you'll get used to it." Sure enough, the itching stopped. And the best part was the next time I visited Mrs. Younger, the back part was braidable. Ever since that time, this previously troublesome portion of hair has entered into a burst of growing and shows no signs of abating.

Funny thing, though. I can't remember what Eunice and I talked about on that first visit. I must have asked her about her family, what her impressions of America were, and how her business was prospering. I, in turn, probably spoke of my radio show, of going to school, and my ever-amusing cat. And doubtless, I had questions about the care of my new style. But nothing of the talk we surely had remains with me, for I was totally entranced with the little bites and tuggings of the comb as it parted and untangled, and the feel of the motions of Mrs. Younger's fingers braiding up and down along my scalp. Whenever her phone rang, I would sneak a rub and think wonderingly to myself: "I'm going to look this good for about a month? Wow! It couldn't be this easy, could it? All I have to do is get up in the morning and step out the door and not do *anything* to my hair? *Wow!*"

Ever since I was a child having to skip swimming classes in the therapeutic pool for disabled and blind children at the small town public school I attended, I had wished in a vague inconsistent way to find a hairstyle or something which would let me sweat, walk in the rain, or hang out in the bathtub or pool or lake till my skin got wrinkly and I wanted to get out. I say vaguely and inconsistently, because back then I knew no way out of this dilemma. It's true that later on in my life, the natural had come. But it never seemed to suit me too well. In any case, once I got my first braids I realized I would no longer have to smell the peculiar, almost acrid odor of metal combs heating and hair frying. And I could forego the fear of being burned by permanents or anything else. That was fine with me. And halleluia, at least as Cobbs and Greer pointed out in their book, *Black Rage,* I could avoid some of the psychological dam-

age that many Black women incur when they try altering their hair to imitate that of white women.

Of course, people are still the same—inevitable and specific in their cruelty—"Your hair is pretty," or "Your dress is pretty." The lines between womanhood and blindness are never supposed to meet. And with Blackness on top of that, what must people be seeing! And although I seldom hear: "*You* are looking nice," I am not the same, even if they are. Since that Saturday in the shop with the wooden floor and squeaky steps, where the heater had to be turned on against the chilly morning, I have always looked forward to the bus ride and the short walk there. Mrs. Younger has not only increased her clientele, other girlfriends of hers from Africa help out with the hair. So it's lovely talking to all of them. And since most of these women are used to me now, we relate as Black sisters who, despite the shortness of time allotted to us, have come together. And though this was not a first step in my growth, mine is actually a case wherein the style of my hair altered the shape of my head within. How many women can say that with satisfaction about *any* beauty treatment they try?

T W E N T Y - T H R E E

◆◆◆

What's a Leg Got to Do with It?

Donna Walton

What's a leg got to do with it? Exactly what I thought when, during a heated conversation, a female rival told me I was less than a woman because I have one leg.

Excuse me. Perhaps I missed something. How could she make such an insensitive comment about something she had no experience with? Was she some expert on disabilities or something? Was she, too, disabled? Had she—like me—fought a battle with cancer that cost her a limb? For a split second, my thoughts were paralyzed by her insensitivity. But, like a defeated fighter who returns to the ring to regain victory, I bounced back for a verbal round with Ms. Thang.

I am woman first, an amputee second and physically challenged last. And it is in that order that I set out to educate and testify to people like Ms. Thang who are unable to discern who I am—a feisty, unequivocally attractive African-American woman with a gimpy gait who can strut proudly into any room and engage in intelligent conversation with folks anxious to feed off my sincere aura.

It is rather comical and equally disturbing how folks—both men and women—view me as a disabled woman, particularly when it comes to sexuality. They have so many misconceptions. Straight women, for example, want to know how I catch a man, while most men are entertained with the idea that because I have one leg sex with me must be a blast.

I have even been confronted by folks who give me the impression that they think having sex is a painful experience for me. Again, I say, What's a leg got to do with it?

For all of those who want to inquire about my sexual prowess but dare not to, or for those who are curious about how I maintain such positive self-esteem when life dealt me the proverbial "bad hand," this story is for you. But those who have a tough time dealing with reality probably should skip the next paragraph because what I am about to confess is the gospel truth.

I like sex! I am very sexual!! I even consider myself sexy, residual limb and all. You see, I was a sexual being before my leg was amputated 19 years ago. My attitude didn't change about sex. I just had to adjust to the attitudes of others.

For example, I remember a brother who I dated in high school — before my leg was amputated — then dated again five years later. The dating ended abruptly because I realized that the brother could not fathom the one-leg thing. When he and I were home alone, he was cool as long as we got hot and bothered with my prostheses on. However, whenever I tried to take off my artificial leg for comfort purposes, he immediately panicked. He could not fathom seeing me with one leg.

I tried to put him at ease by telling him Eva's story from Toni Morrison's novel *Sula*—that "my leg just got tired and walked off one day." But this brother just could not deal. He booked.

On the other hand, my experiences with lesbians have varied; they don't all book right away, but some have booked. Not all are upfront with their feelings 'cuz women are socialized to be courteous, emotional, and indirect, sparing one's feelings. Instead, some tend to communicate their discomfort with my missing limb in more subtle ways. For example, one lesbian I dated did not want to take me out to bars, clubs and other social settings. My lop-sided gait was an embarrassment, and the fact that I use a cane garnered unwanted attention for her. Behind closed doors, she did not have any problems with it. How we would be perceived by trendy lesbians was her main concern.

Conversely, I have had positive experiences with lesbians as well. For instance, I have dated and been in love with women who have been affirming and supportive while respecting my difference. My wholeness has been shaped by all of these experiences. Without hesitation, I can now take off my prostheses, be comfortable hopping around on one-leg and the sex . . . . is still a blast.

How does a woman with one leg maintain such a positive self-esteem in a society where people with disabilities are not valued? Simply by believing in myself. I know you're saying, "That sounds much too hokey." But as I said earlier, this is the gospel truth.

I was 19 years old when my leg was amputated. I was diagnosed with osteogenic sarcoma, bone cancer. During the first five years after my surgery, concentrating on other folks' perceptions of me was the least of my concerns. I was too focused on beating the odds against dying. You see, I was given only a 15% chance of survival — with spiritual guidance and support from my family — I had made the very difficult decision to stop taking my chemotherapy treatments. Doctors predicted that, by halting the dreadful chemotherapy, I was writing my own death certificate. However, through what I believe was divine healing, my cancer was eradicated.

Before this cancerous ordeal, I was not strong spiritually, and my faith was rocked when my leg was amputated because I thought I was to keep my leg. At the time, I could not see past the physical. After my amputation, I was preoccupied with the kinds of crippling thoughts that all the Ms. Thangs of the world are socialized to believe: that I was not going to be able to wear shorts, bathing suits or lingerie; that my womanness was somehow compromised by the loss of a limb.

If you have a disability and are in need of some fuel for your spirit, check out any novel by Toni Morrison ("Sula" is my favorite because of the one-legged grandmother, Eva) or Khalil Gibran's "The Prophet." These resources helped me build self-esteem and deal with my reality.

Ultimately, building positive esteem is an ongoing process. To that end, I am currently producing a motivational video that will outline coping strategies for female amputees.

No matter what your disability or circumstance, you cannot give in to a defeatist attitude. When you do, your battle is lost. There is a way of fighting back. It is called self-esteem.

Believe in yourself, and you will survive — and thrive.

❖❖❖

I Am a Light You Could Read By

Marge Piercy

A flame from each finger,
my hands are candelabra,
my hair stands in a torch.
Out of my mouth a long flame hovers.
Can't anyone see, handing me a newspaper?
Can't anyone see, stamping my book overdue?
I walk blazing along Sixth Avenue,
burning gas blue I buy subway tokens,
a bouquet of coals, I cross the bridge.
Invisible I singe strangers and pass.

Now I am on your street.
How your window flickers.
I come bringing my burning body
like an armful of tigerlilies,
like a votive lantern,
like a roomful of tassels and leopards and grapes
for you to come into,
dance in my burning
and we will flare up together like stars
and fall to sleep.

❖❖❖

Loving Whom We Choose

Lisa Orlando

The struggles of "sexual minorities" within the lesbian and gay and feminist movements have revived interest in issues of sexual freedom. Within our movements such interests seemed, over the years since Stonewall, to have become increasingly confined to our radical margins. Now, however, S/M, man–boy love, butch and femme role-playing, sex workers, cross-dressing, and other sexual behavior are widely discussed in our publications and community meetings, with the result that a renaissance of our early "sex radicalism" seems to be occurring. However, in the midst of all this talk of sex, one sexual practice — bisexuality — is rarely discussed. If we really want a sexually liberating renaissance, we must discuss and rethink bisexuality in the same way that we have other forms of gay "deviance."

In the early days of our movement, many gay liberationists agreed that both homosexual and heterosexual potentials existed in all human beings. They believed that heterosexual culture so vigorously oppresses those who insist on expressing homosexual desire because, as Martha Shelley, one of the first post-Stonewall theorists, wrote, we are heterosexuals' "own worst fears made flesh."* Even later separatist lesbian-feminists like the Furies collective affirmed the inherent bisexuality of human nature. If the feminist and gay liberation movements succeeded, they thought, the gay and straight dichotomy would disappear. Although, as Dennis Altman pointed out, many people would still not *practice* bisexuality, we would nevertheless achieve the "end of the homosexual" as a meaningful category.

Belief in bisexuality as a utopian potential has not always coincided, as it has for Altman, with support for and acceptance of bisexuals. Nevertheless, bisexuals who were active in the earliest days of the gay liberation movement seem to have had little trouble being accepted as gay. But times change. Few gay activists now claim to be striving for a bisexual paradise or to regard bisexuality as a repressed human potential. And while many nonbisexual gays have, as individuals, supported us and encouraged our attempts

---

*Quoted in Dennis Altman, *Homosexual: Oppression and Liberation,* Avon Books, 1971, p. 69.

to organize, the lesbian and gay community abounds with negative images of bisexuals as fence-sitters, traitors, cop-outs, closet cases, people whose primary goal in life is to retain "heterosexual privilege," power-hungry seducers who use and discard their same-sex lovers like so many Kleenex.

These stereotypes result from the ambiguous position of bisexuals, poised as we are between what currently appear as two mutually exclusive sexual cultures, one with the power to exercise violent repression against the other. Others grow out of the popular assumption, contrary to that of early gay liberation, that homosexual and heterosexual *desires* exclude each other. Still others result from lesbian-feminism, which argues that lesbianism is a political choice having little to do with sexual desire *per se*. From this point of view, a bisexual woman "still define[s] herself in terms of male needs"* rather than, as she herself might argue, in terms of her own desires. Since lesbian-feminism equates meeting male needs with supporting male supremacy, it considers bisexual women traitors by definition.

Other factors may have played a role in shifting attitudes toward bisexuals in the lesbian and gay community: the growth of lesbian and gay "lifestyles" and ghettos, the boundaries produced by constructing gay people as a "minority," the development of sexual identity as a political concept; and even, as Cindy Patton has argued, the brief heyday of media-created "bisexual chic" was a factor that trivialized bisexuality as just another fashion.†

But these stereotypes also resonate with some people's personal experience and with the gay subculture lore developed out of collective experience. Most stereotypes reflect some small aspects of reality which they then serve to reinforce. Some bisexuals do act in stereotypical ways, often because we have internalized our social image. And because nonbisexuals view this behavior through the lens of the stereotype, they perceive it as evidence of the truth of the stereotype rather than as an individual action. As more bisexuals refuse to hide our sexual-

ity, as we organize within the gay community, we can better challenge these negative images and demonstrate that they are, like other stereotypes, essentially false. Other gay people will be forced to recognize that as a group bisexuals are no more "promiscuous" or incapable of commitment than anyone else (like many stereotypes of bisexuals, this also runs rampant in the straight world). "Heterosexual privilege" doesn't prevent us from being queerbashed on our way home from the bars or having our children taken away when we come out. We look just like other queers; i.e., we range from blatant to indistinguishable from straights. And many of us not only involve ourselves in lesbian and gay struggles but also identify ourselves primarily with the gay community.

As we challenge people on their more easily disproved beliefs, they may also begin to question whether they perceive their personal experiences with bisexuals in a distorted way. For example, I think we might better explain at least some of the stories about bisexuals who leave their same-sex lovers for heterosexual relationships in the same ways we explain being left, period, rather than as some special form of desertion and betrayal. And if gay people examine the problems we have had with bisexual lovers whose primary relationships are heterosexual, they resemble quite closely the problems we have had in similar "secondary" relationships with homosexuals.

Since most bisexuals are acutely aware of the differences between heterosexual and homosexual relationships, some probably do "settle" for heterosexual relationships, at whatever emotional cost, and for all the reasons one might imagine. I find it as difficult to condemn them as to condemn homosexuals who seek therapy to "become" heterosexual — oppression is ugly and we all want out, whether we seek individual or collective solutions. Other gay people rarely notice, however, that most bisexuals continue to have homosexual relationships *despite* the weight of heterosexist oppression. This can only testify to the fact that heterosexual relationships generate their own problems — and that the power of desire often overcomes that of oppression. Many homosexuals resent the fact that the thoughtless pleasures of a heterosexual relationship always exist as an option for bisexuals and fear that, as homophobia intensifies, more bisexuals will take that option. But "option" seems a strange expression to describe repressing an entire aspect of one's sexuality, and the closet exists as an "option" for *all* queers.

---

*Loretta Ulmschneider for the Furies, "Bisexuality," in *Lesbianism in the Women's Movement*, ed. Nancy Myron and Charlotte Bunch, Diana Press, 1975, p. 86.
†Quoted in Arthur Kroeber, "Bisexuality: Towards a New Understanding of Men, Women, and Their Feelings," *Boston Globe*, October 10, 1983, p. 53.

We all suffer oppression when we choose to express homosexual desire. We may suffer even more when we force ourselves to repress it. And although the experiences differ, we suffer whether, as with bisexuals, our desire might take other paths or whether, as with homosexuals, the only path is total repression. In each of these cases, our suffering results from the power of a homophobic society. We *all* share an interest in assuring that bisexuals make their choices, conscious or not, on the basis of desire rather than oppression. And gay liberation offers the only guarantee that this will happen.

Those who view bisexuals as untrustworthy because of our "options" at least acknowledge that we exist. Others insist that we are the closet cases temporarily stuck in a transitional stage in the coming-out process. I hope that as bisexuals begin to speak for ourselves, we will weaken this notion since many of us have identified as such for years—and lifetimes. I wonder, however, if the power of this belief might not resist such evidence. While I would argue that gay identity is essentially political—something we construct to promote solidarity and oppose our oppression—for many people, gay identity seems to imply that we all naturally possess a *sexual* identity and that this identity just as naturally fits into one of two categories.

Why do so many people who oppose the other forms of madness created and perpetuated by the psychiatric and medical establishment so wholeheartedly embrace the notion of a strict division between heterosexuality and homosexuality, a notion which originated alongside that of homosexuality as disease? As much gay historical research has shown, "homosexuality" as we understand it in the West didn't exist until, with the advent of capitalism, religious ideology began to lose ground and medical ideology took its place. What Christianity saw as a sinful potential in everyone, psychiatry reconceptualized as a sickness which permeated one's being, displacing heterosexual desire. But if we reject the psychiatric definition of homosexuality, why do we cling to the notion of homosexual desire as exclusive? That we do testifies, I think, to the incredible power of our need to fit things into neat dichotomies.

Human beings tend to use dual classification when we think about our world—pairs such as up and down and hot and cold as well as pairs such as human and animal and man and woman, where more value is placed on one term—possibly because such oppositions structure the human mind itself. Many anthropologists believe that when some aspect of a culture gains particular prominence or importance people feel an even stronger need to fit it into such a scheme and will become uneasy in the face of ambiguities. The "disorder" resulting from central features of our lives which we cannot fit into dichotomies with sharp boundaries disturbs us deeply. I suspect that the homosexual and heterosexual dichotomy gained acceptance as both sexuality and "personal identity" became central to our culture. Whether or not this is true, most of us feel threatened when the categories we believe in are challenged, especially if they shape our sense of who we are. Not only do bisexuals contradict a primary set of cultural categories—our culture calls us "decadent" because we refuse to play by the rules, thereby undermining the social "order"—but we challenge many people's personal sense of what constitutes sexual identity. Whether we threaten by introducing a third category or by undermining the notion of categories altogether, we cause enough discomfort that many people deny our existence.

If we wish to develop liberating politics, we must ask, as early gay liberation did, whether our need to classify simultaneously violates the truths of at least some people's desires and plays into heterosexism. Obviously we will never stop classifying; we couldn't speak or even think if we did. But we must be wary of both our obsession with order, with getting rid of "dirt," and our tendency to see the categories we use as natural or simply given rather than as the social and political constructions they are. This is particularly true with those categories which bear the most political weight. But the historically specific categories we adopt in order to think about our world, including our selves, do more than merely describe, or violate the truths of, our desires. They also shape and even create them. We must question as well the whole notion of an essential sexual truth which somehow resides in each of us.

I don't think anyone knows what desire is, where it comes from, or why it takes the general and specific forms it does. I'm inclined to believe that some kind of interaction between a more or less shapeless biological "drive" and a combination of individual experiences and larger social forces creates each of our unique sexualities. But the way we as "modern" people experience them, the mere fact that we experience something we call "sexual identity," is peculiar to our particular culture and historical period. Much current historical research argues that all our talk about "identity crisis" and "finding ourselves," even our very notion of sexuality, would mean nothing to people from another time and place. If both the way we view our selves and the categories into which we fit them are modern social constructions, not timeless truths, I can't view my own sense, however subjectively powerful, that I am "really" *anything* with less than suspicion. The human mind too easily interprets—and reinterprets—anything and everything to fit its current beliefs.

But we still have no better way of describing our experience than by saying that we have discovered what we "really" are. In using the term "really," we acknowledge the experience many people have either of having "always known" or of coming to a place where they finally feel at home. I, too, believe, seventeen years after "discovering" my bisexuality and ten years after relinquishing my lesbian identity, that I am "really" bisexual.

Bisexuality: A Stage

Many exclusive homosexuals *do* experience bisexuality as a stage (as indeed do some heterosexuals). This obviously bolsters the belief that "real" bisexuality doesn't exist. People who have had this experience tend to look back at their old selves with condescension and embarrassment. I suspect that the word "bisexual" triggers unpleasant feelings in many of them which they project on anyone claiming a bisexual identity.

While most self-defined homosexuals and heterosexuals may be correct in seeing their own bisexuality as just a stage, inevitably some people who see themselves as exclusively homosexual or heterosexual will have repressed rather than "grown out of" bisexuality. As some lesbians in the fifties who were neither butch nor femme felt forced to choose, so do some bisexuals. Both sides often exert so much pressure to "make up your mind" and direct so much contempt at people who are unwilling to do so—and most of us are so unaware of bisexuality as a legitimate possibility—that a simple need for acceptance and community often forces people (particularly, and often most painfully, young people) to repress one aspect of their desire. Just as closet queers (also perhaps bisexual) often lead the pack in homophobic attacks,

so may closet bisexuals be the most intensely biphobic. I think this is particularly true among women who came out via lesbian-feminism.

Many women, in fact, who now identify as bisexual, experienced *lesbianism* as a stage. I identified as bisexual before the women's movement, but as happened with many women, consciousness-raising and traumatic experiences fueled an acute anger and disgust with men that led me to lesbianism. Some women became lesbians because "feminism is the theory and lesbianism is the practice."[*] Or they may simply have succumbed to peer pressure (even some heterosexual women "became" lesbians for these reasons). Over the years, many of us, often because of working in political coalitions, have reconnected with the world outside the "women's community" and have discovered our heterosexual desires. We are now attacked for having "gone back into the closet," as traitors, and as self-deceiving fools.

The theoretical and emotional need to keep alive both the notion that all true feminists are lesbians and the belief that no rapprochement with men is possible fuels lesbian-feminist hatred of bisexuals. Many lesbians who oppose other forms of separatism, who work with men politically and have male friends, still see *sexual* separatism as an eternal given. But as political separatism falls into disrepute, sexual separatism also loses its rationale. As many lesbians recognize that class, race, age, etc. may be as powerful sources of oppression as gender and sexual orientation, they also recognize the futility of separatism as more than a stage. Few people—and fewer sexual radicals—really want a movement which forbids us to relate sexually to people whose race, sex, class, physical abilities, age, looks, etc. aren't exactly the same as ours. And many of us also refuse to have our desires and sexual practices dictated by anyone else's idea of "political correctness."

Many bisexuals, like many homosexuals, have never identified with gay politics. But some of us, including many women who have rejected lesbian-feminism, *have* committed ourselves to gay liberation. We see gay identity and solidarity as crucial,

---

[*]The slogan originated with a heterosexual feminist, Ti-Grace Atkinson, who first used it in a speech before the New York chapter of the Daughters of Bilitis, an early homophile organization, in late June 1970. Toby Marotta, *The Politics of Homosexuality,* Houghton Mifflin, 1981, p. 258.

since heterosexism oppresses all gay people, whether homosexual or bisexual, and we can only struggle against it as a self-conscious group. The ambiguous nature of our sexuality needn't imply any ambiguity in our politics. By choosing gay identity we acknowledge that sexuality dominates our identity in a heterosexist world while recognizing that in a nonoppressive society no one would care who we wanted or who our sexual partners were, and sexuality would no longer be so central to our sense of who we are.

Unfortunately, political movements and embattled subcultures have particular difficulty acknowledging ambiguities of any kind. Add to this the current plethora of "ex-lesbians" and we can see what haunts the political unconscious of the lesbian and gay movement. Clearly, the rest of the gay community ignores or ostracizes us at its peril; embattled as we all are, we need all the forces we can muster. Bisexuals often encounter unusual opportunities to confront and contradict homophobia and, if

we have been encouraged to develop a gay consciousness, we will act powerfully and efficiently in such situations.

But if it rejects us, the gay movement loses more than numbers and strategic force. It also loses another opportunity, similar to that offered by other "sexual minorities," to re-examine its commitment to sexual freedom rather than to mere interest-group politics. What would it mean for the gay movement to acknowledge that some people experience their sexuality as a lifelong constant, others as a series of stages, some as a choice, and many as a constant flux? It would certainly mean a drastic reworking of the standard categories which have grounded gay politics over the last decade. And it might mean a renewed commitment to the revolutionary impulse of gay liberation, which, believing that homosexual desire is a potential in everyone, insisted that "gay" is a potentially universal class, since sexual freedom for all people is the ultimate goal of our struggle.

TWENTY-SIX

◆◆◆

The All-American Queer Pakistani Girl

Surina A. Khan

I don't know if my grandmother is dead or alive. I can't remember the last time I saw her—it must have been at least ten years ago, when I was in Pakistan for a visit. She was my only living grandparent, and her health was beginning to fail. Every once in a while, I think she's probably dead and no one bothered to tell me.

I'm completely out of touch with my Pakistani life. I can hardly speak Urdu, my first language; I certainly can't read or write it. I have no idea how many cousins I have. I know my father comes from a large family—eleven brothers and sisters—but I don't know all their names. I've never read the Koran, and I don't have faith in Islam.

As a kid, I remember being constantly reminded that I was different—by my accent, my brown skin color, my mother's traditional clothing, and the smell of the food we ate. And so I consciously Americanized myself. I spent my early childhood perfecting

my American accent, my adolescence affirming my American identity to others, and my late teens rejecting my Pakistani heritage. Now, at the age of twenty-seven, I'm feeling the void I created for myself.

Sometimes I think of what my life would be like if my parents hadn't moved to Connecticut in 1973, when I was five. Most of my family has since moved back to Pakistan, and up until seven years ago, when I came out, I went back somewhat regularly. But I never liked going back. It made me feel stifled, constrained. People were always talking about getting married. First it was, "You're almost old enough to start thinking about finding a nice husband," then, "When are you getting married?" Now I imagine they'd say, with disappointment, "You'll be an old maid."

My family is more liberal than most of Pakistani society. By American standards that translates into conservative (my mother raised money for George

Bush). But I was brought up in a family that valued education, independence, integrity, and love. I never had to worry about getting pressured into an arranged marriage, even though several of my first cousins were — sometimes to each other. Once I went to a wedding in which the bride and groom saw each other for the first time when someone passed them a mirror after their wedding ceremony and they both looked into it at once. That's when I started thinking my family was "modern."

Unfortunately they live in a fundamentalist culture that won't tolerate me. I can't even bring myself to visit Pakistan. The last time I went back was seven years ago, for my father's funeral, and sometimes I wonder if the next time will be for my mother's funeral. She asks me to come visit every time I talk to her. I used to tell her I was too busy, that I couldn't get away. But three years ago I finally answered her truthfully. I told her that I didn't like the idea of traveling to a country that lashed lesbians one hundred times in public. More important, I didn't feel comfortable visiting when she and I had not talked about anything important in my life since I had come out to her.

Pakistan has always been my parents' answer to everything. When they found out my sisters were smoking pot in the late 1970s, they shipped all of us back. "You need to get in touch with the Pakistani culture," my mother would say. When my oldest sister got hooked on transcendental meditation and started walking around the house in a trance, my father packed her up and put her on a plane back to the homeland. She's been there ever since. Being the youngest of six, I wised up quickly. I waited to drop my bomb until after I had moved out of the house and was financially independent. If I had come out while I was still living in my parents' home, you can bet I'd have been on the next flight to Islamabad.

When I came out to my mother, she suggested I go back to Pakistan for a few months. "Just get away from it all," she begged. "You need some time. Clear your head." But I knew better. And when I insisted that I was queer and was going to move to Washington, D.C., to live with my girlfriend, Robin (now my ex-girlfriend, much to my mother's delight), she tried another scare tactic: "You and your lover better watch out. There's a large Pakistani community in D.C., and they'll find out about you. They'll break your legs, mutilate your face." That pretty much did it for me. My mother had just validated all my fears

associated with Pakistan. I cut all ties with the community, including my family. *Pakistan* became synonymous with *homophobia*.

My mother disowned me when I didn't heed her advice. But a year later, when Robin and I broke up, my mother came back into my life. It was partly motivated by wishful thinking on her part. I do give her credit, though, not only for nurturing the strength in me to live by my convictions with integrity and honesty but also for eventually trying to understand me. I'll never forget the day I took her to see a lawyer friend of mine. She was on the verge of settling a lawsuit started by my father before he died and was unhappy with her lawyer. I took her to see Maggie Cassella, a lawyer/comedian based in Hartford, Connecticut, where I was again living. "I presume this woman's a lesbian," my mother said in the car on the way to Maggie's office. "Yes, she is," I replied, thinking, *Oh, no, here it comes again.* But my mother took me by surprise. "Well, the men aren't helping me; I might as well go to the dykes." I didn't think she even knew the word *dyke.* Now, *that* was a moment.

Her changing attitude about my lesbian identity was instilling in me a desire to reclaim my Pakistani identity. The best way to do this, I decided, would be to seek out other Pakistani lesbians. I barely knew any Pakistanis aside from my family, and I sure as hell didn't know, or even know of, any Pakistani lesbians. I was just naive enough to think I was the only one.

It wasn't easy for me even to arrive at the concept of a Pakistani lesbian. Having rejected my culture from a young age, I identified only as a lesbian when I came out, and in my zeal to be all-American, I threw myself into the American queer liberation movement. I did not realize that there is an active South Asian gay and lesbian community in the United States — and that many of us are here precisely because we're able to be queer and out in the Western world.

South Asian culture is rampant with homophobia — so much so that most people in South Asia literally don't have words for homosexuality, which is viewed as a Western phenomenon despite the fact that images of gays and lesbians have been a part of the subcontinent's history for thousands of years. In the temples of Khajuraho and Konarak in India, there are images of same-gender couples — male and female — in intimate positions. One temple carving depicts two women caressing each other, while another shows four women engaged in sexual play. There are also references to homosexuality in the *Kāma-sūtra*, the ancient Indian text on the diversities of sex. Babar, the founder of the Mughal dynasty in India, is said to have been gay, as was Abu Nawas, a famous Islamic poet. The fact is that homosexuality is as native to South Asia as is heterosexuality. But since the culture pressures South Asian women to reject our sexual identity, many South Asian queers living in the United States reject South Asian culture in turn. As a result, we are often isolated from one another.

Despite the odds, I started my search for queer people from South Asia—and I found them, all across America, Canada, and England. Connecting with this network and talking with other queer South Asians has begun to fill the void I've been feeling. But just as it took me years to reject my Pakistani heritage, it will likely take me as long, if not longer, to reintegrate my culture into my life as it is now.

I'm not ready to go back to Pakistan. But I am ready to start examining the hostility I feel toward a part of myself I thought I had discarded long ago.

◆◆◆

CHAPTER FOUR

Relationships, Families, and Households

Losing a close friend, asking for support from family and friends at difficult times, falling in love, moving in with a roommate or partner, holding your newborn baby for the first time, breaking up with a partner of many years, struggling to understand a teenage son or daughter, and helping your mother to die with dignity and in peace are commonplace life events. These ties between us, as human beings, define the very texture of our personal lives. They are a source of much happiness, affirmation, and personal growth as well as frustration, misunderstanding, anxiety, and, sometimes, misery. This chapter looks at personal relationships — between women and men, women and women, parents and children — and the ways in which an idealized notion of family masks the reality of family life for many people in the United States. We argue that families — however they are defined — need to be able to care for their members and that specific forms are much less important than the quality of the relationships between people.

Defining Ourselves Through Connections with Others

As suggested in Chapter 2, personal and family relationships are central to individual development, the definition of self, and ongoing identity develop-

ment. This individual development happens across cultures, though it may not take the same form or have the same meaning in all cultural settings. It involves relying on others when we are very young and later negotiating with them for material care, nurturance, and security; defining our own voice, space, independence, and sense of closeness to others; and learning about ourselves, our family and cultural heritage, ideas of right and wrong, practical aspects of life, and how to negotiate the world outside the home. In the family we learn about socially defined **gender roles**: what it means to be a daughter, sister, wife, and mother, and what is expected of us. In Reading 27 Miriam Louie and Nguyen Louie write about their relationship as mother and daughter. Family resources, including material possessions, emotional bonds, cultural connections and language, and status in the wider community, are also important for the experiences and opportunities they offer children.

How we are treated by parents and siblings and our observations of adult relationships during childhood provide the foundation for our own adult relationships. Fairy tales and romantic stories may end with the characters living happily ever after, but the reality of personal relationships is often very different. Friends and family members may offer rules for dating etiquette. Magazine features and advice columns coach us in how to catch a man (or woman, in the case of lesbian magazines) and how to keep him or her happy once we have. The ups and downs of personal relationships are the material of countless TV talk shows, movies, sit-coms, novels, and pop music. Many women value themselves in terms of whether they can attract and hold a partner. Whole sections of bookstores are given over to books and manuals that analyze relationship problems and teach "relationship skills"; counselors and therapists make a living helping us sort out our personal lives.

Theories About Personal Relationships: Living in Different Worlds?

Popular writers and academics draw on a range of psychological and sociological explanations of relationship dynamics in terms of differences in **gender socialization,** communication styles, and personal power. In real-life situations all these explanations may be useful; for ease of analysis here we look at these theoretical strands separately. Virtually all this theorizing assumes a heterosexual relationship, though some points we raise below may be applicable to lesbians.

Men and Women: Sex Versus Love

Girls and boys generally absorb different messages about relationships from families, peers, and popular culture. Though empirical research is mostly concerned with people of European descent, and therefore limited, anecdotal evidence from conversations and observation suggests that differences in socialization also obtain in other cultural groups. Leaflets addressing date rape on college campuses, for example, warn women students that their dates may well expect sex and that many guys have been taught to see sex as "scoring," whereas young women are more likely to see dating as a way of developing a caring relationship. Indeed, date rape has escalated to alarming proportions: one in four American college women is said to be a victim of rape or attempted rape (Boston Women's Health Book Collective 1992). Skeptics counter that such figures are highly inflated and that many women who claim to have been raped

blame their dates for their own poor judgment in having sex (Paglia 1990; Roiphe 1994). One of the myths about rape is that it is perpetrated by strangers in dark alleyways, though most women are raped by men they know. Other myths are that women want to be raped; that if they stay out late, wear sexy clothes, or get drunk or stoned they are asking for it; that "No" does not mean "No." It is important to note that, over the past twenty-five years or so, many women, including rape-crisis center activists, have challenged the idea that rape is fundamentally about sex and have redefined it as an issue of violation and the abuse of power (Brownmiller 1975; Griffin 1986).

Consensual sex is one of the very few ways for people to make intimate connections in this society, especially men, many of whom do not express emotion easily. Shere Hite (1994), for example, found that for men, dating and marriage are primarily about sex, and that they often shop around for varied sexual experiences. For Hite's women respondents, expressing emotion through sexual intimacy and setting up a home were usually much more important than they were for men. Hite attributes much of the frustration in personal relationships to these fundamentally different approaches. She argues that many women give up on their hope for an emotionally satisfying relationship and settle for companionability with a male partner, while devoting much of their emotional energy elsewhere: to their children, work, or other interests. Some women, perhaps described as "women who love too much," try hard to make an unsatisfactory relationship work (Norwood 1986). Their efforts are explained psychologically in terms of their low self-esteem and willingness to make excuses for their partners' insensitivity and lack of consideration for them. As intimate heterosexual relationships are currently structured, Hite claims, they will be a source of struggle for women who need to resign themselves to some kind of compromise. At the same time she sees women as "revolutionary agents of change" in relationships, working with men to renegotiate this intimate part of their lives. In the readings section, Naomi Wolf takes up the issue of "radical heterosexuality" (Reading 28), as do Carolyn Reyes and Eric DeMeulenaere (Reading 29).

Cross-Cultural Communication —
Speaking a Second Language

Basing her work on the premise that boys and girls grow up in essentially different cultures, sociolinguist Deborah Tannen (1990) analyzes everyday conversations between men and women to make sense of the "seemingly senseless misunderstandings that haunt our relationships" (p. 13). She does not claim that differences in conversational style explain all the problems that may arise in relationships between women and men, and she acknowledges that "psychological problems, the failures of love and caring, genuine selfishness — and real effects of political and economic inequity" may also be important (p. 18). But men and women often accuse each other of these things when they are simply "expressing their thoughts and feelings, and their assumptions about how to communicate, in different ways" (p. 17). By taking a sociolinguistic approach, she argues, one can explain the dissatisfactions many women and men feel in their relationships, "without accusing anyone of being crazy or wrong" (p. 17). Boys' socialization with peers involves jockeying for status in a group; from this experience men learn to see themselves as individuals in a hierarchical social order in which they are either one up or one down. Thus, for men, conversations are negotiations about independence. Girls, by contrast, learn to make connections with a few close friends and later, as adult women, see themselves as individuals in a network of connections, where conversations are negotiations about closeness. Tannen comments that all individuals need closeness and independence, but women tend to focus on the former and men the latter. These differences give women and men different views of the same situation, the root of many misunderstandings in relationships. Partners in heterosexual relationships, she notes, are "living with asymmetry" and each can benefit from learning the other's conversational styles and needs (p. 287). Tannen and Hite both comment on the significance of heterosexual women's friendships, as described by Andrea Canaan in Reading 31. From time to time U.S. women's magazines observe that often a woman's closest emotional ties are with a woman friend, even if they are both married, and that such friendships provide the intimate connection that many women do not have with their partners. John Gray, the author of several best-sellers, including *Men Are from*

Mars, Women are from Venus, also makes the argument that men and women have been socialized differently and have different styles of communication (1994). He assumes that women as a group are naturally giving and caring and that men as a group are naturally "wired up" to be providers, an assumption we reject, favoring a **social-constructionist** view of gender as something learned rather than innate (see Chapter 1).

Inequalities of Power

Personal relationships always include an element of power, though in more egalitarian relationships this shifts back and forth. Our experience of personal relationships as adults often has a lot to do with our experiences as children and the ways in which our parents, siblings, teachers, and other adults used power, rules, and punishments in relationship with us. Hilary Lips (1991) describes this power imbalance in terms of "the principle of least interest" (p. 57), a concept taken from social exchange theory. The person who has the least interest in a relationship — in a heterosexual relationship, often the man — has the most power in it. His moods and needs will tend to be dominant. Women, instead of thinking about themselves, will focus more on what men need and whether they are all right. Men negotiate emotional distance by, for example, calling when it suits them, breaking dates, withdrawing affection, threatening violence, or opposing the woman's desire for a monogamous relationship — if that is what she wants.

Though personal relationships are, by definition, intimate, each person brings to them all of her or his identity — the micro, meso, and macro aspects — what Tannen calls the "real effects of political and economic inequity." The relative power positions of women as a group and men as a group in the wider society are thus crucial factors in personal relationships. These include differences in socialization and in one's sense of agency, efficacy, entitlement, and personal status as a man or a woman. These power relations, which operate at the institutional, or macro, level, are often played out in the relationship, even when the partners are not aware of it. People who are in a subordinate position in some way — through disability, race, or gender, for example — always know more about the dominant group than the other way around. A White person in a relationship with a person of color may objectify his or her partner as "exotic," may unconsciously make racist comments or inappropriate assumptions and criticisms about the partner, may have little respect for aspects of the partner's culture, or may simply fail to see how his or her own white-skin privilege creates a sense of entitlement and confidence that pervades all daily interactions. Similarly, some men consider themselves superior to women, and this is reflected in the relationship as protectiveness, condescension, lack of respect and emotional support, bad manners, or power plays. From time to time, men's magazines, newsmagazines, and TV talk shows make this issue of power explicit by promoting the idea that men need to reclaim the power they have lost to women in recent years, both personally and in the wider society (Segell 1996).

The Ideal Nuclear Family

For psychologists and sociologists the family is a key social institution in which children are nurtured and socialized. In much public debate and political rhetoric the family is touted as the centerpiece of American life. This idealized family, immortalized in the 1950s TV show "Leave it to Beaver," consists of a heterosexual couple, married for life, with two or three children. The father is the provider while the wife/mother spends her days running the home. This is the family that is regularly portrayed in ads for such things as food, cars, cleaning products, or life insurance, which rely on our recognizing — if not identifying with — this symbol of togetherness and care. It is also invoked by conservative politicians who hearken back to so-called traditional family values. The copious academic and popular literature on the family emphasizes change — some say breakdown — in family life. Conservative politicians and religious leaders attribute many social problems to broken homes, dysfunctional families, and moral decline, citing divorce rates, teen pregnancy rates, numbers of single-parent families, large numbers of mothers in the paid workforce, a lack of religious values, and violence. In a *New York Times* article on single mothers, the steady increase in illegitimacy rates since 1952 was called "a predictable metaphor for the fraying of America's collective moral fiber" (Usdansky 1996).

Although this mythic family makes up only a small proportion of U.S. families today, much of the literature on U.S. families assumes homogeneity. The prevalence of this ideal family image has a strong ideological impact and serves to both mask and delegitimize the real diversity of family forms. It gives no hint of the range of family forms, the incidence of family violence, or conflicts between work and caring for children.

Cultural and Historical Variations

The ideal family, with its rigid gender-based division of labor, has always applied more to White families than to families of color. As bell hooks (1984) argues, many women of color and working-class White women have always had to work outside the home. Barbara Omolade (1986) describes strong female-centered networks linking African-American families and households, where single mothers support one another in creating stable homes for their children. She challenges official criticism that this kind of family is "dysfunctional." Eleanor Palo Stoller and Rose Campbell Gibson (1994) note that "when children are orphaned, when parents are ill or at work, or biological mothers are too young to care for their children alone other women take on childcare, sometimes temporarily, sometimes permanently" (p. 162). Children are raised in multigenerational families, by divorced parents who have remarried, by adoptive parents, single parents (usually mothers), or grandparents. One or both parents may have a disability. Lesbians and gay parents have children from earlier heterosexual relationships. Single women (not all of whom are lesbians) have children through alternative insemination. Some families are split between countries through work, immigration, and war. Many adults in the United States live alone. Lesbians and gay men have established networks of friends who function like family.

Besides providing for the care and socialization of children, families in the United States historically were also productive units. Before the onset of industrialization, work and home were not separated, as happened under the factory system, and women were not housewives but workers. Angela Davis (1983a) cites the following description of domestic work in the colonial era:

> A woman's work began at sunup and continued by firelight as long as she could hold her eyes open. For two centuries, almost everything that the family used or ate was produced at home under her direction. She spun and

dyed the yarn that she wove into cloth and cut and hand-stitched into garments. She grew much of the food her family ate, and preserved enough to last the winter months. She made butter, cheese, bread, candles, and soap and knitted her family's stockings.

(p. 225)

Thus, housework was directly productive in a home-based economy. In addition, women produced goods for sale — dyed cloth, finished garments, lace, netting, rope, furniture, and homemade remedies. Enslaved African women were involved in such production for their owners and sometimes also for their own families. Native American women were similarly involved in productive work for their family and community, as described in contemporary times by Mary Petersen in Chapter 2. Under such a family system both parents could integrate child care with their daily tasks, tasks in which children also participated. Indeed, childhood was a different phenomenon, with an emphasis on learning skills and responsibilities as part of a community, rather than on play or schooling.

Chinese immigrant life in the United States was very different from these earlier family experiences. At first only Chinese men were allowed to enter the United States – to build roads and railroads, for example — creating a community of bachelors. Later Chinese women were also permitted entry, and the Chinatowns of several major cities began to echo with children's voices for the first time. Many shopkeeping and restaurant-owning families today — some of them recent immigrants, others the children or grandchildren of immigrants — continue to blend work and home.

Marriage, Domestic Partnership, and Motherhood

Young people in the United States currently face fundamental contradictions concerning marriage and family life. Marriage is highly romanticized: the partners marry for love and are expected to live happily ever after. Love marriages are a relatively recent phenomenon. Although most families in the United States no longer arrange a daughter's marriage, they usually have clear expectations of the kind of man they want her to fall in love with. The ideal of marriage as a committed partnership seems to hold across sexual orientation, with women looking for Mr. or Ms. Right. Marriage and motherhood are often thought to be an essential part of a woman's life, the status to strive for, even if she chooses to keep her own name or rarely uses the coveted title Mrs. People may not refer to unmarried women as "old maids" or "on the shelf" as much as in the past, but there is often still a stigma attached to being single in many cultural groups. Women marry for many reasons, following cultural and religious precepts. They may believe that marriage will make their relationship more secure or provide a stronger foundation for their children. There are material benefits in terms of taxes, health insurance, pension rights, ease of inheritance, and immigration status. It is the conventional and respected way of publicly affirming one's commitment to a partner and being supported in this commitment by family and friends, as well as societal institutions. However, under the excitement and romance of the wedding and despite the fact that many partnerships are thriving, marriage as an institution is taking a buffeting, mainly because of changes in the economy and changing ideas of women's role in society.

Compared with their mothers or grandmothers, fewer U.S. women are marrying, or those who do are marrying later, though they may be involved in committed relationships that last longer than many marriages. Though some research suggests that the vast majority of young people want to marry, a growing number of them see marriage as financially unattainable for a couple who might have to depend on the income of a man without a college degree. Others oppose marriage as the institutionalization of social and economic inequalities between men and women. As Naomi Wolf notes in Reading 28, under English and subsequently U.S. law, a husband and wife were one person in law; married women and children were literally the property of their husbands and fathers. Not for nothing was it called wed*lock*. Marriage is still, at root, a legal contract, though intertwined with social, economic, theological, and emotional aspects. Only a representative of the state can legally marry heterosexual couples, for example. Even now, according to the National Clearinghouse on Marital and Date Rape (1993), rape in marriage is not a crime in nineteen states in the United States, while thirty-one states recognize marital rape only under certain circumstances. Demands for gay marriage in the interests of equal treatment for lesbians, gay men, and heterosexual couples are an interesting counterweight to feminist critiques of marriage as inherently patriarchal, which we explore below. Through concerted lobbying and major national demonstrations, lesbians and gay men have emphasized the validity of their families. Lesbians and gay men, together with heterosexual couples who have chosen not to marry, have campaigned for the benefits of "domestic partnership" — to be covered by a partner's health insurance, for example, or to be able to draw the partner's pension if he or she dies. A number of corporations, city councils, and universities have instituted domestic partner arrangements, and others will probably follow.

College-educated women in their twenties, thirties, and forties have grown up with much more public discussion of women's rights than did their mothers, and with expanded opportunities for education and professional work. Those who work in corporate or professional positions have more financial security in their own right than did middle-class housewives of the 1950s, for example, and are less interested in what Stacey (1996) calls "the patriarchal bargain." Older women, born in the 1920s and brought up during the Great Depression of the 1930s, often valued material security with a man who would be a good provider above emotional closeness or sexual satisfaction. Nowadays, many middle-class women expect much more intimacy in personal relationships than did their mothers.

Like marriage, motherhood is also currently undergoing change. In 1994, 38 percent of women fifteen to forty-four years old had never been married. Of this group, 42 percent were childless and 20 percent had given birth to at least one child (U.S. Census Bureau 1996).* In 1993, 31 percent of the live births

in the United States were to unmarried women. The percentages varied significantly by race: among Chinese- and Japanese-American mothers, 7 percent and 10 percent; among Native American and Puerto Rican mothers, 56 percent and 59 percent; and among African-American mothers 69 percent (Department of Health and Human Services 1996). Generally, more affluent families have fewer children across all racial groups. The **fertility rate,** the number of children born to women between fifteen and fifty-four, for Mexican-American women (sixty-one per thousand) is about twice that of other groups (U.S. Census Bureau 1996). Children of color are less likely than White children to survive infancy and childhood. Although the national infant mortality rate declined at a rate of 3 percent between 1950 and 1991, the disparity between Black/White has increased from 1.6 in 1950 to 2.2 in 1991, and is not expected to decrease; Native American infants had the highest rate of death from sudden infant death syndrome and birth defects (Singh and Yu 1995).

At the same time, more than 25 percent of women between thirty and thirty-four years of age had no children in 1990, compared with 16 percent in 1976. Most are childless on purpose, despite the recent idea, popularized in the media, that women are controlled by a "biological clock," ticking away the years when conception is possible. Many of these women describe themselves as child-free rather than childless, an important shift in emphasis highlighting that this is a positive choice for them (Ireland 1993). Luker (1996) argues that, contrary to popular stereotypes, teen pregnancy rates were higher in the 1950s than they are now, that teenagers — aged fifteen–nineteen — make up less than a third of all unmarried mothers, and that two-thirds of teenage mothers are eighteen or nineteen. Fewer young women than in the fifties and sixties have "shotgun" weddings triggered by pregnancy, and fewer babies are being given up for adoption — 21 percent of babies born to unmarried women between 1965 and 1972, compared with 4 percent in 1982 through 1988 (Usdansky 1996).

Because women are daughters, we all have some perspective on motherhood through the experience of our own mothers. Many people regard motherhood as the ultimate female experience and disapprove of women who do not want to be mothers, especially if they are married. Magazines and advertising images show happy, smiling mothers who dote on their

---

*Official statistics are a key source of information but limited for discussion of diversity, as they are usually analyzed according to three main categories only: White, Black, and Hispanic. "Hispanic" includes Puerto Ricans, Cubans, Mexican-Americans, and people from Central and South America. Some reports give a separate category for Native Americans and Native Alaskans, or for Asians and Pacific Islanders, another very heterogeneous group for whom there are little data at a national level. Data on many social issues are not usually analyzed by class, another serious limitation. We have tried to be as inclusive as possible; sometimes this is limited by the availability of adequate data.

children and buy them their favorite foods, cute clothes, toys, and equipment. Rearing children is hard work, often tedious and repetitious, requiring humor and patience. Many women experience contradictory emotions including fear, resentment, inadequacy, and anger about motherhood despite societal idealization of it and their own hopes or expectations that they will find it unreservedly fulfilling.

Adrienne Rich (1986c), for example, has argued that it is not motherhood itself that is oppressive to women, but the way our society constructs motherhood. The contemporary image of a young mother — usually White and middle-class — with immaculate hair and makeup, wearing a chic business suit, briefcase in one hand and toddler in the other, may define an ideal for many young women. But it also sets a standard that is virtually unattainable without causing the mother to come apart at the seams — that is, in the absence of a generous budget for convenience foods, restaurant meals, work clothes, dry cleaning, hairdressing, and good-quality child care.

Motherhood has been defined differently at different times. During World War II, for example, when women were needed to work in munitions factories and shipyards in place of men drafted overseas, companies often provided housing, canteens, and child care to support these working women (Hayden 1981). After the war women were no longer needed in these jobs, and such facilities were largely discontinued. Psychologists began to talk about the central importance of a mother's care for the healthy physical and emotional development of children (Bowlby 1963). Invoking the notion of maternal instinct, some asserted that a mother's care is qualitatively different from that of others and that only a mother's love will do. Mothers who are not sufficiently "present" can be blamed for their children's problems. Ironically, mothers who are too present, said to be over-identified with their children and a source of negative pressure, are also blamed. Despite the fact that there are more mothers of young children in the paid workforce today than ever before, working mothers, especially women of color, risk being called unfit and perhaps losing their children to foster homes or state agencies if they cannot maintain some conventionally approved standard of family life. In the early 1990s, a series of news reports describing low-quality child-care facilities, including some cases where children were said to have been sexually abused, contributed to the anxiety of working mothers. Cultural ideas about who makes a bad mother are most germane to custody cases. In 1994, for example, a full-time Michigan University student lost custody of her child because the judge decided that she would not be sufficiently available to care for the child properly. The father was awarded custody, even though his mother would be the one to take care of the child because he worked full time. This decision was overturned on appeal. But in a 1996 case involving a lesbian mother, a Florida appeals court judge ruled that the father — who had served eight years in prison for murdering his first wife — would make a better parent than the mother (Navarro-Mireya 1996).

Motherhood has been a persistent rationale for the unequal treatment of women in terms of access to education and well-paid, professional work, though it has not impeded the employment of African-American women, for example, as domestics and nannies in White people's homes, or of White working-class women in factories. Not all today's older women were able to choose whether or not to stay out of the paid workforce when their children were young, despite the popular and scholarly rhetoric advocating full-time motherhood.

A Haven in a Heartless World?

The idealized family is assumed to provide a secure home for its members, what Lasch (1977) has called "a haven in a heartless world." For some this is generally true. Yet many marriages end in divorce, and a significant number are characterized by violence and abuse. For many women and children — in heterosexual and lesbian families — home is not a safe place but one where they experience emotional or physical violence through beatings, threats, or sexual abuse, as described by Caroline Bridges (Reading 35) and Minnie Bruce Pratt (Reading 36). Public information and discussion of this "private" issue have gradually grown over the past twenty-five years or so, pushed along by the steady work of shelters for battered women and dramatic public events like the trial of football star O. J. Simpson, accused of killing his wife, Nicole Brown Simpson. Deciding to leave an abusive partner is often difficult emotionally and practically, especially for women who are dependent on their partners financially or for their immigration status. An abusive relationship shatters a woman's self-confidence and sense of self-worth. Many are ashamed to admit that their partners beat them, or they think they deserve it. They may still have loving feelings for their partners or may fear violent reprisals from them or the disapproval of their family or religious group. Women often blame themselves for family violence, thinking that if only they worked harder, made more money, were more loving, more understanding, smarter, funnier, or sexier, their partners would stop hurting them or their children. Occasionally, women kill abusive partners in self-defense, seemingly their only way out. An immigrant woman whose visa (or "green card") application is based on a family connection has to rely on a close family member to petition for a visa on her behalf. This procedure may take several years depending on the country in question (Young 1997). Such women are very vulnerable if they are in an abusive relationship, as Deanna Jang points out in Reading 37. They often do not challenge or report the abuse for fear that their husbands will withdraw the visa petition. The Violence Against Women Act of 1994 allows the spouse of a U.S. citizen or permanent resident to self-petition for immigrant status by showing that she is residing in the United States and entered the marriage in good faith, that she has been battered or subjected to "extreme cruelty" during the marriage, and that she would experience "extreme hardship" if she were deported (Young 1997).

Family violence is sometimes explained in micro-level terms as personal dysfunction or an unhealthy relationship. Psychological explanations may also invoke a culture of violence that violent families perpetuate. Macro-level factors such as racism, working conditions, unemployment, poverty, or the loss of status and cultural roots that may accompany immigration also affect family relationships from the outside. This is not to excuse men and women who abuse their partners or children but to provide a wider context for understanding family violence. Effective solutions need to take these macro-level factors into account. The fact that the many shelters for battered women in the United States are always crowded should be evidence enough that the idea of home as a safe haven is a myth, and unless many aspects of contemporary life are changed, these shelters will, unfortunately, continue to be full. Indeed, more shel-

Family Violence

- Up to 50 percent of all homeless women and children in this country are fleeing domestic violence. Approximately 1 out of every 25 elder persons is victimized annually. Of those who experience domestic elder abuse, 37 percent are neglected and 26 percent are physically abused. Of those who perpetrate the abuse, 30 percent are adult children of the abused person.

- As violence against women becomes more severe and more frequent in the home, children experience a 300 percent increase in physical violence by the male batterer.

- Sixty-two percent of sons over the age of 14 were injured when they attempted to protect their mothers from attacks by abusive male partners. Women are 10 times more likely than men to be victims of violent crime in intimate relationships.

Source: National Coalition Against Domestic Violence

ters are needed, and those that exist need to be more accessible to women with disabilities, women of color, immigrant women, and lesbians. Abuse of children, exemplified in Dorothy Allison's novel *Bastard Out of Carolina* (1992), is another aspect of family life that has gradually become a public issue through the efforts of incest survivors, counselors, and feminist advocates. Though father-daughter incest is talked about more often, brother-sister incest is also common. Many abused children appear to block out memories of what happened to them, and these may not surface again until their adult years, when they experience flashbacks, nightmares, panic attacks, or pain. Skeptics have called this *false memory syndrome*. Research shows that sexual abuse in childhood may seriously affect a person's ability to trust close friends and lovers, form intimate relationships as an adult, enjoy sex, or experience orgasm. Many women who are homeless, in jail, or on medication for depression are survivors of childhood sexual abuse.

Juggling Home and Work

More U.S. women, especially mothers, are currently in the paid workforce than ever before. Many women work part-time jobs with low pay and no benefits. This is particularly stressful for single parents, most of whom are women, especially if they do not have a strong support network. Even with two adults working, many families find it hard to make ends meet. Although middle- and upper-class families have the money to hire help in the home—nannies, maids, or carers for the elderly—and may send their children to boarding schools and summer camps, most families, whether there are two wage earners or one, continually juggle the demands of their jobs with running a home and family responsibilities. As we noted above, this is one of the greatest strains on contemporary family life and a defining life experience for most working women, many of whom do a **second shift**—coming home to household chores after working outside the home. Women who live with husbands or male partners generally do more of the routine housekeeping than the men. According to a *New York Times* and *CBS News* survey of teenagers conducted in 1994, for example, most girls expected to marry, work outside the home, and share household responsibilities equally with their partners. Only 58 percent of the boys interviewed expected that their wives would work outside the home, compared with 86 percent of the girls. The boys did not see themselves doing what they considered "women's work," particularly cooking, cleaning, and child care. Some of the girls interviewed saw this difference in terms of boys wanting to be "manly" and powerful at home and anticipated "a lot of fights" negotiating the relationships they want. Most women spend seventeen years of their lives, on average, taking care of children, and eighteen years looking after their elderly parents or their husband's parents. In reality these periods overlap, usually when the children are in their teens. An additional factor complicating daily life is the high divorce rate, which makes for shared child-care arrangements between parents and stepparents.

Breaking Up, Living Alone

The idealized family image does not include divorce or widowhood. Making a marriage or committed relationship "work" is complex and involves some combination of loving care, responsibility, communication, patience, humor, and luck. Material circumstances may also have a significant impact, especially over the longer term. Having money, food, personal security, a home, reliable and affordable child care, and additional care for elderly relatives, being willing and able to move for a job or a chance to study, and having good health are examples of favorable circumstances. A negative factor that especially affects young African-American women and Latinas is that roughly 30 percent of young African-American and Latino men between eighteen and twenty-five are caught up in the criminal justice system.

The couple may look to each other as friends, partners, and lovers, and expect that together they can provide for each other's material and emotional needs and fulfill their dreams. In addition to experiencing the joy and satisfaction of sharing life on a daily basis, the partnership may also bear the brunt of work pressures, money worries, changing gender roles, or stress from a violent community, as well as difficulties due to personal misunderstandings, different priorities, or differing views of what it means to be a husband or a wife. These stresses and difficulties are compounded when there are children. Half of U.S. marriages end in divorce, usually initiated by women, for reasons of incompatibility, infidelity, mistreatment, economic problems, or sexual problems. Many women experience the breakup with a mixture of fear, excitement, relief, and a sense of failure. They almost always suffer a serious drop in their standard of living immediately after divorce—hence the saying, "Poverty is only a divorce away"—whereas men's standard of living goes up (Peter-son 1996). Usually mothers retain custody of the children even though fathers may see them on weekends or during school vacations. Relatively few fathers pay regular child support, and in any case child support rates are set too low to be realistic. If a woman receives Aid to Families with Dependent Children (AFDC), child support paid by a father goes directly to the government. Children are usually affected emotionally and educationally by the ups and downs of parents' marital difficulties. Though a divorce may bring some resolution, children may have to adjust to a new home, school, neighborhood, a lowered standard of living, or a whole new family set-up complete with stepparent, and stepbrothers or sisters.

Most divorced or widowed men marry within a year of the end of their previous relationship, often marrying women younger than themselves. Women wait longer to remarry, and fewer do. The majority of older men are married, while the majority of older women are widows. Women in all racial and ethnic groups outlive men in those same groups, though most people of color have a shorter life expectancy than White people. On average, African-American women, for example, are widowed at a younger age than White women. Women alone over sixty-five years of age make up one of the poorest groups in the country — together with single mothers. We take up the issue of poverty in more detail in Chapter 6. Being old and alone is something that women often fear, though some older women feel good about their relative autonomy, especially if they are comfortable financially and have support from family members or friends.

Immigration and the Family

The image of the ideal nuclear family says nothing about how this family happens to be in the United States in the first place. Since 1952, U.S. immigration law and policy have allowed family members to join relatives in this country. As noted above, this can be a lengthy process, and many families are split between the United States and their native countries. In Reading 32 Anne Mi Ok Bruining writes about this experience as someone who was adopted by a U.S. family.

Women who are recent immigrants may be more affected by the customs of their home country, though younger immigrant women see coming to the U.S. partly in terms of greater personal freedom, as do many young women born here to immigrant parents. Differing aspirations and expectations for careers, marriage, and family life between mothers and daughters may lead to tensions between the generations, as exemplified in Amy Tan's novel *The Joy Luck Club* (1989). According to Stoller and Gibson (1994), many older Asian-American women suffer both economic hardship and cultural isolation in this country. Recent elderly immigrants are also affected by cultural isolation, especially if they do not know English and their children and grandchildren are keen to become acculturated. First-generation immigrants who hold traditional views of family obli-

gations, for example, may be disappointed by the treatment they receive from their Americanized children and grandchildren.

Feminist Perspectives on Marriage and the Family

There is a sense in which marriage and family life are so "normal," so much a part of our everyday lives, that many of us rarely stop to think much about them. Feminists often challenge commonplace beliefs about these bedrock social institutions that people may not even know they hold. Marriage and the family are crucially important in feminist theory, and as we argue above, constitute a contested terrain in public discourse.

Challenging the Private/Public Dichotomy

A core idea in much U.S. political thought is that there is a dichotomy between the private and personal (dating, marriage, sexual habits, who does the housework, relationships between parents and children) and the public (religion, law, business). According to this view, these two spheres, although they affect each other, are governed by different rules, attitudes, and behavior. The family, for example, is the only place where love, caring, and sensitivity come first. How a man treats his wife or children, then, is a private matter. A woman's right to an abortion in the United States — despite many restrictions in practice — also rests on this principle of the right to privacy. A key aspect of much feminist theorizing and activism has been to challenge this public vs. private dichotomy and to explain the family as a site of patriarchal power summed up in the saying "The working man's home is his castle." Every man may not be the most powerful person in the family, yet this is a culturally accepted idea. Such power may operate in relatively trivial ways — as, for example, when Mom and the kids cater to Dad's preferences in food or TV shows as a way of avoiding a confrontation. Usually, as the main wage earner and "head" of the family, men command loyalty, respect, and obedience. Some resort to violence or sexual abuse, as mentioned above. White, middle-class feminists like Betty Friedan (1963), writing about her dissatisfactions with suburban life and the boredom of being a full-time homemaker, which she described as "the problem which has no name," identified motherhood as a major obstacle to women's fulfillment. By contrast, working-class women—White women and women of color name racism, a lack of well-paying jobs, and a lack of skills or education, not motherhood, as obstacles to their liberation.

Given the lower status of women in society, many feminists point to marriage as a legal contract between unequal parties. As Okin (1989) notes, the much-repeated slogan "the personal is the political" is "the central message of feminist critiques of the public/private dichotomy" (p. 124). She lists four ways in which the family is a political entity:

1. Power is always an element of family relationships.

2. This domestic sphere is governed by external rules—for example, those concerning marriage and divorce, marital rape, or child custody.

3. It is in the family that much of our early socialization takes place and that we learn gender roles.

4. The division of labor within the family raises practical and psychological barriers against women in all other spheres of life.

(pp. 128–33)

The Family and the Economic System

Other feminist theorists see the family as part of the economic system and emphasize its role in the **reproduction of labor** (Dalla Costa and James 1972; Benston 1969). In this highly unsentimental view, marriage is compared to prostitution, where women trade sex for economic and social support. The family is deemed important for society because it is responsible for producing, nurturing, and socializing the next generation of workers and citizens, the place where children first learn to be "social animals." This includes basic skills like language and potty training and social skills like cooperation and negotiation with others or abiding by rules. Women's unpaid domestic work and child care, though not considered productive work, directly benefit the state and employers by turning out functioning members of society. The family also cares for its adult members by providing meals and clean clothes, as well as rest, relaxation, love, and sexual intimacy, so that they are ready to face another working day—another aspect of the reproduction of labor. Similarly, it cares for people who are not in the workforce, those with disabilities, the elderly, or the chronically ill. Still other theorists explain the family in terms of patriarchal power linked to a capitalist system of economic relations, with much discussion of exactly how these two systems are connected, and how the gendered division of labor within the family first came about (Hartmann 1981; Jaggar 1983; Young 1980).

Policy Implications and Implementation

Many feminist scholars, policy makers, and activists have followed through on their analyses of women's roles in the family by taking steps to implement the policies they advocate. They have set up crisis lines and shelters for battered women and children across the country and made family violence and childhood sexual abuse public issues. They have campaigned for higher wages for women, job training, and advancement, which we discuss further in Chapter 6. They have argued for shared parental responsibility for child care, including flexible work schedules, paid parental leave for both parents, payment of child support, after-school programs, and redrawing the terms of divorce such that, in the event of divorce, both post-divorce households would have the same standard of living. Dorothy Dinnerstein (1976) and Nancy Chodorow (1978), for example, see shared parenting as essential to undermining current gender roles, under which many men are cut off, practically and emotionally, from the organic and emotional concerns of children and dissociated from life processes. Above all, these feminists have campaigned for good-quality child care subsidized by government and employers, on site at big workplaces, and they have organized community child-care facilities and informal networks of mothers who share child care. Though some of these efforts have been successful, there is still a great deal to be accomplished if women are not to be penalized for having children, an issue we discuss in Chapter 6.

Though policy makers and politicians often declare that children are the nation's future and greatest resource, parents are given little practical help in caring for them. The editors of *Mothering* magazine pulled no punches when they asked:

> Why is the United States the only industrial democracy in the world that provides no universal pre- or postnatal care, no universal health coverage; . . . has no national standards for child care; makes no provision to encourage at-home care in the early years of life; . . . has no explicit family policies such as child allowances and housing subsidies for all families; and has not signed the United Nations Convention on the Rights of the Child—a dubious distinction shared with Iraq, Libya, and Cambodia?
>
> *(Brennan, Winklepleck, and*
> *MacNamee 1994, p. 424)*

At the same time First Lady Hillary Clinton (1996), adopting an African proverb, argues that "it takes a village to raise a child." Susan Moller Okin (1989) notes that so few U.S. politicians have raised children that it seems almost a qualification for political office not to have done so.

As Stacey (1996) argues, how "family" is defined is also a political matter. Many policy makers, politicians, and commentators still seek to enforce the idealized nuclear family model. Feminist researchers and activists need to argue for the validity of all family forms. The form is not the issue. What matters is that parents and other adults are supported in raising children with love and security. Many local community organizations, religious groups, and health projects across the country are involved in this. Parents, Families, and Friends of Lesbians and Gays (PFLAG) is an example, with chapters in many areas.

Toward a Redefinition of Family Values

Elevating the ideal of the nuclear, two-parent family is a major contradiction in contemporary U.S. society, as we argue above. Regardless of its form, the family should:

> care for the family members, emotionally and materially;

promote egalitarian relationships among the adults, who should not abuse their power over children;

share parenting between men and women, so that it is not the province of either sex;

do away with a gendered division of labor;

teach children nonsexist, antiracist, anticlassist attitudes and behavior and the values of sustainability and connectedness to others;

pass on cultural heritage; and

influence the wider community.

Relationships Between Equals

As a result of the major U.S. political movements of the past four decades—for civil rights, women's rights, and gay/lesbian rights—many people, particularly women, have understood the connection between inequality in interpersonal relationships and that among groups. For personal relationships to be more egalitarian, as far as possible the partners should have shared values or compatible nonnegotiables, have some compatible sense of why they are together, and experience power in the relationship as fluid, moving back and forth. They also need to be committed to a clear communication process and be willing to work through difficulties with honesty and openness. If the relationship is to last, it must be flexible and able to change over time so that both partners can grow individually as well as together. Few of us have much experience to guide us. Indeed, most people have experienced and observed unequal relationships—at home, in school, and in the wider community—which give us little basis for change.

Shared Parenting

Though children, it is hoped, are a great source of pleasure and satisfaction, women generally bear much more responsibility for children than do men. We argue that caring for family members should not be an individual problem or only a woman's problem but an issue for the wider society. Adrienne Rich (1986c), for example, advocated thinking of pregnancy and childbirth, a short-term condition, quite separately from child rearing, a much longer-term responsibility. We noted above various changes that would bring shared parenting closer to being a reality.

Teaching Children Nonsexist, Antiracist, Anticlassist Attitudes

Currently the family is a key institution for teaching gender roles, though this may not be done in the same way across different cultural groups. Many African-American mothers, for example, emphasize self-confidence, skills, cultural heritage, and a sense of capability and strength in raising children so that they will have practical abilities and inner resources to cope with the institutionalized racism of the wider society. As members of the dominant group, White children often have very little consciousness of "whiteness." Poor children may not know they are poor until they go to school or mix with those from higher income-brackets. Middle-class children often learn classist attitudes about poorer children, expressed, for example, in criticism of their unfashionable clothes, pushy manners, or nonstandard language. Children learn about gender very early, from everyday observation, toys, games, TV shows, and cartoons, and the way adults interact with them. Current gender roles are required by the gendered division of labor. We see this as inherently limiting to both women and men, a caricature of human potential. Though nonconforming behavior is acceptable in small children, girls can be tomboys for only so long before they are pressured to be more ladylike. Similarly, boys are usually discouraged from playing with dolls or dressing up, often out of fear that this behavior will cause them to grow up to be gay. Transgressive gender behavior in heterosexual adults is equally, or maybe even more, challenging to conventional attitudes. Even if a family encourages assertive girls or gentle boys, the children have to deal with gendered reality in school. A family committed to redefining family values will need to negotiate them with the community it is a part of and seek out appropriate schooling, if possible.

Susan Moller Okin (1989) argues that for society to be just, all social institutions must be just, including the family. We argue that the family must be a source of security for its members, an element in constructing a secure and sustainable future. A sustainable future means that we, in the present generation, must consider how our actions will affect people of future generations. A useful reference here is the Native American "seventh generation" principle: the community is responsible for those not yet born, and because of this, whatever actions are taken in the present must not jeopardize the possibility of well-being seven generations to come. How would we have to restructure our relationships as well as other social institutions in order to honor that principle?

In reading and discussing this chapter, consider the following questions:

1. What do you expect/hope for in a personal relationship?

2. What conversations would you like to have with young men/women your age about relationships? Why are these topics important?

3. What is the connection between sex and love?

4. What are all the ways you know to be intimate without having sex?

5. Is it easy or difficult to meet someone you like and are attracted to and whom you respect?

6. Are you in love now? How can you tell?

7. What are your nonnegotiables in a relationship? What are you willing to compromise on?

8. How does power manifest itself in your relationships with family members, friends, dates, or lovers?

9. Do you think a heterosexual relationship can be emotionally egalitarian? What would that be like? Does it matter to you? Why?

10. Should intimate relationships be monogamous? Why/Why not?

11. Do you have friends or dates with people from a racial/ethnic/cultural group different from your own? If so, how did you meet? How have your differences been a factor in your friendship or relationship?

12. How do you define family? Whom do you consider family in your own life?

13. Have you been affected by domestic violence? How?

14. Is your family affected by refugee or immigrant status?

15. How do macro-level institutions—in particular the government, media, and organized religion—shape people's relationships and family lives?

16. Why should there be gay marriage? Where do you stand on this issue?

17. If women are to have more equal treatment within the family, what kinds of changes in male attitudes and behavior will be needed also? How might this happen?

◆◆◆

TWENTY-SEVEN

The Conversation Begins

Miriam Ching Yoon Louie and Nguyen Louie

A Mother's Story

My daughter, Nguyen, was born March 6, 1975, two days before International Women's Day. The Third World Women's Alliance was in charge of organizing a big celebration, and I had to drop off programs and files to another organizer en route to the hospital. My husband, Belvin, was there coaching and taking pictures during the birth, and I was so happy when Nguyen arrived. We named her after Nguyen Thi Dinh, the head of the women's union in Vietnam, who started the armed struggle against French colonialism. Twelve years later, during a women's peace conference in Moscow in 1987, I had the thrill of meeting Madame Nguyen Thi Dinh, by then a salt-and-pepper-haired grandmother. When I showed her a picture of Nguyen, she squeezed my hand and said, "I feel like she is my daughter, too."

I am a third-generation Chinese- and Korean-American, born in Vallejo, California, in 1950, the year the Korean War broke out. My maternal grandfather was a Methodist minister, educated by missionaries in Seoul. He was active in the Korean independence movement while Grandma raised their eleven children. My paternal grandparents came from Guangdong, a province in southern China, and did odd jobs in San Francisco Chinatown. My father upset his family when he married my mother, because she was Korean instead of Chinese.

Vallejo is a naval-shipyard town, and my father worked in the shipyard for over forty years. World War II broke the color line, opening up jobs for minorities in defense industries, but wages were low. To make ends meet, Dad also worked at a Chinese-owned gas station on weekends and moonlighted in a Chinese-owned grocery store at night. Mom took care of us five kids. While I was growing up, my parents fought constantly. As adults we gradually realized that Mom has manic-depression. One of my brothers drank himself to death at twenty-nine; another has had substance abuse problems and a hard time getting a stable job. Half my family can more or less function and get to where they are supposed to be in the morning, and the other half has a real hard time. I suppose we are your typical American working-class dysfunctional family.

After moving out of the projects, we were one of the first minority families to move into another neighborhood in Vallejo. After more black families moved in, some whites began to get hostile. I remember picking up the telephone party line one day and hearing, "Too many niggers are moving into the neighborhood." I thought, "Gee, are they talking about us?" That was my first encounter with racial discrimination. Our Irish-American playmates up the hill called us "Chinks" and "Japs." Mom told us different names we could call whites. One day when they called us "Japs" we called them "Limeys," and they got really mad and broke one of our windows.

When I was a high-school student, a Black Muslim tried to sell me a newspaper on the street, saying, "Hey, they're trying to kill your people in Vietnam." He was way ahead of me. Completely ignorant about Vietnam, I thought, "I'm not Vietnamese." Later my liberal civics teacher raised alternative points of view about the war, which started me thinking. When people at church said, "You know this is a righteous war because those people are Buddhists and we need to

Christianize them," I thought, "This is wrong." That was it for me with the Christian religion. I quit going to church, which made Mom furious.

In 1968 I entered the University of California–Berkeley with scholarships and a Higher Educational Opportunity Program grant—the first person in my family to go to college. It was the height of campus activity at Berkeley. Students rioted in solidarity with the French student movement that summer. In the fall they boycotted classes when the school refused to allow Eldridge Cleaver, then a Black Panther, to teach. In the winter students of color organized the Third World Liberation Front to establish a Third World College, and in the spring others launched the People's Park action. When the police stormed the campus, gassing and beating students, I stopped going to classes, too.

I first met my husband in a freshman chemistry class at Berkeley. We were both trying to avoid getting F's for missing class during the Third World strike. Belvin is second-generation Chinese, and I asked if he had heard about the Asian-American Political Alliance, which later launched the larger Third World Liberation Front, which also included the Black Student Union, MEChA (Movimiento Estudiantil Chicano de Aztlan), and the Native American group. He said, "Nope," and that ended the discussion. That summer we met again at the Third World Board office, where I volunteered as a secretary. My typing was pretty bad, but Belvin stuck up for me. In some organizations women complained about doing only clerical work. In the Asian movement women have always been outspoken leaders who did both the typing and the talking.

Eventually I became so involved in organizing activities that I lost interest in quantitative chemistry tests and premed studies and dropped out of college. When Belvin and I started living together, my mother and I got in a big fight about sex before marriage. We cried and screamed on the phone. Over the years Mom mellowed out so that by the time my sister Beth was in a relationship, Mom advised her, "Don't rush into marriage. Maybe you two should live together first to see if it's going to work." Coming from a family that was active in the Korean independence movement, Mom was open to our activism, whereas Dad, with his conservative Chinese working-class background, advised us, "Don't rock the boat; roll with the punches; don't fight city hall."

Belvin and I went to Cuba together in 1969 as part of the first Venceremos Brigade. (*Venceremos* means "we will win" in Spanish.) We cut sugarcane for two months during the big harvest and met with Fidel Castro. The Cuban Revolution, Vietnam War, China's split with the Soviet Union, student movements in Mexico, Japan, and South Korea—all were events that influenced and radicalized youth-of-color movements in the United States. Our racial identification with these movements opened our eyes to what the United States was doing in the third world and shed light on aspects of our own history as third-world people living "within the belly of the beast."

After Belvin and I had been living together for five years, I got pregnant. My mother said, "Miriam, you always do things ass backward. You're supposed to get married first, then have a baby." We had another big fight about that. In late 1974 I was four months pregnant when our friends and relatives helped us celebrate our marriage with a big lunch buffet at a Chinese restaurant. Nguyen likes to say she was there at the buffet, too, eating chow mein, roast pork, and wedding cake—from the inside. At the time we were under FBI surveillance because of our trip to Cuba. Once on our way to Lamaze classes with pillows under our arms, the FBI showed up on the stairs of our apartment, asking, "Do you want to talk about your trip to Cuba?" "No," we answered, and hurried to class.

When Nguyen was three months old, I took her to a baby-sitter and went to work as an administrative assistant at Asian Manpower Services, a job-training program for new immigrants. When Nguyen was two and a half, I took her to a child-care center in Chinatown that was pretty good. She cried when I left her, which made me feel terrible. Even in the third grade, when she started a new school, Nguyen still burst out crying, "Mom, don't leave me!"

I came into the women's movement by way of the Third World Women's Alliance, shortly before Nguyen was born. Our group did some of the earliest work in this country on the intersection of gender, race, and class, and took up issues ignored by the mainstream women's movement, such as infant mortality, sterilization abuse, abortion access for poor women, affirmative action, and special admissions programs for women of color. The alliance supported women with children because a lot of us had kids. At one point there was a Child Development

Committee, and we always organized child care for meetings and events. When Nguyen was little, she got carted to everything. We took a spread for her to crawl around on at big conferences and demonstrations. When she was six, her brother, Lung San, was born.

My husband and I are pretty close, partly because our work in the movement has given us common experiences and reference points. But we also have had our share of ups and downs. We had a fight about my going back to work after Nguyen was born. He said, "We have to figure out if it's worth your going to work, because of the cost of child care. Maybe it's not worth it." We went back and forth until I said, "How come the price of a baby-sitter is deducted from my salary? How come the cost of the baby-sitter is not deducted from *both* our salaries?" After that I went back to work.

Belvin has always shared the housework and taken care of the kids. He is very responsible, partly because he grew up working in a family-owned Chinese restaurant. He chops vegetables super fast, helps when the kids are stumped on homework, attends parent-teacher conferences, and makes a mean dish of soy sauce pork. I have always worked for nonprofit organizations for low pay; he is the stable earner. He helps my various organizations with computer and campaign work, and lends a hand for special events and demonstrations. He got a Best Corporate Sponsor award for all the garment workers' campaign picket lines he walked. Now, like his father, Lung San helps me leaflet, put out bulk mailings, and inputs supporters on our data base. We brainstorm together on issues, and I badger Belvin to edit my writing. Some men are threatened by women who are active, but not Belvin. Rather, he sees me as a window into different experiences. Many of our friends are single or divorced, lesbian and straight, so as a straight married couple we are an aberration—a dying breed. Friends prophesying the end of the nuclear family call us the dinosaurs.

In 1983 I began working for Asian Immigrant Women's Advocates (AIWA), an organization seeking to empower low-income immigrant women who find themselves working for third-world wages. In 1989 I also started working with the Women of Color Resource Center (WCRC), which includes some good friends from Third World Women's Alliance days. Through AIWA I get to support Asian women workers' struggles for justice, while the WCRC allows me to work with and learn from feisty women-of-color organizers across racial lines. In 1990 I went back to Berkeley to get my BA and in 1991 I studied in Korea for a year while Belvin took care of the kids.

With all the running around we did, Nguyen grew up like a wild weed. If there were meetings at night, Belvin and I took turns taking care of her. Sometimes she would say, "Mommy, I don't want you to go," and I would say, "I have to go." Or she would yell at me as I went out the door. For a period after she turned twelve, we had big fights because she wouldn't do things as I saw fit. It took a while before it dawned on me that she wanted to be more independent. I had to realize that bearing down would only make her rebel against me.

I would have liked to spend more time with my kids while they were growing up. At the time I would not have considered giving up my organizing activities, but now I have some regrets. Nguyen still says, "Hey, Mom, where are you going? Who are you going with? When are you getting back?" Our relationship is something of a role reversal. I jump into things and end up being consumed by different activities, rushing from cause to cause and event to event. I probably get that from the Korean, manic-depressive side of my personality. Nguyen used to try to create some order to pressure me to stick around.

Nguyen has good instincts and is very independent. You can count on her to do the right thing and be at the right place at the right time. Despite having grown up like a weed, she turned out pretty well. I wish she didn't have to agonize so much over her decisions, but she is a critical thinker; she works out things in her own methodical way. Her dad is pretty logical, whereas I am impulsive and often get myself out on a limb. Perhaps because her parents have such strong opinions, she works hard to come up with her own independent perspective on everything. In college she works so hard that she barely sleeps or eats. Sometimes her pop and I tell her not to study so hard, to try to get to more student conferences and demonstrations because that's also what a college education is about. Then we catch ourselves and laugh about the kind of parents we are. Nguyen went up to Boston for a training session for our Garment Workers Justice Campaign and demonstrations against manufacturer Jessica McClintock for corporate responsibility. That made her old mom happy.

I need to slow down because I am getting older. I can't get as much done now as I used to, and I can already tell that menopause is not going to be nice to me. Fortunately, a younger generation of women is coming up that is bringing in new points of view and different issues that we had not considered. I hope they can build on and take advantage of our mistakes and experiences.

I am hopeful for the future. Women in grassroots organizations need more resources and visibility. While the mainstream women's movement is considered to represent us in pursuing important electoral, legislative, and judicial battles, they don't deal with a lot of issues minority women face. The consciousness that the women's movement fought so hard for has filtered into different communities. Now women of color are creating distinct kinds of feminism and organizing relevant to their own communities and experiences. No longer do you have to decide whether your allegiance is to the minority community or to the women's liberation movement. That false dichotomy is absent from the organizations and activists of the new generation.

My definition of feminism has changed over the years. When I worked with the Third World Women's Alliance, I was emphatically not a feminist. I saw feminist ideology as placing gender above class and race, thus rendering working-class women, especially women of color, invisible. Now women of color have crafted feminisms that take into account the many oppressions and challenges they face. I've been in women's groups for over twenty years, and today if people call me a feminist I no longer get uptight about it.

Like anyone else, Nguyen has to deal with her identity and what she wants to be. But in terms of knowing who her people are, where she comes from, and what her culture is, she has a solid foundation. My husband and I handed down our values, either through osmosis at the dinner table or just by our kids' seeing how their parents function—what kind of work we do, whom we respect. Nguyen already has the kind of confidence in the way she looks at the world that took me years to achieve. What I had to fight for, she can assume. She takes for granted the principles of feminism and is secure in her ethnic identity. We've seen her stand up against arbitrary practices by authority figures in school and job settings even when fellow students

and coworkers were afraid to speak out. The girl can hold her own.

It was rewarding to see how things had changed and developed when I went back to school and majored in ethnic studies. For all its ups and downs, that period of ferment in the 1960s was a turning point. Many of us who started out in those movements ended up forming ethnic and women's studies programs and new community-based organizations and campaigns so that this new generation can start from higher ground. I hope Nguyen can do something she really enjoys that will serve the communities and people who are struggling to get by. Whatever she chooses to do, I know she will put all her energy and heart into it.

A Daughter's Story

I am a Chinese-Korean-American young woman. It may be a mouthful, but that is who I am in my entirety. Each identity is an integral part of me that cannot be separated from the others. Because of this, prejudice is something that I have had to deal with all my life. Whenever I am made fun of or discriminated against, I say something and move on, so that I don't have a whole line of resentments following me. In high school this guy in my class would slant his eyes and ask me if he looked Chinese. One day I pushed my eyes together and asked him if I looked black. It became very apparent that he was being stupid. From that day forward, he treated me with respect.

I was born two days before International Women's Day (IWD), on March 6, 1975. This was always a hectic time of year because my mother was busy going to meetings and organizing programs for the IWD event. I resented the fact that it seemed to take precedence over my birthday. I always wanted a full-fledged birthday party with a dozen or so friends, junk food, and presents. Instead, I stayed in daycare with other children whose mothers were members of the Third World Women's Alliance. On my eleventh birthday I was allowed to be part of the IWD event; I gave a speech in front of three hundred people to raise money for a childcare center in Angola. My mother coached me and bought me a purple jumpsuit for the occasion. For the first time, I was actually doing something that might make a difference on the other side of the world. I think I grew more during that five-minute speech than I had during the previous year. That's when I realized why my mother did what she did and why it was important.

My parents were at Berkeley during the sixties. They agitated for the development of ethnic studies, dropped out of school, and protested against the Vietnam War. They were very liberal. They also gave me a lot of freedom to grow on my own. With that flexibility, I didn't feel the need to rebel. I don't really understand the kinds of relationships my girlfriends have with their mothers. Usually their mothers are overprotective, making my friends want to defy them even more. Although my mom and I are not equals, we are best friends. I can talk to her, confide in her, laugh with her, and cry with her.

We weren't always so close. As a young child, I remember telling her I hated her. I was resentful that she didn't have much time to spend with me. I felt closer to my father; he *did* things with me. We watched videos, ate potato chips, played board games, and went for walks together. When my dad brought his paperwork home, I would poke around and ask him what he was doing. My parents were probably gone from home the same amount of time, but I blamed my mother more. I guess it was because I thought my mother was supposed to be around.

When I was six, my mother became pregnant with my brother, Lung San. I was lonely and looked forward to having a sibling to play with, but I didn't expect my parents to spend so much time with him and not with me. Again, I blamed my mother. I tried to run away but made it only to the corner because I wasn't supposed to cross the street. Consequently I was forced to compromise with my parents and accept my new role as a responsible big sister, one who was too mature to have tantrums and run away. By age twelve I preferred to stay home from the conventions my parents went to and take care of my brother. We ate quick and easy meals, like Kraft macaroni and cheese and ramen noodles. After school and on the weekends when my parents were away, I rarely felt burdened with taking care of my brother or doing housework. I enjoyed being the "little mom."

Looking back, I realize that my mother always made sure we had quality time together. My father and I were content to bum around the house, but my mother insisted that we go out and do things. We went on excursions to the Berkeley marina, Golden

Gate Park, and Chinatown, and we took family vacations in Santa Cruz and Hawaii. Although it may sound cheesy, my family is very trusting, loving, and closely knit.

At home we ate a mixture of ethnic and American food. Sometimes my father would fry pork in soy sauce and sugar, sometimes my mother would prepare soft tacos, and other times I would make spaghetti. Most meals were accompanied by rice and kim chee, which is Korean pickled cabbage.

I used to feel pressure to be active in my mother's causes. I felt that I was letting her down if I didn't go to meetings. Being active was the morally right thing to do, but it wasn't always what I wanted to do. I wanted to be a "normal" teenager, to go to the movies or bowling with my friends. Often it seemed like my parents did not have any fun; they were always gone, and they came home exhausted. I wasn't able to see that their work was interesting or worthwhile. To me, it seemed oppressive. Also, I don't like to be pressured into doing things, even if they are "for the best." In a lot of ways I am more conservative than my mom. I often fight change. My mom wants me to get out there and be more active, and sometimes I just don't think I have the time or energy for it. I just want to be myself.

I like the fact that my mom gets an idea into her head and carries through with it. For instance, two years ago she decided to learn how to speak Korean, so she studied abroad at Yonsei University. Sometimes I wish I could do that, but I have a lot of reservations. When I was thirteen my parents sent me to Cuba for a month with an international youth organization. My mother said, "It will open your eyes, and you'll learn so much." But I adamantly did not want to go. My body was changing and I had started to menstruate, and I was insecure and anxious about having to deal with guys or compete with girls on this trip. The mere thought of it terrified me. But my parents were firm; they put me on the plane, and I went.

My parents were right. It was an eye-opening experience. Delegations of young people had come to Cuba from all over the world: Angola, the Soviet Union, Nicaragua. I learned how impoverished some other kids were and the struggles they were going through. When I went home I felt I had a responsibility to do something, to use the information I had gained and become more active. I started out with good intentions, but my resolve dwindled when I went to junior high school. There were many cliques that required being popular and looking cute, and I wanted to be myself. I didn't want to change myself to fit into any clique. Instead, I stayed in the library, and everybody thought I was the nice little Asian girl. I was often lonely and miserable. I hated junior high.

In high school I discovered it was okay to be myself. In fact, it was cool to be an individual. I became secure and comfortable with myself and made a lot of good friends who accepted me for who I was. When I was a sophomore I was a founding member of the Asian Awareness Club. When complaints arose about Asian students getting beaten up and kicked in the hallways, we organized workshops on interracial relationships and Asian stereotypes. Part of what I liked about the club was organizing with my friends and deciding to do it on my own. My parents weren't telling me, "You are going to this meeting and will learn something from it." *I* planned the meetings and the different issues we discussed.

My parents both went back to college when I was in high school. It was hellish for them—having to work, take care of their kids, and maintain honor grades. But their experience made me see that going to college is an opportunity to learn, not just a means to a job. I decided to go to Brown because of its academic diversity and the fact that it offered the flexibility of creating your own major. Also, being at home with my parents was too comfortable; I needed to get out on my own and be more independent. Breaking away from my parents was the hardest thing for me to do. I knew that even though we would see each other in the future, the dynamics of our relationship would change. I would change. But my parents made the transition easier by flying out with me to the East Coast and giving me lots of support.

When I got to Brown, I went through a difficult time. Until I went to college I had never been so aware of my socioeconomic background, but at Brown it seems that the majority of the students have been through private East Coast preparatory schools, and I felt they had the upper hand. I also found it strange to meet so many students whose primary goal is to make money. It seems that many students aspire to be doctors not because they want to help people but in order to have extravagant lifestyles. I was disheartened by this attitude.

The first semester was a struggle for me. My parents stressed that although grades are important, they are not matters of life and death. They never made me feel as though I failed them by getting B's rather than A's. They just said, "Do the best you can." I have learned a lot from my experiences. I know my limitations and can balance my time and priorities better. I still feel the need to work, but the pressure is coming from within myself. And with my parents behind me, I am bound to be a success.

During my first semester, I tacitly went along with the "Asian gravitational pull." It was comfortable and familiar. However, many of the Asians I met grew up in predominantly Caucasian suburbs, and because I grew up in Oakland I found it increasingly difficult to relate. Over the course of the second semester, socioeconomic differences crystallized. I still have a lot of close Asian friends who are Thai, Chinese, Korean, Filipino, and Vietnamese. At the same time, though, I have a lot of close non-Asian friends who are Irish, Jewish, Mexican, and Dominican. I think part of this has to do with the fact that I am Chinese, Korean, and American, and because my parents' friends are of various racial and ethnic backgrounds. At Brown there is a lot of pressure to "stick to your own." But for me, commonalities and true understanding go far beyond race and have to do with cultural, social, and economic complexities.

I am a feminist by my own interpretation: I believe that men and women are equal physically and intellectually; therefore, they are entitled to equal rights, treatment, and respect. I take this for granted, and I immediately assume people are wrong for thinking otherwise. It's almost instinctive. Yet I would never introduce myself as a feminist; I am a Chinese-Korean-American young woman. As such, I must deal with more than uniquely feminist issues. Issues of race, class, and culture are equally important to me. Being a feminist is an integral part of who I am, but it is not all that I am.

At this point in my life, I can't see myself as being as much of an activist as my mother, but activism is definitely a part of me. It's in my blood. I'm not sure whether that's a blessing or a curse. I plan to tap into the activism on campus, but I don't want to devote my life to it. I prefer to deal with things on a personal level. What I want from life is to achieve my maximum potential, to be happy, and to be comfortable. I want to find balance.

Eventually I would like to have the kind of relationship my parents have. They love each other, respect each other, and give each other support, but they are not joined at the hip. They have learned, changed, and grown both individually and "together as one" for the past twenty-five years, and they have encouraged me to do the same. When I went away to college I saw many parts of my mother and my father in myself: the discipline, the curiosity, and the ambition.

You can always hear and know what my mom has to say, whether it is through a bullhorn, a newsletter, or a poem. Her voice is strong, loud, and clear. She's wild; she's out there on her motor scooter. She's in the know. She has traveled around the world and back, working with different organizations and individuals and touching many lives. I am proud to be the daughter of Miriam Ching Louie.

◆◆◆

TWENTY-EIGHT

Radical Heterosexuality

Naomi Wolf

All over the country, millions of feminists have a secret indulgence. By day they fight gender injustice; by night they sleep with men. Is this a dual life? A core contradiction? Is sleeping with a man "sleeping with the enemy"? And is razor burn from kissing inherently oppressive?

It's time to say you *can* hate sexism and love men. As the feminist movement grows more mature and our understanding of our enemies more nuanced, three terms assumed to be in contradiction — radical feminist heterosexuality — can and must be brought together.

Rules of the Relationship

But how? Andrea Dworkin and Catharine MacKinnon have pointed out that sexism limits women to such a degree that it's questionable whether the decision to live with a man can ever truly be free. If you want to use their sound, if depressing, reasoning to a brighter end, turn the thesis around: radical heterosexuality demands substituting choice for dependency.

Radical heterosexuality requires that the woman be able to support herself. This is not to belittle women who must depend financially on men; it is to recognize that when our daughters are raised with the skills that would let them leave abusers, they need not call financial dependence love.

Radical heterosexuality needs alternative institutions. As the child of a good lifetime union, I believe in them. But when I think of pledging my heart and body to a man — even the best and kindest man — within the existing institution of marriage, I feel faint. The more you learn about its legal structure, the less likely you are to call the caterers.

In the nineteenth century, when a judge ruled that a husband could not imprison and rape his wife, the London *Times* bemoaned, "One fine morning last month, marriage in England was suddenly abolished." The phrase "rule of thumb" descends from English common law that said a man could legally beat his wife with a switch "no thicker than his thumb."

If these nightmarish echoes were confined to history, I might feel more nuptial; but look at our own time. Do I want the blessing of an institution that doesn't provide adequate protection from marital rape? That gives a woman less protection from assault by her husband than by a stranger? That assigns men 70 percent of contested child custodies?

Of course I do not fear any such brutality from the man I want to marry (no bride does). But marriage means that his respectful treatment of me and our children becomes, despite our intentions, a kindness rather than a legally grounded right.

We need a heterosexual version of the marriages that gay and lesbian activists are seeking: a commitment untainted by centuries of inequality; a ritual that invites the community to rejoice in the making of a new freely chosen family.

The radical heterosexual man must yield the automatic benefits conferred by gender. I had a lover once who did not want to give up playing sports in a club that had a separate door for women. It must be tempting to imagine you can have both — great squash courts *and* the bed of a liberated woman — but in the mess hall of gender relations, there is *no such thing as a free lunch.*

Radical heterosexual women too must give up gender benefits (such as they are). I know scores of women — independent, autonomous — who avoid assuming any of the risk for a romantic or sexual approach.

I have watched myself stand complacently by while my partner wrestles with a stuck window, an intractable computer printer, maps, or locks. Sisters, I am not proud of this, and I'm working on it. But people are lazy — or at least I am — and it's easy to rationalize that the person with the penis is the one who should get out of a warm bed to fix the snow on the TV screen. After all, it's the very least owed to me *personally* in compensation for centuries of virtual enslavement.

Radical heterosexuals must try to stay conscious — at all times, I'm afraid — of their gender imprinting, and how it plays out in their erotic melodramas. My own psyche is a flagrant *son et lumière* of political incorrectness. Three of my boyfriends had motorcycles; I am easy pickings for the silent and dysfunctional. My roving eye is so taken by the oil-stained persona of the labor organizer that myopic intellectuals have gained access to my favors merely by sporting a Trotsky button.

We feminists are hard on each other for admitting to weakness. Gloria Steinem caught flak from her left-wing sisters for acknowledging in *Revolution from Within* that she was drawn to a man because he could do the things with money and power that we are taught men must do. And some were appalled when Simone de Beauvoir's letters revealed how she coddled Sartre.

But the antifeminist erotic template is *in* us. We would not be citizens of this culture if swooning damsels and abandoned vixens had not been beamed at us from our first solid food to our first vote. We can't fight it until we admit to it. And we can't iden-

tify it until we drag it, its taffeta billowing and its bosom heaving, into the light of day.

I have done embarrassing, reactionary, abject deeds out of love and sexual passion. So, no doubt, has Norman Schwarzkopf. Only when we reveal our conditioning can we tell how much of our self-abasement is neurotic femininity, and how much is the flawed but impressive human apparatus of love.

In the Bedroom

Those are the conditions for the radical heterosexual couple. What might this new creation look like in bed? It will look like something we have no words or images for — the eroticization of consent, the equal primacy of female and male desire.

We will need to tell some secrets — to map our desire for the male body and admit to our fascination with the rhythms and forces of male arousal, its uncanny counterintuitive spell.

We will also need to face our creature qualities. Animality has for so long been used against us — bitch, fox, *Penthouse* pet — that we struggle for the merit badges of higher rationality, ambivalent about our animal nature.

The truth is that heterosexual women believe that men, on some level, are animals; as they believe that we are animals. But what does "animal" mean?

Racism and sexism have long used animal metaphors to distance and degrade the Other. Let us redefine "animal" to make room for that otherness between the genders, an otherness fierce and worthy of respect. Let us define animal as an inchoate kinship, a comradeship, that finds a language beyond our species.

I want the love of two unlikes: the look of astonishment a woman has at the sight of a male back bending. These manifestations of difference confirm in heterosexuals the beauty that similarity confirms in the lesbian or gay imagination. Difference and animality do not have to mean hierarchy.

Men We Love

What must the men be like? Obviously, they're not going to be just anyone. *Esquire* runs infantile disquisitions on "Women We Love" (suggesting, Lucky Girls!). Well, I think that the men who are loved by feminists are lucky. Here's how they qualify to join this fortunate club.

Men We Love understand that, no matter how similar our backgrounds, we are engaged in a cross-cultural (if not practically biracial) relationship. They know that we know much about their world and they but little of ours. They accept what white people must accept in relationships with people of other ethnicities: to know that they do not know.

Men We Love don't hold a baby as if it is a still-squirming, unidentifiable catch from the sea.

Men We Love don't tell women what to feel about sexism. (There's a postcard that shows a dashing young fellow, drawn Love-comix-style, saying to a woman, "Let me explicate to you the nature of your oppression.") They do not presume that there is a line in the sand called "enlightened male," and that all they need is a paperback copy of Djuna Barnes and good digital technique. They understand that unlearning gender oppressiveness means untying the very core of how we become female and male. They know this pursuit takes a lifetime at the minimum.

Sadly, men in our lives sometimes come through on personal feminism but balk at it intellectually. A year ago, I had a bruising debate with my father and brother about the patriarchal nature of traditional religious and literary canons. I almost seized them by their collars, howling "Read Mary Daly! Read Toni Morrison! Take Feminism 101. *No, I can't* explain it to you between the entrée and dessert!"

By spring, my dad, bless his heart, had asked for a bibliography, and last week my brother sent me *Standing Again at Sinai*, a Jewish-feminist classic. Men We Love are willing, sooner or later, to read the Books We Love.

Men We Love accept that successful training in manhood makes them blind to phenomena that are fact to women. Recently, I walked down a New York City avenue with a woman friend, X, and a man friend, Y. I pointed out to Y the leers, hisses, and invitations to sit on faces. Each woman saw clearly what the other woman saw, but Y was baffled. Sexual harassers have superb timing. A passerby makes kissy-noises with his tongue while Y is scrutinizing the menu of the nearest bistro. "There, there! Look! Listen!" we cried. "What? Where? Who?" wailed poor Y, valiantly, uselessly spinning.

What if, hard as they try to see, they cannot hear? Once I was at lunch with a renowned male crusader

for the First Amendment. Another Alpha male was present, and the venue was the Supreme Court lunchroom — two power factors that automatically press the "mute" button on the male ability to detect a female voice on the audioscope. The two men began to rev their motors; soon they were off and racing in a policy-wonk grand prix. I tried, once or twice, to ask questions. But the free-speech champions couldn't hear me over the testosterone roar.

Men We Love undertake half the care and cost of contraception. They realize that it's not fair to wallow in the fun without sharing the responsibility. When stocking up for long weekends, they brave the amused glances when they ask, "Do you have this in unscented?"

Men We Love know that just because we can be irrational doesn't mean we're insane. When we burst into premenstrual tears — having just realized the cosmic fragility of creation — they comfort us. Not until we feel better do they dare remind us gently that we had this same revelation exactly 28 days ago.

Men We Love must make a leap of imagination to believe in the female experience. They do not call women nags or paranoid when we embark on the arduous, often boring, nonnegotiable daily chore of drawing attention to sexism. They treat it like adults taking driving lessons: if irked in the short term at being treated like babies, they're grateful in the long term that someone is willing to teach them patiently how to move through the world without harming the pedestrians. Men We Love don't drive without their gender glasses on.

A Place for Them

It's not simple gender that pits Us against Them. In the fight against sexism, it's those who are for us versus those who are against us — of either gender.

When I was 16, my boyfriend came with me to hear Andrea Dworkin speak. While hearing great feminist oratory in a sea of furious women changed my life, it nearly ended my boyfriend's: he barely escaped being drawn and quartered.

It is time to direct our anger more acutely at the Men We Hate — like George Bush — and give the Men We Love something useful to do. Not to take over meetings, or to set agendas; not to whine, "Why can't feminists teach us how to be free?" but to add their bodies, their hearts, and their numbers, to support us.

I meet many young men who are brought to feminism by love for a woman who has been raped, or by watching their single mothers struggle against great odds, or by simple common sense. Their most frequent question is, "What can I do to help?"

Imagine a rear battalion of committed "Men Against Violence Against Women" (or Men for Choice, or what have you) — of all races, ages, and classes. Wouldn't that be a fine sight to fix in the eyes of a five-year-old boy?

Finally, the place to make room for radical feminist heterosexuality is within our heads. If the movement that I dearly love has a flaw, it is a tendency toward orthodoxies about other women's pleasures and needs. This impulse is historically understandable: in the past, we needed to define ourselves against men if we were to define ourselves at all. But today, the most revolutionary choice we can make is to affirm other women's choices, whether lesbian or straight, bisexual or celibate.

NOW President Patricia Ireland speaks for me even though our sexual lives are not identical. Simone de Beauvoir speaks for me even though our sexual lives are not identical. Audre Lorde speaks for me even though our sexual lives are not identical. Is it the chromosomes of your lovers that establish you as a feminist? Or is it the life you make out of the love you make?

◆◆◆

TWENTY-NINE

Compañeros

Carolyn Reyes and Eric DeMeulenaere

When I saw the white Mustang racing toward us, there was nothing I could do. By the time I yelled, "Watch out!" the car had smashed into ours on Carolyn's side. It was remarkable to me how I cared nothing about my own safety — my sole concern was for Carolyn. Fortunately she only sustained minor wounds that would heal, but the accident reinforced how much I love and depend on Carolyn. It was frightening because it forced me to confront a reality I would prefer to ignore: What would my life be like without Carolyn? I still cannot imagine, but I know how much she means to me. She knows me so well and it is an amazing experience to live in this world with someone who understands, as best as anyone could, what it is like to be me. Even if she cannot solve my problems, she stands by me. She is my comfort when I feel weak or worn out by life. But she also knows when I need to be encouraged to fight or work harder. Her understanding of the world and her ability to examine social realities critically pushes my own social critiques. She has the best sense of humor and makes everyone laugh. I am known as someone who smiles a lot, but the truth is that it is Carolyn who keeps me smiling. We have always struggled with what to call each other not only for political reasons, but because wife, spouse and partner simply do not capture who we are to each other. The term I like best, both politically and emotionally, is *compañera*. Its flavor is more soulful than its English counterpart: companion. Carolyn is *mi compañera*. And I cannot imagine life without her.

Eric had been smiling way before he met me. I could tell he was no novice. It was that smile that I first noticed about him and that lit my journey through my adulthood. Everything I love about Eric can be found in that smile. In his smile lies compassion — his immense capacity to enter into and share in the suffering of others and to be moved to action on their behalf. This is coupled by his deep love for justice — a commitment to a vision of the world as a safe place for all people and to participation in the realization of such a vision. Eric's smile also speaks of his curiosity — of his insatiable hunger for knowledge and understanding of the way the world both is and can be — and of the way that he holds hope and despair in precarious tension. All of these are manifested personally and in his professional life. Eric is unmistakably Eric at all times. Consistency and steadfastness are attributes that he possesses, and loyalty is one of his most outstanding characteristics. Eric is a most faithful friend and lover. I could ask for no better companion through life.

Grace is the first word that comes to mind when reflecting on our relationship. How did we ever come together? How did we get where we are? What is guiding us to where we're going? The more we think about these things, the more we come up short in terms of answers. We've been searching the landscape of our lives for answers, for clues, for explanations, for formulas. But if there is something missing in the equation of our relationship it is a formula.

We met at what may be the most unlikely of places — a small religious liberal arts college in the suburbs of Chicago. I came from a white upper-middle class politically conservative and religious home. I began my youthful rebellion (which continues still) by registering as a Democrat and expressing my disbelief in God. Yet my background had enough momentum to propel me into the college my parents and church thought suitable. I never really felt like I belonged in the college environment in which I found myself, so I took pride in a relentless critique I waged against the school and all that I felt it stood for.

But if mentally I did not belong in that institution, at least my socio-economic class and race matched the unwritten standard. I looked like and spoke like the vast majority of the student body. Carolyn's story was much different. Coming from a low-income Latino family from Miami, she looked, spoke and thought very differently. Racism and sexism on campus slowly worked to push her to the social, political and spiritual edges of the campus. It was here that we found each other and our friendship developed as we vented our frustrations with the ultra-conservative, racist and sexist environment in which we existed.

Back then it didn't occur to me that we would have to negotiate racial or class differences or gender roles. I was aware of many of those differences but had given little thought to the idea that they could play a significant role in our relationship. I had no idea that the power dynamics that were at play at the wider societal level could have a bearing on our micro-level relationship. Neither had I given much thought to the possible social and political statements our relationship would make to the communities to which we belong and to society-at-large. It would be several years before we would hear my sister-in-law's father say to me in congratulatory fashion, *"Estás blanqueando la raza"* (You're whitening the race) when meeting Eric for the first time. It would be quite some time before I would face the disap-

proving looks from progressive people of color who count me as yet another traitor who is "sleeping with the enemy." It would take a lot less time for Eric to gain status among white liberals who believe his being in a relationship with a woman of color is an admirable and "down" reality.

Yet society affects even the most personal areas of our lives. We have clearly rejected societal expectations for our relationship in terms of gender roles, but in so doing we have often been just as controlled by those expectations when we try to live in opposition to them. It is fine for Carolyn to handle the finances and for me to do the laundry, for instance. But Carolyn's enjoyment of washing dishes and my greater knowledge about automotive mechanics often makes us feel uneasy. Whenever we notice ourselves or each other acting in traditional ways in terms of sex roles, we pause to critically examine why we're doing what we're doing. Are we sure we really want to be doing this or are we somehow giving in to societal pressures and expectations? The time and energy expended in this process reminds us that those forces continue to have some power in our lives — to some degree controlling us even though we are explicitly trying to break free from their constraints.

No place do we face societal constraints more directly than in our families. A pattern has evolved during our visits to Miami, and always in Eric's presence, in which both of my sisters-in-law publicly bemoan being married to Latino men. During these visits, when Eric cooks or washes the dishes, my sisters-in-law will often comment on my luck in finding such a helpful and supportive white man because they believe Latino men don't help much around the house. They praise Eric profusely for "helping" me and explain, "Eric, you just don't understand Latino men. They just don't do that," completely unaware of their internalized sexism and racism. They later go on to comment, "American [read "white"] men are the best!" Eric and I try to explain the dangers of generalizing from their experiences, but regardless of our words, these experiences fit their preconceived ideas and they continue to fail to see that sexism knows no ethnic boundaries and that there are men from all backgrounds who attempt to defy the stereotypical roles into which they have been socialized.

While my mother shares my sisters-in-law's perceptions, our relationship also makes her uncomfortable. She agrees that I am lucky to have such a helpful and caring man in my life but fears that I am too controlling and not supportive enough of him. When either of us goes out, whether to dance clubs or school events, unaccompanied by the other partner, my mother criticizes me for not supporting him. Eric is a high-school history teacher and I am finishing up my Masters degree in Social Work. There is something about our independence — and mine in particular — that does not sit well with her. In fact, it is my independence, in thought and action, that has caused her to label me *de carácter fuerte* ("of strong character" — not a positive characteristic for a woman) and *dominante* (domineering). While my assertiveness is labeled domineering, Eric's more easygoing attitude makes him seem "wrapped-around my finger." *No hay nada mas feo que una mujer que domine a un hombre* (There's nothing uglier than a woman who dominates a man), I can hear her say. We're both quite certain that if the opposite were true it would go unchallenged.

In addition to our families expecting us to live out traditional gender roles, they also confront us with issues regarding race. Most of Carolyn's family's stereotypes about my whiteness, although unfair and restricting, are nevertheless intended to be positive. Such positive intentions are often lacking on the part of my family, however. My aunt's grimace at our bringing black beans for a Christmas dinner is just one of the many ways that Carolyn's culture is devalued in my family.

While my relatives seek to embrace Carolyn as part of the family, they fail to see why she might be reluctant to fully accept the welcome. My brother, in particular, believes that Carolyn and I are overly sensitive about issues of race and gender and feels frustrated that he has to be careful about everything he says. He has frequently argued that if Carolyn is offended by his words or actions it is because she is "hypersensitive." He accepts that he says things at times that we might find inappropriate, but he never intends to be hurtful. "Why can't you guys let anything slide?" he challenges when our frequent confrontations lead to tension and bitterness. While he has matured and changed in his level of consideration for Carolyn and people of color in general, problems still arise and both Carolyn and he continue to be hurt. This raises an important question for me. My brother wants very badly that we do not challenge him on everything he says that we find problematic. Carolyn and I want very badly that my brother stop saying — and more importantly, thinking — sexist and racist

things. Given my relationship to Carolyn, what should my relationship to my brother be?

If Carolyn met someone like my brother in a different context, she would not choose to develop a relationship with him. But because he is my family it makes it very difficult. Holidays are very difficult times for us. Carolyn would prefer to avoid my family because even if nothing inappropriate is said, her ethnic and class background make her feel like an outsider. More importantly, she experiences a sense of otherness which no one understands nor even recognizes. And although she recognizes that my family is friendly and generous to her, this creates an incredible tension for her and makes her visits with my family miserable. I, however, am an insider and remain close to my family. I feel very comfortable with them, and I look forward to seeing them. How do I support and protect Carolyn while at the same time maintaining my relationship with my family? I see that Carolyn feels like an outsider in my family. Yet I also understand how her reluctance to accept my family's embrace hurts them. If both are my community, whose pain do I embrace? What does my stand against racism mean if the person closest to me has to struggle with her status in my own family?

These questions troubled me in an incident with my uncle. He and my aunt live in a small town, predominantly white, and align themselves with the religious Right. In the first interaction Carolyn had with my uncle, the subject of race came up. Speaking from his military experiences, he boldly argued that "Blacks are okay one on one; it's when you get them in groups that they're a problem." Since then, Carolyn has understandably avoided virtually all contact with my uncle and his family. But my brother will be having a wedding in their town soon, and my parents are planning to move there after retirement. What are my responsibilities in dealing with these situations?

Such unanswered questions affect us because we are both isolated from each other's experiences. In these situations, I am an insider while Carolyn feels like an outsider. We are also isolated from each other in our individual struggles with identity. I cannot give Carolyn a sense of what it means to be Cuban. Her ethnic identity is best affirmed and supported, obviously, by people within her own ethnic community. More recently, I have also come to realize that Carolyn can be of limited assistance to me in my struggle to understand how I should live in the world as a white man who seeks to be anti-sexist and anti-racist.

Developing an awareness of this reality was painful because we realized that we could not meet a very major need for each other. We came to understand the value of sharing our lives with people whose identities more closely resemble our own. Thus we have been forced to think seriously about what it means to share our lives together as people whose backgrounds and identities are very different. While there are insights to be gained from our differences, it is clear that our differences have their disadvantages as well.

Given the difficulties we have experienced in loving across the boundaries of race, class and gender, why do we bother? Why continue to struggle? My initial response to these questions is to explain that I have never been a stranger to struggle. I am reminded of my grandmother, who raised me, and who when asked how she was doing on any given day, would often respond, *"Aqui, en la lucha."* (Here, in the struggle.) Her statement was, to me, a declaration that life is, in essence, a struggle. It was less a statement of resignation than a recognition of her position in the world and a testament to her survival. Struggle, I learned early on, is not to be feared or avoided at any cost; rather it is to be embraced as a part of living.

My next response is to talk about the things with which we started this paper: comfort, encouragement, humor, compassion, and loyalty. The bottom line is that we have love, joy and respect in this relationship, and that this fits into the vision we share of the world as a safe and nurturing place for all people. Early on we agreed upon a definition of love we found in a popular psychology book: the willingness to extend oneself for the growth of another. This is what we have committed to in our relationship in which power — and the rights and responsibilities that come with it — is shared. It is the extension of *two* individuals toward each other, across boundaries. It is our vision of love; it is our vision for the world.

THIRTY

Unimagined September

Lynore B. Gause

*We choose not fully knowing what we have chosen,
nor what we haven't.
Choice is a hand that spins a top
in a whirling spectrum across floor and foundation,
releasing us into a realm we could not have imagined.*

I

My story is about the gradual revelation that leads to new choices, the choosing itself, and the challenging and unforeseen transition into new contexts as I released myself from several central components of a previous life. I focus on the interplay between the constructs of church and family, their contributions to my history and consequently my still-emerging identity. Over decades, I wove and then unwrapped the fabric of marriage, house–home, church, job and community — threads I valued — to pursue a more profound descent into self. This meant giving up the shell of safety, structure and expectations and moving like an immigrant into a new land. To use another image, I took the puzzle of my life, tossed it high into the air, watched the pieces fall and knew I had to put them back together. But I discovered as they began to land that of course they were no longer the same shape. Questions pattern the reshaping experience: Who was I then, who am I now and who do I want to be? How do I hold on to the fruits of the past even as the present and plans for the future shift and change in my grasp. The hope and goal of integration is central and persistent. The process is intense, like simultaneous death and birth, creating tremendous waves of grief and glimmerings of joy.

The life-vision for many women in my generation, born at the advent of the Second World War, was to follow a simple, defined path and stay on it until death. Variations were often determined by a default system based on the presence or absence of a man. An underlying assumption, reinforced by institutional pressure, was that a choice made was for life whether or not you changed. And no one expected you to, except perhaps to lose your shape, your hair color or a loved one. Religion provided structure and values that kept Catholic girls in place. Those were the days when the priest faced the altar, and boys with straight backs got to ring the bells as if they were golden dusters. I would kneel with my chin resting on the pew and wonder why I couldn't do that. Was it because, in the whispered words of the Mass, I was not worthy? And did that have something to do with the fact that I could not stand up to pee? I felt left out and envious. I knew that women were burned in the Middle Ages for dressing like men, but the priest and the boys serving him were wearing gowns like women and not suffering at all. I was bewildered.

Our model, the Virgin Mary, was someone who said yes at an early age and didn't look back. We were told to be "Mary-like." We knew her as a statue with molded face and veiled hair standing on a stone cloud. What an astounding and mysterious idea—a virgin told she was going to have a baby but not to worry! It chiseled forbidden thoughts in my head about the workings of her body. So how was I to act like Mary? Go barefoot? Cover my body and hair? Be agreeable, especially to angels? Never have sex, and accept any baby that might come along. The nuns put in charge of us and these questions told us to pray for God's will. Their lessons constrained and contained, and over many years I began to seep from under the form they pressed over me. A girl from the past couldn't compete with the girl and woman inside, pushing to take a shape of her own.

With the shaping of my adolescent self came the anxiety of figuring out what I wanted to do when I grew up. Becoming a nun was an option valued more by the sisters than by parents. Virginity was promoted as a higher life and still fit "the man in your life" model by having Jesus be your spouse—wedding gown and all! A vocation to the religious life offered escape from the adolescent pain of not knowing who you were and the opportunity to never find out. I spent a lot of time thinking and praying in the mahogany school chapel. When I finally talked to my mother about it she was not pleased and sent me to talk to my father. His answer to my prayers was a brief response while he was painting the porch ceiling: "I'd rather you shot yourself."

That turned out to be a limited idea. I knew my decision would cause more trouble between my already troubled parents: Protestant father and Catholic mother. Getting married was pushed by my mother, a reader of The Bride Page in the "Los Angeles Times." After college when I left home for Oakland she sent me newspaper clippings that unfolded like origami to a betrothed's winning smile and other marital triumphs, slipped between the lips of an envelope. Those girls are now yellow at the edges, some divorced, some remarried, ghosts to me and minor occupants of the attic nudged aside by thirty years of my life outside an envelope.

I wanted children and liked boys and men (as they came to be known). But my Catholic high school and college were for women (as they came to be known), and so my social and intellectual development was primarily in a female environment. I loved my girl friends with enthusiasm and loyalty. There was something about the energy and excitement of being with them that led me to look up the word "homosexuality" in the dictionary in my late teens. But it didn't describe how I felt either. In high school, I looked forward to spending an overnight with my best friend and was so happy to be with her I couldn't sleep. I wanted to feel the touch of her foot against mine. My mother didn't like me to sleep over because she said I didn't sleep well and didn't like that we shared Clare's double bed. When I contemplated entering the convent, I took the Minnesota Multiphasic Personality Inventory and worried that it would detect my intense feelings for girl friends—feelings so diffuse in my uninformed body and mind as not to be identifiable by me. I came out high on the Fantasy Scale and decided I'd better cut down on day-dreaming!

However, before entering the state of Holy Matrimony, my education was continued through such events as the annual college retreat where the celibate wisdom of Father Collins on having sex during your period was spattered on me from the podium: "For Heaven's sake, Ladies, if your husband wants It— GET OUT THE RUBBER SHEET." He stood center stage, flashing his white gown, the star at my Catholic college on a hill in a corner of Hollywood near "Divine." We sat stiffly for this bloody tirade, like tin figures in the window of an old toy train, driven by a Holy Engineer of sex drives and bodily fluids. He had nothing to worry about as back then we rode in the caboose. His grip of language carried on a venerable tradition of holding women down, flat on the rails to prevent our desires from marring the road-bed of manly needs, or delay the holy prerogative to huff and puff over an obedient woman who must give the husband what he wants and dissolve into a crimson puddle because God says so.

The message about the loss of self was further enforced and went like this: You will sacrifice your body, the particulars of which you are never to gaze upon, nor touch unnecessarily because you would commit masturbation, or some variety of impurity outlined in the Girl's Guide to an Examination of Conscience. Coveting your body is not possible, for it is to be saved for someone else, either God or man. Having no awareness of your body, and therefore being worthy and pure, you are to please your hus-band whenever he wants It, in and out, day or night, up or down. You are to be prepared and pliable like the pillow on which he lies. In this way, you and he will become One. And the One shall be him. Obey him with sweet subservience, for it is in giving that you receive the fruit of his loins, whether or not it's what you had in mind. You will be handed from fa-ther to husband like an unspoiled garment. The soul you cannot hope to call your own, shall be merged in joyful acceptance of the sacred plan as illuminated by me, your priestly father who will deliver you over with pomp into circumstances beyond your control.

I met and fell in love with a very fine and bright Catholic man. Our first child was conceived two weeks after our wedding. Quick conceptions were highly desirable then (post-wedding, of course) and birth control was a sin (still is). I quit teaching school two months before the baby was born. The photo-graphs of Dave's Ph.D. graduation show him proudly holding his son and the degree. At the end of the summer of 1963 we moved across the country for two post-doctoral years and in 1965 had our first daugh-ter. This was followed by a year in Amsterdam in the house of another academic couple with three chil-dren who had gone to the States. Several years later we heard Anneka had left her husband and chil-dren to live as a lesbian. Dutch women were among the earliest feminist revolutionaries of the sixties and were taking paths new to me. I remember we were stunned and mystified by her decision, but also curious.

By the fall of 1966 we were settled at an Ivy League college. I taught school for half a day until our second daughter was born. In the following years we raised our family in a diverse community with a strong neighborhood and friendship network. I worked in a student services program at the uni-versity for two years and did some very intermittent part-time work, but basically I did volunteer work and was a full-time mother until I went to graduate school at the age of 40. In 1987 our youngest daugh-ter graduated from high school and left for a year in England. As we drove back from Kennedy airport I was sobbing and said to my husband that the chil-dren were the most unambivalent relationship of my life. I knew that I was saying something significant to him about the two of us.

Our involvement in liberal Catholic movements kept us close to the church, but when our oldest daughter was ready for First Communion in 1972, I was getting Sunday morning depressions. That was a marker for my increasing discontent with the church that had been a primary source of continuity in my life, and it was emerging in a broader context of social unrest. The Women's Movement challenged my feelings and behavior and was de-stabilizing. Fortunately, we were able to join an experimental, non-territorial parish established by the bishop. In 1978 I became the first woman chairperson, and from that time on women were prominent in the leader-ship. When we returned from a sabbatical year in France in 1981, we re-engaged with our parish. Many of the women were becoming more disheartened about the church's treatment of women. I was angry and in my imagination saw priests in blackened suits and white collars who covered their intentions like hoods and forced us down with gloved hands in a watery asylum, an anti-baptism. They would occa-sionally offer us a slice of air and then plunge us back into a sea of frustration and hopelessness. I pictured women at the bottom, supine in death, stacked in layers on which we stood and from which we were pushing as if they were altars under our feet. I started a group called Spirited Women which met for rituals and support. My anger and discontent increased. We demonstrated in front of the Cathedral for several years, did press releases and television interviews. We were trying to push beyond the past, as we howled at absurdities and clamored with impatience. We sought new footing as the old stream slipped away, and held onto one another, not born alone but joined by the waters of a new kind of baptism.

In 1987, when Dave and I returned from another sabbatical, the parish was in crisis. The bishop was disturbed by our creative independence including extensive efforts to use non-sexist language (and no doubt by our female leadership). After many tumultuous months of trying to resolve the problems, we were closed down. It was a devastating loss for my husband and me: the death of a family community and a unique force for creative and meaningful worship and social justice in the state. Along with another woman, I assumed some leadership in working towards a creative solution for keeping us together. That format lasted for awhile but basically there was an exodus. For some, it had been the last stop on the way out of the church, and it seems to have been so for me. I felt hypocritical and couldn't be part of it anymore. It no longer was consistent with who I was. I left and grieved. It was a deeply distressing time for us as Dave identified more with the traditions and institutions of the church. It coalesced our differences about abortion and the church's attempt to control women's bodies, the hierarchical system, the leadership role of women and religious practice. We had been practicing Catholics during the years of our parenting. As the years passed I sometimes didn't want to go to Sunday Mass but still felt the pressure of the "Sunday obligation." After all, we had grown up being told that not to go was a sin. A pertinent issue was being a good example to the children, and I wanted to avoid conflict with my husband as well. Finally, though, I couldn't go to Mass for the church or for him.

My husband was afraid that if we didn't go to church together, our marriage would be threatened. We might not be able to negotiate such a central and de-stabilizing change. I thought it wasn't so, and in fact, my choice reduced the tension and anger within me and between us. Yet, I now see it as one of the many complex forces which held us together. Letting go contributed to the unraveling of our relationship, but there were multiple, related factors including the changing world about us, and my internal processes and impetus toward growth.

II

In the late '70s, in the middle of our marriage of over thirty years, I fell in love with a woman. I went into shock at the suddenness and ease with which this happened. But I also recall the elevated and sunlit state I entered as I stood in a small medieval stone chapel in France on the rim of a soft pool of light from the stained glass and said in self-recognition: "It's me. God. It's Lynore." That was a gift which has stayed with me. The ensuing struggle was not about who I was but about how to live with the consequences. It created a tremendous internal conflict as I was torn between the relationship, the implications of loving a woman and the family I had helped to create. After a brief initial phase of thinking I would leave with the children, I knew I didn't want to do that. I loved much about my husband and had no ambivalence about the family we'd created. I had expected to be married all my life. There were missing elements, including a lack of energy and communication on some levels, but I appreciated many things, including the shared parenting, his support of my education and writing and opportunities that I had no vision for giving to myself outside of marriage. True, he was more traditional and conventional, but a good person. The relationship offered some sharing and companionship, a sense of belonging and protection against the outside world. I was not ready.

I remember it was in the last days of February when we took a Sunday afternoon walk in our neighborhood with a space between us. There was a 2:30 slowness under the sun but cold enough to remind us that winter would hold on. The snow was gone, if only for a day, and everything once hidden was exposed. I walked next to a chain link fence as if I was searching for something, and he reviewed the latest departmental meeting. Alongside my moving feet I scanned the sidewalk and found a penny, ticket stubs and faceless trash caught in the fence. Just as my foot was above a dead possum, Dave warned me. I leapt, grabbed his arm, babbled in disgust at the pink tail and its open mouth caked with blood as if its tiny teeth had turned on it. As we rounded the corner I clutched him and knew it felt good to need someone, to have someone keep the possums from me.

My internal conflict was heightened by the fact that I was unable to tell Dave about this love for a woman. Early in the experience I woke up one night and felt like I was dying. It was an anxiety attack, but also a message. I found that I couldn't have a sexual relationship with two people. With difficulty I told him I couldn't have sex with him for awhile and that began a time of tension and distancing. As one way to address my turmoil, I entered therapy for a year and encouraged him to do likewise. We did some very brief couples therapy but my secretiveness made it almost useless, and I didn't trust anyone in our small city with the unique issue we had. Finally I was able to tell him what was going on, but my anxiety was so great I had to hide under the blankets as I spoke. He was relieved to know what all the tension and avoidance was about and was not harsh towards me. He must have repressed a lot of anger and hurt. Over several months I broke off my relationship and felt great sadness and guilt that I had caused my lover and my family such pain. At that time I looked less at my own hurt. Dave and I tried to be good parents, but I know the children suffered from the cloud of this unspoken problem and conflict. My family had always been central to me and I reinvested energy as we reconstructed a new marriage.

Encountering an identity and needs outside of marriage threatened everything that shaped my existence, including my values: a sense of responsibility, loyalty, family, home, friendship, community, tending to others and pleasing them. So in the following years I almost managed to repress those sexual/emotional aspects of myself which caused both upset and happiness. The joy and sense of recognition that emerged in that first relationship became supplanted by the will to continue in the life I had. But I knew that I loved women sexually, that it felt natural to me, although identifying with the word "lesbian" took much longer. I responded to the lack of role expectations and the ease of affection without it being interpreted as a sexual expectation. Sexual orientation was not just about orgasms, which I could have just fine with a man. It was about the blend of profound emotional and physical connection, and I missed that. I told Dave I never wanted to put anyone through that again — myself included. But returning to heterosexual sex was the hardest thing I had ever done. After I came to love a woman, I felt like my world, flat as a table, had tipped, and I slid down the face of it to cling on the corners, my legs hanging free just before I slid over the edge and into the surface of the other side. In the decision to return, I scaled back up the glacier and hoped it would level out into a place I could remain.

When the five of us went to France for a year in 1981, it followed upon almost two years of reflection and turmoil. I had been in graduate school full time and had to decide whether to go with my husband on his sabbatical. I was both drawn to and reluctant about the idea because it meant giving up something I had worked hard to achieve — a renewed

sense of vocational direction and the pleasures of new knowledge and colleagues. Should I split the family and have all or some of the children go with him? Should I take one of the children, go to England (where they spoke English) and try to do some work related to my field with occasional family visits? I had neither the energy or will to do something so complicated. More importantly, if I didn't go to France, I felt it would be the final strain on the family and the whole system would fall apart. I am grateful for my decision to accompany him, as for a time we had a close and simple structure for sharing and healing our individual and collective wounds. We had quiet evenings and travel and the kind of bonding which can come from being in a different world. I created a reading list for myself, took photographs, wrote and studied French.

Upon my return, I finished school, and there followed thirteen years of family life for which I have no regrets. In that time, I developed anemia due to fibroids combined with excessive periods. After hemorrhages, I had a hysterectomy and transfusions. From that time on I had intermittent bouts of not feeling well and five years later developed Chronic Fatigue Syndrome after getting the flu. I've wondered if I got CFS because my immune system was suppressed by the stress of the conflict within me. In any event, I pursued my social work, wrote poetry, enjoyed friends, theater and home. Dave wrote books and articles, lectured around the world, and sometimes we shared those experiences together. Our children graduated from college, lived abroad, played music, got graduate degrees, married. In the late winter of 1993 I began to feel low as I considered the prospect of being married for the next thirty years, the first 30 years soon to be celebrated. I was about to turn 54.

In September I experienced those feelings and needs that I never wanted to face again and knew that if I wanted to act on them I had to leave.

I remember those beautiful September days, so filled with grief. The next door neighbors gave us some grapes from their untamed vineyard outback, a purple jungle of leopard eyes. The seeds were caught in the soft casings of orchid gel suffused with light. They demanded a choice: chew, spit or swallow. I couldn't face the challenge and put them aside while Dave and I broke off hope and future from the stem of our marriage. The light enveloping the seeds grew dim, like fireflies held too long in a jar. As we talked, the grapes released their light and wept wild juices, and on a wet morning, when overnight, summer turned to fall, I dumped them into the compost and they stared back at me, the sightless eyes of wild animals.

Leaving was the worst experience of my life, and it continues in intermittent waves of grief. In the midst of re-occurring pain and questioning I knew that I had to keep on moving through.

Within a year I had left my home, job, community, friends, therapist and moved to another state where I could be near the new person I loved. I knew I was letting go of too much at once, but I was trying to find another way.

I had put aside those interconnecting elements which support existence and identity. I lacked a church and an experience of faith and prayer. I missed my home beyond all imagining. It was a symbol of the old life. I had created the space with antiques from our families and artifacts of our time together. The walls vibrated with the past: calling to me, reaching for me like spirits. I thought many times about going back to my familiar world and relationship. A sustaining force was my children, their spouses and the birth of my granddaughters—a gift of life in what was a period of change, loss, depression and several foot surgeries. Standing strong without the backdrop and foundation of my familiar world was hard. New choices and my old history knocked against each other as I spun out into a new and uncertain life.

The woman with whom I was involved was ten years younger, had never been married, and did not understand my experience as a mother and the depth of connection and bonds my family life had created. I grieved the loss of my husband—a chosen loss, but nevertheless a great one. I lived with the hope of transformation into a new way of being family. In this, Dave and the children were remarkably patient although each was experiencing adjustments and strong feelings. Basically, my children said: "Mom, we love you and want you to live an honest life and be happy." My problems and those of my lover, combined with the complex situation, were too much to withstand, and our relationship came to an end.

Now, after several years of struggle, I am going through with a divorce, something I wish I didn't have to face. Dave and I spent Christmas with our children, and it is our shared commitment to them and an ongoing regard for each other which gives

me hope that I can integrate my old life with a new one. Many times I've said to myself: "Why am I going through this?" It has to be about something essential. Why would I risk everything that means so much to me? To put it simply: it is about who I am, my soul.

> *I could more easily thread a river through a needle*
> *than go back along the path I've come.*
> *There is no undoing what I sewed into the fabric of*
> *that autumn*
> *after I ripped open the seam of life in the last days of*
> *summer.*
> *Just before I wrap myself in sleep, a thought spirals*
> *like thread:*
> *Have I cut the cloth when it was better whole?*
> *Swatches of life drift like leaves, settle on the reeds*
> *of your hair*
> *and I know I will continue to cut a new pattern*
> *from the cloth of my heart.*

My concern about the future is represented by this experience. It was almost November, almost dark, the last of the leaves falling in silent chant, like the deer hoofs that crossed the Parkway and the path of my car on a curve leading to 495. Muted in color and almost invisible, the doe slipped into a triangle of trees like a slender stream swallowed by a cave, her return to open terrain uncharted, her survival the other side of dark, uncertain.

I have returned to the community I left three years ago. As I create a new life and a new living space, I think about the meaning of it all. I find that I am taking the objects I love—full of the history of the past—and my recent quest and blending them together. I remind myself that the richness and goodness of the past does not have to be denied or negated. I want to integrate it within my new home and in myself. I am creating a place where I can experience the joy and comfort of being with myself, and I am creating a gathering place where my family and friends can experience the joy and comfort of being together. Among these friends is a woman I have grown to love. Her background is similar to mine and she too is in the process of ending a marriage which she also valued. Now we are on a shared journey of separation as she continues a process of clarification about her future. It is hard to wait for the unknown, but I live in hope as I move ahead with my life. The familiar foundations of church and family are gone or in transformation as I am released into a realm I could not

have imagined. After a lifetime of labor and longing
I am born into myself, both newborn and midwife.

> *In the middle years of transit*
> *I pushed my head against the encircling flesh of fear,*

> *stretched beyond encasements of mind and body,*
> *tore free of the limits, my eyes open and stunned*
> *by the searing light of sameness, and breathed*
> *yes yes yes.*

THIRTY-ONE

◆◆◆

Girlfriends

Andrea R. Canaan

You know, the kind of woman friend you
can be a girl with.
You know what I mean a woman you giggle
with one minute and can be dead serious
the next.
The kind of friend that you can be a bitch
with and she thinks that you were being
a bitch just then, and tells you so.
The kind of friend that you usually
tell all to and when you forget to tell
her some secret that you have been holding
and casually mention it to her, you are
surprised that you hadn't told her.
You know, the kind of friend that you can
go out with and it's not always dutch.
The kind of woman friend that you
play with and sleep with and go to
the movies with and gossip half the day
or night with and argue politics with and
never agree yet always agree with . . . you know?
The kind of friend that you keep secrets
for and with and can be P.I. with, in fact
you both insist upon it.
I mean the kind of friend that you laugh
and cry with over some woman breaking your
heart even though this is the fourth time
this year it's happened, and she will hold
you and let you wail
just like it was the very first time your
heart was ever broken.
The kind of woman that will leave
no stone unturned to find out why she hurt
your feelings even if she didn't mean to and
especially if she did.
The kind of friend that you will accept
an apology from graciously even when you feel
now that you might have been being hypersensitive that day and revel in the knowing
that someone cares so much how you feel and
you don't have to worry about monogamy or
polygamy or which side of the bed is yours
or nothing.
The kind of woman friend that you can tell
how your lover done you so wrong and she
doesn't get mad when you don't do all those
things you swore you would.
The kind of friend that you can get
mad with or strongly disagree with or lose
it with and she will not give up on you
or stop loving you.
The kind of friend that will give
you space to fall in love even though your
new affair is taking the spontaneity out
of her being able to pop over or to
call you late about some small bit of
info to hear your voice and be assured
about some fear that you can not
yet name.
The kind of friend that doesn't get mad
until she has not seen or heard from you
for two solid weeks and then she comes
over or calls and cusses your ass out for days
and then you go out for an ice cream cone.
I mean the kind of friend that stays mad
with the people that fuck over you long
after you have forgiven them.
The kind of friend that
allows you to wallow in self pity for
just so long and then gives you a swift
kick.

The kind of friend that close or far apart
she will be there for you, the distance wiped
away instantly to meet some outside enemy or
trouble.

I mean the kind of woman who always honors
what is private and vulnerable for you.

You know, I mean girlfriends.

THIRTY-TWO

◆◆◆

To Omoni, in Korea

Anne Mi Ok Bruining

Just before falling
asleep you appear before
me, I, slipping

off the foggy edge
into restless oblivion
a vague *nyo* figure hovering
a few inches from my bedroom curtain

then with a brilliant
light
behind the lids of my eyes

oh the glaring
sight of you, the soft
hazy words
of *hangul* sing

to me the sweet notes
of a once familiar song
now harboring only
the mournful *um-ok*
of unremembered memories.

I am your daughter
your child, dear *yo-ja*
I myself a *yo-ja* now
whimpering and crying
to you still
feeling the child
like yearnings
from a previous life when

I feel the comforting
pyong-hwa of your steady
self and am quieted
by the soothing
strokes and caressing
touches and rocking

of your body as I fall
asleep in your arms.

I see your dark, ghostly
sa-mang eyes, moist and lined·
from the invisible scars
of an incomplete motherhood
perhaps you still mourn.

Your almost black hair
streaked with white
from
go-saeng of giving me up
and not surviving
the loss after all.

Yet, I see you
no-ryok and resilient
as the warrior
fighting the battle
to survive
in me

when you were alive
before I was left behind
yong-won on the grey, cement
City Hall steps in Seoul
you were living before

my years of sleeping
on a tiny, thin mattress
with dozens of other
children, each clutching
her only possession, a doll
or a broken toy

within the cold, grey walls
of the orphanage
you had a *ttal*

who learned to never
feel *shin-tak*
or wonder aloud about you
after I was adopted
while the questions surfaced
into silence.

I feel neither the regret
nor the anger, and no,
it isn't the pain, nor the cruelty
but a longing *hae-mang* I ache

when we do meet someday
I have abandoned
bitter resentment
I see the *sa-shil* of your tears
touch your face
feel your pain

that what you feel is a small
element of *cha-bu-sim*
and all of our unspoken
questions will be
answered in the reality
of realizing that

the moment I will miss
you the most will be
when I give birth
to my future *ttal*.

Then the circle will be
complete, and a gift
of *ae-jeong* will have entered
into this mortal world
for us, *Omoni*.

> **nyo** female
> **hangul** our native "Korean" language
> **um-ok** music
> **yo-ja** woman
> **pyong-hwa** peace
> **sa-mang** death
> **go-saeng** hardship
> **no-ryok** strength
> **yong-won** forever
> **shin-tak** trust
> **hae-mang** hope
> **sa-shil** truth
> **cha-bu-sim** pride
> **ttal** daughter
> **ae-jeong** love
> **omoni** (birth) mother

After thirty-six years Mi Ok was found by her birth mother in Seoul, Korea. Mi Ok now lives and works in Korea and is reconnecting with her birth mother, who is alive and well.

THIRTY-THREE

◆◆◆

Loving Across the Boundary

Ann Filemyr

Nubian, our puppy, scratches and whines at the bedroom door. Essie sits bolt upright in bed crying out: "What time is it?" Groggy, I squint at the clock, "Almost seven—"

"Granny was supposed to wake us up at six!"

"Maybe she forgot—" I hustle into my bathrobe at the insistent scratching on the door, "I've got to let Nubi out—"

"Granny never forgets to wake us," Essie mutters under her breath as she scrambles out of the tangled sheets.

I race down the stairs, "Granny! GRANNY!"

I find her body on the cold kitchen floor, but she is gone. I can feel her spirit lifting up and out into the golden morning light filtering through the grand old maples that surround the farmhouse. Despite the utter peace in the room, I panic.

"Essie! Essie Carol!" I scream up the stairs to my partner.

Granny's breath is gone, but her body remains. A line from the book *Daughters of Copper Woman* circles through my mind, *"And she left her bag of bones on the beach. . . ."* Sun crowds the kitchen and the golden maple leaves gleam in October light. Essie flies barefoot across cold linoleum, cradling Granny in her arms, the first sob rising in our throats.

Granny was wearing the tee shirt I had given her from my trip to Brazil. Beneath a little refrain in Portuguese about protecting the rainforest for all the forest creatures was a brown-skinned elf with a green leaf hat. It reminded me of Granny's love for the forest, for the "red-birds" (cardinals) and "loud-mouth crows," for the gentle deer. She would wait all day just to catch a glimpse of them, moving from one window to the next or taking the short trail up to Sunset Hill to sit on her bench, waiting, watching for the deer.

Granny had on the green stretch pants Essie had given her, and pinned to the inside of her pants were her house keys. She always carried her keys when she went out on the paths surrounding the wooded farmhouse where we lived. She loved to take her cane and her cat and go out for a morning walk before we left for work. When she didn't have pockets, she would pin her keys to the inside of her pants just in case in our morning rush to get to work we would leave and lock her out; of course, we never did.

Granny had made her bed that morning. She was dressed and ready for her Monday morning walk. But instead of the familiar stroll, Granny had traveled where we could not follow. We shared a long, sad look. Essie's face crumpled in pain. . . .

In the hospital emergency room we wept, our heads bent over Granny's body. Stroking back her wavy black hair (even at 79 her hair had not turned white) we sighed and pleaded. Two years earlier in ICU the doctors had told us she was gone. Her heart would not hold a steady beat. They pointed to the monitor above her unconscious body to show us the erratic yellow line, the uneven blip across the screen. Only the machines kept her breathing. We said no. It was her second heart failure in three months that winter of 1991, but we had plans for our shared lives—Granny, Essie and me. We were anticipating spring. . . .

Granny regained her strength that time. But that was March 1991 and this was October 1993. The doctor nodded to us and spoke with her strong Pakistani accent, "She looks happy. She had a long life. She would die one day." Then she left us alone, but the nurse on duty asked us a million questions about "the body"—about funeral arrangements—about

donating organs—about contacting "the family"—we could not respond.

We *are* the family—an elder with her two granddaughters. This is our story of love, though now we are the body of women weeping. Granny was ours to care for, we had taken her into our daily lives because we loved her, and now she is sleeping, and we cannot wake her.

Skin color marked Essie as the one who belonged to Granny. The nurse nodded and smiled at me, "It's so nice of you to stand by your friend at a time like this."

Where else would I be? Granny was my grandmother, too. She loved me like no one else in my life: she loved me fiercely. She knew I had stepped across the line in North America which is drawn across the center of our faces to keep us separate—to keep the great grandchildren of slavekeepers from the great grandchildren of slaves. When she met me as Essie's "friend" twelve years earlier, she had watched me closely, but then she accepted me into her household and into her family. As the elder, her acceptance meant acceptance. She recognized my love for her granddaughter and would say to me, "People talk, but you hold your head up. You walk tall. The Lord sees what you're doing for my granddaughter, how you help her with her son. He sees how you stick together and help each other out." As far as Granny was concerned it was the *quality of our caring* not our sexuality that mattered. In this she was far wiser than most.

For the past three years we had lived together in Yellow Springs, sharing meals and dishes. She would sometimes pull out her old photo albums and tell her stories, laughing at memories of wild times out dancing with her friends in the juke joint or riding horses with her cousin on her father's ranch or traveling cross country in the rig with her husband and his magical black cat when he worked as a truckdriver. Rich, warm memories, and I would sip my coffee and imagine her days and nights. What sustained her? Love—no doubt. Love and greens and cornbread—good food. That's what she craved. And the kitchen was her favorite room next to her bedroom.

She had been raised in the fields and farms of the south. When I was deciding whether or not to take the job in Ohio, Granny was part of the decision-making process. Moving back to the country after four decades in the city felt like coming full circle to her. She said she wanted to come with us. And it was here in Ohio that Granny and I had the luxury of time together to make our own relationship to each other. She would talk to me about "the things white folks do — " how they tend to "put themselves first like they better than other folks — " how foolish they looked on the TV talk shows "tellin' all their business — " or how much she had enjoyed some of the white friends she and her husband once had.

She spoke her mind without embarrassment or apology. I listened. She had survived the jim crow laws of the south. She had survived segregation and desegregation. She kept a gun under her pillow she called "Ole Betsy" in case someone would try to break in or "mess with her." Granny paid attention to details as a matter of survival. She prided herself on the subtle things she observed in watching how people acted and how they treated one another. She would interpret everything: tone of voice, a simple gesture, the hunch of someone's shoulders. She always knew when someone felt sad or tired. You didn't have to say anything. She comforted. She sympathized. She was extremely skilled at making others feel loved, feel noticed, feel good about themselves. But if Essie had not been in my life it is doubtful that I would have ever known this remarkable woman, her namesake, Essie (Granny) Hall.

When I moved in with Essie in 1982, my nomadic tendencies were pulling at me, urging me to convince Essie that it was a perfect time for us to relocate to another city. I had lived in Milwaukee for two and a half years, for me that was long enough. I'd found a new love, an important someone in my life. It seemed like the perfect time to move on with my new partner. But Essie's life was described and defined by different currents. She had roots. She had family. She told me, "I will be here as long as Granny needs me." I was shocked. My feet carried me freely; I fought against family attachments. Was this difference cultural? Personal? Both? But now I have grown to respect and appreciate this way of being, this way of belonging. Is it a middle-class white cultural tendency to break free, to move on, to move up, to move out? Certainly the bonds of family and of commitment were far stronger for Essie than for me. One of the greatest gifts in my life has been that she shared her son and grandmother with me.

I wanted to tell the emergency room nurse all of this. I held Essie Carol in my arms as she cried. I wanted to scream, "Here we are, can't you see us? Lovers and partners holding each other in a time of crisis — What do you need for proof?" . . .

Sunday mornings Granny listened to gospel preachers on her old radio, rocking and clapping to the music. When we weren't home, she'd get up and dance through the rooms of the house, tears flowing freely as she sang outloud. We'd catch her and tease her. Once Granny hung a plastic Jesus in the bathroom; he had his hands folded in prayer and flowing blonde locks thrown back over his shoulders. Essie groaned, "A white man on the bathroom wall!" She took it down and tried to explain to Granny everybody did not worship the same way she did.

We were not only a multiracial household, but one that held different spiritual beliefs. Essie followed a path she had first been introduced to by Granny's mother, her great-grandmother, Caroline Kelly Wright, affectionately known as Ma. Ma wore her hair in long braids and had been called "the little Indian" most of her life. She had married a freed African slave, but she herself was Blackfoot. Ma smoked a pipe and prayed to the sun. Essie remembered as a child the whole family would gather in Ma's bedroom facing East. The dawn's pale light would begin to appear through the open window only a few city blocks from the enormous freshwater ocean called Lake Michigan. Everyone listened as Ma prayed aloud over the family, telling all secrets, opening up all stories, praying to Creator to provide answers, to help guide them to find their purpose in life and hold to it, to be strong. Everything was said on these Sunday mornings and tears fell as Ma blew her smoke toward the light of the rising sun.

Ma had delivered Essie during a wild January blizzard. Ma was a midwife, herbalist, neighborhood dream interpreter, the community sage and soothsayer. If the term had been as popular then as it is now, Ma would have been honored as a shaman. Essie remembers the Baptist preacher visiting their house and saying to Ma, "I'll pray for you, Miz Caroline," and Ma responding, "You can't pray for me, but I can pray for you."

At the age of eight after a preacher had singled her out to stand up and read the Bible as a punishment for something she hadn't even done, Essie told her great-grandmother that she did not want to attend church anymore. Ma agreed. So Essie had little patience for Granny's Christianity. She was especially offended by refrains such as the "Good Master" and would try to point out to Granny how Black

Christian faith was a result of slavery, the product of an enforced cultural genocide. Essie would try to "educate" Granny about the ways slaves were punished for trying to hold on to older beliefs, such as the care and worship of the ancestors or relating to land and nature as an expression of the Sacred. Of course this didn't work, and I would try to negotiate peace settlements between the two generations, between the two Essies, between the centuries, between the ancestors and the youth. Neither one of them really listened to me. I would take the younger Essie aside and tell her, "Leave Granny alone. You're not going to change her." And the younger Essie would retort, "But she's trying to change me!" . . .

[A]t the funeral the man in the black suit did his best. He tried to save us. He opened the doors of the church and urged us to enter. He forgot about the corpse in the casket behind him, and he called the stray flock home. White men and Black men held each other in the back row. White women held Black women in the front row. And in between were all shades of brown and pink, young and old, from four week old Jade, the last baby Granny had blessed, to Mrs. Cooper, Granny's phone buddy. They had spoken everyday on the phone for a year. Granny adored "Cooper" as she called her, though they had never met in person. Here we sat in rows before an open casket: all colors, ages, sexualities, brought together by a mutual love for an exceptional person. As some of Essie's family members called out urgently, encouraging the preacher with *Amen* and *Yes, Lord* others ignored the eulogy, attending to their own prayers.

At the funeral we sat side by side in the front row in dark blue dresses. Essie's sister and son sat on the other side of her. We wept and held each other's hands. If Granny loved us for who we were then we weren't going to hide our feelings here. Certainly there were disapproving glances from some family members, but not all. During the decade we lived in Milwaukee, we had shared childcare and holidays, made it through illnesses and the deaths of other beloved family members — what else qualifies someone as family? Yet despite this, I knew there were those who despised my presence for what I represented was the alien. I was the lesbian, and I was white. For some my presence was an inexcusable reminder of Essie's betrayal. She had chosen to be different, and I was the visible reminder of her difference. For some this was a mockery of all they valued, but she did not belong to them so they could control

her identity. Granny knew this, and Granny loved her because she had the strength to be herself.

My family is liberal Democrat, yet my mother once said to me that my choice to love other women would make my life more difficult. She wanted to discourage me from considering it. She said, *I would tell you the same thing if you told me you loved a Black man.* I was then nineteen. It struck me as curious that to love someone of the same sex was to violate the same taboo as to love someone across the color line. In the end I chose to do both. Does this make me a rebel? Certainly if my attraction was based initially on the outlaw quality of it, that thrill would not have been enough to sustain the trauma of crossing the color line in order to share love. The rebellious young woman that I may have been could not make sense of the other story, the story of her darker-skinned sister, without a willingness to question everything I had been raised to accept as "normal," without an active analysis of the politics of racial subjugation and institutionalized white male supremacy. And without personal determination, courage, a refusal to be shamed, a sheer stubbornness based on our assumption that our lives held unquestionable worth as women, as women together, as women of different colors together, despite the position of the dominant culture — and even at times the position of the women's community — to diminish and deny us, we would not have been able to make a life together.

I have participated in and been witness to a side of American life that I would never have glimpsed if Essie had not been my partner. The peculiar and systematic practice of racial division in this country has been brought into sharp focus through many painful but revealing experiences. By sharing our lives, our daily survival, our dreams and aspirations, I have been widened and deepened. It has made me much more conscious of the privileges of being white in a society rigidly structured by the artificiality of "race."

One of the first awakenings came near the beginning of our relationship when her son came home with a note from the school librarian that said, "Your overdue books will cost 45 cents in fines. Irresponsible handling of school property can lead to problems later including prison." I was shocked — threatening a nine year old boy with prison because of overdue books? I couldn't imagine what that librarian was thinking. Did she send these letters home with little white boys and girls? I wanted to call the school and confront her. Essie stopped me by telling me a number of equally horrifying stories about this school so we agreed to take Michael out.

We decided that Michael, who had been staying with Granny and Daddy Son and attending the school near their home during the week, should move in full-time with us. Essie worked first shift at the hospital, and I was a graduate student at the university. She left for work at 6 A.M., and I caught the North Avenue bus at 9:30. I would be able to help Michael get to school before I left for the day. We decided to enroll Michael in our neighborhood school.

The neighborhood we lived in was one of the few mixed neighborhoods in the city. It formed a border between the rundown urban center and the suburbs on the west side. The neighborhood school was across an invisible boundary, a line I did not see but would grow to understand. Somewhere between our house and this building, a distance of approximately six blocks, was a color line. A whites-only-no-Blacks-need-apply distinctly drawn and doggedly patrolled. We scheduled a visit with the principal, and when both of us appeared the next morning, we observed a curious reaction. Though polite, she was absolutely flustered. She could not determine who to direct her comments to. She looked from Essie's closely cropped black hair to my long loose wavy hair, from cream skin to chocolate skin, and stammered, "Who — who is the mother?"

"I am," said Essie.

"I'm sorry," was the reply. "We have already reached our quota of Black students in this school."

"Quota? We live in this neighborhood," I replied. "This is not a question of bussing a child in. He lives here."

She peered at the form we had filled out with our address on it. Then responded coldly, "We are full."

"That's ridiculous," I objected.

"Are you telling me that my child is not welcome to attend the fourth grade in your school?" Essie asked icily.

"We simply don't have room."

Essie stood up and walked out of the room without another word. I wanted to scream. I wanted to force the principal to change her mind, her politics, her preoccupation with the boundaries defined by color. I sat there staring at her. She refused to meet my eyes. I said slowly, "This will be reported to the Superintendent and to the school board," and walked out following Essie to the car.

We scheduled a meeting at the school administration to register a formal complaint and find Michael another school. I was furious. We were tax payers. These are public schools. How can he be refused entrance? How can a child be denied because of some quota determined by an administrator somewhere? I was naive in matters of race.

I would have to say all white people are naive about the persistence of the color line. We prefer naiveté — in fact we insist on it. If we, as white people, actually faced the entrenched injustice of our socioeconomic system and our cultural arrogance, we might suffer tears, we might suffer the enormous weight of history, we might face the iceberg of guilt which is the underside of privilege. We might begin to glimpse our losses, our estrangement from others, our intense fear as the result of a social system that places us in the precarious position of the top. We might be moved to call out and protest the cruelty that passes for normal behavior in our daily lives, in our cities, and on our streets. . . .

Nothing in my life, my education, my reading, my upbringing, prepared me to straddle the color-line with Essie under the Reagan years in Milwaukee, a post-industrial city suffering economic decline and social collapse. The rigidly entrenched division of social power by race and the enormously draining limitations we faced on a daily basis began to tear at the fabric of our daily survival. I began to experience a kind of rage that left me feeling as sharp as broken glass. I was in this inner state when we finally arrived in the long quiet corridors of the central administration of Milwaukee Public Schools.

We were ushered into an office with a man in a suit sitting behind a desk. He could have been an insurance salesman, a loan officer, or any other briefcase-carrying decision-making tall white man in a position of power and control. We were two women of small build and modest dress, but we were carrying the larger presence — righteous anger. We sat down. I leaned across his desk and challenged him to explain to us why Michael had been refused admittance into the school of our choice. He back-pedaled. He avoided. He dodged. Essie suddenly said, "I am finished. I am taking my child out of school," and stood up.

I snapped my notebook closed, signaling the end of the conversation. The man had never asked me who I was. Did he assume I was a social worker? a family member? a friend? a lawyer? a journalist?

Had it even crossed his mind that he was looking at a pair of lovers, at a family, at the two acting parents of this child? For the first time he looked worried, "I am sure we can find an appropriate school for your son. Tell me his interests. We'll place him in one of our specialty schools."

We hesitated.

"I'll personally handle his registration," he seemed to be pleading with us. He looked from Essie to me wondering who his appeal would reach first.

We settled on a school with a square of wild prairie, the environmental science specialty school. It was a half hour bus ride from our home. Michael liked the school, but we did not feel completely victorious. How could we? Though we had challenged the system, these policies and practices which place undue emphasis on the color of a child's skin had not been changed. The school system simply accommodated us, perhaps fearing our potential to cause widespread dissent by giving voice to the intense dissatisfaction of the African American community with the public school system. We compromised — perhaps exhausted by the constant fight against feeling invisible and powerless. It was not just that Michael was Black. It was also that his family consisted of a white woman and a Black woman, and regardless of our commitment to him, we were not perceived as a valid family unit though we functioned as a family. . . .

It is heartbreaking to raise an African American boy in the U.S. From an early age he is taught that others fear him. He is taught that he is less than. He is taught that his future is defined by certain streets in certain neighborhoods, or that the only way out is through musical or athletic achievement. Michael played basketball and football. He wrote raps and performed them to the punctuated beat of electronic keyboards and drum machines. When it was fashionable, he would breakdance on the living room floor. He had a few good years in school, but by and large school did not satisfy his quest for knowledge, nor did it provide him with creative avenues for self-expression. . . .

There were so many things I could not do for Michael. I could not clothe him in transparent skin to prevent him from being pre-judged by color-conscious teachers who would label him inferior. I could not surround him with safety on the street corner where he waited for his school bus. One grisly morning in November he came home shaking. He and a small boy had been shot at while waiting on a familiar corner two blocks from the house. It was 7:30 A.M. While he was preparing to attend school, boys his age were shooting guns out of car windows hoping to kill somebody in order to get into a gang so they could make money.

On that gray morning, the capitalist notion of success as the acquisition of material wealth appeared for what it is: an absolute perversion of human dignity. Yet white American culture persists in holding material affluence as the highest symbol of achievement. The way this plays out in the lives of people of color and those who love them can be summed up in one word: cruelty. We suffer for a lack of basic resources because of the hoarding, the feverish consumerism, and the complete lack of concern by people who have more than they will ever possibly need. Fashion crimes, ganking, children beating and killing other children to acquire the stingy symbols of status in a society devoid of real meaning — this is what happens on the city streets of the richest nation in the world.

I could not keep Michael from the bullets. I could not move him out into the suburbs where another kind of violence would confront him daily, those who would question his presence and limit his right to move freely from one house to the next. I could not close his eyes to the terror he would see in his friends when death visited among them. I could not hold him against the rage he held inside. A rage that thundered through the house pulverizing everything in its path, terrifying me, tearing at his mother.

What could we say to him about how to live on the mean streets of a bully nation? We did not live on those same streets even though we lived in the same neighborhood. His experience, my experience, his mother's experience — we walked out of the front door into three separate worlds. Worlds we did not define or control except in how we would respond to them. Michael watched the hours I spent typing, writing, scratching out, rewriting. He watched the transformations his mother carried out with color on canvas, making lumps of cold clay into warm red altar bowls with her naked hands. He saw that we took our pain and rage, our grinding frustration and radiant hope, and made something out of it that gave us strength. Michael is still writing, making music, performing in his own music videos. He sees himself as an artist as we see ourselves; this is the thing that has carried us through.

The Westside where we bought a home had always been a working class neighborhood where people invested in their sturdy brick and wood frame houses planting roses in their green squares of grass. The neighborhood had been built in the teens and twenties by German immigrants who took a certain pride in quality. These homes had fireplaces and stained glass windows, beautifully crafted built-in bookshelves and beveled mirrors. Only a few generations earlier, there was safety and prosperity here. Waves of immigrants—Greek, Polish, Hasidic Jews, African Americans coming North to work in the factories, shared these streets. I can remember walking into the corner bakery and the Greek woman behind the counter asked Essie and I if we were sisters. It was possible there at that time. Blood was shared. Love between the races happened. We laughed and nodded, "Yes—yes, we're sisters." In these moments we utterly and joyfully belonged together.

My friends who lived on the Eastside of the city rarely came to visit after I moved in with Essie. It was as if I had moved to the other side of the moon. . . . I trusted white women less and less as friends because they could not be counted on when things got tough. They tended to retreat. Race issues are ugly and hard, but if white women who want to fight male supremacy can't stand up to their own fears around the issue of color and simultaneously fight white supremacy, how can they really undertake the work of women's liberation? Certainly without an analysis and willingness to deal with race, there is no depth to the commitment. It is simply a get-ahead strategy for a particular middle class white female minority. Today I feel there is a greater commitment to address issues of racism within the feminist movement, but most of the voices I hear are still women of color. . . .

White women are conditioned to stay put, even rebellious daughters who love other women rarely cross the road that divides the races. Any woman who engages in a serious relationship—as friend or family, as lover, or mother to daughter—with a woman of a different shade of skin will find this relationship demanding a deeper vulnerability than any other as long as race relationships continue to be fraught with tension. But if we settle for a divided nation, we settle for social rigidity and police brutality, we settle for ignorance and stereotypes, we settle for emptiness and fear.

I am still learning how to confront racism when I see it, how to educate my friends without alienating them, how to ask for what I need in terms of support. It has been a rare occurrence, but a joyful one, for us to find other mixed-race lesbian couples. When we begin to talk about how difficult it is, we discover certain patterns and find solace that we are not alone. But why should we suffer for being ourselves and finding ourselves in the borderless culture between races, in the undefined space where wakefulness is necessary for survival, where honest communication and self-reflection must replace the simple recipes of romance. . . .

Few of us born in the Americas can trace our bloodline with impunity. So many of our ancestors have been erased or invented as need be. I know very few family names that have not gone without at least one attempt at revision—to anglicize it—simplify it—discard the ethnic or cultural baggage of a *ski* or *stein* or other markers of race/ethnic identity. One who is raised as part of an unwanted people will shift the identity to become acceptable. Note the number of Chippewa and Menominee people in Wisconsin with French last names. One Chippewa man explained to me how in every neighborhood his family adopted another identity: Mexican when living on the Southside, French on the Eastside. Only back up on the reservation could they say aloud their true names. . . .

How many of us are of African descent? Slavery was challenged in part because of the enormous outcry against the "white slave children." Children of enslaved African women who were the result of forced sex with slavemasters ended up on the auction block. Some of these children looked just like the "free" children of "free" European-American mothers. Obviously there was a tremendous outcry resulting from the confusion that the rationale for chattel slavery was based on a strict hierarchy of skin color as the basis of privilege. How could they justify selling these children that by all appearances looked white even if the mother was a light-skinned African American slave? White men in the South parented children on both sides of the yard: women they took as wives, and women who worked the fields. The brown and pale children were half-brothers and half-sisters related by blood through the father. This simple truth was denied, and these children were taught to never consider themselves as one family. There is no doubt that many of us have relatives we never considered before. Part of my work has been beginning to claim these unnamed Ancestors as family.

The day after I wrote that paragraph, I visited my parents. It was a week before Christmas, and I was planning to spend the day with my two grandmothers and my parents for Mimi's birthday. While in my parent's home, I asked about an old photo album that I remembered from childhood. My mother commented that it had recently surfaced from the jumble of daily life and brought it into the kitchen. Tin types and daguerreotypes, family photographs spanning 1850–1900. Fifty years of Walkers, my mother's father's family.

That night, back in the city, stretched across the guest bed at a friend's house, I slowly turned the pages. There are my Ancestors, among the first generation here from the British Isles. Aunt Mary and Uncle Tom Walker. By pulling the photographs out and inspecting the little leather and brass book, I discovered they settled in Clinton and Seaforth, Ontario. I knew these relatives had lived in Canada, but hadn't known they lived between Lakes Huron, Erie and Ontario! All of the faces were unfamiliar, stiff, caught in frozen poses over a century ago. A few of the photographs I remembered from my childhood, especially the sad-faced child in the unusual robe with straight cropped black hair and Asian eyes. For the first time it occurred to me that this could be the face of a native child — not European at all! Who is this child? Then a particularly striking face caught my attention. A young woman gazed confidently, intently, at what? Her hair hung around her wide face and high cheekbones in thick black ringlets, her full lips barely open, her strong chin — this is a woman of African descent. Who is she to me? She wore a gold hoop earring and a checkered bow over a satin dress. With one arm resting against an upholstered pillow, she posed proudly. Why had I never heard of her before?

I live near Wilberforce College, one of the oldest historically Black colleges in the U.S., which was founded by slaveowners who wanted to train their half-white children in the trades. A friend who used to work there told me a story about a white male teacher at the college who became an important ally to his students. He assisted the African American sons and daughters of slaveowners to escape slavery by helping them relocate to Ontario, Canada after

graduation rather than returning them to the South to work for their fathers. Is this woman the daughter of those students of Wilberforce? Is she my great-aunt or a distant cousin or great-great grandmother?

No one in my family seems to know much about these faces, these people, these lives, and how they relate to us. . . . If I am supposed to be a proud daughter of the colonizing English and the migrating Irish, why can't I also be a proud daughter of the Anishinabeg or Haudenausaunee, two of the indigenous peoples of this Great Lakes region, as well as a proud daughter of the African Diaspora? In America the idea of Europe was created, as if my English Ancestors weren't trying to dominate my Irish Ancestors. Why can't we talk about our truly diverse heritages? Nothing has been passed down in my family of these darker-skinned faces in my family's picture album. Is the refusal to see ourselves as something other than Northern European based in a fearful grasping after shreds of white-skinned privilege? What do we lose if we acknowledge our connection? What do we gain?

Granny kept a photo album. The pictures were important. Some were tattered and worn out, but they mattered. They held the faces of relatives — cousins, aunts, sisters — men in fine hats and women in silk dresses looking into the camera, into the future. In the album is a small square black and white snapshot of two plump white babies seated outdoors on a stuffed armchair. The Kelly boys. Irish. Part of the family. Essie remembers her great-grandmother telling her children, grandchildren and great-grandchildren, "These are your cousins." I bet those white boys don't show the dark faces of their cousins to their kin. . . .

The tight little boxes of identity defined by our society keep the building blocks of political and economic power in place. How can we gender-bend, race-cross, nature-bond, and love ourselves in our plurality enough to rebel against the deadening crush of conformity? Is it a crisis of the imagination which prevents us from extending compassion beyond the boundaries of limited personal experience to listen *and be moved to action by* stories of injustice others suffer. How can we extend the boundaries of our own identities so that they include "the other"? If we have any hope for the future of life, how can we expand our sense of self to include other people as well as beings in nature? The structure of our society is articulated by separation and difference. How do we challenge this by living according to a sense of connection not alienation?

For us, for Essie and I, the greatest challenge has been inventing ourselves as we went along for we could not find a path to follow. Where are our foremothers? Light and Dark women who held each other's hands through childbirth and child-raising? Who stood side by side and loved each other refusing to budge despite everybody's objections? Who pooled their measly resources together to make sure there was food and heat and light enough for everyone's needs? I want to know them. I want to hear their stories. I'll tell them mine. This is the first time anyone has asked me to write anything about the twelve years we have shared.

Despite the absence of role models, we share specific Ancestors, disembodied presences gliding through our lives like a sudden breeze teasing the candle flame on the altar; secret-keepers who come under guard of moonlight, carrying apple baskets full of fresh fruit which they drop into our sleeping; we wake up before dawn with the sweet taste on our lips of good dreams and lucky numbers. We have our shared Ancestors to thank, and we are fortunate to count Granny among them.

◆◆◆

THIRTY-FOUR

Shattering Two Molds
Feminist Parents with Disabilities

Carol J. Gill and Larry A. Voss

We are two persons with extensive physical disabilities who have raised a nondisabled son. Countering the stereotype of people with disabilities as childlike, fragile, and suffering, we have nurtured and, we believe, nurtured powerfully. With wonder and relief, we have watched our child's development into a generous, emotionally open, strong, and socially responsible adult. It was not a snap. All three of us waged a long struggle against society's devaluation of human difference to get to this place.

Our war against ableist beliefs began in childhood when we acquired our disabilities in the 1950 polio epidemic. We used braces and wheelchairs and would have had little problem attending our neighborhood school if not for architecture and its real foundation: attitudes. In those days before the disability rights movement, we were barred from mainstream life. No ramps or elevators were installed to ensure our access. Instead, we were bussed miles each day to a "special" school with similarly displaced children.

Undoubtedly, these experiences laid the groundwork for our acceptance of a feminist perspective. We acquired a deep suspicion of unequal treatment and stereotyping in any form. In high school, we identified with the civil rights struggle. In college,

our rejection of sexism took definite shape. For Carol, the conscious decision to participate in the women's movement grew from classroom discussion of the work of Greer, Friedan, and Steinem. For Larry, it grew out of heated ideological debates between men and women in radical student collectives during the antiwar movement.

When Larry married a woman from this movement (his first marriage), he found daily life to be a mixture of new and traditional gender roles. During most of the marriage, his partner, who was not disabled, worked as an intensive care nurse while Larry completed his education. Although they shared household duties according to preferences as well as Larry's disability limitations, it was expected that his partner would cook and perform "housewife" chores after coming home from her job.

The decision to have a baby, on the other hand, was planned to be as joint a venture as possible. Larry remained by his wife's side during her prenatal exams and, long before it was accepted practice, he participated in the birth of his son in the hospital delivery room. He remembers this experience as ecstasy and agony — the incomparable joy of watching his child's birth and his sense of helpless horror as the emerging head made an audible tear in his wife's tissues. That painful moment registered clearly in Larry's consciousness — a factor, perhaps, in his later diligence in shouldering childcare duties.

Larry, in fact, became the primary parent. As is true of most children of disabled parents, Brian had little trouble adapting to his father's wheelchair and unconventional strategies for accomplishing daily tasks. When Larry's marriage foundered, he had no intention of parting with his son, then a toddler. Although it was for men to get custody of children in divorces, and even rarer for disabled persons, Larry fought to keep Brian with him and won.

Single parenthood was a rich and difficult time for them. Although Larry's sister and mother helped baby-sit, he experienced the loneliness and weight of responsibility that many single parents face. Additionally, there were unique physical and social difficulties. Unemployed and without child support, Larry could afford neither personal assistance nor adequate accessible housing. Consequently, errands such as grocery shopping became all-day feats of endurance. After driving home from the store, he would be forced to leave his wheelchair at the top of the stairs, crawl down the steps several times to his basement apartment and up again, hauling each bag of groceries followed by the baby, and then drag his wheelchair down the steps so he could get back into it and put groceries away!

Even more exhausting were the social hurdles. Strangers as well as family members challenged Larry's decision to keep his child, citing both gender- and disability-based concerns. Brian's first teachers suggested he was being shortchanged by not having a mother or nondisabled parent. (Brian's biological mother moved out of state and maintained very limited contact with him.) Neighborhood children teased or grilled him about his "wheelchair father" and asked why he had no mother. People who knew nothing about Larry's parenting skills would cluck over Brian's misfortune and tell him that having a "crippled daddy" was his cross to bear.

Although we — Carol and Larry — knew each other superficially while attending the same "special" high school, our paths did not cross again until a mutual friend brought us together at the time of Larry's divorce. After several years of intense and romantic friendship, we married.

At first, Brian was thrilled about Carol joining the family. Even before the wedding, which took place when he was seven, he insisted on calling her "Mom."

But once it was official, he was ambivalent. Due both to her disability and her feminism, Brian's "new mother" was anything but the traditional nurturing figure people had told him he needed. She was physically incapable of performing many of the cooking and household chores mothers were supposed to do. She was not conventionally pretty. She was unexpectedly strong in communicating her ideas and affecting household decisions. She was even unwilling to change her name when she got married.

Not that Brian had been raised to be sexist. He had a father who baked cookies, cared for a home, brushed his lover's hair, and became an elementary school teacher. He also knew Larry's fondness for baseball, tools, and macho action movies. Father and son openly shared hugs and kisses between bouts of arm wrestling. Larry's philosophy of child-rearing, like his philosophy of education, stressed openness. He had always been pleased that Brian's early years were fairly non-sex-typed. He had let the toddler's strawberry blond hair grow to shoulder length undaunted by family predictions of gender confusion. He admired Brian's eclectic taste in toy trucks and stuffed animals as well as his drawings of kittens, nudes, Army tanks, Spiderman and posies.

But despite Larry's efforts to raise a child liberated from all the "isms," Brian was exposed to and affected by the sexism and ableism (not to mention racism, ethnocentrism, and heterosexism) of the surrounding culture. Dealing with this in addition to the typical tensions of stepparenting introduced a great deal of struggle into our family life.

It is hard for us to separate where our parenting was guided by feminism or by our experience and values as disabled persons. We believe in both notions of a women's culture and a disabled people's culture. Further, we believe the overlap of cultural values in the two communities is significant. Both feminist analysis and the disability independent living philosophy embrace values of interdependence, cooperative problem-solving, flexibility/adaptability, and the importance of relationships in contrast to traditional male values of autonomy, performance, competition, dominance, and acquisition.

By necessity, a guiding principle of our partnership has always been unfettered cooperation. There has been no "women's work" or "men's work." From the start, we negotiated most tasks of life by deciding who could do it, who was good at it, who wanted to do it, who had time, who needed help, etc. Larry's arm strength meant he had kitchen duty. Carol's greater physical limitations meant she organized the lists and schedules. In our professional jobs, we alternated being the major breadwinner. Everything from lovemaking to getting out of the car was an exercise in cooperation and respect — an orchestration of timing, assistance, and down-to-earth tolerance.

Our parenting was similarly orchestrated. As the only one who could drive, Larry did the car-pooling. Carol's math acuity made her the homework authority. Larry did more of the "hands-on" parenting jobs: cuddling, restraining, washing, roughhousing. Carol nurtured by story-telling, instructing, reprimanding, discussing, and watching endlessly ("Mom, watch this!").

We both did an enormous amount of talking. Larry explained and lectured. Carol questioned motivations and articulated feelings. We even entered family counseling during several difficult times to talk some more. Reflecting back on it, we realize one of the central themes of all this talking was nurturance: caring for and being responsible for people, animals, plants, and the environment. Larry encouraged empathy in Brian through questions like, "How do you think you would feel if that happened to you?" Carol nudged Brian to write notes and make gifts for family members. We gave him regular chores to do for the family and engaged him in many rescues of abandoned and injured stray animals.

Another major theme was prejudice and unfairness. Disability rights and women's rights were frequent topics in our household. Carol often directed Brian's attention to surrounding events, attitudes, and images that contributed to women's oppression, e.g., *Playboy,* sadistic images in rock videos, crude jokes. Most of the time, Brian would roll his eyes and protest that Carol could find sexism in anything. Larry usually backed her up but sometimes he lightened the tension by joining Brian in teasing Carol about her unwillingness to take her menfolk's last name. This was a family joke that ironically conveyed both affection and respect for Carol and got everyone to smile.

We also did a lot of the standard things most people do to raise a nonsexist son, from respecting his need to cry, to encouraging his interests and talents regardless of their traditional "gender appropriateness." Again, this lent a certain eclecticism to Brian's activities which included sports, cooking, ceramics, drawing, music, reading, swimming and surfing, collecting, etc. On both feminist and paci-fist grounds,

we tried to avoid the most destructive "macho" stuff. For example, at his request, we enrolled Brian in a karate class. But when we discovered the instructor tested each boy's mettle by getting the class to take turns punching him in the stomach, Larry pronounced it barbaric and encouraged Brian to drop out, which he did. We also kept Brian out of formal team sports run by zealous competitive coaches and pressured him not to join the military when the gung-ho recruiters tried to nab him in high school.

Although we often held little hope that our battle against the "isms" was making an impact, like other parents, we now see that children do pay attention. Brian is now 22 and spontaneously uses words like "sexism" when critiquing the world. He is also our only relative who consistently uses Carol's proper name in introductions and addressing mail. He is comfortable in the friendship of both men and women. He loves sports and still hugs his childhood stuffed dog when he's sick. He has argued for the rights of women, people with disabilities, and other minorities.

Brian has shared his life for four years with a woman who also has strong goals and opinions. They have found a way to support each other, argue, and give space as needed. Like us, they are lover, companion, and family — equals. Seeing them interact is the great payoff to all our years of struggle. We enjoy watching our son laundering his partner's delicate sweaters or lovingly constructing her sandwiches. We listen to him express the depth of his feelings and respect for her. (Yes, he is a talker like his parents!) They have negotiated their course with cooperation, nurturance, and concern about unfairness. They want to have a family, they want to protect the earth.

When we told Brian about writing this piece, we asked his permission to tell the story of our family. He was enthusiastic and helped us reminisce about the past. One of his recollections confirmed how much he had been affected by the equity in his parents' relationship. He told us that sometimes as a child when he would answer the family telephone, callers would ask to speak to the "head of the house." Brian remembers his natural response to this request was to ask "Which one?" Then he and the caller would have a confusing discussion about which parent was needed on the phone. He said it was always simpler when only one of us was home because then the choice was clear: he would just summon whichever "head of the house" happened to be present!

◆◆◆

THIRTY-FIVE

Lisa's Ritual, Age 10

Grace Caroline Bridges

Afterwards when he has finished
lots of mouthwash helps
to get rid of her father's cigarette taste.
She runs a hot bath
    to soak away the pain
        like red dye leaking from her
           school dress in the washtub.

She doesn't cry.
When the bathwater cools she adds more hot.
She brushes her teeth for a long time.

Then she finds the corner of her room,
curls against it. There the wall is
hard and smooth
as teacher's new chalk, white
as a clean bedsheet. Smells
fresh. Isn't sweaty, hairy, doesn't stick
to skin. Doesn't hurt much
when she presses her small backbone
into it. The wall is steady
while she falls   away:
    first the hands   lost

arms dissolving   feet gone
    the legs   dis-   jointed
      body cracking down
        the center like a fault
      she falls inside
        slides down like
dust   like kitchen dirt
        slips off
the dustpan into
        noplace

  a place where
nothing happens,
nothing ever happened.

When she feels the cool
wall against her cheek
she doesn't want to
come back. Doesn't want to
think about it.
The wall is quiet, waiting.
It is tall like a promise
only better.

◆◆◆

Reading Maps: One

Minnie Bruce Pratt

Yesterday Nettie in my office talked about summer
school, her geography course, how before she hadn't
really known where she was, whether she went
east or south to get to the beach, didn't know
how to read a map, Ezra always did that.
She said, *I never had any need to read
a map, every place I go it's already charted.*

I drive to work down the boulevard. The way
does not lead through trees, no dark crossed limbs
sprouting green flesh. Over my head
a grey net hangs, suspended, lines

from Duke Power wired from pole to pole.
I have learned what to expect at every turn.
The morning headlines again have read *WOMAN
KILLED:* wild chase across town, her car
forced off the road by a truck, her husband,
a sergeant from the army base, with a rifle. She ran
into the woods. He followed and shot her in the
    head,
walked back to his pickup, drove away.

I want to drive away from this town. At my back
to the north men fall from the sky. Parachutes

burst open like nylon morning glories.
In the webbing men jerk at lines to float
closer to their targets. *If I had an M-16*
I could go shoot them down.

> To my left
the Putt-Putt course is open. On zig-zags
of green indoor-outdoor carpet, young men
demonstrate their skill to girlfriends: how to hit
a small ball into a hole curbed by painted brick.
I think of my lovers who have been raped. *I could*
castrate each man there.

> On my right, women
shop at the Winn-Dixie between walls of stacked
> cans.
G.I. wives stand in the cash register line
with ladies from Lakeshore Drive who will not
> speak.
If I drove the car through the window they would
speak, open mouths, stare at nothing
left of the plate glass but a corner of webbed cracks.

Two miles ahead, at the corner where the boule-
> vard runs
into Hay Street, is a church, empty now. *With*
> *spare gas*
in a jug, rags, I could roll a ball of fire
under the porch. Tomorrow there might be no pulpit,
no door for women to enter, to turn down the aisle
toward narrow pew.

> But at that corner other women
still walk for a living, down where I have sat
> stopped
at a red light, seen a woman step to the double
yellow line, straighten the black seam of a stocking,
pull her skirt, purple silk parachute, up
over her head. *I thought she hid in her hand*
a grenade, ready to blow up the man and herself.
Then the light changed; the street looked the same.

I will not drive downtown today. I am afraid
there has been no change, that my anger and
> despair
may ignite like a mass of oiled rags. *I might*
walk into an intersection and burst into flames.

I turn left after A & H Cleaners,
rebuilt from the bombing five years back,
first business owned by a Black man on the avenue.
Behind the red sign, gold letters, promises
of one-hour service, Black women press
knife-sharp creases into army fatigues.

White men I despise already have been here
> with fire.
I see their image in my rear-view mirror,
see my own burning, the will to violence.

I want us all to change; yet I drive to work
the same way every morning, doors locked,
windows rolled up, afraid. *I want to roll my anger*
like a tank over terrain I do not control.
I forget that I have resisted, that I have imagined
how to travel a different way.

> I turn left
at Filter Plant Road, past the telephone pole
with kudzu snaking green up its guy wires.

When I get to work, the papers on my desk lie
ruled by thin blue lines, scrawled over
with tendrils of pencil and ink: *I had to get this job*
to leave my husband. For weeks I could not think
what to put in the white spaces on the applica-
> tion blank,
years of never knowing where I was,
years of marriage when he drove and I tried
to read the map, to see my body in relation
to the space around me, to find it on the diagram:
green boundaries for grassland, forest, parks,
yellow for cities, red for Indian reservation
or military base, red lines for scenic routes,
grey for time zones. *I had no belief*
that I could get myself from here to there.
I would say left for right until at some intersection in Colorado or Georgia he would reach
over and take the map. I did not try
to take it back. I did not know I was angry

until I began to talk to other women, get directions
from them on how to meet. They called me: voices
> travelled
over the phone, spiralled into the labyrinth, my
> inner ear
that sat like a snail, listening. They repeated
turns and streets. I wrote their words down,
then propped the sheet of paper on the seat
> beside me
as I drove,

> once for hours on Bragg Boulevard
to find Johnson Road by the cleaners in Bonnie
> Doone.
At a red light I stopped short of a carload of men:
paratroopers out on the town could slash lines
finer than wrinkles on a woman's face, or fasten

her genitals with copper wire to their battery.
   I had
to locate women friends.

                         I began to guess
at turns. Landmarks blurred, perhaps remembered
by my guide in a different pattern, perhaps not
      clearly seen
by me in the rain, yellow light from massage parlors
streaking the windshield. I slowed down to read
my map under moving streetlights. I was
      determined
to find the house where women met to tell
our secrets, pieces of life torn out, hidden,
or almost thrown away. *If I could find them,*
they might show me the way out.

                         That night
I refused to be lost and got to Denise's apartment.
The words on my scrap of paper matched the
      address
on the door: *Grand Prix Drive, 2105-C.*
Inside six women sat in a maze of chrome and
      plexiglass.
They looked like me; I didn't trust them.
As we talked, the windows rattled: not thunder
      but artillery.
The woman across from me looked directly at me;
blue shadows painted around her eyes did not hide
her glance; her jaw tensed under its camouflage
      of rouge.
She opened her mouth and began to speak.

The room shifted around me to other places
as we hunted our fragments scattered on the
      scorched earth,
men's land, as we gathered the bones of memory:
how her mother forgot the five years before electroshock,
how she moved out and her boyfriend burned
her clothes and books in the front yard, how the rapist
held a lighter to her hair, how my husband chopped
up the kitchen chairs with an axe and burned them.
I saw the ashes in the back yard when I got home,
what was left of three red chairs; I was glad
it wasn't the remains of me and the children.

In the narrow kitchen I told him I did not want
the place he gave me in the world as it was.
He spoke of change, of going from here to there
with me. *I did not want to leave him behind;*
I did not want to be in the same room when he spoke
with the mouth I had loved for nine years, with
      the voice

I had hated when it cracked like bones breaking
      from anger.
He was the same man who shared two small boys,
      the laundry,
dishes, the man who smashed a bowl on the counter
beside me, left a fist of blue fragments on red tile,
the man who leaned with me against the yellow
      wall
and cried, his tears streaking my cheek, the same
      man,
in a three-piece suit, who asked, smiling,
about the revolution while I fixed a mimeograph
      machine
on the kitchen table.

            I wanted to slash his face
with the bread knife. I did not raise my voice.
My hand kept on turning the crank. Sheets
of cheap paper stared up from the floor, lines
slightly blurred, stubborn, black as charcoal:
"Marriage Equality Act 1976,"
"Joanne Little Acquitted," "New book:
Mama Doesn't Live Here Any More," "Lesbian
film: Jan Oxenberg's Home Movie."

When I finally yelled and he shoved me against
      the stove,
out the door, it was like any of our drives together,
like sex: one minute I was in my own body, the next,
outside myself, displaced, while he took control.
After I hit the floor of the back porch, I saw
my family at the far end of the kitchen, looking
at me as if I were at the wrong end of a telescope,
he rigid as a granite marker at a boundary,
the children crying, flesh of my flesh, their faces
not yet hardened, looking at me flat on my back
in the geography of power. I felt the grab of his
      hands on
my arm, the hands that had rubbed my aching back.

The porch cement was cool under my bleeding arm;
I thought I might just lie there on the quiet slab.
I could smell the back yard, the dusty smell
of sasanquas, the rotting leaves gone to earth,
smell of the memory: all living things
change themselves. *He could be different*
but he wasn't. I would be.
I got to my feet. Behind me the back steps
led into the night, into terror and unknown ventures.

I moved out when, fingers sweated around
a ball-point pen, I made myself real
enough on paper to get this job and leave him.

Now I live alone just off the boulevard.
Early in the morning I watch the shadow of pine
needles brush fine lines over my bedroom wall.
I wonder about my charred and smoking heart:
what grows in a burned-over forest. Sometimes
    I sleep
with a lover, my bed an island in the water of night.
With my hand between her breasts, near her heart,
I dream of a place green, flourishing, where we
live safe. At meetings I look for women
who look at me. Our glances catch, like the wind
and seeds poised in the open milkweed pod.

Tonight as I leave work, as streetlights arc
pink over the boulevard, I hardly remember
    the dream.
The evening headlines read WOMAN'S CHARRED
BODY SHOVED INSIDE INCINERATOR. I pass a
    white woman
driving a Continental, a Black woman in the
    backseat.
I meet my neighbor Sheila on her way to third shift.
To feed herself and three children she delivers
pizza, passes between barracks lined up like tanks,
balances herself between rows of soldiers saying
Baby come on and *Don't talk that way to a lady.*
She's never liked the way the place is laid out
but she knows how to get around. *But I want to go*

outside this landscape, drive right off the map.
I don't know the next turn. The street
looks the same as any other day I wanted to
    change it,

on my right, the cement block building marked
topless, stenciled with naked women. A man
in khaki enters; in ten years, he may turn
and show me the face of one of my sons.
And what will I do then? What then, what now?

I can only resist the need to destroy
that spreads anger and despair heavy as asphalt
through my veins, makes me a road driven over
    by violence,
makes me a map of someone else's world.
I will remember that I have learned to travel
a different way.

                Five years ago I was afraid
to cross town; tonight I drive down the boulevard
to a room where snakeplants grow from the wall,
where I eat green-fleshed avocado, and I talk
to women who sketch quick lines over the paper
ridges of a napkin. Our faces have begun to wrinkle,
our eyes are webbed in lines. We trace the anger
flying through our bodies back to its point of origin.
We locate forbidden places, the kind marked
    dangerous
swamp, unknown territory on the old charts.
We plot change. We love one another.
Our bodies become lodestones to the future.
    We imagine
a place not marked yet on any map. Between us
words tremble and veer, like the iron needle
of a compass, a guide to what we are making real.

1981

THIRTY-SEVEN

Asian Immigrant Women Fight Domestic Violence

Deanna L. Jang

Domestic violence occurs in all communities, and the Asian community is no exception. The lack of statistics regarding the incidence of domestic violence in the Asian community is reflective of this fact as well as other factors, such as the inaccessibility of services for non-English or limited English speaking women, the underutilization of the social or governmental services by Asians, and the need for community education in the Asian community regarding domestic violence.

The profiles of Asian and Pacific battered women are similar to battered women in general. Often they have traditional views of the woman's role as wife and mother, the feeling of isolation, low self-esteem, a belief that the abuse may be justified, are financially and emotionally dependent on the batterer, and have a greater fear of the problems of survival outside the family than the violence inside the family. However, because of the immigrant nature of the Asian and Pacific community, these women also face barriers of language, culture and immigration status.

Asian Immigration

U.S. immigration laws for Asia were not liberalized until 1965, when Congress passed amendments to the Immigration and Nationality Act that ended racist national origin quotas and affirmed family reunification as the cornerstone of U.S. immigration policy. For the Asian community this was the first opportunity in decades for reunification. Of the 270,000 visas currently issued annually, Mexico and five Asian countries, including China, Hong Kong and the Philippines, receive the highest number of visas.

The history of U.S. immigration policy is a reflection of the U.S. need for cheap labor. Early Asian immigrants were men who came to build railroads, dig mines or work in the fields. Today, women and children make up approximately two-thirds of legal immigrants and immigrant women are more able to find jobs in the "hidden" service sectors. Employees in the service, garment, or light manufacturing industries are disproportionately Asian women. Isolated in this country without a command of the language, culture, social and legal systems, these women are often subject to discrimination based on sex, race and immigration status. All too often, they are forced to endure substandard working conditions and are vulnerable to exploitation. Many Asian women immigrate via marriage to a U.S. citizen who they have met in their home country or in the United States. Because of the U.S. military bases in Asia, many Asian women have married U.S. servicemen. Since World War II, nearly 250,000 Asian and Pacific women have married servicemen. Studies indicate that there is a higher incidence of domestic violence within military families. Reasons may include isolation, the culture of military training which emphasizes physical force and obedience to authority, and the high rate of alcoholism.

Cheap labor and marriage, however, do not fully encompass the reasons why Asian women immigrate to the U.S. Some are fleeing economic or political repression. Others immigrate with their entire family or join a family already here, sometimes after long periods of separation due to war or legal restrictions. Finally, there are also an alarming number of "mail-order" bride companies that play on the stereotypes of Asian women as passive, noncomplaining servants and/or exotic sex objects. These sexist and racist stereotypes, reinforced by the media, prevail in Western society and encourage the use of violence against Asian women.

Constant Fear

The common stereotype of an undocumented immigrant or "illegal alien" is that of a Mexican male farmworker who illegally crosses the border. Few studies on the magnitude of undocumented Asians exist. In addition, there are a number of undocumented Asian women who may have entered legally as visitors, students, fiancees, or workers and became undocumented after their temporary visas expired or after their conditional residency terminated, even though they may be married to U.S. citizens or permanent residents. Therefore, an undocumented immigrant woman who is also the victim of battering suffers even greater hardships than other immigrant women. In constant fear of deportation and, in most cases, the resulting fear that she may lose her children, she will heed her partner's threat to call the INS if she leaves him or reports him to the police.

"When my husband married me, he continually talked about my becoming a citizen. He told me he had hired a lawyer, that my application for citizenship was taken care of . . . Today my immigration status is expired and a mess." (*A Community Secret: The Story of Two Filipinas*, by Jacqueline R. Agtuca)

With the passage of the Immigration Reform and Control Act (IRCA) in 1986, many immigrant women found fewer legal and social resources to draw upon in their continuous struggle to provide for themselves and their families. Although IRCA offered legalization to thousands of undocumented persons, its main provision was employer sanctions. The employer sanctions provision, opposed by civil rights and immigrant rights organizations, imposes monetary and criminal penalties on employers who hire undocumented workers. Under IRCA, employees must provide proof of work authorization (that they are lawfully residing in the United States and have permission from INS to work) to any employer who hires them after the date of IRCA's passage. Employees hired prior to this date were "grandfathered" in and did not have to provide any documentation of work.

Employer sanctions have served to further disenfranchise an already disempowered community. IRCA legalized their nonemployment, their nonentitlement to public benefits, and their systematic exploitation in the workplace. The General Accounting Office, in its final report on the impact of employer sanctions, found widespread discrimination against Latinos and Asians. "Grandfathered" employees became "trapped" in exploitative working conditions because they cannot work anywhere else. Women, particularly those working in the least regulated industries such as the garment industry, became even more vulnerable to wage discrimination and sexual and racial harassment.

Without work authorization, a battered undocumented woman who has left her batterer will have even greater difficulty obtaining employment and gaining financial independence. She is likely to find only the jobs which are offered by unscrupulous employers who subject their workers to low wages and poor working conditions and threaten deportation if the workers resist. In addition, IRCA's provisions further discourage immigrants from seeking public benefits, even when they are entitled to receive them for themselves or their children who are U.S. citizens.

Economically Trapped

In addition to the fear of deportation, undocumented women may find themselves economically trapped in battering relationships because they are precluded from most public benefits and must find employment without work authorization. While some battered Asian immigrant and refugee women seek help from social services in the Asian community and from domestic violence programs, few turn to the criminal justice system or use the civil legal system for help. They fear that the police or government agency will report them or their spouses to INS. On a local level, advocates for the rights of immigrants and refugees have addressed this problem by lobbying local government to pass resolutions or ordinances which bar city officials and local law enforcement from turning over persons to the INS, from providing names and addresses to the INS, or from generally assisting in the arrest, deportation or detention of individuals.

No clear spokesperson or organization advocating for this disenfranchised community of immigrant women exists. Thus, the goal of advocates for immigrant women is to raise these issues to the civil rights, immigrants' rights, women's and other organizations and to form a broader coalition for the rights of immigrant women. Already, local groups for the rights of immigrant women have formed in San Francisco, New York, Los Angeles and Honolulu.

Battered Asian immigrant women, particularly those who are undocumented and/or are dependent upon a battering husband to obtain legal status, have few legal remedies available to them. Therefore, it is crucial for immigrant rights, women's rights and battered women's advocates to coordinate efforts and create a responsive advocacy and service network that addresses the overwhelming challenges faced by immigrant women in a post-IRCA environment. Networking and coalition building efforts should focus on creating multifaceted strategies that range from public policy advocacy to community outreach and public education on domestic violence, the need for accessible, culturally appropriate services and the rights of immigrant women.

◆◆◆

CHAPTER FIVE

Living in a Global Economy

In September 1995 more than thirty thousand women from virtually every country in the world gathered in Huairou, China, to discuss the many issues and problems faced by women and girls around the world today, and to work together for change (see Reading 8 in Chapter 1). This was the forum for nongovernmental organizations (NGOs) and was the largest meeting of women in history. A two-hour bus ride away, at the official United Nations Fourth World Conference on Women in Beijing, some five thousand delegates discussed what their governments are doing to improve women's lives and negotiated an official U.N. document, the *Platform for Action* (Wong 1995).

There were nearly five thousand workshops listed in the NGO Forum schedule. Among the discussions about literacy and the education of women and girls, nutrition and health care for infants and adults, the need for clean water in many rural areas of the world, the need for jobs or guaranteed livelihood, the plight of millions of refugees, disability rights, violence against women, sexual freedom, solar stoves, and prostitution, to take just a few examples, one theme was repeated again and again: the effects on women and girls of the globalization of the economy, and the inequality between the rich countries of the world, often located in the Northern Hemisphere, and the poorer countries of the Southern. This seemingly abstract issue affects everyone and underlies many other problems.

To understand the situations and experiences of women in the United States, it is important to know something of women's lives and working conditions worldwide and the ways we all participate in, and are affected by, the global economy. It is against this global economic background that women's activism for economic and social justice takes place. This chapter takes this wider angle of view, with nation as an additional analytical category together with gender, race, and class. The film *The Global Assembly Line* is an excellent introduction to the topic, and readers are urged to see it, if possible, in conjunction with reading this chapter.

The Global Factory

In the past thirty years or so, electronic communications and air transport have made it increasingly possible for corporations to operate across national boundaries, a practice that is likely to become even more prevalent in the future. Now a company based in the United States, such as Nike, Playtex, IBM, or General Motors, can have much of its manufacturing work done overseas—in, for example, South Korea, Taiwan, Mexico, the Philippines, Guatemala, or Europe—by workers who are paid much lower wages than U.S. workers. This organization of work results in inexpensive consumer goods for the U.S. market, particularly clothing, toys, household appliances, and electronic equipment. Thus, our lives are dependent on the labor of a myriad of people in a vast global network.

Roughly 90 percent of the workers in this **off-shore production** are young women in their late teens and early twenties. Some countries, like the Philippines and China, have established Export Processing Zones (EPZs), where transnational corporations (TNCs) set up factories making products for export to Europe, North America, and Japan. In Mexico this is done through *maquiladoras* — factories that make goods on contract to a "parent" company, as described by Maria Patricia Fernandez-Kelly in Reading 38. In 1996 Mexican women in Tijuana started working for Samsung (a South Korean firm) at about $50 for a forty-five-hour week (DePalma 1996). Women in Haiti are working for eleven cents an hour making "Pocohontas" pajamas for J.C. Penney. Aside from paying far lower wages than they would pay to U.S. workers, such companies experience fewer restrictions on their operations. Even in countries like Mexico, with protective labor and environmental legislation, these regulations are often not enforced in relation to the operations of transnational corporations. Thus, workers experience oppressive working conditions and suffer health problems such as stress from trying to make the assigned quotas, illnesses from lint and dust in textile factories, and poor eyesight from hours spent at microscopes. In addition, women are often subject to sexual harassment by male supervisors. When workers complain and organize to protest such dire conditions, they are often threatened that the plants will close and move elsewhere; indeed, this has sometimes happened. For example, Nike has moved some of its production from South Korea, where women have campaigned for better wages and working conditions, to Indonesia and the southern part of China, thereby pitting workers in one country against those in another. Cynthia Enloe describes this process in Reading 39.

Many thousands of U.S. workers have been laid off through automation or the movement of jobs overseas. Fewer and fewer products are made in the United States. A U.S. car, such as the Pontiac Le-Mans, for example, sells for about $20,000. Of this, $6,000 goes to South Korea for labor and assembly; $3,500 goes to Japan for advanced components such

as engines and electronic systems; $1,500 goes to Germany for design engineering; and $1,400 goes to other countries for small components, marketing, and data processing. Only $7,600 of the $20,000 selling price, just over one-third, stays in U.S. hands, split among stockholders, executives, managers, distributors, and car assembly workers. For corporate managers it is more profitable to organize car production this way (Global Exchange n.d.). With a lack of manufacturing jobs, the job market in the United States is becoming increasingly polarized between professional jobs and low-paying service work — flipping burgers at McDonald's for example — that offers no benefits or job security. Rising unemployment, or underemployment — where people are overqualified for the jobs available — has had devastating social and economic effects in older manufacturing cities like Detroit, Cleveland, and Pittsburgh, and in newer electronic industries like California's Silicon Valley.

These changes are not random or isolated but part of a wider system of capitalist economics. In practice there is no "pure" capitalism; rather, the system is a mixture of corporate and government decisions that provide the foundation for business operations. Governments levy taxes that may be used to alleviate poor social conditions. Government and corporate elites share assumptions about what makes the economy successful. In extreme circumstances governments may sanction the use of police or military force against workers who strike for better pay and working conditions. Governments of some small countries may have operating budgets smaller than those of transnational corporations, a situation that makes control of the corporations difficult. For instance, according to a report from Conference Board, a U.S. business research group, the operating budget of Exxon is larger than that of South Africa, the budget of Matsushita larger than that of the Philippines, and Daimler-Benz's larger than Pakistan's (World Citizen News 1992). It is useful to consider the underlying principles of this economic system.

The Profit Motive

Companies compete with one another to sell their services and products, and they stay in business only as long as it is profitable or while governments are willing to subsidize them, as happens, for example, with agriculture and defense industries in the United States. If enough people can afford to buy gold faucets or to change their cars every six months, these things will be produced regardless of whether ordinary people have an adequate diet or somewhere to live. Women in Taiwan or Malaysia, for example, spend their working lives producing more and more goods for the U.S. market even if their own daily survival needs are barely met.

Consumerism, Expansionism, and Waste

To expand, companies have to produce more products, develop new products, and find new markets and new needs to supply. The concept of "need" is a tricky one. Many of the things we think we need are not absolute necessities but contrived needs generated by advertising or social pressure. Some needs are also context specific. It is doubtful whether every household in an urban area in the U.S. with extensive public transportation needs a car, but a car is probably required in a rural area for basic necessities like getting to work, as there is unlikely to be adequate, if any, public transportation. This economic system is intrinsically wasteful. Companies have little or no responsibility to workers left stranded, or for polluted land and water they leave behind when, for example, car assembly plants close down in Detroit, or Mattel moves its Barbie doll factory to Malaysia.

The Myth of Progress

There is an assumption that economic growth is the same as "progress"—a much more complex concept with economic, intellectual, social, moral, and spiritual dimensions. This equation often leads people in a highly material society like the United States to value themselves primarily in terms of the money they make and the things they own. At a national level, too, it leads to an emphasis on material success and material security, with support for government policies that facilitate profit making regardless of social costs.

Emphasis on Immediate Costs

The business definition of costs—the immediate costs of raw materials, plant, payroll, and other operating expenses—is a narrow one. It does not take into account longer-term considerations like the effects of production on the environment or workers' well-being. Government regulation of pollution, for example, is frequently resisted by corporations on the grounds that it will increase costs and drive them out of business. In the nineteenth century European and North American factory owners said the same thing about proposals to abolish child labor and reduce working hours to an eight-hour day, both of which were implemented through legislation.

The Global Economy
Complex Inequalities

Our economic system generates profound inequalities within countries — of wealth, material comfort, safety, opportunities, education, social standing, and so on. Members of wealthy elites in Brazil, Saudi Arabia, Indonesia, Germany, South Africa, and the United States, to take a few random examples, often have more in common with one another than they do with many of their fellow citizens. Poor people living in Oakland, Detroit, or the south Bronx have rates of illiteracy and infant mortality as high as poor people in parts of Africa, Latin America, and the Caribbean. This has led some commentators to talk of "the third world within the first world" as a way of emphasizing inequalities within countries, and drawing connections among poor people worldwide, overwhelmingly people of color.

These inequalities are enhanced in a global economy, which produces inequalities between rich and poor nations. Workers in one country are pitted against those in another, as mentioned in the articles that follow, and this generally erodes their bargaining power. The internationalization and mobility of **capital,** or property and means of production, calls for an international labor movement to standardize wages and working conditions. The fact that standards of living and wage rates differ from country to country means that this process of moving work and factories around the world is likely to continue and to become increasingly complex. In addition to U.S.-based corporations, Japanese, European, and South Korean firms also operate in other countries, seeking lower wages, better tax breaks, and other financial incentives.

What's in a Name?

The various overlapping terms used in the discourse on the global economy offer a convenient shorthand but often obscure as much as they explain.

First World, Second World, Third World

These terms refer to countries that can be roughly grouped together according to their political alliances and economic status. The "First World" refers to North America, Western Europe, Australia, New Zealand, and Japan. The "Second World" includes Russia and countries of Eastern Europe. The "Third World" includes most of Asia, Latin America, Africa, and the Caribbean. There is an assumption of a hierarchy built into this terminology, with First World countries superior to the rest. Some Native Americans and indigenous peoples in Latin America, Australia, and New Zealand use the term "first nations" to emphasize the fact that their ancestral lands were colonized and settled by Europeans. Some environmentalists use the term "Fourth World" to refer to a scattered collection of small-scale, environmentally sound projects, suggesting an alternative economic and political model. Some commentators use the term "Two-Thirds World" to draw attention to the fact that the majority of the world's population (approximately 68 percent) lives in Asia, Latin America, Africa, and the Caribbean.

Developed, Undeveloped, Underdeveloped, Developing, Maldevelopment

These terms refer to economic development, assuming that all countries will become industrialized like North America and Western Europe. Ranging these terms on a continuum from "undeveloped" to "developed" suggests that this process is linear and the best way for a nation to progress. Indeed, economic growth is often unquestioningly assumed to be synonymous with progress. This continuum masks the fact that much of the wealth of developed countries comes from undeveloped countries and is a key reason for their lack of economic development. Vandana Shiva (1988) emphasizes this connection by using the term "devastated" instead of "underdeveloped" economies. Other commentators speak of "maldevelopment" to refer to exploitation of undeveloped countries by developed.

East/West; North/South

The division between East and West refers to a political and military division between North America and Western Europe — the West — countries which, despite differences, have stood together against the East — the old Soviet Union and Eastern Europe. Clearly this notion of East and West excludes many countries in the Western and Eastern Hemispheres. This distinction also obscures the similarities between these blocs, which are both highly industrialized with massive military programs. Some writers use the terms North/South to distinguish between rich and poor countries; "rich" in this context usually means rich with cash rather than with land, resources, or people's skills, creativity, and hard work.

Legacies of Colonialism

Current inequalities between countries are often based on older inequalities resulting from colonization. Britain, for example, ruled India, Ghana, Kenya, Nigeria, Pakistan, and Hong Kong. France had colonial possessions in Algeria, Senegal, Togo, and Vietnam. Though the details varied from place to place and from one colonial power to another, several factors were central to this process:

> the imposition of legal and political institutions;
>
> cultural devastation and replacement of language;

International Economic Institutions and Trade Agreements

In recent years several groups of countries have joined together, forming trading blocs such as the Economic Community of West African States (ECOWAS) and the European Union (EU), and agreements such as the North American Free Trade Agreement (NAFTA). The goal of these regional institutions is to strengthen the economies of the member countries, although the various countries may not all have the same economic power or influence in the group.

The World Bank

Headquartered in Washington D.C., the World Bank was set up in 1944 to provide loans for reconstruction after the devastation of World War II and to promote development in countries of the South, where the bank's emphasis has been on major, capital-intensive projects such as roads, dams, hydroelectric schemes, irrigation systems, and the development of large-scale, chemical-dependent, cash-crop production. The bank's investors are the governments of rich countries who make money on the interest on these loans. Because the World Bank assigns voting power in proportion to the capital provided by its shareholders, its decisions are dominated by the governments of the North, and its policies are in line with their concerns.

International Monetary Fund (IMF)

Also based in Washington, the IMF is an international body with 140 member countries. It was founded at the same time as the World Bank to promote international trade and monetary cooperation. It makes loans to governments for development projects and in times of severe budget deficits. France, Germany, Japan, Britain, and the United States have over 50 percent of the votes, which are allocated according to financial contribution to the fund. If member countries borrow from the fund, they must accept a range of conditions, such as structural adjustment programs, and must put export earnings above any other goal for the country's economy.

General Agreement on Tariffs and Trade (GATT)

This trade agreement was started after World War II to regulate international trade. Since its inception, over a hundred nations, responsible for four-fifths of world trade, have participated in the

psychological dimensions such as internalized racism; and

distortions of the economy with dependence on a few agricultural products or raw materials for export.

Colonial powers extracted raw materials — timber, minerals, and cash crops — which were processed into manufactured goods in the colonial centers for consumption there and for export. During the second half of the twentieth century virtually all former colonies have gained political independence but have remained linked to their colonizers — politically through organizations like the British Commonwealth and economically through the activities of established firms in operation since colonial times, from the more recent activities of transnational corporations, and by loans from governments and banks of countries of the North (that is, the rich countries of the developed world). Many members of the new political and business elites were educated at prestigious universities in colonial capitals. Whether the handover of political power was relatively smooth or accompanied by turmoil and bloodshed, newly independent governments have been under pressure to improve living conditions for their populations and have borrowed capital to finance economic development. This is illustrated diagrammatically in the New Internationalist "route map" in Reading 40. This combination of circumstances has led many commentators to characterize the continuing economic inequalities between rich and poor countries as **neocolonialism.** The United States is part of this picture because of its colonial relationships with the agreement. The latest round of GATT negotiations, which began in 1986, significantly changed the agreement in response to transnational corporations' demand for a reduction of import tariffs, in what Nader (1993) described as "an unprecedented corporate power grab" (p. 1). (The changed agreement was adopted by the United States in 1994). Transnational corporations will pay fewer tariffs on the goods they move around the world — data, components, partly finished products, and goods ready for sale. Proponents argued that a global market and free trade mean global prosperity. Labor organizers, environmentalists, and consumer advocates who opposed these changes in GATT argued that governments would lose tax income from imports; that countries like the United States, where wage rates and benefits are high in international terms, would be likely to lose jobs; and that legislation protecting workers and the environment might be set aside or ruled to be an unlawful limitation on the operations of corporations. A new GATT ruling body, the Multilateral Trade Organization (MTO), consisting of trade experts, will review breaches of the rules and sanction countries accordingly. This change in GATT establishes a new, unelected international institution over which member nations and their peoples have no democratic control.

North American Free Trade Agreement (NAFTA)

This agreement among the United States, Canada, and Mexico, established in 1994, allows for greater freedom of movement of jobs and products among the three countries. Its proponents argued that these countries needed to collaborate to remain as competitive internationally as the economically powerful European Union and Pacific Rim trading groups. Like GATT, NAFTA was discussed in terms of a liberalization of trade but is in effect a liberalization of capital expansion, again serving the interests of transnational corporations against opposition in all three countries from labor, environmentalists, and consumers. Proponents argued that NAFTA would create more jobs in the United States, though this has not been the case; indeed, some U.S. companies — including General Electric, Procter and Gamble, Mattel, Scott Paper, and Zenith — have laid off workers because of NAFTA (Malveaux 1995).

Philippines, Hawai'i (now a state), and Puerto Rico (a colony), the strength of the dollar as an international currency, and the fact that key international institutions like the World Bank and the International Monetary Fund have their headquarters in the United States and are heavily influenced by U.S. investments and policies.

External Debt

All countries are involved in international trade, buying and selling goods and services. Currently many countries pay more for imports than they earn in exports, leading to external debt, or a balance of payments deficit. Over $1.3 trillion is jointly owed by governments of Latin America, Asia, Africa, and the Caribbean to Northern governments and commercial banks. In 1991 the sixteen major borrowers in Latin America owed a total of $420 billion, a situation that has not changed significantly since then (O'Reilly 1991). The United States, too, has an overall budget deficit. This was $290 billion in 1992, dropping to $164 billion in 1995 because of major budget economies (Sivard 1996).

Repayment of Loans Partly because countries of western Europe and North America have serious balance-of-payments problems themselves, they have pressured other debtor countries to repay loans. Like a person who acquires a second credit card to cover the debt on the first, a country may take out additional loans to cover interest repayments on earlier ones, thus compounding its debt. This situation is complicated by the fact that loans usually have to be repaid in hard currency that can be exchanged on world currency markets: U.S. dollars, Japanese yen, British pounds, French francs, Swiss francs, and German marks. To repay the loans, debtor nations have to sell goods and services that richer countries want to buy or that can earn hard currency from poorer countries. These include raw materials (hardwoods, oil, copper, gold, diamonds), cash crops (sugar, tobacco, coffee, tea, tropical fruits and flowers), illegal drugs and drug-producing crops (coca, marijuana, opium poppies), and weapons. Debtor countries may also earn foreign exchange by encouraging their people to work abroad as construction workers or maids or to become mail-order brides. They may lease land for foreign military bases or trash dumps that take toxic waste from industrialized countries, or they may develop their tourist assets — sunny beaches, beautiful landscapes, and "exotic" young women and children who are recruited into sex tourism.

Structural Adjustment Programs   In addition to selling goods and services to offset their external debt, debtor nations have also been under pressure from the World Bank and the IMF to make stringent changes in their economies to qualify for new loans. The aim of such structural adjustment programs is to increase the profitability of the economy. Required measures include

cutting back government spending on health, education, child care, and social welfare provisions;

cutting government subsidies and abolishing price controls, particularly on food, fuel, and public transportation;

adding new taxes, especially on consumer goods, and increasing existing taxes and interest rates;

selling nationalized industries, or at least a majority of the shares, to private corporations, often from outside the country;

reducing the number of civil servants on the government payroll;

improving profitability for corporations through wage controls, tax breaks, loans, and credit, or providing infrastructure by building ports, better roads, or rail transportation;

devaluing local currency to discourage imports and encourage exports; and

increasing the output of cash crops, by increasing yields and/or increasing the amount of land in cash crop production.

Though not required to do so by the World Bank, the Reagan, Bush, and Clinton administrations all adopted similar policies for use in the United States, and they were enshrined in the "Contract with America" introduced by the Republican Congress in 1994. Such policies are in line with global economic restructuring with the goal of increasing corporate profitability. Examples include the deregulation of air transport and the privatization of public utilities and aspects of the prison industry. In addition, these administrations restructured government spending by making reductions in the government workforce and cuts in, for example, Medicaid, Medicare, and welfare programs.

Implications of the Debt Crisis for Women   Despite women's increased opportunities for paid work in urban areas and export-processing zones in Asia, Latin America, and the Caribbean, the external debt crisis and structural adjustment programs have had a severe impact on women's lives and livelihoods. Cuts in social services and health care, often already woefully inadequate, have increased women's responsibilities for child care, health, and family welfare. Cuts in government subsidies for food and other basic items and devaluation of local currencies have reduced women's wages and doubly reduced their buying power. Women's wages fell by as much as 50 percent in many countries during the 1980s (Steinberg 1989). The emphasis on cash crops at the expense of subsistence crops has devastating environmental consequences and makes subsistence agriculture — very often the responsibility of women — much more difficult. Growing cash crops on the flatter land, for instance, pushes subsistence farmers to use steep hillsides for food crops, which is harder work and often less productive and which increases soil erosion. Clearing forests to plant cash crops or raise cattle, as McDonald's has done in parts of Central and Latin America, for example, also increases soil erosion and reduces the supply of fuel wood, which further adds to women's daily burden of work (Dankelman and Davidson 1988; Sen and Grown 1987; Shiva 1988). Other consequences of the debt cri-

sis include an increase in the number of people seeking work overseas as temporary migrant workers or
permanent immigrants; increasing unemployment
and underemployment, with growth in the exploitative and unregulated informal sector of the economy
(such as sweatshops and work in homes); an increase
in the number of students who have to drop out of
school and college due to financial pressures; and a
general increase in poverty and hardship.

Debt Cancellation   Between 1982 and 1990 $160 bil-
lion was transferred from Latin America to the developed world in debt repayments (O'Reilly 1991),
but this was only the interest on 50 percent of their
loans (George 1988). Since the mid-1980s African
governments have transferred $2 billion more to the
IMF in interest payments than they have received
in new loans (Beresford 1994). In 1982, Mexico announced that it could not repay its debt, and subsequently other countries suspended their repayments
throughout the 1980s. This led to much political and
financial debate concerning the legitimacy of debts
owed by countries of the South to the North.

    Many activist organizations in both the devel-
oped nations and the debtor countries support debt
cancellation. They argue that much of the money
borrowed has benefited only upper-class and professional elites or has gone into armaments, nuclear
power plants, or luxuries such as prestige buildings,
especially in urban areas. As summed up in the lyrics
to *Ode to the International Debt:* "Guns you can't eat,
And buildings you can't live, And trinkets you can't
wear, It is a debt not owed by the people" (Reagon
1987). In some countries, large sums of money borrowed by governments were kept by corrupt politicians and businesspeople and then reinvested in the
lender countries. As the authors of the Caribbean
Association for Feminist Research and Action Newsletter argue in Reading 41, poor people have rarely
benefited from such investments and should not be
held responsible for this debt. Susan George (1988)
claims that "cancellation would turn recipient countries into financial pariahs" who would not be able
to borrow further loans. She argues that the goals of
a debt campaign "should be to get money and the
political power that goes with it directly into the
hands of the poor majorities, bypassing the elites, and
insofar as possible, the State; and to ensure much
greater popular control over the development process" (p. 20).

Implications of Global Economic Inequalities

In principle inequality is unjust. Some people's freedom and comfort cannot be bought at the expense
of other people's oppression, degradation, and poverty. More pragmatically, inequality is a continual
source of violence and conflict. On an international
level it is one of the main causes of war; on a community level it can lead to alienation, anger, violence,
theft, and vandalism.

Connections to U.S. Policy Issues

Two issues of national importance in the United
States that are greatly affected by global inequalities
are immigration and drugs. Vast differences in living standards between the United States and many
other countries are a source of continuing pressure for
immigration into this country (Ong, Bonacich, and
Cheng 1994), as argued by Saskia Sassen in Reading
42. These same inequalities also drive the international drug trade, a lucrative earner of hard currency
for producer countries as well as for those who pro-
cure and sell illegal drugs or launder drug money
(Lusane 1991). It is important to understand the
global economic forces driving the drug trade and
pressures for immigration and to recognize the inadequacy of control measures that do not address
underlying causes.

    Discussion of the drug trade is beyond the scope
of this book, but we consider the issue of immigration here, building on the brief history of immigration law and policy included in Chapter 2. The ten
years from 1986 to 1996 have seen controversial and
acrimonious debate in the United States over immigration along with a range of new legislation, like
the 1996 Illegal Immigration Reform and Immigrant
Responsibility Act, which aims to control it. Anti-
immigration politicians and countless media reports
have invoked the specter of "alien hordes" poised on
the borders, ready to overrun the country, take jobs
away from the native born, and drain the welfare
system. Wendy Young (1997) counters this perception,
arguing that undocumented people "typically fill
service-sector jobs and are ineligible for most benefits, even though they pay $7 billion annually in taxes
and social security contributions. Moreover, 85% of
immigrants come to the United States through legal
channels" (p. 9). In 1995, 54 percent of documented

immigrants to the United States were women (Immigration and Naturalization Service 1996).

At the heart of much of this debate are racism and xenophobia. White people particularly see the country changing demographically with the arrival of more people from Asia, Mexico, and Central and South America. This poses a threat to the dominance of "the Anglo-Saxon part of America's culture" (Holmes 1995b). Such fears have provided leverage for a greatly increased INS budget and tighter border control, especially along the long land border with Mexico, which has been strongly fortified (Ayres 1994), as described by Leslie Marmon Silko in Reading 43. When Congress is cutting government funding for virtually all agencies except the military, it is significant that the INS has received an increase of $1 billion since 1994, bringing its 1996 budget to $2.6 billion (Freedberg 1996).

The distinction between legal and illegal immigrants has been drawn more sharply. According to Young (1997), in 1981 "the Attorney General estimated that the number of undocumented migrants in this country had grown to 8–10 million" (p. 7); she notes that undocumented migration is currently estimated at some 300,000 people each year. Undocumented women entering the United States are often subject to sexual harassment and rape in the process, including assaults by INS border patrols (Light 1996). The 1986 Immigration Act introduced sanctions against employers, making it illegal to hire knowingly undocumented workers, with fines for those who violate the law. This controversial program was intended to eliminate the "pull" factor of jobs attracting undocumented migrants into the country. Illegal immigrants are hired at low wages by agricultural growers, construction firms, landscaping and cleaning businesses, and the garment industry, for example, as well as by private individuals as maids and baby-sitters. Evidence indicates that employer sanctions have been ineffective; employers are not always prosecuted, and if they are, they tend to consider the relatively small fines as a hazard of doing business. However, as Young (1997) observes, "numerous studies have shown that employer sanctions have caused employment discrimination against U.S. citizens and permanent residents who look or sound 'foreign.' Some employers will avoid hiring such individuals rather than risk being subjected to sanctions and fines" (p. 8).

Increasing numbers of undocumented workers have been deported throughout the 1990s (Holmes 1995a), and legal immigrants have applied for citizenship in record numbers in response to growing controversy over immigration and moves to deny legal immigrants access to government supports. It is likely that migration policy will continue to be a contentious issue in the United States, particularly in states like California, Florida, New York, and Texas with large proportions of immigrants.

International Alliances Among Women

At international feminist meetings and conferences, such as the NGO Forum in September 1995, these global inequalities are central to many discussions. Women from countries of the South invariably challenge those from the North to take up the issue of external debt and structural adjustment with our governments and banks. Women's organizations worldwide are concerned with economic issues, including economic development, loans to start small businesses, and other job opportunities for women, as well as the lack of government spending on health care, child care, or care for the elderly.

Some U.S. feminist organizations focus their work on women's rights in this country, which is understandable, as earlier gains are being eroded. But the separation of domestic and foreign policy masks crucial connections and continuities and can lead to an insularity and parochialism on the part of women in the United States, an important aspect of the ignorance that comes with national privilege. In the context of trade agreements like GATT and NAFTA, Mary McGinn, the North American coordinator for Transnationals Information Exchange, comments, "Unfortunately, most U.S. women's advocacy groups took no position on GATT. But clearly, all women have a lot to lose: expanded freedom for multinational corporations jeopardizes social justice everywhere" (McGinn 1995, p. 15).

In order to build more effective international campaigns and alliances, women in the North need to learn much more about the effects of corporate and government policies on women in Asia, Africa, Latin America, and the Caribbean, and to understand the connections between these women's situations and our own (Bunch 1987). This is the importance of international gatherings like the NGO Forum at Huairou or the U.N. *Platform for Action*, which criticizes structural adjustment programs; advises cuts in military spending in favor of social spending; urges women's participation at all peace talks and in all decision-making affecting development and environment; confronts violence against women; calls for measuring women's unpaid work; and refers to "the family" in all its various forms.

(Morgan 1996, p. 20)

United Nations documents have to be ratified by the governments of individual countries to be accepted as national policy. Even if governments do not ratify them—and the U.S. on several occasions has not—they are still useful for activists in their attempts to hold governments accountable and to show what others have pledged to do for women and girls. Wangari Maathai, coordinator of the Kenyan Women's Green Belt, comments:

It's very hard to push governments on issues that affect all aspects of society, let alone those that affect women. But the U.N. document has given us a tool with which to work. Now it's up to the women to push their issues into the boardrooms where political and economic decisions are made by those who did not even bother to come to Beijing.

(Quoted in Morgan 1996, p. 18)

In the United States the White House committed itself to establish a President's Interagency Council on Women to plan for implementation of the *Platform for Action* in this country, through heightening awareness of domestic violence, tackling the threats to women's health, improving workplace conditions for women with a focus on equal pay, promotion policies, and balancing work and family, removing barriers to the education of women and girls, increasing women's access to credit and economic empowerment, and getting the administration to ratify the U.N. Convention on the Elimination of All Forms of Discrimination against Women, which was adopted by the U.N. in 1979 but has not yet been ratified by the U.S. government. Various women's organizations are lobbying for this commitment to be honored. The Women's Environment and Development Organization (WEDO), together with the Center for Women Policy Studies, initiated a twelve-point "Contract with Women of the U.S.A." based on the U.N. *Platform for Action*, endorsed by hundreds of organizations and thousands

of individuals during 1996, including women state legislators from all fifty states. WEDO is also collating information from many countries to see what steps have been taken to implement the *Platform for Action*. Many women in the United States who attended the NGO Forum spoke to public meetings, religious organizations, women's groups, and school and college classes about their impressions, and brought back a heightened understanding of global linkages to their ongoing organizing efforts. The Women of Color Resource Center (Berkeley, California), for instance, has put the globalization of the economy at the top of its agenda. The group states: "Global economics was at the top of the Beijing agenda; it is now at the top of ours as well" (1996, p. 2).

The Seeds of a New Global Economy

In Latin America, the Caribbean, Africa, and Asia, thousands of workers' organizations, environmentalists, feminists, and religious groups are campaigning for better pay and working conditions and for economic development that is environmentally sound (Braidotti et al. 1994; De Oliveira et al. n.d.; Leonard 1989), and they are protesting the poverty caused by external debt. Some of these organizations have links with similar organizations and networks in countries of the North that advocate that we in the United States learn more about the global economy and the impact of global inequalities on people's lives and livelihoods. They also urge us to live more simply: to recycle materials, wear secondhand clothing, barter for things we need, establish collectives and cooperatives, engage in socially responsible shopping and investing, and buy directly from farmers and craft workers. Specific projects include dialogue projects linking workers of the North and South, such as North-South Dialogue of the American Friends Service Committee's Latin American/Caribbean Program; campaigns urging a debt amnesty for countries of the South, such as initiated by Oxfam and Christian Aid; campaigns to get institutions to stop buying World Bank bonds, such as that by Global Exchange; direct trading between producers and craftspeople in the South and consumers in countries of the North, such as Pueblo to People and Global Exchange; Third World study tours, such as Global Exchange; and direct support through work brigades such as those in Cuba and Nicaragua.

In the 1960s and 1970s those active in U.S. movements for liberation and civil rights made theoretical and practical connections with anticolonial struggles in such countries as South Africa, Vietnam, Cuba, Angola, and Mozambique. In the late 1990s these international linkages are crucial, not merely, as Angela Davis (1997) remarked, "as a matter of inspiration or identification, but as a matter of necessity," because of the impact of the globalization of the economy.

In thinking about the issues raised in this chapter, consider the following questions:

1. Look at the labels in your clothes and on all products you buy. Where were they made? Do you know where these countries are? Look at maps if you don't know.

2. What does it mean to say "Made in the USA"?

3. Why does this issue of the global economy matter to people living in the United States? What does it tell us about structural privilege (which we may not know we have and may not want)? If some of this material is new to you, why do you think you have not learned it before?

4. How does global inequality reinforce racial prejudice and institutionalized racism in the United States?

5. Do you need all that you currently own? List everything you need to sustain life. Which items from this list do you need to buy? Which might you make yourself, share, or barter with others?

6. How do you define wealth, aside from material possessions? List all the ways you are enriched.

7. How do you define "success" in terms of your own life?

8. How do you define security in general? At this point in your life? As you grow older?

9. Does wealth equal political power? Are rich people always in the **power elite** — the group that influences political and economic decisions in the country? Who makes up the power elite in the United States?

10. How do people in elite positions justify the perpetuation of inequalities to others? To themselves? How are the ideologies of nationalism, racial superiority, male superiority, and class superiority useful here?

11. This very difficult issue will be with us for a long time and this material can sometimes seem overwhelming. How do these issues make you feel?

12. What can you do to transform negative and disempowering feelings into action?

13. What alternatives to the current economic systems do you know of? Can you think of others?

THIRTY-EIGHT

◆◆◆

Maquiladoras
The View from Inside

María Patricia Fernández-Kelly

What is it like to be female, single and eager to find employment at a maquiladora? Shortly after arriv-

---

As part of the fieldwork for her study of the *maquiladora* industry in Mexico, anthropologist Maria Patricia Fernandez-Kelly worked in a textile factory in Ciudad Juárez.

ing in Ciudad Juárez and after finding stable lodging, I began looking through the pages of newspapers hoping to find a "wanted" ad. My intent was to merge with the clearly visible mass of women who roam the streets of industrial parks of Ciudad Juárez searching for jobs. They are, beyond doubt, a distinctive feature of the city, an effervescent expression of the conditions that prevail in the local job market.

My objectives were straightforward: I was to spend from four to six weeks applying for jobs and obtaining direct experience about the employment policies, recruitment strategies and screening mechanisms used by companies in the process of hiring assembly workers. Special emphasis would be given to the average investment of time and money expended by individual workers in trying to gain access to jobs. In addition, I was to spend an equal amount of time working at a plant, preferably at one involved in the manufacture of apparel.

With this I expected to learn more about working conditions, production quotas and wages at a particular plant. In general both research stages were planned as exploratory devices that would elicit questions relevant to the research project from the perspective of workers themselves.

In retrospect, it seems odd that the doubt as to whether these goals were feasible or not never entered my design. However, finding a job at a maquiladora is not a self-evident proposition. For many women, actual workers, the task is not an easy one. This is due primarily to the large number of women they must compete with. Especially for those who are older than twenty-five years of age the probability of getting work in a maquiladora is low. At every step of their constant peregrination women are confronted by a familiar sign at the plants, "No applications available," or by the negative response of a guard or a secretary at the entrance of the factories. But such is the arrogance of the uninformed researcher. I went about the business of looking for a job as if the social milieu had to comply with the intents of my research rather than the reverse. Moreover, I was pressed for time. It was indispensable that I get a job as quickly as possible.

By using newspapers as a source of information for jobs available, I was departing from the common strategy of potential workers in that environment. As my own research would show, the majority of these workers avail themselves of information by word of mouth. They are part of informal networks which include relatives, friends and an occasional acquaintance in the personnel management sector. Most potential workers believe that a personal recommendation from someone already employed at a maquiladora can ease their difficult path.

This belief is well founded. At many plants, managers prefer to hire applicants by direct recommendation of employees who have proven to be dependable and hard-working. For example, at Electro Componentes de Mexico, the subsidiary of General Electric and one of the most stable maquiladoras in Juárez, it is established policy not to hire "outsiders." Only those who are introduced personally to the manager are considered to fill up vacancies.

Such a policy is not whimsical. It is the result of evaluations performed on a daily basis during the interactions between company personnel and workers. By resorting to the personal linkage, managers attenuate the dangers of having their factories infiltrated by unreliable workers, independent organizers and "troublemakers." . . .

On the other hand, the resemblance of a personal interest in the individual worker at the moment of hiring enables management to establish a bond often heavily colored by paternalism. From the point of view of workers this is a two-faceted proposition. Some complain of the not unusual practice of superintendents and managers who are prone to demand special services, for example, overtime, in exchange for personal favors: a loan, an exemption from work on a busy day when the presence of the worker at home is required by her children, and so on. As in other similar cases, personal linkages at the workplace can and will be used as subtle mechanisms to exert control.

Workers, in turn, acknowledge a personal debt to the individual who has hired them. In the majority of cases, commitment to the firm is not distinct from the commitment to a particular individual through whom access to employment presumably has been achieved. A job becomes a personal favor granted through the kindness of the personnel manager or the superintendent of a factory. . . .

Only those who are not part of tightly woven informal networks must rely on impersonal ways to find a job. In this situation are recently arrived migrants and older women with children, for whom the attempt to find maquiladora employment may be a new experience after many years spent caring for children and the home. In objective terms my own situation as a newcomer in Ciudad Juárez was not markedly different from that of the former. Both types of women are likely to be found in larger numbers in the apparel manufacturing sector.

This is not a random occurrence. One of the basic propositions in the present work is that differences in manufacturing activity are related to variations in the volume of capital investments. In turn this combined variable determines recruitment strategies. Therefore different types of persons are predominately employed in different manufacturing sectors. Ciudad Juárez electronics maquiladoras, for example, tend to employ very young, single women. This is, in effect, a preferred category of potential workers from the point of view of industry.

Workers, on their part, also prefer the electronics sector, which is characterized by the existence of large stable plants, regular wages and certain additional benefits. In contrast, the apparel manufacturing sector is frequently characterized by smaller, less stable shops where working conditions are particularly strenuous. Because of their low levels of capital investment, many of these shops tend to hire personnel on a more or less temporary basis. The lack of even the smallest of commitments to their employees and the need to maintain an elastic work force to survive as capitalist enterprises in a fluctuating international market forces management to observe crude and often ruthless personnel recruitment policies.

One of such firms was Maquiladoras Internacionales. . . .

Attached to the tent-like factory where women work from 7:30 A.M. to 5:00 P.M. from Monday to Friday there is a tiny office. I entered that office wondering whether my appearance or accent would elicit the suspicion of my potential employers. The personnel manager looked me over sternly and told me to fill out a form. I was to return the following morning at seven to take a dexterity test.

I tried to respond to the thirty-five questions contained in the application in an acceptable manner. Most of the items were straightforward: name, age, marital status, place of birth, length of residence in Ciudad Juárez, property assets, previous jobs and income, number of pregnancies, general state of health, and so on. One, however, was unexpected: What is your major aspiration in life? I pondered briefly upon the superfluous character of that inquiry given the general features of the job sought. . . .

The following morning I was scheduled to take an on-the-job test. I assumed that this would consist of a short evaluation of my skills as a seamstress. I was to be proven wrong. At 7 A.M. I knocked at the door of the personnel office where I had filled out the application the day before. But no one was there yet. I peeked into the entrance of the factory in a state of moderate confusion. A dark-haired woman wearing false eyelashes ordered me to go in and promptly led me to my place. Her name was Margarita and she was the supervisor.

I had never been behind an industrial sewing machine of the kind I confronted at this time. That it was old was plain to see; how it worked was difficult to judge. An assortment of diversely cut denim parts was placed on my left side while I listened intently to Margarita's instructions. I was expected to sew patch-pockets on what were to become blue jeans. Obediently, I started to sew. The particulars of "unskilled" labor unfolded before my eyes.

The procedure involved in this operation required perfect coordination of hands, eyes and legs. The left hand was used to select the larger part of material from the batch next to the worker. Upon it, the pocket (swiftly grabbed by the right hand) had to be attached. There were no markers to guide the placement of the pocket on its proper place. This was achieved by experienced workers on a purely visual basis. Once the patch-pocket had been put on its correct position, the two parts had to be directed under a double needle while applying pressure on the machine's pedal with the right foot.

Because the pockets were sewed on with thread of a contrasting color, it was of peak importance to maintain the edge of the pocket perfectly aligned with the needles so as to produce a regular seam and an attractive design. Due to the diamond-like shape of the pocket, it was also indispensable to slightly rotate the materials three times while adjusting pressure on the pedal. Too much pressure inevitably broke the thread or resulted in seams longer than the edge of the pocket. Even the slightest deviation from the needles produced lopsided designs which had to be unsewed and gone over as many times as necessary to achieve an acceptable product. According to the instructions of the supervisor, once trained, I would be expected to sew a pocket every nine to ten seconds. That is, between 360 and 396 pockets every hour, between 2,880 and 3,168 every shift.

For this, velocity was a central consideration. The vast majority of apparel manufacturing maquiladoras operate through a combination of the minimum wage and piecework. At the moment of being hired, workers receive the minimum wage. During 1978 this amounted to 125 pesos a day (approximately $5.00). However, they are responsible for a production quota arrived at by time-clock calculations. Workers receive slight bonus payments when they are able to fulfill their production quotas on a sustained basis throughout the week. In any case they are not allowed to produce less than 80% of their assigned quota without being admonished. And a worker seriously endangers her job when unable to improve her level of productivity.

At Maquiladoras Internacionales a small blackboard indicated the type of weekly bonus received by those able to produce certain percentages of the quota. These fluctuated between 50.00 pesos (approximately $2.20) for those who completed 80% to 100.00 pesos (about $4.40) for those who accomplished 100%. Managers call this combination of steep production quotas, minimum wages and modest bonuses, "incentive programs."

I started my test at 7:30 A.M. with a sense of embarrassment about my limited skills and disbelief at the speed with which the women in the factory worked. As I continued sewing, the bundle of material on my left was renewed and grew in size, although slowly. I had to repeat the operation many times before the product was considered acceptable. But that is precisely what was troubling about the "test." I was being treated as a new worker while presumably being tested. I had not been issued a contract and, therefore, was not yet incorporated into the Instituto Mexicano del Seguro Social (the National Security System). Nor had I been instructed as to working hours, benefits and system of payment.

I explained to the supervisor that I had recently arrived in the city, alone, and with very little money. Would I be hired? What was the current wage? When would I be given a contract? Margarita listened patiently while helping me unsew one of many defective pockets, and then said, "You are too curious. Don't worry about it. Do your job and things will be all right." I continued to sew aware of the fact that every pocket attached during the "test" was becoming part of the plant's total production.

At 12:30 during the thirty-minute lunch break, I had a chance to better see the factory. Its improvised aura was underscored by the metal folding chairs behind the sewing machines. I had been sitting in one of them during the whole morning, but not until then

did I notice that most of them had the well-known emblem of Coca-Cola painted on their backs. I had seen this kind of chair many times in casual parties both in Mexico and in the United States. Had they been bought or were they being rented from the local concessionary? In any event they were not designed in accordance to the strenuous requirements of a factory job, especially one needing the complex bodily movements of sewing. It was therefore necessary for women to bring their own colorful pillows to ameliorate the stress on their buttocks and spines. Later on I was to discover that chronic lumbago was, and is, a frequent condition among factory seamstresses.

My curiosity did not decrease during the next hours, nor were any of my questions answered. At 5 P.M. a bell rang signaling the end of the shift and workers quickly prepared to leave. I marched to the personnel office with the intent of getting more information about a confusing day. But this time my inquiry was less than welcome. Despite my over-shy approach to the personnel manager, his reaction was hostile. Even before he was able to turn the disapproving expression on his face into words, Margarita intervened with energy. She was angry. To the manager she said, "This woman has too many questions: Will she be hired? Is she going to be insured?" And then to me, "I told you already we do piecework here; if you do your job you get a wage, otherwise you don't. That's clear isn't it? What else do you want? You should be grateful! This plant is giving you a chance to work! What else do you want? Come back tomorrow and be punctual."

This was only the first in a number of application procedures that I underwent. Walking about the industrial parks while following other job-seekers was especially informative. Most women do not engage in this task alone. Rather they do it in the company of friends or relatives. Small groups of two or three women looking for work may be commonly seen in the circumvicinity of the factories. Also frequent is the experience of very young women, ages between sixteen and seventeen, seen in the company of their mothers. . . .

At the times when shifts begin or end, the industrial parks of Juárez form a powerful visual image as thousands of women arrive in buses, taxi-cabs and *ruteras* while many others exit the factories. During working hours only those seeking jobs may be seen wandering about. Many, but not the majority are "older women." They confront special difficulties due both to their age and to the fact that they often support their own children. These are women who, in most cases, enter the labor force after many years dedicated to domestic chores and child-care. The precipitant factor that determines their entry into the labor force is often the desertion by their male companions. The bind they are placed in at that time is well illustrated by the experience of a thirty-one year old woman, the mother of six children: "I have been looking for work since my husband left me two months ago. But I haven't had any luck. It must be my age and the fact that I have so many children. Maybe I should lie and say I've only one. But then the rest wouldn't be entitled to medical care once I got the job." Women often look for jobs in order to support their children. But being a mother is frequently the determining factor that prevents them from getting jobs.

In early June, 1978, Camisas de Juárez, a recently formed maquiladora was starting a second (evening) shift. Until then it had hired approximately 110 workers operating in the morning hours. As it expanded production, a new contingent of workers had to be recruited. Advertisements to that effect appeared in the daily newspapers. I responded to them. So did dozens of other women.

Camisas de Juárez is located in the modern Parque Industrial Bermúdez. On the morning that I arrived with the intent of applying for a job, thirty-seven women had preceded me. Some had arrived as early as 6 A.M. At 10 the door which separated the front lawn from the entrance to the factory had not yet been opened. A guard appeared once in a while to peek at the growing contingent of applicants, but these were given no encouragement to stay on, nor was the door unlocked.

At 10:30 the guard finally opened the door and informed us that only those having personal recommendation letters would be permitted to walk inside. This was the first in a series of formal and informal screening procedures used to reduce the number of potential workers. It was an effective screening device: Thirteen women left immediately, as they did not have the letter of recommendation alluded to by the guard. Others tried to convince him that although they had no personal recommendation, they "knew" someone already employed at the factory. It was through the recommendation of these acquaintances that they had come to apply for a job.

One of them, Xochitl lacked both a written or verbal recommendation but she insisted. She had with her a diploma issued by a sewing academy. She was hopeful that this would work in her favor. "It is better to have proof that you are qualified to do the job than to have a letter for recommendation, right?" I wondered whether the personnel manager would agree.

Indeed her diploma gave Xochitl claim to a particular skill. But academies such as the one she had attended abound in Ciudad Juárez. For a relatively small sum of money they offer technical and vocational courses which presumably qualify young men and women for skilled work. However in an environment lacking in employment opportunities, their value is in question. In many cases maquiladora managers prefer to hire women who have had direct experience on a job or those who are young and inexperienced but who can be trained to suit the needs of a particular firm. As one manager put it to me, "We prefer to hire women who are unspoiled, that is, those who come to us without preconceptions about what industrial work is. Women such as these are easier to shape to our own requirements." . . .

We waited upon the benevolence of the guard who seemed unperturbed by the fluctuating number of women standing by the door. To many of us he was the main obstacle lying between unemployment and getting a job from someone inside the factory in a decision-making position. If only we could get our foot in, maybe there was a chance. . . . The young man dressed in uniform appeared to the expectant women as an arrogant and insensitive figure. I asked him how long he had worked there. With the air of one who feels he has gained mastery over his own fate he answered, "Uy! I've been working here for a very long time, I assure you: almost two years."

To me his words sounded a bit pathetic. But Beatríz and Teresa, two sisters of twenty-three and nineteen years of age, respectively, were not pleased by his attitude. Their patience had been exhausted and their alternating comments were belligerent: "Why must these miserable guards always act this way? It would seem that they've never had to look for a job. Maybe this one thinks he's more important than the owner of the factory. What a bastard!" But their dialogue failed to elicit any response. Guards are accustomed to similar outbursts.

Teresa wanted to know whether I had any sewing experience. "Not much," I told her, "but I used to sew for a lady in my hometown." "Well, then you're very lucky," she said, "because they aren't hiring anyone without experience." The conversation having begun, I proceeded to ask a similar question, "How about you, have you worked before?"

Yes, both my sister and I used to work in a small shop on Altamirano Street in downtown Juárez. There were about seventy women like us sewing in a very tiny space, about twenty square meters. We sewed pants for the minimum wage, but we had no insurance.

The boss used to bring precut fabric from the United States for us to sew and then he sold the finished products in El Paso. When he was unable to get fabric we were laid-off; sent to rest without pay! Later on he wanted to hire us again but he still didn't want to insure us even though we had worked at the shop for three years.

When I was sixteen I used to cut thread at the shop. Afterwards one of the seamstresses taught me how to operate a small machine and I started doing serious work. Beatríz, my sister, used to sew the pockets on the pants. It's been three months since we left the shop. Right now we are living from the little that my father earns. We are two of nine brothers and sisters (there were twelve of us in total but three died when they were young). My father does what he can but he doesn't have a steady job. Sometimes he does construction work; sometimes he's hired to help paint a house or sells toys at the stadium. You know, odd jobs. He doesn't earn enough to support us.

I am single, thanks be to God, and I do not want to get married. There are enough problems in my life as it is! But my sister married an engineer when she was only fifteen. Now she is unmarried and she has three children to support. They live with us too. Beatríz and I are the oldest in the family, you see, that's why we really have to find a job. . . .

At that point Beatríz intervened. I asked whether her husband helped support the children. Her answer was unwavering: "No, and I don't want him to give me anything, not a cent, because I don't want him to have any claim or rights over my babies. As long as I can support them, he won't have to interfere." I replied, "But aren't there better jobs outside of maquiladoras? I understand you can make more money working at a *cantina*. Is that true?"

Both of them looked at me suspiciously. Cantinas are an ever present reminder of overt or concealed prostitution. Teresa said,

That is probably true, but what would our parents think? You can't stop people from gossiping, and many of those cantinas are whorehouses. Of course, when you have great need you can't be choosy, right? For some time I worked as a waitress but that didn't last. The supervisor was always chasing me. First he wanted to see me after work. I told him I had a boyfriend, but he insisted. He said I was too young to have a steady boyfriend. Then, when he learned I had some typing skills, he wanted me to be his secretary. I'm not stupid! I knew what he really wanted; he was always staring at my legs. So I had to leave that job too. I told him I had been rehired at the shop although it wasn't true. He wasn't bad looking, but he was married and had children. . . . Why must men fool around?

At last the guard announced that only those with previous experience would be allowed to fill out applications. Twenty women went into the narrow lobby of Camisas de Juárez, while the rest left in small quiet groups. For those of us who stayed a second waiting period began. One by one we were shown into the office of the personnel manager where we were to take a manual dexterity test. The point was to fit fifty variously colored pegs into fifty similarly colored perforations on a wooden board. This had to be accomplished in the shortest possible time. Clock in hand, the personnel manager told each woman when to begin and when to stop. Some were asked to adjust the pegs by hand, others were given small pliers to do so. Most were unable to complete the test in the allotted time. One by one they came out of the office looking weary and expressing their conviction that they wouldn't be hired.

Later on we were given the familiar application form. Again, I had to ponder what my greatest aspiration in life was. But this time I was curious to know what Xochitl had answered. "Well," she said, "I don't know if my answer is right. Maybe it is wrong. But I tried to be truthful. My greatest aspiration in life is to improve myself and to progress." . . .

After completing the application at Camisas de Juárez there was still another test to take. This one consisted of demonstrating sewing skills on an industrial machine. Again many women expressed doubts and concern after returning to the lobby where other expectant women awaited their turn. In the hours that had been spent together a lively dialogue had ensued. Evidently there was a sense that all of us were united by the common experience of job seeking and by the gnawing anxiety that potential failure entails. Women compared notes and exchanged opinions about the nature and difficulty of their respective tests. They did not offer each other overt reassurance or support, but they made sympathetic comments and hoped that there would be work for all.

At 3:30 P.M., that is, seven hours after the majority of us had arrived at the plant, we were dismissed. We were given no indication that any of us would be hired. Rather we were told that a telegram would be sent to each address as soon as a decision was made. Most women left disappointed and certain that they would probably not be hired.

Two weeks later, when I had almost given up all hope, the telegram arrived. I was to come to the plant as soon as possible to receive further instructions. Upon my arrival I was given the address of a small clinic in downtown Ciudad Juárez. I was to bring two pictures to the clinic and take a medical examination. Its explicit purpose was to evaluate the physical fitness of potential workers. In reality it was a simple pregnancy test. Maquiladoras do not hire pregnant women, although very often these are among the ones with greater need for employment. . . .

Having been examined at the clinic, I returned to the factory with a sealed envelope containing certification of my physical capacity to work. I was then told to return the following Monday at 3:30 P.M. in order to start work. After what seemed an unduly long and complicated procedure, I was finally being hired as an assembly worker. For the next six weeks I shared the experience of approximately eighty women who had also been recruited to work the evening shift at Camisas de Juárez. Xochitl, Beatríz and Teresa had been hired too.

On weekdays work started at 3:45 P.M. and it ended at 11:30 P.M. At 7:30 P.M. a bell signaled the beginning of a half-hour break during which workers could eat their dinner. Some brought homemade sandwiches, but many bought their food at the factory. Meals generally consisted of a dish of *flautas* or *tostadas* and carbonated drinks. The persistence of inadequate diets causes assembly workers numerous gastric problems. On Saturdays the shift started at 11:30 A.M. and it ended at 9:30 P.M. with a half-hour break. We worked in total forty-eight hours every week and earned the minimum wage, that is, 875 pesos per week; 125 pesos per day; an hourly rate of approximately $0.60. . . .

From the perspective of workers, medical insurance is as important as a decorous wage. This is particularly true in the case of women who have children in their care. Thus, it was not surprising to find out that some new workers at Camisas de Juárez were there mainly because of the *seguro*. Maria Luisa, a twenty-nine-year-old woman told me, "I don't have a lot of money, but neither do I have great need to work. My husband owns a small restaurant and we have a fairly good income. But I have four children and one of them is chronically sick. Without insurance medical fees will render us poor. That's the main reason why I am working."

As do the majority of garment maquiladoras, Camisas de Juárez operates by a combination of piecework and the minimum wage. Upon being hired by the plant every worker earns a fixed wage. However, all workers are expected to fulfill production quotas. On the first day at the job I was trained to perform a particular operation. My task was to sew narrow biases around the cuff-openings of men's shirts. As with other operations I had performed before, this one entailed coordination and speed. . . .

As for the production quota, I was expected to complete 162 pairs of sleeves every hour, that is, one every 2.7 seconds, more than 1,200 pairs per shift. It seemed to me that to achieve such a goal would require unworldly skill and velocity. In six weeks as a direct production operator I was to fall short of this goal by almost 50%. But I was a very inexperienced worker. Sandra, who sat next to me during this period, assured me that it could be done. It wasn't easy, but certainly it could be done. . . .

The factory environment was all-embracing, its demands overwhelmed me. Young supervisors walked about the aisles asking for higher productivity and encouraging us to work at greater speed. Periodically their voices could be heard throughout the work place: "Faster! faster! Come on girls, let us hear the sound of those machines!" They were personally responsible before management for the efficiency of the workers under their command.

Esther, who oversaw my labor, had been a nurse prior to her employment in the factory. I was intrigued by her polite manner and her change of jobs. She dressed prettily, seeming a bit out of place amidst the heated humdrum of the sewing machines, the lint and the dispersed fabric that cluttered the plant. She told me it was more profitable to work at a maquiladora than at a clinic or a hospital.

Esther saw her true vocation as that of a nurse, but she had to support an ill and aging father. Her mother had died three years earlier, and although her home was nice and fully owned, she was solely responsible for the family debts. Working at a factory entailed less prestige than working as a nurse, but it offered a better wage. She was now earning almost one thousand pesos a week. As a nurse she had earned only a bit more than half that amount. From her I also learned, for the first time, about the dubious advantages of being a maquiladora supervisor.

As with the others in similar positions, Esther had to stay at the plant long after the shift ended and the workers left. Very often the hours ran until one in the morning. During that time she verified quotas, sorted out production, tried to detect errors and, not seldom, personally unseamed defective garments. With the others she was also responsible for the preparation of shipments and the selection of material for the following day's production. In other words, her supervisory capacities included quality control and some administrative functions.

When productivity levels are not met, when workers fail to arrive punctually or are absent, or when there is trouble in the line, it is the supervisor who is first admonished by management. Thus, supervisors occupy an intermediary position between the firm and the workers, which is to say that they often find themselves between the devil and the deep blue sea.

As with the factory guard, supervisors and group leaders are frequently seen by workers as solely responsible for their plight at the workplace. Perceived abuses, unfair treatment and excessive demands are thought to be the result of supervisors' whims rather than the creature of a particular system of production. That explains, in part, why workers' grievances are often couched in complaints about the performance of supervisors.

But while supervisors may be seen by workers as close allies of the firms, they stand at the bottom of the administrative hierarchy. They are also the receivers of middle and upper management's dissatisfaction, but they have considerably less power and their sphere of action is very limited. Many line supervisors agree that the complications they face in their jobs are hardly worth the differences in pay. . . .

The Organization of Labor in the Factory

The pressures exerted by supervisors at Camisas de Juárez were hard to ignore. Esther was considerate and encouraging: "You're doing much better now. Soon enough you'll be sewing as fast as the others." But I had doubts, as she was constantly asking me to repair my own defective work, a task which entailed an infinite sense of frustration. I began to skip dinner breaks in order to continue sewing in a feeble attempt to improve my productivity level. I was not alone. Some workers fearful of permanent dismissal also stayed at their sewing machines during the break while the rest went outside to eat and rest. I could understand their behavior; their jobs were at stake. But presumably my situation was different. I had nothing to lose by inefficiency, and yet I felt compelled to do my best. I started pondering upon the subtle mechanisms that dominate will at the workplace and about the shame that overwhelms those who fall short of the goals assigned to them.

The fact is that as the days passed it became increasingly difficult to think of factory work as a stage in a research project. My identity became that of the worker; my immediate objectives those determined by the organization of labor at the plant. Academic research became an ethereal fiction. Reality was work, as much for me as for the others who labored under the same roof.

These feelings were reinforced by my personal interactions during working hours. I was one link in a rigidly structured chain. My failure to produce speedily had numerous consequences for others operating in the same line and in the factory as a whole. For example, Lucha, my nineteen-year-old companion, was in charge of cutting remnant thread and separating the sleeves five other seamstresses and I sewed. She also made it her business to return to me all those parts which she felt would not meet Esther's approval. According to her she did this in order to spare me further embarrassment. But it was in her interest that I sewed quickly and well; the catch in this matter was that she was unable to meet her quota unless the six seamstresses she assisted met theirs.

Therefore, a careless and slow worker could stand between Lucha and her possibility to get a weekly bonus. The more a seamstress sewed, the more a thread cutter became indispensable. As a consequence, Lucha was extremely interested in seeing improvements in my level of productivity and in the quality of my work. Sometimes her attitude and exhortations verged on the hostile. As far as I was concerned, the accusatory expression on her face was the best work incentive yet devised by the factory. It was not difficult to discern impinging tension. I was not surprised to find out during the weeks spent at Camisas de Juárez that the germ of enmity had bloomed between some seamstresses and their respective thread cutters over matters of work.

Although the relationships between seamstresses and thread cutters were especially delicate, all workers were affected by each other's level of efficiency. Cuffless sleeves could not be attached to shirts. Sleeves could not be sewed to shirts without collars or pockets. Holes and buttons had to be fixed at the end. Unfinished garments could not be cleaned of lint or labeled. In sum, each minute step required a series of preceding operations effectively completed. Delay of one stage inevitably slowed up the whole process.

From the perspective of the workers, labor appeared as the interconnection of efficiently performed individual activities rather than as a structured imposition from above. Managers are nearly invisible, but the flaws of fellow workers are always apparent. Bonuses exist as seemingly impersonal rewards whose access can be made difficult by a neighbor's laziness or incompetence. As a result, complaints are frequently directed against other workers and supervisors. The organization of labor at any particular plant does not immediately lead to feelings of solidarity.

On the other hand, common experiences at the workplace provide the basis for dialogue and elicit a particular kind of humor. In this there is frequently expressed a longing for relief from the tediousness of industrial work. One of Sandra's favorite topics of conversation was to reflect upon the possibility of marriage. She did so with a witty and self-deprecatory attitude.

She thought that if she could only find a nice man who would be willing to support her, everything in her life would be all right. She didn't mind if he was not young or good-looking, as long as he had plenty of money. Were there men like that left in the world? Of course, with the children it was difficult, not to say impossible, to find such a godsend. Then again, no one kept you from trying. But not at the maquiladora. All of us were female. Not even a lonely engineer was to be found at Camisas de Juárez. One could die of boredom there.

However, the fact that there weren't men around at the plant had its advantages according to Sandra. At many factories men generally occupied supervisory and middle- and upper-management positions. Sandra knew many women who had been seduced and then deserted by engineers and technicians. In other cases women felt they had to comply with the sexual demands of fellow workers because they believed otherwise they would lose their jobs. Some were just plain stupid. Things were especially difficult for very young women at large plants like RCA. They needed guidance and information to stay out of trouble, but there was no one to advise them. Their families had too many problems to care. . . .

Fortunately, there were the bars and the discotheques. Did I like to go out dancing? She didn't think so; I didn't look like the kind who would. But it was great fun; we should go out together sometime (eventually we did). The Malibú, a popular dancing hall, had good shows. But it was tacky and full of kids. It was better to go to the Max Fim, and especially the Cosmos. The latter was always crowded because everyone liked it so much. Even people from the other side (the United States) came to Juárez just to visit Cosmos. Its décor was inspired by outerspace movies like Star Wars. It was full of color and movement and shifting lights. They played the best American disco music. If you were lucky you could meet a U.S. citizen. Maybe he would even want to get married and you could go and live in El Paso. Things like that happen at discotheques. Once a Jordanian soldier in service at Fort Bliss had asked her to marry him the first time they met at Cosmos. But he wanted to return to his country, and she had said no. Cosmos was definitely the best discotheque in Juárez, and Sandra could be found dancing there amidst the deafening sound of music every Saturday evening.

The inexhaustible level of energy of women working at the maquiladoras never ceased to impress me. How could anyone be in the mood for all-night dancing on Saturdays after forty-eight weekly hours of industrial work? I had seen many of these women stretching their muscles late at night, trying to soothe the pain they felt at the waist. After the incessant noise of the sewing machines, how could anyone long for even higher levels of sound? But as Sandra explained to me, life is too short. If you don't go out and have fun you will come to the end of your days having done nothing but sleep, eat and work. And she didn't call that living. . . .

◆◆◆

THIRTY-NINE

The Globetrotting Sneaker

Cynthia Enloe

Four years after the fall of the Berlin Wall marked the end of the Cold War, Reebok, one of the fastest growing companies in United States history, decided that the time had come to make its mark in Russia. Thus it was with considerable fanfare that Reebok's executives opened their first store in downtown Moscow in July 1993. A week after the grand opening, store managers described sales as well above expectations.

Reebok's opening in Moscow was the perfect post-Cold War scenario: commercial rivalry replacing military posturing; consumerist tastes homogenizing heretofore hostile peoples; capital and managerial expertise flowing freely across newly porous state borders. Russians suddenly had the "freedom" to spend money on U.S. cultural icons like athletic footwear, items priced above and beyond daily subsistence: at the end of 1993, the average Russian earned the equivalent of $40 a month. Shoes on display were in the $100 range. Almost 60 percent of single parents, most of whom were women, were living in poverty. Yet in Moscow and Kiev, shoe promoters had begun targeting children, persuading them to pressure their mothers to spend money on stylish, Western sneakers. And as far as strategy goes, athletic shoe giants have, you might say, a good track record. In the U.S. many inner-city boys who see basketball as a "ticket out of the ghetto" have become convinced that certain brand-name shoes will give them an edge.

But no matter where sneakers are bought or sold, the potency of their advertising imagery has made it easy to ignore this mundane fact: Shaquille O'Neal's Reeboks are stitched by someone; Michael Jordan's Nikes are stitched by someone; so are your roommate's, so are your grandmother's. Those someones are women, mostly Asian women who are supposed to believe that their "opportunity" to make sneakers for U.S. companies is a sign of their country's progress—just as a Russian woman's chance to spend two month's salary on a pair of shoes for her child allegedly symbolizes the new Russia.

As the global economy expands, sneaker executives are looking to pay women workers less and less, even though the shoes that they produce are capturing an ever-growing share of the footwear market. By the end of 1993, sales in the U.S. alone had reached $11.6 billion. Nike, the largest supplier of athletic footwear in the world, posted a record $298 million profit for 1993—earnings that had nearly tripled in five years. And sneaker companies continue to refine their strategies for "global competitiveness"—hiring supposedly docile women to make their shoes, changing designs as quickly as we fickle customers change our tastes, and shifting factories from country to country as trade barriers rise and fall.

The logic of it all is really quite simple; yet trade agreements such as the North American Free Trade Agreement (NAFTA) and the General Agreement of Tariffs and Trade (GATT) are, of course, talked about in a jargon that alienates us, as if they were technical matters fit only for economists and diplomats. The

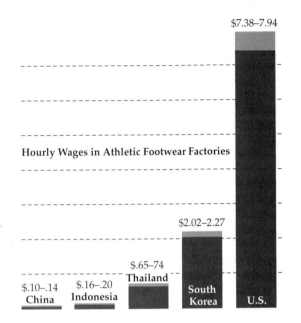

$7.38–7.94

Hourly Wages in Athletic Footwear Factories

$2.02–2.27

$.65–74
Thailand

$.10–.14 $.16–.20
China   **Indonesia**

**South
Korea**

U.S.

bottom line is that all companies operating overseas depend on trade agreements made between their own governments and the regimes ruling the countries in which they want to make or sell their products. Korean, Indonesian, and other women workers around the world know this better than anyone. They are tackling trade politics because they have learned from hard experience that the trade deals their governments sign do little to improve the lives of workers. Guarantees of fair, healthy labor practices, of the rights to speak freely and to organize independently, will usually be left out of trade pacts—and women will suffer. The recent passage of both NAFTA and GATT ensures that a growing number of private companies will now be competing across borders without restriction. The result? Big business will step up efforts to pit working women in industrialized countries against much lower-paid working women in "developing" countries, perpetuating the misleading notion that they are inevitable rivals in the global job market.

All the "New World Order" really means to corporate giants like athletic shoemakers is that they now have the green light to accelerate long-standing industry practices. In the early 1980s, the field marshals commanding Reebok and Nike, which are both

U.S.-based, decided to manufacture most of their sneakers in South Korea and Taiwan, hiring local women. L.A. Gear, Adidas, Fila, and Asics quickly followed their lead. In short time, the coastal city of Pusan, South Korea, became the "sneaker capital of the world." Between 1982 and 1989 the U.S. lost 58,500 footwear jobs to cities like Pusan, which attracted sneaker executives because its location facilitated international transport. More to the point, South Korea's military government had an interest in suppressing labor organizing, and it had a comfortable military alliance with the U.S. Korean women also seemed accepting of Confucian philosophy, which measured a woman's morality by her willingness to work hard for her family's well-being and to acquiesce to her father's and husband's dictates. With their sense of patriotic duty, Korean women seemed the ideal labor force for export-oriented factories.

U.S. and European sneaker company executives were also attracted by the ready supply of eager Korean male entrepreneurs with whom they could make profitable arrangements. This fact was central to Nike's strategy in particular. When they moved their production sites to Asia to lower labor costs, the executives of the Oregon-based company decided to reduce their corporate responsibilities further. Instead of owning factories outright, a more efficient strategy would be to subcontract the manufacturing to wholly foreign-owned—in this case, South Korean—companies. Let them be responsible for workers' health and safety. Let them negotiate with newly emergent unions. Nike would retain control over those parts of sneaker production that gave its officials the greatest professional satisfaction and the ultimate word on the product: design and marketing. Although Nike was following in the footsteps of garment and textile manufacturers, it set the trend for the rest of the athletic footwear industry.

But at the same time, women workers were developing their own strategies. As the South Korean pro-democracy movement grew throughout the 1980s, increasing numbers of women rejected traditional notions of feminine duty. Women began organizing in response to the dangerous working conditions, daily humiliations, and low pay built into their work. Such resistance was profoundly threatening to the government, given the fact that South Korea's emergence as an industrialized "tiger" had

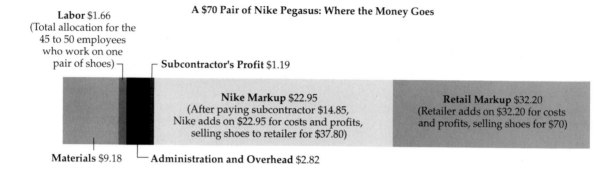

A $70 Pair of Nike Pegasus: Where the Money Goes

Labor $1.66
(Total allocation for the
45 to 50 employees
who work on one
pair of shoes)

Subcontractor's Profit $1.19

Nike Markup $22.95
(After paying subcontractor $14.85,
Nike adds on $22.95 for costs and profits,
selling shoes to retailer for $37.80)

Retail Markup $32.20
(Retailer adds on $32.20 for costs
and profits, selling shoes for $70)

Materials $9.18

Administration and Overhead $2.82

depended on women accepting their "role" in growing industries like sneaker manufacture. If women reimagined their lives as daughters, as wives, as workers, as citizens, it wouldn't just rattle their employers; it would shake the very foundations of the whole political system.

At the first sign of trouble, factory managers called in government riot police to break up employees' meetings. Troops sexually assaulted women workers, stripping, fondling, and raping them "as a control mechanism for suppressing women's engagement in the labor movement," reported Jeong-Lim Nam of Hyosung Women's University in Taegu. It didn't work. It didn't work because the feminist activists in groups like the Korean Women Workers Association (KWWA) helped women understand and deal with the assaults. The KWWA held consciousness-raising sessions in which notions of feminine duty and respectability were tackled along with wages and benefits. They organized independently of the male-led labor unions to ensure that their issues would be taken seriously, in labor negotiations and in the pro-democracy movement as a whole.

The result was that women were at meetings with management, making sure that in addition to issues like long hours and low pay, sexual assault at the hands of managers and health care were on the table. Their activism paid off: in addition to winning the right to organize women's unions, their earnings grew. In 1980, South Korean women in manufacturing jobs earned 45 percent of the wages of their male counterparts; by 1990, they were earning more than 50 percent. Modest though it was, the pay increase was concrete progress, given that the gap between women's and men's manufacturing wages in Japan,

Singapore, and Sri Lanka actually *widened* during the 1980s. Last but certainly not least, women's organizing was credited with playing a major role in toppling the country's military regime and forcing open elections in 1987.

Without that special kind of workplace control that only an authoritarian government could offer, sneaker executives knew that it was time to move. In Nike's case, its famous advertising slogan — "Just Do It" — proved truer to its corporate philosophy than its women's "empowerment" ad campaign, designed to rally women's athletic (and consumer) spirit. In response to South Korean women workers' newfound activist self-confidence, the sneaker company and its subcontractors began shutting down a number of their South Korean factories in the late 1980s and early 1990s. After bargaining with government officials in nearby China and Indonesia, many Nike subcontractors set up shop in those countries, while some went to Thailand. China's government remains nominally Communist; Indonesia's ruling generals are staunchly anti-Communist. But both are governed by authoritarian regimes who share the belief that if women can be kept hard at work, low paid, and unorganized, they can serve as a magnet for foreign investors.

Where does all this leave South Korean women — or any woman who is threatened with a factory closure if she demands decent working conditions and a fair wage? They face the dilemma confronted by thousands of women from dozens of countries. The risk of job loss is especially acute in relatively mobile industries; it's easier for a sneaker, garment, or electronics manufacturer to pick up and move than it is for an automaker or a steel producer. In the case of South Korea, poor women had moved from rural villages into the cities searching for jobs to support not only themselves, but parents and siblings. The exodus of manufacturing jobs has forced more women into the growing "entertainment" industry. The kinds of bars and massage parlors offering sexual services that had mushroomed around U.S. military bases during the Cold War have been opening up across the country.

But the reality is that women throughout Asia are organizing, knowing full well the risks involved. Theirs is a long-term view; they are taking direct aim at companies' nomadic advantage, by building links among workers in countries targeted for "development" by multinational corporations. Through sustained grassroots efforts, women are developing the skills and confidence that will make it increasingly difficult to keep their labor cheap. Many are looking to the United Nations conference on women in Beijing, China, this September [1996], as a rare opportunity to expand their cross-border strategizing.

The Beijing conference will also provide an important opportunity to call world attention to the hypocrisy of the governments and corporations doing business in China. Numerous athletic shoe companies followed Nike in setting up manufacturing sites throughout the country. This included Reebok — a company claiming its share of responsibility for ridding the world of "injustice, poverty, and other ills that gnaw away at the social fabric," according to a statement of corporate principles.

Since 1988, Reebok has been giving out annual human rights awards to dissidents from around the world. But it wasn't until 1992 that the company adopted its own "human rights production standards" — after labor advocates made it known that the quality of life in factories run by its subcontractors was just as dismal as that at most other athletic shoe suppliers in Asia. Reebok's code of conduct, for example, includes a pledge to "seek" those subcontractors who respect workers' rights to organize. The only problem is that independent trade unions are banned in China. Reebok has chosen to ignore that fact, even though Chinese dissidents have been the recipients of the company's own human rights award. As for working conditions, Reebok now says it sends its own inspectors to production sites a couple of times a year. But they have easily "missed" what

subcontractors are trying to hide — like 400 young women workers locked at night into an overcrowded dormitory near a Reebok-contracted factory in the town of Zhuhai, as reported last August in the *Asian Wall Street Journal Weekly.*

Nike's cofounder and CEO Philip Knight has said that he would like the world to think of Nike as "a company with a soul that recognizes the value of human beings." Nike, like Reebok, says it sends in inspectors from time to time to check up on work conditions at its factories; in Indonesia, those factories are run largely by South Korean subcontractors. But according to Donald Katz in a recent book on the company, Nike spokesman Dave Taylor told an in-house newsletter that the factories are "[the subcontractors'] business to run." For the most part, the company relies on regular reports from subcontractors regarding its "Memorandum of Understanding," which managers must sign, promising to impose "local government standards" for wages, working conditions, treatment of workers, and benefits.

In April, the minimum wage in the Indonesian capital of Jakarta will be $1.89 *a day* — among the highest in a country where the minimum wage varies by region. And managers are required to pay only 75 percent of the wage directly; the remainder can be withheld for "benefits." By now, Nike has a well-honed response to growing criticisms of its low-cost labor strategy. Such wages should not be seen as exploitative, says Nike, but rather as the first rung on the ladder of economic opportunity that Nike has extended to workers with few options. Otherwise, they'd be out "harvesting coconut meat in the tropical sun," wrote Nike spokesman Dusty Kidd, in a letter to the *Utne Reader.* The all-is-relative response craftily shifts attention away from reality: Nike didn't move to Indonesia to help Indonesians; it moved to ensure that its profit margin continues to grow. And that is pretty much guaranteed in a country where "local standards" for wages rarely take a worker over the poverty line. A 1991 survey by the International Labor Organization (ILO) found that 88 percent of women working at the Jakarta minimum wage at the time — slightly less than a dollar a day — were malnourished.

A woman named Riyanti might have been among the workers surveyed by the ILO. Interviewed by the *Boston Globe* in 1991, she told the reporter who had asked about her long hours and low pay: "I'm happy working here.... I can make money and I can make friends." But in fact, the reporter discovered that Riyanti had already joined her coworkers in two strikes, the first to force one of Nike's Korean sub-contractors to accept a new women's union and the second to compel managers to pay at least the minimum wage. That Riyanti appeared less than forthcoming about her activities isn't surprising. Many Indonesian factories have military men posted in their front offices who find no fault with managers who tape women's mouths shut to keep them from talking among themselves. They and their superiors have a political reach that extends far beyond the barracks. Indonesia has all the makings for a political explosion, especially since the gap between rich and poor is widening into a chasm. It is in this setting that the government has tried to crack down on any independent labor organizing—a policy that Nike has helped to implement. Referring to a recent strike in a Nike-contracted factory, Tony Nava, Nike representative in Indonesia, told the *Chicago Tribune* in November 1994 that the "troublemakers" had been fired. When asked about Nike policy on the issue, spokesman Keith Peters struck a conciliatory note: "If the government were to allow and encourage independent labor organizing, we would be happy to support it."

Indonesian workers' efforts to create unions independent of governmental control were a surprise to shoe companies. Although their moves from South Korea have been immensely profitable [see chart], they do not have the sort of immunity from activism that they had expected. In May 1993, the murder of a female labor activist outside Surabaya set off a storm of local and international protest. Even the U.S. State Department was forced to take note in its 1993 worldwide human rights report, describing a system similar to that which generated South Korea's boom 20 years earlier: severely restricted union organizing, security forces used to break up strikes, low wages for men, lower wages for women — complete with government rhetoric celebrating women's contribution to national development.

Yet when President Clinton visited Indonesia last November, he made only a token effort to address the country's human rights problem. Instead,

he touted the benefits of free trade, sounding indeed more enlightened, more in tune with the spirit of the post-Cold War era than do those defenders of protectionist trading policies who coat their rhetoric with "America first" chauvinism. But "free trade" as actually being practiced today is hardly *free* for any workers—in the U.S. or abroad—who have to accept the Indonesian, Chinese, or Korean workplace model as the price of keeping their jobs.

The not-so-new plot of the international trade story has been "divide and rule." If women workers and their government in one country can see that a sneaker company will pick up and leave if their labor demands prove more costly than those in a neighbor country, then women workers will tend to see their neighbors not as regional sisters, but as competitors who can steal their precarious livelihoods. Playing women off against each other is, of course, old hat. Yet it is as essential to international trade politics as is the fine print in GATT.

But women workers allied through networks like the Hong Kong-based Committee for Asian Women are developing their own post-Cold War foreign policy, which means addressing women's needs: how to convince fathers and husbands that a woman going out to organizing meetings at night is not sexually promiscuous; how to develop workplace agendas that respond to family needs; how to work with male unionists who push women's demands to the bottom of their lists; how to build a global movement.

These women refuse to stand in awe of the corporate power of the Nike or Reebok or Adidas executive. Growing numbers of Asian women today have concluded that trade politics have to be understood by women on their own terms. They will be coming to Beijing this September [1995] ready to engage with women from other regions to link the politics of consumerism with the politics of manufacturing. If women in Russia and Eastern Europe can challenge Americanized consumerism, if Asian activists can solidify their alliances, and if U.S. women can join with them by taking on trade politics — the post-Cold War sneaker may be a less comfortable fit in the 1990s.

This article draws from the work of South Korean scholars Hyun Sook Kim, Seung-kyung Kim, Katherine Moon, Seungsook Moon, and Jeong-Lim Nam.

FORTY

Life or Debt?

New Internationalist

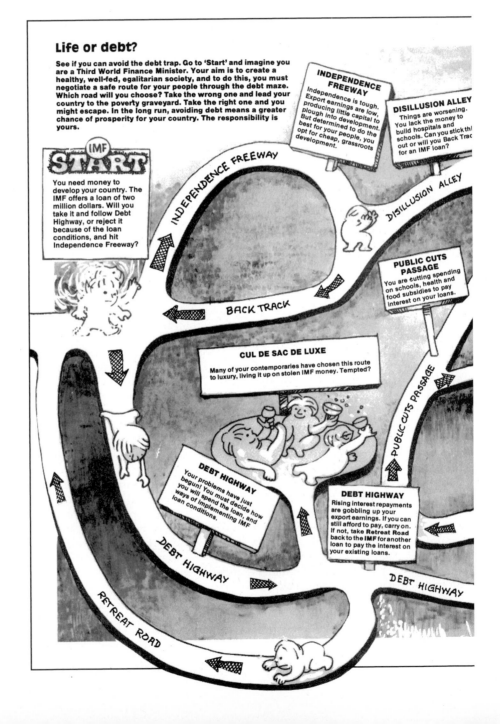

Life or debt?

See if you can avoid the debt trap. Go to 'Start' and imagine you are a Third World Finance Minister. Your aim is to create a healthy, well-fed, egalitarian society, and to do this, you must negotiate a safe route for your people through the debt maze. Which road will you choose? Take the wrong one and lead your country to the poverty graveyard. Take the right one and you might escape. In the long run, avoiding debt means a greater chance of prosperity for your country. The responsibility is yours.

INDEPENDENCE FREEWAY

Independence is tough. Export earnings are low, producing little capital to plough into development. But determined to do the best for your people, you opt for cheap, grassroots development.

DISILLUSION ALLEY

Things are worsening. You lack the money to build hospitals and schools. Can you stick this out or will you Back Track for an IMF loan?

IMF START

You need money to develop your country. The IMF offers a loan of two million dollars. Will you take it and follow Debt Highway, or reject it because of the loan conditions, and hit Independence Freeway?

PUBLIC CUTS PASSAGE

You are cutting spending on schools, health and food subsidies to pay interest on your loans.

CUL DE SAC DE LUXE

Many of your contemporaries have chosen this route to luxury, living it up on stolen IMF money. Tempted?

DEBT HIGHWAY

Your problems have just begun! You must decide how you will spend the loan, and ways of implementing IMF loan conditions.

DEBT HIGHWAY

Rising interest repayments are gobbling up your export earnings. If you can still afford to pay, carry on. If not, take **Retreat Road** back to the **IMF** for another loan to pay the interest on your existing loans.

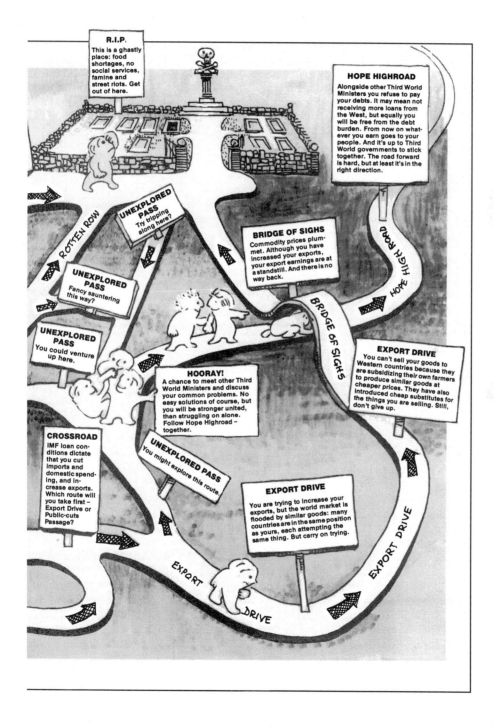

R.I.P.
This is a ghastly place: food shortages, no social services, famine and street riots. Get out of here.

HOPE HIGHROAD
Alongside other Third World Ministers you refuse to pay your debts. It may mean not receiving more loans from the West, but equally you will be free from the debt burden. From now on whatever you earn goes to your people. And it's up to Third World governments to stick together. The road forward is hard, but at least it's in the right direction.

ROTTEN ROW

UNEXPLORED PASS
Try tripping along here?

BRIDGE OF SIGHS
Commodity prices plummet. Although you have increased your exports, your export earnings are at a standstill. And there is no way back.

UNEXPLORED PASS
Fancy sauntering this way?

HOPE HIGH ROAD

UNEXPLORED PASS
You could venture up here.

BRIDGE OF SIGHS

EXPORT DRIVE
You can't sell your goods to Western countries because they are subsidizing their own farmers to produce similar goods at cheaper prices. They have also introduced cheap substitutes for the things you are selling. Still, don't give up.

HOORAY!
A chance to meet other Third World Ministers and discuss your common problems. No easy solutions of course, but you will be stronger united, than struggling on alone. Follow Hope Highroad – together.

CROSSROAD
IMF loan conditions dictate that you cut imports and domestic spending, and increase exports. Which route will you take first – Export Drive or Public-cuts Passage?

UNEXPLORED PASS
You might explore this route.

EXPORT DRIVE
You are trying to increase your exports, but the world market is flooded by similar goods: many countries are in the same position as yours, each attempting the same thing. But carry on trying.

EXPORT DRIVE

EXPORT DRIVE

◆◆◆

FORTY-ONE

The Debt Crisis
Who Really Owes Whom?

Caribbean Association for Feminist Research and Action

Africa, Asia, Latin America and the Caribbean are all suffering in similar manner from the policies applied by the IMF and World Bank for the "development" of these regions. The same "structural adjustment" policies are being applied everywhere: devaluations that put up the prices of food, housing, transportation, clothing, books, etc.; wage freezes which make it impossible to cope with the rapidly increasing cost of living; massive breakdown of social services such as health and education; no consultation with the ordinary people whose living conditions are the most affected by these policies; repression of people's protest; and the confinement of decision-making to elites within the local populations. In this model, development is about big projects that serve big business. For example, on the three continents, hundreds of thousands of indigenous peoples are being moved from their lands to make way for huge dams to service the enterprises of multinational corporations while ordinary people have no access to clean drinking water.

Women across all the regions are the main burden-bearers of this "development." In the Caribbean, they are the ones employed in the Export Processing Zone (EPZ) factories which are the main "solution" offered. The idea that a woman's wage is supplementary to that of some man is being used to justify paying the women extra low wages. In actual fact, in the Caribbean, as in Africa, Asia and Latin America, women's income and labour are critical to family survival. Faced with the deepening economic crisis, women must work longer and longer hours of overtime to make ends meet, and also do more work at home so as not to spend cash, or to make up for declining social services. With less leisure time for themselves, their children, their families, and their social relationships, the quality of life declines. Despite the women's efforts, thousands of children have had their life chances damaged by these policies, and the effect will be felt for generations to come. In 1989, for example, Jamaica recorded the lowest ever percentage of passes in the Caribbean

Examinations Council (CXC) Exams. This is a direct result of the high cost of books and school materials; the low morale of teachers as a result of grossly inadequate pay; and the fact that parents have less and less time to see to their children as they fight the desperate battle for survival. This increased desperation is a direct result of IMF conditionalities placed on loans made to the governments.

Who Is NOT Suffering?

While the quality of life is getting worse for ordinary people, the banks and corporations are flowing with funds. While we have been suffering, U.S. and other corporations have had record profits during the 1980s, particularly since 1987.

Where Does All This Money Come From?

With all this talk about Third World debt, it may come as a surprise to learn that we are subsidising the U.S. and other western banks and big companies, and not the other way round. In 1988–89, US$50 billion more went out from the Third World in profits than what we got in loans, investments, etc. Over the last three years, the net "capital outflow," as it is called, was US$120 billion.

This money does not stay in our countries to contribute to our own development. We need money for this. How do the banks respond? They rush to give us "loans." So then our governments have to put out more (capital plus interest) to pay them back. Furthermore, they can increase the interest rates whenever they wish; then we have to pay back even more.

In reality, the root of the problem lies in the historical colonial relationship between the South ("Third World") and the North ("developed countries"), where the South was colonised mainly to provide cheap raw materials and labour for the profit-oriented machineries of the North. The North sets the prices, and the priority is to get what they need at the cheapest possible rate.

In the late 1970s, this exploitation took on a new phase because there was extra money in the big banks from increased petroleum profits from which the multinational corporations were the main ones to benefit. Of course, small countries which had no oil suffered from this. Then came the banks with their petrodollars to "bail us out," but only if our governments would allow the companies to have a free hand to exploit us through cheap labour, no taxes, no price controls, no unions, etc. The economic situation of the poor countries has therefore gone from bad to worse. But WHO REALLY OWES WHOM?

The Debt Squeeze

Our governments feel powerless to fight the banks and the corporations, so they squeeze us instead, by cutting back social services and by levying more and more taxes on the majority of us. All over the Caribbean, we are seeing more taxes being placed on the backs of the poor rather than on the rich: taxes on traders (also called hucksters, higglers, etc.), VAT (Value Added Tax), consumption taxes, etc.

When taxes are not enough, the IMF and the World Bank and the big foreign corporations that they serve say, "We will accept your land, your successful enterprises, your hotels, in exchange for the debt." This is what they call "debt-equity swaps." In this way, they get our governments to sell out our countries to them.

Debt of Selected Caribbean Countries (US$)

Jamaica	4,048m
Trinidad & Tobago	1,860m
Guyana	1,039m
Haiti	957m
Barbados	650m
St. Vincent and the Grenadines	59m

(Source: WorldBank Debt Tables 1989)

Much of what we owe is due to the changes in interest rates; in other words, we are paying for money we never actually got.

What Are People Doing About This?

There has been resistance all over the Third World.

In the Caribbean, there have been riots and demonstrations in Jamaica, the Dominican Republic, Venezuela, Trinidad and Tobago, Haiti and Guyana. Women in particular have had to confront harassment and brutality from customs officers and police all over the region in their efforts to expand and increase their informal trading activity to maintain themselves and their families. In many of our territories, state forces have driven them from the streets, destroying their stalls, and relocated them away from the areas where it is easiest to get sales. Prostitutes have also come under fire. None of the authorities have concerned themselves very much with the conditions that drive women more and more to these activities.

The women traders have responded with a variety of strategies. In Caracas, Venezuela, traders lay out goods on oil-cloths. When the police sirens are heard, goods are scooped into a bundle in the twinkling of an eye, and disappear into all kinds of hiding places. Minutes after the police leave, the goods are out again. In Africa, traders in Accra, the capital of Ghana, were forcibly removed from the streets. In response, they took to sitting at the roadside with brooms — sweeping at least is a legitimate activity! On the brooms, they tied strips of cloth or other indicators of the goods they had to sell. Interested buyers would come by and sit as if in conversation. They would absent-mindedly fondle the item they wanted to purchase. Purchaser and trader would then walk to where the goods were hidden.

Women have also been organising themselves into vendors' associations, housing groups, co-operatives, etc. The non-governmental organisations (NGOs) of the South and the North, including women's groups, are building links to share experiences, to develop strategies, and to inform people about the reasons for the sharpened economic crisis. NGOs are also beginning to discuss alternatives to the IMF/World Bank prescription which has turned out to be medicine which kills us while they grow fat selling it to us. There is a growing view that the debt should not be paid, and that the money should be used instead to promote regional and inter-regional development which locates people as the main focus of development.

◆◆◆

Immigrants in a Global Economy

Saskia Sassen

Current immigration policy in developed countries is increasingly at odds with other major policy frameworks in the international system and with the growth of global economic integration. All highly developed countries have received rapidly growing numbers of legal and undocumented immigrants over the last decade; none has found its immigration policy effective. These countries are opening up their economies to foreign investment and trade while deregulating their financial markets. In developed countries, the emergence of a new economic regime sharply reduces the role of national governments and borders in controlling international transactions. Yet the framework of immigration policy in these countries remains centered on older conceptions of the nation-state and of national borders.

How can immigration policy account for the facts of rapid economic internationalization and the corresponding transformation of national governments? This is the subject I briefly discuss here.

Shift in Global Economy

The 1980s saw a major shift in the global economy. In that decade, the developed countries opened their economies to foreign investment, international financial markets, and imports of goods and services; deregulation and internationalization of a growing range of economic activities became hallmarks of economic policy. As economic doors have opened to others, many developing countries have implemented export-oriented growth strategies. Export-manufacturing zones and the sale of once-public sector firms on world markets became key venues for this internationalization.

Global economic trends engendered a new framework for national economic policy-making. This new framework is evident in the formation of regional trading blocks: the U.S.-Canada Free Trade Agreement, the European Community (EC), the new trading blocks being formed in Southeast Asia as well as the proposed NAFTA agreement. At the heart of this framework is a new conception of the role of national borders. Borders no longer are sites for imposing levies. Rather, they are transmitting membranes guaranteeing the free flow of goods, capital and information. Eighteenth-century concepts of free trade assumed freedom of movement between distinct national economies: 21st-century concepts of free trade are about an economy which is itself global, and about governments that coordinate rather than control economic activities.

To be sure, neither the old border-wall nor the nation-state has disappeared. The difficulties and complexities involved in this transformation are evident in the many obstacles to the ratification of the Uruguay Round of the GATT talks, which aims at further opening economies to the circulation of services. But the relentless effort to overcome these difficulties also signals the pressure to depart from an old conception of national economic policy and the emergence of a new conception of how economic activity is to be maximized and governed.

The framework for immigration policy in the highly developed countries, on the other hand, is still rooted in the past. Immigration policy has yet to address global economic integration in the 21st century and its implications. Border-control remains the basic mechanism for regulating immigration—an increasingly troubled effort given new policies aimed at opening up national economies, such as the lifting of restrictions on foreign investment, the deregulation of financial markets, and the formation of financial free zones in major cities. Those policies amount to a partial denationalizing of national territory for the flow of capital, and they in turn globalize certain sectors of the workforce, notably the high-level transnational professional and managerial class.

Moreover, the policy framework for immigration treats the flow of labor as the result of individual actions, particularly the decision to migrate in search of better opportunities. Such a policy puts responsibility for immigration on the shoulders of immigrants. Policy commentary which speaks of an immigrant "influx" or "invasion" treats the receiving country as a passive agent. The causes for immigration appear to be outside the control or domain of receiving countries; immigration policy becomes a decision to be more or less benevolent in admitting immigrants. Absent from this understanding is the notion that the international activities of the governments or firms of receiving countries may have contributed to the formation of economic linkages with emigration countries, linkages that may function as bridges not only for capital but also for migration flows. That older view emphasizes individual "push" factors and neglects systemic linkages.

The worldwide evidence shows rather clearly that there is considerable patterning in the geography of migrations, and that the major receiving countries tend to get immigrants from their zones of influence. This holds for countries as diverse as the U.S., France or Japan. A transnational analysis of immigration contributes to its redefinition and allows us to see migrations as happening within global systems. The periods known as Pax Britanica and Pax Americana are but two representations of such transnational systems. The formation of systems for the internationalization of manufacturing production, or the formation of regional trading blocks, are other instances. These systems can be characterized in a multiplicity of ways: economic (the Atlantic economy of the 1800s, the EC, NAFTA); politico-military (the colonial systems of several European countries, U.S. involvement in Central America); transnational war zones (formation of massive refugee flows as a result of major European wars); cultural-ideological zones (impact in socialist countries of the image of Western democracies as offering the "good life").

Recent developments in Japan capture the intersection of economic internationalization and immigration. They also illuminate the intersection of immigration policy and reality. Japan's closed door policy has not prevented a growing influx of immigrants. Nor has its 1990 immigration law, which opens up the country to high-level foreign workers but closes it to all low-wage workers, kept out the latter. Furthermore, despite a strong anti-immigration culture, immigrants have become incorporated into various labor markets and have begun to form immigrant communities in major cities in Japan. A detailed exploration of the dynamic at work provides useful insights into immigration processes.

What makes the disparity between the framework for immigration policy and the facts of the world economy particularly urgent is that all highly developed countries have experienced sharp increases in migration of both legal and undocumented immigrants. In some countries there is a resurgence of immigration after inflows had fallen sharply in the 1970s: this is the case for Germany and Austria. In other countries, notably the U.S., immigration policy opened up the country in 1965, yet in the 1980s, the number of entries doubled compared with the 1965–1980 period. Still other countries are becoming immigration countries for the first time in their contemporary histories: this is the case with Italy and Spain, long-time emigration countries, and with Japan, a nation of deep anti-immigration beliefs and policies.

Discard Old Notions

A detailed analysis of cross-country immigration patterns suggests that some key notions about immigration may be inadequate, particularly the notion that the developed countries may be facing a massive invasion of people from less developed countries. These cross-country regularities suggest that there is more room for effective and equitable policies than the imagery of "invasion" allows:

1. **Emigration is a minority event in demographic terms.** Except for terror-driven refugees, we now know that most people are reluctant to leave their home villages or towns: For example, most people in Mexico have not gone to the U.S. A minority is determined to come no matter what; while a gray area of potential emigrants may or may not leave, depending on pull factors; but the vast mass of people in a poor country are not likely to emigrate.

2. **There is considerable return migration** except when the military/political situation in countries of origin makes it unsafe. For example, we now know that about 60 percent of Italians who left for the U.S. around the turn of the century returned to Italy.

3. Rather than an uncontrolled "invasion," what we see over time is a **tendency towards the formation of permanent settlements** for a variable share of immigrants, but never all. This tendency is likely even when there are high return rates and even when a country's policies seek to prevent

permanent settlement. We see this happening in all countries receiving immigrants, including such extremely closed countries as Japan and Saudi Arabia, as well as in the more liberal Western nations.

4. No matter what the political culture and the particular migration policies of a country, **"illegal" immigration has emerged as a generalized fact in all Western economies in the post World War II era,** including Japan. This has raised a whole set of questions about the need to rethink regulatory enforcement and the sites for such enforcement.

5. **Immigration is a highly differentiated process:** it includes people seeking permanent settlement and those seeking temporary employment who want to circulate back and forth. One important question is whether recognizing these differences might facilitate the formulation of policy today. There is a growing presence of immigrants who are not searching for a new home in a new country; they think of themselves as moving in a cross-country and even global labor market. We know that when illegal immigrants are regularized, they often establish permanent residence in their country of origin and work a few months in the immigration country, an option that becomes available when they can circulate freely.

Towards New Policies

How should the new reality shape our thinking about immigration? A more comprehensive approach can provide more analytic and empirical footholds towards a better understanding of migration and towards more effective policy. The various transnational economic, cultural, political systems now evident in the world all tend to have very specific geographies. They are not planet-wide events, but occur in the relation of cities to cities, or in production chains linking factories in rather remote areas of developing countries to manufacturing and distribution centers in developed countries. Considerable migration flows within these new geographies for economic transactions. By understanding the nature of these geographies we can understand where to intervene for regulatory purposes. Further, international migrations themselves are patterned in geographic, economic and temporal terms. These two types of patterning provide maps within which to search for new policies to regulate immigration.

If immigration is partly an outcome of the actions of the governments and major private economic actors in receiving countries, the latter could conceivably recognize the migration impact of such actions and make decisions accordingly. For instance, economic policies that facilitate overseas operations of firms, particularly in developing countries, should recognize the migration impact of such operations. Economic internationalization suggests that the responsibility for immigration may not be exclusively the immigrant's. Refugee policy in some countries does lift the burden of immigration from the immigrant's shoulders. U.S. refugee policy, particularly for Indochinese refugees, does acknowledge partial responsibility on the part of the government. Clearly, in the case of economic migrations, such responsibility is far more difficult to establish, and by its nature far more indirect. As governments increasingly coordinate rather than contain economic activity, their role in immigration policy, as in other aspects of political economy, becomes elusive. Despite this complexity, the responsibilities for the consequences of globalization do not disappear. If economic internationalization contributes to migration flows, recognition of this fact can only help in designing more effective immigration policy.

◆◆◆

FORTY-THREE

The Border Patrol State

Leslie Marmon Silko

I used to travel the highways of New Mexico and Arizona with a wonderful sensation of absolute freedom as I cruised down the open road and across the vast desert plateaus. On the Laguna Pueblo reservation, where I was raised, the people were patriotic despite the way the U.S. government had treated Native Americans. As proud citizens, we grew up believing the freedom to travel was our inalienable right, a right that some Native Americans had been denied in the early twentieth century. Our cousin, old Bill Pratt, used to ride his horse 300 miles overland from Laguna, New Mexico, to Prescott, Arizona, every summer to work as a fire lookout.

In school in the 1950s, we were taught that our right to travel from state to state without special papers or threat of detainment was a right that citizens under communist and totalitarian governments did not possess. That wide open highway told us we were U.S. citizens; we were free. . . .

Not so long ago, my companion Gus and I were driving south from Albuquerque, returning to Tucson after a book promotion for the paperback edition of my novel *Almanac of the Dead*. I had settled back and gone to sleep while Gus drove, but I was awakened when I felt the car slowing to a stop. It was nearly midnight on New Mexico State Road 26, a dark, lonely stretch of two-lane highway between Hatch and Deming. When I sat up, I saw the headlights and emergency flashers of six vehicles—Border Patrol cars and a van were blocking both lanes of the highway. Gus stopped the car and rolled down the window to ask what was wrong. But the closest Border Patrolman and his companion did not reply; instead, the first agent ordered us to "step out of the car." Gus asked why, but his question seemed to set them off. Two more Border Patrol agents immediately approached our car, and one of them snapped, "Are you looking for trouble?" as if he would relish it.

I will never forget that night beside the highway. There was an awful feeling of menace and violence straining to break loose. It was clear that the uniformed men would be only too happy to drag us out of the car if we did not speedily comply with their request (asking a question is tantamount to resistance, it seems). So we stepped out of the car and they motioned for us to stand on the shoulder of the road. The night was very dark, and no other traffic had come down the road since we had been stopped. All I could think about was a book I had read—*Nunca Más*—the official report of a human rights commission that investigated and certified more than 12,000 "disappearances" during Argentina's "dirty war" in the late 1970s.

The weird anger of these Border Patrolmen made me think about descriptions in the report of Argentine police and military officers who became addicted to interrogation, torture and the murder that followed. When the military and police ran out of political suspects to torture and kill, they resorted to the random abduction of citizens off the streets. I thought how easy it would be for the Border Patrol to shoot us and leave our bodies and car beside the highway, like so many bodies found in these parts and ascribed to "drug runners."

Two other Border Patrolmen stood by the white van. The one who had asked if we were looking for trouble ordered his partner to "get the dog," and from the back of the van another patrolman brought a small female German shepherd on a leash. The dog apparently did not heel well enough to suit him, and the handler jerked the leash. They opened the doors of our car and pulled the dog's head into it, but I saw immediately from the expression in her eyes that the dog hated them, and that she would not serve them. When she showed no interest in the inside of our car, they brought her around back to the trunk, near where we were standing. They half-dragged her up into the trunk, but still she did not indicate any stowed-away human beings or illegal drugs.

Their mood got uglier; the officers seemed outraged that the dog could not find any contraband, and they dragged her over to us and commanded her to sniff our legs and feet. To my relief, the strange violence the Border Patrol agents had focused on us now seemed shifted to the dog. I no longer felt so strongly that we would be murdered. We exchanged looks—the dog and I. She was afraid of what they might do, just as I was. The dog's handler jerked the leash sharply as she sniffed us, as if to make her perform better, but the dog refused to accuse us: She had an innate dignity that did not permit her to serve the murderous impulses of those men. I can't forget the expression in the dog's eyes; it was as if she were embarrassed to be associated with them. I had a small amount of medicinal marijuana in my purse that night, but she refused to expose me. I am not partial to dogs, but I will always remember the small German shepherd that night.

Unfortunately, what happened to me is an everyday occurrence here now. Since the 1980s, on top of greatly expanding border checkpoints, the Immigration and Naturalization Service and the Border Patrol have implemented policies that interfere with the rights of U.S. citizens to travel freely within our borders. I.N.S. agents now patrol all interstate highways and roads that lead to or from the U.S.-Mexico border in Texas, New Mexico, Arizona and California. Now, when you drive east from Tucson on Interstate 10 toward El Paso, you encounter an I.N.S. check station outside Las Cruces, New Mexico. When you drive north from Las Cruces up Interstate 25, two miles north of the town of Truth or Consequences, the highway is blocked with orange emergency barriers, and all traffic is diverted into a two-lane Border Patrol checkpoint—ninety-five miles north of the U.S.-Mexico border.

I was detained once at Truth or Consequences, despite my and my companion's Arizona driver's licenses. Two men, both Chicanos, were detained at the same time, despite the fact that they too presented ID and spoke English without the thick Texas accents of the Border Patrol agents. While we were stopped, we watched as other vehicles—whose occupants were white—were waved through the checkpoint. White people traveling with brown people, however, can expect to be stopped on suspicion they work with the sanctuary movement, which shelters refugees. White people who appear to be clergy, those who wear ethnic clothing or jewelry and women with very long hair or very short hair (they could be nuns) are also frequently detained; white men with beards

or men with long hair are more likely to be detained, too, because Border Patrol agents have "profiles" of "those sorts" of white people who may help political refugees. (Most of the political refugees from Guatemala and El Salvador are Native American or mestizo because the indigenous people of the Americas have continued to resist efforts by invaders to displace them from their ancestral lands.) Alleged increases in illegal immigration by people of Asian ancestry means that the Border Patrol now routinely detains anyone who appears to be Asian or part Asian, as well.

Once your car is diverted from the Interstate Highway into the checkpoint area, you are under the control of the Border Patrol, which in practical terms exercises a power that no highway patrol or city patrolman possesses: They are willing to detain anyone, for no apparent reason. Other law-enforcement officers need a shred of probable cause in order to detain someone. On the books, so does the Border Patrol; but on the road, it's another matter. They'll order you to stop your car and step out; then they'll ask you to open the trunk. If you ask why or request a search warrant, you'll be told that they'll have to have a dog sniff the car before they can request a search warrant, and the dog might not get there for two or three hours. The search warrant might require an hour or two past that. They make it clear that if you force them to obtain a search warrant for the car, they will make you submit to a strip search as well.

Traveling in the open, though, the sense of violation can be even worse. Never mind high-profile cases like that of former Border Patrol agent Michael Elmer, acquitted of murder by claiming self-defense, despite admitting that as an officer he shot an "illegal" immigrant in the back and then hid the body, which remained undiscovered until another Border Patrolman reported the event. (Last month, Elmer was convicted of reckless endangerment in a separate incident, for shooting at least ten rounds from his M-16 too close to a group if immigrants as they were crossing illegally into Nogales in March 1992.) Or that in El Paso, a high school football coach driving a vanload of his players in full uniform was pulled over on the freeway and a Border Patrol agent put a cocked revolver to his head. (The football coach was Mexican-American, as were most of the players in his van; the incident eventually caused a federal judge to issue a restraining order against the Border Patrol.) We've a mountain of personal experiences like that which never make the newspapers. A history professor at U.C.L.A. told me she had been traveling by train from Los Angeles to Albuquerque twice a month doing research. On each of her trips, she had noticed that the Border Patrol agents were at the station in Albuquerque scrutinizing the passengers. Since she is six feet tall and of Irish and German ancestry, she was not particularly concerned. Then one day when she stepped off the train in Albuquerque, two Border Patrolmen accosted her, wanting to know what she was doing, and why she was traveling between Los Angeles and Albuquerque twice a month. She presented identification and an explanation deemed "suitable" by the agents, and was allowed to go about her business.

Just the other day, I mentioned to a friend that I was writing this article and he told me about his 73-year-old father, who is half Chinese and had set out alone by car from Tucson to Albuquerque the week before. His father had become confused by road construction and missed a turnoff from Interstate 10 to Interstate 25; when he turned around and circled back, he missed the turnoff a second time. But when he looped back for yet another try, Border Patrol agents stopped him and forced him to open his trunk. After they satisfied themselves that he was not smuggling Chinese immigrants, they sent him on his way. He was so rattled by the event that he had to be driven home by his daughter.

This is the police state that has developed in the southwestern United States since the 1980s. No person, no citizen, is free to travel without the scrutiny of the Border Patrol. In the city of South Tucson, where 80 percent of the respondents were Chicano or Mexicano, a joint research project by the University of Wisconsin and the University of Arizona recently concluded that one out of every five people there had been detained, mistreated verbally or nonverbally, or questioned by I.N.S. agents in the past two years.

Manifest Destiny may lack its old grandeur of theft and blood — "lock the door" is what it means now, with racism a trump card to be played again and again, shamelessly, by both major political parties.

"Immigration," like "street crime" and "welfare fraud," is a political euphemism that refers to people of color. Politicians and media people talk about "illegal aliens" to dehumanize and demonize undocumented immigrants, who are for the most part people of color. Even in the days of Spanish and Mexican rule, no attempts were made to interfere with the flow of people and goods from south to north and north to south. It is the U.S. government that has continually attempted to sever contact between the tribal people north of the border and those to the south.*

Now that the "Iron Curtain" is gone, it is ironic that the U.S. government and its Border Patrol are constructing a steel wall ten feet high to span sections of the border with Mexico. While politicians and multinational corporations extol the virtues of NAFTA and "free trade" (in goods, not flesh), the ominous curtain is already up in a six-mile section at the border crossing at Mexicali; two miles are being erected but are not yet finished at Naco; and at Nogales, sixty miles south of Tucson, the steel wall has been all rubber-stamped and awaits construction likely to begin in March. Like the pathetic multimillion-dollar "antidrug" border surveillance balloons that were continually deflated by high winds and made only a couple of meager interceptions before they blew away, the fence along the border is a theatrical prop, a bit of pork for contractors. Border entrepreneurs have already used blowtorches to cut passageways through the fence to collect "tolls," and are doing a brisk business. Back in Washington, the I.N.S. announces a $300 million computer contract to modernize its record-keeping and Congress passes a crime bill that shunts $255 million to the I.N.S. for 1995, $181 million earmarked for border control, which is to include 700 new partners for the men who stopped Gus and me in our travels, and the history professor, and my friend's father, and as many as they could from South Tucson.

---

*The Treaty of Guadalupe Hidalgo, signed in 1848, recognizes the right of the Tohano O'Odom (Papago) people to move freely across the U.S.-Mexico border without documents. A treaty with Canada guarantees similar rights to those of the Iroquois nation in traversing the U.S.-Canada border.

It is no use; borders haven't worked, and they won't work, not now, as the indigenous people of the Americas reassert their kinship and solidarity with one another. A mass migration is already under way; its roots are not simply economic. The Uto-Aztecan languages are spoken as far north as Taos Pueblo near the Colorado border, all the way south to Mexico City. Before the arrival of the Europeans, the indigenous communities throughout this region not only conducted commerce, the people shared cosmologies, and oral narratives about the Maize Mother, the Twin Brothers and their Grandmother, Spider Woman, as well as Quetzalcoatl the benevolent snake. The great human migration within the Americas cannot be stopped; human beings are natural forces of the Earth, just as rivers and winds are natural forces.

Deep down the issue is simple: The so-called "Indian Wars" from the days of Sitting Bull and Red Cloud have never really ended in the Americas. The Indian people of southern Mexico, of Guatemala and those left in El Salvador, too, are still fighting for their lives and for their land against the "cavalry" patrols sent out by the governments of those lands. The Americas are Indian country, and the "Indian problem" is not about to go away.

One evening at sundown, we were stopped in traffic at a railroad crossing in downtown Tucson while a freight train passed us, slowly gaining speed as it headed north to Phoenix. In the twilight I saw the most amazing sight: Dozens of human beings, mostly young men, were riding the train; everywhere, on flat cars, inside open boxcars, perched on top of boxcars, hanging off ladders on tank cars and between boxcars. I couldn't count fast enough, but I saw fifty or sixty people headed north. They were dark young men, Indian and mestizo; they were smiling and a few of them waved at us in our cars. I was reminded of the ancient story of Aztlán, told by the Aztecs but known in other Uto-Aztecan communities as well. Aztlán is the beautiful land to the north, the origin place of the Aztec people. I don't remember how or why the people left Aztlán to journey farther south, but the old story says that one day, they will return.

♦♦♦

CHAPTER SIX

Work, Wages, and Welfare

Virtually all women in the world work. They are farmers, artists, craft workers, factory workers, businesswomen, maids, baby-sitters, engineers, secretaries, soldiers, teachers, nurses, sex workers, journalists, bus drivers, lawyers, therapists, waitpersons, prison guards, doctors, cashiers, airline pilots, executives, sales staff, professors, carpenters, dishwashers, filmmakers, mail carriers, dancers, homemakers, mothers, and wives. Many find satisfaction and challenge, even enjoyment, in their work; for others it is a necessary drudgery. This chapter looks at women's experiences of work in the United States, how work is defined in this country, the effects of changes in the economy over the last thirty years, women's wages, and income supports for women without paid work. We argue that economic security is fundamental to women's well-being.

Defining Women's Work

According to dictionary definitions, the English word *economy* comes from two Greek words: *oikos,* meaning "house," and *nemo,* meaning "to manage." Thus, economy can be understood as managing the affairs of the household, and beyond the household, of the wider society. Modern-day professional economists make a distinction between "productive" and "unproductive" work, however, which is not implied in this original definition. So-called productive work is done for money; work not done for money is defined as unproductive. By this analysis, a woman who spends her day making meals for her family, doing laundry, finding the schoolbooks and football shoes, packing school lunches, making beds, washing the kitchen floor, remembering her mother-in-law's birthday, changing diapers, waiting in for the TV repair person, taking the toddler to the park, walking the dog, meeting the older children after school, making calls about an upcoming PTA meeting, changing the cat litter, paying bills, and balancing her checkbook is not involved in productive work (Waring 1988). A United Nations study released in Nairobi, Kenya in 1985 at the end of the International Decade on Women (1975–85) stated that women do 75 percent of the world's work; they earn 10 percent of the world's wages and own 1 percent of the world's property (Pharr 1988, p. 9). Worldwide, then, most of women's work is unpaid and hence unproductive.

Leith Mullins (1997) distinguishes four kinds of women's work: paid work in the formal sector; reproductive work, including housework and raising children as well as paid work taking care of children, the elderly, and the sick; work in the informal sector, which may be paid under the table or in favors returned; and transformational work, volunteering in community organizations, professional groups, and clubs of all kinds. As we discussed in Chapter 4, one

Economic Inequalities

- In the 1,500 biggest companies in the United States, men are 95 percent of the senior managers. (*Women . . . A World Survey*, Ruth Sivard, 1995.)

- The wealth of the world's 358 billionaires exceeds the combined annual incomes of countries that are home to 45 percent of the world's population (*London Guardian*, 16 July 1996, p. 11).

- The average CEO in the United States makes about 149 times the average factory worker's pay.

- Eighteen percent of U.S. workers with full-time jobs earned wages below the poverty level in 1992.

- Since 1973 the number of U.S. children living in poverty has grown by 50 percent; now 22 percent grow up poor, and the number is rising (Richard Barnet, *Nation*, 19 December 1994, p. 754).

- Net growth in the number of U.S. jobs provided by Fortune 500 companies since 1980: 0 (*In Context*, no. 31, spring 1992, p. 5).

- An estimated 250 million children between the ages of 5 and 14 work full and part time in countries of the South (U.N. International Labor Report).

- Nike CEO Philip Knight's personal fortune is estimated at $5.2 billion; Michael Jordan has a $20 million endorsement deal; a pair of Air Jordans retails generally around $135 per pair. Women workers in Indonesia who make Nikes earn $2.20 per day (Global Exchange 1997).

greatly overrepresented in low-paying jobs. In a survey of top corporations, women accounted for 37.2 percent of employees, 16.9 percent of managers, and 6.6 percent of executive management (U.S. Bureau of the Census 1996). As Tucker (1996) remarked, "You do not have to look to Venus or Mars to find the difference in men and women. Just look at their paychecks" (p. 3). Most women in the workforce do "women's work" in service and administrative support jobs, as secretaries, waitresses, and health aides. They work in day-care centers, elder-care facilities, garment factories, food processing, retail stores, restaurants, laundries, and other women's homes. In addition to earning low wages, such workers are often treated badly by employers, as Hattie Gossett points out in Reading 48. Women in professional jobs tend to be elementary school teachers, social workers, nurses, and health-care workers. There is an emphasis on caring for and serving others in many of these jobs; some may also require being on display and meeting dominant beauty standards.

In the idealized nuclear family described in Chapter 4, middle-class women were not expected to be wage earners, and despite the fact that they were responsible for all the tasks we outline above, many said of themselves, "I don't work; I'm just a housewife." The implication has often been, for both middle-class women and those on welfare, that they are lazy or work-shy, as if raising children and housekeeping were not work.

Women in the U.S. Workforce

As pointed out in Chapter 5, the economy of the United States is undergoing fundamental changes because of automation in manufacturing and office work and the movement of jobs overseas. Many U.S. companies have laid off workers, sometimes by the thousands, as they scramble to downsize their operations as a way to cut costs and maintain, or even increase, profits. Innovations such as ATMs, voice mail, salad bars, and self-service gas stations, to name a few everyday examples, all mean fewer jobs. One result has been a growing inequality in earnings between people in professional and technical positions and those without college educations who are working low-income jobs. Despite the influx of relatively inexpensive consumer goods into the United States, especially clothing and electronic items from "global factories" around the world, it has become much

effect of the gendered division of labor in the home has been a similar distinction between women's work and men's work in the paid workforce.

Although in recent years some women have broken into professions and jobs that were once the preserve of men, much paid work in the United States is still divided along gender lines, and women are harder for many families to make ends meet. Several factors have made it imperative that more and more women become income earners. Rents and housing payments, health insurance, and the cost of college tuition, for example, have increased. Much manufacturing, such as car assembly and related engineering work, which was relatively well paid and largely done by men, has been automated or moved out of the United States. Divorce has increased, and many fathers pay little or no child support.

According to the U.S. Department of Labor (1993), in 1992, 57.8 percent of women in the U.S. were in the paid workforce, the highest rate ever, and women accounted for 45 percent of all workers. Labor force participation was highest for women in the 35–44 age group (77 percent), who were closely followed by those aged 25–34 (74 percent) and 45–54 (73 percent). Of older women, 47 percent between 55 and 64 years of age are employed; the rate for younger women (16–19 years) is similar (49 percent). Teenage women, especially African-Americans and Latinas, experience very high unemployment rates (37.2 percent and 26.4 percent, respectively). Most women work full time, but 25 percent hold part-time jobs. Two-thirds of all part-time workers (66 percent) are women. A small percentage of working women are self-employed (5.5 percent) in business, health and legal services, or wholesale and retail trade. The more education a woman has, the more likely she is to have the skills employers are looking for and to be employed. Among women aged 25–54 in 1992, 51 percent of those with less than four years of high school were income earners; for high school graduates this rose to 74 percent, and for women with four or more years of college, to 84 percent. Even with a college education, however, and equivalent work experience and skills, women are far less likely than men to get to the top of their professions or corporations, and they are halted by unseen barriers, such as men's negative attitudes to senior women and low perceptions of their abilities, training, and skills. This barrier has been called a **glass ceiling.** Women can see what the senior positions in their company or their field look like, but few women reach them.

Data examining the relationship between employment and marital status show that 74 percent of divorced women are in the paid labor force, as are 65 percent of single, never-married women and 59 percent of married women with spouses present. Two-thirds of U.S. women with children under eighteen are in paid employment (67 percent). Fifty-eight percent of mothers with preschoolers and 55 percent of mothers with children under three are income earners. Black mothers are more likely to be in the paid workforce than White or Latina mothers. Although 18 percent of all families were maintained solely by women in 1992, the detailed figures show a wide disparity based on race. Forty-seven percent of Black families, 24 percent of Latino families, and 14 percent of White families were maintained by women.

Women's Wages: The Effects of Gender, Race, Class, and Disability

The best-paid jobs for women are as lawyers, physicians, pharmacists, engineers, computer analysts, and scientists, but many more women earn minimum wage. Ida Castro, acting director of the Women's Bureau of the U.S. Department of Labor, comments that "society needs to really look critically at the value given to work performed predominantly by women," and cites child-care workers, home-care attendants, and nursing home workers as persons who earn the minimum wage but do the vitally important work of looking after children and older people (Angwin 1996). Women on average earn roughly seventy cents for every dollar that men earn on average. This gap has slowly narrowed in the past two decades, partly because women's wages are improving but also because men's wages are falling. The average salary of a Black woman college graduate in full-time work is less than that of a White male high school drop-out. Women with disabilities earn much less than non-disabled women, partly because so few women with disabilities have college degrees. Women of color with disabilities earn less than White women with disabilities.

According to Census Bureau data in 1991, average earnings for year-round full-time workers were as follows:

All women	$20,553
White women	20,794
Black women	18,720
Latinas	16,244
All men	29,421
White men	30,266
Black men	22,075
Latinos	19,771

Working wives contribute significantly to household income. According to the U.S. Department of Labor (1993), in 1991, the average income of married couples with both partners in the paid workforce was $48,169, 60 percent higher than families in which the wife was not earning; in the latter, the average income was $30,075. On divorce, the income of a mother and her children drops drastically from its predivorce level. More than 75 percent of divorced mothers with custody of their children are employed. Many fathers (more than 50 percent by some estimates) pay little or no child support. The average weekly income of families maintained by women was $385 in 1992, compared with $779 for two-earner families and $519 for families maintained by men. For White single mothers the average was $409; this fell to $341 for Latina single mothers and $328 for Black single mothers. Bear in mind that averages always conceal extremes. Many women and men earn less than the average figures cited above and less than the official **poverty level,** which in 1996, was $12,000 for a family of three.

Discrimination Against Working Women: Sexual Harassment, Age, and Disability

Sexual Harassment   According to the American Federation of State, County and Municipal Employees (AFSCME), sexual harassment is "a serious problem for over two-thirds of working women and some working men" (AFSCME 1988). It is defined by the federal Equal Opportunity Commission Guidelines as

unwelcome sexual advances, requests for sexual favors and other verbal or physical conduct of a sexual nature when

1. Submission to such conduct is made either explicitly or implicitly a term or condition of employment;

2. Submission to or rejection of such conduct by an individual is used as the basis for employment decisions affecting such individual; or,

3. Such conduct has the purpose or effect of unreasonably interfering with an individual's work performance or creating an intimidating, hostile or offensive working environment.

Sexual harassment at work can include verbal abuse, visual abuse, physical abuse, and rape and is against the law. In 1986 the first case concerning sexual harassment (*Meritor Savings Bank v. Vinson*) reached the Supreme Court and established that sexual harassment includes the creation of a hostile or abusive work environment. The Court also held that the appropriate question is not whether the victim tolerated the harassment "voluntarily" but whether it was "unwelcome." The testimony of Anita Hill in November 1991 before a Senate Judiciary Committee considering the confirmation of Clarence Thomas to the Supreme Court made this issue a lead story for virtually every TV talk show, magazine, and newspaper in the country (Morrison 1992). As women talked about their experiences of sexual harassment, its very widespread nature was publicly acknowledged. Employers hastily set up workshops and seminars for their staffs, mindful of the costs of losing sexual harassment lawsuits. Public figures who were sued for sexual harassment in 1996 include Senator Bob Packwood, who was forced by his Republican colleagues to resign his Senate seat, and President Clinton. It is important to note that the federal law against sexual harassment applies only to behavior in the workplace or in schools, not to sexual intimidation and abuse in other situations.

Age Discrimination   One effect of corporate downsizing and layoffs is that a growing number of older, experienced workers are unemployed. They are too young to retire but often considered too old or too expensive to hire. For women over forty, particularly, age complicates the job search. It takes longer for such women to find new work than it does men, and their new jobs usually pay less than they were earning before or are part time. There are several myths about older women in the workforce: it is not cost-effective to hire an older woman; she will be hard to train and is likely to have difficulty with new technology; her insurance costs will be higher than for a younger person; and she will not have a strong commitment to work. According to the American Association of Retired Persons (n.d.), none of these myths are borne out by research findings.

Discrimination Against Women with Disabilities In Reading 49, Harilyn Rousso describes the work of Carol Ann Roberson, a vocational rehabilitation counselor who is quadriplegic as a result of polio. Nancy Russo and Mary Jansen (1988) note that women with disabilities have not participated in the "women's employment revolution" (p. 229). They argue that people with disabilities are generally stereotyped as dependent, passive, and incompetent, qualities that are also often attributed to women. More African-American women and Latinas report a work disability, a disabling condition that makes them unable to work outside the home, than do White women. Work disabilities are more prevalent among older women. At the same time, many women with disabilities that keep them out of the paid workforce do their own cooking, laundry, and housekeeping. Increasing numbers of students with disabilities are going to college. They tend to be older (36 percent are thirty-five or older) and married, financially independent, and/or veterans. In 1993, 6 percent of all undergraduates reported having some kind of disability, with the most common related to orthopedic conditions (37 percent), health conditions (20 percent), hearing (18 percent), sight (11 percent), and speech (7 percent) (*Mainstream* 1997). Women with disabilities generally have much lower educational attainment than nondisabled women, which bars them from entering higher-paying professional work. They may have missed a lot of school as children or not have been provided with relevant special education programs. Vocational schools and rehabilitation programs for women who suffer a disability after completing their education also tend to channel them into dependent roles within the family, or to low-paid "women's work" in the labor force. Added to these limitations are the prejudices and ignorance of employers and coworkers and the ableist attitudes of this culture. Women with disabilities may also have to make what Mudrick (1988) describes as "significant and sometimes costly special arrangements" (p. 246) to maintain their employment, such as transportation or extra help at home.

Balancing Home and Work

Until the 1950s many companies would not hire married women, and there is still a fear that married women will be less committed to their work than men. In Chapter 4 we discussed the difficulties many women face, juggling paid work and family responsibilities. Despite some men's involvement in housekeeping and child care, women are overwhelmingly responsible for raising children and running the home. Inadequate or unaffordable child care and difficulties in taking time off work to care for a sick child, for example, make many working women's lives extremely stressful and difficult. By some estimates, parents spend 40 percent less time with their children than they did thirty years ago, because of other pressures (Brennan, Winklepleck, and Mac-Namee 1994, p. 373).

Flextime, Part-Time Work, Home Working, and the Mommy Track In Reading 44 Jeannine Ouellette Howitz describes her experiences of juggling work and caring for children. Mothers in the paid workforce may try to find a job with hours that are compatible with children's school schedules. This might mean working jobs that allow some flexible scheduling, seeking part-time work, or working at home — whether sewing, minding children, or "tele-commuting." Thanks to innovations like fax-modems, electronic mail, and pagers, home working is currently touted for professional and corporate workers as a way to work flexible hours with greater personal freedom and no stressful commute. This may alleviate the problem of child care for some professional families and greatly help the commuter marriage, but for garment workers and child-care providers, who account for the majority of home workers, the pay is poor and there are no benefits. Garment workers on piecework rates put in long hours, often working into the night. They are also isolated from one another, which makes it much more difficult to improve their pay through collective bargaining.

Another solution to the problem for professional women, put forward in the late 1980s, was that firms adopt a "mommy track." Professional women who wanted career advancement comparable to that of men would either not have children or would somehow manage their lives so as to combine having children with working long hours, attending out-of-town meetings, taking little vacation time, and doing whatever the job demanded. Otherwise they could "opt" for the mommy track and be recompensed accordingly.

Child Care Child care is a family's fourth highest expense, after housing, food, and taxes. For some women who want to work, the cost of child care is prohibitive, even if they can find suitable child-care providers. Federal and state governments, employers, and labor unions offer some assistance to child-care providers and parents in the form of tax credits, grants to child-care programs, on-site care in the case of some large employers, provisions for child care as part of a benefits package, flextime, and leave for family emergencies, such as sickness. Taken overall, these provisions are woefully inadequate. It is particularly difficult to obtain child care for the hours before and after school and during school vacations. Head Start programs, for example, which offer preschool education to low-income children, are usually available only for a half day and serve approximately 17 percent of eligible children. The Family and Medical Leave Act of 1993 provides for leave in family emergencies like the birth of a child or illness of a family member, but it covers only firms with fifty or more workers, and the leave is unpaid. Most workers cannot take advantage of full unpaid leave without severe financial hardship.

Another aspect of this issue is the working conditions for child-care workers, the vast majority of whom are women who work in their own homes or at child-care centers and preschool programs. Although parents often struggle to afford child care, child-care workers are poorly paid. Many are not paid overtime; they do not receive health insurance or paid vacations. Even fewer have retirement plans. Child-care workers, on average, earn less than animal caretakers, parking lot attendants, and garbage collectors (National Commission on Working Women 1989). Low pay and difficult working conditions mean that turnover among these workers is high.

The Second Shift   Women employed outside the home still carry the main responsibility for housework and raising children and are left with very little time for themselves (Stanhope 1996). Although this is particularly acute for single parents, many women living with men also do more housework and child care than their partners (Mainardi 1992). Undoubtedly, this pattern varies among couples and perhaps also at different stages in their lives. Arlie Hochschild (1990) has estimated that women in the labor force work a second shift of at least fifteen hours a week more than men, or an extra month of twenty-four-hour days over a year, and argues that men need to do more in the home. A 1990 Virginia Slims Opinion Poll uncovered great resentment among women over housework. "Fully 52 percent of wives said they feel resentful about how little their husband does at home" (Brennan, Winklepleck, and MacNee 1994, p. 395). In households where men are present, housework is often divided along gendered lines. Husbands and fathers take care of the car, do yard work and household repairs, and take out the trash. Women usually have major responsibility for food shopping, meals, laundry, and child care. These tasks have to be done every day and take more time and emotional energy than "men's" tasks. Negotiating household responsibilities and the stress of juggling home and paid work is a key source of friction in many families. Middle-class households pay cleaners, maids, and baby-sitters, which helps to free middle-class women from the time crunch and stress of balancing home and work. These domestic workers are usually paid low wages without benefits. In seeking greater freedom for themselves, middle-class women thus find themselves perpetuating poor working conditions for poorer women.

Organized Labor

Historically, the male-dominated labor movement has been weak in pressing for changes that would benefit women workers, and women have not been taken seriously as labor leaders. Some male workers were hostile to women in the workforce, fearing for their own jobs and their authority as breadwinners. In support of women in unions, the Coalition of Labor Union Women (CLUW) has four main goals: to organize the unorganized, to promote affirmative action in the workplace, to stimulate political action and legislation on women's issues, and to increase the participation of women in their unions. The coalition emphasizes such issues as equal pay, child care, universal access to health care, and reproductive freedom. It aims to educate working women about their rights, to provide training in dealing with management, and to prepare women for union leadership positions.

Workers usually make significant gains in wage levels and working conditions when they are members of a labor union, but currently the majority of women in the U.S. workforce are not union members. This is partly due to the decline of unions nationally in recent decades. Also many women work in jobs that are hard to unionize, such as retailing or the fast food business, where they are scattered at many separate locations. In Reading 50 Katie Quan confounds the conventional wisdom that immigrant women are difficult to organize as she recounts her experience of a major strike in New York's Chinatown garment district in 1982, involving twenty thousand young Chinese women. The United Farm Workers of America (UFW), founded by Cesar Chavez and Dolores Huerta, has pressured growers to sign union contracts to improve the pay and working conditions of its members — women and men — many of whom are migrant workers and immigrants to the United States whose health is continually compromised by chemical pesticides. The UFW has called for boycotts of non-organic table grapes, and now strawberries, which are heavily sprayed with pesticides, as a means of leverage in its struggle with growers.

The Working Poor Organized labor also calls attention to low wages, a contributory factor in the raise in the minimum wage in 1996. In public debate poor people are usually assumed to be on welfare, masking the reality of life for the many working poor, whose wages are below or near the poverty level. This includes legal immigrants, who often start off at the bottom of the employment hierarchy. Marion Graham describes her experiences of low-waged work in Reading 52. Some people with very low incomes are working minimum-wage jobs, and others work part time or seasonally. They may be involved in the informal economy as maids, baby-sitters, or gardeners, for example, doing home work for the garment trade, fixing cars, carrying and selling small amounts of drugs, getting money for sex, selling roses at off-ramps. Others work in sweatshops, which are also unregulated in terms of wages, hours, and conditions of work; these are on the rise in many major U.S. cities and often employ undocumented workers. In the mid-1990s there were several media exposés of clothing companies whose subcontractors operate sweatshops, including The Gap, Macy's, and Mervyn's. The Union of Needletrades, Industrial and Textile Employees (UNITE) has organized demonstrations outside department stores to encourage shoppers to boycott brands that use sweatshop labor. In 1996 Asian Immigrant Women Advocates, after a three-year campaign, won a significant agreement from Jessica McClintock to improve labor practices. Starting in the mid-1980s, Fuerza Unida, composed mainly of Mexican-American women workers, organized against Levi Strauss over the closing of its San Antonio plant and the loss of their jobs to Costa Rica. Guess workers have filed a class-action lawsuit against Guess and sixteen of its contracting shops for "systematic violations of basic labor laws" (Sharf 1997).

Affirmative Action Labor unions, as well as many women's organizations and civil rights organizations, also support affirmative action in employment, introduced as part of the Civil Rights Act of 1964 to improve job possibilities for women, people of color, and military veterans, whose opportunities in education, job training, and hiring are not equal to those of White men. Affirmative action is not a quota system, as is often claimed; it is not reverse discrimination, and it is not a system for hiring unqualified people. The need for and desirability of affirmative action policies — which have benefited White women more than any other group — have been called into question increasingly in the 1990s and have been the subject of public campaigns. The affirmative action policy for state agencies in California was overturned in a ballot initiative in 1996. Similar attempts in other states are not far behind.

Challenges of the Global Economy A great challenge for organized labor in the future is the continued impact of the globalization of the economy on the availability of work, wage rates, working conditions in the United States, and continued pressure for immigration into this country. As capital becomes increasingly international in its movements, labor will need to become increasingly international in its strategies. This country has a vital tradition of labor organizing, including actions in support of workers in other countries. Although circumstances have changed, there is much to be learned from this history that can be applied today (Cobble 1993; Milkman 1985).

Pensions, Disability Payments, and Welfare

For women who cannot work because of illness, age, or disability, for those who are made redundant or who cannot leave their children, there is a complex patchwork of income-support measures and means-tested allowances provided by federal and state governments and private pension plans. Community organizations, particularly religious organizations, also provide much-needed informal support to poor people. Before the Great Depression of the 1930s, when the economy collapsed and many thousands were suddenly destitute, there was a commonly held belief that poverty was due to laziness and that there was plenty of work available for those willing to roll up their sleeves and get on with it. But the severity of the collapse, which put so many poor people on bread lines, desperate to feed their families, called for government intervention in the labor market to protect people from the worst effects of the booms and slumps of the economy. This provided the impetus and the political justification for the establishment of Social Security and Medicare programs under the Social Security Act of 1935.

These programs are based on people's relationship to work and are rooted in the principle of the work ethic. Older people can claim pensions because they have already done their share and paid into the Social Security fund during their working lives; people with disabilities may be excused if they are not able to work as long or as vigorously as nondisabled people; those who are laid off because of plant closures or other company changes can usually claim unemployment benefits for a few months while they look for other jobs. Such people are considered "deserving" in contrast to the "undeserving," meaning those who are young and able-bodied but who "simply don't want to work," as is often said in the 1990s, no less than in the 1930s. This distinction underlies two kinds of benefits: one is based on the concept of social insurance, which allows individuals to draw from an insurance fund to which they have contributed during their working lives; the other is based on the concept of public assistance, under which the needy are given "means-tested" allowances.

Significantly for women today, this Social Security legislation was designed to assist the ideal nuclear family, where the male head of the household was in regular, full-time, paid employment until his death or retirement, and the woman was a full-time homemaker. More than fifty years later most U.S. families are not of this type, and women's benefits are adversely affected because their employment histories, upon which payments are calculated, are usually not the same as men's.

Pensions and Retirement

Retirement pensions are a crucial source of income for older people, but women generally receive significantly lower pension payments than men. Pensions are based on wage levels while the person was working and on the number of years in employment. This assumes that only paid work is productive work, so no amount of housekeeping or caring for children and elderly relatives will count. As we mentioned above, women generally earn lower wages than men and are more likely to work part time and to move in and out of the workforce as they balance paid work with raising children and family responsibilities. Currently, few part-time jobs provide health insurance or a pension plan. When women retire, many have to rely on a Social Security pension that will be lower than that for most men, because women were not able to contribute as much to it during their working lives. Because work and retirement are defined according to the labor market experiences of White middle-class men, this penalizes not only many women but also men of color and people with disabilities. Poor or working-class men have lower wages, fewer benefits, and less job security and are more likely to have suffered occupational injury than middle-class men and women. Poor women and men of color often have to piece together an income, depending on seasonal or part-time work, sometimes working informally for cash or favors returned. These factors make them less able to retire from paid work completely when they are older.

A new stereotype of affluent older people in ads for cruises, cars, vitamins, health insurance, and hearing aids suggests that all older people are physically fit and enjoying their retirement. As noted by Stoller and Gibson (1994), this is a welcome change from negative images of elderly people, but it deflects attention from those who are poor. These authors found that 11.4 percent of people over sixty-five in the United States have incomes below the poverty line, but this figure rises to 20 percent for Latinos and 31 percent for African-Americans. For elderly African-Americans living alone the poverty rate increases to 60 percent (p. 55). Because of broken treaties and oppressive policies, elderly Native Americans as a group have the lowest incomes and the worst housing in the country. At the same time, many of these older people provide valuable services for themselves and others: participating in community organizations, helping family and friends, looking after children, maintaining and repairing their homes, and doing daily cooking, cleaning, and other housework. Stoller and Gibson point out that the advantages of a job with good pay and benefits, a comfortable home, and stimulating opportunities tend to accumulate across the life course. Similarly, disadvantages may also accumulate, producing large differences in economic resources, and often also in health, in old age (p. 107).

The country's elderly population will rise dramatically in the next two decades as baby boomers now in their middle years reach retirement age. The elderly will also be a much larger proportion of the population than previously, giving rise to the notion of the affluent older person collecting unearned benefits at the expense of less affluent younger workers. There is concern over the future of the Social Security system, as a larger number of people will be drawing pensions than will be paying into it. Some, claiming that Social Security will become bankrupt, with nothing left for those who are now young, have gone so far as to call for its privatization. Others argue that Social Security can be fixed with relatively modest increases in contributions in the short term, rather than by wholesale privatization (Lieberman 1997).

Disability Payments

For reasons similar to those we outlined above in connection with pensions, women with disabilities also receive less from public income support than do men with disabilities (Mudrick 1988). As a result, fewer women with disabilities are able to claim Social Security Disability Insurance (DI), which was designed with the needs of working men in mind, and must rely on the Supplemental Security Income program (SSI), which is subject to a means test for eligibility and greater bureaucratic scrutiny, often demeaning. Some disabled elderly people may choose disability benefits over Social Security pensions, depending on their work histories. The future of income support for people with disabilities is likely to be influenced by two opposing trends: the growing political clout of the disability rights movement and the desire of many politicians to cut government spending, especially for welfare.

Welfare

Aid to Families with Dependent Children (AFDC) is what people usually mean when they say "welfare," which has become an especially controversial issue in recent years. In Reading 52 Chrystos describes the experience of being on welfare, and in Reading 51 Mimi Abramovitz and Fred Newton dispel several common myths about welfare recipients. Many people think that the majority of welfare mothers are Black with large families. In 1994, of AFDC recipients 38 percent were White, 37 percent, Black, 17 percent, Latina, 2.8 percent, Asian, and 1.4 percent, Native American (Martinez 1996, p. 62). Welfare currently accounts for approximately 1 percent of the federal budget, and 2–3 percent of states' budgets. However, AFDC is being cut following the enactment of the Personal Responsibility and Work Opportunity Reconciliation Act of 1996, signed into law by President Clinton against the opposition of many welfare rights organizations and advocates for poor women and children, such as the National Welfare Rights Union and many local campaigns like Survivors Inc. (Roxbury, Mass.) and the Coalition for Basic Human Needs (Cambridge, Mass.). States are instituting time limits for AFDC payments of two years or less and are insisting that mothers go back to full-time education or work. The challenge, of course, will be to find jobs for them in this shrinking labor market, and this is one of the great contradictions of this issue. These women will generally be competing for low-paid "women's work" that may not pay much more than AFDC and will be competing against other low-paid workers. They will also need affordable child care, a major obstacle for most working mothers.

It is important to note here that many people in this society receive some kind of government support, be it through income-tax deductions for homeowners, medical benefits for those in the military, tax breaks for corporations, agricultural subsidies to farmers, government bailouts to savings and loans companies, or government funding for high-tech military-related research conducted by universities and private firms. This is often not mentioned in discussions of welfare, but it should be.

Feminist Approaches to Women's Work and Income

Comparable Worth

Feminist researchers and policy analysts have been concerned with women's overall working conditions and women's labor history (Amott 1993; Amott and Matthaei 1996; Bergmann 1986; Jones 1985; Kessler-Harris 1990; Zavella 1987). They have questioned why the job market is segregated along gender lines and have challenged traditional inequities in pay between women and men. These may be partly explained by differences in education, qualifications, and work experience, but part of this wage gap is simply attributable to gender. This has led to detailed discussion of the **comparable worth** of women's jobs when considered next to men's jobs requiring comparable levels of skill and knowledge. Why is it, for example, that secretaries or child-care workers, who are virtually all women, earn so much less than truck drivers or mail carriers, who are mainly men? What do wage rates say about the importance of a job to the wider society? What is being rewarded? Advocates for comparable worth have urged employers to evaluate employees without regard to gender, race, or class, but in terms of knowledge and skills needed to perform the job, mental demands or decision making involved in the job, accountability or the degree of supervision involved, and working conditions, such as how physically safe the job is (Tong 1989). Such calculations reveal many discrepancies in current rates of pay between women's work and men's work. Indeed, if pursued, this line of argument opens up the thorny question of how to justify wage differentials at all.

Feminization of Poverty

Feminist researchers have also pointed to the **feminization of poverty** (Dujon and Withorn 1996; Abramovitz 1996; Sidel 1996). The two poorest groups in the United States are women raising children alone and women over sixty-five living alone. According to the Children's Defense Fund, roughly one quarter of U.S. children are currently living in poverty, and more children are abused, neglected, committing suicide, running away, and living without health insurance than was the case twenty years ago (Brennan, Winklepleck, and MacNee 1994). *Poverty* is a complex term with economic, emotional, and cultural dimensions. One may be emotionally impoverished but materially well-off, for example, and vice versa. Poverty also needs to be thought about in the context of costs — for housing, food, transportation, health care, child care, and clothes needed to go to work — and the social expectations of this materialist culture. Many poor children in the United States today clamor for Nikes, for example, in response to high-pressure advertising campaigns.

There is no consistent national policy in the United States designed to lift people out of poverty. Katha Pollitt (1994) argues forcefully that welfare is a feminist issue

> because it weakens women's dependence on men. It means that pregnant women can choose to give birth and keep their babies even if abandoned by their boyfriends and families; it means that battered women can leave abusive men, and miserable working-class wives, like their middle-class sisters, can get a fresh start without reducing their children to starvation. It protects women at a time when the patriarchal family is disintegrating, and that is why family-values conservatives hate it, even though opposition to welfare forces them to laud employed mothers, whom — in another part of the policy forest — they usually attack.
> *(p. 45)*

Marxist theorists of the economy used to see women as a reserve army of labor to be brought into the workforce when necessary, as, for instance, during World War II. More recently such theorists note that currently it is women workers who are specifically hired for export production in the Third World. They are paid low wages and also valued by employers as "docile" and "dexterous." Maria Mies (1986) argues that this international division of labor divides the world into producers and consumers. Third World women producers are linked to First World women consumers through commodities bought by the latter. This division renders many women and men in the First World expendable as far as paid work is concerned; hence the high unemployment rates for young people of color in the United States.

Impact of Class

A key concept in any discussion of work, income, and wealth is class. Janet Zandy describes her experiences of working-class family life in Reading 54. In the United States today, most people describe themselves as "middle class," a term that includes a very wide range of incomes, occupations, levels of security, and life situations. Indicators of class include income, occupation, education, culture and language, neighborhood, clothes, cars, and, particularly important, unearned wealth. As we noted in Chapter 2, some people raised in a working-class community may have a middle-class education and occupation later in life and a somewhat mixed class identity as a result. A woman's class position is often linked to that of her father and husband. For Marxists, a person's class is defined in relation to the process of economic production—whether he or she works for a living. There is currently no politically accepted way for most people to make a livelihood except by working for it, and in this society work, in addition to being an economic necessity, carries strong moral overtones. Note that this same principle is not applied to those among the very rich who live on trust funds or corporate profits. In much public debate in the United States class is more of a psychological concept—what we think and feel about our class position—than an economic one. Poverty is often explained as resulting from individual low self-esteem, laziness, or dysfunctional families, as we pointed out in Chapter 1. In public discourse on inequality, race is invariably emphasized at the expense of class. Government census data, for example, are analyzed for racial differences much more than for class differences, which gives the impression that race is the most salient disparity among people. In practice race and class overlap, but greater attention to class differences would show different patterns of inequality. It would also show more similarities and more of a basis for alliances between people of color and White people who are economically disadvantaged.

Policy Implications and Activist Projects

Feminists have tackled the issue of women and work from many angles. In addition to working for comparable worth in wage rates, they have encouraged women to return to school to improve their educational qualifications, opposed sexual harassment on the job, campaigned for decent, affordable child-care arrangements, exposed the dangers of occupational injury and the health hazards of toxic work environments, and advocated for women in senior positions in all fields, and that math, science, and computer education be more available and effective for girls. The "Take Our Daughters to Work Day" initiated by the Ms. Foundation, for example, exposes girls to jobs they may know little about and provides role models for them, which can have a powerful impact. Several organizations have worked to open up opportunities for women to enter well-paying trades such as carpentry and construction, including Women in the Building Trades (Jamaica Plain, Mass.), Minnesota Women in the Trades, and Northern New England Tradeswomen (Barre, Vt.). Many local groups help women to start small businesses, utilizing existing skills. The Women's Bean Project (Denver) and the Navaho Weaving Project (Kykotsmovi, Ariz.) are group projects that promote self-sufficiency.

Promoting Greater Economic Security for Women

A lack of jobs, low wages, low educational attainment, having children, and divorce all work against women's economic security and keep many women in poverty, dependent on men, or both. As we concluded in Chapter 4, an aspect of security and sustainability for family relationships involves equal opportunities and responsibilities for parenting, which in turn means a redefinition of work. Yet if current workplace trends continue, many young people in the United States—especially young people of color—will never be in regular, full-time employment in their lives. Politicians and businesses promote almost any venture—building convention centers, ballparks, jails and prisons and maintaining obsolete military bases—on the argument that it will create jobs. Changes in the economy force us to confront some fundamental contradictions that affect women's work and the way work is thought about generally:

What should count as work?

Does the distinction between "productive" and "unproductive" work make sense?

How should work be rewarded?

How should those without paid work, many of them women, be supported?

How can the current inequalities between haves and have-nots be justified?

Is the work ethic useful? Should it be redefined?

Is materialism the mark of success?

Years ago, pushed by the impact of the Great Depression of the 1930s, social commentators saw great potential for human development promised by (then) new technologies like telephones, Dictaphones, and washing machines, by means of which people could provide for their needs in a relatively short time each week. The British philosopher Bertrand Russell (1935), for example, favored such "idleness" as an opportunity to become more fully human, to develop oneself in many dimensions of life. Recognizing that this could not happen if material living standards had to keep rising, he put forth a modest notion of what people "need." He also understood that these kinds of changes would require political imagination and will.

In the 1990s, people in many inner-city areas of the United States are faced with a related challenge: how to make a living if there are no jobs. Grace Lee Boggs (1994) and James Boggs (1994), together with others in Detroit, for example, are exploring how communities can support one another now that the auto industry has all but abandoned the city. Neighborhood businesses, community bartering schemes, and community currencies like Ithaca HOURS all suggest possibilities. Participants in Ithaca HOURS (in Ithaca, New York) trade their time and skills for Ithaca money, where one hour is the equivalent of $10. In effect they buy goods and services with their own labor. This system helps people to connect with one another rather than making them competitors. Since its start in 1991, some $50,000 worth of Ithaca HOURS have recirculated in the local community buying goods and services worth an estimated $2,000,000 (Glover 1997).

As you read and discuss this chapter, think about the following:

1. What are your experiences of work?

2. What have you learned through working? About yourself? About other people's lives? About the wider society? How did you learn it? Who were your teachers?

3. What have you wanted to change in your work situations? What would it take to make these changes? What recourse do you have as a worker to improve your conditions of work?

4. What types of productive activity (paid and unpaid) do you expect to be involved in over the next ten or twenty years?

5. How might pension policies be changed to reflect the range of productivity of women across the life course?

6. What are the work experiences of your mother and grandmother? What opportunities did they have? What choices did they make? What differences do you notice between your own life and theirs at the same age?

7. What resources do you want to have available to you in old age?

◆◆◆

FORTY-FOUR

Reflections of a Feminist Mom

Jeannine Ouellette Howitz

I am seven months pregnant, slithering along my kitchen floor. The ruler I clutch is for retrieving small objects lost in the dust jungle beneath my refrigerator. After several swipes I come up with a pile of dirt and a petrified saltine, so I get serious and press my cheek against the floor, positioning my left eye just inches from the target zone. I spot it — the letter "G," a red plastic refrigerator magnet. "Here it is!" I cry, hoisting myself up to offer this hard-won prize to So-

phie, my momentarily maniacal toddler. Her face collapses into a sob as she shrieks, "NOT THAT ONE!"

Sophie is 22 months old, and in the final stages of potty training, which I remember as I feel a gush of warm and wet on my outstretched leg. Wet clothes bring more tears (hers, not mine), and I quickly strip off her clothes, then pull off my own with one hand while I slice and peel an apple with the other. I might have barely enough time while she eats to run upstairs, grab dry clothes, and toss the dirty ones into the basket before I'm urgently missed.

That was how I came to be standing in the middle of my kitchen with the magnificence of my naked abdomen hanging low and wide on a clammy June afternoon. The sweat of my exertion had just begun trickling between my breasts when the phone rang. It was an old friend with whom I'd been out of touch for a while. I panted hello, eyeing Sophie as she climbed up and out of her booster chair to totter precariously on the table top. "What are you doing home?" my friend wanted to know. "Don't you work at all anymore?"

Don't you work at all anymore? Again and again since entering the life phase which positioned my work in the home, I have encountered the judgments, however unconscious, of those whose definition of work excludes most of what I do. The same system that discounts my labor scoffs at its rewards, which, like my productivity, are impossible to measure by conventional standards. By limiting our view to one which allows only for paid employment, usually only that located outside the home, to be included in the understood meaning of the word "work," we support the process through which all that we do and all that we are as women is ultimately devalued and despised.

Like most labels applied to women's roles, "working mother" is extremely inaccurate and defeating, because it foolishly implies that there is another type of mother: the non-working variety. Being a mother is work. On the other hand, it is equally absurd to call mothers who are not employed outside the home "full-time mothers," as this unfairly suggests that employed mothers are only mothers part-time. Ridiculous as they are, these labels go largely unchallenged, even by many feminists. They are a sinister trap, imprisoning women in feelings of inadequacy about whatever roles we have chosen or been required to perform.

The same process that forces a woman to say "I don't work" when she performs 12 to 16 hours of unpaid labor every single day at home ultimately transforms most female-dominated professions into mere chores that women and men alike come to consider less desirable and important than other types of work. Once stamped with the kiss of death "women's work," we can forget entitlement to the same respect and fair wages a man would get for equivalent labor.

Before motherhood, I sold advertising at a newspaper, with hopes of working my way into editorial.

However, my sales performance exceeded standards, and I was quickly promoted to a well-paying position in management which required me to build a classified department from the ground up. I forged ahead until my daughter was born, when, after reexamining our options, my husband and I decided one of us should stay home with her. Although he was happily working in his chosen field, John's income as a schoolteacher was half that of mine, which rendered him the financially logical choice for at-home parenthood. But it was I who jumped at the chance, albeit scary, to shift the gears of my career and of my life.

When my maternity leave was up, I told the publishers that I wouldn't be returning to the office. Surprisingly, they offered me the chance to bring my daughter to work with me. I was thrilled; those long days at home with an infant weren't exactly what I had imagined. I discovered that although I didn't always enjoy my job, I did enjoy the recognition it provided me — something I found was not a part of the package for home-working moms. While my sister spoke with unveiled envy about all the reading and writing I would now be accomplishing, in reality I was lucky if I brushed my teeth. So I took the deal.

Seven weeks old on her first day at work, Sophie fascinated the staff as only a newborn can. A two-minute trip to the copier often turned into a half-hour social ordeal as one person after the next stopped to exclaim over her. She was a great diversion for a young and predominantly single staff. I had no idea, as a new mother, how fortunate I was to have an extroverted baby. It was my own introverted nature that suffered from the constant sensory bombardment. I was uncomfortably aware of my special status, and fighting a losing battle to hide how much time it actually took to care for Sophie on the job.

In a culture where women feel guilty to call in sick to work when a child is sick, it was tremendously difficult to be in an office setting, drawing a full salary, and to say, "Sophie's crying now — this phone call, this meeting, this project, whatever it is, will have to wait." In a society that expects workers to give 150 percent dedication to the job, and considers motherhood a terrible detriment to productivity, it was incredibly stressful and even painful at times to experience such a personal conflict in a very public setting when the two worlds collided.

For six months, I toted a baby, a briefcase, and a diaper bag back and forth from home to my office, which at first housed the crib and swing, after which came the walker, the play gym, and the toy box—not to mention the breast pump equipment and mini-diaper pail. I could hardly see my desk, let alone get to it. Not that it mattered, because by that time I wasn't doing any work that required a desk. It had gotten crazy, and I knew it. The circles under my eyes and my continued weight loss told me it was time for a change.

I explored every alternative I could think of, from researching and visiting daycares to negotiating with my employers for a part-time or home-based position, or a combination of the two. However, my key position on the management team required a full-time presence in the office.

Offering my resignation was an extremely difficult decision, particularly in light of my gratitude for the progressive opportunity to have my daughter on-site. My employers and I finally agreed to view my departure as the beginning of an indefinite unpaid leave that left the door open for my possible return at some unpredictable future date.

A two-month notice allowed me to finish up the last big sales project of the quarter, while my daughter was cared for by a neighbor. I got an unforgettable taste of the superwoman syndrome, rising at 5 A.M. and dashing out the door by 6 to drop Sophie off and commute an hour to the office for a grueling nine-hour day. This was followed by a long drive in Minnesota winter rush-hour traffic to pick my daughter up and go home, and was topped off with a couple of frantic hours that my husband and I spent getting everyone fed and Sophie bathed and to bed so that we could start all over again after what felt like a quick catnap. Relief overcame me as my last day at the office arrived, and I packed my diaper bags for good.

Our plans had always included my return to full-time paid employment upon our children's entry to school, which meant that, for the benefit of our financial solvency, we should have another baby quickly if at all. We chose "quickly," and shortly after our daughter's first birthday I was pregnant again.

I started stringing for our local newspaper, rushing out to city council and school board meetings as soon as my husband dragged himself through the door at seven o'clock. I got paid a measly 25 dollars a story, but since the meetings were at night and I could write the stories at home, I didn't have to pay for childcare. Moreover, it was the first time I saw

my writing published; it signaled a turning point for me as I finally made the leap from advertising to editorial.

Since then, I've stuck to what I'm passionate about as I navigate the uncertain waters of these transitional years. I've redefined my priorities, and am using this time to lay the groundwork for a career that is going to work for me long after my children are grown. Like the many women who grow home businesses while growing young ones, I've discovered meaning in my personal work that was previously absent.

These days, since I do perform paid work from home, I could have an easy answer to "Don't you work at all anymore?" I could say that I am a freelance writer working at home. It's true, and since I know, based upon my own research, that it gains me a great deal more respect in the eyes of the asker than saying that I'm home with the kids, I'm tempted to offer it up. But I won't because every time I do, I'm perpetuating a system that defines work only in terms of what men have traditionally been paid to do, and discounts most of what women have traditionally done for centuries.

I have to make perfectly clear when I say that I work at home, I'm talking about the childcare and the home maintenance activities which utilize my talents as a manager, nurturer, healer, wise woman, acrobat . . . and retriever of small objects lost in the dust jungle beneath my refrigerator. Otherwise, people automatically dismiss these activities and conjure up a false image of an orderly day spent at the computer doing paid work. This strain toward clarity requires a lot more effort than calling myself a full-time mom, or proclaiming that I'm taking time off to be with my kids (motherhood is not a vacation), or worst of all, concurring that no, "I really don't work at all anymore." It demands concentration and patience, but it can be done.

We must find new words, or new combinations of and meanings for old words that more accurately reflect our reality. When we don't—when we resign ourselves to the old words that apportion us less worth than we deserve because it's less awkward and just plain easier—we are validating a description of ourselves that we know to be false. This danger is like that of looking into a fun house mirror, without challenging the falsehood of the contorted stranger staring back at you. Eventually, you're going to believe what you see is you, and that twisted version of yourself becomes the only truth you know.

◆◆◆

FORTY-FIVE

Ruminations of a Feminist Aerobics Instructor

Alisa L. Valdés

Just saying my title is enough to make most people laugh: feminist aerobics instructor. Huh? It's like being a fascist poet. People think you just can't. One day several years ago as I impelled my step class to eat whatever they wanted whenever they wanted, to love their thighs no matter what size, I was overwhelmed by all the uniquely American, female contradictions confronting me. The women in the class just stared at me with these blank, nearly hostile eyes. Hello? What part of "low-fat" didn't I understand? Couldn't I see how fat they were? What kind of aerobics instructor was I, anyway?

The answer was easy: a twenty-something, lower-middle-class musician/writer/social critic cum feminist aerobics instructor with big college loan payments and, therefore, a big, two-sided problem.

Part of the problem is this: In a lecture she gave at the Boston Public Library in 1991, the year of my emerging feminism, Gloria Steinem pointed out that women are a permanent underclass in the United States of America; because of our economic inequity, we comprise a third-world nation within the borders of our own developed country. There is no argument. In 1991, women still earned only seventy-one cents to every dollar earned by a man, and a college-educated woman could (and still can) expect to earn the same as or less than her male colleague with only a high school diploma. If we are ever going to progress, we are going to have to achieve economic equality. Period.

In New York City, aerobics instructors, feminist and otherwise, earn between thirty-five and forty-five dollars an hour.

The second part of my problem is roughly this: In 1986, nutritionist Laurel Mellin did a study through the University of California at San Francisco called "Why Girls as Young as Nine Fear Fat and Go on Diets to Lose Weight." Probably we don't need to know much more than the title to feel depressed, but in this study fifty percent of the nine-year-olds, and nearly eighty percent of the ten- and eleven-year-olds, had "put themselves on a diet because they thought they were too fat." According to some experts, eating dis-

orders were "the disease" of the seventies and have only been getting worse since then, despite being eclipsed by AIDS since the mid-eighties. And this: Studies show that seventy-five percent of adult women in this country think we are too fat, though only twenty-five percent of us actually weigh more than the standards set forth by Metropolitan Life's weight tables. And of course, there's always America's favorite doll, Barbie, by Mattell. If a woman of Barbie's proportions existed, she wouldn't be able to walk, breathe or digest food.

When I first started teaching aerobics I was fifteen years old. I did it for extra money and for a free membership to a health club. I'm not going to lie: I also did it to counter the geek factor of my adolescent existence. I was teased endlessly as a child for being overweight (*fatty fatty two-by-four, can't fit through the kitchen door* was my name), and once I actually lost weight, my parents wouldn't let me be a high school cheerleader like my best friends, Staci and Nana. Instead, they insisted that I go into band. Being a teenage aerobics instructor was a way for me to fight back on both fronts.

Even then I made about eight dollars an hour, which was great compared to the three and change I had earned wearing a greasy orange-and-brown uniform as a cashier at a local restaurant.

In early 1988, at the age of seventeen, I moved to Boston to study saxophone at the Berklee College of Music. One of the first things I did after arriving was secure a job for myself as an aerobics instructor at New England Aerobics and Nautilus, a women's gym a few blocks from school. My peers at Berklee were eighty-five percent male, so it was a good balance for me to enter that sweaty female domain where I could stand in front of the class and command and connect. The gym was one of the few places on earth where I actually felt I possessed an irrefutable degree of power. It hadn't occurred to me yet to analyze why so many brilliant, professional women were wasting so many hours every week hopping around in leotards. All I knew then was that it was a great job with good money, lots of other women, loud music and a kind of ritualized dancing that I got to choreograph.

As fun and American as lite beer, buffalo wings and fried cheese.

Gradually, and somewhat to my astonishment, I became a *professional* instructor. By my senior year of college I had actually carved out a secondary career for myself in the aerobics industry in Boston, which was good since not too many jazz saxophonists or poets were making enough bread to pay back a loan such as the twenty-three thousand dollars I suddenly owed after graduation (no thanks to Uncle Reagan). I was teaching at the city's top clubs — places populated by women who carried attaché cases and men in ties, places with names like the Sky Club, Healthworks, the Squash Club and Boston Health and Swim Club — and getting about twenty-five dollars an hour for my perspirational efforts. Other friends from school were working as cashiers at Tower Records or as security guards at the Hines Convention Center, barely breaking minimum wage. I felt lucky.

I even invested in a license to train other instructors for the Aerobics and Fitness Association of America, one of the two major certification organizations in the country, and was soon able to make about three hundred dollars an hour for private clinics. I taught step, funk, Latin, high- and low-impact, body sculpting and stretch. I even entered an aerobics competition in 1992 with a male partner, and we grinned and bounced our way to second place in the New England regionals.

Soon I was heading the aerobics program at a club near Tufts University; at twenty-three I had my own office, a good salary and power over a whole staff of instructors, and I was presenting a master class at the Boston MetroSports Fitness Expo. People in the industry knew my name. Disc jockeys made free tapes for my classes. Reebok invited me to sit on its instructor board to help design its 1993 line of shoes. Reebok, Nike and Rykä shoe companies gave me freebies, just for being a good instructor. And I could pay back my loans. Though I kept telling myself I was really still a feminist, a musician and a writer, I was becoming a career instructor — sweating more, practicing less, writing less — and it was almost comfortable.

Almost, except for the gnawing ache of betrayal. I had read Alice Walker. I knew better than to encourage women's obsession with their appearance, including my own. I knew better than to freak out at my own cellulite, staying late after work to pump iron to make it go away. I knew better than to stand skinny in front of a room full of self-doubting women and ac-

tually say to them, "Okay, let's tone up." I had betrayed myself, betrayed my dreams; most of all I had betrayed my gender. But it was almost as if I, who spent the first years of my life in a housing project and have been living hand-to-mouth ever since, had no choice. The world had rewarded "Hispanic female" me not for being a writer or musician, but for being an aerobics instructor. I was a cheerleader after all, and I hadn't even noticed. Like many other women who bought the fitness lie, I had been duped into believing there was strength in, well, fat loss. Eventually, my conscience got the better of me. I quit everything fitness-oriented in Boston, packed my bags and moved to New York City to try to be a feminist writer and musician for real. At first it was groovy, but it was only a matter of time before my credit was canceled and the phone company lawyers were threatening me.

I landed a prestigious unpaid internship at the *Village Voice*, but ended up having to leave early and quite sloppily because I was also teaching fifteen to twenty aerobics classes a week to pay my bills. Commuting two hours a day, practicing my saxophone, writing consistently and holding down two jobs was too much; I just couldn't handle the pressure. The physical and emotional stress overwhelmed me: I was physically sick all the time, I slept on the bus home, I craved several boxes of doughnuts at once. So I quit the *Voice* when I really wanted to quit teaching. But there was no money at the *Voice*, and women, remember, are a permanent, albeit fit, underclass in our society.

Before long, I was a full-time aerobics instructor again, this time in Manhattan, at places with names like the Jeff Martin Studio, Molly Fox Fitness and Crunch Fitness, places that had articles written about them in those "women's" magazines, right next to articles about sticking to your diet or ten ways to make Him find you sexy again. I watched as my lifelong dream of being a professional feminist writer slipped through my fingers and back into my spandex and sneakers, all because I needed to pay for a roof over my head and the food in my stomach. I realized that only the children of the rich are able to afford to be entry-level journalists for the progressive publications of our nation. The poor become, well, cheerleaders for the status quo. Give me a "Y"! (Why!)

And that is my problem.

I say I was a cheerleader after all, and a part of me grimaces. I've tried hard to hold on to a shred of feminist dignity in all this jumping around. I made it a goal to battle the common misconception about aerobics instructors — that we are nothing but airheads in thongs.

I rationalized this femifitness philosophy in many ways. I grew convinced that there is actually a great deal of raw, primal energy and force in a room full of women moving together in time; a few of the editors from the *Voice,* feminists all of them (well, Pagliaesque, cutesy, Voicey, Madonna feminists at any rate), took classes at one of the studios I worked for. In real life, I reminded myself, women take aerobics classes in shorts and T-shirts; it is only on television that they all wear tights and thongs. And only on the ESPN programs that air in sports bars at eleven in the morning do aerobics instructors grin wildly and stick their asses in the air.

That dignified instructor part of me thought men, including Woody Allen, had sexified and bubblefied the image of aerobics instructor in order to claim ownership of one of our society's few appealing areas where men simply are not welcome. I thought, What could honestly be more frightening to men than a room full of capable, professional women moving together, in sync, unaware of anything but themselves and each other? Only Hillary Rodham Clinton and a truly lesbian orgy, perhaps.

And I found intellectual polemics to support my misdirected theory. In 1989 Roberta Pollack Seid wrote that "ten years ago vigorous exercise was seen as the province primarily of young men. Today women have smashed the sex barrier that once excluded them from this 'male' domain."[*] Right on, part of me gurgled over the water fountain. Not only had we smashed the barriers, but through our organized dance exercise, we had also created a girls' club where women work for women and make money off of and for women (albeit with a sociopolitically skewed agenda).

Iris Marion Young, a professor from the University of Pittsburgh who has written extensively on gender differences in motility in our society, wrote that there are "certain observable and rather ordinary ways in which women in our society typically comport themselves and move differently from the ways that men do."[†] She documents that we take proportionally shorter steps than men do, keep our arms in close to us when we walk (whereas men swing freely) and stand with our legs closer together. She argues that the cliché way boys and girls throw a ball differently is an outward manifestation of an across-the-board social conditioning to female inferiority; and she adds that until a human can trust her body to actually comport itself in the direction of its possibilities, the possibilities will remain overlooked. The aerobics studio, then, I told myself, is one of the few places women let go of these inhibitions and trust their bodies to move *big.* By hopping and squatting hundreds of women throughout the week, I was moving women toward self-realization.

Young also writes that in everyday life women "fail to summon the full possibilities of our muscular coordination, position, poise, and bearing."[††] I knew the high of that endorphin-assisted moment in the middle of each class when women summon the very core of their strength, and I had seen it shine. Maybe that's why I taught, because seeing and directing a room full of women who were summoning their full possibilities was a charge, even if the motive was ultimately less than feminist.

Finally, both Young and my hero Robin Morgan have argued that consciousness as a human being is related not to the intellect alone, but also to the body; the body is the vehicle through which everything comes to and goes from us. I think that maybe this is why I taught, as well: to dance, to connect with my body in a tangible way so that I could better connect with my intellect and assist others in doing the same. The process of strengthening the body could also strengthen women's ability to achieve our goals. Never mind that often those goals — to achieve a flat tummy, to fit into that tiny wedding dress, to lose ten pounds before going to Club Med to find Mr. Right — do not exactly subvert patriarchy. Creating a psychological space where women could move, really move, was the thrill. Teaching was my way of doing battle with the one idea expressed by Simone de Beauvoir that I vehemently disagreed with: that the female body is ultimately a burden. I tried to bring joy and movement into that body. In a word, I backwardly justified what I did as empowerment.

Interestingly, Young points out that her research does not include "movement that does not have a

---

[*]Roberta Pollack Seid, *Never Too Thin: Why Women Are at War with Their Bodies* (New York: Prentice Hall, 1989), p. 8.
[†]Iris Marion Young, *Throwing Like a Girl and Other Essays in Feminist Philosophy and Social Theory* (Bloomington: Indiana University Press, 1990), p. 143.

[††]Young, p. 145.

particular aim—for example, dancing." Ah. But dancing, aerobic dancing in particular, does have an aim, and this is where all of my aerobi-feminist convictions have turned on me. The aim, usually, is to be thin and beautiful, or as one of my fifty-year-old clients wrote on her release form, "to be 21 years old, 115 pounds, and Beautiful [sic]."

Women's fitness as we now know it truly is our newest patriarchal religion, based in principle as much on ritualized pain and suffering as any of the Judeo-Christian ones that came before it. No wonder nobody trusts Jane Fonda anymore. Fitness is a rigid religion of style, as debilitating and oppressive for many as a corset. Anorexics fill my classes like worshipers in a church, and no one stares. Other instructors starve themselves and do cocaine for energy with a regularity that would surprise many of their admirers. *She's so thin*, the members whisper admiringly in the locker room, *she looks great.* "In earlier centuries," writes Seid, "people who exhibited such mastery over hunger were categorized either as saints or as possessed by the devil, or, like the sixteenth-century Fasting Girl of Couflens, they were regarded as marvels whom travelers flocked to see. Today, that awe has become a horrified fascination, not because of the rarity of the phenomenon, but because of its increasing commonplaceness."*

So by the time I reached twenty-three, I really began to think about my priorities. Might it be worth going into debt to attend graduate school, just so that one day I could pull myself away from the contradictions? I thought about myself, about my assisting

other women to betray their potential. And it was a great relief to finally recognize the female obsession with thinness and fitness as an extension of the hurt we suffer at the hands of a patriarchal society, a society that even convinces us to hurt ourselves, so that we are kept from the real business of our lives.

I had to battle the hurt. I'd go into debt. I did. I am. Two years later I owe nearly forty thousand dollars in loans, but I have a gig as a staff writer for the *Boston Globe*, because my graduate degree from Columbia, while it might not have helped my writing, convinced some editors I was made of the right stuff.

This debt, the one I will have to feed from my bank account for the next couple of decades, is what happened to me because of my second-class citizenship and economic disadvantage. I was distracted for a time from the more serious pursuit of actually hustling to make a living as a writer and musician.

The *Globe* has given me a biweekly fitness column, something I find ironic but challenging. I try to avoid fueling fitness obsession. I've written columns on kid-friendly gyms, community centers that have programs for seniors, how to use objects in the home to strengthen muscles—anything that doesn't evoke spandex. I understand now that the gym has really become just another painful way we are all distracted from the serious business of our lives.

It seems that no matter how close I have gotten to empowerment through the modern fitness industry—women bosses and coworkers, good salary, the opportunity to connect with and help other women—there is still the knowledge that none of us, instructors or members, will ever reach our real goals playing by the rules of that industry, no matter how many inches we shed, no matter how much money we make.

---

*Seid, p. 21.

◆◆◆

FORTY-SIX

Tuna Fish

Barbara Garson

The conversations . . . are based on verbatim quotes. The characters are real. They are not creations or composites. The only thing I've done is to change people's names for their peace of mind and for my own.

Astoria, Oregon, is a town of ten thousand that sits on stone steps above the Columbia, just where it rolls into the Pacific. The town was first settled by one of Jacob Astor's fur-trading parties. Later it was settled by Scandinavian immigrants, many of them Finns, who came to fish. To this day most everyone in Astoria still does a little fishing, or puts their time in at one of the fish canneries.

Though it's August, the height of the salmon season, the big canneries have been letting out early. No one knows exactly what time they'll be let off. The time cards the women wear on their backs at Bumble Bee may be punched at 1:42 or 1:48 or 1:54. (Everything goes in tenths of the hour.) Whatever time it is, it will be too early for those who make their whole living at the cannery, though the youngsters who work for the summer may welcome the early release.

In every tavern in town there's the usual speculations: "It's just a bad season"; "It's the mercury they found near the docks"; "By God, we finally fished out the whole Columbia." These may be the long-range reasons for a declining catch, but the women in the canneries, those who face facts, know that the short-range reason for the short hours this summer is the contract they signed two years ago, a contract that was supposed to benefit the fulltime workers at the expense of the seasonal help.

"It's the 'casual workers' clause," a few women will say, as adamantly as others avoid the issue. "And the strike didn't settle a thing."

But the casual workers (now called probationary workers) clause is a complicated story which I only came to understand slowly. So perhaps I'd better let it unravel for the reader as it did for me.

Since nobody knows exactly what time the skinners and the cleaners will run out of fish, I waited at Bumble Bee's main plant starting at 1 P.M. I sat on a curb in the smelly yard next to a whiney-eyed man of thirty-two. He told me that he had been a photographer for *Life* magazine, that he knew Lawrence Ferlinghetti and that he was waiting for his girl friend Starlein, who was a tuna cleaner.

Starlein was one of the first cleaners out, after the skinners. She still had her white smock on, just like all the other women. But she came out undoing her white head scarf. She was already shaking her brown wavy hair free by the time she got to us. Most of the other women drove or walked home through town in their uniforms, with the white head scarves, knotted squarely in the front, covering every bit of hair.

Starlein's boyfriend hung on her from behind with his head dangling over her shoulder as he introduced us. I think it may have embarrassed or annoyed her. But I'm not sure, and no one else seemed to care.

Starlein was eighteen and pretty. She had a dreamy look when she talked or listened. She said she would be perfectly happy to tell me about her job.

"What do you do in the cannery?" I asked.

"I clean tuna," she said. "The loins come past me on a belt. [Loins are the skinned, headless, tailless, halved or quartered pieces of fish.] I bone the loin and take out the dark meat—the cat food. I put the clean loins on the second belt, the cat food on the third belt and I save my bones. You're not allowed to dump any garbage till the line lady okays it. Because that's how they check your work. They count your bones and see if they're clean."

"Do you talk a lot to the other women?" I asked.

"Not really," she answered.

"What do you do all day?"

"I daydream."

"What do you daydream about?"

"About sex."

"I guess that's my fault," her boyfriend apologized proudly.

"No, it's not you," she said. "It's the tuna fish."

I asked quite curiously what she meant.

"Well first it's the smell. You've got that certain smell in your nose all day. It's not like the smell out here. Your own fish next to you is sweet. And then there's the men touching you when they punch the tags on your back and maybe the other women on the line. But it's mostly handling the loins. Not the touch itself, because we wear gloves. But the soft colors. The reds and the whites and the purples. The most exciting thing is the dark meat. It comes in streaks. It's red-brown. And you have to pull it out with your knife. You pile it next to your loin and it's crumbly and dark red and moist like earth.

"You're supposed to put the cat food on the belt as you finish each loin. But I hold it out to make as big a pile of dark meat as I can."

"Well," I said, "aside from liking the dark meat, what do you think of your work?"

"I don't think about it," she said. "When I get there I put on the apron—we each have a plastic apron with our name in felt pen—and go to the line and wait for the buzzer. The first fish comes along and I pull it off the belt. [She made a heavy movement to show me.] And I just do it."

"I try not to look at the clock so the time will pass more quickly. When I do sometimes I'm surprised at how it went but more often I look and it's not even two minutes later. But there's not that much to complain about. When you're really into it you don't notice it. And then it feels so good when you pull a loin with a big dark vein of cat food.

"I knew it would be dull and boring when I came here. But I had no idea of the sensuous things I would feel just from cleaning fish. I came just to make some money fast."

"How much do you make?" I asked.

"I get something like $2.70 an hour, I think. They don't tell you exactly and I never asked. Mine is lower now because I'm on probation."

"Oh," I asked, "what did you do?"

"Oh no. It's just a thing. When you first come you don't get your real salary."

"How long does it last?" I asked.

"I don't know. But I don't think I'll stay that long."

"How do you get along with the older women?"

"The other women they're very nice. They show you how to tie up the scarves and how to get a good knife. And the line ladies don't bother you much either. At first they're on your back, always counting your bones or checking your cat-food pile. But when they see you're a good worker they don't bother you."

"Are you a good worker?" I asked.

"Sure, what else is there to do. Besides, I like to see how much cat food I can pile up." . . .

I was beginning to understand the casual workers controversy a little better. At their contract negotiations in 1971, the Amalgamated Meat Cutters and Butcher Workmen (Local P-554) had accepted the suggestion of the Columbia River Salmon and Tuna Packers Association that they create a category of "casual worker."

It was not a very new idea. Many canneries have a classification for seasonal workers who get lower pay and fewer benefits. It frequently happens that the casual workers become the majority and the regular employees are whittled down to a few full-time skilled workers and maintenance crew.

The clause accepted in Astoria called for about fifty cents an hour less for workers who stayed under four months. It passed without too much objection. (The summer workers aren't around when the contract is negotiated.) It didn't take long for the permanent women workers to see how the new clause would affect them.

The summer after the negotiations, the cannery was crowded with casual workers. There were jam-ups at the sinks, there weren't enough boards to stand on, there was barely enough room at the tables. But it wasn't really such a great season. People were actually being let off early. Even after the summer there didn't seem to be so much frozen tuna to pack.

Some people felt that the short hours in the summer—and the rest of the year—were because so much of the tuna had been processed by the plethora of summer workers at fifty cents an hour less. Of course some people always blame everything on the company's machinations. Others tend to blame it on the salmon run, the pollution, the will of God.

At the next negotiations there was enough feeling against the casual workers clause to cause a six-week strike. The settlement eliminated the "casual worker" and introduced a new "probationary worker." This was the summer to see whether the new term really made any difference.

Mary Hyrske lives in a tidy little house with a Christian fish symbol at the door.

She's sixty-one and she's worked for Bumble Bee for twenty-five years. She's been a cleaner, a skinner, a salmon slimer, a liver picker and now she takes the viscera out of the tuna.

"I tell young people when they're so tired and bored and disgusted, 'Every day gets better and better. Take it from me.'"

"Are the young people very different these days?" I asked.

"Not really. No. They want to do the best work they can. But they stick up for themselves to the bosses in a way we never would. They have their individual rights. Which is why I admire them."

I asked her if the pace of the work at the plant had changed very much over the years.

"Years ago we worked to help the other member out. You did a few extra fish and let it go towards someone else's quota. It wasn't hard for me to do a little extra. And I always felt, when I get older, then let someone else help me out. That's what the union would tell us. Bud, he was the union man here in 1950, he'd say, 'Do a few extra for the older workers.'"

I asked what if everyone slowed down a little for the older workers.

"Oh no, you can't do that. They know how many you can do. You just have to help your union brother and sister.

"But that just doesn't go anymore. Each one seems to be out for themselves. But I say what is life if you can't help one another out?"

And Mary told me how she had helped a young girl out that summer.

"I had a little Oriental girl, couple of months ago, come pick livers with me. [The viscera are used for fertilizer but the livers are kept out for cat food.]

"She was a sweet little Oriental girl and wanted to do it right. It wasn't but a couple of minutes before she was milking the livers right. There's a way of getting your hands around the liver so it slips right off. 'Milk it! Don't pick it!' our boss yells. If you pick it it comes off in pieces. Well she was getting it just right.

"Suddenly she turns around and says, 'Oh, I'm getting sick to my stomach.'

"'Oh that's not unusual,' I said. 'Honey, turn around, look at the water in the faucet, take three strong breaths and you'll be O.K.'

"It happened a couple of times. I tried to talk to her to keep her mind off it. By the end of the day she could do it fine.

"It's not the fish smell that actually bothers you. It's when you catch a whiff of perfume or deodorant, like from one of the tours going through. It brings the fish odor out."

Some of the younger girls had told me that there were older workers who would tell a line lady, "She's talking and not working" or "Look, she's chewing gum." I asked Mary what she thought of that as a union steward.

The tattling she agreed could get pretty bad. Most of the grievances she handled as steward were not strictly against the company. More often a member felt slighted because someone with less seniority was getting more overtime, or they felt they were bypassed for a bathroom break because someone else took too long.

"Would you complain," I asked, "if someone were breaking a rule?"

"I never would," she answered with great conviction. "I feel as union members we should protect our fellow workers. I would individually speak to my sister of the union and say, 'I'm not a line lady or a boss, but it's not our policy to chew gum.' And if I found a cigarette butt on the floor in the bath-room, I'd pick it up myself before the boss could make an issue."

Mary told me that she had been interested in the union before she had her family. She was inactive while the children were growing up but then became active again, though she wasn't a steward at the moment.

"I feel everyone should be involved and come to the meetings so they could understand and fight for their rights. But they don't come and then after the negotiations they feel the union pulled the wool over their eyes."

I asked how the casual workers clause had been accepted.

"Mr. Bugas explained to the negotiating committee — I wasn't on it; I was on the executive committee — how Bumble Bee needed a casual worker. I was opposed to it when I first heard of it. Mr. Mintron, I think his name was, from the international, he said that the older workers would benefit because all the pension funds from the casual workers would go into the retirement fund.

"I felt as an older worker it would benefit me, but I hated to see all the youngsters come back and take a cut like that.

"But Mr. Mintron, he said that the executive committee should vote for it here so we could present it to the members and let them discuss it."

"Did you speak against it at the membership meeting?" I asked.

"Well, Mr. Mintron, he didn't give us a chance to speak at the membership meeting. It wasn't that kind of a meeting. It was a meeting where the different members of the negotiating committee got up to speak about why it was a good contract. And I wasn't on the negotiating committee.

"But we had seventy-nine nevertheless. The vote was about seventy-nine to three hundred and fifty. But a day later everyone realized what the casual workers clause would do.

"I really don't understand how Mr. Mintron could bring up a casual workers clause and not speak against it himself."

I asked Mary if she was badly set back by the shorter hours. Another long-time worker, a skinner, had showed me her recent paychecks. There was nothing over $188 for the two-week period.

But it hadn't been too bad for Mary. Her husband worked at the Bumble Bee cold storage plant and the men were not as affected by the casual workers.

"Besides," she said, "we have to take it as it comes. We have to depend on the man from above. Salmon used to be plentiful years ago, but there were no tuna. When we run out of tuna he'll send something else." It's true there was pollution, and the casual workers clause and new laws against commercial fishing on the Columbia but . . . "If we have faith, I'm sure we'll have fish."

Nan Cappy lived way out of town in a small house on a big piece of land with a "For Sale" sign.

The kids were playing outside and I almost didn't recognize Nan when she stuck her head out of the door without her white head scarf. Now I saw that her brown hair was short-cropped and curled close around her head. Her nose and chin were small and pointy and her eyes were large and earnest.

Nan was from Detroit originally. She had had a lot of different jobs in her time. She'd worked in a dime store, a cafeteria, a bank, she'd even been a roller-skating messenger at a big studio in Hollywood.

Her husband had brought her here to the Northwest, which she loved and never wanted to leave. "The day we were married we had a family of four," she said. "My one and his three."

He is a log boomer for Crown Zellerbach. She has worked for Bumble Bee for the last four years.

Nan began telling me how things were changing at Bumble Bee.

"When I was first being trained if you just lifted your eyes up the line ladies would say, 'They're watching you' or 'Be careful. They're on the floor today.'

"I thought maybe they had a closed TV system. It was two weeks before I found out that 'they' meant the bosses, the men from the office.

"When I first came if you asked a question, said a single thing, the answer was always, 'Cannery workers are a dime a dozen.' That was the favorite line-lady expression.

"But in the last two years it's harder to get workers and it's harder to push those kids around. They're not so desperate for a job.

"The company is especially lax in the summer now. But they tighten up with the regular crew in the winter.

"I remember they had an efficiency expert, Bert, here one winter. He tried to keep everyone from talking. If he saw anyone talk he'd separate them. So I started talking to the other women wherever he put me. Even with the ones who didn't speak English. Finally he put me at the end of line B with two vacant spaces on one side and a pole on the other. So just to annoy him, I started talking to the pole.

"He was a bug about gum chewing too. People were getting letters in the mail, they looked like they came from the courts: 'First Offense — Gum Chewing,' 'Second Offense — Gum Chewing.'

"He's gone now, but every winter they have some kind of tightening up.

"The line ladies have to get out their line quotas, you know. So they figure out who they can push — the ones who really need the job. And believe me they push them. They're on their backs. 'There's too much white in your cat food. . . . Your loins aren't clean. . . . You haven't done your quota. You'll have to count bones.' And it gets on your nerves.

"Me I don't let them push. I'm a medium-speed worker whether anyone's watching or not.

"The line lady will come over and say, 'Oh come on now, I need fish' or 'Hey, I wanna finish this all up by three.'

"I said to one the other day, 'I'm working as fast as I can. You can take it or leave it.'

"She left it I guess because ten minutes later I was put on another line."

"Is it really a punishment to be put on another line?" I asked.

"No. Not necessarily. But you feel like a kid in school being stepped out by the monitor.

"Now some women can't work any faster no matter how much they're pushed. They just get upset. You can see their eyes tearing. Others speed up and those are the ones the line ladies will go for. I have this one friend, the line lady will always come over and say, 'Haven't you come back from vacation yet?' or 'I see it's still break time for you.' And Cless will speed up, cursing and saying, 'Goddamn, I'll show her.' But she's speeded up. She knows what's happening but she can't help it."

"What if you all slow down together?" I asked.

"The line ladies know right away if there's a slowdown. They'd just make you all count bones."

"Why is counting bones so awful?" I asked.

"For one thing they stand over you. And it's the same as being moved. Everyone knows you're being punished. No one likes to be punished or yelled at.

"Like one day Dick Fengs came over to me and he says, 'Spit it out!' Now it just happens I don't chew gum. So I says, 'Spit what out?' He says, 'Your gum.' I opened up my mouth real wide. He saw I had no gum, I'm sure. But he just says, 'Spit it out!' and walks away.

"The next day I got a pink slip. I tore it up right in front of him.

"He came over once and told me I was smoking in the bathroom. I said, 'But I don't smoke' (which I don't). He just says, 'Skin fish!' and he walks away. What can I do?

"I suppose I could go to the union but . . ." And here a genuine sigh forced its way out. Then she resumed her storytelling.

"One day someone passed out in the place. They stretch them out in the locker room when that happens. When they come to they ask them if they want to stay or go home and they usually say 'I'll stay' and just go right back.

"Well this one woman Violla fainted at nine-thirty and she was really sick. But her house was out of the city limits. So they said, 'We can't have someone take the time off to take her home.' It looked like they were just going to leave her there for all day. So I said, 'All right. I'll punch out and drive her home and punch back in.'

"So Fengs says, 'No. I'm sorry.'

"So I says, 'O.K. Then I'm going home for the day.'

"Then he says, 'All right. But be right back and don't stop.' Just for that I stopped for a cup of coffee.

"It's that kind of thing that makes you feel bitter. Why should you put out for them? Why should I care about a line lady who's rushing around saying she wants her fish by three-twelve? Why should you put out when you're nothing to them as soon as you stop skinning fish? You're not even as good as a machine, because they wouldn't leave a broken machine just sitting on a bench in the locker room.

"I remember once I got banged on the head with a crate of fish by a fish dumper. It didn't hurt at first but later it was bothering me. I said, 'Roach'—he's the timekeeper—'would you please record an accident.' He says, 'You know the dumper has the right of way.'

"I says, 'O.K., I know, but just write it down if something happens.'

"He says, 'Go to the line lady.' So I go to the line lady. And she says, 'Don't you know the dumper has the right of way?'

"'Look,' I said. 'I'm just asking you to write it down in case I wake up paralyzed. At least I want

an industrial accident reported. We can argue whose fault it was later.'

"Why must they do that? Why does the line lady think it's her job to make you feel like you're in the wrong all the time?

"A couple of those line ladies are kind of decent women too. But you know, they have a meeting every Friday to discuss the troublemakers. One of them even keeps a book where she writes down anyone who gives her any lip. . . . No, I never saw it, but she told me about it, as a kind of warning I guess."

I asked Nan if the women ever take action together when something seems unfair. She thought a bit.

"Oh yes, yes! One time. Every single skinner stood together once and we went to the union. Maybe because it was a matter of money," she added a little cynically.

"It was the company policy for years, and it was in the contract I believe, that if any skinners were working on large fish then all of the skinners were given a C punch—you know, on the cards on our backs. [A C punch is about nine cents an hour more than a B punch.] Well Mr. Bert Greene, our good old efficiency expert, noticed it and brought it up.

"One day there were two lines working on large fish—they're very heavy to haul and turn over, which is why more money—and the other lines are working on smaller fish. They had punched us all with a C punch as usual. Half an hour later they came by and punched all the lines down to a B punch except the one line that was left with large fish.

"We called the union on break. And naturally they told us that we were right but 'go ahead and work the job.' We went down to the union after work, all twenty-two of us.

"The business agent, Stella, told two of us to write it up. Then she told us we could have a meeting with Mr. Bugas. 'I want you to listen,' she said. 'We'll hear his point of view and we'll have another chance to answer.'

"Well Bugas was furious. He told us that under no circumstances was anyone going to be paid for big fish while they worked on small fish, not for any reason! I wonder what size fish he gets paid for.

"Well there was another meeting and again we were not supposed to talk. They did all the talking and it dragged on for weeks. Finally Stella says, 'It's in the contract but the company won't give it. But we're here to take up any other cause.'

"Well if we hadn't gone to the union in the first place but all twenty-two of us went into the office as angry as we were . . . but, when the women have a grievance they call the union.

"It's odd because once the women all stuck together against the union and the company. But that was for the men. The fishermen put up a picket. They wanted higher prices from the companies for the fish.

"Our union rep was out there telling us we had to cross. Bugas was foaming at the mouth ordering us to cross. Everyone told us it was an illegal picket line. But only a handful went in. Less than enough for one line. Maybe fifteen out of four hundred. Even the union stewards stayed out.

"But you see, that was a strike for the men.

"You know once I went into the office and said I wanted to train for the job of gitney driver. One of those little trucks the men use to lift and haul the crates of fish. I had watched all the men's jobs carefully and this was the one where you never had to do any heavy lifting.

"But the manager says 'Sorry, if a gitney driver drops a box off he'd have to get out and pick it up. And that could weigh more than thirty-five pounds.'

"Well I never saw that happen so I said, 'That must be rather rare. And if it does happen I could ask someone to help me lift it back.' You see that's the thing about the men's jobs. You're not standing there stuck at the line with a knife in one hand and a fish in the other. You could turn around and help someone.

"But he says, 'No. You might have to lift more than thirty-five pounds.' And he takes out the union contract. 'See it's right there. You can't lift more than thirty-five pounds.'

"I didn't bother to go to the union on that one.

"A lot of us feel the company has bought the union. Of course this woman Stella is elected. But no one ever runs against her.

"Last time a man was going to run against her. And I was for him. But out of the blue, a week before the election the company offered him a better job. Out of the blue.

"We told him he should run anyway but he said the new job paid much better than business agent. So Stella was elected again with no one running against her."

"Why didn't you run?" I asked.

"I considered it. But I couldn't have. It turns out there's a rule that you have to have attended a majority of union meetings throughout the year. And you have to be nominated a month before and this was only a week before. So . . ."

Nan was fingering a swelling chord in her neck. When she talked about the union she had none of the gusto she had when she talked about her skirmishes with line ladies or with Fengs.

I asked her about the casual workers clause.

"I spoke against it two years ago. I said we'd be working short shifts all summer. But the union said I was wrong. They'd never find enough people to fill the place up.

"Now some of those women think, 'Why should a kid get what I've worked for?' And Bugas plays upon that. And the others, they just believe the company and the union. It's like banging your head against the wall. That's when I really want to quit."

And then with despair and pain and pity:

"The union has done it to these women so many times. So many times . . .

"They finally got themselves together to strike. A six-week strike. (Leave it to our union to have a contract that expires before the season so you can strike for a month without hurting the company.) But those women struck for six weeks. And the union comes back with this probationary workers thing. They get thirty cents an hour less until four hundred and eighty hours. But we won, they say. There's no more casual workers.

"I could have told the women to hold out. That the company would still fill the place up with as many casual workers as they wanted. But what's the use? Why should they keep on striking when no matter what they do the union will still sell them out?"

I could see Nan's throat throbbing.

"I feel it's useless. Every contract time we'd have to fight the company *and* the union. That's when I feel like quitting."

I could feel the knot tightening in her neck. I could sense her anguish at being "used" and I wanted to say something to ease it.

Actually most of the women I talked to knew they were being used by the company and sold out by their union. But they had all evolved some funny little philosophy to explain why it had to be that way, or why they shouldn't pay any attention.

I wondered why Nan, who had worked at Bumble Bee for four years, was not better insulated by cynicism or fatigue against the humiliations of the job.

I liked Nan Cappy in her angular earnestness. I almost wanted to say, "Wait! I'll get a job here and we'll really organize this place."

But I was a reporter, so I just thanked her for her time, and the fresh-picked berries and the pleasant afternoon my little girl spent with her little girl.

◆◆◆

FORTY-SEVEN

He Works, She Works, but What Different Impressions They Make

Have you ever found yourself up against the old double standard at work? Then you know how annoying it can be and how alone you can feel. Supervisors and coworkers still judge us by old stereotypes that say women are emotional, disorganized, and inefficient. Here are some of the most glaring examples of the typical office double standard.

The family picture is on HIS desk:
Ah, a solid, responsible family man.

The family picture is on HER desk:
Hmm, her family will come before her career.

HIS desk is cluttered:
He's obviously a hard worker and busy man.

HER desk is cluttered:
She's obviously a disorganized scatterbrain.

HE'S talking with coworkers:
He must be discussing the latest deal.

SHE'S talking with coworkers:
She must be gossiping.

HE'S not at his desk:
He must be at a meeting.

SHE'S not at her desk:
She must be in the ladies' room.

HE'S having lunch with the boss:
He's on his way up.

SHE'S having lunch with the boss:
They must be having an affair.

HE'S getting married.
He'll get more settled.

SHE'S getting married:
She'll get pregnant and leave.

HE'S having a baby:
He'll need a raise.

SHE'S having a baby:
She'll cost the company money in maternity benefits.

HE'S leaving for a better job:
He recognizes a good opportunity.

SHE'S leaving for a better job:
Women are undependable.

HE'S aggressive.

SHE'S pushy.

HE'S careful.

SHE'S picky.

HE loses his temper.

SHE'S bitchy.

HE'S depressed.

SHE'S moody.

HE follows through.

SHE doesn't known when to quit.

HE'S firm.

SHE'S stubborn.

HE makes wise judgments.

SHE reveals her prejudices.

HE is a man of the world.

HE isn't afraid to say what he thinks.

HE exercises authority.

HE'S discreet.

HE'S a stern taskmaster.

SHE'S been around.

SHE'S opinionated.

SHE'S tyrannical.

SHE'S secretive.

SHE'S difficult to work for.

FORTY-EIGHT

◆◆◆

the cleaning woman/labor relations #4

Hattie Gossett

the doctors knew.

the lab people knew.

the secretaries knew.

the volunteers knew.

the patients knew.

the clinic was moving to a new spot and would be closed for a while and everybody knew ahead of time.

everybody except the cleaning woman.

she only found out on closing day.

i dont know why no one thought to tell you before this the woman doctor said to the cleaning woman over the phone annoyance all up in her voice at being asked by the cleaning woman why they hadnt given her an earlier notice.

i dont know why no one thought to tell you. anyway i have patients now and have no time for you.

it was the cleaning womans dime so she went for broke. but i am dependent on the salary you pay me and now suddenly it wont be there she protested. wouldnt it be fair to give me some kind of severance pay?

severance pay! shrieked the woman doctor. look she snapped you havent been with us that long. only a few weeks. besides i have help at home you know and i . . .

its like this the cleaning woman interrupted not wanting to hear about the doctors help at home (at least not what the doctor was going to say) when

you work for a salary you need some kind of reasonable notice when its going to be discontinued so you can prepare yourself. how would you like it if you were in my place?

the woman doctor then tried to offer the cleaning woman a job in the new clinic plus a job in her own new private office but neither of these jobs would start for some weeks. she never did say how she would feel being in the cleaning womans place. the cleaning woman realized she was dealing with people who really didnt care about her. as far as they were concerned she could starve for those few weeks. she wondered how long you would have to work for these people before it was long enough for them to tell you at least 2weeks ahead of time that they were closing. how long is long enough?

forget it the cleaning woman told the woman doctor. she was pissed. she didnt like knowing that she was being shafted and that there wasnt anything she could do. when do you want me to bring back your keys? because she cleaned at night or very early in the morning she had keys to the clinic.

as soon as the woman doctor said anytime in a somewhat startled voice the cleaning woman hung up. she didnt slam down the phone. she put it down gently. but she didnt say goodbye or have a nice day.

damn the cleaning woman said to herself after she had hung up. here these people are supposed to be progressive and look at how they act. here they are running an alternative clinic for lesbians and gays and straights and yet they treat their help just as bad as the american medical association fools treat theirs. are they really an alternative she asked herself.

sure they treat their help bad herself answered laughingly.

the cleaning woman looked up a little surprised because she hadnt heard herself come in. now herself sat down and started eating some of the cleaning womans freshly sliced pineapple.

what do you mean girlfriend the cleaning woman asked herself.

have you forgotten that every sister aint a sister and every brother aint a brother herself began. where did you get this pineapple? its really sweet and fresh.

come on now. dont play games. tell me what you mean the cleaning woman said.

look herself said. some of these sisters and brothers aint nothing but secondhand reprints out of the bidness as usual catalogue in spite of all their tongue flapping to the contrary. and these secondhand reprints can be worse than the originals. like they have to prove that they know how to abuse

people even more coldheartedly than the originals do. its getting harder and harder to tell the real alternatives from the rank rapscallions. of course everybody else on the staff knew that the gig was moving but you. in their book you aint nothing no way.

what could the cleaning woman say?

herself was right once again and the cleaning woman tried to tell herself this but that girl didnt hear anything cuz she had already tipped on out taking the last piece of pineapple with her.

so the cleaning woman laughed for a minute. then she stopped brooding over those fools at the clinic.

she got on the phone and started lining up some more work.

later she sat down and wrote this story which she put in the envelope with the clinic keys. she wrote the woman doctors name on the front of the envelope cuz she wanted to be sure the woman doctor would be able to share the story. at the bottom of the story the cleaning woman put not to be copied or reproduced by any means without written permission from the author.

cuz one monkey sho nuff dont stop no show.

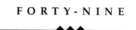

FORTY-NINE

Carol Ann Roberson
Vocational Rehabilitation Supervisor

Harilyn Rousso

Carol Ann Roberson, a supervisor of rehabilitation counseling at the Rusk Institute for Rehabilitation Medicine, which is part of the New York University Medical School, questions a southern black man, trying to find out about his background and what kind of work he likes to do. He is aphasic, which means he has difficulty speaking. At his second interview, he brought Carol Ann a piece of cotton to illustrate what he picked at his job. Carol Ann got him a job in a restaurant kitchen where he began washing lettuce, eventually working his way up to making pies. Then he became a hotel dishwasher. Now he is a bellhop at a New York City hotel, making about $350 a week.

Carol Ann, who is quadriplegic as a result of polio and uses a motorized wheelchair, provides job counseling to people with a range of disabilities. As a first step, she encourages her clients to fantasize about the type of work they might like to do. For example, she asks them

> to write down the kinds of things that they like to do. Then we pull out the qualities from these things that they find enjoyable. For instance, you discover that the person enjoys doing things alone, or maybe he or she prefers to be with lots of people. Then you make a sheet of the

pros and cons of fifteen or so jobs that the client has heard about from family and friends and thinks he or she might like. You go through the list and ask, "What do you think you would like about these jobs and what do you think you would hate." And then you pull out the qualities from that and as you go along you begin to find that you have some issues to look at in terms of what kind of work is the person really interested in.

Carol Ann counsels both recently disabled people and those who have had disabilities from birth. For the last two and one-half years, she has also worked with cancer patients who are undergoing rehabilitation. She helps them deal with the reaction of others to their cancer when they return to work after operations, chemotherapy, or radiation treatments. In addition to her direct work with clients, Carol Ann supervises six other rehabilitation counselors. She meets with them weekly to review their work with clients, brainstorm problems, strengthen their counseling skills, and ensure that they meet reporting and other agency requirements.

Before she was hired for this job, Carol Ann graduated from Hunter College, and then earned a master's degree in social work in a two-year program at New York University. Although she was never trained as a rehabilitation counselor, she gained her certification in the field by passing a written examination developed and administered by the National Commission on Rehabilitation Counselor Certification. The more typical route is for a person to obtain a master's degree in rehabilitation counseling, which is also a two-year program, and then to take the certification exam, although not all jobs require certification in order to practice. The beginning salary for a rehabilitation counselor is $15,000 to $18,000. A supervisor can earn as much as $35,000 to $40,000.

Carol Ann got polio when she was five years old. The disease, also called infantile paralysis, damages nerve cells in the spinal cord. Until a vaccine was developed by Dr. Jonas Salk in the 1950s, polio epidemics were common. Carol Ann's illness left her arms and legs paralyzed.

There were a number of people on my block in Brooklyn who had gotten polio. This was right before Salk [the vaccine] came out and in fact there was a major epidemic in the Midwest. One of the reasons that they believe my dis-

ability is as severe as it is, is because there were no ambulances with respirators [devices to help keep a patient breathing] to take me to the Sister Kenny facility [a special hospital for polio patients located in New Jersey]. They just let me stay at City Hospital. All the ambulances with respirators had gone out west to take care of the epidemic out there.

The oldest of four children in an Italian family, Carol Ann grew up on Manhattan's Lower East Side. Once she became disabled, her fear was always that her parents would move to some inaccessible new place in the suburbs.

At one point—I was about eleven—my parents were thinking about buying a house. I can remember praying and wishing and doing all sorts of things so they would never buy it because the house was way out in Queens somewhere. All I could think was, "I am going to be stuck on this little block in Queens with a tree, and I'll never be able to do anything." Because I was close to the Village [Greenwich Village, a Manhattan neighborhood], close to my friends, and uptown, I could go and do whatever I wanted to, once I got my motorized wheelchair when I was ten.

Carol Ann played with several close friends in her neighborhood. For the most part, they adapted to her limitations, often in very creative ways. According to Carol Ann:

When we played jump rope, they would tie one end of the rope to my chair rather than have someone else turn it, so that I really participated. Or if we played a game like skelzey [where you go from box to box on a chalk board you make up on the ground], someone would shoot my bottle cap when it was my turn.

Carol Ann describes her parents as extremely overprotective. They were reluctant to let her go out of the house by herself or even with her friends for fear that she would fall out of her wheelchair or be hurt in other ways. However, Carol was quite adventuresome and social; she loved to be out exploring the world with her friends. So she had to figure out ways to work around her parents' fears. Carol says she really appreciated what one girlfriend did. She "crossed the street with my wheelchair 150 times when the street had been freshly cemented to prove that she could cross with me — through the wheelchair track marks — so my mom would let me go to the movies with a group of kids." Often Carol found herself "doing things first and telling my mother later" in order to do the things she wanted to do. Eventually, her parents became less fearful.

In the 1950s, when Carol began school, mainstreaming was unheard of. Disabled kids didn't go to school with nondisabled kids. So Carol Ann was bussed away from her neighborhood to an elementary school with a class for disabled children.

> I was bussed every day. I lived the closest to the school, but they took the kids who lived furthest away home first so I was one of the last ones to be dropped off. That meant that I travelled around. If I got out of school at two o'clock, I would get home at five o'clock. It was horrible.

Carol also spent part of her elementary school years on home instruction, which meant that a teacher came to her house once or twice a week to provide lessons in all the different subjects.

At home, Carol had fewer hours of instruction than she would have received had she attended school, and no opportunity to learn with other children. If bussing was difficult, so was being required to stay home.

Carol's parents were concerned that she was not receiving as good an education as her nondisabled friends. So they joined forces with parents of other disabled children to push the Board of Education to provide more and better schools for children with disabilities. In high school, Carol Ann was again bussed, but she was mainstreamed into the school, except for homeroom. The school had an elevator and was basically accessible. Carol Ann took whatever courses she wanted. Usually she took her own notes with a pencil in her mouth. Or she remembered the materials and wrote it down after the class. Occasionally, she would bring carbon paper and ask someone to take notes for her. Unfortunately, Carol Ann could not participate in extracurricular activities because she had to leave immediately after school on the bus. In the summer, however, she went to camp with other young people with disabilities. This was a good experience because "there was a real feeling of participating with other people, and not being different." She also got involved in crafts and singing.

After high school, Carol Ann attended Manhattan Community College and then entered Hunter College. She says she attended Manhattan Community College because she couldn't convince any other school to take her.

> The way that I originally got in was I wrote to then-Senator Keating and said I really wanted to go to school and the Office of Vocational Rehabilitation (OVR) would not provide me with transportation. My feeling was either they pay for me now for the next four years, or they could pay for me for the rest of my life [with benefits] because that was what was going to happen. It was a brand new school, and I graduated with the first class after two years.

Then Hunter College accepted her, but not without reservations. The administration at Hunter did not want to give her any "special accommodations."

> Hunter originally would not take me. Then they said that if I ever asked anyone to help me go to the bathroom, or do anything, they would expel me from school. I was ushered into the dean's office and told this. It was so devastating. Each time I remember it I get goose bumps, it was so horrible. I mean, it's scary to go to a school in the beginning, to think you're going to meet people and worry about whether you are going to be as good as they are, and then to be told you better not want to go to the bathroom!

While she was still at Manhattan Community College, some of Carol's friends applied for a work-study program (combining a part-time job with classes) and persuaded her to apply along with them. Carol told them, "You've got to be crazy. They're never going to hire me to do anything." But they persisted, telling her she should at least give the counselor in charge of the program "a chance to say no."

> Mr. Chase [the counselor at the school] really looked and said to me: "If you can find a work placement near where you live, we'll sponsor you there." And so I went around and he called around and someone had a contact with the Educational Alliance, a tremendous old settlement house, three blocks from my house. And that's how I got my job as a lounge aide there. It was just answering phones, watching that no one

stole the balls at the pool table, and that the radio was not too loud. This job eventually led to more responsible positions, and was a big factor in my decision to go into social work. Then, when I was in social work school, they said they couldn't find a field work replacement [an internship] for me in my second year. That's when I suggested the Educational Alliance because I was still working there. You're not supposed to work while you're in social work school, but I had gotten a taste of the good life and I wasn't going to give that up.

Carol Ann met her husband Carl at the Educational Alliance while he was working with a youth program. They started off as friends and their relationship kept growing.

Carl and Carol Ann have now been married for fifteen years, and they have two daughters, Nicole and Giovanna, ages thirteen and eleven. Family life hasn't always been easy. Carl is black and Carol Ann is white. At first, Carol Ann's parents found it hard to accept her husband. They were concerned about the racial differences. Also, because of the severity of her disability, her parents had never expected her to get married. While they thought she would have a career, they could not imagine her living independently from them. They didn't believe that Carl or any husband would be willing or able to provide her with all the physical assistance that she needed. Carol acknowledges that she had similar fears at first.

How much could I ask this man to do for me? I needed so much help. On the other hand, I recognized that everyone tends to overlook what I can give. Disabled people are never seen as being able to give; they're only seen as being able to get.

And both she and her parents had some initial worries about her having children.

When my kids were younger, I can remember always being afraid. If something happened to Carl, someone would possibly take my kids away from me because the expectation might be that I couldn't do it alone.

When Carol announced she was pregnant with her second child, her mother's response was, "Are you crazy?! Why would you do such a thing?" Carol Ann's mother was afraid she would never be able to manage with two children. Carol Ann's response was to get angry at her mother. She felt that she and Carl should be entitled to make the same decisions about the number of children they wanted as any other couple.

In fact, they figured out a way to manage which has become increasingly popular today. They decided that Carl would quit his job and become a househusband, staying home with the children full-time, while Carol Ann continued to work and support the family. They divided tasks within the home. For example, Carol Ann was the disciplinarian and the more organized one.

In raising her children, Carol Ann found alternative ways to parent.

With my kids I learned to read upside down. I couldn't hold the book so they could sit on my lap and read with me. They could sit in front of me and hold the book, facing them — so I learned to read upside down and I can do it pretty well. It's not a skill I'm going to use all the time, but it certainly is a skill that helped in terms of doing a functional thing with my children.

Time and experience put to rest any fears Carol Ann had about being a parent. People too often concentrate only on the physical aspects of childrearing; Carol Ann learned she had a lot more to offer her children.

One of the therapists at work was saying to me, "Your kids are so terrific. You really did a good job. They are beautiful and I don't just mean physically. They're beautiful people. And I think that's partially because you work at those other kinds of things that sometimes people leave out because they are so into the physical."

Carol Ann often wonders how people see her and her husband.

I think people have questions when they see us together. I'd love to be in their minds. They think, "What is he doing with her, and what does he get from being with her? Is he a saint?" Carl *is* a special person, but not because he's done this supposedly humanitarian thing of marrying me, a disabled woman. It has more to do with who he is as a person and how easily he can get past the exterior of anyone. I've seen him in the elevator talk to people who no one else has talked to in years. That's the kind of person he is.

There are men out there who come on to every woman, but when they get to me, it is a totally different relationship. While on the one hand, a come-on is not exactly what I want, on the other, I wonder how they see me. I am not the ideal of physical beauty, at least not the one that is in vogue. They probably think that I cannot give anything. They have a limited view of what giving and a loving relationship are all about.

When asked what advice she would give to teenage girls with disabilities, Carol Ann says:

Don't be afraid to explore and try. If it doesn't work, it doesn't work—but O.K., so you tried.

It's just like anybody else. Things are not always going to go the way you want them to go, and that's not necessarily because you have a disability. That's because that's the way life is; it's tough sometimes. Things don't always work out. If you take a chance, it might not work out, but it *could.* And it wouldn't work out if you didn't take the chance.

Author's Note: Since this chapter was written, Carol Ann Roberson has moved to a new position as the Director of the Mayor's Office for the Handicapped in New York City. This office, which has a staff of forty people, serves as the link between the disabled community and city government. Carol Ann oversees new legislation, new ideas, and a range of services and activities of benefit to people with disabilities.

FIFTY

◆◆◆

Organizing Immigrant Women in New York's Chinatown
An Interview with Katie Quan
Ruth Milkman

One of the most celebrated events in women's labor history is the "Uprising of the 20,000," the huge garment workers' strike that took place during 1909 and 1910 in New York City. This legendary "girls' strike," which transformed the International Ladies' Garment Workers' Union (ILGWU) into a modern industrial union, demonstrated the previously untapped potential for militancy among young female Jewish and Italian immigrant workers, and dramatically challenged the conventional stereotypes of the era, which constructed women workers as passive and uninterested in unionism. As Samuel Gompers said in 1910: "The strike. . . brought to the consciousness of the nation a recognition of . . . the extent to which women are taking up with industrial life, their consequent tendency to stand together in the struggle to protect their common interests as wage earners, the readiness of people in all classes to approve of trade-union methods in behalf of working women, and the capacity of women as strikers to suffer, to do, and to dare in support of their rights."*

In 1982, another labor struggle shook the New York garment industry. Once again, twenty thousand women workers took to the streets to defend their rights. As in 1909, the strike leaders were young immigrant women — always the bulk of the garment industry's work force. This time, however, they were not Jewish and Italian, but Chinese women. In contrast to the situation in 1909, at the start of the 1982 strike, the workers involved were already union members. They belonged to Sportswear Local 23–25

---

*This is from Gompers' report to the 1910 convention of the American Federation of Labor, cited in Louis Levine's classic history of the ILGWU, *The Women's Garment Workers: A History of the International Ladies' Garment Workers' Union* (New York: B. W. Huebsch, 1924), p. 166.

of th
overv

T
nese
ment
decli
acced
conc
itself
ing i
"Am
job l
enin
in th
took
tanc
to ga
Loca
on t
and
in pa
tow

deca
less
isola
tieth
has
Yet i
mov
tem
tent
wor
U.S.
day
the
gar
wor
inte

con
Cal
wh
org
197
stri
ove
a su
per

Nobody *wanted* to work at home, that I ever met. They would get out of the situation as soon as they could find somebody to take care of their kids.

RM: Did people ever bring their children to the factories?

KQ: Yes, that was another alternative. It was also pretty dangerous and more than once we heard of kids falling out of the windows of the lofts. When we were starting our day care organizing, we went to this one building and workers on several floors told us in a very hushed voice that just the week before a kid had fallen out of a window. Other women arranged private baby-sitting, but you know in the New York tenements, private baby-sitting's often not the best. For instance, I had a girl-friend who took her kid to this old lady who had nine cribs in her tenement apartment. My friend says, "God, if there's a fire, which one does she take first?" Sometimes also the parents would just lock up the kids at home, where they could get into all kinds of mischief. There were no really good alternatives. So we decided to organize around the issue.

It wasn't so easy to do. In the beginning, I really wasn't prepared for organizing women with young children. I had organized in my shop, I had organized tenants, I had organized Chinese restaurant workers, but I still wasn't prepared for the experiences that I had then. Organizing young women with kids turned out to be real different from organizing men. With the Chinese restaurant workers, who had unionized just before this, and who were all men, if you'd have a meeting, they'd basically come on time. Of course, you'd have to hold the meeting where they wanted it, and at the times they wanted to meet. I had meetings at my house at one o'clock in the morning be-cause that's when all the waiters get off work. Also you couldn't interfere with them going to the racetrack—and in fact if you wanted cards signed you went to the racetrack to look for them on their off days. But still, the men were much more used to dealing with matters out-side of household matters. They didn't do the kinds of things that would happen routinely in day care organizing.

With the women, you'd set a meeting for one o'clock, and people would come in at two, three, whenever the kids got up from naps. And they brought the kids with them. They didn't want to meet when it was a cold season, because the kids would catch each other's colds. They didn't want to meet, obviously, when it was raining and snowing because they didn't want to bring their kids in on the sub-way in bad weather. And when we finally managed to have a meeting, it was hard to keep it focused. They'd talk in one sentence about day care and then, in the same sentence, they'd start talking about their kids, about changing diapers and all that stuff. I'd always have to drag the discussion back to day care. It was so frustrating in the beginning because you'd set out to accomplish something for a certain meeting and you'd just feel like you'd never get there. So I started calling people up the night before, after the kids were asleep, and basically going through the whole meet-ing, you know, when I could just talk to them one-on-one. I had to go through the whole meeting ahead of time with each person. Then by the time we got together, we could just agree upon what was going on. But I'd never had to do that before in mixed situations or with men only.

Also, besides myself, there was just one other person who spoke English. The others didn't, and they weren't really educated that well even in Chinese. Most of them had just a couple of years of schooling. So things that you needed for an organizing campaign, like writing press releases and stuff like that—we didn't do much of it in the beginning. In the end, yes, we learned how to do it, but this was a huge effort. Also, we were not used to going and talking with union officials, or day care ex-perts, both of whom were very intimidating to us. We were a different class of person and we weren't used to talking with big shots. Basic things like language and knowledge of the sys-tem make a big difference. I'm thinking about a group of women we're organizing right now who are all English-speaking. Some of them are black, some are Hispanic, and some are white. One or two are immigrants, but mostly they're not. And they're so much more able to do things for themselves. If I just say, "Write a letter to the Board," they come up with a letter. They'd say, "Okay, we're going to have this demonstration, we've got to get so-and-so to support us." So they'd write down which organizations they wanted to get support from and then they'd go out and get it. Whereas with the immigrant women you would have to basically go with them each time. It gets into a whole lot of things—like transportation, for instance, often they don't know how to get around.

With the day care organizing, our whole idea was that, well, we are Chinese members and Chinese members contribute $3.5 million in dues to the union each year. So the union should do this for us. But none of us were active members of the union, none of the people in the union knew who we were. I used to go to union meetings and say some things in the meetings sometimes, but I was never a shop steward, I was never active in the union in any way. And I didn't know anybody who was.

We decided that they were not going to take us seriously unless we proved the need for day care. We had a press conference to launch the whole thing. It was big news, all over the newspapers. We had babies in our arms crying and stuff. Then we circulated a petition and we got about three thousand signatures in ten days. We went up and down the factories using the bosses' P.A. systems to say what we were there for, and about 99 percent of the people in every shop signed. After we got people to sign the petition, we took it to the union. The union's response was that we didn't have to go around and have a petition signed, because the union is for day care. "Why couldn't you've just come talk to us?" they said. And in fact Local 23–25, the local that most of the Chinese belong to, had looked into day care earlier. They even sent a couple of people down to Philadelphia to look at the day care center down there, but they had figured out that there wasn't enough money and so they just dropped the idea. But once we made it a very pressing issue, Jay Mazur, then the manager of Local 23–25, formed a committee composed of civic leaders and people who

were knowledgeable about day care. Susan Cowell was the union staff person assigned to it. She made it happen as far as the administrative side went. She found out that the city agency that administered the city child care centers was looking for models other than just strictly government-financed day care. And because of what we had done, all the community hype that we had gotten over this thing, the employers wanted to show that they were good guys, too. So they had a fundraising banquet and raised about $30,000. The union got this put aside as seed money for the day care center, and it became a cooperative effort between the union and the employers. We found out that there was a day care center that had been built in Chinatown in the mid-1970s, but it had never opened because of lack of funding. The building was occupied by some city department, but it had all these day care facilities. So the site was there. The pieces came together very well. The center opened in late 1983 and had its formal dedication in January 1984, about three years after we started our campaign.

RM: This is basically a story of cooperation between the union and the employers. Yet right in the middle of it came the 1982 strike, which was a dramatic example of exactly the opposite. How did the strike come about? How could the two take place at the same time?

KQ: In 1982, the union contracts were up for renewal. In New York they have master agreements, so everybody's contract is up at the same time. The union negotiated a contract with the manufacturers and then went on to negotiate a contract with the contractors' association. All the Chinatown sportswear contractors belonged to the association, they made up about 70 percent of the contractors in it. At some point, the Chinese contractors balked because they said the contract was negotiated without representation from them. They said it was discriminatory, and they refused to sign the contract. So the workers were faced with the possibility of losing their union benefits. The contractors had assumed that they could get the workers to side with them, both being Chinese. They thought that the Chinese workers would stick with the Chinese bosses, but it didn't work like that. The Chinese workers were not that dumb! They said, "You're talking about—here go my medical benefits, what's my family supposed to do? I've worked nineteen years and next year I get to retire. You're saying I can't collect my pension? Forget this!" At the same time, they wanted to reduce holidays by three and to do some other outrageous things.

The response of the workers destroyed the myth that Chinese workers don't stand up for their rights because they work for Chinese bosses or because they're from the same part of China, or related in some way—the idea that national interests prevail over class interests. I really don't think that it's too helpful to make overly broad generalizations. There are situations where national interests are more important than class interests, but it depends on the issue and on the way it's organized. You can appeal to either interest to promote whatever you want to promote. I think that it's possible to use issues of ethnicity in organizing workers as workers. And probably in some cases, where ethnic identity is very strong, it's just about essential to do it. But that doesn't mean that ethnicity is overridingly more powerful than class under all circumstances.

Anyway, after the contractors refused to sign, the union sent out letters to workers asking if they wanted to be on a committee to fight for the contract, and they got five thousand postcards back. But then they never put the committee together. They never had a meeting until I forced the issue by saying, "Well, we have this committee. When did you have a meeting?" So on the spot, they set up a meeting for us. I brought my whole shop and that was a really big shock at that time. It was all the seamstresses, fifty of us. We all went up to the union office. This was no small feat because we worked in Chinatown, we had to take the subway and walk a couple of long blocks to get to the union office on Twenty-eighth Street. There were another four or five other people there from other shops, but it was mainly us. They went through the list of demands and said what the union was doing, and the workers in my shop wanted to know what we could

do. Someone came up with the idea that we should help leaflet. So at five o'clock the next day, everybody put down what they were working on and left their seats. We all went to the corner where the leaflets were supposed to be distributed, took the leaflets and started handing them out. It was great! I had a girlfriend who worked in Chinatown who passed by and was handed a leaflet by this middle-aged Chinese lady. Later she says to me, "My God, it's so different! Usually, it's us giving leaflets to them. Now, they're giving leaflets to us!" And so everybody in my shop did this.

The next day, the union called up on the telephone and they said, "Over at the radio station they need somebody to talk on the radio as to why the workers want a union." I told a couple of the key people in our unit and they said, "Well, let's all go." So, at two o'clock in the afternoon, we just all left and went to the radio station. It was on the Bowery, two or three stories up, and the staircase was only about three feet wide, and you've got fifty people just crowding, lining the stairways and down on the street. The head of the radio station got really upset at first, he thought we were having a demonstration against him. And you know, it was the first time any of us had been on the radio. It was funny, they had this big mike on a boom, and it was very intimidating. We got all nervous, but it was good, we did it, and then we went back to work.

Everybody was talking about the strike. It was on the radio that's piped into the factories, and it was being debated in the Chinese newspapers and everything. The whole community was talking about it. People were calling each other at night to talk about it on the phone. You would meet people in the stores shopping for vegetables and you'd hear about it. People would be talking about it on the subways. It was really the talk of the town. And overwhelmingly the workers were pissed off at the bosses and wanted the union contract. Our shop was no exception, we'd talk about it. And they told me that I should go call Jay Mazur and I should tell him we want a union contract and we want a strike and we don't care if we don't have strike benefits. We've got to have a union contract. So I would call Jay and I would tell him what the workers were saying and he would just listen very intently; this happened for days on end. I was telling him we should strike.

At that time I went to work for the union to prepare for a strike for a couple of weeks. The union was doing some things to try to bring forward some of the more active people. They put a number of people on staff who were active, and we had meetings in the Chinatown office and in the Roosevelt Auditorium in Union Square. To think about organizing twenty thousand people was not an easy task, especially if you start from ground zero. But you know, everybody was galvanized. Some people even went on wildcats. They walked out when their boss said they weren't going to sign the contract and they came up to the union office. Meanwhile, we were preparing frantically. We were making picket signs and banners and all this. And the union had a big rally in the heart of Chinatown, in Columbus Park. Fifteen to twenty thousand people were at that rally. It was just huge, and it was all these Chinese garment workers. There they were with their picket signs and their hats and everything. We got some militant women up there from some of the shops to give some really dynamite speeches and it was really, really inspiring. It was something that all of us were proud to be a part of. And after that, the union began to go around and sign individual contracts with individual employers. Instead of dealing with the contractors' association, the union decided to try to get them to sign individual contracts, which most of them did. But by the deadline that the union had set, there were still 75 to 100 employers who had not signed, out of 450 in Chinatown. So we had another big rally and a march through Chinatown and then we set up picket lines in front of shops that hadn't signed. The workers were told, "If the name of your shop is on that sign, then your shop is on strike and don't go up there." It only took a morning; by one o'clock all the rest had signed up. This was really, really fantastic!

Everybody learned a lot from the strike. The bosses learned, well, you can't mess with the garment workers. As the Chinese say,

"When the fire burns to the hairs on your skin, then they'll really move." And the union leaders saw that the Chinese workers do fight, whereas they may have had their doubts because maybe they thought that the bosses' appeal based on ethnicity may have worked, or that they're women, they don't speak English, so therefore they won't fight—all these myths. But this really showed the union leaders that the Chinese women do fight and that they have to be much more responsive to what the Chinese workers need. As far as the Chinese workers are concerned, we stunned ourselves as well, you know. Remember how I was telling you how difficult it is just to put one piece-rate struggle together? You face an awful lot of that in your everyday life and you think, "Well, god, I can't even get these people together to sit down and wait for a few pennies more on a piece rate—how are we going to be able to do this?" But people really came out and came forward.

All this happened the summer after we had presented petitions about day care to the union. And it was after the strike that we started to get great response on the day care issue. It wasn't a straight connection, but the idea that the Chinese workers were important to the union and the union really had to do what it could to look after the welfare of the Chinese workers was made obvious by that whole struggle. At the same time, the employers were looking for some way to make themselves look good under those circumstances. And so the whole idea of cooperating with the union to provide funding for this day care center came up when both sides were looking for ways to mend the fences.

RM: What was the impact of all this on the garment workers' union itself, and on the composition of its leadership? For a long time the ILGWU leadership has been dominated by native-born males, even though the membership is made up mainly of immigrant women. Has that changed?

KQ: Well, the successful outcome of the 1982 strike really showed that the union could and would fight in the interests of Chinese garment workers. To that extent, it gained renewed respect among the members and also in the community at large. More people began to turn to the union as spokesperson for the garment workers and began to include the union in all kinds of community coalitions. Also, a number of women joined the staff of the union at about this time. And over the years they have provided leadership to the Chinese rank-and-file members.

Immediately after the strike, we were looking for some vehicle to keep some of these marvelous people who had come forward during the strike and who were there every night to do phone banking, and who were there every night to do poster making and so forth. We wanted to find some way to keep in touch and we formed the Chinese Chorus of the ILGWU. A couple of us really had wanted to form a women's committee within the union, but that had met with some disapproval in some sectors of the local leadership, so we decided to go easy for a while. Eventually, Kathy Andrade, who had been on the Hispanic Committee of the Coalition of Labor Union Women for many years, pressed us to form a Chinese committee of CLUW, which we did. The Chinese Committee of CLUW became a training ground for a number of rank-and-file activists, and it was really formed to promote the idea of Chinese women workers as being strong

and a force to be reckoned with, vis-à-vis the larger labor community, vis-à-vis the Chinese community, and also vis-à-vis the women's movement. We had very big contingents on Labor Day, we had women's health seminars, we had cooking classes. We'd go to City Hall and protest against gentrification and get petitions signed against police brutality, and participate in peace marches in Washington—just a variety of things. I could really see a big difference between somebody who'd been in CLUW for a while and somebody who hadn't. There's just so much more they knew about trade unionism, about other broader issues—there was almost no comparison. We had this core of twenty people who had put themselves out in many different areas, in political areas and community-wide areas, going beyond just the day-to-day thing of sewing in the factories. At the same time, CLUW helped these women become leaders in the factory. Some of them became shop stewards, about five or six of them are now on the Executive Board of Local 23–25, and out of that group one or two became staff people later on, after the first batch of us did. And down the road I think we'll see some more promoting of leadership out of this group of women. . . .

F I F T Y - O N E

◆◆◆

Challenging AFDC Myths with the Facts

Mimi Abramovitz and Fred Newton

MYTH: Women on welfare have large families.

FACT: The typical welfare family is a mother and two children, slightly less than the size of the average family in the United States. Forty-two percent of AFDC families have only one child, thirty percent have two. In the 1980's, AFDC covered less than 60 percent of poor children in the U.S., down from 80 percent in the early 1970's.

COMMENT: AFDC families, like other families in the U.S., are getting smaller.

MYTH: Once on welfare, always on welfare. Welfare is a trap from which few escape.

FACT: More than 70 percent of women on welfare stay on the rolls for less than two years and only 8 percent stay on for more than eight years. . . . research on intergenerational welfare use has not been able to establish that daughters of welfare mothers necessarily end up on welfare too. Some do, some do not.

COMMENT: It is very hard for children of poor women to escape poverty, especially in the current economy with its falling wages and rising unemployment.

MYTH: Setting a time limit on welfare participation is needed to get AFDC mothers to work.

FACT: Since many AFDC mothers already work when they can, time limits are unnecessary and unduly punitive. Getting tough on welfare may win votes but it hurts poor women.

COMMENT: Instead of mandatory work for welfare mothers, we need an expanding domestic economy and a government commitment to job creation. Without adequate work, time limit proposals are merely more sophisticated measures to punish women for their poverty.

MYTH: Women on welfare have "kids for money." Eliminating AFDC will put an end to non-marital births.

FACT: Despite years of research, studies have found no link between AFDC grant and births outside of marriage. Indeed, non-marital births are no more frequent in high benefit states and no greater in states with rising grant levels than in states with flat or falling AFDC payments. The states provide about $79 a month per additional child.

COMMENT: Neither AFDC nor the tax deduction for dependent children are rewards for having children. Rather, these income supplements recognize the value of children to society and the high cost of raising children. The U.S. is the only industrial nation other than South Africa and Japan that does not provide families with an automatic grant for every child.

MYTH: If poor women only married, they would not be poor.

FACT: Family composition does not cause poverty. Although two incomes are clearly better than one, the poor tend to be poor before, during and after they tie the knot.

COMMENT: Marriage is not an effective anti-poverty strategy for women.

FIFTY-TWO

◆◆◆

Dear Mr. President

Chrystos

I am a woman with 3 children   a husband who
    has been out of work
for 18 months & no place to go
I am one of 400 families
Emergency Housing has turned away this month
The 399 others are no consolation to me
This is an emergency
Mr. P. I am a mother of two who lives with my
    mother
who can no longer work
Someone reported to welfare that I was working
My checks have been temporarily stopped pending
    investigation
I think my ex-boyfriend's mother called them
    for spite
because I don't have a job
although I have submitted over 200 resumes in
    the last year & a half
We got evicted   Emergency Housing can't find
    us anything
This is an Emergency
Hey Mr. Prez   My boyfriend was beating me &
    the kids so bad
I just had to get out before one of us was killed
The battered women's is full & so is emergency
    housing

The worker said she'd already turned away 378
   this month
We're living in my car & cooking at my mother's
   studio apartment
in the old people's housing   This is an
   emergency
400 times a month in one city that bothers to try &
   fix it

times 2 years
is a class of people
It is worse in other towns
When we have no place to live
Dear Mr. Pay Attention now
we are not in economic recovery
We are   an emergency

◆◆◆

FIFTY-THREE

Working Your Fingers to the Bone

Marion Graham

I was born in Boston, the youngest of a four-girl family. When I was 13, my father's firm went bankrupt and he found himself out of a job. My family were so ashamed they wouldn't tell their friends that they had to move from the suburbs to a three-decker in Boston, even though they weren't really poor. Now I know a lot of people who would love to move out of the projects into a three-decker.

In 1960 I got married. I left my good job with the telephone company when I was pregnant with my first child, in 1961. I really looked forward to being home with my children. Nobody worked that I knew. During the '60s I was always pregnant when everybody was out rebelling against everything. I was too pregnant to rebel, so I have to rebel now! I have five kids. They are now 35, 32, 31, 30, and 27.

When I saw how my marriage was disintegrating, I did work at home for marketing research companies, and I did typing for college students, just to try to make money. I had planned for two or three years to get a divorce before I did. But I never had the money to do it. I knew I had to have a job in order to save the money to go to a lawyer. I couldn't leave the kids; there was no daycare. Finally, I had to go on welfare because my husband did not pay enough support, and sometimes he did not pay at all.

When I started working full-time again, I thought it was going to be wonderful, that I wasn't going to be poor anymore. I was going to be away from the bureaucracy; they couldn't call me in anytime they wanted to. Even then, though, I still earned so little

that I was eligible for a housing subsidy, Medicaid, and food stamps. I remember at the time being ashamed to let people where I worked know that I was poor enough for food stamps. And I hated that.

About three years ago they came out with some new "poverty line," that's what they called it, and they decided I earned too much for most of those other benefits. I only grossed something like $8,600 at the time, but it was still too much for them, so they cut me off. I still had the same needs I had before, but suddenly I was no longer poor. I guess I was supposed to be proud.

Since then I got a raise, so I thought things would be O.K., but then I lost my housing subsidy because I earned too much. I ended up having to take an apartment that cost exactly seven times what I had paid with a subsidy. My rent came to half of my net pay. Just the rent. After that sometimes I would get to work but not be able to pay for lunch. I had my subway tokens, but no money to eat. Every week they take something different out of my salary. Life insurance, disability insurance, union dues, retirement benefits are all good, but you don't get much to live on. Now, finally, I can buy *Woman's Day* and *Family Circle* magazines — that used to be my dream.

How you dress for work, the hours and flexibility, transportation, whether you can bring a lunch — all these nitty-gritty things make a big difference in how you can live on a low salary. You just cannot afford to take some jobs even if they sound interesting because you have to spend too much money on clothes or transportation. It's sad. I couldn't afford to work at a place where I had to dress up, for instance. You can't "dress for success" on a secretarial salary. It's an invisible poverty.

You think you're not poor because you are working, so you don't even ask for the information about benefits you need. And nobody tells you that you might be eligible, because they think you are working and all set. Also, it is even harder to ask for things from your family, because if you are working you should have the money. I feel bad, though, that I don't have more chance to help my family. I can't afford it, even though I'm working.

The average pay in my union of clerical and hospital workers is not much above poverty for a woman who is trying to raise a family. When people need childcare they have to pay for it, and they can't afford it. I don't need childcare, but the health insurance, which I had to wait two years for, costs a lot. And I couldn't get it for my son, who has suffered from juvenile diabetes since he was very young.

Not having money affects everything about how you feel. I used to feel lousy about myself. I thought I was supposed to be set, to have a slice of the American pie. Now I was a big person and I worked and everything, and I was supposed to get there. But instead I found myself just with a job and no money. When I reached 40 I was so depressed.

Now I have learned that I am not alone, that it is not my fault. The average secretary around here is just over the line for many benefits, but we still have expenses we can't meet. That makes some women, who don't understand how it works, take it out on women on welfare. They blame them for getting something they can't have, instead of blaming the rules, which keep them from getting anything. Some secretaries may think, "I am better off than they are," instead of seeing how we have similar problems. But they are afraid of the label that would be put on them if they identified with welfare. I don't do that because I have been there and I know both, and I know that none of it is good. It's bad to be on welfare, and it is bad to be working and have no money.

As secretaries here we have worked hard to do things together so that we can know each other as people, because at work we are all separated in our individual little offices. We go on picnics together, or to dinner, just to get to know each other. Although they don't pay us much, they act like we can never be absent or the world will fall apart, so we have to cover for each other, and we can't do that if we don't know each other. I keep saying, "If we are so important, why don't they pay us more?" But they don't, so we have to help each other.

◆◆◆

FIFTY-FOUR

Liberating Memory

Janet Zandy

It is Parents' Weekend, a minor ritual in academic institutions. This particular Sunday in early October 1963, my father has to work the weekend shift at his chemical plant and cannot attend. I am disappointed because he is not there, but say nothing. I am a freshman scholarship student and a commuter. I live at home with my parents and sister. My mother and I drive together to Parents' Weekend activities scheduled for parents who have weekends.

We arrive overdressed and feel a discomfort we do not voice. We follow the crowd and sit on the damp steps of an amphitheater carved out of old Watchung Mountain stone. Within a decade much

of the mountain will be leveled for parking lots, but today it is a shaded and beautiful outdoor theater. We listen to the welcoming remarks of some college administrator. Neither of us feels welcomed. I see in my mother's face a hidden sadness; I feel a shame I try to deny.

This is not a memory of continuation or development. It is a memory of rupture. The discrepancy between what my mother and I felt and the scene that was played out could not be acknowledged. We had intense feelings but we didn't have the language to identify and affirm them. We could only push the feelings down and go home.

Today, I cope with middle-aged memory blocks. I forget familiar names, repeat stories, blank out whole days. Old, acute shards of memory crowd out the short-term data and demand attention. I remember that Sunday thirty years ago because I cannot forget the consciousness of discontinuity between the two great loves of my childhood: my family and school. I loved school *almost* as much as I loved my parents. But, the more schooling I got, the more separate I felt from them. It is an old working-class story.

We didn't have a telephone until I was eleven years old. Even after the phone was a black fixture, there wasn't a lot of planning or scheduling. Calendars were there to keep track of birthdays, anniversaries, and deaths. Everything else just happened. My childhood was noisy. Company, usually relatives and rarely friends (who needed friends when there were so many relatives?) would stop by, never quite unexpectedly, on the way to other places. Out would come the coffee and cake, and the joking, teasing, and visiting continued until everyone was too tired or too full. When I was in high school and college and needed quiet to study, I would retreat to the basement, working at my old black desk, wrapped in a blanket during the damp, winter months. I was always excused to study.

My parents were conscious of the value of education to their daughters' future. They both had had to quit school after the ninth grade to get a job and give their pay to the family. My mother was the oldest daughter of ten children; my father was one of seven children. This is not counting the siblings who did not reach adulthood. There was a great sense of obligation on my father's side of the family; a great sense of responsibility and pleasure on my mother's side.

My father's Italian family lived in Hoboken, an enclave of first- and second-generation Italians who antagonistically shared the same crowded streets with third-generation Irish. They stubbornly kept Italian traditions of food and religion, but spoke English at home in order to help their children make it in America. I remember one uncle much touted within the family for having a white-collar job and working on Wall Street. He said little and kept his eyes down. The other five brothers were blue collars. My aunt, the only daughter, married late for an Italian girl and died giving birth to her tenth child. My grandmother outlived several children and died at ninety. She was always carefully dressed, manipulative with her children and their spouses, and insistent that her many grandchildren kiss her on the lips. For most of her long adult life she was a widow. Her husband, the grandfather I never met, left one morning for work and never returned home alive. He was a passenger in a car that was struck head on and he was killed instantly. The accident happened on Route 3 near what is now the Meadowlands, a stadium and racetrack, but what was then a thick marshland where crabs with low toxicity were netted by urban fishermen. By the 1950s and 1960s these marshes became one long garbage dump. As kids, my sister and I would roll up the car windows as fast as we could to beat the stench on Route 3. Heading east, it is the road that has the best view of the beautiful New York City skyline — on clear days.

My father hung out with my mother's oldest brother and that's how he got to meet my mother, avoid Hoboken, and spend a lot of time in Jersey City. My father was very smart, and always acutely felt the absence of what he called "the sheepskin." I remember the story of his stolen education. When my father was living at home in Hoboken, something happened one day that brought everyone to the street side windows — perhaps it was a parade, a peddler, or a fight. While everyone's heads were poked out the window and their backs were turned, someone came into the apartment and stole the money that was supposed to be for Carlos's education. I say *story*, because even as a child I had a hard time believing that one.

So much of the goodness and generosity that is as much a part of my childhood as uncertainty and loss stems from my mother's family. My mother's mother died shortly after I was born. Anna was the daughter of a rabbi whose family lived along the German/Austrian border. She was sent to New York City as a child to stay with distant relatives. Whether the decision to send her to America was an act of rescue or oppression is hard to say. She told stories of having to hide in the skin of a cow when soldiers came into her village. No one explained why. She was apparently sent to America to be a servant in the home of wealthier relatives. One day, she was distracted while she was hanging clothes on the roof of the building where she lived. She fell. She recovered from that fall, but while she was recuperating she met Albert, an immigrant from Italy. Perhaps he gave her the first attention she had had in a long time. In one sudden shift, before she was sixteen, she was a mother, a wife, and an orphan. Her Orthodox parents in Europe lit candles, tore their clothes, and sat shivah. She was dead, but not dead. She never learned to read and write, but her children always praised her ability to travel all over New York City and the boroughs by reading the subway lights. Mostly, though, she stayed at home and worked — the daily battle against dirt in crowded spaces, cooking on a wood stove, scrubbing clothes on a washboard, giving birth to fourteen children, feeding the neighborhood "poor souls" — she worked. Many Sunday afternoons of my childhood were spent at the Jewish cemetery where we would place stones on her grave and visit.

Anna's inheritance to her children and grandchildren was a bone-deep knowledge of what it meant to be shut out. The aunts and uncles, brothers and sisters, trusted each other a lot more than they trusted institutions or any promises of the American Dream. They practiced an unpoliticized and unnamed socialism. Whoever had extra that particular week, month, or year shared it with the others. It came in the form of continuous, spirited, gift giving. My mother never shopped for my sister and me without "taking care" of some of the cousins. My uncle just happened to stop at the house after a trip to the butcher. When the aunts baked, the trays of cookies and cakes were for the Family, never just their own smaller household. No one asked . . . it was expected that each would recognize the other's need. And it was expected that any stranger who was on the arm of a member of the family would be heartily welcomed. I used to think that the same five-dollar bill was in constant circulation, only enclosed in different happy birthday, anniversary, and get well cards. Until the time came for braces, a car that worked, and a college education, it never occurred to me that my own family did not have much money.

Since they never had to be concerned with monetary accumulation or investment, there was space for play. They were gamblers. The aunts played the numbers. They would call each other and discuss numbers that figured in their dreams. Every once in a while, a number hit — for a few dollars. The uncles played the horses. In the days when there was no such thing as off-track betting, they would take the bus to the Big A, or Belmont, or contact their book-

ies. I remember one uncle giving me tightly folded pieces of paper to take to a local candy store. The guy behind the counter of this tiny, dirty shop was fat, cigar-chewing, and not particularly delighted to see children. I handed the paper to him. Sometimes I got a Three Musketeers bar for my efforts, most times not. Such was my short career as a runner. On Saturday afternoons my grandfather would demand absolute silence; uncles, aunts, and children would come to a complete stop so that the radio could be turned on and the race results heard. Every now and then a particular set of horses would win, place, and show, but usually there was just a flash of anger, something thrown at the radio, and then everyone would continue where they left off. On those occasions when I accompanied my uncles to the track, I noticed they were less interested in the physical animals and more interested in their scratch sheets. Sometimes they didn't even watch the race. What they loved was the luck . . . the thrill of risk . . . the possibility of momentary freedom from care . . . a chance to take care of the family . . . not the money, but the luck . . . the great promise . . . the charm . . . the dare and the desire . . . the Luck.

My protected, loving childhood and adolescence halted with my father's unexpected death in 1965 at the age of forty-nine. I cannot recover what is not completely lost. He would fit no stereotype of white maleness. Without an education or many models, he figured out a way to defy the worst in his own culture without abandoning it. He used his meager allowance from the paycheck he handed my mother to buy books for his daughters. Even in our tiny dwelling, our privacy was always respected. He shared all the domestic chores, and enjoyed his woodwork and garden. I never heard him utter a racist or sexist epithet. His life should have been longer. If he had had a physically safe work life, it might have been.

I was very slow to make that particular connection. It is too late now to piece together a causal relationship between his work at the chemical plant and the sudden cancer, embolism, and death. Despite the deep tiredness he carried from his shift work, my father seemed strong and healthy. He was hurt, occasionally, but never sick. Now and then, there was an accident at the chemical plant, some spillage, a minor explosion, and he would be sent home, the red burn marks tattooed on his chest.

Long defunct, Trubeck Laboratories was once located on Route 17 near where it crosses Route 3. It manufactured expensive perfumes. Instead of Christmas turkeys, the men who worked there got little bottles of Shalimar and White Shoulders. There must have been "family days" since I remember walking inside the plant, holding my hand to my nose to block the acrid smell, noticing the open drums, the pipes, the noise of dripping chemicals. That smell touched everything my father owned or wore. I can smell it still. I often wonder how many of the men who worked at Trubeck Labs—before even the minimal restrictions of OSHA on the chemicals, the toxicity, the penetrating smell—survived.

My father was my intellectual companion and he was gone. I have no memory of my junior year in college but the transcript says I got straight A's. My college studies and my time at home were completely severed. I was so slow. I thought knowledge worth learning was inside the library, the classroom, and my professors' minds, not at home. There was no intellectual space to make sense of my private pain. Women, labor, black, and ethnic studies did not exist; there were no occasions to glimpse shared struggle. We learned the Anglo-American story and were implicitly told that was *the* story.

I graduated from college, found a job teaching high school English, and for two years lived at home with my mother and gave her my pay. I read Martin Buber, Nietzsche, Tillich, Gurdjieff, and Jung—but not Marx—looking for answers. I left for graduate school, protested the Vietnam War—a source of great tension in the family since all my uncles "served" in other wars at other times—married because my mother would disapprove of "living together," and became a mother and a feminist. Before I read the great feminist texts of the 1970s, it was the lived experience of delivering and caring for a child day after day, alone, that made me question knowledge in a profound way. I had bouts of anger, depression, and debilitating migraine headaches. Days and days were locked inside a punishing migraine. I had trouble speaking and could barely answer the telephone.

As an act of self-rescue, I joined community women's study groups and the editorial collective of *New Women's Times,* one of the early U.S. radical women's newspapers. Learning about women within the circle of other women enabled me to find a public voice. I was still angry, but now I understood why—at least partially. As we read *Sisterhood Is*

Powerful, Of Woman Born, Mary Daly, Kate Millet, and Redstockings, we, collectively, began to construct the categorical differences of gender. We signed our letters "In Sisterhood" with good faith, as we began to test what "woman" meant in relation to race and class. Perhaps it was 1978 or 1979; we might have been reading a historical novel by a Black woman writer. I blurted out, "Well, slavery is gone; it's much better now." The only African-American woman in our study group, whose love for me I have never questioned, replied, "Easy for you to say, Miss Janet." Wilma Campbell reminded me that even though neither one of us may have a lot of money to spend in a downtown department store, it is not likely that the store detective will follow me.

The dream of a common language and the power to connect seemed to dissolve during my infrequent visits home to my mother. My female relatives tell me now that my mother was always "proud" of me. But too many conversations ended in constricted silence. My head was so much in theoretical radical feminism that I could not even see the conditions of my mother's life. And all she could see was the daughter she used to know. My mother worked in a greasy-spoon luncheonette serving heavy lunches to working people. Everyone in town knew Millie and wanted to have their sandwiches made by her. For all the years she worked there, I never once went in, sat down, and had a cup of coffee with her. Connections are easier to make in books. I could not replicate my mother's life—nor would she want me to—but I could find a way to affirm it without sacrificing my intellectual work. And that's when I began to collect and edit working-class women's writings.

For fifteen years I worked as an adjunct teacher of composition and literature in a local community college. At first, the part-time work seemed satisfactory because it enabled me to care for my children during the day and work evenings and weekends. As a child, I had never had a babysitter who was not a relative, and so day care for young children was not part of my inherited family epistemology. I was able to sustain this because my husband is an engineer who earns a middle-class paycheck. My students at the community college were familiar to me in their language, their attitudes about work, their values and relationships. Many of my full-time colleagues mocked these students for their malapropisms, their lack of class. Of course, these students did not lack *class.* Class was obviously inscribed on their fatigued bodies and in their desire for associate degrees that might earn them a little more take-home pay. What they lacked was the power of class definition. They also lacked the wanna-be-patrician, bourgeois sensibilities cultivated and nurtured in the greenhouses of graduate English departments.

At the community college I learned two profound lessons: how it was possible to connect lived working-class experience to the study of literature and how to organize and struggle for change. I developed and taught a course called Working-Class Literature and I organized adjunct faculty.

My usual zigzag movement between experience and theory became more focused. It was 1981–82 and I was publishing in feminist journals and newspapers, and claiming a public voice. The intellectual ground that was once my formal education was broken up. In the fissures and recesses I began to develop an alternate ground of being that promised location inside the dislocation. Without naming it, I was acting on Foucault's assertion that "knowledge is not just made for understanding; it is made for cutting." In the past, the cutting had been in the power of the owning class to cut down, literally, the lives of working people—but also, I came to realize, in the power of language and the academic elite to cut out working-class studies and sever workers from their own history and culture. It was time to cut in another direction.

I taught working-class literature to working-class students. I realize now that without overt autobiographical references, I was uncovering/recovering the integrity of my own working-class family life to produce curricula, texts, and cultural criticism. Here was a legitimate, powerful alternative to acculturation, nostalgia, or assimilation. I quickly found that the most difficult problem in developing a curriculum of working-class studies is the enormity of the subject. (This is not a problem, of course, for those who do not concede that working-class culture exists.) I organized my course around the interplay of three powerful pronouns: I, they, and we. Who tells the story? Who mediates it? And what is missing? I began with personal narratives, often oral histories, and ask students to do their own work autobiographies and interviews along the Studs Terkel *Working* model. We looked at writing of *witness*—the work of the next generation or the informed insider to tell the stories that were not voiced. We read Harriette

Arnow's *The Dollmaker* and Maxine Hong Kingston's *China Men,* tracing the long journeys of "DP's"—displaced persons—in the land of broken promises. We looked at Lewis Hine photographs, listened to the music of coal miners, read contemporary poetry by working-class women, and studied episodes of resistance in the film *Salt of the Earth* and recovery in Leslie Marmon Silko's *Ceremony.* I grouped texts, photographs, music, and films in a montage that included differences of gender, race, and ethnicity around questions central to suppressed histories: What kind of work is going on here? Who controls it? Who profits from it? I wanted students to discover not only neglected texts, but also those conditions which thwart and suppress the production of culture. I was allowed to do this because I was a harmless adjunct.

If working-class culture becomes exclusively an object of study, and not a means of study, the larger struggle is lost. My intellectual work gave me political courage. I also knew that I had nothing to lose. When a full-time position finally opened after nine years as an adjunct, I applied, but was not given an interview. I tasted my own invisibility. I did not like the taste. I took Joe Hill's advice and started to organize.

I shared the labor of meetings, phone calls, letters, petitions, questionnaires, research, and talking, talking, talking with another longtime part-timer, Chris Munson, and a sympathetic female union president, Judy Toler, who was never reelected after supporting us. We won our first raise in ten years and representation at the union bargaining table. We made small gains, securing mail boxes, the right to assign our own textbooks, and inclusion in the college directory. I published a front page article in a Rochester newspaper and pushed for voting and meeting privileges in my own department. I became an outspoken critic of academic work exploitation at conferences and meetings. I had not lost my pungent working-class tongue. When I began adjunct teaching in 1972 I earned $875 a course; when I left fifteen years later as an adjunct associate professor, I was earning $400 more a course. I still had no benefits, no retirement, and no guarantee that I would actually teach the course I prepared. When the next full-time opening came up, I was not surprised when I was again not invited to interview for the job.

Opportunities for praxis in class struggle are available behind the academic gate; one does not have to travel to Wigan Pier. But it does mean confronting uncomfortable questions: how does my work rest on the labor of others? how can I use my power to practice democracy in the workplace? The increasing use of adjunct faculty is a piece of a larger labor story; white and blue collars blur in a common history of being overworked and underpaid. To be an adjunct is to be an academic "other," a category for academic managers, a flexible object, a thing. In the dynamic of this work relationship, I caught a tiny glimpse of the reality of my parents' work and that of so many others. I also learned there are alternatives to liberal humanism with its emphasis on individuality and its naive faith in progress. I was cutting my way back home.

CHAPTER SEVEN

◆◆◆

Women's Health

Health, healing, and learning how our bodies work are all issues of major concern to women, helping us to take care of ourselves and others more effectively. Although women make up a majority of health care providers in clinics, doctors' offices, nursing homes, and hospitals, professionalization and the medicalization of health care have given doctors — mostly White men — authority in medical matters. In times gone by, women made teas, tinctures, oils, and salves and gave baths and massages to heal sickness and alleviate pain. Some women still study the medicinal properties of plants and treat many complaints with herbal remedies (Perrone, Stockel, and Krueger 1989). Currently, the medical care available to women in the United States is dominated by drug treatments and surgery. Women's health conditions vary greatly depending on individual factors like diet, exercise, smoking, stress, or violence, as well as macro-level factors such as race and class. This chapter reviews data about women's health, discusses the economic basis of the U.S. medical industry, and considers ways to move the emphasis in medical care away from an overreliance on drugs and surgery to a more balanced conception of health. Health is related to many aspects of our lives, and the chapters on body politics, relationships and family, work, and the environment are also relevant here.

Causes of Death for Women: Effects of Race and Class

Like many of the issues covered in this book, health is both a personal concern and a political issue. It is also somewhat intangible — a complex mix of physical, mental, emotional, and spiritual states of well-being. The transition from health to illness is often gradual and rather subjective. By contrast, death is a more clearly defined event and is used as an indicator — though admittedly rather crude — of the health of the population.

Like men, women in the United States are most likely to die from heart disease or cancer, followed by strokes, pneumonia, pulmonary diseases, accidents, and diabetes. Overall men have higher cancer rates than women. In all racial groups, however, women aged thirty to fifty-four have higher rates than men of the same age because of the high incidence of breast and gynecological cancers. Among women, cancer is the most common among White women, though the death rate from cancer is highest in Alaska Native women (National Cancer Institute 1996). Heart disease is 44 percent lower for Asian-American women than for White women. Among the top ten causes of death for African-American women and Latinas are conditions connected to pregnancy and childbirth, not found in the top ten causes of death for White women. Significantly more (25 percent more) African-American women die in their twenties than do White women of that age as a result of HIV/AIDS, maternal mortality, drug use, and homicide. Native American women aged fifteen to twenty-four show a 50 percent higher death rate than White women of the same age for similar reasons. In Reading 60 Frederica Daly provides a detailed historical, legal, and economic context for her discussion of Native American women's health, which, she notes, is among the worst in the country. Taken as a whole, the health of African-American women, Native American women, and Latinas is significantly worse than that of White women and Asian-American women.

Breast Cancer. This affects one woman in nine nationwide, though there are much higher incidences in certain geographical areas, as noted by Rita Arditti and Tatiana Schreiber in Reading 57. Breast cancer is the most frequently diagnosed cancer among all women, though Vietnamese women living in the United States have higher rates of cervical cancer (National Cancer Institute 1996). The incidence of breast cancer increases with age, though African-American women are more likely than White women to get it at younger ages. Fewer Black women get cancer than White women, but their mortality rate is 28 percent higher, presumably because they wait longer than White women to seek medical treatment. Though there is some controversy about the effectiveness of mammograms, they are generally recommended for women in their forties for early detection of breast cancer. Women with more education are more likely to know about this screening procedure, and are more likely to have insurance to cover it and to be registered with a doctor who encourages it (Taueber 1991). Research suggests that even when Black women have insurance, doctors are less likely to suggest mammograms. White women with cancer also get what the literature refers to as "more aggressive" treatment than Black women, meaning that Black women are not told about all relevant treatment options, given the full range of tests, or always prescribed the most effective medications. Lois Lyles writes about cancer in the family in Reading 55.

Hypertension. This is a major risk factor for heart disease and stroke, the first and third leading causes of death for women. During 1988–91, the prevalence of hypertension for African-American women was 31 percent, for Mexican-American women 22 percent, and for White women 21 percent (National Cen-

ter for Health Statistics 1996). According to Krieger and Sidney (1996), more African-Americans than White people have high blood pressure, a fact attributable to stress related to racism.

Diabetes. Three times as many African-American women as White women have diabetes, and more die from it than do White women. Similarly, Latinas have a significantly higher incidence of diabetes, especially Puerto Ricans and Mexican-Americans (Torre 1993). Native American rates for diabetes are twice as high as the rate for the United States as a whole and have risen significantly in the past forty years (Daly 1994).

Tuberculosis. Compared with people in the United States as a whole, Native Americans are four times as likely to have tuberculosis, an infectious disease prevalent in the late nineteenth and early twentieth centuries and usually associated with poverty and poor living conditions (Daly 1995).

HIV/AIDS. For younger people (twenty-five to forty-four) complications from HIV/AIDS were the leading cause of death in 1993; in that year women's deaths increased more than men's, and African-American women's and Latinas' more than White women's. Forty percent of all AIDS patients under thirteen in New York are Latino (Torre 1993). Women have not been diagnosed as early as men because their symptoms are not so clear-cut and doctors were less likely to look for symptoms of HIV/AIDS in women. Moreover, because there were fewer women involved in clinical trials, they did not receive the better treatment that men received.

Stress. Common stressors include such things as new demands, sadness, or fear due to the death of somebody we love or need, ending or beginning a new relationship, starting a new job, having a baby, and moving. In addition, financial insecurity, job loss, illness, and being discriminated against because of race or culture cause stress, especially for poor people and people of color.

Domestic Violence. Women of all race and class groups who are beaten by their partners or suffer emotional violence are subject to an ongoing health hazard. (For more on this issue, see Chapter 4.)

Reproductive Health

The ability to become pregnant and have a baby is one of the most fundamental aspects of women's lives. A woman becomes pregnant for many reasons:

she wants to have a child; she wants to experience pregnancy and childbirth; she believes it will make her a "real" woman; she hopes it will keep her relationship together or make her partner happy. Some women are pregnant by accident, others as a result of being raped. Having a child is a profoundly personal experience, usually with far-reaching consequences for the mother's life, and it is also a public issue. The government has an interest in the numbers of children born, who their parents are, whether they are married, whether they are teens, poor, or recent immigrants. This interest is reinforced by, and also influences, dominant notions of what kinds of women should be mothers. For some women — especially teenagers, lesbians, and mothers receiving welfare — there may be a serious tension between the personal event of pregnancy and societal attitudes to it. African-American women have consistently tried to be self-determining in their reproductive lives despite having been used as breeders by slaveholders and despite subsequent systematic state interventions to control their fertility (Dula 1996). Dula also argues that the state is interested in the literal reproduction of labor power — producing more workers and citizens — and in keeping down the birthrates of women of color so as to reduce the number of people of color.

Infant Mortality

The number of infants who die in their first year is an important indicator of infant and maternal health. Infant mortality is commonly a result of low birth weight, poor nutrition, inadequate prenatal care, the mother's level of education, and her overall health, whether due to poor diet, stress, smoking, drinking and drug use, or HIV/AIDS. Infant mortality in babies born between 1983 and 1991 showed Chinese-Americans with the lowest rate (5.1 deaths per 1,000 live births), White infants (7.4), Hawai'ian and Puerto Rican infants (10.4), Native Americans (12.6), and African-American babies with the highest rate (17.1) (National Center for Health Statistics 1996). More African-American babies than babies from other groups are HIV positive and more Native American babies suffer from fetal alcohol syndrome.

Controlling Fertility

Women's fertility is both a blessing and a liability, and many women in the United States want to con-

trol their fertility — perhaps to limit the number of children they have, to avoid pregnancy with a particular partner, to postpone pregnancy until they are older, or to avoid it altogether — or to have the freedom to bear children. To do this they need some combination of sex education that is accurate and culturally appropriate; affordable and reliable birth control; safe, legal, affordable abortion; prenatal care and care through childbirth; health care for children to decrease infant mortality; and alternative insemination. In addition they need good general health care and widespread cultural acceptance that they have a right to control their lives in this way. As argued by Marsha Saxton in Reading 63, women with disabilities must also fight for the right to have children in the face of a dominant view that they are nonsexual beings who could not cope with being mothers (see also Finger 1990).

Birth Control　Barrier methods like condoms and diaphragms have been used for many years. In the 1960s the intrauterine device (IUD), often called the coil, was introduced despite severe unwanted side effects for some women, such as heavy bleeding, pain, and cramps. The pill, introduced around the same time, was the first chemical contraceptive to be taken every day. It affects the whole body continuously, as do Depo-Provera (an injectable contraceptive) and Norplant (implanted under the skin). Currently, poor African-American and Native American women and Latinas are much more likely than White women to be encouraged to use these long-acting contraceptives. Official policy seeks to limit their pregnancies and assumes that these women would be unreliable using other methods, thereby continuing the long connection between birth control and eugenics. Depo-Provera is currently used in the United States though previously banned because of its many side effects. The Black Women's Health Network, the National Latina Health Organization, and other women's health advocates are currently calling for its withdrawal as unsafe and are also calling attention to the fact that many women using Norplant are having difficulty finding anyone to remove it. In addition, these methods compound many of the health problems suffered by poor women of color, including hypertension, diabetes, and stress. A new barrier method is the female condom, a loosely fitting, polyurethane (not latex) pouch with a semiflexible plastic ring at each end that lines the vagina. Ideally it allows women more control over their reproduction. The pregnancy rate with normal use of the female condom is expected to be similar to the rate with use of the male condom, though early findings show that it is between 21 percent and 26 percent, compared with a 13 percent failure rate for the male condom. This has been attributed to lack of familiarity with its use (www.halcyon.com/elf/altsex/contra.html).

Abortion   Attitudes toward abortion have varied greatly from one society to another. Historically, the Catholic Church, for example, held the view that the soul did not enter the fetus for at least forty days after conception and allowed abortion up to that point. In 1869, however, Pope Pius IX declared that life begins at conception, and thus all abortion became murder in the eyes of the Church. In the United States up until the mid-nineteenth century women were allowed to seek an abortion in the early part of pregnancy before they felt the fetus moving, a subjectively determined time, referred to as the quickening. After the Civil War more restrictive abortion laws were passed, partly to increase population and partly to shift authority over women's reproductive lives to the medical profession. By 1900 the only legal ground for an abortion was to save the life of the mother. Many women were forced to bring unwanted pregnancies to term in poverty, illness, or appalling personal circumstances. Thousands died trying to abort themselves or at the hands of "backstreet" abortionists. Some upper- and middle-class women found doctors to perform safe abortions for a high price, though they and the doctors risked prosecution if they were found out. Women with knowledge of herbs or medicine tried to help other women. The Jane Collective organized a clandestine feminist abortion service in the Chicago area in the early 1970s. In 1973, the landmark case *Roe vs. Wade* made abortion legal, though despite that decision, the right to have an abortion has continued to be contested. In 1977, the Hyde Amendment withdrew state funding for abortion for poor women as the first of many restrictions, which include rules requiring waiting periods and parental consent. The 1970s' feminist demand for "Free Abortion on Demand" was modified in the 1980s to "A Woman's Right to Choose," in the face of increasingly violent protests in support of fetal rights at abortion clinics, the bombing of clinics, and attacks on doctors known to perform abortions as part of their practice (Petchesky 1990). The Freedom of Access to Clinic Entrances Act, 1994, has reduced harassment outside clinics, but licensing by the Federal Drug Administration (FDA) of RU-486, the so-called morning-after pill, will change the landscape of abortion politics. White feminists made abortion the centerpiece of their reproductive rights activism in the 1980s, but for women of color it was a relatively minor concern.

Sterilization Abuse   Sterilization abuse, rather than the right to abortion, has been a concern of poor women, especially women of color, for many years (Davis 1983a). Sterilization, without women's full knowledge or under duress, has been a common practice in the United States for poor Latina, African-American, and Native American women. Currently, sterilization is federally funded under the Medicaid program and is free on demand to poor women.

Teen Pregnancy   More U.S. teenagers than ever before are having sex at younger ages, despite the risk of contracting sexually transmitted diseases and HIV. However, unintended teen pregnancies have risen for White women but have stayed relatively the same for Black women. In many cases the fathers of these babies are considerably older than the young women. According to syndicated columnist Ellen Goodman, "two out of every three teenage mothers are impregnated by a man over 20" (1996, p. A17). Twenty percent of the fathers are at least six years older than the mothers. Babies born to teens present a tremendous responsibility for young women and their families. Many community programs seek to prevent teen pregnancy, although sex education in schools and programs to distribute condoms, to prevent the spread of HIV/AIDS as much as pregnancy, have run into opposition from some parents, school boards, and conservative religious groups. Sara Ruddick writes about sex education in Reading 61.

Sexually Transmitted Disease (STD)   Sexually transmitted diseases affect some 10 million people each year (Boston Women's Health Book Collective, 1992), but women and infants disproportionately bear their long-term effects (Centers for Disease Control and Prevention 1996). The term STD refers to more than twenty diseases, including herpes, genital warts, crab lice, chlamydia, gonorrhea, syphilis, and HIV. With the exception of gonorrhea, all STDs are increasing at an alarming rate. One reason for this is that women often do not have any symptoms or, if they do, the symptoms are mistaken for something else. Sexually transmitted diseases can affect how a woman feels about her body and her partner and can make her infertile or more susceptible to other diseases.

Toxic Hazards   Working in toxic workplaces is a serious health hazard for many poor women and disproportionately for women of color. Some companies have kept women out of the most hazardous work — often the highest paid among blue-collar jobs — or required that they be sterilized first, to avoid being sued if these workers later give birth to babies with disabilities (Chavkin 1984).

Medicalization of Reproductive Life

Childbirth   Before there were male gynecologists, midwives helped women through pregnancy and childbirth (Ehrenreich and English 1978). As medicine became professionalized in the nineteenth century, gynecology and obstetrics developed as an area of medical specialization. Doctors eroded the position of midwives and ignored or scorned their knowledge as "old wives tales." Largely for the convenience of the doctor, women began to give birth lying on their backs, perhaps the hardest position in which to deliver a child. Forceps and various pain-killing medications were widely used. From the 1950s onward cesarean sections (C-sections) became more common, often for the doctors' convenience or from fear of malpractice suits. In 1990 22.7 percent of births in the United States were C-sections, the highest rate in the world (National Women's Health Network 1992). The past twenty years have seen a further extension of this medicalization process as doctors monitor pregnancy from the earliest stages with a battery of new techniques such as amniocentesis, sonograms, and ultrasound. Although this technology allows medical practitioners, and through them, pregnant women, to know details about the health and condition of the fetus, as well as its sex, it also changes women's experiences of pregnancy and childbirth and can erode their knowledge of and confidence in their bodily processes. In Reading 62,

Joy Harjo describes changes in women's experiences of childbirth.

Menopause   Another aspect of this medicalization process concerns menopause. This natural life process is increasingly treated as a disease rather than as a series of complex bodily and emotional changes. Many middle-aged women are advised to take hormone-replacement therapy (HRT) for the rest of their lives to control the symptoms of menopause (Klein and Dumble 1994).

Reproductive Technologies   Technologies like in vitro fertilization (IVF), in which a woman's eggs are fertilized by sperm outside her body and the fertilized embryo is then implanted into her womb, are an important new development. They push the medicalization of pregnancy and childbirth one step further and hold out the hope that infertile couples or postmenopausal women will be able to have children. Bearing a child as a surrogate mother under contract to an infertile couple is one way a relatively poor young woman, usually White, can earn $10,000 or so, plus medical expenses, for nine months' work. Fertility clinics also need ovum donors and seek to harvest the eggs of young, college-educated women from a range of specified racial and ethnic groups. Infertility treatments so far have had a spectacularly low success rate, and they are very expensive. They are aimed at middle- and upper-middle-class women as a way of widening individual choice. Infertility may stem from a range of causes such as sexually transmitted diseases, the effects of IUDs, delayed childbearing, and occupational and environmental factors. Infertility rates are lower in the 1990s than in previous decades, but this issue has a higher profile nowadays because of technological developments.

These reproductive technologies open up an array of economic, legal, and moral questions (Hubbard 1990). Are they liberating for women? for which women? and at what costs? Some feminists have argued that women's biology and the ability to reproduce have been used to justify their social and economic subordination. Shulamith Firestone (1970), for example, was convinced that women's liberation requires freedom from biological reproduction and looked forward to developments in reproductive technology that would make it possible for a fetus to develop outside the womb. This is in stark contrast to

Katz-Rothman (1986) and the myriad women who believe that if women lose their ability to reproduce they lose a "quintessential female experience" (p. 111). Other feminist critics of reproductive technologies focus on their invasiveness and consumers' lack of power over and knowledge about these methods, as compared with that of medical experts or "medocrats" (Arditti, Klein, and Minden 1984; Corea 1985, 1987; Stanworth 1987).

Health and Aging

The health of women in middle age and later life is partly linked to how healthy they were when they were younger. The effects of stress, poor nutrition, smoking, or not getting enough exercise build up over time. Exposure to toxic chemicals, the physical and emotional toll of pregnancies, accidents, injuries, and caring for others all affect our health as we grow older. A lifetime of poverty often translates into poor health later in life.

On average, women in the United States live longer than men, with a life expectancy of 79 years for women and 72.3 years for men. The majority of old people in the United States are women, who account for 60 percent of those aged 65 and over and 72 percent of the population over the age of 85 (Brennan, Winklepleck, and MacNee 1994). African-American women have a life expectancy of 73.9 years, significantly lower than that of White women (79.6 years) but much higher than that of African-American men (64.9 years), while Asian-Americans of both sexes live several years longer than Whites (National Center for Health Statistics 1996). If African-Americans live to be 85, they often live longer than Whites. Of course, the mere fact of living longer says nothing about the quality of a person's life, and older women suffer higher rates of disabling diseases such as arthritis, Alzheimer's, diabetes, deafness, cataracts, broken bones, digestive conditions, and osteoporosis than do men (Doyal 1995). Women over 45 use hospitals less often than men do, reflecting a basic health difference between the sexes: men are more likely to have fatal diseases, whereas women have chronic conditions that worsen with age. These lingering diseases seriously affect the quality of women's lives. Older women often have to accept the fact that they need support and care. They have to face their changed looks, physical limitations, and the

loss of independence and loved ones on a daily basis, which calls on their emotional and spiritual resources, including patience, forbearance, optimism, and religious faith. Older women's health is also adversely affected by caring for their sick partners when they themselves are old and sick.

Mental and Emotional Health

Mental Illness in Women: Difficulties of Diagnosis

Women are overrepresented among people with some sort of mental illness and are most likely to be diagnosed with depression. Men are most likely to be diagnosed with alcohol- and drug-related conditions. There are many problems with diagnostic categories, however, and a great deal of room for interpretation based on individual and cultural factors. The American Psychological Association did not drop homosexuality from its list of mental disorders until 1973. Lesbianism was thought to be caused by dominant mothers and weak fathers or conversely, by girls' having exclusively male role models. Those who "came out" in the 1950s and 1960s risked being sent to psychotherapists or mental institutions for a "cure." Since the 1980s, young women who do not conform to traditional gender roles may be diagnosed with "gender identity disorder," as described by Daphne Scholinski in Reading 64.

Hopelessness and anger at one's life circumstances — which may include childhood sexual abuse, rape, domestic violence, poverty, homelessness, or simply dull routines — are not irrational reactions. Women's symptoms can seem vague to doctors, who may not really try to find out what is troubling them. In Reading 58, Nechas and Foley discuss this issue in connection with alcohol abuse. Even when understood by doctors, women's traumas and difficulties are not easy to cure. According to the U.S. Department of Health and Human Services (1996), in 1990–92, almost 50 percent of all women between fifteen and fifty-four had experienced symptoms suggestive of a psychiatric disorder at some time in their lives; however only 55 percent of them had ever received mental health treatment. More women than men attempt suicide, but men are more likely to use guns and to be successful, whereas women tend to use drug overdoses and are often found before their attempts are fatal. Mental hospital patients represent a relatively small proportion of those who are suffering mentally and emotionally. In general, women are admitted to mental hospitals as inpatients in roughly the same numbers as men. Women aged 25–44 are more likely than women in other age groups to be admitted to a psychiatric hospital.

One reason why more women are classified as having mental illness may be that the proportion of women seeking help for personal or emotional problems is twice as high as it is for men. It increases with educational attainment for both men and women. For both men and women, more persons who were formerly married seek help than do those currently married or never married. Employment is also a factor here, with a higher percentage of men and a slightly higher percentage of women who are unemployed seeking help (Dargan 1995). However, one cannot infer from these data that everyone who "seeks help" is doing so voluntarily; sometimes seeing a counselor or therapist is required by a social service agency or is a condition of probation. Voluntarily seeking help for emotional problems is linked to one's ability to pay, finding a suitable therapist, and cultural attitudes toward this kind of treatment.

Many people of all classes and racial groups attempt to deal with the pain and difficulty of their lives through drugs and alcohol. In Reading 60, Frederica Daly notes that rates of alcoholism, homicide, and suicide among Native Americans are significantly higher than the national rates. In the United States drug addiction is generally thought of as a crime rather than as a health issue. We discuss it further under the topic of crime and criminalization in Chapter 8, but we also see it as a symptom of stress brought on by the pressures of life, often caused by social and economic inequality. There are far fewer drug-treatment programs than required, and fewer for women than for men.

Feminist Perspectives on Mental Illness

A number of feminist writers have argued that contemporary approaches to mental distress, as illness, can be harmful to women (Chesler 1972; Ehrenreich and English 1978; Russell 1995; Showalter 1987; Ussher 1991). Russell (1995) briefly traces the history of definitions of madness from medieval Europe, where it was thought of as a combination of error and sin. During the seventeenth century, economic crises and rising unemployment in Europe prompted local officials to build houses of confinement for beggars, drunks, vagabonds, and other poor people and petty criminals, as well as for those who were thought mad. Through the eighteenth and nineteenth centuries psychiatry gradually developed as a new medical specialty, and asylums in Europe and the United States were headed by doctors, who theorized that much mental distress experienced by women was due to their reproductive capacities and sexuality. Hysteria, thought to be due to a disturbance of the womb, became a catchall category to describe women's mental illness. (The English word *hysterical* comes from the Greek word *husterikos*, meaning "of the womb.") Showalter (1987) and Chesler (1972) show how definitions of madness have been used to suppress women's creativity, education, and political involvement. Nineteenth-century White upper- and middle-class women who wanted to write, paint, travel, or speak out in public on issues of the day were assumed by their husbands—and by psychiatrists—to be insane. Charlotte Perkins Gilman's powerful fictional work *The Yellow Wallpaper,* for example, describes this experience and was written as a result of having lived through it. In the twentieth century depression and premenstrual syndrome (PMS) have replaced "hysteria" as stock phrases used in describing mental illness in women.

Feminist writers offer scathing critiques of the alleged objectivity of much contemporary mental health theorizing and of the value judgments and blatant sexism involved in many diagnostic categories like depression, behavioral disorders, and personality disorders which affect women more than men. Symptoms for these disorders are often very general, vague, and overlapping, and, according to Russell (1995), there is little agreement among practitioners as to what conditions are indicated by the symptoms. She questions the assumption that there is a biological or neurological basis for mental distress and argues that drug therapies based on this assumption have very mixed results in practice. Rather, she points to many external factors affecting women's mental equilibrium, including childhood sexual abuse, domestic violence, restricted educational or economic opportunities, and pressure to look beautiful, to be thin, to be compliant wives and long-suffering mothers, any of which could reasonably make women depressed or "crazy." Fallon (1994) notes that young White women from middle- and upper-middle-class families currently suffer from eating disorders such as anorexia and bulimia in what are described as epidemic proportions, especially on college campuses. This condition is less common for women of color and is relatively unknown outside industrialized countries, all factors that point to its cultural basis.

Medical Care: Business As Usual?

Since the seventeenth century, Western thought has consistently viewed organic, bodily processes as separate from those of the mind. The Western medical model separates physical, mental, emotional, and spiritual states of well-being and focuses on illness and disease rather than on the wholeness of people's lives, often treating symptoms rather than causes (Candib 1995). For example, though stressors generated by racism are a strong influence in the hypertension that disproportionately affects African-Americans, the medical response is to treat the symptoms with medication, rather than to involve doctors, patients, and the wider society in combating racism. Similarly, many women are prescribed antidepressants rather than being empowered and supported in changing their life circumstances. Kat Duff (1993) comments: "Our concepts of physical and psychological health have become one-sidedly identified with the heroic qualities most valued in our culture: youth, activity, productivity, independence, strength, confidence, and optimism" (p. 37). This Western medical model also contributes to fantasies of immortality to be achieved by life-prolonging surgeries and drug treatments, as well as expensive cosmetic surgeries.

Because medical care is provided on a fee-paying basis in the United States, the medical industry has many of the characteristics of any business venture (see the discussion of the global economy in Chapter 5). Hospitals are bought and sold like factories. Hospitals, nursing homes, and clinics that cannot balance their books are forced to lower their standards of treatment or are taken over by more profitable companies. The emphasis is on hi-tech treatments, particularly drug therapies and surgery, as these are the most profitable for drug companies and manufacturers of medical equipment. Although most people have benefited from vaccines and antibiotics,

and the use of drugs and surgery may improve the lives of cancer patients, give relief from constant arthritic pain, or restore good vision to elderly people with cataracts, this overall emphasis has severely skewed the range of treatments available. It has led to an overproduction of intensive-care equipment, for example, while many people, especially the poor, have little access to the most rudimentary medical services. Vincente Navarro (1993) notes that 65 percent of medical expenditures in the United States go to *curing* disease even though more people — especially women — suffer from chronic conditions for which *caring* is the more appropriate mode of treatment. This emphasis on drugs, surgery, and hi-tech procedures also shapes public policy through the testing and use of new drugs, the routine use of mammograms in breast cancer screening, sonograms and amniocentesis in pregnancy, and the prevalence of hysterectomies and births by cesarean section.

Paying for Medical Care

How we pay for medical care as a nation and who can afford it are questions much discussed in recent years, especially in connection with proposals for a national health plan put forward by President Clinton in his first term of office. This plan was successfully opposed by medical insurers, some doctors, and the American Medical Association, who convinced enough voters, editorial writers, and members of Congress that standards of care would inevitably decline under a nationalized health system. The United States is the only industrialized country in the world, except South Africa, that does not have such a system.

Although 70 percent of people in the United States do have some kind of private medical insurance (U.S. Bureau of the Census 1996), this often covers only emergencies and hospitalization. Only 7 to 8 percent of participants in group plans are fully covered for hospital maternity charges. Over 5 million women of reproductive age have private insurance that does not cover maternity care at all, and some 550,000 babies a year are born to uninsured mothers, many of them teens (Brennan, Winklepleck, and MacNee 1994). Adela de la Torre (1993) notes that only 60 percent of Latinas initiate prenatal care in the first trimester of pregnancy, at least in part because they lack insurance coverage; by contrast, 80 percent of White women seek early prenatal care. Women's Wellness programs are currently a profitable screening service provided by hospitals, though many insurance policies do not cover them, and they are not always culturally sensitive for all women's needs, especially women of color, women with disabilities, and lesbians. For most people who have private medical insurance (61 percent), this is employment-related. The figures for men and women with private coverage are very similar. Twenty-five percent of the population receive government coverage — Medicaid or Medicare. More women (11.7 percent) have government coverage than men (8.3 percent), reflecting Medicaid eligibility criteria that focuses on mothers and children, and the greater numbers of women among the elderly who rely on Medicare. Cuts in Medicaid and Medicare during the 1990s mean that some of these people have lost medical coverage altogether or in part. In 1995, 15 percent of the U.S. population was uninsured. This rose to 30 percent for those in the $14,000 to $25,000 income group and to 35 percent among people with the lowest family income (less than $14,000). In the highest income group ($50,000 or more), only 6 percent had no health-care coverage. Young adults between the ages of eighteen and twenty-four constituted the highest proportion (28 percent) of uninsured among age groups (National Center for Health Statistics 1996). These statistics may be misleading, since they do not distinguish those with coverage for only part of the year from those insured the entire year, and since some people are insured by more than one plan.

During the calendar years 1991 and 1992, those with medical coverage for less than twelve months made up approximately 20 percent of the population, with slightly more men (22 percent) in that group than women (19 percent). Analyzed by race, these data show approximately 19 percent Whites, 28 percent African-Americans, and 41 percent Latinos with no insurance (U.S. Bureau of the Census 1996). These people are concentrated in small businesses with low rates of unionization or are working part time or on a temporary basis. Immigration status is another factor affecting the rate of medical coverage. In 1995, a higher proportion of immigrants (33 percent) than those born in the United States (13.6 percent) was without health-care insurance. Among the immigrants, naturalized citizens had a coverage rate

more than double that of noncitizens — 40 percent versus 16 percent. Poor immigrants were even worse off, with 52 percent of them uninsured (National Center for Health Statistics 1996). Recent immigrants are often employed in low-paying jobs without benefits. It is not surprising, then, to note that states with large immigrant populations have the highest proportion of uninsured people: Arizona, California, Louisiana, New Mexico, and Texas (National Center for Health Statistics 1996). Since the mid-1990s, changes in government policy have sought to bar undocumented people and some legal immigrants from public health-care services, including emergency care. Women may risk jeopardizing their work and residence in the United States if they seek medical care for themselves or their children.

Managed Care

Hospitals, health maintenance organizations (HMOs), and nursing homes increasingly use a managed-care approach. In 1994 almost half the people in the United States with medical insurance were enrolled in a managed-care plan. Ellen Freudheim (1996) defines this as "a comprehensive approach to health care delivery that encompasses planning and coordination of care, patient and provider education, monitoring of care quality, and cost control" (p. 155). It works on a prepayment system: if the care provided costs more than the prepayment, the HMO loses money. Though the managed-care approach started out with an emphasis on prevention and coordination among providers, there is always pressure to lower costs in order to increase profits. Treatment tends to be parceled out according to preset formulas that may not meet individual needs. As childbirth became medicalized, for example, women used to be hospitalized for a week or more. This was gradually cut back by insurers to the point where many women had to go home after only one night (increased to two in 1996). Medicaid is moving to a managed-care approach, though working out the cost of care for the elderly or chronically sick is difficult. In Reading 59, Annette Dula creates the character of Miss Mildred, an elderly African-American woman, to make the point that people are not standardized machines and that they need medical care that is appropriate physically, emotionally, culturally, and financially.

Other Barriers to the Use of Medical Services

Other barriers to people's use of medical services, beyond those imposed by managed care and lack of insurance, include fear of treatment, transportation difficulties, long waiting times, not being able to take time off work or losing pay for doing so, child-care responsibilities, language and cultural differences, and residential segregation, which may mean that there are few medical facilities in some communities of color or rural communities. Most inner cities have large teaching hospitals that treat local people, predominantly people of color, in their emergency rooms, but this treatment may be slanted toward the educational needs of the hospital's medical students rather than to the health needs of the patients. Taken overall, women visit doctors and other health practitioners more often than men do. In 1992, on average, for people between the ages of fifteen and sixty-four, women made 66 percent more visits than men. African-Americans tend to be diagnosed or seek treatment later than Whites for many chronic diseases, which may reduce the effectiveness of treatment and their ability to survive. Once under medical treatment, they receive what official reports describe as "less aggressive" treatment than Whites.

Gender and Race Bias in Medical Research

Despite the relative frequency of women's visits to the doctor, however, there is a clear male bias in medical knowledge (Candib 1995). Most doctors in the United States are White, upper-middle-class men, and a meager 13 percent of government research funds is spent on women's health (Doyal 1995). Federal law now requires that women and minorities be included in research, but it will be a long time before this makes a big difference to the state of medical knowledge. Heart disease, which affects both men and women, was thought of as a man's disease for many years. As a result, it has been studied much more than breast cancer. Research samples have mainly consisted of White men even when women's illnesses were being studied. Preliminary testing of antidepressant medications — prescribed mainly to women — was done only on men, despite evidence suggesting a difference in the drugs' effects between men and women. Research into health problems that men and women share is done on men and made to seem universal, not accounting for specific factors that might affect women differently. For example, the NIH-sponsored, five-year Physicians Health Study concerning the effects of aspirin on heart disease used a sample of 22,071 men and no women, even though heart disease is also the number one killer of women (Nechas and Foley 1994). Recommended drug treatments are also tested on men and then prescribed for women on the assumption that they will be equally effective, though whether this is so is not known (Nechas and Foley 1994). Though women now make up one of the fastest-growing groups to contract HIV/AIDS, there has been very little research specifically concerning women and AIDS. Similarly, there is little research on the long-term effects of birth control pills, estrogen-replacement therapy prescribed for menopausal women, or safe, reliable forms of contraception. In general, too little is known about the particular health needs of women of color, older women, women with disabilities, and lesbians.

Caring for People with Disabilities and Chronic Illness: A Labor of Love?

An aspect of health that generally affects women much more than men is caring for relatives and friends with disabilities and chronic illness. Many of these people rely on others to provide meals, shop, do laundry, clean, help with personal care such as bathing and dressing, and give emotional support, love, and encouragement. Over 3 million women in the United States provide personal assistance to family members who are sick or disabled, and over 10 million women provide care to people outside their own households, usually their elderly parents and their husbands' elderly parents. This caretaking of elders may go on for as much as fifteen years and often overlaps with the women's other responsibilities — holding jobs, taking care of growing children, and managing homes. This regimen can be very trying; it involves physical and emotional stress and added expense and can seriously affect the quality of life and health for women in their middle years, who may have to give up opportunities for education, social life, or leisure-time activities. These women may be reluctant and resentful at times but accept their situation as part of what it means to be a good wife or daughter. It is important to recognize that the carers also need care.

Health As Wellness
Requirements for Good Health

Health is not just the absence of illness, as implied by the medical model described above. Feeling well involves a complex mix of physical, mental, and emotional factors, as suggested in Reading 55 by Kat Duff, who was diagnosed with chronic fatigue immune dysfunction syndrome (CFIDS) some years ago. Many aspects of life are not under our control. For example, living in damp housing or near a busy freeway or polluted industrial area, working in hazardous factories and mines, being exposed to toxic pesticides in agricultural work, doing repetitive tasks all day, and sitting in the same position for long periods of time are all aspects of daily life that can compromise one's health. The many newspaper and magazine articles that focus on individual lifestyle factors — diet, cigarette smoking, weight, exercise, and a positive attitude to coping with stress — urge us to take more personal responsibility for our health. Although this is valuable advice, lifestyle is only part of the story, as is made clear in Reading 57. There Rita Arditti and Tatiana Schreiber present data on links between breast cancer and environmental contamination. Cancer research efforts that focus on individual neurological or genetic factors miss this crucial environmental connection.

Health requires clean water, air, and food, adequate housing, safety and security, healthy working conditions, and emotional and material supports. Thus, seemingly unconnected issues like poverty, racism, and sexism are also health issues. Illness is not just a series of symptoms to be eliminated but an indicator that our bodies are telling us something important. Many critics of the current medical system differentiate health care from medical treatment and argue that the medical model, with its emphasis on high-tech equipment and procedures, drug treatments and surgeries, does not adequately protect or promote health.

Feminist Approaches to Wellness

Because many women's health needs are not currently met under this system, feminist health practitioners and advocates urge a fundamental shift in emphasis toward a more holistic system of health care, which recognizes that physical, emotional, and mental health are intimately connected and which emphasizes self-education, prevention, self-help, alternative therapies, a restructuring of medical financing, and a wider provision of basic facilities. As a means to this end, and depending on their view of the cause of the problem, some groups concentrate on changing current health policies while others choose to work with self-help projects on the grounds that this is a more effective use of their time and resources. Still other groups have been active in opposing Operation Rescue and other so-called pro-life organizations that have tried to close down clinics where abortions are performed.

Self-Education and Preventive Care Preventing illness through self-education has low priority in the United States, and beyond basic immunization for infants and some minimal sex education for teens, it has generally been left to interested practitioners, organizations like the American Cancer Society, or self-help health-care projects. It involves learning to listen to our bodies and becoming more conscious of what they can tell us; learning to eat well and to heal common ailments with home remedies; taking regular exercise; quitting smoking; doing breast self-exams; and practicing safe sex. Self-education and preventive care also include various types of self-help, such as programs dealing with substance abuse or codependence. Many of these, like Alcoholics Anonymous, Al-Anon, Narcotics Anonymous, and other twelve-step programs, have been successful in helping people change negative habits and attitudes, though they usually do not address macro-level factors like institutionalized racism, sexism, and heterosexism. A self-help approach also means taking a greater degree of personal responsibility for one's health and being able to make informed decisions about possible remedies and treatments, rather than simply consuming services. Finally, preventive care encompasses all the creative activities and projects, like dancing, music, poetry, sports, and homemaking, that give us joy and make us feel alive.

Alternative Therapies Therapies such as acupuncture, homeopathy, deep tissue massage, and chiropractic care that do not rely on drug treatments and surgery may be highly beneficial for a range of complaints. Although they have been scorned as quackery by many mainstream medical practitioners, they are being used more often, sometimes in conjunction with Western medicine. At present most alternative therapies are not financially accessible even for people with medical insurance, as they are not routinely covered, and they are usually available only in larger cities.

Reform of Health Care Financing   As mentioned above, a proposal for a national health plan put forward by President Clinton in his first term of office was abandoned because of lack of political, financial, and professional support. Many advocates for women's health argue for a fundamental change in the way health care is paid for. In May 1993, for example, the Women's Convergence for National Health Care, attended by over five hundred women from twenty states, called for a universal health-care plan to provide equal access, comprehensive benefits, freedom to choose doctors and other caregivers, health education and prevention, reproductive health, public accountability, and progressive, fair financing (Baker 1993). Participants argued that universal health care is a major component of a social justice agenda.

Feminist Health Projects   These projects have been active since the early 1970s. Examples include courses in women's health, informal self-health groups like the Bloomington Women's Health Collective (Bloomington, Ind.), women's health centers (e.g., in Concord, N.H. and Burlington, Vt.); campaigns for reproductive rights (e.g., National Abortion Rights Action League and regional affiliates) or public funding for breast cancer research and treatment (e.g., Women's Community Cancer Project, Cambridge, Mass.); and national organizations like the Black Women's Health Project (Atlanta), the National Asian Women's Health Organization (San Francisco), the National Latina Health Organization (Oakland), the National Women's Health Network (Washington, D.C.) and the Native American Women's Health and Education Resource Center (Lake Andes, S. Dak.). The Boston Women's Health Book Collective's *Our Bodies, Ourselves* first started as mimeographed notes for a course in women's health and was later developed for publication. A key emphasis of this women's

health movement is a recognition of the politics of health and illness and that individual health is inescapably linked to macro-level factors.

Feminist perspectives, research, lobbying, and policy making have significantly changed how women's health is perceived and how women are treated as patients. There is still a great deal to be done before quality health care is available to all women in this country.

As you read and discuss this chapter, consider the following questions:

1. How do you know when you're healthy? Sick?

2. How can you learn more about your own body and your health?

3. What can/do you do to take care of yourself? List the steps.

4. Where can women go to keep healthy in your community?

5. What are considered legitimate health-care practices? By whom? Why?

6. What is a health crisis? For an individual person? At the national level?

7. Who should pay for health care? How?

8. How does an individual, family, or society construct definitions of illness?

9. How do we, as a society, decide which illnesses are more important than others? Which merit a collective response?

10. Who benefits from these decisions? Who loses?

11. When is it useful to call something a health problem and when not? How are these decisions made?

12. What are your assumptions about pregnancy, childbirth, and parenting? How do they relate to your own experience?

13. How do you define reproductive health? Reproductive rights?

◆◆◆

FIFTY-FIVE

Towards an Ecology of Illness

Kat Duff

I'm sprawled across my bed, as if thrown aimlessly aside. The trappings of illness surround me: twisted tissues and covers, half-empty glasses of water (one with a fly floating in it), and plastic pill bottles, spilling. I watch clouds of dust swim through the slanting rectangle of light from my window as the afternoon creeps away. I've been sick for over a year now with CFIDS (chronic fatigue immune dysfunction syndrome); it's best described as a flu that never goes away. There is no cure as yet, only the remedy of rest for a few years. So I spend twelve hours a day in bed—sleeping, reading, ruminating and wondering: what is the matter? Where did this begin and where is it going?

One of the oddities of being sick is that you suddenly remember all the other times you've been sick: the childhood diseases, stomach flus, chest colds, allergic reactions, food poisonings, sunstrokes . . . the list goes on and on. Illness weaves through our lives with surprising regularity; it is no less central to the human condition than sexuality is, though we hardly give it the same attention. Memories of illness fade quickly under the glare of health, dropping into the muddled background of life, only to reappear with the onset of yet another illness. Now that I'm sick, it seems that all of the many and varied illnesses of my life are simply crests on the waves of an ocean that lies beneath the surface of my world, something like a watertable of the soul.

Illness is a world of its own, a foreign yet familiar landscape, existing within the cosmos we inherit as human beings, not unlike an alpine meadow or a coral reef. But there are few maps of this invisible geography, as if it were circled by the waters of forgetfulness, or the thick impenetrable mists of fairytale lore. We hear from doctors about disease but rarely from the sick themselves. The experience of illness defies description and often escapes language altogether. "English," wrote Virginia Woolf, "which can express the thoughts of Hamlet and the tragedy of Lear, has no words for the shiver or the headache." So, illness remains a wilderness—beyond our grasp, strangely forbidding and forever a mystery—de-

spite its continuing presence in our lives. And like an alpine meadow or a coral reef, it may well play an important role in the ecology of the whole.

One thing is certain; no one chooses to get sick. In fact, we avoid it "like the plague" with our rituals and regimens of healthy living. Illness chooses us, instead, for its own inscrutable reasons. We are caught, unsuspecting, by the onset of symptoms, and often feel attacked, persecuted, even slain, by this hungry hunter we call disease; then we are dragged, like Persephone, into the underworld of sickness. As we "become sick," sickness becomes us and redefines us; so we say we are not ourselves anymore. I lose my usual interests immediately, even before the fever or cough arrives. A kind of existential ennui rises in my bones like flood waters, and nothing seems worth doing: making breakfast, getting to work on time or even making love. That's when I know I'm succumbing to the influence of illness. I slip, like fluid through a porous membrane, into the nightshade of my solar self, where I'm tired of my friends, I hate my work, the weather stinks and I'm a failure.

Sometimes I ask myself: why didn't I realize this before? Inevitably, some sure voice from the depths of my illness replies: "you've been fooling yourself."

That sure voice fills me with a shuddering awe I've come to associate with moonless nights, pounding surf and other such imposing presences. She holds no allegiance to my preferred self-concepts and proud accomplishments; in fact, she rather enjoys replaying recent events in a humiliating light during those long, insufferable afternoons. That sure voice remembers everything I've forgotten, overlooked or denied: my original purposes, deflected desires and persisting failures. These are what Virginia Woolf called the "wastes and deserts of the soul" that appear "when the lights of health go down." I often emerge from the encounter feeling very small, bound by the circle of my own limitations, and beset by the handmaidens of illness: doom, depression and despair.

Romanian philosopher E. M. Cioran once wrote that "illness confers the experience of the terrible." Since I've been sick, I have come close to some truly terrifying possibilities: that I'm dying, that some part of my father (who molested me when I was a baby) wants me dead, and that the nuclear research lab nearby is emitting radiation that is killing all of us, slowly. My friends call it paranoia, in the ready optimism and confidence that health confers, and so do I on my brightest days; but at other times I wake up in a cold sweat sure that it's absolutely true and I'm doomed.

Frankly, I find it very difficult to reconcile the contrary visions of health and illness, or even hold them both in my mind at once. They slip away from each other like oil and water. It's like trying to remember bitter cold of winter in the midst of a sweltering August heat wave. Our brains are not well-equipped for such exercises, and yet something compels us to make the effort.

It has been said that illness is an attempt to escape the truth. I suspect that it's actually an attempt to remember the whole truth, to remember all of ourselves. For illness is not just something that happens to us, like a sudden sneeze or passing storm; it's part of who we are all the time. We carry within ourselves all of the diseases we've had, and many we will have in the future, as genetic inclinations, damaged organs, hidden bacteria and sleeping cancer cells. We just forget in the heyday of health. The longer I'm sick the more I realize that illness is to health what dreams are to waking life — the reminder of what's forgotten, the bigger picture working toward resolution.

There is, perhaps rightly so, an invisible rope that separates the sick from the well, so that each is repelled by the other, like magnets reversed. The well venture forth to accomplish great deeds in the outside world, while the sick turn back into themselves and commune with the dead; neither can face the other without the uncomfortable intrusion of envy, resentment, fear or horror. Frankly, from the viewpoint of illness, healthy people seem ridiculous, even a touch dangerous, in their blinded busyness, marching like soldiers to the drumbeat of duty and desire.

Their world, to which we once belonged, and will again most likely, seems unreal, like some kind of board game that could fold up at any minute. Carl Jung reported that after his heart attack the world suddenly appeared to be a ruse at best ("like a painted curtain"), a prison at worst. He despaired of getting well and having to "convince myself all over again that this was important!" We drop out of the game when we get sick, leave the field and desert the cause. I often feel like a ghost, the slight shade of a person, floating through that world, but not of it. The parameters of my world are different altogether.

Space and time lose their definitions in the unmarked sea of illness. We wake from a nap to wonder where am I? On the train to San Francisco or at Grandmother's house? Maybe both, for opposites co-exist in the underworld of illness. We are hot and cold at once, unable to decide whether to throw off the blankets or pile more on, while something tells us our lives are at stake. Sometimes I feel heavy as a sinking ship, and other times light as a ghost rising from the wreckage.

Time stretches and collapses, warping like a record left in the sun. Ten seconds can seem like an hour of torture in acute pain; while whole lifetimes can squeeze into a few moments when we wake from sleeping or fall in a faint. Past and future inhabit the present, like threads so tangled the ends cannot be found. Many years ago I had a curious experience when I was sick with a fever in a tiny efficiency apartment in Santa Fe. I was drifting in and out of sleep when a host of images swept before me like a flock of birds: a long list of the addresses of my life, the kitchen windows and back stoops I have loved, the stars of the Big Dipper turning overhead, all the cardboard boxes carried in and out of my homes, the stars of the Big Dipper resting on the horizon. Suddenly I knew (and don't ask me how) that I didn't have to keep moving every two years, as I had always done. I saw the skin of my restlessness rise from my body like the thin film of fog over water at dawn and disappear. Sure enough, the next move was my last.

The underworld of illness is full of such impossible events, strange visitations and unexpected transformations. When I was sick with dysentery in India, a Hindu holy man in orange appeared in the corner of my hotel room and sent waves of healing through my ragged body; a friend of mine saw Mother Mary rise up out of her garbage can during an allergic reaction to mold. The universes revealed by illness defy the rules of ordinary reality and share in the hidden logic of dreams, fairytales and the spirit realms mystics and shamans describe. There is often the feeling of exile, wandering, searching, facing dangers, finding treasures. Familiar faces take on the appearance of archetypal allies and enemies. Small ordinary things, like aspirin, sunshine or a glass of water, become charged with potency, the magical ability to cure or poison. Dreams assume a momentous authority. No wonder many tribal peoples consider illness to be one of the most powerful means of revelation available to humankind.

At the very start of my illness, when I still thought it was a simple flu, I dreamt that someone asked me what was wrong and I answered, calmly, "I'm dying." Then the scene switched to my backyard where beautiful blue morning glories were climbing up to the sky. I woke from that dream with a great clarity; I knew I was very sick and better get help, but more importantly, I realized I was in sacred territory, undergoing changes so profound and promising that could only be likened to dying.

Illness is a taste of death, after all, a practice in dying for the living, a visit to the limbos and bardos usually reserved for the recently deceased. There is the slow grind of discomfort and weakness that dissolves desire and cuts us loose; we sink into a private reality of pain, memory and shifting awareness, ruminating upon the tangled knots of our lives. Sometimes there is talk, a sudden urgency, that makes no sense to others; the sick and the dying alike make fervent apologies and stark accusations. And there is the reverberating isolation of enduring pain and luminous revelations that cannot be shared. No wonder we fear for our lives when we fall ill, speak of being "more dead than alive" when we are sick, and "returning from the dead" when we get well.

Death, in its guise as the destroyer, is the active agent in illness. It provokes and exasperates our strengths and weaknesses until something — one's faith in God, overweaning sense of responsibility, good cheer or strong heart — gives way, cut down by the scythe of the grim reaper. No one returns from an operation, accident or illness exactly the same; there is a bitterness (or compassion), strength (or fragility), faith (or despondency) that was never there before. Illness is a small death that prepares us for the bigger life — and death — ahead. It's an initiation of sorts, taking us from one stage of life and level of awareness to the next. In fact, serious illnesses follow the stages and requirements of traditional ceremonies — isolation, suffering, death and resurrection — with remarkable fidelity.

Last year, I dreamt that I went to the doctor for tests. She took a sample of my saliva and returned to say the lab could not run the tests because they found my father's semen in my saliva; I would have to keep returning for tests until the semen was gone, so I could sign the Declaration of Independence. At the time, I knew the dream was referring to the residues of my incest experiences; what I didn't fully realize was that my illness was the way my body would eject the poison. In the months that followed, I had several episodes of sudden nausea, violent shaking and vomiting, reliving the terrors of my infancy; my body moved, of its own accord, to spit out my father's semen. These flashbacks frightened me terribly and left me exhausted; they rank among the most difficult experiences I've ever endured. And yet, in their wake, I felt extraordinarily calm and strangely radiant, as if bathed in light.

Illness is such a good vehicle for eliminating toxins, the ingrained poisons of our physical, mental and emotional anguish. In fact, many Asian and tribal peoples perceive sickness to be a manifestation of the body's wisdom, cleansing us of the bad habits and misunderstandings we've somehow accumulated. The Cherokee, for example, consider sickness a "purifying experience," intended to "return us to our path of destiny and spirit," as Dr. Lewis E. Mehl, a Cherokee himself, explained. And it works this exorcism of sorts through the very features we find so distasteful in the sick: the bad breath, runny noses and oozing sores, the coughing, spitting, crying and vomiting.

Illness, like death, is a dirty, messy vegetative process. The microscopic organisms responsible for most disease — fungi, bacteria and parasites — actually do the work of decay. They break down the order of systems into a disarray of parts, translating dead matter into essential nutrients, to feed the next generation; and our warm, moist anaerobic insides provide the perfect environment for their invisible labors. In a fever my insides feel like soup on the stove, or compost in the bin, seeping and settling. I shudder, shiver and sweat, and drink vast quantities of liquid — all of which work to soften the rigid and eliminate the unnecessary. This is the sacred alchemy of nature we witness every fall, in the sinking of sap, the dropping of leaves, the scattering of seed. It is the "way of the seeded earth," to use a phrase from Joseph Campbell, to sacrifice old life for new in the great chain of life. From this perspective, disease and death are not failures of life; they are part of a cycle of life; in fact, the very means of its continuation.

These powers of decay operate with the ruthless detachment of all scavengers. They don't care whether you are fat or skinny, good or bad, eating low-fat yoghurt or steaks every night; they just do the work that's required — transformation — to restore equilibrium to an imbalanced world. One of the most unexpected discoveries I've come upon during my two years of "rest" is that illness is not just a private affair; it reflects a larger disorder and attempts to remedy it.

Most indigenous peoples consider the illness of an individual to be symptomatic of an imbalance in the larger community of life, an indication that some violation of nature has occurred, which has not been righted; therefore someone is sick, the rains don't come, or the people fight among themselves. Even the ancient Greeks, already far removed from their tribal roots, believed that illness could result from the crimes of one's ancestors or collective transgressions, as well as personal fault. For the physical world is fragile and very susceptible to human actions in this understanding; it must be carefully tended with patience and love. A single strand pulled out of place can tear the web apart, hurting one's family, the community, and the cosmos itself, for generations to come. That's why so many healing ceremonies of indigenous peoples, from the African Yoruba or the Arctic Inuit, involve the entire community.

How, one might ask, does the mining of uranium in northern Arizona, relate to the rising incidence of leukemia throughout the U.S., as many tribal elders of the four corners area insist? This is my understanding of the way it works. Whenever the natural order is violated, feelings of shame and responsibility are evoked, so that wrongs may be righted and the single strand rewoven into the web. Originally, shame carried a sense of the sacred, the great Mystery which infuses all life, instilling reverence and humility. It served to remind us human beings, so prone to hubris, that we are not God, that we have and will make mistakes, encouraging us to acknowledge those mistakes and remedy them as best we can. However, after centuries of institutionalized violence, during which the gods and goddesses of the natural way were buried and replaced by the laws of political orders, shame has been split from its sacred roots. Now it rests as the pervasive sense of being wrong or bad, unworthy or unfit, that afflicts so many sensitive, abused and oppressed peoples.

At this point, shame rarely lands on the shoulders of those who commit the transgressions: the corporate polluters, wife-beaters or keepers of apartheid, and all of us who disregard the life of another. We, of the post-industrial cultures of the West, are so convinced of our separateness, so numb to our own original pain, so bound to inflict upon others what we cannot feel (in the name of practicality, progress, even love) that we are incapable of accepting the shame and responsibility of our actions. As a result, shame floats free of the shameless trespassers and lands upon the trespassed, those who are treated shamefully — the women, children and old people, the underclassed and outcast — who come to manifest the symptoms of distress and disease, becoming the sacrifices. As my dream made so graphically clear, my father's semen — the effects of his transgressions and those of our ancestors — has ended up in my mouth, and I must do something about it in order to be free.

That dream triggered a sequence of events which have showed me how my illness relates to crimes of my ancestors, and how to free myself from that legacy. When my doctor returned with her news from the lab (in the dream) she handed me a questionnaire to fill out about my illness which included several questions about my family history and genetics. At first they seemed irrelevant, but after answering the questions I began to suspect there was more to this business of genes and ancestry than I had realized. That dream led to others about my ancestors on my father's side of the family, who settled in Minnesota in the 1860s, when the native peoples (the Dakota) were being driven off the land. In one of these dreams the basement walls of my grandmother's house (which stood next door to ours on the land settled by my ancestors) were painted with images of imperialism: German soldiers marching in unison, Spanish conquistadors on horseback with shining helmets.

As a result of these dreams, I became preoccupied with figuring out how my great-great grandfather had acquired the land I grew up on. My father told me he bought it from another white man who, in turn, had received it the year before from the state, after the "Sioux Uprising" (read massacre) of 1862; but something seemed wrong, very wrong, about it. So I decided to consult a shaman, since shamans are specially trained to discern far-reaching lines of causation in illness.

He told me first off that I was "a sacrifice dying so that others may live." Many Dakota had starved or frozen to death when they were displaced from the land my ancestors settled, their ancestral homeground, he explained. Those deaths made a big gash in the land and my body is the wound. Something like a curse or a requirement was laid upon my family at that time, that each generation would get smaller and smaller (which it has) until it died out altogether, unless a sacrifice was made. If I did not wish to be that sacrifice, he added, I should honor the Dakota who died and make offerings to them, so that the ill will generated by that tragedy could be transformed into benevolence. He helped me to do that (I can't describe how without diminishing the power and effectiveness of those actions) and since then I have felt relieved of a certain heaviness, the sense that I didn't deserve to be alive, that's been with me as long as I can remember. Now, just over a year later, I'm mostly recovered.

Yes, the sins of the father are visited upon the children, and onto the seventh generation, as many Native American traditions attest. The Bible calls it "blood guilt," psychologists have named it the "genealogical shadow." Deepak Chopra, an M.D. who is well-versed in ayervedic medicine, speaks of "ghosts of memory" which affect our immune systems and foster illness. I suspect that the psyches and bodies of 20th century Americans are crowded and overflowing with these "ghosts of memory" so implicated in disease, because we as a people are so oriented towards progress and eager to escape the burdens, complications and contradictions of continuity. It's the American way (as exemplified by my ancestors, but also by my own life) to leave one's home and past behind to start a new life on the great frontier . . . leaving a terrible — and toxic — trail of unfinished business.

Perhaps that's why sick people and survivors of all kinds so often insist upon remembering the dead and forgotten, and why descendants of the Dakota who survived the Wounded Knee Massacre of 1890 journeyed by foot and by horseback to the grave site one hundred years later, across hundreds of miles through subzero temperatures, to offer prayers, burn

sage and receive the apology of South Dakota Governor George Mickelson. The Dakota, like many other tribes, have repeatedly asked for an apology from the U.S. government for the atrocities of the past in the recognition that our lives and well-being, as red and white peoples, depend upon the mending of those wounds.

The Indo-European root for the word "cure" means "to sorrow for something," and I have yet to meet the sick person who doesn't sorrow deeply for something — the breakdown of a marriage, an early death in the family, or the nameless innocents slaughtered in war. A good friend of mine, who came down with CFIDs after visiting Nicaragua, says it broke her heart to see how our government is destroying that country and that's why she's sick. Our bodies bear the untold lessons and scars of history; as we suffer our wounds in the extremities of illness they become our offerings, our means of realizing and remembering what is right, what is needed, to bring our lives and our world back into balance. I love to see what people do when (and if) they recover from serious illness; there is often an urgency towards some kind of action to set things right. The father of a friend apologized to all his children for his years of absence after a heart attack. Another friend quit her job with the state after a mastectomy to paint full time. A veteran suffering from the effects of Agent Orange is planting trees for every American who died in Vietnam.

When I first got sick, I looked for a cure; now I realize that my illness *is* the cure, or part of the cure, for something much bigger than I. My experience has born out the truth of these words by poet Demetria Martinez: "A wound is not something to cure, but something to listen to and see with." It's "a way out, a way in."

F I F T Y · S I X

◆◆◆

Cancer in the Family

Lois Lyles

Waiting for New Year's: The Hospital

"Lois, I guess you'd better not look at this," my mother says. Humped over and sitting on the edge of the hospital bed, she begins unbuttoning her pajama top. The nurse is already drawing the green, floor-length curtain that makes a cubicle of the area around each bed in the double-occupancy room.

Now the bed next to my mother's is temporarily vacant, so she has the luxury of sleep undisturbed by the groaning of the miserably ill women who, on various occasions during my mother's stay, have been bedded in the room.

"All right," I agree. I swing the massive wooden door shut, and leave the nurse alone with my mother to begin the examination of my mother's chest. Standing at the picture window at the corridor's end, I let the sun's rays burnish my face. The corridor is sticky with the caramel tones of high-volume Spanish. I turn and see, for the first time, the inhabitant of the room which has a pink "Special Precautions" warning placard protruding from its doorway. At the comfortable distance of six feet, the patient is chatting with his guard. The AIDS victim is young — no older than twenty-five, surely. He wears five-and-dime slippers of brown corduroy, and his slight body is clothed in pajamas too thin for December. In a lemon-yellow face, brown eyes and cherry lips move with animation as he speaks. I wonder at his apparent vitality, at his so terribly menaced youth, and at the fierce voracity of the disease which will snap up his life — more quickly, perhaps, than my mother's illness will consume hers.

Several mornings later, as my mother is dressing herself in preparation for her discharge from the hospital, I speak with a nurse outside my mother's room.

"Is there any special care my mother will require once she is home?"

The nurse gazes at me questioningly, pityingly. "No. One of Mrs. Lyles' main difficulties is coming to terms with her illness. For example, I tried to get her to look at the mastectomy scar in the mirror while I was with her, and she refused."

What can I do but nod? How does one "come to terms" with the loss of a part of one's body? How does one "come to terms" with the loss, creeping closer and closer, of one's life?

Cousin David is with Dad and me this New Year's Day, helping to pack Mama's things so that she can be brought home. The checkout time was to be eleven A.M., but because I had misunderstood this and had not gotten Mama dressed on time, we are late. Dad is bullying Mom and the nurse about the difficulty of finding a pharmacy open to fill Mom's prescriptions on a holiday; about her unreadiness to leave; about everything. He is a tall, husky man barking at a trembling, shrunken rag of a woman. Standing, he leans over her and shouts

at her bowed head as she sits wearily on the hospital bed.

Dad and David load the steel hospital trolley with Mama's belongings, and the two men are off down the hall. Mama tells me she needs her glasses, stockings. I run down the hall and tell Dad.

"Your mother is crazy," he declares. "She's got everything she needs."

"You're rushing her!" My head is blazing.

He retorts that she is off her head. Then he shambles off with the triple-shelved trolley, packed with cardboard boxes of pajamas, underwear, toiletries; with the greeting cards and potted plants of well-wishers.

"Stop, let me look just a minute!"

On the middle shelf, I find her glasses, shoved in a corner beneath a piece of embroidery tightened over a small hoop. Next my hands dive into a blue nylon duffel bag and rescue her balled-up stockings.

Back in her room, I help her finish dressing. Her legs, eased with painful slowness into the stockings, are shriveled tan sticks. An orderly comes, helps her into a wheelchair. He rolls her slowly into the corridor and down the hall.

Now missing is the pink sign that has flagged the door on the right-hand side of the hall, not far from my mother's room. "Precautions Warranted in Handling Blood and Body Fluids," the sign had read. The young Latino AIDS victim, whose room has been guarded by blue-uniformed men, is gone — where?

I walk a few paces behind my mother. Her pigeon-like, hump-shouldered, wasted body is garbed in a cardinal-red coat, which is new, and of plush wool. A cheap white knitted cap covers her head. Her clothing combines a main theme of jaunty, coruscatingly vivid color with pallid off-notes suggesting poverty and defeat. She is a picture which seems to corrade all my senses. Midway down the hall, in the room occupied by two middle-aged black men, a radio belts out the blues.

New Year's Night: The House

Sound the alarm! Raise the windows high — our screams should rocket into the silent night. Let the hue and cry tear like wildfire through the streets where Christmas lights still festoon the houses, warmly painting the dark. Get the neighbors up from their peaceful beds. Cry what I cry — come by here, somebody! Why should we, as though disgraced, keep our hands over our mouths, conceal my mother's suffering and our grief, tell friends and neighbors all is well? Why should we lock our doors, and keep still within, while we burn alive from this invisible conflagration? Help! Cancer! Cancer! Cancer!

Eating

And what will the cancer have to eat, of my mother's sparrow body? My mother is so little, five feet five, flesh dwindling before our eyes; ninety, it looks like she weighs — what will the cancer have to eat? Her feet, size six and a half; give my shoes to the Goodwill, she says, nobody but Jean got feet little as mine, and Jean's so glamorous, she'd never wear 'em.

Mama's face is gaunt and her eyes are huge and frightened — brown squirrel eyes. The only big thing on her is her hips. When she is bedridden, I look at her hips and think, *I came from there.* We have the same shape, she and I: small-breasted, big-hipped. She is so little, haggard, and frightened; what will the cancer have to eat?

Cancer eats us all. Dad cooks cheeseburgers with a crisp bacon garnish one night. The cold meat sits out after the meal, a white grease congealing on each patty. The meat is left on the kitchen counter two days. There is little time to cook, and to monitor the storage of food. I ask Mama if the hamburgers are safe to eat, if Ahmed can have them for dinner on the third day. She always knew such things, I could always ask. Who will I have to ask after she is gone?

She says yes, let him have one. With misgivings, I feed it to my son, twelve-year-old Ahmed; there is nothing else for supper. Early the next morning I hear him vomiting behind the closed bathroom door.

When the ambulance comes the first time the pork chops for dinner are thawing on the kitchen counter. No time to put them away. When it comes down to cooking them, hours and hours later, after the crisis (the stroke Mama suffered), I am scared the meat is spoiled.

Dad stops at the Burger King when we are on the way back from the emergency room, Mama wrapped up in a white blanket on the front seat. At the house, I put Mama to bed while Ahmed and Dad sit in the kitchen, eating burgers and fries. I don't eat. Ahmed soon stops eating and goes to bed. I whisper to him

in the dark of his room: "What's wrong?" He says the night in the emergency ward waiting room put him off his food.

Sometimes, at night, from my own bedroom (across the hall from Ahmed's), I hear peculiar sounds, human, coming from the darkened room of the child.

Sleep

Cancer hath murdered sleep. I wake three or four times per night, remembering there is no reason I should arise the next day to another dawn of grief.

Cancer hath murdered sleep. Mama is plagued by insomnia. And even if she were not, her sleep would be destroyed — at her physician's orders. Even if she is asleep at midnight, or at two A.M., or at five A.M., or at ten A.M., I must wake her — not for just one medication at each of these times, but sometimes for two, three, or four pills. The hard, round, shiny pill (Slow-K) is my particular enemy; it sticks in her throat. When I try to stab its shell with a fork, to shatter it into manageable fragments, it dances around its nest, a china saucer. Ampicillin, a white gritty substance encased in a gelatinous red capsule which easily breaks apart, is more friendly. But there are others, some of which must be taken with food; and it is an additional agony for her to eat a cracker, or to drink a glass of milk, at one of the wolf hours. After her second stroke, I must try to mash the pills and get her to lick the crumbs of medicine from my fingers.

When she cries at being awakened, I (and sometimes Ahmed, who is always concerned, always ready to enter the room and help) tell her firmly, "Do your job. Take your pills." My heart blisters as I deliver this instruction. Sometimes she moans, "I'm so tired. I just want to rest, forever."

Scar Tissue

Tap, tap, tap. Lightly my knuckles meet the smooth blond wood of the door to the master bedroom.

"Mom, the nurse is here." I make my voice soft.

"All right, Lois. Come in."

I enter, followed by the heavy-set, ebony-skinned nurse. "Mom, this is the visiting nurse, Mrs. Hutchins."

"Call me Elizabeth, please." She smiles, opening her large mouth wide and showing the gap between her front teeth. Did the gap-toothed Wife of Bath look this robust, friendly, hearty? I hope so.

My mother smiles back from her perch at the head of the bed. She is sitting up, ready, involved.

"I want to check the scar on your breast to see that the flesh is healing properly and the sutures are intact," Elizabeth says.

"Lois, perhaps you had better go out while she does this," my mother says. I note the "perhaps," the question in her tone. I am guessing that she wants me to look, to know, to accept. To accept her.

"Mama, I don't have to leave, unless you are certain you want me to," I maintain. I put my hands on my hips and stand at the foot of the bed, facing her.

"All right. Stay." She nods, and begins unbuttoning her out-of-style polyester knit shirt with garish ribbons of chartreuse and neon orange twirling across a solid black background.

Shirt and brassiere fall to the bedspread, and I am seeing. A raw wind batters the inside of my chest and threatens to stop my breath. But I try to make my voice low and calm when I speak. With the nurse, I look, I point. Elizabeth says, "Healing nicely. Look — no pus, no bleeding, no infection. Those are the danger signs to watch out for."

"Yes, the tissue looks clean and healthy," I say. I nearly gag on the last word. Healthy? My mother is dying!

I wanted to say something positive, to help her. Something positive, to strike down in myself, the fright that rose like nausea to the throat, at the sight of that scar.

It is a good scar. No traces of infection. But what a mutilation! Not the loss of the breast, merely. At her age, when the breast has lost its apple-like roundness, its suppleness and firmness, it is no longer a symbol of beauty and eroticism, anyway. (I suppose not — not being a woman of sixty, how would I know? And who is to say what makes a body beautiful?) My mother's remaining breast is an elongated, soft cone, not a globe. And with the removal of the other breast, something more than beauty, however it might be defined, has been cut away. Maybe the loss has been of self-respect. When she was a girl, she was unquestionably beautiful. In middle age, she still carried beauty — the idea of beauty — about her eyes and mouth, like a flame — and her body at least was whole. But *now. . . .*

Much of the muscle near the armpit has been excised, so that a crater, in shape and texture, lies where

her breast was. Instead of the smooth, parchment-colored skin which is properly hers, she must view a brown, waffled crust, edged all around by tiny black threads. She is held together with the kind of stitch which she, who taught me sewing when I was about age ten, would have called "over and under."

Nurse Elizabeth examines the skin graft on my mother's right thigh. The thigh scar is not yet actually a scar. The plastic surgeon took a patch of skin about ten inches long by six wide to cover the hole left by the missing breast. Now the graft, a raw, furious pink, gleams under its clear plastic dressing.

I am pleased that my mother seems cheered by my calm, objective appraisal of the results of her surgery. But I am quivering inside, with an ague I cannot still, as I look at her and think, *She has been a soldier in some dubious battle.*

My mother had a lump in her breast for over a year and told nobody until the lump was the size of a tennis ball and the pain became unbearable. She was reared during the Depression, when maladies of all kinds went untreated because sick people had no money to pay the doctor. Her life has been a long struggle to amass enough money to enable her family to live with dignity. Her general rule has been: Don't waste money on doctors. If you are sick, try to bear up and last the sickness out.

Recently I asked Mama, "Why didn't you tell a doctor about the lump in your breast?"

She replied, crying, "I thought it would go away!"

Nurse is winding up. "Mrs. Lyles, you got your wig yet?" she kindly asks. "You know when the radiation treatments begin, your hair's gonna fall out. Plus, the chemotherapy will often make you very sick, just like the radiation. There is a nausea medication you can get in suppository form. You will need that because sometimes you will not feel like eating, and other times you will not be able to keep anything in your stomach."

I cringe inside. What was it Dad said? *Minnie's got a long, hard road to travel, and she knows it.*

The nurse folds her hands as she stands at the foot of the bed, giving more quiet, kind forewarnings to my mother, who now buttons her blouse.

"You will have good and bad days. Sometimes you'll feel O.K. Other days you'll be so low you want to cry all the time. If you want to cry, cry. But remember, I'll want to see you smile, sometimes, too. I can't take too much of that crying." Elizabeth grins, and my mother grins back.

Elizabeth and I walk toward the kitchen, just down the hall from the master bedroom. She tells me, "One thing to remember about the cancer patient is the importance of attitude. Your mother will get depressed at times, but try to encourage her to have hope. After all, who knows? There may be a cure."

I nod, definitely in agreement about the importance of hope; nevertheless, I feel glum about where to look for it. What cure could fly here in time to save Mama?

"Respect is important, too. Always listen to the patient and respect her needs."

I nod vigorously.

A woman's face, sporting glasses, pops around the corner of the doorway to the kitchen. The woman is middle-aged and elegantly coiffed; her hair is short, tightly-curled, and of an improbable shade of brown not much darker than that of her light, reddish-brown complexion.

"Lois?" she says, in a high-pitched, florid voice. Seeing my amazed stare as she enters the kitchen, she gives my name the inflection of a question, rather than a greeting.

"Yes?" I ask coldly.

"Don't you know who I am?"

I shake my head. Who is this? And upstairs, too, where Mama is expecting nobody!

"I'm *Norma*!" she remarks emphatically, as though there is no reason I should not know; no reason anybody alive should not know.

"Oh." My voice, dull, offers no welcome.

It is a cousin, on my father's side — second cousin? third? I cannot recall. In any other circumstances I gladly would have thrown her the "long time no see" bit; would have exchanged familial inquiries and traditional courtesies with her. But now, all courtesy is blotted out by the question mounting large in my head: Why did he let her come up here? Mama doesn't want anybody to know she has cancer! My nerves are on fire.

"Perhaps you'd better go back downstairs awhile," I tell Norma, as I unceremoniously grasp her forearm and propel her toward the stairs. Over my shoulder I tell the nurse, "Let's talk again next time you come. I'll see you out. Thanks for your help."

Elizabeth smiles. The three of us go downstairs and I let the nurse out. Norma, looking befuddled, sits down on the couch adjacent to Dad's recliner. As soon as the nurse is gone I turn on Dad. His feet are on a level with his head as he lies back in the chair, but when I start screaming, the thick carpet sounds the thump! of his stockinged feet as he sits upright.

"So Norma is here, is she? Why did you send her upstairs? You knew the nurse was up there, looking at Mom! Don't you have any respect? You know how sick she is! Why would you do that?"

He gapes, then leaps to his feet.

"What's happening up there? Has she had a relapse, to make you carry on like this? Norma, something terrible must've happened to Minnie, to send Lois off."

"Oh, no!" With my index finger, I stab at him repeatedly. "Nothing terrible's happened, and I haven't gone off. But I'll tell you one thing. And I'm a tell it right here, in front of your kin. I'm a tell you 'bout yourself." I am panting with the rage that has flamed up in me from my entrails to my head and that has brought me a terrific release from the fear of him I have known practically my whole life. I am about to do what, in our family, is unforgivable — put the family business in the street.

"You're a terrible person!" I shout. "You don't respect Mama, and you never have. I hate your guts!" My final shout carries me out of the livingroom, back up the stairs, and into my mother's room.

"You know what he did? Norma was up here, on her way back into your room! And the nurse not even gone yet! I am so angry!" Waves of blood assault my brain. My breathing comes fast, fast, fast. "I've never been so angry in my life." Pant, pant, pant. "I told him, too! I said I hated his guts!"

"Lois, Lois." My mother lies back on the bed. Her voice is low: soothing and reproachful simultaneously. "You told him that?"

"Yeah, I told him. And I needed to have told him a long time ago." My stomach feels hot, but my head feels light and free.

I have spoken my mind to him at last. My mother is going, and with her the standard of conduct that has kept a vise on my lips. If she is going to die, I need not try to act quiet, tame, and ladylike any more; I need not try to keep peace in the family for her sake any longer. I need not be afraid of my father any longer, as she has been afraid, and has taught me to be afraid, of the man who for decades has raged and bullied us all into silence. I am miserable at my mother's dying, but fiercely content at the realization that with that terrible event, my deepest self has begun to be born.

◆◆◆

FIFTY-SEVEN

Breast Cancer
The Environmental Connection
Rita Arditti with Tatiana Schreiber

Today in the United States we live in the midst of a cancer epidemic. One out of every three people will get some form of cancer and one out of four will die from it. Cancer is currently the second leading cause of death; it is estimated that by the year 2000 it will become the primary cause of death. It is now more than two decades since the National Cancer Act was signed, yet the treatments offered to cancer patients are the same as those offered fifty years ago: surgery, radiation and chemotherapy (or slash, burn and poison, as they are called bitterly by both patients and increasingly disappointed professionals). And in spite of sporadic optimistic pronouncements from the cancer establishment, survival rates for the three main cancer killers—lung, breast and colorectal cancer—have remained virtually unchanged.

In the sixties and seventies environmental activists and a few scientists emphasized that cancer was linked to environmental contamination, and their concerns began to make an impact on public understanding of the disease. In the eighties and nineties, however, with an increasingly conservative political climate and concerted efforts on the part of industry to play down the importance of chemicals as a cause of cancer, we are presented with a new image of the disease. Now it is portrayed as an individual problem which can only be overcome with the help of experts, and then only if one has the money and know-how to recruit them for one's personal survival efforts. This emphasis on personal responsibility and lifestyle factors has reached absurd proportions. People with cancer are asked "why they brought this disease on themselves" and why they don't work harder at "getting well."

While people with cancer should be encouraged not to fall into victim roles and to do everything possible to strengthen their immune system (our primary line of defense against cancer), it seems that the socio-political and economic dimensions of cancer have been pushed completely out of the picture. "Blaming the victim" is a convenient way to avoid looking at the larger environmental and social issues that frame individual experiences. Here we want to talk about environmental links to cancer in general and to breast cancer in particular, the kinds of research that should be going on, why it's not happening and the political strategies needed to turn things around.

Extensive evidence exists to indicate that cancer is an environmental disease. Even the most conservative scientists agree that approximately 80% of all cancers are in some way related to environmental factors. Support for this view relies on four lines of evidence: 1. the dramatic differences in the incidence of cancer between communities; i.e., incidence of cancer among people of a given age in different parts of the world can vary by a factor of ten to a hundred; 2. changes in the incidence of cancer (either lower or higher rates) in groups that migrate to a new country; 3. changes in the incidence of particular types of cancer over time; and 4. the actual identification of specific causes of certain cancers (like the case of betanaphthylamine, responsible for an epidemic of bladder cancer among dye workers employed at du Pont factories). Other well-known environmentally linked cancers are lung cancer (linked to asbestos, arsenic, chromium, bischloromethyl ether, mustard gas, ionizing radiation, nickel, polycyclic hydrocarbons—in soot, tar and oil—and of course, smoking); endometrial cancer, linked to estrogen use; thyroid cancer, often the result of childhood exposure to irradiation; and liver cancer, linked to exposure to vinyl chloride.

The inescapable conclusion is that if cancer is largely environmental in origin, it is largely preventable.

Our Environment Is a Health Hazard

"Environment" as we use it here includes not only air, water and soil, but also our diets, medical procedures, and living and working conditions. That means that the food we eat, the water we drink, the air we breathe, the radiation to which we are exposed, where we live, what kind of work we do and the stress that we suffer—these are responsible for at least 80% of all cancers. For instance, under current EPA regulations as many as 60 cancer-causing pesticides can legally be used in the most commonly eaten foods. Some of these foods are allowed to contain 20 or more carcinogens, making it impossible to measure how much of the substances a person actually consumes. The 1958 Delaney clause which banned the deliberate addition to foods of *any* level of carcinogens, was revoked in 1988, depriving consumer groups of the possibility for legal action. As Rachel Carson wrote in *Silent Spring* in 1962, "This piling up of chemicals from many different sources creates a total exposure that cannot be measured. It is meaningless, therefore, to talk about the 'safety' of any specific amount of residues." In other words, our everyday food is an environmental hazard to our health.

Recently, a study on the trends in cancer mortality in industrialized countries has revealed that while stomach cancer has been steadily declining, brain and other central-nervous-system cancers, breast cancer, multiple myeloma, kidney cancer, non-Hodgkins lymphoma, and melanoma have increased in persons aged 55 and older.

Given this context, it is not extreme to suspect that breast cancer, which has reached epidemic proportions in the U.S., may be linked to environmental ills. In 1992, estimates are that 180,000 women will develop breast cancer, and 46,000 will die from it. In other words, in the coming year nearly as many women will die from breast cancer as there were American lives lost in the entire Vietnam War. Cancer is the leading cause of death among women ages 35–54, with about a third of these due to breast cancer. Breast cancer incidence data meet three of the four lines of reasoning linking it to the environment: 1. the incidence of breast cancer between communities can vary by a factor of seven; 2. the risk for breast cancer among populations that have migrated becomes that of their new residence within a generation, as is the case for Japanese women who have migrated to the United States; and 3. the incidence of breast cancer in the United States has increased from one in twenty in 1940 to one in nine in the nineties.

A number of factors have been linked to breast cancer: a first blood relative with the disease, early

onset of menstruation, late age at first full-term pregnancy, higher socio-economic status, late menopause, being Jewish, etc. However, for the overwhelming majority of breast cancer patients (70–80%), their illness is not clearly linked to any of these factors. Research suggests that the development of breast cancer probably depends on a complex interplay among environmental exposures, genetic predisposition to the disease, and hormonal activity.

Research on the actual identification of causal factors, however, is given low priority and proceeds at a snail's pace. We still don't know, for example, the effects of birth control pills and the hormone replacement therapy routinely offered to menopausal women. Hormonal treatments are fast becoming the method of choice for the treatment of infertility, while we know nothing about their long range effects. And, the standard addition of hormones into animal feed means that all women (and men) are exposed to hormone residues in meat. Since there is general consensus on the importance of estrogen metabolism for the induction of breast cancer, hormonal interventions (through food or drugs) are particularly worrisome.

A startling example of the lack of interest in breast cancer prevention is the saga of the proposed study on the supposed link between high fat diets and breast cancer. The "Women's Health Trial," a 15-year study designed to provide conclusive data about the high fat–cancer link, was denied funding by the National Cancer Advisory Board despite having been revised to answer previous criticisms, and despite feasibility studies indicating that a full scale trial was worth launching. Fortunately, it now appears that the study will be part of the Women's Health Initiative, a $500 million effort that will look at women's health issues. That is a success story that is a direct result of women's activism and pressures from women's health groups across the country.

But even if the high fat–breast cancer correlation is established, it is unlikely to fully explain how breast cancer develops. The breast is rich in adipose cells, and carcinogens that accumulate in these fat tissues may be responsible for inducing cancer rather than the fat itself, or the fat alone. Environmental contamination of human breast milk with PCBs, PBBs and DDE (a metabolite of the pesticide DDT) is a widely acknowledged phenomenon. These fat-soluble substances are poorly metabolized and have a long half-life in human tissue. They may also interact with one another creating an additive toxic effect, and they may carry what are called "incidental contaminants": compounds like dibenzofurans, dioxins, etc., each with its own toxic properties. (The most infamous of the dioxins [2, 3, 7, 8-tetrachlorodibenzo-p-dioxin or TCDD] for instance, is considered to be the most toxic synthetic chemical known to science.)

Among the established effects of these substances are: liver dysfunction, skin abnormalities, neurological and behavioral abnormalities, immunological aberrations, thyroid dysfunction, gastrointestinal disturbances, reproductive dysfunction, tumor growth and enzyme induction. Serious concerns have been raised about the risks that this contamination entails for infants who are breast-fed. But what is outrageous in the discussion about human breast milk poisoning is that little or no mention is made of the possible effects on the women themselves, particularly since it is known that most of these substances have *estrogenic* properties (that is, they behave like estrogen in the body). It is as if the women, whose breasts contain these carcinogens, do not exist. We witness the paradox of women being made invisible, even while their toxic breasts are put under the microscope.

The Pesticide Studies

Very recently some scientists have at last begun to look at the chemical–breast cancer connection. In 1990 two Israeli scientists from Hebrew University's Hadassah School of Medicine, Elihu Richter and Jerry Westin, reported a surprising statistic. They found that Israel was the only country among 28 countries surveyed that registered a real drop in breast cancer mortality in the decade 1976–1986. This was happening in the face of a worsening of all known risk factors, such as fat intake and age at first pregnancy. As Westin noted, "All and all, we expected a rise in breast cancer mortality of approximately 20% overall, and what we found, was that there was an 8% drop, and in the youngest age group, the drop was 34%, as opposed to an expected 20% rise, so, if we put those two together, we are talking about a difference of about 50% which is enormous."[1]

Westin and Richter could not account for the drop solely in terms of demographic changes or improved medical intervention. Instead, they suspect it may have been related to a 1978 ban on three carcinogenic pesticides (benzene hexachloride, lindane,

and DDT) that heavily contaminated milk and milk products in Israel. Prior to 1978, Westin said, ". . . at least one of them [pesticides] was found in the milk here at a rate 100 times greater than it was in the U.S. in the same period, and in the worst case, nearly a thousand times greater." This observation led them to hypothesize that there might be a connection between the decrease in exposure following the ban and the decrease in breast cancer mortality.

The pesticides that were contaminating Israeli milk are known as inducers of a superfamily of enzymes called the cytochrome P450 system. These enzymes can promote cancer growth, weaken the immune system, and destroy anti-cancer drugs. Westin and Richter believe that these induced enzymes could have increased the virulence of breast cancer in women and therefore increased the mortality rates. They speculated that when the pesticides were removed from the diet, there was a situation of much less virulent cancer and the mortality from breast cancer fell.

Westin and Richter are convinced that there is a critical need to increase awareness about environmental conditions and cancer. Health care clinicians, for example, could play an important role in the detection of potential exposures to toxic chemicals that might be missed in large studies. "It's a question of a mindset and of programming and training and activating the medical profession and the health professions to keep their eyes and ears open for such possible associations," said Richter. "This is not necessarily expensive. It's a question of awareness and professional commitment."

This is a refreshing view since it encourages individual physicians to ask questions about work environments, living quarters, dietary habits, etc., that could provide important clues about the cancer–environment connection. Epidemiological studies, as currently conducted, are not that sensitive in identifying low levels of risk, and the long latency periods of some cancers may not be adequately taken into consideration. Needless to say, the relevant questions are not usually asked of cancer patients.

Other studies are beginning to directly measure chemical residues in women who have breast cancer compared to those who don't. Dr. Mary Wolff, a chemist at New York's Mount Sinai School of Medicine recently completed a pilot study with Dr. Frank Falk (then at Hartford Hospital in Hartford, Connecticut) that has just been published in *The Archives* of *Environmental Health*.[2] In this case-controlled study, Falk and Wolff found that several chemical residues from pesticides and PCBs were elevated in cases of malignant disease as compared to non-malignant cases.

The study involved 25 women with breast cancer and the same number of women who had biopsies but did not have breast cancer. The results showed differences significant enough to interest the National Institute for Environmental Health Sciences which will fund a larger study, a collaboration between Wolff and Dr. Paolo Toniolo, an epidemiologist at New York University School of Medicine and one of the authors of a study conducted in Italy on the role of diet in breast cancer. Wolff and Toniolo's new study will look at the level of DDT and its metabolites in the blood samples of 15,000 women attending a breast cancer screening clinic in New York, and it will take into consideration reproductive factors, dietary habits, family history, and hormone levels in the body. This study could provide valuable data clarifying any link to chemical exposures and stimulating further research.

In the U.S., levels of pesticide residues in adipose tissue have been decreasing since the 1970s (following the banning of DDT and decreased use of other carcinogenic pesticides) while the breast cancer rate continues to rise. This observation would seem to contradict the pesticide hypothesis. However, Toniolo points out that the chemicals could act differently at different exposure levels; they are unlikely to act alone; and time of exposure may be important. For example, if a child is exposed during early adolescence, when breast tissue is growing rapidly, the result may be different than exposure later in life.

Radiation and Mammography

Another area that demands urgent investigation is the role of radiation in breast cancer development. It is widely accepted that ionizing radiation causes breast cancer at high doses, while low doses are generally regarded as safe. Questions remain, however, regarding the shape of the dose-response curve, the length of the latency period and the importance of age at time of exposure. These questions are of great importance to women because of the emphasis on mammography for early detection. There is evidence that mammography screening reduces breast cancer

deaths in women age 50 or older. However, Dr. Rosalie Bertell, (director of the International Institute of Concern for Public Health, author of *No Immediate Danger: Prognosis for a Radioactive World* (Book Publishing Co., TN, 1985) and well-known critic of the nuclear establishment) raises serious questions about mammography screening.

In a paper entitled, "Comments on Ontario Mammography Program" Bertell criticized a breast cancer screening program planned by the Ontario Health Minister in 1989. Bertell argued that the program, which would potentially screen 300,000 women, was a plan to "reduce breast cancer death by increasing breast cancer incidence." She presented an independent risk-benefit assessment of the program and concluded that even if breast cancer deaths were reduced, only a very small number of the lives saved would be exclusively due to the screening. The overwhelming majority of the cancers could have been detected by other means, including monthly self-examination. She added that a significant number of women (163) would have unnecessary breast surgery due to the program and a very high number (10,000) would have retests because of false positive mammographies. Despite these criticisms the program was put into place and is now ongoing.

Bertell's critique of mammography is supported by a recent multi-million dollar Canadian study on 90,000 women that looked at cancer rates between 1980 and 1988.[3] The study has yet to be released, but preliminary results show that for women aged 40 to 49, mammograms have no benefits and may indeed harm them: 44 deaths were found in the group that received mammograms and 29 in the control group. The study also suggests that for women aged 50 to 69, many of the benefits attributed to mammography in earlier studies "may have been provided by the manual breast exams that accompanied the procedure and not by the mammography," as Bertell noted in her paper. Not surprisingly, the study has been mired in controversy. As study director Dr. Anthony Miller remarked, "I've come up with an answer that people are not prepared to accept."

According to Bertell, the present breast cancer epidemic is a direct result of "above ground weapons testing" done in Nevada between 1951 and 1963, when two hundred nuclear bombs were set off and the fallout dispersed across the country. Because the latency period for breast cancer peaks at about 40 years, this is an entirely reasonable hypothesis.

Other studies have looked at the effect of "low-level" radiation on cancer development. A study investigating the incidence of leukemia in southeastern Massachusetts found a positive association with radiation released from the Pilgrim nuclear power plant. (The study was limited to cases first diagnosed between 1978 and 1986). In adult cases diagnosed before 1984, the risk of leukemia was almost four times higher for individuals with the greatest potential for exposure to the emissions of the plant. Other types of cancer take a greater number of years to develop, and there is no reason to assume that excessive radiation emission was limited to the 1978–1986 time frame. In other words, it is entirely possible that as follow up studies continue, other cancers, (including breast cancer) will also show higher rates.

In the last few years, questions have also arisen about the possible biological effects of electromagnetic fields. Studies looking at EMF and childhood leukemia are inconclusive, but two studies on telephone company and electrical workers have raised the possibility of a connection between EMF exposure and breast cancer *in males*. Genevieve Matanoski of Johns Hopkins University studied breast cancer rates in male New York Telephone employees between 1976 to 1980, and observed a dose-response relationship to cancer. There were two cases of breast cancer, a very high number for such a small group. Breast cancer in men is rare; in the U.S. the annual incidence is 1 in 100,000, as compared to 110 in 100,000 for women.

Another study, by Paul Demers and others at the Hutchinson Cancer Research Institute in Seattle, Washington, also found a strong correlation between male breast cancer and jobs that involved exposure to EMFs. They reported that ". . . men whose jobs involved some exposure to EMFs were nearly twice as likely to have breast cancer as men with no exposure, and men likely to have the highest exposures — electricians, utility linemen, and power plant workers — had six times the risk of developing breast cancer as men who worked in occupations with no EMF exposure," (as quoted by Dr. Robert Pool in *Science*). Individuals exposed at least 30 years prior to diagnosis and earlier than age 30 were at higher risk than other EMF-exposed workers. According to Dr. Robert Pool, EMFs can produce changes in the cellular metabolism, including changes in hormone production, protein synthesis and iron flow across cell membranes.

Ironically, most of the studies on EMF exposure have been done on men, while EMFs are generated by household appliances and video display terminals largely used by women.

The Surveillance Theory

Current theory supports the concept that cancerous mutations are a common phenomenon in the body of normal individuals and that the immune system intervenes before mutated cells can multiply. Known as the "surveillance" theory of cancer, the basic premise is that cancer can develop when the immune system fails to eliminate mutant cells. Carcinogenic mutations can be induced by radiation or chemicals, for instance, and if immunological competence is reduced at a critical time, the mutated cells can thrive and grow.

Given the apparent importance of the immune system in protecting us from cancer, we ought to be concerned not only with eliminating carcinogens in our environment, but also with making certain that our immune systems are not under attack. Recent evidence that ultraviolet radiation depresses the immune system is therefore particularly ominous. At a hearing on "Global Change Research: Ozone depletion and Its Impacts" held this past November by the Senate Committee on Commerce, Science, and Transportation, a panel of scientists reported that ozone depletion is even more serious than previously thought.

According to the data, the ozone layer over the U.S. is thinning at a rate of 3–5 percent per decade, resulting in increased ultraviolet radiation which "will reduce the quantity and quality of crops, increase skin cancer, *suppress the immune system,* and disrupt marine ecosystems" (our emphasis). (The report also states that a 10 percent decrease in ozone will lead to approximately 1.7 million additional cases of cataracts per year, world-wide, and at least 250,000 additional cases of skin cancer.) As the writers make chillingly clear, since this is happening literally over our heads, there is no place we can run.

Dioxin, (an extremely toxic substance that has been steadily building up in the environment since the growth of the chlorinated chemical industry following World War II) can disrupt the immune system. "Free radicals" created by exposure to low-level radiation can also cause immune system abnormalities. In other words, our basic mechanisms of defense against cancer are being weakened by the chemical soup in which we are immersed.

It follows that an intelligent and long range cancer prevention strategy would make a clean environment its number one priority. Prevention, however, has a low priority in our national cancer agenda. In 1991, only 17% ($293 million) of the total budget of the NCI was spent on primary prevention. Research on the cellular mechanism of cancer development, where much of the "prevention" effort goes, does not easily get translated into actual prevention strategies. With respect to breast cancer, of $92.7 million allotted in 1991 for breast cancer research, only $11 million was spent on prevention, a shockingly low figure for a disease that represents more than 15 percent of cancers diagnosed each year.[4]

In his 1989 exposé of the cancer establishment, *The Cancer Industry,* Ralph Moss writes that until the late '60s the cancer establishment presented the view that "cancer is . . . widely believed to consist of a hereditable, and therefore genetic" problem. That line of thinking is still with us, but with added emphasis on the personal responsibility we each have for our cancers (smoking and diet), and little or no acknowledgment of the larger environmental context. In a chapter appropriately named "Preventing Prevention" Moss provides an inkling of why this is so.

The close ties between industry, the National Cancer Advisory Board and the President's Cancer Panel, two of the most influential groups determining our national cancer agenda, are revealing. Through most of the eighties, for example, the chairman of the President's Cancer Panel was Armand Hammer, head of Occidental International Corporation. Among its subsidiaries is Hooker Chemical Company, implicated in the environmental disaster in Love Canal. Moss, formerly assistant director of public affairs at Memorial Sloan-Kettering Cancer Center (MSKCC), outlines the structure and affiliations of that institution's leadership. MSKCC is the world's largest private cancer center and the picture that emerges borders on the surreal: in 1988, 32.7% of its board of overseers were tied to the oil, chemical and automobile industries; 34.6% were professional investors (bankers, stockbrokers, venture capitalists). Board members included top officials of drug companies — Squibb, Bristol-Myers, Merck — and influential members of the media — CBS, the New York Times, Warner's communications, and Reader's Digest — as well as leaders of the $55 billion cigarette industry.

Moss's research leaves little doubt about the allegiances of the cancer establishment. Actual cancer prevention would require a massive reorganization of industry, hardly in the interest of the industrial and financial elites. Instead of preventing the generation of carcinogenic and toxic waste, the strategy adopted by industry and government has been one of "management." But as Barry Commoner, director of the Center for the Biology of Natural Systems at Queens College, in Brooklyn, New York, put it rather succinctly, "The best way to stop toxic chemicals from entering the environment is to not produce them."[5]

Instead, the latest "prevention" strategy for breast cancer moves in a completely different direction. A trial has been approved that will test the effect of a breast cancer drug (an anti-estrogen, tamoxifen) in a healthy population, with the hope that it will have a preventive effect. The trial will involve 16,000 women considered at high risk for breast cancer and will be divided into a control group and a tamoxifen group. The National Women's Health Network (a national public-interest organization dedicated solely to women and health) is unequivocal in its criticism of the trial. Adrienne Fugh-Berman, a member of the Network Board, wrote in their September/October 1991 newsletter, "In our view the trial is premature in its assumptions, weak in its hypothesis, questionable in its ethics, and misguided in its public health ramifications." The criticisms center around the fact that tamoxifen causes liver cancer in rats, liver changes in all species tested, and that a number of endometrial cancers have been reported among tamoxifen users. Berman points out that approving a potent, hormonal drug in healthy women and calling that "prevention" sets a dangerous precedent. This drug-oriented trial symbolizes, in a nutshell, the paradoxes of short-sighted cancer prevention strategies: they use more drugs to counteract the effect of previous exposures to drugs, chemicals or other carcinogenic agents. It is a vicious circle and one that will not be easily broken.

Grassroots Pressure Is Essential

In the mid-eighties, women living on Long Island learned that Nassau and Suffolk counties had a breast cancer rate 13–14% higher than the state average (since that time statistics indicate an even more dramatic "hot spot" for breast cancer in Nassau County). When journalist Joan Swirsky learned that a major study would be undertaken to look for associations, she was at first pleased, but in no time found herself in the role of activist, as she discovered flaws in the study design.

From her column in *The Women's Record,* Swirsky noted that the original study (a joint effort of the state Health Department and SUNY-Stony Brook) "omitted at least two important environmental variables — the source of drinking water and proximity to toxic dumpsites."[6] Because of the questions she and other women raised, the study was redesigned twice. When it was finally released in 1991, it was inconclusive but indicated that environmental factors do not account for Long Island's high breast cancer incidence. Instead, residents were told, their cancers were probably attributable to affluence, or diet and that no further research was called for.

Partly in response to the study, a group of Long Island breast cancer survivors and their supporters formed a group called "One in Nine." (The name was based on Nassau County's breast cancer rate which has since become the national average.) Women were enraged at being told that this was "the end" of the issue and met several times with the NY Department of Health, pointing out that their counties are actually areas of mixed income, and at the same time, neighboring affluent counties have not been found to have particularly elevated breast cancer rates. Marie Quinn, founder of the group commented, "Is water studied enough? . . . Electromagnetic fields, dishes that take in TV and radio waves? . . . how about homes that have been built on top of waste dumps that have been closed . . . areas where there were factories years ago, [and] dumped toxic materials. . . . I don't think that these things have been examined closely enough."

Swirsky and members of One in Nine are now demanding that other unexplored variables (such as electromagnetic fields, actual chemical levels in drinking water, hormones in meat, observed "clusters" etc.) be considered. The State Dept. of Health recently "promised" to find a way to address these concerns. Swirsky's criticisms were instrumental in helping other women to speak out and to try to make public officials accountable for their actions.

Cancer, Poverty, Politics

It is ironic that women in Long Island are being told that their high breast cancer rates are due to their af-

fluent lifestyle, when breast cancer is on the rise (both incidence and mortality) among African-American women, hardly an "affluent" population. The African American Breast Cancer Alliance of Minnesota, organized in October of 1990, has noted this steady increase and the limited efforts that have been made to reach African-Americans with information and prevention strategies. People of color often live in the most polluted areas of this country, where factories, incinerators, garbage and toxic waste are part of the landscape. Native American nations are particularly targeted by waste management companies that try to take advantage of the fact that "because of the sovereign relationship many reservations have with the federal government, they are not bound by the same environmental laws as the states around them."[7]

Poverty and pollution go hand in hand. The 1988 Greenpeace report *Mortality and Toxics along the Mississippi River* showed that the "total mortality rates and cancer mortality rates in the counties along the Mississippi River were significantly higher than in the rest of the nation's counties" and that "the areas of the river in which public health statistics are most troubling have populations which are disproportionately poor and black." These are also the areas that have the greatest number of toxic discharges. Louisiana has the dubious distinction of being the state with the most reported toxic releases — 741.2 million pounds a year. Cancer rates in the Louisiana section of the "Chemical Corridor" (the highly industrialized stretch of river between Baton Rouge and New Orleans) are among the highest in the nation. Use of the Mississippi River as a drinking water source has been linked to very high rates of cancer in Louisiana. The rates of cancer of the colon, bladder, kidney, rectum and lung all exceed national averages.[8] Louisiana Attorney General William J. Guste, Jr., has criticized state officials who claimed that people of color and the poor *naturally* have higher cancer rates. You can't "point out race and poverty as cancer factors" said Guste, "without asking if poor people or blacks . . . reside in less desirable areas more heavily impacted by industrial emissions."[9]

It follows that African-American women, living in the most contaminated areas of this country, would indeed be showing a disproportionate increase in breast cancer incidence. However, widespread epidemiological studies to chart such correlation have not been undertaken. For instance, given the evidence implicating pesticides in the development of breast cancer, it would seem imperative to study migrant (and other) farm workers who have been exposed to such chemicals.

Like One in Nine, other women's groups around the country have started organizing to fight the breast cancer epidemic. A National Breast Cancer Coalition was founded in 1991. Its agenda is threefold: to increase the funding for research, organize and educate. All the recently organized groups consider prevention a priority, and one of their tasks will undoubtedly entail defining what effective prevention really means. In Massachusetts, the Women's Community Cancer Project, which defines itself as a "grassroots organization created to facilitate changes in the current medical, social, and political approaches to cancer, particularly as they affect women," has developed a Women's Cancer Agenda to be presented to the federal government and the NCI. Several of its demands address prevention and identification of the causes of cancer. The group will be asking for endorsements of its agenda from organizations and individuals working in the areas of environmental health, women's rights and health care reform. This effort will provide a networking and organizing tool bringing together different constituencies in an all out effort to stop the cancer epidemic.

Cancer is and needs to be seen as a political issue. The women's health movement of the '70s made that strikingly clear and gave us a roadmap to the politics of women's health. In the '80s, AIDS activists have shown the power of direct action to influence research priorities and treatment deliveries. In the '90s, an effective cancer prevention strategy demands that we challenge the present industrial practices of the corporate world, based solely on economic gains for the already powerful, and that we insist on an end to the toxic discharges that the government sanctions under the guise of "protecting our security." According to Lenny Siegel, research director of the Military Toxic Network, the Pentagon has produced more toxic waste in recent years than the five largest multinational chemical companies combined, between 400,000 and 500,000 tons annually.

Indeed, if we want to stop not just breast cancer, but all cancers, we need to think in global terms and build a movement that will link together groups that previously worked at a respectful distance. At a world-wide level, the Women's World Congress for a Healthy Planet that met in Miami this past November (attended by over 1500 women from 92 countries from many different backgrounds and perspectives), drafted a position paper, *Agenda 21,* that will be presented at the 1992 United Nations Earth Summit conference in Brazil. It articulates women's positions on the environment and sustainable development that stress pollution prevention, economic justice and an end to conflict resolution through war and weapons production, probably the greatest force in destroying the environment.

On February 4, 1992, a group of 65 scientists released a statement at a press conference in Washington, D.C. entitled, "Losing the 'War Against Cancer'— Need for Public Policy Reforms" that calls for an amendment to the National Cancer Act that would "re-orient the mission and priorities of the NCI to cancer causes and prevention." The seeds of this movement have been sown. It is now our challenge to nourish this movement with grassroots research, with demonstrations, and with demands that our society as a whole take responsibility for the environmental contamination that is killing us.

Endnotes

1. "The Israeli Breast-Cancer Anomaly," Jerome B. Westin and Elihu Ricter. Annals of the New York Academy of Science, *Trends in Cancer Mortality in Industrial Countries.* Edited by Devra Davis and David Hoel. 1990. pp. 269–279.

2. "Pesticides and Polychlorinated Biphenyl Residues in Human Breast Lipids and Their Relation to Breast Cancer," Frank Falk, Andrew Ricci, Mary S. Wolff, James Gobold and Peter Deckers. *Archives of Environmental Health.* March/April, 1992. Vol. 47 no. 2, 143–146.

3. "Debate rages over study on breast cancer" by Robin Harvey. *The Toronto Star,* August 11, 1991. A 13.

4. Figures were obtained from the budget office of the National Cancer Institute.

5. Quoted in Greenpeace Toxics, non-dated two page article entitled "US Industry's Toxic Chemical Dependency: Causes, Effects and the

Cure." For more information, write to: Greenpeace, 1436 U Street, NW, Washington DC 20009.

6. "Breast Cancer Update." *The Women's Record.* October 1988, by Joan Swirsky.

7. "Dances with Garbage" by Conger Beasley, Jr. *E* magazine, November/December 1991. See also, *We Speak for Ourselves—Social Justice, Race and Environment,* The Panos Institute, December 1990.

8. From *We all live downstream—The Mississippi River and the National Toxic Crisis.* Greenpeace report, by Pat Costner and Joe Thomton, December 1989.

9. *Greenpeace* magazine. Oct/Nov/Dec 1991, page 12, "Baton Rouge, Louisiana."

◆◆◆

FIFTY-EIGHT

Fallen Women
Alcoholics and Drug Abusers
Eileen Nechas and Denise Foley

These days, the biggest challenge facing Julianne Harris (not her real name) is getting her four-month-old twins to settle down for a nap. She relishes that hour or so of peace and tranquility, a rare treat in a day jam-packed with diapers, feedings, and bathings. But for Julianne, a twenty-nine-year-old former bookkeeper and Joan Lunden look-alike, it's a challenge she embraces with joy and optimism. Indeed, she sails through her days with confidence and energy, the picture of young motherhood, a baby perched on each jean-clad hip.

But up until a few years ago, Julianne faced a different kind of daily existence, one she endured alone and in an alcoholic haze. Her days were spent sprawled on the sofa with a glass in one hand and the TV remote control in the other. She didn't even bother to eat. "At my worst, the only thing I managed to do was walk to the liquor store to replenish my supply," she says, "and I would think I had accomplished a lot." Over a period of seven years she saw her life spiral out of control, fueled by the 2 gallons of vodka that she downed each week.

Although her family suspected that she probably drank too much, they didn't know the extent of it. Like so many women alcoholics, Julianne remained hidden to them, her friends, her co-workers, even her doctor. She became one of the millions of closet drinkers, overwhelmed by guilt and shame, shunned by society and ignored by medicine and research.

Although 40 percent of those who abuse alcohol or drugs are women, it's easy for them to remain virtually unnoticed, like so much dirt swept under a carpet. In fact, they feel like dirt much of the time. Like Julianne Harris, most chemically dependent women must contend with the disgust and repulsion of family and friends. In fact, those reactions often reinforce an addicted woman's reluctance to admit to a problem or to seek help for it. "I would make excuses so I didn't have to be around other people," says Julianne. "I didn't want to see their looks of disapproval. I knew I had a problem, but I didn't want anyone else to know. It was too humiliating."

The scientific community has hardly been more open-minded. Traditionally, substance abuse has been regarded almost entirely as a male affliction, an unfortunate assumption that has compounded the invisibility problem for addicted women. Researchers, who have had little interest in studying those who didn't fit the "norm," simply excluded women from their studies or just averaged their data in with the men's. Indeed, of the more than 110,000 substance abusers studied by various researchers over a period of thirty years, only about 7 percent (8,000) were women. Even when looking for possible hereditary predisposition, researchers have more often chosen to study the biological connections between sons and their alcoholic parents, disregarding whether the findings would be applicable to daughters of alcoholics. And because recovery programs have been studied using only addicted men, they have remained insensitive to the special needs of addicted women.

What little is known about substance abuse in women has only served to underscore the desperate need for more research. Women alcoholics, for example, develop severe liver disease after a shorter period of time than men drinkers do and after consuming far less alcohol, although no one has bothered to find out why. The disease progresses faster, too. More women than men die from cirrhosis of the liver, the most common health complication of alcoholism. According to the National Institute of Alcohol Abuse and Alcoholism, women alcoholics have death rates 50 to 100 percent higher than those of male alcoholics. A greater percentage of female alcoholics die from suicides, alcohol-related accidents, and circulatory disorders.

Women are also at an increased risk of developing multiple addictions, far more so than men. Women are prescribed two-thirds of all psychoactive drugs, such as Valium and Librium, and are more likely to be prescribed excessive dosages. Indeed, 25 percent of women in treatment for alcoholism have serious prescription drug problems as well.

Apparently the interest of the scientific community has yet to be stirred to any significant degree. In 1990, for example, the National Institute of Alcohol Abuse and Alcoholism spent under $7 million on research related to women out of a total budget of $132 million, while pleas from those who study and treat women with chemical dependencies are largely ignored. When research money is spent, most goes to studies of the role of drugs and alcohol on women's reproductive functions or on the influence of substance abuse on women's positions as wives and mothers. The research community, as it does in other arenas, fails to recognize that "women are more than just baby carriers and care givers," says substance abuse researcher Tonda Hughes, Ph.D., R.N., of the University of Illinois. The effect of alcohol and drugs on women themselves, on their psychological and physical health, remains unmapped ground as do the social and economic pressures that influence their addictive behaviors. As long as both interest and money remain in short supply, chemical dependencies in women will continue to be ignored, underreported, underdiagnosed, and most definitely undertreated. Consequently, it will be decades or longer before knowledge of the causes, risk factors, long-term effects, and treatment of addictions in women approaches that of men's.

The Stigma of the Female Addict

In society's eyes, women are still held to a higher code of conduct than men. They are seen as the gatekeepers of social standards and morality. Excessive drinking is simply incompatible with that narrow view. No one likes a drunk, but when the drunk is a woman, she is despised. In ancient Roman times, women who were caught drinking were put to death by stoning or starvation. Although the penalty for drinking isn't death anymore, it's still torture for most women. Indeed, drunken women are labeled as fallen women, dangerously promiscuous, and generally out of control. Snubbed by society and riddled with guilt, they are driven into hiding, becoming closet drinkers, like Julianne Harris, or secret pill poppers or both.

Not so for men, however. In typical double-standard fashion, a drunken man is not only tolerated, but is either viewed as "macho" by his buddies or excused with a wink and a boys-will-be-boys attitude. Julianne, who used to play in a coed softball league, says that she eagerly guzzled beer with the guys until she noticed the dirty looks shot her way. "They made it clear that drinking the way *they* did wasn't ladylike."

But by far the most damaging stigma that women who drink or use drugs must contend with is that of sexual promiscuity. The prevailing attitude is that women who drink excessively become far more sexually aggressive. Yet the research simply does not support that notion, no matter how popular it remains. One study showed, for example, that only 8 percent of 1,000 women surveyed said they became less particular about their choice of sexual partner when they had been drinking. And the proportion hardly varied whether the women were light or heavy drinkers. Instead, the majority of the women reported that they were the targets of sexual aggression by men who had been drinking.

This stereotype of promiscuity among women who drink is not only inaccurate, says psychiatry professor Sheila B. Blume, M.D., of the State University of New York at Stony Brook, it results in promoting the sexual victimization of drinking women. In other words, if she drinks, "well, she's just asking for it."

Studies have shown that she gets it, too. In one survey that compared alcohol-dependent women with nondrinking women, 16 percent of the alcoholic women reported being raped, whereas none of the nonalcoholic women had been.

Women who drink in bars are particularly vulnerable to victimization even if they are not themselves heavy or problem drinkers. Julianne Harris says that men often became more brazen when she was out drinking. "They became less afraid to make the first move. Once when I was drunk, a man took advantage of me. It wasn't rape, but I still felt so dirty afterward. It made me want to drink more just to hide the pain," she says, her voice growing soft with embarrassment.

Sadly, women who abuse alcohol or drugs are likely to believe the low opinion that many have of them. "Since the chemically dependent woman grows up in the same society as the rest of us, she applies these stereotypes to herself," says Blume, who also treats alcoholics at South Oaks Hospital in Amityville, New York. When she fails to meet society's standards, she is acutely aware of her own failures, reacting with extreme guilt and shame. Harris says that people called her a slut when she was drunk even though there was no reason for that. Or they'd say "I was just a drunk. It was bad enough to be called a drunk, but *'just* a drunk' made me feel even more diminished and worthless."

The effect of these social stigmas is to drive addicted women into hiding, into invisibility. Indeed, alcoholic women are much more likely to drink alone, at home, early in the mornings or on weekends, and to go to great lengths to hide their problems from themselves and others. Julianne Harris used to make some excuse to go to her room or to the basement or wherever she had stashed a bottle of vodka, and there, alone and hidden away from disapproving stares, she would drink. "Sometimes I'd pour vodka into a glass and put it behind the microwave oven," she recalls. "Since I was always alone in the kitchen when I cooked, I could sip from my secret source without fear of discovery. But when the house was empty, I would drink all day."

Slipping Through the Cracks

The fact is that it's far too easy for women addicted to alcohol or drugs to remain in hiding. It's as if no one

cares enough to even look for them, and in a sense that's true. The existing systems that expose men with addictions and get them into treatment programs don't necessarily work for women. That's because they were all designed with the male substance abuser in mind. It's *his* behavior when he drinks or uses drugs that has been used as the model for detection. Women simply don't follow the same behavior patterns that men do when they're addicted.

When men have chemical dependency problems, they are more likely to have trouble on the job or trouble with the law. Women, because they are more likely to drink alone and at home are, consequently, far less likely to be caught driving under the influence, drunk at work, or making a public scene. Not surprisingly, employee assistance programs, drunk driver rehabilitation programs, and public intoxication programs are all heavily male dominated. Indeed, the male-to-female ratio among the latter two programs is nine to one. Adds Blume, "Employee assistance programs, which use impaired job performance as a problem indicator and job jeopardy as a motivator, have also been more successful with men."

Families, too, whether intentional or not, often undermine any efforts the addicted member makes to seek treatment. Julianne Harris's family tried to get her committed to a mental hospital, a choice *they* felt was more respectable for their upper-class daughter than the drug rehab program she preferred, which they equated with street junkies. Sadly, studies have shown that about 25 percent of women's families are actually opposed to their seeking treatment of any kind, contributing to these women's invisibility and prolonging their addictions. Aware of and sensitive to the social stigmas associated with female substance abuse, these families fear exposure of their shameful secret. Or more selfishly, they may not want to lose the services of the person who also happens to be the primary family caretaker.

Drug-dependent women are also far more likely to be divorced or separated, so the only people who might be aware of their problem are their own children, and the kids are not about to turn in the people who care for them. Besides, women fear losing custody of their children if they acknowledge that they need help for an addiction — with good reason. In some states, a woman who is addicted to drugs or alcohol is legally labeled as a child abuser or child neglecter. Paradoxically, a woman who continues her dependency without seeking help does not have to face this charge. By remaining invisible, she gets to keep her children, although it comes at the expense of her own recovery efforts. Only the state of New York has recognized what a disincentive this rule is for women who want to kick their habits. There, a woman who is participating in a treatment program is not automatically assumed to be an abusive or neglectful parent, at least not without additional evidence.

When women do decide to seek help, it's usually because of trouble with their health or trouble with their families. But unlike the drunk driver and public intoxication programs that favor the needs of men addicts, there are no public assistance programs for the marriage or health problems that are more consistent with women's addictions. The best these women can hope for is that the people they most often turn to — their doctors, health clinics, or even family and social service agencies — will somehow detect their drug or alcohol problems. In fact, divorce lawyers could be good at detecting chemical dependencies in their women clients if they would allow themselves to do so, claims Blume.

What *about* doctors? Who could be better equipped to uncover the hidden alcoholic than a doctor talking face to face with his or her patient? Although this sounds perfectly logical, it simply doesn't happen — not nearly as often as it should, considering that diagnosing ills is what doctors are trained to do. Yet physicians are often reluctant to diagnose *this* particular problem, especially in their women patients, because they're as aware of the negative stereotypes as everyone else is. In surveys, doctors admit that they often shy away from alcoholic patients because evaluating them, confronting them with their suspicions, and then managing their cases all take large blocks of time, the same excuse many use for not diagnosing patients who are victims of domestic violence.

Doctors are at a disadvantage. Like battered women, women with chemical dependencies are more likely to visit their doctors with vague symptoms such as headaches, anxiety, or insomnia. And, like victims of domestic violence, they leave with a prescription for Valium or some other sedative rather than what they really need — a referral to a drug treatment program. It's the vigilant and concerned doctor who can see through the facade. Julianne Harris's doctor was fooled every time. No matter what illness drove her to the doctor, she'd always mention

something about being under a great deal of stress, which, she says, was a complete lie. "I would say that for the past two weeks I've really been drinking a lot. I'd never tell him that I'd been drinking heavily for the past five years. The doctor always took my word for it and never probed further." Instead, Julianne would occasionally receive a prescription for Valium for her so-called stress problem.

Granted, doctors don't have a great deal to go on in their quest to identify a substance abuser. Alcohol screening tests, for example, sound like a good idea. But even if these screening devices were used all the time (which they're not), they're still bound to miss a proportion of women with addictions, because the tests were developed for and tested on men. The Michigan Alcoholism Screening Test, for example, was tested on men at first, and then repeated with another group of people, only 5.5 percent of whom were women, says chemical dependency researcher Tonda Hughes, Ph.D. A shorter version of the same scale (called the Short Michigan Alcoholism Screening Test) was also originally tested on only male subjects. Although some questions have been changed to incorporate women's life experiences, they are still more geared to uncovering men with addictions than women. Questions about getting into fights or arguments, for example, or drinking-related arrests, trouble at work, or being hospitalized due to alcohol problems are not nearly as relevant for women as they are for men, she says.

Neither are the questions that ask the patient if they ever drink first thing in the morning or before noon. Though women whose addiction is limited to alcohol might be detected with that line of questioning, those are still the patterns more typical of men alcoholics. The fact is, alcoholic women are twice as likely to combine their alcoholism with a dependence on sedative drugs, so they may be more inclined to start their days with Valium or other tranquilizers. Indeed, women who have multiple addictions may not touch a drop of alcohol until the evening hours.

A clinician who asks his women patients how much alcohol they drink each day may also be missing the ones with problems. Studies show that women who drink excessively consume only about *half* what their male counterparts do, although both have the same level of impairment. Until recently, doctors blamed body water content for the difference. According to that theory, because women have less body water than men do, alcohol becomes more concentrated in their systems. But there's more to it than that. When researchers finally got around to studying alcohol metabolism in both men *and* women, they uncovered the most important difference. They found that women have far less of the stomach enzyme that breaks down alcohol, gastric alcohol dehydrogenase, than men do. This enzyme decreases the availability of alcohol to the whole body, so that the less of this enzyme there is, the more intoxicated the person becomes. Because women have less of the enzyme, more alcohol enters their systems. Alcoholic women, the researchers found, have virtually none of this alcohol-metabolizing enzyme.

In spite of this new knowledge, the charts and tables that are used to calculate blood alcohol levels have yet to be revised. Those tables are designed to determine when it's safe to drive by taking into account the number of drinks a person has had, body weight, and time elapsed since the last alcoholic beverage. But those tables still apply to men only, so regardless of what they say, women would be well advised to consume half the amount of alcohol recommended as safe on the charts before attempting to get behind the wheel.

Treatment Insensitivity

When women manage to emerge from the shadows of alcohol or drug addictions and attempt treatment programs, they are likely to find the road to recovery a particularly difficult and lonely one. Detection systems have failed women so completely that there are from four to ten times as many men as women being treated for their addictions, even though addicted men outnumber addicted women only two to one. Vast numbers of women with dependencies still go untreated, whereas those who do get help are forced to participate in programs that have been designed with the male addict in mind.

As in other areas of medical research, women have been systematically neglected, particularly by those who study treatments for alcoholism and other drug dependencies. Researchers have relied almost entirely on male volunteers, and the results are simply generalized to both men and women, a process that does nothing to advance the knowledge of women's addictions or how best to treat them.

"It's like operating in a vacuum," says addictions therapist Marsha Vannicelli, Ph.D., of Harvard University Medical School. "Maybe the study results based on men do apply, and then again, maybe they don't."

Because men have been the ones most often studied, they have also become the standard or norm against which women are measured whether women fit that particular picture of "normal" or not. Most often, of course, they don't. Instead, women are relegated to what's called a special population group, a designation that allows those who design treatment programs to exclude their needs in favor of the needs of those all-purpose standard setters—white males. In that way researchers, policy makers, and doctors can leave existing programs as they are whether they work for all their patients or not.

For women, they are often quite problematic. Male-based treatment programs commonly fail to recognize the importance of the excessive guilt and shame that women suffer, to understand the impact of women's life experiences on their addictions, and to treat them as grown-up individuals who want and need to take responsibility for their lives. Julianne Harris, for example, went through three different rehab programs over a period of one and a half years and fell off the wagon each time before finding a therapist who was sensitive to her style of coping.

As with many women alcoholics, Harris found the therapy strategies used by her counselors to be confrontational rather than supportive, a method that has proven to suit men's behavior patterns much more than women's, says Hughes. Women are already so shamed and demoralized by their addictions that a confrontational approach is counterproductive for them, diminishing their already low self-esteem even further. Typically, says Julianne, the therapist would "scream at the group and tell us that we were idiots. They wanted us to get angry and yell right back to get it out of our systems," she says. In all the groups she participated in, nearly every man did just that. In fact, they got so worked up that she expected to see fist fights break out. "But the men really seemed to get something out of it; you could see that they felt better afterward, relieved," she says. "The women, though, would completely shut down. They'd start to cry and simply freeze and not be able to speak at all. I always felt worse about myself after those sessions and would dread each and every one."

Male-based treatments also tend to discount or trivialize the impact of women's social and economic experiences on the development of their chemical dependencies. Women are not just rationalizing when they relate the onset of their addiction problems to life events such as divorce, sexual abuse, joblessness, or childbirth, says Blume, and those events need to be addressed for treatment to be successful. Julianne's drinking, for example, began as an antidote to the humiliation of discovering her first husband in bed with their next-door neighbor. But it progressed rapidly to needing alcohol to boost her confidence for everyday situations, too, even something as routine as picking up the phone to call about a potential job. Yet, the programs she participated in didn't seem interested in her personal story. "The impression I got was that they had heard it all before many, many times, and so they didn't have to listen to what I thought or felt. Instead, they just wanted to tell me what the problem was and then give me the standard treatment."

Just as detrimental to successful treatment outcomes are the stereotypes and false beliefs that many therapists themselves have of chemically dependent women. The fact is, therapists hold the same negative attitudes as society in general. Women, particularly addicted women, are considered weak and therefore needing extra protection. Julianne found, for example, that the rehab programs tended to treat her as if she were a helpless child who needed constant tending. "It was as if, because I was a woman, I couldn't be trusted on my own to follow the program and do what was expected," she says.

Though therapists may believe that they are being supportive and helpful, the effect is anything but that. Says Vannicelli, "In my experience I have found that many women patients, and alcoholic women in particular, need to learn a different message about themselves, namely, that they are or have the potential to be competent, mature women and that they are not doomed to be helpless little girls forever." Indeed, Julianne says that it felt good to take responsibility for herself. "To say, wait a minute, I can do this. If I really want to stop drinking, then it's up to me. Being successful was the best confidence builder."

Chemically dependent women have also been falsely stereotyped as being sicker and harder to treat than their male counterparts. The fact is, however, that women *appear* sicker or less motivated to recover only if they are compared against the male standard. In actuality, of fifty-one studies that compared the treatment outcomes of both sexes, forty-three showed no difference between men and women, seven showed that women had done better than men, and five showed that men had done better than women.* The notion that women have a poorer response to treatment is simply not supported by the existing research, says Vannicelli, who reviewed thirty years' worth of medical literature. "If anything, the weight of the evidence seems to lean slightly in the opposite direction."

And that's with treatment programs designed specifically for the chemically dependent male. What if there were programs sensitive to women's needs? What if there were programs that provided child care for those who needed it; that took women's social and economic status into consideration; that addressed the greater guilt and shame that women experience; that offered supportive rather than the male-oriented confrontational strategies; that included vocational training to improve women's employment opportunities; that worked on assertiveness training and building up long beaten-down self-esteem; that compared results with what's typical for women, not men? Would the outcomes be even better? The truth is, practically no research has been done to find out. Nobody even knows for sure if women do better in all-female groups rather than the more traditional mixed-sex groups, whether a female therapist is better for women than a male therapist, or whether individual counseling is better than group therapy.

"If treatment is done the right way, women respond well, too," says Julianne Harris, who says a day doesn't go by that she doesn't feel blessed. She had her turnaround, which has given her a new life, filled with hope "and diapers," she laughs. But she lost valuable time—most of her twenties—in her search for the right treatment. "I was lucky that I found someone who listened to me," she says. "But I shouldn't have had to find that someone in the Yellow Pages."

---

*The number of studies adds up to more than fifty-one because some studies reported data on more than one sample.

◆◆◆

FIFTY-NINE

The Life and Death of Miss Mildred
An Elderly Black Woman
Annette Dula

Who is the elderly black woman? What do health care workers need to know about her life when they treat her for her numerous chronic ailments? What social factors are important when those chronic illnesses ultimately require decisions about withholding or withdrawing treatment? What must health care providers consider when they approach African American elderly to find out whether they have designated a power of attorney or documented their preferences in case they become incompetent? What are the implications of the Patient Self-Determination Act (PSDA) for elderly African Americans and members of other ethnic populations who also have disproportionately poor health outcomes?

This paper presents the life story of an elderly black woman in the rural south. It is a story about Miss Mildred's history, family, community, work, religion, health, and death. I focus on the elderly black woman simply because she is more likely to live beyond the age of 65 than her male counterpart. Miss Mildred is a composite of elderly black women in the rural southern community where I grew up: They are my mothers, grandmothers, aunts, great aunts, and cousins. They are blood and nonblood relatives. This narrative attempts to link the life, the chronic illnesses, and the death of a black elderly woman.

I have chosen to present a life story because many health care workers do not know the elderly black woman outside the private office, the emergency room, or the clinic. Because what they know about elderly blacks comes from the experts, this paper attempts to let Miss Mildred speak for herself. After all, she is the expert on her life. If one listens carefully, it is clear what she thinks* about her illnesses, her folk health beliefs, her health care providers, life-sustaining therapies, and her approaching death.

Certainly, it is the responsibility of health practitioners—as specified by the PSDA—to educate elderly blacks about advance directives. It is equally, perhaps even more, important to educate elderly blacks so that they themselves can participate in managing and controlling their illnesses, thereby improving the current quality of their lives. Before health care providers can effectively educate, however, they must have a firm grasp of the life challenges that elderly African Americans have faced at every stage of their lives: They must learn about and then understand and accept the culture. To do this, they need to enter the world of the elderly black patient and . . . enter that world cautiously. So let us now enter the world of Miss Mildred.

In the black community, traditionally, the elderly black woman sits on a throne of grace, emanating an aura of dignity that permeates her being. She is respected for her wisdom, admired for her strength, and honored for her contributions to the health and well-being of both the black family and its community. She is tapped as a valuable resource and a knowledgeable advisor because of her life experiences. Her presence provides a "certain steadiness, a calming effect on younger adults and young middle-aged adults as they are moving through the critical periods of adult development." She is an upright, upstanding member of the community; her very presence has served as a buttress against racism and discrimination. She plays a critical role in imparting values on work, education, religion, and family and community responsibility.

She is never referred to by her first name; she is Miss Mildred[†] to non-family members, Sister

---

*In Miss Mildred's story, references are included to substantiate Miss Mildred's reflections.

[†]Regardless of marital status, adult or elderly black women in the south are called "Miss." Hence, throughout this narrative, "Miss Mildred" rather than "Mrs. Mildred" is used. Also, "Aint" is a synonym for "Aunt" used extensively in some southern communities.

Mildred to her age peers and church ladies, and Aint Mildred to her dozens of younger relatives. She is called Big Mama by her grandchildren, her great grandchildren, and all the other blood and nonblood relatives that she has raised and cared for over the years. Almost never is she called just "Mildred."

Her beautiful flower garden with the snapdragons, zinnias, and azaleas is the talk of the neighborhood. She still cans, or "puts up," apples, blackberries, peaches, and tomatoes — all harvested from her own garden with her own hands. At church fetes, members line up to make sure they get some of Sister Mildred's famous fried chicken and deep-dish peach cobbler.

She is somewhat overweight, but *no one* in the community would have the nerve to call her fat. One of her church Sisters might dare to say, "You looking right healthy, Sister Mildred. Life must be treating you pretty good."

Sister Mildred might piously, yet playfully, reply, "Yes Sister, the Lord's been right good to me. I can't complain. If he calls me tomorra, I'm ready to go. And Sister, I hope you can say the same thing, too." And under her breath, she might be heard to mumble indignantly, "Don't you be getting all se-ditty and uppity on me, Tillie Mae. I knowed you before you became a Christian — when you wasn't nothing but a old fast gal, giving your life to the devil."

Elderly black women have a very strong faith; they believe in the Lord with all their hearts. They may show it inside or outside the church. As active church participants, they sing in the choir, teach Sunday School, or head a missionary group. Indeed, they are more active than elderly black males. Elderly black women occupy a most respected role as elders of the church and loudly extol the glory and the grace of God through shouting. They have given to the church all their lives, and when they become sick, the church gives back to them. The church provides some material sustenance, particularly in hard economic times or in sickness. Most of all, however, it provides spiritual sustenance.

Indeed, the older they get, the more religious elderly black women often become. A friend of mine recently said to me, "Chile, every time I go home,

Mama done got more religious than she was the last time I was home. One of these days, she's going to fly right off to heaven."

There is another group of elderly black women who do not spend so much time in the church, perhaps because of poor health, employment requirements, or lack of transportation. But their faith is just as strong. They pray and read the bible frequently, listen to religious radio, and watch religious TV. They have been faithful supporters of evangelical ministers like Oral Roberts, Jimmy Swaggart, Jim Bakker, and Billy Graham for a good number of years. Even if they cannot attend church services regularly, they do manage to attend the bigger and more famous of the traveling church revivals and camp meetings. Elderly black women contribute financially to the church, even though their income is meager.

Although Sister Mildred may have little, she will share her food and visit with the infirm and others doing less well than she. As she puts it "I ain't got much, but the Good Lord done said that we got to help them that needs help. We got to give food to the hungry, visit the old folks and the lonely folks, and minister to the sick. Don't matter what color they is neither. We're all God's children."

Outside the black community, there is a different portrait of the elderly black woman. There, she is often seen just as a poor old black auntie or as an uneducated, domineering matriarch. Her main interactions in the white community are as a patient in the health care system and as a domestic in private or public service.

A number of surveys reveal that she thinks that her health is poor. If she is not doing too poorly, she may still be working in a private white household; some studies show that 72% of employed blacks over the age of 55 work as service workers in private homes and businesses. Although her health care provider and employers may recognize her strength, they do not often see her dignity, her nobility, her beauty, or her importance to her family and the black community.

She may not speak standard English very well, and most likely she has not received formal education beyond the eighth grade. Public school education in the pre-war south revolved around the picking of cotton, the cutting of sugar cane, the harvesting of tobacco, and the explicit and purposeful exclusion of blacks from equal education.

Miss Mildred cooks for the white folks and does a bit of light cleaning. She does not work nearly as hard as she did when she first started working for the Braehills. (She's been working for them off and on for the past four decades.) Over the years, she has worked as hard as any man or woman: She has picked cotton and tobacco; she has nursed white children; she has worked as a domestic worker for several white families; she has washed and ironed white folks' laundry in her own home. (Of all her jobs, she preferred taking in laundry, because working at home meant that she could be her own boss.)

"I even worked in a textile mill and in a furniture factory back in the 60s, when they first began letting us women work the shifts. That was the time I said I wasn't going to be no maid for white folks no more. But I had to quit both them jobs. Those chemicals and dust made me dizzy and sick to the stomach. So I had to go back to work for Miss Braehill."

Things have changed a lot since she first started working for Miss Braehill. In fact, Miss Mildred's white folks treat her pretty decently now, except at holidays. On Thanksgiving and Christmas, they expect her to bake ten cakes and ten pies and cook enough food for all Miss Braehill's relatives who come in for the holidays.

"It ain't so easy for me to do all that cooking nowadays. My bunions hurt me sometimes. I sure get mighty tired when I have to stand up for a long time. But Miss Braehill is pretty good to me. Since I got old she hired somebody else to do most of the cleaning. Now she even lets me leave early on holidays with hardly no fuss a'tall. After all these years, it finally come to her mind that I've got to spend some time with my own family and my own children on holidays. I remember in the old days, I used to hate it real bad when Christmas would fall on a Sunday. That meant I couldn't go to church. And that pained me a heap."

Sister Mildred started her own Thanksgiving dinner this year about a week before the holiday, so all the food was prepared by Thanksgiving day. She cooked candied yams, a 20-pound turkey, two sweet potato pies, 20 pounds of chitlins cooked with hot peppers, potato salad, a pork roast, some buttermilk biscuits, and collard greens seasoned with ham hocks and fat back.

"I know I ain't supposed to be eating these foods. And I done cut back on them some. These is the foods that make your blood hot, and rich, and thick. That's when you get "high blood." High blood is a disease that done killed lots o' us black folks. Now, you can cool down and thin the blood if you take a little bit of garlic water, or lemon juice, or vinegar. That's what my herb doctor told me to do. And I believe it works. But you've got to stop eating pork and grease. That's the hard part, 'cause that's what us old folks was raised on. The chitlins, and the ears, and the tails was the parts o' the pig that the white folks didn't want."

Miss Mildred invited all of her family to Thanksgiving dinner. They include her two remaining blood sisters and five middle-aged children. Only ten of the grandchildren came to dinner, but 20 great grandchildren showed up at Big Mama's. Uncle Boy was there too. He has no blood family, but the ladies in the community look out for him and make sure he has at least one good hot meal every day.

All the grandchildren and great grandchildren call Sister Mildred "Big Mama." Big Mama and Daddy Joe raised their nine children, two grandchildren, and the two Jones kids. The Jones kids lost their parents in the big fire of 1945. They didn't have anyplace to go, so Big Mama took them in. Aint Hominy still lives with Big Mama. Nobody knows where she came from — she just showed up one day and started living with the family. Now she is family. Thirty years later, Miss Hominy and Sister Mildred have the big house to themselves, except when somebody needs a place to stay.

Although the black family structure is showing signs of stress, it has traditionally been the strongest African American institution. One function of the black family has been to act as a buffer against the stress of living in a racist society. The African American family includes nuclear, extended, and augmented family forms. Strong kinship bonds in which relatives and friends support and reinforce one an-other are based on African heritage and the slavery experience. Often, a multigenerational family lives under the same roof. It is likely that our composite elderly woman lives in a multigenerational family. Some of those members are relatives, and some are not, but it doesn't matter. They are all considered family.

Sister Mildred has been feeling poorly lately. In fact, she hasn't felt too good ever since she had that operation 2 years ago. They took out her gallbladder. If she had had her druthers, she would not go back to Miss Braehill's. Lord knows she hasn't felt like it. She likes Miss Braehill; she is a nice white lady. The other day, Sister Mildred told Miss Hominy, "I'm so tired. I been cleaning up after white folks nigh on 60 years now. But I needs to take care of my burial. So I needs to keep working."

Miss Mildred had thought about retiring but decided, "Us poor colored women can't retire; that's what white folks do. We just keep on working and getting sicker and sicker. And then we die.

"Sister Hominy, at my funeral, I want you to make sure they put some gladiolas on top o' the hearse that carries m' body. I get a little bit o' money from the government, but honey, you know it ain't much. But one thing's for sure. I ain't got to ask nobody for nothing. I been paying two dollars a week for my burial ever since I turned 50. Soon's I die, Ebony Funeral Home's going to put up two thousand dollars for my burial. I done picked out and paid for my tombstone and a little plot o' land over in Freedman cemetery. Don't want none of the kin folks to have to put me away.

"I been planning for my death a long time. I know the Lord is coming after me soon. And I'm gonna be ready to go. I want to be buried in that pretty white dress my baby grand-daughter give me two years ago. I ain't never wore it but twice. I want little Donna — how old is she now? 'Bout 30, I reckon — I want her to sing 'I am Climbing Jacob's Ladder.' That sure is a pretty song."

No matter how poor they may be, many elderly black folks have a little burial insurance on the side.

"I still has to pay for some of my medicine and I have to pay for it out o' that little bit o' money that I get from the government and from Miss Braehill. I also set a little money aside each month for the herb doctor. But if I don't have the money, she doctors me just the same."

Although Miss Mildred has been working since she was 11 years old, for the most part, none of her employers have contributed to her Social Security fund. She does receive Supple-mental Security Income (SSI), which is pretty meager but keeps the wolf from the door. She doesn't quite understand that Medicare and Medicaid business. Medicaid is supposed to be for poor folks and Medicare for old folks. But even with Medicaid and Medicare help, it is still hard for Miss Mildred to pay for all of her health care needs. Still, she thinks, "Things is much better for us elderly since Mama died. Didn't have no Medicare and Medicaid to help the elderly then. But even if things is better for us than they used to be, I don't believe colored folks get the same care that white folks get."

Yes, Sister Mildred *has* been feeling poorly lately. It is all she can do to drag herself out of bed everyday and do her housework and put in a few hours at Miss Braehill's. But she isn't quite ready to tell the family how lowly she's been feeling lately. Black elderly describe ill-ness according to their ability to perform the activities of daily living: cooking their meals, cleaning their homes, doing their laundry, shopping, and going to the bathroom without aid. Although they may consider themselves in poor health, they do not regard themselves as really ill until they are no longer able to function on their own.

Sister Mildred will go see Dr. McBee. She doesn't think that Doc McBee is helping her much but since Dr. McBee likes her, Sister Mil-dred humors the doctor a little bit. "Dr. McBee treats me real good. But she ain't so good at explaining things. She uses these big words, and I don't know a bit more what she's talking about. She told me I had a tumor in my lung that was going to kill me. I didn't know she was talking about cancer until one of my grand-children asked me if it was malignant. (I didn't know what that word meant either.) I don't know why them doctors can't just come on out and use plain language. Sometimes *she* don't understand things too good neither. One time my hip was hurting me real bad, and she wanted me to tell her what the pain was like. Now the only thing I could think of was that time I fell off the old mule and got kicked in the side. I told the doctor it had hurt so much that I liked to uh' died.

"And that fool doctor, much as I like her, thought I was saying I wanted to kill myself. That's when she asked me if I knew what euthanasia is. First I thought it had something to do with young people — youthanasia. When she told me what euthanasia is, I looked at her like she was crazy. I was kind of surprised that she even brought it up, since sometimes black folks can be mighty touchy about white folks trying to get rid of us. Maybe she went to one of them conferences that she's always going to and they told her to talk to her patients about these things. They sure didn't teach her how to talk to me about it though.

"But you know what? Ever since we talked about it, looks like every time I turn on the TV, somebody's talking about euthanasia, and doctors helping kill off old and sick folks. Well, I ain't seen them ask nary a elderly black on none of them TV shows and news programs what they thought about euthanasia. I believe the Lord will take me away when it's time to go. Ain't nobody going to hurry me along. You got to be careful what you tell these doctors. Even the good ones.

"Now, McBee's been talking about a living will. I'm kinda confused. I thought about signing that thing. But I didn't know whether they was going to try to kill me by not giving me good doctoring, or keep me alive on them machines, or keep me doped up on them medicines. I just ain't sure about this living will thing. I don't want to be kept alive on no machines. To tell you the truth, I wouldn't put it past them doctors to kill me off anyhow. Well, I don't really think McBee would kill me off, but she ain't the only doctor that tends me. So I ain't about to make it easy for them. I done told Sister Hominy what I want done if I get to the place that I can't talk for myself. That

way the doctors can't play God and decide that I done lived long enough. Them doctors think a pore old colored lady ain't got no sense a'tall. Well, I'm here to tell'em different.

"Chile, they had Sister Johnny doped up so bad that she did not know nothing. Lordy, it was pitiful to see her. She couldn't do nothing for herself. If the family hadn't come in and combed her hair and greased her skin, why, she'da looked like nobody cared nothing about her. The nurses tried to do right, but they don't know how to take care of colored people's skin and hair. Sister Johnny woulda just died of pure dee shame if she coulda knowed that she was messing all over herself. And them nurses, honey. If they was busy, they'd just let her lay in her own mess. I do declare, I don't want to be no burden to nobody. But I don't want them to kill me off, neither. I'm afraid if I sign that living will thing, them doctors will use that piece of paper to kill me off.

"My blood has been real high, and the medicine that Dr. McBee give me just ain't working. So I been goin' to the herb doctor over in WestEnd and she's been treating my high blood. She told me to take some garlic for my high blood. And I been rubbing my side in alcohol and camphor for that pain that I been having for so long. My sugar's been high, too. My eyesight is bad because of the diabetes; I don't read nothing but the Bible and the newspaper these days. McBee is worried that I am going to get glaucoma and go blind. Well, I'm a bit worried about that, too. Even if I ain't got long for this world, I want to see it while I'm here.

"She didn't help me none, neither, when she told me twice as many black people die each year from sugar diabetes than white people. I don't know why she's telling me all this stuff, 'cause I ain't going nowhere till the Lord calls me. She just caused me to have an attack of 'high-pertension.' I don't care what them doctors say, there ain't nothing you can do for high-pertension except to stop worrying and try to get your nerves under control."

Miss Mildred has also been "bleeding from down below." She told her granddaughter that it was like having a period again. It sure is a nuisance, particularly since she had thought that her bleeding was all done with. Now Sister Mildred thinks that if she can just get through Christmas dinner, she will go see Dr. McBee the next day. She has decided that as a last resort, once it became clear that the herb doctor's medications weren't working either. She knows that Dr. McBee will find time to see her. She always does.

Miss Mildred has made it through Christmas dinner, but just barely. It was obvious to other members of the family that Sister Mildred was not herself. She seemed to be in a lot of pain. And she had to take to the bed a couple of times to rest a bit.

"I'm just tired," she told the family when they all tried to make her go the emergency room of the hospital. "I ain't going to no doctor tonight. I just needs me some rest. Besides, the doctor can't do me no good. But I'll go tomorrow if ya'll will quit pestering me. All this aggregation is sure to kill me off. There won't be no need to worry about the doctors doing it."

After a family discussion, they have decided that 16 year-old BettyeLou will stay with her great grandmother and Miss Hominy that night, in case Big Mama has to go to the hospital.

In her heart of hearts, Miss Mildred does not want to go to the doctor this time. She is afraid that she will be hospitalized, and for Miss Mildred, the hospital is a place for old people to go and die. She'd rather die at home. She is getting along in age; she'll be 85 years old come Valentine's Day. That is already longer than most black folks live. She knows her time is coming soon, and she has no regrets. All in all, she has had a good life. And she is ready. Most of her friends have already "gone home." She is tired, too, and about ready to go and see her husband Daddy Joe and her own Mama and Papa.

She thinks to herself, "Daddy Joe sure was a good man. He worked real hard for me and the young'uns. But they beat him to death back in 1959. I always told Daddy Joe that his big mouth was going to get him kilt. Them policemen said he had a heart attack in the jail house. Humph! I knows they beat him to

death. And there weren't nothing I could do about it. Yes, I'm tired and I'm ready to move on where there ain't no more sickness, and meanness, and racial hatred."

Miss Mildred goes back and forth to and from the hospital several times over the next few months. Although her condition has noticeably deteriorated, collapses in cognition have not occurred. She has been approached on several occasions by her physician, who has requested that she "legalize" her treatment preferences through an advance directive. Dr. McBee understands that Miss Hominy is an informal proxy and that informal directives may be just "as ethically compelling as any formal document." But since Miss Mildred had so many relatives, her provider is afraid there will be some difficulties and lack of family consensus in carrying out Miss Mildred's wishes. Miss Mildred — after careful consultation with Miss Hominy, her siblings, her youngest daughter, and her pastor — finally agrees to document her preferences. She formally designates Miss Hominy as her proxy. She particularly lets it be known that food and water — whether artificially administered or ingested through the mouth — are to be provided under all conditions.

"Food and water ain't medication. I don't care how they give it to you. If you take away food and water from a person, you might as well kill 'em. I ain't saying that they have to do every blessed thing. I just want them to respect me and give me good care. Why, you'd give even a thirsty dog some water, wouldn't you? I just want the doctors and the nurses and all these young people learning how to be doctors to treat me just as good as they do the white patients. Like the Good Book say, 'Give comfort to all the sick, not just to some o' them.'"

It has been a couple of weeks since Miss Mildred signed the advance directive. She is certainly getting weaker and weaker each day, but her mind is still clear. She has spent some time in the intensive care unit, but now she is back on the floor. She wonders whether she has been returned to the floor because they have given up on her. She's heard that they do that sometimes — to make room for white patients. But to be fair, she doesn't really think Doc McBee would let them abandon her, just like that. After all, wasn't it Doc McBee who got the hospice people to come over every day when she was home?

Miss Mildred doesn't feel too good within herself about how she is being treated. Since she has come back from intensive care, she feels that the nurses and doctors are just waiting for her to die. They are kind enough; it just seems that they have already disengaged themselves from her, they don't seem to care anymore whether she is comfortable or not. When she signed that living will, they'd been oh so careful to promise her that she would get good care and comfort.

Miss Mildred has her good days and her bad days. Yesterday, she choked on her phlegm. BettyeLou cleared the phlegm from Big Mama's mouth and kept her lips and tongue moistened with a wet cloth. The worst part, though, was when she had to go to the toilet. Usually someone in the family is around to help her. But every now and then she has to depend on the staff. She does not mind using the bedpan if she only has to make water, but it is a matter of self-respect and pride to get up and go to the toilet for a bowel movement. Thank God she can still get to the bathroom, even though she needs a little help. That morning, though, she'd rung and rung, but no one had come to see about her. That was the straw that broke the camel's back. That was when she decided that she would just tear up that darn advance directive.

One of the nurses finally showed up, cheerily inquiring, "Hi there, Hon. How are we doing this morning?"

Big Mama, with all the dignity and iciness that she could muster, answered, "I don't know how *we* are doing, Nurse, but I want you to go and get me that living will that I signed and bring it here to me so that I can tear it up. Maybe then I can get some attention. Ain't nobody paid no attention to me since I signed that thing."

Miss Mildred decides that she wants to spend as much of her remaining time as possible in her own home among friends and family, who are honored and happy to take care of her. Dr. McBee makes arrangements for her to be as comfortable as possible. Different hospice workers spend a couple of hours with her every day. Dr. McBee also manages to find time to drop in each day or so, just to check up on her state and to chat with her. (After all, Mildred has been her patient for 25 years.)

The community will prepare itself and the family for her death; they will talk about all the good Miss Mildred has done, the people she has helped, the wise counsel she has given. They will joke about how she loved to go fishing almost as much as she loved to go to church. The few old friends who are still living will bring her food (which she will pretend to eat) and sit with her for a spell. Neighbors, friends, or family will clean her house; others will make sure she has clean sheets every day. And the younger ones will comb, brush, and braid her hair daily. Friends and family will come in and sit up with Miss Mildred—all night if it seems necessary. She will never be left alone. When she dies, someone in the community will most likely be with her to help her cross over into the other land.

Conclusion

Miss Mildred should not be regarded as a stereotype of the elderly black woman. Although a great many elderly black women are religious, live in southern states, and are surrounded by family and friends, a sizable portion do not fit that mold. Many do bask in the warmth and love of family, friends, church, and community, but some live alone in dangerous and poor urban neighborhoods—without either kin or social, psychological, and spiritual support.

Nor should the elderly black woman be romanticized. There is nothing romantic about having a nutritionally deficient diet or living in unhealthy and substandard housing with the constant threat of utility shutoffs or even evictions and homelessness, as is the case for many elderly black women and men. Whatever lens one uses to try to understand their life situations, it is clear that elderly blacks, as a group, are sicker and poorer than any other adult group in this country.

I have presented the life story of an elderly black woman because her biography is insufficiently appreciated, and because she is more likely than the black man to live long enough to be considered elderly. Although there may be other portraits, I have tried to present one picture of an elderly black woman's life — one that is embedded in a matrix of family, religion, and community. It is a profile in which health disparities in access, inequalities in health status, and end-of-life discussions cannot be considered apart from historical, social, and economic aspects of life. We have seen that Miss Mildred is an example of an important and respected member of a multigenerational extended family that includes both blood relatives and members who are not related. When decisions about life and death are being made, various family members will be involved. For the health care practitioner who is unfamiliar with black culture, it may be difficult to sort out who is who. She may not know that "Mamma Sis," "Aunt Tubby," "Aint Sister," and "Elizabeth" are all the same person.

After the family, religion is the most important institution in the biographies of many elderly black women and is intricately tied to family life. Religious involvement provides not only spiritual succor, but also social life, practical information, and political consciousness.*

If an elderly black woman is 75 years old, she has probably been working for at least 60 of those years, yet has not accumulated wealth or assets. Furthermore, she is unlikely to be enrolled in supplementary medical insurance or to receive Social Security benefits, and she may have only a vague understanding of the intricacies of Medicare and Medicaid. Small SSI payments do little to ameliorate her poverty. Therefore, she may still be employed part-time as a service worker, not because she wants to work but because she needs to supplement her income. If she is among the few elderly blacks enrolled in supplementary medical insurance, some of her small earned income will go to pay for that coverage.

The elderly black woman understands white middle-class people because she has been the recipient of intimacies that the white mistress would not

even tell her best friend. Because of race, class, and ethnicity barriers, however, health care practitioners do not know the elderly poor black outside the clinical setting. To morally intervene in the lives of their patients, providers need to understand those patients' culture, including family and community norms. They need to be familiar with the life stories of their patients, for it is through stories that we get to walk in other people's shoes. Stories open our eyes to other people's ethical dilemmas and dramas surrounding life and death. In a health care system in which the providers are mostly white and the sickest people are elderly African Americans, a larger sense of each patient's story will improve the quality of the everyday practice of medicine as well as the quality of communication with the person who is ill or approaching death.

As we see with Miss Mildred, differences in use of language contribute to misunderstanding and distrust. Health care workers may use unfamiliar terms and medical jargon that Miss Mildred is unlikely to understand. Conversely, the physician is likely to misconstrue or simply fail to understand what Miss Mildred considers the plainest description of her experience. Understanding and appreciating life histories can go a long way to eliminating the distrust that many elderly blacks may have for the health care system.

Miss Mildred teaches us that the elderly black woman is a proud and independent being. She is used to taking care of others — not being taken care of. She is used to doing things for herself. One of her greatest fears in life is that she will be a burden to her family, friends, and community. She would rather die than do that. Preparation for and control of one's own death have always been a part of black culture. There are accounts in black history and literature in which death is preferable to life. The idea of controlling the circumstances of one's death does not necessarily contradict the image of a self-sufficient elderly black woman. Rather, the difficulty will be in persuading her that health care providers and the larger society are just as committed to improving access to care and reducing health disparities based on race as they are to getting her to execute a living will. Only then will she be convinced that the living will is neither an excuse to kill her off by stopping treatment prematurely or to prolong her life beyond God's will, but rather simply a tool to protect her rights and preferences.

---

*Langston Hughes, highly acclaimed African American author, pointed out that many of the old Negro spirituals were really calls for political action. For example, "Swing Low, Sweet Chariot," is a song about a "chariot of freedom from slavery," not about a "chariot of death."

♦♦♦

SIXTY

Perspectives of Native American
Women on Race and Gender

Frederica Y. Daly

Any examination of Native Americans is made difficult because they are not an integral people, even though the United States government and Native Americans themselves often act and write as if they were. Native Americans constitute well over five hundred recognized tribes, which speak more than two hundred (mostly living) languages. Their variety and vital cultures notwithstanding, the official U.S. policy unreflectively, and simply, transforms them from Indians to "Americans" (Wilkinson 1987). Some consideration will be given to their unifying traditions, not the least of which are their common history of surviving genocide and their strong, shared commitment to their heritage.

Any discussion of Indian people requires a brief review of the history of the violent decimation of their populations as well as the massive expropriation of their land and water holdings, accomplished with rare exception with the approval of American governments at every level. To ignore these experiences prevents us from understanding the basis for their radical and profound desire for self-determination, a condition they enjoyed fully before the European incursions began.

The five hundredth anniversary of the so-called discovery of America was met by protests from large groups of indigenous North and South Americans. Vine Deloria, in *We Talk, You Listen* (1990), writes that some Indians had wanted to celebrate 11 October as, "Indians discover Leif Ericson and Christopher Columbus Day" (111). He goes on to pinpoint the critical dilemmas depending on whose eyes determine the history that is written. The discovery by Columbus, from the Native American point of view, involved the invasion of their land and its continuing occupation. In the brief historical account that follows I have drawn mainly from Charles Wilkinson's *American Indians, Time, and The Law* (1987), Vine Deloria and Clifford M. Lytle's *American Indians, American Justice* (1983), and Francis P. Prucha's *The Indians in American Society* (1985).

Historical Overview

Indian history, since the European invasion in the early sixteenth century, is replete with incidents of exploitation, land swindle, enslavement, and murder by the European settlers. The narration includes well-documented, government-initiated, biological warfare, which included giving Indians clothing infected with smallpox, diphtheria, and other diseases to which Indians were vulnerable. Starvation strategies were employed, with forced removal from their lands and the consequent loss of access to basic natural resources, example, the Cherokee and Choctaw experiences in the famous "trail of tears."

Wilkinson as well as Deloria and Lytle assert that Indian history is best understood when presented within a historical framework established by four major, somewhat overlapping, periods. The events dominate federal policy about Indians, subsequent Indian law, and many of the formational forces described in Indian sociology, anthropology, and culture.

Period 1: 1532–1828

This period is described by Europeans as one of "discovery" and is characterized by the conquest of Indians and the making of treaties. The early settlers did not have laws or policies governing their relationships with the indigenous tribes until the sixteenth-century theologian, Francisco de Vitorio advised the king of Spain in 1532 that the tribes should be recognized "as legitimate entities capable of dealing with the European nations by treaty." As a result, writes Deloria, treaty making became a "feasible method of gaining a foothold on the continent without alarming the natives" (1970, 3). Deloria explains further that inherent in this decision was the fact that it encouraged respect for the tribes as societies of people and, thus, became the workable tool for defining intergroup relationships. By 1778 the U.S. government entered into its first treaty, with the Delaware

Indians, at which point the tribe became, and remains, the basic unit in federal Indian law.

The early decision by Vitorio to recognize the legal entity of the tribe no doubt was instrumental in the rejection of one of the early attempts at "scientific" racism. During the decade just before the end of the nineteenth century, the American Bureau of Ethnology, in Washington, D.C., "proposed as an official policy the theory of polygenesis — the multiple creation of the races — and argued that the separate creation of the non-white races accounted for innate inferiority of Blacks and Indians" (Prucha 1985, 6). Prucha writes that Thomas McKinney of the Bureau of Indian Affairs (BIA) rejected polygenesis and held firmly to monogenesis. While the polygenesist theory was rejected by those government officials acting in the interest of Indians, the non-Indian mainstream continued to view Indians and their cultures as inferior. Prucha asserts, "They contrasted the pre-literate Indian societies with the accomplishments of their own society and judged the Indian languages generally worthless even though of scientific interest" (8).

By this time, however, an official paternalism characterized both the language and the actions of the government in its dealings with Indians. Prucha reports that three tribes were told: "The Great White Spirit has ordained that your Great Father and Congress should be to the Red Man, as Guardian and Fathers. . . . Soon you shall be at a permanent home from which there will be no danger of your moving again, you will receive their full benefit" (1985, 17). Furthermore, Chief Justice Marshall had also defined the Indian Nations as "domestic dependent nations." But even if paternalism and their legal status somewhat shielded them from the academized racism of the American Bureau of Ethnology, Indians had already long since learned that the "Great White Father" and the Congress, racist or otherwise, had a devastating deceitfulness all their own.

Period 2: 1828–87

The second period, beginning little more than a few decades before the Civil War, witnessed massive removal of Indians from their ancestral lands and subsequent relocation, primarily because of their resistance to mainstream assimilation and the "missionary efforts" of the various Christian sects.

Early in his presidency Andrew Jackson proposed voluntary removal of the Indians. When none

of the tribes responded the Indian Removal Act of 1830 was passed. The act resulted in the removal of the tribes from the Ohio and Mississippi valleys to the plains of the West. "Nearly sixteen thousand Cherokees walked from Georgia to Eastern Oklahoma . . . the Choctaws surrendered more than ten million acres and moved west" (Deloria and Lytle 1983, 7). Soldiers, teachers, and missionaries were sent to reservations for policing and proselytizing purposes, activities by no means mutually exclusive and which represented the full benefit of the act as far as the tribes were concerned. Meanwhile, discovery of gold (especially "strikes" on or near Indian land) in the West, coupled with the extension of the railroad, once again raised the "Indian Problem." But at this point, with nowhere else to be moved, Indian tribes were even more in jeopardy, setting the basis for the third significant period.

Period 3: 1887–1928

During the final years of the nineteenth century offering land allotments seemed to provide a workable technique for assimilating Indian families into the mainstream. The Dawes Act of 1887 proposed the formula for allotment. "A period of twenty-five years was established during which the Indian owner [of a specified, allotted piece of reservation property] was expected to learn proper methods of self-sufficiency, e.g., business or farming. At the end of that period, the land, free of restrictions against sale, was to be delivered to the allottee" (Deloria and Lytle 1983, 9). At the same time the Indian received title to the land and citizenship in the state.

The Dawes Act and its aftermath constitute one of the most sordid narratives in American history involving tribal peoples. Through assimilation, swindling, and other forms of exploitation, more than ninety million acres of allotted land were transferred to non-Indian owners. Furthermore, much of the original land that remained for the Indians was in the "Great American Desert," unsuitable for farming and unattractive for any other kind of development. During this same period, off-reservation boarding schools began to be instituted, some in former army barracks, to assist in the overall program of assimilation, and the Dawes Act also made parcels of reservation land available to whites for settlement. The plan to assimilate the Indian and thereby eradicate the internal tribal nations caused immense misery and enormous economic loss. But as we know, it failed. Phyllis Old Dog Cross, a nurse of the North Dakota Mandan Tribe, mordantly puts it, "We are not vanishing" (1987, 29).

Period 4: 1928–Present

The fourth period is identified by Wilkinson especially as beginning just before the Depression in 1928. It is characterized by reestablishment of tribes as separate "sovereignties" involving moves toward formalized self-government and self-determination, and cessation, during World War II, of federal assistance to the tribes.

Prucha reminds us that, with the increased belief in the sciences in the 1920s and the accompanying beliefs that the sciences could solve human problems, attitudes toward Indians hardened. At this point the professional anthropologist began to be sent and be seen on the reservations to study and live with the people, alongside the missionaries. The changing attitudes continued into the 1930s with the Roosevelt administration. It was during this period that John Collier became commissioner of Indian Affairs, and the reforms of the Indian Reorganization Act of 1934 invalidated the land allotment policies of the Dawes Act, effectively halting the transfer of Indian land to non-Indians. As Deloria indicates, the Reorganization Act provided immense benefits, including the establishment and reorganization of tribal councils and tribal courts.

After about a decade of progress the budgetary demands of World War II resulted in deep reductions in domestic programs, including assistance to the tribes. John Collier resigned in 1945 under attack from critics and amid growing demands in Washington to cancel federal support for Indians. The writer Simon Ortiz describes the period as a time when the intent of U.S. public policy was that "Indians were no longer to be Indians" (quoted in Swann and Krupat 1987, 191).

Deloria writes that Senator Watkins of Utah was "firmly convinced that if the Indians were freed from federal restrictions, they would soon prosper by learning in the school of life those lessons that a cynical federal bureaucracy had not been able to instill in them" (1970, 18). He was able to implement his convictions during the Eisenhower administration into the infamous Termination Act of 1953, in con-

sequence of which several tribes in at least five states were eliminated. In effect, as far as the government was concerned, the tribes no longer existed and could make no claims on the government. Contrary to its original intent as a means of releasing the tribes from their status as federal wards under BIA control, the Termination Act did just the opposite, causing more loss of land, further erosion of tribal power, and literally terrorizing most of the tribes with intimidation, uncertainty, and, worst of all, fear of the loss of tribal standing.

Deloria quotes HR Doc. 363 in which, in 1970, President Nixon asserted, "Because termination is morally and legally unacceptable, because it produces bad practical results, and because the mere threat of termination tends to discourage greater self-sufficiency among Indian groups, I am asking the Congress to pass a new concurrent resolution which would expressly renounce, repudiate, and repeal the termination policy" (1970, 20). This firm repudiation by Nixon of the termination policy earned him the esteem of many Indian people, in much the same way that presidents Kennedy and Johnson are esteemed by many African Americans for establishing programs designed to improve their socioeconomic conditions.

From the Nixon administration through the Carter administration tribal affairs were marked by strong federal support and a variety of programs aimed at encouraging tribal self-determination. The Indian Child Welfare Act of 1978, which gave preference to Indians in adoptions involving Indian children and authorized establishment of social services on and near reservations, was one of the major accomplishments of this period.

Prucha believes that the tribes' continued need for federal programs is an obstacle to their sovereignty. He asserts that dependency persists but that no one knows how to eliminate it (1985, 97). Deloria insists that Indians are citizens and residents of the United States and of the individual states in which they live and, as such, "are entitled to the full benefits and privileges that are offered to all citizens" (246).

As a country, we have failed to acknowledge our despicable treatment of the Indians. This failure continues to exist in the world of science and remains a source of grave concern to Indians. An Indian leader, on the occasion of a reburial ceremony of bones at a sacred site, prayed for the time when science would stop viewing Indians as "specimens." It is hoped that the Indian quest for self-determination and proper respect will be realized, and with it will come our healing as a nation as well. There exists a tremendous need to help the U.S. public begin to understand the real significance of Indian history. The recent elaborate celebrations of the half-millennium anniversary of the arrival of Columbus in America failed wretchedly to respond to this need.

Contemporary Native American Women and Sexism

I have just presented a very abbreviated statement of the general, post-European influx historical experiences of Indians in America, drawing from the research and insights of lawyers and social scientists. Without this introduction it would be difficult to understand Native American women and their contemporary experiences of sexism and racism.

Although many tribes were matrilineal, Indian women were seldom mentioned prominently in the personal journals or formal records of the early settlers or in the narratives of the westward movement. They were excluded from treaty-making sessions with federal government agents, and later ethnologists and anthropologists who reported on Indian women frequently presented distorted accounts of their lives, usually based on interviews with Christianized women, who said what they believed would be compatible with the European worldview. Helen Carr, in her essay in Brodzki and Schenck's *Life-Lines: Theorizing Women's Autobiographies*, offers some caveats about the authenticity of contemporary autobiographies of Indian women, when they are written in the Euro-American autobiographical tradition. She cautions that, in reading the autobiographies collected by early anthropologists, we need to be "aware that they have been structured, consciously or unconsciously, to serve particular 'white' purposes and to give credence to particular white views" (1988, 132).

Ruby Leavitt, writing in Gornick and Moran's *Women in Sexist Society,* states: "Certainly the status of women is higher in the matrilineal than the patrilineal societies. Where women own property and pass it on to their daughters or sisters, they are far more influential and secure. Where their economic role is important and well defined . . . they are not nearly so

subject to male domination, and they have much more freedom of movement and action" (1972, 397).

We do not learn from social scientists observing Indian communities that women also were the traders in many tribes. With this history of matrilinealism and economic responsibilities it is not surprising that some Indian women deny the existence of an oppressed, nonparticipatory tribal female role. Yet just as other North American women, they are concerned with child care needs, access to abortion, violence against women, and the effects of alcoholism on the family, all symptomatic of sexism experiences. They are also aware of these symptoms as prevalent throughout our society in the United States; they do not view them as specifically Indian related.

Bea Medicine, Lakota activist, anthropologist, and poet *as quoted* in the preface of *American Indian Women — Telling Their Lives,* states "Indian women do not need liberation, they have always been liberated within their tribal structure" (1984, viii). Her view is the more common one I have encountered in my readings and in conversations with Native American women. In the middle 1970s Native American women who were in New York City to protest a U.S. treaty violation, in a meeting to which they had invited non-Indian women, were adamant that they did not need the "luxury of feminism." Their focus, along with that of Indian men, concerned the more primary needs of survival.

The poet, Carol Sanchez, writes in *A Gathering of the Spirits,* "We still have Women's societies, and there are at least thirty active woman-centered Mother rite cultures existing and practicing their everyday life in that manner on this continent" (1984, 164). These groups are characterized by their "keeping of the culture" activities.

Medicine and Sanchez concur about the deemphasis of the importance of gender roles in some tribes as reflected in the "Gia" concept. *Gia* is the word in the Pueblo Tewa language which signifies the earth. It is also used to connote nurturance and biological motherhood. The tribal core welfare role, which can be assumed by a male or a female, is defined by the tribe in this Gia context. To be a nurturing male is to be the object of much respect and esteem, although one does not act nurturing to gain group approval. Swentzell and Naranjo, educational consultant and sociologist, respectively, and coauthors, write, "The male in the gia role is a person who guides, advises, cares, and universally loves and encompasses all." The authors describe the role, saying, "The core gia was a strong, stable individual who served as the central focus for a large number of the pueblo's members . . . [for example], 'she' co-ordinated large group activities such as marriages, feast days, gathering and preparing of food products, even house building and plastering" (1986, 37). With increasing tribal governmental concerns the role of core group Gia has lessened, "so that children are no longer raised by the core group members" (39). Interestingly, the Gia concept is being used currently by social ecologists. For them it parallels the notion of Mother Earth and corresponds with the increasingly widespread understanding of the earth as a living organism.

Charles Lange, in *Cochiti — A New Mexico Pueblo, Past and Present,* says: "Among the Cochiti, the woman is boss; the high offices are held by men, but in the households and in the councils of the clans, woman is supreme. . . . She has been arbiter of destinies of the tribe for centuries" (1959, 367). The important role performed by the "Women's Society," Lange continues, includes "the ceremonial grinding of corn to make prayer meal" (283). Compatible with women's having spiritual role assignments is the fact that in some tribes the gods are women — example, in the matrifocal Cherokee and Pueblo nations Corn Mother is a sacred figure.

A Cheyenne saying reflects the tribe's profound regard for women: "A nation is not conquered until the hearts of its women are on the ground. Then it is done, no matter how brave its warriors, nor how strong its weapons" (Kutz 1988, 143–58). Historically, in some tribes women were warriors and participated in raiding parties. The Apache medicine woman and warrior Lozen lived such a role and was the last of the women warriors (Kutz 1988, 143–58). Paula Gunn Allen, in *The Sacred Hoop* (1986), notes that "traditional tribal lifestyles are more often gynocratic . . . women are not merely doomed victims of Western progress; they are also the carriers of the dream. . . . Since the first attempts at colonization . . . the invaders have exerted every effort to remove Indian women from every position of authority, to obliterate all records pertaining to gynocratic social systems and to ensure that no Americans . . . would remember that gynocracy was the primary social order of Indian America" (2–3). Later she alludes to the regeneration of these earlier roles: "Women

migrating to the cities are regaining self-sufficiency and positions of influence they had held in earlier centuries" (31). "Women's traditions," she says, "are about continuity and men's are about change, life maintenance/risk, death and transformation" (82).

When Indian women deny having experienced sexism they seem mainly to be referring to their continuing historical roles within their tribes, in which they are seen as *the keepers of the culture.* There exists a general consensus that the powerful role of tribal women, both traditionally and contemporarily, is not paralleled in the non-Indian society. Additionally, they allude to the women serving in various tribes as council members, and they point to such prominent, well-known leaders as Wilma Mankiller, chief of the Oklahoma Cherokee Nation; Verna Williamson, former governor of Isleta Pueblo; and Virginia Klinekole, former president of the Mescalero Apache Tribal Council.

Contemporary Native American Women and Racism

The relentless system of racism, in both its overt and covert manifestations, impacts the lives of Indian women; most are very clear about their experiences of it, and they recognize it for what it is. Although many are reticent about discussing these experiences, a growing number of Native American women writers are giving voice to their encounters with racism.

Elizabeth Cook-Lynn, a poet and teacher with combined Crow, Creek, and Sioux heritage, writes about an editor who questioned her about why Native American poetry is so incredibly sad. Cook-Lynn describes her reaction in her essay "You May Consider Speaking about Your Art," published in the anthology *I Tell You Now:* "Now I recognize it as a tactless question asked out of astonishing ignorance. It reflects the general attitude that American Indians should have been happy to have been robbed of their land and murdered" (1987, 60–61).

In the same anthology Linda Hogan, from the Chickasaw Tribe in Oklahoma, writes with concern about the absence of information about Native American people throughout the curricula in our educational systems: "The closest I came to learning what I needed was a course in Labor Literature, and the lesson there was in knowing there were writers who lived similar lives to ours. . . . This is one of the ways that higher education perpetuates racism and classism. By ignoring our lives and work, by creating standards for only their own work" (1987, 243). Earlier she had written that "the significance of intermarriage between Indian and white or between Indian and black [has not] been explored . . . but the fact remains that great numbers of apparently white or black Americans carry notable degrees of Indian blood" (216). And in Brant's *Gathering of the Spirit* Carol Sanchez says "To be Indian is to be considered 'colorful,' spiritual, connected to the earth, simplistic, and disappointing if not dressed in buckskin and feathers" (1984, 163).

These Indian women talk openly about symptoms of these social pathologies, example, experiencing academic elitism or the demeaning attitudes of employees in federal and private, nonprofit Indian agencies. Or they tell of being accepted in U.S. society in proportion to the lightness of skin color. The few who deny having had experiences with racism mention the equality bestowed upon them through the tribal sovereignty of the Indian nations. In reality the tribes are not sovereign. They are controlled nearly completely by the U.S. Department of Interior, the federal agency that, ironically, also oversees animal life on public lands.

Rayna Green, a member of the Cherokee nation, in her book *That's What She Said* (1984), makes a strong, clear statement about racism and sexism: "The desperate lives of Indian women are worn by poverty, the abuse of men, the silence and blindness of whites. . . . The root of their problem appears attributable to the callousness and sexism of the Indian men and white society equally. They are tightly bound indeed in the double bind of race and gender. Wasted lives and battered women are part of the Indian turf" (10). It is not surprising to find some Indian men reflecting the attitudes of the white majority in relating to Indian women. This is the psychological phenomenon found in oppressed people, labeled as identification with the oppressor.

Mary Tallmountain, the Native Alaskan poet writes, in *I Tell You Now* (1987) that she refused to attend school in Oregon because her schoolmates mocked her "Indianness": "But, I know who I am. Marginal person, misfit, mutant; nevertheless, I am of this country, these people" (12). Linda Hogan describes the same experience, saying, "Those who are privileged would like for us to believe that we are in some way defective, that we are not smart enough,

not good enough" (237). She recalls an experience with her former employer, an orthodontist, whom she says, "believed I was inferior because I worked for less than his wife's clothing budget or their liquor bill . . . and who, when I received money to attend night school and was proud, accused me of being a welfare leech and said I should be ashamed" (242). In her poem "Those Who Thunder" Linda translated the experience into verse:

> *Those who are timid are sagging in the soul,*
> *And those poor who will inherit the earth*
> *already work it*
> *So take shelter you*
> *because we are thundering and beating on floors*
> *And this is how walls have fallen in other cities.*
> *(242)*

In the United States we do not know one another, except from the stereotypes presented in the media. As a result, there is the tendency to view people of a differing group vicariously, through the eyes of media interpreters.

Louise Erdrich and Michael Dorris, both Indian and both university professors and eminent writers, reported in Bill Moyer's *World of Ideas* (1989): "We had one guy come to dinner, and we cleaned our house and made a nice dinner, and he looks and says, kind of depressed, 'Do you always eat on the table?'" (465). They used the example to demonstrate how people "imagine" (as distinguished from "know") Indians on the basis of movie portrayals, usually as figures partially dressed or dressed in the fashion of the nineteenth century and typically eating while seated on the ground. It is difficult to form accurate perceptions of the people and worldview of another group. Carol Sanchez seems to challenge us to do just that when she asks us not to dismiss Native Americans and then asks, "How many Indians do you know?" (163). How many of you in this audience know one? Ten? More than ten?

The reports in the media in May 1993 of a strange illness striking people living on reservation land in the Four Corners area bordering Arizona and New Mexico rapidly produced fear of Navajo people by many, because the illness was dubbed a "Navajo disease." The fear became blatant discrimination in some instances. Two typical cases — one in which a group of Navajo schoolchildren were "uninvited" to a program by their California host school and another in which a group of tourists visiting Gallup, New Mexico, actually put on gas masks — were reported in New Mexico's largest newspaper, the *Albuquerque Journal*. To combat these inaccuracies about the disease and its origins New Mexico TV stations initiated and continued to air public service announcements featuring Navajo children explaining the symptoms of the illness, now identified as Hantavirus, along with strong statements to the effect that it is neither caused by nor restricted to Navajo people.

The health departments of New Mexico, Arizona, Colorado, and Utah, working in concert with appropriate agencies of the federal government, have identified the disease, linking it to exposure to rodent excrement. They issued warnings and have initiated programs of rodent control. Similarly, during the early stages of the outbreak Navajo medicine men linked the illness to the year's unusually abundant piñon crop, which caused an increase in the pest population. The tourist industry continued to anticipate a negative impact on business in the Southwest because of summer visitors having associated the illness with one of the area's major tourist attractions, the Indian people.

Sanchez charges non-Indians with the wish to have Indians act like whites, so they will be more acceptable to whites, another example of accommodation, assimilation. She is describing the attitude cited by the young child care worker who said to me, "They like our food, our drum music, our jewelry, why don't they like us!?" Activist Winona La Duke, of the Ojibwa Tribe and by profession an economist, asserts in her offering in *Gathering of the Spirits*: "As far as the crises of water contamination, radiation, and death to the natural world and her children are concerned, respectable racism is as alive today as it was a century ago . . . a certain level of racism and ignorance has gained acceptance . . . in fact respectability . . . we either pick your bananas or act as a mascot for your football team . . . in this way, enlightened people are racist. They are arrogant toward all of nature, arrogant toward the children of nature, and ultimately arrogant toward all of life" (65–66). And in the same book again Kate Shanley, Assiniboine Sioux and literary scholar, wrote: "The time has come for Indian women and Indian people to be known on our own terms . . . this nuclear age demands new terms of communication for all people. Our survival depends on it" (215). There is hope

that newly shared terms of communication will lead to new understanding and common insights to a more balanced history.

Continuing Tensions

That since the sixteenth century the history of Native Americans is one of racist oppression has become an integral part of contemporary historical understanding. Indian women are speaking with increasing frequency and force about their experiences of the double jeopardy of racism and sexism. I wish now to consider three factors that continue to contribute to serious tensions within the tribes and between the tribes and the so-called dominant culture. The factors are, first, the tension within the Indian community between accommodation and traditionalism; second, the erosion of tribal life which is resulting in what has become known as cultural marginality; and third, the problems that arise because of conflicts between reservation law and federal and state laws.

Tensions Within the Indian Community

Indian People who wish to retain their identity and culture by continuing reservation life have constantly to struggle with choices regarding adaptation to the dominant culture. They realize that extremism in either direction will result in destruction of their ways of life. Those who resist any adaptation will be made to do so involuntarily, and those who accept "white men's ways" completely and without modification by that very fact forgo their heritage. For well over a century governmental policy favored assimilation and the concomitant dissolution of Indian tribal existence. Real estate value and greed for precious natural resources were crucial motivating factors throughout the period. Indians simply were in the way of the invaders' efforts to amass money.

To a certain degree the situation remains the same today. A California Indian cited the tensions between the Indians who live on reservations and the people who live in the surrounding communities. He reported that the dismissal and erasure of a group, even in subtle ways, is psychologically destructive. Verna Williamson, former governor of the Isleta Pueblo in New Mexico, stated that she was determined to bring an open and accountable spirit to the Isleta government, and that determination led her to run for office. Her vision of a progressive tribal government, co-operative with county, state, and federal agencies, resulted in her being attacked at times by her sup-porters as well as her opponents. In many ways she remained a traditionalist who presented and fos-tered programs to strengthen and teach traditional beliefs. But she also brought to the people new con-cepts such as legal advocacy training. She justified her accommodation strategies in the following state-ment: "The encroaching outside world cannot be ig-nored; its complexities affect the Pueblo's future . . . and the cultural influences from the Anglo commu-nities . . . threaten the rich pueblo tradition" (quoted in 1988, 5). Even though she recognized the danger to the tradition, her opponents feared that her ac-commodation to external community ways neces-sarily would erode the Pueblo way of life.

At the Flathead reservation in Montana attempts are under way to "revive the traditional Salish cul-ture and preserve the rugged land from develop-ment" (1990, 54). Attempts to protect the Indian land for future generations is buttressed by the tradi-tional, nearly universal Indian belief that we do not own the land, that we are simply caretakers of it and will pass it on to future generations. Thus, how the land is used can become an issue of deep tension between strict traditionalists and those who want to assimilate contemporary economic development thinking into tribal life and institutions. Likewise, nearly universally held precepts include the prevail-ing rights of the tribe over individual rights and the discouragement of aggression and competitiveness, which are seen as threats to tribal harmony and sur-vival. Phyllis Old Dog Cross, a Sioux and a nurse, speaking at a health conference in Denver in 1987, stated: "The need not to appear aggressive and com-petitive within the group is still seen among contem-porary Indians . . . even quite acculturated Indians tend to be very unobtrusive. . . . [If not,] they receive strong criticism . . . also anything that would seem to precipitate anger, resentment, jealousy was . . . discouraged, for it is believed that tribal group har-mony is threatened" (1987, 20).

Acknowledging their need for self-sufficiency as reductions in federal funding continue, the tribes are searching intensively for economic solutions. Some have introduced organized gambling onto the reser-vations and the leasing of land to business corpora-tions; others are considering storage on reservation

land of toxic wastes from federal facilities. Many of these measures are resisted, especially by tradition-alists within the tribes, who see them as culturally destructive.

Erosion of Tribal Life: Cultural Marginality

Cultural marginality is increasingly experienced by Indian people because of the confusion resulting from ambiguities about what defines Indian iden-tity, individually and tribally. The questions "Who is an Indian?" and "What is a tribe?" no longer per-mit neat unequivocal answers.

Different tribes have different attitudes toward people of mixed heritage. In some a person with white blood may be accepted, while a person with some African-American blood may or may not be identified as Indian. Indian women, if they marry non-Indians, may or may not be identified within their tribes as Indians. To be a member of a tribe a person must meet that tribe's requirements. Many tribes require proof of a person's being one-sixteenth or one-quarter or more of Indian descent to receive tribal affiliation.

This question becomes more complicated when the issue is "Who is an 'Indian Artist'?" and it be-came even more confusing with the signing on 29 November 1990 of Public Law 101-644 by President George Bush. Entitled "The Indian Arts and Crafts Act," the law requires the artists to prove their "na-tive heritage."

Halleah J. Tsinhnahjinnie, of Seminole, Creek, and Navajo heritage, writes: "I am concerned when a law regulates identity. I am reminded of the numbers tat-tooed on the arms of Jewish people; I am reminded of the vicious witch hunts of the McCarthy period; I am reminded of the ethnic cleansing of Bosnia" (1993, 13). This law is divisive and imposes the racist concerns of their oppressors on Native Americans, keeping current the old and useless blood quantum witch hunt.

A group or an individual may qualify as an In-dian for some federal purposes but not for others. A June 1977 statement by the U.S. Department of La-bor on American Indian women reads: "For their 1970 Census, the Bureau included in their question-naire the category, 'American Indian,' persons who indicated their race as Indian. . . . In the Eastern U.S., there are certain groups with mixed white, Negro, and Indian ancestry. In U.S. censuses prior to 1950, these groups had been variously classified by the enumerators, sometimes as Negro and sometimes as Indian, regardless of the respondent's preferred racial identity." LeAnne Howe, writing in Paula Gunn Allen's *Spider Woman's Granddaughters,* says "Halfbreeds live on the edge of both races . . . you're torn between wanting to kill everyone in the room or buying them all another round of drinks" (1989, 220).

Paula Gunn Allen, of the Laguna Pueblo tribe and a professor of literature, in her essay in *I Tell You Now,* writes: "Of course I always knew I was an Indian. I was told over and over, 'Never forget that you're an Indian.' My mother said it. Nor did she say, 'Remember you're part Indian.'" (1987, 144).

Conflicts Between Tribal and Other Governmental Laws

The Bureau of Indian Affairs, which has specific oversight responsibilities for the reservations, has played, at best, an ambivalent role, according to its very numerous critics. There have been many rumors of mishandled funds, especially of failure of funds to reach the reservations. It is the source of endless satire by Indian humorists, who, at their kindest, refer to it as the "Boss the Indian Around" department. By federal mandate the BIA is charged with coordinating the federal programs for the reservations. Originally, it was a section of the War Department, but for the last century and a half it has operated as part of the Department of the Interior.

Continuing skirmishes occur over violations of reservation land and water rights. Consequently, the tribes continue to appeal to the Supreme Court and to the United Nations for assistance in redressing federal treaty violations. When these cases are made public they become fodder for those who continue to push for the assimilation of Indians into the dominant society as well as for the ever-present cadre of racial bigots.

Federal law and policy have too often been paternalistic, detrimental, and contrary to the best interests of the Indian people. Further, the federal dollar dominance of the tribes has a controlling interest on Indian life. Levitan and Johnston conclude that, "for Indians, far more than for any other group, socio-economic status is a federal responsibility, and the success or failure of federal programs determines the quality of Indian lives" (1975, 10).

To receive eligibility for government services requires that the person live on or near a reservation, trust, or restricted land or be a member of a tribe recognized by the federal government. To be an Indian in America can mean living under tribal laws and traditions, under state law, and under federal laws. The situation can become extremely complex and irksome, for example, when taxes are considered. The maze and snarl of legalese over such questions as whether the Navajo tribe can tax reservation mineral developments without losing its "trust status" and accompanying federal benefits would defeat, and does, the most ardent experts of jurisprudence. And the whole question of income tax for the Indian person living on a reservation and working in a nearby community requires expertise that borders on the ridiculous.

University of New Mexico law professor Fred Ragsdale, describing the relationship of reservation Indians with the federal government, compares it to playing blackjack: "Indians play with their own money. They can't get up and walk away. And the house gets to change the rules any time it wants" (1985, 1).

The outlawing of certain Indian religious practices occurred without challenge until the 1920s, when the laws and policies prohibiting dancing and ceremonies were viewed as cultural attacks. With the passage of the Indian Civil Rights Act in 1964 Indians have been able to present court challenges to discrimination based on their religious practices. Members of the North American Church use peyote, a psychoactive drug, in their ceremonies. Many consider their religion threatened by the recent Supreme Court ruling that removes First Amendment protection of traditional worship practiced by Native Americans.

The negative impact of the 1966 Bennett freeze, a federally attempted solution to the bitter Navajo-Hopi land dispute, continues to cause pain to the Hopi, who use this 1.5 million-acre land mass for grazing, and to the Navajo, many of whom have resided on this land for generations. Sue Ann Presley, a *Washington Post* reporter, describes the area as being among the poorest in the nation and notes that the people living there are prohibited by law from participating in federal antipoverty programs. She reports that 90 percent of the homes have neither electricity nor indoor plumbing, and home repairs are not permitted. She quotes Navajo chair, Peterson Zah: "There are many Navajos who want to live in what we call the traditional way. But that does not mean they want to live with inadequate sewers, unpaved roads, no running water or electricity and under the watchful eye of the Hopi Tribe" (1993, B1). The forced removal of some of the Navajos from this area to border town housing caused a tremendous increase in the number of people who sought mental health treatment for depression and other disorders, according to the clinical observations of Tuba City, Arizona, psychologist Martin Topper.

Discussion

So, what does that narrative information have to do with scientific practice? What does it have to do with scientists and educators?

Drs. Lila Wallis and Perri Klass, in *Lear's*, an upper-class "woman's magazine," in October 1989, accused the medical establishment, doctors and researchers, of practicing "MACHO MEDICINE." Their remarks were neither flip nor random, and they documented their accusations with research evidence. If their accusations are that the physical health of U.S. white women is seriously underattended, what does that imply for minority women in general and American Indian women in particular? Wallis and Klass write that, in the area of medicine, "women have been a variant, a deviation from the concept of the human norm" (1989, 68).

Robert Hadley, a psychologist at the University of California–Los Angeles, in a letter in a 1990 issue of *American Psychologist,* condemns such gender bias in research. "Research biased by social stereotypes is faulty because it violates *general* principles of good science. Social bias is the content of the violations rather than their substance" (1990, 73).

In "Indian country" the Indian Health Service is entrusted with the care of Indians. Yet tensions created in the community by economic deprivations, sexism, racism, and federal and state interferences impact negatively on both the community health and individual health of Indian people. Historically, Native Americans have experienced medical treatment indignities and have concerns regarding the professional methods of direct inquiry, note taking, picture taking (the use of X-rays, for example), and

forced separation from their families during hospital and clinic visits. For most health is a condition resulting from living in harmony with one's body, one's community, and the natural world.

Paula Gunn Allen writes: "When a community is out of balance for whatever nearest reason, its most sensitive members are most likely to suffer in their bodies and minds . . . their very sensitivity on psychic and spiritual levels makes them lightning rods, drawing the disharmony to themselves and grounding it, rendering it far less harmful to the larger community" (1991, 169). Differences in worldviews therefore result in markedly different causal factors being attributed to the same illness by Native Americans and Indian Health Service officials and other professional medical personnel. "There are powerful arguments advanced in the Indian community," Allen continues, "that many of us suffer from a variety of immune system disorders and other chronic debilitations because we are earth's children, and as she endures monstrous patriarchal abuse, we suffer as well, sharing in her pain and disease and in that way ameliorating its devastation and bringing some respite to her" (169).

The Indian Health Service supplies health data on Indian clients, and, since its transfer to the Public Health Service in 1955, improvements have occurred. Even so, according to a study published in 1987, "The health status of American Indians and Alaska Natives still lags behind that of the general population" (Stuart 1987, 95). Paul Stuart reports that accidents, alcoholism, homicide, and suicide among Native Americans are significantly above the national rate, and the death rate from diabetes has also increased.

The Navajo word for *cancer* means "sore that never heals." This sore that never heals is of great concern to Native American women living on reservations, many of whom live in areas close to uranium mining areas and the Los Alamos National Laboratories. Many have expressed suspicions because of the number of women in their immediate families diagnosed with cancer. They wonder about the proximity of the mines and the potential for contamination of their water supply. Many of these women are not monitored yearly with scheduled mammograms and pelvic examinations. As if this alone were not cause for concern, a study reported in a 1993 issue of the *New England Journal of Medicine* reports that male doctors in general are less likely to refer their female patients for these examinations.

Alcohol-related illnesses and alcoholism play significant roles in the early death of Indians; one-third of Indians die before age forty-five, according to a congressional study reported in the 18 May 1989 issue of the *Albuquerque Journal.* The Indian Health Service spends a mere 3 percent of its budget on alcohol abuse programs, according to the same study. Many of the Indians who die before age forty-five are children, whose deaths are caused by drivers under the influence of alcohol. Despite the impact of the phenomenon, the Indian Health Service does not encourage its staff to do research in this area, about which so little is known.

Alcoholism is not as prevalent in Native American women as in Native American men, yet for both the numbers affected are very high. Phillip May reports, "When behaviors which are alcohol-related are examined Indians in the United States have higher rates of death from accidents, cirrhosis of the liver, homicide, and suicide" (1989, 105). May further states that fetal alcohol syndrome was found to be the leading major birth defect among southwestern Native Americans but says this problem "is one concentrated in a small number of heavy drinking women" (106). Native American novelist and essayist Michael Dorris has written about this problem, as he encountered and attempted to live with it, in his adopted son (*The Broken Cord* [1989]). Dorris has made many educational public appearances to express his concern about the high rate of alcohol-related birth defects among Native Americans. Both the Indian Health Service and the tribes have developed programs to educate their communities about the dangers of alcohol use during pregnancy.

My own experience treating Native American clients regularly included their acknowledgment of alcoholism's multifaceted problems. Most of them were motivated to cooperate during treatment, although maintaining sobriety during weekends posed enormous difficulties for many. Of those who were successful many were members of the Native American Church and were involved in nondrinking group activities. Most of the Native Americans attributed their drinking to peer pressure, needing to "numb out," or getting away from problems by drinking to unconsciousness. None of them said they liked to drink, and environmental stress appeared to be the root cause of their problem drinking.

While many professionals have described very positive attitudes about participation in the Native American Church and recommended it to their clients, the Supreme Court recently decided that the First Amendment does not protect traditional worship by Native Americans. As a result, this indigenous adjunct to therapy is threatened by limiting the religious freedom of these people.

Conclusions

This closing decade of the twentieth century, as a promise for continuing scientific discovery and almost geometric progress, offers a special framework as a time for healing. The healing should be aligned with bias-free hope, and it should be as universally inclusive as possible. I think it a modest suggestion to say that it could well start with sharper identification and diagnosis by the scientific community of Native American women's experience of sexism and racism. Studies showing the impact of the privileged culture and dominant race on the development of Native Americans deserve continued exposure and extended development. We need medical research that investigates the health conditions and illnesses of minorities, including Native American women, whose general health status has to be among the worst in America.

Culturally significant alcoholism treatment measures need to be developed and tested along with studies on fetal alcohol syndrome. Traditional treatment approaches utilizing cooperative and nurturing values need to be investigated and formally studied under the sponsorship of the new department of Alternative Medicine, whose first director is a Native American professional with an advanced degree in medicine. And the impending national health plan, which aims to provide basic health care to all Americans, needs to contain provisions for Native Americans in general and women in particular which answer past inadequacies and preclude continuation of practices that support or are supported by racism and sexism.

The development of new theories must include appropriate, representative definitions of the total population, free of gender bias and not derived disproportionately from the observation of middle-class white men and women. Curriculum offerings with accurate and comprehensive historical data about gender-specific Native American experiences are needed. This kind of expanded scholarship seems to me a natural and obvious priority of our scientists, who now in a special way understand themselves to be on the threshold of a new era, that of the truth seekers of the twenty-first century.

References

Allen, P. G. 1986. *The Sacred Hoop.* Boston: Beacon Press.

———. 1987. "The Autobiography of a Confluence." In *I Tell You Now,* ed. B. Swann and A. Krupat. Lincoln: University of Nebraska Press, 141–54.

———, ed. 1989. *Spider Woman's Granddaughters.* Boston: Beacon Press.

———. 1991. *Grandmothers of the Light: A Medicine Woman's Sourcebook.* Boston: Beacon Press.

Bataille, G., and K. Sands. 1984. *American Indian Women — Telling Their Lives.* Lincoln: University of Nebraska Press.

Bergman, R. 1971. "Navajo Peyote Use: Its Apparent Safety." *American Journal of Psychiatry* 128:6.

Canby, W. C. 1981. *American Indian Law.* St. Paul, Minn.: West Publishing.

Carr, Helen. 1988. "In Other Words: Native American Women's Autobiography." In *Life-Lines: Theorizing Women's Autobiographies,* ed. Bella Brodzki and Celeste Schenck. Ithaca, N.Y.: Cornell University Press, 131–53.

Cook-Lynn, E. 1987. "You May Consider Speaking about Your Art." In *I Tell You Now,* ed. B. Swann and A. Krupat. Lincoln: University of Nebraska Press, 55–63.

Daly, F. 1980. "Relocation as a Mental Health Issue." Paper presented at the University of New Mexico, Psychiatry Department.

———. 1987. "Women and Alcohol." Paper presented at VA Medical Center, the University of New Mexico, Psychiatry Department.

Deloria, V. 1970. *We Talk, You Listen.* New York: Dell Publishing.

Deloria, V., and C. Lytle. 1983. *American Indians, American Justice.* Austin: University of Texas Press.

Dorris, M. 1989. *The Broken Cord.* New York: Harper and Row.

Erdrich, Louise, and M. Dorris. 1989. "Interview." in *Bill Moyers: A World of Ideas,* ed. B. S. Flowers. New York: Doubleday, 460–69.

Francis, D. 1990. "You, Your Doctors, and the Health Care System." *Every Woman's Health.* Garden City, N.Y.: Guild America.

Glasrud, B., and A. Smith, eds. 1982. *Race Relations in British North America, 1607–1783.* Chicago: Nelson-Hall.

Gornick, V., and B. Moran, eds. 1972. *Women in Sexist Society.* New York: Signet.

Green, R. 1984. *That's What She Said.* Bloomington: University of Indiana Press.

Hadley, R. 1990. "Sexism in Research Is Not Only Sexism." *American Psychologist* 45:73.

Hogan, L. 1987. "The Two Lives." In *I Tell You Now,* ed. B. Swann and A. Krupat. Lincoln: University of Nebraska Press, 231–49.

Howe, L. 1989. "An American in New York." In *Spider Woman's Granddaughters,* ed. P. G. Allen. Boston: Beacon Press, 212–20.

Journal Staff. 1993 July 21. "Suspected Hantavirus Patient Now in Satisfactory Condition." *Albuquerque Journal,* 1.

Katz, W. 1986. *Black Indians: A Hidden Heritage.* New York: Atheneum.

Klass, P., and L. Wallis. October 1989, "Macho Medicine." *Lears,* 65–68.

Kress, S. 1993. "One of the Few." *Crosswinds* 5:9.

Kutz, J. 1988. *Mysteries and Miracles of New Mexico.* Corrales, N.M.: Rhombus Publishing.

La Duke, Winona. 1988. "They Always Come Back." In *A Gathering of Spirit,* ed. B. Brant. Ithaca, N.Y.: Firebrand Books, 62–67.

Laird, C. 1975. *Encounter with an Angry God.* Banning, Calif.: Malki Museum.

Lange, C. 1959. *Cochiti — A New Mexico Pueblo, Past and Present.* Austin: University of Texas Press.

Levitan, S., and W. Johnston. 1975. *Indian Giving.* Baltimore: Johns Hopkins University Press.

Lurie, N., et. al. 1993. "Preventive Care for Women — Does Sex of Physician Matter?" *New England Journal of Medicine* 8:12.

May, P. 1989. "Alcohol Abuse and Alcoholism among Native Americans: An Overview." *Alcoholism in Minority Populations.* Springfield, Ill.: Charles C. Thomas.

Munar, D. 1988. "Verna Williamson — First Woman Governor." *Albuquerque Women in Business News* 5:3–5.

Old Dog Cross, P. 1987. "What Would You Want a Caregiver to Know about You?" *The Value of Many Voices Conference Proceedings,* 29–32.

Perrone, B., H. Stockel, and V. Kruger. 1989. *Medicine Women, Curanderas, and Women Doctors.* Norman: University of Oklahoma Press.

Presley, S. 18 July 1993. "Restrictions Force Deprivations on Navajos." *The Washington Post,* G1–G2.

Prucha, F. 1985. *The Indians in American Society.* Berkeley: University of California Press.

Ragsdale, F. 1985. Quoted in Sherry Robinson's "Indian Laws Complicate Development." *Albuquerque Journal,* 1.

Rosen, L. 1976. *American Indians and the Law.* New Brunswick, N.J.: Transaction Books.

Sanchez, Carol. 1984. "Sex, Class and Race Intersections: Visions of Women of Color." In *A Gathering of Spirits,* ed. B. Brant. Ithaca, N.Y.: Firebrand Books.

Scott, J. 1989. *Changing Woman—The Life and Art of Helen Hardin.* Flagstaff, Ariz.: Northland Publishing.

Sewell, C. M. 1993. *Outbreak of Acute Illness—Southwestern United States.* June. New Mexico Department of Health memo.

Shaffer, P. January/February 1990. "A Tree Grows in Montana." *Utne Reader,* 54–63.

Stuart, P. 1987. *Nations within a Nation—Historical Statistics of American Indians.* Westport, Conn.: Greenwood Press.

Swentzell, R., and T. Naranjo. (1986). "Nurturing the Gia." *El Palacio* (Summer–Fall): 35–39.

Tallmountain, M. 1987. "You Can Go Home Again: A Sequence." In *I Tell You Now,* ed. B. Swann and A. Krupat. Lincoln: University of Nebraska Press, 1–13.

Topper, Martin. 1979. "Mental Health Effects at Navajo Relocation in the Former Joint Use Area." Paper presented at University of New Mexico, Psychiatry Department.

Tsinhnahjinnie, H. 1993. "Proving Nothing." *Crosswinds* 5:9, 13.

Tuchner, A., ed. 1990. *Bill Moyers—A World of Ideas.* Vol. 2. 267–84.

U.S. Department of Labor. 1977, June. *Memo on American Indian Women.* Washington, D.C.: U.S. Government Printing Office.

Wallis, L., and P. Klass. 1989. "Macho Medicine." *Lear's* (October): 65.

Wilkinson, C. 1987. *American Indians, Time, and the Law.* New Haven, Conn.: Yale University Press.

Wrone, D., and R. Nelson, eds. 1973. *Who's the Savage? A Documentary History of the Mistreatment of the Native North Americans.* Greenwich, Conn.: Fawcett.

SIXTY-ONE

◆◆◆

Educating for Procreative Choice
The "Case" of Adolescent Women
Sara Ruddick

The "sex education" I imagine for adolescents—just barely imaginable in the current climate of repression and fear—starts in early childhood and carries at least through high school. Throughout the years students are encouraged to speak of their sexual experiences; write, paint, or dramatize them; and read and watch whatever is interesting or helpful in making sense of what they have felt and observed. Through their reading and self-expressions they learn to depict particular sexual acts as hurtful, repellent, or merely boring. Equally they learn to name without shame their curiosities and distinctive sources of sexual pleasure—homo-, hetero-, and auto-erotic. Although they are encouraged to defend themselves, with the help of their teachers, against intrusion or cruelty, they postpone judgment on their own desires, except in the special case that they themselves not only dream of, but act out, cruel and hurtful desires.

This sex education, as I imagine it, would foster memory and honest speech. Crucial to honesty, and probably its consequence, would be a critical wondering at the sexual division of wage labor, domestic work, and power and nurturance within the adolescents' homes and culture. Girls — and also boys — would discuss fears of abandonment and compulsions to please that confound their power to refuse as well as their capacity to own and therefore enjoy their sexual pleasures. Boys — and also girls — would explore the ways that the alleged privileges of masculinity, especially in a context of social abuse or deprivation, become personally burdensome, conductive to violence, and distracting from the power to act. Young women and men would critically scrutinize their culture's myths about masculinity and femininity that legitimate particular sexual practices but rule out others. In particular, the homophobia that seems to pervade the fantasies of adolescents in many classes and cultures would be explored for its connections to a fearful need to prove one's heterosexuality, sometimes through violence against the different other, often through causing or displaying a gender-confirming pregnancy. And in the safety of the classroom all children would describe sexual violence and abuse they have witnessed or suffered.

S I X T Y - T W O

◆◆◆

Three Generations of Native American Women's Birth Experience

Joy Harjo

It was still dark when I awakened in the stuffed back room of my mother-in-law's small rented house with what felt like hard cramps. At 17 years of age I had read everything I could from the Tahlequah Public Library about pregnancy and giving birth. But nothing prepared me for what was coming. I awakened my child's father and then ironed him a shirt before we walked the four blocks to the Indian hospital because we had no car and no money for a taxi. He had been working with another Cherokee artist silk-screening signs for specials at the supermarket and making $5 a day, and had to leave me alone at the hospital because he had to go to work. We didn't awaken his mother. She had to get up soon enough to fix breakfast for her daughter and granddaughter before leaving for her job at the nursing home. I knew my life was balanced at the edge of great, precarious change and I felt alone and cheated. Where was the circle of women to acknowledge and honor this birth?

It was still dark as we walked through the cold morning, under oaks that symbolized the stubbornness and endurance of the Cherokee people who had made Tahlequah their capital in the new lands. I looked for handholds in the misty gray sky, for a voice announcing this impending miracle. I wanted to change everything; I wanted to go back to a place before childhood, before our tribe's removal to Oklahoma. What kind of life was I bringing this child into? I was a poor, mixed-blood woman heavy with a child who would suffer the struggle of poverty, the legacy of loss. For the second time in my life I felt the sharp tug of my own birth cord, still connected to my mother. I believe it never pulls away, until death, and even then it becomes a streak in the sky symbolizing that most important warrior road. In my teens I had fought my mother's weaknesses with all my might, and here I was at 17, becoming as my mother, who was in Tulsa, cooking breakfasts and preparing for the lunch shift at a factory cafeteria as I walked to the hospital to give birth. I should be with her; instead, I was far from her house, in the house of a mother-in-law who later would try to use witchcraft to destroy me.

After my son's father left me I was prepped for birth. This meant my pubic area was shaved completely and then I endured the humiliation of an enema, all at the hands of strangers. I was left alone in a room painted government green. An overwhelming antiseptic smell emphasized the sterility of the hospital, a hospital built because of the U.S. government's treaty and responsibility to provide health care to Indian people.

I intellectually understood the stages of labor, the place of transition, of birth—but it was difficult to bear the actuality of it, and to bear it alone. Yet in some ways I wasn't alone, for history surrounded me. It is with the birth of children that history is given form and voice. Birth is one of the most sacred acts we take part in and witness in our lives. But sacredness seemed to be far from my lonely labor room in the Indian hospital. I heard a woman screaming in the next room with her pain, and I wanted to comfort her. The nurse used her as a bad example to the rest of us who were struggling to keep our suffering silent.

The doctor was a military man who had signed on this watch not for the love of healing or out of awe at the miracle of birth, but to fulfill a contract for medical school payments. I was another statistic to him; he touched me as if he were moving equipment from one place to another. During my last visit I was given the option of being sterilized. He explained to me that the moment of birth was the best time to do it. I was handed the form but chose not to sign it, and am amazed now that I didn't think too much of it at the time. Later I would learn that many Indian women who weren't fluent in English signed, thinking it was a form giving consent for the doctor to deliver their babies. Others were sterilized without even the formality of signing. My light skin had probably saved me from such a fate. It wouldn't be the first time in my life.

When my son was finally born I had been deadened with a needle in my spine. He was shown to me—the incredible miracle nothing prepared me for—then taken from me in the name of medical progress. I fell asleep with the weight of chemicals and awoke yearning for the child I had suffered for, had anticipated in the months proceeding from his unexpected genesis when I was still 16 and a student at Indian school. I was not allowed to sit up or walk because of the possibility of paralysis (one of the drug's side effects), and when I finally got to hold him, the nurse stood guard as if I would hurt him. I felt enmeshed in a system in which the wisdom that had carried my people from generation to generation was ignored. In that place I felt ashamed I was an Indian woman. But I was also proud of what my body had accomplished despite the rape by the bureaucracy's machinery, and I got us out of there as soon as possible. My son would flourish on beans

and fry bread, and on the dreams and stories we fed him.

My daughter was born four years later, while I was an art student at the University of New Mexico. Since my son's birth I had waitressed, cleaned hospital rooms, filled cars with gas (while wearing a miniskirt), worked as a nursing assistant, and led dance classes at a health spa. I knew I didn't want to cook and waitress all my life, as my mother had done. I had watched the varicose veins grow branches on her legs, and as they grew, her zest for dancing and sports dissolved into utter tiredness. She had been born with a caul over her face, the sign of a gifted visionary.

My earliest memories are of my mother writing songs on an ancient Underwood typewriter after she had washed and waxed the kitchen floor on her hands and knees. She too had wanted something different for her life. She had left an impoverished existence at age 17, bound for the big city of Tulsa. She was shamed in a time in which to be even part Indian was to be an outcast in the great U.S. system. Half her relatives were Cherokee full-bloods from near Jay, Oklahoma, who for the most part had nothing to do with white people. The other half were musically inclined "white trash" addicted to country-western music and Holy Roller fervor. She thought she could disappear in the city; no one would know her family, where she came from. She had dreams of singing and had once been offered a job singing on the radio but turned it down because she was shy. Later one of her songs would be stolen before she could copyright it and would make someone else rich. She would quit writing songs. She and my father would divorce and she would be forced to work for money to feed and clothe four children, all born within two years of each other.

As a child growing up in Oklahoma, I liked to be told the story of my birth. I would beg for it while my mother cleaned and ironed. "You almost killed me," she would say. "We almost died." That I could kill my mother filled me with remorse and shame. And I imagined the push-pull of my life, which is a legacy I deal with even now when I am twice as old as my mother was at my birth. I loved to hear the story of my warrior fight for my breath. The way it was told, it had been my decision to live. When I got older, I realized we were both nearly casualties of the system, the same system flourishing in the Indian hospital where later my son Phil would be born.

My parents felt lucky to have insurance, to be able to have their children in the hospital. My father came from a fairly prominent Muscogee Creek family. *His* mother was a full-blood who in the early 1920s got her degree in art. She was a painter. She gave birth to him in a private hospital in Oklahoma City; at least that's what I think he told me before he died at age 53. It was something of which they were proud.

This experience was much different from my mother's own birth. She and five of her six brothers were born at home, with no medical assistance. The only time a doctor was called was when someone was dying. When she was born her mother named her Wynema, a Cherokee name my mother says means beautiful woman, and Jewell, for a can of shortening stored in the room where she was born.

I wanted something different for my life, for my son, and for my daughter, who later was born in a university hospital in Albuquerque. It was a bright summer morning when she was ready to begin her journey. I still had no car, but I had enough money saved for a taxi for a ride to the hospital. She was born "naturally," without drugs. I could look out of the hospital window while I was in labor at the bluest sky in the world. I had support. Her father was present in the delivery room — though after her birth he disappeared on a drinking binge. I understood his despair, but did not agree with the painful means to describe it. A few days later Rainy Dawn was presented to the sun at her father's pueblo and given a name so that she will always be recognized as a part of the people, as a child of the sun.

That's not to say that my experience in the hospital reached perfection. The clang of metal against metal in the delivery room had the effect of a tuning fork reverberating fear in my pelvis. After giving birth I held my daughter, but they took her from me for "processing." I refused to lie down to be wheeled to my room after giving birth; I wanted to walk out of there to find my daughter. We reached a compromise and I rode in a wheelchair. When we reached the room I stood up and walked to the nursery and demanded my daughter. I knew she needed me. That began my war with the nursery staff, who deemed me unknowledgeable because I was Indian and poor. Once again I felt the brushfire of shame, but I'd learned to put it out much more quickly, and I demanded early release so I could take care of my baby without the judgment of strangers.

I wanted something different for Rainy, and as she grew up I worked hard to prove that I could make "something" of my life. I obtained two degrees as a single mother. I wrote poetry, screenplays, became a professor, and tried to live a life that would be a positive influence for both of my children. My work in this life has to do with reclaiming the memory stolen from our peoples when we were dispossessed from our lands east of the Mississippi; it has to do with restoring us. I am proud of our history, a history so powerful that it both destroyed my father and guarded him. It's a history that claims my mother as she lives not far from the place her mother was born, names her as she cooks in the cafeteria of a small college in Oklahoma.

When my daughter told me she was pregnant, I wasn't surprised. I had known it before she did, or at least before she would admit it to me. I felt despair, as if nothing had changed or ever would. She had run away from Indian school with her boyfriend and they had been living in the streets of Gallup, a border town notorious for the suicides and deaths of Indian peoples. I brought her and her boyfriend with me because it was the only way I could bring her home. At age 16, she was fighting me just as I had so fiercely fought my mother. She was making the same mistakes. I felt as if everything I had accomplished had been in vain. Yet I felt strangely empowered, too, at this repetition of history, this continuance, by a new possibility of life and love, and I steadfastly stood by my daughter.

I had a university job, so I had insurance that covered my daughter. She saw an obstetrician in town who was reputed to be one of the best. She had the choice of a birthing room. She had the finest care. Despite this, I once again battled with a system in which physicians are taught the art of healing by dissecting cadavers. My daughter went into labor a month early. We both knew intuitively the baby was ready, but how to explain that to a system in which numbers and statistics provide the base of understanding? My daughter would have her labor interrupted; her blood pressure would rise because of the drug given to her to stop the labor. She would be given an unneeded amniocentesis and would have her labor induced — after having it artificially stopped! I was warned that if I took her out of the hospital so her labor could occur naturally my insurance would cover nothing.

My daughter's induced labor was unnatural and difficult, monitored by machines, not by touch. I was shocked. I felt as if I'd come full circle, as if I were watching my mother's labor and the struggle of my own birth. But I was there in the hospital room with her, as neither my mother had been for me, nor her mother for her. My daughter and I went through the labor and birth together.

And when Krista Rae was born she was born to her family. Her father was there for her, as were both her grandmothers and my friend who had flown in to be with us. Her paternal great-grandparents and aunts and uncles had also arrived from the Navajo Reservation to honor her. Something *had* changed.

Four days later, I took my granddaughter to the Saguaro forest before dawn and gave her the name I had dreamed for her just before her birth. Her name looks like clouds of mist settling around a sacred mountain as it begins to speak. A female ancestor approaches on a horse. We are all together.

SIXTY-THREE

◆◆◆

Reproductive Rights
A Disability Rights Issue
Marsha Saxton

In recent years, the women's movement has broadened its definition of "reproductive rights" to include not only abortion, but all aspects of sexuality, procreation, and parenthood. The priorities of the National Abortion Reproductive Rights Action League also reveal this broader agenda: protecting adolescent reproductive health, preventing unintended pregnancy and sexually transmitted disease, eliminating restrictive or coercive reproductive health policies, and promoting healthy pregnancy and early childhood health.

Some women may take for granted birth control, reproductive health care, and sex education, forgetting that people with different life experiences based on class, race, or physical or mental ability may not have access to these fundamental aspects of reproductive freedom. But for people with disabilities, *all* the reproductive rights are still at stake.

For centuries, the oppression of people with disabilities has denied us "choice": choice about who should be regarded as "a sexual being," who should have babies, which babies should be born, which babies should be allowed to live after they're born, who should raise these babies into adulthood. These choices were made, for the most part, by others. People with disabilities are beginning to demand a say in these decisions now that the Americans with Disabilities Act (ADA) has forced the public to perceive our issues as civil rights issues. In the decades to come, we hope to see a transformation in the public's perception of disability and of people with disabilities. The issue of reproductive rights can serve as a catalyst for this transformation.

The stereotype of asexuality is slowly lifting. There are now a few disabled characters in the popular literature and media who are portrayed as sexual beings participating in intimate activities. (Some of these movie personalities, such as actress Marlee Maitlin, themselves are deaf or have physical disabilities. However, most disabled characters on TV or in the movies are still played by non-disabled actors.)

New and complex issues are emerging in regard to disability and procreation. Many relate to new developments in reproductive technologies. Others reflect changing social values. What follows is a discussion of how these new issues affect people with disabilities.

Reproductive Health Care

Because of patronizing attitudes about disabled people, many medical practitioners and health care facilities do not consider offering reproductive health care services to their patients who have disabilities. Many people with disabilities or with chronic illness, because of the "preexisting condition" exclusion in most health insurance, have been denied access to *any* health care, not only reproductive health care. There are few medical or nursing schools that offer any training on the reproductive health of people with disabilities. Only in the last five years has there been any research on the effects of various birth control methods for people with different kinds of disabilities or chronic illness, and these studies are limited, often focusing only on spinal cord injury. Even people with the more common disabling conditions like diabetes, arthritis, or multiple sclerosis have little or no information about whether they should or shouldn't use particular methods of birth control.

In Chicago, a group of disabled women have created a "disability accessible" gynecological clinic through the Chicago Rehabilitation Institute and the Prentice Women's Hospital, staffed with practitioners who have been trained to serve disabled women. The Health Resource Center for Women with Disabilities is unique. One day a week, it offers accessible core gyn services for women with disabilities and now serves more than 200 women. The staff includes nurse practitioners and midwives; and a nurse who has a disability has been hired. The clinic program plans to expand its resources to include a project director to monitor clinic services and to oversee a library with health-related videos and publications. It will also add an 800 telephone number staffed by a woman with a disability to respond to questions about accessible health care services. The center has initiated research directed at documenting the medical experiences of women with disabilities and improving services for traditionally underserved populations, including developmentally disabled, learning disabled, and mentally retarded women.

Sex Education

Disabled children and adults need information about dating, sex, menstruation, pregnancy, birth control, AIDS, and other sexually transmitted diseases. Attitudes have changed, and increasingly, parents and educators are recognizing that disabled children need sex education. But this is not the norm. Disabled chil-

dren are still often overprotected by adults who don't know how to teach them about "the facts of life." Questions such as the following tend to provoke confusion: how can blind children be given information about gender anatomy? How should retarded children be told about AIDS? How can deaf children, children who use wheelchairs, or any child who may have felt the stigma of disability be encouraged to interact positively with non-disabled and disabled peers and to learn positive sexual self-esteem? Many disabled adults never received important information about sex. They are vulnerable to confusing or dangerous misinformation and serious difficulties with their own sexuality, difficulties that result not from actual physical limitations but simply from exclusion from information and experience.

Marriage Disincentives

In the United States, people with disabilities who receive certain kinds of Social Security or Medicaid benefits are discouraged from getting married by threat of reduced or eliminated benefits. These "marriage disincentives" (like "employment disincentives," which discourage disabled people from employment by threat of reduced medical coverage) reveal the serious disability discrimination fundamentally built into our disability policies. If an SSI (Supplemental Security Income) recipient marries, his or her spouse's earnings are considered income, thus reducing the recipient's benefits, jeopardizing essential medical and personal care attendant services, and often placing enormous financial burden on the couple to finance prohibitively expensive services or equipment. The current law has the effect of forcing people with disabilities to accept "living together" as temporary sweethearts rather than an adult, community-sanctioned marriage. A recent attempt by disability rights advocates to urge Donna Shalala of the federal Department of Health and Human Services to legislate a more equitable system failed. While the outward rationale for the law is to save taxpayer money on people who could be supported by a spouse (based on the assumption that two can live as cheaply as one), social scientists and disability rights activists suspect that drafters of these marriage disincentive laws were also intending to thwart marriage and potential procreation for disabled people.

"Reproducing Ourselves"

The very idea of disabled persons as parents scares some people and exposes discriminatory attitudes that might otherwise remain hidden. Acceptance of disabled people as parents simply requires the larger community's acceptance of us as human beings. By denying our rights to be mothers and fathers, it is not only our competence to care for our young, but our very existence, our desire to "reproduce ourselves," that is forbidden.

In late 1991, TV news anchor Bree Walker, who has a genetic disability and who was pregnant, became the brunt of a call-in radio talk show when the host Jane Norris asked listeners, "Should disabled people have children?" Callers aired their opinions about whether Walker should have her baby or, as Norris posed the question, "Is it 'fair' to bring a child with a disability into the world?" The incident became the focal point of the disabled women's community's challenge to the idea that people with disabilities should not be born.

Qualifications for Parenthood

The Earls are a married Michigan couple, both severely disabled with cerebral palsy. They had a baby, Natalie, and sought assistance from the Michigan Home Help Program in providing physical care for the infant. Their desire to raise their own child and to demonstrate their competence as loving parents was thwarted by state regulations that bar the personal care assistant (PCA) of a disabled client from touching the client's child during paid work hours. One result of this regulation seems to be that disabled people who rely on the PCA program for help in daily living cannot have children.

Of course, people with disabilities must take seriously the responsibilities of adult sexuality and the potential for pregnancy and parenthood. We must also educate ourselves, the disability community, and our families and friends about what it means to be a parent and be disabled. And we must be prepared to take on the discriminatory policies of a variety of institutions: medical, social services, legal, and media. But we must also do battle within ourselves. We must overcome the voices we've internalized that say, "You can't possibly do this, you can't be good parents, and you don't deserve the benefits or the assistance required to raise your own children."

In Berkeley, California, an agency called Through the Looking Glass offers the first program specifically designed to assist parents with disabilities in skills development, community resources, and peer support. Looking Glass also publishes a newsletter, which can be ordered at [2198 Sixth St., Suite 100, Berkeley, CA 94710].

Custody Struggles

Tiffany Callo is a young woman who wanted to raise her newborn son. Because of her cerebral palsy, the California Department of Social Services challenged her ability to care for the child. Armed with lawyers and court orders, the department refused to allow her to demonstrate her parenting skills in an appropriate environment that would enable her to show the creative approaches she had developed to handle the baby. *Newsweek* reporter Jay Mathews picked up her story, and Callo became a spokesperson for the cause of mothers with disabilities who fight for the right to raise their own children. Social service and child protection agency professionals need training and awareness to allow them to perceive the *abilities* of disabled parents, not only the stereotyped limitations.

Adoption

A large number of children adopted or waiting for adoption are disabled. Many disabled adults were adopted or placed in foster homes. It is still largely the case that adoption agencies do not consider disabled people as prospective parents for either disabled or non-disabled children. We need to challenge this stereotype that people with disabilities cannot be good adoptive parents. A few adoption agencies are changing policies, allowing disabled people to adopt, and in some cases even encouraging disabled adults to adopt children with disabilities. For example, Adoption Resource Associates in Watertown, Massachusetts, has taken a special interest in prospective disabled parents and makes specific mention in their brochure that they do not discriminate on the basis of disability in their placement services.

Sterilization Abuse

Consider this story of a woman with a psychiatric disability: "When I was twenty, I got pregnant by my boyfriend at the state mental school. Of course, there was no birth control for patients. We weren't allowed to have sex, but it went on all the time, even between patients and attendants. A doctor forced my mother to sign a paper giving me an abortion, even though I wanted to give up the baby for adoption. When I woke up, I found out I had had a hysterectomy. Maybe I couldn't take care of the baby then, but nobody even asked me what I wanted to do, or what I hoped for when I got older."

When a guardian or medical professional decides that people labeled retarded, mentally ill, or with other disabilities should not be parents, sterilization without consent may occur. Often, guardians or other decision makers who intervene on behalf of these disabled people have little exposure to the Independent Living Movement, or other community disability resources. As disabled people, we need to be empowered to make our own decisions regarding sexuality and procreation.

Abortion

Women with disabilities have reported significant difficulties with regard to abortion. These include being pressured to undergo an abortion because it is assumed that a disabled woman could not be a good parent, or, conversely, being denied access to abortion because a guardian decides the woman was incapable of making her own reproductive choices. Sometimes, after birth, a disabled woman's child is taken away from her. Women with disabilities experience the same kinds of abortion access difficulties as non-disabled women, but these difficulties are often magnified by disability discrimination.

Prenatal Screening

Scientific advances in the field of genetics have created technologies that can detect an increasing number of genetic conditions in the womb. While the general public seems to regard this medical technology as a wonderful advance and a way to reduce the incidence of disability and improve the quality of life, people with disabilities often have a very different view. As revealed in the Bree Walker case mentioned above, the unchallenged assumption often accompanying the use of these screening tests is that the lives of people with genetically related disabilities (such as muscular dystrophy, Down syndrome, cystic fibrosis, sickle cell anemia, and spina bifida) are simply not worth living and are a burden that families and society would rather not endure. The options to abort a fetus who might die early in life, or to abort in order to preclude the birth of a child with severe disabilities, are framed as "reproductive options." But in this era of health care cost containment, the notion of controlling costs by eliminating births of disabled babies may become a requirement, rather than an option. Then it ceases to be reproductive freedom and becomes quality control of babies — eugenics. The availability of these tests reinforces these notions, and the tests are actually marketed to women and to health care providers on this basis. Women are increasingly pressured to abort a fetus identified as disabled. Real choice must include the right to bear children with disabilities.

We in the disabled community must voice our ideas about selective abortion and attest to the true value of our lives. Only when a valid picture of the quality of our lives is available can prospective parents make choices about the use of tests for genetic disabilities in fetuses.

The Reproductive Rights Movement

The women's movement has begun to reach out to women with disabilities as a group. Women's organizations have begun to understand and challenge their own discriminatory attitudes and behaviors. More and more events in the women's movement are beginning to be wheelchair accessible and interpreted for the hearing impaired. But we have a long way to go to make the women's community fully welcoming of disabled people. This is a good time to get involved and share our thinking and energies. To be fully integrated into society, we must get involved and take leadership in all movements, and the movement for reproductive health care and real choice is an especially important one for people with disabilities to take on.

As disabled people, we have unique perspectives to share. Our views can enlighten everyone about the fundamental issues of sexuality and reproduction. We have gained much knowledge and experience with medical intervention, asking for and effectively managing help, dealing with bureaucracy, and fighting for access and power. Other controversial issues to which we can contribute our thinking include surrogate motherhood, population concerns, birthing technologies, artificial insemination, and *in vitro* fertilization.

The movement for reproductive rights needs to include people with disabilities as much as disabled people need to be included in the movement.

SIXTY-FOUR

◆◆◆

Human Rights Violations Based on Gender Identity and Sexual Orientation
Testimony to the International Tribunal on Human Rights Violations Against Sexual Minorities. Oct. 17, 1995. New York City

Daphne Scholinski

My name is Daphne. I am 29 years old and currently live as an artist/writer in San Francisco, California. I am here today as a surviving, living testimony, and to give voice to the experience of many lesbian, gay, bisexual youth and young people who do not conform to traditional gender roles. Thousands of us continue to be stripped of dignity and brutalized by psychiatric abuse in institutions or are struggling to survive after psychiatric incarceration. I must stress *Living,* because many never make it this far, due to high suicide rates resulting from this abuse or the internalized fear and shame of their experiences.

Most of my childhood I was mistaken for a boy. Constantly in need of defense for my self expression, I spent a lot of time hiding. I would be asked, "Why don't you try to look more like a girl?" I couldn't even if I tried. Throughout grammar school and into junior high school, I was continually abused verbally and physically by my family, teachers, and peers for being too masculine. In my defense I frequently needed to fight with people and eventually was forced out of social activities or refused to go to events because of the stress it created for me. I became angry and rebellious. Resulting from a background of abusive and unsupportive family members, teachers, counselors, and peers, I eventually gave in to the depression caused by these circumstances, and at the urging of doctors and teachers, my parents had me institutionalized.

So in 1981, at the age of 14, I was labeled "mentally ill" and confined to the psychiatric ward of Michael Reese Hospital in Chicago, Illinois. I was later transferred to Forest Hospital in Des Plaines, Illinois and then to the Constance Bultman Wilson Center in Faribault, Minnesota—losing four entire years of my youth. I was admitted for reasons of: depression, not adjusting well to adolescence, not attending school, suicidal thoughts and gestures, but most specifically, as they put it, for lacking signs of being a "sexual female." The initial comment given to my parents was, "people in your daughter's condition usually spend the rest of their lives in mental institutions."

My primary diagnosis was "gender identity disorder." Although the American Psychiatric Association removed homosexuality from its official list of mental disorders in 1973, the U.S. mental health system remains an extremely hostile environment for lesbian, gay, and bisexual youth, who are still routinely viewed by child and adolescent psychiatrists as "emotionally disturbed" and in need of aggressive psychiatric treatment "to prevent adult homosexuality."

The doctors attempted to "cure" me of "prehomosexuality" and any wish they thought I had of being a boy. This was based on assumptions due to my "choice of clothing, friendship patterns, and career goals." Much of my so called "treatment" consisted of pressure to conform to norms of heterosexuality and femininity. I was being forced to try to be more feminine. I was to become more concerned with my appearance, and more "obsessive about impressing boys." The goals set for me were: "learn about make-up; dress more like a girl; curl and style hair; and spend quality time learning about girl things with female peers—like, what boys like, etc."

These attempts to force me to be what they thought I should be were failing. So they saw me as a failure, I was never going to be a "normal female." I was on a "point system," and received points for "good behavior" and lost points for "bad behavior." You needed these points to receive "privileges"; like being able to walk to meals unescorted, watch a movie, make a phone call, or even to shower without someone watching you, or leave your room. Having no privileges was not only embarrassing but torturous. You had no escape. I would spend months never leaving my unit, never going to the bathroom without someone staring at me (which I must add was not always by female attendants). Stretches of solitary confinement, heavy medication, physical restraint and horror stories from staff became routine. Though I don't remember if I ever received shock treatments, I witnessed it and it was one of the most terrifying things I have ever seen. I lived with people who claimed to be Jesus and angrily accused me of "stealing their bones." The woman who lived next door to me screamed over and over again "I want to die, let me die!" And I was supposed to be maintaining my sanity? I was growing up in a mental hospital.

Beginning at the age of 14 and continuing until I was 18 years old, I was in three different hospitals. I was subjected to abuse all around me; feeling deserted by my family and left in a mental hospital with extremely "disturbed" adults who yelled, teased and abused me. One of the first statements ever made to me by a patient was while I was in seclusion. She walked right up to the little window in the door, looked in and said, "I think I'm going to have to kill you." I was sexually molested by a male in his late 20s while I was restrained and helplessly strapped to my bed, not to mention how many times I had patients masturbating around me. I was physically assaulted countless times by out of control patients. Staff were sometimes equally as violent. Restraining was often painful. All I would have to do is get a little angry, maybe just call someone a name, and I would get thrown to the floor with my arm twisted

so far behind my back that I feared it would be broken. This was usually followed by a shot of Thorazine, a powerful tranquilizer that would put me to sleep for the rest of the day, only to awaken in seclusion, often without any memory of how I got there. A staff person once held his foot on top of my head while he said "shut up you fucking crazy ass queer," and then yelled for help to calm me down because he felt I was "out of control." None of this was ever dealt with, instead I would have to continually be accused of insanity for my actions, while I believed I was responding very *sanely* to a very *insane* situation.

Stranded in a place where you can not win, everything you do becomes a symptom of something. If you stand or pace, you are hyperactive. If you sit you are withdrawn. If you say you need help, you are looking for attention. If you say you do not need help, you are in denial. I was to explore, in therapy, my "feelings related to the opposite sex." The goals of treatment at this time were stated as: "Elimination of depression, and for the patient to come to terms with herself, as a sexual female." They described my relationship with my best friend as "an expression of a fixated level of sexuality that was being acted out." Nothing about our friendship was out of the ordinary. But because of my "masculine manner" we became suspected of "acting gay" and presumed to be sexual, which we never were. They never believed us. We were forced to be restricted from each other. We were not allowed to speak about each other, to each other; we could not even make eye contact without being punished.

I would spend my entire "treatment" never really dealing with my depression or the symptoms resulting from the abuses from parents, teachers, peers, or previous psychiatric interactions. Instead I was immediately targeted for my "sexual identity" as the problem and the only "thing" that needed resolution. Each and every day was reinforcement that I WAS THE PROBLEM. The silence around the issues of abuses forced me to believe that I deserved it. The idea being that only if I changed, became more feminine, more beautiful, more "acceptably heterosexual," that then there would be no reasons for anyone to treat me poorly, and then I would no longer need to be depressed and could go on to lead a "happy normal life." I was defeated from the beginning.

I had been sentenced to an adolescence spent surrounded by white walls and lab coats. Quite a punishment for a 14 year old who was really showing the typical signs of growing up gay in a heterosexual society.

It was not until 2½ years into my treatment that my parents (specifically my mother) became aware of the intent of the institution and my doctors. When my mother said she thought I might be gay, the doctor responded, "Oh no, don't worry about that. We'll take care of that." She specifically told them not to treat me for that. She believed that her wishes would be respected and followed. I was never aware of this conversation taking place, but once you are behind those closed doors, nobody knows what is really going on. You become a prisoner of that system. I can tell you my treatment never did change.

Every hospital came with the highest of recommendations, but conditions were grossly inadequate for an adolescent. In the first institution I was on a unit of approximately 30 people, and only 4 other patients were under 18. The rest of the patients were much older, ranging from the age of my parents to older than my grandparents. Some patients had already been there for years. There is no hierarchy of sanity. Meaning, everyone is treated the same, no matter how sane or insane you are, or people think you are. I believed this was not only my future, but my only future.

In the end my parents would be convinced that the hospital saved my life; after all I am alive aren't I? While I believe it was necessary to remove me from my home, taking away my freedom, dignity, and any ounce of self-respect was not the answer. I was dying there, they killed my spirit, and no progress was being made. I was ready to live and die there, until, three years into my treatment, an intern looked me in the eyes and said, "What are you doing here? You are so sane." Up to that point the thought never crossed my mind that I could be sane, they could be wrong, and I could be free. I will never forget that moment, that spark that this woman alone created in me, so that I could finally believe in myself.

I was finally released 5 days after my 18th birthday, when they were unable to legally keep me, and conveniently as my insurance had run out and would no longer cover my "treatment." In total, my treatment cost over one million dollars. One month after my million dollar insurance policy ran out, my father received a bill for fifty thousand dollars.

Is it not totally absurd, attempting to prove that which is not provable? The charge of insanity. No matter how hard you try, you cannot convince them of your sanity. I am afraid I will have to wear this mark on my forehead for the rest of my life. This scar follows me like a shadow, watching my every move, every thought. Is it possible for anyone to understand what it is like to be at the mercy of people who at any moment can exercise their authority, their "expert" opinions, their "god complex" over you? That with one swift mark of a pen, they can write the orders that will change your life forever?

We need to create a safe space for us to continue breaking the silence that has allowed this issue to be ignored for far too long and has prevented this issue from receiving the attention it urgently requires; and that clearly identifies homophobic psychiatric abuse as a violation of the most basic human rights. This includes: personal dignity, bodily integrity, and individual autonomy.

I was left traumatized by homophobic counseling and "treatments." Damaged, silenced, and discarded; with emotional scars that will take a lifetime to dissolve. Being labeled and treated as mentally ill simply because of who I am has had long-term disabling effects that have prevented me from speaking out about my experiences. While some have remained incarcerated in the mental health system into adulthood, and others are lost to suicide or other forms of self-directed violence, there are the ones who like me have been silenced by shame and the overwhelming fear of being further stigmatized or discriminated against as a former mental health patient. When you have had your sanity challenged, you always have something to prove. I have often felt so overwhelmed by the tremendous difficulty of surviving and attempting to build a life in the aftermath of extreme trauma.

It is now eleven years later; I realize that I was not supposed to survive. I realize that my "treatment" was designed to leave me with only two options: either change or do not exist. Some might say change would have been easy; I mean "act straight," get discharged, and then go on with your life. But it would have been at that moment of "acting" that I would have surely lost my self. My identity would have disappeared, and then they really would have had someone to "treat." At the time I chose neither, and today, as an artist approaching over 3500 paintings, I have chosen to exist.

◆◆◆

CHAPTER EIGHT

Women, Crime, and Criminalization*

I n recent years, movie audiences have been entertained by a new Hollywood depiction of women
as violent criminals. *Thelma and Louise* (two White
women run from the police after one kills the man
who tried to rape the other), *Set It Off* (four young
Black women in dire straits go on a spree of bank
robberies), and *Bound* (two White lesbians try to
steal $2 million from the Mob), among others, have
introduced images of women — Black and White,
heterosexual and lesbian, working-class and middle-
class — seeking revenge, money, fun, a sense of
being in charge, adventure, and even "liberation"
through criminal activity. Many moviegoers have
reacted with approval and excitement to these images of women breaking out of stereotypical roles,
no longer the moll, sister, mother, or wife of the
main character, a criminal man. In reality, the life
stories of women in the United States who commit crimes and who are caught up in the criminal
justice system are very different. Some steal from
stores, bounce checks, use stolen credit cards, and
use illegal drugs; some are pickpockets, and small-
scale drug dealers; some are simply in the wrong

place at the wrong time. They are disproportionately Latina and African-American, and most are
poor.

The National Context:
"Get Tough on Crime"

The criminalization of women must be understood
in the context of a pro-punishment mind-set fueled
by the "get tough on crime" rhetoric that has proliferated in the United States for the past two decades,
especially during recent years. In the 1988 presiden-
tial election, the Republican candidate George Bush
used the case of Willie Horton, a Black inmate from
a Massachusetts prison who committed murder
while out of prison on the state's furlough program,
to establish street crime — burglary, auto theft, mug-
ging, murder, and rape committed by strangers — as
one of the most important national issues. This tactic implied that Black people, especially men, were
the ones to fear most. Since then, politicians and the
media have reinforced that view by promoting and
reporting on legislation such as the "three-strikes-
you're out" law, which requires a life sentence without parole for three-time felons, and continually
publicizing crime stories, particularly high-profile
cases such as those involving murder and abduction
of children. This trend continues although national

---

*This chapter was written by Barbara Bloom, MSW, Ph.D.,
a criminal justice consultant and researcher specializing
in the development and evaluation of programs serving
girls and women under criminal justice supervision.

and many local crime statistics show a decline in crimes rates.

This "get tough on crime" rhetoric taps into people's sense of futility and fear—especially White people's fear of people of color. People are led to believe that no one is safe from street crime anywhere, but especially around African-American and Latino men, and that everyone labeled "criminal" is an incorrigible street tough or "gangsta." Contrary to this rhetoric, the facts show that women are least safe in their own homes and that the greatest economic losses from crime do not happen on the street. According to Lichtenstein and Kroll (1996), "Society's losses from 'white collar crime' far exceed the economic impact of all burglaries, robberies, larcenies, and auto thefts combined" (p. 20). Nonetheless, high-income criminals who commit such crimes as fraud and embezzlement are not only less likely to be incarcerated but also less likely even to be considered hardened criminals; rather they may be regarded as people who used bad judgment or went "off track." Why, then, is crime being promoted as one of the most serious problems facing this country, and why are women of color the fastest-growing population in the criminal justice system?

Women in the Criminal Justice System

I stood with my forehead pressed as close as possible to the dark, tinted window of my jail cell. The window was long and narrow, the foot-deep wall that framed it made it impossible to stand close. The thick glass blurred everything outside. I squinted and focused, and I concentrated all my attention on the area where my mother said the family would stand and wave. . . . It would be good to see my grandparents and my mother, but it was my daughter I really wanted to see. My daughter who would be two years old in two months.

A couple of minutes passed, and in that small space of time, I rethought my entire life and how it had come to this absurd moment, when I became a twenty-one-year-old girl in jail on a drug charge, a mother who had to wait for someone to bring my own daughter to glimpse me. I could not rub my hands across her fat, brown cheeks, or plait her curly hair the way I like it.

(Gaines 1994, p. 1)

On any given day, over 120,000 women are incarcerated in jails—where people are held before trial and when convicted of a misdemeanor with a sentence of less than one year—and prisons—where people convicted of felony charges and serving more than a one-year sentence are held. Historically, women offenders were ignored by researchers and media reports because their numbers were small in comparison with those of men. For more than a decade, however, the rate of growth in women's imprisonment has far outstripped that of men's, with more than a fivefold increase in the number of women in prison. In 1980, there were roughly 12,000 women in state and federal prisons compared with over 65,000 in 1995 (Bureau of Justice Statistics 1995). Mary Bennett (Reading 65), Shannon Murray (Reading 66), Teresa Luftus (Reading 67), and Nancy Kurshan (Reading 68) describe this experience in the readings that follow.

This dramatic increase in the imprisonment of women has been driven primarily by "the war on drugs" and mandatory sentencing for drug offenses. The majority of female arrests are for drug offenses, such as possession and dealing, and crimes committed to support a drug habit, particularly theft and prostitution, sometimes referred to as drug-related crimes. According to Drug Use Forecasting (DUF) data, more than half of the women arrested test positive for drugs (Bureau of Justice Statistics 1991).

Under current punishment philosophies and practices, women are also increasingly subject to criminalization of noncriminal actions and behaviors. For example, poor and homeless women—many of them mothers—are subject to criminalization as many cities pass ordinances prohibiting begging and sleeping in public places. Another disturbing trend has been the criminalization of HIV-positive women and pregnant drug-addicted women. For example, in 1992, a woman in North Carolina, allegedly HIV-positive, became entangled in the criminal justice system when she went to a public health facility for a pregnancy test. The test was positive, and she was arrested and prosecuted for "failure to follow public health warning." Her crimes were not advising her sexual partners of her HIV status, and not using condoms whenever she had sexual intercourse (Cooper 1992). Though this is an extreme example, it is part of a growing trend, as discussed by Elizabeth Cooper in Reading 69. Pregnant women using illegal drugs are characterized as "evil women" and "bad mothers" who are willing to endanger the health of their unborn children in pursuit of drug-induced highs. There also has been a trend to arrest and prosecute these women for "the 'delivery' of controlled substances to their newborns; their alleged mode of 'delivery' to the newborn is through the umbilical cord between birth and the time the cord is cut" (Cooper 1992, p. 11).

Characteristics of Incarcerated Women

Women prisoners have a host of medical, psychological, and financial problems and needs. Substance abuse, compounded by poverty, unemployment, physical and mental illness, and homelessness, often propels women into a revolving cycle of life inside and outside jails and prisons. They are predominantly single heads of households, with at least two children. They are undereducated and unskilled, with sporadic employment histories. The majority of jailed and imprisoned women were unemployed prior to arrest (53 percent), and only some (23 percent) had completed high school. They frequently have histories of physical and sexual abuse as children, adults, or both. More than 40 percent of women in prisons and in jails reported having been physically or sexually abused at least once at some time in their lives prior to incarceration. Imprisoned women were at least three times more likely than men to have been physically abused and at least six times more likely to have been sexually abused since age eighteen (Bureau of Justice Statistics 1994).

The average age of women in prison is approximately thirty-two years; jailed women are a little younger, with an average age of twenty-nine years. Most are unmarried (46 percent never married) and approximately 80 percent have children, two-thirds of whom are under age eighteen. It is estimated that 165,000 children are affected by the incarceration of their mothers. The majority of those children live with relatives, primarily grandparents, and approximately 10 percent of them are in foster care, a group home, or other social service agency. About 8 percent to 10 percent of women are pregnant when they are incarcerated. For most women under correctional supervision, their problems began as girls. One national study of incarcerated women indicates that nearly half (46.7 percent) had run away from home as girls, and two-thirds of these women ran away more than once (American Correctional Association 1990).

Daily Life of Incarcerated Women

- Women prisoners spend on average 17 hours a day in their cells with 1 hour outside for exercise. By contrast, men prisoners spend on average 15 hours a day in their cells with 1.5 hours outside.

- 80 percent of imprisoned women have children and of those women, 70 percent are single mothers. Prior to imprisonment, 84.7 percent of female prisoners (compared with 46.6 percent of male prisoners) had custody of their children.

- Mothers in prison are less likely to be visited by their children than are fathers because women are sent away to other counties or remote areas of a state more often than men.

- A survey conducted in 38 states revealed that 58 percent of the prisons or jails serve exactly the same diet to pregnant prisoners as to others, and in most cases these meals do not meet the minimum recommended allowances for pregnancy.

- Health care for prisoners is practically nonexistent. It is common practice for prisoners to be denied medical examinations and treatments outright. Incarcerated HIV-infected women have no access to experimental drug trials or to use of new drug protocols.

- It costs more to send a person to prison for a year than to an Ivy League university for a year.

Source: Prison Activist Resource Center 1997.

Incarcerated women use more serious drugs and use them somewhat more frequently than do incarcerated men (Bureau of Justice Statistics 1992). In addition, women are more likely than men to report having used a needle to inject drugs prior to incarceration. The rate of HIV infection is higher for women prisoners than for men prisoners according to the Bureau of Justice Statistics (1994). An estimated 3.3 percent of the women reported being HIV-positive, compared with 2.1 percent of the men. Among prisoners who had shared needles to inject drugs, more women than men were likely to be HIV-positive (10 percent vs. 6.7 percent).

Offenses Committed by Women and Patterns of Arrest

Studies have consistently shown that women generally commit fewer crimes than men and that their offenses tend to be less serious, primarily nonviolent property offenses such as fraud, forgery, and theft, as well as drug offenses (Bloom, Chesney-Lind, and Owen 1994; Gilfus 1992; Pollack 1994). Notwithstanding movie images of violent female criminals, violent offenses committed by women continue to decline. The percentage of women in prison for violent offenses has decreased (three in ten women prisoners in 1991, down from four in ten in 1986), while the proportion of women in prison for drug-related offenses has increased substantially (nearly one in three women prisoners was serving a sentence for drug offenses in 1991; in 1986 that figure was one in eight). When women do commit acts of violence, these are usually in self-defense against abusive spouses or partners (Browne 1987; Bureau of Justice Statistics 1994).

From 1982 to 1991, the number of women arrested for drug offenses increased by 89 percent, in comparison with an increase of 51 percent for men during the same period (Mauer and Huling 1995). Though it is commonly assumed that women addicts engage in prostitution to support their drug habits, their involvement in property crimes is even more common. In a sample of 197 female crack cocaine users in Miami, Inciardi, Lockwood, and Pottieger (1993) found that in the women's last ninety days on the street, 76 percent engaged in drug-related offenses, 77 percent committed minor property crimes, and 51 percent engaged in prostitution (p. 120). Anglin and Hser (1987) found that the women in their sample supported their habits with a variety of crimes. Felony conviction data for most serious offenses from state courts in 1990 illustrate that the highest percentage of women were convicted of fraud, which includes forgery and embezzlement (38 percent), followed by drug possession (17 per-

cent) and trafficking (15 percent) (Maguire, Pastore, and Flanagan 1993, p. 528).

Sentence Length and Time Served

The Bureau of Justice Statistics (1991, 1994) provides some information on the length of women's sentences and the time they actually serve, which is much shorter. The average time served for those released in 1986 was 16 months. Violent offenders served an average of 27 months, property offenders about 13 months, and drug offenders around 14 months. In a 1991 sample, women received somewhat shorter maximum sentences than men but served much less time than men. Half of the female prisoners served a sentence of 60 months or less, whereas half of the men served a sentence of 120 months or less. Twenty-four percent of the female prison population received sentences of less than 36 months. Women drug offenders received an average sentence of 79 months, property offenders 74 months, and violent offenders 178 months. For all female prisoners, the average sentence received was 105 months (Bureau of Justice Statistics 1994).

Because female prisoners tend to receive shorter sentences than men overall, it has been assumed by researchers that women benefit from chivalrous treatment (a so-called chivalry factor) by sentencing judges. Although the chivalry factor does have some statistical support, there is more evidence that women may receive harsher sentences for some crimes, or that women who do not fit traditional female stereotypes — such as butch lesbians — may receive more punitive sentences than men (Chesney-Lind 1987; Erez 1992). When women receive shorter sentences, this is due to gender differences in the offenses for which they are incarcerated, their criminal histories, and the roles they played in the crime, such as whether they were accessories to men or were the "masterminds," and whether they acted alone. On average, women incarcerated in state prisons in 1991 had fewer previous convictions than men, and the crimes of which they had been convicted in the past were less violent (Mauer and Huling 1995).

Race and Class Disparities

Most women in the U.S. criminal justice system are marginalized by race and class. African-American women constitute 46 percent of women prisoners and 43 percent of women in jail, White women 36 percent of women in prison and 38 percent of women in jail, and Latinas 14 percent of women in prison and 16 percent of women in jail. According to the Sentencing Project, from 1989 to 1994, young African-American women experienced the greatest increase in involvement with the criminal justice system of all demographic groups studied. Nationally, between 1980 and 1992 the number of Black women in state and federal prisons grew 278 percent while the number of Black men grew 186 percent; overall the inmate population increased by 168 percent during this period (Mauer and Huling 1995). Women of color are also disproportionately represented on the death rows of this country.

Many crimes committed on Native American reservations are classified as federal offenses, and lawbreakers are held in federal prisons, usually in remote places long distances away from home and hard to get to by public transportation, two factors that increase the isolation of such prisoners.

Racial bias is a factor in arrests, pretrial treatment, and differential sentencing of women offenders. Mann (1995) documents disparity in prison sentences by comparing arrest rates with sentencing rates of women offenders in California, Florida, and New York. She found that, in all three states, women of color, particularly African-Americans, were disproportionately arrested. The few studies that report race-specific differences indicate more punitive treatment of women of color. In their study of one Missouri institution over a sixteen-year period, Foley and Rasche (1979) found that, in general, African-American women received longer sentences (55.1 months) than White women (52.5 months). They also discovered differences based on race in sentencing for the same offense. For example, White women imprisoned for murder served one-third less time than African-American women for the same offense. In a study of gender differences in felony court processing in California in 1988, Farnsworth and Teske (1995) found that White women defendants were more likely to have charges of assault changed to nonassault than were women of color. In 1996 the issue of differential sentencing for cocaine use surfaced as a public issue. Currently the sentences for possession and use of crack cocaine, mainly used by poor people of color, are much higher than sentences for the possession of powdered cocaine, mainly used by middle- and upper-middle-class White people.

The current "war on drugs," initiated by the Reagan administration and continued under Bush and Clinton, has been aggressively pursued in poor urban neighborhoods, especially poor African-American and Latino communities, and in Third World countries, despite the fact that White people make up the majority of drug users and traffickers. A presidentially appointed "drug czar" is responsible for overseeing this policy. Proponents justify massive government intervention as necessary to quell the drug epidemic, gang violence, and "narco-terrorism." However, critics charge that "Blacks, Latinos, and third world people are suffering the worst excesses of a program that violates . . . civil rights, human rights, and national sovereignty" (Lusane 1991, p. 4).

The declared intention to get rid of drugs and drug-related crime has resulted in the allocation of federal and state funding for more police officers on the streets, more federal law enforcement officers, and more jails and prisons, rather than for prevention, rehabilitation, and education. Poor women of color have become the main victims of these efforts in two ways: they are trying to hold their families and communities together while so many men of color are incarcerated, and they are increasingly incarcerated themselves. As Lusane (1991) observes, "The get-tough, mandatory-sentencing laws are forcing judges to send to prison first-time offenders who a short time ago would have gotten only probation or a fine . . . it is inevitable that women caught selling the smallest amount of drugs will do time" (p. 56).

Women Political Prisoners

The International Tribunal on Human Rights Violations of Political Prisoners and Prisoners of War in the United States, held in New York City, December 1990, defined a political prisoner as "a person incarcerated for actions carried out in support of legitimate struggles for self-determination or for opposing illegal policies of the United States government" (Bin Wahad 1996, p. 277). A small but significant group of women in federal prisons is there as a result of such political activities. In Reading 70, Silvia Baraldini, Marilyn Buck, Susan Rosenberg, and Laura Whitehorn describe conditions at the Women's Control Unit in

Marianna, Florida, that houses ninety women, including members of the Puerto Rican Socialist Party, supporters of Native American sovereignty movements, and Black revolutionary movements in the United States and abroad. Silvia Baraldini, who is serving a forty-year sentence, is an Italian citizen, arrested on conspiracy charges arising out of militant political activities in solidarity with national liberation movements, including assisting in the escape of Black activist Assata Shakur. She was active in the women's movement and the anti-Vietnam War movement, and was a supporter of the national liberation movement in Zimbabwe. Laura Whitehorn and Marilyn Buck define themselves as anti-imperialist activists. They were charged with a number of bombings claimed by the Armed Resistance Unit and the Red Guerrilla Resistance (Browne 1996). Susan Rosenberg was involved in the student movement, the anti-Vietnam War movement, and the women's movement. According to Rosenblatt, "she was targeted by the FBI for her support of the liberation of Assata Shakur from prison, and her support of the Black Liberation Army. After going underground in the 1980s she was arrested . . . in 1984, convicted of weapons possession, and sentenced to 58 years" (1996, p. 355). From 1986 to 1988 Silvia Baraldini and Susan Rosenberg were held in the "High Security Unit" (HSU), a specially built underground prison for political prisoners in Lexington, Kentucky. Although this sixteen-bed prison housed no more than six women at a time, it became the center of intense scrutiny by national and international human rights organizations, including Amnesty International, and "became direct proof that political prisoners not only exist in the United States but are the targets of a well-organized counter-insurgency campaign" (O'Melveny 1996, p. 322).

Indeed, since about the mid-1950s, the federal government has operated "counter-insurgency programs," complete with special police forces and lockup facilities, to track, undermine, and destroy left-wing political organizations it deemed radical and militant and to imprison or kill activists. The Federal Bureau of Investigation (FBI) in its Counter Intelligence Programs (COINTELPRO) launched campaigns against the Communist Party in 1954 and subsequently, against the Socialist Workers Party, the Puerto Rican independence movement, the Black Power Movement, particularly the Black Panther Party, and the American Indian Movement (AIM) in the 1960s and 1970s (Churchill 1992). Mumia Abu-Jamal, Leonard Peltier, and Geronimo Pratt were all convicted of murder, though they all claim to have been framed by the FBI. Geronimo Pratt was freed in 1997 after over twenty-five years in prison after a judge ruled that the evidence used to convict him had indeed been tampered with, as both Pratt and prison rights activists had been arguing all along (Booth 1997). Angela Davis, an internationally known scholar and activist, was imprisoned for two years for, and later acquitted of, murder, conspiracy, and kidnapping charges.

Women jailed earlier this century for opposition to government policy were suffragists, whose crime was peacefully picketing the White House in their campaign for votes for women. In 1917, for example, hundreds of suffragists, mainly White, middle-class women, organized pickets around the clock. At first they were ignored by the police. By June they began to be arrested, and in August they received thirty-day and sixty-day sentences for obstructing traffic. A number of those who were jailed went on hunger strikes; they were forcibly fed and threatened with transfer to an insane asylum. They were released the following year by order of President Wilson, and the Washington, D.C., Court of Appeals ruled that their arrests, convictions, and imprisonment were illegal (Gluck 1976). This kind of political action was very different from that of revolutionary organizations committed to self-defense and armed struggle if necessary. But, like the sentences of political women prisoners active in the seventies and eighties, suffragists also received disproportionately long sentences and harsh treatment, clearly intended to discourage this kind of sustained opposition to government policy (Browne (1996, p. 285) notes: "A Ku Klux Klansman, charged with violations of the Neutrality Act and with possessing a boatload of explosives and weapons to be used in an invasion of the Caribbean island of Dominica received eight years. Yet Linda Evans [charged with bombings claimed by militant left-wing groups], convicted of purchasing four weapons with false ID, was sentenced to 40 years—the longest sentence ever imposed for this offense."

Another example of politically-motivated incarceration was the internment of thousands of Japanese-Americans in remote camps following the bombing of Pearl Harbor by Japanese troops during World War II, as described by Rita Takahashi in Reading 71. Most of these people were U.S. citizens, living in West Coast states. They were forced to leave their homes and property, and were kept in the camps for the duration of the war. In Reading 72, Wendy Young describes the experiences of three Chinese women who came to the United States in 1993 to escape China's coercive "one child" family-planning policy and who, in 1997, are still being held in detention by the Immigration and Naturalization Service (INS) under extremely harsh conditions, waiting for decisions on their applications for political asylum.

Theories of Women and Crime

There is a lack of research specifically on women in conflict with the law in the United States. This is partly because until the 1980s far fewer women than men were caught up in the criminal justice system and also because it is difficult for researchers to obtain access to women in prison. Official data collected by the Bureau of Justice is limited and often dates back several years by the time it is published, a limitation of the data cited in this chapter.

Theories of female criminality have been developed primarily from two strands of thought. The first approach is taken by those who attempt to explain female criminality in individual terms. These theories often apply assumptions and stereotypes about the "female psyche" that are blatantly sexist and without much evidence to support their claims. They include biological arguments—for example, that women commit crimes as a result of premenstrual syndrome (PMS)—and psychological notions—that "hysterical" women bahave criminally, or that women are conniving and manipulative, and so resort to using poison rather than a gun to kill a person.

The second approach applies traditional theories of crime, developed to explain male criminality, to women. These include theories of *social learning* (crime is learned), *social process* (individuals are affected by institutions such as the family, school, and peers), and *social structure* (individuals are shaped by structural inequalities), and *conflict theory*, a specific social structure theory, which generally claims that the law is a weapon of social control used by the powerful against the less powerful (Turk 1995).

An apparent increase in female crime in the 1960s and 1970s prompted new theories attributing female criminality to the women's liberation movement. The female offender was identified as its "dark side" (Chesney-Lind 1986). More recently, the phenomenon of girls in gangs has been blamed on the women's movement (Chesney-Lind 1992). Sociologist Freda Adler (1975), for example, proposed that women were committing more violent crimes because the women's movement had created a liberated, tougher class of women, a view that became known as the "masculinity thesis." Similarly, Simon (1975) argued that a rise in women's involvement in property crimes, such as theft, embezzlement, and fraud, was due to women entering previously male occupations, such as banking and business, and to their consequent exposure to opportunities for crime that were previously the preserve of men. This theory is called the "opportunity thesis." Neither of these theses is supported by much empirical evidence.

A third theory of female criminality, the "economic marginalization thesis," posits that it is the absence, rather than the availability, of employment opportunity for women that appears to lead to increases in female crime (Naffine 1987; Giordano 1981). According to this view, most crime committed by women is petty property crime, such as theft, a rational response to poverty and economic insecurity. The increasing numbers of single women supporting dependent children mean that more women may risk the benefits of criminal activity as supplements or alternatives to employment (Rafter 1990). Noting that the majority of female offenders are low-income women who committed non-employment-related crimes, rather than middle- and upper-middle-class professional women who committed employment-related crimes, proponents of economic marginalization theory argue that the feminization of poverty, not women's liberation, is the social trend most relevant to female criminality.

Contemporary feminist research on women and crime, though still in its early stages, has contributed to our understanding of women's experiences on their own terms, not simply by contrasting women's experiences to men's. Feminist scholars have attempted to explain crime, gender differences in crime rates, and the exploitation of female victims from different perspectives. Some view the cause of female crime as originating in male supremacy, which subordinates women through male domination and aggression, and in men's efforts to control women sexually. Such scholars attempt to show how physical and sexual victimization of girls and women can be underlying causes of criminal behavior (Chesney-Lind 1995; Owen and Bloom 1995). They argue that the exploitation of women and girls causes some to run away or to begin abusing drugs at an early age, which often leads to criminal activity.

Other feminists view gender inequality as stemming from the unequal power of women and men in a capitalist society (Connell 1990; Messerschmidt 1986). They trace the origins of gender differences to the development of private property and male domination over the laws of inheritance, asserting that within the current economic system, men control women economically as well as socially. Thus women commit fewer crimes than men because women are isolated in the family and have fewer opportunities to engage in white-collar crimes or street crimes. Since capitalism renders women relatively powerless both in the home and in the economic arena, any crimes they commit are less serious, nonviolent, self-destructive crimes such as drug possession and prostitution. Moreover, women's powerlessness also increases the likelihood that they will be the target of violent acts, usually by men.

Though these feminist theories break some new ground in explaining women's criminal behavior, they do not explain why some women commit crimes and others from the same backgrounds and similar life circumstances do not. Compelling theoretical explanations for women's crime do not yet exist, and further research is needed.

"Equality with a Vengeance": Is Equal Treatment Fair Treatment?

Feminist legal scholars have been very concerned about women's treatment in the criminal justice system. Pollack (1994) asks, are women receiving more equal treatment today? If equal treatment relates to equal incarceration, then the answer appears to be a resounding yes. More women offenders are likely to be incarcerated than at any other time in U.S. history. There is a continuing debate among feminist legal scholars about whether equality under the law is nec-

essarily good for women (Chesney-Lind 1995; Daly 1994). On the one hand, some argue that the only way to eliminate the discriminatory treatment and oppression that women have experienced in the past is to push for continued equalization under the law. Though equal treatment may hurt women in the short run, in the long run it is the only way to guarantee that women will be treated as equal partners economically and socially. For example, MacKinnon (1987) states, "For women to affirm difference, when difference means dominance, as it does with gender, means to affirm the qualities and characteristics of powerlessness" (pp. 38–39). Even those who do not view women as an oppressed group conclude that women will be victimized by laws created out of "concern and affection" and designed to protect them.

Another view maintains that any approach focusing on equality and inequality always presumes that the norm is men. Hence studies of criminal justice always compare the treatment of women with that of men, and men remain the standard against which all are judged (Smart 1995). Some feminist scholars call for a recognition of the differential, or "special" needs of women. Critics of both these positions note that the equal-treatment and special-needs approaches accept the domination of male definitions: equality is defined as having rights equal to those of males, and differential needs are defined as needs different from those of males. Women are the "other" under the law; the bottom line is a male one (Smart 1989).

Although these scholars have identified the limitations of an equal-treatment model in law or in research into legal practices, that model, and the evidence on which it is based, is the centerpiece for sentencing reforms throughout the United States. These gender-neutral sentencing reforms aim to reduce disparities in sentencing by punishing like crimes in the same way. Through this emphasis on parity and the utilization of a male standard, more women are being imprisoned (Daly 1994). New prison beds for women take the place of alternatives to prison, and gender-blind mandatory sentencing statutes, particularly for drug law violations, contribute to the rising numbers of women in prison. A Phoenix, Arizona, sheriff proudly boasted, "I don't believe in discrimination" after he established the first female chain gang in the United States, where women, whose work boots are chained together, pick up trash in downtown Phoenix ("In Phoenix" 1996). This is what Lahey (1985) has called "equality with a vengeance."

Another effect of the equalization approach has been in the types of facilities women are sentenced to. For example, boot camps have become popular with prison authorities as an alternative to prison for juvenile and adult offenders. New York, for instance, operates a boot camp for women that is modeled on those for men. This includes uniforms, shorn hair, humiliation for behaviors considered to be disrespectful of staff, and other militaristic approaches.

Carlen (1989) argues that equality with men in the criminal justice system means more punitive measures applied to women. Instead, she advocates the supervision of women in noncustodial settings in their communities, where they can remain connected with their children and families, and calls for reducing the number of prison beds for women and using nonprison alternatives for all but a few dangerous offenders. She bases her argument on the fact that most women commit nonviolent crimes and are themselves victims of physical, sexual, and emotional abuse. Therefore, she claims, programs that acknowledge women's victimization and support their emotional needs are more appropriate than punitive measures.

The "Prison Industrial Complex"

Public policy, however, is going in the other direction, with an emphasis on incarceration. Currently there are more than 1.5 million people — women and men — in U.S. jails and prisons, an increase of 113 percent since 1985 (Walker 1996). Government funding for the building and operation of new jails and prisons has increased while funding for social services, education, welfare, and housing has been cut.

Some critics of the criminal justice system argue that this current trend has created what they term the "prison industrial complex" (Browne 1996; Davis 1997; Walker 1996). According to Walker (1996), "Over the past 10 years, the construction and servicing of prisons and jails have become a multi-million dollar industry" that is "experiencing huge profits and becoming the growth industry of the 1990s" (p. 4). Profits are being generated not only by architecture firms designing prisons, security companies supplying equipment, and food distribution companies providing food service but also in part, by the direct and indirect exploitation of prisoners. For example, TWA and Best Western (the international motel chain) use prisoners to take calls from customers during times when there is an overflow, such as before holidays and certain vacation periods. This is being done for a number of reasons: it is difficult to attract regular workers for seasonal employment, prisoners do not have to be paid minimum wage or be covered by workers' compensation (a tax employers must pay for regular employees), and they cannot unionize (Lichtenstein and Kroll 1996). Telephone companies also profit because people outside jails and prisons are not allowed to call prisoners directly; prisoners are allowed only to call collect, which is one of the most expensive ways of making telephone calls. Telecommunications industry officials estimate that the corrections communications market generates about $1 billion annually, and it is expected to grow in the future (Walker 1996).

Inside/Outside Connections

The issue of crime and criminality is an important one for women because of the massive increase in the number of women who are serving time in U.S. jails and prisons and because the criminalization of women is one of the most dramatic ways in which gender, race, and class position shape women's lives. Many in this society are shielded from this reality because incarcerated women are literally locked away, behind bars, and out of sight. In many cases, society has given up on them.

The societal assumptions that justify and reinforce this separation between "inside" and "outside" are that these are bad women, perhaps foolishly involved with criminal men, a little crazy from drink, drugs, or the pain of their lives, but that they must have done something *terrible* to end up in jail. Criminal and noncriminal women often share the same life situations. Many have experienced physical, sexual, and emotional abuse, racism, sexism, classism, and other forms of exploitation. An anonymous poet speaks to this connection in Reading 73. Most women who commit crimes are economically marginalized, involved in drug and alcohol abuse, and single heads of households. The crimes they commit reflect their marginalization in our society, and generally are a result of being poor, women of color, or both.

Women who have never been incarcerated can be allies to incarcerated and formerly incarcerated women by getting involved in advocacy organizations, or by attending activities involving former prisoners and activists. Examples include Aid to Incarcerated Mothers (Atlanta), the National Women's Law Center Women's Prison Project (Washington, D.C.), National Network for Women in Prison (San Francisco), and Social Justice for Women (Boston). Women on the outside are working with women prisoners in literacy classes and creative writing projects, such as The Women in Prison Project, sponsored by *Woman's Way* (Utah) and (Boulder, Colo.), or supporting self-help groups run by prisoners, such as Convicted Women against Violence at the California Institution for Women. AIDS awareness programs for people in prison are sponsored by the ACLU National Prison Project (Washington, D.C.) and the AIDS in Prison Project (New York). Advocates for incarcerated women critique the funding priorities of successive administrations that give a higher priority to building more jails and prisons than to education, social services, and welfare; they urge a fundamental redirection of these resources. They also critique the inadequate provision of health care and of educational, therapeutic, and life-skills programs for incarcerated women.

As you read and discuss this chapter, consider the following:

1. Why is there such attention by politicians and the media to street crimes?

2. Why are people so afraid of street crimes?

3. Where is the prison nearest to where you live?

4. What do you know about prison conditions for women?

5. What would compel a woman to think that a jail or prison is the best place for her to be?

6. What laws, if any, have you ever broken? Why? How did you justify this to yourself or others?

7. Do you think the law is always right?

8. When you hear "female criminal," what images come to mind? How did you form your ideas about what a female criminal is? How can you find out if they are really accurate?

9. Consider the readings by Shannon Murray and Teresa Loftus; what conditions outside must these women be facing to think that jail is the best thing that ever happened to them?

10. What can you do on behalf of women in prison?

SIXTY-FIVE

◆◆◆

Cells

Mary Bennett

Cell, brick, cement, bars, walls, hard,
tv's, soaps, stories, tears, no visitors
allowed, lawyers, liars, guards, big,
touch guns, mean fingers, small bed,
green cloth, disinfectant, toilet, sink,
bars, no window, no door, no knob to turn,

no air, no wind, cold, nightmares, screams,
no touch, no touching.

I want to touch someone. I want to hold
that woman who cries every goddamn night.

I WANT TO TOUCH SOMEONE.

◆◆◆

SIXTY-SIX

Shannon's Story

Shannon Murray

I was born in Detroit Lakes, Minnesota on September 21, 1969. I grew up in the Old Colony projects in South Boston. The neighborhoods in them days were quiet. The parents kept to themselves and the children were well behaved. We would play games like kick ball or Red Rover. There was a huge park across the street from the complex with a playground so there was always something to do.

My family consisted of my mother, my stepfather, my older sister Janine, and my younger brother Robbie. We were a close family that showed a lot of affection for each other. My parents were alcoholics so it was a struggle. We made the best of what we had. We weren't any worse off than other families; in some ways we had more. Somehow my parents managed to send me and my younger brother to Catholic school. In this way I felt more fortunate than others.

My sister and I are American Indians. My mother, stepfather, and brother are Irish. It was hard because my sister and I were often singled out. I've always felt different from everyone else at home and at school.

I first started smoking pot and drinking at the age of twelve. By this time, I was more aware of the drug abuse in my neighborhood. The older teens would hang in the hallways smoking pot and drinking. I started to "use" to fit in. It also helped me to escape the feelings I had surrounding my parents' alcoholism.

My first arrest was at the age of 16 for drinking in public. Over the next four years I was able to avoid the arms of the law. I was put into Protective Custody a few times for disorderly conduct. By this time I was drinking and drugging daily. My disease had taken over. I supported my habits by baby-sitting and selling pot. I dropped out of school in the tenth grade because it was getting in the way of me partying the way I wanted to. I had a few jobs here and there but was unable to hold one because they also got in the way of my using.

After I had my daughter Jaquelin at the age of 18, I started smoking coke more and more often. I had used before that but I stopped during my preg-

nancy, only smoking pot because I was more afraid of the effects coke could have on my baby than the effect of pot.

The cocaine caused me to lose custody of my daughter to my parents and eventually my apartment. I couldn't deal with the pain of losing my daughter so I turned to heroin. This led to many arrests for shoplifting and possession. My first incarceration was at the age of 25. I was to do three months with probation upon my release.

I was scared because of the stories I had heard about jail. I just felt alone and cut off from reality. I kept to myself and didn't get involved with any of the programs except going to the AA meetings for my good time. I was released with the intention of never coming back.

About nine months later I was incarcerated again, this time for a year. I kind of welcomed the incarceration. This time I am taking advantage of the time I have here to learn more about myself. Being here has given me the chance to take a good look at my lifestyle and what I need to change. I am in the Recovery Program here and I have taken classes like Peace at Home, HIV Prevention, Voices Within, Graphic Arts, and I tutor for pre-GED.

It is hard being locked up in a man's prison. I feel there are prejudices against women here at the Suffolk County House of Corrections. We don't have yard privileges except for a caged-in area that we are only allowed access to during the summer months. We aren't allowed to work in the kitchen or anywhere else in the prison except for the two floors which hold female inmates. We are only allowed to go to the other parts of the prison during the night for things like the library or computers.

I think poverty has a lot to do with people being incarcerated. Where there is poverty there is a lot of drug abuse and less access to structured programs. I think prejudice has a lot to do with being incarcerated because there aren't many jobs for minorities and people have to resort to crime to get things they need that you aren't able to at low-paying jobs.

I have learned that I want a better way of life and that I really don't want to come back here. I know I need to lead an honest life if I truly want to stay out of prison. I hope to become a productive person in society by taking on my responsibilities. I am afraid of failing but I know if I pick up by first dealing with my addictions then I won't have to resort to criminal behavior.

S I X T Y - S E V E N

◆◆◆

Teresa's Story

Teresa Loftus

My name is Teresa. I was born in Boston in 1962. From there we moved to Quincy, Massachusetts. We had a huge house with a little farm out back and chickens in the basement. The neighborhood was very peaceful and I had a lot of friends. I lived with my Mom and Dad and grandmother on my Mom's side. I have 3 sisters and 2 brothers. My oldest brother died last summer. We all loved each other very much. My two older sisters took care of me and my younger sister while my parents worked. Money was never a problem that I can remember. When we needed something or wanted something my Mom would see to it that we got it. We had about the same income as the people who lived around the neighborhood. We were comfortable. My parents and grandparents came from Sicily. We learned to speak Sicilian before we were taught the English language. We made wine in the cellar and ate all Italian dishes on Sundays. When we went to visit our other grandparents we could have a glass of wine mixed with ginger ale with our pasta and meat dinner. We moved to another town when I was 8 years old. It was a summer resort. In the winter we had only a few neighbors but when the summer came all the houses filled up. We were the only Italians on the street and all the neighbors would love coming over to eat. Our house was always full and my parents and grandparents used to tell everyone to eat. My Dad was feared and respected. I grew up very proud to be Sicilian.

I first used drugs at the age of 8. I walked in on my two older sisters while they were smoking pot. They made me smoke some so that I didn't tell on them. I had my first drink at 7 when my sister got married. I got very drunk and didn't drink again for years. Later I used pot and alcohol because of peer pressure. In later years I went on to coke and heroin. I tried coke for my first time at 18 and heroin at 26. I fell in love with both of them right away. The first time I got arrested I was 19 years old. It was over driving violations. My first incarceration came in 1996. I felt very scared. I had been in and out of police stations for years but never did anything bad enough to land myself in prison. I felt like a failure and a low-life. Once I was inside I felt hopeless and depressed and I put on my tough guy act so no one would mess with me. It really was not who I was but I felt I had no choice if I was going to survive. Women are treated no better than bad children in a man's prison. We are confined to one floor. When we do get the chance to go out it is in a cage. If we look or try to talk with a man we get locked. They give us 5–10 minutes to eat. They only have a spoon or a fork at every meal and no napkins. If we wear anything in our hair to hold it out of our eyes we get locked and they don't provide anything in the canteen for our hair. The place is very overcrowded. Some units have 3 to a two-man room and 4 in the larger rooms. Women are definitely treated much worse than the men. Some meals wouldn't fill a child and the quality of the food is bad. I see a lot of black people in jail. I don't know why that is, except for the fact that their neighborhoods have more of a crime rate and they become easy prey. They seem to be prejudiced and jealous of the white people, but in my eyes we are all the same, some a little luckier than others, that's all. I think poverty has a lot to do with being incarcerated, when you don't have money to have the things necessary to survive you really have no choice but to turn to a life in the fast lane which always ends up in crime, and it's only a matter of time before you get caught.

While being here I have learned that I never want to go through the shame of having my freedom taken away and having to be told when I can eat, sleep, go to the bathroom, how to act and don't act. It has been degrading for me and has left me feeling worthless more than not. When I get out I want to live life again and be a mother to my children. I want to become a productive member of society and do good and help people not hurt them. My fears are that it will all catch up to me again and that I'll end up back in prison or worse, dead. The Recovery Unit has been my only ray of sunshine. It has given me back my self-respect and dignity, and most of all it has given me hope.

SIXTY-EIGHT

◆◆◆

Behind the Walls
The History and Current Reality of Women's Imprisonment
Nancy Kurshan

Prisons serve the same purpose for women as they do for men; they are instruments of social control. However, the imprisonment of women, as well as all the other aspects of our lives, takes place against a backdrop of patriarchal relationships. We refer here to Gerda Lerner's definition of patriarchy: "The manifestation and institutionalization of male dominance over women and children in the family and the extension of male dominance over women in society in general. It implies that men hold power in all the important institutions of society and that women are deprived of access to such power." Therefore, the imprisonment of women in the United States has always been a different phenomenon than that for men; the proportion of women in prison has always differed from that of men; women have traditionally been sent to prison for different reasons; and once in prison, they endure different conditions of incarceration. Women's "crimes" have often had a sexual definition and been rooted in the patriarchal double standard. Furthermore, the nature of women's imprisonment reflects the position of women in society.

In an effort to examine these issues further, this essay explores how prisons have historically served to enforce and reinforce women's traditional roles, to foster dependency and passivity, bearing in mind that it is not just incarcerated women who are affected. Rather, the social stigma and conditions of incarceration serve as a warning to women to stay within the "proper female sphere." Needless to say this warning is not issued equally to women of all nationalities and classes. For this reason, our analysis will also take into account the centrality of race in determining female prison populations, both in the North and the South and pre- and post-Civil War. We believe that white supremacy alters the way that gender impacts on white women and women of color. The final avenue of exploration of this chapter will thus concern the relationship between race and women's imprisonment. We will attempt to show that the history of the imprisonment of women is consistent with Audre Lorde's comment that in "a patriarchal power system where white skin privilege is a major prop, the entrapments used to neutralize Black women and white women are not the same."

As long as there has been crime and punishment, patriarchal and gender-based realities and assumptions have been central determinants of the response of society to female "offenders." In the late Middle Ages, reports reveal differential treatment of men and women. A woman might commonly be able to receive lenient punishment if she were to "plead her belly," that is, a pregnant woman could plead leniency on the basis of her pregnancy. On the other hand, women were burned at the stake for adultery or murdering a spouse, while men would most often not be punished for such actions. Such differential treatment reflected ideological assumptions as well as women's subordinate positions within the family, church, and other aspects of society. Although systematic imprisonment arose with industrialization, for centuries prior to that time unwanted daughters and wives were forced into convents, nunneries, and monasteries. In those cloisters were found political prisoners, illegitimate daughters, the disinherited, the physically deformed, and the mentally "defective."

A more general campaign of violence against women was unleashed in the witch-hunts of 16th- and 17th-century Europe, as society tried to exert control over women by labeling them as witches. This resulted in the death by execution of at least tens of thousands, and possibly millions of people. Conservative estimates indicate that over 80 percent of all the people killed were women. Here in the United States, the witchcraft trials were a dramatic chapter in the social control of women long before systematic imprisonment. Although the colonies were settled relatively late in the history of European witch-hunts, they proved fertile ground for this misogynist campaign. The context was a new colonial society, changing and wrought with conflicts. There were arguments within the ruling alliance, a costly war with the indigenous people led by King Philip, and land disputes. In the face of social uncertainty, unrest and "uncivilized Indians," the Puritans were determined to recreate the Christian family way of life in the wilderness and reestablish the social patterns of the homeland. The success of their project was an open question at the time, and the molding of the role of women was an essential element in the defense of that project.

Hundreds were accused of witchcraft during the New England witchcraft trials of the late 1600s, and at least 36 were executed. The primary determinant of who was designated a witch was gender; overwhelmingly, it was women who were the objects of witch fear. More women were charged with witchcraft, and women were more likely than men to be convicted and executed. In fact, men who confessed were likely to be scoffed at as liars. But age, too, was an important factor. Women over 40 were most likely to be accused of witchcraft and fared much worse than younger women when they were charged. Women over 60 were especially at high risk. Women who were alone, not attached to men as mothers, sisters, or wives were also represented disproportionately among the witches. Puritan society was very hierarchal, and the family was an essential aspect of that hierarchy. According to Carol Karlsen, the Puritan definition of woman as procreator and "helpmate" of man could not be ensured except through

force. Most of the witches had expressed dissatisfaction with their lot, if only indirectly. Some were not sufficiently submissive in that they filed petitions and court suits, and sometimes sought divorces. Others were midwives and had influence over the wellbeing of others, often to the chagrin of their male competitors, medical doctors. Still others exhibited a female pride and assertiveness, refusing to defer to their male neighbors.

Karlsen goes on to offer one of the most powerful explanations of the New England witchcraft trials. She argues that at the heart of the hysteria was an underlying anxiety about inheritance. The inheritance system was designed to keep property in the hands of men. When there were no legitimate male heirs, women inheritors became aberrations who threatened the orderly transmission of property from one male generation to the next. Many of the witches were potential inheritors. Some of them were already widowed and without sons. Others were married but older, beyond their childbearing years, and therefore no longer likely to produce male heirs. They were also "disposable" since they were no longer performing the "essential" functions of a woman, as reproducer and, in some cases, helpmate. Many of the witches were charged just shortly after the death of the male family member, and their witchcraft convictions meant that their lands could easily be seized. Seen in this light, persecution of "witches" was an attempt to maintain the patriarchal social structure and prevent women from becoming economically independent. These early examples of the use of criminal charges in the social control of women may be seen as precursors to the punitive institutions of the 1800s. Up until this time, there were few carceral institutions in society. However, with the rise of capitalism and urbanization come the burgeoning of prisons in the United States. It is to those initial days of systematic imprisonment that we now turn.

The Emergence of Prisons for Women

The relatively few women who were imprisoned at the beginning of the 19th century were confined in separate quarters or wings of men's prisons. Like the men, women suffered from filthy conditions, overcrowding, and harsh treatment. In 1838 in the New York City Jail (the "Tombs"), for instance, there were

42 one-person cells for 70 women. In the 1920s at Auburn Penitentiary in New York, there were no separate cells for the 25 or so women serving sentences up to 14 years. They were all lodged together in a one-room attic, the windows sealed to prevent communication with men. But women had to endure even more. Primary among these additional negative aspects was sexual abuse, which was reportedly a common occurrence. In 1826, Rachel Welch became pregnant while serving in solitary confinement as a punishment and shortly after childbirth she died as a result of flogging by a prison official. Such sexual abuse was apparently so acceptable that the Indiana state prison actually ran a prostitution service for male guards, using female prisoners.

Women received the short end of even the prison stick. Rather than spend the money to hire a matron, women were often left completely on their own, vulnerable to attack by guards. Women had less access to the physician and chaplain and did not go to workshops, mess halls, or exercise yards as men did. Food and needlework were brought to their quarters, and they remained in that area for the full term of their sentence.

Criminal conviction and imprisonment of women soared during and after the Civil War. In the North, this is commonly attributed to a multitude of factors, including men's absence during wartime and the rise of industrialization, as well as the impact of the dominant sexual ideology of 19th-century Victorianism. The double standard of Victorian morality supported the criminalization of certain behaviors for women but not for men. In New York in the 1850s and 1860s, female "crimes against persons" tripled while "crimes against property" rose 10 times faster than the male rate.

Black people, both women and men, have always been disproportionately incarcerated at all times and all places. This was true in the Northeast and Midwest prisons before the Civil War. It was also the case in the budding prison system in the western states, where Blacks outstripped their very small percentage of the population at large. The only exception was in the South where slavery, not imprisonment, was the preferred form of control of African-American people. Yet while the South had the lowest Black imprisonment rate before the Civil War, this changed dramatically after the slaves were freed. This change took place for African-American women as well as men. After the Civil War, as part of the re-entrenchment of Euro-American control and the continuing subjugation of Black people, the post-war southern states passed infamous Jim Crow laws that made newly freed Blacks vulnerable to incarceration for the most minor crimes. For example, stealing a couple of chickens brought three to ten years in North Carolina. It is fair to say that many Blacks stepped from slavery into imprisonment. As a result, southern prison populations became predominately Black overnight. Between 1874 and 1877, the Black imprisonment rate went up 300 percent in Mississippi and Georgia. In some states, previously all-white prisons could not contain the influx of African-Americans sentenced to hard labor for petty offenses.

These spiraling rates in both the North and South meant that by mid-century there were enough women prisoners, both in the North and South, to necessitate the emergence of separate women's quarters. This practical necessity opened the door to changes in the nature of the imprisonment of women. In 1869, Sarah Smith and Rhoda Coffin, two Indiana Quakers, led a campaign to end the sexual abuse of women in that state's prison, and in 1874 the first completely separate women's prison was constructed. By 1940, 23 states had separate women's prisons. The literature refers to these separate prisons for women as "independent" women's prisons. This is ironic usage of the word since they were independent only in their physical construction. In every other way they fostered all forms of dependency in the incarcerated women and were an integral part of the prison system. Although these prisons were not initiated as separate institutions until almost a century after men's prisons, it is not so much this time lag that differentiates the development of prisons for women from those for men. The difference comes from the establishment of a bifurcated (two-part) system, the roots of which can be found in the patriarchal and white supremacist aspects of life in the United States at the time. Understanding this bifurcation is a step towards understanding the incarceration of women in the United States.

On the one hand, there were custodial institutions that corresponded by and large to men's prisons. The purpose of custodial prisons, as the name implies, was to warehouse prisoners. There was no pretense of rehabilitation. On the other hand, there were reformatories that, as the name implies, were intended to be more benevolent institutions that "uplifted" or "improved" the character of the women held there. These reformatories had no male counterparts. Almost every state had a custodial women's prison, but in the Northeast and Midwest the majority of incarcerated women were in reformatories. In the South, the few reformatories that existed were exclusively white. However, these differences are not, in essence, geographical; they are racial. The women in the custodial institutions were black whether in the North or the South, and had to undergo the most degrading conditions, while it was mainly white women who were sent to the reformatories, institutions that had the ostensible philosophy of benevolence and sisterly and therapeutic ideals.

The Evolution of Separate Custodial Prisons for Women

In the South after 1870, prison camps emerged as penal servitude and were essentially substituted for slavery. The overwhelming majority of women in the prison camps were Black; the few white women who were there had been imprisoned for much more serious offenses, yet experienced better conditions of confinement. For instance, at Bowden Farm in Texas, the majority of women were Black, were there for property offenses, and worked in the field. The few white women who were there had been convicted of homicide and served as domestics. As the techniques of slavery were applied to the penal system, some states forced women to work on the state-owned penal plantations but also leased women to local farms, mines, and railroads. Treatment on the infamous chain gangs was brutal and degrading. For example, women were whipped on the buttocks in the presence of men. They were also forced to defecate right where they worked, in front of men.

An 1880 census indicated that in Alabama, Louisiana, Mississippi, North Carolina, Tennessee, and Texas, 37 percent of the 220 Black women were leased out whereas only 1 of the 40 white women was leased. Testimony in an 1870 Georgia investigation revealed that in one instance "There were no white women there. One started there, and I heard Mr. Alexander (the lessee) say he turned her loose. He was talking to the guard; I was working in the cut. He said his wife was a white woman, and he could not stand it to see a white woman worked in such places." Eventually, as central penitentiaries were built or rebuilt, many

women were shipped there from prison farms because they were considered "dead hands" as compared with the men. At first, the most common form of custodial confinement was attachment to male prisons; eventually independent women's prisons evolved out of these male institutions. These separate women's prisons were established largely for administrative convenience, not reform. Female matrons worked there, but they took their orders from men.

Like the prison camps, custodial women's prisons were overwhelmingly Black, regardless of their location. Although they have always been imprisoned in smaller numbers than African-American or Euro-American men, Black women often constituted larger percentages within female prisons than Black men did within men's prison. For instance, between 1797 and 1801, 44 percent of the women sent to New York state prisons were African-Americans as compared to 20 percent of the men. In the Tennessee state prison in 1868, 100 percent of the women were Black, whereas 60 percent of the men were of African descent. The women incarcerated in the custodial prisons tended to be 21 years of age or older. Forty percent were unmarried, and many of them had worked in the past.

Women in custodial prisons were frequently convicted of felony charges; most commonly for "crimes" against property, often petty theft. Only about a third of female felons were serving time for violent crimes. The rates for both property crimes and violent crimes were much higher than for the women at the reformatories. On the other hand, there were relatively fewer women incarcerated in custodial prisons for public order offenses (fornication, adultery, drunkenness, etc.), which were the most common in the reformatories. This was especially true in the South where these so-called morality offenses by Blacks were generally ignored, and where authorities were reluctant to imprison white women at all. Data from the Auburn, New York prison on homicide statistics between 1909 and 1933 reveal the special nature of the women's "violent" crime. Most of the victims of murder by women were adult men. Of 149 victims, two-thirds were male; 29 percent were husbands, 2 percent were lovers, and the rest were listed as "man" or "boy" (a similar distribution exists today). Another form of violent crime resulting in the imprisonment of women was performing "illegal" abortions.

Tennessee Supreme Court records offer additional anecdotal information about the nature of women's violent crimes. Eighteen-year-old Sally Griffin killed her fifty-year-old husband after a fight in which, according to Sally, he knocked her through a window, hit her with a hammer, and threatened to "knock her brains out." A doctor testified that in previous months her husband had seriously injured her ovaries when he knocked her out of bed because she refused to have sex during her period. Sally's conviction stood because an eye-witness said she hadn't been threatened with a hammer. A second similar case was also turned down for retrial.

Southern states were especially reluctant to send white women to prison, so they were deliberately screened out by the judicial process. When white women were sent to prison, it was for homicide or sometimes arson; almost never did larceny result in incarceration. In the Tennessee prison, many of the African-American property offenders had committed less serious offenses than the whites, although they were incarcerated in far greater numbers. Frances Kellor, a renowned prison reformer, remarked of this screening process that the Black female offender "is first a Negro and then a woman—in the whites' estimation." A 1922 North Carolina report describes one institution as being "so horrible that the judge refuses to send white women to this jail, but Negro women are sometimes sent." Hundreds of such instances combined to create institutions overwhelmingly made up of African-American women.

The conditions of these custodial prisons were horrendous, as they were in prisons for men. The southern prisons were by far the worst. They were generally unsanitary, lacking adequate toilet and bathing facilities. Medical attention was rarely available. Women were either left totally idle or forced into hard labor. Women with mental problems were locked in solitary confinement and ignored. But women suffered an additional oppression as well.

> The condition of the women prisoners is most deplorable. They are usually placed in the oldest part of the prison structure. They are almost always in the direct charge of men guards. They are treated and disciplined as men are. In some of the prisons children are born . . . either from the male prisoners or just "others". . . One county warden told me in confidence, "That I near kill that woman yesterday . . ." One of the most reliable women officials in the South told me that in her state at the State Farm for

women the dining room contains a sweat box for women who are punished by being locked up in a narrow place with insufficient room to sit down, and near enough to the table so as to be able to smell the food. Over the table there is an iron bar to which women are handcuffed when they are strapped.

Generally speaking, the higher the proportion of women of color in the prison population, the worse the conditions. Therefore, it is not surprising that the physical conditions of incarceration for women in the custodial prisons were abysmal compared to the reformatories (as the following section indicates). Even in mainly Black penal institutions, Euro-American women were treated better than African-American women.[*]

Early Twentieth Century: Female Reformatories

Reformatories for women developed alongside custodial prisons. These were parallel, but distinct, developments. By the turn of the century, industrialization was in full swing, bringing fundamental changes in social relations: shifts from a rural society to an urban one, from a family to market economy; increased geographic mobility; increased disruption of lives; more life outside the church, family, and community. More production, even for women, was outside the home. By 1910, a record high of at least 27 percent of all women in New York state were "gainfully" employed. Thousands of women worked in the New York sweatshops under abominable conditions.

There was a huge influx of immigration from Southern and Eastern Europe; many of these were Jewish women who had come straight from Czarist Russia and brought with them a tradition of resistance and struggle. The division between social classes was clearly widening and erupted in dynamic labor struggles. For example, in 1909, 20,000 shirt-waist makers, four-fifths of whom were women, went on strike in New York. Racism and national chauvinism were rampant in the United States at the

---

[*]Estelle B. Freedman, *Their Sisters' Keepers: Women's Prison Reform in America, 1830–1930* (Ann Arbor: University of Michigan Press, 1981). Ch. 4, note 44.

turn of the century in response to the waves of immigrants from Europe and Black people from the South. The Women's Prison Association of New York, which was active in the social purity movement, declared in 1906 that:

> If promiscuous immigration is to continue, it devolves upon the enlightened, industrious, and moral citizens, from selfish as well as from philanthropic motives, to instruct the morally defective to conform to our ways and exact from them our own high standard of morality and legitimate industry. . . . Do you want immoral women to walk our streets, pollute society, endanger your households, menace the morals of your sons and daughters . . . ? Do you think the women here described fit to become mothers of American citizens? Shall foreign powers generate criminals and dump them on our shores?*

Also at the turn of the century various currents of social concern converged to create a new reform effort, the Progressive movement, that swept the country, particularly the Northeast and Midwest, for several decades. It was in this context that reformatories for women proliferated. Reformatories were actually begun by an earlier generation of female reformers who appeared between 1840 and 1900, but their proliferation took place during this Progressive Era as an alternative to the penitentiary's harsh conditions of enforced silence and hard labor. The reformatories came into being as a result of the work of prison reformers who were ostensibly motivated to improve penal treatment for women. They believed that the mixed prisons afforded women no privacy and left them vulnerable to debilitating humiliations.

Indeed, the reformatories were more humane and conditions were better than at the women's penitentiaries (custodial institutions). They did eliminate much male abuse and the fear of attack. They also resulted in more freedom of movement and opened up a variety of opportunities for "men's" work in the operation of the prison. Children of prisoners up to two years old could stay in most institu-

tions. At least some of the reformatories were staffed and administered by women. They usually had cottages, flower gardens, and no fences. They offered discussions on the law, academics, and training, and women were often paroled more readily than in custodial institutions. However, a closer look at who the women prisoners were, the nature of their offenses, and the program to which they were subjected reveals the seamier side of these ostensibly noble institutions.

It is important to emphasize that reformatories existed for women only. No such parallel development took place within men's prisons. There were no institutions devoted to "correcting" men for so-called moral offenses. In fact, such activities were not considered crimes when men engaged in them and therefore men were not as a result imprisoned. A glance at these "crimes" for women only suggests the extent to which society was bent on repressing women's sexuality. Despite the hue and cry about prostitution, only 8.5 percent of the women at the reformatories were actually convicted of prostitution. More than half, however, were imprisoned because of "sexual misconduct." Women were incarcerated in reformatories primarily for various public order offenses or so-called "moral" offenses: lewd and lascivious carriage, stubbornness, idle and disorderly conduct, drunkenness, fornication, serial premarital pregnancies, keeping bad company, adultery, venereal disease, and vagrancy. A woman might face charges simply because a relative disapproved of her behavior and reported her, or because she had been sexually abused and was being punished for it. Most were rebels of some sort.

Jennie B., for instance, was sent to Albion reformatory for five years for having "had unlawful sexual intercourse with young men and remain[ing] at hotels with young men all night, particularly on July 4, 1893." Lilian R. quit school and ran off for one week with a soldier, contracting a venereal disease. She was hospitalized, then sentenced to the reformatory. Other women were convicted of offenses related to exploitation and/or abuse by men. Ann B. became pregnant twice from older men, one of whom was her father, who was sentenced to prison for rape. She was convicted of "running around" when she was seven months pregnant. One woman who claimed to have miscarried and disposed of the fetus had been convicted of murdering her illegitimate child. There was also the increasing practice of abor-

---

*Nicole Hahn Rafter, *Partial Justice: Women in State Prisons 1800–1935* (Boston: New England University Press, 1985), pp. 93–94.

tion that accounted for at least some of the rise in "crime against persons."

As with all prisons, the women in the reformatories were of the working class. Many of them worked outside the home. At New York State's Albion Reformatory, for instance, 80 percent had, in the past, worked for wages. Reformatories were also overwhelmingly institutions for white women. Government statistics indicate that in 1921, for instance, 12 percent of the women in reformatories were Black while 88 percent were white.

Record keeping at the Albion Reformatory in New York demonstrates how unusual it was for Black women to be incarcerated there. The registries left spaces for entries of a large number of variables, such as family history of insanity and epilepsy. Nowhere was there a space for recording race. When African Americans were admitted, the clerk penciled "colored" at the top of the page. African-American women were much less likely to be arrested for such public order offenses. Rafter suggests that Black women were not expected to act like "ladies" in the first place and therefore were reportedly not deemed worthy of such rehabilitation.

The program of these institutions, as well as the offenses, was based on patriarchal assumptions. Reformatory training centered on fostering ladylike behavior and perfecting housewifely skills. In this way it encouraged dependency and women's subjugation. Additionally, one aspect of the retraining of these women was to isolate them, to strip them of environmental influences in order to instill them with new values. To this end family ties were obstructed, which is somewhat ironic since the family is at the center of the traditional role of women. Letters might come every two months and were censored. Visits were allowed four times a year for those who were on the approved list. The reformatories were geographically remote, making it very difficult for loved ones to visit. Another thorn in the rosy picture of the reformatory was the fact that sentencing was often open-ended. This was an outgrowth of the rehabilitative ideology. The incarceration was not of fixed length because the notion was that a woman would stay for as long as it took to accomplish the task of reforming her.

Parole was also used as a patriarchal weapon. Ever since the Civil War, there was a scarcity of white working-class women for domestic service. At the same time, the "need for good help" was increasing because more people could afford to hire help. It was not an accident that women were frequently paroled into domestic jobs, the only ones for which they had been trained. In this way, vocational regulation went hand-in-hand with social control, leading always backwards to home and hearth, and away from self-sufficiency and independence. Additionally, independent behavior was punished by revoking parole for "sauciness," obscenity, or failure to work hard enough. One woman was cited for a parole violation for running away from a domestic position to join a theater troupe; another for going on car rides with men; still others for becoming pregnant, going around with a disreputable married man, or associating with the father of her child. And finally, some very unrepentant women were ultimately transferred indefinitely to asylums for the "feeble-minded."

Prison reform movements have been common; a reform movement also existed for men. However, all these institutions were inexorably returned to the role of institutions of social control. Understanding this early history can prepare us to understand recent developments in women's imprisonment and indeed imprisonment in general. Although the reformatories rejected the more traditional authoritarian penal regimes, they were nonetheless concerned with social control. Feminist criminologists claim that in their very inception, reformatories were institutions of patriarchy. They were part of a broad attack on young working-class women who were attempting to lead somewhat more autonomous lives. Women's sexual independence was being curbed in the context of "social purity" campaigns. As more and more white working-class women left home for the labor force, they took up smoking, frequenting dance halls, and having sexual relationships. Prostitution had long been a source of income for poor women, but despite the fact that prostitution had actually begun to wane about 1900, there was a major morality crusade at the turn of the century that attacked prostitution as well as all kinds of small deviations from the standard of "proper" female propriety.

Even when the prisons were run by women, they were, of course, still doing the work of a male supremacist prison system and society. We have seen how white working-class women were punished for "immoral behavior" when men were not. We have seen how they were indoctrinated with a program of "ladylike" behavior. According to feminist criminologists such as Nicole Hahn Rafter and Estelle

Freedman, reformatories essentially punished those who did not conform to bourgeois definitions of femininity and prescribed gender roles. The prisoners were to embrace the social values, although, of course, never to occupy the social station of a "lady." It is relevant to note that the social stigma of imprisonment was even greater for women than men because women were supposedly denying their own "pure nature." This stigma plus the nature of the conditions of incarceration served as a warning to all such women to stay within the proper female sphere.

These observations shed some light on the role of "treatment" within penal practice. Reformatories were an early attempt at "treatment," that is, the uplifting and improvement of the women, as opposed to mere punishment or retribution. However, these reforms were also an example of the subservience of "treatment" to social control. They demonstrate that the underlying function of control continually reasserts itself when attempts to "improve" people take place within a coercive framework. The reformatories are an illustration of how sincere efforts at reform may only serve to broaden the net and extend the state's power of social control. In fact, hundreds and hundreds of women were incarcerated for public order offenses who previously would not have been vulnerable to the punishment of confinement in a state institution were it not for the existence of reformatories.

By 1935, the custodial prisons for women and the reformatories had basically merged. In the 1930s, the United States experienced the repression of radicalism, the decline of the progressive and feminist movements, and the Great Depression. Along with these changes came the demise of the reformatories. The prison reform movement had achieved one of its earliest central aims, separate prisons for women. The reformatory buildings still stood and were filled with prisoners. However, these institutions were reformatories in name only. Some were administered by women but they were women who did not even have the progressive pretenses of their predecessors. The conditions of incarceration had deteriorated miserably, suffering from cutbacks and lack of funding.

Meanwhile, there had been a slow but steady transformation of the inmate population. Increasingly, the white women convicted of misdemeanors were given probation, paroled, or sent back to local jails. As Euro-American women left the reformatories, the buildings themselves were transformed into custodial prisons, institutions that repeated the terrible conditions of the past. As custodial prison buildings were physically closed down for various reasons, felons were transferred to the buildings that had housed the reformatories. Most of the women were not only poor but also were Black. African-American women were increasingly incarcerated there with the growth of the Black migration north after World War I. These custodial institutions now included some added negative dimensions as the legacy of the reformatories, such as the strict reinforcement of gender roles and the infantilization of women. In the end, the reformatories were certainly not a triumph for the women's liberation. Rather they can be viewed as one of many instances in which U.S. institutions are able to absorb an apparent reform and use it for continuing efforts at social control.

Women and Prison Today

. . . What are the conditions women face when they are imprisoned? Women are confined in a system designed, built and run by men for men, according to a fall 1990 issue of *Time Magazine*. Prison authorities rationalize that because the numbers of women have been so relatively low, there are no "economies of scale" in meeting women's needs, particularly their special needs. Therefore, women suffer accordingly, they say. There are a wide range of institutions that incarcerate women and conditions vary. Some women's prisons look like "small college campuses," remnants of the historical legacy of the reformatory movement. Bedford Hills state prison in New York is one such institution; Alderson Federal Prison in West Virginia is another. Appearances, however, are deceptive. For instance, Russell Dobash describes the "underlying atmosphere [of such a prison] as one of intense hostility, frustration, and anger."

Many institutions have no pretenses and are notoriously overcrowded and inadequate. The California Institution for Women at Frontera houses 2,500 women in a facility built for 1,011. Overcrowding sometimes means that women who are being held for trivial offenses are incarcerated in maximum-security institutions for lack of other facilities. Women's prisons are often particularly ill-equipped and poorly financed. They have fewer medical, educational, and vocational facilities than men's prisons. Medical treatment is often unavailable, inappropriate, and inconsistent. Job training is also largely unavailable; when opportunities exist, they are usually traditional female occupations. Courses concentrate on homemaking and low-paid skills like beautician and launderer. Other barriers exist as well. In an Alabama women's prison, there is a cosmetology program but those convicted of felonies are prohibited by state law from obtaining such licenses.

In most prisons, guards have total authority, and the women can never take care of their basic intimate needs in a secure atmosphere free from intrusion. In the ostensible name of security, male guards can take down or look over a curtain, walk into a bathroom, or observe a woman showering or changing her clothes. In Michigan, for instance, male guards are employed at all women's prisons. At Huron Valley, about half the guards are men. At Crane prison, approximately 80 percent of the staff is male and there are open dormitories divided into cubicles. In one section the cubicle walls are only four feet high and there are no doors or curtains on any cubicles anywhere at Crane. The officers' desks are right next to the bathroom and the bathroom doors must be left open at all times. Male guards are also allowed to do body shakedowns where they run their hands all over the women's bodies.

Incarceration has severe and particular ramifications for women. Eighty percent of women entering state prisons are mothers. By contrast 60 percent of men in state prisons are fathers and less than half of them have custodial responsibility. These mothers have to undergo the intense pain of forced separation from their children. They are often the sole caretakers of their children and were the primary source of financial and emotional support. Their children are twice as likely to end up in foster care than the children of male prisoners. Whereas when a man goes to prison, his wife or lover most often assumes or continues to assume responsibilities for the children, the reverse is not true. Women often have no one else to turn to and are in danger of permanently losing custody of their children. For all imprisoned mothers the separation from their children is one of the greatest punishments of incarceration, and engenders despondency and feelings of guilt and anxiety about their children's welfare.

Visiting with children often is extremely difficult or impossible. At county jails where women are awaiting trial, prisoners are often denied contact vis-

its and are required to visit behind glass partitions or through telephones. Prisons are usually built far away from the urban centers where most of the prisoners and their families and friends live. Where children are able to visit, they have to undergo frightening experiences like pat-downs under awkward and generally anti-human conditions. When women get out of prison, many states are supposed to provide reunification services, but in fact most do not. Although even departments of corrections admit that family contact is the one factor that most greatly enhances parole success, the prison system actively works to obstruct such contact.

Reproductive rights are nonexistent for the 10 percent of the women in prison who are pregnant. Massachusetts is one of the few states to provide Medicaid funds for poor women to get abortions, but these funds are unavailable for imprisoned women. All the essentials for a healthy pregnancy are missing in prison: nutritious food, fresh air, exercise, sanitary conditions, extra vitamins, and prenatal care. Women in prison are denied nutritional supplements such as those afforded by the Women Infants and Children (WIC) program. Women frequently undergo bumpy bus rides, and are shackled and watched throughout their delivery. It is no wonder then that a 1985 California Department of Health study indicated that a third of all prison pregnancies end in late-term miscarriage, twice the outside rate. In fact, only 20 percent have live births. For those women who are lucky enough to have healthy deliveries, forced separation from the infant usually comes within 24 to 72 hours after birth.

Many commentators argue that, at their best, women's prisons are shot through with a viciously destructive paternalistic mentality. According to Rafter, "women in prison are perpetually infantilized by routines and paternalistic attitudes." Assata Shakur describes it as a "pseudo-motherly attitude . . . a deception which all too often successfully reverts women to children." Guards call prisoners by their first names and admonish them to "grow up," "be good girls," and "behave." They threaten the women with a "good spanking." Kathryn Burkhart refers to this as a "mass infancy treatment." Powerlessness, helplessness, and dependency are systematically heightened in prison while what would be most therapeutic for women is the opposite — for women to feel their own power and to take control of their lives. Friendship among women is discouraged, and the homophobia of the prison system is exemplified by rules in many prisons that prohibit any type of physical contact between women prisoners. A woman can be punished for hugging a friend who has just learned that her mother died. There is a general prohibition against physical affection, but it is most seriously enforced against known Lesbians. One Lesbian received a disciplinary ticket for lending a sweater and was told she didn't know the difference between compassion and passion. Lesbians may be confronted with extra surveillance or may be "treated like a man." Some Lesbians receive incident reports simply because they are gay.

Many prison administrators generally agree that community-based alternatives would be better and cheaper than imprisonment. However, there is very little public pressure in that direction. While imprisonment rates for women continue to rise, the public outcry is deafening in its silence. Ruth Ann Jones of the Division of Massachusetts Parole Board says her agency receives no outside pressure to develop programs for women. However, around the country small groups of dedicated people are working to introduce progressive reforms into the prisons. In Michigan, there is a program that buses family and friends to visit at prisons. In New York, at Bedford Hills, there is a program geared towards enhancing and encouraging visits with children. Chicago Legal Aid for Imprisoned Mothers (CLAIM), Atlanta's Aid to Imprisoned Mothers, and Madison, Wisconsin's Women's Jail Project are just some of the groups that have tirelessly and persistently fought for reforms as well as provided critical services for women and children.

The best programs are the ones that can concretely improve the situation of the women inside. However, many programs that begin with reform-minded intentions become institutionalized in such a way that they are disadvantageous to the population they are supposedly helping. Psychological counselors may have good intentions, but they work for the departments of corrections and often offer no confidentiality. And of course, even the best of them tend to focus on individual pathology rather than exposing systematic oppression. Less restrictive alternatives like halfway houses often get turned around so that they become halfway in, not halfway out. That is, what we are experiencing is the widening of the net of state control. The results are that women who would not be incarcerated at all wind up under the supervision of the state rather than decreasing the numbers of women who are imprisoned.

Prison Resistance

One topic that has not been adequately researched is the rebellion and resistance of women in prison. It is only with great difficulty that any information was found. We do not believe that is because resistance does not occur, but rather because those in charge of documenting history have a stake in burying this herstory. Such a herstory would challenge the patriarchal ideology that insists that women are, by nature, passive and docile. What we do know is that as far back as 1943 there was a riot in Sing Sing Prison in New York, which was the first woman's prison. It took place in response to overcrowding and inadequate facilities.

During the Civil War, Georgia's prison was burned down, allegedly torched by women trying to escape. It was again burned down in 1900. In 1888, similar activity took place at Framingham, Massachusetts, although reports refer to it as merely "fun." Women rebelled at New York's Hudson House of Refuge in response to excessive punishment. They forced the closing of "the dungeon," basement cells and a diet of bread and water. Within a year, similar cells were reinstituted. The story of Bedford Hills is a particularly interesting one. From 1915 to 1920 there were a series of rebellions against cruelty to inmates. The administration had refused to segregate Black and white women up until 1916, and reports of the time attribute these occurrences to the "unfortunate attachments formed by white women for the Negroes." A 1931 study indicated that "colored girls" revolted against discrimination at the New Jersey State Reformatory.

Around the time of the historic prison rebellion at Attica Prison in New York State, rebellions also took place at women's prisons. In 1971, there was a work stoppage at Alderson simultaneous with the rebellion at Attica. In June of 1975, the women at the North Carolina Correctional Center for Women staged a five-day demonstration "against oppressive working atmospheres, inaccessible and inadequate medical facilities and treatment, and racial discrimination, and many other conditions at the prison." Unprotected, unarmed women were attacked by male guards armed with riot gear. The women sustained physical injuries and miscarriages as well as punitive punishment in lockup and in segregation, and illegal transfers to the Mattawan State Hospital for the Criminally Insane. In February of 1977, male guards were for the first time officially assigned to duty in the housing units where they freely watched women showering, changing their clothes, and performing all other private functions. On August 2, 1977, a riot squad of predominantly male guards armed with tear gas, high pressure water hoses, and billy clubs attacked one housing unit for five hours. Many of the women defended themselves and were brutally beaten; 28 women were illegally transferred to Mattawan where they faced a behavior modification program.

This short exposition of the rebellions in women's prisons is clearly inadequate. Feminist criminologists and others should look towards the need for a detailed herstory of this thread of the women's experience in America.

Conclusion

We began this research in an attempt to understand the ways that patriarchy and white supremacy interact in the imprisonment of women. We looked at the history of the imprisonment of women in the United States and found that it has always been different for white women and African-American women. This was most dramatically true in the social control of white women, geared toward turning them into "ladies." This was a more physically benign prison track than the custodial prisons that contained Black women or men. But it was insidiously patriarchal, both in this character and in the fact that similar institutions did not exist to control men's behavior in those areas. We also saw that historically the more "Black" the penal institution, the worse the conditions. It is difficult to understand how this plays out within the walls of prisons today since there are more sophisticated forms of tracking. That is, within a given prison there are levels of privileges that offer a better or worse quality of life. Research is necessary to determine how this operates in terms of white and African-American female prisoners. However, we can hypothesize that as women's prisons become increasingly Black institutions, conditions will, as in the past, come more and more to resemble the punitive conditions of men's prisons. This is an especially

timely consideration now that Black women are incarcerated eight times more frequently than white women.

Although the percentage of women in prison is still very low compared to men, the rates are rapidly rising. And when we examine the conditions of incarceration, it does appear as if the imprisonment of women is coming more and more to resemble that of men in the sense that there is no separate, more benign, track for women. Now more than ever, women are being subjected to more maximum-security, control units, shock incarceration; in short, everything negative that men receive. We thus may be looking at the beginning of a new era in the imprisonment of women. One observation that is consistent with these findings is that the purpose of prisons for women may not be to function primarily as institutions of patriarchal control. That is, their mission as instruments of social control of people of color generally may be the overriding purpose. Turning women into "ladies" or "feminizing" women is not the essence of the mission of prisons. Warehousing and punishment are now enough, for women as well as men.

This is not to suggest that the imprisonment of women is not replete with sexist ideology and practices. It is a thoroughly patriarchal society that sends women to prison; that is, the rules and regulations, the definition of crimes are defined by the patriarchy. This would include situations in which it is "okay" for a husband to beat up his wife, but that very same wife cannot defend herself against his violence; in which women are forced to act as accessories to crimes committed by men; in which abortion is becoming more and more criminalized. Once in prison, patriarchal assumptions and male dominance continue to play an essential role in the treatment of women. As discussed previously, women have to deal with a whole set of factors that men do not, from intrusion by male guards to the denial of reproductive rights. Modern day women's imprisonment has taken on the worst aspects of the imprisonment of men. But it is also left with the sexist legacy of the reformatories and the contemporary structures of the patriarchy. Infantilization and the reinforcement of passivity and dependency are woven into the very fabric of the incarceration of women.

The imprisonment of women of color can be characterized by the enforcement of patriarchy in the service of the social control of people of color as a whole.

This raises larger questions about the enormous attacks aimed at family life in communities of color, in which imprisonment of men, women, and children plays a significant role. However, since this area of inquiry concerns the most disenfranchised elements of our society, it is no wonder that so little attention is paid to dealing with this desperate situation. More research in this area is needed as there are certainly unanswered questions. But we must not wait for this research before we begin to unleash our energies to dismantle a prison system that grinds up our sisters.

SIXTY-NINE

◆◆◆

When Being Ill Is Illegal
Women and the Criminalization of HIV

Elizabeth B. Cooper

In 1992 in North Carolina a woman was arrested and prosecuted for "failure to follow public health warnings" to advise her sexual partners that she was (allegedly) HIV-positive and to use a condom whenever she had sexual intercourse. The catalyst for her arrest was that she had become pregnant, according to a test performed at a public health facility. This disturbing but so far unique case is certainly the most extreme example of government intrusion into the reproductive activity of HIV-positive women, but it is far from the only one.

Women's, health, and AIDS activists have noted with alarm a number of indications that government and health authorities may be moving toward limiting the civil rights of people who are infected with HIV. Such actions seem to be aimed particularly at seropositive women in their child-bearing years, who are viewed primarily as threats to any children they might bear. These actions are unacceptable, not only because they infringe on the civil rights of one group of citizens, but also because they interfere with the provision of health care and services to people who desperately need them.

C.M.

The North Carolina case involves C.M., an African-American woman in her early 20s, who allegedly has been a prostitute and an active drug user for many years. C.M. has been dependent on government assistance, and, as a result, has sought health care services at the county clinic. She had two successful pregnancies before her third child died shortly after birth. It is alleged that the third child had tested positive for the presence of HIV antibodies and that when C.M. was tested shortly thereafter she also tested positive.

County officials claim they repeatedly warned C.M. that whenever she was to have sexual intercourse, she had to reveal that she was carrying an infectious agent and had to use a condom. County officials further assert that despite repeated warnings, C.M. generally did not comply with their public health order. There is some evidence that C.M. functions at a level slightly above that classified as mentally retarded.

In early 1992, C.M. told a county health nurse that she should be seen by a gynecologist for pain she was having and further thought she might be pregnant. When C.M.'s pregnancy test came back positive, the county sought and obtained a warrant for her arrest. C.M. was prosecuted for failure to follow public health warnings; aside from the statements of the county health officers regarding C.M.'s past behavior, the evidence against her consisted of the fact that she had gotten pregnant. C.M. was sentenced to two years in jail, which she must serve day-for-day. Conviction under any other misdemeanor generally results in serving 15 to 30 days. While her initial case was pending, C.M. had an abortion and a tubal ligation. She has indicated that she took these actions, in part, to appease public health officials. C.M.'s appeal is pending.

It is clear that this prosecution never would have occurred if C.M. had not been poor and had not gotten pregnant. It was the confluence of C.M.'s poverty—necessitating her reliance on the public health system—and her seropositive status that led to her arrest, prosecution, and conviction. A wealthier HIV-positive woman in C.M.'s position surely would not have been treated as a criminal.

Disturbing Trends

In the past few years two disturbing trends have developed that indicate that repressive measures, such as those used against C.M., may increasingly be used against HIV-positive women, particularly those who choose to have children. First, postpartum women increasingly have been arrested and prosecuted for the "delivery" of controlled substances to their newborns; the alleged mode of "delivery" to the newborn is through the umbilical cord between birth and the time the cord is cut.[1] This trend toward seeing pregnant women as "fetal vessels" and as potential antagonists to their fetuses and newborns particularly applies to HIV-positive women, who are often viewed primarily as threats to the health of any children they might bear, while their own significant needs are ignored.

Second, we have recently seen an increase in the criminalization of the behavior of HIV-positive individuals in general. In Michigan and Louisiana, for example, people have been criminally charged for having otherwise consensual sex because they did not reveal their HIV-positive status to their partners. And HIV-positive individuals have been prosecuted for attempted murder for having bitten or spit at law enforcement officials, even though HIV has not been found to be transmitted in this manner. Most recently, in late 1992, a man with AIDS living in upstate New York, was charged with attempted murder for biting an emergency medical technician who was assisting him.

In some cases, the increased criminalization of HIV has been aimed specifically at women. For example, prostitutes in many states are routinely tested for HIV antibodies upon arrest; if they test positive and are arrested again for soliciting, they are subjected to higher bail requirements and enhanced penalties—changing a conviction from a misdemeanor to a felony, for instance. A Colorado law makes prostitution a felony for anyone who is HIV-infected.

Women historically have been unfairly blamed for the spread of infectious illness. For example, female prostitutes have been blamed for the high incidence of sexually transmitted diseases experienced by male military personnel overseas. HIV-positive people generally have been accused of "intentionally" transmitting HIV; and HIV-positive women have been criticized for "selfishly" and "recklessly" bringing harm to any children they may bear.

It would not be surprising, then, to see the merging of these trends toward criminalization and to witness increased restriction and prosecution of HIV-positive women who become pregnant or give birth. Indeed, we have had inklings, even before the arrest of C.M., that this has been going on in various guises for some time.

Repressive Measures

While the rate of increase of AIDS cases has shown signs of slowing in other populations in the United States, it is fast growing among women. For example, although new reported cases for gay men increased from 23,555 in 1990 to 23,745 in 1991, this represented an increase in new cases of just 0.8 percent; for intravenous drug users the number of new cases increased 4.5 percent; in the same time period, the number of women diagnosed with AIDS grew at a rate of almost 14 percent.[2] As a result, women represent an increasingly greater proportion of the people with AIDS in the United States. Women with AIDS are disproportionately women of color; nearly 74 percent of these women are African-American or Hispanic. Women with HIV are also disproportionately low-income or living in poverty.

Among these already disenfranchised populations, the HIV epidemic has hit women of child-bearing age the hardest. In fact, HIV disease is the number one killer of women between the ages of 25 and 44 in New York City; in 1990, the most recent year for which figures are available, it was the sixth greatest killer of women in this age group in the United States.[3] Because of these demographics, many HIV-positive women are faced with the highly personal and often agonizing choice of whether or when to have children, or, if they are already pregnant, whether to continue the pregnancy, knowing that there is a 25 to 30 percent chance that the child would also be infected, that there is a chance they could lose custody of the child, and that they might not live to raise their own child.

Contrary to the assumptions some people make, there is no reason to believe that HIV-positive women choose to have children for any reasons other than those of most women or that seropositive women will not adequately care for their children. In fact, there is every indication that seropositive women, like other women tend to put the well-being of their children ahead of all other concerns they may have.

There is no doubt that if we could wave a magic wand, we would do away with HIV — spare the children and all the others who are touched by it. So far, however, we do not have this kind of magic. So, advocates for people with AIDS as well as health care workers and administrators, legislators, and HIV-positive women themselves must confront the question: how do we deal with the reality that the majority of women who are HIV-infected are in their childbearing years?

Coercive Counseling

Faced with this question, some public health personnel have attempted to preempt the rights of seropositive women to make their own choices, arrogating to themselves this personal prerogative. For example, there are numerous stories of HIV-positive women who have been coerced by health care personnel into either obtaining abortions or being sterilized. In fact, one woman filed suit against a hospital (*Doe v. Jamaica Hospital*) that she alleges virtually forced her to have an abortion against her will.

Ironically, many facilities that provide abortions have erected barriers that interfere with the rights of HIV-positive women to exercise this option. Many such facilities claim that they would need to take greater sterilization precautions when treating HIV-positive women, when, in fact, because it is not always possible to know who may be carrying an infectious agent, they should always be using universal infection control procedures to protect against the transmission of HIV, hepatitis-B, and other blood-borne pathogens. Furthermore, these facilities are generally obliged under state and federal law to provide their services without regard to the client's serostatus.

Mandatory Reporting

Advocates for people with HIV disease have long opposed another policy that may have particular repercussions for women: mandatory reporting by health care workers or laboratories of the names of people who are HIV-infected to state and local surveillance offices. Currently, approximately 26 states have imposed some form of HIV name reporting; the names of people with AIDS are reportable in all states.

Opposition to mandatory reporting is grounded in the understanding that, first, such programs and attendant fears of breaches in confidentiality serve to deter people from obtaining counseling, testing, and health care; and, second, despite government assurances to the contrary, such "list keeping" rarely, if ever, results in getting increased care to people who are HIV-infected.

Although HIV name reporting is a threat to all people who are or perceive themselves to be HIV infected, newborns and their mothers are particularly at risk. For example, Connecticut recently implemented mandatory reporting only for HIV-positive children under 13 years of age; government officials were unable to garner sufficient support to implement such a program for all HIV-positive individuals.

Mandatory Testing

Policy questions regarding who should be reported implicitly and explicitly raise the question of who should be tested. Not surprisingly, pregnant women and newborns, particularly those living in high-incidence areas, are at greatest risk for being subjected to mandatory HIV-testing programs. At least three jurisdictions have seriously considered or temporarily adopted such mandatory testing programs. In New York State, advocates for women with HIV disease, allied with state officials, are fighting ongoing efforts to "un-blind" the state's blinded seroprevalence study of all newborns. In Illinois, the director of public health issued the conflicting recommendations that "newborn infants should be tested at delivery if the mother resides in a high seroprevalence area, the mother's status is not known, and the mother refuses testing for herself. The mother should receive counseling and informed consent should be obtained as a condition of testing the newborn."[4] In San Diego, California, a judge took the extraordinary step of issuing an order allowing government officials to compel the HIV antibody testing of newborns deemed "at risk" for infection because the mother has or is suspected of having engaged in behavior deemed high-risk for transmitting HIV and has refused testing or is unavailable.

AIDS advocates have opposed the mandatory screening of newborns for the presence of HIV for a number of reasons. First, women will rightly view such mandatory programs as selective and repressive; to avoid mandatory testing programs, women will have to avoid the settings in which they are instituted. Thus, imposition of mandatory testing programs will undermine the goal of increasing women's use of health care services for their children and themselves.

Second, a state that implements such programs will have interposed itself between the mother and her child with the message that the state is a better caretaker than the mother. This mode of state intervention is unacceptable, particularly as it sets the stage for broader intrusions of the government into the lives of women and their children. Concern over such intrusion — particularly the removal of children to foster care discourages women from utilizing services that might otherwise be beneficial to them or their families.

Furthermore, mandatory testing for parturient women is unacceptably prejudicial and demeaning. Because newborns carry their mother's antibodies and testing reveals the mother's serostatus rather than that of the infant, mandatory programs would selectively remove the right of informed consent for HIV-antibody screening of parturient women. It would be unconscionable and grossly prejudicial if informed consent — a value so highly regarded in other areas — were dispensed with only for women who have just given birth. Moreover, when providing care and services to newborns becomes more important than caring for both mother *and* child, one must conclude that the institution has reduced its vision of the woman solely to that of carrier and deliverer of the newborn.

Implementation of mandatory, unblinded perinatal HIV testing undoubtedly will be contested as a violation of both federal laws protecting the rights of people with disabilities and any state laws that require proper counseling and specific, written, informed consent prior to testing. States implementing such programs also will need to defend their position that only parturient women as a class are exempted from the principles contained in that law. The state's bur-

den to justify such intrusive measures will be significant. While the goal of getting newborns into care is an important state interest, this objective can be better met through less-intrusive measures, such as voluntary counseling and testing programs and improved access to care for both mother and newborn.

Providing Options

Legal prosecutions of HIV-positive women who become pregnant, such as that of C.M., are among the most severe deprivations of a woman's civil and reproductive rights. Yet even state and local governments that have not gone to this extreme have developed, considered, and adopted measures that severely repress the rights of HIV-positive women. And, unfortunately, as the numbers of HIV-positive women and HIV-positive newborns continue to grow, we can expect to see increased attempts by government and medical officials to interfere in the highly private and personal choices that must be made by seropositive women. But such repressive measures will do nothing to stem the spread of HIV — either horizontally to partners or vertically to newborns — or to reduce the number of women, men, or children who are HIV-infected. In fact, if public clinics are also the source of criminal prosecutions, women will simply avoid them. A doctor, especially a public health officer, cannot also be a prosecutor. Unfortunately, many low-income women have no real choice of where they obtain their health care. The logical result of the repression and prosecution of HIV-positive women is that they will choose to avoid the health care system altogether.

Advocates and care providers for HIV-positive women — and the women themselves — suggest quite different measures. Instead, they propose the availability of informative, non-directive counseling that will truly allow women to choose whether they want to get pregnant or continue an existing pregnancy. Moreover, everyone should be provided with access to HIV-related testing and counseling services; and all women should have the opportunity to consent to (or withhold consent from) the testing of their newborns. Needless to say, women must be provided with full access to health care for themselves and for their families, for both HIV-related and other health concerns.

The most effective, sensitive, respectful, and legally sound approach to stemming the spread of HIV and protecting the health of those already HIV-positive would be to use available resources to increase access to health care services that are geared toward assisting women, not prosecuting them. We cannot allow policy to be developed and resources to be allocated along a line of false distinction between those who are perceived as "innocent" and others who are not. Every family member—and every single individual—must be provided with access to voluntary counseling and testing programs and adequate and appropriate health care. The best approach to preserving and improving the quality of life is the provision of counseling and health care services to all.

Notes

1. Lynn Paltrow, *Criminal Prosecutions Against Pregnant Women: National Update and Overview,*

New York: Reproductive Freedom Project, American Civil Liberties Union Foundation, April 1992.

2. *HIV/AIDS Surveillance Report,* Rockville, MD: Centers for Disease Control, October 1992.

3. Kathleen Stoll, Center for Women Policy Studies; telephone interview, National Center for Health Statistics, Centers for Disease Control, February 1992; Garrett, Laurie, "AIDS Cases in Women are Skyrocketing; 35% Increase Expected This Year in U.S.; Many Unaware of Risk," *New York Newsday,* June 10, 1991, p. 5.

4. Lumpkin, John, "Recommendations for Counseling and Testing Women, Newborns, and Infants for Human Immunodeficiency Virus (HIV) Infection," November 8, 1991. These recommendations have not been finalized or actively enforced. Conversation with Matthew Nosanchuck, Staff Counsel, American Civil Liberties Union of Illinois, December 1992.

◆◆◆

SEVENTY

Women's Control Unit
Marianna, FL

Silvia Baraldini, Marilyn Buck, Susan Rosenberg, and Laura Whitehorn

Shawnee Unit, at the Federal Correctional Institution in Marianna, Florida, was opened by the Federal Bureau of Prisons (BOP) in August 1988, after the small group-isolation experiment at Lexington High Security Unit (HSU) was shut down in response to a lawsuit by prisoners housed there and a national and international campaign. The political and security mission of Shawnee is the same as that of the HSU: to control, isolate, and neutralize women who, for varying reasons, pose either a political, escape, or disruption threat. Neutralization ensures that the women imprisoned here will never leave prison with the full capacity to function. Central to the mission is the understanding that Washington can decide at any point to transfer any female political prisoner or prisoner of war here. The recent transfer of Laura Whitehorn is a case in point.

The unit serves as a public admonishment to those who would challenge the supremacy of the United States—deterrence and isolation are central to its mission. It also serves to maintain control over all women in BOP prisons: 12 women who were targeted as leadership of the recent demonstration against police violence by women at Lexington were transferred here in less than 24 hours.

Once a control unit is set up, it fulfills many needs. The BOP operates Shawnee with some flexibility. Protected witnesses, disciplinary cases, high profile individuals, members of various Colombian cartels, and women with successful escape histories are imprisoned here. What distinguishes them from the political prisoners is their ability to transfer out of Shawnee. Over the past year, there has been a massive movement out of the unit. But political prisoners, despite repeated requests to be transferred, have been excluded from this.

Psychological Control

To wash away the brutal image of the HSU, the BOP has created the deception that life at Shawnee is normal, not designed or manipulated. The physical plant is designed to deflect any concern from the outside about human rights abuses — it looks comfortable and attractive. This appearance is a lie.

The women of Shawnee live in a psychologically assaultive environment that aims at destabilizing women's personal and social identities. This is true of the prison system as a whole; here it has been elevated to a primary weapon, implemented through a physical layout and day-to-day regimen that produce inwardness and self-containment. The unit is a small triangle with a small yard. Within this severely limited space, women are under constant scrutiny and observation. In the unit, cameras and listening devices (the latter are installed in every cell) ensure constant surveillance and control of even the most intimate conversation. Lockdown is not necessary because there is nowhere to go, and individuals can be observed and controlled better while having the illusion of some mobility.

The fences around the yard — the only place where one could have any sense that an outside world existed — were recently covered with green cloth, further hammering into the women the sense of being completely apart and separate. It is one thing to be imprisoned in this tiny isolation unit for a year or two, another to be told one will be here for three more decades — that this small unit will be one's world for the rest of one's life.

Compared to the other federal prisons for women, Shawnee is like being in a suffocating cocoon. What replaces visual stimulation and communication is TV. As in the Marion control unit, there is a TV in every cell — the perfect answer to any complaints about isolation or boredom. TV provides the major link to the world — a link that conveniently produces passivity and inculcates "family values."

The intense physical limitations are compounded by a total lack of educational, training, or recreational programs. At a time when such programs are being

expanded at other women's prisons, here, at the end of the line, women are not worthy of even the pretense of rehabilitation. The geographical location of Shawnee makes contact with family and community an almost impossible task. Gradually, women here begin to lose their ability to relate to the outside world. As time moves on, frustration sets in, accompanied by alienation and despair. The result is the creation of dysfunctional individuals who are completely self-involved, unable to participate in organized social activities, and unprepared for eventual reintegration into life on the outside: women who resist less, demand less, and see each other as fierce competitors for the few privileges allowed.

Competition and individualism become the defining characteristics of personality distortion here. The staff seeks out the most needy personalities and molds them into informants. Unit life has been rocked by a number of internal investigations begun when individual prisoners "confided" in ambitious staff members. Snitching and cooperation are the pillars of the "justice system." Those who refuse to go along are isolated and targeted by those who do. In the tiny world of the unit, this can have a massive effect on one's daily life.

A system of hierarchical privileges governs the unit and destroys any potential unity. Small comforts, such as pieces of clothing, have become the mechanism through which cooperation and collaboration are obtained. The latest wrinkle is the institution of "privileged housing" — the arbitrary designation of a limited number of cells on the upper tier as a reward for acceptable behavior. This is classic behavior modification. The unit is in a constant state of uproar over the daily moves that enforce the fall from privileged status.

White Supremacy and Racism

There are close to 90 women imprisoned at Shawnee: one-third Black women from various parts of the world, one-third Latin women, one-third white women, and a very small number of Native-American women. The numerical balance belies the hegemony of white supremacist ideology. As outside the walls, a permanent conflict exists between Black people and those in power. Prisoners experience and are affected by the sharpening of conflict on the outside and the increasing national oppression experienced by Black people in particular. Events in California have given focus to the discontent and heightened the contradictions. Since May 1992, an unprecedented number of Black women have been put in the hole—more than the total for the past two years. Currently, five women from the unit are in the hole; all are Black. And while the administration says that they do not deal with gangs, "Boyz 'N the Hood" and "Jungle Fever" were banned from the prison after the Aryan Brotherhood protested.

A strict segregationist policy determines who gets the jobs. After four years, no Black women have ever worked for education or recreation, except for janitorial jobs. It has taken as long to place a Black woman in commissary and to promote one woman to be a trainer in the UNICOR* factory. All Black staff have left the unit, eliminating the small cushion they provided. This is significant, as staff in the federal system determine everything from access to family to release conditions.

Racism governs how religion can be practiced. Islam, Judaism, and Native-American religions are either totally ignored or marginalized. One cannot help but notice this, since there is a daily diet of fundamentalist Protestant and Catholic services, seminars and retreats.

Superexploitation of Women's Labor

Like B block at Marion, there is no productive labor at Shawnee besides UNICOR. Unit life is organized to facilitate the functioning of the Automated Data Processing (ADP) factory. Nearly 40 women work here, 12 hours a day and 5 more hours on Saturday. The forced rhythm of this work has made the ADP factory the most profitable UNICOR operation in the BOP for its size. The complete lack of any other jobs, the need for funds, the lack of family support, the enormous expense of living in Shawnee, all push women into UNICOR, into intense competition and into an acceptance of their exploitation. Unlike gen-

eral population prisons, Shawnee prisoners are not even permitted to work in jobs maintaining the physical plant. Removing productive labor is an element in destroying human identity and self-worth.

Increasing Violence, Misogyny and Homophobia

The recent physical attacks by male guards at Lexington, and a similar incident here at Shawnee, illustrate the marked tendency towards using greater force to control women prisoners. While lower security women are being sent to minimum-security facilities, those left in high-security prisons will be more and more vulnerable to physical attack—justified by being characterized by the BOP as "dangerous."

Women in prison are at the very bottom. The misogyny and contempt for women in the society as a whole are compounded by the way the prison system is organized to exploit and utilize women's oppression. The BOP characterizes some women as "dangerous" and "terrorist" (having gone beyond the bounds of acceptable female behavior in the United States), making them the target of particularized repression, scorn, and hatred. To be classified maximum-security is to be seen as less than human, by definition not eligible for "rehabilitation."

All women's prisons operate based on the all-pervasive threat of sexual assault, and the dehumanizing invasion of privacy. Throughout the state and federal prison system in the United States, invasive "pat searches" of women by male guards ensure that a woman prisoner is daily reminded of her powerlessness: she cannot even defend her own body.

In the control unit, there is absolutely no privacy: windows in cell doors (which cannot be covered), patrolling of the unit by male guards, and the presence of the bathrooms in the cells guarantee this. The voyeuristic nature of the constant surveillance is a matter of record: in the past year alone, there have been three major internal investigations of sexual harassment and misconduct by male officers—including rape.

Programs that exist in other women's prisons, addressing the particular needs of women, are deemed frivolous at Shawnee. Most women here are mothers, but no support at all is given to efforts to main-

---

*[Ed note: The federal prison industry.]

tain the vital relationship between mother and child. Similarly, if Shawnee were not a control unit, then education, recreation, religious, and cultural programs should be on a par with those at Lewisburg, Leavenworth, and Lompoc (three men's high-security prisons). But not a single program available in those prisons is available here.

The median age of the women here is 37—a situation distinct from any other women's prison. Nearly everyone is doing more than 15 years; more than 10 women are serving life sentences without parole. Menopause is the main medical problem in the unit. Menopause is an emotional as well as a physiological process. Ignoring this is a pillar of misogynist Western medicine. In the repressive reality of Shawnee, refusal to recognize and treat the symptoms of menopause becomes a cruel means of punishment and an attack on the integrity of one's personality.

Security determines all medical care. Two women who have suffered strokes here were both denied access to necessary treatment in a hospital, a life-threatening decision, made solely for "security reasons."

Intense isolation and lack of activities mean that the loving relationships that provide intimacy and comfort to women in all prisons are of heightened importance here. Until recently, a seemingly tolerant attitude towards Lesbian relationships was actually a form of control. For Lesbian relationships to function without disciplinary intervention by the police, the women had to negotiate with, and in some instances work for, the staff. This tolerance was viewed as necessary because the relationships served as a safety valve for the tensions and anger in the population. As a result of the system of police-sanctioned tolerance, people tended to elevate the individual relationships above any collective alliances that might endanger the administration's rule over the unit.

This situation served to increase the already intense homophobia in the population. A new administration has now ended the tolerance, and Lesbian women are now suffering greater harassment and discrimination. A witch hunt is underway to identify Lesbians and couples engaging in homosexual behavior.

Misogyny and homophobia, together with racism, define conditions here. When coupled with the repressive practices of a control unit, psychological disablement can result—fulfilling the Shawnee mission.

Conclusion

Partly as a result of the astronomic rise in the number of women in prison and the resulting public interest in women's prisons, and partly as a result of the struggle against the Lexington HSU, the BOP has to be very careful not to appear to be brutal in its treatment of women prisoners. The investigations of the HSU by Amnesty International, the Methodist Church, the American Civil Liberties Union and others struck a nerve in Washington. The experiment carried out within the walls of the HSU failed because of the personal and political resistance of those inside and outside the walls. But this defeat did not deter the BOP-stated goals. It just drove them to hide those goals cosmetically behind a veneer of new paint and the momentary elimination of the most notorious abuses. The BOP always denies the truth of its workings. It denies the existence of control units and this unit in particular, not even listing it in the BOP Register of Prisons. Nevertheless, Shawnee is the present women's version of the Marionization of the prison system. The next one is supposed to be opened in North Carolina in 1994. [At the time of publication, this prison has not opened.] The movement should not fall into the trap and ignore the particular control strategy aimed at women. Uncovering and exposing the reality that Shawnee Unit is a control unit will contribute to the movement against all control units.

Anti-imperialist Political Prisoners
Marianna, Florida
Fall 1992

◆◆◆

SEVENTY-ONE

U.S. Concentration Camps and Exclusion Policies
Impact on Japanese American Women
Rita Takahashi

During World War II, most women of Japanese ancestry residing in the United States received the same sentence from their government. Under Executive Order 9066, signed by President Franklin Delano Roosevelt on 19 February 1942, people of Japanese ancestry living on the West Coast were excluded from their communities and incarcerated in concentration camps. The government justified its actions on grounds of "military necessity," although more than two-thirds of the incarcerated people were U.S.-born citizens. The camps were initially established and temporarily operated by the U.S. Army, under the name of the Wartime Civil Control Administration (WCCA). Later, jurisdiction was transferred to a newly-created civilian federal agency, the War Relocation Authority (WRA).

U.S. Incarceration Policy for People of Japanese Ancestry

A documented 120,313 persons of Japanese ancestry fell under the jurisdiction of the WRA. Of this number, 112,603 people were forced to leave their homes and enter U.S. concentration camps in seven states — Arizona, Arkansas, California, Colorado, Idaho, Utah, and Wyoming. A third of those incarcerated were classified as resident "aliens," despite the fact that they lived in the United States for many years prior to World War II. Less than one-third of one percent of all evacuated persons of Japanese ancestry (native and foreign-born) had been living in the U.S. for less than ten years.

"Aliens" of Japanese ancestry were "non-citizens" because of discriminatory laws that made them ineligible for naturalized citizenship. At the time of incarceration, 30,619 (80.2%) of the first generation "aliens" (known as *Isseis*) had resided in the United States for 23 or more years. Almost all *Isseis* had been residents for more than fifteen years, since the 1924 Immigration Act excluded Japan from further immigration to the United States. Only 345 alien Japanese had resided in the U.S. for less than ten years.

Banished individuals had the choice of moving "voluntarily" to inland states (they had about a three-week period to do so), and approximately 9,000 people did this, to avoid being sent to concentration camps. Approximately 4,000 of these "voluntary resettlers" moved to the eastern half of California. This group was subsequently forced to move again when the Government announced that the entire state of California, not just the western half, was off limits to people of Japanese ancestry. Some 4,889 persons "voluntarily" moved to states outside of California (1,963 to Colorado; 1,519 to Utah, 305 to Idaho; 208 to eastern Washington; 115 to eastern Oregon; and the remainder scattered throughout the United States).

This incarceration policy was consistent with previous discriminatory local, state, and federal policies affecting Asian Americans in the United States. Japanese Americans were targeted, in part because of the economic competition they posed in various states, particularly on the West Coast (California, Oregon, and Washington). Many government officials saw World War II as the perfect opportunity to get rid of Japanese Americans from their states, once and for all. For the U.S. government, under President Roosevelt, the war was a good opportunity to institute its assimilation policy and "Americanization" plan: to disperse persons of Japanese ancestry throughout the U.S., in a deliberate plan to break up the "Little Tokyos" and "Japantowns."

The U.S. Constitution calls for equal protection under the law and prohibits deprivation of life, liberty, or property without "due process of law." These "protective" guarantees were suspended in this case, and the Government was able to implement this massive program with few questions asked. Congress sanctioned the plan and the U.S. Supreme Court failed to challenge its constitutionality. Few dared to oppose such a plan, presented as an urgent necessity to secure a nation under what was rhetorically stated as a dire military threat.

Intelligence Reports Dispute "Military Necessity"

Although military necessity and national security were the stated reason and goal for mass incarceration, decision-making elites knew that there was no threat to U.S. security from Japanese Americans. Top officials had access to years of intelligence reports from a variety of sources, including the Department of State, Department of Justice (through the Federal Bureau of Investigation), Navy Intelligence, and Army Intelligence. In October, 1941, Jim Marshall reported:

For five years or more there has been a constant check on both Issei [first generation immigrants from Japan] and Nisei [second generation, U.S.-born persons of Japanese ancestry] — the consensus among intelligent people is that an overwhelming majority is loyal. The few who are suspect are carefully watched. In event of war, they would be behind bars at once. In case of war, there would be some demand in California for concentration camps into which Japanese and Japanese-Americans would be herded for the duration. Army, Navy or FBI never have suggested officially that such a step would be necessary. . . . Their opinion, based on intensive and continuous investigation, is that the situation is not dangerous and that, whatever happens, there is not likely to be any trouble — with this opinion west coast newspapermen, in touch with the problem for years, agree most unanimously.[1]

In an intelligence report submitted in November 1941 (only three months before President Roosevelt signed Executive Order 9066), Curtis Munson, a Special Representative to the State Department, said that:

As interview after interview piles up, those bringing in results began to call it the same old tune. . . . There is no Japanese "problem" on the Coast. There will be no armed uprising of Japanese. . . .[2]

Just two days before President Roosevelt signed Executive Order 9066, the Head of the Justice Department, Francis Biddle, encouraged Roosevelt to say something in defense of persons of Japanese ancestry, and wrote, "My last advice from the War Department is that there is no evidence of planned sabotage."[3]

Despite the evidence presented to President Roosevelt — all confirming that there was no threat that warranted *en masse* incarceration — he proceeded with the incarceration policy. He also maintained a consistent pattern of not "setting the record straight" based on intelligence facts.

Experiences of Japanese American Women

All Japanese American women felt the impact of World War II, and the exclusion policy caused major disruptions and upheavals in their lives. It affected their professional careers, impinged on the ways in which they viewed the world, and changed the course and direction of their lives.

Although the exclusion orders affected all women of Japanese ancestry, their specific experiences varied broadly due to many factors, including residence at the time of the exclusion order, age at the time of incarceration (adult or child), the camp that one went into, the job that one was able to get (inside and outside of camp), the college one was admitted to, the degree of co-operation one exhibited toward the concentration camp administrators, and one's status and socio-economic class.

From 1991 to 1997 this author conducted over 300 interviews with Japanese Americans, all of whom were affected by the U.S. Government's policy to banish, exclude, and incarcerate this population, *en masse,* because of their Japanese heritage. This author discovered that, although the same policies were directed at the entire group, the personal experiences were as diverse as the individuals themselves.

The following discussion represents a sampling of five Japanese American women's experiences during World War II derived from interviews conducted by this writer.[4]

Meriko Hoshiyama Mori

A Teenager Left to Fend for Herself After FBI Picked Up Both Parents

Meriko Hoshiyama Mori, born in Hollywood, California, is the only child of Suematsu Hoshiyama (of Niigata-ken, Japan) and Fuki Noguchi Hoshiyama (of Tochig-ken, Japan). Her parents owned a nursery/

gardening business in West Los Angeles until World War II. Her mother, who taught at a Japanese language school before the war, was picked up and detained by the Federal Bureau of Investigation (FBI) on 22 February 1942. Fuki Noguchi Hoshiyama was among the few women who were picked up by the FBI (she was later released and sent to Santa Anita Assembly Center, a converted race track). She had the presence of mind to collect the personal thoughts of detainees — other Japanese women who were also picked up by the FBI. These quotations, collected at the time of internment, are hand-written in Japanese.

A few weeks later, in March 1942, Meriko Mori's father, who was the Japanese Language School treasurer, was also picked up by the FBI. Consequently, Meriko Mori was left, by herself, to take care of all the family and business matters. She was only nineteen years of age when both parents were picked up.

As a teenager desperate for help, Meriko Mori went to the social welfare office to get aid. According to Mori, they told her that they could do nothing for her because there were no rules or regulations for cases like hers. Therefore, Mori got no assistance from them. Reflecting back on this experience in a letter dated 10 February 1997, Mori wrote:

> When I was left alone, it was a shock, but perhaps not as great as it might have been because by the time my father was picked up, the FBI had come several times, and did not find him at home, because he was at work. I recall the FBI sitting in the car waiting for him to come home . . . although I had said I would be all alone, I recall following them [FBI] to Mr. Hayashida's home a block away where he was picked up. Even now as I write this, tears come to my eyes. It is very difficult to recall unpleasant memories.
>
> My Caucasian neighbors expressed concern and wrote to me in camp. My Japanese neighbors were so concerned [about] their own families and situation of packing, moving, etc. they expressed concern but did not have the time to be involved in my predicament. If my Aunt Maki and Uncle Iwamatsu Hoshiyama did not offer to include me in their family (they had 3 girls and 2 boys), I don't know what I could have done when the welfare department didn't know what to do. To say the least, I was

very fortunate and am forever grateful to Maki and Iwamatsu Hoshiyama.

When the U.S. entered World War II, Meriko Mori was a sophomore at the University of California at Los Angeles. She was surprised that she was treated like an enemy alien, and angered by her exclusion. In the words of her letter (1997):

> I was angry at the U.S. Government for its treatment of a U.S. citizen, and felt forsaken by my country and lost faith in the U.S. . . . we had lost our freedoms on which the country was founded.

Her studies were disrupted when she had to leave for Manzanar Camp, where she was watched and controlled by the U.S. Army's armed guards. In 1997, she thought about her camp experience, and said, "My memories of Manzanar are [that it was a] very hot or cold desert. I recall many sand storms and walking against the wind backwards." This camp, originally established under the U.S. Army's WCCA, later became a WRA camp. While at Manzanar, Mori earned the top salary of $19 a month for her work as a school teacher. Fifty-five years later, in her 1997 letter, Mori addressed the impact of her experiences:

> These experiences have taught me to be self-reliant, independent, resourceful, and aware of how injustices can be perpetrated on innocent victims who are weak and have no voice. We need to be constantly vigilant.

Kiyo Sato-Viacrucis

A Student Who Left Camp for a Midwest School and Who Returned to Stolen Property

Kiyo Sato-Viacrucis was born in Sacramento, California, the eldest of nine children born to Shinji "John" Sato (from Chiba-ken, Japan) and Tomomi "Mary" Watanabe Sato (from Aizuwakamatsu, Fukushima-ken). When World War II broke out, the Sato family was farming in the Sacramento area. Having graduated from Sacramento High School in Spring 1941, Kiyo Sato-Viacrucis was attending Sacramento Junior City College at the time of the incarceration orders.

In May 1942, the Sato family was ordered to go to Pinedale Assembly Center, a WCCA facility set up and run by the U.S. Army. Ironically, while her family was sent to a concentration camp, under armed Army guard, her brother was serving in the U.S. Army. He had volunteered after Pearl Harbor was bombed by Japan, and ended up serving for the duration of the war. When Kiyo Sato-Viacrucis volunteered her services to the military, and when she attempted to gain admission into institutions of higher education, she was rejected. Later she wrote to the institutions, saying: "My brother and others are fighting to uphold democratic principles. I cannot understand that an institution of your standing would have such a policy." She was eventually accepted by Western Reserve University in 1945.

After four and one half months at Pinedale, she and her family were shipped, via train and open army truck, to Poston (Arizona) Camp, which was operated by the newly-established civil federal agency, the WRA. Upon her family's arrival in July 1942, the temperature was 127 degrees Fahrenheit. Viewing all the sage brush and experiencing the heat, Kiyo Sato-Viacrucis literally passed out.

Sato-Viacrucis did what she could to leave Poston quickly. After three and one half months, she managed to depart for Hillsdale College in Michigan. Since the college was located in an inland state, she was released only if she would agree to attend this private Baptist college.

After the West Coast was opened to Japanese Americans, Kiyo Sato-Viacrucis was one of the early returnees to Sacramento in 1945. She found that her family's home had been occupied by unknown and unauthorized persons, and that all their stored goods had been stolen. Further, she saw that the Mayhew Japanese Baptist Church (in Sacramento), which had stored the incarcerated Japanese American's belongings, had been burned to the ground the night before her return.

The incarceration experience had continuous and long-term impact on excludees. Reflecting on the implications for her and other women, Sato-Viacrucis said, "Partly because of our background, we *nisei* women retreated from a hostile world into our shells like turtles. Even after fifty years, we are afraid to come out and tell what happened." Reminiscing in 1997, fifty-five years after the exclusionary policies and programs, she said:

Nisei [U.S.-born and second generation Japanese American] men were able to go to war and be recognized for their heroic efforts, but we *nisei* women were "war casualties" on two fronts. Not only were we not of the right color for the Navy or Air Force, but we were not acceptable by many institutions of higher learning "due to policy." It was certainly devastating to be rejected by the Navy because of my color, and then by Yale, Johns Hopkins, Western Reserve University schools of nursing, again because of their "policy." It is hard to believe that even our country's most prestigious institutions of higher learning succumbed to social pressure. That is scary. It happened so easily; will it happen again?

Yoshiye Togasaki

A Medical Doctor Who Took Her Practice to the Concentration Camps

Yoshiye Togasaki was born in an upstairs room of the Geary Theater, located in San Francisco. She was the fifth of six children born to Kikumatsu Togasaki (from Ibaraki-ken, Japan) and Shige Kushida Togasaki (from Tokyo). In 1892, her mother had been sent to the United States as an activist in the Women's Christian Temperance Union. This Japanese immigrant woman was a most unique person who did not shy away from publicly expressing her opinions and speaking her mind. She had stood out on the streets of San Francisco, preaching Christian doctrine.

When World War II broke out, Yoshiye Togasaki was already established in her profession as a medical doctor. In those days, women doctors — especially women of color — were a small minority. After her December 1921 graduation from Lowell High School in San Francisco, Togasaki attended the University of California, Berkeley, where she received a bachelor's degree in public health in 1929. With her medical doctor's degree from Johns Hopkins University in June 1935, she took an internship at the Los Angeles General Hospital.

In 1938, Togasaki became chief resident for communicable diseases at the L.A. General Hospital. She remained in this position until just six months before the U.S. entered World War II. At the time of the Pearl Harbor bombing, Togasaki was an assistant to the City of Los Angeles's epidemiologist. Because she knew she would be terminated when the war broke out, she resigned.

Togasaki spent time trying to correct public perceptions about Japanese Americans. Because the President of the Council on Churches harangued persons of Japanese ancestry, Togasaki went directly to him to try to change his belief that Japanese Americans were "untrustworthy." According to Togasaki, his mind was rigidly set.

After the incarceration orders were announced, and when it became clear that Manzanar, California, would be one of the WCCA Assembly Centers, Togasaki volunteered to help set it up. She arrived at the camp on 21 March 1942, and remained there until October 1942. Open trenches and hygienic problems were prevalent throughout the camp. According to Togasaki, she worked sixteen hours a day, dealing with public health and medical matters. For her services, she earned a salary of $16 per month. She managed to get scarce medical supplies, such as vaccines, from friends or associates outside the camp.

Due to overwork, Togasaki became ill, so she went to Tule Lake Camp (also in California) to join her two sisters. Because there were few resources to diagnose and care for her illness, she went to San Francisco's Children's Hospital for diagnosis. This was a rare event, since Japanese Americans were supposed to be excluded from the area. After five or six days at Children's Hospital, Togasaki stayed at the home of a doctor friend in San Francisco. In Togasaki's words, "No one complained that a Japanese American was there."

Togasaki worked as a pediatric doctor at Tule Lake, where she worked with Dr. Pedicord, a retired doctor from the Kentucky mountains who had failed to keep abreast of the latest developments in medicine. He stirred up a lot of antagonism around Tule Lake because of his attitude toward Japanese Americans, whom he viewed as inferior, foreign, and un-American. Considered whistle blowers and antagonists, Togasaki and her two sisters, Kazue (an obstetrician) and Chiye were transferred to Manzanar in April 1943. Yoshiye Togasaki remained at Manzanar a few months before she left, in July 1943, for a pediatric position at New York's Bellevue Hospital.

Masako Takahashi Hamada

An Excludee Who "Voluntarily" Moved Inland to Idaho

Masako Takahashi Hamada was born in Seattle, Washington, the sixth of seven children born to Kumato Takahashi and Toshi Kato Takahashi, both of Niigata-ken, Japan. After graduating from Garfield High School, she was studying in Seattle when World War II broke out.

During a three week period in March 1942, Japanese Americans were given the option to "voluntarily" leave their homes in the military exclusion zones (the entire West Coast of the U.S. mainland) and to resettle in an inland state outside the military zones, or be sent to a concentration camp. Masako Takahashi, her mother, and five siblings decided to move and join their oldest brother and his wife in Idaho, where his wife's family [Tamura] resided. Leaving most of their valuable possessions behind, they moved to avoid going into concentration camps. They were among the 305 "voluntary movers" who entered Idaho from the restricted military zones. Another older brother, who was living in Washington at the time of the exclusion, did not move because he was originally unaware of the orders. Consequently, he was incarcerated in a concentration camp.

In the Southern Idaho area where she settled, travel was restricted in certain areas, and "NO JAPS ALLOWED" signs were posted in various businesses, alerting the public that "Japs" would not be served. Of course, it did not matter whether one was a citizen or not; service was denied, regardless. This discriminatory behavior was matched by the Idaho Governor's attitude toward Japanese Americans. Governor Chase Clark openly expressed his aversion to any Japanese American migration into the State of Idaho.

Masako Takahashi and her family faced very tough times in the new area. They struggled to make enough money to live, as they encountered new work environments and life situations. They worked for the E. H. Dewey family, who are related to Colonel W. H. Dewey of Silver City, Idaho. Although her goal, at that time, was to be a dress designer, she spent her days working in the fields, hoeing, weeding, and toiling in the hot sun for minimal rewards.

She and her sister (Yuki) went to Chicago to further their education. After the war, she married an Idaho-born Japanese American veteran of World War II, who served with the 442nd Regimental Combat Team, whose motto was, "Go For Broke." She remained in Idaho, where she served as a nurse for twenty-five years and where she volunteers her services in Mountain Home, Idaho.

Reflecting upon her experiences in a 3 February 1997 letter, Hamada said, "I hope that such a sad [and] shocking experience will never be repeated again in history . . . let us hope that each and every one of us [will] live in peace and harmony."

Tsuru Fukui Takenaka

A Businesswoman Outside the Military Zone Who Faced Government Restrictions

Tsuru Fukui Takenaka was born on 26 August 1900, in Wakayama-ken, Japan. In 1920, after marrying Sennosuke Takenaka in Japan, she came to the United States with her husband who had been working in the U.S. prior to marriage. Upon her arrival in San Francisco, she was detained and quarantined a week by the U.S. immigration authorities at Angel Island. In her words, her immigration detention was "just like jail."

In 1930, she and her husband went to Lovelock, Nevada, and took over the Up-to-Date Laundry from the Nakamuras. They owned and worked in this hand laundry throughout World War II, and they maintained the business for years thereafter. In fact, Tsuru Takenaka continued to work in the laundry until 1990, when she was 90 years of age. During the years at the laundry, she strenuously worked long hours.

The Takenakas did not have to leave their home and go into concentration camps because they were situated in a non-military exclusion zone. Therefore, the family continued to run the laundry business throughout the war. Although some established customers did not return after the start of World War II, the Takenakas remained busy enough to keep their business going. But the military restrictions, imposed during World War II, affected the Takenakas' free movement. They were restricted to a fifty mile radius, and could not go to the closest large town, Reno. Further, according to Tsuru Takenaka, the Reno Mayor was known to harbor anti-Japanese sentiments.

Until after World War II, the Takenaka family was the only Japanese American family in Lovelock, and they did experience some discriminatory treatment. Takenaka's daughter, for example, was not allowed to board a train, and her husband, Sennosuke, was subjected to harassment and "bad" talk when he went to the Persian Hotel and Restaurant in downtown Lovelock.

Final Comments

The World War II experiences of Japanese American women are as varied as the number of people involved. In this paper, only five examples are presented, to illustrate the variety in experience. While some women were already established in their profession (e.g. Togasaki), others were just beginning their careers (e.g. Sato-Viacrucis). Some women owned their own businesses in the non-exclusion areas (e.g. Takenaka), while others were employees. All were affected by their residential location. Some living in the military exclusion zones were subjected to FBI raids (e.g. Mori), and most were forced, *en masse*, to go into concentration camps (Mori, Sato-Viacrucis, and Togasaki). With mandatory removal imminent, some chose to move from military exclusion zones prior to being incarcerated in concentration camps (Takahashi Hamada).

Nearly 40 years after this incarceration policy was instituted, the U.S. Commission on Wartime Relocation and Internment of Civilians (CWRIC) was established, in 1980, to "review the facts and circumstances surrounding Executive Order Number 9066 . . . and the impact of such Executive Order on American citizens and permanent resident aliens." The Commission concluded that these policy decisions were shaped by "race prejudice, war hysteria and a failure of political leadership." In summary, "a grave personal injustice was done." Furthermore,

> The excluded people suffered enormous damages and losses, both material and intangible. To the disastrous loss of farms, businesses and homes must be added the disruption for many years of careers and professional lives, as well as the long-term loss of income and opportunity. . . .

Following these findings, there were years of debate in the U.S. House of Representatives and in the U.S. Senate concerning compensation to those who had suffered this injustice. After many Congressional sessions, compromises, and legislative drafts, the U.S. House of Representatives passed the Civil Liberties Act on 17 September 1987, by a vote of 243 to 141. The U.S. Senate passed a similar bill on 20 April 1988, also after lengthy discussion, by a vote of 69 to 27. To bring the two congressional versions together, a conference bill was worked out between the U.S. House and U.S. Senate leaders. This conference bill passed in the Senate on 17 July 1988 and in the House on 4 August 1988. President Ronald Reagan signed the Civil Liberties Act of 1988 into law on 10 August 1988.

Because the new law was an authorization bill, there was no provision for actual appropriations of $20,000 payments to each eligible individual. In November 1989, President George Bush signed an authorization bill into law, entitling the U.S. Government to pay up to $500 million each fiscal year, up to a total of $1.25 billion. With this entitlement in place, the Government was able to begin payments in October 1990.

The redress policy included provisions for a U.S. Government apology for discriminatory wrongs it committed and for individual monetary compensation. The following letter, signed by President George Bush, accompanied each individual redress check:

A monetary sum and words alone cannot restore lost years or erase painful memories;

neither can they fully convey our Nation's resolve to rectify injustice and to uphold the rights of individuals. We can never fully right the wrongs of the past. But we can take a clear stand for justice and recognize that serious injustices were done to Japanese Americans during World War II.

In enacting a law calling for restitution and offering a sincere apology, your fellow Americans have, in a very real sense, renewed their traditional commitment to the ideals of freedom, equality, and justice. You and your family have our best wishes for the future.

Notes

1. Carey McWilliams. *Prejudice: Japanese-Americans: Symbol of Racial Intolerance.* Hamden, CT: Shoe String Press (Reprint), 1971, p. 114.

2. Curtis B. Munson. "Japanese on the West Coast," reprinted in *Hearings before the Joint Committee on the Investigation of the Pearl Harbor Attack* (79th Congress, 1st Session, Part 6). Washington, D.C.: Government Printing Office, January, 1946, p. 2686.

3. Bill Hosokawa, *Nisei: The Quiet American.* New York: William Morrow and Company, Inc., 1969, p. 277.

4. Quotes from the five women were taken from interviews conducted by Rita Takahashi or from their letters to her.

SEVENTY-TWO

◆◆◆

Three Chinese Women in Search of Asylum Held in U.S. Prisons

Wendy A. Young

Founded in 1989, the Women's Commission for Refugee Women and Children is a nonprofit membership organization that seeks to improve the lives of refugee women and children through a vigorous and comprehensive program of public education and advocacy. Its goal is to secure for refugee women and children around the world the protection, assistance, education, and health care they deserve. Moreover, the Women's Commission promotes the empowerment of refugee women by ensuring that women themselves are the leaders and decision makers in their quest for personal safety and a secure family life.

In December 1996, the Women's Commission for Refugee Women and Children sponsored a delegation to assess conditions of detention for female asylum seekers in the Kern County Lerdo Detention Center in Bakersfield, California. At that time, the Immigration and Naturalization Service (INS) was holding seven Chinese women in detention there. Members of the delegation included experts in immigration, refugees, and social work.

The delegation interviewed three Chinese women,* who had been incarcerated in a variety of county prisons for three and a half years. Two of the women, Chi and Zheng, entered the United States on board the *Golden Venture,* a ship that received extensive media coverage when it ran aground off Rockaway Beach, New York carrying more than 300 Chinese asylum seekers, 23 of whom were women. As far as the delegation could ascertain, the five other Chinese women held in Kern County had been in detention for a similar length of time.

Most of the women have based their political asylum claims on China's coercive family planning policy. Whether their fear of sterilization or punishment for having, or planning to have, more than one child is grounds for asylum has been the subject of much controversy. Both the Bush and Clinton Administrations, as well as the Justice Department's Board of Immigration Appeals and various federal courts, have issued conflicting directives on the issue. Most recently, Congress included a section in the "Illegal Immigration Reform and Immigration Responsibility Act of 1996" (Immigration Act of 1996), signed into law by President Clinton on September 28, 1996, stating that a person fleeing her homeland to escape involuntary family planning shall be deemed to have been persecuted on account of her political opinion.

Because of the confusion on this issue and the Clinton Administration's fear that releasing the Chinese would invite increased "alien smuggling," the Chinese have been subjected to prolonged detention. Many of the women have been transferred from county prison to county prison, caught up in a system they do not understand and losing hope that the United States will answer their dream of freedom.

The Women's Commission for Refugee Women and Children first addressed the situation of the Chinese women in March 1995 when it sponsored a delegation to New Orleans and Bay St. Louis, Mississippi, where the *Golden Venture* women were first detained. The delegation raised serious concerns about the effect prolonged detention was having on the women's mental health. These concerns were even more evident in 1996; the confusion, fear, depression, and anger the women were experiencing had clearly been exacerbated to a point of crisis as a result of their continued incarceration. It was extremely difficult for the 1996 delegation to solicit much information from the women, because they were so distraught when speaking about their experience.

Delegation Findings

Physical Setting

The Bakersfield Lerdo Detention Center is approximately a five-and-a-half hour drive from San Francisco and two hours from Los Angeles. Bakersfield is an isolated community that lacks a strong immigrant or immigrant advocate presence. The prison is located several miles outside of town, and is surrounded by fences and concertina wire.

Although owned and administered by Kern County, the detention center is only used to house federal detainees held by the INS, Marshals Service, or Bureau of Prisons. Kern County is paid approximately $57 per day for each detainee. The overall capacity of the prison is approximately 300 inmates. In contrast to other county prisons visited by the Women's Commission, the Kern County facility does not clearly delineate between space in which women are housed as opposed to men. Instead, detainees are moved around to meet the facility's space needs on any particular day. This means that women may be housed in close proximity to male detainees, although locked doors separate them.

Of the three federal agencies contracting with the facility, the INS uses it most frequently. According to the prison staff, the INS contract allows the county "to keep the lights on." The detention center is used by both the INS San Francisco District Office and the Los Angeles District Office to detain individuals in immigration proceedings. The Chinese women are being held under the jurisdiction of the San Francisco office.

---

*Throughout this report, the women will be referred to as Chi, Zheng, and Su to protect their privacy.

The facility was constructed in the mid-1970s. It contains a variety of cell units of different sizes and levels of security. The Chinese women have been moved from unit to unit depending on the size of the prison population and the needs of the facility. At the time of the Women's Commission's visit, they were housed together in a 12-person cell, which contains six bunk beds. As far as the delegation could tell, the women are not commingled with criminal detainees, and the prison staff stated that it is their practice to house criminal and civil detainees separately. However, one woman had recently been transferred to another building within the complex, which the delegation did not tour. It remained unclear who else was housed in that facility with her.

The prison design and atmosphere are extremely oppressive. The walls are painted a dull yellow and gray, and the floors are cement. Little or no natural light reaches the cells. The large cells have some windows too high for an inmate to look out, while the smaller cells, including the one in which the women had been held for several months, have no natural light. The ventilation seemed poor, as the air was stagnant and smelled bad. The temperature is erratic, a problem acknowledged by the prison staff. The women also complained that their cell is infested with insects that bite them. All detainees wear prison uniforms, and are shackled when they leave the facility.

In December 1995, when the women participated in a 50-day hunger strike to protest their prolonged detention, they were held in isolation in a row of "disciplinary isolation" cells, each of which is approximately 6' by 15' without natural light and with only televisions locked outside each cell for entertainment.

Most disturbing was an isolation cell used to house inmates experiencing behavioral problems, including suicidal tendencies. Approximately 10' by 10', the padded cell is painted brown and dimly lit by an overhead light. The cell is completely bare, lacking a bed, a chair, and even a toilet. Detainees are forced to urinate and defecate in a grate in the middle of the floor. Prison staff reported that detainees held in the cell are checked every 15 minutes, including by psychiatric staff, but that there is no overall limit on how long they can be held there.

The prison also contains holding and processing cells, several attorney visiting rooms, a visiting area where detainees can speak to family members and friends through a glass partition via a telephone, a clinic, and a classroom.

Translation Assistance

Neither the prison staff nor the INS staff posted onsite include full-time trained interpreters. One INS officer speaks Mandarin; however, it did not appear that he attempts to speak with the Chinese detainees in any regular or systematic way, unless the women request his assistance in writing.

Interpretation is also occasionally provided by telephone through AT&T in situations such as medical emergencies or routine examinations. The prison staff also indicated that they sometimes rely on inmates to translate for each other, although they admitted they do not like to do so.

Education

The only education provided in the prison is English as a Second Language (ESL) classes, which are offered through an adult education program in Bakersfield. However, the women detainees are not even provided this service, because there are so few of them. The prison staff said it is open to providing access to volunteer teachers for the women.

Diet

The women complained that the food they are served is geared toward a Latino diet, which is unfamiliar and unappealing to them. They therefore rely on dried ramen noodles that they purchase through the prison commissary to satisfy their hunger. They crave such staples of the Chinese diet as rice.

Meals are served at odd times. Breakfast is scheduled before dawn at approximately 4:00 A.M. Lunch is at 10 A.M., and dinner is at 3:00 or 4:00 P.M. As a result, one woman reported that they are often very hungry in the evening. The prison staff stated that the odd meal times are necessary because of "security concerns."

Both the women and advocates who have had contact with them reported that the water in the facility is undrinkable and "foul smelling." For a time, the women were able to purchase bottled water through the commissary but that service has been discontinued, leaving them with no alternative but to drink the tap water.

The prison has publicly stated that it has fixed the water problem, which is attributable to a high level of hydrogen sulfate, and advocates reported that there has been some improvement. The women indicated that they notice little difference. When the delegation tested the water, it was flat and sulfuric.

Recreation and Exercise

The prison staff reported that the women are allowed outside for three hours a week, for one-and-a-half hours at a time, weather permitting. Su said that they actually had been allowed out 3–4 times per week, after her attorney complained to the facility about the limited outdoor access. This access, however, was often provided during non-daylight hours, such as 6 A.M. or 11 P.M.

The outdoor recreation area is approximately the size of one-fourth a football field and is completely paved, with no grass or trees. It is also fully enclosed with cement walls, over which it is impossible to see, topped by fencing and a roof. It contains a volleyball net and some balls.

The prison contains a small library and a book cart that makes the rounds every Sunday. However, all the literature is in English.

The women reported that they spend their time reading Chinese newspapers that have been donated to them; talking among themselves; writing letters; watching English language television, which is kept on all day long; and sleeping. They reported that they are very bored.

Visitor Access and Isolation

After frequent attempts over the course of several months to obtain permission to visit the Bakersfield facility, the Women's Commission was finally able to interview the Chinese women and tour the facility. The day before its scheduled visit, however, the INS San Francisco District staff indicated that they had revoked this agreement due to ongoing national litigation dealing with INS detention policy. The District cited an INS General Counsel "e-mail" to support its decision. After intervention by the INS Central Office in Washington, DC, however, the visit was rescheduled.

Once in Bakersfield, the delegation was given a thorough tour of the facility and allowed to interview three women. The prison staff answered all questions addressed to them. The delegation, however, was not allowed to interview the INS staff in the San Francisco District Office.

Access to the facility is generally limited by its remote location. Attorneys representing the women have found it difficult to visit their clients because of the amount of time it takes them to travel from San Francisco to Bakersfield. One attorney has managed to make the trip once a month, but at great cost in terms of time.

According to advocates, two of the women have boyfriends who wish to marry them. However, the prison has refused to allow this to happen. One of the men regularly visits his fiancée. The other has been forbidden to visit, as he was expelled for "disturbing the peace." Some of the women have family in the United States, but they live in New York.

Members of a local organization, Voice for Life, have taken a strong interest in the women's situation, and visit the women almost every week. The group has also organized occasional visits from members of the community concerned about the women. The prison staff indicated that the detainees otherwise receive few visitors.

The women have had only limited access to Chinese language religious services. Initially, advocates reported, the prison chaplain refused to allow Chinese-speaking ministers into the facility. Now, a Chinese Baptist minister is allowed to provide a weekly service, but only with the prison chaplain present. He is not allowed to provide individual counseling. When the Women's Commission requested an interview with the Baptist minister, he responded that the chaplain had forbidden him to speak with the delegation.

Health Care

The Bakersfield facility has a nurse on duty 24 hours a day and a doctor on call. The facility maintains a clinic to handle routine medical problems, and transports detainees to the local county hospital in emergency situations.

Chi was very concerned about her health. Since her detention, she has developed high blood pressure, which she attributed to the stress caused by her incarceration. She is currently on medication for the condition. She also said that she has "something growing in her throat." She is confused about the exact nature of this but has been receiving medication for it for over a year. She also reported that her eyes and feet are swelling. In addition, she appeared jaundiced. She expressed anxiety about her condition, and stated that she feared that she would die in prison without seeing her children again.

Su, who is 24 years old, is taking pain killers for stomach problems. She also reported that she had been three months pregnant when she was first picked up by the U.S. Border Patrol. She had been experiencing abdominal and stomach pains for approximately a month prior to this, and said that she was immediately taken to a hospital in San Diego, where she lost the fetus. It was unclear to the delegation whether she had experienced a spontaneous abortion or if she had been given an abortion without her consent. It appeared to the delegation that she was experiencing medical complications with her pregnancy that needed immediate attention. However, Su herself was obviously very confused about why she required an "abortion." She stated that the translation services she received in the hospital were very poor. She reported that she frequently dreams about her child.

Zheng did not report any medical problems. However, she appeared very gaunt, and had a rash on her face.

All the women were exhibiting signs of stress and anxiety. They were feeling tremendous pressure as a result of their fleeing from China, their arduous trip to the United States, and their subsequent incarceration. They were anxious to see their loved ones. They exhibited symptoms of Post-Traumatic Stress Disorder, including intense fear, helplessness, anxiety, social withdrawal, somatic complaints, feelings of ineffectiveness, shame, feeling permanently damaged, and feeling constantly threatened.

All of the women feared the future. Adding to this was the fact that they had seen several of their compatriots removed from the facility without explanation. The delegation confirmed that one woman was moved to a separate building within the Bakersfield complex. At least one was deported, and another was transferred back to New Orleans where she was released. These transfers, however, were never explained to the women left behind.

Chi sobbed as she told the delegation about her nightmare the night before. She reported that she is having problems sleeping and frequently has bad dreams. She was haunted by the notion that she may never see her two children again, including a teenage son who has gone blind during her time in detention. However, she is also ashamed of her detention and fears what her children might think of her. She said, "I feel as if there is something wrong with me when I wear these prison clothes."

Zheng was visibly outraged by her experience in detention. She had been moved from the cell in which the other Chinese women are held into a solitary cell, because she had an argument with a fellow detainee. She was distraught that the prison had failed to move her personal belongings with her, such as letters from home and her commissary purchases. She reported that she was not even able to bring her attorney's telephone number with her.

Su said that "she thinks too much" and constantly worries about her future. Despite their obvious distress, none of the women reported having received mental health care while in detention.

Treatment by the Prison Guards

Other than with each other, the most regular human contact the women have is with the prison staff. The women reported that some of the guards are "nice," while others are "bad" and "rude." Chi stated, "the guards treat me as less than a person." It was obvious to the delegation that the overall atmosphere in the facility was institutional and punitive in nature.

For example, the women are patted down or strip searched (but not cavity searched), every time they return from the outside exercise area. The staff reported that women guards perform these searches on women detainees, but advocates said that men have occasionally filled this function. Advocates indicated that one woman refuses to go outside, because she is so intimidated by these searches. Reportedly, she was subjected to spousal abuse in China.

In addition, the women have been placed in solitary confinement for infraction of minor "rules" of prison. Chi was in solitary for five days, because she failed to use a pencil sharpener properly. Exacerbating this treatment is the fact that no one has explained the facility rules to the women in Chinese, forcing them to learn by trial and error.

Monitoring of the women's residential area is performed by male guards as well as female guards. The staff noted that they are required to have a female guard on duty, but she is not necessarily stationed in the women's cell area. The staff admitted that male guards occasionally see the women showering or dressing, but blamed that on the women "not caring." Screens are provided to block the view of the showers and toilets.

Su complained that a guard used to deny her sanitary napkins. She was forced to use toilet paper. The guard got upset with her for using too much toilet paper, shoved her, and then placed her in disciplinary isolation for 15 days.

The prison staff indicated that the women must request sanitary napkins on an as-need basis. One male guard said that male guards are uncomfortable with the whole issue, and that they give the women as many napkins as they request, stating, "We are typical guys. We don't like to talk about it. We don't care as long as they don't turn the napkins into art work or use them to plug up the toilets."

Access to Counsel and Asylum Proceedings

Attorneys can visit their clients in Bakersfield at any time. However, as previously mentioned, their access is effectively limited by the remote location of the detention center. This is particularly troublesome due to the complexity of the law forming the basis of the women's asylum claims.

The INS occasionally will transport a detainee to San Francisco to meet with an attorney if the attorney so requests and a van is transporting detainees there for other reasons. Attorneys representing the women, however, reported that this service was discontinued for the women for some time because the INS claimed there were too few women to merit it.

In order to communicate with their attorneys, therefore, the women must rely primarily on telephone calls. However, all outgoing calls must be made collect. Attorneys cannot call into the facility even to convey a message to their client that they should call them.

The delegation was very concerned about one Chinese woman who was moved to San Francisco the day of its visit. Her attorney had not been informed of this transfer.

Not surprisingly, the women are very confused about the status of their cases. Advocates reported that at least one woman has indicated that she will give up and agree to deportation if she is not released by New Year's Day. Others indicated that they will endure detention until their claims are recon-

sidered under the new immigration law, which advocates have informed them might facilitate their release. Advocates stated that one woman was deported to China in October 1996. Although she had initially agreed to her deportation, she tried to reverse her decision after learning of passage of the new law. The INS refused her request and carried out her deportation.

Conclusions and Recommendations

- The prolonged detention of the Chinese women is arbitrary, cruel, and inhumane, and may very well be causing them serious psychological harm. It also violates international standards for the detention of asylum seekers.

- The Chinese women should be immediately released from detention pending the reconsideration of their asylum claims under the Immigration Act of 1996. They should not be held hostage to a legal system that inadequately addresses the basis of their asylum claims nor to concerns about the potential political costs of a further Chinese influx. The new law is clearly intended to facilitate the admission of individuals such as the Chinese women.

- At the very least, the INS should allow refugee organizations that are willing to care for the women to provide them with more suitable housing and the social services necessary to address their needs.

- The INS should discontinue its use of county prisons located in remote areas for the detention of asylum seekers. Ready access to attorneys must be a requirement for any contracted detention space.

- Under no circumstances should women asylum-seekers be penalized on the grounds that there are too few of them and deprived of services made available to male detainees. Education services that are provided to male detainees must be equally provided to the women. Transport to San Francisco for attorney consultations must also be equally available. Anything less constitutes an unacceptable form of discrimination.

- The transfer of detainees from facility to facility should be prevented, unless clearly required to facilitate access to a detainee by her attorney or family. Transfers should not be performed solely for the administrative convenience of the INS.

- The INS must retain ongoing authority over detention space. This includes developing detailed standards for detention that adequately address the special needs of asylum seekers. It also includes frequent and meaningful contact with detainees in its custody.

- The special needs of women asylum seekers must be fully addressed. This includes oversight and monitoring of facility staff to ensure that women are not exposed to any abuse or mistreatment. Only female guards should be assigned to supervise female detainees.

Addendum

Soon after the issuance of this report by the Women's Commission, President Bill Clinton ordered the INS to release the *Golden Venture* Chinese from detention. However, their ordeal is not over, as their claims to asylum still await adjudication. Moreover, the decision to release the *Golden Venture* Chinese was a political one, made in the context of tremendous media coverage and pressure from organizations such as the Women's Commission and concerned members of Congress, rather than a policy change.

Hundreds of women asylum seekers remain in detention, including, ironically, other Chinese who also left their home country to escape its coercive family planning program but who arrived in the United States on other vessels. The need for comprehensive reform of the U.S. detention system continues.

◆◆◆

SEVENTY-THREE

I wake in middle-of-night terror

Anonymous

I wake in middle-of-night terror
next to the warm sleeping body of my lover
yet alone in the conviction that I am in a prison cell
shut away, suddenly, from all that makes my life.
I sense the great weight of the prison
pressing down on the little box of room I lie in
   alone   forgotten.
How often do women awake
in the prison of marriage,
of solitary motherhood
   alone and forgotten
of exhaustion from meaningless work,
of self-despising learned early,
of advancing age
   alone and forgotten.
How many women lie awake at this moment
   struggling as I do against despair,
   knowing the morning will crush us once again
   under the futility of our lives.
And how short a step it is
   — for us — to the more obvious imprisonment
   of bars and concrete
   where our sisters lie
   alone   forgotten

See now, in this middle-of-the-night emptiness
   how little it matters
      whether we wear a convicts ill-made cotton dress
      or a velvet pantsuit —
We are possessions to be bought and sold,
We are children to be curbed and patronized,
We are bodies to be coveted, seized, and rejected
   when our breasts begin to sag,
We are dummies to be laughed at.

   I sense the great weight of the society
   pressing down on the little box of room I lie in
   alone   forgotten
   like my sisters in prison.
If you hear me
   consider
   how the bomb of human dignity
   could be planted outside your cell
   how its explosion could shake
   the foundations of our jail
   and might burst open the door that separates you
   how we might struggle together to be free.

♦♦♦

CHAPTER NINE

Women and the Military

In the United States most people grow up with pride in this country, its wealth, its power, and its superior position in the world. We learn the Pledge of Allegiance, a sense of patriotism, and that our way of life is worth fighting and perhaps dying for. Most families have at least one member who has served in the military. The United States is number one in the world in terms of military technology, military bases, training of foreign forces, and military aid to foreign countries (Sivard 1996). The largest proportion of our federal tax dollars, $627 billion in 1997–98 or 52 percent, supports current and past military operations, including the upkeep of over four hundred bases and installations at home and over two thousand of those abroad, the development and maintenance of weapons systems, pensions for retired military personnel, veterans benefits, and interest on the national debt attributable to military spending (War Resisters League 1997; U.S. Department of Defense 1992). Major companies with household names like Westinghouse, Boeing, and General Electric research and develop weapons systems and military aircraft. War movies are a film industry staple, portraying images of manly heroes. Five out of the six best-selling toys are war toys. G. I. Joe has a new female colleague, a helicopter pilot, dressed in a jumpsuit and helmet and armed with a 9mm Beretta. Even Barbie is in uniform.

The military shapes our notions of patriotism, heroism, honor, duty, and citizenship. President Clinton's avoidance of military service as a young man was heavily criticized by his detractors in both election campaigns, the suggestion being that this was unpatriotic and not fitting for a president of the United States, who is also the commander in chief of the armed forces. Politically, economically, and culturally, the military is a central U.S. institution.

The Need for Women in the Military

Although the vast majority of U.S. military personnel have always been male, the military has needed and continues to need women's support and participation in many capacities (Enloe 1983; Isakson 1988). It needs mothers to believe in the concept of patriotic duty and to encourage their sons, and more recently their daughters, to enlist, or at least to support their desire to do so. It needs women nurses to heal the wounded and the traumatized. It needs wives and girlfriends back home, the prize waiting at the end of war or a period of duty overseas, who live with veterans' trauma or who mourn loved ones killed in action. White, African-American, and Latina women, symbolized by Rosie the Riveter, were needed for the war effort working in shipyards and munitions factories while men were drafted for active service overseas. Currently the military needs women to work in electronics and many other industries producing weapons components, machine parts, tools, uniforms, household supplies, and foodstuffs for military contracts. It needs women working in nightclubs, bars, and massage parlors near foreign bases and ports providing R and R, rest and relaxation, for military personnel, or, as it is sometimes called, I and I, intoxication and intercourse. And the military needs women on active duty, increasingly trained for combat as well as performing more traditional roles in administration, communications, intelligence, or medicine.

Having women in the military to the extent that they are today is a relatively new phenomenon. In 1972, women were only 1.2 percent of military personnel. The following year, after much debate, Congress ended the draft for men, though young men are still required to register for the draft when they turn eighteen. Many left the services as soon as they could, causing a manpower shortfall that has been made up by recruiting women, especially women of color. At the beginning of the fiscal year 1994, 12 percent of the active duty personnel in the U.S. military were women. In 1993, 43 percent of the enlisted women in all services (Army, Navy, Marine Corps, and Air Force) were women of color (34 percent African American, 5 percent Latina, and 4 percent "other"); 20 percent of all women officers were women of color. The Air Force has the highest percentage of women (15 percent), although the Army, being more labor-intensive, has the greatest numbers. Though African-American women make up only 12 percent of the general population, in 1992 they comprised 48 percent of the women in enlisted ranks in the U.S. Army and 20 percent of the women officers.

The Military As Employer

For many of these women the military offers much better opportunities than the wider society: jobs with better pay, health care, pensions, and other benefits, as well as the chance for education, travel, and escape from the crisis-torn inner cities in the United States. It enhances women's self-esteem and confers the status of first-class citizenship attributed to those who serve their country. Military recruiters emphasize security, professionalism, empowerment, adventure, patriotism, and pride. In noting the benefits of army life in the early 1950s, Jean Grossholtz (Reading 76) includes medical services, expanded opportunities, a ready-made community of women, and a sense of self-worth and accomplishment. Margarethe Cammermeyer served as a military nurse for twenty-six years, in the Army, the Army Reserves, and the National Guard; she was the highest-ranking officer to challenge military policy on homosexuality before being discharged in 1992 on the basis of sexual orientation. Her autobiography, excerpted in Reading 77, emphasizes the professionalism, structure, and discipline she experienced in military life and her keen sense of patriotism and duty.

As we argued in Chapter 6, the U.S. labor market has changed markedly over the past three decades or so through automation and the movement of jobs overseas. In addition to a loss of jobs, there are also few sources of funding for working-class women's (and men's) education. Government funding for education and many welfare programs has been increasingly cut back during the 1980s and 1990s, but despite the end of the Cold War, enormous changes in the former Soviet Union, and cuts in U.S. bases and personnel, the U.S. military budget has been maintained at high levels. Women who enter the military are thus going where the money is. Their very presence, however, exposes serious dilemmas and contradictions for the institution, which we explore below. Another contradiction of this situation is the fact that massive government spending on the military diverts funds that could otherwise be invested in civilian job programs and inner-city communities.

Limitations to Women's Equal Participation in the Military

Support for women's equality within the military is based on a belief in women's right to equal access to education, jobs, promotion, and authority in all aspects of society, and to the benefits of first-class citizenship. Women's rights organizations, such as the National Organization for Women, have campaigned for women to have equal opportunity with men in the military, as have women military personnel and key members of Congress like former Representative Pat Schroeder, who was on the Armed Services Committee for many years. After years of pressure women who served in Vietnam were honored with a memorial in Washington, D.C. This advocacy and recognition, together with women's changing position in society, have also affected social attitudes. In the Persian Gulf War, for example, military women were featured in headline news stories around the country. Saying good-bye to their families as they prepared to go overseas, they were portrayed as professional soldiers as well as mothers.

Women's equal participation in the military is limited in several ways, however; these include limits on combat roles, a lack of access to some military academies, the effects of a general culture of racism, sexism and sexual harassment, and the ban on being openly lesbian.

Women in Combat Roles

Although women served in the U.S. military during World War II, the Korean War, and the Vietnam War, it was generally as nurses and administrators. The influx of women into the military in the past twenty-five years and the question of whether to train women for combat have exposed a range of stereotypical attitudes toward women on the part of military commanders, Pentagon planners, and members of Congress, depending on the degree to which they believe that combat is male. War making is increasingly a high-tech, push-button affair, as exemplified in the bombing missions of the Gulf War, but old attitudes die hard. Combat roles are dangerous and demanding. Many argue that women are not physically strong enough, are too emotional, and lack discipline or stamina. They will be bad for men's morale, it is said, and will disrupt fighting units because men will be distracted if a woman buddy is hurt or captured. The country is not ready for women coming home in body bags.

Women in the military tend to have better performance records than men, according to Enloe (1993). Military planners face a dilemma. They need women to make up the shortfall in personnel; at the same time they hold sexist or condescending notions about women. What counts as combat in modern warfare is not as simple as it might seem, however, and definitions of "the front" and "the rear" change with ad-

vances in military technology. Communications and supply, defined as noncombat areas where women work, are both likely targets of attack. In 1993 the rule barring women from dangerous jobs was changed, though some exceptions were preserved. Women can work on combat ships and jet planes but not in submarines or in direct offensive combat on the ground. Restricting women from combat roles has been a way of limiting their career advancement, as senior positions often require combat experience.

Officer Training: Storming the Citadel

In 1975 Congress mandated that the three military academies were to admit women. Researching the experiences of the first women to enter the U.S. Military Academy at West Point, Yoder (1989) noted the severe pressure on these women to do well. They were a highly visible, very small minority, tokens in what had been constructed as an exclusively male institution. They faced tough physical tests designed for men; they were out of the loop in many informal settings and were routinely subjected to sexist notions and behavior by male cadets who did not accept them as peers. As a result, for the first four years at least, the dropout rate for women was significantly higher than it was for men, a fact that could be used by policy makers to justify exclusionary practices. Yoder concluded, however, that these women were not competing on equal terms with men, and she argued for changes in evaluation criteria and the overwhelmingly male culture of the Academy, an increase in the number of women entering the Academy, and greater commitment to women's full participation at an institutional level. More recently, women have entered other military academies like the Citadel and Virginia Military Institute with similarly mixed success. In January 1997, two of the first four women at the Citadel withdrew because of intolerable harassment (Applebome 1997).

Sexism and Misogyny

Added to this chilly climate for women are overt sexual harassment and sexual abuse. An internal report from the Naval Academy, compiled by the Women Midshipmen Study Group and released in October 1990, noted that sexual harassment of female students was widespread. "The lack of acceptance [of female students] has created an environment in which steady low-level sexual harassment passes as nor-mal operating procedure" (*Rocky Mountain News*, 1990, p. 35). Most victims do not complain, the re-port noted, for fear of reprisals. Even when women do report sexual harassment to superior officers, the majority of their complaints have been dismissed or ignored. After hearing testimony from servicewomen in 1992, following public disclosures of sexual ha-rassment, indecent assault, and indecent exposure at the Tailhook naval aviators' conference at the Las Vegas Hilton the previous year, a Senate Committee estimated that as many as 60,000 women had been sexually assaulted or raped while serving in the U.S. armed forces. Senator Dennis DeConcini com-mented, "American women serving in the Gulf were in greater danger of being sexually assaulted by our own troops than by the enemy" (Walker 1992, p. 6). In the fall of 1996 this issue surfaced publicly again, when women at the Aberdeen Proving Grounds Ordnance Center in Maryland complained of being sexually harassed and raped by drill sergeants during training. As part of its investigations into these allegations, the Army set up a toll-free hotline, which took four thousand calls in the first week relating to harassment at many military facilities (McKenna 1996/1997). *Time* magazine reporter Eliz-abeth Gleick described this issue as an abuse of power by superiors, threatening "to undermine the thing that many in the military hold sacred: the chain of command" (1996, p. 28). Interviewed for the ABC weekly news program *20/20*, Alan Cranston, former U.S. Senator from California, suggested three reasons for the intensity of sexual abuse in the mili-tary: men feeling threatened by women coworkers, the general "macho" military culture, and the fact that many military personnel have easy access to guns (Walters and Downs 1996). As the investiga-tion spread, military commanders did their best to attribute any misconduct to "a few bad apples." Brigadier General Robert Courter, for example, com-mander of the 37th Training Wing at Lackland Air Force Base, was quoted as saying, "There are going to be incidents, but where we have those cases, we take action. . . . I feel certain the American people can be confident that their sons and daughters are going to be safe in the Air Force" (Military sex scan-dal 1996, p. A15). At the same time, many who op-pose women's participation in the military have claimed that such incidents support their view that the military is, indeed, no place for women.

Racism

Although the armed services were officially inte-grated in 1948, decades before desegregation in the southern states, racism, like sexism, is still a common occurrence in the military between individuals and at an institutional level. In 1994, a House Armed Services Committee investigation uncovered serious problems with institutionalized racism throughout the armed forces and warned about skinhead and other extremist activity on four military bases vis-ited by investigators. In December 1995, for exam-ple, two African-American civilians were random victims, shot and killed by three White G. I.s, de-scribed in press reports as right-wing extremists, from the Army's 82nd Airborne Division at Fort Bragg, North Carolina (Citizen Soldier 1996). In De-cember 1996 two African-American airmen at Kelly Air Force Base (Texas) talked to the media about a racist incident in which they were taunted by men wearing pillowcases resembling Ku Klux Klan hoods and said that they were dissatisfied with the Air Force's response to their complaints (2 Black airmen 1996). Undoubtedly, racist attitudes and comments also affect women of color in the military.

Sexual Orientation

A final area of limitation for women—and men—in the military concerns sexual orientation. The Pen-tagon considers homosexuality incompatible with military service, and a series of regulations have pre-cluded lesbians and gay men from serving openly, despite their continuing presence as officers and en-listed personnel. In Reading 76 Jean Grossholtz notes the contradiction implicit in this policy: the military is based on male bonding, yet homosexuality is banned. Thousands of gay men and lesbians have been discharged over the years in what she refers to as "purges." Margarethe Cammermeyer (1994) notes that in June 1992 the General Accounting Office re-ported that fourteen hundred military personnel who had been trained for military service were dis-charged each year between 1980 and 1991, at an es-timated cost of $494 million, not including the cost of investigations (p. 293). During his first presiden-tial election campaign President Clinton promised to lift the ban on gays in the military when he came into office in 1992. Concerted opposition from the Pentagon and many politicians made this politically impossible, however, and some argue that current policy, summed up as "Don't ask, don't tell," is not much different than before. "Homosexual conduct," defined as homosexual activity, trying to marry someone of the same sex, or acknowledging one's homosexuality, is grounds for discharge. A number of lesbians and gay men have challenged this policy in court. Gay rights organizations, like the National Gay and Lesbian Task Force and Gay, Lesbian, and Bisexual Vets of America, continue to raise this issue as an example of lesbians' and gay men's second-class citizenship.

The Impact of the U.S. Military on Women Overseas

The worldwide superiority of the United States—in political, economic, and military terms—is sustained by a wide network of U.S. bases, troops, ships, submarines, and aircraft in Europe, Asia, Latin America, the Caribbean, the Persian Gulf, and the Pacific. This U.S. presence relies on agreements with each particular government. In return the military may pay rent for the land it occupies. Some local people may be employed directly on the bases; many others work in nearby businesses patronized by U.S. military personnel. We consider four ways that U.S. military policies and bases abroad affect women: through militarized prostitution, through their responsibility for mixed-race children fathered by G. I.s, through crimes of violence committed by G. I.s, and through the harmful effects of atomic tests.

Militarized Prostitution

As a way of keeping up the morale of their troops, military commanders have long tolerated, and sometimes actively encouraged, women to live outside military camps to support and sexually service the men. With U.S. bases positioned strategically around the globe, especially since World War II, militarized prostitution has required explicit arrangements between the U.S. government and those of the Philippines, Japan (Okinawa), Thailand, and South Korea, for example, where many women work in bars and massage parlors, "entertaining" G. I.s (Enloe 1990, 1993; Sturdevant and Stoltzfus 1992). As a way of protecting the men's health, women who work in bars must have regular medical exams, on the as-

sumption that they are the source of sexually transmitted diseases. If the bar women fail such tests, they are quarantined until they pass. They usually earn better money than they can make in other ways, though this may be harder as they grow older. By creating a class of women who are available for sexual servicing, the governments attempt to limit the sexual demands of U.S. military personnel to specific women and specific locations. Despite the low opinion many of their people have of bar women, their work is the linchpin of the subeconomy of the "G. I. Towns" adjoining the bases, and many people, including store owners, salespeople, bar owners, restaurateurs, cooks, pimps, procurers, cab drivers, and security men, are in business as a result of their work. Some of the bar women are able to send money to their aging parents or younger siblings, an important part of being a good daughter, especially in countries with few social services or welfare supports. Occupational dangers for the women include psychological violence, rape, and beatings from some of their customers; health risks from contraceptive devices, especially I. U. D.s; abortions; AIDS and other sexually transmitted diseases; drug use; and a general lack of respect associated with this stigmatized work. Despite the incursions of transnational corporations, there are few options for women's economic development in rural areas in South Korea and the Philippines, and there is a need for income-generating projects that pay decent wages. Kathleen Barry (1995) argues that "military prostitution buys off women with higher wages than they can earn in the industrial wage labor sector," and is, in effect, "a dumping ground . . . between the patriarchal family structure and the industrializing labor force" (p. 163).

Mixed-Race Children Fathered by G. I.s

Many bar women and former bar women in Okinawa (Japan), South Korea, the Philippines, and Vietnam have Amerasian children, an important and often-neglected group. Some of these people, born during the Korean War or Vietnam War, are now in their thirties and forties; others are young children born to women recently involved with G. I.s stationed in South Korea or Okinawa. Most of them have been raised in poverty, further stigmatized by their mothers' occupation and their own mixed heritage. According to Okazawa-Rey (1997), many of the mothers of Amerasian children in South Korea had serious relationships with the children's fathers. Yu Bok Nim (1990), who founded a shelter, My Sister's Place, for Korean women involved with G. I.s, notes that some three thousand marriages currently take place each year between Korean women and U.S. military personnel. Most of the men, however, simply leave. They may turn out to be already married in the United States—a fact they had not thought necessary to mention—or they just disappear. Many of the children of these unions have not had much schooling as a result of poverty and intimidation and harassment from their peers. In South Korea, Amerasians whose fathers are African-American may gain some acceptance only by doing well in stereotypically Black spheres like sports and music. Some of the girls become bar women like their mothers. A relatively small number of such children are adopted by U.S. families, but this is expensive and not possible for children whose births have not been registered.

Crimes of Violence Against Women

The behavior of U.S. troops in other countries is governed by agreements between the U.S. government and the host government. Usually U.S. military personnel who commit crimes against civilians are dealt with, if at all, through military channels rather than the local courts. In many cases G. I.s are not held responsible for crimes they commit. Sometimes they are simply moved to another posting. This is a highly contentious issue, especially for those who do not support the U.S. military presence in their countries. In South Korea, for example, the National Campaign for Eradication of Crime by U.S. Troops in Korea was founded in 1993, growing out of a coalition of groups composed of women, students, labor, religious people, and human rights activists that formed to protest the brutal murder of a young woman, Yoon Kum E, the previous year. The campaign collects information about crimes committed against Korean civilians by U.S. military personnel and cites a South Korean Assembly report that estimated 39,542 such crimes between 1967 and 1987, including murders, brutal rapes and sexual abuse; incidents of arson, theft, smuggling, fraud, and traffic offenses; an outflow of P.X. (on-base department store) merchandise, and a black market in U.S. goods (Ahn 1996). This information is not known by many in the United States and is rarely publicized

here. This customary silence, however, was broken in the fall of 1995 when a twelve-year-old Okinawan girl was abducted and raped by three U.S. military personnel. This incident is one of many; its brutality and the victim's age were important factors in generating renewed outrage at the presence of U.S. bases by many Okinawans (Okazawa-Rey and Kirk 1996).

Atomic Testing

In the 1950s and early 1960s the United States military, as well as those of Britain and France, undertook a series of atomic tests in the Pacific, which irradiated whole islands and contaminated soil and water for generations to come. The U.S. military conducted tests in Micronesia, which it administered as a United Nations Strategic Trust Territory, supposedly as a step toward the political independence of the islanders. Many Micronesian women have since given birth to children with severe illnesses or disabilities caused by radiation, including some "jellyfish babies" without skeletons who live only a few hours (de Ishtar 1994; Dibblin 1989). Pacific Island women and men have contracted several kinds of cancer as a result of their exposure to high levels of radioactive fallout. Given the long-lasting effects of atomic material in the food chain and people's reproductive systems, these disabilities and illnesses are likely to last for many generations. Film footage of the U.S. tests, included in newsreels for U.S. audiences, described the islanders as simple people, indeed, as happy savages (O'Rourke 1985). In 1969, some years after the partial Test Ban Treaty (1963), which banned atomic tests in the atmosphere, the United States ended its Trusteeship of Micronesia. Henry Kissinger, then secretary of state, was highly dismissive of the indigenous people in his comment: "There's only 90,000 people out there, who gives a damn?" (Women Working for a Nuclear-Free and Independent Pacific 1987). Many in Pacific Island nations see these atomic— and later nuclear—tests, which France continued until 1996, as imperialist and racist. Various activist organizations are campaigning for a nuclear-free and independent Pacific and see U.S. military bases in Hawai'i and Guam, for example, and the activities of the U.S. Pacific fleet as a serious limitation on their sovereignty and self-determination (Trask 1993). Meanwhile, women take the lead in trying to keep their families and devastated communities together.

Women's Opposition to the Military

Early Peace Organizations in the United States

Activist organizations oppose the presence and impact of U.S. military bases in many countries, including those mentioned above. This opposition is sometimes based on nationalism, sometimes on arguments for greater self-determination, local control of land and resources, with more sustainable economic development. Women often play a key role in these organizations.

In the United States, too, although many women have supported and continue to support the military in various ways, there is a history of women's opposition to militarism and war with roots in Quakerism and the nineteenth-century suffrage and temperance movements. Julia Ward Howe, for example, remembered as the author of the Civil War song "The Battle Hymn of the Republic," was involved in the suffrage movement as a way of organizing women for peace. In 1873 she initiated Mothers' Day for Peace on June 2, a day to honor mothers, who, she felt, best understood the suffering caused by war. Women's peace festivals were organized in several U.S. cities, mainly in the Northeast and Midwest, with women speakers who opposed war and military training in schools. The Philadelphia Peace Society was still organizing in this way as late as 1909 (Alonso 1993). During the 1890s many women's organizations had peace committees that were active in the years before U.S. entry into World War I. In 1914 the Women's Peace Party was formed under the leadership of Carrie Chapman Catt and Jane Addams. Despite difficulties of obtaining passports and war-time travel, over one thousand women from twelve countries, "cutting across national enmities," participated in a Congress of Women in the Hague, Holland, in 1915, calling for an end to the war. The congress sent delegations to meet with heads of state in fourteen countries and influenced press and public opinion. A second congress at the end of the war proposed an ongoing international organization: the Women's International League for Peace and Freedom (WILPF), which is active in forty-two countries today and maintains an international base in Geneva, Switzerland (Foster 1989). Among the participants at the second congress were Mary Church Terrell, a Black labor leader from the United States, and Jeanette Rankin, the first U.S. congresswoman and the only member of congress to vote against U.S. involvement in both world wars. In the 1950s and again in the 1960s, more U.S. women than men opposed the Korean War and Vietnam War. Women Strike for Peace, founded in 1961and still active through the 1980s, was initially concerned with the nuclear arms race, as well as the Vietnam War (Swerdlow 1993). These organizations attracted members who were overwhelmingly White and middle-class, though many women of color have an antimilitarist perspective, as exemplified by Linda Hogan and Sonia Sanchez, in Readings 80 and 83.

Feminist Antimilitarist Perspectives

Women's opposition to militarism draws on a range of theoretical perspectives, which we discuss briefly below. In any particular organization several of these perspectives may provide the basis for activism, but it is useful to look at them separately here to clarify different and sometimes contradictory positions.

Women's Peaceful Nature   Although some women—and men—believe that women are "naturally" more peaceful than men, there is no conclusive evidence for this. Differences in socialization, however, from infancy onward, lead to important differences in attitudes, behavior, and responsibilities in caring for others. In electoral politics since 1980 these differences have been described as creating a "gender gap," under which more women than men oppose high military budgets and environmental destruction and support socially useful government spending (Abzug 1984). Many who oppose the military see the current division of labor in society between men's and women's roles as a fundamental aspect of military systems, whereby men (and now a few women) "protect" women, children, and older people. They ask: Can we afford this dichotomy? Where does it lead? Those who support women's equal access to social institutions argue that everyone should have the opportunity to join the military and take on roles formerly reserved for men. Opponents argue that the abolition of war is dependent on changing this division of labor, with men taking on traditional women's roles and caring for infants and small children, the elderly, and the sick (Dinnerstein 1989).

Maternalism   Some women see their opposition to war mainly in terms of their responsibility to protect and nurture their children; they want to save the lives of both their own children and the children of "enemy" mothers. In the early 1980s, for example, when the U.S. and Soviet militaries were deploying more powerful nuclear weapons, Susan Lamb, who lived near USAF Greenham Common in England, a nuclear base, put it this way:

> I've got two young children, and I've taken responsibility for their passage into adulthood. Everyone tells me they are my responsibility. The government tells me this. It is my responsibility to create a world fit for them to grow up in. I can't say I'm responsible for my children not catching whooping cough and not responsible for doing anything about the threat of annihilation that hangs over them every minute of the day.
> *(Quoted in Cook and Kirk 1983, p. 27)*

Although this approach can sentimentalize motherhood, it is also powerful because mothers are behaving according to their roles and it is difficult for the state to suppress them. They expose contradictions: that the state, through militarism, does not let them get on with their job of mothering.

Diversion of Military Budgets to Socially Useful Programs   Another argument put forward by peace activists—women and men—concerns government spending. The Women's International League for Peace and Freedom (U.S. Section) publishes a Women's Budget, which shows how a 50 percent reduction in military expenditures and redistribution of those funds could provide for social programs that benefit women and their families. Cuts in funding for nuclear weapons, chemical and biological weapons, and U.S. troops, ships, and aircraft carriers around the world, they argue, could fund job-training programs, public housing, education, urban development, environmental cleanup, and AIDS research, for example. They would enable cuts in Medicaid, food stamps, and child nutrition programs to be restored.

The Military As a Sexist and Racist Institution   Opposition to the military also turns on the argument that, by its very nature, the military is profoundly antifeminist and racist and is fundamental to political systems that oppress women and peoples of color. Its ultimate effectiveness depends on people's ability to see reality in oppositional categories: us and them, friends and enemies, kill or be killed.

Human and Financial Costs of War

- Since 1900, there have been 250 wars and 109,746,000 war-related deaths, more than the combined populations of France, Belgium, Netherlands, and the four Scandinavian countries. In the 1980s, civilians constituted 74 percent of those killed.

- World military expenditure in 1995 amounted to $1.4 million per minute, despite a decline during the previous 5 years.

- Between 1990 and 1995, over three-fourths of arms sales by the United States to developing countries went to nations where citizens had no right to choose their own government.

- The cost of one Stealth bomber—$2,200,000,000—could supply family planning services to 120 million women.

- The cost of a multiple launcher rocket system loaded with ballistic missiles (a long-range self-propelled artillery weapon widely used in the Gulf War), at $29,000,000, could supply one year's basic rural water and sanitation services for 2,000,000 people in developing countries.

- In Cambodia, one of every 236 people is an amputee; there are as many land mines planted there as there are people (estimated 10 million mines and 9.9 million people).

Source: Sivard 1996.

To this end it is organized on rigidly hierarchical lines, demanding unquestioning obedience to superiors. Although the military uses women's labor in many ways, as mentioned above, it does so strictly on its own terms. The military environment also fosters violence against women. The higher incidence of domestic violence in military families than in nonmilitary families and crimes of violence against women committed near military bases in the United States and overseas are not coincidences but integral aspects of military life and training. Moreover, though not publicly sanctioned, rape is a weapon of war (Peterson and Runyan 1993; Rayner 1997).

This opposition focuses not only on how the military operates but also on militarism as an underlying system and worldview based on the objectification of "others" as enemies, a culture that celebrates war and killing (Reardon 1985). The Women's Pentagon Action, for example, identified militarism as a cornerstone of the oppression of women and the destruction of the nonhuman world. Thousands of women surrounded the Pentagon in November 1980 and again in 1981. They protested massive military budgets; the fact that militaries cause more ecological destruction than any other institutions; the widespread, everyday culture of violence manifested in war toys, films, and video games; the connection between violence and sexuality in pornography, rape, battering, and incest; and the connections between militarism and racism. This was no routine demonstration but a highly creative action organized in four stages: mourning, rage, empowerment, and defiance, culminating in the arrest of many women who chose to blockade the doors of the Pentagon (King 1983). The Unity Statement of the Women's Pentagon Action is included as Reading 82. At an Okinawan rally on violence and human rights violations against girls and women in September 1995, a women's declaration pointed to military training as a systematic process of dehumanization which turns "soldiers into war machines who inflict violence on the Okinawan community, only a chain-link fence away" (Okinawa women act against military violence 1996, p. 7). These activists see crucial connections between personal violence and international violence, both based on the objectification of others. Cynthia Enloe's concept of a constructed militarized masculinity fits in here (1990, 1993b). Citing the sexual assault of women at the Tailhook meeting of Navy aviators in 1991, the general incidence of sexual assault on military women, men's resistance to women in combat, and fears about openly gay men and lesbians in the military, she argues that the U.S. military is based on very specific notions of "militarized masculinity" (Enloe 1993b). Thus, women in combat roles threaten the manliness of war and the very nature of militarism as male.

Women who oppose militarism have very different perspectives from those who enter the military. They may also have different class positions and more opportunities for education and work. Liberal feminists criticize feminist peace activists for being classist and racist in their condemnation of the military as an employer when working women, especially women of color, have few employment options. The Unity Statement of the Women's Pentagon Action, for example, also argues for equality between men and women but against participation in the military for either sex. Peace activists also argue that the military is no place for gay men and lesbians. Jean Grossholtz in Reading 76 writes that, ironically, it was her involvement in the military, seeing casualties of the Korean War, that changed her views and led her to become a peace activist later in life. Barbara Omolade (1989) notes the contradictions of militarism for people of color in the United States, many of whom support the military because it provides economic opportunities that are lacking in civilian society. Military personnel of color fight for the United States, a country where they are oppressed. The people they fight against and are trained to kill are other people of color in various parts of the world — Vietnam, Grenada, Libya, Panama, and Iraq — to take examples from the past several decades. Combatants of color are more likely to be killed than their White counterparts, as happened in Vietnam.

Redefining Adventure, Power, and Security

Antimilitarist activists have well-developed critiques of militarism as philosophy and institution. To rework the recruiters' slogan, they do not believe that joining the army is being all you can be. Yet military recruitment ads promise security, challenge, professionalism, empowerment, exhilaration, adventure, and pride for the individual who enlists. How can these concepts be redefined so that they are not limited to military activities? Feminist writings on power and empowerment are relevant here (see, for example, Starhawk 1987; Plant and Plant 1992; Shields 1994).

Antimilitarists believe that a world that will sustain the lives of individuals, as well as communities and nations, must be built on the security of respect for differences of gender, race, and culture, not the creation of enemies; that the world's resources should be devoted to people's basic needs — housing, feeding, and schooling everyone; that gross inequalities between rich and poor countries and between rich and poor people within countries must be eradicated. Peace is not just an absence of war, and there can be no peace without justice. They believe in cultures that are generative rather than materialistic, where people recognize and appreciate that we are nurtured and sustained by the earth's wealth and that we need to live in sustainable ways. This view includes security for the individual—a major reason why women in the United States are currently drawn to enlist in the military—but this individual security also involves security at the meso and macro levels, for communities and nations (Boulding 1990; Reardon 1993). They think about the process of de-militarization—in economic, political, and practical terms and in terms of masculinity and the reconstruction of gender relations. They may work at practical projects that embody some small piece of this larger vision—teaching conflict resolution in schools; working as healers, on rape crisis lines, or in shelters for victims of domestic violence; establishing community gardens and alternative economic projects, or working with Amerasian children in South Korea or the Philippines. Women involved in antimilitarist work also imagine alternatives, exemplified in several of the writings we have included here. This redefinition of security is not an issue for women only, of course. Long-standing organizations like the War Resisters League and Jobs with Peace, and the conversion of military bases and technology are also salient here. Much more needs to be done in this direction and against the conventional wisdom that the military is an inevitable fact of life as well as a major source of jobs in many states.

A crucial question for the future concerns security and safety for individuals, communities, and nations. Currently notions of security usually rely on strength and force: building walls, gates, and fences; locking people up, keeping them in or out; carrying mace, buying guns, stockpiling weapons, and maintaining the military budget. These are all ways of separating people and maintaining hierarchies of haves and have-nots, people who are dominant and those who are inferior. It is leading to a world that is increasingly militarized, where people generally feel less, not more, secure.

As you read and discuss this chapter, think about the following questions:

1. What purposes does the military serve in this society?

2. Who joins the military? Why?

3. Why has the issue of gays in the military surfaced as an issue of mainstream U.S. politics in the 1990s?

4. What kinds of service could you imagine as an alternative to military service?

5. What makes you feel safe/unsafe at home? At school? In your community? On the streets? In communities you don't know? In cities or the countryside?

6. What can you do to improve your sense of safety/security in these different settings?

7. How do you view conflict?

8. How do you usually resolve conflicts or serious differences of opinion with your family? Your friends and peers? Teachers? Employers?

SEVENTY-FOUR

◆◆◆

Looking for New Opportunities

Monique Corbin

My name is Monique Corbin and I am seventeen years old. I was born and raised in San Francisco. My ethnicity is Filipino and African American. Culturally, I was raised as a Filipino, but I feel more like an American. I do not feel tied down to any of my nationalities. I attend Philip and Sala Burton Academic High School located in the city. My favorite subjects are En- glish and history. My least favorite subject is math. Math just seems so boring to me. There is nothing to debate about in math. Whatever it is, just is, and that's that. I consider that a strange concept.

During the fall before graduation, I thought about my life after high school. My grades in sophomore and junior years were not college material, and even if I were accepted I do not think I would have the discipline to study, do my homework, or even get to class on time. I also thought about the rising cost of college tuition. I could buy a car for the cost of college tuition. I then remembered my father telling me that after he graduated high school he went into the military. I have always admired people in uniform, especially men. The uniform symbolizes that the person is representing and fighting for our country. It also shows that he or she worked hard to get where they are, and reflects a strong pride.

I thought by joining the military I could finally get the breaks I need. I would get freedom from my parents and from San Francisco. I would also receive an education and learn discipline. I tend to be hyperactive, and sometimes have trouble concentrating; I also procrastinate so don't complete things I start; and I sometimes don't obey my parents like I should. The discipline I would get in the military would help me focus, get things done, and better obey people in authority.

I weighed the positives and the negatives of college and the military, and the military won. The trouble now was deciding which branch of service I should go into. I considered the Marines, but when I heard that boot camp was for three months, that totally scared me away. And I thought about the Air Force. My father influenced me to take that route because he had been in the Air Force. I picked the Air Force because to me it was the main branch that emphasizes education and also trains you in career fields. In the future I want to be a politician and work in advertising, or some other business field. While in the service, I want to do office work (except recruiting) or something in the medical field.

What I hope to gain from the military experience is discipline, proper education, and a better sense of myself. I also hope to gain pride, not only for myself but for my country. Right now America has a bad rep. I want to do my part to improve our image around the world.

SEVENTY-FIVE

◆◆◆

The Women in Blue

Melinda Smith-Wells

The advertising slogan says: "The United States Air Force, a great way of life!" Is it really? I beg to differ.

In order to fuel the war-fighting machine, and advance its economic and political goals, our government — the government I provide "muscle" for — embarked on a media campaign to attract young, adventurous dreamers like me. It has enticed and entrapped many.

"I promise to defend, honor and protect my country and fellow countrymen with my life, until the day that I die." In the early morning hours six years ago, in South Carolina, I swore to uphold and defend The Constitution of the United States against all enemies, foreign and domestic. In making this promise, I relinquished a substantial portion of my liberty to ensure that others would be able to have and enjoy their own. I did not foresee what the future had in store for me on that fateful morning that

seems so long ago. Unaware of the consequences, I jumped in feet first, hoping to be successful and to achieve something great. Unfortunately, I seem to have landed in something bad.

Recruiting? I didn't need that; my father was "in." I thought I was doing the right thing at the time — securing my future and giving myself the opportunity to advance and excel in life. I wanted the finer things that life has to offer: education, training, travel, money: things that many only dream of. I must admit that I have received these things, more or less, but not the quality I was promised, and at a cost I didn't think would be so high.

I am a twenty-five-year old woman of Portuguese-Puerto Rican ancestry, struggling to juggle my studies to attain a Bachelor of Arts Degree in Business Administration while serving as an active duty military member. Currently, I am a Maintenance Scheduler. I schedule maintenance for the various aircraft and support equipment in the Air Force inventory. During my six-year military career I have been stationed at three different Air Force bases in the U.S.: Homestead AFB, Florida; McCord AFB, Washington; and Beale AFB, California. I have had the opportunity to travel to South Korea and England on temporary duty.

The military has affected my personal life in two ways. First, I don't know my husband as well as I'd like to because I constantly go on temporary assignments to various locations. This can be very stressful on a relationship because it keeps us apart for six months at a time or longer. There are times when we need each other, but due to the circumstances we can't be together. We have been married for nearly four years, but have only spent 2.5 years together. Second, I don't have any "true" friends with whom to socialize. Once you get to the point where you consider someone a friend, either one of you may be moved to a different location. You have to get used to people leaving, and the transient nature of the "business."

The "trials and tribulations" of military life have definitely had an effect on me and many other women that I have worked with. Sexual harassment has been and always will be a sensitive issue in all organizations because of the narrow-minded, insecure individuals that exist in our world. In the military, sexual harassment—regardless of what the establishment says—is very much alive and well. In my experience, the military leadership tends to look the other way when it comes to this issue. I think they feel that "boys will be boys," and women should accept this because the military is a man's world.

Oh yes, when you see incidents like "Tailhook" or those involving the Army training instructors, those of you on the outside might say, "the military will get to the bottom of this and resolve these matters." Don't be naïve enough to think that happens. The military will resolve matters in the media but not in the various units around the military world. What the leadership does is to send out memorandums or have a 1–2 hour "crash training course" on sexual harassment as if this will eliminate the problem! Does that resolve the matter? What do you think? It's just another piece of training for people to brush aside.

If you should go so far as to file a sexual harassment complaint you may put your career in jeopardy. These matters are supposed to be confidential but they eventually get out. When they do, you walk around with a stigma attached to you. You become labeled a "bitch or whore" who wanted it to happen and couldn't handle it when it did. "You brought it upon yourself because you shouldn't walk around here looking and smelling nice." That's a great environment to live and work in, huh!

Although my overall experiences in the Air Force have been livable, I do not wish to endure them again for the simple fact that my military experience has not met my expectations. Budget cuts have had an intense impact on the quality of military life. Yes, the military offers educational benefits to its members if you can fit the classes into your hectic work schedule. Medical benefits have become nothing more than medical insurance, and the quality of care we receive is adequate at best. Then there are ongoing senseless changes, and the ongoing conversations and actions regarding sexual harassment.

Some of the "intangible benefits" of the military are achieving self-discipline and maturity. You must have both of these to keep from losing your composure, and maybe cursing someone out. It is very tough to do. Many military members judge your intelligence and ability by how many stripes you have on your sleeve instead of looking at you as an individual, and what you demonstrate through your work and conversation.

A disadvantage of the military is that military members are not compensated for the work we do. Can you actually put a price on someone's life and liberty? No, you can't, but you can show them through the compensation they receive that they are a respected, valuable, and integral part of this nation. The military robs a person of their dignity and individuality. Your thoughts and actions are not your own. You have to focus on the mission and not on your own personal agenda. There are times when you are given an assignment and told how to do it, but the instructions you've been given are wrong. You can't deviate because the person who gave you the assignment has more stripes than you. The worst part is that when it comes out in the wash that the job was done wrong, who gets blamed—you. You are manipulated like a puppet on a string in a never-ending play.

I will not continue pursuing the military as a career after my enlistment ends, nor would I recommend it to other adventurous women because it's not what you are led to believe it is. I recommend that young women take the time to assess their lives and determine what they truly want for themselves and their future. There are other options out there, and you should weigh them all before you make a decision that can have a lasting effect on the rest of your life.

In the military there is a gap between perception and reality that can be compared to the myth of "The Great American Dream": something that never really existed, or not the reality of your own experience. If it sounds too good to be true, then it probably is.

◆◆◆

The Search for Peace and Justice
Notes Toward an Autobiography

Jean Grossholtz

I was standing in the sunlight on Pennsylvania Avenue watching the passing gays and lesbians, relishing the color, the noise, and the excitement. I saw them coming around the corner, men and women many in uniform carrying signs, "I'm gay and I served." I watched them as they passed, the pride in their faces, the confidence in their step. And suddenly there I was marching, tears streaming down my face, holding the hand of another woman beside me. Here I was, a 65-year-old dedicated peace activist, who had put my body on the line in such out of the way places as the Seneca Army Base, Greenham Common, and Diablo Canyon. I, who had courted federal prison and spent time in many jails for peace, was marching with the military for the rights of Gays to serve in an institution I found distasteful in the extreme. But it was an institution in which I served for four years, nine months, and five days through the Korean War. It was an institution that had meant my personal survival, had honed my political passions to a fine level of anger, had given me a deep and everlasting commitment to end war.

Confused, conflicted, and still a strong lesbian political activist, I walked beside my newfound friend as we traded stories of the purges, the fears, the betrayals by our own and others as we had sought to survive in a hostile environment. I remembered sitting paralyzed in the mess hall while non-commissioned officers who outranked me discussed the dangers of getting too close to the "troops." I knew this was aimed at me. I had just returned from a weekend of love and lust with one of my "troops."

It did not matter that I knew some of them were guilty of the same infractions. I was in danger and they were warning me.

It took some time to understand those warnings before I began to hear them. The Lieutenant who made fun of me for walking with my arm around my friend. "Childish," she called it, "high school," not the behavior of a grown woman and a non-commissioned officer. The Captain who mentioned a missing light bulb as a means of casually warning me there was to be a surprise bed check. There were many such warnings as we all did our best to be decent people in an atmosphere of constant betrayal. This way surely madness lies, this occupation of a totally alien space where what one was and wanted to be was denied and hidden and yet ever present.

So there I was marching in the Gay Pride March for a Simple Matter of Justice, reliving those old fears and betrayals, the times I denied, the times I turned my back as others felt the wrath of the Army's purging. This was an important moment. Did I really want to honor the right to serve in this institution? Was I marching for the right of women, of lesbians to join this killing machine?

I had grown up committed to the organization of the working class. I grew up believing in freedom and justice. I read about the strikes of the women textile workers in Lawrence in 1912, and shed real tears when I read of the awful things that happened to strikers. I read of the Pullman Company and their private police and the murdered men at Haymarket in Chicago in 1894. I read of the government's and businessmen's fears of anarchism and the scapegoating of two foreign-born working men, Sacco and Vanzetti. Account after account of those martyred for justice made me understand that capitalism grew in this country at great cost to ordinary people, to the workers whose labor made it all possible. And I dreamed of playing that role, of being the one burnt at the stake or beheaded. Overhearing my father talking with his friends, I learned of the Industrial Workers of the World and their dream of one big union for all the working class. I fell in love with the words of these men and women. Elizabeth Gurley Flynn and Joe Hill and Big Bill Haywood of the Industrial Workers of the World. Nicknamed the Wobblies by some Chinese workers unable to pronounce the "W" these organizers moved around the country lending their skills to local leadership, integrating grass roots groups, trying to build one big union. Throughout middle school and high school I chased after stories of these grand ideas of equality and justice.

I joined the Army, as did most of the women I met in the Women's Army Corps, to get out of what looked to me a dead end street. I was 17 years old and going nowhere, with nothing but drinking and living from one shit-level job to the next in my future. I had read enough war novels to know that the men in the Army were not all establishment puppets. I knew some of the people in the Army were the same people who walked the picket lines outside of factories. I did not make the connection between the Army, the state, and the destruction of the IWW. I only knew I had to get somewhere, go somewhere where I would be able to read, to think about these people and their ideas, to find people who used these words this way.

And I had another, deeper, darker secret for leaving my home town, I was a freak. I lusted after women. I did not like boys, could not relate to them except as friends, did not want to marry, or be what the women around me seemed to want. In the small town where I went to high school I was driven crazy by my inability to fit in, to even try, make an attempt. I did not know the words dyke, lesbian. I learned of homosexual and I heard people referring to sick people they called "queer" and I knew that was me. I had hopes and hints there were others like me. When I finally met one such, she was already going into the Army and she convinced me there would be others like us there.

But the driving force was economic. With a high school education all I could do was waitress, wash dishes, work in the laundry, stand all day on an assembly line. I had spent much of my life in small towns or on a farm; I was unused to being cooped up, unused to routine. I drifted from one job to another, failing as a waitress, having a brief happy fling for some months as a short order cook when the male cook got sick. Mostly it was jobs that were killing me, that I could not keep because my anger and despair led me to outraged rebellion. The middle-aged women who stood all day on an assembly line repeating the same movement endlessly hour after hour, having to ask permission to go to the toilet, tried to comfort me. They understood only that we had no choice, that the world offered only this to poor and uneducated people. When I raged they gave me cookies, when I spoke of strikes they laughed. My heart hurting, my body aching, my mind numbed, I would eventually explode at the foreman, the factory superintendent, the product we were making. And I would be fired and move to another factory to repeat the experience.

The Army saved me. Although it led me to some heavy drinking for a time, it also led me to reject that life full force and to see some hope in moving beyond this past to something new. For the first time we had medical care, good food, warm clothes. For many of us our first visit to the dentist. (I credit the Army for the fact that alone of all my siblings I still have real teeth at the age of 67.) I had the first medication for my chronic stomach ulcers that I never had a name for before. We laughed about our uniforms but it was for some of us the first time we were not in danger of being laughed at, criticized for what we wore and how we wore it. We had social services we never thought possible. The Army was the biggest welfare state in the world and it took great care of us. And in the end it gave me the GI Bill and a college education.

We complained and raged against the Army's peculiar ways of trying to break our spirit but all of us secretly gloried in our new wealth and were shamed into lying about our pasts, making up stories that were nowhere near true. We would tell Dick and Jane stories of loving fathers who wore suits and carried briefcases, of mothers smiling and young-looking, of little white houses with shutters and pets. And when one of us would tell the truth of the shopworn mother, the abusive father, the rape by a brother, the fights over money, we would sit together in silence, loving one another and knowing we were all afraid to speak out as she had done, afraid to make ourselves so vulnerable.

I learned that I could be somebody. That I could do all the things they asked of me, that I could stand up against the harshest, most angry of my peers and survive. A lieutenant, angry at me and humiliated because I knew more than she did about what was happening in the world, set me impossible tasks over and over until I was made into a zombie by tiredness and lack of sleep. And I still led my platoon and won good soldier awards. I was a good teacher, a popular leader. I began to see there was a way to have integrity, to be able to live as I really was. Not at first, at first I lied, I passed myself off as what I was not, indeed never wanted to be. I tried on different faces of myself searching for the one that fit. The Army allowed me that space, that time. As long as I did my duty. And that proved easy.

I learned how to act in concert with others. I learned the discipline that group activity required. Much of what the Army thrived on struck me as dumb and not worth paying attention to. The Army demanded total unquestioned obedience. They called it discipline, and punished infractions with idiotic penalties. For example, once, for arguing with an officer, I was sent to remove all the coal from the coal bin, scrub the bin, and put all the coal back. I found this ridiculous. If I thought someone was wrong I needed to say so. Sometimes this worked in my favor and allowed me to blossom, at other times it caused me grief and I paid for my inattention to the Army's rules.

Over time I realized that people liked me, that I was smart, that the Army appreciated me despite all my rebellions. I was sent to Leadership School and the entire unit showed me they thought this was a fine idea, that I was worthy of respect as a leader.

I was sent to Leadership School in Carlisle Barracks, Pennsylvania. There I met some wonderful historians who told us stories of the battles and generals of the Civil War. I fell in love with the history and with the ease which these men told the stories of Grant and Meade and Robert E. Lee and calvary charges across peach orchids. And then I saw the pictures, the dead strewn across the battlefields. And I remembered Walt Whitman who had become the poet of my liberation, of my becoming.

I learned to teach everything from map-reading to first aid to current events. I grew daily more confident, less confused. I met women who had been to college and we talked of many things. I learned to read the *New York Times*, not knowing then how much it was misshaping and confusing my principled politics of the working class. I was sent to a detachment working with an engineering battalion in the woods of Wisconsin and I became a newspaper editor. Me, the farm girl, editing an Army newspaper. I found myself at the heart of some of the more important activities of the camp.

I learned about war. War had been something I'd read about, something that people became heroes in. And a hero I wanted to be. I did not like the killing. Felt instinctively it was wrong and that nothing would justify it or ever make me take a weapon against another human being. I had grown up with brothers and fathers hunting, hunting for meat for our food. I could not stand the smell of them when they returned—the smell of fresh blood and dead animals. I did not eat the meat they brought so proudly. I did not look at the carcasses as they carved them up and canned the results. Still I wanted to be a hero. I did not altogether reject the idea of armies in battle, of enemies.

After I had been in the Army for a few months, the United States began what they called "a police action" against North Koreans. This reaction started with a movement by North Koreans across the border with South Korea. But 1950 was the height of the Cold War frenzy. Washington was in turmoil over who had "lost" China to the Communists. The inside view in Washington was that the border crossings and troop movements in the North were a precursor of a massive, Soviet-backed invasion. This never happened. Instead the Americans, failing to stop at just policing the border, invaded North Korea and headed for Manchuria. In response, the People's Republic of China entered the war and drove the Americans from the North in a massive and bloody retreat.

A small peacetime army was suddenly increased. Thousands of new recruits were brought in, trained, and sent to Korea. Many died within days of landing at Inch'on. One young man I met from Kansas had lied about his age, entered the Army at 17, was dead on his eighteenth birthday.

As the U.S. Generals pushed to the border, proclaiming victory, the terrible retreats, the terrible killing fields of the North came to haunt us. Pictures of young men, their feet wrapped in blankets, their eyes hollow with horror. "They brought their dead out," the generals crowed, as if that were a victory. I lay many nights in my cot listening to Taps and remembering the strong young men learning engineering skills in the woods of Wisconsin. I could no longer countenance war. I no longer wanted to be a hero. I wanted to stop war, this war, all wars.

I was transferred from Wisconsin to Fitzsimmons General Hospital in Denver and the wounded came flooding back. As editor of the Hospital newspaper, my job was ostensibly to tout the patriotism of these young men. I had considerable freedom until I printed a story about the limited blood supply and then I was put under tighter rein.

As I haunted the wards talking with these men, I came to see what war was really about. I saw that the bravery I had identified with saving one's buddies, was really the result of a foolish, meaningless slaughter. The broken bodies of the young men I met in those hospitals, were the reverse image of the sweating healthy young men I had seen training in Wisconsin. I knew that I had to organize my life to destroy the idea that war and dying in war was glorious. This blatant disrespect for life was wrong.

The Army taught me that whatever else was true, war was never an answer to any political issue; that politicians and the Generals were not good judges of reality.

But the Army taught me also that I could not love my own kind. For many years I lived in fear and shame. Shame, because what I wanted was so far from what I was supposed to want. Shame, as I saw other WACS seeking private hideouts to live out their realities while maintaining a public posture rejecting that very reality. This option did not appeal to me, it demanded that I think of myself as less than what I was, what I wanted to be. Not being able to talk to each other honestly, not being able to be anything together, they turned to drink. I saw them drinking themselves into an oblivion where shame would be stilled and they could act on their feelings and for some brief moments forget the pain of their unac-ceptable existence. I could not do this. I felt confused, alienated from those who hated queers and those who would not admit to being queer except when drunk. I was unable to find a center for myself.

As confidence in my own abilities grew, confidence in who I was emerged and I came to understand that the Army's war on homosexuals was wrong, that there was nothing the matter with me that a little healthy acceptance wouldn't cure. I recognized an eerie similarity between the Army's relentless attack on homosexuality, the total rejection of love of your own sex, and the constant insistent bonding with your unit, your buddies. The Army runs on love for your buddies, the willingness to lay down your very life for the group.

The Army's internal war against homosexuality is a warning not to go too far, not to put your faith in individuals but in the unit. And the unit is the Army. Men must be willing to die for the Army, to see their manhood as coming out of the barrel of a gun and its use. It is our national idea of heroism. How many times have we seen U.S. Presidents (Ronald Reagan most especially) visiting caskets in an airplane hangar and declaring these were heroes. Sometimes men who only happened to be at the wrong end of the barracks when a "terrorist" ran his explosive-laden truck into the gate, or when an airplane crashed inadvertently. Heroes simply for being there. No one saw the heroism of the women left as single heads of family back home who still managed to raise their kids and keep them out of poverty in the face of terrible odds. If you put on a uniform you are a hero, you are somebody, you are your nation's finest. Even if you are treated like a pile of shit everywhere you go and are roughed up, discriminated against, called names, within the Army. Such a contradiction—love your buddy like your brother, do not love another man.

The Army's vicious, continuous, almost holy crusade against homosexuals, the periodic purges of the WAC Detachments, and the continuous challenges to gay men were all means by which the Army kept its control. Gendered identities made men into soldiers willing to kill for their commanders, and women into either the girl back home or whores. There was no place for anyone who challenged these assumptions. A real man, a soldier, abjures homosexuals even as he learns to put his hope, trust and daily livelihood in his buddies, his unit, his commander. Study what happens to men in battle. Read the war novels by men from every war. They are driven nearly crazy with fear and grief before they can turn to help one another, to express their love physically. How can this clearly "men loving men" organization keep its militaristic pose without undercutting the very thing it is built on?

The Army's relentless pursuit of homosexuals is one way a gendered power structure is kept in place. If women can be competent, active public agents, and men can access that part of themselves which shares the softer, life-enhancing qualities of womanness, what will happen to the killing force, to the automatic disciplined response to orders?

After I left the Army I watched the madness of the Korean war continue as the United States embarked upon a massive war economy, engaged in a worldwide contest with the "Evil Empire," the Soviet Union. I used the GI Bill to enter college and then went on to graduate school. I studied international relations, and political economy, I became a specialist on Southeast Asian politics.

I came to know that the war machines were created not really to be used because that would be the end of the world, but to press the Soviets to spend their resources, to spend to bankruptcy. Meanwhile American corporations feeding at the military trough, developed technology to enter world markets at a great advantage, selling military equipment and technology developed at the taxpayer's expense. This military machine, now released by the fall of the Soviet Union, can be used to secure and guarantee the resources of a new global economic order. From Korea to Vietnam, Grenada, Afghanistan, and Kuwait, the American Army is used to keep imperialism solidly in place. Without the Soviet Army to oppose them, the U.S. military can freely intervene. The global success of the international capitalist economic system is ultimately guaranteed by that military force.

Years after I had left the Army, after I had earned a Ph.D. in Political Science, another American government entered into another war, reminiscent of the Korean War: Vietnam. An area of the world in struggle against colonial rule, a country also divided by international fiat into north and south. And again a U.S.-generated incident and a military response, and once again young men, barely out of basic training

sent to die and Generals chortling about how brave they were, how fine, counting up the numbers they killed as if at a football match.

And I now took to the streets and found myself many times on the opposite side of the Army. Standing holding hands with my colleagues staring into the faces of young men and women frightened by us and worried about their own self-esteem.

I began standing at the gates of Westover Air Base in Massachusetts with a remarkable woman named Frances Crowe. At first we were alone but in time others joined us. Other actions followed, lying in the streets to stop the buses taking the new draftees, blocking the doors of the New York Stock Exchange, surrounding the Pentagon, being dragged to police buses and jails. I learned remarkable strength as we faced our fears of what would happen, of how we would behave when threatened by the police. I sat through endless meetings processing and planning, and nights on church floors with hundreds of others, catching what little sleep we could before an action. I experienced wonderful togetherness in jail cells. And eventually there were the women's peace camps at Seneca and at Greenham Common. Public spaces where women met freely and as equals, seeking a new way of being, a new way of making decisions, a new way of resisting injustice. This it seemed to me was the real beginning of something new, something with hope for a different future.

I have seen women create community; create, without structured authority, large-scale actions and projects. These actions were not without problems and not, in the end, without being somewhat co-opted. But we did create and maintain organized effort whether to bring attention to Cruise missiles stored at the Seneca Army Base or to keep constant attention on the delivery of Cruise missiles to Greenham. Communities formed, the discipline of consensus decision-making was accepted, and we learned to appreciate ourselves and each other as women. The Women's Peace Camps had their days of glory, of achievement, and to all who came there, something remains, the possibility, maybe only the hope, that another way of living, of making decisions, of sharing in a common life can happen. Those of us who experienced the camps changed our lives. We could hope for an alternative. Even if we had not found it altogether.

Later in New England I joined a wondrous group of women called the Women of Faith. We did monthly actions against the nuclear submarines and their D5 missiles being constructed at Electric Boat in Connecticut. We marched and demonstrated at each launching, sometimes getting arrested, sometimes simply doing guerrilla theater. But each month we did some action. Dancing at the gate one morning at 6:30, we shut down the missile business for 28 minutes and were inordinately proud of it. Another time we invaded their offices, several times we chained ourselves to gates or blockaded entrances.

We would think up our next action while we were waiting arraignment in the holding cell or sitting waiting as part of the support group in the courtroom. The night before the planned action we would meet to make signs, plan the press coverage, assign tasks. We would meet in a church or a private home near our action. For a couple of years we worked together without tension or friction, bringing new women into our group and learning how to talk to the media, handle the jail situation. What broke us up was some of the changes in the military situation and internal disruption caused by one new woman's inability to accept consensus. Until that time we had worked without a slip. Proving that it can be done.

I found some of the same camaraderie, the same sense of belonging to something bigger than one's self, the same willingness to accept others' decisions, as I found in the Army and this time aimed at peace, at justice, and at the creation of political community.

So why was I marching in a parade proclaiming the right of queers to serve in the military? What did I hope to accomplish by this? How did it fit with my peace activism?

I was marching along with hundreds of others to say "Yes, I was there. You can no longer deny my existence. Silencing me and all these others was useless because we know and you know what you are up to. Those of us in uniform are not just robots wound up and set out to kill and be killed at the bidding of the world economic order. We have lives that you do not approve of, we have thoughts and values that reject yours."

So I was marching for all of this, to challenge the Army's gendered system of power, to challenge its failure to honor the love of men and women for each other, to force them to change that reality. Because if they acknowledge the existence of queers in their ranks, in their leadership, and among those who make the decisions that vote them budgets, then they can no longer adhere to that male ideology of exclusion and machoism. Those qualities that have been assigned to women, the experiences and perceptions of women can not so simply be dismissed. The Army as a male hierarchical institution is weakened.

And I was marching because I wanted to put the lie to all that we have been told was not possible, was dangerous. Contrary to what we are told, I have seen that this country can provide all the necessities of life, housing, food, clothing, health care, and education to hundreds of thousands of people in a very short time. An enormous army was assembled, housed, fed, and clothed in a very short time for the Korean War and again for the Vietnam War. Despite all we have heard of the dangers of the welfare programs and helping people out of trouble, the country did not go bankrupt, those people did not become lazy or valueless. Providing young people with all the necessities of life and good health made them strong and efficient.

Contrary to the claim that we only act out of individual self-interest, I have seen men and women put the good of the community above their own individual wishes. I have seen that men and women can think collectively about how to live together and get a job done. And I have seen them do this despite, not because of, the barbarous discipline.

Equality and justice, my lifelong dreams, are not to be found in fighting, in militarism. Killing people does not bring peace. There are other ways to create common commitments, a willingness to put one's body on the line, the courage to take risks.

It is here we must start to remake the world.

S E V E N T Y - S E V E N

◆◆◆

Choosing Your Battle

Margarethe Cammermeyer

After my enlistment in 1961, my advancement in the military proceeded exactly on schedule (one of the delightful aspects about such a splendidly rigid institution is that if you do what you're supposed to, the system does what it's supposed to). I was promoted from recruit to private, then to private first class, and finally commissioned as a second lieutenant.

My world was still very small. It consisted of school and the military. The social upheaval that began in the 1960s didn't really affect me. You're sheltered from the world when you're in school, just as in many ways you're protected when you're in the military. And for me, the additional benefit of having enlisted was that I didn't have to make any decisions about what I was going to do tomorrow. It was all taken care of. I liked that. It was good not to have to worry about where I was going to live, or where my job would be. I happily said, "Take me where you want, and let me learn to be an adult, without having to make other decisions." In a way, I was relinquishing responsibility; at the same time this life fit my lack of emotional maturity. I was being taken care of.

As an Army student nurse I received my first military commendation, the Good Conduct Medal, for hospital work and some recruiting I'd performed. When it was pinned on my uniform it had the full, intended effect. I was tremendously proud.

Beyond being praised and regularly promoted (hallmarks of the military regime), I was paid seventy-eight dollars a month—a handsome amount in those days. It was wonderful to be paid to go to school. With this regular income, I saved enough money to make two important purchases. First, I bought my mother a washer and dryer, so she could stop doing laundry by hand. She was delighted with the gift, and I was proud to have the autonomy and the income to help make her life a little easier.

Then I bought my first car: a gorgeous big black four-door 1957 Mercury. It had sleek lines with contrasting white fins protruding off the back end. The seats were leather, and the windows and gears were operated by push buttons (an innovation in those days). It was an absolute dream car. Owning it, driving it, showing off its power and style delighted me tremendously. I wasn't just at peace with myself, I was ready to go. Army, here I come!

After graduation, the only thing that stood between me and the military was passing a two-day state board nursing examination. This was the culmination of all my college and hospital training. The multiple-choice questions covered every aspect of nursing. After the test, my classmates and I dragged ourselves out of the exam center in Baltimore, so sure that we were going to fail that we made plans to get together to study for the next time the test would be given. The six weeks of waiting for the results went slowly—with fears surfacing from my earlier failure in school. Then, finally, the Army notified me I was to report for active duty. I had passed the state board examination. I was ecstatic.

The preparation was over; my career was truly beginning. I waited eagerly at my parents' home in Bethesda for my orders. Any day they would arrive and I would begin my military life. Any day I would put on my uniform, pack my bag, report for duty—and finally take my place in my new world.

"Any day" came on Sunday evening, July 22, 1963. *The* telegram arrived at the door. My orders—even the phrase was impressive. Impatiently I opened *the* telegram. I read it. I read it again. I read it a third time. My heart stopped. I didn't know what to do. These were my orders:

TC 220. BY ORDER SA FOL RSG DIR. WP TDN. FOR TVL COSTS TO AND PD AT TDY

Margarethe Cammermeyer served as an officer in the U.S. Armed Forces for twenty-six years. These excerpts from her book, *Serving in Silence,* focus on her early years as an Army nurse.

STA ONLY 2142020 32–29 P2450–21 22 25
S99–999. FOR ALL OTHER COSTS 2142010
01–1231-1233. EFF UPON EXPR PRESENT
LV. TDY ENR TO STU DET, MFSS BAMC
(3410–02) FT SAM HOUSTON, TEX. REPT
DATE: NST 0730 HRS 23 JUL 63.

The telegram told me other things as well, an entire page of instructions. All in capital letters and commanding abbreviations and acronyms. After searching the page for clues, I decided I'd been ordered to Fort Sam Houston—but when? How? If I didn't find out, I might disobey the first orders of my career.

There had to be a solution. I couldn't get hold of my recruiter—it was Sunday night. Where were military matters best analyzed and understood? And where was I most likely to find someone on duty even on a Sunday? The Pentagon, of course. I worked up my courage, dialed the Pentagon, and asked to speak to the officer in charge. He abruptly got on the line. Flustered, hardly able to explain my reason for calling, I finally convinced him to translate the telegram. He must have considered me an absolute idiot. After all, the Pentagon had a few other obligations—like managing troops and planning for war—that were more important than deciphering a telegram for a young nurse. But at the time, it was the only thing I knew to do. And it worked. He told me what I needed to know. I was on my way.

I made travel plans so I would arrive and report for active duty no sooner than 7:30 A.M., July 23, 1963, to the Medical Field Service School, Brooke Army Medical Center, at Fort Sam Houston, Texas. Though I had no idea about military protocol or what to do once in uniform, I got out my manual that described each style of uniform and opened it on the dresser. It showed the correct positioning of all insignias and medals. Now I went to work.

I spent hours ironing my cord uniform. No longer used today, cord was the type of fabric—a lightweight, green-and-white cotton weave—that was made into a smart-looking skirt-and-blouse outfit. Once every wrinkle was out, and each crease looked sharp and perfect, I placed the brass just as it was in the manual photograph. The simple gold lieutenant's bars went parallel, one-half inch from the top shoulder seam and centered. The Nurse Corps

caduceus was placed on the right lapel, perpendicular to the floor and three quarters of an inch from the edge. The U.S. insignia was centered on the left lapel and parallel to the floor. The name tag went over the right breast across from the top buttonhole and anatomically adjusted as necessary. The second lieutenant's bar graced the cap one inch from the front crease on the right side. Everything was in its proper position. I compared myself in uniform to the picture in the manual—perfection. I looked beautiful.

I went out to show my mother. I don't know what pleased her more—my new look as an officer or my own excitement. By now, she and my father were allies of my decision to become a soldier. They had watched me thrive since my enlistment, and defended my new career if friends or colleagues questioned it. Mother agreed the uniform suited me very well, laughing as I paraded around, and teasing, "Come down to earth, prima donna."

But on the way to the airport, perfectly attired as an officer, I felt strange. I looked the part, but could I act it? This was just the second time I had been out in such a public place as a second lieutenant. I had dressed in my uniform to fly on standby status when I visited Aagot in Portland, Oregon, earlier in the summer (military personnel received special airline rates). Then, as now, I was plagued with questions. What was the protocol for behavior? Where and when should I salute? And whom? My duty was to salute first anyone senior to me whether in the Army, Navy, Air Force, or Marines. That was my duty—but would I be able to tell who was senior to me? I didn't know how to read insignias—there were so many. What if I mistakenly saluted an enlisted person? That would be totally wrong. The enlisted person had to initiate the salute, but what if that didn't happen? My anxiety rising, I reached the airport. As I entered the terminal, I didn't know whether to take off my cap or leave it on. I left it on, hoping I wasn't committing a grave error. As I waited for the plane, I decided it was the time and place to take evasive action. I scanned the airport, determined to avoid other military people. Every time people in uniform approached, I turned my eyes away. But when they had passed and were at a safe distance, I'd peek to see what they did with their hats and how they acted when they met others in uniform. I felt like an impersonator.

That was soon to change. The Army has a systematic process for reshaping the identity of each person. Not only do you get a new preface to your name (lieutenant), new clothing (uniforms), new behaviors (marching and saluting), but you also learn a new language (abbreviations and acronyms). It is accomplished in only ten weeks, and it's called basic training.

My transformation occurred at Fort Sam, as we called it. I arrived on time, with the rest of my fellow trainees, exactly as ordered, and went directly to billeting to receive my housing assignment. For the duration of basic training, we all stayed in sparse officers' quarters.

Arriving on a military post, I always feel as if I've been picked up and set down again in a foreign culture — a culture somewhere back in time. The terrain is invariably flat. This is best for parades, of course. It also allows everybody to be, quite literally, on the same plane. Roads are more economical to build and it's easier to move equipment and vehicles quickly and safely on a flat landscape. And aesthetically it's very pleasing. The lawns are vast and green. The buildings are elegantly stoic, without ingenious designs — very straight lines, very pragmatic. Every square inch is used because every square inch is needed. The symmetry in the landscape and architecture is mirrored by the meticulously maintained grounds, where vehicles never exceed the posted speed and people in fine uniforms calmly, diligently go about their work. In this place of picturesque serenity, a wonderful thing happens: impersonators are turned into officers.

At Fort Sam all high-ranking officers live in Victorian-style wooden residences. Other officers and enlisted are billeted in simple brick houses, duplexes, and barracks. From there, a half-mile-long parade field, framed by rows of elegant trees, stretches up to the imposing Brooke Army Medical Center.

In the center of it all, surrounded by the vast green lawn of the parade field, stand the flagpole and the cannon. Every morning, on every Army post, including Fort Sam, reveille is sounded. I always made sure to be outside at 0600 hours to be a part of this awakening ritual. The cannon goes off and everything on post stops. Talk about bowing to Mecca — this is the military equivalent. If you're outside anywhere on the post — even if you're a civilian — once the cannon

goes off, you stop. If you're in a car, you stop the car and get out; if you're marching or walking, you halt. The national anthem begins, and everyone stands and salutes in rapt attention in the direction of the flag while it is raised. At sundown, the reverse ritual occurs with the lowering of the flag at retreat.

All these elements of military life — from the uniformity of the architecture to the defining rituals and behaviors — serve to create a sense of shared values and purposes that are vital and comforting. For example, the salute. Such a central part of military life, it is the focus of the first obligation we faced. As soon as we got on the post, we were told that military honor requires each new officer to perpetuate a cardinal rule: to give the first enlisted person who salutes you a dollar. This happened to me the first day as I walked to my quarters. After I returned the salute, I gave the enlisted man a dollar, and blushed, because he now knew I was a green "butter bar" — as the bearer of the gold-colored insignia of the second lieutenant bar is termed. The initiation was over and it had its effect. I was a member of this group, connected in gestures, rituals, and dress.

A salute is a greeting. On one level, it's the subordinate's respect for the senior rank. But it's much more than that. The salute creates a humanizing connectedness. Here are two people walking on the same street who are forced by tradition to say hello, in a society that normally is segregated by hierarchy and nonfraternization between officers and enlisted personnel. The discipline of it changes a person in good ways. I can tell who's been in the military even if they're not in uniform. Out in the civilian world, walking along the street, if I have direct, unhesitant eye contact with a stranger who says hello, we both know we have a common military history, are connected, and share a world.

Our immersion in military life continued in the classroom. My class of incoming members of the Army Nurse Corps studied the structure of the Army, the symbols of unit sizes and corps, the developments of battle plans. We learned the configuration of platoons, companies, battalions, batteries, and armies. As medical personnel, we learned about battle casualties, requirements for beds and supplies, medical resources, and the skills of each specialist and technician on the battlefield. In addition to the battlefield scenario, there were lectures on the care of soldiers and their families during peacetime. Most of the on-site work we did at Brooke Army Medical Center was to learn that inescapable aspect of all military service: paperwork. . . .

For some, military discipline is too confining. To be told what to wear, how to wear it, what to do, where and when to do it, relieves a person of the small decisions of daily life to such a degree that some feel there is no self left. But that's not true. Trivia are eliminated so your entire attention can be directed to what matters: your mission. A nurse's mission in the Army is to conserve the fighting force and to perform that duty with honor and integrity. Those of us who

stayed and embraced these values grew strong in this strenuously consistent environment.

The military's most potent weapon is the belief that we are more alike than we are different. That is the way to marshal our best impulses and actions for the greater good. Go to one parade and you'll understand — a thousand fall in and march as one. We don't get caught up in our differences. But that beautiful precision takes training. Lots of training. That's why the parade field is the centerpiece of the military post. . . .

SEVENTY-EIGHT

◆◆◆

An Appeal for the Recognition of Women's Human Rights

Okinawa Women Act Against Military Violence

The verdict in the trial of the three U.S. military personnel accused of seizing and raping a young Okinawan girl on September 4, 1995, was handed down by the Fukuoka High Court, Naha District Court today, just six months after the incident occurred. We have confirmed the fact that the young girl involved strongly desired that such a thing should never again occur, and as a result, this trial took place and the verdict was handed down today.

Although the trial made clear the crime committed by the three military personnel, it did not address the issue of the violent nature of the military system, an issue that must be examined closely. We must accept major responsibility for society's failure to examine this issue, despite the courage shown by this young girl. U.S. military personnel are not stationed in Okinawa as individuals. We must press for the examination of the reality that these military personnel are trained in violence, murder, and destruction by the U.S. military forces. Otherwise, this kind of incident will continue to produce further victims in the future.

Moreover, this court verdict was handed down by a Japanese legal system which was put in place

in Okinawa after Okinawa's reversion to Japan, a system which views rape more lightly than robbery. We have to make clear the limitations of the present legal system. The length of the sentence handed down is viewed as being very light in comparison with the severity of the physical and mental suffering experienced by the young girl and her family, and when compared to other young girls and women who have suffered similarly. Throughout the 50-year-long U.S. military presence in Okinawa, we have suffered unending human rights violations at the hands of U.S. military personnel, especially those extreme acts directly against women. Such acts have occurred both before and after this incident. We feel that revising the Japanese law in order to achieve the recognition of women's full human rights and the establishment of women's right to sexual self-determination is an urgent priority.

We have just returned from a two-week America Peace Caravan (February 3–17), in which we appealed to American citizens concerning the U.S. military presence in Okinawa and the resulting human rights violations against women and children. As a result we were able to reconfirm the violent nature of the U.S. military system, and to discover specific avenues for working toward the removal of military bases and military forces from Okinawa.

Based on the above, we, the members of the "Okinawan Women Act Against Military Violence," appeal on the following issues, and call upon women both throughout Japan and the rest of the world to join us in this task:

- A full investigation of all past U.S. military crimes and human rights violations committed against women and girls;
- The ultimate withdrawal of all military bases and military forces, and until that is achieved,

an ongoing program of human rights education for all military personnel;

- Revision of the present Japanese law to recognize the human rights of women and their right to sexual self-determination;
- The creation of a social climate in which women are free to appeal, including the legal, municipal administration, medical care and education systems.

We shall continue our efforts in order to achieve the above.

March 7, 1996

◆◆◆

SEVENTY-NINE

What Are the Alternatives to a Military Base?
Alma Bulawan and the Women of BUKLOD*

Presently, there are significant questions being raised about the continued existence of the U.S. bases here in our country. Many consultations are also being held in order to discuss these questions. At first glance, the primary problem and stumbling block would be the loss of work for the large numbers of Filipinos who work inside the base.

This issue is being seriously considered by the government and the large and strong sectors of the country. I wish to make known to everyone that there is one more sector that is in need of an alternative if the bases leave. This sector is the 9,000 women who work in the hospitality industry.[1] I am

here therefore because I want to pass on to everyone, and to you, the fact that there is a responsibility to make decisions about their serious needs. Please listen for a moment and consider what the women in this trade would like to have passed on.

Based on our questions and our knowledge as of now, one alternative to the U.S. bases is to make a free port at Olongapo City. We believe that this is not the answer to our situation and that, rather, the situation would become even worse. If many different ships came into port, there would simply be different kinds of customers—a situation that would induce many more women to work in the hospitality trade. This would add to the loss of suitable ways of caring for and control of foreigners who arrive.

One more alternative being considered is an industrial complex. This would mean that the women would work in factories. This is a possible answer to the situation if the regulations and conditions were just: for example, a proper salary, time away from the job for the different duties and responsibilities of women, benefits that respond to the situation of women, support for their needs in caring for their

---

*This statement, based on discussions with women in Olongapo, was written by Alma Bulawan, a staff member at BUKLOD and formerly a waitress in a club, to present at a consultation on alternatives to U.S. bases in the Philippines.

[1] The figure of 9,000 used here refers to registered women in Olongapo. Estimates of the number of registered and unregistered women together are around 16,000.

children and families, and the assurance that management would not make assessments according to high levels of education and experience. If this is not accomplished, nothing will change because the work in the factories will only lead to exasperation and frustration; and if the earnings are not sufficient, it is possible that the women will return to what they did before.

Our questioning indicated that if the government provided an alternative, a number of women would like to have some capital in order to start a small business. Perhaps this is one of several possible solutions to the problem and should be studied in detail. If so, there are additional considerations that need to be addressed: drawing from our limited experience, we know that many of the women who borrow even a small amount of capital are not able to repay it. There are at least three reasons for this: first, lack of business experience; second, lack of knowledge about the system of business dealings; and third, perhaps, a certain lack of responsibility. If there were capital available for business loans, proper training and experience would have to be provided as well. The training and experience should respond to the entirety of what is needed for the advancement of women. These are the following:

1. Consciousness raising so that the women may understand that it is not right to lose one's choice of livelihood and also feel forced to barter this valuable resource (sexual labor) in order just to eat and stay alive.

2. Training about the rights and responsibilities of women.

3. Focus on an understanding of reproductive health and other health training.

4. The importance of nationalism and self-reliance.

5. Education and training in business: being careful, orderly, and clean; saving for the future; and recognizing the importance of work and one's fellow human beings.

Equally as important as education and experience is the methodology of implementation. The methodology must be suitable to the progress of the women's consciousness.

Finally, and perhaps of greatest importance, is the eradication of society's low regard for the women who have been forced to work in the hospitality trade. We must all endeavor to accept them without exception and without doubt as valuable members of the country of the Philippines.

When all this has been accomplished, we will be able to say that there are genuine alternatives for our women in Olongapo.

EIGHTY

◆◆◆

Black Hills Survival Gathering, 1980

Linda Hogan

Bodies on fire
the monks in orange cloth
sing morning into light.

Men wake on the hill.
Dry grass blows from their hair.
B52's blow over their heads
leaving a cross on the ground.
Air returns to itself and silence.

Rainclouds are disappearing
with fractures of light in the distance.
Fierce gases forming,
the sky bending
where people arrive
on dusty roads that change
matter to energy.

My husband wakes.
My daughter wakes.
Quiet morning, she stands
in a pail of water
naked, reflecting light
and this man I love,
with kind hands
he washes her slim hips,
narrow shoulders, splashes
the skin containing
wind and fragile fire,
the pulse in her wrist.

My other daughter wakes
to comb warm sun across her hair.
While I make coffee I tell her
this is the land of her ancestors,
blood and heart.
Does her hair become a mane
blowing in the electric breeze,
her eyes dilate and darken?

The sun rises on all of them
in the center of light
hills that have no boundary,
the child named Thunder Horse,
the child named Dawn Protector

and the man
whose name would mean home in Navajo.

At ground zero
in the center of light we stand.
Bombs are buried beneath us,
destruction flies overhead.
We are waking
in the expanding light
the sulphur-colored grass.
A red horse standing on a distant ridge
looks like one burned
over Hiroshima,
silent, head hanging in sickness.
But look
she raises her head
and surges toward the bluing sky.

Radiant morning.
The dark tunnels inside us carry life.
Red.
Blue.
The children's dark hair against my breast.
On the burning hills
in flaring orange cloth
men are singing and drumming
Heartbeat.

EIGHTY-ONE

◆◆◆

Women's Budget

Women's International League for Peace and Freedom

The distribution of federal payments is heavily weighted toward military expenditures. Investments in programs that guarantee a social safety net for low-income people, fund vital local services, and enrich the infrastructure of the country are seriously underfunded. In addition to the kinds of investments listed below, the government could enhance women's economic potential through policies such as full employment, a guaranteed adequate annual income, an increase in the minimum wage, universal access to health care, and the guarantee of child care for all who need it.

High levels of military spending are particularly damaging to women's economic prospects because women are severely under-represented in the military and in military contractor jobs, and because military spending creates fewer jobs than civilian spending. When the government spends money in the military sector, spending on consumer goods, state and local governments, schools, health care, and day care lose out, all sectors that have high concentrations of women. One billion transferred from military spending to civilian investment would create a net gain of 6,800 jobs, which means that a $350 billion transfer from military to civilian spending would create over 2 millions jobs in five years.

Investments of $350 billion could be made in social investments over five years through military cuts. . . . Following are examples of investments that could be made:

Education   **$40 billion**
Increase funding for Head Start, Compensatory Education, Student Aid, enforcement of the Women's Educational Equity Act

Infrastructure   **$45 billion**
Increase spending for highways, bridges and airports, Mass Transit, Amtrak, Wastewater Collection and Treatment

Environment   **$20 billion**
Increase funding for Superfund cleanup, Municipal Solid Waste Program, Groundwater Protection, Forestry and Conservation, Renewable Energy and Energy Conservation

Housing   **$55 billion**
Increase investment in Public Housing and support services for the homeless

Income Support   **$60 billion**
Increase investment in Child Care, Aid to Families with Dependent Children (AFDC), Supplemental Security Income, Low-Income Energy Assistance, Unemployment Compensation

Health Care   **$50 billion**
Expand Medicaid, increase funding for Maternal and Child Health Block Grant, Community and Migrant Health Centers, the Family Planning Program, the Child Immunization Program, Office of Research on Women's Health

Nutrition   **$20 billion**
Expand the Women's, Infant's and Children's Program (WIC), the Older Americans Act Nutrition Programs, School Breakfast, Child Care, and Summer Food Programs, and Food Stamps

Employment & Training   **$25 billion**
Increase funding for the Economic Dislocation and Worker Act, Senior Community Services Employment Program, Occupational Safety and Health Administration (OSHA), the Wage and Hour Administration, and new initiatives to provide training targeted for low-income women

Special Women's Programs   **$15 billion**
Increase funding for Violence Against Women Act, Older Americans Act, Displaced Homemakers Self-sufficiency Act, transition programs and services for women entering the job market, the Women's Bureau

International Relations   **$20 billion**
Increase funding for U.S. development assistance for women, support goals of the Fourth World Conference on Women, pay debt to UN and increase contribution

Total Investments   **$350 billion**

Which Would You Choose?
The ballistic missile defense ("Star Wars") program ($91 billion) **OR** *Provide early education for 740,000 children under Head Start for 26 years?*

◆◆◆

Unity Statement

Women's Pentagon Action

We are gathering at the Pentagon on November 16 because we fear for our lives. We fear for the life of this planet, our Earth, and the life of the children who are our human future.

We are mostly women who come from the northeastern region of our United States. We are city women who know the wreckage and fear of city streets, we are country women who grieve the loss of the small farm and have lived on the poisoned earth. We are young and older, we are married, single, lesbian. We live in different kinds of households: In groups, families, alone, some are single parents.

We work at a variety of jobs. We are students, teachers, factory workers, office workers, lawyers, farmers, doctors, builders, waitresses, weavers, poets, engineers, homeworkers, electricians, artists, blacksmiths. We are all daughters and sisters.

We have come here to mourn and rage and defy the Pentagon because it is the workplace of the imperial power which threatens us all. Every day while we work, study, love, the colonels and generals who are planning our annihilation walk calmly in and out the doors of its five sides. They have accumulated over 30,000 nuclear bombs, at the rate of three to six bombs every day. They are determined to produce the billion-dollar MX missile. They are creating a technology called Stealth — the invisible, unperceivable arsenal. They have revised the cruel old killer, nerve gas. They have proclaimed Directive 59 which asks for 'small nuclear wars, prolonged but limited.' The Soviet Union works hard to keep up with the United States initiatives. We can destroy each other's cities, towns, schools and children many times over. The United States has sent 'advisors,' money and arms to El Salvador and Guatemala to enable those juntas to massacre their own people.

The very same men, the same legislative committees that offer trillions of dollars to the Pentagon have brutally cut day care, children's lunches, battered women's shelters. The same men have con-

cocted the Family Protection Act which will mandate the strictly patriarchal family and thrust federal authority into our home life. They are preventing the passage of ERA's simple statement and supporting the Human Life Amendment which will deprive all women of choice and many women of life itself.

We are in the hands of men whose power and wealth have separated them from the reality of daily life and from the imagination. We are right to be afraid.

At the same time our cities are in ruins, bankrupt; they suffer the devastation of war. Hospitals are closed, our schools deprived of books and teachers. Our Black and Latino youth are without decent work. They will be forced, drafted to become the cannon fodder for the very power that oppresses them. Whatever help the poor receive is cut or withdrawn to feed the Pentagon which needs about $500,000,000 a day for its murderous health. It extracted $157 billion dollars last year from our own tax money, $1,800 from a family of four.

With this wealth our scientists are corrupted; over 40% work in government and corporate laboratories that refine the methods for destroying or deforming life. The lands of the Native American people have been turned to radioactive rubble in order to enlarge the nuclear warehouse. The uranium of South Africa, necessary to the nuclear enterprise, enriches the white minority and encourages the vicious system of racist oppression and war.

The President has just decided to produce the neutron bomb, which kills people but leaves property (buildings like this one) intact. There is fear among the people, and that fear, created by the industrial militarists is used as an excuse to accelerate the arms race. 'We will protect you . . .' they say, but we have never been so endangered, so close to the end of human time.

We women are gathering because life on the precipice is intolerable. We want to know what anger in these men, what fear, which can only be satisfied by destruction, what coldness of heart and ambition drives their days. We want to know because we do

---

Statement from 1980.

not want that dominance which is exploitative and murderous in international relations, and so dangerous to women and children at home — we do not want that sickness transferred by the violent society through the fathers to the sons.

What is it that we women need for our ordinary lives, that we want for ourselves and also for our sisters in new nations and old colonies who suffer the white man's exploitation and too often the oppression of their own countrymen?

We want enough good food, decent housing, communities with clean air and water, good care for our children while we work. We want work that is useful to a sensible society. There is a modest technology to minimize drudgery and restore joy to labor. We are determined to use skills and knowledge from which we have been excluded — like plumbing or engineering or physics or composing. We intend to form women's groups or unions that will demand safe workplaces, free of sexual harassment, equal pay for work of comparable value. We respect the work women have done in caring for the young, their own and others, in maintaining a physical and spiritual shelter against the greedy and militaristic society. In our old age we expect our experience, our skills, to be honored and used.

We want health care which respects and understands our bodies. Physically challenged sisters must have access to gatherings, actions, happy events, work. For this, ramps must be added to stairs and we must become readers, signers, supporting arms. So close, so many, why have we allowed ourselves not to know them?

We want an education for children which tells the true story of our women's lives, which describes the earth as our home to be cherished, to be fed as well as harvested.

We want to be free from violence in our streets and in our houses. One in every three of us will be raped in her lifetime. The pervasive social power of the masculine ideal and the greed of the pornographer have come together to steal our freedom, so that whole neighborhoods and the life of the evening and night have been taken from us. For too many women the dark country road and the city alley have concealed the rapist. We want the night returned: the light of the moon, special in the cycle of our female lives, the stars and the gaiety of the city streets.

We want the right to have or not to have children — we do not want gangs of politicians and med-

ical men to say we must be sterilized for the country's good. We know that this technique is the racists' method for controlling populations. Nor do we want to be prevented from having an abortion when we need one. We think this freedom should be available to poor women as it always has been to the rich. We want to be free to love whomever we choose. We will live with women or with men or we will live alone. We will not allow the oppression of lesbians. One sex or one sexual preference must not dominate another.

We do not want to be drafted into the army. We do not want our young brothers drafted. We want *them* equal with us.

We want to see the pathology of racism ended in our time. It has been the imperial arrogance of white male power that has separated us from the suffering and wisdom of our sisters in Asia, Africa, South America and in our own country. Many North American women look down on the minority nearest them: the Black, the Hispanic, the Jew, the Native American, the Asian, the immigrant. Racism has offered them privilege and convenience; they often fail to see that they themselves have bent to the unnatural authority and violence of men in government, at work, at home. Privilege does not increase knowledge or spirit or understanding. There can be no peace while one race dominates another, one people, one nation, one sex despises another.

We must not forget the tens of thousands of American women who live much of their lives in cages, away from family, lovers, all the growing-up years of their children. Most of them were born at the intersection of oppressions: people of color, female, poor. Women on the outside have been taught to fear those sisters. We refuse that separation. We need each other's knowledge and anger in our common struggle against the builders of jails and bombs.

We want the uranium left in the earth and the earth given back to the people who tilled it. We want a system of energy which is renewable, which does not take resources out of the earth without returning them. We want those systems to belong to the people and their communities, not to the giant corporations which invariably turn knowledge into weaponry. We want the sham of Atoms for Peace ended, all nuclear plants decommissioned and the construction of new plants stopped. That is another war against the people and the child to be born in fifty years.

We want an end to the arms race. No more bombs. No more amazing inventions for death.

We understand all is connectedness. We know the life and work of animals and plants in seeding, reseeding and in fact simply inhabiting this planet. Their exploitation and the organized destruction of never to be seen again species threatens and sorrows us. The earth nourishes us as we with our bodies will eventually feed it. Through us, our mothers connected the human past to the human future.

With that sense, that ecological right, we oppose the financial connections between the Pentagon and the multinational corporations and banks that the Pentagon serves. Those connections are made of gold and oil. We are made of blood and bone, we are made of the sweet and finite resource, water. We will not allow these violent games to continue. If we are here in our stubborn thousands today, we will certainly return in the hundreds of thousands in the months and years to come.

We know there is a healthy, sensible, loving way to live and we intend to live that way in our neighborhoods and our farms in these United States, and among our sisters and brothers in all the countries of the world.

E I G H T Y - T H R E E

◆◆◆

Reflection After the June 12th March for Disarmament

Sonia Sanchez

I have come to you tonite out of the depths
   of slavery
   from white hands peeling black skins over
   America;
I have come out to you from reconstruction eyes
   that closed on black humanity
   that reduced black hope to the dark
   huts of America;
I have come to you from the lynching years —
   the exploitation of blk/men and women by
   a country that allowed the swinging of
   strange fruits from southern trees;
I have come to you tonite thru the
   Delaney years, the Du Bois years, the
   B. T. Washington years, the Robeson
   years, the Garvey years, the
   Depression years, the you can't eat
   or sit or live just die here years,
   the Civil rights years, the black power
   years, the blk Nationalist years, the
   Affirmative Action years, the liberal
   years, the Neo-conservative years;

I have come to say that those years
   were not in vain — the ghosts of our
   ancestors searching this american dust for
rest were not in vain — black women
walking their lives in clots were not
in vain — the years walked
sideways in a forsaken land were not
in vain;
I have come to you tonite as an equal,
   as a comrade, as a Black woman
   walking down a corridor of tears,
   looking neither to the left or the right,
   pulling my history with bruised
   heels,
   beckoning to the illusion of America,
   daring you to look me in the eyes to
   see these faces — the exploitation of a
   people because of skin pigmentation;
I have come to you tonite because no people
   have been asked to be modern day people
   with the history of slavery, and still
   we walk — and still we talk — and
   still we plan — and still we hope and
   still we sing;
I have come to you tonite because there are
   inhumanitarians in the world. They are not
   new. They are old. They go back into history.
   They were called explorers, soldiers, mercenaries,
   imperialists, missionaries, adventurers —

but they looked at the world for what
it would give up to them and they violated
the land and the people, they looked
at the land and sectioned it up for
private ownership, they looked at the
people and decided how to manipulate
them thru fear and ignorance, they looked
at the gold and began to hoard and
worship it;
I have come to you because it is time
for us all to purge capitalism from
our dreams, to purge materialism
from our eyes, from the planet earth
to deliver the earth again into the hands
of the humanitarians;
I have come to you tonite not just for the stoppage
of nuclear proliferation — nuclear
plants — nuclear bombs — nuclear
waste — but to stop the proliferation
of nuclear minds, of nuclear generals,
of nuclear presidents, of nuclear scientists, who
spread human
and nuclear waste over the world;
I come to you because the world needs to be
saved for the future generations who must
return the earth to peace — who will not
be startled by a man's/a woman's skin
color;

I come to you because the world needs sanity
now, needs men and women who will
not work to produce nuclear weapons,
who will give up their need for excess
wealth and learn how to share the
world's resources, who will never
again as scientists invent again just

for the sake of inventing;
I come to you because we need to turn our
eyes to the beauty of this planet, to the
bright green laughter of trees, to the beautiful
human animals waiting to smile their
unprostituted
smiles;
I have come to you to talk about our inexperience
at living as human beings — thru death marches
and camps,
thru middle passages and slavery
and thundering countries raining hungry faces;
I am here to move against
leaving our shadows implanted on the
earth while our bodies disintegrate in
nuclear lightning;
I am here because our scientists must
be stripped of their imperialist dreams;
I am here between the voices of our ancestors
and the noise of the planet,
between the surprise of death and life;
I am here because I shall not give the
earth up to non-dreamers and earth molesters;
I am here to say to YOU:

My body is full of veins
like the bombs waiting to burst
with blood.
We must learn to suckle life not
bombs and rhetoric
rising up in redwhiteandblue patriotism;
I am here. And my breath/our breaths
must thunder across this land
arousing new breaths. New life.
New people, who will live in peace
and honor.

◆◆

CHAPTER TEN

Women and the Environment

In the past twenty-five years many people in the United States have become increasingly concerned with environmental issues. Hazardous industrial production processes have affected the health of workers and people who live near, or downwind, of industrial areas. Industrial pollutants, chemical pesticides and fertilizers, and wastes from nuclear power plants and uranium mines are seeping into the groundwater in many parts of the country. Homes and schools have been built on land once used for toxic dumps. Deforestation, global warming, and the disappearance of hundreds of species are also hallmarks of vast environmental destruction worldwide. In the United States, legislation has been introduced to reduce pollution and to preserve wilderness areas and the habitats of endangered species; recycling has become more commonplace; "Green," or environmentally safe, products, such as paper goods made from recycled paper or biodegradable soaps and detergents, are increasingly available. Given the enormous scale of the environmental crisis, however, these are small steps that do not begin to touch the heart of the problem, though as we discuss below, there are many views as to what the heart of the problem is. United States environmental activists probably agree, however, that the greatest threat to environmental security worldwide comes from the waste-producing, industrialized, militarized economies of the North, especially North America, Europe, and Japan.

In the United States the environmental crisis affects men as well as women, of course, but in terms of environmental health, women and children show the effects of toxic pollution earlier than men do, either because of low body weight, or because women's bodies become what some have termed "unhealthy environments" for their babies (Nelson 1990). A significant number of babies without brains have been born to women on both sides of the Rio Grande, a river polluted by U.S.-controlled maquiladora industries on the Mexican side. (Working conditions in these maquiladoras, or subassembly plants, are described in more detail in Chapter 5.) Contact with pesticides has led to poor health for many women farmworkers in the United States and to chronic illnesses or severe disabilities for their children. Several firms have tried to keep women of child-bearing age out of the most noxious production processes — often the highest paid — or to insist that they be sterilized, lest women sue them later for fetal damage (Chavkin 1984). Children's health in the United States is also compromised by environmental factors such as lead in paints and gasoline, air pollution, traffic hazards, and violence that often involves the use of handguns, with significant differences between those living in inner cities and those in suburban neighborhoods (Hamilton 1993; Phoenix 1993). The Akwesasne Mothers' Milk project in upstate New York, founded by Katsi Cook and described in Reading 87, is a Native American research project that was started in response to women's concern that their breastmilk might be toxic, and that breast-feeding, supposedly the best way to nurture infants, could expose them to pollutants from the very beginning.

Many more women than men are involved in campaigning on behalf of environmental issues at a grassroots level. We do not see women as somehow closer to nature than men, as is sometimes argued, or as having an essentially nurturing, caring nature. Rather, we see women's environmental activism as an extension of their roles as daughters, wives, and mothers, caring for families and communities. Because of the gendered division of labor between home and work, women have a long-standing history of involvement in community organizing: campaigning against poor housing conditions, high rents, unsafe streets, lead in gasoline, toxic dumps, and so on. Ideally, taking care of children and other family members should be everyone's responsibility, as we argue in Chapter 4. We see organizing around environmental issues as part of this responsibility.

Theoretical and Activist Perspectives

Many theories grow out of and inform experience. Women who are concerned about environmental degradation mainly draw on three different theoretical and activist perspectives: deep ecology, ecofeminism, and environmental justice. These are not unitary perspectives, though here we emphasize points of comparison between them rather than their internal variations.

Deep Ecology

Deep ecology is a term coined by Norwegian philosopher Arne Naess and taken up in the United States by Devall and Sessions (1985). It is premised on two fundamental principles: self-realization for every being and a "biocentric" equality among species. Many environmental activists in the United States who are drawn to deep ecology are critical of more mainstream environmental organizations that focus on lobbying and legislation to improve air and water quality or to protect wilderness areas and endangered species. Though these efforts have contributed to growing public concern about environmental degradation, they are slow; they are cast in human-centered terms and invariably compromised by corporate interests. Earth First! is an activist network that exemplifies principles of deep ecology in practice. It has gained public recognition through direct action, particularly in opposition to the logging of old growth forests in the Pacific Northwest and northern California (Davis 1991; List 1993).

At its worst, deep ecology is sometimes reduced to a rather simplistic view of the world in which nature is "good" and people are "bad." Deep ecologists argue for reducing human population, reducing human interference in the biosphere, and reducing human standards of living. As its name implies, Earth First! is more interested in saving the earth than in safeguarding the human population. This has led to arguments that, for example, if AIDS didn't exist it would have had to be invented, or that starving people in Africa should be left to die so that the human population can be brought back into balance with the carrying capacity of the land (Thropy 1991). Deep ecologists value the preservation of nature in and of itself rather than for any benefit such preservation affords to humans. Nature is often seen in terms of romance: the virgin, feminized wilderness is vulnerable, innocent, and weak, and protecting "her" draws on old macho, militaristic iconography (King 1987). Wilderness is not thought of as the homeland of indigenous people but as a special place where people (at least athletic, nondisabled people, usually male) can get close to an "experience" of nature. Critics of U.S. deep ecology oppose its people vs. nature stance and argue that nature is not something far away, to be encountered on weekend hikes or occasional camping trips. Everyone is connected to nature in the most mundane but profound way: through the air we breathe, the water we drink, and the food we eat, as embodied human beings in a continuum of life.

The biocentric view also prevails within the largely White bioregional movement, which emphasizes decentralization, agricultural and economic self-sufficiency within bioregions, and a strongly developed attachment to place (Andruss, Plant, C., Plant, J., and Mills 1990; Berg 1993; Sale 1985). Many ecofeminists and environmental justice activists are critical of this strand of bioregionalism. It does not analyze the structures of dominance among people in capitalist, patriarchal societies. It does not appear to be specifically committed to women's liberation or to opposing racism and has no principles for dealing with social and economic inequality within a bioregion. There is the assumption that decentralized, small-scale, regional structures and a shift from a human-centered to a biocentered perspective will solve all problems. Without an explicit social ethics this seems highly unlikely.

Ecofeminism

The term **ecofeminism** was first used by a group of French feminists who founded the Ecology-Feminism Center in 1974, and was based on their analysis of connections between masculinist social institutions and the destruction of the physical environment (d'Eaubonne 1994). A few years later groundbreaking work in the United States by Susan Griffin (1978) and Carolyn Merchant (1980) also put forward a central insight of ecofeminism, the connection between the domination of women and the domination of nature. These authors pointed to the ways in which Western thought and science from the time of Francis Bacon has seen nonhuman nature as wild and hostile, so much matter to be mastered and used:

> For you have to but follow and . . . hound nature in her wanderings, and you will be able when you like to lead and drive her afterward to the same place again. . . . Neither ought a man make scruple of entering and penetrating into these holes and corners, when the inquisition of truth is his whole object.
>
> *(Quoted in Merchant, 1980, p. 168)*

In Western thought nature is often feminized and sexualized through imagery such as "virgin forest," "the rape of the earth," and "penetrating" the wilderness. Vandana Shiva (1988) notes that in the Western model of development sources, living things that can reproduce life — whether forests, seeds, or women's bodies — are turned into resources to be objectified, controlled, and used. This makes them productive in economic terms. In this view, a forest that is not logged, a river that is not fished, or a hillside that is not mined, is unproductive (Waring 1988). A core point in ecofeminist analysis involves the concept of dualism, where various attributes are thought of

in terms of oppositions: culture/nature; mind/body; male/female; civilized/primitive; sacred/profane; subject/object; self/other. Val Plumwood (1993) argues that these dualisms are mutually reinforcing and should be thought of as an interlocking set. In each pair, one side is valued over the other. Culture, mind, male, civilized, for example, are valued over nature, body, female, primitive, which are thought of as "other" and inferior. Plumwood argues that dualism is the logic of hierarchical systems of thought — colonialism, racism, sexism, or militarism, for example, which rely on the idea of otherness, enemies, and inferiority to justify superiority and domination. Ecofeminism links concerns with racism and economic exploitation to the domination of women and nature.

Such a broad approach is open to many interpretations and ideas for activism. The first ecofeminist conference in the United States, entitled "Women for Life on Earth," was held in Amherst, Massachusetts as a response to the near-meltdown at the Three Mile Island nuclear power plant in 1980. One outcome of the conference was the Women's Pentagon Action, a major demonstration against militarism in the early 1980s, discussed in more detail in Chapter 9. Currently, ecofeminism is explored and developed through newsletters and study groups, college courses, animal rights organizing, and long-term women's land projects. Some ecofeminist writers and researchers work with local activist groups or contribute to national and international debates. Significant examples include the National Women's Health Network's research and organizing around industrial and environmental health (Nelson 1990), critiques of reproductive technology and genetic engineering by the Feminist Network of Resistance to Reproductive and Genetic Engineering (Mies and Shiva 1993), and the Committee on Women, Population, and the Environment, which critiques simplistic overpopulation arguments that focus only on countries of the South rather than also addressing the overconsumption of the North (Hartmann 1995; Mello 1996). Women's Environment and Development Organization coordinated a major international conference in 1991 to work out a women's agenda (Agenda 21) to take to the U.N. Conference on the Environment and Development in Rio de Janeiro in June 1992. This group also was an active participant in the NGO Forum in China in 1995, as we noted in Chapter 5.

Charlene Spretnak (1990) embraces the eclectic nature of U.S. ecofeminism and notes its varied roots in feminist theory, feminist spirituality, and social ecology. This diversity in ecofeminist approaches raises the question of whether there is a sufficiently consistent, intellectually coherent ecofeminist perspective, and many academics claim that there is not. Some women of color argue that, as with U.S. feminism in general, ecofeminism emphasizes gender over race and class; others argue that it focuses on abstract ideas about women and nature rather than on practical issues with a material base. Left-wing radicals, some environmentalists, and many academics reject ecofeminism as synonymous with goddess worship, or on the grounds that it assumes women are essentially closer to nature than men. Joni Seager (1993), for example, develops a feminist understanding of environmental issues but does not use the term *ecofeminism* to describe her work. We argue that an ecological feminism can, and should, integrate gender, race, class, and nation in its analyses and that its powerful theoretical insights can, and should, translate into activism. At present U.S. ecofeminism is very much the preserve of writers and scholars, albeit those who are often on the margins of the academy in part-time or temporary positions. Although this may lead to an activism of scholarship — by no means insignificant, as suggested above — it does not often connect directly with the reality of life for many women organizing around environmental issues.

Environmental Justice

The people most affected by poor physical environments in the United States are women and children, particularly women and children of color. Many women of color and poor White women are active in hundreds of local organizations campaigning for healthy living and working conditions in working-class communities, communities of color, and on Native American land, which are all disproportionately affected by pollution from incinerators, toxic dumps, pesticides, and hazardous working conditions in industry and agriculture (Bullard 1990; Bullard 1993; Hofrichter 1993; Szasz 1994). Data

show a strong correlation between the distribution of toxic wastes and race, which has been termed **environmental racism** (Lee 1987). The theory of environmental racism and the movement for **environmental justice** draw on concepts of civil rights, under which all citizens have a right to healthy living and working conditions. Organizationally, too, the environmental justice movement has roots in civil rights organizing, as well as in labor unions, Chicano land-grant movements, social justice organizations, and Native American rights organizations. Its tactics include demonstrations and rallies, public education, research and monitoring of toxic sites, preparing and presenting expert testimony to government agencies, reclaiming land through direct action, and maintaining and teaching traditional agricultural practices, crafts, and skills. Examples of local organizations include West Harlem Environmental Action (New York), the Center for Third World Organizing (Oakland, California), and the Southwest Organizing Project (Albuquerque, New Mexico). Local organizations embrace different issues depending on their memberships and geographical locations. Some are primarily concerned to stop the location of toxic waste dumps or incinerators in their neighborhoods, an approach sometimes dubbed the Not-In-My-Back-Yard (NIMBY) syndrome. Most groups are quick to see that it is not enough to keep hazards out of their own neighborhoods if this means that dumps or incinerators will then be located in other poor communities. This has led to coordinated opposition on a local and regional level. Examples of this environmental justice perspective and the work of such organizations are described by Bouapha Toommaly (Reading 86), Mililani Trask (Reading 88), and Mary Pardo (Reading 89).

Besides opposing hazardous conditions, the environmental justice movement also has a powerful reconstructive dimension involving sustainable projects that intertwine ecological, economic, and cultural survival. Examples include Tierra Wools (northern New Mexico) where a workers' cooperative produces high-quality, handwoven rugs and clothing and organically fed lamb from its sheep (Pulido 1993); the Native American White Earth Land Recovery Project in Minnesota, which produces wild rice, maple sugar, berries, and birch bark (LaDuke 1993); and many inner-city community gardening projects producing vegetables for local consumption (Hynes 1996; Warner 1987).

Although very few local environmental issues are exclusively the concern of women, women form the majority of local activists in opposing such hazards as toxic dumps. As noted, women have a history of community organizing. This activism may also be given special impetus if they have sick children or become ill themselves. Illnesses caused by toxics are sometimes difficult to diagnose and treat because they affect internal organs and the balance of body functioning, and symptoms can be mistaken for those of other conditions. Women have been persistent in raising questions and searching for plausible explanations for such illnesses, sometimes discovering that their communities have been built on contaminated land, as happened at Love Canal, New York, for example, or tracing probable sources of pollution affecting their neighborhoods (Gibbs 1995). They have publicized their findings and taken on governmental agencies and corporations responsible for contamination. In so doing they are often ridiculed as "hysterical housewives" by officials and reporters and their research trivialized as emotional and unscholarly. By contrast, others — Nelson (1990), for example — honor this work as kitchen table science. In October 1991 women were 60 percent of the participants at the First National People of Color Environmental Leadership Summit in Washington, D.C. The conference adopted a statement called "Principles of Environmental Justice," included here as Reading 85. Many urban gardeners in northern cities are elderly African-American women like Rachel Bagby, whose work is described in Reading 92. In rural areas women work on family subsistence garden plots, planting, harvesting, and processing fruits and vegetables for home use. Some know the woods or backcountry areas in great detail, as ethnobotanists, because they go there at different seasons to gather herbs for medicinal purposes. Among Mexican-Americans, for example, *curanderas* — traditional healers — continue to work with herbal remedies and acquire their knowledge from older women relatives (Perrone 1989).

In 1989 the Citizens' Clearinghouse for Hazardous Wastes organized a conference to address women's experiences as environmental activists (Zeff, Love, and Stults 1989). Excerpts from the conference report are included in Reading 90. When women become involved with environmental justice organizing, they are suddenly caught up in meetings, maybe traveling to other towns and cities and staying away overnight. They spend much more time, and money, on the phone than before. They are quoted in the local papers or on the TV news. They often face new challenges, balancing family responsibilities, perhaps struggling with their husbands' misgivings about their involvement, or facing the tensions of being strong women in male-dominated communities. Women activists see their identity as women integrated with their racial and class identities, with race and/or class often more a place of empowerment for them than gender. While recognizing gender subordination, they are not interested in separating themselves from the men in their communities and frame their perspectives, as women, in class- and race-conscious ways.

Connectedness and Sustainability

Underlying and implicit in these various perspectives are ideas of connectedness, relationship, respect, and responsibility: among people, nonhuman species, and the natural world. The activists mentioned in this chapter all work from their sense of relationship and responsibility to maintain these connections, or to remake them where they have been severed. Together such projects and movements draw on alternative visions and strategies for sustainable living, however small-scale and fragile they might be at present. At root this is about taking on the current economic system and the systems of power — personal and institutional — that sustain and benefit from it, working to transform relationships of exploitation and oppression.

The idea of sustainability is often invoked but means very different things to different people. For corporate economists, for example, it means sustained economic growth that will yield sustained profits; for ecologists it involves the maintenance of natural systems — wetlands, forests, wilderness, air and water quality; for environmentalists it means using only renewable resources and generating low, or nonaccumulating levels of pollution (Pearce, Markandya, and Barbier 1990). Many concerned with environmental economics note the contradiction between the linear expansionism of current capitalist economies and long-term sustainability (Henderson 1991; O'Connor 1994). Maria Mies (1993) notes that for countries of the South to follow the development model of the industrial North there would need to be two more worlds: one for the necessary natural resources and the other for the waste. A more sustainable future for both North and South means rethinking current economic systems and priorities and emphasizing ecologically sound production to meet people's basic needs. It implies local control over transnational corporations, reduction of poor countries' foreign debt, and making money available for development that is ecologically sound, as we suggested in Chapter 5. At a local level in the United States it implies support for community gardens, farmers' markets, credit unions, and small-scale worker-owned businesses and markets, as we suggested in Chapter 6. It means valuing women's unpaid domestic and caring work, a key aspect of sustaining home and community life (Mellor 1992; Waring 1988). Mellor notes that this work is geared to biological time. Children need feeding when they are hungry; sick people need care regardless of what time of day it is; gardens need planting in the right season. She argues that, given a gendered division of labor, "women's responsibility for biological time means that men have been able to create a public world that largely ignores it," a world "no longer rooted in the physical reality of human existence" (pp. 258–59). A sustainable future must be based in biological time and will require emotional as well as physical and intellectual labor.

To create such a future will also mean changing current definitions of wealth that emphasize materialism and consumerism. A broader notion of wealth includes everything that has the potential to enrich a person and a community, such as health, physical energy and strength, safety and security, time, skills, talents, wisdom, creativity, love, community support, a connection to one's history and cultural heritage, and a sense of belonging. This is not a philosophy of denial or a romanticization of poverty, though it does involve a fundamental **paradigm shift,** or change of perspective, in a country—indeed, a world—so dominated by the allure of material wealth. Writers included in this chapter all implicitly or explicitly argue for a profound change in attitudes, in which human life and the life of the natural world are valued, cared for, and sustained.

Reading 91 by Maria Mies and Reading 92 by Rachel Bagby give examples.

As you read and discuss this chapter, ask yourself these questions:

1. How familiar are you with the place you live now? What kinds of things do you know about it? What would you like to know? How can you find out?

2. Is there a farmers' market in your area?

3. Are there community gardens in your area?

4. Where does your waste food go? Do you have access to a compost pile or worm box?

5. What are the main environmental issues in your area?

6. What are the main environmental organizations in your area?

7. What do you know about the culture of the Native people who live, or lived, where you live now?

8. What are the main illnesses in your area? Are they linked to environmental causes?

9. Have you been involved in a "subsistence project" in the sense that Maria Mies uses this term? How successful was it? Why/why not?

10. How does thinking holistically, rather than dualistically, change one's perceptions and actions?

11. Do you consider yourself a "conscious" consumer? What kinds of factors do you take into account before buying things?

12. How can you do some of the things you want to do at a lower cost? How can you use less energy or other resources? Less time?

13. Think about the practical projects mentioned in the readings for this chapter. What resources were used by the people involved? What worldviews are implicit in their actions?

14. What is your vision of a sustainable future?

◆◆◆

EIGHTY-FOUR

Where You At?
A Bioregional Quiz

Leonard Charles, Jim Dodge, Lynn Milliman, and Victoria Stockley

What follows is a self-scoring test on basic environmental perception of place. Scoring is done on the honor system, so if you fudge, cheat, or elude, you also get an idea of where you're at. The quiz is culture-bound, favoring those people who live in the country over city dwellers, and scores can be adjusted accordingly.

1. Trace the water you drink from precipitation to tap.

2. How many days till the moon is full? (Slack of two days allowed.)

3. What soil series are you standing on?

4. What was the total rainfall in your area last year (July-June)? (Slack: 1 inch for every 20 inches.)

5. When was the last time a fire burned your area?

6. What were the primary subsistence techniques of the culture that lived in your area before you?

7. Name five native edible plants in your region and their season(s) of availability.

8. From what direction do winter storms generally come in your region?

9. Where does your garbage go?

10. How long is the growing season where you live?

11. On what day of the year are the shadows the shortest where you live?

12. When do the deer rut in your region, and when are the young born?

13. Name five grasses in your area. Are any of them native?

14. Name five resident and five migratory birds in your area.

15. What is the land use history of where you live?

16. What primary ecological event/process influenced the land form where you live? (Bonus special: what's the evidence?)

17. What species have become extinct in your area?

18. What are the major plant associations in your region?

19. From where you're reading this, point north.

20. What spring wildflower is consistently among the first to bloom where you live?

◆◆◆

Principles of Environmental Justice

The First National People of Color Environmental Leadership Summit

October 24–27, 1991
Washington, D.C.

Preamble

We, the people of color, gathered together at this multinational People of Color Environmental Leadership Summit, to begin to build a national and international movement of all peoples of color to fight the destruction and taking of our lands and communities, do hereby re-establish our spiritual interdependence to the sacredness of our Mother Earth; to respect and celebrate each of our cultures, languages and beliefs about the natural world and our roles in healing ourselves; to insure environmental justice; to promote economic alternatives which would contribute to the development of environmentally safe livelihoods; and, to secure our political, economic and cultural liberation that has been denied for over 500 years of colonization and oppression, resulting in the poisoning of our communities and land and the genocide of our peoples, do affirm and adopt these Principles of Environmental Justice:

1. *Environmental justice* affirms the sacredness of Mother Earth, ecological unity and the interdependence of all species, and the right to be free from ecological destruction.

2. *Environmental justice* demands that public policy be based on mutual respect and justice for all peoples, free from any form of discrimination or bias.

3. *Environmental justice* mandates the right to ethical, balanced and responsible uses of land and renewable resources in the interest of a sustainable planet for humans and other living things.

4. *Environmental justice* calls for universal protection from nuclear testing, extraction, pro

duction and disposal of toxic/hazardous wastes and poisons and nuclear testing that threaten the fundamental right to clean air, land, water, and food.

5. *Environmental justice* affirms the fundamental right to political, economic, cultural and environmental self-determination of all peoples.

6. *Environmental justice* demands the cessation of the production of all toxins, hazardous wastes, and radioactive materials, and that all past and current producers be held strictly accountable to the people for detoxification and the containment at the point of production.

7. *Environmental justice* demands the right to participate as equal partners at every level of decision-making including needs assessment, planning, implementation, enforcement and evaluation.

8. *Environmental justice* affirms the right of all workers to a safe and healthy work environment, without being forced to choose between an unsafe livelihood and unemployment. It also affirms the right of those who work at home to be free from environmental hazards.

9. *Environmental justice* protects the right of victims of environmental injustice to receive full compensation and reparations for damages as well as quality health care.

10. *Environmental justice* considers governmental acts of environmental injustice a violation of international law, the Universal Declaration On Human Rights, and the United Nations Convention on Genocide.

11. *Environmental justice* must recognize a special legal and natural relationship of Native Peoples to the U.S. government

through treaties, agreements, compacts, and covenants affirming sovereignty and self-determination.

12. *Environmental justice* affirms the need for urban and rural ecological policies to clean up and rebuild our cities and rural areas in balance with nature, honoring the cultural integrity of all our communities, and providing fair access for all to the full range of resources.

13. *Environmental justice* calls for the strict enforcement of principles of informed consent, and a halt to the testing of experimental reproductive and medical procedures and vaccinations on people of color.

14. *Environmental justice* opposes the destructive operations of multi-national corporations.

15. *Environmental justice* opposes military occupation, repression and exploitation of lands, peoples and cultures, and other life forms.

16. *Environmental justice* calls for the education of present and future generations which emphasizes social and environmental issues, based on our experience and an appreciation of our diverse cultural perspectives.

17. *Environmental justice* requires that we, as individuals, make personal and consumer choices to consume as little of Mother Earth's resources and to produce as little waste as possible; and make the conscious decision to challenge and reprioritize our lifestyles to insure the health of the natural world for present and future generations.

Adopted, October 27, 1991
The First National People of Color
    Environmental Leadership Summit
Washington, D.C.

E I G H T Y - S I X

◆◆◆

Asians and Pacific Islanders in the Environment

Bouapha Toommaly

My name is Bouapha Toommaly. I am from one of the Laotian tribal groups called Khmmu. We are considered the indigenous people of Laos. In fact, when we talk in the Khmmu language about Native Americans we call them the Khmmu of America.

We have had a hard time moving from the hills of Laos to Richmond. One day our folks were farmers and hunters — just like their ancestors — and the next day we were fighting a war for the United States, running into Thai refugee camps, and then taking a jet plane to the U.S.

As our people moved into many parts of the U.S. they heard through the grapevine about Richmond's weather. They heard about the jobs, and they moved because grandma and grandpa were already living here — the last reason is why my family moved from San Francisco to the East Bay. It is important for us to be near our extended family because Laotians are used to living in small villages.

I thought that this situation was unique to my family. Then I learned that across many urban areas around the country, Southeast Asian refugees have settled in the poorest and most environmentally sick areas of their cities and they suffer alongside their African American and Latino neighbors. I don't think this stuff happened by chance.

We are overlooked because of our small numbers and because we don't speak English. Don't overlook us, we have lived off of the land for hundreds of years. We know some things about taking care of the land. To this day Laotian women still like to grow their own vegetables in their small yards and men in our community still go fishing in our toxic bay to put food on the table. Richmond should be clean enough so we can continue to think of the land and water as good things, not poisonous things.

I think we have a special role as indigenous people to teach people to respect the land, air, and water so that no matter where we live we can be healthy and happy.

◆◆◆

EIGHTY-SEVEN

Breastmilk, PCBs and Motherhood
An Interview with Katsi Cook, Mohawk
Winona LaDuke

About fifteen years back, Katsi Cook, a Mohawk woman had a dream she couldn't forget. Katsi (pronounced "Gudgi") dreamt she was swimming in the St. Lawrence River. The river, which she had known all her life, has always been central to the Mohawk people. For generations, the Mohawks have relied on the river for fish, food and transportation. But, today, they are often warned not to fish or harvest at all. The river is now full of poisons.

"As I swam, I felt myself making a promise to the river and to myself as a mother, to do what I could to help clean this wonderful waterway that means so much to our Indian people," she said. "I did not know then how exactly I might help in this work, but I knew I would do something." Katsi has worked to fulfill her dream by initiating several projects — work which carefully nourishes the link between women, the environment and the river, and work which summons strength to advocate on behalf of each.

In Canadian terms, the Akwesasne Mohawk reservation has been singled out from 63 Native communities located in the Great Lakes Basin as the most contaminated. A dubious honor. On the American side things aren't much better. A General Motors Plant (the GM-Massena Central Foundry) may prove to be the biggest PCB dump site yet uncovered. The insidious chemical is known to cause brain, nerve, liver, and skin disorders in humans and cancer and reproductive disorders in laboratory animals. Five PCB saturated lagoons and a number of sludge pits dot GM's 258 acre property, adjacent to the reserve. In 1983, the General Motors site was placed on the national priorities list of the EPA (the list of the most hazardous waste sites in the US, called the "Superfund List"), and was fined $500,000 for violation of federal environmental laws.

All of this is little consolation to the Mohawk People who live down stream and downwind from the GM site. A place called "Containment Cove" (the conflux of the Grass River and the St. Lawrence) seems to be the hotbed of contamination. Put it this way: 50 parts per million of PCBs in the soil is considered to be hazardous waste. Sludge and vegetation at the bottom of "Containment Cove" showed up at 3000 parts per million, and a snapping turtle was found with 3067 parts per million of PCB contamination. It's no wonder the Mohawks are concerned.

Elizabeth Herne Cook, Katsi's grandmother, delivered many of the children in the community. Following in her footsteps, Katsi is a trained midwife. "My concern grew when women I was encouraging to breastfeed, began to fear that their breastmilk might be contaminated," Katsi explained. "The fact is, **that women are the first environment.** We accumulate toxic chemicals like PCBs, DDT, mirex, HCBs, et cetera, dumped into the waters by various industries. They are stored in our bodyfat and are excreted primarily through breastmilk. What that means, is that through our own breastmilk, our sacred natural link to our babies, they stand the chance of getting concentrated dosages. We were flabbergasted."

Katsi, and a group of women banded together to form the Akwesasne Mothers Milk Project. After a series of organizing meetings, and beginning to understand the scope of the challenge they were facing, the women decided to seek scientific help. In the fall of 1984, the search for answers led to the offices of wildlife pathologist Ward Stone at the New York State Department of Environmental Conservation and to the Chemist Brian Bush's laboratory at the Wadsworth Center for Labs and Research at the New York State Department of Health. The cooperation resulting from these meetings led to a full investigation of the food chain at Akwesasne; including: fish, wildlife, and human breastmilk. The Women and scientists together wrote a proposal to the National Institute of Environmental Health Sciences and the Center for Disease Control. The proposal was selected as one of eleven Superfund Studies funded by Congress, and is the only project dealing with human health. The Akwesasne Mother's Milk Project was founded on the idea that Native Women "ourselves, would be organizers, participants and investigators, not merely research projects."

The Breastmilk Study

There are around fifty Mohawk women who participate in the study each year, or about a third of the new mothers each year on the reservation. Each woman was identified through the network established by the Mother's Milk project. The mothers were contacted about two to four weeks after giving birth, and were asked to complete a questionnaire concerning fish consumption and other dietary habits. A so-called "control group" of approximately the same number of women from elsewhere in rural New York was also studied for comparison. Each of the women provided breastmilk samples.

And, using some highly sophisticated scientific techniques, the researchers involved are capable of breaking down the chemicals in the breastmilk to up to sixty-nine separate PCB compounds, called "cogeners." These are something like a PCB fingerprint which can help trace which PCBs from the GM plant site have made their way through the environment and into the Mohawk women's breastmilk. Everything is done very carefully to secure the best possible data. Another set of data is now being collected from umbilical cord blood and urine samples. All told, the draft report is due this fall, and will cover 168 breastmilk, cord blood, and urine samples.

What will they find? It is likely that the Mohawk women will have some elevated levels of PCB con-

tamination in their breastmilk. "I've got myself .108 parts per billion (ppb) of mirex (a flame retardant), 22 ppb of PCBs, .013 ppb of HCBs and 13.947 ppb of DDE (a pesticide related to DDT) in my breastmilk," Katsi says, acknowledging the concern. "This report however is going to the women first, it is their right, and they are the ones who are in control of the study, and of their bodies."

There is no question that elevated levels of PCB contamination can harm humans. Two large "poisonings" of PCBs occurred in Japan (1968) and Taiwan (1979), when PCB contaminated cooking oil was consumed by local people. Signs of PCB toxicity, as noted in studies on these poisonings included newborns with low birth weights, pigmentation of gums, nails, noses, and other concerns. (The babies born to women who had consumed the contaminated oil were called "cocoa colored babies" because of the pigmentation.) A rash was highly prevalent in the breastfed children. There has been however, no study of the impact of low-level contamination. That is part of why this study is so important. It is also important for a number of other reasons.

"Some scientists are saying that our women shouldn't breastfeed; I disagree," Katsi says emphatically. "Virtually every woman on the planet carries a body burden of PCBs and other toxics in her breastmilk. It is a potentially alarming issue coming at a time when at a community level, we are doing everything we can to get mothers to breastfeed again. For their health, and the health of their children. Besides," Katsi adds, "if that argument gets carried any further, it says 'we might as well tell them to stop having babies,' and from an Indian point of view, that's totally unacceptable."

Breastfeeding is a natural continuation of the relationship between mother and baby during pregnancy, labor, and birth. This is the most traditional and natural form of infant nutrition, and is without question "best for baby." Dr. Allan Cunningham, Associate in Clinical Pediatrics at Columbia University reports that based on observations (of a non-Indian control population), "I would expect seventy-seven hospital admissions for illness during the first four months of life for every 1000 bottle fed infants. A comparable figure for breastfed infants is five hospital admissions."

As the Mother's Milk Project explains in their literature, "A decline in the practice of breastfeeding in Native American communities is one of the most serious nutritional problems of the Indian people. Babies raised on substitutes to mother's milk risk digestive problems, allergies, and have an increased risk for developing diseases in adulthood such as obesity, and diabetes. Mothers who do not nurse their infants at all, . . . risk another pregnancy, and a short birth interval . . . In a community with poor water quality, a very high unemployment rate, and a poor economic status, bottle feeding may be an invitation to tragedy. It is also a great deal more expensive."

Instead, Katsi and the other women involved in the project continue to counsel women to breast-feed. "The benefits still offset the risks, by far," she says, explaining, and indeed, there has been some controversy over this. The very thought that breast-milk might be contaminated causes serious anxiety and psychological problems in many breastfeeding women. The only study done on the social problems caused the victims (PCB contaminated women in Michigan — 1973) found that 61% of those sampled felt guilt and feared they had harmed their child's normal growth and development. Most felt inadequate, and had lower self esteem. (On the other hand, some women responded positively, they breastfed even more, hoping that the natural immunities encouraged by breastmilk would help their babies out.) Overall, what is clear to women like Katsi, is that the social and psychological impacts, are underestimated, and need to be carefully deliberated in any discussion. Lower self esteem, and a loss of confidence can be easily transformed into less breast-feeding, and without question, that loss of both the physical, and the psychological bonding, poses a risk to babies.

First Environment

The agenda of the project is not just to document the connection between women and the environ-ment. The interest of the project is to clean up the environment. "We as women and mothers are our children's first environment. This consciousness empowers women and communities to respond to environmental degradation caused by industrial overdevelopment and community underdevelopment. In our own situation at Akwesasne for example, temporary leadership in governing councils may not provide for any total cleanup of a landfill. This means," Katsi continues, "there may be potential exposure of our future generations. The analysis of Mohawk mother's milk shows that our bodies are in fact, a part of the landfill."

They have a long battle ahead with General Motors, especially considering that at present, GM plans on cleaning up portions of the site only to 500 ppm PCBs — which the company contends is acceptable for industrial sites. What Katsi and other Mohawk people contend is that most industrial sites are not in a residential area. "Besides," Katsi adds, "we've got to face Alcoa and Reynolds as well. They've got PCBs too, and we need to make sure that the General Motors clean up sends a clear signal to them." These issues will affect all the people in the St. Lawrence River Valley, not just the Mohawks.

To address the longer term issues, the Akwesasne project has undertaken a newsletter called "First Environment," around the theme of the womb as the first environment for the baby, and the link between women, infants and the earth. Katsi hopes to use this to increase communication to Native communities in the Great Lakes and St. Lawrence River basin, about the project, and to encourage people to become informed and active participants in the environmental and family issues in their area. The essence of Katsi's work seems to be that Native women are not research subjects, but are in fact playing an active role in making a future for the generations to come.

◆◆◆

EIGHTY-EIGHT

Native Hawaiian Historical and Cultural Perspectives on Environmental Justice

Mililani Trask

When you ask a Hawaiian who they are, their response is "Keiki hanau o ka aina, child that is borne up from the land." I am a Native Hawaiian attorney. I also have the great honor and distinction, and the great burden and responsibility, of being the first elected Kia'Aina of Ka Lahui Hawai'i, the sovereign nation of the Native Hawaiian people, which we created ourselves in 1987.

It's a great pleasure and honor for me to be here to address a group such as yourselves, such a momentous occasion, the first time that the people of color will gather to consider the impacts on our common land base.

I thought I would begin by giving a little bit of history about Hawaii Nei because many people are not aware of the crisis there and the status of the Native Hawaiian people. As we approach the United Nations' celebration of the discoverers, we are celebrating not only the arrival of Columbus but also of Cortez and Captain Cook. In Hawaii Nei we are celebrating 500 years of resilient resistance to the coming of the "discoverers."

In 1778 Captain James Cook sailed into the Hawaiian archipelago. He found there a thriving Native community of 800,000 Native people, living in balance on their lands, completely economically self-sufficient, feeding and clothing themselves off of the resources of their own land base. Within one generation, 770,000 of our people were dead — dead from what is called "mai haole, the sickness of the white man," which Cook brought: venereal disease, flu, pox, the same tragic history that occurred on the American continent to Native American Indians and the Native people of Central and South America.

In 1893 the United States Marines dispatched a group of soldiers to the Island of Oahu for the purpose of overthrowing the lawful kingdom of Hawaii Nei. Prior to 1893, Hawaii was welcomed into the world family of nations and maintained over 20 international treaties, including treaties of friendship and peace with the United States. Despite those in-

ternational laws, revolution was perpetrated against our government, and our lawful government overthrown. In two years we will mark the hundredth anniversary of when we had the right to be self-determining and self-governing.

In 1959, Hawaii was admitted into the Union of the United States of America. There were great debates that occurred in Washington, DC that focused on the fact that people were afraid to incorporate the Territory of Hawaii because it would become the first state in the union in which white people would be a minority of less than 25 percent. That was the reason for the concern when those debates were launched. In 1959, when Hawaii became a state, something happened that did not happen in any other state of the union. In all of the other states, when the U.S. admitted that state into the union, America set aside lands for the Native people of those states, as federal reserves. Today there is a policy that provides that Native Americans should be self-governing, should be allowed to maintain their nations, should be allowed to pass laws, environmental and otherwise, to protect their land base. That did not occur in the State of Hawaii. In the State of Hawaii in 1959, the federal government gave our lands to the state to be held in trust, and gave the Native Hawaiian people, of which there are 200,000, the status of perpetual wardship. We are not allowed to form governments if we are Native Hawaiian; we are not allowed to control our land base. To this day our lands are controlled by state agencies and utilized extensively by the American military complex as part of a plan designed by Hawaii's Senator Daniel Inouye.

In 1987 we decided to exercise our inherent rights to be self-governing. The Hawaii Visitors Bureau declared 1987 the Year of the Hawaiian for a great tourist and media campaign. We took a look at our statistics: 22,000 families on lists waiting for land entitlements since 1920; 30,000 families dead waiting for their Hawaiian homelands awards; 22,000 currently waiting. We thought to ourselves, how are *we* going to celebrate 1987? And we decided that the time had come to convene a constitutional convention to resurrect our nation and to exert our basic and inherent rights, much to the dismay and consternation of the state and the federal government, and certainly to the shock of Senator Inouye.

We have passed a constitution that recognizes the right and the responsibility of Native people to protect their land base and to ensure water quality, because Western laws have been unable to protect the environment. We decided to lift up and resurrect our nation in 1987, passing our constitution, and we are proceeding now to come out, to announce that we are alive and well, and to network with other people.

I have come to announce that a state of emergency exists with regards to the natural environment of the archipelagic lands and waters of Hawaii, and also a state of emergency exists with regards to the survival of the Native people who live there and throughout the Pacific basin. We have many environmental injustices and issues that need to be addressed; most of them have dire global consequences. The expansion of the United States military complex presents substantial threats to our environment.

Right now on the Island of Hawaii and on the Island of Kauai, Senator Inouye is pressing for what he calls the "space-porting initiative," which we all know to be Star Wars. It will distribute large amounts of toxic gases, it will scorch the earth beyond repair and, most importantly and offensive to us, the lands that have been chosen are lands set aside by the Congress in 1920 for the homesteading of Hawaiian people. These are the lands that are pursued on the Island of Hawaii.

Our response to that is "kapu Ka'u." Ka'u is the district; kapu is the Hawaiian way for saying, "It is taboo." We cannot allow desecration of sacred lands, desecration of historic properties that are the cultural inheritance of our people to be converted for the military complex and for the designs of those who would further the interests of war against others. It is an inappropriate use of Native lands.

Other Threats

The United States Navy continues its relentless bombing of Kahoolawe Island. Not only have they denuded the upper one-third of that island, but as they have blasted away the lands, trees and shrubs, all that silt has come down to the channels between Kahoolawe and Maui Islands, the channels that are the spawning grounds of the whales that migrate every year to Hawaii Nei.

We now have information coming from Lualualie on the Island of Oahu that there is a very high incidence of leukemia and other cancers among the Hawaiian children who live there. We believe that this is due to electromagnetic contamination. In Lualualie the United States military is taking control of 2,000 acres of Hawaiian homelands, lands set aside by the Congress to homestead our people. These lands were taken over and converted for a nuclear and military storage facility. Ten years ago, in 1981, they issued a report saying that there's electromagnetic radiation there. After the report was issued all the military families were moved out of the base, but nobody told the Hawaiian community that lives in the surrounding area. We have taken it to the Western courts, we have been thrown out, because the court ruled that Native Hawaiians are wards of the state and the federal government. Therefore, Native Hawaiians are not allowed standing to sue in the federal courts to protect our trust land assets. We are the only class of Native Americans, and the only class of American citizens, that are not allowed access to the federal court system to seek redress of grievances relating to breach of trust.

Ka Lahui Hawai'i is pleased and proud to join all of the other Pacific Island nations in opposing the federal policy which is being perpetrated by Mr. Bush and Senator Inouye identifying the Pacific region as a national sacrifice area. What is a national sacrifice area? I did some legal research and I found out that national sacrifice areas usually occur on Indian reservations or in black communities. They are areas that the nation identifies primarily for the dumping of toxic wastes. As the Greens celebrate in Europe what they perceive to be an environmental victory in forcing America to remove its nuclear and military wastes from Europe, we in the Pacific region have been told that Johnston Island and other Pacific nations have been targeted for storage and dumping. We will not allow that and we will continue to speak out against it.

Tourist Evils

Tourism and its attendant evils continue to assault our island land base. Hundreds of thousands of tourists come to Hawaii every year. They are seeking a dream of paradise. They drink our water, they contaminate our environment. They are responsible for millions of tons of sewage every year, which is deposited into the Pacific Ocean. And, in addition, they are taking lands from our rural communities.

Tourism perpetuates certain Western concepts of exclusive rights to land. Tourists don't like to see other people on their beaches. Tourists don't like to allow Native people to go and fish in the traditional ways. And, because of toxification of the ocean due to release of sewage in Hawaii, there are many places where you can no longer find the reef fish. You cannot go there and take the opihi, the squid, or take the turtle, because they're gone now. So in the few remaining areas where there are fish, the state and federal governments have imposed public park restrictions to prevent Native people from going there to lay the net and take the fish. If the fish are taken out, what will the tourists see when they put on their snorkels? Native people are not allowed to fish so that tourists can view through their goggles what remains of the few species we have because their own tourist practices destroyed all the rest of the bounty of our fisheries.

Tourists need golf courses; golf courses need tons of pesticides, herbicides and millions of tons of water. Hawaii is an island ecology, we do not get fresh water from flowing streams. All the water that falls from the rain in Hawaii is percolated through the lava of the islands and comes to rest in a central basal lens underneath our island. As the rains percolate down they bring with them all the herbicides and pesticides that have been used for years by agribusiness: King Cane, Dole Pineapple, United States military. Already on the island of Oahu we have had to permanently close two of our drinking wells because of toxification. Nobody in the State of Hawaii or the Hawaii Visitors Bureau is going to tell you that at the present time there are 30 contaminants in the drinking water in the State of Hawaii.

The specter of geothermal development lays heavily upon our lands. For 25 years the United States and its allies have been developing geothermal energy in Hawaii. It is destroying the last Pacific tropical rain forest on the Island of Hawaii, Wao Kele o Puna Forest, sacred to the lands of Tutu Pele, our Grandmother Pele, who erupts and gives birth to the earth. This is her home, yet this is the place where they are developing geothermal. And as it proceeds, Native people are denied their basic right to worship

there. We have taken this case to the United States Supreme Court. It was struck down along with the Native American freedom of religion cases because the court ruled that religious worship in America must be "site-specific." If you take the Akua, if you put God in the building, American courts will understand. But if you take God and say, "The earth is the Lord's and the fullness of it, the Black Hills of South Dakota, the lands and forests of Tutu Pele," American courts do not understand.

This past year we have had two geothermal explosions in the State of Hawaii. Despite the fact that we were in court to stop geothermal development while the Civil Defense removed 1,000 families and a state of emergency was declared, the governor and representatives of these developers issued press statements celebrating the explosion. They said it demonstrated that there was a great deal more energy they could harvest than initially anticipated. Their press releases ceased 48 hours after the explosion when it was reported that Hawaii had now recorded its first prenatal death as a result of geothermal toxicity. That case will proceed to court but I can tell you one thing: there is no jury award, no amount of Kala (the white man's dollar) that will compensate the family that lost that child. There's no dollar figure for that kind of loss.

International fishing practices, gill netting and drift netting, are genocide in the sea. As a result of these practices, the Native fisheries are diminished and depleted. In some areas our marine fisheries are depleted to the point that we can no longer harvest that resource.

What is the appropriate response to this environmental and human outrage? In Hawaii Nei we have undertaken to address these things through sovereignty and the basic exertion of the rights of Native people to govern and control their own land base. These are political issues, certainly. But they spring from a very ancient source, a source within our heart, a source that all Natives and people of color understand: our relationship in the global context. As Hawaiians say, "Keiki hanau o ka cuna, child that is borne up from the land," understanding that there is an innate connection to the earth as the Mother. We are called upon now as the guardians of our sacred lands to rise up in the defense of our Mother. You don't subdivide your Mother, you don't chop her body up, you don't drill, penetrate and pull out her lifeblood. You protect and nurture your

Mother. And the Hawaiian value for that is aloha ai'na, love for the land, malama ai'na, care and nurturing for the land. It is reciprocal. It gives back to the Native people. Our people know that the Akua put us here on this earth to be guardians of these sacred lands. It is a God-given responsibility and trust that a sovereign nation must assume if it is to have any integrity. And so we in Ka Lahui have undertaken this struggle. Environmental racism is the enemy. The question is, What is our response? What really is environmental justice? I'll tell you one thing I learned in law school at Santa Clara. Do you know how they perceive and teach justice, the white schools of this country? A blind white woman with her eyes covered up by cloth, holding the scales of justice. And if you look at it, they're not balanced. The Native scale and the environmental scale are outweighed by other priorities.

Well, environmental justice is not a blindfolded white woman. When I saw the woman with the scales of justice in law school, I thought to myself, "You know, if you blindfold yourself the only thing you're going to do is walk into walls." You are not going to resolve anything. And that's where we are with Western law. I know that there are many attorneys here and others who are working on environmental cases. I support them. We have received a great deal of support from attorneys working in environmental law. But do not put your eggs in the basket of the blind white lady. We must try other approaches.

In closing, I would like to say in behalf of myself and the Hawaii delegation that we are very renewed in coming here, and that when we return to Hawaii in two or three days we will have good news to share with our people, that we have come ourselves these many thousands of miles, that we have looked in the faces of people of color, that we have seen there, in their hearts and in their eyes, a light shining, a light of commitment, a light that is filled with capacity and a light that is filled with love for the Mother Earth, a light that is the same that we have in our hearts.

I try to do one thing whenever I finish speaking. I try to leave the podium by telling people what the motto of Ka Lahui Hawai'i is, the motto of our nation that we're forming now. I find it to be very applicable to the situations that we are in. We are facing a difficult struggle. Every bit of commitment and energy is needed to save our Mother Earth and to insure the survival of our people and all of the species of the earth. It is a difficult row to hoe. There is going to be a great deal of strife and a great deal of pain. But we must proceed; we have no alternative. This is the same position that the native people of Hawaii Nei found themselves in 1987 when we committed to resurrecting our national government. And at the time that we passed that constitution we also adopted a motto. It is a motto that I think you might want to live by as we proceed in this environmental war that we are waging. That motto is: "A difficult birth does not make the baby any less beautiful."

◆◆◆

EIGHTY-NINE

Mexican American Women Grassroots Community Activists
"Mothers of East Los Angeles"
Mary Pardo

The relatively few studies of Chicana political activism show a bias in the way political activism is conceptualized by social scientists, who often use a narrow definition confined to electoral politics. Most feminist research uses an expanded definition that moves across the boundaries between public,

electoral politics and private, family politics; but feminist research generally focuses on women mobilized around gender-specific issues. For some feminists, adherence to "tradition" constitutes conservatism and submission to patriarchy. Both approaches exclude the contributions of working-class women, particularly those of Afro-American women and Latinas, thus failing to capture the full dynamic of social change.

The following case study of Mexican American women activists in "Mothers of East Los Angeles" (MELA) contributes another dimension to the conception of grassroots politics. It illustrates how these Mexican American women transform "traditional" networks and resources based on family and culture into political assets to defend the quality of urban life. Far from unique, these patterns of activism are repeated in Latin America and elsewhere. Here as in other times and places, the women's activism arises out of seemingly "traditional" roles, addresses wider social and political issues, and capitalizes on informal associations sanctioned by the community. Religion, commonly viewed as a conservative force, is intertwined with politics. Often, women speak of their communities and their activism as extensions of their family and household responsibility. The central role of women in grassroots struggles around quality of life, in the Third World and in the United States, challenges conventional assumptions about the powerlessness of women and static definitions of culture and tradition.

In general, the women in MELA are longtime residents of East Los Angeles; some are bilingual and native born, others Mexican born and Spanish dominant. All the core activists are bilingual and have lived in the community over thirty years. All have been active in parish-sponsored groups and activities; some have had experience working in community-based groups arising from schools, neighborhood watch associations, and labor support groups. To gain an appreciation of the group and the core activists, I used ethnographic field methods. I interviewed six women, using a life history approach focused on their first community activities, current activism, household and family responsibilities, and perceptions of community issues. Also, from December 1987 through October 1989, I attended hearings on the two currently pending projects of contention—a proposed state prison and a toxic waste incinerator—and participated in community and organizational meetings and demonstrations. The following discussion briefly chronicles an intense and significant five-year segment of community history from which emerged MELA and the women's transformation of "traditional" resources and experiences into political assets for community mobilization.

The Community Context: East Los Angeles Resisting Siege

Political science theory often guides the political strategies used by local government to select the sites for undesirable projects. In 1984, the state of California commissioned a public relations firm to assess the political difficulties facing the construction of energy-producing waste incinerators. The report provided a "personality profile" of those residents most likely to organize effective opposition to projects:

> middle and upper socioeconomic strata possess better resources to effectuate their opposition. Middle and higher socioeconomic strata neighborhoods should not fall within the one-mile and five-mile radii of the proposed site. Conversely, older people, people with a high school education or less are least likely to oppose a facility.

The state accordingly placed the plant in Commerce, a predominantly Mexican American, low-income community. This pattern holds throughout the state and the country: three out of five Afro-Americans and Latinos live near toxic waste sites, and three of the five largest hazardous waste landfills are in communities with at least 80 percent minority populations.

Similarly, in March 1985, when the state sought a site for the first state prison in Los Angeles County, Governor Deukmejian resolved to place the 1,700-inmate institution in East Los Angeles, within a mile of the long-established Boyle Heights neighborhood and within two miles of thirty-four schools. Furthermore, violating convention, the state bid on the expensive parcel of industrially zoned land without compiling an environmental impact report or providing a public community hearing. According to James Vigil, Jr., a field representative for Assemblywoman Gloria Molina, shortly after the state announced the site selection, Molina's office began informing the community and gauging residents' sentiments about it through direct mailings and calls to leaders of organizations and business groups.

In spring 1986, after much pressure from the 56th assembly district office and the community, the Department of Corrections agreed to hold a public information meeting, which was attended by over 700 Boyle Heights residents. From this moment on, Vigil observed, "the tables turned, the community mobilized, and the residents began calling the political representatives and requesting their presence at hearings and meetings." By summer 1986, the community was well aware of the prison site proposal. Over two thousand people, carrying placards proclaiming "No Prison in ELA," marched from Resurrection Church in Boyle Heights to the 3rd Street bridge linking East Los Angeles with the rapidly expanding downtown Los Angeles. This march marked the beginning of one of the largest grassroots coalitions to emerge from the Latino community in the last decade.

Prominent among the coalition's groups is "Mothers of East Los Angeles," a loosely knit group of over 400 Mexican American women. MELA initially coalesced to oppose the state prison construction but has since organized opposition to several other projects detrimental to the quality of life in the central city. Its second large target is a toxic waste incinerator proposed for Vernon, a small city adjacent to East Los Angeles. This incinerator would worsen the already debilitating air quality of the entire county and set a precedent dangerous for other communities throughout California. When MELA took up the fight against the toxic waste incinerator, it became more than a single-issue group and began working with environmental groups around the state. As a result of the community struggle, AB58 (Roybal-Allard), which provides all Californians with the minimum protection of an environmental impact report before the construction of hazardous waste incinerators, was signed into law. But the law's effectiveness relies on a watchful community network. Since its emergence, "Mothers of East Los Angeles" has become centrally important to just such a network of grassroots activists including a select number of Catholic priests and two Mexican American political representatives. Furthermore, the group's very formation, and its continued spirit and activism, fly in the face of the conventional political science beliefs regarding political participation.

Predictions by the "experts" attribute the low formal political participation (i.e., voting) of Mexican American people in the U.S. to a set of cultural "retardants" including primary kinship systems, fatalism, religious traditionalism, traditional cultural values, and mother country attachment. The core activists in MELA may appear to fit this description, as well as the state-commissioned profile of residents least likely to oppose toxic waste incinerator projects.

All the women live in a low-income community. Furthermore, they identify themselves as active and committed participants in the Catholic Church; they claim an ethnic identity—Mexican American; their ages range from forty to sixty; and they have attained at most high school educations. However, these women fail to conform to the predicted political apathy. Instead, they have transformed social identity—ethnic identity, class identity, and gender identity—into an impetus as well as a basis for activism. And, in transforming their existing social networks into grassroots political networks, they have also transformed themselves.

Transformation As a Dominant Theme

From the life histories of the group's core activists and from my own field notes, I have selected excerpts that tell two representative stories. One is a narrative of the events that led to community mobilization in East Los Angeles. The other is a story of transformation, the process of creating new and better relationships that empower people to unite and achieve common goals.

First, women have transformed organizing experiences and social networks arising from gender-related responsibilities into political resources. When I asked the women about the first community, not necessarily "political," involvement they could recall, they discussed experiences that predated the formation of MELA. Juana Gutiérrez explained:

> Well, it didn't start with the prison, you know. It started when my kids went to school. I started by joining the Parents Club and we worked on different problems here in the area. Like the people who come to the parks to sell drugs to the kids. I got the neighbors to have meetings. I would go knock at the doors, house to house. And I told them that we should stick together with the Neighborhood Watch for the community and for the kids.

Erlinda Robles similarly recalled:

> I wanted my kids to go to Catholic school and from the time my oldest one went there, I was there every day. I used to take my two little ones with me and I helped one way or another.

I used to question things they did. And the other mothers would just watch me. Later, they would ask me, "Why do you do that? They are going to take it out on your kids." I'd say, "They better not." And before you knew it, we had a big group of mothers that were very involved.

Part of a mother's "traditional" responsibility includes overseeing her child's progress in school, interacting with school staff, and supporting school activities. In these processes, women meet other mothers and begin developing a network of acquaintanceships and friendships based on mutual concern for the welfare of their children.

Although the women in MELA carried the greatest burden of participating in school activities, Erlinda Robles also spoke of strategies they used to draw men into the enterprise and into the networks:

At the beginning, the priests used to say who the president of the mothers guild would be; they used to pick 'um. But, we wanted elections, so we got elections. Then we wanted the fathers to be involved, and the nuns suggested that a father should be president and a mother would be secretary or be involved there [at the school site].

Of course, this comment piqued my curiosity, so I asked how the mothers agreed on the nuns' suggestion. The answer was simple and instructive:

At the time we thought it was a "natural" way to get the fathers involved because they weren't involved; it was just the mothers. Everybody [the women] agreed on them [the fathers] being president because they worked all day and they couldn't be involved in a lot of daily activities like food sales and whatever. During the week, a steering committee of mothers planned the group's activities. But now that I think about it, a woman could have done the job just as well!

So women got men into the group by giving them a position they could manage. The men may have held the title of "president," but they were not making day-to-day decisions about work, nor were they dictating the direction of the group. Erlinda Robles laughed as she recalled an occasion when the president insisted, against the wishes of the women, on scheduling a parents' group fundraiser—a breakfast—on Mother's Day. On that morning, only the president and his wife were present to prepare breakfast. This should alert researchers against measuring power and influence by looking solely at who holds titles.

Each of the cofounders had a history of working with groups arising out of the responsibilities usually assumed by "mothers"—the education of children and the safety of the surrounding community. From these groups, they gained valuable experiences and networks that facilitated the formation of "Mothers of East Los Angeles." Juana Gutiérrez explained how preexisting networks progressively expanded community support:

You know nobody knew about the plan to build a prison in this community until Assemblywoman Gloria Molina told me. Martha Molina called me and said, "You know what is happening in your area? The governor wants to put a prison in Boyle Heights!" So, I called a Neighborhood Watch meeting at my house and we got fifteen people together. Then, Father John started informing his people at the Church and that is when the group of two to three hundred started showing up for every march on the bridge.

MELA effectively linked up preexisting networks into a viable grassroots coalition.

Second, the process of activism also transformed previously "invisible" women, making them not only visible but the center of public attention. From a conventional perspective, political activism assumes a kind of gender neutrality. This means that anyone can participate, but men are the expected key actors. In accordance with this pattern, in winter 1986 an informal group of concerned businessmen in the community began lobbying and testifying against the prison at hearings in Sacramento. Working in conjunction with Assemblywoman Molina, they made many trips to Sacramento at their own expense. Residents who did not have the income to travel were unable to join them. Finally, Molina, commonly recognized as a forceful advocate for Latinas and the community, asked Frank Villalobos, an urban planner in the group, why there were no women coming up to speak in Sacramento against the prison. As he phrased it, "I was getting some heat from her because no women were going up there."

In response to this comment, Veronica Gutiérrez, a law student who lived in the community, agreed to accompany him on the next trip to Sacramento. He also mentioned the comment to Father John Moretta at Resurrection Catholic Parish. Meanwhile, representatives of the business sector of the community and of the 56th assembly district office were continuing to compile arguments and supportive data against the East Los Angeles prison site. Frank Villalobos stated one of the pressing problems:

> We felt that the Senators whom we prepared all this for didn't even acknowledge that we existed. They kept calling it the "downtown" site, and they argued that there was no opposition in the community. So, I told Father Moretta, what we have to do is demonstrate that there is a link (proximity) between the Boyle Heights community and the prison.

The next juncture illustrates how perceptions of gender-specific behavior set in motion a sequence of events that brought women into the political limelight. Father Moretta decided to ask all the women to meet after mass. He told them about the prison site and called for their support. When I asked him about his rationale for selecting the women, he replied:

> I felt so strongly about the issue, and I knew in my heart what a terrible offense this was to the people. So, I was afraid that once we got into a demonstration situation we had to be very careful. I thought the women would be cooler and calmer than the men. The bottom line is that the men came anyway. The first times out the majority were women. Then they began to invite their husbands and their children, but originally it was just women.

Father Moretta also named the group. Quite moved by a film, *The Official Story,* about the courageous Argentine women who demonstrated for the return of their children who disappeared during a repressive right-wing military dictatorship, he transformed the name "Las Madres de la Plaza de Mayo" into "Mothers of East Los Angeles."

However, Aurora Castillo, one of the cofounders of the group, modified my emphasis on the predominance of women:

> Of course the fathers work. We also have many, many grandmothers. And all this IS with the support of the fathers. They make the placards and the posters; they do the security and carry the signs; and they come to the marches when they can.

Although women played a key role in the mobilization, they emphasized the group's broad base of active supporters as well as the other organizations in the "Coalition Against the Prison." Their intent was to counter any notion that MELA was composed exclusively of women or mothers and to stress the "inclusiveness" of the group. All the women who assumed lead roles in the group had long histories of volunteer work in the Boyle Heights community; but formation of the group brought them out of the "private" margins and into "public" light.

Third, the women in "Mothers of East L.A." have transformed the definition of "mother" to include militant political opposition to state-proposed projects they see as adverse to the quality of life in the community. Explaining how she discovered the issue, Aurora Castillo said,

> You know if one of your children's safety is jeopardized, the mother turns into a lioness. That's why Father John got the mothers. We have to have a well-organized, strong group of mothers to protect the community and oppose things that are detrimental to us. You know the governor is in the wrong and the mothers are in the right. After all, the mothers have to be right. Mothers are for the children's interest, not for self-interest; the governor is for his own political interest.

The women also have expanded the boundaries of "motherhood" to include social and political community activism and redefined the word to include women who are not biological "mothers." At one meeting a young Latina expressed her solidarity with the group and, almost apologetically, qualified herself as a "resident," not a "mother," of East Los Angeles. Erlinda Robles replied:

> When you are fighting for a better life for children and "doing" for them, isn't that what mothers do? So we're all mothers. You don't have to have children to be a "mother."

At critical points, grassroots community activism requires attending many meetings, phone calling, and door-to-door communications—all very labor-intensive work. In order to keep harmony in the "domestic" sphere, the core activists must creatively integrate family members into their community activities. I asked Erlinda Robles how her husband felt about her activism, and she replied quite openly:

> My husband doesn't like getting involved, but he takes me because he knows I like it. Sometimes we would have two or three meetings a week. And my husband would say, "Why are you doing so much? It is really getting out of hand." But he is very supportive. Once he gets there, he enjoys it and he starts in arguing too! See, it's just that he is not used to it. He couldn't believe things happened the way that they do. He was in the Navy twenty years and they brainwashed him that none of the politicians could do wrong. So he has come a long way. Now he comes home and parks the car out front and asks me, "Well, where are we going tonight?"

When women explain their activism, they link family and community as one entity. Juana Gutiérrez, a woman with extensive experience working on community and neighborhood issues, stated:

> Yo como madre de familia, y como residente del Este de Los Angeles, seguiré luchando sin descanso por que se nos respete. Y yo lo hago con bastante cariño hacia mi comunidad. Digo "mi comunidad," porque me siento parte de ella, quiero a mi raza como parte de mi familia, y si Dios me permite seguiré luchando contra todos los gobernadores que quieran abusar de nosotros. (As a mother and a resident of East L.A., I shall continue fighting tirelessly, so we will be respected. And I will do this with much affection for my community. I say "my community" because I am part of it. I love my "raza" [race] as part of my family; and if God allows, I will keep on fighting against all the governors that want to take advantage of us.)

Like the other activists, she has expanded her responsibilities and legitimated militant opposition to abuse of the community by representatives of the state.

Working-class women activists seldom opt to separate themselves from men and their families. In this particular struggle for community quality of life, they are fighting for the family unit and thus are not competitive with men. Of course, this fact does not preclude different alignments in other contexts and situations.

Fourth, the story of MELA also shows the transformation of class and ethnic identity. Aurora Castillo told of an incident that illustrated her growing knowledge of the relationship of East Los Angeles to other communities and the basis necessary for coalition building:

> And do you know we have been approached by other groups? [She lowers her voice in emphasis.] You know that Pacific Palisades group asked for our backing. But what they did, they sent their powerful lobbyist that they pay thousands of dollars to get our support against the drilling in Pacific Palisades. So what we did was tell them to send their grassroots people, not their lobbyist. We're suspicious. We don't want to talk to a high-salaried lobbyist; we are humble people. We did our own lobbying. In one week we went to Sacramento twice.

The contrast between the often tedious and labor-intensive work of mobilizing people at the "grassroots" level and the paid work of a "high-salaried lobbyist" represents a point of pride and integrity, not a deficiency or a source of shame. If the two groups were to construct a coalition, they must communicate on equal terms.

The women of MELA combine a willingness to assert opposition with a critical assessment of their own weaknesses. At one community meeting, for example, representatives of several oil companies attempted to gain support for placement of an oil pipeline through the center of East Los Angeles. The exchange between the women in the audience and the oil representative was heated, as women alternated asking questions about the chosen route for the pipeline:

> "Is it going through Cielito Lindo [Reagan's ranch]?" The oil representative answered, "No." Another woman stood up and asked, "Why not place it along the coastline?" Without thinking of the implications, the representative responded, "Oh, no! If it burst, it would endanger the marine life." The woman retorted, "You value the marine life more than human beings?" His face reddened with anger and the hearing disintegrated into angry chanting.

The proposal was quickly defeated. But Aurora Castillo acknowledged that it was not solely their opposition that brought about the defeat:

> We won because the westside was opposed to it, so we united with them. You know there are a lot of attorneys who live there and they also questioned the representative. Believe me, no way is justice blind. . . . We just don't want all this garbage thrown at us because we are low-income and Mexican American. We are lucky now that we have good representatives, which we didn't have before.

Throughout their life histories, the women refer to the disruptive effects of land use decisions made in the 1950s. As longtime residents, all but one share the experience of losing a home and relocating to make way for a freeway. Juana Gutiérrez refers to the community response at that time:

> Una de las cosas que me caen muy mal es la injusticia y en nuestra comunidad hemos visto mucho de eso. Sobre todo antes, porque creo que nuestra gente estaba mas dormida, nos atrevíamos menos. En los cincuentas hicieron los freeways y así, sin más, nos dieron la noticia de que nos teníamos que mudar. Y eso pasó dos veces. La gente se conformaba porque lo ordeno el gobierno. Recuerdo que yo me enojaba y quería que los demás me secundaran, pero nadie quería hacer nada. (One of the things that really upsets me is the injustice that we see so much in our community. Above everything else, I believe that our people were less aware; we were less challenging. In the 1950s — they made the freeways and just like that they gave us a notice that we had to move. That happened twice. The people accepted it because the government ordered it. I remember that I was angry and wanted the others to back me but nobody else wanted to do anything.)

The freeways that cut through communities and disrupted neighborhoods are now a concrete reminder of shared injustice, of the vulnerability of the community in the 1950s. The community's social and political history thus informs perceptions of its current predicament; however, today's activists emphasize not the powerlessness of the community but the change in status and progression toward political empowerment.

Fifth, the core activists typically tell stories illustrating personal change and a new sense of entitlement to speak for the community. They have transformed the unspoken sentiments of individuals into a collective community voice. Lucy Ramos related her initial apprehensions:

> I was afraid to get involved. I didn't know what was going to come out of this and I hesitated at first. Right after we started, Father John came up to me and told me, "I want you to be a spokesperson." I said, "Oh no, I don't know what I am going to say." I was nervous. I am surprised I didn't have a nervous breakdown then. Every time we used to get in front of the TV cameras and even interviews like this, I used to sit there and I could feel myself shaking. But as time went on, I started getting used to it.
>
> And this is what I have noticed with a lot of them. They were afraid to speak up and say anything. Now, with this prison issue, a lot of them have come out and come forward and given their opinions. Everybody used to be real "quietlike."

She also related a situation that brought all her fears to a climax, which she confronted and resolved as follows:

> When I first started working with the coalition, Channel 13 called me up and said they wanted to interview me and I said OK. Then I started getting nervous. So I called Father John and told him, "You better get over here right away." He said, "Don't worry, don't worry, you can handle it by yourself." Then Channel 13 called me back and said they were going to interview another person, someone I had never heard of, and asked if it was OK if he came to my house. And I said OK again. Then I began thinking, what if this guy is for the prison? What am I going to do? And I was so nervous and I thought, I know what I am going to do!

Since the meeting was taking place in her home, she reasoned that she was entitled to order any troublemakers out of her domain:

> If this man tells me anything, I am just going to chase him out of my house. That is what I am going to do! All these thoughts were

going through my head. Then Channel 13 walk into my house followed by six men I had never met. And I thought, Oh, my God, what did I get myself into? I kept saying to myself, if they get smart with me I am throwing them ALL out.

At this point her tone expressed a sense of resolve. In fact, the situation turned out to be neither confrontational nor threatening, as the "other men" were also members of the coalition. This woman confronted an anxiety-laden situation by relying on her sense of control within her home and family — a quite "traditional" source of authority for women — and transforming that control into the courage to express a political position before a potential audience all over one of the largest metropolitan areas in the nation.

People living in Third World countries as well as in minority communities in the United States face an increasingly degraded environment. Recognizing the threat to the well-being of their families, residents have mobilized at the neighborhood level to fight for "quality of life" issues. The common notion that environmental well-being is of concern solely to white middle-class and upper-class residents ignores the specific way working-class neighborhoods suffer from the fallout of the city "growth machine" geared for profit.

In Los Angeles, the culmination of postwar urban renewal policies, the growing Pacific Rim trade surplus and investment, and low-wage international labor migration from Third World countries are creating potentially volatile conditions. Literally palatial financial buildings swallow up the space previously occupied by modest, low-cost housing. Increasing density and development not matched by investment in social programs, services, and infrastructure erode the quality of life, beginning in the core of the city. Latinos, the majority of whom live close to the center of the city, must confront the distilled social consequences of development focused solely on profit. The Mexican American community in East Los Angeles, much like other minority working-class communities, has been a repository for prisons instead of new schools, hazardous industries instead of safe work sites, and one of the largest concentrations of freeway interchanges in the country, which transports much wealth past the community. And the concerns of residents in East Los Angeles may provide lessons for other minority as well as middle-class communities. Increasing environmental pollution resulting from inadequate waste disposal plans and an out-of-control "need" for penal institutions to contain the casualties created by the growing bipolar distribution of wages may not be limited to the Southwest. These conditions set the stage for new conflicts and new opportunities, to transform old relationships into coalitions that can challenge state agendas and create new community visions.

Mexican American women living east of downtown Los Angeles exemplify the tendency of women to enter into environmental struggles in defense of their community. Women have a rich historical legacy of community activism, partly reconstructed over the last two decades in social histories of women who contested other "quality of life issues," from the price of bread to "Demon Rum" (often representing domestic violence).

But something new is also happening. The issues "traditionally" addressed by women — health, housing, sanitation, and the urban environment — have moved to center stage as capitalist urbanization progresses. Environmental issues now fuel the fires of many political campaigns and drive citizens beyond the rather restricted, perfunctory political act of voting. Instances of political mobilization at the grass-roots level, where women often play a central role, allow us to "see" abstract concepts like participatory democracy and social change as dynamic processes.

The existence and activities of "Mothers of East Los Angeles" attest to the dynamic nature of participatory democracy, as well as to the dynamic nature of our gender, class, and ethnic identity. The story of MELA reveals, on the one hand, how individuals and groups can transform a seemingly "traditional" role such as "mother." On the other hand, it illustrates how such a role may also be a social agent drawing members of the community into the "political" arena. Studying women's contributions as well as men's will shed greater light on the networks dynamic of grassroots movements.

The work "Mothers of East Los Angeles" do to mobilize the community demonstrates that people's political involvement cannot be predicted by their cultural characteristics. These women have defied stereotypes of apathy and used ethnic, gender, and class identity as an impetus, a strength, a vehicle for political activism. They have expanded their — and our — understanding of the complexities of a political system, and they have reaffirmed the possibility of "doing something."

They also generously share the lessons they have learned. One of the women in "Mothers of East Los Angeles" told me, as I hesitated to set up an interview with another woman I hadn't yet met in person,

You know, nothing ventured nothing lost. You should have seen how timid we were the first time we went to a public hearing. Now, forget it, I walk right up and make myself heard and that's what you have to do.

◆◆◆

NINETY

Empowering Ourselves
Women and Toxics Organizing

Robbin Lee Zeff, Marsha Love, and Karen Stults

Health Effects

The environmental justice movement would not exist today were we not concerned about the devastating health effects on our families from exposure to toxic wastes. We got involved because we want justice for ourselves and others who have already been harmed. We're concerned about protecting families against future harm from incinerators, leaking landfills and other sources of hazardous waste contamination. Involuntary exposure to toxic substances is a form of persecution. We will no longer be victims to environmental persecution.

Since environmentally induced illness is such an overwhelming reality in all of our lives, we have devoted a large portion of this publication to the subject of health effects. . . . Three women who have faced the consequences of the environmental poisoning of their families and their communities tell their stories. Then we discuss the emotions we feel as we deal with illness and, finally, some obstacles and solutions for dealing with the health effects of toxic exposure.

Penny Newman

Penny Newman is a long-time veteran in the grassroots movement against toxics and a leader of Concerned Neighbors in Action of Riverside, California. Penny was one of the first to work with Lois Gibbs at Love Canal to discover that hazardous waste was in everyone's backyard. Penny is one of the key activists at the Stringfellow Acid Pits site in Riverside, California. She is now the western regional field organizer for CCHW [Citizens Clearinghouse for Hazardous Wastes].

"I Didn't Know the Danger."

We chose to move to our community because we thought it was the place to raise our kids. The small town atmosphere, the rural countryside, was the kind of place we wanted to be. I knew that when you go house hunting, you find out about the schools in the neighborhood. But I didn't know then that I had to ask whether the community had a toxic dump.

This community is near a Class 1 hazardous waste site. On the site there are volatile organics, TCE, DDT, the heavy metals. We have radiation. We have everything at Stringfellow. I didn't know it then.

When we moved there, I was three months pregnant. At $5\frac{1}{2}$ months I miscarried. Eric was conceived just a few months after that. Eric was born 6 weeks premature. He had a lot of allergies from the very beginning and was always a fairly fragile child. It was routine not to sleep at night, because you lay there listening for his breathing. At any time you might have to rush him to the hospital for his injections.

"The Doctors Didn't Know What Was Wrong."

When Eric started school, instead of things getting better, like everybody told me he would, "he'd outgrow the asthma," he just got worse. We went through a year of really severe abdominal pains and the doctors just didn't know what was going on. Eric went through all kinds of tests. They finally said it was an epileptic stomach. It had to be a teacher who was putting pressure on Eric at school. That seemed really strange to me, because he had a very laid-back teacher.

One night he had to have emergency surgery. They thought it was appendicitis, but it wasn't. So they did exploratory surgery and took out Eric's gall bladder. They decided that's what it was. A six year old with a gall bladder problem! So unusual, they wrote articles in medical journals about him. On top of this, Eric was diagnosed as having a congenital defect which required being in braces. Eric also had no vision in one eye. They classified it as "lazy eye," but it wasn't quite that. So we went through a period of braces, glasses and an eye patch. He knocked out teeth, because he kept falling with his braces. He looked like a battered child. Every time we took him out, I'd have to say, "No, I really don't beat this kid." It was very embarrassing.

After the gall bladder surgery Eric seemed to do a little better. Every time the flu came around he wasn't drastically ill. Every time a cold came around he wouldn't be out of school for two weeks.

Shawn was always the healthy kid. I finally thought, "Aha, we've got one that is going to make it." Until he started school. The school is ¾ of a mile from the site. Shawn started with asthma, which he didn't have as a younger child. He seemed to develop it very quickly, as I did, because I had started working at the school. His skin would crack open and ooze. And he had ear infections, continuous ear infections.

"The Officials Didn't Tell Us."

In 1978, we had overflows from the site. They pumped 800,000 gallons of chemicals into the community. It flowed down the street and the flood canal, which goes directly behind the elementary school. It overflowed into the playground. The state officials didn't tell anyone they were doing this. They didn't want to panic the public.

The school district found out and decided they should do something. They didn't want to close the school, because they would lose state financing, based on the average daily attendance rates. So they set up an evacuation plan. They told the staff, "If you hear one bell, take the kids down to buses. If you hear two bells, it will be too late; the dam will be broken. Put the kids on the desks and hope for the best." The staff was instructed not to tell parents.

So we were sending our kids off to school every day, and the kids played in the puddles, as all kids do. They didn't know that they shouldn't be playing in that water; they thought it was rain water. We had foam in the community which they kept telling us was agricultural foam. The kids could actually make beards out of it. They put the foam on their faces.

"Doctors Ended Up Adding to the Problem."

After that, Shawn began having neurological symptoms — the blurred vision, the headaches. The headaches would get so bad he would just scream. It didn't do any good to put him in a dark room; it didn't do any good to give him aspirins. And then he'd start in with dizzy spells to the point of really being nauseous. And you'd actually have to hold on to him, so he could see he wasn't moving. He was in the 4th grade.

We went through two years of tests on him. It was probably the biggest nightmare I'd ever gone through. At that point I really began to hate doctors. They ended up adding to the problem rather than helping it, by telling a 4th grader that he had brain damage without giving him any explanation. By telling him later on that he was just doing it to get attention. They said this to a young man in his formative years.

Shawn graduated into junior high school, which is out of that immediate area. Things began to subside a bit. He was put on phenobarbital. And we never figured out if it was the medication or just removing him from the area. But he seemed to improve a little bit. However, he never, from that 4th grade period on, never did well in school again, as he used to. And Shawn had been recommended for the gifted program. He was extremely bright and very well coordinated. But he wasn't any more. Clearly there was a change. He noticed it more than I did. He became very conscious of it, to the point that he didn't want to participate in sports any more because he couldn't do things that he used to be able to do. He has also told me he simply can't concentrate.

"The State Says There Are No Significant Health Effects."

In the last year we've started having testing done, as part of our lawsuit. And despite what the state has said in their epidemiological studies — and our community has been studied like a zoo by the state — they kept saying there were no significant health effects. But we got ahold of an internal memo, where they outlined health effects that included an increase in cancer, urinary tract infections, respiratory problems, ear infections, heart problems. But they considered this "no significant health impact." A young man with terrific potential. That potential is reduced. They'll never be able to give that back to him.

I look back now and think: How stupid could I have been? But I just never made the connection. And it wasn't until we got a list of all the chemicals and their health effects that I started reading and thinking, "My God, that's Eric's problem, that's Shawn's problem."

"People Were Scared."

My kids are not the sickest kids in our community. They are considered pretty healthy kids. For a long time people didn't even want to discuss what was going on, because they were scared. Some suspected, mainly because of skin problems. You could see the rashes; you could see the sores. Sores that didn't respond to treatment. And so people would talk about that. The things they wouldn't talk about were the suicide tendencies of their kids, or the really emotional state that some of the people were in. They didn't talk about the reproductive problems they were having. And a lot of it was that they didn't associate those problems with those chemicals.

It's frightening to have a doctor go through this whole list of things that are wrong. And knowing that there are not any doctors around us who are even going to acknowledge that it's happening, much less provide treatment. That's a real problem. What do you do with people by telling them they have these problems and not being able to offer them any help?

Luella Kenny

Luella Kenny joined the grassroots movement for environmental justice in 1978 when her son

Jon died from chemical exposure at Love Canal. Luella remains active as a member of CCHW's Board of Directors, the chairperson of the Love Canal Medical Trust Fund, and as a consultant to grassroots groups nationwide.

I was one of the original activists at Love Canal. And I'm ashamed to say that the only thing that got me involved was because my son died, because he was playing in his own backyard. Otherwise I was just as complacent as the next person and didn't pay attention to what was going on.

Yet back in 1978 my 7-year-old son suddenly became ill. And I was too busy running back and forth from the hospital to pay attention. I knew that 1/10th of a mile from my house there was a lot of ruckus going on. People were protesting.

Both my husband and I are in the sciences. We went to the medical library and started reading. Jon had a kidney disease, known as nephrosis. We found out that this disease could be triggered if you're exposed to chemicals. I was told not to worry about it.

But 4 months later this little 7-year-old boy died. The members of the Love Canal Home Owners Association were interested because the death occurred in the immediate neighborhood. And New York State said that they were going to investigate Jon's death. Ironically, I worked for the New York State Dept. of Health for 29 years. I was very trusting. I thought this was what we should do. We should investigate it.

"The Commissioner of Health Didn't Look Me in the Eye."

It's not very easy for a mother to have to read her son's autopsy report and to try and deal with the officials. I thought it was important to know what had happened, so I sat down with the Commissioner of Health of New York State and tried to go over this autopsy report. Typical of most officials, his head down, not looking me straight in the eye, he had the nerve to tell me that little boys have the tendency to pick their nose and therefore they get bloody noses, not because they are exposed to chemicals. Nothing happens to little boys' kidneys because they are exposed to chemicals; it's because they play football and they fall down and rupture them.

Children have a gland called the thymus gland. It is what determines immune response. It usually disappears when children are 14 years old. The autopsy report indicated that Jon's thymus was already shrunk. In the medical journals, all of the animal studies showed that a shrunken thymus is an indicator of exposure to dioxin. That's what was in our backyard. Dioxin.

Who would have thought that my other son who was 10, was anorexic because of the appetite-suppressing chemicals at the creek? Who would have thought that the hundreds and hundreds of warts that were all over his body which we constantly had to have removed, who would have thought it was due to chemical exposures?

"Don't Be Intimidated by Doctors."

I had worked in the scientific field, and yet I was given stupid answers. I was considered an hysterical housewife. But the officials didn't address the issues any better when I tried to approach them without emotion. Because they are not ready to accept it.

I want to make one last point. Don't be intimidated by doctors. They are not gods. And don't take what they say. You have to go out and search for what you know is true. Don't let them focus only on cancer and miscarriages, which are the obvious things. David Axelrod, the Health Commissioner told me, "Collect yourself, go back home, start your life again." It's impossible. This is 9 years later. I've started my life again, but certainly not in the direction he told me to.

Patty Frase

Born and raised in Jacksonville, Arkansas, Patty first became involved in the toxics issue when she lost her parents to toxics-related illnesses. Patty now lives in Benton, Arkansas, and directs the Environmental Congress of Arkansas which works on a variety of issues such as hazardous waste incineration, deep well injection, and landfills.

"Don't Trust Government and Industry Research Studies."

When I hear these stories I get so angry. I want to go out and grab these doctors and throw them in the pit. I want to take them out there and let them drink our water.

We have "independent" studies we're supposed to rely on. The majority of those studies are funded by the chemical companies. So they're going to have a study that says, "It's o.k. Don't worry about what's in your landfill. There is nothing wrong with your landfill."

"CDC: Center for Diffusing Citizen Concern."

The government studies are also bogus. We just have to start out knowing that the Centers for Disease Control, the EPA, or any of these regulatory agencies are not telling the truth. When they come your way, tell them to go away. Tell them, "We don't need your studies." You don't need their studies, because then you are countering more than you were before they got there. Because now they are reinforcing that you're crazy. But you're not crazy; there is nothing wrong with you.

Some of the things that go on with the CDC and the EPA are so incredible that it's hard to believe that we're the ignorant ones. The CDC and the EPA came to town and said, "We're going to do you a favor. You've been asking for all this stuff, so we're going to test 10 people that have died in your community. We're going to do liver samples. We're going to do brain samples. We're going to do intestinal samples. We're going to do it all."

My Congressman's office calls me two weeks later and says, "Patty, I don't think you want that. You're the control group for Times Beach, Missouri." So I called the CDC and I asked them if this was true. And I called the press, like crazy. The next day the study was cancelled. Thank goodness. We were supposed to be the control group. We were. Our contamination level was just as high, if not higher, in some parts of our community, than Times Beach. They evacuated Times Beach at the 1 part per billion (ppb) level. Some of our homes have 2.8 ppb, 3.7 ppb, 4.6 ppb.

Don't let any of them tell you anything, because it's all b.s. The CDC was supposed to test for 10 chemicals. There were no established background levels for these chemicals, so they compared the levels of these chemicals with DDT, DDE, etc. So that they can show you that you're crazy.

The CDC got up at a press conference with an autopsy report, and they say 508 ppb 3,5 dichlorophenyl, 2,4,5,T. This is the autopsy of a little baby. A baby that's never eaten anything. Been on canned formula. Canned formula. The CDC holds up the autopsy report and a can of mothballs and says "These children are no more contaminated than if they ate these moth balls." They took the warning labels off the moth balls, and they held them up in front of us hysterical housewives to justify to us idiots that the children are no more contaminated than if they swallowed moth balls.

"They Don't Know How to Handle Us Hysterical Housewives."

They don't know how to handle us emotional people, which is wonderful. I thank God they don't, because otherwise we'd never win. I'm glad I'm hysterical. Now they're putting sociologists and psychologists in the field to come deal with us crazy people, us emotional people.

Health Effects: Obstacles and Solutions

Obstacles

Emotional Responses to Health Effects   Handling a serious illness in the family is difficult. Environmentally caused illnesses are all the more tragic and difficult for families because they are less understood, harder to treat, and caused by corporate carelessness. It is especially stressful for women since we are the primary caretakers of the ill family member. Whether we are dealing with illness or death, in ourselves or in others, we feel many emotions: denial, sadness, fear, and anger.

> **Denial:** You deny the death, hoping to cheer others up. You become a bit hard. You close off your feelings as you see someone dying.
>
> We are the strong ones. We have no one to break down with. We cannot show remorse, cry or be sad with our groups, whenever we feel like it. Most times, when it is time to cry, we are the ones helping others to express their grief, enabling the process, rather than participating in it for ourselves. As organizers we are involved in the recovery, the moving on.
>
> **Sadness:** Yet it's hard to keep being pumped up. You're losing still another person in your support group. We have delivered eulogies

to beloved community leaders and have felt the loss of the entire community and have expressed that with sadness.

> Death of children at a site is the most devastating. We have children ourselves and when we counsel others on the loss of a child, we are reminded of our own child's vulnerability. We own the problem twice.
>
> **Fear:** It's terrifying. You wonder who's next.
>
> **Anger:** I really had to work off my anger. My daughter was contaminated and had symptoms and I was contaminated and exposed to the chemicals. "I'm going to get these people," I thought, "they just can't do this to me and get away with it." I wanted to get them back.

Solutions

It's o.k. to be emotional. Warm and caring people feel emotions. In our work, we are reclaiming the role of women as healers and nurturers. Acknowledge your emotions and let your sadness, anger, and fear lead you to ACTION.

Obstacles

Physicians' Lack of Knowledge on Illnesses Due to Toxic Exposure   Your local family physician is not likely to know anything about toxic chemicals. Medical students receive only 4 hours of training on this subject in 4 years of medical school.

Solutions

It's our job to educate our doctors, so that they know what questions to ask us and how to treat our families when we become ill. Shortly after this conference CCHW began a newsletter called "Environmental Health Monthly" which is sent to doctors across the country to educate them about environmental health issues. Contact CCHW to get your local doctors on the mailing list.

Obstacles

Too Much Emphasis on Cancer   Scientists and government agencies who study our communities have not validated all the types of health effects that may occur. In their view there's only a problem if a population shows up with cancers and reproductive problems. They are not so quick to acknowledge or accept, for example, neurological damage or immune system dysfunction.

Solutions

Be persistent. Don't give up. Trust your instincts. We are being forced to be living experiments of chemical exposure. If you believe there's a real problem which they're not acknowledging, don't accept what they tell you. Contact CCHW for advice about what to do.

Obstacles

Experts   The environmental science field is not all that big. The same "experts" get called in to evaluate communities all over the country. Some of them do good work, but some of them do not. Many "experts" have bad reputations with environmental groups because they act more like "hired guns" than scientists and professionals.

Solutions

Let CCHW know of your experiences dealing with scientists and other experts. CCHW will keep a "Hit List" of names of people to avoid. If they are brought to your community, just say, "No thanks, we're not co-

operating until this person is replaced." Try to check an expert's credentials and find out which other communities they have worked in. Call those communities to find out what kind of job they did. A national network of sympathetic doctors and industrial hygienists has also been created to help exposed workers and their families deal with work-related health problems. These professionals may be helpful to our local groups. Contact CCHW for more information.[*]

Obstacles

Intimidation of Scientific Language   Lots of scientific and medical terms are thrown at us by government agencies and scientists who study our communities. Learning the language they use and knowing how they operate can be confusing and difficult.

Solutions

CCHW has a science department that can help you decipher technical reports and studies. There are books available for community groups that make science accessible to everyone. These books describe how epidemiological surveys are done and how to conduct your own health survey.

---

[*]P. O. Box 6806, Falls Church, VA 22040. (703) 237-2249

◆◆◆

NINETY-ONE

From Garbage to Subsistence

Maria Mies

Phase 1: From students' movement to squatter movement: The Sozialistische Selbsthilfe Köln (SSK) is one of the oldest self-help initiatives in Cologne (Germany); its beginning dates back to the Students Movement in the early 1970s. Inspired by Herbert Marcuse's argument that the "revolution," the alternative to capitalist, industrial society, could no longer be expected from the working class in industrialized, affluent societies, but rather from drop-outs, marginalized groups and the colonized in the Third World, a group of students in Cologne initiated a scheme

whose objective was to give shelter to youngsters who had run away from authoritarian homes, remand homes or even prisons. They claimed that they could offer a better education and better prospects for life to these young people than could the establishment institutions. Their initiative was originally called *Sozialpädagogische Sondermassnahme Köln* (Special Social-Pedagogical Measures, Cologne) and they laid down a set of principles according to which anybody would be accepted in their commune. Initially, the project was supported by the Social Welfare Department of the Municipality of Cologne, who not only gave a house to the SSK but also agreed to pay the same amount for a boy or a girl, which they would have paid to a remand home. Eventually however, it became evident that this project was too expensive for the municipality. Moreover, neighbours began to protest against the SSK, which accepted everybody, including alcoholics and drug addicts.

When, in 1974, the Social Welfare Department decided to close down the SSK, the group, which then consisted of about 100 people, found temporary political asylum in the *Fachhochschule Köln* in the Department of Social Pedagogy and Social Work.

The question then arose of whether the SSK could survive without the municipality's financial support. About 30 people decided to continue the SSK and to depend only on their own work and the help of friends and sympathizers. They henceforth changed the name to: Sozialistische Selbsthilfe Köln (Socialist Self-Help, Cologne, SSK) and laid down a series of strict rules for all who wished to become members. The most important of these were:

- No money is accepted from the state, not even social welfare money. Self-reliance is the main principle.

- Everybody, men and women must work for the livelihood of all. Every morning this work is distributed by the whole commune.

- All income is pooled and distributed equally.

- No violence (beating, harassing etc.) is allowed within the SSK.

- No drugs and alcohol are allowed.

- Everybody must participate in political work and actions.

- The SSK has no leadership. All problems are discussed in plenary sessions and decisions are taken according to the consensus principle.

The SSK-commune saw these rules and principles not only as necessary for their own survival but also as the beginning of a truly socialist society in which both the capitalist and the centralist and bureaucratic socialist models of society, then prevailing in Eastern Europe, were to be transcended. They saw their own commune as a model of such a society.

For their livelihood the SSK did various odd jobs, such as: transporting coal; collecting and re-selling old furniture, clothes or household equipment; repair jobs; cleaning houses; gardening, and so on. They virtually lived off the garbage of our rich society.

The SSK's political activities centered around the problems created by the modernization strategy of the commercial community and the city planners, which penalized mainly the poor, the elderly, and foreign workers. Due to this policy of transforming the city centre of Cologne into a complex of banks, insurance and business centres, older and cheaper housing areas were destroyed and their inhabitants pushed to the (more expensive) city periphery. For many years the SSK-commune was in the forefront of the squatter movement in Cologne, which fought against the destruction of old, cheap neighbourhoods.

Another important political struggle centered around the inhuman conditions which prevailed in many state-run psychiatric clinics. By publicly exposing these conditions and offering shelter in their commune to patients who had run away from these institutions, they initiated a wide critical debate on Germany's psychiatric system, forced the authorities to close one of the more notorious clinics and start reforming the others.

In these and many other political struggles the SSK's strength lay in its potential for quick, direct, non-bureaucratic action, innovative publicity by means of wall-newspapers, a direct link between action and reflection, and their commitment to live by their own strength and be open to all the downtrodden, the social 'garbage' of our industrial society. Over the years the SSK became well-known and through its struggles gained considerable power. The bureaucrats in Cologne Town Hall feared SSK exposures and often gave in to their demands. Five new SSK centres, which followed the same principles, were eventually created in the region around Cologne.

Phase 2: From Chernobyl to the ecology question and the discovery of subsistence: About 1986, after the meltdown at Chernobyl, the SSK-commune became aware of the ecology problem. They began to question their model of socialism and asked themselves what was its use in an environment poisoned and polluted by radioactivity and other toxic wastes of industrial society. They held many discussions on how to change the SSK in order to contribute to a more ecologically sound society. But they failed to arrive at a consensus, and the organization faced a grave crisis, while several members left the commune.

Around this time my friend Claudia v. Werlhof and I organized a conference at the Evangelische

Akademie, Bad Boll—Die Subsistenzperspektive, ein Weg ins Freie (The Subsistence Perspective—a Path into the Open). The conference's objective was to bring together activists and theoreticians from the women's movement, the alternative and ecology movements and the Third World in order to clarify our ideas about a possible common strategy or perspective: The Subsistence Perspective. Three members of the SSK were also invited because I felt that they had practised this perspective for years. This conference later proved to have indeed opened a 'path into the open' for the SSK, because not only did the three activists discover the global interconnections between their own work and the ideals and such diverse movements as a peasants' movement in Venezuela, the peoples' struggles against modernization and industrialization in Ladakh, the Chipko movement in India, but they also discovered the richness encapsulated in the concept subsistence. They realized that it encompassed what they had been aspiring to during all those years. In an SSK brochure called 'Land in Sight' Lothar Gothe (one of SSK's founders) and Maggie Lucke defined the concept as follows:

> The word (subsistence) is derived from the Latin word *subsistere*, which has several meanings: "to stand still, to make a halt, to persist, to resist, to stay back, to remain backward." Today the word means: "to be able to live on (by) the basic (minimum) necessities of life" or: "to exist and sustain oneself by one's own strength."

Today we include all these meanings and connotations when we talk of the Subsistence Perspective as the way out, the emergency exit out of our blockaded, overgrown, industrial society.

To live according to the guiding star of subsistence means no longer to live off the exploitation of the environment or of foreign peoples. For human life it means a new balance between talking and giving, between each one of us and other people, our people and other peoples, our species and the other species in nature. . . .*

Phase 3: From garbage to compost: The Subsistence Conference at Bad Boll not only meant the discov-

ery of a new guiding concept but also the beginning of a new process in which their old utopia could be re-created within a new ecological framework. Through a friend present at this conference, the three SSK activists came into contact with a biologist, Peter van Dohlen who had developed a method to make compost out of organic kitchen waste in closed containers. He had tried in vain to persuade the Green Party of Cologne to propagate this compost-technology, which was particularly appropriate for cities. When the three activists met Peter it was a meeting of people who, left to themselves, had begun to despair and saw no way out of their crisis. But by coming together and exchanging ideas a new and creative process started which is still on-going. To make a long story short: the technology developed by Peter provided the SSK with a new type of meaningful, self-sustaining ecological work, while for him, here at last were people who grasped the significance of his compost-making technology and, as a collective, were ready to work to make it function. Having adapted an old oil container for compost-making, the SSK people collected kitchen garbage from their neighbourhood in Gummersbach and experimented with it. The result was excellent: within three weeks kitchen garbage could be transformed into compost. In addition they also learned Jean Paine's method, whereby biomass from tree branches, shrubs and hedges is used not only to generate heat in a bio-generator but can also be used to restore soil fertility.

At the same time, in accordance with their principles of combining practical, manual subsistence work with political work, the SSK approached the municipal authorities in cities and towns where they had branches, and demanded contracts for SSK groups to make compost out of household organic waste. They demanded to be paid a sum equal to that paid by citizens for the dumping of their household garbage—at present this is almost 300DM per ton. The struggle for contracts lasted several years, but the SSK had already begun work and their compost project gained more and more support from the people.

The political significance of this project is that a new, cheap, people-controlled ecological technology was developed to return the bio-mass (kitchen garbage) back to the soil as compost, instead of simply dumping or burning it, and thus further polluting the environment. From the beginning, Lothar Gothe clearly saw the strategic importance of the waste problem to which industrial society has no

---

*Gothe, Lothar and Maggie Lucke, *Land in Sight*, Cologne, 1990.

solution. What consumerist society calls waste to be rid of as soon as possible, is raw material for a newly emerging waste disposal industry; the more waste produced the better for this industry. The main waste-disposal industrialist in the area who holds a monopoly of this industry, Edelhoff, had contracts with all the municipalities to collect all household waste, including organic waste. The SSK, by claiming this waste which constitutes about 40 per cent of the household garbage, effectively resisted the privatization and the destruction of valuable bio-mass, a common resource, for the sake of profit-making.

Today the SSK has composting contracts in Cologne and four other towns and municipalities. It is noteworthy that the municipal council of Gummersbach has agreed to change its contract with Edelhoff and to extend the SSK's contract to 400 more households. The municipal authorities have apparently begun to understand that the industrial disposal of waste and kitchen garbage cannot be a solution. Despite their initial resistance they are now in favour of such groups as the SSK.

Phase 4: From compost to subsistence agriculture: From the beginning the SSK had stressed the interconnections between the various problems with which they dealt: joblessness; the ecology problem; the inanity of most work; a sense of futility; loneliness; health problems; lack of dignity and recognition; overconsumption and addictions, and so on. Therefore also in their practical, political work similar also synergetic solutions should be sought.

A logical continuation of the composting process was that some SSK-groups began to look around for land, for compost belongs to the land, as Lothar Gothe said. At first the SSK sold the compost in Green shops, to gardeners and others, but it became clear that not enough city- or townspeople needed or wanted it. What then to do with the compost?

A piece of waste land in a valley called 'Duster Grundchen' was therefore acquired — privately purchased but used communely. For the first time some SSK members who, so far, knew only an urban existence began to work on the land; cleaning; laying out an experimental plot; looking after the bio-generator, and so on. For the first time these urbanites began to experience the joy of doing hard, manual but ecologically meaningful work on the land, in co-operation with nature. Some of the SSK Gummersbach's younger members were so enthusiastic that they would walk 15 km from Gummersbach to work in this valley.

For Lothar Gothe the question was, could this ecological subsistence work be accepted not only by the SSK members but eventually provide a solution for society at large? Because only if people began to *understand* the significance and the need for this work on the land and to *enjoy doing it* could this approach have a future. *The combination of work as a burden and work as pleasure* is a necessary precondition for healing both the earth and society.

Work in the Duster Grundchen, the logical continuation of the strategy of consumption critique, the use of organic garbage for compost-making, began to reveal the interconnected character of the holistic social and ecological approach we called "subsistence perspective."

It not only sparked off a new sense of enthusiasm, enjoyment, meaningfulness, political and personal purpose in SSK members and others, particularly some younger people, but also a new wave of reflection, theorizing and political creativity. In a paper produced in this process of action and reflection sent to the chairman of the local authority (Regierungspräsident), Lothar Gothe pointed out that neither the government nor any official party had succeeded in solving so many interrelated problems in one single project, namely: combining ecological with social problem-solving; healing the earth as well as people and communities by creating meaningful work, giving a new sense of purpose to socially marginalized women and men; developing a new, appropriate technology out of discarded, obsolete objects; recultivating wasteland; re-establishing a new community-sense among people who are concerned and feel responsible for the future of life on this planet; and finally, creating new hope not only for those directly involved in the project but for many who have lost a sense of orientation.

It is this project's *synergic* character which was not planned but which developed out of necessity and which guarantees its survival. Had it been developed as a monocultural one-issue project, planned by experts, it could not have survived.

Guided by the subsistence perspective and the need to get enough hay for the animals, the next step was to buy an old farmhouse and repair the old equipment for subsistence production. At the same time the group secured a contract for composting the kitchen garbage for a series of villages. This compost is used as fertilizer in the new fields and gardens where experimental organic farming is carried out to produce vegetables for the SSK workers on the farm. Chickens, pigs, ducks, goats, sheep and a horse which pulls a cart to collect garbage, are kept on the farm. At present about six to eight people can live by this subsistence work.

Conclusion

In summarizing the main features of the subsistence perspective which has informed and inspired the initiatives described above, as well as many ecological and feminist grassroots movements . . . we can see that these struggles for survival are a practical critique not only of an aggressive, exploitative, ecologically destructive technology, but of commodity-producing, growth-oriented capitalist, or socialist industrial systems. Although none of these movements, initiatives, communities have spelt out a full-fledged explicit new utopia for an ecologically sound, feminist, non-colonial, non-exploitative society there is enough evidence in their practice and theory to show that their concept of a "good society" differs from the classical Marxian utopia. While Marx and his followers saw capitalism as the "midwife" of the "material base" upon which a socialist society could be built, these movements and initiatives demonstrate their rejection of the universal supermarket as a model of a better society, even if it was equally accessible to all. Neither do they accept Engel's statement that what is good for the ruling class should be good for everybody. These women's and men's concept of what constitutes a "good life," of "freedom" is different, as is their concept of economics, politics and culture. Their utopia may not yet be spelt out explicitly, but its components are already being tested in everyday practice, it is a potentially *concrete utopia*. What are the main characteristics of this subsistence perspective?

1. The aim of *economic activity* is not to produce an ever-growing mountain of commodities and money (wages or profit) for an anonymous market but the creation and re-creation of *life,* that means, the satisfaction of fundamental human needs mainly by the production of use-values not by the purchase of commodities. Self-provisioning, self-sufficiency, particularly in food and other basic needs; regionality; and decentralization from a state bureaucracy are the main economic principles. The local and regional re-

sources are used but not exploited; the market plays a subordinate role.

2. These economic activities are based on new *relationships:* a) to *nature:* nature is respected in her richness and diversity, both for her own sake and as a precondition for the survival of all creatures on this planet. Hence, nature is not exploited for the sake of profit, instead, whenever possible, the damage done to nature by capitalism is being healed. Human interaction with nature is based on respect, co-operation and reciprocity. Man's domination over nature — the principle that has guided Northern society since the Renaissance — is replaced by the recognition that humans are part of nature, that nature has her own subjectivity.

b) *Among people.* As man's domination over nature is related to man's domination over women and other human beings a different, non-exploitative relationship to nature cannot be established without a change in human relationships, particularly between *women and men.* This means not only a change in the various *divisions of labour* (sexual division; manual/mental and urban/rural labour, and so on) but mainly the substitution of money or commodity relationships by such principles as reciprocity, mutuality, solidarity, reliability, sharing and caring, respect for the individual and responsibility for the "whole." The need for *subsistence security* is satisfied not by trust in one's bank account or a social welfare state, but by trust in the reliability of one's community. A subsistence perspective can be realized only within such a network of reliable, stable human relations, it cannot be based on the atomized, self-centred individuality of the market economy.

3. A subsistence perspective is based on and promotes participatory or grassroots democracy — not only in so far as political decisions *per se* are concerned, but also with regard to all economic, social and technological decisions. Divisions between politics and economics, or public and private spheres are largely abolished. The personal is the political. Not only the parliament but also everyday life and life-style are battlefields of politics. Political responsibility and action is no longer expected solely from elected representatives but assumed by all in a communal and practical way.

4. A subsistence perspective necessarily requires a multidimensional or synergic problem-solving approach. It is based on the recognition that not only

the different dominance systems and problems are interconnected, but also that they cannot be solved in isolation or by a mere technological fix. Thus social problems (patriarchal relations, inequality, alienation, poverty) must be solved together with ecological problems. This interconnectedness of all life on earth, of problems and solutions is one of the main insights of ecofeminism.

5. A subsistence perspective demands a new paradigm of science, technology and knowledge. Instead of the prevailing instrumentalist, reductionist science and technology—based on dualistic dichotomies which have constituted and maintain man's domination over nature, women and other people—ecologically sound, feminist, subsistence science and technology will be developed in participatory action with the people. Such a grass roots, women and people-based knowledge and science will lead to a re-evaluation of older survival wisdom and traditions and also utilize modern knowledge in such a way that people maintain control over their technology and survival base. Social relations are not external to technology but rather incorporated in the artefacts as such. Such science and technology will therefore not reinforce unequal social relationships but will be such as to make possible greater social justice.

6. A subsistence perspective leads to a reintegration of culture and work, of work as both burden and pleasure. It does not promise bread without sweat nor imply a life of toil and tears. On the contrary, the main aim is happiness and a fulfilled life. Culture is wider than specialized activity exclusive to a professional elite—it imbues everyday life.

This also necessitates a reintegration of spirit and matter, a rejection of both mechanical materialism and of airy spirituality. This perspective cannot be realized within a dualistic worldview.

7. A subsistence perspective resists all efforts to further privatize, and/or commercialize the commons: water, air, waste, soil, resources. Instead it fosters common responsibility for these gifts of nature and demands their preservation and regeneration.

8. Most of the characteristics in the foregoing would also be appropriate to the conception of an ecofeminist society. In particular, the practical and theoretical insistence on the interconnectedness of all life, on a concept of politics that puts everyday practice and experiential ethics, the consistency of means and ends, in the forefront. And yet, the two

examples previously documented are not feminist projects in the narrow sense in which this term is often understood, namely, all-women initiatives in which men have no role to play. In fact, the initiators of these projects were men. In the ecofeminist movement there are many examples of women-only projects and initiatives. But the question is: can we conceive of a perspective for a better future society by concentrating only on women, or by building all-women islands within a capitalist-patriarchal ocean? As ecofeminists emphasize overcoming established dualisms and false dichotomies, as they want to put the interdependence of all life at the centre of a new ethic and politics, it would be quite inconsistent to exclude men from this network of responsibility for the creation and continuation of life. Ecofeminism does not mean, as some argue, that women will clean up the ecological mess which capitalist-patriarchal men have caused; women will not eternally be the *Trümmerfrauen* (the women who clear up the ruins after the patriarchal wars). Therefore, a subsistence perspective necessarily means men begin to share, *in practice,* the responsibility for the creation and preservation of life on this planet. Therefore, men must start a movement to redefine their identity. They must give up their involvement in destructive commodity production for the sake of accumulation and begin to share women's work for the preservation of life. In practical terms this means they have to share unpaid subsistence work: in the household, with children, with the old and sick, in ecological work to heal the earth, in new forms of subsistence production.

In this respect it is essential that the old sexist division of labour criticized by the feminists in the 1970s—that is, men become the theoreticians of the subsistence perspective while women do the practical work—is abolished. This division between mental and manual labour is contrary to the principles of a subsistence perspective. The two examples documented above are significant in this respect, in so far as they demonstrate that men have begun to see the importance of the need to overcome this dichotomy.

9. Moreover, if the dichotomy between life-producing and preserving and commodity-producing activities is abolished, if men acquire caring and nurturing qualities which have so far been considered women's domain, and if, in an economy based on self-reliance, mutuality, self-provisioning, not women alone but men too are involved in subsistence

production they will have neither time nor the inclination to pursue their destructive war games. A subsistence perspective will be the most significant contribution to the de-militarization of men and society. Only a society based on a subsistence perspective can afford to live in peace with nature, and uphold peace between nations, generations and men and women, because it does not base its concept of a good life on the exploitation and domination of nature and other people.

Finally, it must be pointed out that we are not the first to spell out a subsistence perspective as a vision for a better society. Wherever women and men have envisaged a society in which all—women and men, old and young, all races and cultures—could share the "good life," where social justice, equality, human dignity, beauty and joy in life were not just utopian dreams never to be realized (except for a small elite or postponed to an after-life), there has been close to what we call a subsistence perspective. Kamla Bhasin, an Indian feminist who tried to spell out what "sustainable development" could mean for all women in the world lists a number of principles of sustainability similar to the features of a subsistence perspective. It is clear to her, as it is to many women

and men who are not blind to the reality that we live in a limited world, that sustainability is not compatible with the existing profit- and growth-oriented development paradigm. And this means that the standard of living of the North's affluent societies cannot be generalized. This was already clear to Mahatma Gandhi 60 years ago, who, when asked by a British journalist whether he would like India to have the same standard of living as Britain, replied: "To have its standard of living a tiny country like Britain had to exploit half the globe. How many globes will India need to exploit to have the same standard of living?"* From an ecological and feminist perspective, moreover, even if there were more globes to be exploited, it is not even desirable that this development paradigm and standard of living was generalized, because it has failed to fulfill its promises of happiness, freedom, dignity and peace, even for those who have profited from it.

---

*Quoted by Kamla Bhasin, "Environment, Daily Life and Health: Women's Strategies for Our Common Future." Speech at Fifth International Congress on Women's Health, Copenhagen, 25 August 1992, p. 11.

NINETY-TWO

◆◆◆

Daughters of Growing Things

Rachel L. Bagby

This essay tells of an ongoing effort to maintain mutually nurturing relationships with nature, human and elemental, in the midst of a low- and no-income urban village community of about 5,000 people. *Webster's New World Dictionary* reserves the use of the word *village* for certain types of living units located in the country. Yet, despite its location within the city of Philadelphia, the area on which this essay focuses meets every other qualification listed under "village community" in that it is comprised of a group of houses, is larger than a hamlet, functions as a self-governing political unit, and has several half-acre plots that are worked by the community.

Philadelphia Community Rehabilitation Corporation (PCRC) is the institution through which this work is accomplished. Momma — Rachel Edna Samiella Rebecca Jones Bagby — is the woman who founded it. PCRC's operating budget is financed from the $4,000 in rents collected each month, a yearly bazaar (complete with prizes for the best sweet potato pie), and a seemingly infinite number of chicken dinners, plant sales, and bus trips to Atlantic City. It employs a regular staff of three to five and numerous independent contractors. Every summer a handful of teenagers get their first work experience there. Its "repeopling" program has renovated and rented more than fifty formerly vacant homes and created a twelve-unit shared-house.

And then there are the gardens, the focus of this essay.

The material was culled from more than forty cassette recordings of phone conversations between me and Momma — between Northern California and North Philadelphia, Pa. — over the past 3 years. It is essential to have Momma tell her stories in her own, inimitable voice. While the interview format comes close, we are still working on a hybrid form of prose and musical notation that will do the rhythms and melodies of her speech justice. What may seem to be misspellings and grammatical errors are intentional, ways of honoring Momma's voice. Much of her power in the community comes from her *way* with people. Much of that way is communicated in her manner of speaking.

DAUGHTER: How much land do you have?

MOTHER: I think it's about 5 acres. I imagine if you measured it, it would be about 5 acres. All the different lots we have.

DAUGHTER: And how do you choose your lots for the gardens?

MOTHER: We didn't choose the lots. We just got the lot that we could get. These were empty lots, in other words. Rather than to grow weeds, we just begged the city to let us have them. And we paid for some of them, too. [At a cost of about $500 per half acre.] Some of them are really ours; we own.

DAUGHTER: So these were empty lots?

MOTHER: They were all empty lots, yes, and we just got them, we asked for them in order to make the place look better than growing a whole lot of weeds. We just grow something that's more useful — food and flowers. Make it beautiful. And the food is outta sight. Rather than to grow weeds. Why sit and grow weeds when you can do something with it? So this is what we did, and it's working, and it's spreading. We have a meeting now every month.

DAUGHTER: We'll come back to the meetings. First tell me how much food you get from the garden.

MOTHER: Out of that garden? We made more tomatoes than we could use and still have tomatoes coming out of our ears. Green peppers, too. And we still have them.

DAUGHTER: So what did you do? Can them?

MOTHER: Yeah, we canned them. And the tomatoes are canned. Remember I told you? Tomatoes are canned, the peppers are canned, and I have a lot of the greens canned. Vegetables we don't buy. Peas we dried. We still got dried peas. California black eyes. And it yields a lot because, see, what you do is as fast as one crop get through, you plant another one until the frost falls. In the winter, we can't plant; before then we plant winter greens. We plant okra, then we plant potatoes; we plant cucumber; and then we plant carrots. You know, so we just put different things in as food. We just keep things going until the frost falls.

DAUGHTER: So you rotate the crops?

MOTHER: We rotate the crops. That's how you yield more. Right now, we're planting some seeds, as soon as, next week we'll be planting seeds so we can set them outdoors when the weather breaks.

DAUGHTER: How did you have to prepare the land? And what was the original shape? Wasn't there glass and bottles and all that?

MOTHER: We just took hoes and rakes and stuff and raked it. Dug it as deep as the plants will grow, and raked all that stuff and put it out.

DAUGHTER: What?

MOTHER: We dug with something called a grub hoe and just paid some boys for just going in and digging it up. Tole them, "Just dig it as deep as the food will grow."

DAUGHTER: How deep is that?

MOTHER: About as deep as my leg.

DAUGHTER: So that if you stood up, your waist would be at the cement?

MOTHER: My knee would be in the ground.

DAUGHTER: So we're talking maybe 2 feet?

MOTHER: Yeah, 2 or 3 feet. What we did, we did that and then we asked for top soil and had folks go out in the park and get the horse manure from the park.

DAUGHTER: What park?

MOTHER: Woodside Park, right here. You remember Woodside Park! The stables — the drippings from the horses. Stable compost, they call it. Stable manure. It's one of the largest parks in the United States! That's right! See, when you come, you're in such a hurry you forgot all the good parts. All you see is these raggedy places. But there are some good parts.

DAUGHTER: I know Momma. The best part in Philadelphia is *you!*

MOTHER: Well . . . There are some good parts. Anyway, that's where we get the compost. We go out there and get it and it don't cost anything. Just go out there and haul it.

DAUGHTER: It's free.

MOTHER: Yeah. You don't pay for that! It's there for the getting. It makes such good dirt. You heap it up, all that stuff. That's how your crop grows.

DAUGHTER: Now, you said you paid some boys to do it.

MOTHER: We had two or three boys and we paid the men to dig it up for us. We didn't have a plow. I know how we used to do it in the South, turn it with the turnplow and two horses. But we didn't have the turnplow here, so we just paid the men to dig it up and dig it deep and they had to dig it right.

DAUGHTER: How long did they work on this?

MOTHER: It didn't take them long. Took 'em like 2 days.

DAUGHTER: And you paid some young boys to work on it, too?

MOTHER: Yes, about $3 an hour even.

DAUGHTER: So they were employed for that little bit. How old were they?

MOTHER: One was—I think the best worker was 14. His name was Joey, I think. I can't remember his name. I called him Joey.

DAUGHTER: So after they turned it, they plowed it up and then hauled out all that they dug up?

MOTHER: No, we took the rake and raked up what wasn't too good. Raked up as much as we could. They, you set it out and they picked it up, then you paid them to get rid of it is what we did.

DAUGHTER: There's still glass and stuff down there, but the food just grows around it?

MOTHER: That's what I'm saying. That's what we did.

DAUGHTER: Then you got the horse drippings?

MOTHER: We got that from the horse stables before we raked up the place and had it all chopped up in there together.

DAUGHTER: Oh, I see. So first you turned it by digging it up, then you put the drippings down and turned it all up together?

MOTHER: Right. Then chop it up again.

DAUGHTER: Who did the planting?

MOTHER: Well, I supervised the planting.

DAUGHTER: Who helped you?

MOTHER: Most everybody helped.

DAUGHTER: Women, men, about how many people?

MOTHER: Six of us.

DAUGHTER: Do you plant from seeds?

MOTHER: You plant from seeds, some of them were planted from seeds and some of them were plants we bought. The ones that we couldn't get enough plants up from seeds we bought.

DAUGHTER: What did you buy?

MOTHER: Red cabbage and carrots, more or less we bought those seeds. And all the herbs, I bought those seeds. But see, once you plant them, you don't plant them the next year.

DAUGHTER: They just come back?

MOTHER: Yes. Now I did say *all.* I'm wrong, because thyme you don't plant anymore, the peppermint you don't plant, so many of the stuff you don't plant anymore. You just plant it one time and it comes back every year.

DAUGHTER: And you timed it all based on the moon?

MOTHER: Yes. I always plant according to the moon. According to that, I plant. According to the light I know when to plant.

DAUGHTER: So how much did it cost for . . . ?

MOTHER: Oh! I forgot!

DAUGHTER: I know Momma, just try to estimate for seeds and . . .

MOTHER: I think the tools were quite expensive.

DAUGHTER: Let me ask you the full question, all right? The whole question is, how much did it cost for the seeds, the plants, the hoes, the other equipment that you got, paying the boys? How much do you think all that cost?

MOTHER: Well, the land was about $1,000 for the land. And we put the fence up. I think that wire fence was $1,300—cyclone fence. Then we used the boys 2 days and I paid them, that was $3 an hour. There was two boys, $3 an hour for 16 hours. The seeds run you less than a dollar a pack, you know, and I didn't get but one pack each because I had about five or six different herbs, so that's what the seeds are.

DAUGHTER: But you got other plants.

MOTHER: The plants will run you about $1.50 to $2.00. Say, about $10 worth of plants. That's not the seeds, though. The seeds were about $5 for all the seeds, say, $10 for the seeds. That's just an estimate, now.

DAUGHTER: And the equipment?

MOTHER: Well, we bought . . . We don't have to buy equipment every year. We bought about $200 worth of equipment, but we don't buy that every year.

DAUGHTER: Well, you don't buy the land or the fence every year either. It looks like your yearly cost is $20 for the seeds and plants.

MOTHER: Yes, you can put about $20 or $25 for the year. For the seeds themselves, and the plants. They just use the equipment over and over again.

DAUGHTER: That $25 feeds how many people for how long?

MOTHER: About twelve households for one season. When spring comes, you start all over again.

DAUGHTER: So it feeds you for the fall and the winter, doesn't it?

MOTHER: Yeah, that's one season. During the summer we eat a lot out of there. We don't have to can it.

DAUGHTER: So it feeds you year round? Vegetables.

MOTHER: Yeah. Vegetables year round. I told you. Vegetables we don't buy.

DAUGHTER: That's a big savings, Momma.

MOTHER: I'm trying to get these folks to realize that.

DAUGHTER: What happens at your meetings? You said the meetings have been growing.

MOTHER: We trying to get them to realize how much they save by doing this. And spread it. Because the city has so many vacant lots so they can plant these things. This is what we're trying to get them to do and show them the value of having, of doing this. We see so many of them lazy, they say they can't do, but you *can* do it.

DAUGHTER: You say the meetings have been getting bigger?

MOTHER: Yes. I think the meetings have been getting larger and more valuable.

DAUGHTER: How many people come to the meetings?

MOTHER: We had forty-nine last week.

DAUGHTER: And you're meeting once a week?

MOTHER: Once a month.

DAUGHTER: Who comes to these meetings?

MOTHER: Just people that're interested in planting gardens. Neighborhood people. And now we're letting them see how the food looks canned.

DAUGHTER: That's what you do in your meetings? What else do you do? It sounds like a real educational program.

MOTHER: That's what it is! See how it look canned, and also how it tastes.

DAUGHTER: You give them samples?

MOTHER: Yes. I just thought of that out of my head, you know, but it's a lot of work.

DAUGHTER: How many meetings have you had?

MOTHER: We had one last month. And this month we'll have another one. We plan to have one every month.

DAUGHTER: You're building up to planting season? How did you get people interested before, since you've just started the meetings? This is the first time you've had them, right?

MOTHER: This is the first time I started the meetings.

DAUGHTER: You just go around and talk to people?

MOTHER: Like door-to-door campaigning. Door-to-door education.

DAUGHTER: You are such a jewel on this planet, Momma. You are wonderful!

MOTHER: (*Quietly*) What do you mean?

DAUGHTER: What do you mean what do I mean? You really are. I don't know. It's real unusual what you're doing and you're helping people and you're keeping that connection between the Earth and people and . . .

MOTHER: You know what? (*Laughs*) We help ourselves when we help others. You can't help yourself unless you, you have to help somebody, too.

DAUGHTER: Tell me a little about your background. *I* know it. *You* know it, but tell me again so I can get it on this tape.

MOTHER: See, what give me the idea to do this, is I just got sick and tired of walking by weeds. Absolutely a disgrace to me. Instead of growing weeds, if weeds can grow where there's nothing but cement and bricks and stuff, if weeds can grow in there, something else can grow also. And you have the weeds taller than I am. People be afraid to go by Twenty-first

Street. That's where we had to go to go to the store, and people would snatch pocketbooks and run over you, and you couldn't find them in the weeds. So that's how we got started with that. Now, when I was home, I came up on the farm . . .

DAUGHTER: Home where?

MOTHER: South Carolina. I came up on a farm. My father was a farmer. And I loved it. We grew our stuff there. I really loved it. To sit there and get in a field of watermelon and walk on watermelons from one end to the other. I thought it was fun.

DAUGHTER: To walk on them? And they wouldn't bust?

MOTHER: When they were smaller, you know. When they get ripe, they get tender.

DAUGHTER: You mean when they're smaller, they're harder?

MOTHER: Yes. And I was little, too. Anyway, what I'm trying to say is he would grow so many watermelons that you could hardly see the ground. That's just how [many] there were. Sweet taters, peanuts, all kinds of beans, white potatoes. So, I learned that he would plant his stuff at a certain time. Some I have forgotten, but he would get the *Farmer's Almanac*. . . .

I plant things in the ground when the sign of the moon . . . you plant the fish. In that *Farmer's Almanac*. Like the carrots. I won't plant carrots from the corner of the moon. I plant like beans and those kind of things that go on top of the ground. Anything underneath, you plant the fish. And peas, you plant them on the twins and your leaves will be hanging with beans and stuff. I'll never forget that, because I used to have to drop that stuff. I used to love to do that, too; drop the seeds in the ground.

I knew how to drop them. I knew how to take my hand and put it in so it won't spread out. I put it in right down and I could bend then, you know, when you're young you can bend, you can buckle. And I would take my hand and put it right down in the ground. I would do an acre or so a day and wouldn't think nothing of it. And I loved it. It's just in me. That's all.

I like to see things grow instead of wasting. And all these vacant lots you can't, you don't have the money to put houses on all them, but you can buy a little dollar worth of seeds and put on them. Can't put houses on them, but you sit and eat stuff that comes from them. Look at the flowers that are so pretty. That sort of thing. So this is what started. And everybody, it's spreading, you know.

DAUGHTER: It's really wonderful Momma. I'm wondering about how Philadelphia Green [a horticultural society devoted to assisting neighborhood revitalization efforts] and how the city [of Philadelphia] got involved. You approached the city, right? The city wasn't doing it at first, right?

MOTHER: No, but then we approached the city to help us, because I found out they could help us do a lot. That's how I got in with them. Anything that I think can give us a hand, because we need a lot of help out here. Anybody that can give us a hand we approach them. The Philadelphia Green can have a lot of things; they can help with the tools, they can send out people to help, now like we don't have those tapes and stuff. They have that and they bring it out and show these different gardens on these tapes and tell you what it's all about.

DAUGHTER: You mean video tapes?

MOTHER: Video tape. They have that, so then they bring it out for us. But if you don't ever ask for it, you won't get it.

DAUGHTER: Philadelphia Green has existed for a while, hasn't it?

MOTHER: See, that started when you were here, because when I was over at ACDC [Advocate Community Development Corporation], I planted the first garden over there. You were in high school and I was there working ACDC.

DAUGHTER: It was 1970?

MOTHER: Yes, something like that. I planted the first garden over there.

DAUGHTER: And Philadelphia Green existed then?

MOTHER: They existed then and I got involved when we first got the plants, the little pots to put flowers on the steps. That was Philadelphia Green. Ever since then. That's how I got started. That's why I worked there as long as I did because I was glad to be involved with people, you know. And these gardens and stuff. Now we have it ourselves. So it's a joy. It's work, but it's a joy, and we're opening a park.

DAUGHTER: What else are you planning?

MOTHER: Well, we're planning to do more gardening. We're trying hard not to slide backward. We're trying to go forwards. Add a little bit more each year.

DAUGHTER: What else are you doing?

MOTHER: Gardening, shared housing, and regular housing. We're also getting tutoring for literacy, starting to teach some people how to read and get jobs. We just started that. That's the tutoring I been wanted. I want to get that going in a big way.

DAUGHTER: Do you still have training programs for kids to get employment?

MOTHER: Yes, we still have that job bank, that's what we call that. So people can get a job. So that's it. And it keeps you going, too, just like those different directions on the *Farmer's Almanac.*

DAUGHTER: Keeps you out of trouble, too.

MOTHER: Well, I never get in too much trouble no way. I have a whole lot I can do. See, I've always been able to keep myself busy. I've never been able to not have anything to do. See, I can sit and crochet. I want to sew. I piece quilts. There's so much you can do. My goodness! If I wasn't doing that [work with PCRC] I'd stay in this house here a month and don't even go to the door and work the whole time.

DAUGHTER: How do you think what you do relates to ecology, relates to the Earth? How do you talk about that?

MOTHER: Well, I talk about it like I always do, 'cause this is where you see the real nature of the universe. The real one, without . . . before it's transformed into different things. Because even children don't have the least idea of the food they eat. What grows in the ground, what grows on top, what good for blood, what good for different things. A lot of adults don't have any idea. So that's how I relate it to everyday living.

   You get firsthand . . . everybody get a firsthand look at real nature. That's how I see it. That's how I love it. You can see it come up, you can see it grow and you see how it grows, and see it dies if you don't take care of it. That tells you something.

DAUGHTER: What does it tell you?

MOTHER: It tells you that if you're not taken care of, tells you, you got to take care of whatever you have. If you don't it will die then, or grow wild like the things in the fields, out in the woods. God has created things to stay alive without being taken care of but you can't try to, like to say, try to tame them. If you try to tame them you have to give them some of that that they get ordinarily. But the Earth is created so that everything should be taken care of.

DAUGHTER: By somebody or something?

MOTHER: By nature, and then if you interfere with it . . .

DAUGHTER: Say that again, the Earth was created . . .

MOTHER: To take care of everything on Earth. It's supposed to be taken care of. That's why, man, they say, has been made the highest of all things, because we're supposed to take care of the things that we cultivate. We're supposed to take care of them. And if we're not going to take care of it let it grow wild, the Earth will take care of it.

DAUGHTER: But if you interfere . . .

MOTHER: Right. If you interfere with it, and we must if we can survive. See, we must interfere because we need these things *to* survive. And it goes around and around. See, we need these things to survive therefore when you plant something you hafta take care of it. If you don't, it'll die. Either you take care of it or leave it alone.

DAUGHTER: What kind of resistance have you met?

MOTHER: People not wantin' to work. They don't want to get their hands dirty. They don't want to, not want to work, what I mean is, you take a lot of mothers don't want to wash the greens, they don't wanna dig down and get the carrots from the ground, they don't want to get the turnips from the ground. That's dirt. When they get it it's in the store and they clean, so to speak. So a lot of them rather go to the store and get it. I say, "How long it's been in that store? You can get it right from here and clean it, put it right in your pot or eat it like it is. Put it in your salad and you get the real, all the vitamins."

   So you have resistance, people say, I can't bend down, can't bend over, or my fingernails too long. They don't tell you that but you look at the fingernails and know they're too long to do any work. So that's the resistance you get. You get a lot of that, 'cause we

are undereducated to the facts. And not just
that, but in a lot of things. We just don't seem
to understand.

But I feel as though our children would better understand how to take care of things and
would have a better feeling of the things around
them, you know. It begins when you're, you
know, small really.

DAUGHTER: Do you work with children a lot in
the garden?

MOTHER: I love to, yes. I generally have them in
there and showing them the grass from the
weeds and from the plants and how it looks
and how they grow, too. The grass grows, too.
The weeds grow, too. That's part of nature.
They say, "What good are they?" This can be a
fertilizer for next year. "What!? Weeds!?" You
let them sit there and rot and that replenish the
Earth. See, everything has a cycle. See, those
the kinda things.

DAUGHTER: How do you get the children in there?

MOTHER: All you have to do is open the gate and
say "Come on children." If I had more strength
I'd have all the kids in there, but I don't have
the strength anymore and I can't get anyone
interested in the children. The mothers say,
yeh, take the children so they can sit down
and look at television. But all the kids that I
have met want to get out there in the garden
and they beg you to let them come in and
help. It takes a lot of time with children. And
I don't have that much time trying to do all
these other things. But I would just have someone to just go with them. I don't have that.
The mothers not interested anymore. "I gotta
look at my soap opera." And they are their
children. "Here, you can take 'em, I gotta
look at my soap opera. I'll give you money.
Take 'em to such and such a thing. You take
'em while I sit and watch my soap opera, or
do anything else." So those opposition you
get now.

DAUGHTER: And what kind of hope do you have?
Even with that opposition, how do you keep
on going?

MOTHER: Faith. I know out of all of that, it may
be one or two that you'll get through to. Even
with one, I'll be thankful. You know. Faith. Just
keep on going. You do that with children, all of
them will not end up in jail. Some of 'em come

out all right. But you don't look for a whole
lot. You don't expect a whole lot.

DAUGHTER: Why do you think that if you show
them the living things that will help them
straighten up?

MOTHER: It helps, it helps them to . . . I think it
will help them to appreciate the beauty of the
Earth, and of nature; we call it mother nature.

DAUGHTER: Do you think it helps them appreciate
the beauty of each other and their abilities?

MOTHER: This is the thing. If you can appreciate
the Earth, you can appreciate the beauty of
yourself. Even if this has beauty, I, too, have
beauty. The same creator created both. And if
I learned to take care of that I'll also take care
of myself and help take care of others. See, taking care of yourself and appreciating yourself
is the first step. But you can't go with a child
and say that. You know, you show 'em this and
they'll say, "ummmm," you know, some of
these other things'll come to them themselves,
or "if this is it, then I, look at me." Then they
won't feel so let down all the time. Sometime
we fail in trying to do that.

DAUGHTER: What do you mean you may fail?

MOTHER: Sometime you may fail, the children
may not get it. They may not. Like I say, you
may get one or two. That's what I mean. I am
who I am whether I'm black, blue, or brown.
I'm a human being. Therefore, I stand for just
as much right as you stand for although my
color is different, you see. I'm no less than you
are regardless of my color.

DAUGHTER: You see the children move past some
of that as a result of working?

MOTHER: Yes. Yes. They compare sometimes so
you let them see pictures of other children
working, say, "Well, I can do it as well as he
can do it."

DAUGHTER: You show them pictures of other children working?

MOTHER: Right. And then see that's giving them
confidence in themselves that they can do
things, too, other than throw a ball and bat a
ball. Other than break out people's windows
and curse in the street. "If they can stop and
make things, make a beautiful plant, so can
I." Some of them will stop and say that. And
they'll tell you, "Let's do our garden."

DAUGHTER: Do you have special meetings for children?

MOTHER: Special meetings, special workshops. They don't have the same workshops as the adults. Yes.

DAUGHTER: The organization has special meetings?

MOTHER: For children. We have to.

DAUGHTER: What age groups?

MOTHER: We have all ages.

DAUGHTER: From what? Starting where?

MOTHER: Acch! We have some small 'cause the, uh, the 8-year-old wanna bring the 2-year-old. Some of 'em so little, but we don't turn them away. Long as they can walk and talk, they come. From 3 up. But we don't limit the age group.

DAUGHTER: What's the oldest?

MOTHER: Well, the teenagers get so . . . but we have some teenagers help us with the others though. We have some as long as they in school and don't have a job.

DAUGHTER: And how many children are you working with?

MOTHER: Oh! I don't know.

DAUGHTER: Give me an estimate.

MOTHER: (*Sigh*) Look like to me it's 'bout fifty or more. Because of the fact — uh, it's more than that. But I can't work with the children like I want to. That's the only thing. I want to work with them on a regular basis. Like I would like to work with those children every week. Have just 2 hours or 3 hours every week working with the kids. You'd be surprised to see the difference. With all this stuff going on you have to create agencies that's going to work with the children to help, because in every state of the universe — I don't know 'bout, I haven't read much about the foreign states — there're abandoned children. Because of crack, because of alcohol, or because of this or because of that, you name it.

We gon' have to learn to set up something to work with these kids because outta that, one of those abandoned children you get one or two children, one or two kids that will carry on, that will not use and will not do the stuff that they were abused by. See, because a lot of people think that if you don't beat a child it's not abuse, but there's other ways to abuse chil-dren. And more damaging, or just as damaging. It's a whole lotta ways to abuse children. I know.

DAUGHTER: How often do you meet with the children?

MOTHER: Well, see, it depends. Like right now I'm not meeting with them because I'm with this housing. Usually it's during the summer. But see that isn't the way it's supposed to . . . not like I would like to have it. I would like to have a year-round program for the children. You gotta have a place, you gotta have money, you gotta have those things to do this with. We have a meeting like at Christmas. Last week was a Christmas workshop. Then we have a fall workshop.

DAUGHTER: Special workshops.

MOTHER: Yes. That isn't enough for them.

DAUGHTER: What did you do during the fall workshop?

MOTHER: Fall workshop we had making pump-kins and Thanksgiving. That was the fall work-shop. Making pumpkins and playing in the hay. Things like the old folks do, like they did before. Some children had never seen a bundle of hay and had something like a hay ride, you know, put it up and let you slide down on the hay.

DAUGHTER: Where did you have that?

MOTHER: In the yard, in the garden.

DAUGHTER: As part of the composting?

MOTHER: Right. So see, that was fall, that's just one time. Then we had a workshop for Christ-mas, how you make decorations, that's another time. . . . During the winter, you work from the proceeds of the fall. But it isn't enough to get through. I feel as though if we could work con-stantly with the children we could reach more of them. Now it takes a smart child to remem-ber from this workshop to that workshop how it connects. But see, the majority of them can't get it.

DAUGHTER: What do you mean, "how it connects"?

MOTHER: Okay, we get the pinecones, we only can get the pinecones certain time of year. And we tell them that this pinecone has ma-tured, it's grown, and now we can do this with it. But now how many children gonna remember that when we make them for

Christmas. So then see, it's too big a gap to reach most children now. It's too big a gap between them.

DAUGHTER: So, you want them to see the process, to see the stages?

MOTHER: That's it. It's very sad to me, 'cause they missing so much. It's really sad. Go around, you see all these children in the street, you see all these babies having babies, it's sad. Sad times.

DAUGHTER: So, how do you maintain what you *are* doing with the adults, through all that resistance? I know you said you have those door-to-door campaigns sometimes. But how do you pass their resistance?

MOTHER: Just keep on talking to them and showing them different things.

DAUGHTER: Do you work one-on-one with them?

MOTHER: You have . . . it's better. A lot of times it's better. You get better results to work one-on-one because everyone is different.

DAUGHTER: And what kinds of articles do you read?

MOTHER: Well, like I was reading the article we had in the paper couple Sundays ago 'bout abandoned children and how many children in this state, I was talking about this state, that has been abandoned. And how they were talking about they didn't have enough workers to work closely with these children and how these crack mothers and drunken fathers and crack fathers just put the children out in the street. And just last week, last week?, this week, the mother stole a car and was renting them out to people and sending her son out to make sure the car came back and one 16-year-old find it out and killed the boy. Those kinds of things. . . .

DAUGHTER: So, when you're working with the folks you read them articles like that and . . .

MOTHER: And I say, "Now, this is the type of mother you don't wanna be. You had these children and you have a responsibility whether you take or accept it or not." I say not just mothers have responsibility, fathers, too, but, where the fathers? If you know where the fathers are, you love them so much you won't turn them in. Then if you won't turn them in, you work for your child, that's all. You work and do it.

DAUGHTER: What age group are you talking about?

MOTHER: All these mothers now are having children. Most of 'em are teenagers. Most of 'em are young children. Most of them are babies themselves.

DAUGHTER: And these are the same mothers whose children you get and take to the garden?

MOTHER: Yes, a lot of them. And a lot of these mothers we take to the garden are young. Most of 'em young. I don't think I have an old person with a child that we take to the garden. Most of 'em these young mothers. I can't think of a one.

DAUGHTER: What do you do? How do you get to them? You just go up to their house or what do you do?

MOTHER: And ask them would you like for your child to join, and then the children come and ask you. A lot of them come and ask you.

DAUGHTER: The children do?

MOTHER: Right. Then we go to the house. So I got Helen working with me now and another lady to head up that project. I hope it'll work well. Get the children involved. Went in the block and took every name of a child that wanted to work. And asked to work. You didn't have to ask them. And then went to the mothers and had the mothers to agree and asked them to come and help us. Only two came out. The others had something else to do. They didn't have time to come. "I give you some money but I don't have time." You know. Those kinda things.

DAUGHTER: And how many children were there?

MOTHER: Oh Jesus, we had about twenty-some-odd. 'Round thirty-three or thirty-four children and two parents.

DAUGHTER: And how about the old folks that you do have working on the garden. You go door to door with them, too?

MOTHER: Yeh, some of them like to work in the garden. The older folks.

DAUGHTER: And what do you call older? What age group?

MOTHER: Well, the ones without children mostly. 'Cause I have one lady . . .

DAUGHTER: That's over forty or how old?

MOTHER: Over 40, yeh. Over 40. They come to the garden because they love it. And they never done it before and they say they learning. So they enjoy it. Over 40, I got over 40 up to how old? I think we had a 90-year-old man working in the garden, but he not able to come anymore. But he worked 'til he was 90-something years old. We give him a plaque for being the oldest gardener that we had. And he had the prettiest garden we had.

DAUGHTER: He did now? Was he from the South?

MOTHER: Yep.

DAUGHTER: Do you have a bunch of folks from the South working?

MOTHER: Yes. He couldn't read, but he'd have you to read it to him and he would catch it as you read it and go do just what you say.

DAUGHTER: Read what now?

MOTHER: Like the directions on the paper how you plant? You read it out to him, he won't miss a thing. He go right on and do it.

DAUGHTER: So everybody has a place?

MOTHER: Right. That's it. So that's how it's done, but it takes a lot of time and a lot of . . . When everybody says it's hard because it takes a lot of time. It takes a lot of time with these people to counsel them. It's a lot of time. And you can't do it in a hurry and you can't do it one time and you can't limit the times that you hafta do it. You have to do it until it gets done. That's all.

DAUGHTER: But you do see some results?

MOTHER: Well, yes, you see a good bit of results. I saw a good bit of results this summer when we plant those, were putting those plants out. They said the plants were not gonna stay. The children themselves didn't destroy any of the plants. They watched out for the plants. And they enjoyed the street. They played ball but none of the ball broke those plants. They watched out for it. Close as it is. They watched out for it and that was marvelous.

When you have your vision, that's one step, as you go through one it'll go to the next step. And you follow it, nothing gonna be unturned, everything will work in place.

DAUGHTER: But if you follow it?

MOTHER: Yeh, and keep on praying. Can't stop. Can't stop 'cause too much out here. And a lot of times you may have to change sometimes. Who knows? You know what I mean?

DAUGHTER: You may have to change directions a little bit.

MOTHER: Right. May have to change your directions. So you have to keep in touch always. You have to, have to constantly think it over and . . . you know . . . pray for guidance 'cause you don't know when you have to change. So when time come to change you know to change. 'Cause I pray for my strength and my health and guidance so that I can go 'head. 'Cause I have to pray for the words to be right to go talk to some of these parents 'cause some of them may get insulted. You have to pray for that patience. I pray for that patience and understanding.

DAUGHTER: It takes a lot of patience?

MOTHER: Oh, yeh. Ha! Don't start without patience, honey.

◆◆◆

CHAPTER ELEVEN

Creating Change:
Theory, Vision, and Action

At the end of the nineteenth century, suffragists in the United States were nearing the end of a seventy-year-long campaign for women's right to vote, which was finally won in 1920. This campaign had roots in the nineteenth-century movement for the abolition of slavery. Again in the 1960s, the struggle for racial equality was "midwife to a feminist movement" (Evans 1980, p. 24) as women in the civil rights movement looked more closely at the ways they were oppressed as women and began to take action for women's liberation. In the last one hundred years women in the United States have also won the right to own property in their own names, the right to divorce, and increased access to higher education and the professions. Developments in birth control have allowed women to have fewer babies, and family size is much smaller than it was in the early years of this century. Improved health care and somewhat better working conditions mean that women now live longer than ever before. Women's wage rates are inching closer to men's. Issues like domestic violence, rape, sexual harassment, and women's sexual freedom are public issues. As a group women in the United States are more independent — economically and socially — than ever before.

Although women have broken free from many earlier limitations, this book also shows how much still needs to be done. As we argue in earlier chapters, many aspects of women's lives are subject to

debate and controversy as **contested terrains.** These controversial issues include women's sexuality, reproductive freedom, the nature of marriage and family relationships, the right to livelihood independent of men, and the right to affordable health care. Gains have been made and also eroded, as conservative politicians aided by conservative religious leaders and media personalities attempt to turn the clock back. Suzanne Pharr notes the success of the religious Right in Reading 100 and argues for a revitalized progressive politics, not in the narrow party sense of Republican and Democrat, but in terms of broad-based coalitions and alliances.

Politics is about power: What is it? Who has it? How is it used? Who does it benefit and who is disadvantaged? It is easy to review the details of U.S. women's experiences of discrimination and to come away feeling angry, depressed, hopeless, and disempowered. The interlocking systems that keep women oppressed can seem monolithic and unchangeable. Major U.S. social movements this century — for the rights of working people, the civil rights of peoples of color, women's liberation, disability rights, gay and lesbian rights — have made gains and also seen those gains challenged and attacked.

In this final chapter we consider what is needed to tackle the problems for women that we have identified throughout the book. How can this be done in ways that address underlying causes as well as visible manifestations? More fundamentally, how can we—women and men—build relationships, systems of work, local communities, and a wider world based on sustainability and real security?

Each person needs to find meaning in his or her life. Knowing a lot of facts may be an effective way of doing well on tests and getting good grades, but this kind of knowledge does not necessarily provide meaning. Knowing what matters to you means that you can begin to take charge of your own life, and begin to direct change. This process involves examining your own life, as suggested through the many questions included in each chapter. Unless you examine your own life, you will be absent from your own system of knowledge.

At the opening ceremony for Detroit Summer, 1994—a multicultural, intergenerational youth movement to rebuild, redefine, and re-spirit the city from the ground up—Grace Lee Boggs, a long-time community activist in her eighties and one of the founders of Detroit Summer, quoted Black revolutionary Frantz Fanon: "Each generation must . . . discover its mission. . . . " Boggs (1994) told Detroit Summer participants:

> In the physical work that you do, the "found art" that you create, the connections you make with one another, and in your reflections and discussions on . . . tough questions, you are using your hearts, hands, and heads to create new ways of living.
>
> *(p. 2)*

We draw on this connection of the head, the heart, and the hands in thinking about social change for a secure and sustainable future. These are not separate steps but connected ways of thinking and working that reinforce one another. The process of creating change requires a combination of theoretical insights and understandings, visions of alternatives, and action. The readings in this chapter include a blend of these three aspects.

Using the Head: Theories for Social Change

Throughout this book we have presented information about women's lives and women's own descriptions and analyses of their experiences. The issues, as we have presented them, are multilayered, especially when viewed in terms of the intersections of gender, race, class, and nation. As scholars and editors, we want readers to come away with a clear sense that women's lives are complex and are often affected by contradictory pressures and expectations. As we argued in Chapter 1, facts do not speak for themselves but through the framework in which they are placed. Key points that arise out of Chapters 1–10 provide examples of this. In very summary form they represent our understandings—the understandings on which our ideas for change are based.

- Our personal identities as women—rooted in a complex mix of gender, race, class, culture, and history—shape who we are, how we relate to others, and how we understand the world.

- We are embodied human beings. Through our bodies we sense and experience our sexuality and the world around us. Our bodies connect us to the natural world but are also culturally constructed with reference to ideal standards of beauty. Pressure to conform to this increasingly rigorous standard may block and divert our energies and undermine our self-confidence.

- Through personal and family relationships we learn about ourselves and how to live with others. Seemingly personal issues are also profoundly political. The larger social system affects personal relationships, as well as our situation and opportunities in this society. Women are not equally placed because of differences based on race, class, age, sexuality, disability, and nationality. Moreover, women are not equal to men in many aspects of life.

- The global economy affects work opportunities worldwide.

- More women in the United States are working for wages than ever before. This brings opportunities and responsibilities, especially as most conditions of work are not geared to parenting. The polarization of the job market and greater restrictions on welfare payments to mothers who are not in paid work means that many women barely make a living.

- Women's health has improved overall, though there are differences in health linked to race and class. The health system is not geared to research women's illnesses, to care for chronic illnesses that affect women more than men, or to explore alternative therapies based on the concept of wellness.

- Many more women than ever before are incarcerated, especially poor women of color.

- More women are joining the military as a way to better their situation in life. Others oppose military values and argue for alternative ways of thinking about security.

- Women and children are particularly affected by environmental pollution. Many women are campaigning for clean air, water, and food and for healthy living and work environments.

As we pointed out in Chapter 1, doing something about an issue or a problem requires us to have a theory, an explanation, of what it is. The theory we create directly shapes what we think ought to be done about it. Thus *how* we theorize is a key first step in creating change. When people face difficult problems alone, they can draw only on their own insights. Although these are valuable, they are also likely to be limited. In talking things over with others, we may discover that they are also facing a similar situation or have done so in the past, that their perspective sheds light on things we may have missed, or that they provide a whole different way to think about and understand what we are dealing with. Similarly, as people trying to understand the lives of women, if we only examine the specifics of an issue, examine each issue separately, or use a limited analytical framework, we will end up with limited understandings. For a fuller picture we need to analyze issues individually and together, looking for commonalities, recognizing differences, and using frameworks that illuminate as many parts as possible.

This principle has guided our choices in making the selections for this book. Our theoretical ideas, which run through the earlier chapters — sometimes explicit, sometimes implicit — are summarized here:

- A social-constructionist perspective allows people to see how social and political forces shape our lives and our sense of ourselves in ways we may not have been aware of. It encourages us to focus on the specificity of experience and also the diversity of experiences among people. It allows us to see that situations and structures are not fixed for all time and hence are changeable under the right circumstances.

- How an issue is defined and framed is extremely important. It will affect how people think about the problem, where we look for probable causes, our ideas about what ought to be done about it, and who is likely to become involved.

- In analyzing social situations it is necessary to look at them in terms of micro, meso, macro, and global levels, and to understand how these levels affect one another. Strategies for change need to address all levels of a situation.

- There are many women's activist organizations and projects working on all the issues discussed in this book.

- Efforts to create equal opportunities for women and equal access to current institutions have made a difference in many women's lives, but by themselves they cannot achieve a genuinely secure and sustainable world for women and men because these are not the goals of most institutions.

Theories for social change also involve ideas about how change happens. We see a key role for individuals, as change agents, working with others to envision alternatives and bring them into being through collective action.

Using the Heart: Visions for Social Change

Vision is the second necessary ingredient in creating social change — some idea of a different way of doing things, a different future for humankind, framed by explicit principles around which human relations ought to be organized. Otherwise, as the saying goes, "If you don't know where you're going, any road will get you there."

Visions are about values, drawing from inside ourselves everything we value and daring to think big. The many demands of our busy lives leave most people with little time or opportunity to envision alternatives. In school and college, for example, we are rarely asked to think seriously about our hopes and dreams for our own lives and a more truly human world in which to live. Much of what we do is guided not by our own visions but in reaction to the expectations of others and outside pressures. Social issues, too, are framed in reactive and negative terms. People talk about "antiracism," for instance, not about what a truly multicultural society would be like.

Some people scorn this step as time-wasting and unrealistic. What matters, they say, is to come up with ideas that people feel comfortable with, that businesses will want to invest in, or that fit government programs and guidelines. Tackle something small and specific, something winnable. Don't waste time on grandiose ideas.

Because most of us are not encouraged to envision change, it may take a while to free ourselves from seemingly practical ideas. Our imaginations are often limited to what we know, and we need a full-blown opportunity to break out of our cramped daily routines and habits of thought. Envisioning something different also means putting on hold the voice inside your head that says: Are you *crazy?* This will never work! Who do you think you are? Where will you *ever* get the money? Better keep quiet on this one, people will think you're nuts. . . .

Go ahead. Envision the multicultural society, the women's health project, the community play/read/care program for elders and children, the Internet information business run by inner-city teenagers, the women's taxi service, the intimate relationship of your dreams, your blossoming sexuality. Envision it in as much detail as you can. Think it, see it, taste it, smell it, sing it, draw it, and write it down. Share it with others who you think will be sympathetic to it. This is where you're headed. Now all you need is to create the road. The projects we mention throughout this book, like this book itself, all started this way, as somebody's dream.

Using the Hands: Action for Social Change

Though theories and visions may be extremely interesting and inspiring, by themselves they do not create change; the third essential ingredient is action. Through action, theories and visions are tested, sharpened, and refined to create even more useful theories and more creative visions. In Chapter 1 we referred to Rosenberg's (1988) distinction between *knowing* and *understanding.* Rosenberg further argues that understanding compels us to action, even though we may not initially want to change our habitual ways of thinking and being. When you understand something, you

find that [your] world becomes a different world and that [you] must generate a new way to be in the new world. Since each person's way of being in the world is relatively fixed — and serves as protection against the anxieties of the unknown — integration is extremely hard. To give up a world in which one's life makes sense means undergoing great loss. Yet without the readiness to risk that loss we cannot hope to pursue understanding.

(p. 382)

In previous chapters we mentioned various activist projects, which are all relevant to this discussion. In this chapter, readings by Cynthia Cohen (Reading 98), Elizabeth Compton-Wilson (Reading 99), and Suzanne Pharr (Reading 100) address specific projects. Here we suggest a range of avenues for trying to implement your visions. Some will be more appropriate than others, depending on your goals and theoretical perspectives. Some of the activities we list below may be impossible for you, as students who need to concentrate on getting degrees, to participate in. Progressive social change is a long-term project; there will be plenty to do after you graduate.

- Think of yourself as someone with something valuable and important to say, as someone who can take the initiative and start something you think is important. Think about what you want to do after college, how to live your values and ideals.

- Express your ideas: talk to others; write 'zines, poems, leaflets, speeches, letters to newspaper editors and politicians; put up flyers or posters; organize a film series; paint murals, dance, sing, or perform your ideas.

- Be a conscious shopper. Boycott products made in sweatshops, for example. Buy directly from farmers' markets or craft producers. Spend your money where it will support your values.

- Support women's organizations, environmental groups, antiracist organizations, or gay/lesbian groups by letting them know you appreciate their work, letting others know these groups exist, donating money or something the group needs, volunteering your time, proposing ideas for projects, working as an intern for college credit.

- Work for institutional change. Within your family you may want to stop others from telling sexist or racist jokes, create greater understanding between family members, or develop more egalitarian relationships. At school you may want to set up study groups to work together, support teachers who help you, point out glaring gaps in the curriculum to teachers and administrators, challenge sexual harassment.

- Participate in direct action politics. This includes interrupting, keeping silent, organizing groups of women to walk together at night, defending clinics where abortions are performed, participating in boycotts, picketing, rent strikes, tax resistance. Whatever the setting, take back the Nike slogan. Just Do It!

- Get involved in grassroots organizing. Meet with others and decide what you can do together to tackle some issue of shared concern. Look for allies, resources, funding. This kind of group may have various goals over time, depending on how long it holds together; it provides a place where people can speak out and express themselves, it creates services that people need, and it provides a base from which people can strategize about how to change things that affect them.

- Participate in coalition politics. Consider joining with other groups on an issue of shared concern so as to be more visible and effective. Coalitions are usually short-term efforts that mobilize the maximum number of people around a single issue or a few issues.

- Learn about local and national issues, and use your vote, even if you think there isn't much choice between candidates. The lesser of two evils is still the lesser of two evils. Let your representatives at city, state, and national level know your opinions. Urge them to use their offices to pass appropriate laws and regulations and to speak out in public situations and to the media. Help to elect progressive candidates. Support them if they get into office, and hold them accountable to their election promises. Participate in demonstrations and rallies.

- Learn more about international networks and organizations that are working on issues that concern you. Consider participating in international meetings and bringing the knowledge you gain there to your organizing work back home.

Power and Empowerment

In attempting to make change, to realize visions, people almost always come up against established power relationships and inequalities of power. The term *power* is used in many ways: to describe laundry detergents and body deodorants, to prescribe successful behavior, as with "power dressing" and "power lunching," to refer to key decision makers within society (the power elite), or to describe people having power over the natural environment. In other chapters, we refer to power dynamics between women and men, people in positions of corporate or political power in this society, or the power of the United States in the world.

Popular conceptions of power assume that it is a thing, a scarce commodity to be acquired and used to get what we want or to make others do what we want them to do. Such conceptions also assume relationships of inequality where some are more powerful than others. Where inequalities exist — such as in the family, hierarchical organizations, or oppressive societies — there may be intense power struggles. People in the dominant group make every effort to maintain their power position and those in subordinate groups try to move into positions of power. In patriarchal cultures, for example, men use personal and institutional power to maintain their dominance over women and children. Women, and sometimes children, attempt to shift this power inequality in both direct and subtle ways. Many people focus on the ways in which others exert power over us or on the fact that they have more power than we have. We generally pay less attention to the ways in which we have power over others or more power than others. This is true especially for members of oppressed groups, such as women and peoples of color in the United States, where some fundamental aspect of our existence, if not our identity, is predicated on being "the powerless" in many settings.

Power is also built into social institutions, for example, education, the law, religion, government, or the media, and can be exercised regardless of individual intent or knowledge of its existence (Baron 1970). From this perspective, power is expressed in the values and practices of the institutions that compel people to think, talk, and behave in specific ways. For example, the heterosexist values embedded in our culture and its institutions define the family as a heterosexual couple, legally bound by marriage, and their children. The value attached to this institution is a powerful influence on people and is in itself a pressure to marry. Higher education operates out of values that are overwhelmingly Eurocentric, middle-class, and masculinist. These values uphold particular ways of learning, certain kinds of discourse, and the use of specific language. To succeed in college, a student must subscribe to these values, at least in a minimal way.

Power, then, is the ability to make things happen. Audre Lorde writes of women's personal power in Reading 94. Power also operates at the community, national, and global levels. It is a verb as well as a noun. It is a force that is generated by people in relationship with one another, in specific contexts, and for particular reasons.

Identity Politics

A personal source of confidence and power is knowing who we are. As we discussed in Chapter 2, the development of identity is a crucial process, ongoing through life. Throughout this book many writers talk about their own identity and note significant changes in the way they think about themselves over time. Some mention the difficulties of coming to terms with who they are, the complexities of their contradictory positions, naming things that have happened to them, or breaking the silence surrounding taboo subjects, thoughts, and feelings. They also comment that coming to new understandings about themselves and being able to speak from a place of personal identity and self-knowledge is profoundly empowering.

Identity politics is a politics that puts identity at the center, based on, for example, age, race, ethnicity, or sexual orientation. It usually involves the assumption that this particular characteristic is the most important in the lives of group members and that the group is not differentiated according to other characteristics in any significant way. Identity politics is concerned with wider opportunities — maybe greater visibility and recognition in society, equality, justice, even liberation for ourselves and our group. Our authoritativeness comes from our experience of a shared identity, some common ground of experience that allows a group to say "we." This identity politics is the foundation for many campus organizations, grassroots community groups, religious groups, and national networks.

At the same time, identity politics has serious limitations, as mentioned by Suzanne Pharr in Reading 100. Groups tend to remain separate, focused on their own issues and concerns, often competing with each other for recognition and resources. The language of identity politics gives voice to people's discrimination and oppression. It does not encourage us to think about identity in a more complex way, as a mix of privilege and disadvantage. In Chapter 2 we introduced the idea that most people occupy multiple positions, and that salient aspects of identity may vary significantly depending on the context. An African-American graduate student who is about to receive her Ph.D., for example, may be highly respected by her teachers and peers, regardless of their race or hers. A White man walking past her in the street may insult and curse her because she is Black. Understanding this notion of multiple positionality helps us to see how our personal and group identities are political and how the various identity groups fit together in the wider society. The specific context is crucial. In the public discourse about immigration, for example, there is a fear on the part of White people — usually hinted at rather than stated directly — of being overrun by Asians. When the context shifts to a discussion of peoples of color in the United States, however, Asians become the "model minority," the standard against which African-Americans or Latinos are compared unfavorably. Understanding one's identity involves a recognition of the ways in which one is privileged as well as the ways in which one is disadvantaged, and the contradictions that this raises, as noted by Melanie Kaye/Kantrowitz in Reading 97. With this more nuanced perspective one not only focuses on the circumstances and concerns of one's own group, but can use the complexity of one's identity to make connections to other groups. Thus, a White, middle-class woman with a hearing disability can take all these aspects of her identity and understand her social location in terms of privilege as well as disadvantage. This is important for building effective alliances with others, which we discuss in more detail later.

Overcoming Blocks to Effective Action

Political action does not always work; that is, a chosen course of action may not achieve our original goals. There are many possible reasons for this: inadequate theoretical understandings and analysis of the issues; choosing inappropriate or ineffective strategies; not following through on the course of action; not being able to get enough people involved for this particular strategy to be effective; wrong timing; the failure of the group to work together well enough; the failure of people whom you thought were allies to come through when needed, and so on. The other major reason, of course, is that the opposition — whether this is your sexist uncle, your boss, the university administration, the city school board, or the U.S. Congress — was simply more powerful.

Feeling that an action has failed is disheartening and may lead people to give up, assuming that creating change is hopeless. But action *always* accomplishes something, and in this sense it always works.

At the very least, activism that does not meet your goals teaches you something important. In hindsight, what may seem like mistakes are actually valuable ways to learn how to be more effective in the future. This is what we called "socially lived" theory in Chapter 1. Always evaluate what you did after some activity or event, personally and with the group. If it worked as you hoped, why did it work? What have you learned as a result? If it did not work, why? What will you do differently next time?

Personal blocks to activism may include practical factors like not having enough time or energy, or needing to focus on some other aspect of life. Emotional blocks include guilt — a paralyzing emotion that keeps us stuck — and cynicism — a frustrated idealism that has turned hopeless and bitter. Anger can be a very useful, high-octane fuel if you can channel it in a constructive direction, as Dai Thompson points out in Reading 93. Overextending yourself is not a sign of your commitment to your ideals, and trying to do more than you can, under pressure, is one sure way to burn out quickly. Activism for progressive social change needs patience, humor, creativity, a wide range of skills and resources, an ability to talk to other people, a willingness to listen and to change, a willingness to be reflective, refining your ideas, holding onto your visions.

Building Alliances for Social Change

Although one often hears of the failures, of times when alliances did not work, there have also been effective alliances across lines of difference. We emphasize the importance of such alliances for two reasons. First, the many inequalities among women, mentioned throughout this book, often separate us and make it very difficult to work together effectively. Those with power over us know this and often exploit differences to pit one group against another. Second, progressive social change is a slow process that needs sustained action over the long haul. Effective alliances, based on a deepening knowledge of others and learning whom to trust over time, are necessary for long-term efforts, in contrast to coalition work, where the important thing is to stand together around a single issue, regardless of other differences. Alliances across lines of difference are both a means and an end. Gandhi commented that there is no road to peace; peace *is* the road. Similarly, alliances across lines of difference provide both the process for moving toward, and at the same time some experience of, multicultural society. Gloria Yamato (Reading 96), and Melanie Kaye/Kantrowitz (Reading 97) address aspects of alliance building later in the chapter.

Some Principles for Alliance Building

- Know who you are, what is important to you, what are your nonnegotiables. Know your strengths and what you bring to this shared venture.

- Decide whether you want to be allies with a particular person or group. What do they stand for? What are their values? What are they interested in doing in terms of creating social change? Are they open to the alliance? What is the purpose for coming together?

- Recognize, honor, and accept the ways you are different from the others. You may look different. You may have learned some very different messages from your own community.

- Check out the person or the group as the acquaintance grows. Are they who they say they are? Do they do what they say they believe in? Do you have reason to trust them to be there for you? Judge them by their track records and what actually happens, not by your fears, hopes, or expectations that come from old experiences.

- Commit yourself to communicate. Listen, talk, and listen more. Communication may be through conversations, reading, films, events and meetings, or learning about one another's communities. Work together on projects and support one another's projects. Go into one another's settings as participants, observers, guests. Get to know one another in different settings.

- Share the past. Talk about what has happened to you, whom you've known, what has been important, what you've hoped for. Talk about the ways you've changed. If I

hear something negative about you, is it the "you" you are now?

- Wanting to understand, to hear more, to stay connected requires patience from the inside. It is not an abstract principle imposed from the outside. Allow one another room to explore ideas, share, dream, ramble, make mistakes, change words, be tentative. Hold judgment until you understand what's going on. Ask the other person to say more. Be committed to the process of communication rather than attached to a specific position.

- Honesty is the most important thing. Be authentic and ask for authenticity from others. If this is not possible, what is the alliance worth? Say honestly what you honestly need.

- Keep the process "clean." Call one another on bad things if they happen—preferably with grace, teasing maybe, firmly but gently, so that the other person does not lose face. Don't try to disentangle difficulties when it is impossible to do so meaningfully, but don't use externals (too late, too tired, too busy, too many other items on the agenda) to avoid it.

- Be open to being called on your own mistakes, admitting when you're wrong, even if it is embarrassing or makes you feel vulnerable. Tell the other person when his or her opinions and experiences give you new insights and help you to see things differently.

- Do some people in the group take up a lot of time talking about their own issues and concerns? Are they aware of it? What is the unspoken power dynamic among people? How does privilege based on gender, race, class, sexuality, disability, age, culture, or language play out in this relationship or alliance? Can you talk about it openly?

- What is the "culture" of your group or alliance? What kinds of meetings do you have? What is your decision-making style? If you eat together, what kind of food do you serve? What kind of music do you listen to? Where do you meet? What do you do when you are together? Does everyone in the group feel comfortable with these cultural aspects?

- Work out the boundaries of your responsibilities to one another. What do you want to do for yourself? What do you need others to help with? When? How?

- Look for the common ground. What are the perspectives, experiences, and insights we share?

Impediments to Effective Alliances

Over and over again sincere and committed attempts at building alliances have been thwarted, despite the best of intentions. Several common impediments to creating effective alliances include the following beliefs and behaviors:

Internalized Oppression   This is a learned mindset of subservience and inferiority in oppressed peoples. It is the passive and active acceptance of labels, characteristics, prejudices, and perceptions promoted by the dominant society. Specific behaviors include self-hatred and dislike, disrespect for and hatred of others of the same group, isolation, and being satisfied, even grateful for being allowed to exist (Lipsky 1977; Pheterson 1990).

Internalized Domination   This is a mindset of entitlement and superiority among members of the dominant group, which includes the belief that inequalities are normal; thus those in the dominant group never realize that they are privileged. This belief is often accompanied by the contradictory feelings of self-righteousness and guilt. Behaviors such as always speaking first in group discussions, being unconscious of the large amount of physical and social space one takes up, and automatically assuming leadership roles are some manifestations of internalized domination.

Operating from a Politics of Scarcity   This impediment results from a deeply held, sometimes unconscious, belief that there is not enough of anything—material things as well as nonmaterial things like power, positive regard, popularity, friendship, time—and, more important, that however much

there is, it will not be shared equally. In this view, inequality is simply a given that cannot be changed.

Subscribing to a Hierarchy of Oppression   This involves the placement of one oppressed group in relation to another so that one group's experiences of discrimination, prejudice, and disadvantage are deemed to be worse or better than another's. There is an assumption that these experiences can somehow be measured accurately and that a negative or positive value can be placed on certain kinds of experiences.

Not Knowing One Another's History   Ignorance about other persons' backgrounds often results in drawing incorrect conclusions about their experiences. This prevents us from recognizing the complexity of women's experiences and can hide the ways our experiences are both different and similar.

Creating a Secure and Sustainable World

Throughout the history of this country, countless numbers of women have worked on many fronts to improve women's lives. Some provide direct services, such as counseling, support groups, crisis lines, shelters, training schemes, and so forth. Others become advocates to reform the existing social, political, and economic institutions so more women will have increased opportunities within these institutions. Still others have the goal of transforming those institutions and establishing values that are fundamentally different from those now in place. We call this third kind of effort at social change a transformational movement, in which one of the main goals is to change the core interpersonal, community, and societal values, not simply to alter or add to existing ones.

Providing services to women in need and reforming existing institutions to make them more responsive to those who are excluded are crucially important in the overall work of progressive social change and have made a difference to generations of women. The challenge for the future is to continue to expand this work. Given the many insecurities of life for women and for men, and the growing threat to the planet itself from increasing industrialization, militarization, and ecological devastation, what sense does it make for women to seek an equal piece of what Ynestra King (1993, p. 76) has called this "rotten and carcinogenic" pie? In previous chapters we assume a fundamental interdependence between people as an absolute given. We see sustainability in terms of egalitarian relationships, redefined family values, supportive communities, livelihood, wellness, positive notions of security, ecological balance, and hope for the future.

In Reading 103 Grace Lee Boggs notes that this is both an exciting and daunting time in human history, and concludes, "For our own well-being, for the health and safety of our communities, our cities and our country, we need to accept the awesome responsibility of creating new ways of . . . living . . ." (1994, p. 2).

For her, this conviction comes from fifty years of community activism in Detroit, where once-thriving auto plants and other industries have virtually disappeared, leaving much of the city derelict. For Starhawk (Reading 102), a similar conviction comes from her belief in an earth-based spirituality.

This book is about U.S. women's lives and the kind of world we need to create for women's empowerment, development, and well-being. This world will be based on notions of security and sustainability, as we have suggested here. The project of human development — for both women and men — is one that has been in process for a very long time. Over time there have been important gains as well as serious setbacks. It is our challenge to take the next steps in this process. How can we settle for anything less?

As you read and discuss this chapter, think about these questions:

1. What is your theory of social change? How did you arrive at this view? What are your assumptions about how people and societies change? What do you think needs changing, if anything?

2. Have you ever been involved in a social-action project? What was your experience like? If you have not, why not?

3. Have you ever tried to establish and maintain an ongoing relationship, friendship, or working partnership with someone from a background very different from your own? What happened? What did you learn from that experience? What would you do differently, if anything?

4. If you have had such a relationship, why did you become involved in the first place? Was that a good enough reason? Why or why not? If you never have, why not?

5. What do you know about the history of the various groups you are a member of? What do you know about groups that are not your own? How does knowing this history help, and how does not knowing it hinder you in making alliances across lines of difference?

6. What is your vision of a secure and sustainable personal relationship? Community? Society? World?

NINETY-THREE

◆◆◆

Anger

Dai R. Thompson

Anger is not a pretty emotion. And, in spite of a lot of rhetoric to the contrary, it is still not very well accepted even in women's communities, unless, perhaps, its source is rage against men. But anger is real, whatever its source. And it is strong. It can immobilize. It can twist a person's life into a warped mess

completely out of touch with reality. It can turn inward, leading to severe depression and even suicide. On the other hand, anger can be a major force behind an individual's desire to accomplish. But even that productive aspect of anger can lead to serious burn-out problems. Anger is, then, a part of almost all of our lives. If it remains unacknowledged, it can rarely be successfully sublimated for any long period of time, and it can be disastrous to both the individual and those around her.

Anger felt by women because of our disabilities is rarely accepted in women's communities, or anywhere else for that matter. Disabled or not, most of us grew up with media images depicting pathetic little "crippled" children on various telethons or blind beggars with caps in hand ("handicap") or "brave" war heroes limping back to a home where they were promptly forgotten. Such individuals' anger was never seen, and still rarely is. Instead of acknowledging the basic humanity of our often-powerful emotions, able-bodied persons tend to view us either as helpless things to be pitied or as Super Crips, gallantly fighting to overcome insurmountable odds. Such attitudes display a bizarre two-tiered mindset: it is horrible beyond imagination to be disabled, but disabled people with guts can, if they only try hard enough, make themselves almost "normal." The absurdity of such all-or-nothing images is obvious. So, too, is the damage these images do to disabled people by robbing us of our sense of reality.

The reasoning behind such attitudes is certainly hard to understand. When able-bodied persons are temporarily sick or encumbered by a broken leg or a patched eye, it is understood they will be grouchy or out-of-sorts or childish. But if an individual happens to be disabled in any permanent or long-term way, the rules of the game suddenly switch. The permanent inability to perform a major life function, such as hearing or seeing or walking, seems to require silent endurance of often-excruciating pain, patience far beyond any normal human capacity, quiet acceptance of architectural and attitudinal barriers, and groveling gratitude for the pittances doled out by various welfare agencies. Unlike the temporarily ill, we who are permanently disabled are not supposed to be, do not in fact have the right to be, angry or even upset about all the things we can't or aren't allowed to do. Even non-disabled women willing to acknowledge our disabilities and even, perhaps, our right to be angry, caution us not to express our anger because most able-bodied persons just can't handle it. It's okay to be angry about rape or pornography or wife abuse or the KKK or the whole Nuke situation; it does not seem to be okay to get mad because your peers refuse to acknowledge

the barriers they constantly help erect to shut out their disabled sisters.

It is not fun to be disabled. Being disabled is not a "challenge" we voluntarily undertake. Nor is it that we are merely "differently-abled." We are disabled; there are just some things that we can't do, at least not as quickly or easily as other people. Sure, the rehabilitation therapists and many disabled individuals have devised ingenious methods and gadgets for accomplishing all kinds of things our disabilities would not otherwise allow us to do. But being fluent in sign language or lip reading still does not give a person the ability to hear. Being able to use a prosthesis does not give someone back her lost leg. And certainly finally being deinstitutionalized does not automatically return to an individual her dignity or all the time she has lost behind bars. For probably all of us, at least at times, being disabled hurts. Even if the larger community would adopt totally fair and appropriate attitudes toward people with disabilities, this would still not eliminate the sense of loss, the frustration, and indeed the anger we feel just because we are disabled.

Non-acceptance of us and our needs, especially by the women's community, is destructive. We have trouble getting others to acknowledge even our most obvious problems such as the need for accessibility or interpretive services. How then can we make them deal with our emotional reality as well? How can we make others understand our anger, our frustrations, all those numerous bits and pieces of our lives that are different because we do happen to be disabled? Women's communities often refuse to give any credibility to our anger and may even trash us if we try to express it. Not surprisingly, such attitudes make us even more angry. And this, in turn, makes us even less acceptable to the able-bodied world.

Because we are disabled, many of us have pretty low self-esteem. Our physical appearance, for example, often does not fit any traditional standards: we fit neither "mother" nor "whore" images found in the straight world, and we are certainly often a far cry from the strong, tough dyke model. The very definition of being disabled means that we cannot do one or more basic life functions. This inability to do what others take for granted can also be extremely demoralizing. Added to our actual limitations are additional ones able-bodied persons frequently impose on us.

Women labelled mentally retarded are often considered to be incapable of ever working or living independently or even being sexual. Not fitting into the "American ideal"—having to put up with certain functional limitations, and having to cope with often-ludicrous stereotypes—can result in very depressed egos.

Self-image problems differ considerably, of course, depending on the type and origin of an individual's disability. Women disabled later in life may have fairly intact egos developed in disability-free childhoods. They do not, then, usually display the life-long self-esteem problems found in many women born with disabilities who grew up feeling isolated and rejected by almost everything and everyone around them, often including their own families.

But women disabled as adults do have to deal with a different set of problems that can often be just as anger provoking. Having experienced a life free of limitations for decades perhaps, most newly-disabled women cannot help but feel an often-overwhelming sense of loss and anger at all the things they cannot now do that they once used to. And their frustration often increases as those around them fail to understand the enormous changes they must make in even the simplest of daily tasks. In an effort to cheer up newly-disabled people, friends and relatives often try to point out the positive: even if you can't walk anymore, you can still use your hands; I know you can't read, but how 'bout all those wonderful recordings they make for the blind now; or—a real favorite—at least your mind is still intact. Positive thinking can, of course, be quite useful and is an important part of any successful rehabilitation program. But if a newly-disabled woman is constantly surrounded by only those spouting worn-out "it could be worse" cliches, she is likely to develop a very strong urge to strangle them all. Little Mary Sunshine types often mean well. But nothing they can say or do can make that disability disappear. It's there, and it's real, and it must be coped with.

Getting used to a new disability involves many things which vary, naturally, depending on the type and extent of the disability: getting through the initial diagnosis and rehabilitation period; making necessary adjustments in living space, modes of transportation, work possibilities, financial arrangements; trying to deal with numerous changes in personal, family, and sexual relationships. Most of these problems are, of course, a daily part of any disabled woman's life. But unlike those who have been trying to cope since early childhood, newly-disabled women often find their previously well-ordered lives have suddenly been turned upside down. They not only have to deal with their new limitations, but often also with the additional emotional losses caused by sudden and often drastic changes in self-image, feelings of independence, and their relationships with almost everyone around them.

Sometimes it's hard for birth-disabled women to understand the often out-of-control anger and frustration newly-disabled women feel. After all, they've had to deal with such limitations all their lives. At least previously able-bodied women had a chance at decent, unsegregated education. A chance to grow up with at least fairly healthy self-images, often a much easier chance to establish careers, develop financial security, meet potential lovers, have children. Of course, some women born with disabilities are lucky enough to enjoy these same experiences. But, even so, they probably had to fight a lot harder to get, as the saying goes, half as far. And so, the complexities of our anger grow.

Competing for who's got it worse is really not going to accomplish anything for anyone. It just feeds anger and division among all of us. But the desire to create a truly unified disabled community cannot negate the lack of understanding that does, indeed, foster this anger. And like the anger all disabled women feel, at times, towards this ignorant, inaccessible society, the anger felt by those disabled at different times in their lives is also quite real, and will not go away easily or automatically. And it must be acknowledged by all parties involved if any kind of solution is ever going to be found.

There is also a different kind of in-house dispute in the disabled community that can be equally frustrating and anger-provoking. This is based on a rarely-acknowledged but very real hierarchy that ranks people according to the "acceptability" of their disability. An individual's position in this hierarchy is generally determined by how well that person fits into society's "norm." In other words, the less disabled you look, the higher your rank. And this reasoning frequently applies in both the able-bodied and disabled communities.

Use of this hierarchy within the disabled community may well, of course, be just a reflection of able-bodied attitudes, similar to once-prevalent rankings in the Black community based on a preference for lighter-colored skin. The urge to "pass" is apparently fairly universal. But whether it's a reflection of able-bodied views or not, this hierarchy is often adopted by people with disabilities and it can thus become one more part of the anger cycle for those considered less acceptable.

The rungs on this ladder of conformity are not based just on type of disability. Rather they can vary considerably even within a single disability: the essential criteria depend on how closely an individual meets society's standards of appearance and behavior. For example, proponents of comprehensive learning programs for deaf children, which include sign, feel that strictly-oral curriculums unnecessarily limit children in order to try to force them to appear as non-disabled as possible. Lip readers seem to be high on the scale of acceptability; sign users are not. By the same reasoning, individuals with mobility problems often choose to suffer needless pain or to limit their lives needlessly rather than use any kind of mobility aid. Individuals with cerebral palsy can be seen all along the ladder, depending on how serious their communication and motor coordination problems are.

Probably the lowest on the general hierarchy of disability, set up by the able-bodied society and mirrored in the disabled community, are those individuals labelled mentally ill or mentally retarded. Both groups are still routinely referred to as incompetents, vegetables, basket cases, and, thanks to the media, dangerous threats to society. Frequently considered to be "better off" in institutions, we are often drugged up, locked away, shocked out of our minds, and totally rejected by both the able-bodied and otherwise-disabled communities.

Internalized attitudes about hierarchies are not the only things that help create barriers within the disabled community. Some factors which foster such feelings are very understandable and hence are even harder to overcome than mere prejudice. Once again, the whole issue comes from a vicious circle of inaccurate labeling which causes anger which, in turn, leads to a strong desire to separate into distinct disability groups. The fact that individuals with mental disabilities are frequently shunned by those with physical or sensory ones is a prime example of this problem. People with learning disabilities, for example, are often labelled as mentally retarded be-

cause of the difficulties they have communicating. Naturally such individuals fight very hard to be recognized as the intelligent, competent people they are. To then develop alliances with mentally retarded people can, therefore, be enormously threatening. Likewise, those who begin to develop multiple sclerosis or other hard-to-diagnose disabilities frequently have their problems dismissed as purely psychiatric in nature. Fighting such dismissals and the denials of treatment and financial help because of them can often go on for years, building up enormous resentment. It is not surprising, then, that such people feel a strong desire to clearly separate themselves from those whose disabilities are, indeed, psychiatrically-based.

Issues like these are very complex and not easy to solve. But they are also very real and can be extremely anger-provoking when, for example, physically-disabled women refuse to even acknowledge their mentally-disabled sisters' existence.

The same kind of reasoning applies to barriers erected between disabled people because of their sex, race, religion, educational level, socio-economic background or current financial status. The latter can be particularly frustrating since it usually relates directly to the disability itself. Some disabled individuals, frequently those from more "acceptable" racial, religious and socio-economic backgrounds, are lucky enough to enjoy financial security thanks to decent jobs, substantial gains from lawsuits or insurance policies, or solid support from well-to-do families. Such individuals often display little understanding of their sisters who are dependent on the whims of government agencies for even their most basic needs. The demeaning and increasingly fruitless nature of the application and renewal process for Social Security and other entitlements can be one of the most anger-provoking barriers experienced by disabled individuals. And yet disabled people who have never had to go through such demoralizing procedures often seem to have no understanding of their sisters who must. So individuals on welfare find themselves doubly frustrated and angry at both the system itself and others who refuse to understand.

All these vicious cycles, then, tend to turn onward and inward, perpetuating and often deepening the anger felt by women with disabilities. Anger at being disabled at all, anger at being ostracized by society as a whole and by the women's community in particular, anger at the disabled community itself for judging individuals by their economic status or the type and origin of their disabilities. This anger grows strong as the cycles continue and it is not going to disappear either quickly or easily.

But slowly and surely, attempts can, and are, being made to dissipate this anger and so reduce its ability to further handicap women with disabilities. An absolutely essential beginning step in any such process is, of course, recognizing and giving credibility to the anger. Disabled women must learn to understand their own anger, and to accept that it is both reasonable and justified. It is lousy to be disabled and it is perfectly healthy and normal to feel that way, at least occasionally. The trick, however, is to learn how to control that anger so it does not become a liability in and of itself. Those with more acceptable disabilities, or those on a more sound economic footing, must examine the source of their prejudice against their sisters, recognize how harmful it can be, and then begin to discard their outmoded attitudes. On the other hand, those on the outs by hierarchy or finances must also try to understand why their prejudiced sisters feel and act the way they do. No one should be asked to accept discrimination from anyone. But recognizing its origin can make it a bit easier to deal with while the afflicted ones are getting their acts together.

And, of course, the able-bodied must begin tearing down the numerous physical, attitudinal and other barriers they have placed in front of the people who happen to be disabled. Those of us who are disabled must learn to cope with the anger-provoking reality that all those many barriers are not going to come tumbling down all at once, as unjust, unfair and just plain infuriating as they are. It is not easy to constantly have to work our lives around the multitude of obstacles this society has put in our way. But it is also not very helpful, to ourselves or anyone else, to just sit around and scream at the injustice of it all. We need to find effective coping mechanisms to help us keep sane and strong. For some, political action may be useful. For others, a support group may help. There are numerous possibilities. The important thing is to find a way to survive.

NINETY-FOUR

◆◆◆

Uses of the Erotic
The Erotic As Power
Audre Lorde

There are many kinds of power, used and unused, acknowledged or otherwise. The erotic is a resource within each of us that lies in a deeply female and spiritual plane, firmly rooted in the power of our unexpressed or unrecognized feeling. In order to perpetuate itself, every oppression must corrupt or distort those various sources of power within the culture of the oppressed that can provide energy for change. For women, this has meant a suppression of the erotic as a considered source of power and information within our lives.

We have been taught to suspect this resource, vilified, abused, and devalued within western society. On the one hand, the superficially erotic has been encouraged as a sign of female inferiority; on the other hand, women have been made to suffer and to feel both contemptible and suspect by virtue of its existence.

It is a short step from there to the false belief that only by the suppression of the erotic within our lives and consciousness can women be truly strong. But that strength is illusory, for it is fashioned within the context of male models of power.

As women, we have come to distrust that power which rises from our deepest and nonrational knowledge. We have been warned against it all our lives by the male world, which values this depth of feeling enough to keep women around in order to exercise it in the service of men, but which fears this same depth too much to examine the possibilities of it within themselves. So women are maintained at a distant/inferior position to be psychically milked, much the same way ants maintain colonies of aphids to provide a life-giving substance for their masters.

But the erotic offers a well of replenishing and provocative force to the woman who does not fear its revelation, nor succumb to the belief that sensation is enough.

The erotic has often been misnamed by men and used against women. It has been made into the confused, the trivial, the psychotic, the plasticized sensation. For this reason, we have often turned away from the exploration and consideration of the erotic as a source of power and information, confusing it with its opposite, the pornographic. But pornography is a direct denial of the power of the erotic, for it represents the suppression of true feeling. Pornography emphasizes sensation without feeling.

The erotic is a measure between the beginnings of our sense of self and the chaos of our strongest feelings. It is an internal sense of satisfaction to which, once we have experienced it, we know we can aspire. For having experienced the fullness of this depth of feeling and recognizing its power, in honor and self-respect we can require no less of ourselves.

It is never easy to demand the most from ourselves, from our lives, from our work. To encourage excellence is to go beyond the encouraged mediocrity of our society. To go beyond the encouraged mediocrity of our society is to encourage excellence. But giving in to the fear of feeling and working to capacity is a luxury only the unintentional can afford, and the unintentional are those who do not wish to guide their own destinies.

This internal requirement toward excellence which we learn from the erotic must not be misconstrued as demanding the impossible from ourselves nor from others. Such a demand incapacitates everyone in the process. For the erotic is not a question only of what we do; it is a question of how acutely and fully we can feel in the doing. Once we know the extent to which we are capable of feeling that sense of satisfaction and completion, we can then observe which of our various life endeavors bring us closest to that fullness.

The aim of each thing which we do is to make our lives and the lives of our children richer and more possible. Within the celebration of the erotic in all our endeavors, my work becomes a conscious decision—a longed-for bed which I enter gratefully and from which I rise up empowered.

Of course, women so empowered are dangerous. So we are taught to separate the erotic demand from most vital areas of our lives other than sex. And the lack of concern for the erotic root and satisfactions of our work is felt in our disaffection from so much of what we do. For instance, how often do we truly love our work even at its most difficult?

The principal horror of any system which defines the good in terms of profit rather than in terms of human need, or which defines human need to the exclusion of the psychic and emotional components of that need—the principal horror of such a system is that it robs our work of its erotic value, its erotic power and life appeal and fulfillment. Such a system reduces work to a travesty of necessities, a duty by which we earn bread or oblivion for ourselves and those we love. But this is tantamount to blinding a painter and then telling her to improve her work, and to enjoy the act of painting. It is not only next to impossible, it is also profoundly cruel.

As women, we need to examine the ways in which our world can be truly different. I am speaking here of the necessity for reassessing the quality of all the aspects of our lives and of our work, and of how we move toward and through them.

The very word *erotic* comes from the Greek word *eros*, the personification of love in all its aspects—born of Chaos, and personifying creative power and harmony. When I speak of the erotic, then, I speak of it as an assertion of the lifeforce of women; of that creative energy empowered, the knowledge and use of which we are now reclaiming in our language, our history, our dancing, our loving, our work, our lives.

There are frequent attempts to equate pornography and eroticism, two diametrically opposed uses of the sexual. Because of these attempts, it has become fashionable to separate the spiritual (psychic and emotional) from the political, to see them as contradictory or antithetical. "What do you mean, a poetic revolutionary, a meditating gunrunner?" In the same way, we have attempted to separate the spiritual and the erotic, thereby reducing the spiritual to a world of flattened affect, a world of the ascetic who aspires to feel nothing. But nothing is farther from the truth. For the ascetic position is one of the highest fear, the gravest immobility. The severe abstinence of the ascetic becomes the ruling obsession. And it is one not of self-discipline but of self-abnegation.

The dichotomy between the spiritual and the political is also false, resulting from an incomplete attention to our erotic knowledge. For the bridge which connects them is formed by the erotic — the sensual — those physical, emotional, and psychic expressions of what is deepest and strongest and richest within each of us, being shared: the passions of love, in its deepest meanings.

Beyond the superficial, the considered phrase, "It feels right to me," acknowledges the strength of the erotic into a true knowledge, for what that means is the first and most powerful guiding light toward any understanding. And understanding is a handmaiden which can only wait upon, or clarify, that knowledge, deeply born. The erotic is the nurturer or nursemaid of all our deepest knowledge.

The erotic functions for me in several ways, and the first is in providing the power which comes from sharing deeply any pursuit with another person. The sharing of joy, whether physical, emotional, psychic, or intellectual, forms a bridge between the sharers which can be the basis for understanding much of what is not shared between them, and lessens the threat of their difference.

Another important way in which the erotic connection functions is the open and fearless underlining of my capacity for joy. In the way my body stretches to music and opens into response, hearkening to its deepest rhythms, so every level upon which I sense also opens to the erotically satisfying experience, whether it is dancing, building a bookcase, writing a poem, examining an idea.

That self-connection shared is a measure of the joy which I know myself to be capable of feeling, a reminder of my capacity for feeling. And that deep and irreplaceable knowledge of my capacity for joy comes to demand from all of my life that it be lived within the knowledge that such satisfaction is possible, and does not have to be called *marriage*, nor *god*, nor *an afterlife*.

This is one reason why the erotic is so feared, and so often relegated to the bedroom alone, when it is recognized at all. For once we begin to feel deeply all the aspects of our lives, we begin to demand from ourselves and from our life-pursuits that they feel in accordance with that joy which we know ourselves to be capable of. Our erotic knowledge empowers us, becomes a lens through which we scrutinize all

aspects of our existence, forcing us to evaluate those aspects honestly in terms of their relative meaning within our lives. And this is a grave responsibility, projected from within each of us, not to settle for the convenient, the shoddy, the conventionally expected, nor the merely safe.

During World War II, we bought sealed plastic packets of white, uncolored margarine, with a tiny, intense pellet of yellow coloring perched like a topaz just inside the clear skin of the bag. We would leave the margarine out for a while to soften, and then we would pinch the little pellet to break it inside the bag, releasing the rich yellowness into the soft pale mass of margarine. Then taking it carefully between our fingers, we would knead it gently back and forth, over and over, until the color had spread throughout the whole pound bag of margarine, thoroughly coloring it.

I find the erotic such a kernel within myself. When released from its intense and constrained pellet, it flows through and colors my life with a kind of energy that heightens and sensitizes and strengthens all my experience.

We have been raised to fear the *yes* within ourselves, our deepest cravings. But, once recognized, those which do not enhance our future lose their power and can be altered. The fear of our desires keeps them suspect and indiscriminately powerful, for to suppress any truth is to give it strength beyond endurance. The fear that we cannot grow beyond whatever distortions we may find within ourselves keeps us docile and loyal and obedient, externally defined, and leads us to accept many facets of our oppression as women.

When we live outside ourselves, and by that I mean on external directives only rather than from our internal knowledge and needs, when we live away from those erotic guides from within ourselves, then our lives are limited by external and alien forms, and we conform to the needs of a structure that is not based on human need, let alone an individual's. But when we begin to live from within outward, in touch with the power of the erotic within ourselves, and allowing that power to inform and illuminate our actions upon the world around us, then we begin to be responsible to ourselves in the deepest sense. For as we begin to recognize our deepest feelings, we begin to give up, of necessity, being satisfied with suffering and self-negation, and with the numbness which so often seems like their only alternative in our society. Our acts against oppression become integral with self, motivated and empowered from within.

In touch with the erotic, I become less willing to accept powerlessness, or those other supplied states of being which are not native to me, such as resignation, despair, self-effacement, depression, self-denial.

And yes, there is a hierarchy. There is a difference between painting a back fence and writing a poem, but only one of quantity. And there is, for me, no difference between writing a good poem and moving into sunlight against the body of a woman I love.

This brings me to the last consideration of the erotic. To share the power of each other's feelings is different from using another's feelings as we would use a kleenex. When we look the other way from our experience, erotic or otherwise, we use rather than share the feelings of those others who participate in the experience with us. And use without consent of the used is abuse.

In order to be utilized, our erotic feelings must be recognized. The need for sharing deep feeling is a human need. But within the european-american tradition, this need is satisfied by certain proscribed erotic comings-together. These occasions are almost always characterized by a simultaneous looking away, a pretense of calling them something else, whether a religion, a fit, mob violence, or even playing doctor. And this misnaming of the need and the deed give rise to that distortion which results in pornography and obscenity — the abuse of feeling.

When we look away from the importance of the erotic in the development and sustenance of our power, or when we look away from ourselves as we satisfy our erotic needs in concert with others, we use each other as objects of satisfaction rather than share our joy in the satisfying, rather than make connection with our similarities and our differences. To refuse to be conscious of what we are feeling at any time, however comfortable that might seem, is to deny a large part of the experience, and to allow ourselves to be reduced to the pornographic, the abused, and the absurd.

The erotic cannot be felt secondhand. As a Black lesbian feminist, I have a particular feeling, knowledge, and understanding for those sisters with whom I have danced hard, played, or even fought. This deep participation has often been the forerunner for joint concerted actions not possible before.

But this erotic charge is not easily shared by women who continue to operate under an exclusively european-american male tradition. I know it was not available to me when I was trying to adapt my consciousness to this mode of living and sensation.

Only now, I find more and more women-identified women brave enough to risk sharing the erotic's electrical charge without having to look away, and without distorting the enormously powerful and creative nature of that exchange. Recognizing the power of the erotic within our lives can give us the energy to pursue genuine change within our world, rather than merely settling for a shift of characters in the same weary drama.

For not only do we touch our most profoundly creative source, but we do that which is female and self-affirming in the face of a racist, patriarchal, and anti-erotic society.

◆◆◆

NINETY-FIVE

An Open Letter to the Women's Movement

Barbara Macdonald

. . . The following are a few suggestions to all of us for working on our ageism:

• Don't expect that older women are there to serve you because you are younger — and *don't think the only alternative is for you to serve us.* . . .

• Don't believe you are complimenting an old woman by letting her know that you think she is "different from" (more fun, more gutsy, more interesting than) other older women. To accept the compliment, she has to join in your rejection of old women.

• Don't point out to an old woman how strong she is, how she is more capable in certain situations than you are. Not only is this patronizing, but the implication is that you admire the way she does not show her age, and it follows that you do not admire the ways in which she does, or soon will, show her age.

• If an old woman talks about arthritis or cataracts, don't think old women are constantly complaining. We are just trying to get a word in edgewise while you talk and write about abortions, contraception, pre-menstrual syndromes, toxic shock, or turkey basters.

• Don't feel guilty. You will then avoid us because you are afraid we might become dependent and you know you can't meet our needs. Don't burden us with *your* idea of dependency and *your* idea of obligation.

• By the year 2000, approximately one out of every four adults will be over 50. The marketplace is ready now to present a new public image of the aging American, just as it developed an image of American youth and the "youth movement" at a time when a larger section of the population was young. Don't trust the glossy images that are about to bombard you in the media. In order to

sell products to a burgeoning population of older women, they will tell you that we are all white, comfortably middle class, and able to "pass" if we just use enough creams and hair dyes. Old women are the single poorest minority group in this country. Only ageism makes us feel a need to pass.

• Don't think that an old woman has always been old. She is in the process of discovering what 70, 80, and 90 mean. As more and more old women talk and write about the reality of this process, in a world that negates us, we will all discover how revolutionary that is.

• Don't assume that every old woman is not ageist. . . .

• If you have insights you can bring to bear from your racial background or ethnic culture — bring them. We need to pool all of our resources to deal with this issue. But don't talk about your grandmother as the bearer of your culture — don't objectify her. Don't make her a museum piece or a woman whose value is that she has sacrificed and continues to sacrifice on your behalf. Tell us who she is now, a woman in process. Better yet, encourage *her* to tell us.

NINETY-SIX

◆◆◆

Something About the Subject Makes It Hard to Name

Gloria Yamato

Racism — simple enough in structure, yet difficult to eliminate. Racism — pervasive in the U.S. culture to the point that it deeply affects all the local town folk and spills over, negatively influencing the fortunes of folk around the world. Racism is pervasive to the point that we take many of its manifestations for granted, believing "that's life." Many believe that racism can be dealt with effectively in one hellifying workshop, or one hour-long heated discussion. Many

actually believe this monster, racism, that has had at least a few hundred years to take root, grow, invade our space and develop subtle variations . . . this mind-funk that distorts thought and action, can be merely wished away. I've run into folks who really think that we can beat this devil, kick this habit, be healed of this disease in a snap. In a sincere blink of a well-intentioned eye, presto — poof — racism disappears. "I've dealt with my racism . . . (envision a laying on of hands) . . . Hallelujah! Now I can go to the beach." Well, fine. Go to the beach. In fact, why don't we all go the beach and continue to work on the sucker over there? Cuz you can't even shave a little piece off this thing called racism in a day, or a weekend, or a workshop.

When I speak of *oppression*, I'm talking about the systematic, institutionalized mistreatment of one group of people by another for whatever reason. The oppressors are purported to have an innate ability to access economic resources, information, respect, etc., while the oppressed are believed to have a corresponding negative innate ability. The flip side of oppression is *internalized oppression*. Members of the target group are emotionally, physically, and spiritually battered to the point that they begin to actually believe that their oppression is deserved, is their lot in life, is natural and right, and that it doesn't even exist. The oppression begins to feel comfortable, familiar enough that when mean ol' Massa lay down de whip, we got's to pick up and whack ourselves and each other. Like a virus, it's hard to beat racism, because by the time you come up with a cure it's mutated to a "new cure-resistant" form. One shot just won't get it. Racism must be attacked from many angles.

The forms of racism that I pick up on these days are 1) aware/blatant racism, 2) aware/covert racism, 3) unaware/unintentional racism, and 4) unaware/self-righteous racism. I can't say that I prefer any one form of racism over the others, because they all look like an itch needing a scratch. I've heard it said (and understandably so) that the aware/blatant form of racism is preferable if one must suffer it. Outright racists will, without apology or confusion, tell us that because of our color we don't appeal to them. If we so choose, we can attempt to get the hell out of their way before we get the sweat knocked out of us. Growing up, aware/covert racism is what I heard many of my elders bemoaning "up north," after having escaped the overt racism "down south." Apartments were suddenly no longer vacant or rents were outrageously high, when black, brown, red, or yellow persons went to inquire about them. Job vacancies were suddenly filled, or we were fired for very vague reasons. It still happens, though the perpetrators really take care to cover their tracks these days. They don't want to get gummed to death or slobbered on by the toothless laws that supposedly protect us from such inequities.

Unaware/unintentional racism drives usually tranquil white liberals wild when they get called on it, and confirms the suspicions of many people of color who feel that white folks are just plain crazy. It has led white people to believe that it's just fine to ask if they can touch my hair (while reaching). They then exclaim over how soft it is, how it does not scratch their hand. It has led whites to assume that bending over backwards and speaking to me in high-pitched (terrified), condescending tones would make up for all the racist wrongs that distort our lives. This type of racism has led whites right to my doorstep, talking 'bout, "We're sorry/we love you and want to make things right," which is fine, and further, "We're gonna give you the opportunity to fix it while we sleep. Just tell us what you need. 'Bye!!" — which *ain't* fine. With the best of intentions, the best of educations, and the greatest generosity of heart, whites, operating on the misinformation fed to them from day one, will behave in ways that are racist, will perpetuate racism by being "nice" the way we're taught to be nice. You can just "nice" somebody to death with naïveté and lack of awareness of privilege. Then there's guilt and the desire to end racism and how the two get all tangled up to the point that people, morbidly fascinated with their guilt, are immobilized. Rather than deal with ending racism, they sit and ponder their guilt and hope nobody notices how awful they are. Meanwhile, racism picks up momentum and keeps on keepin' on.

Now, the newest form of racism that I'm hip to is unaware/self-righteous racism. The "good white" racist attempts to shame Blacks into being blacker, scorns Japanese-Americans who don't speak Japanese, and knows more about the Chicano/a community than the folks who make up the community. They assign themselves as the "good whites," as opposed to the "bad whites," and are often so busy telling people of color what the issues in the Black, Asian, Indian, Latino/a communities should be that they don't have time to deal with their errant sisters and brothers in the white community. Which means that people of color are still left to deal with what the "good whites" don't want to . . . racism.

Internalized racism is what really gets in my way as a Black woman. It influences the way I see or don't see myself, limits what I expect of myself or others like me. It results in my acceptance of mistreatment, leads me to believe that being treated with less than absolute respect, at least this once, is to be expected because I am Black, because I am not white. "Because I am (*you fill in the color*)," you think, "life is going to be hard." The fact is life may be hard, but the color of your skin is not the cause of the hardship. The color of your skin may be used as an excuse to mistreat you, but there is no reason or logic involved in the mistreatment. If it seems that your color is the reason, if it seems that your ethnic heritage is the cause of the woe, it's because you've been deliberately beaten down by agents of a greedy system until you swallowed the garbage. That is the internalization of racism.

Racism is the systematic, institutionalized mistreatment of one group of people by another based on racial heritage. Like every other oppression, racism can be internalized. People of color come to believe misinformation about their particular ethnic group and thus believe that their mistreatment is justified. With that basic vocabulary, let's take a look at how the whole thing works together. Meet "the Ism Family," racism, classism, ageism, adultism, elitism, sexism, heterosexism, physicalism, etc. All these ism's are systemic, that is, not only are these parasites feeding off our lives, they are also dependent on one another for foundation. Racism is supported and reinforced by classism, which is given a foothold and a boost by adultism, which also feeds sexism, which is validated by heterosexism, and so it goes. You cannot have the "ism" functioning without first effectively installing its flip-side, the internalized version of the ism. Like twins, as one particular form of the ism grows in potency, there is a corresponding increasing in its internalized form within the population. Before oppression becomes a specific ism like racism, usually all hell breaks loose. War. People fight attempts to enslave them, or to subvert their will, or to take what they consider theirs, whether that is territory or dignity. It's true that the various elements of racism, while repugnant, would not be able to do very much damage, but for one generally overlooked key piece: power/privilege.

While in one sense we all have power, we have to look at the fact that, in our society, people are stratified into various classes and some of these classes have more privilege than others. The owning class has enough power and privilege to not have to give a good whinney what the rest of the folks have on their minds. The power and privilege of the owning class provide the ability to pay off enough of the working class and offer that paid-off group, the mid-

dle class, just enough privilege to make it agreeable to do various and sundry oppressive things to other working-class and outright disenfranchised folk, keeping the lid on explosive inequities, at least for a minute. If you're at the bottom of this heap, and you believe the line that says you're there because that's all you're worth, it is at least some small solace to believe that there are others more worthless than you, because of their gender, race, sexual preference . . . whatever. The specific form of power that runs the show here is the power to intimidate. The power to take away the most lives the quickest, and back it up with legal and "divine" sanction, is the very bottom line. It makes the difference between who's holding the racism end of the stick and who's getting beat with it (or beating others as vulnerable as they are) on the internalized racism end of the stick. What I am saying is, while people of color are welcome to tear up their own neighborhoods and each other, everybody knows that you cannot do that to white folks without hell to pay. People of color can be prejudiced against one another and whites but do not have an ice-cube's chance in hell of passing laws that will get whites sent to relocation camps "for their own protection and the security of the nation." People who have not thought about or refuse to acknowledge this imbalance of power/privilege often want to talk about the racism of people of color. But then that is one of the ways racism is able to continue to function. You look for someone to blame and you blame the victim, who will nine times out of ten accept the blame out of habit.

So, what can we do? Acknowledge racism for a start, even though and especially when we've struggled to be kind and fair, or struggled to rise above it all. It is hard to acknowledge the fact that racism circumscribes and pervades our lives. Racism must be dealt with on two levels, personal and societal, emotional and institutional. It is possible — and most effective — to do both at the same time. We must reclaim whatever delight we have lost in our own ethnic heritage or heritages. This so-called melting pot has only succeeded in turning us into fast food-gobbling "generics" (as in generic "white folks" who were once Irish, Polish, Russian, English, etc., and "black folks," who were once Ashanti, Bambara, Baule, Yoruba, etc.). Find or create safe places to actually *feel* what we've been forced to repress each time we were a victim of, witness to or perpetrator of racism, so that we do not continue, like puppets, to act out the past in the present and future. Challenge oppression. Take a stand against it. When you are aware of something oppressive going down, stop the show. At least call it. We become so numbed to racism that we don't even think twice about it, unless it is immediately life-threatening.

Whites who want to be allies to people of color: You can educate yourselves via research and observation rather than rigidly, arrogantly relying solely on interrogating people of color. Do not expect that people of color should teach you how to behave nonoppressively. Do not give into the pull to be lazy. Think, hard. Do not blame people of color for your frustration about racism, but do appreciate the fact that people of color will often help you get in touch with that frustration. Assume that your effort to be a good friend is appreciated, but don't expect or accept gratitude from people of color. Work on racism for your sake, not "their" sake. Assume that you are needed and capable of being a good ally. Know that

you'll make mistakes and commit yourself to correcting them and continuing on as an ally, no matter what. Don't give up.

People of color, working through internalized racism: Remember always that you and others like you are completely worthy of respect, completely capable of achieving whatever you take a notion to do. Remember that the term "people of color" refers to a variety of ethnic and cultural backgrounds. These various groups have been oppressed in a variety of ways. Educate yourself about the ways different peoples have been oppressed and how they've resisted that oppression. Expect and insist that whites are capable of being good allies against racism. Don't give up. Resist the pull to give out the "people of color seal of approval" to aspiring white allies. A moment of appreciation is fine, but more than that tends to be less than helpful. Celebrate yourself. Celebrate yourself. Celebrate the inevitable end of racism.

◆◆◆

NINETY-SEVEN

Jews, Class, Color, and the Cost of Whiteness

Melanie Kaye/Kantrowitz

asleep: dream. i walk down the street wearing shorts and a t-shirt and the new earrings my ex-lover just gave me for my birthday. i pass two young hip-looking women.

she's all japped out, *they say. about me. i cringe, self-conscious.*

then i look down at my shorts & t-shirt. i'm not even dressed up, except for the earrings. suddenly i understand that no matter what i wear i will be perceived as "all japped out."

When I wake I realize I've never heard the expression. But I know exactly what it means.

Awake: vision. I walk down 106th street, a big wide street, in the mostly Puerto Rican and Dominican neighborhood where I live, after 25 years away from New York. I spot a man I've seen before on Broadway, asking for money. He's out in the street, shaking his fist at cars, gesturing as if in a silent

movie—he looks like he's shouting and no words come out, or at least I can't hear them. He moves in jerky, violent spurts so that when he veers toward the sidewalk, people scatter, afraid. I watch him for a bit, afraid he'll hurt himself, wondering if I should do something. I walk into the copy shop I sometimes use. Everyone's speaking Spanish. I don't, and so I ask, "Do you speak English?" Yes. I discuss the problem with the man behind the counter. We go out into the street and watch. We decide to phone 911, the emergency number.

First question they ask: *is he white black or hispanic?* Like the new baby question: *boy or girl?* Asian doesn't even exist.

White, I say, knowing it's only because he's white that I can phone cops on his behalf. If he were Black or Latino, I'd be afraid of how they'd treat him. I keep walking towards Broadway. So does the silently cursing man. He miraculously crosses Broadway to the traffic island without incident and plunks down on a park bench, one of two white men on the Upper West Side asking for money. I watch for a while. No police car arrives.

Awake: more vision. Last night on Broadway I saw the man who had asked me and Helena for money, and I ran across the street against the light and dangerously close to traffic to get away. He scares me. A couple of weeks ago we were walking home, we were almost on my block, 106th between Amsterdam and Columbus, where no one ever asks for money because no one assumes anyone east of Amsterdam has any money. We told him, sorry, not today. I had just given money to two different people, and Helena had three dollars to her name.

By the time we reached the end of the block he'd circled back, stood in front of us, asking again. *You know, I don't want to rob or anything but I just might have to,* he says.

I'm not about to respond, but he keeps talking. *I don't want to be like this, asking for money on the street, but you know I need money, and I don't want to rob or anything. . . .* Finally Helena gives him a dollar.

It seems that he came back to us, rather than the dozen other people on the street, because he (a black man) assumes we have money (we're white) and will be afraid (we're women). The truth is, we are neither moneyed nor afraid, and we give (Helena) or not (me) for our own reasons. The truth also is, he's desperate and we're not.

The next night I'm walking home by myself, late, and there he is, practically in front of my building. He approaches, extends his hand. *I'm sorry about last night,* he says. We shake hands, smile. Then he says, *but I need some money again, could you give me some?*

Late and dark. I don't want to stand there going through my pockets and especially taking out my wallet. Most of all I'm disturbed that he knows me. I am afraid of him becoming mine: *my beggar.* I don't want to be responsible for him. I don't want him to expect anything from me. Half the movies I've ever seen rise up in me, and I know if this were a movie I'd run into him every day for a week and at the end of the week he'd stab me. Everyone watching would recognize the heavy symbolism.

I shove aside the racist movie images. I say, *I can't give you money today*—and now I am stuck with my lie. I could give something. But I want to keep moving, get home.

He demands, *I need money.*
I can't . . .
I need . . .
I can't . . .
I need . . .
until finally I say, *hey man, I dig it but do you hear me?*

He nods. We both know I'm lying, that I'm the one who gets to say yes or no. We say goodnight, smile.

Let me walk you around my neighborhood. On 106th street at Broadway, people of all colors and ages shopping, walking, sitting at street cafes, waiting for buses, heading for the subway, wheeling children in strollers. But notice the people, and there are many, stretched out asleep on the benches and even on the sidewalks—winter is harsh here and still they're in the street, sometimes without shoes—the people shaking cups, asking, *can you spare some change,* saying, *I'm very hungry, can you give me something, even a quarter.* They're almost all African American men, a few women, also African American. Look at the taxi drivers. Step into one of the hundreds of small shops, restaurants, groceries, stationery shops that line Broadway. I see owners and often their families, and hired clerks: Asian, Indian, Arab, Latino, Greek, Jewish, sometimes Caribbean Black. Rarely are they African American. Practically all of them speak English wrapped in the vowels and consonants of their mother tongue, which is not English; except their kids, teenagers who help out after school and Saturdays, as I used to help out in my parents' store, are fluently bilingual, perfect English, as well as rapid-fire Chinese, Korean, Spanish. . . . They will go to college, their kids will probably lose their language, their culture. This is the American dream.

South of 96th street the balance of color shifts from brown to white, Latino to yuppie. Gentrified, white graduates of elite colleges live in buildings with swimming pools and elaborate doormen, views of the George Washington bridge—men and women in their twenties whose parents, or trust funds, bought them apartments costing maybe a million dollars.

There are lots of old Jews, surviving still in their rent-controlled apartments that will probably turn co-op when they die. Lots of harried thirty-somethings and forty-something Jewish women and men, their Jewishness visible only to those familiar with the intricacies and codes of New York Jews. They had their kids late, they split economically between upper middle and middle, and politically between liberals and radicals. Some are insistent about sending their kids to public schools, and some have given up on the public schools, refusing, in their words, to sacrifice their kids to a principle. They are professionals who live on schedules so tight that any unforeseen disruption is a minor disaster. To cope with the stress of life by the clock, and because they were raised to, or have taught themselves to, expect some joy and fulfillment in life, they see therapists, acupuncturists, chiropractors, and belong to health clubs where they work out and stay in shape. On the Upper West Side (and all over New York City) class shows in well-developed calves and trim forms. Fat is sloppy. Fat is poor. I am sure that the average weight in my immediate neighborhood among the women is 15 pounds higher than 15 blocks south.

One more thing: in my immediate neighborhood, when you see women with children, they tend to be the same color, brown to black. A few blocks west or south, when I see a woman and child of the same color, I'm almost surprised; the norm is women of color caring for white children, what I've come to think of as the underbelly of feminism. Most of the women are immigrants. Some of the children are Jews.

Let me adjust the lens, for accuracy. Not all Jews are professionals (45% are working class or poor); not all African Americans are homeless or poor, generation after generation (though a full third live below the poverty line). Not all whites are yuppies, New York is not the nation, and the Upper West Side is not even all of New York.

For example, I recently visited Seattle; at the Asian community health clinic, the brochures come in ten different languages for clients from Hong Kong and the hills of Laos (imagine in the early part of this century, a "European" clinic had to serve Irish, Poles, Italians, Slavs, Greeks, Jews, and Swedes, from farms and *shtetlekh*, from Sicily, Dublin, Paris and Prague). In Seattle the homeless are white men, and anti-racist coalitions include Jews as a matter of course, because skinheads and other white supremacist groups mustering forces in Idaho target Jews and people of color. Or in New Mexico, where I used to live and where I still return as often as I can, the poor are Native American and after them, Chicano/a; Anglos buy up the

beautiful old adobes; the issues are development and ecology, water table first and foremost. In Maine and Vermont, where I also have lived, and which share with New Mexico and Mississippi the honor of being the poorest states in the union, the poor are mostly white, nationally invisible because small-town and rural and the only news that counts happens in the big cities, where media thrive. For rural and small-town residents, the issues are not street violence; there are few streets and hardly anyone is anonymous, though women and children endure and resist violence in their homes. Rural issues are development and agriculture; the question is whether all food production will rest in the hands of a few multinational corporations.

But whatever is coming apart in the nation is doing so to some extent in New York first. When the public schools are essentially abandoned; when thousands upon thousands of people have no place to live, and everyone who does carries key rings heavy with metal, for the two to five locks required to simply get in one's apartment; when the threat of rape and other street violence against women controls our every decision about where to go, how long to stay, how much it will cost, and how much anxiety we can tolerate; when hate crimes of all kinds are on the rise, this is the future of our nation if something doesn't change. A recent survey found that even in rural areas, nearly half the people encounter on a daily basis people with no place to live. This is the human cost of our nation's priorities.

In the early and mid-eighties, I was working out some thoughts on racism and anti-semitism, heavily influenced by these places I'd lived, and by my friends, many of whom were women of color, from both poor/working- and middle-class families, and white poor and working-class women. The way the debate was being framed as Black-Jewish or even Black-white obscured, I felt, the issue of class and the complexity of race. I wrote about the ways racism played out very differently against the various peoples of color—Chinese, Japanese, Arab, Native American. . . . I wrote about why I saw anti-Semitism as a form of racism, meaning racist ideology. This last seemed like a truism to me; the camps of Europe were revealed three months before I was born. And in New Mexico, Maine, Vermont, I was certainly an alien. And I said then, the difficulty some people have in grasping anti-Semitism as a serious concern and as a form of racism is that it hasn't kept Jews poor. (In fact, anti-Semitism often claims that all Jews are rich.) I also saw what was getting called Black-Jewish conflict as a mutual scapegoating—Jews were getting blamed for white racism and Blacks for christian anti-Semitism—as well as obscured class conflict.

But I have come to believe that this analysis needs to be pushed further. I am troubled, for example, by analogies between Asians and Jews, between Arabs and Jews, not because these analogies are not valid—with the difference that Asians almost always look Asian, while Jews and Arabs may often pass. What troubles me is this: while class and general principles of race-hate are illuminated by these analogies, something else gets obscured: the intransigence and virulence of oppression of African Americans . . . and something else.

The structure of apartheid is useful to contemplate here, not because things in the U.S. are so fixed and clear; they're not. But let me pursue the analogy. South Africa has not two racial categories, but three: white, black and colored. It's the particular buffer zone of colored that I want to examine. Colored are those who will never be white but at least aren't black. Colored are those who have more access to higher status and all that implies—better housing, jobs, education, health, leisure, safety, respect. I want to suggest that in many places in the U.S., Japanese, Korean, and some Chinese, Indians and Pakistanis, Arabs and lighter-skinned or wealthier Latinos get to be colored. Sometimes Caribbean Blacks, by virtue of their accent, their education, the strength of growing up as the majority, also get to be colored. And African Americans, I want to suggest, are not the only "blacks," though they are the most visible. Many Latinos are black—dark in color—and also those most Indian of Chicanos, tracked in the lowest social and economic status. Immigrants from Southeast Asia hold some of the hardest, worst-paying jobs in the nation. And in the Southwest and sometimes Northwest, where there are few African Americans, native Americans are kept the lowest of the low, and every cruel stereotype of inferiority shows up in local racist culture.

As I've said, these categories are not totally fixed. There is a certain permeability that characterizes the class-race system in the U.S., a certain amount of passing—literally, for those with skin light enough, who shed their accents, language, culture; and ap-

proximately, for those who, laboring under the heavy burden of racism, through luck and extraordinary heroism and sometimes through hardness against their own people, still squeak through. Clarence Thomas rises up from poverty to hobnob with the white male club called the Senate precisely by abandoning his people's concerns.

The point of this white/colored/black classification is not to violate the hope of solidarity among people of color by dividing them, but to recognize divisions that exist and must be named in order to bridge them. The Iraqi-Black conflicts in Detroit; Korean-Black in Flatbush and L.A.; Cuban-Black in Miami. Conflicts which a generation ago often were Jewish-Black because they are in part the inevitable result of who owns what in whose community, and who is poor, and who is accessible.

You could say, as my sister did when I was sharing these thoughts with her, aren't you talking about class? Yes and no. I'm talking about *caste as access to class*, as representing the probability either of moving up or standing still. And in the years of Reagan and Bush, standing still means things get worse.

Let me meander for a moment in the swamp of class. Top down, billionaires, millionaires: control and power; wealth so beyond the needs of one person, one family, it staggers the mind; here we find unlimited access to health care, comfort, resources; mostly WASP. 70% of Congress comes from this class. While most white people aren't in it, most people in it are white, some Jews.

Middle class includes low-level managers, social workers, small shopkeepers, and teachers—K-12, secondary school, junior college, university—as well as business people, doctors, lawyers, and other professionals with incomes of $200,000 a year and more ($200,000, the dividing line under Reagan/Bush, between the rich getting richer and everyone else getting poorer). When a class category includes both those piling up assets and those applying for food stamps, we should recognize an obsolete term and come up with something else. Here is where we find over half the Jews in the U.S., spread throughout the category, and a fair number of people of color, mostly represented at the lower end of the class.

Working class is also problematic as an economic category. The nonunionized women in the chicken factories, Black in the South, white in Maine; Asians and Latinas in the endlessly transforming, infinitely stable New York City sweatshops once worked by Italian and Jewish women: these are working-class, and, as we see, part of the problem with the category is gender. Working class also includes the racially diverse members of the UAW, the men whose sons used to be guaranteed the best paid laboring jobs in the U.S.—but today Michigan, heart of the auto industry, endures 35% unemployment. Working class excludes the endemic poor, the poor without a prayer of breaking out of it, not those who perform backbreaking work of past generations of immigrants but those who can find no work at all, or can only find work that pays so badly that, for example, women with children can't afford to give up welfare to earn money that will all get swallowed by childcare costs. They are African American, Latino, Native American, Asian. As for the rural white poor, because there are no jobs, their children leave for the cities, become essentially immigrants, and in the cities their white skin serves them in finding work—but, like other immigrants, they lose their culture. Working class spans well-paid unionized fields, many of which are now threatened because of automation, and because successful unionization has challenged owners' greed and sent manufacturing jobs abroad to pay workers less and maximize profits. Whole industries abandon communities of workers who have served them for generations; even keypunch work which requires English is shipped to Ireland (lest we miss the dominance of class/poverty as theme, and mistake it entirely for race/color), because Irish women are so poor as to demand so little. The two fields of labor still growing in the U.S., the hardest to organize and the worst paid, are office work and the service industry, including maids and restaurant workers.

Who does this office and service work? Women. People of color, especially immigrants, a replenishing, flexible pool of cheap labor, thankful to work hideously long hours for little money, because it is more than they had, and because they came here, often, not for their own betterment but for their children's. And so they groom their kids to escape the parents' lives, to assimilate, much as I, raised passionately pro-union, was groomed to escape the working class, and even the lower-middle-class shopkeeping existence at which my parents had succeeded.

It is precisely this access to better-paid working-class jobs or lower-middle-class small business opportunities, along with access to education for the next generation, that characterizes the experience of "colored" in the U.S. It is precisely this lack of better working-class jobs and small business opportunities along with systematic disadvantaging and exclusion by the educational system, that characterizes the experience of "blacks" in the U.S. Sherry Gorelick's *City College and the Jewish Poor* describes how City College was created as a path to upward mobility to distract the radical Jewish poor from the revolutionary class struggle predicted by Marx; the path of higher education was taken by thousands and thousands of poor and working-class Jews. But college was free for us, and there was room, if not at the top, then certainly in the middle. Where are the free colleges now? Private colleges cost more than $20,000 a year. And where is room in the middle, when even the middle is suffering?

This shared economic disaster could and should unite most people across lines of color. But the illusory protection of "whiteness" offers a partial escape route toward which anyone who can scrambles. This desire to identify with whiteness, as well as bigotry and fear, blocks solidarity.

In this white-colored-black scheme, where are the Jews?

Of the groups I've named as targeted by a general hate I'll call race-hate, Jews are the closest to white. Many would say we are white, and indeed a common-sense visual response suggests that many of us are.

But listen to the prophet James Baldwin: "No one was white before he/she came to America," Baldwin wrote in the mid-eighties.* "It took generations, and a vast amount of coercion, before this became a white country . . . "

> It is probable that it is the Jewish community— or more accurately, perhaps, its remnants— that in America has paid the highest and most extraordinary price for becoming white. For the Jews came here from countries where they were not white, and they came here in part because they were not white; and incontestably— in the eyes of the Black American (and not only in those eyes) American Jews have opted to become white. . . .

---

*James Baldwin, "On Being 'White' and Other Lies" *Essence* (April, 1984).

Now, the point is not for us, Jews, to escape the category "white," to evade confronting our own racism, nor is it to insert ourselves artificially into a category of oppression, as sometimes happens in our movements where oppression in some puny paradoxical way confers privilege. It is to recognize a continuum where we are the closest of the coloreds to white, or the closest of the whites to colored.

This is hardest to see in New York City, where Jews can hardly be called a minority. If there is the diaspora and Eretz Yisroel, I have come to think of New York as a third category, somewhere between the two. "I'm in exile from Brooklyn," I used to joke, but it's no joke. Jews in New York City, except for select neighborhoods, experience the luxury of normality. To assume christianity in New York is to be hopelessly provincial. In New York one finds Jewish culture on a broad spectrum: orthodox, secular, lesbian and gay, Sephardic, Yiddishist, feminist. . . . The paradoxical result is a majority of Jews who operate without consciousness of their Jewishness. It's not an issue. Anti-Semitism is occasional, focused, and historical, and in recent years, for New Yorkers, has been associated mostly with African Americans. Quite the opposite from what's going on in the farm belt, the Northwest, and the South, where alliances between Jews and people of color are obvious to everyone.

Yet I'm suggesting that progressive Jews recognize our position in between colored and white, a source of tension but also of possibility. I can envision a powerful coalition between Jewish and Asian women, against the JAP stereotype. I can also envision a nightmare coalition between Jewish and Asian men against affirmative action. The challenge is to build progressive coalitions not only among the coloreds but between the coloreds and the blacks, and between these and the economically struggling whites — and then to expand still further. The issue of hate crimes, for example, can unite Jews with people of color, and with lesbians and gays; and we should insist on the legal — and moral — classification of violence against women as a hate crime. That will be a powerful coalition indeed.

What I want to focus on is this: in James Baldwin's phrase, "the extraordinary price of becoming white."

Many of us chose, or had chosen for us, a white path. A path of assimilation, of passing, often accompanied by extreme cultural loss. How many of us speak or read Yiddish or Ladino or Judeo-Arabic?

What do we know of our own histories, our literature, our music, our cultural diversity, our rich traditions? What do we know beyond or besides the now-usual sources of American Jewish identity, which are, in a nutshell, religion, Israel, and the Holocaust. Nothing wrong with these sources — but as the sum total of Jewish identity, this is limited. Where does this restricted focus leave secularists or confirmed diasporists? What happens when we disagree, as we do, about solutions to the Israeli-Palestinian conflict? How does this restricted focus help us create and strengthen an authentic Jewish American identity? How does it enable us to see the Holocaust in a context of Jewish history, the tragedy of which was not only the destruction of millions of lives — as though that were not tragedy enough — but also the destruction of a rich and varied culture.

It's called assimilation. We, like others who pass or partly pass, can choose where to direct our allegiance: upward and whitening, restricting our Jewishness to that which assimilation increasingly demands, *a Jew at home, a "man" in the streets,*[*] white people who go to Jewish church, i.e., synagogue; or we can deepen both our identity and our affiliation, with the other "others," the outsiders: the coloreds and the blacks.

Think about shedding whiteness. I don't mean to pretend that Jews who are white endure the same visual vulnerability as people of color; though we should recognize that many Jews, especially outside the U.S., simply *are* people of color, that the definition of Jews as automatically "European" is incorrect. In addition, many Sephardi and also many Ashkenazi Jews are sufficiently dark to be readily perceived, at least in the South and in the heartland, as people of color. Think also about the Hasids; think about wearing a Jewish star, or other item that identifies you as a Jew; think about never taking it off. Think about driving through Mississippi.

So: is fighting anti-Semitism a diversion from fighting racism? Do we think we can fight anti-Semitism without fighting racism? Do we think Jews can be safe within a white supremacist society?

I do not. I believe, along with a great many other Jews, that a color/class barrier means injustice, and

---

[*] The phrase was used to characterize the "modern" Jew of the European Enlightenment.

our culture teaches us to pursue justice. I also believe that a color/class barrier threatens Jews, in two ways:

1. Because race hate will never exclude us. As long as the world is divided into us and them, minorities are vulnerable. Fascism is on the rise. In our century, can we be naive about the danger?

2. Because the particular nature of anti-Semitism, which defines Jews as money, as powermongers — especially marks us as scapegoats for the abuses of capitalism, and we are living through a time of rampant abuse.

It's also a hard time to be talking about the abuses of capitalism, when it seems that so many people living under communism have rejected it, or tried to. Even allowing for lies and misperceptions, the American left is going through something as massively disruptive to our way of describing and envisioning the world as were the fifties' exposés of Stalinism on one hand, and persecutions by McCarthy on the other. I know that some of us who came to adulthood calling Lyndon Baines Johnson a fascist have a perspective problem, one which Reagan and Bush have helped us address. But we have not yet dealt, even theoretically, with the re-emergence in Europe and the former Soviet Union of toxic nationalism, nor with the dazzling speed with which internationalization of capital is matched by internationalization of labor: "guest workers" in Germany, Kuwait, Saudi Arabia; "illegals" in the U.S. What do national boundaries or national identity mean at this century's end?

Jews with any sense of history are scanning the airwaves for disaster. What I think we must keep poised in response to our knowledge that communism as practiced has failed; *so has capitalism.* We cannot accept what we have as tolerable. It's not okay that, in the richest country in the world, millions are without health care. It's not okay that one out of five children grows up in poverty, or that the figure for Black children is one out of two.

The rich get richer. And who does the dominant culture blame? Jews; Asians, especially Japanese; Arabs; foreigners; let's face it, "the colored" get blamed for various contributions to economic disaster; for controlling the economy, or making money on the backs of the poor; for raising the price of oil; for stealing or eliminating jobs (by importing goods or exporting production); for taking the jobs. African Americans, Latinos, Native Americans, "the blacks," get blamed for urban violence and chaos, for drugs,

for the skyrocketing costs and failures of social programs. That is, coloreds get blamed for capitalism's crimes; blacks for capitalism's fallout. Do I need to point out who escapes all blame?

When we are scapegoated we are most conscious of how we feel humiliated, alienated, and endangered. But the other function of scapegoating is at least as pernicious. Scapegoating protects the source of the problem we are being scapegoated for, the vicious system of profit and exploitation, of plenty and scarcity existing side by side.

And let me address briefly, because it is the glaring omission so far, the pain and difficulty many of us have experienced from hearing about or facing anti-Semitism from African Americans. How are we supposed to be allies? people ask, not unreasonably.

But I want us to understand a few things. First, just as a racist remark by Jackie Mason does not reveal the inherent racism of all Jews, let us not assume that an anti-Semitic remark by Leonard Jeffries, or by ten Leonard Jeffries, reveals the heart of the African American community. We need to recognize the destructive role played by the media in fanning the flames of the "Black-Jewish Conflict." Cornel West, bell hooks, Richard Green, Barbara Christian, Henry Louis Gates, Marian Wright Edelman, Nell Painter, Albert Raby. . . . Why are these names not as well known outside the African American community as the names of Louis Farrakhan or Leonard Jeffries? Are they, in their diversity and dynamism, less representative of the African American community?

Second, no more than racism in the Jewish community should surprise us, should we be surprised by anti-Semitism in the christian and Muslim communities, which includes African Americans. Nor should we be surprised by racism among people of color against each other. We all learn the same lies about one another. Part of our work is untangling these lies.

I want to make one last point about Jews and class, and this is about privilege and power. Hatred, chauvinism, oppression always function to keep people from their power, to mute their strength. Because they're laboring under heavier odds. Because they're taught to feel bad about themselves.

Anti-Semitism has a peculiar edge because the myth is that we're too powerful, too rich, and much too pushy. I began with my dream, where displaying a simple gift of earrings, walking down the street daring to feel okay, means: *she's all japped out.* Any particle of this that we absorb makes us afraid of our strength, loath to use our power, embarrassed by the relative economic and social success of Jews as a people, afraid it will be used against us (and it will).

Jewish progressives often buy into this scheme of contempt for "most Jews," assumed to be uniformly well off, or they experience a nostalgic longing for the time when Jews were authentically the right class, that is, poor and working-class.

I think we need to look critically at this attitude. First, because it erases working-class Jews and poor Jews. Second, because it writes off the political energy and concerns that exist sometimes apart from class, the ripe possibilities for coalition of feminist Jews, of lesbian and gay Jews, of Jewish educators and cultural workers, of Jewish seniors, and on and on, not to mention Jews who see anti-Semitism for what it is, a form of race hate which must be fought along with other forms of race hate, and those who are simply hungry for economic and social justice. Who do not wish to spend our lives deciding whether or not to give quarters or dollars to other human beings who need more than we can possibly give; who do not wish to abandon the cities with their fabulous human variety because of the stresses of economic inequality, alienation, and violence; who still believe a better way is possible.

Third, because this attitude of contempt for Jews who are not poor, which is, after all, a form of inter-nalized anti-Semitism, ignores the fact that education, choice, comfort are all valuable. One cannot walk the streets of any of our cities, see people living in cardboard boxes or wrapped in torn blankets, and not appreciate the material basis for human existence. The problem is not relative Jewish success. The problem is a severe class system that distributes success so unequally.

Used well, education, choice, even comfort, can strengthen people, individually and collectively. As for money—let me say the dirty word—nothing gets done without it. The question is, what do we do with our education, our choice, privilege, skills, experience, passion for justice: our power. Don't racism and anti-Semitism make you sick? Doesn't hatred scare you? Don't you feel at least a little desperate about the way things are going unless something intervenes?

I think Jews need to gather our power, make it visible, and use it right. I'm sick of the more conservative wing of the Jewish community speaking for all of us. Everyone knows that Jews are all over progressive movements, what I've come to think of as the political diaspora. Maybe our task is to ingather the Jews, just a little, into a new civil and human rights coalition, in which we are present and visible as Jews. It means being proud of our collective strength, confident that we can use it right. Someone will always call us pushy. Isn't it time to really push?

◆◆◆

NINETY-EIGHT

Common Threads
Life Stories and the Arts in Educating for Social Change
Cynthia Cohen

Introduction

The Oral History Center for Education and Action, (OHC), a community organization currently located at the Center for Innovation in Urban Education at Northeastern University in Boston, uses oral history methods and the arts for the purpose of strengthening communities. Our work is informed by a strong multi-cultural and anti-racist perspective; it is de-signed to facilitate the kinds of understanding needed to build alliances across differences.

The OHC's model is based on the idea that everyone has an important story to tell. It emphasizes an attentive quality of listening, that can be transformative for both the listener and the teller. It also integrates the arts, in ways that nourish people's imagination, validate diverse cultures, and reach large audiences. The model evolved out of two projects I coordinated under the auspices of The Cambridge Arts Council, in 1980 through 1982: The Cambridge Women's Oral History Project (CWOHP) and the Cambridge Women's Quilt Project (CWQP). This article describes those two projects, as well as others the OHC sponsored during the years when I was its director, from 1982 through 1990.

The Cambridge Women's Oral History Project

In the CWOHP, high school students collected stories from their own and other's cultural communities. We chose the theme "transitions in women's lives" because the young women themselves were undergoing many transitions, and also because it could embrace the experience of women from all groups in the city, including recent immigrants. The young women conducted interviews (mostly in English, but also in Haitian Creole, Portuguese and Spanish), indexed tapes, and created a visual exhibit incorporating photographic portraits, excerpts of oral narrative, and brief biographies. Working with the staff of the project, they created a slide-tape show "Let Life Be Yours: Voices of Cambridge Working Women," which focuses on the theme of work in women's lives. "Let Life Be Yours" asks a question. How have women's cultural and economic backgrounds affected their ability to make choices in their lives? Answers can be found in the women's stories.

> Antonia Cruz, a recent immigrant from Puerto Rico: "My father wanted to take me out of school, because it was too expensive, he said. They were poor, they took me out of school in the fifth grade."

> Addie Eskin, a Jewish woman born near Boston: "'What do you mean you have to go to high school, what do you have to go to high school for?' she said. 'Your father is very sick, what do you think, you're gonna go to school and hold your hand out?' And I said, 'Auntie, if I have to wear this middy blouse for the next four years, I'm going to graduate from high school.'"

> Henrietta Jackson, a black woman born in Cambridge: "One of the newspapers called Cambridge High and Latin School, and asked the office practice teacher if she had any good student who might want a few hours every day after school in the newspaper office. I was considered one of the fastest typists and I went with two other girls. I was rejected immediately. And she called them and she was practically told they weren't quite ready for a black person. She said that it will be a long time before there won't be this kind of unfair treatment of a person whose only fault is that she happens to have a black face."

> Catherine Zirpolo, an Italian woman born in Boston: "1914. I was fortunate, I didn't have to go to work . . . being an only child. . . . When I became of age to go to high school, I wasn't a bit interested in high school. I wanted to be an actress even then. . . . "

When the older women who participated in the Cambridge Women's Oral History Project told stories about the obstacles they faced, they revealed inspiring spiritual strength. The project's political message (i.e. opposing oppression based on race, class and gender) is all the more powerful because their language is personal and accessible, devoid of rhetoric. In evaluation interviews at the end of the project, the young women involved reported that their participation in the project had changed their ideas about older people, about the study of history, and about working with women:

> Books are dull, but this way I get enjoyment out of history. . . . Winona and I have had really different lives. She's black and I'm white; I have more opportunities with education, work, and money. She's religious. There's a strength about her, so it's nice to talk to her. She's the kind of inspiring person that makes us want to go out and read and read good books and take it in. She makes you see how somebody can be at peace with things. Part of this is kind of making up for what I couldn't find from my own grandmother.

> The people changed my opinions a lot. . . . Older people are pretty active in the community; they have a lot to say, most of them. They are just older, not feeble or anything. I used to see them like stereotypes, as people who sat back and watched the world go by. But they have a big part while it goes by. I never realized that.

I got a lot out of seeing women work together. It gives you a sense of self-respect, a sense that I'm a valuable person. You see women working together and taking each other seriously and you know it's there and you know it should be there all the time.

Since it's completion in 1984, "Let Life Be Yours" has been translated into Portuguese, Haitian Creole and Spanish. It has been used as the basis for community education programs on women's history, multicultural issues, older people's lives, and oral history methods.

The Cambridge Women's Quilt Project

The Oral History Center's second major project involved sixty women and girls, ranging in age from eight to eighty, working in collaboration with two fabric artists to create images from their lives in fabric. The project was designed as a study of the historical, social and cultural factors that influenced changes in women's lives. Also we intended to reflect on quilt-making: its function in women's lives, and its relationship to oral tradition. Through the project, we were able to enact the very subjects we were studying. For instance, many women and girls found that their participation in the project was itself producing changes in their lives. As has been a part of the American quilting bee tradition historically, participants in the project shared medical and political information, reflected together on their relationships with boys and men, and gained perspective on the decisions they were facing. They felt themselves becoming part of a community.

The fabric artists supported each woman to create her own image of a story from her own life. One was about braiding a daughter's hair and another about a great-grandmother quilting. Others were about lighting Sabbath candles, dressing up to go to church, riding a donkey in Haiti, making wine in Italy, the dream of walking freely outside at night, hitchhiking throughout Europe and Africa, making life rafts during World War II, giving birth at home, reading alone in one's bedroom, reading to a group of neighborhood children, a childhood picking cotton in the South and a childhood dream of becoming a ballerina.

Our respect for each woman's expression was put to the test when one woman depicted in her quilt patch a child, pants rolled down, being spanked by his parent. When asked to document something important for history, this participant had chosen to represent "a time when parents cared enough about their children to set limits, to punish them when necessary." Other participants were upset by the expression of what they took to be violent: not only the spanking itself, but the humiliation of the child, with his bare bottom exposed. Through discussion, compromise was reached: the patch remained, but re-stitched with rolled-up pants.

In other ways too, the project created a congruence between the content and methods of our inquiry. For instance, women and girls depicted women weaving rugs, making lace and quilting, and here we were, making a quilt. Several patches honored women as bearers of traditional food ways: a Jamaican aunt carrying fruits home from market on her head, a Mennonite grandmother baking a cherry pie, and an Irish Nana heating tea. As we shared traditional foods and recipes at our potlucks, we were enacting as well as documenting this dimension of women's experience.

A total of 52 fabric images were sewn into two vibrant quilts. Some of the participants tape recorded interviews about the meaning of each patch; these oral narratives were edited into a catalog. Finally, a group of younger women worked with singer/songwriter Betsy Rose to compose a ballad, sung to a traditional Portuguese melody, based on the stories of the quilt patches. The ballad became the audio background for a slide-tape on the making of the quilts.

Informal conversations as well as the more formal sharing of stories in interviews were understood to be an important aspect of the projects. As one participant said,

People who came were very shy and really, you couldn't see a visible importance about their lives. But once the little quilt square opened it was like they came alive. Everybody was so enthusiastic and one story led to another. . . . Maybe the most important thing about the quilt project was that the women who did it enjoyed each other and talked to each other. . . . There was no performance, and no being performed. Everybody is on stage. Everybody's the song. Everybody's the story teller.

Since their completion in 1982, the quilts have been exhibited in the neighborhoods of the city, at local festivals, and in libraries, stores, churches, schools and cultural and social service organizations. They have traveled to several other New England cities, and as far away as The International Women's Forum in Nairobi, Kenya, and to meetings of the Belize Rural Women's Association in Central America. In one of our most engaging exhibits, viewers of the quilts at the Boston Children's Museum could use nearby computer terminals to call up edited versions of the interview narratives according to a number of different categories.

Common Threads

As we watched women and girls from different ethnic communities interacting as they sewed the quilts, it became clear that fabric arts were familiar media in which many women felt comfortable expressing themselves. In fact, many of the participants in the quilt project were steeped in the skills and customs of rich fabric traditions such as Portuguese lace-making, Haitian embroidery, African-American appliqué quilting, as well as knitting, crocheting and sewing. Activities using fabric gave women and girls the chance to feel a sense of accomplishment for their skills (generally unacknowledged, even within their own communities), and to learn about one another's lives and cultures.

We used these insights to design Common Threads, an exhibit and series of events which highlighted the stories and work of ten traditional and contemporary fabric artists, each from a different local ethnic community. The exhibit, displayed at a branch of the local library and in the high school, consisted of samples of fabric art such as lace, embroidery, batik, appliqué and crochet, along with the life stories of the women who created the pieces. At several events, members of English-as-a-Second-Language classes and others in the community were invited to bring their own fabric work and other crafts, and to share stories about their lives and their work.

Following the exhibit, the OHC collaborated with several local organizations to sponsor a visit to Cam-

bridge of two Chilean *arpilleristas,* women who use small burlap tapestries to depict the harsh realities of daily life under the dictatorship of Augusto Pinochet. One of the *arpilleristas,* for instance, used a series of her tapestries to document her ten year search for her son, detained by the military police shortly after Pinochet came to power. Many of the community women who participated in Common Threads and the Cambridge Women's Quilt Project attended a workshop with the arpilleristas, making an immediate connection through their common interest in storytelling through fabric. The following year, the OHC built on this awareness by sponsoring our own Stories-in-Fabric workshop, and the resulting tapestries were taken to the International Women's Forum in Nairobi, Kenya.

Because the Common Threads exhibit was temporary, we created a slide-tape show, which explores the social, political, economic and artistic meanings of fabric art in the lives of women. The slide show has been used in educational programs with groups of older people, fabric artists and students of women's history.

Lifelines

In addition to conducting women's oral history projects in community settings, the OHC also collaborated with teachers to adapt its model to a classroom context. Lifelines was a curriculum development project, designed to support fifth through eighth grade and bilingual teachers to incorporate oral history into on-going Social Studies and Language Arts curricula. Two teachers, for example, worked with students on labor history projects. In one case, students created a visual exhibit combining excerpts of interviews with parents and older workers with statistical analyses of the shifting economic base of the city. In the other classroom, students interviewed six women who worked in Cambridge factories during the 1930's and 1940's, and produced an illustrated timeline, visual exhibit, and slide-tape show about the changing patterns of women's work in the Depression, World War II, and the post-war eras. Three Lifelines classes explored topics in family and ethnic studies.

The arts were especially important in a Lifelines project in a Haitian bilingual class. The project was designed specifically to enhance self-esteem. The Haitian students were at the bottom of the social hierarchy at their school. They were teased about their language, their body odor, the possibility of being carriers of AIDS. These assaults on their integrity were sustained while they were struggling to learn a new language, to adjust to separation from members of their families, and often while they were recovering from the political violence and the extreme poverty that had led their families to leave the island whose landscape and culture they still cherished.

Students who had been in the U.S. for just two or three years interviewed Haitian adults who worked in careers of interest to the children. As they began to hear the stories of the adults of their own community validated and celebrated in their classroom, there began an outpouring of expression from them: stories and especially pictures of their lives in Haiti and their bewildering encounters with an American city. With help from a student intern from Harvard, the students created a slide-tape show, "We Are Proud of Who We Are," in which they narrated the stories told them by adults. They also worked with a storyteller to prepare performances of their own narratives. The children's stories and artwork, exhibited in the school corridors, provided contexts for relationship-building between the teachers and administrators in the school's monolingual program and the Haitian children. In subsequent years, students created notecards embellished with their drawings of images from their lives, and sold the cards to raise funds for an eye clinic in Haiti. The entire school participated in that effort, and later a group traveled to Haiti to visit a sister school. Through this project, the students began to realize the possibilities inherent in their own expression, and to understand that they were not only documentors, but makers, of history.

A Passion for Life: Stories and Folk Arts of Palestinian Women

During the same years we were working in collaboration with the Cambridge Public School on Lifelines, one of the women drawn to our Stories-in-Fabric series became involved in the OHC. Her name was Feryal Abbasi Ghnaim, and she worked as a traditional Palestinian embroiderer. Her interests and skills helped define our next major oral history project, A Passion for Life: Stories and Folk Arts of Palestinian and Jewish Women. The project was designed to explore whether stories and folk arts could be used to facilitate communication not just across differences, but across the chasm created by long-standing political conflict and violence.

The project's final exhibition displayed the stories of eight Jewish and Palestinian women, along with objects of folk expression, such as baskets, embroidered dresses, family photographs and cooking utensils. Eighteen public events preceded and accompanied the exhibition; these ranged from sessions of sharing recipes, songs, dance and visual arts, to a theoretical discussion on the role of folk arts in communities in crisis and a workshop on challenging stereotypes of Arab and Jewish people. The members of the project's Directions Committee, which consisted of both Jewish and Palestinian women and others, wrote at the time that we were looking for modes of expression which would invite people in conflict to reach beneath their defenses and their fears, so they could come to recognize each other's humanity:

> In spite of our many differences, we believe there is wisdom in the perspectives of women, who are striving day to day, sometimes under harsh oppression, to create their lives and to recreate culture and community for their children. There is value in the stories of these regular common people who do the mundane but richly detailed work of sowing seeds and harvesting fruits, preparing foods and cleaning homes, fixing remedies and stitching cloth, selling goods and listening to the stories people share when they come together to celebrate, to grieve and to pass on traditions.

> The stories and works of art in our exhibition include descriptions of the tragedy of the Palestinian Diaspora and the oppression of Palestinian people under Israeli occupation. They speak to the terrible persecution which Jewish people have endured throughout history, most horrifyingly manifested in Europe during World War II.

> We bring these stories together in one exhibition not to suggest any simple parallels, but to create a vision broad enough to embrace them all. As we listen to stories from

both Jewish and Palestinian women, we share feelings of sadness and anger, sometimes outrage. We believe that nothing excuses acts of inhumanity. Has the world not seen enough of families divided, homes and communities destroyed? Have there not been enough precious heirlooms confiscated, people imprisoned, children murdered? How can this fragile fabric of our lives, which we and our mothers and our grandmothers have stitched so carefully—note by note, spoonful by spoonful, caress by caress, story by story—be so brutally torn to shreds?

We engage with this work out of a deep love for our own traditions and an appreciation for the richness of the others'.

We recognize the deep-seated fears of both Palestinian and Jewish people. We are work-ing towards a world in which we all are safe to preserve and develop our cultures. We are inspired by the passion for life which permeates these women's stories and their art: the impulse to create beauty, to nourish children, to take risks, to resist oppression, to celebrate community; and the determination to survive, both physically and spiritually, against forces of brutality and destruction.

Take inspiration from these stories to reach out to each other with openness and respect. Let them motivate you to take a stand for justice and to work for peace.

A Passion for Life proved to be more difficult than we ever could have imagined at the outset. Sometimes it seemed to be little more than a snarl of ethical dilemmas, demanding relationships and intense emotions. At times, both Feryal and I, the project's co-directors, felt pressured by members of our families and communities to withdraw from the project. Key people from both communities chose not to participate, and in a couple of cases, backed out at the last minute. In retrospect, it seems like a miracle that we ever managed to bring the eight women's stories under one roof, even for just a couple of months.

Among the many conflicts we needed to resolve in the course of the project, the most contentious were misunderstandings about language, and our lack of awareness of the meanings and resonances of specific words for members of each other's communities. For many Palestinians, for instance, the word "peace," unless immediately followed by the word "justice," had come to signify a criticism of Palestinian resistance to the Israeli occupation. It was a kind of a code, understood by many Jewish people, who had themselves come to perceive the word "justice" as pro-Palestinian. The word "1948" also resonated very differently for members of each community. For Palestinians, 1948 is the year of the *nakba*, or disaster. It is the year of the dispersion, when many Palestinians were dispossessed of their land, the year when the fabric of their lives was permanently rent. Nineteen-forty-eight is the year of the massacre of the citizens of Deir Yessin, a Palestinian village plundered by members of two Jewish right-wing terrorist organizations. Thousands of Palestinians fled from their homes in fear of a repetition of Deir Yessin. For most Jewish people, on the other hand, 1948 marks the creation of the state of Israel, a time of rejoicing in the fulfillment of a dream of a homeland—a symbol that evokes images of security, justice, democracy, and the possibility of a post-Holocaust renewal. It isn't just that one group views the history as victors and the other as a people defeated, but that each places the events of the year within a different frame of historical reference.

The most problematic and emotionally charged meanings were encoded in the phrase "The Holocaust." The emotional resonances which surround the memory of the holocaust, the politically motivated abuses of holocaust imagery by both sides, and the disparate meanings which are attached to the word may be among the central barriers to Palestinian-Jewish reconciliation. While most Palestinians and Jews understand each others' readings of the words "peace" and "justice," often they are unaware of the different resonances of references to the holocaust. For most Jews of Eastern European background, The Holocaust is a sacred memory. Less than fifty years ago, a third of the Jewish people were killed, and this fact still defines communal reality.

What happened in Europe—the systematic obliteration of thousands of communities; the destruction of Yiddishkeit as a living culture; the challenge to Jewish understanding of God, and justice and faith; the magnitude of the suffering and the devastation underscoring the meaning of being homeless in the world—all of this is the context in which contemporary Jews of European heritage came to define their individual and collective identity.

From a Palestinian perspective, "the holocaust" is what they have repeatedly heard as an excuse for the inexcusable brutality and injustice to which they have been subjected. European and American guilt about it was a major factor in turning world opinion to support the Zionist claim to Israel. Palestinian people feel that they are being made to suffer for Europe's crimes, and that somehow the significance of their own suffering diminishes when it is compared to the holocaust. A Palestinian friend once said to me: "Don't put me beside a Holocaust survivor; I feel like nothing. How can my suffering compare?"

While Jewish people feel a need to honor the memory of the Holocaust by retelling the story and by bearing witness to the tragedy, many Palestinian people are weary of hearing the story. "Why do they have to tell us this story?" asked Feryal. "We are the ones who are suffering now." The documentaries and fictional renditions of the Holocaust story on TV often culminate with hopeful references to the new state of Israel, accompanied by images which either demonize Arabs or render their true experience invisible. These are especially painful because of the media's relative silence about Palestinian history and culture, its muteness about Palestinian suffering and legitimate needs for security.

Throughout A Passion for Life, in spite of these misunderstandings of words, there were moments when Palestinian and Jewish people began to understand each other's point of view, to feel each other's suffering, to recognize themselves in each other's aspirations. This happened through hearing each other's stories, and seeing and appreciating each other's artistic work. After hearing the stories of Palestinian women who had become friends, one Jewish woman acknowledged for instance that she had never realized that Jewish people in Israel were living in the actual dwellings which had once belonged to Palestinian families. One Palestinian woman said that although she had known about the Holocaust before, she had never truly felt the enormity of it. After seeing Feryal describe the symbols in her embroidery, an older Jewish man, a committed supporter of Israel, commented that he had never realized that Palestinian women were telling stories in their embroidery.

Often, A Passion for Life seemed like an enormous landscape, clouded by terror and confusion. It often seemed that what we were attempting was actually impossible. But, all along, there were moments when the terrain would shift, creating new contours of possibility. These openings, made possible by our caring for each other and by the power of stories and the arts, enlarged our imagination and deepened our yearning for reconciliation. These were the moments that sustained us in our work. Once after a particularly difficult phase of the project, Feryal and I spoke together at a gathering of people from both communities. She showed her beautiful tapestry of a Palestinian woman holding aloft a dove. In its beak is an envelope carrying this message:

> Women of the world: Women love peace to raise their children in, so why don't you make peace your number one goal? I as a Palestinian know intimately that there are two kinds of peace. 1) Peace that is built on the bodies of those brutalized and murdered to silence their calls for their just rights; 2) peace which comes from understanding a people's suffering, sitting down with them to genuinely solve and resolve their problems, so that justice and equality can be the code of the land, not death and suffering.
>
> Why don't we, women, raise our voices high and strong in the service of true peace to preserve our children, our future as human beings? I ask you to support my call for true peace for my people. We are not subhumans. We are people with history and civilization. We are mothers and fathers and children. We have had enough killing and Diaspora. I smuggled my dreams in my hidden wishes and crossed the ocean in hope for peace; for my Palestinian sisters who lost their children in wars and who have been widowed at an early age. I ask you for true peace for my people.

I followed Feryal by reading an excerpt from the extraordinary autobiography of Heda Margolius Kovaly, in which she recounts the events of her life in Prague from 1941 through 1968:

> Three forces carved the landscape of my life. Two of them crushed half the world. The third was very small and weak, and, actually, invisible. It was a shy little bird hidden in my rib cage an inch or two above my stomach.

Sometimes in the most unexpected moments the bird would wake up, lift its head, and flutter its wings in rapture. Then I too would lift my head because, for that short moment, I would know for certain that love and hope are infinitely more powerful than hate and fury, and that, somewhere beyond the line of my horizon there was life indestructible, always triumphant.

The first force was Adolf Hitler; the second was Iosif Stalin. They made my life a microcosm in which the history of a small country in the heart of Europe was condensed. The little bird, the third force, kept me alive to tell the story.

When I finished reading Kovaly's words, Feryal leaned over and pointed to the dove in her tapestry. "You see," she whispered, "it's the same bird."

The Oral History Center for Community Education and Action is located at The Center for Innovation in Urban Education, 403 Richards Hall, Northeastern University, Boston, MA 02115. Oral history resources mentioned in this article can be ordered from The OHC by mail or by phone: 617-373-4814, or fax: 617-373-8482. Requests can also be directed to the author, c/o The Department of Education, University of New Hampshire, Durham, NH 03824.

NINETY-NINE

◆◆◆

The Anti-Violence Coalition of Kentucky
An Experience in Alliance-Building
Elizabeth Wilson-Compton

Bowling Green, Kentucky 1996

Western Kentucky University's campus spreads itself out along a steep hill and reminds the onlooker that they are in Kentucky. Pine trees sporadically show themselves among the majestic oaks and maples, and thick, rich bluegrass covers the lawns. Once a Normal School for teachers, Western is now a state university that actively recruits people of diverse backgrounds to fill its faculty positions as well as seeking diversity among its student body. WKU has a Women's Studies Department, an African American Studies Department, and an International Studies Department, complete with a progressive recruitment of foreign students. I have been at Western since the summer of 1994 and, until I attended a conference in Washington, D.C. in spring 1996 on "Building Alliances and Coalitions," I believed it to be a great place for my children to grow up. Now, I realize that it is a great place to begin changing before my children grow up.

I ended up receiving the skills to change my part of the world in a very unexpected way. While between classes reading the postings on a bulletin board, I saw a letter about the Women as Leaders Conference, an enrichment seminar sponsored by the Washington Center in Washington, D.C. The idea of a "girls only" vacation in D.C., highlighted by academic work, appealed to me. So I applied and was accepted into the program. A scholarship covered most of my expenses, freeing up my finances to explore the sights of the city.

The sights I ended up being most enthralled with, however, were free. I spent a great deal of time standing, walking, or just sitting and watching people of the Capitol. Suddenly, political awareness was not something I studied in a "Controversial Issues" class, and the concerns of African Americans, Native Americans, gay and lesbian people, people with disabilities, and Asian Americans were not just words on a page, they were an integral part of policy and life. I visited the buildings where the American Indian Movement had holed up in protest of continual broken promises from our government. I walked on the grass where civil rights marches took place and, more recently, where a mass wedding of gays and lesbians was held. I could almost feel the heat from the bras that burnt in protest of our paternalistic government when I stood on the steps of the Supreme Court building.

Still, even more inspiring were the people of D.C. The women I met really cared about equality, some of them had dedicated their entire lives to it. Blacks and whites walked down Pennsylvania Avenue and laughed together. Men and women in the traditional dress of their native countries or tribes walked, unnoticed, among the crowds. I was deeply affected by the contrast between this city and mine, and it moved something in me that had been stirring for a long time.

I lay in my hotel room that night and thought about what I had seen. I acknowledged that, had I not gone out of my way to take classes that forced me to look at other people's perspectives — American Institutions and Minorities, Psychology, Honors, and Sociology classes — I might not have noticed these differences so clearly. However, I felt dumbfounded about how to bring this knowledge home in a real way. Simply retelling my experience would be no more effective than having my friends and family read a book. I wanted them to *feel* the experience of seeing life, all aspects of it, through someone else's eyes.

At the conference I learned about tools to catalyze change and the yearning within me to give this empowerment, especially to other women, became overwhelming. The following is an excerpt from my journal:

> The women here are all strong. At home I
> felt special because I was strong. That my up-
> bringing or something in my mother caused
> me to be different. But I am not different. I
> have just been given the opportunity to see
> things through a wider lens. I didn't come to
> school to get my MRS and I have closed myself
> off to the women who have, but if I can show
> them what I see, lend them the experiences
> that bring about insight, maybe we can all be
> strong — Together.

I began to develop a strategy. I would form a coalition of people and organizations to put on a Clothesline Display Project. We would call it The Anti-Violence Coalition of Kentucky. The Clothesline Display Project, a visual display of T-shirts created by victims of violence, their friends, or family members,

had been successfully initiated in over 250 cities since its inception in the early eighties. Like the founders, I wanted to bring attention to the problem of violence and the ability of women to survive; but I also had other dreams for this project: Strength, solidarity, and insight.

Back home, I sat in the lobby of the Plaza Hotel, less than two weeks after my return from D.C., waiting for Marlice Pillow, the Director of our local spouse abuse shelter. Marlice was a very classy lady who exuded strength and tenacity, and who had led many alliances and mentored many people throughout her life. We went to a seat in the dining room and I told her about my past (I had been in an abusive marriage that robbed me of my childhood as well as my high school education) and about the Clothesline Project itself.

"I see this as a chance to draw women into this project who have not been involved with much before. For them to experience the empowerment of helping others and to work with different people on an important issue. I may be being idealistic, but I think this could be the start of bringing about a change in some of the women who only come to school to get married. Women with enormous potential who cannot see beyond today, or their boyfriend, or whatever keeps them from being like those women I met in D.C.," I said enthusiastically.

Marlice smiled and said many encouraging things. That lunch, alongside the image of the sixteen women in my small group in Washington, gave me the strength that I was too excited to realize I would need over the next few months.

After meeting with Marlice and the Director of the Rape Crisis Center, Phyllis Millstaugh, I began calling organizations and people that I believed would be interested in the project. My first letdown occurred within the first week when I called the Pregnancy Help Center. In organizing my list of contacts I had included Black, white, pro-life, pro-choice, Republican, Democrat, straight, gay, conservative, liberal, and neutral organizations. I expected some to refuse, as the national Clothesline Display Project included "women assaulted because of their sexual orientation," but I was still hurt by the director's response.

"I'm sorry Miss, what was it? Wilson?" he asked.

"Wilson-Compton," I replied, knowing full well that even my hyphenation was an offense to many conservatives.

"Yes, well. I really don't think we would be interested. It sounds like your agenda is a little too feminist/political for us."

"My mother is a pastor and I have worked with affiliates of yours. Do you know Dena in Somerset?" I queried, feeling insulted, but trying to draw on my personal past to engage him in dialogue.

I tried to draw him into the conversation and he thawed a little. "Yes, I know Dena well," he said with some warmth, but went on to say, "Listen, why don't you drop off the information and we'll call you if we're interested." Of course, he wasn't interested, nor were any of the other thirty Christian organizations I called.

I refused to let it get me down. I went out to the abuse center and talked with Marlice for about an hour and toured the facilities, fascinated and distracted. Later, I put the picture of my small group in the front of my day-runner and started calling prospective board members and sponsors again. The Plaza Hotel was our first corporate sponsor, then Women's Studies, and the list grew. Eventually we raised over $1000 in cash and over $500 in supplies.

I sat at my computer working one morning when the phone rang. It was Larry Calliout, head of the Christian Fellowship of Faculty/Staff (CFFS) of WKU. CFFS is a very visible group on campus that takes out a full page ad twice a year, announcing its membership roster. Larry told me that CFFS wanted to throw their hat into the ring as board members AND sponsors! I discussed my problems in getting a response from the Christian community with Larry at length and he encouraged me to keep trying. He and I talked two or three more times over the course of the next few months and he sent representatives to several board meetings.

Another phone call brought the news that Marlice had died from a long-term illness. Though our friendship had been very brief, this discovery cut me to the quick. Marlice's treatment of me had been nothing short of inspiring and her contribution to the coalition had been profound. I let myself cry openly for a long time, concentrating on the enormity of this loss to our community. She had served as the first female police officer, a faculty member at Western, and in various other positions before coming to the spouse abuse shelter. Her wide influence was attested to by the diverse crowd at her funeral, and we decided to dedicate the Bowling Green

Clothesline Display Project to her. She had left us with a hard, but worthy, act to follow.

As the coalition gathered steam we were a diverse group partly due to Marlice's influence. Our board included an openly gay man, a lesbian, a Native American Christian, an atheist, a male social worker (sporting an earring), several women (including a police officer, myself (sporting an eye-ring), several older members, one who was 19, and working closely with us was Take Back the Night, a predominantly black group on our campus. Volunteers came from all walks of life and all segments of the college and community. We had counselors from a Christian firm, from the Rape Crisis and Spouse Abuse Centers, and from the Campus Counseling Service. We set up booths at the Kentucky Victims Advocate Conference, the International Festival, and the National Coming Out Day celebration on campus.

At those sessions, women, and more than a dozen men, who created shirts talked with us and touched us with stories too horrible to repeat, but too profound to forget. One incident I remember vividly was that of an eighteen-year-old gay man who had been raped by another man. Words failed me as he told his story. All I could do was hold him. Another story came from my relatives in northeastern Kentucky. My cousin had found a ten-year-old girl raped and sodomized. Many mothers stopped by our predisplay booths and talked to us. A local eight-year-old girl had been recently kidnapped from her yard. People were frightened for their children. Women from the Spouse Abuse Center created shirts in their therapy sessions. One was on a white, one-piece infant outfit and read "No, no, please don't hurt me." This shirt had a powerful impact on the crowds at our displays — one downtown and one on campus. Young white couples picked up brochures on how to talk to their kids about abuse and about a local drop-in daycare center. Children wore bear stickers that said "Stop Child Abuse." Black women stopped and took brochures; Asian women used an interpreter to talk with me briefly. Women from all walks of life and all backgrounds shared stories and concerns, and made T-shirts for themselves or someone they knew.

I made a shirt too. My shirt had a weeping willow drawn on it and said "My Family Tree Is a Weeping Willow: Grandpa raped his daughters and beat daddy. Daddy raped my sister and beat us all. Brother raped me and my sister." At the bottom I wrote a promise to my children that the cycle stops with me. Another promise I make to them everyday is that I will show them the world through the widest possible lens. I don't mind being the only white family in the Martin Luther King Jr. Day march. I don't mind having my house broken into and my life threatened because gay men and lesbians are welcome in my home. I don't mind being out of place or feeling different. *That is the essence of building alliances, that is the essence of change. And only when we are willing to leave the security of the known and venture into the "other" do we stretch and grow and learn.* And somewhere along the road we look back and realize that the greatest thing we have learned is that we can work together and that each of us has a unique and valuable contribution to give.

At the end of the conference in Washington, our group performed a skit where a wire hanger was shaped into a woman's figure and each member of our group brought up a personal item (glasses, keys, scarf, . . .) and attached it to the woman as I read the following. This "model woman" is who we must all aspire to be, as the alliance begins inside of us.

Mysterious Woman

Numerous, seemingly unrelated parts go into her
  construction.
A bit of wit from her mother.
A bit of self-esteem from her teacher.
Humility, through failures she dares not forget.
Bigotries she hopes to erase.
Sunsets which bring her a glimpse of serenity.
Wars, which force upon her rage.
Injustices which bring her unrest.
Internal conflicts whose resolutions change her
  very appearance,
and somewhere — before the final artwork is
  unveiled —
A sense that all that is wrong,
all that is painful,
all that causes others to cry out in desperation
  or hunger,
fear or loneliness,
ALL THAT IS . . .
Can be irrevocably altered . . .
by her.

She is the homeless mother.
She is the woman in Africa whose genitals were
  mutilated during childhood.

She is the woman who kicked at the bricks of the
  Berlin wall.
She is the self-conscious fourth grader.
She is the political prisoner.
She is the girl from the suburbs.
She is a hundred shades of brown.
She is the hope.
She is the salvation.
She is the leader.
The woman — she, my friend, is YOU.

Since October, when the Clothesline Display Project was packed into boxes (until next year), I have become more active in the newly re-formed Lesbian/Bisexual/Straight/Gay Alliance, where I am putting what I have learned to work for that organization. "What I learned" encompasses both my acquired knowledge from The Washington Center's Women As Leaders Seminar and the more subtle things I learned from my experiences with the Anti-Violence Coalition. The suggestions that follow are a synthesis of the two.

Learn About People Who Are Different from You You cannot work with people from different backgrounds if you have no knowledge of those backgrounds. A few books or a couple of multiculturalism classes will give you a great start. You will probably find that some cultures or issues interest you more than others; that is fine. Understand that any culture or issue you understand well will give you the tools to communicate with members of that group or persons interested in that issue MUCH better than if you are simply tolerant. A good example is the issue of Christianity here in Bowling Green. Though I am now an atheist, I grew up in a Christian home and attended Bible School for two years. There have been numerous occasions where displaying my knowledge of the Bible, my understanding of modern theology, or my simply mentioning that I went to Bible School has opened communications with colleagues. I was not "selling out" or advocating their position, I was simply showing them that I understood their point of view. This is a powerful tool, to be sure.

Ask Questions If you don't understand someone's argument, whether they are siding with you or not, ask them open-ended questions in a neutral manner. An example would be, "Really Nancy? That's an interesting way of looking at the euthanasia issue. What makes you see it as a breach of the doctor's contract?" "Can you elaborate?" is another great opener. If you are hostile — in tone or body language — then the person will respond defensively. Defensiveness is the quickest way to end all communication.

Stay on Task   If you are working on school reform, abortion issues have no place in your meeting. Do not bring side issues up, and quickly change the subject when they are brought up. This can be difficult, but I have found it helpful to say things like, "we're getting a little off track here," or "that brings up a number of issues, maybe after the meeting you could discuss it, but for right now, we need to vote on. . . ." I often make a joke after tense moments like these, sometimes making a joke of the intervention itself. "Okayyyyy kids. If talking about abortion will solve our staffing problem, I'm all for it, but otherwise — help, help, help!!" Having served as VP of Protocol for LBSGA, the primary job of which was to keep things on-task, I recognize that *this can be the single hardest problem in alliances.*

Be Organized, but Flexible   Never come to a meeting without an agenda. If you have an issue to contend with, make up several suggestions beforehand (calling members for suggestions is very helpful and builds one-on-one communication) and introduce them, asking for feedback/further suggestions. I strongly recommend not making any major decisions without doing this, though. You want as many people in on the decision making as possible. *If people do not feel like their opinion is valued (this means being flexible and listening intently to their comments), they will not continue in alliance with you.*

Look for Strengths in Odd Places   We tend to count on the most outspoken people the most, but I have found that people who are not a part of the main group represented (usually Anglo-Saxon, abled, heterosexual, men from the middle class) are far less outspoken. While this trend is changing in some areas (e.g., women represent much of the anti-violence work I do), it is holding fast in most. I try very concertedly to draw out people who are quiet and I intentionally assign them duties. I have met with great success on this front. A case that comes to mind is a shy young man I am working with in LBSGA. Aside from his shyness, his inexperience and tendency to act or speak in socially inappropriate ways cause him to be overlooked for leadership/responsibility roles. After some discussion with him, he confessed that he would like to do more for the group (his shyness faded within a year of becoming a member, but the other problems persisted). Two weeks ago we voted him in as my assistant and I assigned him as stage manager for an upcoming benefit concert. The belief I have shown in him has not been unwarranted, as he has attended the meetings faithfully and gotten his tasks done more quickly and accurately than some veteran members. *Some of the best alliances come from having confidence in people's abilities regardless of how they may appear.*

O N E   H U N D R E D

◆◆◆

Multi-Issue Politics

Suzanne Pharr

At the National Gay and Lesbian Task Force's Creating Change Conference, I was asked to give a luncheon speech to the participants of the People of Color Institute and the Diversity Institute. Right off, I told them that I thought I was an odd choice for these groups because I don't really believe in either diversity or identity politics as they are currently practiced.

Fortunately, people respectfully stayed to hear me explain myself.

First, diversity politics, as popularly practiced, seem to focus on the necessity for having everyone (across gender, race, class, age, religion, physical ability, etc.) present and treated well in any given setting or organization. An assumption is that everyone is oppressed, and all oppressions are equal. Since the publication of the report, "Workforce 2000," that predicted the U.S. workforce would be made up of 80% women and people of color by 2000, a veritable growth industry of "diversity consultants" has arisen to teach corporations how to "manage" diversity. With integration and productivity as goals, they focus on the issues of sensitivity and inclusion — a human relations approach — with acceptance and comfort as high priorities. Popular images of diversity politics present people holding hands around America, singing "We Are the World."

I have a lot of appreciation for the part of diversity work that concentrates on making sure everyone is included because the history of oppression is one of excluding, of silencing, of rendering people invisible. However, for me, our diversity work fails if it does not deal with the power dynamics of difference and go straight to the heart of shifting the balance of power among individuals and within institutions. A danger of diversity politics is becoming a tool of oppression by creating the illusion of participation when in fact there is no shared power. Having a presence within an organization or institution means very little if one does not have the power of decision-making, an adequate share of the resources, and participation in the development of the workplan or agenda. We as oppressed people must demand much more than acceptance. Tolerance, sympathy and understanding are not enough, though they soften the impact of oppression by making people feel better in the face of it. Our job is not just to soften blows but to make change, fundamental and far-reaching.

Identity politics, on the other hand, rather than trying to include everyone, brings together people who share a single common identity such as sexual orientation, gender, or race. Generally, it focuses on the elimination of a single oppression, the one that is based on the common identity; i.e., homophobia/ heterosexism, sexism, racism. However, this can be a limited, hierarchical approach, reducing people of multiple identities to a single identity. Which identity should a lesbian of color choose as a priority — gender, race or sexual orientation? And does choosing one necessitate leaving the other two at home? What do we say to bisexual or biracial people? Choose, damnit, choose??? Our multiple identities allow us to develop a politic that is broad in scope because it is grounded in a wide range of experiences.

There are positive aspects of organizing along identity lines: clarity of single focus in tactics and strategies, self-examination and education apart from the dominant culture, development of solidarity and group bonding, etc. Creating organizations based on identity allows us to have visibility and collective power, to advance concerns that otherwise would never be recognized because of our marginalization within the dominant society.

However, identity politics often suffers from failing to acknowledge that the same multiplicity of oppressions, a similar imbalance of power, exists within identity groups as within the larger society. People who group together on the basis of their sexual orientation still find within their groups sexism and racism that have to be dealt with — or if gathering on the basis of race, there is still sexism and homophobia to be confronted. Whole, not partial, people come to identity groups, carrying several identities. Some of the major barriers of our liberation movements to being able to mount a unified or cohesive strategy, I believe, come from our refusal to work directly on the oppressions — the fundamental issues of power — within our own groups. A successful liberation movement cannot be built on the effort to liberate only a few and only a piece of who we are.

Diversity and identity politics are responses to oppression. In confronting oppressions, we must remember that they are more than people just not being nice to one another: they are systemic, based in institutions and in general society, where one group of people is allowed to exert power and control over members of another group, denying them fundamental rights. Also, we must remember that oppressions are interconnected, operating in similar ways, and that many people experience more than one oppression.

I believe that all oppressions in this country turn on an economic wheel; they all, in the long run, serve to consolidate and keep wealth in the hands of the few, with the many fighting over crumbs. Oppressions are built in particular on the dynamic intersection of race and class. Without work against economic injustice, against the excesses of capitalism, there can be no deep and lasting work on oppression. Why? Because it is always in the best interest of the dominators, the greedy, to maintain and expand oppression — the feeding of economic and social injustice.

Unless we understand the interconnections of oppressions and the economic exploitation of oppressed groups, we have little hope of succeeding in a liberation movement. The religious Right has been successful in driving wedges between oppressed groups because there is little common understanding of the linkages of oppressions. Progressives, including lesbians and gay men, have contributed to these divisions because generally we have dealt with only single pieces of the fabric of injustice. We stand ready to be divided. If, for example, an organization has worked only on sexual identity issues and has not worked internally on issues of race and gender, then it is ripe for being divided on those issues.

The Right has had extraordinary success in using homosexuality as a wedge issue, dividing people on the issues clustered around the Right's two central organizing points: traditional family values and economics. An example is their success in using homosexuality as a way to organize people to oppose multicultural curricula, which particularly affects people of color and women; while acting to "save the family from homosexuals," women and people of color find themselves working against their own inclusion. If women's groups, people of color and lesbian and gay groups worked on gender, race and sexual identity issues internally, then perhaps we would recognize the need for a coalition and a common agenda for multicultural education.

An even more striking example is how the Right, in its "No Special Rights" campaign, successfully plays upon the social and economic fears of people, using homosexuality as the wedge issue, and as the *coup de grace*, pits the lesbian and gay community against the African-American community. Ingeniously, they blend race, class, gender and sexual identity issues into one campaign whose success has profound implications for the destruction of democracy.

In summary, the goal of the "No Special Rights" campaign is to change the way this nation thinks about civil rights so that the groundwork is laid for the gradual elimination of civil rights. This is not an easy idea to present to the general public in a straightforward manner. Therefore, the religious Right has chosen homosexuality and homophobia to open the door to thinking that is influenced by racial hatred and its correlatives, gender and class prejudice.

Depending upon the persuasion of racism, sexism and homophobia, the religious Right seeks these basic twisted and distorted changes in our thinking about civil rights:

1. **They suggest that** civil rights do not already exist in our Constitution and Bill of Rights; they are a special category for "minorities" such as people of color and women. The religious Right refers to these people as having "minority status," a term they have invented to keep us focused on the word **minority.** Most people think of minorities as people of color. Recently in Oregon, signs appeared that read, "End Minority Status." They did not specify gay and lesbian: the message was about **minorities** and what that so-called "status" brings them.

2. **Then they say that** basic civil rights are themselves "Special Rights" that can be given or taken away by the majority who has ordinary rights, not "special rights."

3. **They argue that** "Special Rights" should be given to people based on deserving behavior and hardship conditions (especially economic) that require special treatment. In their words, people who "qualify" for "minority status."

4. **Then they introduce the popular belief that** "Special Rights" given to people of color and women and people with disabilities have resulted in the loss of jobs for deserving, "qualified" people through affirmative action and quotas. This introduces the notion that rights for some has an economic cost for others; therefore the enhancement of civil rights for everyone is not a good thing.

5. **They argue that** lesbians and gay men have no hardship conditions that would require extending "Special Rights" to them. Further, homosexuals **disqualify** themselves from basic civil rights because, by the nature of who they are, they exhibit bad behavior. They do not, according to the Right's formula, "qualify" for "minority status."

6. **Then there is the pernicious connection:** There are other people who already have "Special Rights" who exhibit bad behavior and prove themselves undeserving as they use and deal drugs and commit crimes of violence and welfare fraud. The popular perception is that these are minorities. However, the Right also extends its description of the undeserving to those who bear children outside of two-parent married families, women who

choose abortion, and even those who receive public assistance.

7. **And finally, their logical and dangerous conclusion:** because giving "Special Rights" to undeserving groups is destroying our families, communities and jobs for good people, who deserves and does not deserve to be granted "Special Rights" should be put to the popular vote and good, ordinary citizens allowed to decide who gets them and who gets to keep them.

Clearly, the religious Right understands the interconnection among oppressions and in this campaign plays directly to that interweaving of racism, sexism, classism and homophobia that is virtually impossible to tease apart. To see this campaign as single issue, i.e., simply about lesbians and gay men, is to ensure defeat of our efforts in opposing it. It has to be responded to as the multi-issue campaign that it is. If the "No Special Rights" campaign is successful, everyone stands to lose.

The question, as ever, is what to do? I do not believe that either a diversity or identity politics approach will work unless they are changed to incorporate a multi-issue analysis and strategy that combine the politics of inclusion with shared power. But, you say, it will spread us too thin if we try to work on everyone's issue, and ours will fall by the wayside. In our external work (doing women's anti-violence work, working against police brutality in people-of-color communities, seeking government funding for AIDS research, etc.), we do not have to work on "everybody's issue" but how can we do true social change work unless we look at all within our constituency who are affected by our particular issue? People who are infected with the HIV virus are of every race, class, age, gender, geographic location, yet when research and services are sought, it is women, people of color, poor people, etc., who are usually overlooked. Yet today, the AIDS virus rages on because those in power think that the people who contract it are dispensable. Are we to be like those currently in power? To understand why police brutality is so much more extreme in people-of-color communities, we have to understand why, even within that community, it is so much greater against poor people of color, prostituted women and gay men and lesbians of color. To leave any group out leaves a hole for everyone's freedoms and rights to fall through. It becomes an issue of "acceptable" and "unacceptable" people, deserving and undeserving of rights.

Identity politics offers a strong, vital place for bonding, for developing political analysis, for understanding our relationship to a world that says on the one hand that we are no more than our identity, and on the other, that there is no real oppression based on the identity of race or gender or sexual identity. Our challenge is to learn how to use the experiences of our many identities to forge an inclusive social change politic. The question that faces us is how to do multi-issue coalition building from an identity base. The hope for a multi-racial, multi-issue movement rests in large part on the answer to this question.

Our linkages can create a movement, and our divisions can destroy us.

Internally, if our organizations are not committed to the inclusion and shared power of all those who share our issue, how can we with any integrity demand inclusion and shared power in society at large? If women, lesbians and gay men are treated as people undeserving of equality within civil rights organizations, how can those organizations demand equality? If women of color and poor women are marginalized in women's rights organizations, how can those organizations argue that women as a class should be moved into full participation in the mainstream? If lesbian and gay organizations are not anti-racist and feminist in all their practices, what hope is there for the elimination of homophobia and heterosexism in a racist, sexist society?

When we grasp the value and interconnectedness of our liberation issues, then we will at last be able to make true coalition and begin building a common agenda that eliminates oppression and brings forth a vision of diversity that shares power and resources. In particular, I think there is great hope for this work among lesbians and gay men. First, we must reconceptualize who we are and see ourselves not as the wedge, not as the divisive, diversionary issue of the religious Right—but as the bridge that links the issues and people together. If we indeed represent everyone—cutting across all sectors of society, race, gender, age, ability, geographic location, religion—and if we develop a liberation politic that is transformational, that is, that eliminates the power and dominance of one group over another within our own organizations—we as old and young, people of color and white, rich and poor, rural and urban lesbians and gay men can provide the forum for bringing people and groups together to form a progressive, multi-issue, truly diverse liberation movement. Our success will be decided by the depth of our work on race, class and gender issues.

Instead of the flashpoint for division, we can be the flashpoint for developing common ground, a common agenda, a common humanity. We can be at the heart of hope for creating true inclusive, participatory democracy in this country.

O N E   H U N D R E D   O N E

◆◆◆

Power, Authority, and Mystery
Ecofeminism and Earth-Based Spirituality

Starhawk

Earth-based spirituality is rooted in three basic concepts that I call immanence, interconnection, and community. The first — immanence — names our primary understanding that the Earth is alive, part of a living cosmos. What that means is that spirit, sacred, Goddess, God — whatever you want to call it — is not found outside the world somewhere — it's in the world: it *is* the world, and it is us. Our goal is not to get off the wheel of birth nor to be saved from something. Our deepest experiences are experiences of connection with the Earth and with the world.

When you understand the universe as a living being, then the split between religion and science disappears because religion no longer becomes a set of dogmas and beliefs we have to accept even though they don't make any sense, and science is no longer restricted to a type of analysis that picks the world apart. Science becomes our way of looking more deeply into this living being that we're all in, understanding it more deeply and clearly. This itself has a poetic dimension. I want to explore what it means when we really accept that this Earth is alive and that we are part of her being. Right now we are at a point where that living being is nearly terminally diseased. We need to reverse that, to turn that around. We really need to find a way to reclaim our power so that we can reverse the destruction of the Earth.

When we understand that the Earth itself embodies spirit and that the cosmos is alive, then we also understand that everything is interconnected. Just as in our bodies: what happens to a finger affects what happens to a toe. The brain doesn't work

without the heart. In the same way, what happens in South Africa affects us here: what we do to the Amazon rain forest affects the air that we breathe here. All these things are interconnected, and interconnection is the second principle of Earth-based spirituality.

Finally, when we understand these interconnections, we know that we are all part of a living community, the Earth. The kind of spirituality and the kind of politics we're called upon to practice are rooted in community. Again, the goal is not individual salvation or enlightenment, or even individual self-improvement, though these may be things and *are* things that happen along the way. The goal is the creation of a community that becomes a place in which we can be empowered and in which we can be connected to the Earth and take action together to heal the Earth.

Each of these principles — immanence, interconnection, and community — calls us to do something. That call, that challenge, is the difference between a spirituality that is practiced versus an intellectual philosophy. The idea that the Earth is alive is becoming an acceptable intellectual philosophy. Scientists have conferences on the Gaia hypothesis without acknowledging that this is exactly what people in tribal cultures, what Witches, shamans, and psychics, have been saying for thousands of years. But there's a difference between accepting it as a scientific philosophy and really living it. Living with the knowledge that the cosmos is alive causes us to do something. It challenges us. Earth-based spirituality makes certain demands. That is, when we start to understand that the Earth is alive, she calls us to act to preserve her life. When we understand that everything is interconnected, we are called to a politics and a set of actions that come from compassion, from the ability to literally feel *with* all living beings on the Earth. That feeling is the ground upon which we can build community and come together and take action and find direction.

Earth-based spirituality calls us to live with integrity. Once we know that we're all part of this living body, this world becomes the terrain where we live out spiritual growth and development. It doesn't happen anywhere else, and the way we do it is by enacting what we believe, by taking responsibility for what we do.

These values are not limited to any particular tradition. They can be found in many, many different spiritual traditions and within many different political groups. For me, they come out of my tradition, which is the Pagan tradition, the Wiccan tradition, the old pre-Christian Goddess religion of Europe. We have a certain perspective that I believe can be valuable politically and that is, in some way, linked to what I see ecofeminism and the Green movement attempting. It's not that I think everyone has to be a Witch to be an ecofeminist, or that all Greens should be Witches — pluralism is vitally important in all our movements. It's that I do feel that Pagan values and perspectives can make important contributions to ecofeminist analysis and organizing.

A Pagan perspective might influence our approach to action. For example, I've participated in many political actions and organizations over the past 15 years. There have been times when it's been very exciting. In 1981, 1982, and 1983 the Livermore Action Group (LAG) was active in the Bay Area. We were constantly blockading, demonstrating, risking arrest, and mobilizing large numbers of people.

What happened to LAG, though, is very interesting. At a certain point — in fact, after what was really our strongest, most solid and successful action in 1983 — things began to fall apart. Organizing began to get harder and harder, and we were never able to organize a large, cohesive action again. At the same time this was happening to LAG — and we were having meeting after meeting, asking, "Where did we go wrong?" — the same thing was happening to the peace movement in general. Everybody was asking, "What's wrong? Why are we burning out?"

In 1981 and 1982 we were very much focused on the Cruise and Pershing missiles, which were going to be deployed in Europe. There was a strong sense that if we didn't prevent the deployment from happening, that would be it. Russia would go to launch on warning, which meant that computers with approximately a 6-minute margin for error would essentially be in charge of blowing the world up. It made people more than nervous: we were terrified. This was a great impetus for action. If ever there was a time to put your personal life aside, to put your body on the line, to get dragged away, to go to jail, this was it. So our organizing was apocalyptic. Every meal, we feared, was the Last Supper. Without realizing it, we were acting out a Christian myth, expecting the end of the world, the end of time.

Of course, what happened is that the missiles went in, in spite of all the times we went to jail. And that's the way that political organizing and action often work. You go out, twelve hundred people performing civil disobedience, holding solidarity for 2 weeks, but President Reagan doesn't wake up the next day and say, "Gee, all these people are in jail. They're so sincere. They must have a point." It doesn't work that way.

But then, five years later, after long negotiations, Reagan and Gorbachev decide to take those missiles out of Europe. That is a victory, a victory that is the fruit of the organizing that we did all those years. But this kind of victory is not one we're going to see immediately. This is where the Pagan perspective comes in.

What Witches and Pagans do is practice magic. I like the definition of magic that says, "Magic is the art of changing consciousness at will." I also think that's a very good definition of political change — changing consciousness on a mass scale in this country. And one of the things we learn when we practice magic is that the results don't necessarily happen immediately. They unfold over time, and they always unfold in surprising ways, which is why we talk about our spiritual tradition in terms of mystery rather than answers and dogma and certainty. We talk about what it is we don't know and can only wonder about and be amazed at.

There is a certain way that magic works: it is, in a sense, a technology. When we want to do something, to change consciousness, for example, we first need an image of the change we want to create. We need a vision.

The same is true for political work. If we want to change consciousness in this nation, we first need to have a vision in our minds of what we want to change it into. We need to have an image, and we need to create that image and make it strong. And we need to direct energy and, in some way, ground it in reality.

The vision we want to create must also reflect a different model of power, one rooted in our understanding of the Earth as alive. We live in a system where power is *power-over,* that is, domination and control; it is a system in which a person or group of people has the right to tell other people what to do, to make their decisions, to set standards they have to live up to. The system may be overtly coercive, like a prison, or it may be benign on the surface, but it is still a system of power. And we internalize the system of domination. It lives inside us, like an entity, as if we were possessed by it.

Ecofeminism challenges all relations of domination. Its goal is not just to change who wields power, but to transform the structure of power itself. When the spirit is immanent, when each of us is the Goddess, is God, we have an inalienable right to be here and to be alive. We have a value that can't be taken away from us, that doesn't have to be earned, that doesn't have to be acquired. That kind of value is central to the change we want to create. That's the spell we want to cast.

The way we can embody that vision, can create the living image of that value, is in the groups we form and the structures we create. In some ways, especially in the Bay Area, we often have done this well. That is why so many people found organizing around Livermore and Diablo empowering. The Livermore Action Group and the Abalone Alliance (which organized the blockade at the Diablo nuclear power plant) were structured around small groups that worked by consensus. Now consensus can drive you out of your mind with frustration sometimes, but there is a very important principle in it. That is, everyone in the group has power, and everyone has equal power because everyone has value. That value is accepted, it's inherent, and it can't be taken away.

Along with the decision-making process goes a real care for the process that we use with each other. We listen to each other, we let each person have a say and hear each other and recognize that different people's opinions may be important, even if we disagree with them. Feminist process, as we call it, creates a strong sense of safety, and it changes people. I've known people in LAG who've said that their lives were profoundly changed by living for the first time in a society in which what they said was heard and considered important.

In a sense, that kind of decision making and organizing becomes a ritual. A ritual really is any kind of an intentional act we create that deepens our sense of value. The real heart of any ritual is telling our stories, that is, listening to each other and telling the sacred stories that we may have heard, that have been handed down and distilled from many people's experience, and telling the stories of our own experience.

Groups often seem to be most empowering when they are small. Only in a relatively small group can we really know each other as individuals. That's why LAG was organized in affinity groups, which are small, and why Witches are organized in covens, which traditionally have no more than thirteen members. When a group gets too large, people begin to become faceless. At the same time, small groups can also come together and form networks and coalitions and act together in larger ways. But the real base is always a small community of people who know and value each other personally.

We also need to have a sense of safety. A lot of people will say, "I feel unsafe in this group," meaning "I'm afraid someone's going to hurt my feelings." The truth is that someone will — someone always does — you can count on it. When we're honest, when we really interact with each other, there are always times when our needs or our style or our ways of communicating don't mesh. But when we each feel sure of our value to the group, conflict need not be devastating.

But real safety comes from something else. The groups we create and the ways we organize also have to be sustainable. If we weren't living in a state of denial all the time, the whole idea of sustainability would clearly be our first priority. How is it that we can live in a world where we use the Earth in ways that are destroying it and not worry? We all know we have to breathe; we all know we have to drink water; we all know we have to eat food; and, we all know it's got to come from somewhere. So why isn't the preservation of the environment our first priority? It makes such logical sense that it's irritating to have to say it.

In order to put the environment on the national agenda, we have to organize, but we also need to embody the principle of sustainability in our own groups. I think one of the flaws in our organizing, for example, in that period in the early 1980s, was exactly the apocalyptic sense coming out of that unconscious Christian myth that the end of time was near.

From a Pagan perspective, there is no end of time. Time is a cycle, and cycles come around and they go around and come back again. Our goal isn't to burn ourselves out as martyrs. Our model is the Earth, and the seed that is planted and springs up, grows, loses life, is planted and comes up again and again and again.

That, I think, is the kind of model we need for our politics. We need to see the process of changing our society as a lifetime challenge and commitment. Transforming consciousness so that we can preserve and sustain the Earth is a long-term project. We need the communities we create around that task to be sustainable. There are going to be times when we're active and it's exciting and we're obsessed by action, and there are going to be times when we pull back and nurture ourselves and heal and take care of ourselves. There are times when each of us gives a lot to a group, and times when each should get something back from the group, times when the giving and taking in a group balance out. Nobody should be stuck always having to be the leader, the organizer, or the one who pulls it all together. These tasks should rotate. And nobody should get stuck being the nurturer, the one everyone complains to, the mediator, the one who smooths everything over.

It is true that sometimes doing political work involves making sacrifices, and it may involve suffering. It's also true that around the world, people are suffering tremendously right now because of the policies of this country, the historical decisions and choices this country has made. We have to oppose and change these policies, and to do that we have to be willing to take risks. But sometimes in the nonviolence movement there's a kind of idealization of suffering. And I don't think that serves us. It comes out of the fantasy that people will see us suffering for our cause, be impressed by our nobility and sincerity, and be attracted to join and suffer with us.

Gandhi was a great man, but his ideas don't always fit for a lot of us, particularly for women. Gandhi said we have to accept the suffering and take

it in. Women have been doing that for thousands and thousands of years, and it hasn't stopped anything much — except a lot of women's lives. In some ways, it's also not ecological. Rather than absorb the violence, what we need to do is to find some way to stop it and then transform it, to take that energy and turn it into creative change. Not to take it on ourselves.

The actual unsung truth about a lot of organizing is that it feels really good, and that's why people do it, again and again and again. It feels good because when we're actually organizing and taking action to stop the destruction of the Earth, we're doing an act of healing and we are free. There are few times when we are free in this culture and this is one of them. We need to speak about the joy and wildness and sense of liberation that comes when we step beyond the bounds of the authorities to resist control and create change.

Finally, I think that the spell we need to cast, the model we need to create, has to be open to mystery, to the understanding that we don't know everything about what's going on and we don't know exactly what to do about it. The mystery can be expressed in many ways. For one person it might be expressed through ritual, through celebration, chanting, and meditation; in some groups it might be expressed through humor, through making fun of what everybody else is doing. In some groups it might be expressed both ways. We can't define how a group or individual is going to experience it, but we can attempt to structure things so that we don't have dogmas and party lines, so we remain open to many possibilities of the sacred.

These are some ideas of how we build communities and what kinds of communities we might want to create. The other question is what we're going to organize these communities around. It's hard to get people together in a vacuum. One of the things that plagues our movements is that when we start looking at what's really going on with the Earth and the people on it, it's overwhelming. All the issues seem so important that it's very, very hard to know what to focus on, and we can easily get fragmented.

I had dinner recently with a man named Terry Gips who heads a group called the International Alliance for Sustainable Agriculture. He was telling me that he'd come to the conclusion that we have about 3 years to turn around the environmental destruction or it'll be too late. He had expressed this idea to his friends and reactions were so bad that he'd decided not to talk about it any more. People got very depressed. I could understand that because I'd gotten terribly depressed myself.

I said, "Well, I don't know if it's useful to think in those terms. When you said 'three years,' it didn't sound like enough time. It reminds me of that period in the early 1980s when we thought we had to get rid of those missiles now or never. At the same time, if you really believe that, what do we need to do? Do we need to smash capitalism in 3 years and totally transform society? I don't think we can do that."

He said, "No. Actually, there are some very concrete things to do in the next 3 to 5 years—however long we might have—that would reverse the destruction enough to give us time to make the deeper kinds of changes and transformations we need to make." He sat there talking, and I started thinking, and we came up with a campaign for turning the tide.

So this is what I think we should do, and, if I were setting an ecofeminist or a Green agenda, this is how I would organize it, the beginning of which I look at as a sort of magic circle.

Illustrated are the tree of life and the magic circle. The magic circle is a circle of the elements: air, fire, water, and earth. The tree has roots and a core, a center, a heart that's the same as the circle, and it has branches. If we think about it, all of these issues that we see as being so interconnected can fit into that magic circle.

For example, let's talk about air. The ozone layer has holes in it and is rapidly being depleted. We should be organizing around this issue if we want our food crops and ocean plankton to survive, if we want to preserve the viability of the Earth. And such organizing has already had some success. Du Pont, which manufactures 25 percent of the world's chlorofluorocarbons, has voluntarily decided to phase out production. Several states, including Minnesota, are considering bills to ban these substances, and some fast-food franchises are phasing out packaging made from these substances. But even with these changes, the ozone will continue to diminish since chlorofluorocarbons remain in the Earth's atmo-sphere for up to 80 years. Yet these positive steps show us that public pressure can bring about important changes.

Another air issue is the destruction of tropical rain forests. If you wonder why I put that under air, it's because these forests are the lungs of the world. They are being cut down, and they are key to systems that

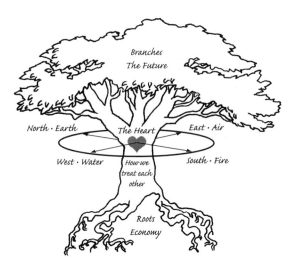

regulate the Earth's weather patterns. There *should* be an international commission on the rain forest, and there should also be pressure on institutions like the World Bank and the International Monetary Fund to stop funding the destruction of rain forests. A lot of the destruction comes as rain forests are cut down so cattle can graze and our fast-food restaurants can turn out hamburgers. That's another thing we can organize around. A boycott of one fast-food chain, Burger King, convinced it to stop buying rain forest beef.

Now look at fire: we have nuclear issues. Nuclear power—what do we do with all that waste? Nuclear weapons, we should be working to ban them. Fire represents energy, and we need renewable sources of energy. We need our money put into those sources rather than into things that pollute and kill.

There are also important water issues. Acid rain is also killing trees and forests. Canada wanted some very simple things from us, like smoke scrubbers and curbs on acid rain, and then-President Reagan refused. We need to set standards and see that they're enforced. (Bush's new proposals sound good but actually lack strict standards.) We need to be talking about groundwater pollution. In Minnesota, "Land of a Thousand Lakes" as the license plate says, wells were tested and 39 percent were found to be contaminated; similar statistics exist for many areas. We also need to stop the pollution of the ocean, the oil drilling off the coasts, the depletion of fisheries, and the killing of whales.

Then, of course, there's the Earth. One of the things that would push us toward sustainable agriculture would be simply to stop subsidizing pesticides, which we do now in a lot of very subtle ways. For example, if a pesticide is banned, who is it that pays for storing and destroying it? It's us. It's our tax money, not the company that produces it. In California beekeepers lose thousands of dollars every year to pesticides. The government reimburses them, but the pesticide companies should be paying the price. It's estimated that there are four pesticide poisonings a minute, three-fourths of them in the Third World. We could make it uneconomical to poison the Earth and the human beings who grow and eat the food the Earth produces. We could make alliances with the United Farmworkers of America, who've been calling for a boycott of grapes and focusing attention on pesticide issues and labor practices.

We also need to preserve sacred lands such as Big Mountain and end the destruction of indigenous peoples and cultures. If the Earth is sacred to us, we must preserve the wilderness that's left because that's the place we go for renewal, where we can most strongly feel the immanence of the Goddess.

Also with Earth go feeding the hungry, sheltering the homeless. One of the advantages of seeing issues as integrated, rather than fragmented, is that it can help us avoid false dichotomies. For example, environmental issues *are* social justice issues, for it is the poor who are forced to work directly with unsafe chemicals, in whose neighborhoods toxic waste incinerators are planned, who cannot afford to buy bottled water and organic vegetables or pay for medical care. Environmental issues are international issues, for we cannot simply export unsafe pesticides, toxic wastes, and destructive technologies without poisoning the whole living body of the Earth. And environmental issues are women's issues, for women sicken, starve, and die from toxics, droughts, and famines, their capacity to bear new life is threatened by pollution, and they bear the brunt of care for the sick and the dying, as well as for the next generation.

Environmental issues cannot be intelligently approached without the perspectives of women, the poor, and those who come from other parts of the globe, as well as those of all races and cultural backgrounds. To take only one example, we cannot responsibly approach questions of overpopulation without facing questions of women's power to make decisions about their own reproduction, to challenge traditional roles and restrictions.

If we approach any issue without taking into account the perspectives of all those it affects, we run the risk of accepting false solutions, for example, that famine or AIDS are acceptable answers to population problems. From a Pagan point of view, such "solutions" are entirely unethical because the ethics of integrity prevents us from accepting a solution for someone else that we are unwilling to accept for ourselves.

False solutions are also dangerous because they divert our attention from the real forces with which we must contend. Like an illusionist's tricks, they distract us from seeing what is really going on and from noticing what really works and what doesn't. What really works to stem population growth is not mass death — wars, famines, and epidemics have produced, at most, a ripple in the rising tide. What works is increasing the security of life for those who are already alive and, especially, increasing women's power and autonomy, women's control over our own bodies and access to work and economic compensation independent of our role in procreation. Feminists have been saying this for a long time, and environmentalists need to listen or their analysis will remain fragmented and shortsighted.

Unless we understand all the interconnections, we are vulnerable to manipulation. For example, we are often told that to end hunger we must sacrifice wilderness. But what will work to end hunger is not the further destruction of natural resources within the same system of greed and inequality that has engendered hunger. In their book, *World Hunger: Twelve Myths* (New York: Grove Press, 1986), Frances Moore Lappé and Joseph Collins make the point that people are hungry not because there isn't enough food in the world, but because they are poor. To end hunger we must restore control over land and economic resources to those who have been disenfranchised by the same forces that destroy, with equal lack of concern, the life of a child or a tree or an endangered species, in the name of profit.

And so we come to the roots of the tree — our economic base. Our economy reflects our system of values, in which profit replaces inherent value as the ultimate measure of all things. If we saw ourselves as interconnected parts of the living being that is the Earth, of equal existential value, we could no longer justify economic exploitation.

Our economy is one of waste. The biggest part of that waste is that it's an economy of war, which is inherently wasteful. We need to transform that into an economy that is truly productive and sustainable.

To do that we need economic justice — economic democracy as well as political democracy.

Then we can support the branches of the tree, which reach out into the future, touching upon such issues as caring for our children, education, and the values that we teach people. Protecting the future also involves challenging potentially dangerous technologies like genetic engineering. It means basing our decisions, plans, and programs on our obligation to future generations.

In the heart of the tree, the center, is how we treat each other. To work on any of these issues, we must transform the power relationships and the hierarchies of value that keep us separate and unequal. We must challenge the relations of domination between men and women, between light people and dark people, between rich people and poor people; we must do away with all of those things that my friend Luisah Teish calls the "Ism brothers." Then we can really begin treating each other with that sense that each one of us has inherent value, that nobody's interests can be written off and forgotten.

These are the ways I see the issues as being interconnected. Ultimately, to work on any one of them, we need to work on all of them. To work on all of them, we can start at any place on that circle or part of the tree. What I would envision ecofeminist groups saying is: "Let's do it. Let's turn the environmental destruction around. Let's have a movement we call Turning the Tide and commit ourselves to it. Not as a short-term thing that we're going to do for a year and then burn out, but as a way of transforming and changing our lives."

We can begin this long-term commitment by first getting together with people in a small way and forming our own action groups, our own circles for support, which can take on their own characters and their own personalities. Maybe you will form a circle where members take off their clothes and go to the beach and dance around and jump in the waves and energize yourselves that way. And then you'll all write letters to your congresspersons about the ozone condition. Maybe somebody else will form a circle in their church where members sit on chairs and meditate quietly and then go out to Nevada and get in the way of the nuclear testing. But whatever we do, our spirituality needs to be grounded in action.

Along with seeing issues as interconnected, we need to all be able to envision new kinds of organizing. We need to envision a movement where our first priority is to form community, small groups centered around both personal support and action, and to make that what people see as their ongoing, long-term commitment. We don't have to commit ourselves to some big, overall organization. We can commit ourselves to eight other people with whom we can say, "We can form a community to do political and spiritual work and find support over a long period of time." Then our communities can network and form organizations around issues and around tasks as needed, and can dissolve the larger organizations and networks when they're not needed.

I want to end with my vision of where this might all bring us. It's an optimistic one because, ultimately, I do believe that we can do it. We really can turn the tide — we can reverse the destruction of the Earth.

And so the time comes when all the people of the earth
can bring their gifts to the fire
and look into each other's faces
unafraid

Breathe deep
Feel the sacred well that is your own breath, and look
look at that circle
See us come from every direction
from the four quarters of the earth
See the lines that stretch to the horizon
the procession, the gifts borne
see us feed the fire
Feel the earth's life renewed
And the circle is complete again
and the medicine wheel is formed anew
and the knowledge within each one of us
made whole
Feel the great turning, feel the change
the new life runs through your blood like fire
and all of nature rises with it
greening, burgeoning, bursting into flower
At that mighty rising
do the vines rise up, do the grains rise up
and the desert turns green
the wasteland blooms like a garden
Hear the earth sing
of her own loveliness
her hillock lands, her valleys
her furrows well-watered
her untamed wild places
She arises in you
as you in her
Your voice becomes her voice

Sing!
Your dance is her dance
   of the circling stars
   and the ever-renewing flame
As your labor has become her labor
Out of the bone, ash
Out of the ash, pain

Out of the pain, the swelling
Out of the swelling, the opening
Out of the opening, the labor
Out of the labor, the birth
Out of the birth, the turning wheel
   the turning tide

ONE HUNDRED TWO

◆◆◆

Each Generation Must Discover Its Mission

Grace Lee Boggs

Opening Ceremony, Detroit Summer '94

This summer is the 30th anniversary of Mississippi Freedom Summer, the program/movement which inspired Detroit Summer. In a recent documentary, entitled *Freedom on My Mind*, Endesha Ida Mae Holland tells the story of how Mississippi Summer changed her life. After being raped by a white man at the age of 11, she had dropped out of school and become a prostitute. When the volunteers from the North arrived in Mississippi in 1964, she responded at first by looking for customers but then decided to stay on as a volunteer because, as she put it, "The movement said to me I was somebody." Today she is a well-known playwright.

That is what a Movement does. It tells individuals that they are somebody, that they can make a difference. A Movement creates hope, it empowers human beings, advances them to a new plateau of consciousness and self-consciousness, creativity and social responsibility. The main reason for the violence among young people today is that there is no Movement to inspire and empower them. So their lives and the lives of others seem meaningless. That is why your volunteering for Detroit Summer is so significant. You are planting the seeds for a Movement.

In the 1960s everybody in the Movement carried around this little book: THE WRETCHED OF THE EARTH by Frantz Fanon. "The Handbook for the Black Revolution that is changing the shape of the world." My favorite quote is on page 206:

Each generation must out of relative obscurity discover its mission, and fulfill or betray it.

Thirty years ago the mission before this country was the abolition of discrimination and segregation. The young people of the 60s fulfilled that mission. True, racism still exists in many forms, but due in no small part to the youth of Mississippi Freedom Summer the Civil Rights Act of 1964 was passed, making discrimination and segregation illegal.

Your mission today is much more challenging. 30 years ago blacks in the South were lynched for trying to register to vote. But there were plenty of jobs. Today all over the United States our cities have been turned into wastelands because corporations have gone multinational, exporting jobs overseas in order to make more profit with cheaper labor. At the same time millions of jobs have been eliminated by Hi-Tech. So young people can no longer drop out of school in 9th grade and go to work in the plant making enough money to get married and raise a family. As a result, in many neighborhoods the only economy is the drug economy.

Ten years ago most people believed the lie that it was only the unskilled and uneducated whose jobs were being eliminated but that there would be plenty of good service and information industry jobs for those who went to college. However, since the late 1980s IBM, Xerox, Kodak and similar corporations are downsizing like crazy, laying off or "shedding" millions of workers to the point where a cartoon last year showed college graduates in cap and gown walking across the platform to receive a placard reading "Will work for food" rather than a diploma.

30 years ago racial oppression was the main contradiction facing this country. Today the contradictions we face are economic, social and environmental, and they are all tied together. How do we make a living? How do we rebuild our social ties with one another? How do we produce for our material needs without at the same time producing the pollutants and toxic wastes which are destroying our land, air and water and increasing the rates of cancer, respiratory diseases and birth defects, especially in communities of color and of poor people.

We can't depend upon Ford, GM, IBM and outside investors for jobs. Even when or if they invest in our cities and communities, we know that they will pick up and leave as soon as they see an opportunity to make more money elsewhere. We can't go back to the days when the Korean, Vietnam and cold wars provided plenty of jobs for our parents and grandparents and the United States dominated the world economically and militarily. But even if we could, we know things that our parents and grandparents didn't know. We know that while folks were making what they thought was a good living, our families and communities were falling apart because people were thinking mainly of a good living in terms of accumulating more material things. We also know that while folks were making what they thought was a good living, the petrochemical industries they were working in were producing life-threatening pollutants and carcinogenic wastes. For example, a recent study links the growing rate of breast cancer to the organochlorines that are produced in the manufacture of pesticides, petrochemicals, plastics and paper. And scientists are increasingly concerned that the depletion of our rain forests — which is linked to our pursuit of an ever higher standard of living — may unleash new organisms even deadlier than the AIDS virus.

What kind of technology would be the most beneficial in human and environmental terms? Up to now it has been assumed that Hi-Tech is just as inevitable as sunrise and sunset. But we can no longer evade the environmental and social consequences of Hi-Tech — the toxic wastes from petrochemical production, the nuclear waste which, understandably, no community or state wants to store; and the millions of human be-

ings, no longer needed in Hi-Tech production, who are being stored in prisons and other institutions because the only outlet for their energies and imagination is anti-social violence.

We don't have to accept the dictatorship of Hi-Tech. Human beings can make the decisions as to when and where to use Hi-Tech, Low-Tech or Intermediate Tech, or a mix of these, on the basis of what best develops people and communities and at the same time maintains the health of our ecosystem. Petrochemical production has been in existence for only a hundred years; nuclear energy for only 50. For thousands of years before that great civilizations have been built without them.

We also don't have to accept the dictatorship of a global economy. Most people assume that Free Trade and the world market are as sacred and unquestionable as Motherhood and apple pie. But why should human beings be cannon fodder for global economic war? Why should the purpose of American education be the preparation of American youth to compete with Japanese or West German youth? Why can't the purpose of our economic and educational system be the development of our people and our communities and our country? Instead of producing for export, instead of importing our food and clothing, why can't we begin producing for our own needs, thus creating a safer, healthier, more Self-Reliant society?

As we approach the 21st century, these are the very tough and very real questions we have to grapple with and the choices we have to make if we want to cut back on crime and violence, homelessness, cancer and birth defects. We can't leave these decisions to multinational corporations who we now know have no loyalty to our communities or even to this country — or to the politicians who serve these corporations.

For our own well-being, for the health and safety of our communities, our cities and our country, we need to accept the awesome responsibility of creating new ways of making a living, new ways of producing for our material needs and new ways of daily living that reestablish our sacred connection to Mother Earth and to one another. We can no longer look at a job only in terms of how much money it pays; we can no longer think only of ourselves and the hell with the rest of the world. As Tom Goldtooth said to the People of Color Environmental Leadership Summit in 1991, "We have to look at our personal life, our dreams, our goals for ourselves and our family. Do we want that shiny, brand new car? That big house out in the suburbs?"

There are no quick or easy answers to these questions. Twenty years ago the Black Panthers captured the imagination of people all around the country with the saying, "If you're not part of the solution, you're part of the problem." In becoming a Detroit Summer volunteer you have become part of the solution. In the physical work that you do, the "found art" that you create, the connections you make with one another and with people in the community, and in your reflections and discussions on these tough questions, you are using your hearts, hands and heads to create new ways of living.

Glossary

This glossary contains many of the key concepts found in this book. The first time the concept is used in the text it is shown in **bold.** Refer to the definitions here to refresh your memory when you come across them again later.

able-bodyism Attitudes, actions, and institutional practices that subordinate people with disabilities.

adultism Attitudes, actions, and institutional practices that subordinate young people on the basis of their age.

ageism Attitudes, actions, and institutional practices that subordinate elderly persons due to their age.

alliance Working with others, as a result of a deepening understanding of one another's lives and experiences.

analytical framework A perspective that allows one to analyze the causes and implications of a particular issue, rather than simply describing it.

anti-Semitism Attitudes, actions, and institutional practices that subordinate Jewish people (the term *Semite* is used also to refer to some Arabs).

biological determinism A general theory holding that a group's biological or genetic makeup shapes its social, political, and economic destiny. This view is used to justify women's subordination, or the subordination of peoples of color on the argument that they are biologically or genetically different from, and usually inferior to, men or White people.

capitalism An economic system in which most of the **capital**—property, raw materials, and the means of production (including people's labor)—and goods produced are owned or controlled by individuals or groups—capitalists. The goal of all production is to maximize profit making.

classism Attitudes, actions, and institutional practices that subordinate working-class and poor people on the basis of their economic condition.

coalition Usually a short-term alliance of organizations in which the important strategy is to stand together to achieve a specific goal or set of goals around a particular issue, regardless of other differences among the organizations.

commodification The process of turning people and intangible things into things, or commodities, for sale; an example is the commodification of women's bodies through advertising and cultural practices.

comparable worth A method of evaluating jobs that are traditionally defined as men's work or women's work—in terms of the knowledge and skills required for a particular job; the mental demands or decision making involved; the accountability or degree of supervision involved; and working conditions, such as how physically safe the job is—so as to eliminate inequities in pay based on gender.

conscientization A methodology for understanding reality, or gaining a "critical consciousness," through group dialogue, critical analysis and examination of people's experiences and conditions that face them, which leads to action to transform that reality (Freire 1989).

contested terrain An area of debate or controversy, in which several individuals or groups attempt to impose their own views or meanings on a situation.

502

criminalization The process of turning people's circumstances or behaviors into a crime, such as the criminalization of mothers with HIV/AIDS or homeless people.

cultural relativism The view that all "authentic" experience is equally valid and cannot be challenged by others. For example, White-supremacist views of Ku Klux Klan members are seen to be equally as valid as those held by antiracist activists. There are no external standards or principles by which to judge people's attitudes and behaviors.

culture The values, symbols, means of expression, language, and interests of a group of people. The **dominant culture** includes the values, symbols, means of expression, language, and interests of people in power in this society.

discrimination Differential treatment against less powerful groups (such as women, the elderly, or people of color) by those in positions of dominance.

ecofeminism A philosophy that links the domination of women with the domination of nature.

environmental racism The strong correlation between the distribution of toxic wastes and race; the movement for **environmental justice** draws on concepts of civil rights, whereby all citizens have a right to healthy living and working conditions.

essentialism The view that people have some inherent essence, or characteristics and qualities, that define them. Some people argue, for example, that women are essentially more caring and nurturing than men.

eugenics The White-supremacist belief that the human race can be "improved" through selective breeding.

feminization of poverty Women and children constitute the vast majority of poor people in the United States and throughout the world, a result of structural inequalities and discriminatory policies that do not address this issue.

fertility rate The number of children born to women between fifteen and fifty-four, considered by official census reports to be the child-bearing years.

gender socialization The process of learning the attitudes and behaviors that are considered culturally appropriate for boys or girls.

gendered division of labor A division of duties between men and women under which women have the main responsibility for home and nurturing and men are mainly active in the public sphere. Also referred to as **gender roles.**

glass ceiling An unseen barrier to women's promotion to senior positions in the workplace. Women can see the senior positions in their company or field, but few women reach them because of negative attitudes toward senior women and low perceptions of their abilities and training.

global level of analysis A term used to describe the connections among people and among issues as viewed from a worldwide perspective.

heterosexism Attitudes, actions, and institutional practices that subordinate people on the basis of their gay, lesbian, bisexual, or transgender orientation.

ideology Ideas, attitudes, and values that represent the interests of a group of people. The dominant ideology comprises the ideas, attitudes, and values that represent the interests of the dominant group(s). Thus, for example, the ideological role of the idealized nuclear family is to devalue other family forms.

internalized oppression Attitudes and behavior of some oppressed people that reflect the negative, harmful, stereotypical beliefs of the dominant group directed at oppressed people. The behaviors include holding negative beliefs about people in their own group. An example of internalized sexism is the view of some women that they and other women are inferior to men, which causes them to adopt oppressive attitudes and behaviors toward women.

liberal feminism A philosophy that sees the oppression of women as a denial of equal rights, representation, and access to opportunities.

macro level of analysis A term used to describe the relationships among issues, individuals, and groups as viewed from a national perspective.

marginality The situation in which a person has a deep connection to more than one culture, community, or social group but is not completely able to identify with or be accepted by that group as an insider. For example, bisexual, mixed-race/mixed-culture, and immigrant peoples often find themselves caught between two or more social worlds.

marginalization   Attitudes and behaviors that relegate certain people to the social, political, and economic margins of society by branding them and their interests as inferior, unimportant, or both.

matrix of oppression   The interconnections among various forms of oppression. People can be privileged along certain dimensions of life and disadvantaged on others.

medicalization   The process of turning life processes, like childbirth or menopause, into medical issues, where the dominant model is based on sickness. Thus, menopause becomes an illness to be treated by medical professionals with formal educational qualifications and accreditation. By the same token, experienced midwives are considered unqualified because they lack these credentials.

meso level of analysis   A term used to describe the relationships among issues, individuals, and groups as viewed from a community, or local, perspective.

micro level of analysis   A term used to describe the connections among people and issues as seen from a personal or individual perspective.

militarism   A system and worldview based on the objectification of "others" as enemies, a culture that celebrates war and killing. This worldview operates through specific military institutions and actions.

militarized masculinity   A masculinity constructed to support militarism, with an emphasis on heroism, physical strength, lack of emotion, and invulnerability (Enloe 1990, 1993).

misogyny   Woman-hating attitudes and behavior.

neocolonialism   Continuing economic inequalities between rich and poor countries that originated in colonial relationships.

objectification   Attitudes and behaviors by which people are treated as if they were "things." One example is the objectification of women through advertising images.

objectivity   A form of understanding in which knowledge and meaning are believed to come from outside oneself and are presumably not affected by personal opinion or bias.

offshore production   Factory work or office work performed outside the United States—for example, in Mexico, the Philippines, or Indonesia—that is done for U.S.-based companies.

oppression   Prejudice and discrimination directed toward whole socially recognized groups of people and promoted by the ideologies and practices of all social institutions. The critical elements differentiating oppression from simple prejudice and discrimination are that it is a group phenomenon and that institutional power and authority are used to support prejudices and enforce discriminatory behaviors in systematic ways. Everyone is socialized to participate in oppressive practices, either as direct and indirect perpetrators or passive beneficiaries, or—as with some oppressed peoples—by directing discriminatory behaviors at members of one's own group.

paradigm shift   A complete change in theoretical perspective.

patriarchy   A family, social group, or society in which men hold power and are dominant figures. Patriarchal power in the United States plays out in the family, the economy, the media, religion, law, and electoral politics.

post-modern feminism   A type of feminism that repudiates the broad-brush "universal" theorizing of liberalism, radical feminism, or socialism, and emphasizes the particularity of women's experiences in specific cultural and historical contexts.

poverty level   An income level for individuals and families that officially defines poverty.

power elite   A relatively small group—not always easily identifiable—of key politicians, senior corporate executives, the very rich, and opinion makers such as key media figures who influence political and economic decisions in the country. Although this group shifts over time, and according to the issue, it is relatively closed.

praxis   Reflection and action upon the world in order to transform it; a key part of socially lived theorizing.

prejudice   A closed-minded prejudging of a person or group as negative or inferior, even without personal knowledge of that person or group, and often contrary to reason or facts; unreasonable, unfair, and hostile attitudes toward people.

privilege   Benefits and power from institutional inequalities. Individuals and groups may be privileged without realizing, recognizing, or even wanting it.

public vs. private dichotomy   The view that distinguishes between the private and personal (dating, marriage, sexual habits, who does the housework, relationships between parents and children) and the public (religion, law, business). Although these two spheres affect each other, according to this view they are governed by different rules, attitudes, and behavior.

racism   Racial prejudice and discrimination that are supported by institutional power and authority. In the United States, racism is based on the ideology of White (European) supremacy and is used to the advantage of White people and the disadvantage of peoples of color.

radical feminism   A philosophy that sees the oppression of women in terms of patriarchy, a system of male authority, especially manifested in sexuality, personal relationships, and the family.

reproduction labor   Women's unpaid domestic work in producing, nurturing, and socializing the next generation of workers and citizens; caring for adult members by providing meals and clean clothes, as well as rest, relaxation, love, and sexual intimacy, so that they are ready to face another working day.

second shift   Responsibilities for household chores and child care after having already done a full day's work outside the home mostly done by women.

sexism   Attitudes, actions, and institutional practices that subordinate women because of their gender.

situated knowledge   Knowledge and ways of knowing that are specific to a particular historical and cultural context.

social control   Attitudes, behaviors, and mechanisms that keep people in their place. Overt social controls include laws, fines, imprisonment, and violence. Subtle ones include ostracism and withdrawal of status and affection.

social constructionism   The view that concepts that appear to be concrete, immutable, and often solely biological, such as gender, race, and sexual orientation, are defined by human beings operating out of particular cultural contexts and ideologies. The definitions are systematically transmitted, and attitudes and behaviors purported to be appropriate are learned through childhood socialization and life experience. In this view, for example, heterosexuality is something learned — socially constructed — not innate.

social institutions   Institutions such as the family, education, the media, organized religion, law, and government.

social location   The social features of one's identity incorporating individual, community, societal, and global factors such as gender, class, ability, sexual orientation, age, and so on.

socialist feminism   A view that sees the oppression of women in terms of their subordinate position in a system defined as both patriarchal and capitalist.

speciesism   Attitudes, actions, and institutional practices that subordinate nonhuman species; usually used in discussions of environmental and ecological issues.

state   Governmental institutions, authority, and control. This includes the machinery of electoral politics, lawmaking, government agencies that execute law and policy, law enforcement agencies, and the military.

subjectivity   A form of understanding in which knowledge and meaning come from oneself and one's own experiences.

sustainability   The ability of an ecologically sound economy to sustain itself by using renewable resources and generating low or nonaccumulating levels of pollution. A more sustainable future means rethinking and radically changing current production processes, as well as the materialism and consumerism that support excessive production.

theory   An explanation of how things are and why they are the way they are; a theory is based on a set of assumptions, has a perspective, and serves a purpose.

References

Abramovitz, M. 1996. *Regulating the lives of women*. Rev. ed. Boston: South End Press.

Abzug, B. 1984. *Gender gap: Bella Abzug's guide to political power for American women*. Boston: Houghton Mifflin.

Adler, F. 1975. *Sisters in crime: The rise of the new female criminal*. New York: McGraw-Hill.

Agarwal, B. 1992. The gender and environment debate: Lessons from India. *Feminist Review* 18(1): 119–57.

Ahn, I. S. 1996. Great army, great father. In *Great army, great father*, edited by T. H. Yu. Seoul, South Korea: Korean Church Women United.

Aisha. 1991. Changing my perception. *Aché: A Journal for Lesbians of African Descent*, 3(3): 28–29.

Alexander, J., and C. T. Mohanty, eds. 1997. *Feminist genealogies, colonial legacies, democratic futures*. New York: Routledge.

Allison, D. 1992. *Bastard out of Carolina*. New York: Dutton.

Alonso, H. H. 1993. *Peace as a women's issue: A history of the U.S. movement for world peace and women's rights*. Syracuse, N.Y.: Syracuse University Press.

American Association of Retired Persons. N.d. *America's changing work force: Statistics in brief*. Washington, D.C.: American Association of Retired Persons.

American Correctional Association. 1990. *The female offender: What does the future hold?* Washington, D.C.: St. Mary's Press.

American Federation of State, County, and Municipal Employees. 1988. *Stopping sexual harassment: An AFSCME guide*. Washington, D.C.: American Federation of State, County, and Municipal Employees.

American Friends Service Committee. 1989. *AFSC perspectives on the employer sanctions provisions of the Immigration Reform and Control Act of 1986*. Philadelphia: American Friends Service Committee.

American Heritage Dictionary. 1993. 3d ed. Boston: Houghton Mifflin.

Amott, T. 1993. *Caught in the crisis: Women and the U.S. economy today*. New York: Monthly Review Press.

Amott, T., and J. Matthaei. 1996. *Race, gender, and work: A multicultural economic history of women in the United States*. Rev. ed. Boston: South End Press.

Anderson, M. L., and P. H. Collins, eds. 1995. *Race, class, and gender: An anthology*. 2d ed. Belmont, Calif.: Wadsworth.

Andre, J. 1988. Stereotypes: Conceptual and normative considerations. In *Racism and sexism: An integrated study*, edited by P. S. Rothenberg. New York: St. Martin's Press.

Andruss, V., C. Plant, J. Plant, and S. Mills. 1990. *Home!: A bioregional reader*. Philadelphia: New Society.

Anglin, M., and Y. Hser. 1987. Addicted women and crime. *Criminology* 25: 359–94.

Angwin, J. 1996. Pounding on the glass ceiling. *San Francisco Chronicle*, 24 November, p. C3.

Applebome, P. 1997. Citadel's president insists coeducation will succeed. *New York Times*, 14 January, p. A1.

Arditti, R., R. D. Klein, and S. Minden, eds. 1984. *Test-tube women: What future for motherhood?* Boston: Pandora Press.

Ayres, B. D., Jr. 1994. U.S. crackdown at border stems illegal crossings. *New York Times*, 6 October, pp. A1, A14.

Baker, B. 1993. The women's convergence for national health care. *The Network News,* July/August, 1, 3.

Baron, H. M. 1970. *The web of urban racism.* In *Institutional racism in America,* edited by L. L. Knowles and K. Prewitt. Englewood Cliffs, N.J.: Prentice-Hall.

Barry, K. 1995. *The prostitution of sexuality: The global exploitation of women.* New York: New York University Press.

Bentson, M. 1969. The political economy of women's liberation. *Monthly Review* 21(4): 13–27.

Beresford, D. 1994. *London Guardian,* 20 July, p. 11.

Berg, P. 1993. Growing a life-place politics. In *Radical environmentalism: Philosophy and tactics,* edited by J. List. Belmont, Calif.: Wadsworth.

Bergmann, B. R. 1986. *The economic emergence of women.* New York: Basic Books.

Bernstein, R., and S. C. Silberman, eds. 1996. *Generation Q.* Los Angeles: Alyson.

Bin Whahad, D. 1996. Speaking truth to power: Political prisoners in the United States. In *Criminal injustice: Confronting the prison crisis,* edited by E. Rosenblatt. Boston: South End Press.

Bird, C. 1995. *Lives of ours: Secrets of salty old women.* New York: Houghton Mifflin.

Bird, C., and S. W. Briller. 1969. *Born female: The high cost of keeping women down.* New York: Pocket Books.

Blauner, R. 1972. *Racial oppression in America.* New York: Harper & Row.

Bloom, B., M. Chesney-Lind, and B. Owen. 1994. *Women in California prisons: Hidden victims of the war on drugs.* San Francisco: Center on Juvenile and Criminal Justice.

Boggs, G. L. 1994. Fifty years on the left. *The Witness,* May, 8–12.

Boggs, J. 1994. *What can we be that our children can see?* Detroit: New Life.

Booth, W. 1997. Ex-Black Panther freed. *Washington Post,* 11 June, p. A1.

Bordo, S. 1993. *Unbearable weight: Feminism, Western culture, and the body.* Berkeley: University of California Press.

Boston Women's Health Book Collective. 1992. *The new our bodies, ourselves.* New York: Simon & Schuster.

———. 1994. *The new ourselves growing older.* New York: Simon & Schuster.

Boulding, E. 1990. *Building a civic culture: Education for an interdependent world.* Syracuse, N.Y.: Syracuse University Press.

Bowlby, J. 1963. *Child care and the growth of love.* Baltimore: Penguin Books.

Braidotti, R., E. Charkiewicz, S. Häusler, and S. Wieringa. 1994. *Women, the environment and sustainable development: Towards a theoretical synthesis.* London: Zed Books.

Brennan, S., J. Winklepleck, and G. McNee. 1994. *The resourceful woman.* Detroit: Visible Ink.

Bright, S., and J. Blank, eds. *Herotica 2: A collection of women's erotic fiction.* New York: Plume.

Brown, B. R. D. 1996. White North American political prisoners. In *Criminal injustice: Confronting the prison crisis,* edited by E. Rosenblatt. Boston: South End Press.

Browne, A. 1987. *When battered women kill.* New York: The Free Press.

Browne, J. 1996. The labor of doing time. In *Criminal injustice: Confronting the prison crisis,* edited by E. Rosenblatt. Boston: South End Press.

Brownmiller, S. 1975. *Against our will: Men, women, and rape.* New York: Simon & Schuster.

Bullard, R. D. 1990. *Dumping in Dixie: Race, class, and environmental quality.* Boulder, Colo.: Westview Press.

———, ed. 1993. *Confronting environmental racism: Voices from the grassroots.* Boston: South End Press.

Bunch, C. 1986. *Passionate politics: Essays 1968–1986.* New York: St. Martin's Press.

Bureau of Justice Statistics. 1991. *Special report: Women in prison in 1986.* Washington, D.C.: U.S. Department of Justice.

———. 1992. *Women in jail in 1989.* Washington, D.C.: U.S. Department of Justice.

———. 1994. *Special report: women in prison in 1991.* Washington, D.C.: U.S. Department of Justice.

———. 1995. *Census of state and federal adult correctional facilities.* Washington, D.C.: U.S. Department of Justice.

Burke, P. 1996. *Gender shock: Exploding the myths of male and female.* New York: Anchor Books.

Bury, J., V. Morrison, and S. McLauchlan, eds. 1992. *Working with women with AIDS.* New York: Routledge.

Butler, J. 1990. *Gender trouble: Feminism and the subversion of identity.* New York: Routledge, Chapman, & Hall.

Cammermeyer, M. 1994. *Serving in silence.* New York: Viking.

Candib, L. 1995. *Medicine and the family: A feminist perspective.* New York: Basic Books.

Caplan, P., ed. 1987. *The cultural construction of sexuality.* London: Tavistock Publications.

Carlen, P. 1989. Feminist jurisprudence, or women-wise penology. *Probation Journal* 36(3): 110–14.

Centers for Disease Control and Prevention. 1996. *Sexually transmitted disease surveillance.* Atlanta: U.S. Department of Health and Human Services.

Chambers, V. 1995. Betrayal feminism. In *Listen up: Voices from the next feminist generation,* edited by B. Findlen. Seattle: Seal Press.

Chapkis, W. 1986. *Beauty secrets: Women and the politics of appearance.* Boston: South End Press.

Chavkin, W. 1984. *Double exposure: Women's health hazards on the job and at home.* New York: Monthly Review Press.

Chesler, P. 1972. *Women and madness.* New York: Avon.

Chesney-Lind, M. 1986. Women and crime: A review of the literature on the female offender. *Signs: Journal of Women in Culture and Society* 12(1): 78–96.

———. 1987. Female offenders: Paternalism reexamined. In *Women, the courts and equality,* edited by L. Crites and W. Hepperle. Newbury Park: Sage.

———. 1995. Rethinking women's imprisonment: A critical examination of trends in female incarceration. In *Women, Crime, and Criminal Justice,* edited by B. R. Price and N. Sokoloff. New York: McGraw-Hill.

Chodorow, N. 1978. *Reproduction and mothering: Psychoanalysis and the sociology of gender.* Berkeley: University of California Press.

Churchill, W. 1992. Introduction: The Third World at home. In *Cages of steel: The politics of imprisonment in the United States,* edited by W. Churchill and J. J. Vander Wall. Washington, D.C.: Maisonnueve Press.

Clinton, H. R. 1996. *It takes a village and other lessons children teach us.* New York: Simon & Schuster.

Cobble, D. S., ed. 1993. *Women and unions: Forging a partnership.* Ithaca, N.Y.: ILR Press.

Collins, P. H. 1990. *Black feminist thought: Knowledge, consciousness, and the politics of empowerment.* Boston: Unwin Hyman.

Connell, R. W. 1990. The state, gender, and sexual politics: Theory and appraisal. *Theory and Society,* 19(4): 507–44.

Cook, A., and G. Kirk. 1983. *Greenham women everywhere: Dreams, ideas, and actions from the women's peace movement.* Boston: South End Press.

Cooper, E. 1992. When being ill is illegal: Women and the criminalization of HIV. *Health/PAC Bulletin,* Winter, 10-14.

Corea, G. 1985. *The mother machine: Reproductive technologies from artificial insemination to artificial wombs.* New York: Harper & Row.

———. 1987. *Man-made women: How reproductive technologies affect women.* Bloomington: Indiana University Press.

Dalla Costa, M., and S. James. 1972. *The power of women and the subversion of the community.* Bristol, England: Falling Wall Press.

Daly, F. 1994. Perspectives of Native American women on race and gender. In *Challenging racism: Alternatives to genetic explanations,* edited by E. Tobach and B. Risoff. New York: The Feminist Press.

Daly, K. 1994. *Gender, crime, and punishment.* New Haven: Yale University Press.

Daly, M. 1976. *Gyn/ecology: The metaethics of radical feminism.* Boston: Beacon Press.

Dankelman, I., and J. Davidson. 1988. *Women and the environment in the Third World.* London: Earthscan.

Dargan, C. A. 1995. *Statistical record of health and medicine.* Detroit: Gale Research.

Davis, A. Y. 1983a. Racism, birth control, and reproductive rights. In *Women, race, and class.* New York: Vintage Books.

———. 1983b. *Women, race, and class.* New York: Vintage Books.

———. 1997. A plenary address. Paper presented at conference, Frontline Feminisms: Women, War, and Resistance, 16 January, at University of California, Riverside.

Davis, J., ed. 1991. *The Earth First! reader: Ten years of radical environmentalism.* Salt Lake City: Peregrine Smith Books.

d'Eaubonne, F. 1994. The time for ecofeminism. In *Ecology,* edited by C. Merchant. Atlantic Highlands, N.J.: Humanities Press.

de Beauvoir, S. 1973. *The second sex.* New York: Vintage Books.

de Ishtar, Z. 1994. *Daughters of the Pacific.* Melbourne: Spinifex Press.

De Oliveira, O., T. De Barbieri, I. Arriagada, M. Valenzuela, C. Serrano, and G. Emeagwali. N.d. *Alternatives: The food, energy, and debt crises in relation to women.* Bangalore, India: DAWN.

DePalma, A. 1996. Why that Asian TV has a "Made in Mexico" label. *New York Times,* 23 May, p. D1.

Devall, B., and G. Sessions. 1985. *Deep ecology: Living as if nature mattered.* Salt Lake City: Smith Books.

Diamond, I., and G. F. Orenstein, eds. 1990. *Reweaving the world: The emergence of ecofeminism.* San Francisco: Sierra Club Books.

Dibblin, J. 1989. *The day of two suns: U.S. nuclear testing and the Pacific Islands.* New York: New Amsterdam Books.

Dinnerstein, D. 1976. *Sexual arrangements and the human malaise.* New York: Harper & Row.

———. 1989. Surviving on earth: Meaning of feminism. In *Healing the wounds,* edited by J. Plant. Philadelphia: New Society Publishers.

DNA Testing: A new military invasion. 1996. *Citizen Soldier.* Available from Citizen Soldier, 175 Fifth Ave., #2135, New York, NY 10010.

Doyal, L. 1995. *What makes women sick: Gender and the political economy of health.* New Brunswick, N.J.: Rutgers University Press.

Duff, K. 1993. *The alchemy of illness.* New York: Pantheon.

Dujon, D., and A. Withorn, eds. 1996. *For crying out loud: Women's poverty in the United States.* Boston: South End Press.

Dula, A. 1994. The life and death of Miss Mildred: An elderly Black woman. *Clinics in Geriatric Medicine* 10(3): 419–30.

———. 1996. An African American Perspective on Reproductive Freedoms. Panel on Reproduction, Race, and Class at the Third World Congress of Bioethics, Feminist Approaches to Bioethics, November, San Francisco.

Dziemianowicz, J. 1992. How we make the stars so beautiful. *McCall's,* July, 105.

Echols, A. 1989. *Daring to be bad: Radical feminism in America 1967–1975.* Minneapolis: University of Minnesota Press.

Edison, L. T., and D. Notkin. 1994. *Women en large: Images of fat nudes.* San Francisco: Books in Focus.

Ehrenreich, B., and D. English. 1973. *Witches, midwives, and nurses: A history of women healers.* Old Westbury, N.Y.: Feminist Press.

———. 1978. *For her own good: 150 years of the experts' advice to women.* Garden City, N.Y.: Anchor/Doubleday.

Ehrenreich, B., E. Hess, and G. Jacobs. 1986. *Remaking love: The feminization of sex.* New York: Anchor/Doubleday.

Eisenstein, Z. R. 1979. *Capitalism, patriarchy, and the case for socialist feminism.* New York: Monthly Review Press.

———. 1988. *The female body and the law.* Berkeley: University of California Press.

Enloe, C. 1983. *Does khaki become you? The militarization of women's lives.* Boston: South End Press.

———. 1990. *Bananas, beaches, bases: Making feminist sense of international relations.* Berkeley: University of California Press.

———. 1993a. *The morning after: Sexual politics at the end of the cold war.* Berkeley: University of California Press.

———. 1993b. The right to fight: A feminist Catch-22. *Ms.,* July/August, 84–87.

Erez, E. 1992. Dangerous men, evil women: Gender and parole decision making. *Justice Quarterly* 9(1): 105–27.

Eridani. 1992. Is sexual orientation a secondary sex characteristic? In *Closer to home: Bisexuality and feminism,* edited by E. R. Weise. Seattle: Seal Press.

Evans, S. 1980. *Personal politics.* New York: Vintage Books.

Fallon, P., ed. 1994. *Consuming passions: Feminist perspectives on eating disorders.* New York: Guilford.

Faludi, S. 1991. *Backlash: The undeclared war against women.* New York: Crown.

Farnsworth, M., and R. Teske, Jr. 1995. Gender differences in felony court processing: three hypotheses of disparity. *Women and Criminal Justice* 6(2), 23–44.

Federal Bureau of Investigation. 1992. *Uniform Crime Reports 1991.* Washington, D.C.: U.S. Department of Justice.

Federation of Feminist Health Centers. 1995. *A new view of a woman's body.* 2d ed. Los Angeles: Feminist Health Press.

Feinberg, L. 1993. *Stone butch blues.* Ithaca, N.Y.: Firebrand Books.

———. 1996. *Transgender warriors: Making history from Joan of Arc to RuPaul.* Boston: Beacon Press.

Ferguson, M., and J. Wicke, ed. 1992. *Feminism and postmodernism.* Durham, N.C.: Duke University Press.

Ferreyra, S., and K. Hughes. 1991. *Table manners: A guide to the pelvic examination for disabled women and health care providers.* San Francisco: Sex Education for Disabled People and Planned Parenthood Alameda.

Fineman, M. A. 1994. *The public nature of private violence: The discovery of domestic abuse.* New York: Routledge.

Finger, A. 1990. *Past due: A story of disability, pregnancy, and birth.* Seattle: Seal Press.

Firestone, S. 1970. *The dialectics of sex: The case for feminist revolution.* New York: Morrow.

Foley, L., and C. Rasche. 1979. The effect of race on sentence, actual time served and final disposition of female offenders. In *Theory and research in criminal justice,* edited by J. Conley. Cincinnati: Anderson.

Foster, C. 1989. *Women for all seasons: The story of W.I.L.P.F.* Athens, Ga.: University of Georgia Press.

Fox-Genovese, E. 1994. Beyond individualism: The new Puritanism, feminism, and women. *Salmagundi* 101(2): 79–95.

Frankenberg, R. 1993. *White women, race matters: The social construction of whiteness.* Minneapolis: University of Minnesota Press.

Fraser, L. 1997. *Losing it: America's obsession with weight and the industry that feeds it.* New York: Dutton.

Freedberg, L. 1996. 1,000 more agents will be sent to the border. *San Francisco Chronicle,* 9 February, p. A3.

Free Trade vs. Fair Trade. N.d. Available from Global Exchange, 2017 Mission St., Rm. 303, San Francisco, CA 94110.

Freire, P. 1989. *Pedagogy of the oppressed.* New York: Continuum.

Freudenheim, E. 1995. *Healthspeak: A complete dictionary of America's health care system.* New York: Facts on File.

Friedan, B. 1963. *The feminine mystique.* New York: W. W. Norton.

Fuchs, L. 1990. The reaction of Black Americans to immigration. In *Immigration reconsidered,* edited by V. Yans-McLaughlin. New York: Oxford University Press.

Gaines, P. 1994. *Laughing in the dark: From colored girl to woman of color—a journey from prison to power.* New York: Anchor Books.

Garber, M. 1992. *Vested interests: Cross-dressing and cultural anxiety.* New York: HarperPerennial.

George, S. 1988. Getting your own back: Solving the Third World debt crisis. *New Statesman & Society,* 15 July, 20.

Gibbs, L. 1995. *Dying from dioxin: A citizens' guide to reclaiming our health and rebuilding democracy.* Boston: South End Press.

Gilfus, M. 1992. From victims to survivors: Women's routes of entry and immersion into street crime. *Women and Criminal Justice* 4(1), 62–89.

Giordano, P., S. Kerbel, and S. Dudley. 1981. The economics of female criminality. In *Women and crime in America,* edited by L. Bowker. New York: Macmillan.

Gleick, E. 1996. Scandal in the military. *Time,* 25 November, 28–31.

Glover, P. 1997. Ithaca HOURS makes social change pay: "Print money locally and make revolution globally." *Resist* 6(4): 3.

Gluck, S. 1976. *From parlor to prison: Five American suffragists talk about their lives.* New York: Vintage Books.

Goodman, E. 1996. Predators and jailbait. *San Francisco Chronicle,* 21 February, p. A17.

Gray, J. 1992. Men are from Mars, women are from Venus. New York: HarperCollins.

Griffin, S. 1978. *Woman and nature: the roaring inside her.* San Francisco: Harper Colophon.

———. 1986. *Rape: The politics of consciousness.* 3d ed. San Francisco: Harper & Row.

Hall, L. 1996. Eating salt. In *Names we call home: Autobiography on racial identity,* edited by B. Thompson & S. Tyagi. New York: Routledge.

Hamilton, C. 1993. Coping with industrial exploitation. In *Confronting environmental racism: Voices from the grassroots,* edited by R. Bullard. Boston: South End Press.

Harne, L., and E. Miller, eds. 1996. *All the rage: Reasserting radical lesbian feminism.* New York: Teachers College Press.

Hartmann, B. 1995. Dangerous intersections. *Political Environments* no. 2 (summer): 1–7. Publication of the Committee on Women, Population and the Environment, Hampshire College, Amherst, Mass.

Hartmann, H. 1981. The unhappy marriage of Marxism and feminism: Towards a more progressive union. In *Women and revolution: A discussion of the unhappy marriage of Marxism and feminism,* edited by L. Sargent. Boston: South End Press.

Hayden, D. 1981. *The grand domestic revolution: A history of feminist designs for American homes, neighborhoods, and cities.* Cambridge, Mass.: MIT Press.

Henderson, H. 1991. *Paradigms in progress: Life beyond economics.* Indianapolis: Knowledge Systems.

Hesse-Biber, S. J. 1991. Women, weight, and eating disorders: A socio-cultural analysis. *Women's Studies International Forum* 14(3): 173–91.

Hill, J. 1993. Outrageous acts. Unpublished class assignment, Antioch College.

Hite, S. 1994. *Women as revolutionary agents of change: The Hite Report and beyond.* Madison: University of Wisconsin Press.

———. 1995. *Hite report on the family: Growing patriarchy.* New York: Grove Press.

Hochschild, A. R. 1990. *The second shift.* New York: Avon Books.

Hofrichter, R., ed. 1993. *Toxic struggles: The theory and practice of environmental justice.* Philadelphia and Gabriola Island, B.C.: New Society Publishers.

Holmes, S. A. 1995. Ousters of undocumented immigrants set a record. *San Francisco Chronicle,* 28 December, p. A13.

———. 1995. The strange politics of immigration. *New York Times,* 31 December, p. E3.

hooks, b. 1984. *Feminist theory: From margin to center.* Boston: South End Press.

Hubbard, R. 1989. Science, facts, and feminism. In *Feminism and science,* edited by N. Tuana. Bloomington: Indiana University Press.

———. 1990. *The politics of women's biology.* New Brunswick, N.J.: Rutgers University Press.

Humm, A., ed. 1992. *Feminisms: A reader.* New York: Harvester Wheatsheaf.

Hurtado, A. 1996. *The color of privilege: Three blasphemies on race and feminism.* Ann Arbor: The University of Michigan Press.

Hynes, P. 1996. *A patch of Eden.* White River Junction, Vt.: Chelsea Green.

Inciardi, J., D. Lockwood, and A. Pottieger. 1993. *Women and crack cocaine.* New York: Macmillan.

Ireland, M. S. 1993. *Reconceiving women: Separating motherhood from female identity.* New York: Guilford Press.

Isakson, E., ed. 1988. *Women and the military system.* New York: St. Martin's Press.

Jaggar, A. M. 1983. *Feminist politics and human nature.* Totowa, N.J.: Rowman & Allanheld.

Jones, J. 1985. *Labor of love, labor of sorrow: Black women, work, and the family, from slavery to present.* New York: Vintage Books.

Katz, J. N. 1995. *The invention of heterosexuality.* New York: Plume.

Katz-Rothman, B. 1986. *Tentative pregnancy: Prenatal diagnosis and the future of motherhood.* New York: Viking.

Kessler-Harris, A. 1990. *A woman's wage: Historical meanings and social consequences.* Lexington: University Press of Kentucky.

King, Y. 1983. All is connectedness: Notes from the Women's Pentagon Action, USA. In *Keeping the peace,* edited by L. Jones. London: The Women's Press.

———. 1987. Letter to the editor. *The Nation.* Dec. 12, pp. 702, 730–31.

———. 1991. Reflection on the other body: Difference, disability and identity politics. Unpublished paper.

———. 1993. Feminism and ecology. In *Toxic struggles: The theory and practice of environmental justice,* edited by R. Hofrichter. Philadelphia and Gabriola Island, B.C.: New Society.

Klein, R., and L. J. Dumble. 1994. Disempowering midlife women: The science and politics of hormone replacement therapy (HRT). *Women's Studies International Forum* 17(4): 327–43.

Kohl, H. 1992. *From archetype to zeitgeist: Powerful ideas for powerful thinking.* Boston: Little Brown.

Krieger, N., and S. Sidney. 1996. Racial discrimination and blood pressure: The CARDIA study of young black and white adults. *American Journal of Public Health* 86(10): 1370–78.

Kruttschnitt, C. 1980–81. Social status and sentences of female offenders. *Law and Society Review* 15(2): 247–65.

LaDuke, W. 1993. A society based on conquest cannot be sustained: Native peoples and the environmental crisis. In *Toxic struggles: The theory and practice of environmental justice,* edited by R. Hofrichter. Philadelphia and Gabriola Island, B.C.: New Society.

Lahey, K. 1985. Until women themselves have told all they have to tell. *Osgoode Hall Law Journal* 23(3): 519–41.

Lakoff, R. T., and R. L. Sherr. 1984. *Face value.* Boston: Routledge & Kegan Paul.

Lasch, C. 1977. *Haven in a heartless world: The family besieged.* New York: Basic Books.

LaVigne, P. 1989. "Take a little off the sides": Baby boomers boost plastic surgery biz. *Utne Reader,* September/October, 12.

Lee, C. 1987. *Toxic wastes and race in the United States.* New York: New York Commission for Racial Justice United Church of Christ.

Lehrman, K. 1993. Off course. *Mother Jones,* September/October, 45–55.

Leonard, A., ed. 1989. *SEEDS: Supporting women's work in the Third World*. New York: The Feminist Press.

Lichtenstein, A. C., and M. A. Kroll. 1996. The fortress economy: The economic role of the U.S. prison system. In *Criminal injustice: Confronting the prison crisis*, edited by E. Rosenblatt. Boston: South End Press.

Lieberman, T. 1997. Social Security: The campaign to take the system private. *The Nation*, 27 January, 11–16, 18.

Light, J. 1996. Rape on the border. *The Progressive*, September, 24.

Lips, H. 1991. *Women, men, and power*. Mountain View, Calif.: Mayfield.

Lipsky, S. 1977. Internalized oppression. *Black Re-emergence*, Winter, 5–10.

List, P. C., ed. 1993. *Radical environmentalism: Philosophy and tactics*. Belmont, Calif.: Wadsworth.

Lord, S. A. 1993. *Social welfare and the feminization of poverty*. New York: Garland.

Lorde, A. 1984. Uses of the erotic: The erotic as power. In *Sister outsider*. Freedom, Calif.: The Crossing Press.

Luebke, B. F., and M. E. Reilly. 1995. *Women's studies graduates: The first generation*. New York: Teachers College Press.

Luker, K. 1996. *Dubious conceptions: The politics of teenage pregnancy*. Cambridge, Mass.: Harvard University Press.

Lusane, C. 1991. *Pipe dream blues: Racism and the war on drugs*. Boston: South End Press.

MacKinnon, C. 1987. *Feminism unmodified: discourse on life and law*. Cambridge, Mass.: Harvard University Press.

———. 1991. From practice to theory, or what is a white woman anyway? *Yale Journal of Law and Feminism* 4(13–22), 1281–1328.

Maguire, K., A. L. Pastore, and T. Flanagan, eds. 1993. *Sourcebook of Criminal Justice Statistics, 1992*. Washington, D.C.: U.S. Department of Justice.

Maher, F. A., and M. K. T. Tetreault. 1994. *The feminist classroom*. New York: Basic Books.

Mainardi, P. 1992. The politics of housework. *Ms.*, May/June, 40–41.

Mainstream. 1997. 15(2): 14–16.

Malveaux, J. 1995. NAFTA's broken promises. *San Francisco Examiner*, 17 September, p. E2.

Mann, C. R. 1995. Women of color and the criminal justice system. In *The criminal justice system and women*, edited by B. R. Price and N. J. Sokoloff. New York: McGraw-Hill.

Martin, G. 1986. *Socialist feminism: The first decade*. Seattle: Freedom Socialist.

Martinez, L. A. 1996. Women of color and reproductive health. In *Dangerous intersections: feminist perspectives on population, immigration, and the environment*, edited by T. Reisz and A. Smith. Amherst, Mass.: Committee on Women, Population, and the Environment, Hampshire College.

Mauer, M., and T. Huling. 1995. *Young black Americans and the criminal justice system five years later*. Washington, D.C.: The Sentencing Project.

McCarthy, C., and W. Crichlow, eds. 1993. *Race, identity, and representation in education*. New York: Routledge.

McGinn, M. 1995. How GATT puts hard-won victories at risk. *Ms.*, March/April, 15.

McIntosh, P. 1988. *White privilege and male privilege: A personal account of coming to see correspondences through work in women's studies*. Wellesley, Mass.: Center for Research on Women, Wellesley College.

McKenna, T. 1996/1997. Military culture breeds misogyny. *Women against military madness*, December/January, 1.

Mello, F. V. 1996. Population and international security in the new world order. *Political Environments* no. 3 (Winter/Spring): 25–26. Publication of the Committee on Women, Population and the Environment, Hampshire College, Amherst, Mass.

Mellor, M. 1992. *Breaking the boundaries: Towards a feminist green socialism*. London: Virago Press.

Merchant, C. 1980. *The death of nature: Ecology and the scientific revolution*. San Francisco: Harper & Row.

Messerschmidt, J. W. 1986. *Capitalism, patriarchy, and crime: Toward a socialist feminist criminology*. Totowa, N.J.: Rowman & Littlefield.

Mies, M. 1986. *Patriarchy and accumulation on a world scale: Women in the international division of labor*. London: Zed Books.

———. 1993. The need for a new vision: The subsistence perspective. In *Ecofeminism*, edited by M. Mies and V. Shiva. London: Zed Books.

Mies, M., and V. Shiva. 1993. *Ecofeminism*. London: Zed Books.

Military sex scandal extends to Air Force base. 1996. *San Francisco Chronicle*, 15 November, p. A15.

Milkman, R., ed. 1985. *Women, work, and protest: A century of U.S. women's labor history*. London: Routledge & Kegan Paul.

Mills, J. 1986. *The underground empire: Where crime and governments embrace.* New York: Doubleday.

Mitchell, J. 1990. Women: The longest revolution. In *Women, class, and the feminist imagination,* edited by K. V. Hansen and I. J. Philipson. Philadelphia: Temple University Press.

Mohanty, C., A. Russo, and L. Torres, eds. 1991. *Third World women and the politics of feminism.* Bloomington: Indiana University Press.

Moraga, C., and G. Anzaldua, eds. 1983. *This bridge called my back: Writings by radical women of color.* New York: Kitchen Table Press: Women of Color Press.

Morgan, R. 1996. Dispatch from Beijing. *Ms.,* January/February, 12–15.

Morrison, T., ed. 1992. *Race-ing, justice, en-gendering power: Essays on Anita Hill, Clarence Thomas, and the construction of reality.* New York: Pantheon.

Mudrick, N. R. 1988. Disabled women and the public policies of income support. In *Women with disabilities: Essays in psychology, culture, and politics,* edited by M. Fine and A. Asch. Philadelphia: Temple University Press.

Mullins, L. 1997. *On our own: Race, class, and gender in the lives of African American women.* New York: Routledge.

Musil, C. M., ed. 1992. *The courage to question: Women's studies and student learning.* Washington, D.C.: Association of American Colleges.

Nader, R. 1993. *The case against free trade.* San Francisco: Earth Island Press.

Naffine, N. 1987. *Female crime: the construction of women in criminology.* Boston: Allen & Unwin.

Naidus, B. 1993. *One size does not fit all.* Littleton, Colo.: Aigis Publications.

National Cancer Institute. 1996. *SEER monograph: Racial/ethnic patterns of cancer in the United States, 1988–1992.* Washington, D.C.: National Cancer Institute.

National Center for Health Statistics. 1996a. *Health United States, 1995.* Hyattsville, Md.: Public Health Service.

National Center for Health Statistics. 1996b. *Monthly vital statistics report on final mortality, 1994.* Hyattsville, Md.: National Center for Health Statistics.

National Commission on Working Women. 1989. *Women, work, and childcare.* Washington, D.C.: Wider Opportunities for Women.

National Women's Studies Association. 1994. *NWSA directory of women's studies programs, women's centers, and women's research centers.* College Park, Md.: National Women's Studies Association.

Navarro, M. 1996. Lesbian loses court appeal for custody of daughter. *New York Times,* 31 August, p. A7.

Navarro, V. 1993. *Dangerous to your health: Capitalism in health care.* New York: Monthly Review Press.

Nechas, E., and D. Foley. 1994. *Unequal treatment: What you don't know about how women are mistreated by the medical community.* Philadelphia: Temple University Press.

Nelson, L. 1990. The place of women in polluted places. In *Reweaving the world: The emergence of ecofeminism,* edited by I. Diamond and G. Orenstein. San Francisco: Sierra Club Books.

Nestle, J., ed. 1992. *The persistent desire: A femme-butch reader.* Los Angeles: Alyson.

Nicholson, L., ed. 1990. *Feminism/postmodernism.* New York: Routledge.

Nike: Just don't *do it.* 1997. Special report available from Global Exchange, 2017 Mission St., Rm. 303, San Francisco, CA 94110.

Norwood, R. 1986. *Women who love too much.* New York: Pocket Books.

O'Connor, M., ed. 1994. *Is capitalism sustainable?: Political economy and the politics of ecology.* New York: Guilford Press.

Odubekun, L. 1992. A structural approach to differential gender sentencing. *Criminal Justice Abstracts* 24(2): 343–60.

Okazawa-Rey, M. 1997. Amerasians in GI town: The legacy of U.S. militarism in South Korea. *Asian Journal of Women's Studies* 3: 1.

Okazawa-Rey, M., and G. Kirk. 1996. Military security: Confronting the oxymoron. *CrossRoads* 60: 4–7.

Okin, S. M. 1989. *Justice, gender, and the family.* New York: Basic Books.

Okinawa women's America peace caravan. 1996. Unpublished program. February 3–17. Naha City, Okinawa: Okinawa Women Act Against Military Violence.

O'Melveny, M. 1996. Lexington Prison High Security Unit: U. S. political prison. In *Criminal injustice: Confronting the prison crisis,* edited by E. Rosenblatt. Boston: South End Press.

Omolade, B. 1986. *It's a family affair: The real lives of Black single mothers.* New York: Kitchen Table: Women of Color Press.

———. 1989. We speak for the planet. In *Rocking the ship of state: Toward a feminist peace politics,* edited by A. Harris and Y. King. Boulder, Colo.: Westview Press.

Ong, P., E. Bonacich, and L. Cheng. 1994. *The new Asian immigration in Los Angeles and global restructuring.* Philadelphia: Temple University Press.

O'Reilly, B. 1991. Cooling down the world debt bomb. *Fortune,* 20 May, 123.

O'Rourke, D. 1985. *Half life: A parable for the nuclear age.* Video.

Owen, B., and B. Bloom. 1995. Profiling women prisoners. *The Prison Journal* 75(2): 165–85.

Paglia, C. 1990. *Sexual personae: Art and decadence from Nefertiti to Emily Dickinson.* New Haven: Yale University Press.

Pearce, D., A. Markandya, and E. B. Barbier. 1990. *Blueprint for a Green economy.* London: Earthscan.

Perrone, B., H. H. Stockel, and V. Kreuger. 1989. *Medicine women, curanderas, and women doctors.* Norman: University of Oklahoma Press.

Petchesky, R. 1990. *Abortion and woman's choice: The state, sexuality, and reproductive freedom.* Rev. ed. Boston: Northeastern University Press.

Peterson, R. R. 1996. Re-evaluation of the economic consequences of divorce. *American Sociological Review* 61(3): 528–53.

Peterson, V. S., and A. S. Runyan. 1993. *Global gender issues.* Boulder, Colo.: Westview Press.

Pharr, S. 1988. *Homophobia: A weapon of sexism.* Inverness, Calif.: Chardon Press.

Pheterson, G. 1990. Alliances between women: Overcoming internalized oppression and internalized domination. In *Bridges of power,* edited by L. Albrecht and R. M. Brewer. Philadelphia and Gabriola Island, B. C.: New Society Publishers.

Phoenix, J. 1993. Getting the lead out of the community. In *Confronting environmental racism,* edited by R. D. Bullard. Boston: South End Press.

In Phoenix chain gangs for women. 1996. *New York Times,* 28 August, p. C1.

Plant, C., and J. Plant, eds. 1992. *Putting power in its place: Create community control!* Philadelphia and Gabriola Island, B.C.: New Society Publishers.

Plumwood, V. 1993. *Feminism and the mastery of nature.* New York: Routledge.

Pollack, J. 1994. The increasing incarceration rate of women offenders: Equality or justice? Paper presented at Prisons 2000 Conference, Leicester, England.

Pollitt, K. 1994. Subject to debate. *The Nation,* July 11, 259(2), p. 45.

Prison Activist Resource Center. 1997. *Women in prison.* Fact sheet prepared by Prison Activist Resource Center, Berkeley, Calif.

Pratt, M. B. 1995. *S/he.* Ithaca, N.Y.: Firebrand Books.

Pulido, L. 1993. Sustainable Development at Ganados del Valle. In *Confronting environmental racism: Voices from the grassroots,* edited by R. Bullard. Boston: South End Press.

Quindlen, A. 1994. Feminism continues to grow and reach and affect us all. *Chicago Tribune,* 21 January, sec. 1, p. 21.

Rafter, N. 1990. *Partial justice: Women, prisons and social control.* New Brunswick, N.J.: Transaction.

Raymond, J. 1994. *The transsexual empire: The making of the she-male.* 2d ed. New York: Teachers College Press.

Rayner, R. 1997. Women in the warrior culture. *New York Times Magazine,* 22 June, pp. 24–29, 40, 49, 53, 55–56.

Reagon, B. J. 1987. *Ode to the international debt.* Boston: Songtalk.

Reardon, B. A. 1985. *Sexism and the war system.* New York: Teachers College Press.

———. 1993. *Women and peace: Feminist visions of global security.* Albany, N.Y.: SUNY Press.

Reynolds, M. 1992. *Erotica: Women's writing from Sappho to Margaret Atwood.* New York: Fawcett Columbine.

Rich, A. 1986a. Compulsory heterosexuality and lesbian existence. In *Blood, bread, and poetry.* New York: W. W. Norton.

———. 1986b. *Of woman born: Motherhood as experience and institution.* 10th anniversary ed. New York: W. W. Norton.

Roberts, M. M., and T. Mizuta, eds. 1993. *The reformers: Socialist feminism.* London: Routledge/Thoemmes Press.

Roediger, D. R. 1991. *The wages of whiteness: Race and the making of the American working class.* New York: Verso.

Roiphe, K. 1993. *The morning after: Sex, fear, and feminism.* Boston: Little Brown.

Rosenberg, A. 1988. The crisis in knowing and understanding the Holocaust. In *Echoes from the Holocaust: Philosophical reflections on a dark time,* edited by A. Rosenberg and G. E. Meyers. Philadelphia: Temple University Press.

Rosenblatt, E., ed. 1996. *Criminal injustice: Confronting the prison crisis.* Boston: South End Press.

Russell, B. 1935. *In praise of idleness and other essays.* New York: W. W. Norton.

Russell, D. 1995. *Women, madness, and medicine.* Cambridge, England: Polity Press.

Russo, N. F., and M. A. Jansen. 1988. Women, work, and disability: Opportunities and challenges. In

Women with disabilities: Essays in psychology, culture, and politics, edited by M. Fine and A. Asch. Philadelphia: Temple University Press.

Sale, K. 1985. *Dwellers in the land, the bioregional vision.* San Francisco: Sierra Books.

Seager, J. 1993. *Earth follies: Coming to feminist terms with the global environmental crisis.* New York: Routledge.

Segell, M. 1996. The second coming of the Alpha male: A prescription for righteous masculinity at the millennium. *Esquire,* October, 74–82.

Sen, G., and C. Grown. 1987. *Development, crises, and alternative visions: Third World women's perspectives.* New York: Monthly Review Press.

Sharf, J. 1997. Guess again: Sweatshop violations continue. *Jews for economic and racial justice,* Bulletin 33. Available from JREC, 64 Fulton St., #605, New York, N.Y. 10038.

Shields, K. 1994. *In the tiger's mouth: An empowerment guide for action.* Gabriola Island, B.C.: New Society Publishers.

Shiva, V. 1988. *Staying alive: Women, ecology and development.* London: Zed Books.

Showalter, E. 1987. *The female malady: Women, madness, and English culture, 1830–1980.* London: Virago.

Sidel, R. 1996. *Keeping women and children last: America's war on the poor.* New York: Penguin Books.

Simon, R. 1975. *Women and crime.* Lexington, Mass.: Lexington Books.

Singh, G. K., and S. M. Yu. 1995. Infant mortality in the United States: Trends, differentials, and projections, 1950 through 2010. *American Journal of Public Health* 85(7): 957–64.

Sivard, R. L. 1995. *Women . . . a world survey.* 2d ed. Washington, D.C.: World Priorities.

———. 1996. *World military and social expenditures 1996.* 16th ed. Washington, D.C.: World Priorities.

Smart, C. 1989. *Feminism and the power of law.* London: Routledge & Kegan Paul.

———. 1995. *Law, crime, and sexuality: Essays in feminism.* London: Sage.

Smelser, N. 1994. *Sociology.* Cambridge, Mass.: Blackwell.

Smith, B., ed. 1983. *Home girls: A black feminist anthology.* New York: Kitchen Table: Women of Color Press.

Spretnak, C. 1990. Ecofeminism: our roots and flowering. In *Reweaving the world: The emergence of ecofeminism,* edited by I. Diamond & G. Orenstein. San Francisco: Sierra Club Books.

Stacey, J. 1996. *In the name of the family: Rethinking values in the postmodern age.* Boston: Beacon Press.

Stanworth, M., ed. 1987. *Reproductive technologies.* Cambridge, England: Cambridge University Press.

Starhawk. 1987. *Truth or dare: Encounters with power, authority, and mystery.* San Francisco: Harper & Row.

Steinberg, J. 1989. At debt's door. *Ms.,* November, 78.

Steinem, G. 1983. *Outrageous acts and everyday rebellions.* New York: Holt, Rinehart, & Winston.

Stonequist, E. V. 1937. *The marginal man: A study in personality and cultural conflict.* New York: Scribner & Sons.

Stoller, E. P., and R. C. Gibson, eds. 1994. *Worlds of difference: Inequality in the aging experience.* Thousand Oaks, Calif.: Pine Forge.

Sturdevant, S., and B. Stoltzfus. 1992. *Let the good times roll: Prostitution and the U.S. military in Asia.* New York: New Press.

Sward, S. 1997. S.F. Police panel puts off FBI proposal. Feds want to team up to fight terrorism. *San Francisco Chronicle,* 16 January, p. A18.

Swerdlow, A. 1993. *Women strike for peace: Traditional motherhood and radical politics in the 1960s.* Chicago: University of Chicago Press.

Szasz, A. 1994. *Ecopopulism, toxic waste and the movement for environmental justice.* Minneapolis: University of Minnesota Press.

Takaki, R. 1987. *Strangers from a different shore: Perspectives on race and ethnicity in America.* New York: Oxford University Press.

Tan, A. 1989. *The joy luck club.* New York: G. P. Putnam's Sons.

Tannen, D. 1990. *You just don't understand: Men and women in conversation.* New York: Morrow.

Taueber, C. 1991. *Statistical handbook on women in America.* Phoenix: Oryx Press.

This Bud's for you. No, not you, her. 1991. *Business Week,* 4 November, 86.

Thompson, B. W. 1994. *A hunger so wide and so deep.* Minneapolis: University of Minnesota Press.

Thropy, M. A. 1991. Overpopulation and industrialism. In *Earth First! reader,* edited by J. Davis. Salt Lake City: Peregrine Smith Books.

Torre, A. de la. 1993. Key issues in Latina health: Voicing Latina concerns in the health financing debate. In *Chicana critical issues,* edited by N. Alarcon, R. Castro, E. Perez, B. Pesquera, A. S. Riddell, and P. Zavella. Berkeley: Third Woman Press.

Trask, H. 1993. *From a native daughter.* Monroe, Maine: Common Courage Press.

Tuana, N., ed. 1989. *Feminism and science.* Bloomington: Indiana University Press.

Tucker, C. 1996. Women's practical vote for Clinton. *Chicago Tribune,* 9 November, p. 3.

Turk, A. T. 1995. Transformation versus revolutionism and reformism: Policy implications of conflict theory. In *Crime and public policy: Putting theory to work,* edited by H. Barlow. Boulder, Colo.: Westview.

2 black airmen allege racial discrimination. 1996. *San Francisco Chronicle,* 4 December, p. A9.

Tyagi, S. 1996. Writing in search of a home: Geography, culture, and language in the creation of racial identity. In *Names we call home,* edited by B. Thompson and S. Tyagi. New York: Routledge.

Unnecessary Cesarean sections: Halting a national epidemic. 1992. *The Network News,* November/December, 7.

U.S. Bureau of the Census. 1996. *Statistical abstract of the United States: 1996.* 116th ed. Washington, D.C.: U.S. Bureau of the Census.

U.S. Department of Defense. 1992. *Department of defense worldwide list of military installations (major, minor, and support).* Washington, D.C.: U.S. Department of Defense.

U.S. Department of Labor. 1993. *Facts on working women* (No. 93-2). Washington, D.C.: U.S. Department of Labor.

U.S. Immigration and Naturalization Service. 1996. *Immigration to the United States in Fiscal Year 1995.* Washington, D.C.: U.S. Immigration and Naturalization Service.

Usdansky, M. L. 1996. Single motherhood: Stereotypes vs. statistics. *New York Times,* 11 February, p. E4.

Ussher, J. 1991. *Women's madness.* Hemel Hempstead, England: Harvester Wheatsheaf.

Walker, J. 1996. The prison industrial complex. *RESIST Newsletter* 5(9): 4–6.

Walker, M. 1992. Sex attacks "rife" on U.S. servicewomen. *London Guardian,* 2 July, p. 6.

Walters, B., and H. Downs. 1996. 20/20, November 15. New York: American Broadcasting Company.

Warner, S. B. 1987. *To dwell is to garden: A history of Boston's community gardens.* Boston: Northeastern University Press.

War Resisters League. 1997. *Where your income tax money really goes: The United States federal budget for fiscal year 1998.* New York: War Resisters League.

Waring, M. 1988. *If women counted: A new feminist economics.* New York: Harper & Row.

Weise, E. R., ed. 1992. *Closer to home: Bisexuality and feminism.* Seattle: Seal Press.

Wider Opportunities for Women. 1989. *Women, work, and childcare.* Washington, D.C.: Wider Opportunities for Women.

Will the new corporations rule the new world order? 1992. *World Citizen News,* March, 9.

Wittig, M. 1992. *The straight mind and other essays.* Boston: Beacon Press.

Wolf, N. 1991. *The beauty myth.* New York: Doubleday.

Wolf, N. 1993. *Fire with fire: The new female power and how it will change the 21st century.* New York: Random House.

Women of Color Resource Center. 1996. Solicitation letter to donors, December. Berkeley, Calif.: Women of Color Resource Center.

Women harassed at Naval Academy. 1990. *Rocky Mountain News,* 10 October, p. 35.

Women Working for a Nuclear Free and Independent Pacific, ed. 1987. *Pacific women speak.* Oxford, England: Green Line.

Wong, L. 1995. U.N. women's conference platform for action. *Sojourner,* October, 7.

Yans-McLaughlin, V., ed. 1990. *Immigration reconsidered.* New York: Oxford University Press.

Yen, M. 1989. Refusal to jail immigrant who killed wife stirs outrage. *Washington Post,* 10 April, p. A3.

Yoder, J. 1989. Women at West Point: Lessons for token women in male-dominated occupations. In *Women: A feminist perspective,* edited by J. Freeman. Mountain View, Calif.: Mayfield.

Young, I. 1980. Socialist feminism and the limits of dual systems theory. *Socialist Review,* 10(2–3): 174.

Young, W. A. 1997. Women and immigration. Unpublished manuscript produced for Women's Commission for Refugee Women and Children, Washington, D.C.

Yu, B. N. 1990. Voices of hope and anger: Women speak out for sovereignty and self-determination. *Listen ReaLoud: News of Women's Liberation Worldwide* 10(1–2): 20. Philadelphia: Nationwide Women's Program, American Friends Service Committee.

Zavella, P. 1987. *Women's work and Chicano families: Cannery workers of the Santa Clara Valley.* Ithaca, N.Y.: Cornell University.

Zeff, R., M. Love, and K. Stults, eds. 1989. *Empowering ourselves: Women and toxics organizing.* Falls Church, Va.: Citizens Clearinghouse for Hazardous Wastes.

Zinn, H. 1995. *People's history of the United States: 1492–present.* Rev. and updated ed. New York: HarperPerennial.

Credits

MIMI ABRAMOVITZ and FRED NEWTON, "Challenging AFDC Myths with the Facts" excerpted from myths and facts compiled by Mimi Abramovitz and Fred Newton. Available for $1.50 by writing to The Bertha Capen Reynolds Society, Columbus Circle Station, P. O. Box 20563, New York, NY 10023. Used with permission.

MAYA ANGELOU, "Phenomenal Woman" from *And Still I Rise* by Maya Angelou. Copyright © 1978 by Maya Angelou. Reprinted by permission of Random House, Inc.

RITA ARDITTI with Tatiana Schreiber, "Breast Cancer: The Environmental Connection." Article reprinted with permission from the *Resist Newsletter,* May/June 1992, published by Resist, Inc., 259 Elm St., Somerville, MA 02144. Resist has been funding social change since 1967.

RACHEL L. BAGBY, "Daughters of Growing Things" from *Reweaving the World.* Copyright © 1990 by Irene Diamond and Gloria Orenstein. Reprinted with permission of Sierra Club Books.

SILVIA BARALDINI, MARILYN BUCK, SUSAN ROSENBERG, and LAURA WHITEHORN, "Women's Control Unit: Marianna, FL." Used with permission of Prison News Service.

MARY BENNETT, "Cells" from *A Gathering of Spirit* edited by Beth Brant, Firebrand Books, Ithaca, New York. Copyright © 1984 by Beth Brant.

GRACE LEE BOGGS, "Each Generation Must Discover Its Mission." Used with permission of the author.

GRACE CAROLINE BRIDGES, "Lisa's Ritual, Age 10" from *Resourceful Woman* edited by Shawn Brennan and Julie Winklepleck. Copyright © 1994 Visible Ink Press. All rights reserved. Reproduced by permission.

ANNE MI OK BRUINING, "To Omoni, in Korea" from *Making Face, Making Soul/Haciendo Caras: Creative and Critical Perspectives by Feminists of Color.* Copyright © 1990 by Gloria Anzaldúa. Reprinted with permission from Aunt Lute Books (415) 826-1300.

ALMA BULAWAN and THE WOMEN OF BUKLOD, "What Are the Alternatives to a Military Base?" from *Let the Good Times Roll: Prostitution and the U.S. Military in Asia.* Copyright © 1992 by Saundra Pollock Sturdevant and Brenda Stoltzfus. Reprinted by permission of The New Press.

CHARLOTTE BUNCH, "Not by Degrees: Feminist Theory and Education" from *Passionate Politics* by Charlotte Bunch. Copyright © 1987 Charlotte Bunch. Reprinted by permission of St. Martin's Press, Inc.

MARGARETHE CAMMERMEYER, "Choosing Your Battle" from *Serving in Silence* by Margarethe Cammermeyer. Copyright © 1994 Margarethe Cammermeyer. Used by permission of Viking Penguin, a division of Penguin Books USA, Inc.

ANDREA R. CANAAN, "Girlfriends" from *Making Face, Making Soul/Haciendo Caras: Creative and Critical Perspectives by Feminists of Color.* Copyright © 1990 by Gloria Anzaldúa. Reprinted with permission from Aunt Lute Books (415) 826-1300.

CARIBBEAN ASSOCIATION FOR FEMINIST RESEARCH AND ACTION, "The Debt Crisis: Who Really Owes Whom?" from *CAFRA News,* March–May 1990. Used with permission of CAFRA.

JEANNINE OUELLETTE HOWITZ, "Reflections of a Feminist Mom." Used with permission of the author. Jeannine Ouellette Howitz is the author of *Mama Moon,* a children's picture book about a mother and daughter sharing knowledge of the feminine power of birth. She is the editor of *Minnesota Parent,* a regional journal devoted to the voices of mothers, fathers, and children. Jeannine lives and writes in Center City, Minnesota with her husband John, and their three small children.

RUTH HUBBARD, "Science, Facts, and Feminism" from *Hypatia,* vol. 3, no. 1, Spring 1988. Reprinted by permission of the author.

AÍDA HURTADO, "Theorizing by Feminists of Color" from *The Color of Privilege* by Aída Hurtado. Copyright © 1996 The University of Michigan Press. Reprinted by permission of the publisher.

DEANNA L. JANG, "Asian Immigrant Women Fight Domestic Violence" from *CrossRoads,* March 1994. Reprinted by permission of the publisher.

MELANIE KAYE/KANTROWITZ, "Jews, Class, Color, and the Cost of Whiteness" from *The Issue Is Power: Essays on Women, Jews, Violence and Resistance.* Copyright © 1992 by Melanie Kaye/Kantrowitz. Reprinted with permission from Aunt Lute Books (415) 826-1300.

SURINA A. KHAN, "All American Queer Pakistani Girl." Used with permission of the author. She is an Associate Analyst at Political Research Associates, a think tank and research center that monitors authoritarian, antidemocratic movements. She has contributed to the *Boston Phoenix, Sojourner,* the *Washington Blade, Gay Community News,* and the *Harvard Gay and Lesbian Review,* among other publications.

NANCY KURSHAN, "Behind the Walls: The History and Current Reality of Women's Imprisonment." Reprinted by permission of Nancy Kurshan. She has been a political activist for the past 30 years. Through her activities in the political movements of the 1960s she developed an understanding of the racist nature of the prison system, as well as the important role prisons play in the containment of social change. Ms. Kurshan is a founding member of the Committee to End the Marion Lockdown (CEML) which has been organizing to abolish control unit prisons since 1985. You can contact her at CEML, P. O. Box 57812, Chicago, IL 60657.

WINONA LADUKE, an interview with Katsi Cook, "Breastmilk, PCBs and Motherhood." First published in *Indigenous Woman.* Reprinted by permission of Winona LaDuke, Katsi Cook and Indigenous Women's Network.

MEREDITH LEE, "Outrageous Acts." Used with permission of the author.

AUDRE LORDE, poem reprinted from "Age, Race, Class, and Sex" in *Sister Outsider: Essays and Speeches* by Audre Lorde, Freedom, CA: The Crossing Press. Copyright © 1984 Audre Lorde. Used with permission of the publisher; "Uses of the Erotic: The Erotic as Power" reprinted from *Sister Outsider: Essays and Speeches* by Audre Lorde, Freedom, CA: The Crossing Press. Copyright © 1984 Audre Lorde. Used with permission of the publisher.

MIRIAM CHING LOUIE and NGUYEN LOUIE, "The Conversation Begins" from *Conversation Begins: Mothers and Daughters Talk AB* by Christina Baker-Kline and Christina Looper Baker. Copyright © 1996 by Christina Looper Baker and Christina Baker-Kline. Used by permission of Bantam Books, a division of Bantam Doubleday Dell Publishing Group, Inc.

LOIS LYLES, "Cancer in the Family." Reprinted from *Wings of Gauze* by Barbara Bair and Susan E. Cayleff, eds., Wayne State University Press, 1993. Copyright © 1993 by Barbara Bair and Susan E. Cayleff, eds. Used by permission of Wayne State University Press.

BARBARA MACDONALD, "Do You Remember Me?" and an excerpt from "An Open Letter To The Women's Movement" in *Look Me in the Eye* by Barbara Macdonald with Cynthia Rich, San Francisco: Spinsters Ink, 1983. Available from Spinsters Ink, 32 East First Street, #330, Duluth, MN 55802. Reprinted by permission.

LISA SUHAIR MAJAJ, "Boundaries: Arab/American" from *Food for Our Grandmothers,* Joanna Kadi, ed., with permission from the publisher, South End Press, 116 St. Botolph St., Boston, MA 02115.

MARIA MIES, "From Garbage to Subsistence" in *Ecofeminism* by Maria Mies and Vandana Shiva. Copyright © 1993 Maria Mies and Vandana Shiva. Used with permission of Zed Press.

RUTH MILKMAN, "Organizing Immigrant Women in New York's Chinatown: An Interview with Katie Quan." Reprinted from *Women and Unions: Forging a New Partnership,* ed. Dorothy Sue Cobble, pp. 281–298. Copyright © 1993 by Cornell University. An IRL Press

Used with permission of International Gay and Lesbian Human Rights Commission.

SONIA SHAH, "Presenting the Blue Goddess: Toward a National Pan-Asian Feminist Agenda" from *The State of Asian-America,* Karin Aguilar-San Juan, ed. Copyright © 1994 South End Press. Used by permission of the publisher.

LESLIE MARMON SILKO, "The Border Patrol State." Reprinted with the permission of Simon & Schuster from *Yellow Woman and a Beauty of Spirit: Essays on Native American Life Today* by Leslie Marmon Silko. Copyright © 1996 by Leslie Marmon Silko. Originally appeared in *The Nation.*

STARHAWK, "Power, Authority, and Mystery: Eco-feminism and Earth-Based Spirituality" from *Reweaving the World,* edited by Irene Diamond and Gloria Orenstein. Copyright © 1990 by Irene Diamond and Gloria Orenstein. Reprinted with permission of Sierra Club Books.

CAROL TARLEN, "White Trash: An Autobiography" in *Calling Home: Working-Class Women's Writing, An Anthology,* J. Zandy, ed. Rutgers University Press, 1990. Used by permission of the author.

DAI R. THOMPSON, "Anger" from *With the Power of Each Breath,* Susan Brown et al., eds., Cleis Press, 1985. Used with permission of the publisher.

BOUAPHA TOOMMALY, "Asian and Pacific Islanders in the Environment" from *APEN Voices,* Fall 1995, Volume 2, Number 1, newsletter of the ASIAN PACIFIC ENVIRONMENTAL NETWORK. Used with permission.

MILILANI TRASK, "Native Hawaiian Historical and Cultural Perspectives on Environmental Justice" from *Race, Poverty and the Environment,* vol. 3, no. 1, Spring 1992. For inquiries, call (415) 561-3331. Used with permission of Race, Poverty and the Enviorment and the author.

ALISA L. VALDÉS, "Ruminations of a Feminist Aerobics Instructor" from *Listen Up: Voices from the Next Feminist Generation,* Barbara Findlen, ed., Seal Press, Seattle, WA. Copyright © 1995 by Barbara Findlen. Used with permission of the publisher.

DONNA WALTON, "What's a Leg Got to Do with It?" Used with permission of the author.

NAOMI WOLF, "Radical Heterosexuality." Used with permission of the author.

WOMEN'S INTERNATIONAL LEAGUE FOR PEACE AND FREEDOM, "The Women's Budget." Reprinted from the *Women's Budget,* Special Edition, February, 1996, produced by the Women's International League for Peace and Freedom.

NELLIE WONG, "When I Was Growing Up" from *This Bridge Called My Back: Writings by Radical Women of Color.* Copyright © 1983 by Cherríe Moraga and Gloria Anzaldúa, eds. Reprinted by permission of Nellie Wong and Kitchen Table: Women of Color Press, P. O. Box 40-4920, Brooklyn, NY 11240-4920.

MERLE WOO, "Letter to Ma" from *This Bridge Called My Back: Writings by Radical Women of Color,* Cherríe Moraga and Gloria Anzaldúa, eds. Copyright © 1983 Cherríe Moraga and Gloria Anzaldúa, eds. Reprinted by permission of the author and of Kitchen Table: Women of Color Press, P. O. Box 40-4920, Brooklyn, NY 11240-4920. Merle Woo is a writer and educator in Women's Studies and active in Radical Women and the Freedom Socialist Party.

MAIJUE XIONG, "An Unforgettable Journey" from *Hmong Means Free,* Sucheng Chan, ed. Copyright © 1994 by Temple University. Reprinted by permission of Temple University Press.

GLORIA YAMATO, "Something about the Subject Makes It Hard to Name" in *Changing Our Power: An Introduction to Women Studies,* J. Whitehorse Cochran, D. Langston, and C. Woodward, eds. Kendall/Hunt, 1988. Used by permission of the author.

JANET ZANDY, "Liberating Memory." Used with permission of the author. Janet Zandy is an Associate Professor of Language and Literature at RIT. She is the editor of *Calling Home: Working-Class Women's Writings* (Rutgers University Press, 1990), *Liberating Memory: Our Work and Our Working-Class Consciousness* (Rutgers University Press, 1995), a special issue of *Women's Studies Quarterly* on "Working-Class Studies" (The Feminist Press, Spring/Summer 1995) and other articles on class, women's writings, and the curriculum. She is an advocate of working-class studies and General Editor of *Women's Studies Quarterly.*

ROBBIN LEE ZEFF, MARSHA LOVE, and KAREN STULTS, eds. "Empowering Ourselves: Women and Toxics Organizing" from *Empowering Ourselves: Women and Toxics Organizing* R. L. Zeff, M. Love and K. Stults, eds. Reprinted by permission of Citizens Clearinghouse for Hazardous Wastes, Center for Health, Environment, and Justice.